כֶּתֶר ירושלים

מחזור קורן לשבועות • נוסח אשכנז
The Koren Shavuot Maḥzor • Nusaḥ Ashkenaz

THE MILLER EDITION

מחזור קורן לשבועות
THE KOREN SHAVUOT MAHZOR

WITH INTRODUCTION, TRANSLATION AND COMMENTARY BY

Rabbi Lord Jonathan Sacks

FOREWORD BY

Rabbi Shalom Baum and
Rabbi Leonard Matanky

•

KOREN PUBLISHERS JERUSALEM

The Koren Shavuot Maḥzor
The Miller Edition
Nusaḥ Ashkenaz, First North American Hebrew/English Edition, 2016

Koren Publishers Jerusalem Ltd.
POB 4044, Jerusalem 91040, ISRAEL
POB 8531, New Milford, CT 06776, USA

www.korenpub.com

The creation of this Maḥzor was made possible with the generous support of
Torah Education in Israel.

Standard Size, Hardcover, ISBN 978-965-301-818-1
Compact Size, Hardcover, ISBN 978-965-301-819-8

SHUA2

Printed in PRC

The Miller Edition

of the

KOREN SHAVUOT MAḤZOR

*is dedicated
to the memories of our parents*

Martin M. Miller, ז״ל
מרדכי מיכל בן יונה

Florence Miller, ז״ל
גיטע פרומע בת ברוך מרדכי

Sigmund Brief, ז״ל
שמעון בן צבי הלוי

Itta Brief, ז״ל
איטה בת בן־ציון

*May they continue to inspire and serve as models
for our children, grandchildren,
and their families.*

Renée and Matthew Miller
Jerusalem, Sivan 5776 (June 2016)

The Miller Edition

of the

KOREN SHAVUOT MAḤZOR

is dedicated

to the memories of our parents

Martin M. Miller, ז״ל
מרדכי בן זלמן ע״ה

Florence Miller, ז״ל
פעריל בת משה זאב הלוי ע״ה

Sigmund Brief, ז״ל
שמעון בן צבי הלוי

Ita Brief, ז״ל
איטא בת דוב בער

May they continue to inspire and serve as models
for our children, grandchildren,
and their families

Renée and Mathew Miller
Jerusalem, Sivan 5776 (June 2016)

CONTENTS

זמן מתן תורתנו
The time of the giving of our Torah

Why does the Torah not explicitly associate the holiday of Shavuot with the giving of the Torah? The answer, says the Maharal, lies in the fact that Shavuot is a *ḥag* – a holiday on which we celebrate and rejoice. An explicit association of Shavuot with the giving of the Torah would constitute a commandment to rejoice about our having received the Torah. But happiness cannot be legislated – it must originate within us. Salvation from slavery is marked by Pesaḥ, and God's protection in the wilderness which we celebrate on Sukkot is obvious grounds for joy. Receiving the Torah might not appear to the casual observer as a reason to rejoice. It was left to the Jewish people, as a community and as individuals, to reach this conclusion on our own, to appreciate and celebrate the privilege of *Matan Torah* (Rabbi Yehuda Amital, זיל). It is our hope that this *Koren Shavuot Maḥzor*, with its elucidating translations and thought-provoking commentaries, will help *Klal Yisrael* reach the understanding of the enormity of the gift we have received, enabling us to rejoice as that gift warrants.

We could not have embarked on this project without the moral leadership and intellectual spark of Rabbi Lord Jonathan Sacks. Rabbi Sacks provides an invaluable guide to the liturgy through his remarkable introduction, translation, and commentary. His work not only clarifies the text and explains the teachings of our sages, but uniquely and seamlessly weaves profound concepts of Judaism into the reality of contemporary life. It was our distinct privilege to work with Rabbi Sacks to create a Maḥzor that we believe appropriately reflects the complexity and depth of Jewish prayer.

The Rabbinical Council of America has long been the moral and professional voice of traditional Orthodoxy in North America. The publication of this Maḥzor marks Koren's first association with the RCA; this endorsement has great meaning for us and we thank Rabbi Leonard Matanky, Rabbi Shalom Baum and Executive Director Rabbi Mark Dratch under whose leadership the RCA has grown and expanded its activities for the benefit of the religious life of Jews everywhere.

◄ We only

We only hope that all these contributions are matched by the scholarship, design, and typography that have been hallmarks of Koren Publishers Jerusalem for more than fifty years. Koren is privileged to have a small, but remarkably talented team of consummate and dedicated professionals. Rabbi David Fuchs supervised the textual aspects of the work. Rachel Meghnagi edited the English texts and Efrat Gross the Hebrew texts. Jessica Sacks supplied the superb translations of *Megillat Rut*, the Torah readings, and many of the *piyutim*. The text of the *mishnayot* for *Tikkun Leil Shavuot* was taken from the Noé edition of the *Koren Talmud Bavli*, with commentary and elucidation by Rav Adin (Even-Israel) Steinsaltz. Rabbi Eli Clark contributed the informative and useful Halakha Guide. We thank Esther Be'er for assembling and typesetting the texts.

This new edition of the Koren Maḥzor continues the Koren tradition of making the language of prayer more accessible, thus enhancing the prayer experience. One of the unique features of the Maḥzor is the use of typesetting to break up a prayer phrase-by-phrase – rather than using a block paragraph format – so that the reader will naturally pause at the correct places. No commas appear in the Hebrew text at the end of lines, but in the English translation, where linguistic clarity requires, we have retained the use of commas at the end of lines. Unlike other Hebrew/English *maḥzorim*, the Hebrew text is on the left-hand page and the English on the right. This arrangement preserves the distinctive "fanning out" effect of the Koren text and the beauty of the Koren layout.

We hope and pray that this Maḥzor, like all our publications, extends the vision of Koren's founder, Eliyahu Koren, to a new generation, to further *Avodat HaShem* for Jews everywhere.

Matthew Miller, Publisher

Jerusalem, 5776 (2016)

FOREWORD

Unlike the holidays of Sukkot or Pesaḥ, the holiday of Shavuot, as celebrated in a post-Temple era, lacks the majesty of distinctive mitzvot and customs. For there is no Shavuot equivalent of a seder or a sukka, a matza or a lulav. Rather, Shavuot is centered on the memory of the pageantry of the offering of the first fruits and awesome revelation at Sinai.

As such, the nature of the spoken or printed word, of prayer to God and remembrances of glories long ago are in the forefront of our Shavuot experience. It is for this reason that a Shavuot maḥzor carries such significance. Because it is within the words of the maḥzor that we create mental images of events beyond our experiences, and connect to the past. Whether it is the ninety verses of *Akdamut*, that begin with Creation and take us on a journey through angelic praises and human suffering, or the Torah readings that recall the Temple service and the glory of Sinai, the maḥzor is our guide to creating both memory and meaning.

Yet, the meaning of Shavuot can also be discovered within our daily prayer, via the *Birkot HaTorah* recited each morning. While on the surface, these opening prayers may be categorized simply as blessings for mitzvot, similar to other *berakhot* that precede other mitzvot, Rabbi Mordekhai Yaffe in his halakhic masterpiece, the *Levush* (אורח חיים סימן מז), rules that they are in fact *Birkot HaNehenin* – blessings of worldly enjoyment. In fact, he argued that the first *berakha* – "לַעֲסוֹק בְּדִבְרֵי תוֹרָה, To engage in study of the words of Torah" – is the *Berakha Aḥarona*, the concluding blessing, to the previous day's learning, while the more familiar "אֲשֶׁר בָּחַר בָּנוּ מִכָּל הָעַמִּים, Who has chosen us from all the peoples," is the *berakha* for the coming day's study.

However, beyond the halakhic detail of this position, there is a critical lesson – that the study of Torah is one of the great pleasures of this world. In fact, Rabbi Avraham Bornstein in his classic introduction to *Eglei Tal* argues that unlike other mitzvot that are not given for the purpose of pleasure, the study of Torah is unique in that its goal is to bring joy to the student.

Rabbi Joseph Soloveitchik categorized Torah study as an "object of joy" and therefore even if one didn't derive pleasure from its study, it would still be a forbidden activity on days of mourning.

◄ The Rabbinical

The Rabbinical Council of America is very proud to partner with Koren Publishers Jerusalem in the presentation of this magnificent new maḥzor. It is our hope and prayer that together with the soaring translation and commentary, our thoughts will be transported to the time of God's revelation at Sinai, and our prayers will be filled with the glory of Torah – as our motto expresses, לְהַגְדִּיל תּוֹרָה וּלְהַאְדִּירָה.

Rabbi Shalom Baum, President of RCA
Rabbi Leonard Matanky, Past President of RCA
Adar Sheni 5776 (March 2016)

INTRODUCTION

THE GREATEST GIFT:
Essays on the themes and concepts of Shavuot

by
RABBI LORD
JONATHAN SACKS

INTRODUCTION

THE GREATEST GIFT

1. The Enigma of Shavuot

Shavuot is a riddle wrapped in a mystery inside an enigma.

It is the only festival in the Torah without a specific date in the Jewish calendar. We know exactly when Pesaḥ and Sukkot occur. The same is true for Rosh HaShana and Yom Kippur. Each has its given day or days in the cycle of the year. Not so Shavuot. Nowhere does the Torah say that we should celebrate it on such-and-such a day in a specific month. Instead it says: "And you shall count seven complete weeks from the day following the first day of the festival, when you brought the omer as a wave-offering … And you shall proclaim on that day – it shall be a sacred assembly for you: you may not perform any laborious work" (Lev. 23:15–21). The text in Deuteronomy is even less specific: "Count for yourselves seven weeks; when the sickle begins to cut the standing grain" (Deut. 16:9).

Not only does the Torah not specify a date: for a prolonged period, until the calendar was fixed by calculation in the fourth century, it could fall on three *different* days, depending on whether in any given year Nisan and Iyar were both short months of twenty-nine days, or both long, of thirty days, or one was long, the other short. If both were long, Shavuot fell on the fifth of Sivan. If one was long and one short, it was celebrated on the sixth, and if both were short, it occurred on the seventh. This makes it difficult to understand how it could be a commemoration of any historical event, since events happen on particular days of the year, while Shavuot did not.

These, though, are minor problems when it comes to dating Shavuot. The larger problem lies in the phrase the Torah uses to describe the day on which the seven-week count begins. Above, we translated it as "the day following the first day of the festival." However, the text actually says *mimoḥorat haShabbat*, literally "the day after the Sabbath." Reading the phrase literally, this means Sunday, from which it follows that Shavuot, the fiftieth day, also falls on a Sunday. This gave rise to an extraordinary range of interpretations, reflecting the deep schisms in Jewish life in the late Second Temple period between Pharisees and other groups like the

◀ Boethusians

Boethusians, Sadducees, Samaritans and the Qumran sect of the Dead Sea Scrolls.

Later in the age of the Geonim, from the eighth century onward, a similar controversy arose between the followers of the rabbis and the Karaites. The Pharisees and the rabbis held, as we do, that there is an Oral tradition, the *Torah shebe'al peh*, of equal authority with the Torah's written text, the *Torah shebikhtav*. That tradition said that in this case, "the day after the Sabbath" means "the day after the first day of the festival," which, being a day of rest, could also be called Shabbat.

The other groups, denying the oral tradition, held that the "Shabbat" was to be construed literally. For them the Omer – the sheaf of the wave offering – was to be offered on a Sunday, and Shavuot fell on Sunday seven weeks later. The Boethusians, Sadducees and Karaites understood the phrase as "the day after the Shabbat *during* Pesaḥ." The Qumran sect understood it to refer to the Shabbat *after* Pesaḥ. Both the sect and the Book of Jubilees (second century BCE) had a fixed solar calendar, according to which Shavuot always fell on the fifteenth of Sivan. The Jews of Ethiopia held a fourth view, understanding it to mean the last day of the festival, so for them Shavuot fell six days later than for the Pharisees and rabbis.

The result was chaos, at least one mark of which is still evident today in the institution known as *Yom Tov sheni shel galuyot*, the second day of the festival observed outside Israel. Often this is thought of as the result of the ancient system by which the new moon was determined, month by month, on the basis of eye-witness testimony. No one could tell in advance of the court's decision when the new month would begin. Immediately the month had been fixed, messengers were sent out to notify communities, and since it took them a long time to make the journey, Diaspora communities had to keep festivals for two days because of the doubt as to whether the previous month was long or short.

In fact, the real reason is significantly different. During the Second Temple period there was no need for a second day even in Babylonia because the decision of the court was conveyed that night by the lighting of a series of bonfires that stretched from Israel to Babylonia. However, as a result of controversies about the calendar, one of which was about the determination of the date of Shavuot, the bonfires were sabotaged. Thereafter, the news had to be conveyed by messengers instead (Mishna,

◄ *Rosh HaShana*

Rosh HaShana 2:2). So the second day owes its existence not to the absence of a system of rapid communication, but rather to a lack of unity and mutual respect within the Jewish people itself. Ironically, serving one God did not always create one nation.

The second strange fact about Shavuot is that nowhere does the Torah link it to a specific historical event. Pesaḥ recalls the exodus from Egypt. Sukkot is a reminder of the forty years in the desert when the Israelites lived in temporary dwellings. Shavuot is given, explicitly in the Torah, no such historical dimension. We know it as *zeman matan torateinu*, "the time of the giving of our Torah," the anniversary of the revelation at Mount Sinai. But this identification appears nowhere in the Torah or elsewhere in Tanakh. Only in the Talmud (see for example, *Pesaḥim* 68b, among others) do we begin to find this connection.

What is more, until the fourth century, as we have seen, Shavuot could occur on the fifth, sixth or seventh of Sivan. So whichever date the Torah was given, Shavuot did not necessarily fall on that day. Nor was there agreement as to which day the Torah was in fact given. The Talmud records a dispute between the other sages and Rabbi Yose. The sages held that it was given on the sixth of Sivan. Rabbi Yose disagreed and argued that it was given on the seventh (*Shabbat* 86b; see page 171). His view could not be lightly dismissed, since Rabbi Yose had a reputation for clarity and precision that often gave his rulings authority (*Eiruvin* 46b; *Gittin* 67a). It follows that, at least in Israel where Shavuot is observed for only one day, the sixth of Sivan, in Rabbi Yose's view Shavuot falls *not* on the day the Torah was given, but the day before.

So, according to the written sources, biblical and post-biblical, there was intense debate as to when Shavuot is celebrated and why. That is what makes the study of this particular festival so fascinating, for the conflict of interpretations has to do not just with the wording of the Torah and its connection with historical events. It has to do with one of the most fundamental questions of all: what it is to be a Jew and why. Shavuot will turn out to be, among other things, the festival of Jewish identity.

CELEBRATING THE LAND

One fact emerges with great clarity from the biblical sources. Shavuot is an agricultural celebration. Exodus calls it the "time of the first wheat

◂ harvest

harvest" (Ex. 23:16). Numbers calls it "the day of the first fruits" (Num. 28:26). Deuteronomy defines the start of the seven-week count as "when the sickle begins to cut the standing grain" (Deut. 16:9). Leviticus 23 interrupts its account of holy days to add, immediately after giving the details of Shavuot, a command that has nothing to do with festivals: "And when you reap the grain of your land, do not finish reaping the corner of your field, and do not collect the fallen remnants of your harvest: you must leave them for the poor and for the stranger." This is the practice vividly described in the book of Ruth. Whenever Shavuot is mentioned in the Torah, we can almost smell the fragrance of fields, feel the open air, and see the harvested grain. It is supremely the farmers' festival.

According to one Talmudic passage (*Menaḥot* 65a), this was the logic behind the sectarians' practice of always celebrating Shavuot on a Sunday. Challenged by Rabban Yoḥanan ben Zakkai as to why, unlike all the other festivals, Shavuot should have a fixed day in the week rather than in the month, an elderly Boethusian gave the explanation that Moses was "a lover of Israel." Realizing that after seven exhausting weeks in the field, farmers would be tired, he (or rather, God) had compassion on them and gave them a long weekend! Since Shavuot, unlike Pesaḥ and Sukkot, lasts for only one day, ensuring that it always fell on Sunday gave weary farmers two consecutive days of rest.

However, the problem remains. Pesaḥ and Sukkot are also agricultural and seasonal. Pesaḥ is the festival of spring. Sukkot is the festival of ingathering, the autumn harvest. But each also had a historical dimension. That is what made these festivals unique in the ancient world. Every society had agricultural festivals. There was nothing odd in seeing God in nature. None before Israel, though, had seen God in history or regarded collective memory as a religious obligation. It may therefore have been that Shavuot also had a historical dimension from the outset, but one that had to do with the land. It was the day that celebrated the gift of the Promised Land.

This is purely speculative, but it is supported by several considerations. First is the seven-week countdown that we find in no other festival. The obvious analogy is with the seven-year cycle of *shemitta*, the year of release, culminating in the fiftieth or Jubilee year. These had primarily (though not exclusively) to do with fields, produce, agricultural labor

◄ and the ownership

and the ownership of land. The count was set in motion by the offering of the Omer from the first of the barley harvest, while on Shavuot itself the key offering was two loaves of bread from the wheat harvest. So the seven weeks were the time when the people were most conscious of God's blessing in "bringing forth bread from the earth." R. Yehuda HeḤasid (Germany, twelfth–thirteenth century) suggested that the fifty-day count was instituted because people were so busy and preoccupied in the fields that they might otherwise forget to celebrate the festival on time. It was the obvious time to celebrate the land promised, and blessed, by God.

Second, there is an obvious lacuna in the pilgrimage festivals themselves. Pesaḥ is about the start of the journey from Egypt. Sukkot recalls the forty years of the journey itself. What is missing is a festival celebrating journey's end, the arrival at the destination. Logic would suggest that this was Shavuot. Interestingly, this is what it became again in the kibbutzim during the early years of the modern state. Secular Israelis re-appropriated Shavuot precisely as a celebration of the land.

Third, the theme of the Mosaic books as a whole is *the promise of the land*. In Genesis, God makes the promise seven times to Abraham, once to Isaac and three times to Jacob. Jewish history begins with Abraham leaving his family and traveling to "the land that I will show you" (Gen. 12:1). The rest of the Torah from Exodus to Deuteronomy is about the Israelites' journey from Egypt toward it. If the gift of the land is the supreme divine promise, it would be extraordinary *not* to have a festival marking its fulfillment.

Fourth, the book of Joshua tells us that it was *the act of eating the grain of the land* that made the Israelites vividly aware that the wilderness era had ended. We read that "They ate of the produce of the land on the day after the Pesaḥ, matzot and roasted grain, on that very day. And the manna ceased [to come down] the next day, when they ate of the produce of the land, and the children of Israel no longer had manna; they ate of the crops of the land of Canaan that year" (Josh. 5:11–12). The manna stopped, in other words, on the day that became fixed as the offering of the Omer that began the seven-week count to Shavuot. Historically, therefore, the new grain each year was a reminder of how the Israelites first tasted the produce of what Moses described as "a land of wheat and barley" (Deut. 8:8).

◀ We know

We know precisely how this history was celebrated. The Torah defines Shavuot as "the festival of the first fruits," and tells us that on bringing first fruits to the central Sanctuary, each farmer was to make a declaration:

"My father was a wandering Aramean, and he went down into Egypt… And the Egyptians dealt cruelly with us and oppressed us, and imposed hard labor on us… And the LORD brought us out of Egypt with a strong hand and an outstretched arm… He brought us to this place and gave us this land, a land flowing with milk and honey; and now I bring the first fruits of the soil that You, LORD, have given me." (Deuteronomy 26:5–10)

We are familiar with this passage because, for at least the last two thousand years, it has occupied a central place in the Haggada on Pesaḥ, but its original context was the bringing of first fruits to the Temple on Shavuot. *The first regular historical declaration made by the people as a whole had to do with the gift of the land.* This then is the most likely historical dimension of the festival during some periods of the biblical age. It was the day when once a year, coupled with an act of thanksgiving for the grain harvest, the Israelites came to the Temple and told the story of their arrival at the land itself. It was when the nation gave expression to the sense of gratitude Moses believed they ought to have:

For the LORD your God is bringing you into a good land – a land with brooks, streams, and deep springs gushing out into the valleys and hills; a land of wheat and barley, vines and fig trees, pomegranates, olive oil and honey; a land where bread will not be scarce and you will lack nothing… You will eat and be satisfied, then you shall bless the LORD your God for the good land He has given you. (Deuteronomy 8:7–10)

This was traditionally understood as the biblical source of the command to say Grace after Meals, but it is not impossible that it was also the basis for an annual celebration on Shavuot. This, to repeat, is pure conjecture. What gives it force, however, is that were it not so, there would have been no annual celebration of the single most important fact about Israel's existence as a nation, namely that it lived in the land given

◄ by God

by God in fulfillment of the promise He had made to their ancestors at the dawn of their history. Neither Pesaḥ nor Sukkot are about this. They are festivals of exodus and exile. Shavuot completes the cycle by being the festival of homecoming. That was its historical dimension, made explicit in the *Vidui bikkurim*, the declaration accompanying the first fruits, and symbolized in the two loaves of wheat that were the special offering of Shavuot.

If so, we can understand two longstanding customs of Shavuot: eating dairy food and decorating the synagogue with flowers and foliage. The milk recalls the phrase most associated with Israel – "a land flowing with milk and honey" – that appears no fewer than fifteen times in the Torah. The flowers and foliage recall God's blessing if the people follow Him: "I will give grass in your field for your cattle, and you shall eat and be satisfied" (Deut. 11:15).

It would also follow that the three pilgrimage festivals correspond to three different kinds of bread. Pesaḥ is about "the bread of oppression" our ancestors ate in Egypt. Sukkot is about the manna, the "bread from heaven" they ate for forty years in the wilderness, the sukka itself symbolizing the clouds of glory that appeared just before the manna fell for the first time (Ex. 13:21; 16:10). Shavuot, with its offering of "two loaves" (Lev. 23:17), is about the bread of freedom made with the grain of the land itself. So it might once have been. But something happened that decisively changed people's understanding of the day itself.

EXILE AND IDENTITY

What changed was that Israel lost the land. In 722 BCE Assyria conquered the northern kingdom and transported its population, known to history as the Lost Ten Tribes. In 597 BCE Babylonia defeated Judah, the kingdom of the south, taking its king and other leaders captive. In 588–586 BCE it attacked again, this time, after a prolonged siege, destroying the Temple. In the book of Lamentations we can still sense the trauma, undiminished by time.

You cannot celebrate the land when you have lost it. You cannot rejoice over the produce of the fields if the fields are no longer yours. You cannot thank God for the gift of home when you are in exile. "How can we sing the LORD's song on foreign soil?" asked the people, weeping by the waters of Babylon (Ps. 137:4). All the hopes that had accompanied Abraham's descendants since he and Sarah began their journey to the Promised Land lay in ruins. It was the worst crisis of the biblical age.

It was then that a curious feature of Israelite history played a decisive role. In the normal experience of nations, first comes the land and only then, the law. People settle a region. They evolve from group to clan to tribe. They take up agriculture. They build villages, then towns and cities, then nations and sometimes empires. Only relatively late in this process do structures of governance emerge and with them, laws governing relationships in society. The "where" precedes the "how." When it comes to the history of nations, connections with the land are primal, visceral. Legislation is secondary and contingent.

In Israel's case, uniquely, it was the other way around. First came the law, and only then the land. At Mount Sinai, a mere seven weeks after leaving Egypt, the Israelites underwent a unique experience that transformed their identity. They made a covenant with God. They accepted Him as their sovereign. They pledged themselves to live by His laws. This was their foundational moment as a body politic.

The consequence could not have been more far reaching. *If the law preceded the land, then even when they lost the land, they still had the law. If the covenant came before they had achieved political independence as a territorial state, it might still be in force even when they had lost their independence and state.* That is what God had promised even before they entered the land. The terrifying curses at the end of Leviticus contain a remarkable promise:

> Yet in spite of this, when they are in the land of their enemies, I will not reject them or abhor them so as to destroy them completely, breaking My covenant with them. I am the LORD their God. (Leviticus 26:44)

That became the message of all the prophets who lived through or foresaw conquest and exile. "Where is your mother's certificate of divorce with which I sent her away?" asked God through Isaiah (Is. 50:1). Only if the sun, moon and stars cease to shine, said Jeremiah in God's name, will Israel cease to be a nation (Jer. 31:34–35). "I shall open your graves and lift you out of your graves, My people; I shall bring you to the land

◀ of Israel

of Israel," said God through Ezekiel in his chilling vision of the nation as a valley of dry bones (Ezek. 37:12).

In Babylonia, through individuals like the prophet Ezekiel, the exiles began to understand that they had lost their country but they still had the covenant. They were still God's people. He was still their King. That was when the Torah became, in Heinrich Heine's famous words, "the portable homeland of the Jew." It was their country of the mind, their extraterritorial landscape, their metaphysical refuge. The Torah was the record of their past and their assurance of a future. Never have a people owed more to a book.

What happened in the Babylonian exile we do not know but we can reasonably infer. It was there that they rediscovered Torah as the key to Jewish identity. We know this because of what happened when two major Jewish figures, Ezra the scribe and Nehemiah the politician-administrator, left Babylon to return to Israel in the mid-fifth century BCE. Dismayed at the low ebb of Jewish life, they undertook an initiative with far-reaching consequences. They assembled a national gathering at the Water Gate in Jerusalem and conducted the first-recorded adult education seminar in history.

The book of Nehemiah describes how Ezra stood on a wooden platform in the Temple courtyard and read Torah to the people:

> Ezra opened the book. All the people could see him because he was standing above them; and as he opened it, the people all stood up. Ezra praised the Lord, the great God; and all the people lifted their hands and responded, "Amen! Amen!" Then they bowed down and worshiped the Lord with their faces to the ground. The Levites... instructed the people in the Law while the people were standing there. They read from the Book of the Law of God, making it clear and giving the meaning so that the people understood what was being read. (Nehemiah 8:5–8)

Shortly thereafter, the people formally rededicated themselves to the covenant. It was the start of a movement that gathered pace over the next five hundred years, turning Jewry into the people of Torah for whom, when the Temple was destroyed a second time, scholars took

◄ the place

the place of priests and prophets, and study became a substitute for acrifice.

What Ezra and Nehemiah understood was that the spiritual battle was ultimately more consequential than the military one. This became clear in the second century BCE, when the Seleucid Greeks under Antiochus IV attempted to force the pace of Hellenization, banning the public practice of Judaism and introducing pagan practices into the Temple. The Maccabees, a pietistic group led by the sons of an elderly priest, Mattityahu, fought back and won, rededicating the Temple in the ceremony we still commemorate on Ḥanukka.

However, their successors, the Hasmonean kings, rapidly became Hellenized themselves, choosing Greek names and combining kingship with priesthood in a way incompatible with the separation of powers implicit in the Bible. It was probably at this time that a group of priests disgusted by what they saw as the corruption of the Temple decided to leave Jerusalem and live in seclusion in Qumran, the sect we have come to know through the Dead Sea Scrolls.

The religious fragmentation of Jewry in the last days of the Second Temple was extreme and tragic. The people were religiously divided, says Josephus, into Sadducees, Pharisees and Essenes. The Pharisees themselves were fragmented to the point at which the sages said that the split between the schools of Hillel and Shammai threatened to divide the Torah into two (*Sotah* 47b; *Sanhedrin* 88b). A political rift grew among the population as to whether to live with or rebel against the increasingly repressive Roman rule. There were moderates, zealots, and terrorists known as the Sicarii. Josephus, an eye-witness of those events, paints a terrifying picture of Jews inside the besieged Jerusalem more intent on fighting one another than the enemy outside. A house divided against itself cannot stand, and so Jerusalem fell again, as it was to do a third time sixty-five years later with the failure of the Bar Kokhba revolt.

These were devastating blows, and unlike the Babylonian exile, this time there were no prophets to offer a compelling vision of imminent hope. It was the end of Israel as an actor on the historical stage for almost two thousand years. Tradition has left us a famous story about how Rabban Yoḥanan ben Zakkai arranged to have himself smuggled outside the besieged city and taken to Vespasian, the Roman general leading the

◀ campaign

campaign. Correctly predicting that the general would soon be made Caesar, he extracted a promise in return: "Give me the academy of Yavneh and its sages" (*Gittin* 56b). This became the best-known memory of Jewish survival after catastrophe. From here onward Judaism would become a religion of teachers, schools and houses of study, the faith of a people dedicated to the book, not the sword.

The years following the destruction of the Second Temple proved to be the definitive test as to which form of Judaism would survive the loss of the land and its institutions. Within a remarkably short time, the Sadducees had disappeared along with the Qumran sectarians. We hear no more of the Essenes. The Samaritans persisted but in small numbers. The survivors were the rabbis, heirs to the Pharisees, who saw Torah study as a higher religious experience than even prayer and who created in the form of the Mishna, the Jerusalem and Babylonian Talmud, and the halakhic and aggadic midrashim, a heavenly city of the mind. Celebrating scholarship, "dispute for the sake of Heaven" (Ethics of the Fathers 5:21) and intense focus on the divine will as translated into halakha, they became co-architects with the Torah itself of the rich, variegated and intensely detailed universe of Jewish law. Thus Jewry survived, despite persecutions, expulsions, and occasional sectarian schisms, until the late eighteenth century.

It was an astonishing achievement. The rabbis achieved what no other leadership group has done in all of religious history. They had shaped a way of life capable of surviving in the most adverse environments, turning every setback into a catalyst for new creativity. It was they who spoke of Shavuot as *zeman matan torateinu*, the "time of the giving of our Law (Torah)," the anniversary of the revelation and covenant at Mount Sinai.

Life is lived forward but understood only backward, in retrospect. It was in the aftermath of the two great historical catastrophes, the Babylonian conquest and the failed rebellion against Rome, that the nature of Jewish history became clear. *The law did not exist for the sake of the land.* It was the other way round: *the land existed for the sake of the law.* It was in order that the Israelites should create a sacred society of justice and compassion that God gave Israel the land. You do not need a territorial base to encounter God in the private recesses of the soul, but you do

◀ need a land

need a land to create a society in which the Divine Presence is real in the public square.

It was only when they lost the land but knew they still had the Torah that Jews fully realized that this is what Shavuot had been about from the very beginning.

THE DAY OF COVENANT

There is evidence that Shavuot was, from the outset, the anniversary of the giving of the Torah.

First, on all the several views as to the date of Shavuot, it took place in the third month, and there is only one significant event in the Torah that happened then. The Israelites arrived at the Sinai desert "on the third new moon" after they had left Egypt (Ex. 19:1). There then follows a series of exchanges between Moses and God, and Moses and the people, each of which involved ascending and descending the mountain. God then told Moses to tell the people to prepare for a revelation that would take place on the third day. Then we read, "On the third day, in the early morning – thunder and lightning; heavy cloud covered the mountain, there was a very loud sound of the shofar, and all of the people in the camp quaked" (Ex. 19:16). There are different ways of calculating the chronology of these events, but the revelation at Sinai clearly took place in the third month, and there is only one festival in the third month: Shavuot.

Nor can we doubt the centrality of the Sinai event. We can see this by the sheer space the Torah dedicates to it. The Israelites arrived at Sinai at the beginning of Exodus 19, and not until Numbers 10:11, "On the twentieth day of the second month of the second year," did they leave. *They spent less than a year at Sinai, but the Torah devotes approximately one third of its entire text to it,* while passing over thirty-eight of the forty wilderness years in silence other than to record the places where the Israelites stopped. It would be astonishing if this event were not commemorated in the Jewish calendar while a relatively minor feature of the wilderness years, the fact that the Israelites lived in *sukkot*, booths, has a seven-day festival dedicated to it.

There is other evidence. We read in the second book of Chronicles about how King Asa, after cleansing the land of idols, convened a national covenant renewal ceremony:

◄ They assembled

They assembled at Jerusalem *in the third month* of the fifteenth year of Asa's reign... They entered into a covenant to seek the LORD, the God of their ancestors, with all their heart and soul... They *took an oath* to the LORD with loud acclamation, with shouting and with trumpets and horns. All Judah rejoiced about the oath because they had sworn it wholeheartedly. They sought God eagerly, and He was found by them. So the LORD gave them rest on every side. (II Chronicles 15:10–15)

The fact that the ceremony was held in the third month suggests that it coincided with Shavuot, and that the festival itself was associated with the covenant at Mount Sinai. There is even a hint in the text of an early association between the word *Shavuot*, "weeks," and *shevua*, "oath," used here to mean commitment to the covenant.

Then there is the fascinating evidence of the Book of Jubilees. This is a text written in the middle of the second century BCE, author unknown but almost certainly a priest, which retells the whole of biblical history in terms of fifty-year, jubilee cycles. It was not accepted as part of Tanakh, but it occasionally records traditions unknown elsewhere, and that is the case here. According to Jubilees (6:15–19), Shavuot was first celebrated *by Noah* to celebrate the covenant God made with him, and through him with all humanity, after the flood. "For his reason it has been ordained and written on the heavenly tablets that they should celebrate the Festival of Weeks during this month, once a year, to renew the covenant each and every year" (6:17). Jubilees goes on to say that God made His covenant *with Abraham* on the same date in the third month (14:20). Thus there was an early tradition that held that Shavuot was supremely the covenant-making and renewal day for all three biblical covenants between God and human beings: with Noah, Abraham, and the Israelites in the days of Moses.

R. David Zvi Hoffman (*Commentary to Leviticus*, vol. 2, 158–168) adds that the rabbinical name for the festival – *Atzeret*, or in Aramaic, *Atzarta* – meaning "assembly" or "gathering," may be related to Moses' own description of the day the Torah was given as *Yom haKahal*, "the day of the assembly" (Deut. 9:10, 10:4, 18:16). He also suggests that the reason the Torah relates the festivals to historical events is simply to explain why we perform certain acts, such as sitting in a booth on Sukkot. Since Shavuot has no distinctive mitzva, it needed no historical explanation. As to why

◀ there is no

there is no distinctive mitzva on Shavuot, he argues that it is to emphasize that at Sinai the Israelites "saw no image; there was only a voice" (Deut. 4:12). There is no symbolic action that could capture the experience of hearing the voice of the invisible God.

Why then, if Shavuot is the anniversary of the covenant at Sinai, does it not have a fixed date in the calendar? The answer was set out by Nahmanides in his Commentary to the Torah (Lev. 23:36). The relationship between Shavuot and Pesaḥ, he says, is like that between Shemini Atzeret and Sukkot. In both cases there is a count of seven – seven days in the case of Sukkot, seven weeks in the case of Pesaḥ and the counting of the Omer – followed by a concluding festival. That is how he understands *Atzeret*, the name the Torah gives to the eighth day of Sukkot, and that the rabbis called Shavuot, deriving it from the verb ע-צ-ר meaning "stop, close, cease, conclude." Though both are festivals in their own right, both celebrate the end of something; they are not stand-alone celebrations. They are defined in terms of what went before.

Thus the days of counting the Omer between Pesaḥ and Shavuot are like Ḥol HaMo'ed, the intermediate days of a festival. *Pesaḥ and Shavuot are the beginning and end of a single extended festival.* That is why Shavuot is not given a date in the Jewish calendar because what matters is not what day of the week or month it falls but the fact that it marks the conclusion of the seven weeks initiated by the Omer. That, in fact, is why the Oral tradition held that the Omer begins not on a Sunday (the literal meaning of "the day following the rest day") but after the first day of Pesaḥ, because the Omer is not a free-standing institution but the start of a seven-week count linking Pesaḥ to Shavuot.

The nature of that link was stated at the very beginning of the exodus narrative, when Moses met God at the burning bush. God told Moses his mission and then said, *"And this will be the sign to you that it is I who have sent you: When you have brought the people out of Egypt, you will worship God on this mountain"* (Ex. 3:12). The exodus from Egypt, in other words, was only the beginning of a process that would reach its culmination when the people worshiped God at Mount Sinai.

Pesaḥ and Shavuot are inseparable. Revelation without the exodus was impossible. But exodus without revelation was meaningless. God did not bring the people out of Egypt only to leave them to the hazards of

◂ fate

fate. They were His people, "My child, My firstborn, Israel," as He told Moses to say to Pharaoh (Ex. 4:22).

Why then the forty-nine days? Maimonides and the *Zohar* give subtly different explanations. The *Zohar* (*Emor*, 97a) sees the giving of the Torah at Sinai as a marriage between God and the people. Just as a bride must purify herself by keeping seven "clean" days and then going to the *mikveh*, so the Israelites, defiled by the impurities of Egypt, had to keep seven "clean" weeks, each day purifying one of the forty-nine combinations of *sefirot*, the sacred emanations linking creation with God.

Maimonides says that since the giving of the Torah was anticipated by the Israelites as the supreme culmination of the exodus, they counted the days "just as one who expects his most intimate friend on a certain day counts the days and even the hours" (*Guide for the Perplexed*, III:43).

The most significant hint, though, lies in the name tradition gave to Pesaḥ: *zeman ḥeruteinu*, "the time of our freedom." Freedom in Judaism means more than release from slavery: individual freedom. It means law-governed liberty, "the rule of laws not men": collective freedom. Thus the Israelites did not achieve freedom on Pesaḥ when they left Egypt. They acquired it on Shavuot when, standing at the foot of the mountain, they accepted the covenant and became a holy nation under the sovereignty of God. That is why Pesaḥ and Shavuot are not two separate festivals but the beginning and end of a single stretch of time – the time it took for them to cease to be slaves to Pharaoh and to become instead the servants of God.

FORGETTING AND REMEMBERING

The real question is not when or why Shavuot became *zeman matan torateinu*, "the time of the giving of our Torah." It is, rather, why it ever ceased to be.

At the core of Israel's collective memory, at the heart of its self-definition, is the idea that faithfulness to the covenant at Sinai is its raison d'être and the key to its survival and flourishing. That is the moral of almost every book in Tanakh and the burden of all the prophets. They, especially Amos, Hosea, Isaiah and Jeremiah, told the people candidly and with great passion that faithlessness to God would lead to military defeat and political disaster. The closer this came, the more the prophets

◀ were ignored

were ignored, culminating with Jeremiah who was ridiculed, mocked, insulted, abused, sentenced to death and thrown into a pit for telling the people what they did not want to hear.

The story we read in Tanakh of the centuries in which the Israelites were in possession of the land, from the time of Joshua to the Babylonian conquest, is not a happy one. Time and again the people find themselves drawn to the local gods and to pagan practices, and this goes hand in hand with political corruption, the abuse of power, sharp practices in business and mistreatment of the poor. Amos speaks of those who "have sold for silver those whose cause was just, and the needy for a pair of sandals, trampling the heads of the poor into the dust of the ground" (Amos 2:6–7). Isaiah declares, "Your rulers are rogues and cronies of thieves, every one avid for presents and greedy for gifts; they do not judge the cause of the orphan and the widow's cause never reaches them" (Is. 1:23).

To be sure, there were reforming kings – among them Asa, Jehoshaphat, Hezekiah and Josiah – but the impression we receive is that their efforts, however well-intentioned, were too little, too late. Repeatedly in the narratives of Israel's and Judah's kings, we read the verdict that "he did evil in the eyes of the LORD." The overriding question that comes to mind when reading the Hebrew Bible is: why did the people so often ignore the warnings of the prophets, the teachings of Moses and the lessons of their own history? Isaiah well expresses this sense of amazement when he says, "An ox knows its owner, an ass its master's crib: Israel does not know, My people take no thought" (Is. 1:3). Animals know to whom they belong; Israel sometimes forgets.

It should be obvious from every syllable of Jewish history, the prophets say, that faith and fate, loyalty and liberty, go hand in hand. Yet the people continue to ignore the message. Ironically, one of the few instances in Tanakh where an entire people heeds the words of a prophet occurs in the book of Jonah, where the people concerned are Israel's enemies, the Assyrians in the military city of Nineveh.

Why was it so hard to persuade people that idolatry was their weakness and faith in the God of Abraham and the covenant of Sinai their strength? Because we are seeing history with hindsight. We have read the book. We know how it ends. At the time it did not seem that way at all.

One passage sheds light on the whole era of Israel's kings. It occurs

◀ in the book

in the book of Jeremiah. The prophet had been warning the people that they faced disaster. If they continued on their present course they would be conquered by the Babylonians and the result would be national catastrophe. So it happened. Jerusalem and Judah lay in ruins. Now, once again, he addresses the people, begging them finally to acknowledge their error and return to God. Defiantly, the people refuse:

> "We will not listen to the message you have spoken to us in the name of the LORD. We will certainly do everything we said we would: We will burn incense to the Queen of Heaven and will pour out libations to her just as we and our ancestors, our kings and our officials did in the towns of Judah and in the streets of Jerusalem. *At that time we had plenty of food and were well off and suffered no harm. But ever since we stopped burning incense to the Queen of Heaven and pouring out libations to her, we have had nothing and have been perishing by sword and famine."*
> (Jeremiah 44:16–18)

As far as the people were concerned, as long as they served idols (the Queen of Heaven was probably Ishtar, the Mesopotamian goddess of fertility, love and war), they prospered. When they stopped doing so (the reference is probably to the reforms of Josiah) they began to suffer. We need to let these words sink in.

There is no immediate short-term correlation between faithfulness to God and national success in the arena of history. That is the problem. Jeroboam II was one of the northern kingdom's most successful kings. He reigned for forty-one years and "restored the boundaries of Israel from Lebo Hamath to the Dead Sea" (II Kings 14:25). Yet he "did evil in the eyes of the LORD" (ibid. 24), perpetuating the sins of his namesake, Jeroboam son of Nebat. Manasseh, Hezekiah's son, reversed the religious reforms of his father and reintroduced idolatry into the kingdom, leading the people astray "so that they did more evil than the nations the LORD had destroyed before the Israelites" (II Kings 21:2). He is also said to have "shed so much innocent blood that he filled Jerusalem from end to end" (ibid. 16). Yet he ruled, apparently, successfully, for fifty-five years, while his grandson, Josiah, one of Tanakh's most righteous kings, died prematurely in battle.

◄ A contemporary

A contemporary observer would have understood why Jeremiah was unheeded, and why people resented the bad news he brought. The Talmud (*Sanhedrin* 102b) tells us that King Manasseh appeared to Rav Ashi in a dream. The rabbi had been about to deliver a lecture on how evil a king he had been. In the dream, the king said to the rabbi, "Had you been there at that time, in that place, you would have caught hold of my coat-tails and followed me." Only in retrospect does the truth of a prophet's words become apparent.

There is a technical name for this phenomenon: the J-curve effect. This says that the result of any necessary correction to a trend – from devaluing a currency to revolution against a repressive regime – will initially be negative and only subsequently positive. Things get worse before they get better. Psalm 92, the "song for the Sabbath day," tells us that the wicked grow like grass, the righteous like a tree. In the short term, evil flourishes, but not in the long. The essence of prophecy is that it is long term. While others are at ease, the prophet sees the coming cataclysm. While others are traumatized and grief-stricken, the prophet sees the distant consolation.

The prophet will always be at a disadvantage vis-à-vis the large cast of false prophets and flattering courtiers who tell rulers what they want, not what they need, to hear. The reply of the people to Jeremiah was, within its own terms, devastating. If you are looking for an immediate correlation between sanctity and success, repentance and reward, you will look in vain. That is the fact with which Israel's prophets wrestled for much of their lives. Bad things happen to good people, while evildoers flourish. That troubled Jeremiah and Job and all who sought to discern God's justice through the mists of history and circumstance.

For most of the biblical era, land seemed primary and law secondary. It was far easier, on Shavuot, to thank God for the fields and the food than for the Torah and its obligations and restraints. That is what makes the history of Shavuot so telling an insight into the state of the collective Jewish soul. It is one of the ironies of Jewish history that its most creative periods of spirituality occurred before they possessed the land, in the days from Abraham to Moses, or when they were exiled from it, after the Babylonian conquest, and then again after defeat at the hand of Rome.

◄ By contrast

By contrast, when they had both land and independence they tended to lapse into idolatry and civil strife. The era of the judges ended in chaos and civil war. In the age of monarchy, after the reign of a mere three kings, the kingdom split in two. The Hasmoneans, who had started as religious purists, soon became Hellenized and corrupt. Moses was right in his visionary speeches in Deuteronomy. The real challenge, he said, would not be slavery but freedom; not the privations of the wilderness but the affluence of home. As Paul Johnson put it in his *A History of the Jews*, "In self-government and prosperity, the Jews always seemed drawn to neighboring religions, whether Canaanite, Philistine-Phoenician or Greek. Only in adversity did they cling resolutely to their principles and develop their extraordinary powers of religious imagination, their originality, their clarity and their zeal."

It took the Babylonian exile to produce Ezra and Nehemiah, and the Roman conquest to yield Yoḥanan ben Zakkai and the academy at Yavneh. Only after a sequence of tragedies culminating in the defeat of the Bar Kokhba revolt and the ensuing Hadrianic persecutions, did the people hear again the original message of Shavuot, that it was not just about grain and first fruits, but about the way of life by which they had covenanted to live more than a thousand years before.

We who were born after the Holocaust know that Divine Providence is not always waiting in the wings, ready to intervene in history and save us from our enemies and ourselves. The connection between faith and fate is deeper and more demanding than that. What the prophets knew and the people sometimes forgot was that Israel is a small country in a region of large empires and brutal politics. Only if its people believe in something greater than themselves will they become stronger than themselves, which they will need to be to survive. Jews became the eternal people because of their faith in the eternal God. Without this, they would almost certainly have gone the way of their neighbors, the Canaanites, Jebusites and Perizzites, the Moabites and Edomites, and even great empires like Assyria and Babylon.

For this reason Shavuot was, for a long time, the hardest of festivals to appreciate. It was easy to celebrate the land, difficult to rejoice in the demanding covenant they had made with God when they had nothing but water from a rock, manna from heaven, and the desert as a home. Yet

◀ this always

this always was the source of their strength: that unforgettable moment at an otherwise unmemorable mountain, when God gave the people His word, and they gave Him theirs: "All that the LORD has spoken, we shall perform."

PEOPLE OF THE BOOK

There are moments when you can see an entire civilization reimagining itself. That is what happens in a Talmudic vignette about the life of King David (*Shabbat* 30b). Once, says the Talmud, David asked God to tell him when he would die. God refused to answer, saying that no one is granted this knowledge. "Then at least tell me," said David, "on which day of the week I will die." "You will die," said God, "on Shabbat." Thenceforth, every Shabbat, David spent the whole day in study.

When the scheduled moment came for him to die, the Angel of Death found him engaged in uninterrupted learning: "His mouth did not cease from study." As long as this continued, the angel discovered he had no power over him, so he devised a stratagem. He made a rustling sound in a nearby tree. Climbing a ladder to see what was making the noise, David slipped and fell. For a moment, as he was falling, no Torah came from his lips. At that moment, the angel took his soul and he died.

Simple though it is, this story tells us what had changed in Jewish life. For the rabbis David was no longer primarily the military hero, victor of Israel's greatest battles, or the astute politician, or even the man who initiated the plan to build the Temple. He had become a sage. The battles he fights are in the mind. His home has become a house of study.

David had become a new kind of symbol for an old-new people that no longer predicated itself on a land, a king, an army, a Temple, sacrifices and a priesthood, but lived instead in synagogues, schools and academies. So long as the Jewish people never stops studying, the story intimated, the Angel of Death has no power over it. Jews had become, in the most profound sense, people of the book, of Shavuot, of Sinai. Theophrastus, a pupil of Aristotle, called them "a nation of philosophers." In the first century, Josephus could write, "Should any one of our nation be asked about our laws, he will repeat them as readily as his own name. The result of our thorough education in our laws from the very dawn of intelligence is that they are, as it were, engraved on our souls."

◀ Ezra

Ezra and Nehemiah's public reading of the Torah had set in motion a profound change in Jewish life, one whose early details are hard to come by because of the shortage of literary materials from Jewish sources between the fourth and second centuries BCE. But we can take up the story with Shimon ben Sheṭaḥ in the first century BCE. Until then education had largely taken place within the family. Shimon ben Sheṭaḥ established the first national educational system in Israel, creating schools throughout the country for sixteen- and seventeen-year-olds. This was not entirely successful, and around 63–65 CE, Joshua ben Gamla established a more comprehensive structure, later described by the Talmud in these words:

> May the name of that man, Joshua ben Gamla, be blessed, because, were it not for him, the Torah would have been forgotten from Israel. For at first, if a child had a father, his father taught him, and if he had no father, he did not learn at all. ... They then made an ordinance that teachers of children should be appointed in Jerusalem... Even so, however, if a child had a father, the father would take him up to Jerusalem and have him taught there, and if not, he would not go up to learn there. They therefore ordained that teachers should be appointed in each prefecture, and that boys should enter school at the age of sixteen or seventeen. However, if the teacher punished them they used to rebel and leave the school. Eventually Joshua ben Gamla came and ordained that teachers of young children should be appointed in each district and each town, and that children should enter the school at the age of six or seven. (*Bava Batra* 21a)

This was the first system of its kind in the world. The Talmud also contains the world's first regulations about teacher provision and class size. As H.G. Wells noted in his *Outline of History*, "The Jewish religion, because it was a literature-sustained religion, led to the first efforts to provide elementary education for all children in the community." By contrast, universal compulsory education did not exist in England until 1870. There was nothing remotely similar in the ancient world. Even the great academies of ancient Greece were confined to an elite. Rabbinic Judaism set itself to achieve a society of universal literacy. Paul Johnson

◂ calls it

calls it an "ancient and highly efficient social machine for the production of intellectuals."

Quite how deeply the passion for education went can be seen in the following law. The Torah rules that someone found guilty of manslaughter was to be exiled to one of the Cities of Refuge. The rabbis ruled that *if a student is exiled, his teacher must go with him* – not because he shares in the blame, but because the Bible says that the exiled person shall live, "and *life without a teacher is not life*" (Maimonides, *Hilkhot Rotze'aḥ* 7:1 following *Makkot* 10a). When the fourth-century teacher Rava found one of his students late for class because he was praying slowly he said, "You are forsaking eternal life for the sake of life in the here-and-now" (*Shabbat* 10a). Study was a religious experience higher than prayer, because in prayer we speak to God, but in study we learn to hear God speaking to us.

To a degree unrivaled by any other culture, Jews became a people whose very survival was predicated on the school, the house of study, and life as a never-ending process of learning. A community that had made no provision for the Jewish education of its children, ruled the rabbis, was to be excommunicated until teachers have been appointed, because "the world only exists in virtue of the sound of children at their studies" (*Shabbat* 119b). When does the obligation to study begin? asks Maimonides, and answers, "As soon as a child can talk." When does it end? "On the day of death" (*Laws of Torah Study* 1:6, 10).

So, throughout the ages, Jewish communities made education their first priority. The fees of poorer children, and sometimes the salaries of teachers, were paid for by the community. The funds were raised by taxes, or obligatory contributions on being called to the Torah, or house-to-house collections. In twelfth-century France, Rabbeinu Tam ruled that where there was a shortage of funds for education, money designated for other purposes could be diverted to schools and teachers.

At a time when their neighbors were often illiterate, Jews lived a life devoted to study, and gave the seats of honor in the synagogue to scholars. A twelfth-century monk, one of Abelard's disciples, wrote that "A Jew, however poor, if he had ten sons, would put them all to letters, and not for gain as the Christians do, but for the understanding of God's law; and not only his sons but his daughters."

◄ The quality

The quality of education varied from country to country and from century to century, but until the modern era there was virtually no Jewish community, however small, without its own school and teachers. Benjamin of Tudela, traveling in Provence in 1165, could report that in Posquieres, a town of a mere forty Jews, there was a great yeshiva. Marseilles, whose Jewish population numbered three hundred, was "a city of *geonim* [outstanding scholars] and sages."

In fifteenth-century Spain, where Jews were facing constant persecution, the 1432 Valladolid Synod established taxes on meat and wine, circumcisions, weddings and funerals, to create a fund to establish schools in every community where there were fifteen householders.

In the *shtetl* (small township) in Eastern Europe, learning conferred prestige, status, authority and respect. Men of wealth were honored, but scholars were honored more. In their study of the *shtetl*, *Life is with People*, Zborowski and Herzog describe the impact this made on the Jewish family:

> The most important item in the family budget is the tuition fee that must be paid each term to the teacher of the younger boys' school. "Parents will bend the sky to educate their son." The mother, who has charge of household accounts, will cut the family food costs to the limit if necessary, in order to pay for her son's schooling. If the worst comes to the worst, she will pawn her cherished pearls in order to pay for the school term. The boy must study, the boy must become a good Jew – for her the two are synonymous.

These values had been part of Judaism from the beginning. In Genesis, God says of Abraham, "For I have chosen him, *so that he will instruct his children* and his household after him to keep the way of the LORD…" (Gen. 18:19). Abraham was chosen to be a father and a teacher. In two of the key passages of Jewish faith, the first and second paragraphs of the Shema, Moses placed education at the heart of Jewish life: "Teach them [these words] repeatedly to your children, speaking of them when you sit at home and when you travel on the way, when you lie down and when you rise" (Deut. 6:7). But it took crisis – defeat and exile – to bring this value back to the fore.

◄ Few have

Few have put more eloquently than Jacob Neusner what Jews remembered and Shavuot taught: "Civilization hangs suspended, from generation to generation, by the gossamer strand of memory. If only one cohort of mothers and fathers fails to convey to its children what it has learned from its parents, then the great chain of learning and wisdom snaps. If the guardians of human knowledge stumble only one time, in their fall collapses the whole edifice of knowledge and understanding."

In their darkest moments Jews rediscovered this ancient truth. It was the giving of the Torah at Sinai on the first Shavuot that proved to be the gift of eternity.

2. What Happened at Sinai?

The scene was terrifying. There was a storm: thunder and lightning. Thick cloud covered the mountain. Fire blazed. A shofar sounded. The mountain shook and the earth trembled. Something immense was about to happen. It seemed as if the world were shaking to its foundations. The event that day at Sinai when God revealed Himself to an entire people was a "singularity" – less an event in time than an event that transformed time. As Maimonides wrote: we struggle to understand it and fail because there was nothing to compare it to, before or since (*Guide for the Perplexed*, II:33).

Einstein taught that light – even time itself – is distorted, curved, as it travels in close proximity to the sun. Something like that can be observed in the Torah as it approaches the moment when a group of escaping slaves met God at a mountain in the desert, and there their destiny was born. Time slows almost to a standstill.

By contrast, the book of Genesis covers the whole of time past from the birth of the universe to the descent of Jacob's children to Egypt. Deuteronomy, the book of Moses' visions at the end of his life, charts time future from the Israelites' entry into the Promised Land to the furthermost horizon of their not-yet-written history. The first half of Exodus and the second half of Numbers track the Israelites' forty-year, forty-two-stage journey from Egypt to the bank of the Jordan. But their stay at Sinai takes up fifty-nine chapters, from Exodus 19 to Numbers 10, including the whole of Leviticus, despite the fact that they were there for less than a year. As an object accelerates toward the speed of light,

◄ time decelerates

time decelerates. So, judging by the metronome of biblical prose, it was at Sinai.

The descriptions of the giving of the Torah in Tanakh focus largely on externalities. "You came near and stood at the foot of the mountain while it blazed with fire to the very heavens, with black clouds and deep darkness" said Moses (Deut. 4:11). "The earth shook, the heavens poured, the clouds poured down water. The mountains quaked before the LORD," sang Deborah (Judges 5:4–5, see also Ps. 68:8–9). Yet, when something similar happened to Elijah centuries later, standing on the same mountain (1 Kings 19), the Bible makes it clear that God was not in the whirlwind or the earthquake or the fire but in a "still, small voice," a sound on the edge of silence (v. 12). As Moses himself emphasized, at Sinai, "You saw no image; there was only a voice" (Deut. 4:12).

What was unique, transfiguring and still hard to understand was that the nation, as a nation, heard the voice of God. God spoke – not just to a prophet, not in a vision or a trance, not as a sound within the soul but as an event in public space and time. As a brilliantly ambiguous phrase in Deuteronomy (5:19) puts it, it was a *kol gadol velo yasaf*, a great voice that was *never* heard again, and that was *ever* heard again (Rashi, ad loc.). It happened once but it reverberated for all time.

The rabbis debated as to exactly what the Israelites heard (*Shir Ha-Shirim Raba* 1:2:2; *Pesikta Rabbati* 22). Some said they heard all ten commands, others that they heard only the first two, yet others that they heard all ten but as a single burst of sound that Moses had to decode, word by word. Some said that they heard not only what was eventually written on the tablets of stone and set out in the Written Torah but also what the oral tradition would eventually infer from each word and phrase on the basis of its interpretive principles.

One thing, though, is clear from both the Exodus and Deuteronomy accounts. The sound was of almost unbearable intensity. The Israelites clamored around Moses begging him to ask God to stop: "You speak to us and we shall listen, but let God not speak to us, lest we die" (Ex. 20:16). When a voice from beyond the universe enters the universe the result is both terrifying and transformative. Yet though we cannot say what happened or how, we can at least hypothesize as to why. *The voice of Revelation was intimately related to the voice of Creation.* The God who

◄ said, "I

said, "I am the LORD your God, who brought you out of the land of Egypt, from the slave-house," was the God who said, "Let there be light," and there was light. To understand this, we have to go back to the beginning of the biblical account of humankind and ask why Judaism is a religion of holy words and God-given law.

The pagan cultures of ancient times and today's science-based atheism have one thing in common. They hold that all that exists is bounded by the physical, essentially material world of nature. The ancients spoke of the gods of the sun, the moon, the sea, the storm, the famine, the flood, the wind and the rain. Today scientists speak of the strong and weak nuclear force, cosmic antigravity, quantum fluctuations and the six mathematical constants that make the universe the size and shape it is. Where the ancients saw random, capricious fate, science sees the opposite: the ordered regularity of nature charted by cosmology, physics, chemistry and biology. But for neither is there a concept of *revelation*. What we know is, in the broadest sense, what we see. Reality is bounded by what we, given the current state of technology, can detect and measure.

Judaism, however, is about meaning, and meaning is something we hear, not see. It is about what makes us human, and why we behave the way we do, and why we so often destroy what is most precious. These are things that cannot be reduced to atoms, particles and forces. Judaism speaks, above all, of a monumental series of encounters between human beings and a reality beyond the quantifiable and predictable, a reality that is to the universe what the soul is to the body. The question of questions is therefore: how can we relate to something so utterly beyond us?

The biblical answer, astonishing in its beauty and simplicity, is that the meeting between us and God is like the meeting between two persons, myself and another. I can see your body but I cannot feel your pain. How then can I enter your world? Through words. You speak, I listen. I ask, you answer. We communicate. Language is the narrow bridge across the abyss between soul and human soul. So it is between us and the Soul of the universe. Revelation takes place through speech. That is what happened at Sinai. Infinity spoke and the world trembled. In the silence of the desert the Israelites heard the voice of God.

Why, if God spoke at the beginning of time, did He need to speak in the midst of time? The answer lies in what the Bible sees as the most

◄ fateful event

fateful event in the history of the world. God, having created a being in His image, gave it freedom. But the being He created was physical, and thus subject to desires that conflict with those of others. So began the long, bitter, brutal story of humankind.

God created order and gave humans freedom. Humans then proceeded to create chaos. That is the story of Adam and Eve, Cain and Abel and humanity before the Flood – a world of *freedom without order*. After the Flood, humans created empires that had social stability, but they did so by depriving others of their liberty. That is the biblical story from the Tower of Babel to the Egypt of the Pharaohs. The result was *order without freedom*. How then can order and freedom coexist? The whole of Judaism is an answer to that question, and all of Jewish history is a commentary to it.

The biblical answer is *law*: not physical, scientific law, the law of cause and effect that applies to mindless particles on a micro- or macro-scale, but moral, ethical and spiritual law: the law that speaks to human beings in full acknowledgment of their freedom. That is why God spoke at Sinai. Creating a mindless universe, implies the Torah, is easy. In Genesis, it takes a mere thirty-four verses. Creating a social order in which free human beings act justly and compassionately, is difficult. That is why the story of Sinai takes fifty-nine chapters. At the beginning of time God spoke the laws that frame the natural universe. At Sinai He spoke the laws that shape the moral universe, inviting the Israelites to construct a society that would serve as a pilot project for humanity as a whole.

The humans God addressed in the desert were liberated slaves. They knew what it was to be treated as less-than-fully-human. That was now behind them. God spoke – and it was essential that He did so not to an elite, but to everyone, men, women and children. He told them that though He was the God of all humanity ("the whole earth is Mine," Ex. 19:5), He was willing to risk His own profile in history by linking His name with theirs. He was offering them a covenant that if followed would – in priestly terminology – turn them into "a kingdom of priests and a holy nation" (Ex. 19:6). In prophetic language, He would "betroth them in righteousness and justice, loving-kindness and compassion" (Hos. 2:21). In the vocabulary of wisdom, He would give them statutes that would be their "wisdom and understanding in the eyes of the nations" (Deut. 4:6).

◄ For it is

For it is law, voluntarily accepted, conscientiously practiced, studied, meditated on, internalized, taught by parents to children across the generations, spoken of "when you sit at home and when you travel on the way, when you lie down and when you rise," a law transcending all earthly principalities and powers, that alone reconciles freedom and order. It is only by voluntary self-restraint, born of learned habits of law-abidingness, that we preserve our own freedom while at the same time extending it to others. That is what God spoke at Sinai.

What proof do we have that this really happened; that what the Israelites heard that day was indeed the voice of God? Religion is not science. The revelation of the One *beyond* space and time *within* space and time is not an empirical event demonstrable by experiment or describable within the normal parameters of history. Yet we are not without evidence. Among the unpublished papers found in his desk after he died in 1778, Jean-Jacques Rousseau left the following fragment:

But an astonishing and truly unique spectacle is to see an expatriated people, who have had neither place nor land for nearly two thousand years, a people mingled with foreigners, no longer perhaps having a single descendant of the early races, a scattered people, dispersed over the world, enslaved, persecuted, scorned by all nations, nonetheless preserving its characteristics, its laws, its customs, its patriotic love of the early social union, when all ties with it seem broken. The Jews provide us with an astonishing spectacle: the laws of Numa, Lycurgus, Solon are dead; the very much older laws of Moses are still alive. Athens, Sparta, Rome have perished and no longer have children left on earth; Zion, destroyed, has not lost its children.

They mingle with all the nations and never merge with them; they no longer have leaders, and are still a nation; they no longer have a homeland, and are always citizens of it... Any man whosoever he is, must acknowledge this as a unique marvel, the causes of which, divine or human, certainly deserve the study and admiration of the sages, in preference to all that Greece and Rome offer of what is admirable in the way of political institutions and human settlements. (Rousseau, *Cahiers de brouillons, notes et extraits*, no. 7843, Neuchâtel)

◀ The laws

The laws the Israelites received from God that day at Sinai did indeed become their "wisdom and understanding in the eyes of the nations." They transformed a small, fractious and otherwise undistinguished nation into a people who outlived empires and permanently enlarged the moral landscape of humankind.

TORAH FROM HEAVEN

The revelation at Mount Sinai was not just a religious event. It was a *political* event of a unique kind. It was the birth of a nation. Throughout Genesis, the heirs of Abraham had been an extended family. At the beginning of Exodus we hear them for the first time described as an *Am*, a "people." Pharaoh says, "Look, *the people of the children of Israel* are too many and powerful for us" (Ex. 1:9).

What made them a people were many things. There was kinship: they were all descendants of Jacob. There was culture: they were shepherds which made them suspect to the Egyptians. There was history: they were newcomers to the land, their origins lay elsewhere. Above all, there was shared suffering. Isaiah Berlin noted that it is usually a sense of an injustice done to one's people that is the crucible in which nations are formed. Israel became a people in Egypt, bound by *brit goral*, a covenant of shared fate.

At Sinai, however, they became an *eda*, a body politic. God invited them to become a "kingdom of priests... a holy nation" (Ex. 19:6) – the first mission statement of the Jewish people, perhaps the first of any nation anywhere. The covenant they agreed to then became their written constitution as citizens in the republic of faith under the sovereignty of God.

It is the last phrase that is crucial here: "under the sovereignty of God." It is sometimes thought that the Ten Commandments were a moral revolution in humankind. This is not so in the sense usually understood. It did not take divine revelation to tell humans that they must not murder, or rob, or give false testimony in court. Humans have always known this. Cain was punished by God for killing his brother Abel, but God had not yet commanded, "Do not murder." Every rational moral rule has been binding on humans since they first appeared on earth, said Rabbeinu Nissim (*Derashot HaRan* 1). It is not here that the originality of Sinai lies.

◀ It lies

It lies in something deeper. *The Torah is a sustained critique of the abuse of power.* It is a response to and a reaction against the world's first empires, those of Akkad under Sargon (c.2334 to 2279 BCE, see Gen. 10:8–10) and Egypt under the Pharaohs, where whole populations could be enslaved to further the self-aggrandizing projects ordered by rulers to ensure their earthly and heavenly immortality.

In the ancient world, politics and religion were inseparably intertwined. The head of state was also head of the religion and regarded as semi-divine. Power was projected in the form of monumental buildings, ziggurats, pyramids, palaces, temples and royal tombs. Akkadian kings were identified with the god of their city-state. The Pharaohs were regarded as deities in their lifetime and worshiped after their death. In Babylon, the king was the earthly equivalent of the god Marduk who had established order by his victory over Tiamat, the goddess of chaos. Among the Hittites, the king was high priest and on his death joined the gods. Isaiah speaks caustically about an Assyrian ruler who imagines that "I will ascend to the heavens; I will raise my throne above the stars of God… I will make myself like the Most High" (Is. 14:13–14).

What underwrote such cultures was cosmological myth. There was hierarchy in the heavens – the sun ruled the sky. There was hierarchy in the forest – the lion ruled the beasts. So there was hierarchy in society. Some were born to rule, others to be ruled. That alone is how order is sustained. The Torah is a protest against this entire view of the human condition, on two grounds: first, it turns some people into gods; second, it turns others, the majority, into slaves. The Torah's first and most decisive statement on the subject appears in its opening chapter when it says that God created human beings in His image and likeness (Gen. 1:26–27). All humans, not just rulers, carry within them the image of God, but no human is a god. At best, we – and everyone else – are in His image. There is and must be an absolute boundary between heaven and earth, God and humankind. That, above all, applies to power.

The idea that one human being should exercise power over others is a profound insult to the human condition. This was the sin of Nimrod, instigator of the Tower of Babel according to the Midrash. This is how John Milton describes him in *Paradise Lost*:

◄ O execrable

O execrable son! so to aspire
Above his brethren; to himself assuming
Authority usurped, from God not given:
He gave us only over beast, fish, fowl,
Dominion absolute; that right we hold
By his donation; but man over men
He made not lord; such title to himself
Reserving, human left from human free. (Book XII, lines 64–71)

No human has the right to rule over others against their will. That is what the judge and military hero Gideon meant when the people asked him to become their king. He replied, "I will not rule over you nor will my son rule over you. God will rule over you" (Judges 8:23).

That is what Sinai was about. What the people agreed to was that God alone would be their king, legislator, law-giver. This is the principle known in the rabbinic literature as *kabbalat ol malkhut shamayim*, "acceptance of the yoke of the kingship of heaven." According to the sages, it is what we are doing when we say the first paragraph of the Shema. It is an oath of allegiance to God: "Listen, Israel, the LORD is our God, the LORD alone." Or as we say in the prayer *Avinu Malkenu*, "We have no king but You." The Israelites became "one nation under God."

This is the core meaning of the idea of *Torah min hashamayim*, "Torah from heaven." Later, under the impact of Second Temple sectarianism, then of Christianity and Islam, all of which challenged the Jewish understanding of Scripture, it came to mean much else besides, but its basic meaning is simply this: all law – Torah – comes from God. He is Israel's sole law-giver.

This is what Moses meant when he said: "See: I have taught you rules and laws as the LORD my God has commanded me… What great nation has decrees and laws as perfect as all this Torah that I am setting before you today?" (Deut. 4:5–8). It is what the psalmist means when he says, "He has declared His word to Jacob, His statutes and laws to Israel. He has done this for no other nation; such laws they do not know" (Ps. 147:19–20). Other nations had their gods to whom they prayed, but only Israel had God, not a human being, as their head of state and sole

◀ legislative

legislative authority. Only when kingship is in heaven can there be equality of dignity on earth.

To be sure, in practical terms, this principle came under strain. For several centuries after their entry into the land, Israel was led, temporarily at times of war, by charismatic leaders known as judges, but the book of Judges ends on a negative note. The nation was sliding into social and moral decline. The people came to Samuel, asking him to appoint a king. Reluctantly and at God's bidding, he did so.

Monarchy gave rise to two radically different schools of thought within Judaism. Some saw it as an ideal, especially in the person of David, and later after the experience of exile, in the idea of the Messiah, a Davidic king who would restore Israel's glory and usher in an era of peace (Maimonides, *Laws of Kings* ch. 11). Others were deeply critical of it, precisely because in principle Israel should have no other king but God. In the midrashic work *Devarim Raba* (5:8–11), as well as the medieval commentaries of Ibn Ezra, Rabbeinu Baḥya and Abrabanel, monarchy was seen as a concession to human weakness and the people's wish to be "like all the nations around" (Deut. 17:14). The book of Samuel records God as saying, when the people first asked for a king, "It is Me they have rejected as their King." (I Sam. 8:7).

On either view, however, monarchy as portrayed in Tanakh was unique in the ancient world. First, *the king had no legislative power*. He could institute temporary measures in response to the needs of the time, but not make permanently binding law. Second, *the king had no special status in the religious sphere*. He was not even a priest, let alone chief intermediary with God. Henri Frankfurt, in *Kingship and the Gods*, noted that "The relationship between the Hebrew monarch and his people was as nearly secular as possible in a society wherein religion is a living force." Michael Walzer noted that even in the biblical account of David, the almost-ideal king, "there is no hint of the conventional magnifications of monarchy: no mysteries of state, no divine descent, no royal magic, no healing touch." Third, *kings could be criticized*, by the prophets and by the biblical text itself. There is no parallel for any of this in the ancient world.

Israel was not the only ancient nation to have laws. They all did. Some became famous, for instance the Sumerian Code of Ur-Nammu and the Babylonian Code of Hammurabi. But these were edicts of the king.

◀ Justice

Justice was a common value in the ancient Near East, but the idea that this was the domain of the gods would have struck people as absurd. The gods were capricious, quarrelsome, and did not like human beings at all. As Shakespeare put it in *King Lear*, "Like flies to the wanton boys are we to the gods. They kill us for their pleasure."

In Judaism, law comes from God alone. *Torah min hashamayim*: law is made in heaven. Kings, priests, prophets and sages were empowered to interpret the law and in some cases make enactments to safeguard it, but not to make it or annul it. All earthly authority is subject to the law: this is the basic principle of human equality and the foundation of a free society.

That is what happened at Sinai. Accepting the covenant, the Jewish people became a nation under the direct sovereignty of God, with no other legislative authority. All law, to be valid, must be traceable back to Sinai and the voice of God. There was nothing like this before and – as we saw in the quotation from Rousseau – it survived all vicissitudes of Jewish history. At Sinai God gave the people the gift of law, and it became their constitution of liberty.

SOCIAL COVENANT, SOCIAL CONTRACT

At Sinai, a new kind of politics was born.

From Plato's *Republic* to modern times, political philosophy has focused on power and the state. Judaism has its own theory of the state, but it also has a *political theory of society*, something rare in the history of thought, and to this day a vision unsurpassed in its simplicity and humanity.

The theory of the state and the role of power is signaled in Deuteronomy and described in detail in the book of Samuel. It is about the appointment of a king. We saw in the previous chapter why Judaism is ambivalent about this. Ideally the Israelites should have no other king but God. Nonetheless, God tells Samuel not to refuse to appoint a king but rather to warn the people the high price they will have to pay. Samuel does so. The king, he warns, will take their sons and daughters for his service, appropriate their property for his own use, and much else besides. "When that day comes you will cry out for relief from the king you have chosen, and the LORD will not answer you in that day" (1 Sam. 8:18). The people nonetheless insist: they still want a king. God grants permission, and

Samuel duly anoints Saul. Israel becomes a monarchy. For the first time it has a unified, central government.

Commentators have long been puzzled by the biblical approach to monarchy. If it is disapproved of, why is there a command in the Torah to appoint a king (Deut. 17:14–15)? If it is approved of, why did God say that, in asking for a king, the people were rejecting Him (1 Sam. 8:7)? And why does He tell Samuel to warn the people? A brilliantly simple answer, given by Rabbi Zvi Hirsch Chajes (1805–1855) in his *Torat Nevi'im*, is that Samuel was proposing what Hobbes and Rousseau called a *social contract*.

The idea behind it is this. Without a central power capable of enforcing the rule of law and the defense of the realm, a nation is at risk, internally of anarchy, externally of defeat by a foreign power. Under these circumstances, the people may seek a central power vested with the authority to achieve these ends. But this power can only be brought into being if the people are prepared to hand over certain of their rights of property and liberty so that the king can levy taxes and recruit an army. There is a transfer of rights and powers from the individual to the state. This carries with it the risk that the power thus created will become tyrannical and corrupt. That is the equation Samuel sets out. God gives the people the right to be governed this way, so long as they do so freely and in full knowledge of the price and risk. The Israelites agreed, as Hobbes thought rational individuals always would. Without a central government, which in those days meant a king, life and liberty would be difficult to defend.

It is no accident that this theory, the foundation of modern politics, made its first appearance in the Hebrew Bible – because it was there that the key ideas emerged of the sanctity of life, the dignity of the individual, the integrity of private property and the insistence on freedom as the basis of society. For the first time, no power of one person over another – even a king over his subjects – could be taken as part of the natural order. The biblical revolution was that *no* human hierarchies are self-justifying. Ideally a society should be comprised of free citizens, all equally under the sovereignty of God. All earthly power structures, therefore, are necessary evils. None is written into the fabric of the universe, and none is good in itself.

◄ Yet what

Yet what made the politics of the Hebrew Bible unique was not its theory of the *state* in the days of Samuel, but rather its conception of *society*, which came into existence centuries before, at Mount Sinai. The difference was fundamental. The state was created by a *social contract* among the people. The *eda*, the society, was created by a *social covenant* between the people and God. That is what God proposed and the people accepted at Sinai on the first Shavuot. It was an event unique in the religious history of humankind.

The *outward form* of the agreement was nothing new. Covenants or treaties were a familiar feature of the ancient Near East. Genesis records several such treaties. Abraham made one with Avimelekh, king of Gerar, at Be'ersheva (Gen. 21:27–32). So did Isaac (Gen. 26:28–31). Jacob did so with Laban (Gen. 31:44–54). Besides, God had already made covenants with Noah (Gen. 9) and Abraham (Gen. 17).

What was new at Sinai has become clearer in the light of the discovery in the mid-twentieth century of engraved records of ancient Mesopotamian treaties, among them the "Stele of the Vultures" commemorating the victory of Eannatum, ruler of Lagash in southern Mesopotamia, over the people of Umma, and that of Naram-Sin, king of Kish and Akkad, with the ruler of Elam. Both date from the third millennium BCE, that is to say, before the time of Abraham.

These treaties are of two kinds: between parties of roughly equal power ("parity treaties") and those between a strong one – what today we would call a superpower – and a weak one. These latter are known as "suzerainty treaties", *suzerain* meaning the dominant power in a particular region. The Sinai covenant between God and the Israelites was a suzerainty treaty. Three features, though, made it unique.

First is the fact that *one of the parties was God Himself.* This would have been unintelligible to Israel's neighbors, and remains extraordinary even today. The idea that God might bind Himself to human beings, linking their destiny to His, making them His ambassadors – His "witnesses" – to the world, is still radical and challenging.

Second, the other party to the covenant was not, as it invariably was in the ancient world, a king or ruler, but *the people as a whole.* Their collective participation was essential. It is a point the Torah repeatedly emphasizes: "*All the people* responded as one" (Ex. 19:8); "*All the people* responded

◀ with one

with one voice" (24:3). In the Hebrew text, the phrase "the people" appears seventeen times in Exodus 19 (the covenant proposed), and five times in Exodus 24 (the covenant accepted). This is not democracy in the modern sense, but it is the basis of what Michael Walzer calls "Israel's almost-democracy," and it had lasting implications.

It meant that every Israelite, as party to the covenant, was co-responsible with the people as a whole for its being kept. From this flowed the rabbinic idea of *kol Yisrael arevin zeh lazeh*, "all Jews are responsible for one another" (Rashi, Lev. 26:37 following *Shevuot* 39a), as well as the much later American idea of "We, the people." *It meant that the basis of social order in Judaism is not power but collective responsibility.* Power belongs to God. Responsibility belongs to us.

This meant that every Jew had to know the law and teach it to his or her children. Each had to know the story of his or her people, reciting it at key religious moments in the year. This is covenant politics, based not on hierarchical power but on a shared sense of history and destiny. It is a moral politics, dedicated to creating a just and gracious society honoring the dignity of all, especially the downtrodden, the poor, the powerless and the marginal: the widow, the orphan and the stranger.

The third key feature was God's insistence that Moses had first to secure the people's assent before the revelation could take place. This was essential, for the Bible portrays God not as an overwhelming force but as a constitutional monarch. The supreme power makes space for human freedom. *There is no justified government without the consent of the governed, even if the Governor is Creator of heaven and earth.* The people agree three times (Ex. 19:8; 24:3, 7). Thus the Judaic basis of a free society is not democracy as such. The rule of the majority can lead, as it has many times, to tyranny and the persecution of minorities. Freedom, in Judaism, is based on the consent of the governed and the overarching authority of God-given rules of justice. These establish the moral limits of power.

What happened at Sinai was a covenant, not a contract. Contracts are made between individuals on the basis of self-interest. A contract creates a limited partnership for mutual gain. A covenant creates a more enduring bond of mutual commitment and loyalty. Partners to a covenant have more than self-interest at stake. They have *shared* interests. A covenant

◄ relationship

relationship is one in which the parties come together, each respecting the freedom and dignity of the other, to create together something that neither could achieve alone – love, friendship, loyalty, communication, trust. Covenants create not personal gain but *the common good*, meaning things that only exist in virtue of being shared.

For the Bible the key example of a covenant is marriage, understood as a *bond of identity* between husband and wife. A marriage is held together not by power or mutual advantage but by a moral bond of love and fidelity. Virtually all the prophets compare the bond between God and Israel to a marriage. The significance of Sinai is that, long before the Israelites had a state, they had a society, and they did so because they had a social covenant before they had a social contract. That is why, uniquely, Jews remained a nation even in exile and dispersion. Though they had lost their state, they still had their *eda*, their community of faith. Though they had lost the land, they still had the law.

THE TEN UTTERANCES

What the Israelites heard at Sinai has become known as the "Ten Commandments." But this description raises obvious problems. First, neither the Torah nor Jewish tradition calls them the Ten Commandments. The Torah calls them *aseret hadevarim* (Ex. 34:28), and tradition terms them *aseret hadibrot*, meaning "the ten utterances." Second, there was much debate, especially between Maimonides and Nahmanides, as to whether the first verse, "I am the LORD your God ...," is a command or a preface to the commands (see commentary on page 411). Third, there are not ten commandments in Judaism but 613. Why, then, these but not those?

Light has been shed on all these issues by the discovery, already mentioned, of ancient Near-Eastern suzerainty treaties, most of which share certain features and forms. They begin with a preamble stating who is initiating the covenant. That is why the revelation opened with the words, "I am the LORD your God." Then comes a historical review stating the background and context of the covenant, in this case, "who brought you out of the land of Egypt, from the slave-house."

Next come the stipulations, first in general outline, then in specific detail. That is precisely the relationship between the "ten utterances" and

◀ the detailed

the detailed commands set out in later chapters and books of the Torah. The former are the general outline; the latter, the details. So the "ten utterances" are not commandments as such but an articulation of basic principles. What makes them special is that they are simple and easy to memorize. That is because in Judaism, law is not intended for judges alone. The covenant at Sinai was made by God with an entire people. Hence the need for a brief statement of basic principles that everyone could remember and recite.

Usually they are portrayed as two sets of five, the first dealing with relationships between us and God (including honoring our parents since they, like God, brought us into being), the second with the relations between us and our fellow humans. However, it also makes sense to see them as three groups of three.

The first three – No other gods besides Me, no sculptured images, and no taking of God's name in vain – are about God, the Author and Authority of the laws. The first states that divine sovereignty transcends all other loyalties (No other gods besides Me). The second tells us that God is a living force, not an abstract power (No sculptured images). The third states that sovereignty presupposes reverence (Do not take My name in vain).

The second three – the Sabbath, honoring parents, and the prohibition of murder – are all about the principle of *the createdness of life*. Shabbat is the day dedicated to seeing God as Creator, and the universe as His creation. Honoring parents acknowledges our human createdness. "Do not murder" restates the central principle of the Noahide covenant that murder is not just a crime against man but a sin against God in whose image we are created. So the fourth, fifth and sixth commands form the basic jurisprudential principles of Jewish life. They tell us to remember where we came from if we seek to know how to live.

The third three – against adultery, theft and bearing false witness – establish the basic institutions on which society depends. Marriage is sacred because it is the human bond closest in approximation to the covenant between us and God. The prohibition against theft establishes the integrity of property, which John Locke saw as one of the bases of a free society. Tyrants abuse property rights. The prohibition of false testimony is the precondition of justice. A just society needs more than a structure

◄ of laws

of laws, courts and enforcement agencies. It also needs basic honesty on the part of us all. There is no freedom without justice, and no justice without each of us accepting individual and collective responsibility for truth-telling.

Finally comes the stand-alone prohibition against envying your neighbor's house, wife, slave, maid, ox, donkey, or anything else belonging to him or her. This seems odd if we think of the "ten words" as commands, but not if we think of them as the basic principles of a free society.

The greatest challenge of any society is how to contain the universal phenomenon of envy: the desire to have what belongs to someone else. Rene Girard, in *Violence and the Sacred*, argued that the primary driver of human violence is mimetic desire, that is, the desire to have what someone else has, which is ultimately the desire to be what someone else is. Envy can lead to breaking many of the other commands: it can move people to adultery, theft, false testimony and even murder. It led Cain to murder Abel, made Abraham and Isaac fear for their lives because they were married to beautiful women, and led Joseph's brothers to hate him and sell him into slavery. It was envy of their neighbors that led the Israelites often to imitate their religious practices and worship their gods.

So the prohibition of envy is not odd at all. It is the most basic force undermining the social harmony and order that are the aim of the Ten Commandments as a whole. Not only though do they forbid it; they also help us rise above it. It is precisely the first three commands, reminding us of God's presence in history and our lives, and the second three, reminding us of our createdness, that help us rise above envy.

We are here because God wanted us to be. We have what God wanted us to have. Why then should we seek what others have? If what matters most in our lives is how we appear in the eyes of God, why should we seek anything else merely because someone else has it? It is when we *stop* defining ourselves in relation to God and start defining ourselves in relation to other people that competition, strife, covetousness and envy enter our minds, and they lead only to unhappiness.

Thirty-three centuries after they were first given, the Ten Commandments remain the simplest, shortest guide to the creation of a good society.

◀ *3. Ruth*

3. Ruth: the Book of Loyalty and Love

The story of Ruth is one of the most beautiful in the Bible. It begins in dislocation and grief. Famine leads Elimelekh, together with his wife Naomi and their two sons, to leave their home in Bethlehem, Judah, to go to Moab to find food. There, the sons marry Moabite women, but all three men die, leaving Naomi and her two daughters-in-law childless widows. Naomi decides to return home, and Ruth, who had married her son Maḥlon, insists on going with her. There, in Bethlehem, in a field at harvest time, Ruth meets a relative of Naomi's, Boaz, who acts kindly towards her. Later at Naomi's suggestion, Ruth asks him to act the part of a kinsman-redeemer. Boaz does so, and he and Ruth marry and have a child. The book that begins with death ends in new life. It is a story about the power of human kindness to redeem life from tragedy, and its message is that out of suffering, if transformed by love, can come new life and hope.

The book itself is a literary masterpiece. It owes much of its vividness to the fact that of all books of the Hebrew Bible it has the highest proportion of direct speech to descriptive narrative: fifty-five of its eighty-five verses are in dialogue form. Its four chapters are structured as a chiasmus, a mirror-image symmetry, so that, for example, the end with its account of births and genealogies mirrors the beginning with its recitation of deaths and childlessness. It is held together by a series of key words and recurring themes, among them "return," "redemption," and "blessing." Seven times people bless one another in the book, sustaining the sense that divine providence is at work beneath the surface of events. Not always but often, good things happen to good people, even if they take time.

The practice of reading a megilla on a festival began with the book of Esther on Purim despite the fact that the book itself was one of the last to be canonized. The reason is that without it, there would be no festival. The book records the events the festival commemorates as well as explaining its basic practices. The Talmudic tractate dealing with the day is called not Purim but Megilla. During the Mishnaic and Talmudic period, if you used the word megilla, you meant the book of Esther. Also early was the custom of reading Lamentations on Tisha B'Av: the book of grief on the day of grief.

The custom of reading Song of Songs on Pesaḥ, Ruth on Shavuot

◄ and Ecclesiastes

and Ecclesiastes on Sukkot came later – first mentioned in the tractate of *Soferim* (14:16), dating to the seventh or eighth century. The commentators make two primary connections between Ruth and Shavuot. The first is seasonal. The key events in the book are set during the barley and wheat harvests, the time of the counting of the Omer and Shavuot itself. The second is substantive. Ruth became the paradigm case of a convert to Judaism, and to become a convert you have to enter the covenant of Sinai with its life of the commands: what the Israelites did when they accepted the Torah on the first Shavuot.

There is, though, a deeper dimension. Reading a megilla on the three pilgrimage festivals sets up a field of tensions and associations that function as a profound commentary on the festival itself. They add depth and drama to the day.

All three megillot read on the pilgrimage festivals are about love: the stages of love as we experience it in our growth from youth to maturity to old age. The Song of Songs, read on Pesaḥ, the festival of spring, is about love in the spring: the passion between two lovers that has nothing in it of yesterday or tomorrow but lives in the overwhelming intensity of today. The book is structured as a series of duets between beloved and lover, their voices freighted with desire. There is nothing in it about courtship, marriage, home-building and having children: the world of adult responsibilities. The lovers long simply to be together, to elope.

Ecclesiastes, or Kohelet, read on Sukkot, the festival of autumn, is about love in the autumn of life, as the heat cools, light fades, the leaves fall, and clouds begin to hide the sun. "Live well, with the woman you love," says Kohelet (9:9). This is love as companionship, and it is rich in irony. Kohelet is written as the autobiography of King Solomon, the man who married seven hundred wives and three hundred concubines (I Kings 11:3), and in the end concluded, "And this is what I found: woman is more bitter than death, for she is all traps, with nets laid in her heart; her arms are a prison" (Eccl. 7:26). A thousand wives will not bring you happiness. Faithfulness to one, will.

Ruth is about the love at the heart of Judaism, the love of summer, when the passion of youth has been tamed and the clouds of age do not yet cover the sky. Ruth is about love as loyalty, faithfulness, committing yourself to another in a bond of responsibility and grace. It is about caring

◂ for the other

for the other more than you care about yourself. It is about Ruth setting her own aspirations aside to care for her mother-in-law Naomi, bereaved as she is of her husband and two sons. It is what Boaz does for Ruth. The root א-ה-ב, "love," which appears eighteen times in the Song of Songs, appears in Ruth only once. By contrast, the words ḥesed, loving-kindness, and the verb ג-א-ל, "to redeem," do not appear at all in the Song of Songs, but figure in Ruth respectively three and twenty-four times.

The megillot are framing devices that force us into seeing the festivals themselves in a new light. When we read Song of Songs on Pesaḥ it transforms our understanding of the exodus from a political event, the liberation of slaves, into an elopement and honeymoon, which is precisely how the prophets portray it. The book reminds us of the exodus as Jeremiah saw it when he said, "I remember of you the kindness of your youth, your love when you were a bride; how you walked after Me in the desert, through a land not sown" (Jer. 2:2).

Kohelet turns Sukkot into a philosophical reflection on the sukka as a symbol of mortality, the body as a temporary dwelling. It is the sobering story of how Solomon, wisest of men, sought to deny death by taking refuge in possessions, wives, servants and worldly wisdom, yet at every step he found himself face to face with the brevity and vulnerability of life: "the shallowest breath, it is all but breath" (1:2). Only at the end did he discover that joy is to be found in simple things: life itself, dignified by work and beautified by love.

Ruth likewise invites us to reframe Shavuot, seeing the making of the covenant at Sinai not simply as a religious or political act, but as an act of love – a mutual pledge between two parties, committing themselves to one another in a bond of responsibility, dedication and loyalty. The covenant at Sinai was a marriage between God and the children of Israel. That is how the prophets saw it.

Ezekiel does so using an image drawn from the book of Ruth itself. Ruth, at night, lying at Boaz's feet, asks him to spread his mantle over her (Ruth 3:9). That, says Ezekiel, is what God did for Israel: "'Later I passed by, and when I looked at you and saw that you were old enough for love, I spread the corner of My garment over you and covered your naked body. I gave you My solemn oath and entered into a covenant with you, declares the Sovereign LORD, and you became Mine" (Ezek. 16:8).

◀ It fell

It fell to the prophet Hosea to retell the story of the covenant as an act of love and marriage in wondrous words that Jewish men say each weekday morning as they put on the strap of the tefillin:

> I will betroth you to Me forever;
> I will betroth you to Me in righteousness and justice, loving-kindness and compassion;
> I will betroth you to Me in faithfulness;
> and you shall know the LORD. (Hos. 2:21–22)

The covenant at Sinai was a bond of love whose closest analogue in Tanakh is the relationship between Boaz and Ruth.

One of the most sustained libels in religious history was Christianity's claim that Judaism was a religion not of love but of law; not of compassion but of justice; not of forgiveness but of retribution. The book of Ruth, read on Shavuot, is the refutation. Judaism is a religion of love, three loves: loving God with all our heart, our soul and our might (Deut. 6:5); loving our neighbor as ourselves (Lev. 19:18); and loving the stranger because we know what it feels like to be a stranger (Deut. 10:19).

Judaism is, from beginning to end, the story of a love: the love of God for a small, powerless and much afflicted people, and the love of a people – tempestuous at times to be sure – of a people for God. That is the story of Ruth: love as faithfulness, loyalty and responsibility, and as a marriage that brings new life into the world. That is the love that was consecrated at Sinai on the first Shavuot of all.

THE PERSONAL AND THE POLITICAL

About two biblical books, the sages asked, why were they written? One is Ruth, about which Rabbi Zeira said: "This scroll contains no laws about impurity or purity, forbidden or permitted. Why then was it written? To show how great is the reward of those who perform acts of kindness" (*Rut Raba* 2:14). The other is Genesis. Rashi begins his commentary to the Torah with almost the same question. Why, if the Torah is a book of law, does it begin with creation and the early history of humankind? It should begin with the first law given to the Israelites, which does not appear until the twelfth chapter of Exodus.

Ruth and Genesis have much else in common. In both, "there was a famine in the land." What happened to Elimelekh in the beginning of Ruth, a famine that forced him to leave home, happens four times in Genesis: twice to Abraham, once to Isaac and once to Jacob. In both books, future marriage partners meet as strangers, apparently by chance, in a public place. What happened to Ruth and Boaz happens twice in Genesis, when Abraham's servant encounters Rebecca, and when Jacob meets Rachel.

One passage in particular drives the connection home. In their first encounter amid the alien corn, Boaz says to Ruth: "I have heard what you have done for your mother-in-law, since your husband died; *of how you left your father, your mother, the land of your birth* and came to a people you knew not the day before" (Ruth 2:11). The echo is unmistakable. We are immediately reminded of God's call to Abraham, the first recorded syllables of Jewish time: "*Leave your land, your birthplace and your father's house*, and go to the land that I will show you" (Gen. 12:1). Ruth is portrayed as a female equivalent of Abraham.

To be sure, there are differences. Abraham is responding to a call from God, Ruth to a moral imperative. Yet both are leaving behind all they know: their family, their friends, their country and culture, and both have the courage to journey to a place where they will be seen as strangers, outsiders, aliens. Both, too, are among the Bible's supreme exemplars of ḥesed, love as kindness and as deed.

More substantively, both Genesis and Ruth are preludes, introductions to a new chapter in the history of Israel. The book of Ruth, in its opening and closing words, positions itself precisely within the biblical story. It begins, "Once, in the days when the Judges judged." It ends with the birth of Oved, father of Yishai, father of David, Israel's second and greatest king. The book is a connecting link between two distinct periods of Jewish history, the era of the judges and that of kings. It functions as a preface to the first book of Samuel, which tells of how Israel's monarchy was born. There is even a subtle verbal connection between the two. In the last chapter of Ruth, the townspeople say to Naomi that her daughter-in-law "is better to you than seven sons could be" (Ruth 4:15). In the first chapter of the book of Samuel, Elkanah says to his wife Hannah, "Am I not better to you than ten sons?" (1 Sam. 1:8). The echo connects the two books.

◂ Genesis

Genesis, too, is a prelude, in this case to the story of Israel as a people, its exile and enslavement and its liberation by the hand of God. We can now state the connection between the two books. Genesis is a prelude to the birth of Israel as a *nation*. Ruth is a prelude to the birth of Israel as a *kingdom*. Together the two books make an immensely consequential statement of *the primacy of the personal over the political*.

The Hebrew Bible is largely about politics: kings and their battles, society and its tensions, and the relationship between Israel and neighboring powers. However, Tanakh does not see politics as an end in itself. In this it differs fundamentally from the civic culture of ancient Greece and Rome. There, the polis was the embodiment of all that is best in the people. Service to it was the highest calling.

Judaism, by contrast, is skeptical about politics. It knows all too well the force of Lord Acton's dictum that power tends to corrupt, and absolute power corrupts absolutely. It knows, too, the truth stated by Oliver Goldsmith: "How small, of all that human hearts endure, / That part which laws or kings can cause or cure." Politics in Judaism is a concession to necessity, not an end in itself. In Judaism, people do not exist to serve the state. The state exists to serve the people, and the people exist to serve God.

What Genesis and Ruth tell us is: do not think you can change the world or the human condition by politics and power alone. What matters is about how human beings – ordinary human beings, not just kings, courtiers and commanders – behave toward one another. An empire can have the world's strongest army, yet if it lacks justice and compassion it will eventually crumble.

More important than politics is the way we treat our fellow humans in our day-to-day interactions – and the quality of those relationships will itself be the surest indicator of our relationship with God. *You cannot serve God while exploiting or oppressing your fellow humans.* That is the message of all the prophets, and it is the story of Abraham and Sarah, Ruth, Naomi and Boaz. Love of God and loving-kindness toward our fellows go hand in hand.

The book of Judges ends with the terrible story of a concubine assaulted, raped and killed in the town of Gibeah, a crime that shocks the nation and leads to civil war (Judges 19–21). The episode resembles nothing so much as the story of Sodom (Gen. 19), where the people of the town attempt sexually to assault Lot's two guests. The message could not be more clear: Everything that had happened to the Israelites – the exodus, the wilderness years, the conquest of the land, the miracles and deliverances – did not stop the people of the covenant from lapsing into the worst conduct of their neighbors.

There is no short-cut to freedom. Neither military victories nor divine deliverance can achieve it. Without virtue, politics fails. Without habits of law-abidingness on the part of the people, even God cannot or will not save a nation. A free society depends on the character and virtues of its citizens, their willingness to sacrifice for the sake of others and to take responsibility for the weak and vulnerable, the orphan, the widow and the stranger within the gates. Abraham takes responsibility for Lot. Ruth takes responsibility for Naomi. Boaz takes responsibility for Ruth. They are their brother's and sister's keepers. Society is prior to the state, the family is prior to both, and what sustains them all is *ḥesed,* the kindness that is the mark of human greatness and the sign of those who truly understand what God wants from us.

The simplicity and tenderness of the book of Ruth should not deceive us. Its message is blunt and basic. What would matter in the end about David, whose name is the last word of the book, would not be his military genius or his political vision but the quality of his personal morality. That is a complex story in its own right, but what reverberates across the centuries is the simple fact that Abraham, great-grandfather of the children of Israel, and Ruth, great-grandmother of their greatest king, ruled no nation, performed no miracles and held no formal office. It was their *ḥesed,* their loving kindness, that ultimately transformed the world.

A TALE OF TWO WOMEN

As the book of Ruth hastens to its conclusion, there is a surprise in store. Their child, Oved, turns out to be the grandfather of King David. However, to those with an attentive ear, there is a far greater surprise. When the townspeople congratulate Boaz and Ruth on their marriage, they say "*May your house be like that of Peretz, whom Tamar bore* to Judah growing from the seed that the LORD will give you from this young woman" (4:12).

What have Peretz and Tamar to do with Ruth? They have played no

◂ part in the

part in the narrative. Yet when David's genealogy is set out at the end of the book it begins with Peretz, Boaz's distant ancestor. It is then that the attentive reader goes back to reread the story of Tamar and makes a remarkable discovery. It has so many parallels to that of Ruth that the similarity cannot be accidental.

The story of Tamar is told in Genesis 38. In the previous chapter, Judah had persuaded his brothers to sell Joseph as a slave. He then leaves his brothers and marries a Canaanite woman with whom he has three sons, Er, Onan and Shelah. When Er grows up Judah finds him a wife, Tamar. Tragedy strikes. Er dies. Judah – practicing a pre-Mosaic form of levirate marriage – tells his second son Onan that he must marry his brother's widow so that she can bear a child in memory of her dead husband. Onan resents the fact that the child would be regarded as his brother's, and he "spills his seed." For this he is punished, and he too dies.

Judah tells Tamar that she must "live like a widow" until Shelah is old enough to marry her. But he delays, fearing that his third son too may die. This places Tamar in a situation of living widowhood, unable to marry anyone else because she is bound to her remaining brother-in-law, unable to marry him because of Judah's fear.

Taking destiny into her own hands, she seizes the opportunity when she hears Judah is on his way to Timnah to shear his sheep. Covering her face with a veil, she dresses as a prostitute and positions herself on the route she knows her father-in-law will take. Judah approaches her and sleeps with her. She returns home and removes the disguise. She becomes pregnant. Three months later, her condition is apparent. People tell Judah, who is indignant. She must, he reasons, be guilty of adultery since she is bound to Shelah, whom Judah has kept from her. He orders: "Bring her out and have her burned."

Tamar, however, had prepared for this eventuality. During her deception, she had insisted on a pledge against payment: Judah's seal, cord and staff. By the time Judah sent a messenger to pay her and reclaim the pledge, she had disappeared. Now she produces the items and sends them to Judah with the words, "I am pregnant by the man who owns these." It is a masterly stroke. She has established her innocence without shaming Judah. Judah admits his error. He says, "She is more righteous than me." Eventually she gives birth to twins whom she names Peretz and Zerah.

◄ The stories

JONATHAN SACKS · lxii

The stories of Tamar and Ruth are very different. But they have a number of striking similarities.

- In both cases the story begins with a "going down," the separation of a key character – Judah in Genesis, Elimelekh in Ruth – from the rest of his family or people.
- In both cases the journey is a questionable one. Judah lives among the Canaanites and marries a local woman, despite the fact that Abraham had told his servant to ensure that Isaac, Judah's grandfather, did not do so: "I want you to swear by the LORD, the God of heaven and the God of earth, that you will not get a wife for my son from the daughters of the Canaanites, among whom I am living" (Gen. 24:3). Elimelekh goes to Moab, where his children marry local women despite the apparent biblical prohibition: "No Ammonite or Moabite or any of their descendants may enter the assembly of the LORD, not even in the tenth generation … Do not seek a treaty of friendship with them as long as you live" (Deut. 23:3, 6).
- In both stories two sons die: Er and Onan in the case of Judah; Maḥlon and Kilyon in that of Elimelekh. In each case their names prefigure their fate. Er means "childless," Onan signifies "mourning," Maḥlon means "sickness" and Kilyon "destruction."
- Tamar and Ruth are both childless widows. Both are concerned to have a child out of a sense of duty to "to raise the name of the dead."
- In both cases there are clear obstacles to their doing so. Judah refuses to allow Tamar to marry his third son, Shelah, the natural candidate for levirate marriage (the marriage of a childless widow to her brother-in-law). Naomi tells Ruth there is no chance she will have another child; therefore, she has no chance of marrying within the family.
- In both cases, it is the women themselves who take the initiative in ensuring that nonetheless a child will be born, and that the father will be someone from their husband's family.
- In both cases they do so by a daring act open to misinterpretation. Tamar dresses as a prostitute and positions herself to be seen by Judah. Ruth goes at night to Boaz, uncovers his cloak and sleeps at his feet. In both cases, care is taken so that the men concerned will

◀ not be exposed

not be exposed to shame. Tamar, by taking a pledge from Judah, is able to convince him he is the father of her child without anyone else becoming aware of the fact. Ruth takes care not to be seen going to or from Boaz at night.

▸ In both cases, a non-normative form of levirate marriage is involved. Neither Judah nor Boaz is a brother-in-law. In both cases there is a closer relative to whom the duty applies: Shelah and the anonymous "Such-and-such." Both times, it is the woman who shows the deepest loyalty to her late husband's family and name – more so than Judah or Naomi's anonymous relative.

The family tree lists ten generations from Peretz to the birth of David. A ten-generation genealogy is a highly charged phenomenon in the Bible. There are ten generations from Adam to Noah, and ten from Noah to Abraham. The ten generations from Peretz to David carry the same sense of preordained destiny. The beginning of such a family tree is significant. So too is the seventh, the number associated with holiness. *David's family tree begins with Peretz, the son born to Judah and Tamar. The seventh generation is Oved, the son born to Ruth and Boaz.* The key progenitors of Israel's great and future king are Tamar and Ruth. Theirs are in fact the only stories told in any detail about David's female forebears.

This is astonishing. The heroes in David's background are two women who stand at the very edge of Israelite society. In the biblical era there were no more vulnerable individuals than childless widows. But Tamar and Ruth were in a far worse situation still. They came from groups traditionally despised by the Israelites: the Canaanites and the Moabites. They had no natural place in the society in which they found themselves. *It was these two women, Tamar and Ruth, whose loyalty and steadfastness were the key factors in giving birth eventually to King David,* the man who became king of Israel, united the nation, initiated the plans for building the Temple, and wrote some of the finest poetry in the religious history of humankind.

This is worthy of serious reflection. Otto Rank, in his classic *The Myth of the Birth of the Hero*, points out that there are common elements in the stories told about the heroes of myth. Though raised by lowly adoptive parents, they are of noble birth. They have royal blood or are descended

◂ from the gods

from the gods. The story of David turns this convention on its head. David has the kind of family background most people would seek to hide.

It is exceptionally moving that the Bible should cast in these heroic roles two figures at the extreme margins of Israelite society: women, childless widows, outsiders, aliens. Tamar and Ruth, powerless except for their moral courage, wrote their names into Jewish history as role models who gave birth to royalty – to remind us, in case we ever forget, that true royalty lies in love and faithfulness, and that greatness often exists where we expect it least.

HEALING AN ANCIENT WOUND

The word *tikkun*, as in *tikkun olam*, "mending the world," and *tikkun leil Shavuot*, the custom of staying up and studying Torah all night on the first night of the festival, has a curious history. In Mishnaic Hebrew, that is, until the third century, it meant no more than social order, the rules that made society a safe and predictable place (see Mishna *Gittin*, ch. 4 and 5). In Jewish mysticism it came to mean something more metaphysical: mending the fractures in the universe that made life on earth so full of suffering and injustice, chief symbol of which was the Jewish condition in exile.

According to Rabbi Isaac Luria, the great mystic of the sixteenth century, this had to do with the fact that something had gone wrong with creation itself. The divine light of the first day of creation had proved too intense for the physical vehicles meant to contain it. The vessels had shattered, leaving debris and fragments of light scattered everywhere. Ours, said the mystics, is a broken world, and the fractures are so deep that they affect the Divine Being Itself. Exile is not just a human phenomenon. It represents a rift between God as He is in Himself – the Infinite, the *Ein Sof*, the Without-End – and the *Shekhina*, the Divine Presence, God as He is among us. When Jews went into exile, the *Shekhina* went with them. So we, by our mystical endeavors, have to help heal the fractures in the Divine. Every religious act, if done with sufficient intensity of mind and soul, does something to reunite *Kudsha Berikh Hu*, the Holy One, blessed be He, and *Shekhintei*, His immanent Presence.

There is, though, a third sense of *tikkun* that is not mystical at all but makes powerful sense in terms of the Jewish vision of the world. Bad

◀ things happen

things happen between people. The innocent are harmed. There is envy, jealousy, anger, resentment. There is injustice, oppression, exploitation. The human world is full of tears. If you believe, as polytheists did in the ancient world and some atheists do today, that life is essentially conflict, a Darwinian struggle to survive, then there is nothing odd about a world full of pain. That is how it is. There is no right; only might. Justice is whatever serves the interests of the strong. History is written by the victors. The victims are mere collateral damage of the fight to impose our will on the world or, in the language of the neo-Darwinians, to hand on our genes to the next generation.

That, though, is not how Jews understand it. The natural condition of the world is harmony, like a well-ordered garden or a loving family or a gracious society. That is how it was in the beginning when God made the universe and saw that it was good. God, though, gave humans freedom, and humans often use that freedom to disobey Him. God created order. We create chaos. That is, or would be, the human tragedy if Jews believed in tragedy. But we do not. We believe in hope, and hope has the power to defeat tragedy – as we have the power to mend what we or others have broken.

That is the philosophy that lies behind the central Jewish idea of *teshuva*, meaning "repentance" or "return." Through *teshuva*, we can heal some of the pain we or others have created. Though the concept of *teshuva* does not figure explicitly in the stories of Genesis, it is there nonetheless beneath the surface. Broken relationships are mended. Ishmael, Abraham's child by the slave-woman Hagar, was sent away when he was young, yet we see him standing together with his half-brother Isaac at Abraham's grave. Jacob and Esau, divided by Jacob's act of taking Esau's blessing, meet twenty-two years later and embrace with no evident trace of lingering resentment. Joseph forgives his brothers who sold him into slavery. Genesis ends on a note of reconciliation. There are wounds that can be healed.

Neither Tanakh nor the rabbis, nor even the mystics, called this *tikkun*, but that is what it is: the intensely human ability to repair damaged relationships and restore order to the social world. But what if the moment passes? What if those who did the damage and those who suffered it, are no longer alive? Can what we do in the present mend something broken long ago, before our time? That is one of the subtexts of the book of Ruth, and it applies to two people: Ruth herself, and Boaz.

First, Ruth. She was, we are told no fewer than five times, a Moabite. This raises a powerful question not touched on in the book itself. The Torah explicitly states that "a Moabite shall not come into the congregation of the LORD even to the tenth generation" (Deut. 23:4). The rabbis solved this problem simply and ingeniously. The Hebrew for Moabite, *Moavi*, is masculine not feminine. So the prohibition applies to men not women (*Yevamot* 76b–77a). This, they said, was one of the rulings given "in the days when the judges judged."

There was a reason for this. The Torah explains the original prohibition by saying, "They did not come to meet you with bread and water on your way when you came out of Egypt, and they hired Balaam son of Beor from Pethor in Aram Naharaim to pronounce a curse on you" (Deut. 23:45). The Moabites, the Torah implies, had a natural hostility to the Israelites. They were mean-spirited and worse: they had paid the pagan prophet Balaam to put a curse on them.

Why so? The Torah itself tells a story about this, early in the history of Abraham's family. Leaving his land, birthplace and father's house, Abraham took his nephew Lot with him. In Genesis 13, the first recorded argument within the family, we see the shepherds of Abraham and Lot arguing. They had returned from Egypt rich in sheep and cattle, and there were too many to be grazed in the same area. Abraham suggested to Lot that, rather than quarrel, they should separate, and he offers Lot the choice of where to go.

Lot, seeing the affluence of the Jordan valley, "like the garden of the LORD" (v. 10), chooses to settle there in the town of Sodom. Immediately, though, the Torah adds a warning note. The people of Sodom are "wicked and sinning greatly against the LORD" (v. 13). Soon, Lot's life was in danger. Four neighboring kings attacked Sodom, taking many captives, including Lot. Abraham gathered a force, pursued the invading army, rescued the hostages and returned Lot to his home (Gen. 14).

Five chapters later, two strangers come to visit Lot. They are in fact angels sent to warn him that the town was about to be destroyed. That night all the inhabitants of the town crowd round Lot's house, demanding that he bring out the visitors so that they can be assaulted. Lot refuses

◄ but does

but does something even worse: offers them his daughters. The angels intervene. Smiting the townspeople with temporary blindness, they urge Lot to leave. Lot reports this to his sons-in-law, who treat his remarks like a joke. The angels then force Lot, his wife and daughters to leave and the area is almost immediately destroyed. Against the angels' instructions, Lot's wife looks back and is turned into a pillar of salt, leaving Lot and his two daughters as the sole survivors.

Sheltering in a cave among the mountains, Lot's daughters, suspecting there is no one in the region left alive, decide to get their father drunk and sleep with him. They do so, they become pregnant and eventually give birth. The elder calls her son Moab ("from father"). That is the Torah's account of the origin of the Moabites. They are the outcome of an incestuous relationship, and they have acquired the characteristics of the people of Sodom. They are hostile to strangers, sexually amoral, and the result of a division within the Abrahamic family – Lot's decision to live among the people of the cities of the plain.

Turning now to the story of Ruth, we see certain similarities between it and that of Lot. In both cases there is a man and two women. There is anxiety as to whether there will be a next generation. In both cases it is the women rather than the man who take the initiative, and in both, the man has been drinking. In both, there is an encounter in the dark, at night, and in both a child is born.

The differences, though, are immense. Sodom is a place of hostility to strangers. Ruth's is a story of kindness to strangers. Lot separated from Abraham; Ruth refused to be separated from Naomi. Lot's daughters are licentious. Ruth, alone with Boaz, is chaste. Sodom is a symbol of absence of ḥesed; Ruth is symbol of its presence.

Ruth, in her life and by her example, performs a *tikkun*. Though there is no element of *teshuva* involved, the verb *shuv*, in the sense of "return," appears thirteen times in the book. Something has been healed. By her conduct and character, she shows that not all Moabites lack kindness. They, too, ultimately come from the same family, that of Teraḥ, as Abraham himself. Ruth has redeemed something of the past. Reuniting two long separated branches of the family, her great-grandson became the person who united the nation. That is *tikkun*. By our acts in the present we can heal some of the wounds in the past.

◀ BOAZ

BOAZ AND JUDAH

There is another *tikkun* in the book of Ruth.

There can be no doubt as to why the book was written and included in Tanakh. It ends with the birth of David and a genealogy tracing his descent. Heavily emphasized throughout is its setting in Bethlehem, Judah. Despite the prominence of Joseph in the book of Genesis, and the tribe of Levi – in the form of Moses, Aaron and Miriam – in the rest of the Pentateuch, the kings of Israel descended not from them but from Jacob's fourth son, Judah.

Yet Genesis raises real doubts about Judah's character. Like Elimelekh at the beginning of Ruth, Judah left his brothers, in his case to live among the Canaanites. He married a Canaanite woman. He later used the services of what he took to be a prostitute. He was willing to have his daughter-in-law sentenced to death for a sin she had not committed. Most fundamentally, however, it was Judah who was responsible for selling Joseph into slavery in Egypt. The brothers initially proposed killing him. Reuben, planning later to rescue Joseph, suggested that they threw him in a pit and left him to die. But it was Judah who said the chilling words:

> "*What will we gain* if we kill our brother and cover up his blood? Come, let's sell him to the Ishmaelites and not lay our hands on him; *after all, he is our brother, our own flesh and blood.*" (Gen. 37:26–27)

Note, first, that he did not say, "It is wrong to kill our brother." He said "What will we gain?" if we kill him. This is the language not of principle but pragmatism. Second, he proposed selling Joseph as a slave at the very moment he recognized that "he is our brother, our own flesh and blood." It is as if Judah were echoing Cain when he said, "Am I my brother's keeper?"

To be sure, after his encounter with a righteous woman, Tamar, Judah appears as a changed character. He became, de facto, the leader of the remaining brothers. He was their spokesman in their last great dialogue with the viceroy of Egypt. Faced with the opportunity to repeat the earlier sin, by leaving his brother Benjamin as a slave, he showed that he had changed. He offered himself as a slave, so that Benjamin could go free.

He had repented, but in highly unusual circumstances. Unbeknown to the brothers, the viceroy was in fact Joseph himself, who had been putting

◄ them through

them through a series of trials to see if they acknowledged their guilt and had changed. Was this sufficient to establish that the descendants of Judah would not also share his moral weaknesses, above all his failure to act as his brother's guardian, surely the first requirement of a leader?

One of the powerful techniques of biblical literature is its intertextuality, its use of literary devices to connect one passage with another. This prompts the listener or reader to ask, "Now where have I heard those words before?" We make connections between one text and another, and slowly begin to realise that they are part of a single story, that the later passage is a commentary on the earlier one. There is a dramatic instance in the book of Ruth.

It happens at the first encounter between Ruth and Boaz. Ruth has gone to gather grain in a field belonging to one of Naomi's relatives. We know this because the text tells us so, but Ruth, at this point, does not. He is simply a local landowner, clearly a man of substance but not someone she knows. Boaz, seeing her, asks the overseer of the field who she is, and he tells him, she is a Moabite who came with Naomi. Boaz then goes to speak to her, showing her great kindness and sensitivity. She is profoundly moved, prostrates herself "low, to the ground," and says: "Why is it that I have found favor in your eyes, that you give me recognition [*hakireini*] such as this, when I am a stranger [*nokhriya*]?" (2:10).

What makes this a most unusual sentence is a detail lost in translation. There is a very rare linguistic phenomenon known as a contronym, a word with two meanings that are diametrically opposed. One example in English is "cleave," which means both to split apart and to cling together. Another is "sanction," which means to permit, and the opposite, to forbid and punish. The Hebrew verb נ-כ-ר in some forms means "to recognize," and in others, the opposite: "to be, or act as, a stranger," that is, someone *not* recognized. The appearance in a single sentence of the word in both meanings is arresting and very rare.

There is only one other place in Tanakh where it occurs: when Jacob's sons go to Egypt to buy food during a famine. They come before the viceroy, who is, unknown to them, their brother Joseph:

> When Joseph saw his brothers, he recognized them [*vayakirem*], but he pretended to be a stranger [*vayitnaker*] and spoke harshly

◄ to them

to them. "Where do you come from?" he asked. "From the land of Canaan," they replied, "to buy food." Joseph recognized [vayaker] his brothers, they did not recognize him [hikiruhu]. (Gen. 42:7–8)

To "recognize," in biblical Hebrew, is a complex idea. It is cognitive: "I recognize you" means "I know who you are." But it means something legal and moral also. It says there is kinship between us. We are part, literally or metaphorically, of the same family. I have special duties toward you that I do not have toward everyone. The Torah states, "Do not recognize faces in judgment" (Deut. 1:17). This means, do not let kinship distort the course of justice. From the negative we can infer the positive, that when it comes not to justice but compassion, then to "recognize a face" means to show the kind of care that family members should have to one another. That is why Ruth asks, "Why have I found favor in your eyes that you recognize me?" meaning, Why have you shown me such special treatment?

When she goes on to say, "I am a foreigner," the word she uses, *nokhriya*, is far stronger than the usual biblical word for stranger, *ger*. A *ger* in biblical times was a temporary resident without citizenship rights. *Nokhri*, by contrast, means "an alien, an outsider," someone who does not belong here and would normally be viewed with suspicion and hostility. When Ruth calls herself a *nokhriya*, she is referring to the fact that she is a Moabite, fully aware of the historic tensions between her people and Naomi's.

Returning to Joseph, we see that in its description of the brothers' first encounter in Egypt, the Torah is hinting at something larger than the meeting itself. When Judah said, years earlier, "Let's sell him... after all, he is our brother, our own flesh and blood," he was committing a kind of contronym of the mind. He knew Joseph was his brother, but he treated him like an alien, someone with no claim to his care. What Joseph proceeds to do over the next few chapters is to force the brothers to experience what he himself suffered, to see if this role reversal will get them to understand what they had done wrong. He acts as if they are strangers, for that is how they – specifically Judah – acted toward him.

What we see in Ruth's first encounter with Boaz – the seventh-generation descendant of Judah – is a precise reversal of that earlier scene. She really is an alien, a foreigner, a Moabite, a *nokhriya*. Yet he extends

◄ to her

to her the kindness he would show to a member of his own family: he "recognizes" her. He also immediately explains why. He has heard of what she has done for his relative, Naomi. It would be perfectly understandable if he refused to treat her as a member of the family. She came, after all, from a nation distrusted by Israelites as immoral, cruel, and hostile. But he immediately treats her as a full and respected member of the family.

The intertextual resonance of the verb נ-כ-ר in its two opposite senses tells us that a larger drama is being played out here. Boaz is repairing, redeeming, performing a *tikkun* toward Judah's past. Judah treated his brother as a stranger. Boaz treats a stranger like a member of the family. That is the *tikkun* that had to take place before a descendant of Judah, David, could become a king of Israel.

RUTH AND THE DE-ETHNICIZATION OF JUDAISM

Something happened at Sinai that fundamentally changed the terms of Jewish existence. Until then God's covenant with Abraham had been with his biological descendants. The Abrahamic family was a kinship group, a clan, a tribe. You were born into it. You could not enter it from the outside. To be sure, not every descendant of Abraham was part of it. Isaac was chosen but not Ishmael, Jacob but not Esau. But with Jacob, this ended. All of his children became tribes within the larger family of Israel. The covenant was closed to outsiders.

Hence the concern Abraham and Isaac showed that their children marry within the family. Abraham, sending his servant to find a wife for his son, made him swear that he would not take anyone from among the Canaanites but would go instead "to my country and my own family" (Gen. 24:3–4). When Esau married two Hittite women, it was "a source of grief" to Isaac and Rebecca (Gen. 26:34–35).

Yet as the story unfolds, this principle comes under ever greater strain. Judah married a Canaanite woman. Joseph married the daughter of an Egyptian priest. Moses married the daughter of a priest of Midian. Each of these women, on marriage, surely adopted the religion of their husbands, but there was as yet no formal conversion procedure, nor could there be. The covenant was a family heritage you were born into, not a set of commitments you could choose to adopt.

That changed with the giving of the Torah. Judaism now had a set of

◀ commands

commands that defined it as a way of life. In principle conversion became possible. In some sense, what the Israelites themselves underwent at the time was a kind of conversion (*Yevamot* 46b; *Keritot* 9a). The men were circumcised in Egypt (Josh. 5:5). The people purified themselves before the revelation (Ex. 19:10). At the revelation itself, the people said, "All that the LORD has spoken, we shall perform" (ibid. 8) – essentially the same act that constitutes conversion itself: *kabbalat hamitzvot*, "acceptance of the commandments. Israelite identity became a matter of *assent*, not just *descent*.

There are several instances in Tanakh of outsiders aligning themselves with the fate of Israel, Rahab in the book of Joshua (ch. 2) for example, or Yael in the book of Judges (ch. 4). There is, though, only one episode that resembles a conversion: Ruth's declaration to Naomi, "Wherever you walk, I shall walk; wherever you lie down, there shall I lie. Your people is my people; your God is my God." This subsequently became the model on which conversion was based (*Yevamot* 47a–b). Note that it has two elements: joining both a covenant of fate ("your people is my people") and a covenant of faith ("your God is my God").

This possibility of joining the Jewish people through an act of choice, the voluntary acceptance of religious responsibilities, turned Judaism from an ethnicity into something broader and more open, all the more so in light of the fact that the person who became the role-model for conversion came from Moab, the group whose ethnicity was among the most problematic to the Israelites.

The story of Ruth de-ethnicizes Judaism, as did the covenant at Sinai. Being Jewish ceased to be a race and became a responsibility. This has a bearing on one of the great questions of Judaism: Did God choose the Jewish people because they were special, or did they become special because God chose them? Is Jewish distinctiveness a cause or consequence of election? Are Jews intrinsically, ethnically, spiritually different, or is it living the life of the commandments that makes them so? Is Jewishness a genetic endowment, as it were, or an acquired characteristic?

There is a line of thought in Judaism that suggests that Jews are indeed different: that something special has been passed on to them by the patriarchs and matriarchs and more than a hundred generations of ancestors who kept the faith through all the hardships. We find this in

◂ some passages

some passages of the Talmud and Midrash, the *Zohar*, and the writings of Judah HaLevi and Maharal (R. Judah Loewe) of Prague. The difficulty in this view is how to understand the act of conversion itself. How can someone not ethnically Jewish become so?

Against this stands the view of Maimonides, for whom there is no ontological difference between Jews and gentiles. All humans are in the image of God. All are capable of moral and intellectual greatness. If Jews are close to God it is because of their performance of the commands and the study of Torah. The one refines our character, the other elevates our mind.

Nowhere does Maimonides make the point more emphatically than at the end of his Laws of the Sabbatical Year and the Jubilee. There he explains that the tribe of Levi had no share in the land because they were set apart to serve God and minister to Him. He then adds:

> Not only the tribe of Levi but *every single individual from among the inhabitants of the world* whose spirit moves him and whose intelligence gives him the understanding to withdraw from the world in order to stand before God to serve and minister to Him... such an individual is consecrated to the Holy of Holies and his portion and inheritance shall be in the LORD forever and ever more. The LORD will grant him in this world whatever is sufficient for him, the same as He had granted to the priests and the Levites. (*Hilkhot Shemitta veYovel* 13:13)

This is an extraordinary passage, set right at the center of Maimonides' law code, the *Mishneh Torah* (it is the last law of the seventh of fourteen books), which also begins and ends on a universalistic note.

Maimonides' attitude is made even more clear in his letter to Ovadia, a convert to Judaism who had written to him in some distress, apparently having been told by a rabbi that he could not say words in prayer such as "Our God *and the God of our fathers*," since in his case his father was a gentile. Maimonides had no hesitation in telling him that he may say these words and all others, exactly like a born Jew. Abraham, he writes, is not only the biological "father" of the Jewish people, but also and equally the spiritual father of all who convert to Judaism. There is, says Maimonides, no difference between you and us. What is more, he says, in Egypt, "our

◀ fathers

fathers were mostly idolaters; they had mingled with the pagans in Egypt and imitated their way of life." Therefore, "you should not consider your origin as inferior" to ours: we are both, born Jew and convert alike, descended from those who did not worship the true God. We have all been brought under the wings of the Divine Presence.

He ends the letter on a beautiful note. He quotes a line from Isaiah in which the prophet says that a day will come when "I will pour out My spirit on your offspring, and My blessing on your descendants." At that time:

> Some will say, "I belong to the LORD";
> others will call themselves by the name of Jacob;
> still others will write on their hand, "The LORD's,"
> and will take the name Israel. (Is. 44:5)

The phrase, "Some will say I belong to the LORD," says Maimonides, refers to converts, while "others will call themselves by the name of Jacob" refers to Jews (thus the text in *Letters of Maimonides*, ed. Yitzḥak Sheilat, vol. 1, 231–35). "Do not let your ancestry be a small thing in your eyes," he concludes, "for we are descendants of Abraham, Isaac and Jacob while you derive from Him by whose word the world was created."

Ruth stands as the eternal model of one who made the journey to join the people of the covenant. In her merit, Israel was blessed by King David and the book of Psalms, as it will be, one day, by the Messiah and a world at peace.

4. Shavuot Today

On the face of it, Shavuot is a brief festival with few distinctive practices and, at least as far as the Torah is concerned, no specific historical content. This Introduction has argued otherwise. Shavuot is the festival of Jewish identity, and the controversies to which it gave rise through the ages are evidence of how variously at different times that identity was conceived. The sociologist Peter Berger once defined modernity as a condition of permanent identity crisis. For Jews that is not the mark of modernity: it is our recurring, perennial fate.

For Judaism is not just a set of beliefs and practices. It is also a field

◄ of tensions

of tensions: between the universal and particular, exile and home, priest and prophet, halakha and aggada, rationalism and mysticism, tradition and revolution, acceptance and protest, the walls of the house of study and the stalls of the market-place. Its greatness is that, by and large, it has kept these tensions in play. That is what has given it gifts of survival and creativity unmatched by any other religious tradition in the West.

Shavuot is defined by those tensions. One, as we saw, was that between law and land. Judaism is supremely a religion of the land – the whole of Torah from Abraham to the death of Moses is a journey toward it – and Shavuot was the supreme festival of the land. There were agricultural elements on Pesaḥ and Sukkot also, but Shavuot was the time of the grain harvest and of bringing first fruits to the Temple and declaring: "My father was a wandering Aramean... And the Lord brought us out of Egypt... He brought us to this place and gave us this land, a land flowing with milk and honey."

If Pesaḥ commemorated the beginning of the journey from Egypt, and Sukkot the forty years of the journey, then – so this Introduction has argued – Shavuot celebrated its culmination: the entry into the land itself. On it people recalled not "the bread of oppression our ancestors ate in Egypt," nor the miraculous "bread from heaven" they ate in the desert, but bread made from the grain of the Holy Land itself.

To be sure, it had also from the outset been the festival of the Giving of the Law, seen as the culmination of the seven-week journey that began with Pesaḥ. But every nation had laws, and for much of the biblical era other issues, political, military and cultural, held center stage. The prophets tirelessly argued that without faithfulness to God and justice and compassion to their fellow humans, Israel would eventually suffer a momentous defeat, but all too few were listening, and the reforms of kings like Hezekiah and Josiah proved too little too late.

Only with the experience of the Babylonian exile did people come to see that the law of Israel was unlike that of any other nation – not just because of its content but because of who gave it, when and where. It was given not at Mount Zion in Jerusalem but at Mount Sinai in the desert. The law came before the land. Therefore though they had lost the land, they still had the law. Though they had lost the country, they still had the covenant. The law of Israel was *not* like the law of every other

◄ nation

nation – the decree of kings or the edict of a legislative assembly. It came from God Himself, the Infinite Eternal. Therefore it could never be lost or nullified.

That was when the full significance of Shavuot began to come clear. The real miracle was not the land but the law that preceded the land. Ezra and Nehemiah understood this after the Babylonian exile, as did Rabban Yoḥanan ben Zakkai in the midst of the rebellion against Rome. Without them it is highly doubtful whether Jews or Judaism would have survived.

As we have seen, Shavuot embodies other tensions as well: between covenant and contract, society and state, and the question of whether Judaism is primarily about politics and power or about morality, civil society and the ties that bind us to one another in a community of fate and faith. It is about Ruth and Boaz and the power of *ḥesed* to defeat tragedy and create hope. Not accidentally also, the book of Ruth ends with the birth of David, who made Jerusalem the capital of Israel. Shavuot thus brings together the two mountains that frame Jewish destiny: Mount Sinai in the desert where the Israelites made their covenant with God and Mount Zion in Jerusalem where they worshiped Him in sacrifice and song.

For the better part of two thousand years Jews lost their land, and once again – as it was for the exiles in Babylon – it was Torah that sustained the people as a people, giving them the assurance that one day they would return. So Shavuot has been reborn in our time – first among the early kibbutzim as a festival of the land, and more recently as the festival of the *Tikkun*, the all-night study session that today embraces Jews of all shades of belief and practice, constituting them again as the people of the Book in the land of the Book, hearing again the *kol gadol velo yasaf*, the great sound of Sinai that pierced the desert silence once and continues to reverberate for all time.

To see the crowds converging on the Kotel from all parts of Jerusalem just before dawn, having studied all night and ready now to say *Shema Yisrael* together, as the first rays of the rising sun light the sky with red and gold, is to see one of the miracles of human faith and endurance, and to know how deeply we owe thanks to God who "gave us the Torah of truth, planting everlasting life in our midst."

◄ For in truth

For in truth this always was our greatest gift: the Torah, our constitution of liberty under the sovereignty of God, our marriage contract with Heaven itself, written in letters of black fire on white fire, joining the infinity of God and the finitude of humankind in an unbreakable bond of law and love, the scroll Jews carried wherever they went, and that carried them. This is the Torah: the voice of heaven as it is heard on earth, the word that lights the world.

Acknowledgments

A work of this scope and complexity is a team enterprise, and it has been a privilege to work with some of the most wonderful colleagues anyone could ask for. The team at Koren are outstanding: Matthew Miller, its tireless and visionary driving force, together with Rachel Meghnagi, Jessica Sacks, Rabbi David Fuchs, Efrat Gross, Rabbi Eli Clark and Esther Be'er, each of whom has contributed massively to this work.

I am especially grateful also to David Frei of the London Beth Din and Professor Leslie Wagner for their helpful comments on the Introduction.

My deepest thanks as always are to my wife Elaine, the inspiration of my life, and the human Thou who has taught me to be open to the Divine Thou.

Ultimately, all thanks belong to God who chose us, on the first Shavuot, as His covenantal partners, bestowing on us, in equal measure, love and responsibility. My deepest prayer is that He may help each of us to be equal to that blessing and that task in our time.

Rabbi Lord Jonathan Sacks
Adar Sheni 5776 (March 2016)

מחזור קורן לשבועות

THE KOREN SHAVUOT MAḤZOR

Erev Shabbat and Yom Tov

EIRUV TEḤUMIN

*On Shabbat and Yom Tov it is forbidden to walk more than 2000 cubits (about 3000 feet)
beyond the boundary (teḥum) of the town where you live or are staying when the day begins.
By placing food sufficient for two meals, before nightfall, at a point within 2000 cubits
from the town limits, you confer on that place the status of a dwelling for the
next day, and are then permitted to walk 2000 cubits from there.*

בָּרוּךְ Blessed are You, Lord our God, King of the Universe,
who has made us holy through His commandments,
and has commanded us about the mitzva of Eiruv.

By this Eiruv may we be permitted to walk from this place,
two thousand cubits in any direction.

EIRUV ḤATZEROT

*On Shabbat it is forbidden to carry objects from one private domain to another,
or from a private domain into space shared by others, such as a communal
staircase, corridor or courtyard. If Shavuot falls on Friday, an Eiruv Ḥatzerot is
created when each of the Jewish households in a court or apartment block, before
Yom Tov, places a piece of bread in one of the homes. The entire court or block
then becomes a single private domain within which it is permitted to carry.*

בָּרוּךְ Blessed are You, Lord our God, King of the Universe,
who has made us holy through His commandments,
and has commanded us about the mitzva of Eiruv.

By this Eiruv may we be permitted to move,
carry out and carry in from the houses to the courtyard,
or from the courtyard to the houses, or from house to house,
for all the houses within the courtyard.

---

that joins day and night; *arev*, "a guarantor," who joins another person or
persons in a bond of shared responsibility, and *arev*, "pleasant," the mood
that prevails when people join in friendship. An *eiruv* softens the sharp divide
of boundaries.

An *eiruv teḥumin* is a device that allows us to walk for up to two thousand
cubits beyond the two-thousand-cubit boundary that marks how far we may

ערב שבת ויום טוב

עירוב תחומין

On שבת and יום טוב it is forbidden to walk more than 2000 cubits (about 3000 feet)
beyond the boundary (תחום) of the town where you live or are staying when the day begins.
By placing food sufficient for two meals, before nightfall, at a point within 2000 cubits
from the town limits, you confer on that place the status of a dwelling for the
next day, and are then permitted to walk 2000 cubits from there.

בָּרוּךְ אַתָּה יהוה אֱלֹהֵינוּ מֶלֶךְ הָעוֹלָם
אֲשֶׁר קִדְּשָׁנוּ בְּמִצְוֹתָיו וְצִוָּנוּ עַל מִצְוַת עֵרוּב.

בְּדֵין עֵרוּבָא יְהֵא שָׁרֵא לִי לְמֵיזַל מֵאַתְרָא
הָדֵין תְּרֵין אַלְפִין אַמִּין לְכָל רוּחָא.

עירוב חצרות

On שבת it is forbidden to carry objects from one private domain to another,
or from a private domain into space shared by others, such as a communal
staircase, corridor or courtyard. If שבועות falls on Friday, an עירוב חצרות is
created when each of the Jewish households in a court or apartment block, before
יום טוב, places a piece of bread in one of the homes. The entire court or block
then becomes a single private domain within which it is permitted to carry.

בָּרוּךְ אַתָּה יהוה אֱלֹהֵינוּ מֶלֶךְ הָעוֹלָם
אֲשֶׁר קִדְּשָׁנוּ בְּמִצְוֹתָיו וְצִוָּנוּ עַל מִצְוַת עֵרוּב.

בְּדֵין עֵרוּבָא יְהֵא שָׁרֵא לָנָא לְטַלְטוּלֵי וּלְאַפּוּקֵי וּלְעַיּוּלֵי
מִן הַבָּתִּים לֶחָצֵר וּמִן הֶחָצֵר לַבָּתִּים
וּמִבַּיִת לְבַיִת לְכָל הַבָּתִּים שֶׁבֶּחָצֵר.

EIRUVIN

Eiruvin are halakhic devices relating to Shabbat and the festivals by which
the sages "joined" different domains of space and time. *Eiruv* comes from
the same root (ע-ר-ב, literally: combine or join) as *erev*, "evening," the time

EIRUV TAVSHILIN

*It is not permitted to cook for Shabbat when Shavuot falls on Friday unless
an Eiruv Tavshilin has been made prior to the Yom Tov. This is done by taking
a loaf or piece of matza together with a boiled egg, or a piece of cooked fish
or meat to be used on Shabbat. While holding them, say the following:*

בָּרוּךְ Blessed are You, LORD our God, King of the Universe,
who has made us holy through His commandments,
and has commanded us
about the mitzva of Eiruv.

By this Eiruv may we be permitted
to bake, cook, insulate food, light a flame
and do everything necessary on the festival for the sake of Shabbat,
for us and for all Jews living in this city.

CANDLE LIGHTING

*On Erev Yom Tov, say the following blessing and then light the candles from an
existing flame. If also Shabbat, cover the eyes with the hands after lighting the
candles and say the following blessing, adding the words in parentheses.*

בָּרוּךְ Blessed are You, LORD our God, King of the Universe,
who has made us holy through His commandments,
and has commanded us to light
(the Sabbath light and) the festival light.

בָּרוּךְ Blessed are You, LORD our God, King of the Universe,
who has given us life, sustained us,
and brought us to this time.

---

essential structure of Jewish law that surrounds and protects the holiness of
space and time.

CANDLE LIGHTING
Candle lighting on Shabbat and festivals represents *shelom bayit*, "peace in
the home." The sages say that Adam and Eve were created on the eve of

עירוב תבשילין

It is not permitted to cook for שבת *when* שבועות *falls on Friday unless an* עירוב תבשילין *has been made prior to the* יום טוב. *This is done by taking a loaf or piece of matza together with a boiled egg, or a piece of cooked fish or meat to be used on* שבת. *While holding them, say the following:*

בָּרוּךְ אַתָּה יהוה אֱלֹהֵינוּ מֶלֶךְ הָעוֹלָם
אֲשֶׁר קִדְּשָׁנוּ בְּמִצְוֹתָיו וְצִוָּנוּ עַל מִצְוַת עֵרוּב.

בְּדֵין עֵרוּבָא יְהֵא שָׁרֵא לָנָא
לְמֵיפָא וּלְבַשָׁלָא וּלְאַטְמָנָא וּלְאַדְלָקָא שְׁרָגָא
וּלְמֶעְבַּד כָּל צָרְכַּנָא מִיּוֹמָא טָבָא לְשַׁבְּתָא
לָנוּ וּלְכָל יִשְׂרָאֵל הַדָּרִים בָּעִיר הַזֹּאת.

הדלקת נרות

On ערב יום טוב, *say the following blessing and then light the candles from an existing flame. If also* שבת, *cover the eyes with the hands after lighting the candles and say the following blessing, adding the words in parentheses.*

בָּרוּךְ אַתָּה יהוה אֱלֹהֵינוּ מֶלֶךְ הָעוֹלָם
אֲשֶׁר קִדְּשָׁנוּ בְּמִצְוֹתָיו
וְצִוָּנוּ לְהַדְלִיק נֵר שֶׁל (שַׁבָּת וְשֶׁל) יוֹם טוֹב.

בָּרוּךְ אַתָּה יהוה אֱלֹהֵינוּ מֶלֶךְ הָעוֹלָם
שֶׁהֶחֱיָנוּ וְקִיְּמָנוּ, וְהִגִּיעָנוּ לַזְּמַן הַזֶּה.

walk outside the limits of a town. An *eiruv ḥatzerot* joins multiple homes into a single private domain for the purpose of carrying between them on Shabbat. An *eiruv tavshilin* permits us to prepare food for Shabbat on a festival that immediately precedes Shabbat. All three were instituted to enhance the joy of the festival and the delight of Shabbat without weakening the

Some add:

יְהִי רָצוֹן May it be Your will, LORD our God and God of our ancestors, that the Temple be speedily rebuilt in our days, and grant us our share in Your Torah. And may we serve You there in reverence, as in the days of old and as in former years.   *Mal. 3*

Prayer after candle lighting
(*add the words in parentheses as appropriate*):

יְהִי רָצוֹן May it be Your will, LORD my God and God of my forebears, that You give me grace – me (and my husband/and my father/and my mother/and my sons and my daughters) and all those close to me, and give us and all Israel good and long lives. And remember us with a memory that brings goodness and blessing; come to us with compassion and bless us with great blessings. Build our homes until they are complete, and allow Your Presence to live among us. And may I merit to raise children and grandchildren, each one wise and under-standing, loving the LORD and in awe of God, people of truth, holy children, who will cling on to the LORD and light up the world with Torah and with good actions, and with all the kinds of work that serve the Creator. Please, hear my pleading at this time, by the merit of Sarah and Rebecca, Rachel and Leah our mothers, and light our candle that it should never go out, and light up Your face, so that we shall be saved, Amen.

---

the festivals when in the soft light of the flickering flames, the jagged edges of the week lose their sharpness and we begin to feel the unity of all things in the sensed presence of their Creator.

יְהִי רָצוֹן *May it be Your will.* A beautiful prayer usually said by the woman of the house, invoking the merits and enduring influence of the matriarchs of our people – Sarah, Rebecca, Rachel and Leah – and the courage and devotion of their steadfast love for God and their families. It is a touching summary of the values by which Jewish women through the millennia lived and taught their children.

Some add:

יְהִי רָצוֹן מִלְּפָנֶיךָ יהוה אֱלֹהֵינוּ וֵאלֹהֵי אֲבוֹתֵינוּ, שֶׁיִּבָּנֶה בֵּית
הַמִּקְדָּשׁ בִּמְהֵרָה בְיָמֵינוּ, וְתֵן חֶלְקֵנוּ בְּתוֹרָתֶךָ, וְשָׁם נַעֲבָדְךָ
בְּיִרְאָה כִּימֵי עוֹלָם וּכְשָׁנִים קַדְמֹנִיּוֹת. וְעָרְבָה לַיהוה מִנְחַת
יְהוּדָה וִירוּשָׁלָםִ כִּימֵי עוֹלָם וּכְשָׁנִים קַדְמֹנִיּוֹת: מלאכי ג

Prayer after candle lighting
(add the words in parentheses as appropriate):

יְהִי רָצוֹן מִלְּפָנֶיךָ יהוה אֱלֹהַי וֵאלֹהֵי אֲבוֹתַי, שֶׁתְּחוֹנֵן אוֹתִי (וְאֶת
אִישִׁי/ וְאֶת אָבִי/ וְאֶת אִמִּי/ וְאֶת בָּנַי וְאֶת בְּנוֹתַי) וְאֶת כָּל קְרוֹבַי,
וְתִתֶּן לָנוּ וּלְכָל יִשְׂרָאֵל חַיִּים טוֹבִים וַאֲרֻכִּים, וְתִזְכְּרֵנוּ בְּזִכְרוֹן טוֹבָה
וּבְרָכָה, וְתִפְקְדֵנוּ בִּפְקֻדַּת יְשׁוּעָה וְרַחֲמִים, וּתְבָרְכֵנוּ בְּרָכוֹת גְּדוֹלוֹת,
וְתַשְׁלִים בָּתֵּינוּ וְתַשְׁכֵּן שְׁכִינָתְךָ בֵּינֵינוּ. וְזַכֵּנִי לְגַדֵּל בָּנִים וּבְנֵי בָנִים
חֲכָמִים וּנְבוֹנִים, אוֹהֲבֵי יהוה יִרְאֵי אֱלֹהִים, אַנְשֵׁי אֱמֶת זֶרַע קֹדֶשׁ,
בַּיהוה דְּבֵקִים וּמְאִירִים אֶת הָעוֹלָם בַּתּוֹרָה וּבְמַעֲשִׂים טוֹבִים וּבְכָל
מְלֶאכֶת עֲבוֹדַת הַבּוֹרֵא. אָנָּא שְׁמַע אֶת תְּחִנָּתִי בָּעֵת הַזֹּאת בִּזְכוּת
שָׂרָה וְרִבְקָה וְרָחֵל וְלֵאָה אִמּוֹתֵינוּ, וְהָאֵר נֵרֵנוּ שֶׁלֹּא יִכְבֶּה לְעוֹלָם וָעֶד,
וְהָאֵר פָּנֶיךָ וְנִוָּשֵׁעָה. אָמֵן.

Shabbat, the sixth day, and sinned and were sentenced to exile from Eden on
the same day (*Avot deRabbi Natan* 1). God took pity on them and delayed
the start of their exile by a day so that they were able to spend one day,
Shabbat, in paradise. On that day, said the sages, the sun did not set. It was a
day of light, physical and spiritual, in which the first man and woman experienced the harmony of the universe and of their relationship. The candles
of Shabbat – customarily two, though Jewish law requires minimally one –
symbolize the two aspects of holy time: *zakhor*, "remember" (Ex. 20:8) and
shamor "guard" (Deut. 5:12). They also symbolize man and woman, humanity
and God, heaven and earth, united on this day. Though, since the first humans,
we no longer inhabit paradise, we capture something of it on Shabbat and

Minḥa for Weekdays

אַשְׁרֵי Happy are those who dwell in Your House;   Ps. 84
they shall continue to praise You, Selah!
Happy are the people for whom this is so;   Ps. 144
happy are the people whose God is the LORD.

A song of praise by David.   Ps. 145

I will exalt You, my God, the King, and bless Your name for ever
and all time. Every day I will bless You, and praise Your name for
ever and all time. Great is the LORD and greatly to be praised;
His greatness is unfathomable. One generation will praise Your
works to the next, and tell of Your mighty deeds. On the glorious splendor of Your majesty I will meditate, and on the acts
of Your wonders. They shall talk of the power of Your awesome deeds, and I will tell of Your greatness. They shall recite
the record of Your great goodness, and sing with joy of Your
righteousness. The LORD is gracious and compassionate, slow
to anger and great in loving-kindness. The LORD is good to all,

---

through many streets and across the marketplace throughout the day. He
almost forgets that there is a Maker of the world. Only when the time for the
afternoon prayer comes, does he remember, 'I must pray.' And then, from the
bottom of his heart, he heaves a sigh of regret that he has spent his day on
idle matters, and he runs into a side street and stands there and prays. God
holds him dear, very dear, and his prayer pierces the heavens."

אַשְׁרֵי *Psalm 145. Ashrei*, at the beginning of Minḥa, is an abridged form of
the more extended *Pesukei DeZimra*, the Verses of Praise, of the morning
service. It is a meditation prior to the Amida. The Amida is prayer in its pur-
est form, and it requires *kavana*, a direction of the mind, a focusing of our
thoughts. *Kavana* involves "clearing your mind of all extraneous thoughts,
and seeing yourself as if you are standing before the Divine Presence. Therefore it is necessary to sit for a while before prayer in order to direct your
mind, and then pray gently and pleadingly, not like one who prays as if he
were carrying a burden which he is keen to unload and leave" (Maimonides,

מנחה לחול

אַשְׁרֵי יוֹשְׁבֵי בֵיתֶךָ, עוֹד יְהַלְלוּךָ סֶּלָה:
אַשְׁרֵי הָעָם שֶׁכָּכָה לּוֹ, אַשְׁרֵי הָעָם שֶׁיהוה אֱלֹהָיו:

תְּהִלָּה לְדָוִד
אֲרוֹמִמְךָ אֱלוֹהַי הַמֶּלֶךְ, וַאֲבָרְכָה שִׁמְךָ לְעוֹלָם וָעֶד:
בְּכָל־יוֹם אֲבָרְכֶךָּ, וַאֲהַלְלָה שִׁמְךָ לְעוֹלָם וָעֶד:
גָּדוֹל יהוה וּמְהֻלָּל מְאֹד, וְלִגְדֻלָּתוֹ אֵין חֵקֶר:
דּוֹר לְדוֹר יְשַׁבַּח מַעֲשֶׂיךָ, וּגְבוּרֹתֶיךָ יַגִּידוּ:
הֲדַר כְּבוֹד הוֹדֶךָ, וְדִבְרֵי נִפְלְאֹתֶיךָ אָשִׂיחָה:
וֶעֱזוּז נוֹרְאֹתֶיךָ יֹאמֵרוּ, וּגְדוּלָּתְךָ אֲסַפְּרֶנָּה:
זֵכֶר רַב־טוּבְךָ יַבִּיעוּ, וְצִדְקָתְךָ יְרַנֵּנוּ:
חַנּוּן וְרַחוּם יהוה, אֶרֶךְ אַפַּיִם וּגְדָל־חָסֶד:

MINḤA – AFTERNOON SERVICE

The Afternoon Service corresponds to the daily afternoon sacrifice (*Berakhot* 26b). The *Minḥa*, or "meal-offering," was not unique to the afternoon sacrifice. The afternoon service may have become known as Minḥa because of the verse in Psalms (141:2): "May my prayer be like incense before You, the lifting up of my hands like the afternoon offering [*minḥat arev*]."

The sages (*Berakhot* 6b) attached special significance to the afternoon prayer, noting that Elijah's prayer was answered at this time (1 Kings 18:36). It is easier to pray in the morning and evening as we are about to begin or end our engagement with the world for the day. Minḥa is more demanding. It means that we are turning to God in the midst of our distractions. We are bringing Him into our life when it is maximally preoccupied with other things. Minḥa is the triumph of the important over the urgent, of what matters ultimately over what matters immediately. That is why prayer in the midst of the day has a special transformative power.

The Ba'al Shem Tov said: "Imagine a man whose business hounds him

and His compassion extends to all His works. All Your works
shall thank You, Lord, and Your devoted ones shall bless You.
They shall talk of the glory of Your kingship, and speak of Your
might. To make known to mankind His mighty deeds and the
glorious majesty of His kingship. Your kingdom is an everlasting kingdom, and Your reign is for all generations. The Lord
supports all who fall, and raises all who are bowed down. All
raise their eyes to You in hope, and You give them their food in
due season. You open Your hand, and satisfy every living thing
with favor. The Lord is righteous in all His ways, and kind in all
He does. The Lord is close to all who call on Him, to all who
call on Him in truth. He fulfills the will of those who revere
Him; He hears their cry and saves them. The Lord guards all
who love Him, but all the wicked He will destroy. ▸ My mouth
shall speak the praise of the Lord, and all creatures shall bless
His holy name for ever and all time.

We will bless the Lord now and for ever. Halleluya! *Ps. 115*

---

which include three times the word *Ashrei* ("happy"), the first word of the
book of Psalms; and one at the end, which ends with *Halleluya*, the last
word of the book of Psalms. Thus *Ashrei* is a miniature version of the book
of Psalms as a whole.

Ashrei means "happy, blessed, fruitful, flourishing." It refers not to a temporary emotional state but to a life as a whole. One who is *ashrei* does well and
fares well, living uprightly and honestly, respected by those worthy of respect.
The word is in the plural construct, literally "the *happinesses* of," as if to say
that happiness is not one thing but a harmonious blend of many things that
make up a good life. Psalm 1 gives a vivid picture of such a life:

Happy is one who does not walk in step with the wicked, or stand in the
place of sinners, or sit in the company of mockers, but whose delight
is in the Torah of the Lord, and who meditates on His Torah day and
night. He is like a tree planted by streams of water that yields its fruit
in season and whose leaf does not wither – whatever he does prospers.
(Verses 1–3)

טוב־יהוה לַכֹּל, וְרַחֲמָיו עַל־כָּל־מַעֲשָׂיו:

יוֹדְוּךָ יהוה כָּל־מַעֲשֶׂיךָ, וַחֲסִידֶיךָ יְבָרְכְוּכָה:

כְּבוֹד מַלְכוּתְךָ יֹאמֵרוּ, וּגְבוּרָתְךָ יְדַבֵּרוּ:

לְהוֹדִיעַ לִבְנֵי הָאָדָם גְּבוּרֹתָיו, וּכְבוֹד הֲדַר מַלְכוּתוֹ:

מַלְכוּתְךָ מַלְכוּת כָּל־עֹלָמִים, וּמֶמְשַׁלְתְּךָ בְּכָל־דּוֹר וָדֹר:

סוֹמֵךְ יהוה לְכָל־הַנֹּפְלִים, וְזוֹקֵף לְכָל־הַכְּפוּפִים:

עֵינֵי־כֹל אֵלֶיךָ יְשַׂבֵּרוּ, וְאַתָּה נוֹתֵן־לָהֶם אֶת־אָכְלָם בְּעִתּוֹ:

פּוֹתֵחַ אֶת־יָדֶךָ, וּמַשְׂבִּיעַ לְכָל־חַי רָצוֹן:

צַדִּיק יהוה בְּכָל־דְּרָכָיו, וְחָסִיד בְּכָל־מַעֲשָׂיו:

קָרוֹב יהוה לְכָל־קֹרְאָיו, לְכֹל אֲשֶׁר יִקְרָאֻהוּ בֶאֱמֶת:

רְצוֹן־יְרֵאָיו יַעֲשֶׂה, וְאֶת־שַׁוְעָתָם יִשְׁמַע, וְיוֹשִׁיעֵם:

שׁוֹמֵר יהוה אֶת־כָּל־אֹהֲבָיו, וְאֵת כָּל־הָרְשָׁעִים יַשְׁמִיד:

◂ תְּהִלַּת יהוה יְדַבֶּר פִּי, וִיבָרֵךְ כָּל־בָּשָׂר שֵׁם קָדְשׁוֹ לְעוֹלָם וָעֶד:

וַאֲנַחְנוּ נְבָרֵךְ יָהּ מֵעַתָּה וְעַד־עוֹלָם, הַלְלוּיָהּ:

תהלים קמו

Laws of Prayer 4:16). *Ashrei* is the way we "sit for a while before prayer" in order to direct our mind (*Berakhot* 32b). Therefore, though it may be said standing or sitting, the custom is to say it sitting.

It consists of Psalm 145, chosen for three reasons: (1) It is an alphabetical acrostic, praising God with every letter of the alphabet (except *nun*, missing lest it refer to a verse that speaks about the fall, *nefila*, of Israel). (2) It contains the verse, "You open Your hand, and satisfy every living thing with favor," regarded by the sages as one of the essential features of prayer, namely recognition of our complete dependence on God (*Berakhot* 4b). (3) As the psalm speaks of the joy and serenity of those who trust in God, it fulfills the requirement to pray joyfully (see Rashi, *Berakhot* 31a). Psalm 145 is also the only one of the 150 psalms to be called a psalm (*tehilla*) in its superscription.

Added to Psalm 145 are verses from other psalms: two at the beginning,

HALF KADDISH

Leader: יִתְגַּדַּל Magnified and sanctified may His great name be,
in the world He created by His will.
May He establish His kingdom
in your lifetime and in your days,
and in the lifetime of all the house of Israel,
swiftly and soon –
and say: Amen.

All: May His great name be blessed for ever and all time.

Leader: Blessed and praised, glorified and exalted,
raised and honored, uplifted and lauded
be the name of the Holy One, blessed be He,
beyond any blessing,
song, praise and consolation
uttered in the world –
and say: Amen.

THE AMIDA

*The following prayer, until "in former years" on page 28, is said silently, standing
with feet together. If there is a minyan, the Amida is repeated aloud by the Leader.
Take three steps forward and at the points indicated by ˙, bend the knees at the
first word, bow at the second, and stand straight before saying God's name.*

When I proclaim the Lᴏʀᴅ's name, give glory to our God.   *Deut. 32*
O Lᴏʀᴅ, open my lips, so that my mouth may declare Your praise.   *Ps. 51*

PATRIARCHS

בָּרוּךְ˙ Blessed are You, Lᴏʀᴅ our God and God of our fathers,
God of Abraham, God of Isaac and God of Jacob;
the great, mighty and awesome God, God Most High,

───

represents the dawn of Jewish faith, and Jacob the nighttime of exile, Isaac
represents the afternoon joining of past and future, the unspectacular hero-
ism of Jewish continuity. We are each a link in the chain of generations, heirs

חצי קדיש

ש״ץ יִתְגַּדַּל וְיִתְקַדַּשׁ שְׁמֵהּ רַבָּא (קהל: אָמֵן)
בְּעָלְמָא דִּי בְרָא כִרְעוּתֵהּ
וְיַמְלִיךְ מַלְכוּתֵהּ
בְּחַיֵּיכוֹן וּבְיוֹמֵיכוֹן וּבְחַיֵּי דְכָל בֵּית יִשְׂרָאֵל
בַּעֲגָלָא וּבִזְמַן קָרִיב, וְאִמְרוּ אָמֵן. (קהל: אָמֵן)

קהל וש״ץ: יְהֵא שְׁמֵהּ רַבָּא מְבָרַךְ לְעָלַם וּלְעָלְמֵי עָלְמַיָּא.

ש״ץ יִתְבָּרַךְ וְיִשְׁתַּבַּח וְיִתְפָּאַר וְיִתְרוֹמַם וְיִתְנַשֵּׂא
וְיִתְהַדָּר וְיִתְעַלֶּה וְיִתְהַלָּל
שְׁמֵהּ דְּקֻדְשָׁא בְּרִיךְ הוּא (קהל: בְּרִיךְ הוּא)
לְעֵלָּא מִן כָּל בִּרְכָתָא וְשִׁירָתָא, תֻּשְׁבְּחָתָא וְנֶחֱמָתָא
דַּאֲמִירָן בְּעָלְמָא, וְאִמְרוּ אָמֵן. (קהל: אָמֵן)

עמידה

The following prayer, until קְדְמֹנִיּוֹת *on page 29, is said silently, standing with feet together. If there is a* מִנְיָן, *the* עמידה *is repeated aloud by the* שְׁלִיחַ צִבּוּר. *Take three steps forward and at the points indicated by* ׳, *bend the knees at the first word, bow at the second, and stand straight before saying God's name.*

דברים לב
תהלים נא

כִּי שֵׁם יהוה אֶקְרָא, הָבוּ גֹדֶל לֵאלֹהֵינוּ:
אֲדֹנָי, שְׂפָתַי תִּפְתָּח, וּפִי יַגִּיד תְּהִלָּתֶךָ:

אבות

יבָּרוּךְ אַתָּה יהוה, אֱלֹהֵינוּ וֵאלֹהֵי אֲבוֹתֵינוּ
אֱלֹהֵי אַבְרָהָם, אֱלֹהֵי יִצְחָק, וֵאלֹהֵי יַעֲקֹב
הָאֵל הַגָּדוֹל הַגִּבּוֹר וְהַנּוֹרָא, אֵל עֶלְיוֹן

THE AFTERNOON AMIDA
The sages (*Berakhot* 26b) associated the afternoon Amida with Isaac, who
"went out to meditate in the field toward evening" (Gen. 24:63). If Abraham

who bestows acts of loving-kindness and creates all,
who remembers the loving-kindness of the fathers
and will bring a Redeemer to their children's children
for the sake of His name, in love.
King, Helper, Savior, Shield:
ᵛBlessed are You, LORD,
Shield of Abraham.

DIVINE MIGHT

אַתָּה גִּבּוֹר You are eternally mighty, LORD.
You give life to the dead
and have great power to save.

> *In Israel:*
> He causes the dew to fall.

He sustains the living with loving-kindness,
and with great compassion revives the dead.
He supports the fallen, heals the sick, sets captives free,
and keeps His faith with those who sleep in the dust.
Who is like You, Master of might,
and who can compare to You,
O King who brings death and gives life,
and makes salvation grow?
Faithful are You to revive the dead.
Blessed are You, LORD,
who revives the dead.

> *When saying the Amida silently, continue with "You are holy" on the next page.*

---

requests: for redemption, healing and prosperity, (3) collective material-
political requests: for the ingathering of exiles, the restoration of sovereignty,
and the removal of enemies, and (4) collective spiritual requests: for the
righteous, the rebuilding of Jerusalem, and the restoration of the kingdom
of David. The thirteenth blessing is all-embracing, asking God to hear and
heed our prayer.

גּוֹמֵל חֲסָדִים טוֹבִים, וְקֹנֶה הַכֹּל

וְזוֹכֵר חַסְדֵי אָבוֹת

וּמֵבִיא גוֹאֵל לִבְנֵי בְנֵיהֶם לְמַעַן שְׁמוֹ בְּאַהֲבָה.

מֶלֶךְ עוֹזֵר וּמוֹשִׁיעַ וּמָגֵן.

יּבָּרוּךְ אַתָּה יהוה, מָגֵן אַבְרָהָם.

גבורות

אַתָּה גִּבּוֹר לְעוֹלָם, אֲדֹנָי

מְחַיֵּה מֵתִים אַתָּה, רַב לְהוֹשִׁיעַ

In ארץ ישראל:

מוֹרִיד הַטָּל

מְכַלְכֵּל חַיִּים בְּחֶסֶד, מְחַיֵּה מֵתִים בְּרַחֲמִים רַבִּים

סוֹמֵךְ נוֹפְלִים, וְרוֹפֵא חוֹלִים, וּמַתִּיר אֲסוּרִים

וּמְקַיֵּם אֱמוּנָתוֹ לִישֵׁנֵי עָפָר.

מִי כָמוֹךָ, בַּעַל גְּבוּרוֹת

וּמִי דּוֹמֶה לָּךְ

מֶלֶךְ, מֵמִית וּמְחַיֶּה וּמַצְמִיחַ יְשׁוּעָה.

וְנֶאֱמָן אַתָּה לְהַחֲיוֹת מֵתִים.

בָּרוּךְ אַתָּה יהוה, מְחַיֵּה הַמֵּתִים.

When saying the עמידה *silently, continue with* אַתָּה קָדוֹשׁ *on the next page.*

of our ancestors, guardians of our children's future, remembering God in the midst of time and placing our destiny in His hands.

The Central Blessings. There are thirteen central blessings in the weekday Amida and they are grouped into four sets of three: (1) personal spiritual requests: for knowledge, repentance and forgiveness, (2) personal material

KEDUSHA

During the Leader's Repetition, the following is said standing with feet together, rising on the toes at the words indicated by ⁺.

Cong. then נְקַדֵּשׁ We will sanctify Your name on earth,
Leader: as they sanctify it in the highest heavens,
as is written by Your prophet,
"And they [the angels] call to one another saying: *Is. 6*

Cong. then ⁺Holy, ⁺holy, ⁺holy is the LORD of hosts;
Leader: the whole world is filled with His glory."
Those facing them say "Blessed –"

Cong. then ⁺"Blessed is the LORD's glory from His place."   *Ezek. 3*
Leader: And in Your holy Writings it is written thus:

Cong. then ⁺"The LORD shall reign for ever. He is your God, Zion,   *Ps. 146*
Leader: from generation to generation, Halleluya!"

Leader: From generation to generation we will declare Your greatness,
and we will proclaim Your holiness for evermore.
Your praise, our God, shall not leave our mouth forever,
for You, God, are a great and holy King.
Blessed are You, LORD, the holy God.

The Leader continues with "You grace humanity" below.

HOLINESS

אַתָּה קָדוֹשׁ You are holy and Your name is holy,
and holy ones praise You daily, Selah!
Blessed are You, LORD,
the holy God.

KNOWLEDGE

אַתָּה חוֹנֵן You grace humanity with knowledge
and teach mortals understanding.
Grace us with the knowledge, understanding
and discernment that come from You.
Blessed are You, LORD,
who graciously grants knowledge.

קדושה

During the חזרת הש״ץ, *the following is said standing*
with feet together, rising on the toes at the words indicated by ‸.

ישעיה ו

קהל
then
ש״ץ:
נְקַדֵּשׁ אֶת שִׁמְךָ בָּעוֹלָם, כְּשֵׁם שֶׁמַּקְדִּישִׁים אוֹתוֹ בִּשְׁמֵי מָרוֹם
כַּכָּתוּב עַל יַד נְבִיאֶךָ: וְקָרָא זֶה אֶל־זֶה וְאָמַר,

קהל
then
ש״ץ:
‸קָדוֹשׁ, ‸קָדוֹשׁ, ‸קָדוֹשׁ, יהוה צְבָאוֹת, מְלֹא כָל־הָאָרֶץ כְּבוֹדוֹ:
לְעֻמָּתָם בָּרוּךְ יֹאמֵרוּ

יחזקאל ג

קהל
then
ש״ץ:
‸בָּרוּךְ כְּבוֹד־יהוה מִמְּקוֹמוֹ:
וּבְדִבְרֵי קָדְשְׁךָ כָּתוּב לֵאמֹר

תהלים קמו

קהל
then
ש״ץ:
‸יִמְלֹךְ יהוה לְעוֹלָם, אֱלֹהַיִךְ צִיּוֹן לְדֹר וָדֹר, הַלְלוּיָהּ:

ש״ץ:
לְדוֹר וָדוֹר נַגִּיד גָּדְלֶךָ, וּלְנֵצַח נְצָחִים קְדֻשָּׁתְךָ נַקְדִּישׁ
וְשִׁבְחֲךָ אֱלֹהֵינוּ מִפִּינוּ לֹא יָמוּשׁ לְעוֹלָם וָעֶד
כִּי אֵל מֶלֶךְ גָּדוֹל וְקָדוֹשׁ אָתָּה.
בָּרוּךְ אַתָּה יהוה, הָאֵל הַקָּדוֹשׁ.

The שליח ציבור *continues with* אַתָּה חוֹנֵן *below.*

קדושת השם

אַתָּה קָדוֹשׁ וְשִׁמְךָ קָדוֹשׁ
וּקְדוֹשִׁים בְּכָל יוֹם יְהַלְלוּךָ סֶּלָה.
בָּרוּךְ אַתָּה יהוה, הָאֵל הַקָּדוֹשׁ.

דעת

אַתָּה חוֹנֵן לְאָדָם דַּעַת, וּמְלַמֵּד לֶאֱנוֹשׁ בִּינָה.
חָנֵּנוּ מֵאִתְּךָ דֵּעָה בִּינָה וְהַשְׂכֵּל.
בָּרוּךְ אַתָּה יהוה, חוֹנֵן הַדָּעַת.

דֵּעָה בִּינָה וְהַשְׂכֵּל *Knowledge, Repentance and Forgiveness.* Note the sequence.
First we pray for knowledge and understanding. Without these it is as if we

REPENTANCE

הֲשִׁיבֵנוּ Bring us back, our Father, to Your Torah.
Draw us near, our King, to Your service.
Lead us back to You in perfect repentance.
Blessed are You, LORD,
who desires repentance.

FORGIVENESS

Strike the left side of the chest at °.

סְלַח לָנוּ Forgive us, our Father, for we have °sinned.
Pardon us, our King, for we have °transgressed;
for You pardon and forgive.
Blessed are You, LORD,
the gracious One who repeatedly forgives.

REDEMPTION

רְאֵה Look on our affliction,
plead our cause,
and redeem us soon for Your name's sake,
for You are a powerful Redeemer.
Blessed are You, LORD,
the Redeemer of Israel.

HEALING

רְפָאֵנוּ Heal us, LORD, and we shall be healed.
Save us and we shall be saved,
for You are our praise.
Bring complete recovery for all our ailments,

---

but humility. Knowing how we should live, we come to realize how we fall
short, and this brings us to repentance. Only then do we ask for forgiveness.
We must put in the work of self-understanding and self-judgment before we
can ask God to excuse our lapses.

תשובה

הֲשִׁיבֵנוּ אָבִינוּ לְתוֹרָתֶךָ
וְקָרְבֵנוּ מַלְכֵּנוּ לַעֲבוֹדָתֶךָ
וְהַחֲזִירֵנוּ בִּתְשׁוּבָה שְׁלֵמָה לְפָנֶיךָ.
בָּרוּךְ אַתָּה יהוה, הָרוֹצֶה בִּתְשׁוּבָה.

סליחה

Strike the left side of the chest at °.

סְלַח לֵנוּ אָבִינוּ כִּי °חָטָאנוּ
מְחַל לֵנוּ מַלְכֵּנוּ כִּי °פָשָׁעְנוּ
כִּי מוֹחֵל וְסוֹלֵחַ אָתָּה.
בָּרוּךְ אַתָּה יהוה, חַנּוּן הַמַּרְבֶּה לִסְלוֹחַ.

גאולה

רְאֵה בְעָנְיֵנוּ, וְרִיבָה רִיבֵנוּ
וּגְאָלֵנוּ מְהֵרָה לְמַעַן שְׁמֶךָ
כִּי גוֹאֵל חָזָק אָתָּה.
בָּרוּךְ אַתָּה יהוה, גּוֹאֵל יִשְׂרָאֵל.

רפואה

רְפָאֵנוּ יהוה וְנֵרָפֵא
הוֹשִׁיעֵנוּ וְנִוָּשֵׁעָה, כִּי תְהִלָּתֵנוּ אָתָּה
וְהַעֲלֵה רְפוּאָה שְׁלֵמָה לְכָל מַכּוֹתֵינוּ

travel blind. Judaism is a religion of emotion, but emotion instructed by the mind. Second, understanding should lead us not to intellectual arrogance

---

The following prayer for a sick person may be said here:
May it be Your will, O LORD my God and God of my ancestors, that You
speedily send a complete recovery from heaven, a healing of both soul
and body, to the patient (*name*), son/daughter of (*mother's name*) among
the other afflicted of Israel.

---

for You, God, King, are a faithful and compassionate Healer.
Blessed are You, LORD,
Healer of the sick of His people Israel.

PROSPERITY
בָּרֵךְ Bless this year for us, LORD our God,
and all its types of produce for good.
Grant blessing on the face of the earth,
and from its goodness satisfy us,
blessing our year as the best of years.
Blessed are You, LORD,
who blesses the years.

INGATHERING OF EXILES
תְּקַע Sound the great shofar for our freedom,
raise high the banner to gather our exiles,
and gather us together
from the four quarters of the earth.
Blessed are You, LORD,
who gathers the dispersed of His people Israel.

JUSTICE
הָשִׁיבָה Restore our judges as at first,
and our counselors as at the beginning,
and remove from us sorrow and sighing.
May You alone, LORD,
reign over us with loving-kindness and compassion,
and vindicate us in justice.
Blessed are You, LORD,
the King who loves righteousness and justice.

The following prayer for a sick person may be said here:

יְהִי רָצוֹן מִלְּפָנֶיךָ יהוה אֱלֹהַי וֵאלֹהֵי אֲבוֹתַי, שֶׁתִּשְׁלַח מְהֵרָה רְפוּאָה שְׁלֵמָה
מִן הַשָּׁמַיִם רְפוּאַת הַנֶּפֶשׁ וּרְפוּאַת הַגּוּף לַחוֹלֶה/לַחוֹלָה *name of patient*
בֶּן/בַּת *mother's name* בְּתוֹךְ שְׁאָר חוֹלֵי יִשְׂרָאֵל.

כִּי אֵל מֶלֶךְ רוֹפֵא נֶאֱמָן וְרַחֲמָן אָתָּה.
בָּרוּךְ אַתָּה יהוה, רוֹפֵא חוֹלֵי עַמּוֹ יִשְׂרָאֵל.

בְּרְכַּת הַשָּׁנִים
בָּרֵךְ עָלֵינוּ יהוה אֱלֹהֵינוּ אֶת הַשָּׁנָה הַזֹּאת
וְאֶת כָּל מִינֵי תְבוּאָתָהּ לְטוֹבָה
וְתֵן בְּרָכָה עַל פְּנֵי הָאֲדָמָה
וְשַׂבְּעֵנוּ מִטּוּבָהּ
וּבָרֵךְ שְׁנָתֵנוּ כַּשָּׁנִים הַטּוֹבוֹת.
בָּרוּךְ אַתָּה יהוה, מְבָרֵךְ הַשָּׁנִים.

קִבּוּץ גָּלֻיּוֹת
תְּקַע בְּשׁוֹפָר גָּדוֹל לְחֵרוּתֵנוּ
וְשָׂא נֵס לְקַבֵּץ גָּלֻיּוֹתֵינוּ
וְקַבְּצֵנוּ יַחַד מֵאַרְבַּע כַּנְפוֹת הָאָרֶץ.
בָּרוּךְ אַתָּה יהוה, מְקַבֵּץ נִדְחֵי עַמּוֹ יִשְׂרָאֵל.

הָשַׁבַת הַמִּשְׁפָּט
הָשִׁיבָה שׁוֹפְטֵינוּ כְּבָרִאשׁוֹנָה וְיוֹעֲצֵינוּ כְּבַתְּחִלָּה
וְהָסֵר מִמֶּנּוּ יָגוֹן וַאֲנָחָה
וּמְלֹךְ עָלֵינוּ אַתָּה יהוה לְבַדְּךָ בְּחֶסֶד וּבְרַחֲמִים
וְצַדְּקֵנוּ בַּמִּשְׁפָּט.
בָּרוּךְ אַתָּה יהוה, מֶלֶךְ אוֹהֵב צְדָקָה וּמִשְׁפָּט.

AGAINST INFORMERS

וְלַמַּלְשִׁינִים For the slanderers let there be no hope,
and may all wickedness perish in an instant.
May all Your people's enemies swiftly be cut down.
May You swiftly uproot, crush, cast down
and humble the arrogant swiftly in our days.
Blessed are You, LORD,
who destroys enemies and humbles the arrogant.

THE RIGHTEOUS

עַל הַצַּדִּיקִים To the righteous, the pious,
the elders of Your people the house of Israel,
the remnant of their scholars,
the righteous converts, and to us,
may Your compassion be aroused, LORD our God.
Grant a good reward
to all who sincerely trust in Your name.
Set our lot with them,
so that we may never be ashamed,
for in You we trust.
Blessed are You, LORD,
who is the support and trust of the righteous.

REBUILDING JERUSALEM

וְלִירוּשָׁלַיִם To Jerusalem, Your city,
may You return in compassion,
and may You dwell in it as You promised.
May You rebuild it rapidly in our days
as an everlasting structure,
and install within it soon the throne of David.
Blessed are You, LORD,
who builds Jerusalem.

ברכת המינים

וְלַמַּלְשִׁינִים אַל תְּהִי תִקְוָה

וְכָל הָרִשְׁעָה כְּרֶגַע תֹּאבֵד

וְכָל אוֹיְבֵי עַמְּךָ מְהֵרָה יִכָּרֵתוּ

וְהַזֵּדִים מְהֵרָה תְעַקֵּר וּתְשַׁבֵּר וּתְמַגֵּר וְתַכְנִיעַ

בִּמְהֵרָה בְיָמֵינוּ.

בָּרוּךְ אַתָּה יהוה, שׁוֹבֵר אוֹיְבִים וּמַכְנִיעַ זֵדִים.

על הצדיקים

עַל הַצַּדִּיקִים וְעַל הַחֲסִידִים

וְעַל זִקְנֵי עַמְּךָ בֵּית יִשְׂרָאֵל

וְעַל פְּלֵיטַת סוֹפְרֵיהֶם

וְעַל גֵּרֵי הַצֶּדֶק, וְעָלֵינוּ

יֶהֱמוּ רַחֲמֶיךָ יהוה אֱלֹהֵינוּ

וְתֵן שָׂכָר טוֹב לְכָל הַבּוֹטְחִים בְּשִׁמְךָ בֶּאֱמֶת

וְשִׂים חֶלְקֵנוּ עִמָּהֶם

וּלְעוֹלָם לֹא נֵבוֹשׁ כִּי בְךָ בָּטָחְנוּ.

בָּרוּךְ אַתָּה יהוה, מִשְׁעָן וּמִבְטָח לַצַּדִּיקִים.

בניין ירושלים

וְלִירוּשָׁלַיִם עִירְךָ בְּרַחֲמִים תָּשׁוּב

וְתִשְׁכֹּן בְּתוֹכָהּ כַּאֲשֶׁר דִּבַּרְתָּ

וּבְנֵה אוֹתָהּ בְּקָרוֹב בְּיָמֵינוּ בִּנְיַן עוֹלָם

וְכִסֵּא דָוִד מְהֵרָה לְתוֹכָהּ תָּכִין.

בָּרוּךְ אַתָּה יהוה, בּוֹנֵה יְרוּשָׁלָיִם.

KINGDOM OF DAVID

אֶת צֶמַח May the offshoot of Your servant David soon flower,
and may his pride be raised high by Your salvation,
for we wait for Your salvation all day.
Blessed are You, LORD,
who makes the glory of salvation flourish.

RESPONSE TO PRAYER

שְׁמַע קוֹלֵנוּ Listen to our voice, LORD our God.
Spare us and have compassion on us,
and in compassion and favor accept our prayer,
for You, God, listen to prayers and pleas.
Do not turn us away, O our King,
empty-handed from Your presence,
for You listen with compassion
to the prayer of Your people Israel.
Blessed are You, LORD,
who listens to prayer.

TEMPLE SERVICE

רְצֵה Find favor, LORD our God,
in Your people Israel and their prayer.
Restore the service to Your most holy House,
and accept in love and favor
the fire-offerings of Israel and their prayer.
May the service of Your people Israel
always find favor with You.

---

praying for the *Shekhina* to return to Jerusalem. We must therefore bow
at *Modim* as if we were standing in the presence of the restored *Shekhina*."
(Rabbi Joseph Soloveitchik)

משיח בן דוד

אֶת צֶמַח דָּוִד עַבְדְּךָ מְהֵרָה תַצְמִיחַ

וְקַרְנוֹ תָּרוּם בִּישׁוּעָתֶךָ

כִּי לִישׁוּעָתְךָ קִוִּינוּ כָּל הַיּוֹם.

בָּרוּךְ אַתָּה יהוה, מַצְמִיחַ קֶרֶן יְשׁוּעָה.

שומע תפלה

שְׁמַע קוֹלֵנוּ יהוה אֱלֹהֵינוּ

חוּס וְרַחֵם עָלֵינוּ

וְקַבֵּל בְּרַחֲמִים וּבְרָצוֹן אֶת תְּפִלָּתֵנוּ

כִּי אֵל שׁוֹמֵעַ תְּפִלּוֹת וְתַחֲנוּנִים אָתָּה

וּמִלְּפָנֶיךָ מַלְכֵּנוּ רֵיקָם אַל תְּשִׁיבֵנוּ

כִּי אַתָּה שׁוֹמֵעַ תְּפִלַּת עַמְּךָ יִשְׂרָאֵל בְּרַחֲמִים.

בָּרוּךְ אַתָּה יהוה, שׁוֹמֵעַ תְּפִלָּה.

עבודה

רְצֵה יהוה אֱלֹהֵינוּ בְּעַמְּךָ יִשְׂרָאֵל, וּבִתְפִלָּתָם

וְהָשֵׁב אֶת הָעֲבוֹדָה לִדְבִיר בֵּיתֶךָ

וְאִשֵּׁי יִשְׂרָאֵל וּתְפִלָּתָם בְּאַהֲבָה תְקַבֵּל בְּרָצוֹן

וּתְהִי לְרָצוֹן תָּמִיד עֲבוֹדַת יִשְׂרָאֵל עַמֶּךָ.

Temple Service and Thanksgiving. "As the Jew recites *Retzeh* and beseeches God to accept his sacrifices, he is no longer praying in his local synagogue in Warsaw, Vilna or New York. He is suddenly transported to Jerusalem, and his prayer is transformed into an offering in the Temple. Rabbi Judah HaLevi (*Kuzari* 3:19) highlights that at this juncture in the Amida we are

וְתֶחֱזֶינָה And may our eyes witness Your return
to Zion in compassion.
Blessed are You, LORD, who restores His Presence to Zion.

THANKSGIVING   *Bow at the first nine words.*

מוֹדִים We give thanks to You,
for You are the LORD our God
and God of our ancestors
for ever and all time.
You are the Rock of our lives,
Shield of our salvation
from generation to generation.
We will thank You and
declare Your praise for our lives,
which are entrusted into Your hand;
for our souls,
which are placed in Your charge;
for Your miracles
which are with us every day;
and for Your wonders and favors
at all times, evening,
morning and midday.
You are good –
for Your compassion never fails.
You are compassionate –
for Your loving-kindnesses never cease.
We have always placed our hope in You.

During the Leader's Repetition,
the congregation says quietly:
מוֹדִים We give thanks to You,
for You are the LORD our God
and God of our ancestors,
God of all flesh,
who formed us
and formed the universe.
Blessings and thanks
are due to Your great
and holy name
for giving us life
and sustaining us.
May You continue
to give us life
and sustain us;
and may You gather our
exiles to Your holy courts,
to keep Your decrees,
do Your will and serve You
with a perfect heart,
for it is for us
to give You thanks.
Blessed be God to whom
thanksgiving is due.

וְעַל כֻּלָּם For all these things may Your name be blessed and exalted,
our King, continually, for ever and all time.
Let all that lives thank You, Selah! and praise Your name in truth,
God, our Savior and Help, Selah!
Blessed are You, LORD, whose name is "the Good"
and to whom thanks are due.

וְתֶחֱזֶינָה עֵינֵינוּ בְּשׁוּבְךָ לְצִיּוֹן בְּרַחֲמִים.
בָּרוּךְ אַתָּה יהוה, הַמַּחֲזִיר שְׁכִינָתוֹ לְצִיּוֹן.

הודאה

Bow at the first five words.

מוֹדִים אֲנַחְנוּ לָךְ
שָׁאַתָּה הוּא יהוה אֱלֹהֵינוּ
וֵאלֹהֵי אֲבוֹתֵינוּ לְעוֹלָם וָעֶד.
צוּר חַיֵּינוּ, מָגֵן יִשְׁעֵנוּ
אַתָּה הוּא לְדוֹר וָדוֹר.
נוֹדֶה לְּךָ וּנְסַפֵּר תְּהִלָּתֶךָ
עַל חַיֵּינוּ הַמְּסוּרִים בְּיָדֶךָ
וְעַל נִשְׁמוֹתֵינוּ הַפְּקוּדוֹת לָךְ
וְעַל נִסֶּיךָ שֶׁבְּכָל יוֹם עִמָּנוּ
וְעַל נִפְלְאוֹתֶיךָ וְטוֹבוֹתֶיךָ
שֶׁבְּכָל עֵת
עֶרֶב וָבֹקֶר וְצָהֳרָיִם.
הַטּוֹב, כִּי לֹא כָלוּ רַחֲמֶיךָ
וְהַמְרַחֵם, כִּי לֹא תַמּוּ חֲסָדֶיךָ
מֵעוֹלָם קִוִּינוּ לָךְ.

During the חזרת הש״ץ,
the קהל *says quietly:*

מוֹדִים אֲנַחְנוּ לָךְ
שָׁאַתָּה הוּא יהוה אֱלֹהֵינוּ
וֵאלֹהֵי אֲבוֹתֵינוּ
אֱלֹהֵי כָל בָּשָׂר
יוֹצְרֵנוּ, יוֹצֵר בְּרֵאשִׁית
בְּרָכוֹת וְהוֹדָאוֹת
לְשִׁמְךָ הַגָּדוֹל וְהַקָּדוֹשׁ
עַל שֶׁהֶחֱיִיתָנוּ וְקִיַּמְתָּנוּ.
כֵּן תְּחַיֵּנוּ וּתְקַיְּמֵנוּ
וְתֶאֱסֹף גָּלֻיּוֹתֵינוּ
לְחַצְרוֹת קָדְשֶׁךָ
לִשְׁמֹר חֻקֶּיךָ
וְלַעֲשׂוֹת רְצוֹנֶךָ וּלְעָבְדְּךָ
בְּלֵבָב שָׁלֵם
עַל שֶׁאֲנַחְנוּ מוֹדִים לָךְ.
בָּרוּךְ אֵל הַהוֹדָאוֹת.

וְעַל כֻּלָּם יִתְבָּרַךְ וְיִתְרוֹמַם שִׁמְךָ מַלְכֵּנוּ תָּמִיד לְעוֹלָם וָעֶד.
וְכֹל הַחַיִּים יוֹדוּךָ סֶּלָה, וִיהַלְלוּ אֶת שִׁמְךָ בֶּאֱמֶת
הָאֵל יְשׁוּעָתֵנוּ וְעֶזְרָתֵנוּ סֶלָה.
בָּרוּךְ אַתָּה יהוה, הַטּוֹב שִׁמְךָ וּלְךָ נָאֶה לְהוֹדוֹת.

PEACE

שָׁלוֹם רָב Grant great peace to Your people Israel for ever,
for You are the sovereign LORD of all peace;
and may it be good in Your eyes
to bless Your people Israel
at every time, at every hour, with Your peace.
Blessed are You, LORD, who blesses His people Israel with peace.

The following verse concludes the Leader's Repetition of the Amida.
Some also say it here as part of the silent Amida.

May the words of my mouth and the meditation of my heart   *Ps. 19*
find favor before You, LORD, my Rock and Redeemer.

אֱלֹהַי My God,   *Berakhot*
                                                                   17a
guard my tongue from evil and my lips from deceitful speech.
To those who curse me, let my soul be silent;
may my soul be to all like the dust.
Open my heart to Your Torah and let my soul
pursue Your commandments. As for all who plan evil against me,
swiftly thwart their counsel and frustrate their plans.
   Act for the sake of Your name; act for the sake of Your right hand;
   act for the sake of Your holiness; act for the sake of Your Torah.
That Your beloved ones may be delivered,   *Ps. 60*
save with Your right hand and answer me.
May the words of my mouth and the meditation of my heart   *Ps. 19*
find favor before You, LORD, my Rock and Redeemer.

Bow, take three steps back, then bow, first left, then right, then center, while saying:
May He who makes peace in His high places,
make peace for us and all Israel – and say: Amen.

יְהִי רָצוֹן May it be Your will, LORD our God and God of our ancestors,
that the Temple be rebuilt speedily in our days,
and grant us a share in Your Torah.
And there we will serve You with reverence,
as in the days of old and as in former years.
Then the offering of Judah and Jerusalem will be pleasing to the LORD   *Mal. 3*
as in the days of old and as in former years.

ברכת שלום
שָׁלוֹם רָב עַל יִשְׂרָאֵל עַמְּךָ תָּשִׂים לְעוֹלָם
כִּי אַתָּה הוּא מֶלֶךְ אָדוֹן לְכָל הַשָּׁלוֹם.
וְטוֹב בְּעֵינֶיךָ לְבָרֵךְ אֶת עַמְּךָ יִשְׂרָאֵל
בְּכָל עֵת וּבְכָל שָׁעָה בִּשְׁלוֹמֶךָ.
בָּרוּךְ אַתָּה יהוה, הַמְבָרֵךְ אֶת עַמּוֹ יִשְׂרָאֵל בַּשָּׁלוֹם.

The following verse concludes the חזרת הש״ץ.
Some also say it here as part of the silent עמידה.

תהלים יט
יִהְיוּ לְרָצוֹן אִמְרֵי־פִי וְהֶגְיוֹן לִבִּי לְפָנֶיךָ, יהוה צוּרִי וְגֹאֲלִי:

ברכות יז.
אֱלֹהַי
נְצֹר לְשׁוֹנִי מֵרָע וּשְׂפָתַי מִדַּבֵּר מִרְמָה
וְלִמְקַלְלַי נַפְשִׁי תִדֹּם, וְנַפְשִׁי כֶּעָפָר לַכֹּל תִּהְיֶה.
פְּתַח לִבִּי בְּתוֹרָתֶךָ, וּבְמִצְוֹתֶיךָ תִּרְדֹּף נַפְשִׁי.
וְכָל הַחוֹשְׁבִים עָלַי רָעָה
מְהֵרָה הָפֵר עֲצָתָם וְקַלְקֵל מַחֲשַׁבְתָּם.
עֲשֵׂה לְמַעַן שְׁמֶךָ, עֲשֵׂה לְמַעַן יְמִינֶךָ
עֲשֵׂה לְמַעַן קְדֻשָּׁתֶךָ, עֲשֵׂה לְמַעַן תּוֹרָתֶךָ.
תהלים ס
לְמַעַן יֵחָלְצוּן יְדִידֶיךָ, הוֹשִׁיעָה יְמִינְךָ וַעֲנֵנִי:
תהלים יט
יִהְיוּ לְרָצוֹן אִמְרֵי־פִי וְהֶגְיוֹן לִבִּי לְפָנֶיךָ, יהוה צוּרִי וְגֹאֲלִי:

Bow, take three steps back, then bow, first left, then right, then center, while saying:

עֹשֶׂה שָׁלוֹם בִּמְרוֹמָיו
הוּא יַעֲשֶׂה שָׁלוֹם עָלֵינוּ וְעַל כָּל יִשְׂרָאֵל, וְאִמְרוּ אָמֵן.

יְהִי רָצוֹן מִלְּפָנֶיךָ יהוה אֱלֹהֵינוּ וֵאלֹהֵי אֲבוֹתֵינוּ
שֶׁיִּבָּנֶה בֵּית הַמִּקְדָּשׁ בִּמְהֵרָה בְיָמֵינוּ, וְתֵן חֶלְקֵנוּ בְּתוֹרָתֶךָ
וְשָׁם נַעֲבָדְךָ בְּיִרְאָה כִּימֵי עוֹלָם וּכְשָׁנִים קַדְמֹנִיּוֹת.
מלאכי ג
וְעָרְבָה לַיהוה מִנְחַת יְהוּדָה וִירוּשָׁלָיִם כִּימֵי עוֹלָם וּכְשָׁנִים קַדְמֹנִיּוֹת:

FULL KADDISH

Leader: יִתְגַּדַּל Magnified and sanctified
may His great name be,
in the world He created by His will.
May He establish His kingdom
in your lifetime and in your days,
and in the lifetime of all the house of Israel,
swiftly and soon –
and say: Amen.

All: May His great name be blessed
for ever and all time.

Leader: Blessed and praised,
glorified and exalted,
raised and honored,
uplifted and lauded be
the name of the Holy One,
blessed be He,
beyond any blessing,
song, praise and consolation
uttered in the world –
and say: Amen.

May the prayers and pleas of all Israel
be accepted by their Father in heaven –
and say: Amen.

May there be great peace from heaven,
and life for us and all Israel –
and say: Amen.

*Bow, take three steps back, as if taking leave of the Divine Presence,
then bow, first left, then right, then center, while saying:*
May He who makes peace in His high places,
make peace for us and all Israel –
and say: Amen.

קדיש שלם

ש״ץ: יִתְגַּדַּל וְיִתְקַדַּשׁ שְׁמֵהּ רַבָּא (קהל: אָמֵן)
בְּעָלְמָא דִּי בְרָא כִרְעוּתֵהּ
וְיַמְלִיךְ מַלְכוּתֵהּ
בְּחַיֵּיכוֹן וּבְיוֹמֵיכוֹן וּבְחַיֵּי דְכָל בֵּית יִשְׂרָאֵל
בַּעֲגָלָא וּבִזְמַן קָרִיב
וְאִמְרוּ אָמֵן. (קהל: אָמֵן)

קהל
 וש״ץ: יְהֵא שְׁמֵהּ רַבָּא מְבָרַךְ לְעָלַם וּלְעָלְמֵי עָלְמַיָּא.

ש״ץ: יִתְבָּרַךְ וְיִשְׁתַּבַּח וְיִתְפָּאַר
וְיִתְרוֹמַם וְיִתְנַשֵּׂא וְיִתְהַדָּר וְיִתְעַלֶּה וְיִתְהַלָּל
שְׁמֵהּ דְּקֻדְשָׁא בְּרִיךְ הוּא (קהל: בְּרִיךְ הוּא)
לְעֵלָּא מִן כָּל בִּרְכָתָא וְשִׁירָתָא, תֻּשְׁבְּחָתָא וְנֶחֱמָתָא
דַּאֲמִירָן בְּעָלְמָא
וְאִמְרוּ אָמֵן. (קהל: אָמֵן)

תִּתְקַבַּל צְלוֹתְהוֹן וּבָעוּתְהוֹן דְּכָל יִשְׂרָאֵל
קֳדָם אֲבוּהוֹן דִּי בִשְׁמַיָּא
וְאִמְרוּ אָמֵן. (קהל: אָמֵן)

יְהֵא שְׁלָמָא רַבָּא מִן שְׁמַיָּא
וְחַיִּים, עָלֵינוּ וְעַל כָּל יִשְׂרָאֵל
וְאִמְרוּ אָמֵן. (קהל: אָמֵן)

*Bow, take three steps back, as if taking leave of the Divine Presence,
then bow, first left, then right, then center, while saying:*

עֹשֶׂה שָׁלוֹם בִּמְרוֹמָיו
הוּא יַעֲשֶׂה שָׁלוֹם עָלֵינוּ וְעַל כָּל יִשְׂרָאֵל
וְאִמְרוּ אָמֵן. (קהל: אָמֵן)

Stand while saying Aleinu. Bow at ˙.

עָלֵינוּ It is our duty to praise the Master of all,
and ascribe greatness to the Author of creation,
who has not made us like the nations of the lands
nor placed us like the families of the earth;
who has not made our portion like theirs,
nor our destiny like all their multitudes.
(For they worship vanity and emptiness,
and pray to a god who cannot save.)
˙But we bow in worship
and thank the Supreme King of kings,
the Holy One, blessed be He,
who extends the heavens and establishes the earth,
whose throne of glory is in the heavens above,
and whose power's Presence is in the highest of heights.
He is our God; there is no other.
Truly He is our King, there is none else,
as it is written in His Torah:
"You shall know and take to heart this day   *Deut. 4*
that the LORD is God,
in heaven above and on earth below.
There is no other."

Note the contrast between the first and second paragraphs. The first is a statement of Jewish particularity. We thank God for the uniqueness of the Jewish people and its vocation. We are different. It is not our highest aspiration to be like everyone else. We have been singled out for a sacred mission, to be God's ambassadors, His witnesses, part of a nation that in itself testifies to something larger than itself, to a divine presence in history.

The second paragraph is a no less emphatic prayer for universality, for the day when all humanity will recognize the sovereignty of God. All humans are in God's image, part of God's world, heirs to God's covenant with Noah,

Stand while saying עָלֵינוּ. Bow at ׳.

עָלֵינוּ לְשַׁבֵּחַ לַאֲדוֹן הַכֹּל

לָתֵת גְּדֻלָּה לְיוֹצֵר בְּרֵאשִׁית

שֶׁלֹּא עָשָׂנוּ כְּגוֹיֵי הָאֲרָצוֹת

וְלֹא שָׂמָנוּ כְּמִשְׁפְּחוֹת הָאֲדָמָה

שֶׁלֹּא שָׂם חֶלְקֵנוּ כָּהֶם וְגוֹרָלֵנוּ כְּכָל הֲמוֹנָם.

(שֶׁהֵם מִשְׁתַּחֲוִים לְהֶבֶל וָרִיק

וּמִתְפַּלְלִים אֶל אֵל לֹא יוֹשִׁיעַ.)

׳וַאֲנַחְנוּ כּוֹרְעִים וּמִשְׁתַּחֲוִים וּמוֹדִים

לִפְנֵי מֶלֶךְ מַלְכֵי הַמְּלָכִים, הַקָּדוֹשׁ בָּרוּךְ הוּא

שֶׁהוּא נוֹטֶה שָׁמַיִם וְיוֹסֵד אֶרֶץ

וּמוֹשַׁב יְקָרוֹ בַּשָּׁמַיִם מִמַּעַל

וּשְׁכִינַת עֻזּוֹ בְּגָבְהֵי מְרוֹמִים.

הוּא אֱלֹהֵינוּ, אֵין עוֹד.

אֱמֶת מַלְכֵּנוּ, אֶפֶס זוּלָתוֹ

כַּכָּתוּב בְּתוֹרָתוֹ

וְיָדַעְתָּ הַיּוֹם וַהֲשֵׁבֹתָ אֶל־לְבָבֶךָ

כִּי יהוה הוּא הָאֱלֹהִים בַּשָּׁמַיִם מִמַּעַל וְעַל־הָאָרֶץ מִתָּחַת

אֵין עוֹד:

דברים ד

ALEINU

Aleinu, one of Judaism's great affirmations of faith, is an ancient prayer, originally composed as the prelude to *Malkhiyot*, the verses relating to God's kingship in the Musaf Amida of Rosh HaShana. Only in the twelfth century did it begin to be said daily at the conclusion of each service.

Therefore, we place our hope in You, LORD our God,
that we may soon see the glory of Your power,
when You will remove abominations from the earth,
and idols will be utterly destroyed,
when the world will be perfected
under the sovereignty of the Almighty,
when all humanity will call on Your name,
to turn all the earth's wicked toward You.
All the world's inhabitants will realize and know
that to You every knee must bow
and every tongue swear loyalty.
Before You, LORD our God,
they will kneel and bow down
and give honor to Your glorious name.
They will all accept the yoke of Your kingdom,
and You will reign over them soon and for ever.
For the kingdom is Yours,
and to all eternity You will reign in glory,
as it is written in Your Torah:
"The LORD will reign for ever and ever."   Ex. 15
▸ And it is said:
"Then the LORD shall be King over all the earth;   Zech. 14
on that day the LORD shall be One and His name One."

Some add:

Have no fear of sudden terror or of the ruin when it overtakes the wicked.   *Prov. 3*
Devise your strategy, but it will be thwarted; propose your plan,   *Is. 8*
but it will not stand, for God is with us.
When you grow old, I will still be the same.   *Is. 46*
When your hair turns gray, I will still carry you.
I made you, I will bear you, I will carry you, and I will rescue you.

There is no contradiction between particularity and universality. Only by being what we uniquely are, do we contribute to humanity as a whole what only we can give.

עַל כֵּן נְקַוֶּה לְךָ יהוה אֱלֹהֵינוּ
לִרְאוֹת מְהֵרָה בְּתִפְאֶרֶת עֻזֶּךָ
לְהַעֲבִיר גִּלּוּלִים מִן הָאָרֶץ
וְהָאֱלִילִים כָּרוֹת יִכָּרֵתוּן
לְתַקֵּן עוֹלָם בְּמַלְכוּת שַׁדַּי.
וְכָל בְּנֵי בָשָׂר יִקְרְאוּ בִשְׁמֶךָ
לְהַפְנוֹת אֵלֶיךָ כָּל רִשְׁעֵי אָרֶץ.
יַכִּירוּ וְיֵדְעוּ כָּל יוֹשְׁבֵי תֵבֵל
כִּי לְךָ תִּכְרַע כָּל בֶּרֶךְ, תִּשָּׁבַע כָּל לָשׁוֹן.
לְפָנֶיךָ יהוה אֱלֹהֵינוּ יִכְרְעוּ וְיִפֹּלוּ
וְלִכְבוֹד שִׁמְךָ יְקָר יִתֵּנוּ
וִיקַבְּלוּ כֻלָּם אֶת עֹל מַלְכוּתֶךָ
וְתִמְלֹךְ עֲלֵיהֶם מְהֵרָה לְעוֹלָם וָעֶד.
כִּי הַמַּלְכוּת שֶׁלְּךָ הִיא וּלְעוֹלְמֵי עַד תִּמְלֹךְ בְּכָבוֹד
כַּכָּתוּב בְּתוֹרָתֶךָ

שמות טו
יהוה יִמְלֹךְ לְעֹלָם וָעֶד:

זכריה יד
‹ וְנֶאֱמַר, וְהָיָה יהוה לְמֶלֶךְ עַל־כָּל־הָאָרֶץ
בַּיּוֹם הַהוּא יִהְיֶה יהוה אֶחָד וּשְׁמוֹ אֶחָד:

Some add:

משלי ג
אַל־תִּירָא מִפַּחַד פִּתְאֹם וּמִשֹּׁאַת רְשָׁעִים כִּי תָבֹא:

ישעיה ח
עֻצוּ עֵצָה וְתֻפָר, דַּבְּרוּ דָבָר וְלֹא יָקוּם, כִּי עִמָּנוּ אֵל:

ישעיה מו
וְעַד־זִקְנָה אֲנִי הוּא, וְעַד־שֵׂיבָה אֲנִי אֶסְבֹּל
אֲנִי עָשִׂיתִי וַאֲנִי אֶשָּׂא וַאֲנִי אֶסְבֹּל וַאֲמַלֵּט:

and in the future, as polytheism and atheism reveal themselves to be empty
creeds, all humanity will turn to the One God.

MOURNER'S KADDISH

The following prayer, said by mourners, requires the presence of a minyan.
A transliteration can be found on page 779.

Mourner: יִתְגַּדַּל Magnified and sanctified
may His great name be,
in the world He created by His will.
May He establish His kingdom
in your lifetime and in your days,
and in the lifetime of all the house of Israel,
swiftly and soon – and say: Amen.

All: May His great name be blessed
for ever and all time.

Mourner: Blessed and praised,
glorified and exalted,
raised and honored,
uplifted and lauded
be the name of the Holy One, blessed be He,
beyond any blessing,
song, praise and consolation
uttered in the world – and say: Amen.

May there be great peace from heaven,
and life for us and all Israel – and say: Amen.

Bow, take three steps back, as if taking leave of the Divine Presence,
then bow, first left, then right, then center, while saying:
May He who makes peace in His high places,
make peace for us and all Israel – and say: Amen.

---

synagogue or a house of study and say "May His great name be blessed," the
Holy One, blessed be He, nods His head and says: "Happy is the King who is
thus praised in this house" (*Berakhot* 3a). Note that Kaddish speaks neither of
death nor of the past. It speaks about the future and about peace. We honor
the dead by the way we live. We honor the past by the future we create.

קדיש יתום

The following prayer, said by mourners, requires the presence of a מנין.
A transliteration can be found on page 779.

אבל: יִתְגַּדַּל וְיִתְקַדַּשׁ שְׁמֵהּ רַבָּא (קהל: אָמֵן)
בְּעָלְמָא דִּי בְרָא כִרְעוּתֵהּ
וְיַמְלִיךְ מַלְכוּתֵהּ
בְּחַיֵּיכוֹן וּבְיוֹמֵיכוֹן וּבְחַיֵּי דְכָל בֵּית יִשְׂרָאֵל
בַּעֲגָלָא וּבִזְמַן קָרִיב, וְאִמְרוּ אָמֵן. (קהל: אָמֵן)

קהל
ואבל: יְהֵא שְׁמֵהּ רַבָּא מְבָרַךְ לְעָלַם וּלְעָלְמֵי עָלְמַיָּא.

אבל: יִתְבָּרַךְ וְיִשְׁתַּבַּח וְיִתְפָּאַר
וְיִתְרוֹמַם וְיִתְנַשֵּׂא וְיִתְהַדָּר וְיִתְעַלֶּה וְיִתְהַלָּל
שְׁמֵהּ דְּקֻדְשָׁא בְּרִיךְ הוּא (קהל: בְּרִיךְ הוּא)
לְעֵלָּא מִן כָּל בִּרְכָתָא וְשִׁירָתָא, תֻּשְׁבְּחָתָא וְנֶחֱמָתָא
דַּאֲמִירָן בְּעָלְמָא, וְאִמְרוּ אָמֵן. (קהל: אָמֵן)

יְהֵא שְׁלָמָא רַבָּא מִן שְׁמַיָּא
וְחַיִּים, עָלֵינוּ וְעַל כָּל יִשְׂרָאֵל, וְאִמְרוּ אָמֵן. (קהל: אָמֵן)

Bow, take three steps back, as if taking leave of the Divine Presence,
then bow, first left, then right, then center, while saying:

עֹשֶׂה שָׁלוֹם בִּמְרוֹמָיו
הוּא יַעֲשֶׂה שָׁלוֹם עָלֵינוּ
וְעַל כָּל יִשְׂרָאֵל, וְאִמְרוּ אָמֵן. (קהל: אָמֵן)

MOURNER'S KADDISH

We bring credit to the memory of the dead by doing acts that confer merit
on the living. This especially applies to the saying of Kaddish, since it causes
the congregation to praise God by saying, "May His great name be blessed
for ever and all time." According to the Talmud, whenever Jews enter a

וְחַג הַקָּצִיר֙ בִּכּוּרֵ֣י מַעֲשֶׂ֔יךָ

שמות כג, טז

שִׁבְעָ֥ה שָׁבֻעֹ֖ת
תִּסְפָּר־לָ֑ךְ
מֵהָחֵ֤ל חֶרְמֵשׁ֙ בַּקָּמָ֔ה
תָּחֵ֣ל לִסְפֹּ֔ר
שִׁבְעָ֖ה שָׁבֻעֽוֹת
וְעָשִׂ֜יתָ

חַ֧ג שָׁבֻעֹ֛ת

לַה' אֱלֹהֶ֑יךָ
וְשָׂמַחְתָּ֞ לִפְנֵ֣י ׀ ה' אֱלֹהֶ֗יךָ

דברים טז, ט-יא

Erev Yom Tov

KABBALAT SHABBAT

On weekdays, Ma'ariv begins on page 46.
On the second night of Yom Tov, if also Shabbat, begin here:

מִזְמוֹר A psalm. A song for the Sabbath day.   *Ps. 92*
It is good to thank the LORD
and sing psalms to Your name, Most High –
to tell of Your loving-kindness in the morning
and Your faithfulness at night,
to the music of the ten-stringed lyre and the melody of the harp.
For You have made me rejoice by Your work, O LORD;
I sing for joy at the deeds of Your hands.
How great are Your deeds, LORD,
and how very deep Your thoughts.
A boor cannot know, nor can a fool understand,
that though the wicked spring up like grass
and all evildoers flourish,
it is only that they may be destroyed for ever.
But You, LORD, are eternally exalted.

---

dimensions of Shabbat (that is why on a regular Shabbat the Amida prayers
for evening, morning, and afternoon are different, a phenomenon unique to
Shabbat). There is the Shabbat of the past – Shabbat as a memorial of creation. There is the Shabbat of the present – the Shabbat of revelation when,
resting from work, we encounter the divine presence more acutely than at
other times, and we read the Torah, itself the record of revelation. And there
is the Shabbat of the future, the Messianic Age, when all of humanity will acknowledge the One God, and peace will reign. It is this Shabbat of the future
to which the psalm is dedicated. People will then look back on the history of
suffering that humans have caused one another, and see clearly how, though
the wicked flourished briefly "like grass," in the long run justice prevailed. "A
fool cannot understand" that evil, however invulnerable it seems at the time,

ערב יום טוב

קבלת שבת

On weekdays, מעריב begins on page 47.
On the second night of יום טוב, if also שבת, begin here:

תהלים צב

מִזְמוֹר שִׁיר לְיוֹם הַשַּׁבָּת:

טוֹב לְהֹדוֹת לַיהוה, וּלְזַמֵּר לְשִׁמְךָ עֶלְיוֹן:

לְהַגִּיד בַּבְּקֶר חַסְדֶּךָ, וֶאֱמוּנָתְךָ בַּלֵּילוֹת:

עֲלֵי־עָשׂוֹר וַעֲלֵי־נָבֶל, עֲלֵי הִגָּיוֹן בְּכִנּוֹר:

כִּי שִׂמַּחְתַּנִי יהוה בְּפָעֳלֶךָ, בְּמַעֲשֵׂי יָדֶיךָ אֲרַנֵּן:

מַה־גָּדְלוּ מַעֲשֶׂיךָ יהוה, מְאֹד עָמְקוּ מַחְשְׁבֹתֶיךָ:

אִישׁ־בַּעַר לֹא יֵדָע, וּכְסִיל לֹא־יָבִין אֶת־זֹאת:

בִּפְרֹחַ רְשָׁעִים כְּמוֹ עֵשֶׂב, וַיָּצִיצוּ כָּל־פֹּעֲלֵי אָוֶן

לְהִשָּׁמְדָם עֲדֵי־עַד:

וְאַתָּה מָרוֹם לְעֹלָם יהוה:

KABBALAT SHABBAT / WELCOMING SHABBAT

Our normal service for Kabbalat Shabbat dates back to the sixteenth century and the circle of Jewish mystics in Safed. However, the custom of saying psalms 92 and 93, respectively the psalms for Shabbat and for Friday – the day the first humans were created – goes back many centuries before this. Therefore, when Yom Tov or Ḥol HaMoʼed falls on Shabbat, we say only these psalms, regarded as more obligatory than the other psalms and the song "Come my beloved" (*Pri Megadim* 488:1).

מִזְמוֹר שִׁיר *Psalm 92.* The superscription, "A psalm. A song for the Sabbath day" is part of the psalm itself, testifying to the antiquity of the custom of saying it on Shabbat as part of the Temple service. The connection between it and Shabbat is not immediately clear. The explanation is that there are three

For behold Your enemies, LORD, behold Your enemies will perish;
all evildoers will be scattered.
You have raised my pride like that of a wild ox;
I am anointed with fresh oil.
My eyes shall look in triumph on my adversaries,
my ears shall hear the downfall of the wicked who rise against me.
▸ The righteous will flourish like a palm tree
and grow tall like a cedar in Lebanon.
Planted in the LORD's House,
blossoming in our God's courtyards,
they will still bear fruit in old age, and stay vigorous and fresh,
proclaiming that the LORD is upright:
He is my Rock, in whom there is no wrong.

יהוה מָלָךְ The LORD reigns. He is robed in majesty.   *Ps. 93*
The LORD is robed, girded with strength.
The world is firmly established; it cannot be moved.
Your throne stands firm as of old; You are eternal.
Rivers lift up, LORD, rivers lift up their voice,
rivers lift up their crashing waves.
▸ Mightier than the noise of many waters,
than the mighty waves of the sea is the LORD on high.
Your testimonies are very sure;
holiness adorns Your House, LORD, for evermore.

---

goddess of the primordial sea. Not so, says the psalm. The waters may roar
but God is supreme over all. The universe is the result of a single creative
Intelligence; therefore struggle and combat are not written into its script.
Faith is the ability to hear the music beneath the noise, the order beneath
the seeming chaos.

נָשְׂאוּ נְהָרוֹת *Rivers lift up.* The repetitions in this verse, and the rhythms of
the next, capture in sound the rolling of mighty waves, culminating in the
magnificent, "LORD on high," the great affirmation ringing out above the
sound of the sea.

כִּי הִנֵּה אֹיְבֶיךָ יהוה, כִּי־הִנֵּה אֹיְבֶיךָ יֹאבֵדוּ
יִתְפָּרְדוּ כָּל־פֹּעֲלֵי אָוֶן:
וַתָּרֶם כִּרְאֵים קַרְנִי, בַּלֹּתִי בְּשֶׁמֶן רַעֲנָן:
וַתַּבֵּט עֵינִי בְּשׁוּרָי, בַּקָּמִים עָלַי מְרֵעִים תִּשְׁמַעְנָה אָזְנָי:
צַדִּיק כַּתָּמָר יִפְרָח, כְּאֶרֶז בַּלְּבָנוֹן יִשְׂגֶּה:
שְׁתוּלִים בְּבֵית יהוה, בְּחַצְרוֹת אֱלֹהֵינוּ יַפְרִיחוּ:
עוֹד יְנוּבוּן בְּשֵׂיבָה, דְּשֵׁנִים וְרַעֲנַנִּים יִהְיוּ:
לְהַגִּיד כִּי־יָשָׁר יהוה, צוּרִי, וְלֹא־עַוְלָתָה בּוֹ:

תהלים צג

יהוה מָלָךְ, גֵּאוּת לָבֵשׁ
לָבֵשׁ יהוה עֹז הִתְאַזָּר, אַף־תִּכּוֹן תֵּבֵל בַּל־תִּמּוֹט:
נָכוֹן כִּסְאֲךָ מֵאָז, מֵעוֹלָם אָתָּה:
נָשְׂאוּ נְהָרוֹת יהוה, נָשְׂאוּ נְהָרוֹת קוֹלָם, יִשְׂאוּ נְהָרוֹת דָּכְיָם:
מִקֹּלוֹת מַיִם רַבִּים, אַדִּירִים מִשְׁבְּרֵי־יָם, אַדִּיר בַּמָּרוֹם יהוה:
עֵדֹתֶיךָ נֶאֶמְנוּ מְאֹד, לְבֵיתְךָ נַאֲוָה־קֹּדֶשׁ, יהוה לְאֹרֶךְ יָמִים:

---

has a short life-span. It never wins the final victory. The psalm ends with a
vindication of God's justice.

כְּאֶרֶז...כַּתָּמָר *Like a palm tree… a cedar.* The difference between a date palm
and a cedar is that we benefit from the palm tree while it is alive: we eat its
fruit, we sit in its shade. A cedar is used for its wood. Only when a cedar is
cut down do we realize how tall it was. With the righteous, both of these
are true. While they live, we enjoy their presence: we eat the fruit of their
wisdom, we sit in the shade of their presence. When they are cut down and
are no longer with us, only then do we realize their true stature.

יהוה מָלָךְ *Psalm 93. The LORD reigns.* This psalm is, among other things, a polemic against the world of myth. In many ancient myths there was a struggle
between the god of order and the forces of chaos, represented by the god or

MOURNER'S KADDISH

The following prayer, said by mourners, requires the presence of a minyan.
A transliteration can be found on page 779.

Mourner: יִתְגַּדַּל Magnified and sanctified
may His great name be,
in the world He created by His will.
May He establish His kingdom
in your lifetime and in your days,
and in the lifetime of all the house of Israel,
swiftly and soon –
and say: Amen.

All: May His great name be blessed
for ever and all time.

Mourner: Blessed and praised,
glorified and exalted,
raised and honored,
uplifted and lauded
be the name of the Holy One,
blessed be He,
beyond any blessing, song,
praise and consolation
uttered in the world –
and say: Amen.

May there be great peace from heaven,
and life for us and all Israel –
and say: Amen.

Bow, take three steps back, as if taking leave of the Divine Presence,
then bow, first left, then right, then center, while saying:

May He who makes peace in His high places,
make peace for us and all Israel –
and say: Amen.

קַדִּישׁ יָתוֹם

The following prayer, said by mourners, requires the presence of a מִנְיָן.
A transliteration can be found on page 779.

אבל: יִתְגַּדַּל וְיִתְקַדַּשׁ שְׁמֵהּ רַבָּא (קהל: אָמֵן)

בְּעָלְמָא דִּי בְרָא כִרְעוּתֵהּ

וְיַמְלִיךְ מַלְכוּתֵהּ

בְּחַיֵּיכוֹן וּבְיוֹמֵיכוֹן וּבְחַיֵּי דְּכָל בֵּית יִשְׂרָאֵל

בַּעֲגָלָא וּבִזְמַן קָרִיב

וְאִמְרוּ אָמֵן. (קהל: אָמֵן)

קהל
ואבל: יְהֵא שְׁמֵהּ רַבָּא מְבָרַךְ לְעָלַם וּלְעָלְמֵי עָלְמַיָּא.

אבל: יִתְבָּרַךְ וְיִשְׁתַּבַּח וְיִתְפָּאַר

וְיִתְרוֹמַם וְיִתְנַשֵּׂא וְיִתְהַדָּר וְיִתְעַלֶּה וְיִתְהַלָּל

שְׁמֵהּ דְּקֻדְשָׁא בְּרִיךְ הוּא (קהל: בְּרִיךְ הוּא)

לְעֵלָּא מִן כָּל בִּרְכָתָא וְשִׁירָתָא

תֻּשְׁבְּחָתָא וְנֶחֱמָתָא

דַּאֲמִירָן בְּעָלְמָא

וְאִמְרוּ אָמֵן. (קהל: אָמֵן)

יְהֵא שְׁלָמָא רַבָּא מִן שְׁמַיָּא

וְחַיִּים, עָלֵינוּ וְעַל כָּל יִשְׂרָאֵל

וְאִמְרוּ אָמֵן. (קהל: אָמֵן)

Bow, take three steps back, as if taking leave of the Divine Presence,
then bow, first left, then right, then center, while saying:

עֹשֶׂה שָׁלוֹם בִּמְרוֹמָיו

הוּא יַעֲשֶׂה שָׁלוֹם עָלֵינוּ וְעַל כָּל יִשְׂרָאֵל

וְאִמְרוּ אָמֵן. (קהל: אָמֵן)

Ma'ariv for Yom Tov

BLESSINGS OF THE SHEMA

*The Leader says the following, bowing at "Bless," standing straight at "the Lord." The
congregation, followed by the Leader, responds, bowing at "Bless," standing straight at "the Lord."*

Leader: # BLESS

the Lord, the blessed One.

Congregation: Bless the Lord, the blessed One,
for ever and all time.

Leader: Bless the Lord, the blessed One,
for ever and all time.

*On weekdays, some congregations follow the ancient custom of saying piyutim here.
The piyutim for Ma'ariv, commonly known as Ma'aravot,
are interweaved in the blessings of the Shema.*
*For Ma'aravot for the first night of Shavuot, turn to page 94;
for Ma'aravot for the second night of Shavuot, turn to page 112.*

בָּרְכוּ אֶת יהוה **Bless the Lord.** A call by the leader of prayer to the community
to join him in praising God, in the spirit of the verse, "Magnify the Lord with
me, and let us exalt His name together" (Ps. 34:4). This is a formal summons
to public prayer in the presence of a *minyan*.

בָּרְכוּ **Bless.** We do not bless God; God blesses us. To speak of blessing God as
we do in this prayer means (1) we acknowledge Him as the source of all our
blessings, (2) we humble ourselves in this acknowledgment, (3) we seek to
be vehicles of His blessings by creating the space for them to fill. That space –
humility, self effacement, an opening of the soul to the presence of God – is
what we seek to achieve in prayer.

We bow, some bending the knee, when we say the word *Barekhu*. The
Hebrew word for "knee" is *berekh*. The word for a pool or reservoir of water
is *berekha*. Common to them all is a sense of downward movement – of
genuflection in the case of the body, of water from a spring to a pool, and of

מעריב ליום טוב

קריאת שמע וברכותיה

The ‏שליח ציבור‎ says the following, bowing at ‏בָּרְכוּ‎, standing straight at ‏'ה‎.
The ‏קהל‎, followed by the ‏שליח ציבור‎, responds, bowing at ‏בָּרוּךְ‎, standing straight at ‏'ה‎.

ש"ץ: **בָּרְכוּ**

אֶת יהוה הַמְבֹרָךְ.

קהל: בָּרוּךְ יהוה הַמְבֹרָךְ לְעוֹלָם וָעֶד.

ש"ץ: בָּרוּךְ יהוה הַמְבֹרָךְ לְעוֹלָם וָעֶד.

On weekdays, some congregations follow the ancient custom of saying piyutim here.
The piyutim for ‏מעריב‎, commonly known as ‏מערבות‎,
are interwoven in the blessings of the ‏שמע‎.
For ‏מערבות‎ for the first night of ‏שבועות‎, turn to page 95;
for ‏מערבות‎ for the second night of ‏שבועות‎, turn to page 113.

EVENING SERVICE

Ma'ariv is the prayer associated with Jacob, the man whose greatest encounters with God were at night. At night he had a vision, symbolic of prayer itself, of a ladder stretching from earth to heaven. Awakening from that vision he gave the most profound description of the effect of prayer: "Surely God was in this place and I did not know it" (Gen. 28:16). At night he wrestled with an angel and was given the name Israel, one who "struggles with God and with men and prevails" (Gen. 32:28).

Judaism has known its dawns, its ages of new hope, associated with Abraham. It has known the full brightness of day, its ages of peace and continuity, associated with Isaac's life after the binding. But it has also known its nights. Night is when we take with us the spirit of Jacob, a man who knew fear but was never defeated by it.

בָּרוּךְ Blessed are You, LORD our God, King of the Universe,
who by His word brings on evenings,
by His wisdom opens the gates of heaven,
with understanding makes time change and the seasons rotate,
and by His will orders the stars in their constellations in the sky.
He creates day and night,
rolling away the light before the darkness,
and darkness before the light.
▸ He makes the day pass and brings on night,
distinguishing day from night:
the LORD of hosts is His name.
May the living and forever enduring God rule over us for all time.
Blessed are You, LORD, who brings on evenings.

אַהֲבַת עוֹלָם With everlasting love
have You loved Your people, the house of Israel.
You have taught us Torah and commandments,
decrees and laws of justice.
Therefore, LORD our God, when we lie down and when we rise up
we will speak of Your decrees, rejoicing in the words of Your Torah
and Your commandments for ever.
▸ For they are our life and the length of our days;
on them will we meditate day and night.

---

brought our ancestors from slavery to freedom. These paragraphs are directed
to these three ways through which we come to know God: the wonders of
the natural universe, the teachings of the Torah, and the miracles of Jewish
history.

The Siddur and Maḥzor are the supreme expressions of Jewish faith. For
the most part Jews did not write books of theology; they wrote prayers. In
Judaism we do not speak *about* God; we speak *to* God. We do not *discuss*
faith; we *express* faith. Faith is our relationship with God made articulate in
the words of prayer.

אַהֲבַת עוֹלָם *With everlasting love.* Of all the ways in which God has made Him-

בָּרוּךְ אַתָּה יהוה אֱלֹהֵינוּ מֶלֶךְ הָעוֹלָם

אֲשֶׁר בִּדְבָרוֹ מַעֲרִיב עֲרָבִים

בְּחָכְמָה פּוֹתֵחַ שְׁעָרִים

וּבִתְבוּנָה מְשַׁנֶּה עִתִּים וּמַחֲלִיף אֶת הַזְּמַנִּים

וּמְסַדֵּר אֶת הַכּוֹכָבִים בְּמִשְׁמְרוֹתֵיהֶם בָּרָקִיעַ כִּרְצוֹנוֹ.

בּוֹרֵא יוֹם וָלַיְלָה, גּוֹלֵל אוֹר מִפְּנֵי חֹשֶׁךְ וְחֹשֶׁךְ מִפְּנֵי אוֹר

׳ וּמַעֲבִיר יוֹם וּמֵבִיא לָיְלָה

וּמַבְדִּיל בֵּין יוֹם וּבֵין לָיְלָה

יהוה צְבָאוֹת שְׁמוֹ.

אֵל חַי וְקַיָּם תָּמִיד, יִמְלֹךְ עָלֵינוּ לְעוֹלָם וָעֶד.

בָּרוּךְ אַתָּה יהוה, הַמַּעֲרִיב עֲרָבִים.

אַהֲבַת עוֹלָם בֵּית יִשְׂרָאֵל עַמְּךָ אָהָבְתָּ

תּוֹרָה וּמִצְוֹת, חֻקִּים וּמִשְׁפָּטִים, אוֹתָנוּ לִמַּדְתָּ

עַל כֵּן יהוה אֱלֹהֵינוּ בְּשָׁכְבֵּנוּ וּבְקוּמֵנוּ נָשִׂיחַ בְּחֻקֶּיךָ

וְנִשְׂמַח בְּדִבְרֵי תוֹרָתֶךָ וּבְמִצְוֹתֶיךָ לְעוֹלָם וָעֶד

׳ כִּי הֵם חַיֵּינוּ וְאֹרֶךְ יָמֵינוּ, וּבָהֶם נֶהְגֶּה יוֹמָם וָלָיְלָה.

---

blessing flowing from heaven to earth as we align ourselves with its energies, moving from self-sufficiency and pride to humility in the face of the Infinite.

THE BLESSINGS OF THE SHEMA

The blessings that surround the Shema, evening and morning, are a precisely articulated summary of the three basic elements of Jewish faith: *creation, revelation* and *redemption*. Creation: God is the Author of the universe, Architect of the cosmos. Revelation: God has revealed Himself to us in the form of His word, the Torah, the text of our covenant with Him and our constitution as a holy nation. Redemption: God's interventions in history, as when He

May You never take away Your love from us.
Blessed are You, LORD, who loves His people Israel.

> *The Shema must be said with intense concentration.*
> *When not with a minyan, say:*
> God, faithful King!

The following verse should be said aloud, while covering the eyes with the right hand:

Listen, Israel: the LORD is our God, the LORD is One.

Deut. 6

Quietly: Blessed be the name of His glorious kingdom for ever and all time.

וְאָהַבְתָּ Love the LORD your God with all your heart, with all your soul, and with all your might. These words which I command you

Deut. 6

יהוה אֱלֹהֵינוּ *The LORD is our God.* He alone is our ultimate Sovereign. To be a Jew is to be a citizen in the republic of faith under the sovereignty of God.

יהוה אֶחָד *The LORD is One.* An ultimate unity pervades the diversity of the world. The universe is the expression of a single creative intelligence; therefore its natural state is harmony. We believe that ultimately all humanity will acknowledge the unity of God. Then and only then, will harmony prevail in the affairs of humankind.

בָּרוּךְ שֵׁם *Blessed be the name.* This was the response of the congregation in the Temple when the officiating priest recited the first verse of the Shema (the equivalent of our "Amen"). Though we continue to say it in memory of the Temple, we now say it quietly on account of the Temple's destruction and because it is not part of the biblical text (*Pesaḥim* 56a).

וְאָהַבְתָּ אֵת יהוה אֱלֹהֶיךָ *Love the LORD your God.* Judaism was the world's first civilization to place love at the heart of the moral universe. Not abstract or dispassionate love, but "with all your heart, with all your soul, and with all your might," meaning: with the totality of your being, emotion, intellect and will. Love begets love; love reciprocates love; our love for God is the response to God's love for us.

עַל־לְבָבֶךָ *On your heart.* Rabbi Menaḥem Mendel of Kotzk once asked: "Why does the Torah say that these words should be 'on your heart'? Should it not

וְאַהֲבָתְךָ אַל תָּסִיר מִמֶּנּוּ לְעוֹלָמִים.
בָּרוּךְ אַתָּה יהוה, אוֹהֵב עַמּוֹ יִשְׂרָאֵל.

The שמע must be said with intense concentration.
When not with a מנין, say:

אֵל מֶלֶךְ נֶאֱמָן

The following verse should be said aloud, while covering the eyes with the right hand:

דברים ו

שְׁמַע יִשְׂרָאֵל, יהוה אֱלֹהֵינוּ, יהוה ׀ אֶחָד:

Quietly בָּרוּךְ שֵׁם כְּבוֹד מַלְכוּתוֹ לְעוֹלָם וָעֶד.

דברים ו

וְאָהַבְתָּ אֵת יהוה אֱלֹהֶיךָ, בְּכָל־לְבָבְךָ וּבְכָל־נַפְשְׁךָ וּבְכָל־
מְאֹדֶךָ: וְהָיוּ הַדְּבָרִים הָאֵלֶּה, אֲשֶׁר אָנֹכִי מְצַוְּךָ הַיּוֹם, עַל־לְבָבֶךָ:

---

self known to us, the one that is central is revelation: God's word as recorded in Torah. The history of the Jewish mind is the story of a love affair between a people and a book. Heinrich Heine called the Torah "the portable homeland of the Jew." Wherever Jews went they took Torah with them. Where Torah study was strong Jewish life was strong. This paragraph expresses that love.

On Shavuot in particular it is worth noting how deeply Judaism rejects the opposition between "law" and "love," as if these were two different ways of serving God. They are not. They go hand-in-hand. Law without love is harsh, but love without law leads to favoritism, rivalry and conflict. God reveals Himself to humanity in general, Israel in particular, in the form of law because only law, given, received and observed in love, reconciles the fundamental tension of the human condition, between freedom and order. The violence and chaos of the generation of the Flood represents freedom without order. Oppressive empires such as the Egypt of the Pharaohs represent order without freedom. Law alone, engraved on the heart and practiced until it becomes instinctual, reconciles the two: "I will walk in freedom for I have sought out Your precepts" (Ps. 119:45).

שְׁמַע יִשְׂרָאֵל *Listen, Israel.* Since God's primary revelation is through words, the highest religious act is the act of listening – creating a silence in the soul in which we hear the call of God.

today shall be on your heart. Teach them repeatedly to your children, speaking of them when you sit at home and when you travel on the way, when you lie down and when you rise. Bind them as a sign on your hand, and they shall be an emblem between your eyes. Write them on the doorposts of your house and gates.

וְהָיָה If you indeed heed My commandments with which I charge   *Deut. 11*
you today, to love the LORD your God and worship Him with all your heart and with all your soul, I will give rain in your land in its season, the early and late rain; and you shall gather in your grain, wine and oil. I will give grass in your field for your cattle, and you shall eat and be satisfied. Be careful lest your heart be tempted and you go astray and worship other gods, bowing down to them. Then the LORD's anger will flare against you and He will close the heavens so that there will be no rain. The land will not yield its crops, and you will perish swiftly from the good land that the LORD is

———————————————————————————————

וְנָתַתִּי מְטַר־אַרְצְכֶם בְּעִתּוֹ *I will give rain in your land in its season.* At the end of his life, Moses told the next generation, those who would enter the land, that they would find it "not like the land of Egypt, from which you have come, where you planted your seed and irrigated it by foot as in a vegetable garden. But the land you are crossing the Jordan to take possession of is a land of mountains and valleys that drinks rain from heaven" (Deut. 11:10–11). Unlike the Nile Valley and Delta, it did not have a constant, regular supply of water. In Egypt, the natural instinct is to look down to the river for sustenance. In Israel, dependent on rain, the natural instinct is to look up to heaven.

הִשָּׁמְרוּ לָכֶם פֶּן־יִפְתֶּה לְבַבְכֶם *Be careful lest your heart be tempted.* Throughout the book of Deuteronomy, from which this paragraph is taken, Moses warns the people that their greatest trial was not the wilderness years when they wandered without a home. It would be when they entered the land and became prosperous. The greatest challenge to faith is not poverty but affluence. It is then we are in danger of becoming complacent, forgetting why we are here.

וְשִׁנַּנְתָּם לְבָנֶיךָ וְדִבַּרְתָּ בָּם, בְּשִׁבְתְּךָ בְּבֵיתֶךָ וּבְלֶכְתְּךָ בַדֶּרֶךְ, וּבְשָׁכְבְּךָ וּבְקוּמֶךָ: וּקְשַׁרְתָּם לְאוֹת עַל־יָדֶךָ וְהָיוּ לְטֹטָפֹת בֵּין עֵינֶיךָ: וּכְתַבְתָּם עַל־מְזֻזוֹת בֵּיתֶךָ וּבִשְׁעָרֶיךָ:

וְהָיָה אִם־שָׁמֹעַ תִּשְׁמְעוּ אֶל־מִצְוֹתַי אֲשֶׁר אָנֹכִי מְצַוֶּה אֶתְכֶם הַיּוֹם, לְאַהֲבָה אֶת־יהוה אֱלֹהֵיכֶם וּלְעָבְדוֹ, בְּכָל־לְבַבְכֶם וּבְכָל־נַפְשְׁכֶם: וְנָתַתִּי מְטַר־אַרְצְכֶם בְּעִתּוֹ, יוֹרֶה וּמַלְקוֹשׁ, וְאָסַפְתָּ דְגָנֶךָ וְתִירֹשְׁךָ וְיִצְהָרֶךָ: וְנָתַתִּי עֵשֶׂב בְּשָׂדְךָ לִבְהֶמְתֶּךָ, וְאָכַלְתָּ וְשָׂבָעְתָּ: הִשָּׁמְרוּ לָכֶם פֶּן־יִפְתֶּה לְבַבְכֶם, וְסַרְתֶּם וַעֲבַדְתֶּם אֱלֹהִים אֲחֵרִים וְהִשְׁתַּחֲוִיתֶם לָהֶם: וְחָרָה אַף־יהוה בָּכֶם, וְעָצַר אֶת־הַשָּׁמַיִם וְלֹא־יִהְיֶה מָטָר, וְהָאֲדָמָה לֹא תִתֵּן אֶת־יְבוּלָהּ, וַאֲבַדְתֶּם מְהֵרָה מֵעַל הָאָרֶץ הַטֹּבָה אֲשֶׁר יהוה נֹתֵן לָכֶם:

---

say, 'in your heart'?" He answered: "The human heart is not always open. Therefore the Torah commands us to lay these words *on* our heart, so that when it opens, they will be there, ready to enter."

וְשִׁנַּנְתָּם לְבָנֶיךָ *Teach them repeatedly to your children.* Education is the conversation between the generations. In the only place in the Torah to explain why God chose Abraham to be the bearer of a new covenant, it says, "For I have singled him out so tht he may instruct his children and his posterity to keep the way of the LORD by doing what is just and right" (Gen. 18:19). Educating our children is the first duty of a Jewish parent.

וּקְשַׁרְתָּם...וּכְתַבְתָּם *Bind them ... write them.* Because God is often hidden in this world, we surround ourselves with reminders of His presence.

וְהָיָה אִם־שָׁמֹעַ תִּשְׁמְעוּ *If you indeed heed.* This, the second paragraph of the Shema, was described by the sages as an act of acceptance of the yoke of the commandments, while the first is acceptance of the sovereignty of heaven (Mishna, *Berakhot* 13a). In Judaism, faith is not merely a general state of mind but also and fundamentally a way of life, the life of the commandments. On this, our fate as a nation depends.

giving you. Therefore, set these, My words, on your heart and soul. Bind them as a sign on your hand, and they shall be an emblem between your eyes. Teach them to your children, speaking of them when you sit at home and when you travel on the way, when you lie down and when you rise. Write them on the doorposts of your house and gates, so that you and your children may live long in the land that the LORD swore to your ancestors to give them, for as long as the heavens are above the earth.

וַיֹּאמֶר The LORD spoke to Moses, saying: Speak to the Israelites *Num. 15* and tell them to make tassels on the corners of their garments for all generations. They shall attach to the tassel at each corner a thread of blue. This shall be your tassel, and you shall see it and remember all of the LORD's commandments and keep them, not straying after your heart and after your eyes, following your own sinful desires. Thus you will be reminded to keep all My commandments, and be holy to your God. I am the LORD your God, who brought you out of the land of Egypt to be your God. I am the LORD your God.

True –

The Leader repeats:

▸ The LORD your God is true –

אֱמֶת *True.* The Hebrew word *emet* means more than "truth" in the conventional Western sense of fact as opposed to falsehood. *Emet* also means "being truthful," keeping your word, honoring your commitments. Hence the importance here of connecting past redemption to future deliverance. Indeed the word *emet* itself is composed of the first, middle and last letters of the alphabet, subliminally suggesting a truth continuous through past, present and future. Thus as the Shema segues into the blessing of Redemption, we base our faith in God's future redemption on the basis of the history of the past when He brought us out of Egypt as He said He would. God honors His word. His truth is the basis of our hope.

וְשַׂמְתֶּם אֶת־דְּבָרַי אֵלֶּה עַל־לְבַבְכֶם וְעַל־נַפְשְׁכֶם, וּקְשַׁרְתֶּם אֹתָם לְאוֹת עַל־יֶדְכֶם, וְהָיוּ לְטוֹטָפֹת בֵּין עֵינֵיכֶם: וְלִמַּדְתֶּם אֹתָם אֶת־בְּנֵיכֶם לְדַבֵּר בָּם, בְּשִׁבְתְּךָ בְּבֵיתֶךָ וּבְלֶכְתְּךָ בַדֶּרֶךְ, וּבְשָׁכְבְּךָ וּבְקוּמֶךָ: וּכְתַבְתָּם עַל־מְזוּזוֹת בֵּיתֶךָ וּבִשְׁעָרֶיךָ: לְמַעַן יִרְבּוּ יְמֵיכֶם וִימֵי בְנֵיכֶם עַל הָאֲדָמָה אֲשֶׁר נִשְׁבַּע יהוה לַאֲבֹתֵיכֶם לָתֵת לָהֶם, כִּימֵי הַשָּׁמַיִם עַל־הָאָרֶץ:

במדבר טו

וַיֹּאמֶר יהוה אֶל־מֹשֶׁה לֵּאמֹר: דַּבֵּר אֶל־בְּנֵי יִשְׂרָאֵל וְאָמַרְתָּ אֲלֵהֶם, וְעָשׂוּ לָהֶם צִיצִת עַל־כַּנְפֵי בִגְדֵיהֶם לְדֹרֹתָם, וְנָתְנוּ עַל־צִיצִת הַכָּנָף פְּתִיל תְּכֵלֶת: וְהָיָה לָכֶם לְצִיצִת, וּרְאִיתֶם אֹתוֹ וּזְכַרְתֶּם אֶת־כָּל־מִצְוֹת יהוה וַעֲשִׂיתֶם אֹתָם, וְלֹא תָתוּרוּ אַחֲרֵי לְבַבְכֶם וְאַחֲרֵי עֵינֵיכֶם, אֲשֶׁר־אַתֶּם זֹנִים אַחֲרֵיהֶם: לְמַעַן תִּזְכְּרוּ וַעֲשִׂיתֶם אֶת־כָּל־מִצְוֹתָי, וִהְיִיתֶם קְדֹשִׁים לֵאלֹהֵיכֶם: אֲנִי יהוה אֱלֹהֵיכֶם, אֲשֶׁר הוֹצֵאתִי אֶתְכֶם מֵאֶרֶץ מִצְרַיִם, לִהְיוֹת לָכֶם לֵאלֹהִים, אֲנִי יהוה אֱלֹהֵיכֶם:

אֱמֶת

The שליח ציבור *repeats:*

‹ יהוה אֱלֹהֵיכֶם אֱמֶת

צִיצָת *Tassels.* The third paragraph of the Shema is largely about the command of *Tzitzit*, one of the perennial reminders of God's presence in our lives. Since *Tzitzit* were not obligatory at night (the command is that "you shall see them" and at night they could not be seen), the primary message of the third paragraph at night is its concluding verse, about the exodus. It fulfills the command "so that you will remember the day you left Egypt all the days of your life" (Deut. 16:3). As we will mention in the Haggada, Ben Zoma interpreted the emphatic word "all" to include not just days but also nights (Mishna, *Berakhot* 12b).

וֶאֱמוּנָה – and faithful is all this,
and firmly established for us
that He is the Lᴏʀᴅ our God,
and there is none beside Him,
and that we, Israel, are His people.
He is our King,
who redeems us from the hand of kings
and delivers us from the grasp of all tyrants.
He is our God,
who on our behalf repays our foes
and brings just retribution on our mortal enemies;
who performs great deeds
beyond understanding and wonders beyond number;
who kept us alive, not letting our foot slip;   *Ps. 66*
who led us on the high places of our enemies,
raising our pride above all our foes;
who did miracles for us
and brought vengeance against Pharaoh;
who performed signs and wonders
in the land of Ham's children;
who smote in His wrath all the firstborn of Egypt,
and brought out His people Israel from their midst
into everlasting freedom;
who led His children through the divided Reed Sea,
plunging their pursuers and enemies into the depths.
When His children saw His might,
they gave praise and thanks to His name,
▸ and willingly accepted His Sovereignty.
Moses and the children of Israel
then sang a song to You with great joy,
and they all exclaimed:

"Who is like You, Lᴏʀᴅ, among the mighty?   *Ex. 15*
Who is like You, majestic in holiness,
awesome in praises, doing wonders?"

וֶאֱמוּנָה כָּל זֹאת וְקַיָּם עָלֵינוּ

כִּי הוּא יהוה אֱלֹהֵינוּ וְאֵין זוּלָתוֹ

וַאֲנַחְנוּ יִשְׂרָאֵל עַמּוֹ.

הַפּוֹדֵנוּ מִיַּד מְלָכִים

מַלְכֵּנוּ הַגּוֹאֲלֵנוּ מִכַּף כָּל הֶעָרִיצִים.

הָאֵל הַנִּפְרָע לָנוּ מִצָּרֵינוּ

וְהַמְשַׁלֵּם גְּמוּל לְכָל אוֹיְבֵי נַפְשֵׁנוּ.

הָעוֹשֶׂה גְדוֹלוֹת עַד אֵין חֵקֶר

וְנִפְלָאוֹת עַד אֵין מִסְפָּר.

תהלים סו

הַשָּׂם נַפְשֵׁנוּ בַּחַיִּים, וְלֹא־נָתַן לַמּוֹט רַגְלֵנוּ:

הַמַּדְרִיכֵנוּ עַל בָּמוֹת אוֹיְבֵינוּ

וַיָּרֶם קַרְנֵנוּ עַל כָּל שׂוֹנְאֵינוּ.

הָעוֹשֶׂה לָּנוּ נִסִּים וּנְקָמָה בְּפַרְעֹה

אוֹתוֹת וּמוֹפְתִים בְּאַדְמַת בְּנֵי חָם.

הַמַּכֶּה בְעֶבְרָתוֹ כָּל בְּכוֹרֵי מִצְרָיִם

וַיּוֹצֵא אֶת עַמּוֹ יִשְׂרָאֵל מִתּוֹכָם לְחֵרוּת עוֹלָם.

הַמַּעֲבִיר בָּנָיו בֵּין גִּזְרֵי יַם סוּף

אֶת רוֹדְפֵיהֶם וְאֶת שׂוֹנְאֵיהֶם בִּתְהוֹמוֹת טִבַּע

וְרָאוּ בָנָיו גְּבוּרָתוֹ, שִׁבְּחוּ וְהוֹדוּ לִשְׁמוֹ

‹ וּמַלְכוּתוֹ בְרָצוֹן קִבְּלוּ עֲלֵיהֶם.

מֹשֶׁה וּבְנֵי יִשְׂרָאֵל, לְךָ עָנוּ שִׁירָה בְּשִׂמְחָה רַבָּה

וְאָמְרוּ כֻלָּם

שמות טו

מִי־כָמֹכָה בָּאֵלִם יהוה

מִי כָּמֹכָה נֶאְדָּר בַּקֹּדֶשׁ

נוֹרָא תְהִלֹּת עֹשֵׂה פֶלֶא:

▸ Your children beheld Your majesty
  as You parted the sea before Moses.
  "This is my God!" they responded, and then said:
           "The LORD shall reign for ever and ever."   *Ex. 15*
▸ And it is said,
           "For the LORD has redeemed Jacob   *Jer. 31*
              and rescued him from a power stronger than his own."
  Blessed are You, LORD, who redeemed Israel.

הַשְׁכִּיבֵנוּ Help us lie down, O LORD our God, in peace,
and rise up, O our King, to life.
Spread over us Your canopy of peace.
Direct us with Your good counsel,
and save us for the sake of Your name.
Shield us and remove from us every enemy,
plague, sword, famine and sorrow.
Remove the adversary from before and behind us.
Shelter us in the shadow of Your wings,
for You, God, are our Guardian and Deliverer;
You, God, are a gracious and compassionate King.
▸ Guard our going out and our coming in,
  for life and peace, from now and for ever.
  Spread over us Your canopy of peace.
  Blessed are You, LORD, who spreads a canopy of peace over us,
  over all His people Israel, and over Jerusalem.

---

in the ancient world. We pray for a peaceful night under the protective canopy
of God's sheltering presence.

וְהָסֵר שָׂטָן *Remove the adversary.* In Hebrew, Satan. In Tanakh and Jewish
thought generally, Satan is the counsel for the prosecution in the heavenly
court, the angel who keeps a record of our sins and failings, most famously in
the book of Job. The rabbis identified Satan with the "evil inclination" and the
angel of death, that is, our emotional and physical limitations as embodied

‣ מַלְכוּתְךָ רָאוּ בָנֶיךָ, בּוֹקֵעַ יָם לִפְנֵי מֹשֶׁה
זֶה אֵלִי עָנוּ, וְאָמְרוּ

שמות טו

יהוה יִמְלֹךְ לְעֹלָם וָעֶד:

‣ וְנֶאֱמַר

ירמיה לא

כִּי־פָדָה יהוה אֶת־יַעֲקֹב, וּגְאָלוֹ מִיַּד חָזָק מִמֶּנּוּ:
בָּרוּךְ אַתָּה יהוה, גָּאַל יִשְׂרָאֵל.

הַשְׁכִּיבֵנוּ יהוה אֱלֹהֵינוּ לְשָׁלוֹם, וְהַעֲמִידֵנוּ מַלְכֵּנוּ לְחַיִּים
וּפְרֹשׂ עָלֵינוּ סֻכַּת שְׁלוֹמֶךָ, וְתַקְּנֵנוּ בְּעֵצָה טוֹבָה מִלְּפָנֶיךָ
וְהוֹשִׁיעֵנוּ לְמַעַן שְׁמֶךָ.
וְהָגֵן בַּעֲדֵנוּ
וְהָסֵר מֵעָלֵינוּ אוֹיֵב, דֶּבֶר וְחֶרֶב וְרָעָב וְיָגוֹן
וְהָסֵר שָׂטָן מִלְּפָנֵינוּ וּמֵאַחֲרֵינוּ
וּבְצֵל כְּנָפֶיךָ תַּסְתִּירֵנוּ
כִּי אֵל שׁוֹמְרֵנוּ וּמַצִּילֵנוּ אָתָּה
כִּי אֵל מֶלֶךְ חַנּוּן וְרַחוּם אָתָּה.

‣ וּשְׁמֹר צֵאתֵנוּ וּבוֹאֵנוּ לְחַיִּים וּלְשָׁלוֹם מֵעַתָּה וְעַד עוֹלָם.
וּפְרֹשׂ עָלֵינוּ סֻכַּת שְׁלוֹמֶךָ.
בָּרוּךְ אַתָּה יהוה
הַפּוֹרֵשׂ סֻכַּת שָׁלוֹם עָלֵינוּ וְעַל כָּל עַמּוֹ יִשְׂרָאֵל וְעַל יְרוּשָׁלָיִם.

הַשְׁכִּיבֵנוּ *Help us lie down.* Since there is supposed to be no interruption between redemption (the paragraph ending "who redeemed Israel") and the
formal act of prayer (Amida), this paragraph is regarded as an extension of
the previous one (see 4b). It takes the theme of redemption and translates it
into the here-and-now of night, a time of vulnerability and danger, especially

On Shabbat, the congregation stands and, together with the Leader, says:

וְשָׁמְרוּ The children of Israel must keep the Sabbath,   *Ex. 31*
observing the Sabbath in every generation
as an everlasting covenant.
It is a sign between Me and the children of Israel for ever,
for in six days God made the heavens and the earth,
but on the seventh day He ceased work and refreshed Himself.

The congregation, then the Leader:

וַיְדַבֵּר Thus Moses announced the Lord's appointed seasons   *Lev. 23*
to the children of Israel.

HALF KADDISH

Leader: יִתְגַּדַּל Magnified and sanctified may His great name be,
in the world He created by His will.
May He establish His kingdom
in your lifetime and in your days,
and in the lifetime of all the house of Israel,
swiftly and soon –
and say: Amen.

All: May His great name be blessed for ever and all time.

Leader: Blessed and praised, glorified and exalted,
raised and honored, uplifted and lauded
be the name of the Holy One, blessed be He,
beyond any blessing, song, praise and consolation
uttered in the world –
and say: Amen.

---

souls, beings of flesh and blood, "dust of the earth." We pray, in other words, to be protected not only from external enemies but also from the instincts and desires that lead us to harm others and ourselves. Satan is not, as in some other religious traditions, an independent force of evil. That is dualism, and is incompatible with monotheism.

On שבת, *the* קהל *stands and, together with the* שליח ציבור, *says:*

שמות לא

וְשָׁמְרוּ בְנֵי־יִשְׂרָאֵל אֶת־הַשַּׁבָּת
לַעֲשׂוֹת אֶת־הַשַּׁבָּת לְדֹרֹתָם בְּרִית עוֹלָם:
בֵּינִי וּבֵין בְּנֵי יִשְׂרָאֵל, אוֹת הִוא לְעֹלָם
כִּי־שֵׁשֶׁת יָמִים עָשָׂה יהוה אֶת־הַשָּׁמַיִם וְאֶת־הָאָרֶץ
וּבַיּוֹם הַשְּׁבִיעִי שָׁבַת וַיִּנָּפַשׁ:

The קהל, *then the* שליח ציבור:

ויקרא כג

וַיְדַבֵּר מֹשֶׁה אֶת־מֹעֲדֵי יהוה אֶל־בְּנֵי יִשְׂרָאֵל:

חצי קדיש

ש״ץ יִתְגַּדַּל וְיִתְקַדַּשׁ שְׁמֵהּ רַבָּא (קהל: אָמֵן)
בְּעָלְמָא דִּי בְרָא כִרְעוּתֵהּ
וְיַמְלִיךְ מַלְכוּתֵהּ
בְּחַיֵּיכוֹן וּבְיוֹמֵיכוֹן וּבְחַיֵּי דְּכָל בֵּית יִשְׂרָאֵל
בַּעֲגָלָא וּבִזְמַן קָרִיב
וְאִמְרוּ אָמֵן. (קהל: אָמֵן)

קהל
 וש״ץ
יְהֵא שְׁמֵהּ רַבָּא מְבָרַךְ לְעָלַם וּלְעָלְמֵי עָלְמַיָּא.

ש״ץ יִתְבָּרַךְ וְיִשְׁתַּבַּח וְיִתְפָּאַר וְיִתְרוֹמַם וְיִתְנַשֵּׂא
וְיִתְהַדָּר וְיִתְעַלֶּה וְיִתְהַלָּל
שְׁמֵהּ דְּקֻדְשָׁא בְּרִיךְ הוּא (קהל: בְּרִיךְ הוּא)
לְעֵלָּא מִן כָּל בִּרְכָתָא וְשִׁירָתָא
תֻּשְׁבְּחָתָא וְנֶחֱמָתָא
דַּאֲמִירָן בְּעָלְמָא
וְאִמְרוּ אָמֵן. (קהל: אָמֵן)

THE AMIDA

The following prayer, until "in former years" on page 76, is said silently, standing with feet together. Take three steps forward and at the points indicated by ˙, bend the knees at the first word, bow at the second, and stand straight before saying God's name.

O LORD, open my lips,   *Ps. 51*
so that my mouth may declare Your praise.

PATRIARCHS

˙בָּרוּךְ Blessed are You, LORD our God and God of our fathers,
God of Abraham, God of Isaac and God of Jacob;
the great, mighty and awesome God, God Most High,
who bestows acts of loving-kindness and creates all,
who remembers the loving-kindness of the fathers
and will bring a Redeemer
to their children's children
for the sake of His name, in love.
King, Helper, Savior, Shield:
˙Blessed are You, LORD,
Shield of Abraham.

DIVINE MIGHT

אַתָּה גִבּוֹר You are eternally mighty, LORD.
You give life to the dead
and have great power to save.

> *In Israel:*
> He causes the dew to fall.

(Shabbat), the seventh month (Tishrei), the seventh year (*Shemitta*, the year of release), and the Jubilee at the end of seven cycles of seven years. In the case of the festivals, the basic text of the central prayer is ancient, several of its various parts already mentioned in the Talmud (*Berakhot* 33b, *Pesaḥim* 117b, *Yoma* 87b).

עמידה

The following prayer, until קַדְמֹנִיּוֹת on page 77, is said silently, standing with feet together.
Take three steps forward and at the points indicated by ׳, bend the knees at the
first word, bow at the second, and stand straight before saying God's name.

אֲדֹנָי, שְׂפָתַי תִּפְתָּח, וּפִי יַגִּיד תְּהִלָּתֶךָ:

אבות

יּבָּרוּךְ אַתָּה יהוה, אֱלֹהֵינוּ וֵאלֹהֵי אֲבוֹתֵינוּ
אֱלֹהֵי אַבְרָהָם, אֱלֹהֵי יִצְחָק, וֵאלֹהֵי יַעֲקֹב
הָאֵל הַגָּדוֹל הַגִּבּוֹר וְהַנּוֹרָא, אֵל עֶלְיוֹן
גּוֹמֵל חֲסָדִים טוֹבִים, וְקֹנֵה הַכֹּל
וְזוֹכֵר חַסְדֵי אָבוֹת
וּמֵבִיא גוֹאֵל לִבְנֵי בְנֵיהֶם לְמַעַן שְׁמוֹ בְּאַהֲבָה.
מֶלֶךְ עוֹזֵר וּמוֹשִׁיעַ וּמָגֵן.
יּבָּרוּךְ אַתָּה יהוה, מָגֵן אַבְרָהָם.

גבורות

אַתָּה גִּבּוֹר לְעוֹלָם, אֲדֹנָי
מְחַיֵּה מֵתִים אַתָּה, רַב לְהוֹשִׁיעַ

In ארץ ישראל:
מוֹרִיד הַטָּל

THE AMIDA

On Shabbat and festivals (with the exception of Musaf of Rosh HaShana) the Amida consists of seven blessings. The first three (expressions
of praise) and the last three (expressions of thanks) are as for all Amida
prayers, while the middle blessing is dedicated to the specific sanctity of
the day (*Kedushat HaYom*). Seven is the sign of the sacred – the seventh day

He sustains the living with loving-kindness,
and with great compassion revives the dead.
He supports the fallen, heals the sick,
sets captives free,
and keeps His faith with those who sleep in the dust.
Who is like You, Master of might,
and who can compare to You,
O King who brings death and gives life,
and makes salvation grow?
Faithful are You to revive the dead.
Blessed are You, LORD, who revives the dead.

HOLINESS

אַתָּה קָדוֹשׁ You are holy and Your name is holy,
and holy ones praise You daily, Selah!
Blessed are You, LORD, the holy God.

HOLINESS OF THE DAY

אַתָּה בְחַרְתָּנוּ You have chosen us from among all peoples.
You have loved and favored us.

---

they are all festivals of history. The truths of Judaism are universal; the history
of the Jewish people is not.

> Ask now about the former days, long before your time, from the day God
> created human beings on the earth; ask from one end of the heavens to
> the other. Has anything so great as this ever happened, or has anything
> like it ever been heard of? Has any other people heard the voice of God
> speaking out of fire, as you have, and lived? Has any god ever tried to
> take for himself one nation out of another nation, by tests, by signs and
> wonders, by war, by a mighty hand and an outstretched arm, or by great
> and awesome deeds, like all the things the LORD your God did for you in
> Egypt before your very eyes? (Deuteronomy 4:32–34)

Non-Jewish sages, among them Blaise Pascal, Jean-Jacques Rousseau, Leo
Tolstoy and Winston Churchill, wrote about the uniqueness of the history

מְכַלְכֵּל חַיִּים בְּחֶסֶד, מְחַיֵּה מֵתִים בְּרַחֲמִים רַבִּים

סוֹמֵךְ נוֹפְלִים, וְרוֹפֵא חוֹלִים

וּמַתִּיר אֲסוּרִים

וּמְקַיֵּם אֱמוּנָתוֹ לִישֵׁנֵי עָפָר.

מִי כָמְוֹךָ, בַּעַל גְּבוּרוֹת, וּמִי דּוֹמֶה לָּךְ

מֶלֶךְ, מֵמִית וּמְחַיֵּה וּמַצְמִיחַ יְשׁוּעָה.

וְנֶאֱמָן אַתָּה לְהַחֲיוֹת מֵתִים.

בָּרוּךְ אַתָּה יהוה, מְחַיֵּה הַמֵּתִים.

קדושת השם

אַתָּה קָדוֹשׁ וְשִׁמְךָ קָדוֹשׁ

וּקְדוֹשִׁים בְּכָל יוֹם יְהַלְלוּךָ סֶּלָה.

בָּרוּךְ אַתָּה יהוה, הָאֵל הַקָּדוֹשׁ.

קדושת היום

אַתָּה בְחַרְתָּנוּ מִכָּל הָעַמִּים

אָהַבְתָּ אוֹתָנוּ וְרָצִיתָ בָּנוּ

The first three paragraphs of prayer represent the three patriarchs. The first is about Abraham, the first to heed God's call to leave his land, birthplace, and father's house and begin the journey of faith. The second with its theme of resurrection is associated with Isaac, the child who unflinchingly faced death but was restored to life, an eternal symbol that life is God's gift. The third, about holiness, represents Jacob whose children all continued the covenant and whose descendants became, at Sinai, "a kingdom of priests and a holy nation" (Ex. 19:6), meaning a people dedicated to God, His ambassadors and witnesses to the world.

אַתָּה בְחַרְתָּנוּ *You have chosen us.* This striking emphasis on Jewish singularity is common to all three pilgrimage festivals, Pesaḥ, Shavuot and Sukkot, for

You have raised us above all tongues.
You have made us holy through Your commandments.
You have brought us near, our King, to Your service,
and have called us by Your great and holy name.

On Motza'ei Shabbat:

וַתּוֹדִיעֵנוּ You have made known to us, Lᴏʀᴅ our God,
Your righteous laws,
and have taught us to perform Your will's decrees.
You have given us, Lᴏʀᴅ our God, just laws and true teachings,
good precepts and commandments.
You have given us as our heritage seasons of joy,
holy festivals, and occasions for presenting our freewill offerings.
You have given us as our heritage the holiness of the Sabbath,
the glory of the festival,
and the festive offerings of the pilgrimage days.
You have distinguished, Lᴏʀᴅ our God, between sacred and secular,
between light and darkness,
between Israel and the nations,
between the seventh day and the six days of work.
You have distinguished between the holiness of the Sabbath
and the holiness of the festival,
and have made the seventh day holy above the six days of work.
You have distinguished and sanctified Your people Israel
with Your holiness.

---

guage has a special sanctity. For some this is because it was the language of
creation; for others, Maimonides especially, it was because of the modesty
of its expressions. Robert Frost said that "poetry is what is lost in translation."
Many of the misunderstandings of Judaism have arisen because of the untrans-
latability of many of its key terms into Western languages, influenced as they
were by Greek concepts that are very different from their Judaic counterparts.

וַתּוֹדִיעֵנוּ *You have made known to us.* A form of the Havdala prayer specific
to occasions when a festival falls immediately after Shabbat. The text is
already mentioned in the Talmud (*Berakhot* 33b). Havdala represents a most

וְרוֹמַמְתָּנוּ מִכָּל הַלְּשׁוֹנוֹת
וְקִדַּשְׁתָּנוּ בְּמִצְוֹתֶיךָ
וְקֵרַבְתָּנוּ מַלְכֵּנוּ לַעֲבוֹדָתֶךָ
וְשִׁמְךָ הַגָּדוֹל וְהַקָּדוֹשׁ עָלֵינוּ קָרָאתָ.

_____

On מוצאי שבת:

וַתּוֹדִיעֵנוּ יהוה אֱלֹהֵינוּ אֶת מִשְׁפְּטֵי צִדְקֶךָ
וַתְּלַמְּדֵנוּ לַעֲשׂוֹת חֻקֵּי רְצוֹנֶךָ
וַתִּתֶּן לָנוּ יהוה אֱלֹהֵינוּ מִשְׁפָּטִים יְשָׁרִים וְתוֹרוֹת אֱמֶת
חֻקִּים וּמִצְוֹת טוֹבִים
וַתַּנְחִילֵנוּ זְמַנֵּי שָׂשׂוֹן וּמוֹעֲדֵי קֹדֶשׁ וְחַגֵּי נְדָבָה
וַתּוֹרִישֵׁנוּ קְדֻשַּׁת שַׁבָּת וּכְבוֹד מוֹעֵד וַחֲגִיגַת הָרֶגֶל.
וַתַּבְדֵּל יהוה אֱלֹהֵינוּ בֵּין קֹדֶשׁ לְחֹל
בֵּין אוֹר לְחֹשֶׁךְ
בֵּין יִשְׂרָאֵל לָעַמִּים
בֵּין יוֹם הַשְּׁבִיעִי לְשֵׁשֶׁת יְמֵי הַמַּעֲשֶׂה.
בֵּין קְדֻשַּׁת שַׁבָּת לִקְדֻשַּׁת יוֹם טוֹב הִבְדַּלְתָּ
וְאֶת יוֹם הַשְּׁבִיעִי מִשֵּׁשֶׁת יְמֵי הַמַּעֲשֶׂה קִדַּשְׁתָּ
הִבְדַּלְתָּ וְקִדַּשְׁתָּ אֶת עַמְּךָ יִשְׂרָאֵל בִּקְדֻשָּׁתֶךָ.

_____

of the Jewish people, its survival against the odds and its continuity in the most varied and adverse circumstances. It is said that King Frederick the Great once asked his physician, Zimmermann of Brugg-in-Aargau, "Zimmermann, can you name me a single proof of the existence of God?" The physician considered the matter, and could think of only one answer not open to refutation. His reply: "Your majesty, the Jews." Through its history the singular people bears witness to the single God.

וְרוֹמַמְתָּנוּ מִכָּל הַלְּשׁוֹנוֹת *You have raised us above all tongues.* The Hebrew lan-

On Shabbat, add the words in parentheses:

וַתִּתֶּן לָֽנוּ And You, LORD our God, have given us in love
(Sabbaths for rest and) festivals for rejoicing,
holy days and seasons for joy,
(this Sabbath day and) this day of
the festival of Shavuot,
the time of the giving of our Torah
(with love), a holy assembly
in memory of the exodus from Egypt.

---

a rejoicing in his own stomach…. Rejoicing of this kind is a disgrace to
those who indulge in it. (Laws of Festival Rest 6:18)

This insistence on the *inclusive* nature of festivity – simultaneously a moral,
political, social and spiritual idea – is fundamental to Judaism and to the kind
of community and society we are commanded to create.

זְמַן מַתַּן תּוֹרָתֵֽנוּ *The time of the giving of our Torah.* The connection between
Shavuot and the giving of the Torah at Mount Sinai is not made explicitly in
Tanakh. The Torah calls Shavuot "the festival of the harvest" (Ex. 23:16), "the
festival of weeks" (Ex. 34:22), and "the day of the first fruits" (Num. 28:26).
The first explicit connection in a rabbinic source is in the Talmud (*Pesaḥim*
68b), though Shavuot is already identified with the revelation at Sinai in The
Book of Jubilees several centuries earlier. For an essay on the subject, see
Introduction, page xxiv.

זֵֽכֶר לִיצִיאַת מִצְרָֽיִם *In memory of the exodus from Egypt.* Note that all three pilgrimage festivals involve remembering the exodus. On Pesaḥ we recall and
reenact the exodus itself. On Shavuot we recall the point of the exodus, the
liberation of the Israelites from slavery in Egypt to become God's covenanted
people, "a kingdom of priests and a holy nation" (Ex. 19:6). On Sukkot we
recall the forty-year journey through the desert, when the Israelites lived as
nomads in temporary dwellings, surrounded by God's clouds of glory.

THE FOUR NAMES FOR "FESTIVAL"
The *Kedushat HaYom* blessing uses four different terms to describe the festivals: *mo'ed, ḥag, zeman,* and *mikra kodesh. Mo'ed* comes from the same root as
ed, "a witness." The idea that history is itself a witness to divine redemption

On שבת, add the words in parentheses:

וַתִּתֶּן לָנוּ יהוה אֱלֹהֵינוּ בְּאַהֲבָה
(שַׁבָּתוֹת לִמְנוּחָה וּ)מוֹעֲדִים לְשִׂמְחָה
חַגִּים וּזְמַנִּים לְשָׂשׂוֹן
אֶת יוֹם (הַשַּׁבָּת הַזֶּה וְאֶת יוֹם)
חַג הַשָּׁבוּעוֹת הַזֶּה, זְמַן מַתַּן תּוֹרָתֵנוּ
(בְּאַהֲבָה) מִקְרָא קֹדֶשׁ, זֵכֶר לִיצִיאַת מִצְרָיִם.

---

beautiful way in which we become "partners with the Holy One, blessed be He, in the work of creation," by beginning the week with a ceremony inviting us to share in a key activity in which God engaged when creating the universe. In Genesis 1 the verb ב-ד-ל, "to distinguish, differentiate, separate" occurs five times. So we, too, begin each week with an act of Havdala, separation. Normally the separation is between Shabbat and secular time (ḥol). Here it is between two different forms of holy time, that of Shabbat and that of a festival. The principle, however, remains the same: knowledge ("You have made known to us") is the ability to differentiate one kind of thing from another. The ability to make distinctions is the mark of the educated mind.

שַׁבָּתוֹת לִמְנוּחָה וּמוֹעֲדִים לְשִׂמְחָה *Sabbaths for rest and festivals for rejoicing.* There is a significant difference between rest and joy. Rest renews, joy uplifts. There is no exact English equivalent of the word *simḥa* since it essentially means "joy shared" or "collective celebration." *Simḥa* in Judaism, especially in relation to the festivals, is communal. It must involve everyone, even the poorest and loneliest. The Torah is emphatic in insisting that festive celebration should include "you, your sons and daughters, your male and female servants, and the Levites, the foreigners, the fatherless and the widows who live in your towns" (Deut. 16:14). Maimonides writes:

> While eating and drinking [on a festival], it is one's duty to feed the stranger, the orphan, the widow, and other poor and unfortunate people, for he who locks the doors to his courtyard and eats and drinks with his wife and family, without giving anything to eat and drink to the poor and the bitter in soul – his meal is not a rejoicing in a divine commandment, but

אֱלֹהֵינוּ Our God and God of our ancestors,
may there rise, come, reach,
appear, be favored, heard,
regarded and remembered before You,
our recollection and remembrance,
as well as the remembrance of our ancestors,
and of the Messiah son of David Your servant,
and of Jerusalem Your holy city,
and of all Your people the house of Israel –
for deliverance and well-being,
grace, loving-kindness and compassion,
life and peace,
on this day of the festival of Shavuot.
On it remember us, LORD our God, for good;
recollect us for blessing,
and deliver us for life.
In accord with Your promise of salvation and compassion,
spare us and be gracious to us;
have compassion on us and deliver us,
for our eyes are turned to You
because You, God, are a gracious and compassionate King.

יַעֲלֶה וְיָבוֹא וְיַגִּיעַ *Rise, come, reach* .... A crescendo of eight verbs, signifying the
seven heavenly realms, with God above them all – a spatial metaphor, meaning, may our prayers reach the innermost heart of God. Note the motif of
memory in this paragraph: the root ז-כ-ר appears seven times, and the related
verb פ-ק-ד three times. Judaism is a religion of memory, God's and ours. The
Egyptians memorialized their history by monuments and inscriptions. Our
history is engraved not on walls of stone but on the mind. We live not *in* the
past but *with* the past: it is our satellite navigation system as we travel the
wilderness of time, reminding us where we have come from and where we
seek to go. "People will not look forward to posterity who never look backward to their ancestors" (Edmund Burke). We ask God to remember; God
asks us to remember.

אֱלֹהֵינוּ וֵאלֹהֵי אֲבוֹתֵינוּ

יַעֲלֶה וְיָבוֹא וְיַגִּיעַ וְיֵרָאֶה וְיֵרָצֶה וְיִשָּׁמַע

וְיִפָּקֵד וְיִזָּכֵר זִכְרוֹנֵנוּ וּפִקְדוֹנֵנוּ

וְזִכְרוֹן אֲבוֹתֵינוּ

וְזִכְרוֹן מָשִׁיחַ בֶּן דָּוִד עַבְדֶּךָ

וְזִכְרוֹן יְרוּשָׁלַיִם עִיר קָדְשֶׁךָ

וְזִכְרוֹן כָּל עַמְּךָ בֵּית יִשְׂרָאֵל, לְפָנֶיךָ

לִפְלֵיטָה, לְטוֹבָה, לְחֵן וּלְחֶסֶד וּלְרַחֲמִים

לְחַיִּים וּלְשָׁלוֹם

בְּיוֹם חַג הַשָּׁבוּעוֹת הַזֶּה.

זָכְרֵנוּ יהוה אֱלֹהֵינוּ בּוֹ לְטוֹבָה

וּפָקְדֵנוּ בּוֹ לִבְרָכָה

וְהוֹשִׁיעֵנוּ בּוֹ לְחַיִּים.

וּבִדְבַר יְשׁוּעָה וְרַחֲמִים חוּס וְחָנֵּנוּ

וְרַחֵם עָלֵינוּ וְהוֹשִׁיעֵנוּ

כִּי אֵלֶיךָ עֵינֵינוּ

כִּי אֵל מֶלֶךְ חַנּוּן וְרַחוּם אָתָּה.

is thus embedded in the Hebrew language. Ḥag alludes to the festival offering (ḥagiga) brought at the Temple. Zeman indicates a time dedicated to a
particular event or idea; Pesaḥ to liberation, Shavuot to revelation, Sukkot to
joy. It also conveys the sense of season: Pesaḥ in spring, Shavuot at the time
of first fruits, and Sukkot in the fall. Mikra kodesh means a day made holy by
declaration, that is, by Kiddush, prayer, and the recitation of Hallel. Rabbi
Yaakov Tzvi Mecklenburg (Germany, nineteenth century) understands it
to mean "a call to holiness." Mikra also means sacred Scripture, for these are
days of public gathering when the Torah is read.

On Shabbat, add the words in parentheses:

וְהַשִּׂיאֵנוּ Bestow on us, LORD our God,
the blessings of Your festivals
for good life and peace, joy and gladness,
as You desired and promised to bless us.
(Our God and God of our fathers, find favor in our rest.)
Make us holy through Your commandments
and grant us a share in Your Torah.
Satisfy us with Your goodness, gladden us with Your salvation,
and purify our hearts to serve You in truth.
Grant us as our heritage, LORD our God (with love and favor,)
with joy and gladness, Your holy (Sabbath and) festivals,
and may Israel, who sanctify Your name, rejoice in You.
Blessed are You, LORD,
who sanctifies (the Sabbath and) Israel and the festive seasons.

TEMPLE SERVICE
רְצֵה Find favor, LORD our God,
in Your people Israel and their prayer.
Restore the service to Your most holy House,
and accept in love and favor
the fire-offerings of Israel and their prayer.
May the service of Your people Israel always find favor with You.
And may our eyes witness Your return to Zion in compassion.
Blessed are You, LORD,
who restores His Presence to Zion.

The precise order of the conclusion of this blessing is important. "Israel" comes before "seasons" since it is God who sanctifies Israel, and Israel who consecrates times by fixing the calendar, the first command given to us as a people (Ex. 12:2). Shabbat precedes both, since it was consecrated by God on the seventh day of creation (Gen. 2:1–3), before there was an Israel or a calendar of festivals.

On שבת*, add the words in parentheses:*

וְהַשִּׂיאֵנוּ יהוה אֱלֹהֵינוּ אֶת בִּרְכַּת מוֹעֲדֶיךָ
לְחַיִּים וּלְשָׁלוֹם, לְשִׂמְחָה וּלְשָׂשׂוֹן
כַּאֲשֶׁר רָצִיתָ וְאָמַרְתָּ לְבָרְכֵנוּ.
(אֱלֹהֵינוּ וֵאלֹהֵי אֲבוֹתֵינוּ, רְצֵה בִמְנוּחָתֵנוּ)
קַדְּשֵׁנוּ בְּמִצְוֹתֶיךָ, וְתֵן חֶלְקֵנוּ בְּתוֹרָתֶךָ
שַׂבְּעֵנוּ מִטּוּבֶךָ, וְשַׂמְּחֵנוּ בִּישׁוּעָתֶךָ
וְטַהֵר לִבֵּנוּ לְעָבְדְּךָ בֶּאֱמֶת.
וְהַנְחִילֵנוּ יהוה אֱלֹהֵינוּ (בְּאַהֲבָה וּבְרָצוֹן)
בְּשִׂמְחָה וּבְשָׂשׂוֹן (שַׁבָּת וּ) מוֹעֲדֵי קָדְשֶׁךָ
וְיִשְׂמְחוּ בְךָ יִשְׂרָאֵל מְקַדְּשֵׁי שְׁמֶךָ.
בָּרוּךְ אַתָּה יהוה, מְקַדֵּשׁ (הַשַּׁבָּת וְ) יִשְׂרָאֵל וְהַזְּמַנִּים.

עבודה

רְצֵה יהוה אֱלֹהֵינוּ בְּעַמְּךָ יִשְׂרָאֵל, וּבִתְפִלָּתָם
וְהָשֵׁב אֶת הָעֲבוֹדָה לִדְבִיר בֵּיתֶךָ
וְאִשֵּׁי יִשְׂרָאֵל וּתְפִלָּתָם בְּאַהֲבָה תְקַבֵּל בְּרָצוֹן
וּתְהִי לְרָצוֹן תָּמִיד עֲבוֹדַת יִשְׂרָאֵל עַמֶּךָ.
וְתֶחֱזֶינָה עֵינֵינוּ בְּשׁוּבְךָ לְצִיּוֹן בְּרַחֲמִים.
בָּרוּךְ אַתָּה יהוה, הַמַּחֲזִיר שְׁכִינָתוֹ לְצִיּוֹן.

וְהַשִּׂיאֵנוּ...מְקַדֵּשׁ הַשַּׁבָּת וְיִשְׂרָאֵל וְהַזְּמַנִּים *Bestow on us… who sanctifies the Sabbath and Israel and the festive seasons.*

The root ש-מ-ח, "joy" or "rejoice," appears four times in this paragraph, corresponding to the four times in the Torah where we are commanded to rejoice on the festivals (Lev. 23:40; Deut. 16:11, 14, 15).

THANKSGIVING

Bow at the first nine words.

מוֹדִים We give thanks to You,
for You are the LORD our God and God of our ancestors
for ever and all time.
You are the Rock of our lives,
Shield of our salvation from generation to generation.
We will thank You and declare Your praise for our lives,
which are entrusted into Your hand;
for our souls, which are placed in Your charge;
for Your miracles which are with us every day;
and for Your wonders and favors
at all times, evening, morning and midday.
You are good –
for Your compassion never fails.
You are compassionate –
for Your loving-kindnesses never cease.
We have always placed our hope in You.
For all these things
may Your name be blessed and exalted, our King,
continually, for ever and all time.
Let all that lives thank You, Selah!
and praise Your name in truth, God, our Savior and Help, Selah!
Blessed are You, LORD,
whose name is "the Good" and to whom thanks are due.

PEACE

שָׁלוֹם רָב Grant great peace to Your people Israel for ever,
for You are the sovereign LORD of all peace;
and may it be good in Your eyes to bless Your people Israel
at every time, at every hour, with Your peace.
Blessed are You, LORD,
who blesses His people Israel with peace.

הודאה

Bow at the first five words.

יְמוֹדִים אֲנַחְנוּ לָךְ

שָׁאַתָּה הוּא יהוה אֱלֹהֵינוּ וֵאלֹהֵי אֲבוֹתֵינוּ לְעוֹלָם וָעֶד.

צוּר חַיֵּינוּ, מָגֵן יִשְׁעֵנוּ, אַתָּה הוּא לְדוֹר וָדוֹר.

נוֹדֶה לְּךָ וּנְסַפֵּר תְּהִלָּתֶךָ

עַל חַיֵּינוּ הַמְּסוּרִים בְּיָדֶךָ

וְעַל נִשְׁמוֹתֵינוּ הַפְּקוּדוֹת לָךְ

וְעַל נִסֶּיךָ שֶׁבְּכָל יוֹם עִמָּנוּ

וְעַל נִפְלְאוֹתֶיךָ וְטוֹבוֹתֶיךָ

שֶׁבְּכָל עֵת, עֶרֶב וָבֹקֶר וְצָהֳרָיִם.

הַטּוֹב, כִּי לֹא כָלוּ רַחֲמֶיךָ

וְהַמְרַחֵם, כִּי לֹא תַמּוּ חֲסָדֶיךָ

מֵעוֹלָם קִוִּינוּ לָךְ.

וְעַל כֻּלָּם יִתְבָּרַךְ וְיִתְרוֹמַם שִׁמְךָ מַלְכֵּנוּ תָּמִיד לְעוֹלָם וָעֶד.

וְכֹל הַחַיִּים יוֹדוּךָ סֶּלָה, וִיהַלְלוּ אֶת שִׁמְךָ בֶּאֱמֶת

הָאֵל יְשׁוּעָתֵנוּ וְעֶזְרָתֵנוּ סֶלָה.

יְבָּרוּךְ אַתָּה יהוה, הַטּוֹב שִׁמְךָ וּלְךָ נָאֶה לְהוֹדוֹת.

ברכת שלום

שָׁלוֹם רָב עַל יִשְׂרָאֵל עַמְּךָ תָּשִׂים לְעוֹלָם

כִּי אַתָּה הוּא מֶלֶךְ אָדוֹן לְכָל הַשָּׁלוֹם.

וְטוֹב בְּעֵינֶיךָ לְבָרֵךְ אֶת עַמְּךָ יִשְׂרָאֵל

בְּכָל עֵת וּבְכָל שָׁעָה בִּשְׁלוֹמֶךָ.

בָּרוּךְ אַתָּה יהוה, הַמְבָרֵךְ אֶת עַמּוֹ יִשְׂרָאֵל בַּשָּׁלוֹם.

Some say the following verse.

May the words of my mouth and the meditation of my heart
find favor before You, Lord, my Rock and Redeemer.

Ps. 19

אֱלֹהַי My God,
guard my tongue from evil and my lips from deceitful speech.
To those who curse me, let my soul be silent;
may my soul be to all like the dust.
Open my heart to Your Torah
and let my soul pursue Your commandments.
As for all who plan evil against me,
swiftly thwart their counsel and frustrate their plans.
   Act for the sake of Your name; act for the sake of Your right hand;
   act for the sake of Your holiness; act for the sake of Your Torah.
That Your beloved ones may be delivered,
save with Your right hand and answer me.
May the words of my mouth and the meditation of my heart
find favor before You, Lord, my Rock and Redeemer.

*Berakhot
17a*

Ps. 60

Ps. 19

Bow, take three steps back, then bow, first left, then right, then center, while saying:

May He who makes peace in His high places,
make peace for us and all Israel – and say: Amen.

יְהִי רָצוֹן May it be Your will, Lord our God and God of our ancestors,
that the Temple be rebuilt speedily in our days,
and grant us a share in Your Torah.
And there we will serve You with reverence,
as in the days of old and as in former years.
Then the offering of Judah and Jerusalem
will be pleasing to the Lord as in the days of old and as in former years.

Mal. 3

> On Shabbat, continue with "Then the heavens" below.
> If Yom Tov falls on a weekday, the service continues with Full Kaddish on page 80.

> On Shabbat all stand and say:

וַיְכֻלּוּ Then the heavens and the earth were completed, and all their array.
With the seventh day, God completed the work He had done.
He ceased on the seventh day from all the work He had done.
God blessed the seventh day and declared it holy,
because on it He ceased from all His work He had created to do.

Gen. 2

Some say the following verse.

תהלים יט

יִהְיוּ לְרָצוֹן אִמְרֵי־פִי וְהֶגְיוֹן לִבִּי לְפָנֶיךָ, יהוה צוּרִי וְגֹאֲלִי:

ברכות יז

אֱלֹהַי

נְצֹר לְשׁוֹנִי מֵרָע וּשְׂפָתַי מִדַּבֵּר מִרְמָה

וְלִמְקַלְלַי נַפְשִׁי תִדֹּם, וְנַפְשִׁי כֶּעָפָר לַכֹּל תִּהְיֶה.

פְּתַח לִבִּי בְּתוֹרָתֶךָ, וּבְמִצְוֹתֶיךָ תִּרְדֹּף נַפְשִׁי.

וְכָל הַחוֹשְׁבִים עָלַי רָעָה, מְהֵרָה הָפֵר עֲצָתָם וְקַלְקֵל מַחֲשַׁבְתָּם.

עֲשֵׂה לְמַעַן שְׁמֶךָ, עֲשֵׂה לְמַעַן יְמִינֶךָ

עֲשֵׂה לְמַעַן קְדֻשָּׁתֶךָ, עֲשֵׂה לְמַעַן תּוֹרָתֶךָ.

תהלים ס

לְמַעַן יֵחָלְצוּן יְדִידֶיךָ, הוֹשִׁיעָה יְמִינְךָ וַעֲנֵנִי:

תהלים יט

יִהְיוּ לְרָצוֹן אִמְרֵי־פִי וְהֶגְיוֹן לִבִּי לְפָנֶיךָ, יהוה צוּרִי וְגֹאֲלִי:

Bow, take three steps back, then bow, first left, then right, then center, while saying:

עֹשֶׂה שָׁלוֹם בִּמְרוֹמָיו

הוּא יַעֲשֶׂה שָׁלוֹם עָלֵינוּ וְעַל כָּל יִשְׂרָאֵל, וְאִמְרוּ אָמֵן.

יְהִי רָצוֹן מִלְּפָנֶיךָ יהוה אֱלֹהֵינוּ וֵאלֹהֵי אֲבוֹתֵינוּ

שֶׁיִּבָּנֶה בֵּית הַמִּקְדָּשׁ בִּמְהֵרָה בְיָמֵינוּ, וְתֵן חֶלְקֵנוּ בְּתוֹרָתֶךָ

וְשָׁם נַעֲבָדְךָ בְּיִרְאָה כִּימֵי עוֹלָם וּכְשָׁנִים קַדְמֹנִיּוֹת.

מלאכי ג

וְעָרְבָה לַיהוה מִנְחַת יְהוּדָה וִירוּשָׁלָ͏ִם כִּימֵי עוֹלָם וּכְשָׁנִים קַדְמֹנִיּוֹת:

On שבת*, continue with* וַיְכֻלּוּ *below.*
On יום טוב *which falls on a weekday, the service continues with* קדיש שלם *on page 81.*

On שבת *all stand and say:*

בראשית ב

וַיְכֻלּוּ הַשָּׁמַיִם וְהָאָרֶץ וְכָל־צְבָאָם:

וַיְכַל אֱלֹהִים בַּיּוֹם הַשְּׁבִיעִי מְלַאכְתּוֹ אֲשֶׁר עָשָׂה

וַיִּשְׁבֹּת בַּיּוֹם הַשְּׁבִיעִי מִכָּל־מְלַאכְתּוֹ אֲשֶׁר עָשָׂה:

וַיְבָרֶךְ אֱלֹהִים אֶת־יוֹם הַשְּׁבִיעִי, וַיְקַדֵּשׁ אֹתוֹ

כִּי בוֹ שָׁבַת מִכָּל־מְלַאכְתּוֹ, אֲשֶׁר־בָּרָא אֱלֹהִים, לַעֲשׂוֹת:

*The following until "who sanctifies the Sabbath" below,
is omitted when praying with an occasional minyan or alone.*

The Leader continues:

ME'EIN SHEVA

בָּרוּךְ Blessed are You, LORD our God and God of our fathers,
God of Abraham, God of Isaac and God of Jacob,
the great, mighty and awesome God,
God Most High, Creator of heaven and earth.

The congregation then the Leader:

מָגֵן אָבוֹת By His word, He was the Shield of our ancestors.
By His promise, He will revive the dead.
There is none like the holy God
who gives rest to His people on His holy Sabbath day,
for He found them worthy of His favor to give them rest.
Before Him we will come in worship with reverence and awe,
giving thanks to His name daily, continually, with due blessings.
He is God to whom thanks are due, the LORD of peace
who sanctifies the Sabbath and blesses the seventh day,
and in holiness gives rest to a people filled with delight,
in remembrance of the work of creation.

The Leader continues:

אֱלֹהֵינוּ Our God and God of our ancestors,
may You find favor in our rest.
Make us holy through Your commandments
and grant us our share in Your Torah.
Satisfy us with Your goodness,
grant us joy in Your salvation,
and purify our hearts to serve You in truth.
In love and favor, LORD our God,
grant us as our heritage Your holy Sabbath,
so that Israel who sanctify Your name may find rest on it.
Blessed are You, LORD,
who sanctifies the Sabbath.

The following until מְקַדֵּשׁ הַשַּׁבָּת *below, is omitted when praying with an occasional* מנין *or alone.*

The שליח ציבור *continues:*

ברכה מעין שבע

בָּרוּךְ אַתָּה יהוה, אֱלֹהֵינוּ וֵאלֹהֵי אֲבוֹתֵינוּ
אֱלֹהֵי אַבְרָהָם, אֱלֹהֵי יִצְחָק, וֵאלֹהֵי יַעֲקֹב
הָאֵל הַגָּדוֹל הַגִּבּוֹר וְהַנּוֹרָא, אֵל עֶלְיוֹן, קֹנֵה שָׁמַיִם וָאָרֶץ.

The קהל *then the* שליח ציבור:

מָגֵן אָבוֹת בִּדְבָרוֹ
מְחַיֵּה מֵתִים בְּמַאֲמָרוֹ
הָאֵל הַקָּדוֹשׁ שֶׁאֵין כָּמוֹהוּ
הַמֵּנִיחַ לְעַמּוֹ בְּיוֹם שַׁבַּת קָדְשׁוֹ
כִּי בָם רָצָה לְהָנִיחַ לָהֶם
לְפָנָיו נַעֲבֹד בְּיִרְאָה וָפַחַד
וְנוֹדֶה לִשְׁמוֹ בְּכָל יוֹם תָּמִיד, מֵעֵין הַבְּרָכוֹת
אֵל הַהוֹדָאוֹת, אֲדוֹן הַשָּׁלוֹם
מְקַדֵּשׁ הַשַּׁבָּת וּמְבָרֵךְ שְׁבִיעִי
וּמֵנִיחַ בִּקְדֻשָּׁה לְעַם מְדֻשְּׁנֵי עֹנֶג
זֵכֶר לְמַעֲשֵׂה בְרֵאשִׁית.

The שליח ציבור *continues:*

אֱלֹהֵינוּ וֵאלֹהֵי אֲבוֹתֵינוּ, רְצֵה בִמְנוּחָתֵנוּ.
קַדְּשֵׁנוּ בְּמִצְוֹתֶיךָ וְתֵן חֶלְקֵנוּ בְּתוֹרָתֶךָ
שַׂבְּעֵנוּ מִטּוּבֶךָ וְשַׂמְּחֵנוּ בִּישׁוּעָתֶךָ
וְטַהֵר לִבֵּנוּ לְעָבְדְּךָ בֶּאֱמֶת.
וְהַנְחִילֵנוּ יהוה אֱלֹהֵינוּ בְּאַהֲבָה וּבְרָצוֹן שַׁבַּת קָדְשֶׁךָ
וְיָנוּחוּ בָהּ יִשְׂרָאֵל מְקַדְּשֵׁי שְׁמֶךָ.
בָּרוּךְ אַתָּה יהוה, מְקַדֵּשׁ הַשַּׁבָּת.

FULL KADDISH

Leader: יִתְגַּדַּל Magnified and sanctified
may His great name be,
in the world He created by His will.
May He establish His kingdom
in your lifetime and in your days,
and in the lifetime of all the house of Israel,
swiftly and soon –
and say: Amen.

All: May His great name be blessed
for ever and all time.

Leader: Blessed and praised, glorified and exalted,
raised and honored,
uplifted and lauded be
the name of the Holy One,
blessed be He,
beyond any blessing,
song, praise and consolation
uttered in the world –
and say: Amen.

May the prayers and pleas of all Israel
be accepted by their Father in heaven –
and say: Amen.

May there be great peace from heaven,
and life for us and all Israel –
and say: Amen.

Bow, take three steps back, as if taking leave of the Divine Presence,
then bow, first left, then right, then center, while saying:

May He who makes peace in His high places,
make peace for us and all Israel –
and say: Amen.

קדיש שלם

ש״ץ: יִתְגַּדַּל וְיִתְקַדַּשׁ שְׁמֵהּ רַבָּא (קהל: אָמֵן)

בְּעָלְמָא דִּי בְרָא כִרְעוּתֵהּ

וְיַמְלִיךְ מַלְכוּתֵהּ

בְּחַיֵּיכוֹן וּבְיוֹמֵיכוֹן וּבְחַיֵּי דְּכָל בֵּית יִשְׂרָאֵל

בַּעֲגָלָא וּבִזְמַן קָרִיב

וְאִמְרוּ אָמֵן. (קהל: אָמֵן)

קהל
 וש״ץ: יְהֵא שְׁמֵהּ רַבָּא מְבָרַךְ לְעָלַם וּלְעָלְמֵי עָלְמַיָּא.

ש״ץ: יִתְבָּרַךְ וְיִשְׁתַּבַּח וְיִתְפָּאַר

וְיִתְרוֹמַם וְיִתְנַשֵּׂא וְיִתְהַדָּר וְיִתְעַלֶּה וְיִתְהַלָּל

שְׁמֵהּ דְּקֻדְשָׁא בְּרִיךְ הוּא (קהל: בְּרִיךְ הוּא)

לְעֵלָּא מִן כָּל בִּרְכָתָא וְשִׁירָתָא, תֻּשְׁבְּחָתָא וְנֶחֱמָתָא

דַּאֲמִירָן בְּעָלְמָא

וְאִמְרוּ אָמֵן. (קהל: אָמֵן)

תִּתְקַבֵּל צְלוֹתְהוֹן וּבָעוּתְהוֹן דְּכָל יִשְׂרָאֵל

קֳדָם אֲבוּהוֹן דִּי בִשְׁמַיָּא

וְאִמְרוּ אָמֵן. (קהל: אָמֵן)

יְהֵא שְׁלָמָא רַבָּא מִן שְׁמַיָּא

וְחַיִּים, עָלֵינוּ וְעַל כָּל יִשְׂרָאֵל

וְאִמְרוּ אָמֵן. (קהל: אָמֵן)

Bow, take three steps back, as if taking leave of the Divine Presence,
then bow, first left, then right, then center, while saying:

עֹשֶׂה שָׁלוֹם בִּמְרוֹמָיו

הוּא יַעֲשֶׂה שָׁלוֹם עָלֵינוּ וְעַל כָּל יִשְׂרָאֵל

וְאִמְרוּ אָמֵן. (קהל: אָמֵן)

KIDDUSH IN THE SYNAGOGUE

The Leader raises a cup of wine and says:

Please pay attention, my masters.

בָּרוּךְ Blessed are You, Lord our God, King of the Universe,
who creates the fruit of the vine.

On Shabbat, add the words in parentheses.

בָּרוּךְ Blessed are You, Lord our God, King of the Universe,
who has chosen us from among all peoples,
raised us above all tongues,
and made us holy through His commandments.
You have given us, Lord our God, in love (Sabbaths for rest),
festivals for rejoicing, holy days and seasons for joy,
(this Sabbath day and) this day of
the festival of Shavuot, the time of the giving of our Torah
(with love), a holy assembly in memory of the exodus from Egypt.
For You have chosen us and sanctified us above all peoples,
and given us as our heritage (Your holy Sabbath in love and favor and)
Your holy festivals for joy and gladness.
Blessed are you, Lord,
who sanctifies (the Sabbath,) Israel and the festivals.

On Motza'ei Shabbat, the following Havdala is added.
The Leader lifts his hands toward the flame of the Havdala candle and says:

בָּרוּךְ Blessed are You, Lord our God, King of the Universe,
who creates the lights of fire.

Blessed are You, Lord our God, King of the Universe, who distinguishes between
sacred and secular, between light and darkness, between Israel and the nations,
between the seventh day and the six days of work. You have made a distinction
between the holiness of the Sabbath and the holiness of festivals, and have sanctified the seventh day above the six days of work. You have distinguished and
sanctified Your people Israel with Your holiness. Blessed are You, Lord, who
distinguishes between sacred and sacred.

בָּרוּךְ Blessed are You, Lord our God, King of the Universe,
who has given us life, sustained us, and brought us to this time.

The wine should be drunk by children under the age
of Bar/Bat Mitzva or, if there are none, by the Leader.

קידוש בבית הכנסת

The שליח ציבור *raises a cup of wine and says:*

סַבְרִי מָרָנָן

בָּרוּךְ אַתָּה יהוה אֱלֹהֵינוּ מֶלֶךְ הָעוֹלָם בּוֹרֵא פְּרִי הַגָּפֶן.

On שבת, *add the words in parentheses.*

בָּרוּךְ אַתָּה יהוה אֱלֹהֵינוּ מֶלֶךְ הָעוֹלָם

אֲשֶׁר בָּחַר בָּנוּ מִכָּל עָם

וְרוֹמְמָנוּ מִכָּל לָשׁוֹן, וְקִדְּשָׁנוּ בְּמִצְוֹתָיו

וַתִּתֶּן לָנוּ יהוה אֱלֹהֵינוּ בְּאַהֲבָה

(שַׁבָּתוֹת לִמְנוּחָה וּ) מוֹעֲדִים לְשִׂמְחָה, חַגִּים וּזְמַנִּים לְשָׂשׂוֹן

אֶת יוֹם (הַשַּׁבָּת הַזֶּה וְאֶת יוֹם) חַג הַשָּׁבוּעוֹת הַזֶּה, זְמַן מַתַּן תּוֹרָתֵנוּ

(בְּאַהֲבָה) מִקְרָא קֹדֶשׁ, זֵכֶר לִיצִיאַת מִצְרָיִם.

כִּי בָנוּ בָחַרְתָּ וְאוֹתָנוּ קִדַּשְׁתָּ מִכָּל הָעַמִּים

(וְשַׁבָּת) וּמוֹעֲדֵי קָדְשֶׁךָ (בְּאַהֲבָה וּבְרָצוֹן) בְּשִׂמְחָה וּבְשָׂשׂוֹן הִנְחַלְתָּנוּ.

בָּרוּךְ אַתָּה יהוה, מְקַדֵּשׁ (הַשַּׁבָּת וְ) יִשְׂרָאֵל וְהַזְּמַנִּים.

On מוצאי שבת, *the following* הבדלה *is added.*
The שליח ציבור *lifts his hands toward the* הבדלה *candle and says:*

בָּרוּךְ אַתָּה יהוה אֱלֹהֵינוּ מֶלֶךְ הָעוֹלָם, בּוֹרֵא מְאוֹרֵי הָאֵשׁ.

בָּרוּךְ אַתָּה יהוה אֱלֹהֵינוּ מֶלֶךְ הָעוֹלָם, הַמַּבְדִּיל בֵּין קֹדֶשׁ לְחֹל, בֵּין אוֹר
לְחֹשֶׁךְ, בֵּין יִשְׂרָאֵל לָעַמִּים, בֵּין יוֹם הַשְּׁבִיעִי לְשֵׁשֶׁת יְמֵי הַמַּעֲשֶׂה. בֵּין קְדֻשַּׁת
שַׁבָּת לִקְדֻשַּׁת יוֹם טוֹב הִבְדַּלְתָּ, וְאֶת יוֹם הַשְּׁבִיעִי מִשֵּׁשֶׁת יְמֵי הַמַּעֲשֶׂה
קִדַּשְׁתָּ, הִבְדַּלְתָּ וְקִדַּשְׁתָּ אֶת עַמְּךָ יִשְׂרָאֵל בִּקְדֻשָּׁתֶךָ. בָּרוּךְ אַתָּה יהוה,
הַמַּבְדִּיל בֵּין קֹדֶשׁ לְקֹדֶשׁ.

בָּרוּךְ אַתָּה יהוה אֱלֹהֵינוּ מֶלֶךְ הָעוֹלָם
שֶׁהֶחֱיָנוּ וְקִיְּמָנוּ וְהִגִּיעָנוּ לַזְּמַן הַזֶּה.

*The wine should be drunk by children under the age
of* בר מצווה or בת מצווה *or, if there are none, by the* שליח ציבור.

Stand while saying Aleinu. Bow at ˙.

עָלֵינוּ It is our duty to praise the Master of all,
and ascribe greatness to the Author of creation,
who has not made us like the nations of the lands
nor placed us like the families of the earth;
who has not made our portion like theirs,
nor our destiny like all their multitudes.
(For they worship vanity and emptiness,
and pray to a god who cannot save.)
˙But we bow in worship
and thank the Supreme King of kings,
the Holy One, blessed be He,
who extends the heavens and establishes the earth,
whose throne of glory is in the heavens above,
and whose power's Presence is in the highest of heights.
He is our God; there is no other.
Truly He is our King, there is none else,
as it is written in His Torah:
"You shall know and take to heart this day   *Deut. 4*
that the LORD is God, in heaven above and on earth below.
There is no other."

---

271). It is our task to bear witness to God on earth, to be His ambassadors to
humanity.

   That is the Jewish vocation. At times of paganism it involved the fight
against myth and the idea that the universe was the arena of a cosmic struggle
of heavenly powers, played out on earth in the form of wars, battles, and a
hierarchy of power. At times of secularism it means insisting that the material
universe is not the only, or even the most important dimension in which we
live. There is a world of the spirit to which meaning and freedom – two es-
sentials of our humanity – belong. Judaism has often been the countervoice
in the human conversation, and this has often meant shouldering a heavy
burden, attracting the scorn and sometimes the violence, of others. Yet this

Stand while saying עָלֵינוּ. *Bow at* ‫٭‬.

עָלֵינוּ לְשַׁבֵּחַ לַאֲדוֹן הַכֹּל, לָתֵת גְּדֻלָּה לְיוֹצֵר בְּרֵאשִׁית
שֶׁלֹּא עָשָׂנוּ כְּגוֹיֵי הָאֲרָצוֹת
וְלֹא שָׂמָנוּ כְּמִשְׁפְּחוֹת הָאֲדָמָה
שֶׁלֹּא שָׂם חֶלְקֵנוּ כָּהֶם וְגוֹרָלֵנוּ כְּכָל הֲמוֹנָם.
(שֶׁהֵם מִשְׁתַּחֲוִים לְהֶבֶל וָרִיק וּמִתְפַּלְלִים אֶל אֵל לֹא יוֹשִׁיעַ.)
٭וַאֲנַחְנוּ כּוֹרְעִים וּמִשְׁתַּחֲוִים וּמוֹדִים
לִפְנֵי מֶלֶךְ מַלְכֵי הַמְּלָכִים, הַקָּדוֹשׁ בָּרוּךְ הוּא
שֶׁהוּא נוֹטֶה שָׁמַיִם וְיוֹסֵד אָרֶץ
וּמוֹשַׁב יְקָרוֹ בַּשָּׁמַיִם מִמַּעַל
וּשְׁכִינַת עֻזּוֹ בְּגָבְהֵי מְרוֹמִים.
הוּא אֱלֹהֵינוּ, אֵין עוֹד.
אֱמֶת מַלְכֵּנוּ, אֶפֶס זוּלָתוֹ
כַּכָּתוּב בְּתוֹרָתוֹ
וְיָדַעְתָּ הַיּוֹם וַהֲשֵׁבֹתָ אֶל־לְבָבֶךָ
כִּי יהוה הוּא הָאֱלֹהִים בַּשָּׁמַיִם מִמַּעַל וְעַל־הָאָרֶץ מִתָּחַת
אֵין עוֹד:

דברים ד

עָלֵינוּ *It is our duty.* In the first line of the Shema, the final letter of the first and last words – written, in a Torah scroll, larger than the other letters – spell out the word *Ed*, meaning "witness." The first and last letters of *Aleinu* spell out the same word. This recalls the great passage in Isaiah in which God declares "You are My witnesses…and My servant whom I have chosen…You are My witnesses – declares the LORD – that I am God" (Is. 43:10–12), which the sages interpreted as meaning: "If you are My witnesses, then I am God, but if you are not My witnesses it is as if I were not God" (*Yalkut Shimoni*

Therefore, we place our hope in You, LORD our God,
that we may soon see the glory of Your power,
when You will remove abominations from the earth,
and idols will be utterly destroyed,
when the world will be perfected
under the sovereignty of the Almighty,
when all humanity will call on Your name,
to turn all the earth's wicked toward You.
All the world's inhabitants will realize and know
that to You every knee must bow
and every tongue swear loyalty.
Before You, LORD our God, they will kneel and bow down
and give honor to Your glorious name.
They will all accept the yoke of Your kingdom,
and You will reign over them soon and for ever.
For the kingdom is Yours,
and to all eternity You will reign in glory,
as it is written in Your Torah:
"The LORD will reign for ever and ever."   *Ex. 15*
▸ And it is said:
"Then the LORD shall be King over all the earth;   *Zech. 14*
on that day the LORD shall be One and His name One."

Some add:

Have no fear of sudden terror or of the ruin when it overtakes the wicked.   *Prov. 3*
Devise your strategy, but it will be thwarted;   *Is. 8*
propose your plan, but it will not stand, for God is with us.
When you grow old, I will still be the same.   *Is. 46*
When your hair turns gray, I will still carry you.
I made you, I will bear you,
I will carry you, and I will rescue you.

is the message we are called on to bear witness to, and *Aleinu* expresses it
with great power.

עַל כֵּן נְקַוֶּה לְךָ יהוה אֱלֹהֵינוּ

לִרְאוֹת מְהֵרָה בְּתִפְאֶרֶת עֻזֶּךָ

לְהַעֲבִיר גִּלּוּלִים מִן הָאָרֶץ

וְהָאֱלִילִים כָּרוֹת יִכָּרֵתוּן

לְתַקֵּן עוֹלָם בְּמַלְכוּת שַׁדַּי.

וְכָל בְּנֵי בָשָׂר יִקְרְאוּ בִשְׁמֶךָ

לְהַפְנוֹת אֵלֶיךָ כָּל רִשְׁעֵי אָרֶץ.

יַכִּירוּ וְיֵדְעוּ כָּל יוֹשְׁבֵי תֵבֵל

כִּי לְךָ תִּכְרַע כָּל בֶּרֶךְ, תִּשָּׁבַע כָּל לָשׁוֹן.

לְפָנֶיךָ יהוה אֱלֹהֵינוּ יִכְרְעוּ וְיִפֹּלוּ

וְלִכְבוֹד שִׁמְךָ יְקָר יִתֵּנוּ

וִיקַבְּלוּ כֻלָּם אֶת עֹל מַלְכוּתֶךָ

וְתִמְלֹךְ עֲלֵיהֶם מְהֵרָה לְעוֹלָם וָעֶד.

כִּי הַמַּלְכוּת שֶׁלְּךָ הִיא וּלְעוֹלְמֵי עַד תִּמְלֹךְ בְּכָבוֹד

כַּכָּתוּב בְּתוֹרָתֶךָ

שמות טו יהוה יִמְלֹךְ לְעוֹלָם וָעֶד:

◂ וְנֶאֱמַר

זכריה יד וְהָיָה יהוה לְמֶלֶךְ עַל־כָּל־הָאָרֶץ

בַּיּוֹם הַהוּא יִהְיֶה יהוה אֶחָד וּשְׁמוֹ אֶחָד:

Some add:

משלי ג אַל־תִּירָא מִפַּחַד פִּתְאֹם וּמִשֹּׁאַת רְשָׁעִים כִּי תָבֹא:

ישעיה ח עֻצוּ עֵצָה וְתֻפָר, דַּבְּרוּ דָבָר וְלֹא יָקוּם, כִּי עִמָּנוּ אֵל:

ישעיה מו וְעַד־זִקְנָה אֲנִי הוּא, וְעַד־שֵׂיבָה אֲנִי אֶסְבֹּל

אֲנִי עָשִׂיתִי וַאֲנִי אֶשָּׂא וַאֲנִי אֶסְבֹּל וַאֲמַלֵּט:

MOURNER'S KADDISH

The following prayer, said by mourners, requires the presence of a minyan.
A transliteration can be found on page 779.

Mourner: יִתְגַּדַּל Magnified and sanctified
may His great name be,
in the world He created by His will.
May He establish His kingdom
in your lifetime and in your days,
and in the lifetime of all the house of Israel,
swiftly and soon –
and say: Amen.

All: May His great name be blessed
for ever and all time.

Mourner: Blessed and praised,
glorified and exalted,
raised and honored,
uplifted and lauded
be the name of the Holy One,
blessed be He,
beyond any blessing,
song, praise and consolation
uttered in the world –
and say: Amen.

May there be great peace from heaven,
and life for us and all Israel –
and say: Amen.

Bow, take three steps back, as if taking leave of the Divine Presence,
then bow, first left, then right, then center, while saying:
May He who makes peace in His high places,
make peace for us and all Israel –
and say: Amen.

קדיש יתום

The following prayer, said by mourners, requires the presence of a מנין.
A transliteration can be found on page 779.

אבל: יִתְגַּדַּל וְיִתְקַדַּשׁ שְׁמֵהּ רַבָּא (קהל: אָמֵן)

בְּעָלְמָא דִּי בְרָא כִרְעוּתֵהּ

וְיַמְלִיךְ מַלְכוּתֵהּ

בְּחַיֵּיכוֹן וּבְיוֹמֵיכוֹן וּבְחַיֵּי דְכָל בֵּית יִשְׂרָאֵל

בַּעֲגָלָא וּבִזְמַן קָרִיב

וְאִמְרוּ אָמֵן. (קהל: אָמֵן)

קהל
ואבל: יְהֵא שְׁמֵהּ רַבָּא מְבָרַךְ לְעָלַם וּלְעָלְמֵי עָלְמַיָּא.

אבל: יִתְבָּרַךְ וְיִשְׁתַּבַּח וְיִתְפָּאַר

וְיִתְרוֹמַם וְיִתְנַשֵּׂא וְיִתְהַדָּר וְיִתְעַלֶּה וְיִתְהַלָּל

שְׁמֵהּ דְּקֻדְשָׁא בְּרִיךְ הוּא (קהל: בְּרִיךְ הוּא)

לְעֵלָּא מִן כָּל בִּרְכָתָא וְשִׁירָתָא

תֻּשְׁבְּחָתָא וְנֶחֱמָתָא

דַּאֲמִירָן בְּעָלְמָא

וְאִמְרוּ אָמֵן. (קהל: אָמֵן)

יְהֵא שְׁלָמָא רַבָּא מִן שְׁמַיָּא

וְחַיִּים, עָלֵינוּ וְעַל כָּל יִשְׂרָאֵל

וְאִמְרוּ אָמֵן. (קהל: אָמֵן)

Bow, take three steps back, as if taking leave of the Divine Presence,
then bow, first left, then right, then center, while saying:

עֹשֶׂה שָׁלוֹם בִּמְרוֹמָיו

הוּא יַעֲשֶׂה שָׁלוֹם עָלֵינוּ וְעַל כָּל יִשְׂרָאֵל

וְאִמְרוּ אָמֵן. (קהל: אָמֵן)

*The following poems, on this page and the next, both from the Middle Ages,
are summary statements of Jewish faith, orienting us to the spiritual contours
of the world that we actualize in the mind by the act of prayer.*

LORD OF THE UNIVERSE,
who reigned before the birth of any thing –

When by His will all things were made
then was His name proclaimed King.

And when all things shall cease to be
He alone will reign in awe.

He was, He is, and He shall be
glorious for evermore.

He is One, there is none else,
alone, unique, beyond compare;

Without beginning, without end,
His might, His rule are everywhere.

He is my God; my Redeemer lives.
He is the Rock on whom I rely –

My banner and my safe retreat,
my cup, my portion when I cry.

Into His hand my soul I place,
when I awake and when I sleep.

The LORD is with me, I shall not fear;
body and soul from harm will He keep.

---

way it moves seamlessly from God, Creator of the universe, beyond time and
space, to God who is close and ever-comforting, each day as I sleep and awake.

It thus beautifully crystallizes the central miracle of faith, that God – vaster
than the universe, older than time – is nonetheless closer to us than we are to
ourselves. The final verse, "Into His hand my soul I place," explains the difference faith makes to life. Reality is not indifferent to our existence. We are here
because God wanted us to be. We are surrounded by His love, protected by
His care, held in His everlasting arms. Therefore we can live in trust, not fear.

*The following poems, on this page and the next, both from the Middle Ages,
are summary statements of Jewish faith, orienting us to the spiritual contours
of the world that we actualize in the mind by the act of prayer.*

אֲדוֹן עוֹלָם

אֲשֶׁר מָלַךְ בְּטֶרֶם כָּל־יְצִיר נִבְרָא.

לְעֵת נַעֲשָׂה בְחֶפְצוֹ כֹּל אֲזַי מֶלֶךְ שְׁמוֹ נִקְרָא.

וְאַחֲרֵי כִּכְלוֹת הַכֹּל לְבַדּוֹ יִמְלֹךְ נוֹרָא.

וְהוּא הָיָה וְהוּא הֹוֶה וְהוּא יִהְיֶה בְּתִפְאָרָה.

וְהוּא אֶחָד וְאֵין שֵׁנִי לְהַמְשִׁיל לוֹ לְהַחְבִּירָה.

בְּלִי רֵאשִׁית בְּלִי תַכְלִית וְלוֹ הָעֹז וְהַמִּשְׂרָה.

וְהוּא אֵלִי וְחַי גּוֹאֲלִי וְצוּר חֶבְלִי בְּעֵת צָרָה.

וְהוּא נִסִּי וּמָנוֹס לִי מְנָת כּוֹסִי בְּיוֹם אֶקְרָא.

בְּיָדוֹ אַפְקִיד רוּחִי בְּעֵת אִישַׁן וְאָעִירָה.

וְעִם רוּחִי גְּוִיָּתִי יהוה לִי וְלֹא אִירָא.

אֲדוֹן עוֹלָם *Adon Olam.* One of the simplest and most beautiful hymn-like
celebrations of Jewish faith. It has been attributed to several possible au-
thors, among them Rabbi Sherira Gaon and Rabbi Hai Gaon in the tenth
century. Most scholars however believe it was written by the poet and philosopher Rabbi Solomon ibn Gabirol (born Malaga, Spain, c.1021; died
Valencia, c.1058). Little is known about Ibn Gabirol's life or death, except that
he spent several unsettled years wandering from town to town and that he
died comparatively young. He was the author of a philosophical work, *Mekor
Hayyim* (in Latin, *Fons Vitae*) and was one of the first since Philo ten centuries
earlier, to synthesize Judaism with Greek philosophy. Apart from the limpid
simplicity, what gives *Adon Olam* its power and enduring popularity is the

Most congregations sing Yigdal at this point.

GREAT

is the living God and praised.
He exists, and His existence is beyond time.

He is One, and there is no unity like His.
Unfathomable, His Oneness is infinite.

He has neither bodily form nor substance;
His holiness is beyond compare.

He preceded all that was created.
He was first: there was no beginning to His beginning.

Behold He is Master of the Universe; every creature
shows His greatness and majesty.

The rich flow of His prophecy He gave
to His treasured people in whom He gloried.

Never in Israel has there arisen another like Moses,
a prophet who beheld God's image.

God gave His people a Torah of truth
by the hand of His prophet, most faithful of His House.

God will not alter or change His law
for any other, for eternity.

He sees and knows our secret thoughts;
as soon as something is begun, He foresees its end.

He rewards people with loving-kindness according to their deeds;
He punishes the wicked according to his wickedness.

At the end of days He will send our Messiah,
to redeem those who await His final salvation.

God will revive the dead in His great loving-kindness.
Blessed for evermore is His glorious name!

---

physicality of God; principles 6–9 are about revelation; principles 10–13 are
about divine providence, reward and punishment, and end with faith in the
messianic age and the end of days when those who have died will live again.

Most congregations sing יִגְדַּל at this point.

יִגְדַּל

אֱלֹהִים חַי וְיִשְׁתַּבַּח, נִמְצָא וְאֵין עֵת אֶל מְצִיאוּתוֹ.

אֶחָד וְאֵין יָחִיד כְּיִחוּדוֹ, נֶעְלָם וְגַם אֵין סוֹף לְאַחְדּוּתוֹ.

אֵין לוֹ דְּמוּת הַגּוּף וְאֵינוֹ גוּף, לֹא נַעֲרֹךְ אֵלָיו קְדֻשָּׁתוֹ.

קַדְמוֹן לְכָל דָּבָר אֲשֶׁר נִבְרָא, רִאשׁוֹן וְאֵין רֵאשִׁית לְרֵאשִׁיתוֹ.

הִנּוֹ אֲדוֹן עוֹלָם, וְכָל נוֹצָר יוֹרֶה גְדֻלָּתוֹ וּמַלְכוּתוֹ.

שֶׁפַע נְבוּאָתוֹ נְתָנוֹ אֶל־אַנְשֵׁי סְגֻלָּתוֹ וְתִפְאַרְתּוֹ.

לֹא קָם בְּיִשְׂרָאֵל כְּמֹשֶׁה עוֹד נָבִיא וּמַבִּיט אֶת תְּמוּנָתוֹ.

תּוֹרַת אֱמֶת נָתַן לְעַמּוֹ אֵל עַל יַד נְבִיאוֹ נֶאֱמַן בֵּיתוֹ.

לֹא יַחֲלִיף הָאֵל וְלֹא יָמִיר דָּתוֹ לְעוֹלָמִים לְזוּלָתוֹ.

צוֹפֶה וְיוֹדֵעַ סְתָרֵינוּ, מַבִּיט לְסוֹף דָּבָר בְּקַדְמָתוֹ.

גּוֹמֵל לְאִישׁ חֶסֶד כְּמִפְעָלוֹ, נוֹתֵן לְרָשָׁע רַע כְּרִשְׁעָתוֹ.

יִשְׁלַח לְקֵץ יָמִין מְשִׁיחֵנוּ לִפְדּוֹת מְחַכֵּי קֵץ יְשׁוּעָתוֹ.

מֵתִים יְחַיֶּה אֵל בְּרֹב חַסְדּוֹ, בָּרוּךְ עֲדֵי עַד שֵׁם תְּהִלָּתוֹ.

יִגְדַּל *Yigdal.* A poetic setting of the most famous "creed" in Judaism: Moses Maimonides' Thirteen Principles of Jewish Faith. Faced with a philosophically sophisticated, contemporary Islamic culture, Maimonides felt the need to set out the principles of Jewish faith in a structured way, which he did in his Commentary to the Mishna to *Sanhedrin* 10. So influential was this account that it was summarized, after his death, in both prose and poetry. The prose form, thirteen paragraphs each beginning, "I believe with perfect faith" (אֲנִי מַאֲמִין בֶּאֱמוּנָה שְׁלֵמָה), is printed in most prayer books. The poetic form is *Yigdal.* The first five principles have to do with the unity, eternity, and non-

Ma'aravot

MA'ARIV FOR THE FIRST NIGHT

The recitation of piyutim for Ma'ariv (Ma'aravot) varies among different communities.
Many congregations omit Ma'aravot altogether. On Shabbat, Ma'aravot are not recited.

Each set of piyutim is essentially one long piyut divided into six parts, one part recited
before each of the four blessings of the Shema, and two before the two verses in the
Redemption blessing: "Who is like You, LORD, among the mighty," and "The LORD shall
reign for ever and ever." In many congregations, an additional piyut is recited following
the Ma'aravot, before the concluding blessing, "Who spreads a canopy of peace."

בָּרוּךְ Blessed are You, LORD our God, King of the Universe,
who by His word brings on evenings,
by His wisdom opens the gates of heaven,
with understanding makes time change and the seasons rotate,
and by His will orders the stars in their constellations in the sky.

Piyut grew more or less contemporaneously with the development of *Midrash Aggada*, rabbinic reflection on and commentary to biblical narrative. *Piyut* incorporates much of this material, suggesting that part of its purpose was educational as well as aesthetic. It reminded people of the laws and traditions relating to the day. It may even have been a way of circumventing the bans that occurred from time to time on the public teaching of Judaism.

We do not know the names of the earliest writers of *piyut*. The first we know by name is Yose ben Yose who lived in Israel, probably in the fourth or fifth century. The first great master of the genre, a century later, was Yannai. A century later still came the virtuoso, R. Elazar HaKalir, who brought the art to extreme sophistication, coining new words, developing new literary techniques, and creating, in short phrases and sometimes single words, dense networks of association and allusion. To judge by the complexity and popularity of *piyut*, the communities to which it was addressed were exceptionally literate, testimony to the high levels of education sustained by Jewry even in ages of persecution and poverty.

Not everyone approved of *piyut*. There were notes of dissent from Rav Hai Gaon, Maimonides, Ibn Ezra and others, on a number of grounds: they were unwarranted interruptions; they made the services too long; they are hard to understand; their use of language was uneven and eccentric. Their theology, thought Maimonides, was sometimes suspect. Yet *piyut* survived and thrived. It

מעַרָבות

מעריב לליל יום טוב ראשון של שבועות

The recitation of piyutim for מעריב (מעַרָבות) varies among different communities.
Many congregations omit מעַרָבות altogether. On שבת, מעַרָבות are not recited.

Each set of piyutim is essentially one long piyut divided into six parts, one part recited before
each of the four blessings of the שמע, and two before the two verses in the גאולה blessing:
"יהוה יִמְלֹךְ לְעֹלָם וָעֶד," and "מִי־כָמֹכָה בָּאֵלִם יהוה." In many congregations, an additional
piyut is recited following the מעַרָבות, before the concluding blessing, "וְסַלְהַפּוֹרֵשׂ סֻכַּת שָׁ."

בָּרוּךְ אַתָּה יהוה אֱלֹהֵינוּ מֶלֶךְ הָעוֹלָם
אֲשֶׁר בִּדְבָרוֹ מַעֲרִיב עֲרָבִים
בְּחָכְמָה פּוֹתֵחַ שְׁעָרִים
וּבִתְבוּנָה מְשַׁנֶּה עִתִּים וּמַחֲלִיף אֶת הַזְּמַנִּים
וּמְסַדֵּר אֶת הַכּוֹכָבִים בְּמִשְׁמְרוֹתֵיהֶם בָּרָקִיעַ כִּרְצוֹנוֹ.

PIYUT: THE POETRY OF THE PRAYER BOOK

Jewish prayer is structured around the tension between the fixed and the free, the elements that do not change, and those that do. Historically, the first formulation of Jewish prayer goes back to the time of Ezra and the Men of the Great Assembly, in the fifth century BCE. A second major consolidation occurred in the time of Rabban Gamliel II, after the destruction of the Second Temple. In the absence of sacrifices, prayer assumed greater significance, and it was important for the spiritual unity of the people that they pray the same prayers, at the same time, in the same way.

No sooner had the formal structure been completed than a new type of prayer, *piyut* (the word comes from the same root as "poetry"), began to develop. What makes it different from other prayers is that it is non-obligatory, not part of the halakhic requirement of prayer. *Piyut* was created to augment, adorn, beautify; to reflect more deeply on key points of the service; to bring out in greater depth the distinctive character of specific days; to bring variety to the rhythm and pace of prayer; to inform, educate, and sometimes simply to create a mood. It originated in Israel in the third or fourth century CE, and eventually spread to all major centers of Jewish life. Babylon, Spain, Italy, and Northern Europe all contributed richly to the poetry of the synagogue, and different rites reflect that variety.

He creates day and night, rolling away the light before the darkness,
and darkness before the light.
▸ He makes the day pass and brings on night,
distinguishing day from night:
the LORD of hosts is His name.
May the living and forever enduring God rule over us for all time.

*The overarching theme of the Ma'aravot for Shavuot (on both nights) is the giving of the
Torah and Ten Commandments. The cycle said on the first night includes six parts: five
stanzas of four lines each, and one long piyut (the third part, known as the Zulat). Set
as an alphabetic acrostic, the first stanza describes the drama of Divine Revelation and
references the first commandment – implying that it is a header for the nine others.*

And He *descended*, the Champion of Jacob – God of awesome works,
and spoke in a great tumult, all the ten commands,
I am, He revealed, shining first light upon His people, the Beloved who
makes days pass and brings on nights.

Blessed are You, LORD, who brings on evenings.

Sinai and the giving of the Ten Commandments. Preceding several of the
lines are direct quotations of key words from the account of the revelation
in Exodus 19–20.

וַיֵּרֶד *And He descended.* "The LORD descended to Mount Sinai" (Ex. 19:20) –
a figurative expression. God, beyond space, does not literally ascend or
descend. The word *descend* in this context refers to revelation (Maimonides,
Guide for the Perplexed 1:10). There was thunder, lightning, smoke and fire,
and the mountain itself trembled. The Israelites felt a terrifying, palpable
sense of the closeness of God. It was a unique moment: heaven and earth
seemed almost to touch.

בְּטוּי עֲשֶׂרֶת הַדִּבְּרוֹת *All the ten commands.* Both the Torah (Ex. 34:28; Deut.
4:13, 10:4) and the sages called the laws revealed at Sinai and inscribed on the
tablets, the Ten "Words" or "Utterances" rather than the Ten Commands. For
the significance of this, see Introduction, page xlix.

גִּלָּה וְהֵאִיר *He revealed, shining first light.* A midrash (*Pesikta Rabbati* 21:19)
relates the Ten Utterances at Mount Sinai to the Ten Utterances with which
the universe was created (the ten times it says in Genesis 1, "And God said").
Thus the first utterance, "I am the LORD…" corresponds to the first creative
utterance, "Let there be light." God is the light of the universe.

בּוֹרֵא יוֹם וָלַיְלָה, גּוֹלֵל אוֹר מִפְּנֵי חֹשֶׁךְ וְחֹשֶׁךְ מִפְּנֵי אוֹר

וּמַעֲבִיר יוֹם וּמֵבִיא לָיְלָה, וּמַבְדִּיל בֵּין יוֹם וּבֵין לָיְלָה

יהוה צְבָאוֹת שְׁמוֹ.

אֵל חַי וְקַיָּם תָּמִיד, יִמְלֹךְ עָלֵינוּ לְעוֹלָם וָעֶד.

The overarching theme of the מערבות for שבועות (on both nights) is מתן תורה and עשרת הדיברות. The cycle said on the first night includes six parts: five stanzas of four lines each, and one long piyut (the third part, known as the זולת). Set as an alphabetic acrostic, the first stanza describes the drama of Divine Revelation and references the first commandment – implying that it is a header for the nine others.

וַיֵּרֶד   אֲבִיר יַעֲקֹב נוֹרָא עֲלִילָה

וַיְדַבֵּר   בְּטוּי עֲשֶׂרֶת הַדִּבְּרוֹת בְּהַמְלָה

אָנֹכִי   גִּלָּה וְהֵאִיר לְעַמּוֹ תְּחִלָּה

דּוֹד מַעֲבִיר יוֹם וּמֵבִיא לָיְלָה.

בָּרוּךְ אַתָּה יהוה, הַמַּעֲרִיב עֲרָבִים.

---

remains as a magnificent set of solo intervals in the choral symphony Israel has sung to its Maker, King, Judge, and Redeemer. It is prayer as poetry and poetry as prayer, and its sacred beauty still challenges the mind as it lifts the heart.

MA'ARAVOT: FIRST NIGHT

The *piyut* for the first night was written by Rabbi Joseph Tov Alem ben Samuel Bonfils (eleventh century). Bonfils was born in Narbonne and became rabbi of Limoges in the province of Anjou. He was a distinguished halakhist, known to his contemporaries as Rabbi Joseph the Great, and many of his rulings, especially with regard to communal taxation, were cited by later authorities. His responsa and Bible commentaries are no longer extant, but sixty-two of his *piyutim* survive and were widely adopted by the Jews of France, Germany and Poland. Indeed it was the fact that a scholar of his eminence composed *piyutim* that helped secure their acceptance as a normative feature of the prayer book, despite the opposition. Bonfils wove both halakhic and aggadic traditions into his poetry, and his *piyut* for Shabbat HaGadol, the Shabbat before Pesah, was regarded as a major source in its own right for the laws of Passover (see for example *Tosafot, Pesaḥim* 117b).

The *piyut*, structured as an alphabetic acrostic followed by the name of the composer, *Yosef haKatan bar Shmuel*, is an account of the revelation at Mount

אַהֲבַת עוֹלָם With everlasting love
have You loved Your people, the house of Israel.
You have taught us Torah and commandments,
decrees and laws of justice.
Therefore, Lord our God, when we lie down and when we rise up
we will speak of Your decrees, rejoicing in the words of Your Torah
and Your commandments for ever.
▸ For they are our life and the length of our days;
on them will we meditate day and night.
May You never take away Your love from us.

*The second stanza is based on the next three commandments, culminating in the commandment
of Shabbat, which, like the Torah, is a gift and an expression of God's love for Israel.*

Have no futile, no cursed form of an idol,
do not take the sacred, unfathomable name in vain, or give up its honor.
Remember your eager haste as you keep and glorify the [Shabbat]
laws of pleasantness – and the Gracious One shall remember
for us His everlasting love:

Blessed are You, Lord, who loves His people Israel.

The Shema must be said with intense concentration.
When not with a minyan, say:
God, faithful King!

The following verse should be said aloud, while covering the eyes with the right hand:

Listen, Israel: the Lord is our God,
the Lord is One.

Deut. 6

Quietly: Blessed be the name of His glorious kingdom for ever and all time.

---

universe. When God revealed Himself at Sinai, He did so in language. As
Moses reminded the Israelites, "Then the Lord spoke to you out of the fire.
You heard the sound of words but saw no form; there was only a voice" (Deut.
4:12). Judaism is a religion of holy words. Specifically, using the holy of holies
of language, God's sacred name, for a secular purpose is an act of desecration.

נֹעַם *Pleasantness.* The fourth command, Shabbat, is not merely negative – a
day on which work is forbidden – but also positive, "a delight" (Is. 58:13).

אַהֲבַת עוֹלָם בֵּית יִשְׂרָאֵל עַמְּךָ אָהֵבְתָּ

תּוֹרָה וּמִצְוֹת, חֻקִּים וּמִשְׁפָּטִים, אוֹתָנוּ לִמַּדְתָּ

עַל כֵּן יהוה אֱלֹהֵינוּ בְּשָׁכְבֵּנוּ וּבְקוּמֵנוּ נָשִׂיחַ בְּחֻקֶּיךָ

וְנִשְׂמַח בְּדִבְרֵי תוֹרָתֶךָ וּבְמִצְוֹתֶיךָ לְעוֹלָם וָעֶד

◂ כִּי הֵם חַיֵּינוּ וְאֹרֶךְ יָמֵינוּ, וּבָהֶם נֶהְגֶּה יוֹמָם וָלָיְלָה.

וְאַהֲבָתְךָ אַל תָּסִיר מִמֶּנּוּ לְעוֹלָמִים.

*The second stanza is based on the next three commandments, culminating in the
commandment of שבת, which, like the תורה, is a gift and an expression of God's love for Israel.*

לֹא־יִהְיֶה לָךְ	הֶבֶל תַּבְנִית אֱלִיל נִכְלָם	
לֹא תִשָּׂא	וְתָמִיר קָדְשַׁת שֵׁם נֶעְלָם	
זָכוֹר	זְרִיזוּת מִשְׁפְּטֵי נֹעַם וְסִלְסוּלָם	
	חַנּוּן יִזְכֹּר לָנוּ אַהֲבַת עוֹלָם.	

בָּרוּךְ אַתָּה יהוה, אוֹהֵב עַמּוֹ יִשְׂרָאֵל.

*The שמע must be said with intense concentration.
When not with a מנין, say:*

אֵל מֶלֶךְ נֶאֱמָן

The following verse should be said aloud, while covering the eyes with the right hand:

דברים ו **שְׁמַע יִשְׂרָאֵל, יהוה אֱלֹהֵינוּ, יהוה ׀ אֶחָד׃**

Quietly בָּרוּךְ שֵׁם כְּבוֹד מַלְכוּתוֹ לְעוֹלָם וָעֶד.

דּוֹד *The Beloved (previous page).* The last line of the poetic insertion reconnects with the theme of the paragraph as a whole.

תַּבְנִית אֱלִיל נִכְלָם *Cursed form of an idol.* Not only is the idol cursed, so are those who make it: "All the makers of idols will be put to shame and disgraced" (Is. 45:16).

לֹא תִשָּׂא *Do not take.* The third command, against taking God's name in vain, exemplifies the intense significance of speech in Judaism. With words God created the natural universe. With words we create or harm the social

וְאָהַבְתָּ Love the LORD your God with all your heart, with all *Deut. 6* your soul, and with all your might. These words which I command you today shall be on your heart. Teach them repeatedly to your children, speaking of them when you sit at home and when you travel on the way, when you lie down and when you rise. Bind them as a sign on your hand, and they shall be an emblem between your eyes. Write them on the doorposts of your house and gates.

וְהָיָה If you indeed heed My commandments with which I charge *Deut. 11* you today, to love the LORD your God and worship Him with all your heart and with all your soul, I will give rain in your land in its season, the early and late rain; and you shall gather in your grain, wine and oil. I will give grass in your field for your cattle, and you shall eat and be satisfied. Be careful lest your heart be tempted and you go astray and worship other gods, bowing down to them. Then the LORD's anger will flare against you and He will close the heavens so that there will be no rain. The land will not yield its crops, and you will perish swiftly from the good land that the LORD is giving you. Therefore, set these, My words, on your heart and soul. Bind them as a sign on your hand, and they shall be an emblem between your eyes. Teach them to your children, speaking of them when you sit at home and when you travel on the way, when you lie down and when you rise. Write them on the doorposts of your house and gates, so that you and your children may live long in the land that the LORD swore to your ancestors to give them, for as long as the heavens are above the earth.

וַיֹּאמֶר The LORD spoke to Moses, saying: Speak to the Israelites *Num. 15* and tell them to make tassels on the corners of their garments for all generations. They shall attach to the tassel at each corner a thread of blue. This shall be your tassel, and you shall see it and remember all of the LORD's commandments and keep them, not straying after your heart and after your eyes, following your own sinful desires. Thus you will be reminded to keep all My

דברים ו

וְאָהַבְתָּ אֵת יהוה אֱלֹהֶיךָ, בְּכָל־לְבָבְךָ וּבְכָל־נַפְשְׁךָ וּבְכָל־מְאֹדֶךָ: וְהָיוּ הַדְּבָרִים הָאֵלֶּה, אֲשֶׁר אָנֹכִי מְצַוְּךָ הַיּוֹם, עַל־לְבָבֶךָ: וְשִׁנַּנְתָּם לְבָנֶיךָ וְדִבַּרְתָּ בָּם, בְּשִׁבְתְּךָ בְּבֵיתֶךָ וּבְלֶכְתְּךָ בַדֶּרֶךְ, וּבְשָׁכְבְּךָ וּבְקוּמֶךָ: וּקְשַׁרְתָּם לְאוֹת עַל־יָדֶךָ וְהָיוּ לְטֹטָפֹת בֵּין עֵינֶיךָ: וּכְתַבְתָּם עַל־מְזֻזוֹת בֵּיתֶךָ וּבִשְׁעָרֶיךָ:

דברים יא

וְהָיָה אִם־שָׁמֹעַ תִּשְׁמְעוּ אֶל־מִצְוֹתַי אֲשֶׁר אָנֹכִי מְצַוֶּה אֶתְכֶם הַיּוֹם, לְאַהֲבָה אֶת־יהוה אֱלֹהֵיכֶם וּלְעָבְדוֹ, בְּכָל־לְבַבְכֶם וּבְכָל־נַפְשְׁכֶם: וְנָתַתִּי מְטַר־אַרְצְכֶם בְּעִתּוֹ, יוֹרֶה וּמַלְקוֹשׁ, וְאָסַפְתָּ דְגָנֶךָ וְתִירֹשְׁךָ וְיִצְהָרֶךָ: וְנָתַתִּי עֵשֶׂב בְּשָׂדְךָ לִבְהֶמְתֶּךָ, וְאָכַלְתָּ וְשָׂבָעְתָּ: הִשָּׁמְרוּ לָכֶם פֶּן־יִפְתֶּה לְבַבְכֶם, וְסַרְתֶּם וַעֲבַדְתֶּם אֱלֹהִים אֲחֵרִים וְהִשְׁתַּחֲוִיתֶם לָהֶם: וְחָרָה אַף־יהוה בָּכֶם, וְעָצַר אֶת־הַשָּׁמַיִם וְלֹא־יִהְיֶה מָטָר, וְהָאֲדָמָה לֹא תִתֵּן אֶת־יְבוּלָהּ, וַאֲבַדְתֶּם מְהֵרָה מֵעַל הָאָרֶץ הַטֹּבָה אֲשֶׁר יהוה נֹתֵן לָכֶם: וְשַׂמְתֶּם אֶת־דְּבָרַי אֵלֶּה עַל־לְבַבְכֶם וְעַל־נַפְשְׁכֶם, וּקְשַׁרְתֶּם אֹתָם לְאוֹת עַל־יֶדְכֶם, וְהָיוּ לְטוֹטָפֹת בֵּין עֵינֵיכֶם: וְלִמַּדְתֶּם אֹתָם אֶת־בְּנֵיכֶם לְדַבֵּר בָּם, בְּשִׁבְתְּךָ בְּבֵיתֶךָ וּבְלֶכְתְּךָ בַדֶּרֶךְ, וּבְשָׁכְבְּךָ וּבְקוּמֶךָ: וּכְתַבְתָּם עַל־מְזוּזוֹת בֵּיתֶךָ וּבִשְׁעָרֶיךָ: לְמַעַן יִרְבּוּ יְמֵיכֶם וִימֵי בְנֵיכֶם עַל הָאֲדָמָה אֲשֶׁר נִשְׁבַּע יהוה לַאֲבֹתֵיכֶם לָתֵת לָהֶם, כִּימֵי הַשָּׁמַיִם עַל־הָאָרֶץ:

במדבר טו

וַיֹּאמֶר יהוה אֶל־מֹשֶׁה לֵּאמֹר: דַּבֵּר אֶל־בְּנֵי יִשְׂרָאֵל וְאָמַרְתָּ אֲלֵהֶם, וְעָשׂוּ לָהֶם צִיצִת עַל־כַּנְפֵי בִגְדֵיהֶם לְדֹרֹתָם, וְנָתְנוּ עַל־צִיצִת הַכָּנָף פְּתִיל תְּכֵלֶת: וְהָיָה לָכֶם לְצִיצִת, וּרְאִיתֶם אֹתוֹ וּזְכַרְתֶּם אֶת־כָּל־מִצְוֹת יהוה וַעֲשִׂיתֶם אֹתָם, וְלֹא תָתוּרוּ אַחֲרֵי לְבַבְכֶם וְאַחֲרֵי עֵינֵיכֶם, אֲשֶׁר־אַתֶּם זֹנִים אַחֲרֵיהֶם: לְמַעַן תִּזְכְּרוּ

commandments, and be holy to your God. I am the Lord your
God, who brought you out of the land of Egypt to be your God.
I am the Lord your God.

True –

The Leader repeats:

▸ The Lord your God is true –

וֶאֱמוּנָה – and faithful is all this, and firmly established for us
    that He is the Lord our God,
    and there is none beside Him,
    and that we, Israel, are His people.
    He is our King, who redeems us from the hand of kings
    and delivers us from the grasp of all tyrants.
    He is our God, who on our behalf repays our foes
    and brings just retribution on our mortal enemies;
    who performs great deeds beyond understanding
    and wonders beyond number;
    who kept us alive, not letting our foot slip;   *Ps. 66*
    who led us on the high places of our enemies,
    raising our pride above all our foes;
    who did miracles for us
    and brought vengeance against Pharaoh;
    who performed signs and wonders
    in the land of Ham's children;
    who smote in His wrath all the firstborn of Egypt,
    and brought out His people Israel from their midst
    into everlasting freedom;
    who led His children through the divided Reed Sea,
    plunging their pursuers and enemies into the depths.
    When His children saw His might,
    they gave praise and thanks to His name,
▸ and willingly accepted His Sovereignty.
    Moses and the children of Israel
    then sang a song to You.

וַעֲשִׂיתֶם אֶת־כָּל־מִצְוֹתָי, וִהְיִיתֶם קְדֹשִׁים לֵאלֹהֵיכֶם: אֲנִי יהוה
אֱלֹהֵיכֶם, אֲשֶׁר הוֹצֵאתִי אֶתְכֶם מֵאֶרֶץ מִצְרַיִם, לִהְיוֹת לָכֶם
לֵאלֹהִים, אֲנִי יהוה אֱלֹהֵיכֶם:

אֱמֶת

The שליח ציבור repeats:

‹ יהוה אֱלֹהֵיכֶם אֱמֶת

וֶאֱמוּנָה כָּל זֹאת וְקַיָּם עָלֵינוּ

כִּי הוּא יהוה אֱלֹהֵינוּ וְאֵין זוּלָתוֹ, וַאֲנַחְנוּ יִשְׂרָאֵל עַמּוֹ.

הַפּוֹדֵנוּ מִיַּד מְלָכִים

מַלְכֵּנוּ הַגּוֹאֲלֵנוּ מִכַּף כָּל הֶעָרִיצִים.

הָאֵל הַנִּפְרָע לָנוּ מִצָּרֵינוּ

וְהַמְשַׁלֵּם גְּמוּל לְכָל אוֹיְבֵי נַפְשֵׁנוּ.

הָעוֹשֶׂה גְדוֹלוֹת עַד אֵין חֵקֶר, וְנִפְלָאוֹת עַד אֵין מִסְפָּר

הַשָּׂם נַפְשֵׁנוּ בַּחַיִּים, וְלֹא־נָתַן לַמּוֹט רַגְלֵנוּ:

הַמַּדְרִיכֵנוּ עַל בָּמוֹת אוֹיְבֵינוּ

וַיָּרֶם קַרְנֵנוּ עַל כָּל שׂוֹנְאֵינוּ.

הָעוֹשֶׂה לָּנוּ נִסִּים וּנְקָמָה בְּפַרְעֹה

אוֹתוֹת וּמוֹפְתִים בְּאַדְמַת בְּנֵי חָם.

הַמַּכֶּה בְעֶבְרָתוֹ כָּל בְּכוֹרֵי מִצְרָיִם

וַיּוֹצֵא אֶת עַמּוֹ יִשְׂרָאֵל מִתּוֹכָם לְחֵרוּת עוֹלָם.

הַמַּעֲבִיר בָּנָיו בֵּין גִּזְרֵי יַם סוּף

אֶת רוֹדְפֵיהֶם וְאֶת שׂוֹנְאֵיהֶם בִּתְהוֹמוֹת טִבַּע

וְרָאוּ בָנָיו גְּבוּרָתוֹ, שִׁבְּחוּ וְהוֹדוּ לִשְׁמוֹ

‹ וּמַלְכוּתוֹ בְרָצוֹן קִבְּלוּ עֲלֵיהֶם

מֹשֶׁה וּבְנֵי יִשְׂרָאֵל, לְךָ עָנוּ שִׁירָה.

תהלים סו

In the Zulat, the long piyut before the third part of the Ma'aravot,
the poet pauses in the middle of the account (already interrupted by the
Shema) to enlarge upon the setting of the drama. The final stanza connects
the song of praise sung at the Giving of the Torah, with the Song at the Sea
as referenced in the blessing. The alphabetic acrostic is completed, followed
by an allusion to the poet's name: Yosef HaKatan bar Shmuel.

Toviya [Moses] ascended the heights / and brought down the Law
    crowned in splendor / at Shavuot.

The Rock Himself descended / and gave His people strength / amid thun-
    der and earthquake.

All the trees of the forest / were gripped with trembling and storm winds, /
    and so the hills and mountains,

as He taught the holy people / the order of seasons and months / and the
    numbering of hours.

He loved them above all other nations, / and drew them near to Mount
    Sinai – / God of salvation.

He bore them on eagles' wings – / He who dwells at the crest of heavens – /
    resting on His arms beneath.

When the rebellious kings heard / of the glorious splendor given to a
    people, / their palace walls shook.

Wretched, they bared their heads in shame, / and were marked for execu-
    tion by the Rock / who exacts vengeance.

[Sky,] the glory spread out like a robe, / and the high point of the earth He
    made firm ground – / touched.

---

calendar (Ex. 12:2). As to why this was the first of the commands, given to
the Israelites while they were still in Egypt, R. Avraham Pam said that the
difference between a slave and a free human being is that the former lacks,
while the latter has, control over their time. Mastering time is thus the first
step to freedom.

סוֹרְרִים בְּעֵת שָׁמְעָם *When the rebellious kings heard.* A reference to the tradition
(*Avoda Zara* 2b) that God offered the Torah to other nations but they refused
it; the Israelites alone accepted it.

נִגְעוֹת *Touched.* The revelation at Mount Sinai, the only time God revealed
Himself verbally to an entire nation, was the supreme moment at which,
metaphorically, Heaven came down to earth and the earth was lifted to the
heights of Heaven.

In the זולת, the long piyut before the third part of the מערבות,
the poet pauses in the middle of the account (already interrupted
by the שמע) to enlarge upon the setting of the drama. The final stanza
connects the song of praise sung at מתן תורה, with the Song at the Sea
as referenced in the blessing. The alphabetic acrostic is completed,
followed by an allusion to the poet's name: יוסף הקטן בר שמואל.

טוֹבִיָּה לַמָּרוֹם עָלָה / וְהוֹרִיד דָּת כְּלוּלָה / בְּחַג הַשָּׁבֻעוֹת

יָרַד צוּר בְּעַצְמוֹ / וְנָתַן עֹז לְעַמּוֹ / בִּרְעָמִים וְזֹוָעוֹת

כָּל עֲצֵי הַיַּעַר / אֲחָזוּם חִיל וָסַעַר / וְהָרִים וּגְבָעוֹת

לִמַּד לְעַם קְדוֹשִׁים / סֵדֶר תְּקוּפוֹת וַחֲדָשִׁים / וְחֶשְׁבּוֹן הַשָּׁעוֹת

מִכָּל אֹם חִבְּבָם / וּלְהַר סִינַי קֵרְבָם / אֵל לְמוֹשָׁעוֹת

נְשָׂאָם בְּכַנְפֵי נְשָׁרִים / שֹׁכֵן בְּרוּם אַוֵּרִים / וּמִתַּחַת זְרֹעֹת

סוֹרְרִים בְּעֵת שְׁמָעָם / צְבִי תִּפְאֶרֶת עָם / יִרְגְּזוּן יְרִיעוֹת

עֲלוּבִים חָפוּ רֹאשָׁם / וְלַהֲרֹגָה צוּר הִקְדִּישָׁם / בְּפִרְעַ פְּרָעוֹת

פְּרִישַׂת הוֹד שַׁלְמָה / וּרְקוּעַת גְּבַהּ אֲדָמָה / שְׁתֵיהֶן נוֹגָעוֹת

טוֹבִיָּה *Toviya.* According to midrashic tradition, this was the name given to Moses by his mother Yokheved, based on the phrase, at his birth, that "she saw that the child was good [*tov*]" (Ex. 2:2). The name Toviya appears in Zechariah 6:10. This section, describing the scene at Mount Sinai, is a digression from the rest of the *piyut*, which focuses for the most part on the Ten Commandments.

וְנָתַן עֹז לְעַמּוֹ *Gave His people strength.* The *Mekhilta deRabbi Shimon bar Yoḥai* (19:16) interprets "The Lord gives His people strength" (Ps. 29:10) as a reference to Torah. Jewish strength is spiritual, not physical: "Not by might nor by power, but by My spirit, says the Lord Almighty" (Zech. 4:6).

כָּל עֲצֵי הַיַּעַר *All the trees of the forest.* "the Lord's voice breaks cedars, the Lord shatters the cedars of Lebanon" (Ps. 29:5). The rabbis interpreted this as a reference to the shaking of the world at the time of the giving of the Torah (*Zevaḥim* 116a).

סֵדֶר תְּקוּפוֹת וַחֲדָשִׁים *The order of seasons and months.* The first command given to the Israelites as a nation was to determine the months and thus the Jewish

The Righteous One held the mountain as a dome / over the heads of the
    lovely, the beautiful people / like a barrel, like a tent.
The chosen people heard / the noble laws and statutes / with listening ears.
The Elevated One, in His kindness, protected them / from the hands of all
    their oppressors / and from cruel decrees.
And He sent signs and wonders, / and passed down engraved laws to them /
    with wisdom and knowledge.
He raised their glory skyward, / granting them name and glory / in their
    blessing, their cup of salvation.

    The Savior, the Redeemer, showed them many salvations,
     and crowned them and made them beautiful with the Law of Yekutiel
      [Moses].
    And they sang out words of praise and prayer to the one God;
     they glorified and praised Him – Moses and the people of Israel –

With happiness, with song, with great joy,
and they all exclaimed:
        "Who is like You, LORD, among the mighty?   *Ex. 15*
        Who is like You, majestic in holiness,
        awesome in praises, doing wonders?"

▸ Your children beheld Your majesty
as You parted the sea before Moses.

> *The Ma'aravot were written to accompany a slightly different text of the*
> *Blessings of the Shema, and so congregations which recite them usually alter*
> *the text of the Blessings accordingly. Here, the words "This is the Rock of our*
> *salvation" (on the next page) are reflected in the text of the piyut.*

Honor your parents, with the fifth command He told them,
do not murder any man formed of clay, cutting off a life in anger.
Do not commit adultery – not for any woman of graceful looks,
    devoid of thought. In the company of many, crown the eternal
    Rock of your salvation:

בְּחָכְמָה וּבְדֵעוֹת *With wisdom and knowledge.* "Observe [these statutes] care-
fully, for this is your wisdom and understanding in the eyes of the nations,
who will hear about all these decrees and say, 'Surely this great nation is a
wise and understanding people'" (Deut. 4:6).

צַדִּיק הַר כָּפָה / עָלֵי נָאוָה וְיָפָה / כְּגִגִּית וְכִירִיעוֹת
קָשְׁבוּ עַם בְּחִירִים / חֻקִּים וּמִשְׁפָּטִים יְשָׁרִים / לְאֹזֶן הַשְׁמָעוֹת
רָם בְּחַסְדּוֹ שְׁמָרָם / מִכַּף כָּל צוֹרְרָם / וּמִגְּזֵרוֹת רָעוֹת
שָׁלַח אוֹתוֹת וּמוֹפְתִים / וְהִנְחִילָם דָּתוֹת חֲרוּתִים / בְּחָכְמָה וּבְדֵעוֹת
תִּפְאַרְתָּם הִגְדִּיל לְמַעֲלָה / לְתִתָּם לְשֵׁם וְלִתְהִלָּה
בְּבִרְכַּת כּוֹס יְשׁוּעוֹת.

יְשׁוּעוֹת רַבּוֹת הֶרְאָם פּוֹדֶה וְגוֹאֵל
וְעִטְּרָם וְהִנָּם בְּדַת יְקוּתִיאֵל
סוֹחֲחִים רֶנֶן וְהוֹדָיָה לָאֵל
פֵּאֲרוּ וְשִׁבְּחוּ מֹשֶׁה וּבְנֵי יִשְׂרָאֵל.

בְּגִילָה, בְּרִנָּה בְּשִׂמְחָה רַבָּה
וְאָמְרוּ כֻלָּם

שמות טו

מִי־כָמֹכָה בָּאֵלִם יהוה
מִי כָּמֹכָה נֶאְדָּר בַּקֹּדֶשׁ
נוֹרָא תְהִלֹּת עֹשֵׂה פֶלֶא:

‹ מַלְכוּתְךָ רָאוּ בָנֶיךָ, בּוֹקֵעַ יָם לִפְנֵי מֹשֶׁה

The מערבות ברכות קריאת שמע *were written to accompany a slightly different text of,*
and so congregations which recite them usually alter the text of the Blessings accordingly.
*Here, the words "*זֶה צוּר יִשְׁעֵנוּ*" (on the next page) are reflected in the text of the piyut.*

כָּבֵד   הוֹרֵיךָ בְּדִבּוּר חֲמִישִׁי הִשְׁמִיעָם
לֹא תִרְצָח   קוֹוְצֵי חֹמֶר לְהַכְרִית בְּזַעַם
לֹא תִנְאָף   טוֹבַת חֵן וְסָרַת טַעַם
נֶצַח צוּר יִשְׁעֲךָ הַמְלִיכֵהוּ בְּרָב עַם.

הַר כָּפָה *Held the mountain as a dome.* The sages understood the Torah's statement that the people stood "at the foot of the mountain" (Ex. 19:17) to mean
"underneath the mountain," suggesting that God suspended the mountain
over their heads "like a tub" (*Shabbat* 88a; see page 193).

This is the Rock of our salvation;
[Israel] opened their mouths and exclaimed:

> "The LORD shall reign for ever and ever." *Ex. 15*

▸ And it is said,

> "For the LORD has redeemed Jacob *Jer. 31*
> and rescued him from a power
> stronger than his own."

The text of the following stanza, in which the last of the commandments are described, alludes to an earlier, alternate ending of the Blessing: "King, Rock and Redeemer of Israel" (see commentary below). However, some authorities hold that the words of the actual blessing should not be altered.

Do not steal in secret, lurking in the shadows of the village;
do not testify as a false witness, lying, a violence against
  your fellow.
Do not be envious of your fellow's plenty, of his precious belongings.
  Israel's King and Redeemer stands firm through all the ages.*

Blessed are You, LORD, who redeemed Israel.

Some end the blessing as follows:
Blessed are You, LORD, King, Rock and Redeemer of Israel.

הַשְׁכִּיבֵנוּ Help us lie down, O LORD our God, in peace,
and rise up, O our King, to life.
Spread over us Your canopy of peace.
Direct us with Your good counsel,
and save us for the sake of Your name.

Talmud Yerushalmi (*Berakhot* 1:6) records the first, the Babylonian Talmud (*Pesaḥim* 116b) the second. The reason for the custom of using the Talmud Yerushalmi's ending on festival nights when *piyutim* are said is that most of the early *piyutim* were composed in Israel and were thus incorporated the Israeli ending.

זֶה צוּר יִשְׁעֵנוּ, פָּצוּ פֶה, וְאָמְרוּ

יהוה יִמְלֹךְ לְעֹלָם וָעֶד:

‹ וְנֶאֱמַר

כִּי־פָדָה יהוה אֶת־יַעֲקֹב

וּגְאָלוֹ מִיַּד חָזָק מִמֶּנּוּ:

The text of the following stanza, in which the last of the commandments are described, alludes to an earlier, alternate ending of the Blessing:
"מֶלֶךְ צוּר יִשְׂרָאֵל וְגוֹאֲלוֹ" *(see commentary below). However, some authorities hold that the words of the actual blessing should not be altered.*

לֹא תִגְנֹב   בְּמִסְתָּרִים לֵישֵׁב בְּמַאֲרַב חֲצֵרִים

לֹא־תַעֲנֶה   רֵעַ חָמָס הֱיוֹת עֵד שְׁקָרִים

לֹא תַחְמֹד   שִׁפְעַת רֵעַ וַחֲפָצִים יְקָרִים

מֶלֶךְ יִשְׂרָאֵל וְגוֹאֲלוֹ קַיָּם לְדוֹר דּוֹרִים.*

בָּרוּךְ אַתָּה יהוה, גָּאַל יִשְׂרָאֵל.

Some end the blessing as follows:

בָּרוּךְ אַתָּה יהוה, מֶלֶךְ צוּר יִשְׂרָאֵל וְגוֹאֲלוֹ.

הַשְׁכִּיבֵנוּ יהוה אֱלֹהֵינוּ לְשָׁלוֹם, וְהַעֲמִידֵנוּ מַלְכֵּנוּ לְחַיִּים

וּפְרֹשׂ עָלֵינוּ סֻכַּת שְׁלוֹמֶךָ

וְתַקְּנֵנוּ בְּעֵצָה טוֹבָה מִלְּפָנֶיךָ

וְהוֹשִׁיעֵנוּ לְמַעַן שְׁמֶךָ.

גָּאַל יִשְׂרָאֵל... מֶלֶךְ צוּר יִשְׂרָאֵל וְגוֹאֲלוֹ *Who redeemed Israel... King, Rock and Redeemer of Israel.* The difference between these two endings, "Rock of Israel and its Redeemer" and "who redeemed Israel," reflects an ancient variation between the Jewish communities of Israel and Babylon. The

Shield us and remove from us every enemy,
plague, sword, famine and sorrow.
Remove the adversary from before and behind us.
Shelter us in the shadow of Your wings,
for You, God, are our Guardian and Deliverer;
You, God, are a gracious and compassionate King.
‣ Guard our going out and our coming in,
for life and peace, from now and for ever.
Spread over us Your canopy of peace.

> *The final stanza describes how the people received the Torah,*
> *and prays for a blessing of peace on their descendants.*

And all the people saw and heard the thunder,
came together as one to receive both weighty
    laws and light.
He let them dwell in safety, He who does great things;
    so may He spread His peace over all our communities.

Blessed are You, Lord,
who spreads a canopy of peace
over all His people Israel,
and over Jerusalem.

Continue with "Thus Moses announced" on page 60.

אֲגוּדִים יַחַד *Came together as one.* The Torah emphasizes the unity of the
people as they assented to the covenant: "All the people responded *as one*"
(Ex. 19:8); "The people all responded *with a single voice*" (Ex. 24:3).

וְהָגֵן בַּעֲדֵנוּ, וְהָסֵר מֵעָלֵינוּ אוֹיֵב, דֶּבֶר וְחֶרֶב וְרָעָב וְיָגוֹן

וְהָסֵר שָׂטָן מִלְּפָנֵינוּ וּמֵאַחֲרֵינוּ

וּבְצֵל כְּנָפֶיךָ תַּסְתִּירֵנוּ

כִּי אֵל שׁוֹמְרֵנוּ וּמַצִּילֵנוּ אָתָּה

כִּי אֵל מֶלֶךְ חַנּוּן וְרַחוּם אָתָּה.

◄ וּשְׁמֹר צֵאתֵנוּ וּבוֹאֵנוּ לְחַיִּים וּלְשָׁלוֹם מֵעַתָּה וְעַד עוֹלָם.

וּפְרֹשׂ עָלֵינוּ סֻכַּת שְׁלוֹמֶךָ.

*The final stanza describes how the people received the תורה,
and prays for a blessing of peace on their descendants.*

וְכָל הָעָם רֹאִים וְשׁוֹמְעִים אֶת הַקּוֹלֹת

אֲגוּדִים יַחַד לְקַבֵּל חֲמוּרוֹת וְקַלּוֹת

לְבֶטַח הוֹשִׁיבָם עָשֶׂה גְדֹלוֹת

כֵּן יִפְרֹשׂ שְׁלוֹמוֹ עַל כָּל מַקְהֵלוֹת.

בָּרוּךְ אַתָּה יהוה

הַפּוֹרֵשׂ סֻכַּת שָׁלוֹם עָלֵינוּ וְעַל כָּל עַמּוֹ יִשְׂרָאֵל

וְעַל יְרוּשָׁלָיִם.

Continue with "וַיְדַבֵּר מֹשֶׁה" on page 61.

וְכָל־הָעָם רֹאִים וְשׁוֹמְעִים אֶת־הַקּוֹלֹת *And all the people saw and heard the thunder.*
The Torah states that "All the people saw the thunder", literally "the sounds"
(Ex. 20:15). This was interpreted by the *Mekhilta* and Rashi as meaning that
they experienced synesthesia: they saw what is normally only heard.

MA'ARIV FOR THE SECOND NIGHT

בָּרוּךְ Blessed are You, LORD our God, King of the Universe,
who by His word brings on evenings,
by His wisdom opens the gates of heaven,
with understanding makes time change
and the seasons rotate,
and by His will orders the stars in their constellations in the sky.
He creates day and night,
rolling away the light before the darkness,
and darkness before the light.
▸ He makes the day pass and brings on night,
distinguishing day from night:
the LORD of hosts is His name.
May the living and forever enduring God rule over us for all time.

*The Ma'aravot said on the second night are a cycle of short stanzas
describing the setting of the Giving of the Torah and the
Ten Commandments. Its stichs follow a simple alphabetic acrostic.*

God *descended* to Mount Sinai, / to explicate the Law
to my knowing people,
and He spoke great and awesome words before my very eyes,
unmistakable God who makes His sun pass by before me.

Blessed are You, LORD, who brings on evenings.

בָּאֵר דָּת *To explicate the law.* This line follows the *Mekhilta*, which states that as the Ten Commandments were being revealed, not only did the Israelites hear God's words as recorded in the Torah but also instantly understood the Oral Tradition – the midrashic expositions and halakhic implications – associated with each word.

לְעֵינַי *Before my very eyes.* The words of the revelation themselves became visible: "And all the people saw the sounds" (*Pirkei deRabbi Eliezer* 40; Rashi to Ex. 20:15).

מעריב לליל יום טוב שני של שבועות

בָּרוּךְ אַתָּה יהוה אֱלֹהֵינוּ מֶלֶךְ הָעוֹלָם
אֲשֶׁר בִּדְבָרוֹ מַעֲרִיב עֲרָבִים
בְּחָכְמָה פּוֹתֵחַ שְׁעָרִים
וּבִתְבוּנָה מְשַׁנֶּה עִתִּים וּמַחֲלִיף אֶת הַזְּמַנִּים
וּמְסַדֵּר אֶת הַכּוֹכָבִים בְּמִשְׁמְרוֹתֵיהֶם בָּרָקִיעַ כִּרְצוֹנוֹ.
בּוֹרֵא יוֹם וָלַיְלָה
גּוֹלֵל אוֹר מִפְּנֵי חֹשֶׁךְ וְחֹשֶׁךְ מִפְּנֵי אוֹר
וּמַעֲבִיר יוֹם וּמֵבִיא לָיְלָה
וּמַבְדִּיל בֵּין יוֹם וּבֵין לָיְלָה
יהוה צְבָאוֹת שְׁמוֹ.
אֵל חַי וְקַיָּם תָּמִיד, יִמְלֹךְ עָלֵינוּ לְעוֹלָם וָעֶד.

The מערבות *said on the second night are a cycle of short stanzas describing the setting of* עשרת הדיברות *and* מתן תורה. *Its stichs follow a simple alphabetic acrostic.*

וַיֵּרֶד   אֱלֹהִים עַל הַר סִינַי / בְּאֵר דָּת לִנְבוֹנַי
וַיְדַבֵּר   גְּדֻלּוֹת וְנוֹרָאוֹת לְעֵינַי / דָּגוּל מַעֲרִיב שִׁמְשׁוֹ מִפָּנַי.

בָּרוּךְ אַתָּה יהוה, הַמַּעֲרִיב עֲרָבִים.

MA'ARAVOT: SECOND NIGHT

The piyutim for the second night, like those of the first, are a commentary to the giving of the Torah and the Ten Commandments. They are composed in the form of an alphabetic acrostic, followed by an acrostic of the poet's name, Yitzḥak ben Moshe, about whom nothing else is known. Like those of the first night the lines often begin with a key word taken from the biblical account of the revelation, especially the introductory words of the Ten Commandments.

אַהֲבַת עוֹלָם With everlasting love
have You loved Your people, the house of Israel.
You have taught us Torah and commandments,
decrees and laws of justice.
Therefore, LORD our God, when we lie down and when we rise up
we will speak of Your decrees,
rejoicing in the words of Your Torah
and Your commandments for ever.
▸ For they are our life and the length of our days;
on them will we meditate day and night.
May You never take away Your love from us.

> *I am* God who works wonders, / and brought you
>   out of your imprisonment.
> *Have no* hateful betrayal, worshiping what is arid, / for I have
>   yearned to be revealed to you in love.

Blessed are You, LORD, who loves His people Israel.

The Shema must be said with intense concentration.
When not with a minyan, say:

God, faithful King!

The following verse should be said aloud, while covering the eyes with the right hand:

Listen, Israel: the LORD is our God,
the LORD is One.

Deut. 6

Quietly: Blessed be the name of His glorious kingdom for ever and all time.

וְאָהַבְתָּ Love the LORD your God with all your heart, with all your
soul, and with all your might. These words which I command
you today shall be on your heart. Teach them repeatedly to your

Deut. 6

---

emphasizes the element of betrayal involved in idol worship. Not only does
idolatry involve worshiping false ("arid") gods; it also means being unfaithful
to the relationship of love with which God took His people to be His own
("My treasure among all the peoples," Ex. 19:5). The revelation at Mount

אַהֲבַת עוֹלָם בֵּית יִשְׂרָאֵל עַמְּךָ אָהֶבְתָּ
תּוֹרָה וּמִצְוֹת, חֻקִּים וּמִשְׁפָּטִים, אוֹתָנוּ לִמָּדְתָּ
עַל כֵּן יהוה אֱלֹהֵינוּ בְּשָׁכְבֵנוּ וּבְקוּמֵנוּ נָשְׂיחַ בְּחֻקֶּיךָ
וְנִשְׂמַח בְּדִבְרֵי תוֹרָתֶךָ וּבְמִצְוֹתֶיךָ לְעוֹלָם וָעֶד
כִּי הֵם חַיֵּינוּ וְאֹרֶךְ יָמֵינוּ, וּבָהֶם נֶהְגֶּה יוֹמָם וָלָיְלָה.
וְאַהֲבָתְךָ אַל תָּסִיר מִמֶּנּוּ לְעוֹלָמִים.

אָנֹכִי ⟶ הָאֵל עָשָׂה פֶלֶא / וְהוֹצֵאתִיךָ מִבֵּית כֶּלֶא
לֹא־יִהְיֶה לְךָ זָדוֹן צְמֵאָה לְהַעֲלֶה / חָשַׁקְתִּי בְּאַהֲבָה עָלֶיךָ לְהִגָּלֶה.

בָּרוּךְ אַתָּה יהוה, אוֹהֵב עַמּוֹ יִשְׂרָאֵל.

The שמע must be said with intense concentration.
When not with a מנין, say:

אֵל מֶלֶךְ נֶאֱמָן

The following verse should be said aloud, while covering the eyes with the right hand:

דברים ו
שְׁמַע יִשְׂרָאֵל, יהוה אֱלֹהֵינוּ, יהוה ׀ אֶחָד:

Quietly
בָּרוּךְ שֵׁם כְּבוֹד מַלְכוּתוֹ לְעוֹלָם וָעֶד.

דברים ו
וְאָהַבְתָּ אֵת יהוה אֱלֹהֶיךָ, בְּכָל־לְבָבְךָ וּבְכָל־נַפְשְׁךָ וּבְכָל־
מְאֹדֶךָ: וְהָיוּ הַדְּבָרִים הָאֵלֶּה, אֲשֶׁר אָנֹכִי מְצַוְּךָ הַיּוֹם, עַל־לְבָבֶךָ:

אָנֹכִי הָאֵל *I am God.* A paraphrase of the first commandment. Nahmanides understood this not as a command in itself but a prelude to the commands. God had redeemed His people, liberating them from slavery. In virtue of this, He was to become their Sovereign and Law-Giver. God rules by right, not might.

לֹא־יִהְיֶה לְךָ זָדוֹן *Have no hateful betrayal.* An interpretation of the second command influenced by a central theme in the prophetic literature that

children, speaking of them when you sit at home and when you travel on the way, when you lie down and when you rise. Bind them as a sign on your hand, and they shall be an emblem between your eyes. Write them on the doorposts of your house and gates.

וְהָיָה If you indeed heed My commandments with which I charge *Deut. 11* you today, to love the LORD your God and worship Him with all your heart and with all your soul, I will give rain in your land in its season, the early and late rain; and you shall gather in your grain, wine and oil. I will give grass in your field for your cattle, and you shall eat and be satisfied. Be careful lest your heart be tempted and you go astray and worship other gods, bowing down to them. Then the LORD's anger will flare against you and He will close the heavens so that there will be no rain. The land will not yield its crops, and you will perish swiftly from the good land that the LORD is giving you. Therefore, set these, My words, on your heart and soul. Bind them as a sign on your hand, and they shall be an emblem between your eyes. Teach them to your children, speaking of them when you sit at home and when you travel on the way, when you lie down and when you rise. Write them on the doorposts of your house and gates, so that you and your children may live long in the land that the LORD swore to your ancestors to give them, for as long as the heavens are above the earth.

וַיֹּאמֶר The LORD spoke to Moses, saying: Speak to the Israelites *Num. 15* and tell them to make tassels on the corners of their garments for all generations. They shall attach to the tassel at each corner a thread of blue. This shall be your tassel, and you shall see it and remember all of the LORD's commandments and keep them, not straying after your heart and after your eyes, following your own sinful desires. Thus you will be reminded to keep all My commandments, and be holy to your God. I am the LORD your

---

Sinai was itself an act of love: never before and never since has God spoken to an entire people.

וְשִׁנַּנְתָּם לְבָנֶיךָ וְדִבַּרְתָּ בָּם, בְּשִׁבְתְּךָ בְּבֵיתֶךָ וּבְלֶכְתְּךָ בַדֶּרֶךְ, וּבְשָׁכְבְּךָ וּבְקוּמֶךָ: וּקְשַׁרְתָּם לְאוֹת עַל־יָדֶךָ וְהָיוּ לְטֹטָפֹת בֵּין עֵינֶיךָ: וּכְתַבְתָּם עַל־מְזֻזוֹת בֵּיתֶךָ וּבִשְׁעָרֶיךָ:

דברים יא

וְהָיָה אִם־שָׁמֹעַ תִּשְׁמְעוּ אֶל־מִצְוֹתַי אֲשֶׁר אָנֹכִי מְצַוֶּה אֶתְכֶם הַיּוֹם, לְאַהֲבָה אֶת־יהוה אֱלֹהֵיכֶם וּלְעָבְדוֹ, בְּכָל־לְבַבְכֶם וּבְכָל־נַפְשְׁכֶם: וְנָתַתִּי מְטַר־אַרְצְכֶם בְּעִתּוֹ, יוֹרֶה וּמַלְקוֹשׁ, וְאָסַפְתָּ דְגָנֶךָ וְתִירֹשְׁךָ וְיִצְהָרֶךָ: וְנָתַתִּי עֵשֶׂב בְּשָׂדְךָ לִבְהֶמְתֶּךָ, וְאָכַלְתָּ וְשָׂבָעְתָּ: הִשָּׁמְרוּ לָכֶם פֶּן־יִפְתֶּה לְבַבְכֶם, וְסַרְתֶּם וַעֲבַדְתֶּם אֱלֹהִים אֲחֵרִים וְהִשְׁתַּחֲוִיתֶם לָהֶם: וְחָרָה אַף־יהוה בָּכֶם, וְעָצַר אֶת־הַשָּׁמַיִם וְלֹא־יִהְיֶה מָטָר, וְהָאֲדָמָה לֹא תִתֵּן אֶת־יְבוּלָהּ, וַאֲבַדְתֶּם מְהֵרָה מֵעַל הָאָרֶץ הַטֹּבָה אֲשֶׁר יהוה נֹתֵן לָכֶם: וְשַׂמְתֶּם אֶת־דְּבָרַי אֵלֶּה עַל־לְבַבְכֶם וְעַל־נַפְשְׁכֶם, וּקְשַׁרְתֶּם אֹתָם לְאוֹת עַל־יֶדְכֶם, וְהָיוּ לְטוֹטָפֹת בֵּין עֵינֵיכֶם: וְלִמַּדְתֶּם אֹתָם אֶת־בְּנֵיכֶם לְדַבֵּר בָּם, בְּשִׁבְתְּךָ בְּבֵיתֶךָ וּבְלֶכְתְּךָ בַדֶּרֶךְ, וּבְשָׁכְבְּךָ וּבְקוּמֶךָ: וּכְתַבְתָּם עַל־מְזוּזוֹת בֵּיתֶךָ וּבִשְׁעָרֶיךָ: לְמַעַן יִרְבּוּ יְמֵיכֶם וִימֵי בְנֵיכֶם עַל הָאֲדָמָה אֲשֶׁר נִשְׁבַּע יהוה לַאֲבֹתֵיכֶם לָתֵת לָהֶם, כִּימֵי הַשָּׁמַיִם עַל־הָאָרֶץ:

במדבר טו

וַיֹּאמֶר יהוה אֶל־מֹשֶׁה לֵּאמֹר: דַּבֵּר אֶל־בְּנֵי יִשְׂרָאֵל וְאָמַרְתָּ אֲלֵהֶם, וְעָשׂוּ לָהֶם צִיצִת עַל־כַּנְפֵי בִגְדֵיהֶם לְדֹרֹתָם, וְנָתְנוּ עַל־צִיצִת הַכָּנָף פְּתִיל תְּכֵלֶת: וְהָיָה לָכֶם לְצִיצִת, וּרְאִיתֶם אֹתוֹ וּזְכַרְתֶּם אֶת־כָּל־מִצְוֹת יהוה וַעֲשִׂיתֶם אֹתָם, וְלֹא תָתוּרוּ אַחֲרֵי לְבַבְכֶם וְאַחֲרֵי עֵינֵיכֶם, אֲשֶׁר־אַתֶּם זֹנִים אַחֲרֵיהֶם: לְמַעַן תִּזְכְּרוּ וַעֲשִׂיתֶם אֶת־כָּל־מִצְוֹתָי, וִהְיִיתֶם קְדֹשִׁים לֵאלֹהֵיכֶם: אֲנִי יהוה

God, who brought you out of the land of Egypt to be your God.
I am the LORD your God.

True –

The Leader repeats:
▸ The LORD your God is true –

וֶאֱמוּנָה – and faithful is all this,
and firmly established for us
that He is the LORD our God,
and there is none beside Him,
and that we, Israel, are His people.
He is our King, who redeems us from the hand of kings
and delivers us from the grasp of all tyrants.
He is our God, who on our behalf repays our foes
and brings just retribution on our mortal enemies;
who performs great deeds beyond understanding
and wonders beyond number;
who kept us alive, not letting our foot slip;   Ps. 66
who led us on the high places of our enemies,
raising our pride above all our foes;
who did miracles for us
and brought vengeance against Pharaoh;
who performed signs and wonders
in the land of Ham's children;
who smote in His wrath all the firstborn of Egypt,
and brought out His people Israel from their midst
into everlasting freedom;
who led His children through the divided Reed Sea,
plunging their pursuers and enemies into the depths.
When His children saw His might,
they gave praise and thanks to His name,
▸ and willingly accepted His Sovereignty.
Moses and the children of Israel then sang a song to You.

אֱלֹהֵיכֶם, אֲשֶׁר הוֹצֵאתִי אֶתְכֶם מֵאֶרֶץ מִצְרַיִם, לִהְיוֹת לָכֶם
לֵאלֹהִים, אֲנִי יהוה אֱלֹהֵיכֶם:

אֱמֶת

The שליח ציבור *repeats:*

‹ יהוה אֱלֹהֵיכֶם אֱמֶת

וֶאֱמוּנָה כָּל זֹאת וְקַיָּם עָלֵינוּ
כִּי הוּא יהוה אֱלֹהֵינוּ וְאֵין זוּלָתוֹ
וַאֲנַחְנוּ יִשְׂרָאֵל עַמּוֹ.
הַפּוֹדֵנוּ מִיַּד מְלָכִים
מַלְכֵּנוּ הַגּוֹאֲלֵנוּ מִכַּף כָּל הֶעָרִיצִים.
הָאֵל הַנִּפְרָע לָנוּ מִצָּרֵינוּ
וְהַמְשַׁלֵּם גְּמוּל לְכָל אוֹיְבֵי נַפְשֵׁנוּ.
הָעוֹשֶׂה גְדוֹלוֹת עַד אֵין חֵקֶר, וְנִפְלָאוֹת עַד אֵין מִסְפָּר
הַשָּׂם נַפְשֵׁנוּ בַּחַיִּים, וְלֹא־נָתַן לַמּוֹט רַגְלֵנוּ:
הַמַּדְרִיכֵנוּ עַל בָּמוֹת אוֹיְבֵינוּ
וַיָּרֶם קַרְנֵנוּ עַל כָּל שׂוֹנְאֵינוּ.
הָעוֹשֶׂה לָּנוּ נִסִּים וּנְקָמָה בְּפַרְעֹה
אוֹתוֹת וּמוֹפְתִים בְּאַדְמַת בְּנֵי חָם.
הַמַּכֶּה בְעֶבְרָתוֹ כָּל בְּכוֹרֵי מִצְרָיִם
וַיּוֹצֵא אֶת עַמּוֹ יִשְׂרָאֵל מִתּוֹכָם לְחֵרוּת עוֹלָם.
הַמַּעֲבִיר בָּנָיו בֵּין גִּזְרֵי יַם סוּף
אֶת רוֹדְפֵיהֶם וְאֶת שׂוֹנְאֵיהֶם בִּתְהוֹמוֹת טִבַּע
וְרָאוּ בָנָיו גְּבוּרָתוֹ, שִׁבְּחוּ וְהוֹדוּ לִשְׁמוֹ
‹ וּמַלְכוּתוֹ בְּרָצוֹן קִבְּלוּ עֲלֵיהֶם
מֹשֶׁה וּבְנֵי יִשְׂרָאֵל, לְךָ עָנוּ שִׁירָה.

תהלים סו

The Zulat (see page 104) describes Israel as a bride on her wedding day.

Overwhelming [Israel] was crowned, / adorned and ennobled, /
    on the day the Torah was given;

chosen from all nations, / daughter of three perfect patriarchs, /
    liberated from Put [Egypt].

He drew her along with many miracles – / Master of all creation – /
    and she came to the desert.

He spoke to her very heart – / He who sits upon a throne amid
    myriads – / so that she clung to Him.

He had the third child [Moses] run to them / in the third month
    / after the release of scattered [Israel].

And she longed to take shelter in His shadow, / and so replied
    that she would fulfill, / and made herself beautiful, crowned.

The High and Awesome One set a time for her, / and she con-
    secrated herself for three days – / [Israel] who guards the
    vineyards.

She adorned herself with jewelry, / putting aside her tattered gar-
    ments, / and was perfumed with myrrh.

The Pure One, amid fire and great light, / descended to the
    mountaintop, / and shining Israel quaked.

In clefts of the rock she hid herself, / for fear of the lightning, /
    and the deafening sound.

He crowned her with ornaments, / and maturity had come / for
    that hidden dove.

He taught her how to serve Him, / how to honor Him with all her
    heart, / and the Law became clear.

Her mouth was filled with laughter, / on the day the Law was
    given / that is beautified in everything.

שְׁלִישִׁי *The third child.* A threefold Torah (Torah, Prophets and Writings) was
given by a third child (Moses, younger brother of Miriam and Aaron), in the
third month.

נָבְנוּ שָׁדַיִם לְיוֹנָה מִסְתְּרֶה *Maturity had come / for that hidden dove.* A beautiful
juxtaposition of two phrases, one from Ezekiel, the other from the Song of
Songs. The prophecy in Ezekiel speaks of how God found Israel like a young

The זולת (*see page 105*) *describes Israel as a bride on her wedding day.*

אֵימָה נִכְתָּרָה / עֲדוּיָה וּמְעֻטָּרָה / בְּיוֹם מַתַּן תּוֹרָה

בְּחוּרָה מֵעֲמָמִים / בַּת שְׁלֹשֶׁת הַתְּמִימִים / מִפּוּט וְתָרָה

גֻּרְרָה בְּרֹב נִסִּים / אָדוֹן כָּל הַמַּעֲשִׂים / בָּאָה לַמִּדְבָּרָה

דִּבֶּר עַל לִבָּהּ / יוֹשֵׁב בְּכֵס רְבָבָה / עֵדָיו לְהִתְחַבְּרָה

הֵרִיץ לָהּ שְׁלִישִׁי / בַּחֹדֶשׁ הַשְּׁלִישִׁי / לִיצִיאַת פְּזוּרָה

וְחִמְּדָהּ בְּצִלּוֹ חֲסוּת / וְהֵשִׁיבָה כֵּן לַעֲשׂוֹת / וְנִתְיַפְּתָה נְזוּרָה

זִמְּנָה רָם וְאָיִם / וְנִתְקַדְּשָׁה לִשְׁלֹשֶׁת יוֹם / כְּרַמִּים נְטֵרָה

חֲלָאִים נִתְקַשְּׁטָה / וּבְלָאוֹתֶיהָ פְּשָׁטָה / וּמְמֹר מִקְטְרָה

טָהוֹר בָּאֵשׁ וְזֹהַר / יָרַד לְרֹאשׁ הָהָר / וְנוֹדְעָזְעָה בְרָה

יָשְׁבָה בִּנְקִיקִים / מֵחֶרְדַּת הַבְּרָקִים / וּמִקּוֹל הַהֲבָרָה

כְּלוּלָה בַּעֲדָיִים / נָכְנוּ שָׁדַיִם / לְיוֹנָה מִסְתָּרָה

לֻמְּדָה בַּמֶּה לְעָבְדוֹ / בְּכָל לִבָּהּ לְכַבְּדוֹ / וְהַדָּת נִפְתָּרָה

מָלְאָה פִּיהָ שְׂחוֹק / בְּיוֹם נְתִינַת חֹק / בַּכֹּל מְפֹאָרָה

אֵימָה נִכְתָּרָה **Overwhelming [Israel] was crowned.** A reference to the Talmudic tradition that when the Israelites said, "We will do and we will hear," assenting to the covenant before they knew what it would require of them, each was given two crowns, one for "We will do" and one for "We will hear" (*Shabbat* 88a; see page 194). Note how, in this central section, the poet uses the language of the prophets (Hosea and Ezekiel), Psalms and especially the Song of Songs to evoke the sense of mutual love between Redeemer and redeemed, Law-Giver and law-receivers, God and His people, as if the covenant at Mount Sinai were a wedding. This is the language of tenderness and intimacy, and it pervades much of Tanakh. At Sinai what was revealed was not law as a coercive force merely for the purpose of social order, but rather law-as-love and love-as-law, the Creator revealing to His creations the moral law that brings harmony to the free association of free human beings, much as scientific law underlies the harmony of the universe, the stars and planets in their orbits, and life in its evolving splendor.

And she received precious laws for an inheritance, / to be her
own legacy, / her splendor and her glory.

He elevated [the Torah,] her pearls, / as she girded herself with
strength, / for her business is a good one.

Yes, [the Torah] laid her table, / and her King sat down there, /
and she came to break bread.

[Angels] of fire and water combined / descended from heaven /
to dance all together.

Her Rock, surrounded by celestial beings / is well known in His
gates, [throughout His world,] / for His is the power.

Cassia and aloe – / she was perfumed with song and with praises – /
and swathed in kindness.

Many have done much, / but [Israel,] you surpass them all. / For
this [Torah] are you celebrated.

Lily of the valleys, / she received laws and statutes, / written into
her bridal endowment.

Their number is [611, the numerical value of] "Torah," / plus the
two foremost [spoken directly by God]. / With these, [613 in
all,] are we charged.

> *Do not take* the gravity of God's name in vain: His of the
> awesome deeds. / Unify His name by day and by night.
> *Remember* the great adornment of the delight [that is Shabbat,]
> doubling its bread, / and singing to Your Maker as did
> those who passed through the deep:

---

the others is that the first were spoken by God directly in the first person.
Other sages, however, held that the people heard all ten of the commands
directly from God (*Pesikta Rabbati* 22).

לֹא תִשָּׂא *Do not take.* The poet returns to his enumeration and explication of
the Ten Commandments.

יַחֵד שְׁמוֹ *Unify His name.* By reciting the Shema during the day and at night.

לְכִפְלָה *Doubling its bread.* A reference to the two loaves of bread on Shabbat,
a memory of the double portion of manna that fell on Friday (Ex. 16:5).

נֶחֱמָדִים יְרֻשָּׁה / לִהְיוֹת לָהּ לְמוֹרָשָׁה / לִצְבִי וּלְתִפְאָרָה
סִלְסֵל פְּנִינֶיהָ / חָגְרָה בְעוֹז מָתְנֶיהָ / עֵקֶב טוֹב סַחְרָהּ
עָרְכָה שֻׁלְחָנָהּ / וּמַלְכָּהּ שָׁם חָנָה / וְלַלְחֹם נִסְחָרָה
פְּתוּכֵי אֵשׁ וּמַיִם / יָרְדוּ מִן שָׁמַיִם / לְרַקֵּד בַּחֲבוּרָה
צוּרָהּ תּוֹךְ עִירִין / נוֹדַע בַּשְּׁעָרִים / כִּי לוֹ הַגְּבוּרָה
קְצִיעוֹת וַאֲהָלוֹת / מְבֻשֶּׂמֶת בְּשִׁיר וּתְהִלּוֹת / וְחֶסֶד מְקֻשָּׁרָה
רַבּוֹת עָשׂוּ הֲמוֹנָה / וְאַתְּ עָלִית עַל־כֻּלָּנָה / בְּזֹאת מְאֻשָּׁרָה
שׁוֹשַׁנַּת עֲמָקִים / קַבָּלָה מִצְוֹת וְחֻקִּים / בִּכְתָב הַמֹּהֲרָה
תּוֹרָה מִנְיָנָם / וּשְׁתַּיִם בְּרֹאשׁ בִּנְיָנָם / כֻּהֶיךָ מְזֻהֲרָה.

לֹא תִשָּׂא   טִכּוּס שֵׁם נוֹרָא עֲלִילָה
יַחֵד שְׁמוֹ יוֹמָם וְלַיְלָה
זָכוֹר   כָּלוּל עֹנֶג לְכָפְלָה
לְיוֹצֶרְךָ תָּשׁוֹרֵר כְּעָבְרֵי מְצוּלָה.

girl beginning to show signs of maturity, "And when I looked at you and saw that you were old enough for love, I spread the corner of My garment over you…I gave you My solemn oath and entered into a covenant with you, declares the Sovereign Lord, and you became Mine" (Ezek. 16:6–8). In the Song of Songs (2:14) the Lover (God) says of his beloved (Israel), "My dove in the rock's cleft, in the cliff's shadow" applied by the poet to the Israelites hiding in rock clefts in fear of the thunder and lightning and the shaking of the mountain.

סִלְסֵל פְּנִינֶיהָ *He elevated… her pearls.* Phrases in this and the following lines contain phrases from the passage in Proverbs 31 about *eshet ḥayil*, "the woman of strength," understood here as God's bride, the children of Israel.

תּוֹרָה מִנְיָנָם *Their number is 611.* The numerical value of the word "Torah." The sages say that there are 613 commands in the Torah, 611 of which they received via Moses, but the first two they heard directly from God Himself (*Makkot* 24a). The difference between the first two of the Ten Commandments and

With happiness, with song, with great joy,
and they all exclaimed:

> "Who is like You, LORD, among the mighty?   *Ex. 15*
> Who is like You, majestic in holiness,
> awesome in praises, doing wonders?"

▸ Your children beheld Your majesty
as You parted the sea before Moses.

> *Honor* greatly your father and mother,
> to lengthen your days to eternity.
> *Do not murder* any one formed in My image and your flesh;
> and crown your supernal Rock, as you have said:

This is the Rock of our salvation;
[Israel] opened their mouths and exclaimed:

> "The LORD shall reign for ever and ever."   *Ex. 15*

▸ And it is said,

> "For the LORD has redeemed Jacob   *Jer. 31*
> and rescued him from a power
> stronger than his own."

> *Do not commit adultery* with women who tread the streets,
> smooth-tongued, / to entrap the souls of men in deepest pits.
> *Do not steal* stores of lusted gold, / for the Compassionate One
> will redeem you from your troubles.*

Blessed are You, LORD, who redeemed Israel.

Some end the blessing as follows (see commentary on page 109):
Blessed are You, LORD, King, Rock and Redeemer of Israel.

God in whose image we each are, and a betrayal of our shared humanity since
the human other is, like us, a mortal creature of flesh and blood.

בְּגִילָה, בְּרִנָּה בְּשִׂמְחָה רַבָּה

וְאָמְרוּ כֻלָּם

שמות טו

מִי־כָמֹכָה בָּאֵלִם יהוה

מִי כָּמֹכָה נֶאְדָּר בַּקֹּדֶשׁ

נוֹרָא תְהִלֹּת עֹשֵׂה פֶלֶא:

‹ מַלְכוּתְךָ רָאוּ בָנֶיךָ, בּוֹקֵעַ יָם לִפְנֵי מֹשֶׁה

כַּבֵּד   מְאֹד אָבִיךָ וְאִמֶּךָ / נֶצַח יִרְבּוּ יָמֶיךָ

לֹא תִרְצָח   סָדוּר בְּצַלְמִי וּבְגָלְמֶךָ / עֶלְיוֹן צוּרְךָ הִמְלִיכֵהוּ
כְּנֶאֱמֶךָ.

זֶה צוּר יִשְׁעֵנוּ, פָּצוּ פֶה. וְאָמְרוּ

שמות טו

יהוה יִמְלֹךְ לְעֹלָם וָעֶד:

‹ וְנֶאֱמַר

ירמיה לא

כִּי־פָדָה יהוה אֶת־יַעֲקֹב, וּגְאָלוֹ מִיַּד חָזָק מִמֶּנּוּ:

לְלֹא תִנְאָף   פּוֹעֲמוֹת חוּצוֹת וּמַחֲלִיקוֹת / צוּדוֹת נְפָשׁוֹת
בְּשׁוּחוֹת עֲמֻקּוֹת

לֹא תִגְנֹב   קְבוּצוֹת זָהָב חֲשׁוּקוֹת / רַחוּם יִגְאָלְךָ מִמְּצוּקוֹת.*

בָּרוּךְ אַתָּה יהוה, גָּאַל יִשְׂרָאֵל.

*Some end the blessing as follows (see commentary on page 109):
בָּרוּךְ אַתָּה יהוה, מֶלֶךְ צוּר יִשְׂרָאֵל וְגוֹאֲלוֹ.

סָדוּר בְּצַלְמִי וּבְגָלְמֶךָ *Formed in My image and your flesh.* A lovely expression of
the dual nature of humanity. Murder is a double crime: an offense against

הַשְׁכִּיבֵנוּ Help us lie down, O LORD our God, in peace,
and rise up, O our King, to life.
Spread over us Your canopy of peace.
Direct us with Your good counsel,
and save us for the sake of Your name.
Shield us and remove from us every enemy,
plague, sword, famine and sorrow.
Remove the adversary
from before and behind us.
Shelter us in the shadow of Your wings,
for You, God, are our Guardian and Deliverer;
You, God, are a gracious and compassionate King.
▸ Guard our going out and our coming in,
for life and peace,
from now and for ever.
Spread over us Your canopy of peace.

> *Do not testify* as a false witness, do not lie;
> instead pursue justice in all your ways.
> *Do not be envious* of the pristine beauty of your
> friend's possession. / For you shall lie down
> in the sanctuary where peace reigns;
> for your sleep will fill you with joy.

Blessed are You, LORD,
who spreads a canopy of peace over us,
over all His people Israel,
and over Jerusalem.

Continue with "Thus Moses announced" on page 60.

הַשְׁכִּיבֵנוּ יְהוה אֱלֹהֵינוּ לְשָׁלוֹם

וְהַעֲמִידֵנוּ מַלְכֵּנוּ לְחַיִּים

וּפְרֹשׁ עָלֵינוּ סֻכַּת שְׁלוֹמֶךָ

וְתַקְּנֵנוּ בְּעֵצָה טוֹבָה מִלְּפָנֶיךָ

וְהוֹשִׁיעֵנוּ לְמַעַן שְׁמֶךָ.

וְהָגֵן בַּעֲדֵנוּ

וְהָסֵר מֵעָלֵינוּ אוֹיֵב, דֶּבֶר וְחֶרֶב וְרָעָב וְיָגוֹן

וְהָסֵר שָׂטָן מִלְּפָנֵינוּ וּמֵאַחֲרֵינוּ, וּבְצֵל כְּנָפֶיךָ תַּסְתִּירֵנוּ

כִּי אֵל שׁוֹמְרֵנוּ וּמַצִּילֵנוּ אָתָּה

כִּי אֵל מֶלֶךְ חַנּוּן וְרַחוּם אָתָּה.

◦ וּשְׁמֹר צֵאתֵנוּ וּבוֹאֵנוּ לְחַיִּים וּלְשָׁלוֹם מֵעַתָּה וְעַד עוֹלָם.

וּפְרֹשׂ עָלֵינוּ סֻכַּת שְׁלוֹמֶךָ.

לֹא־תַעֲנֶה שְׁקָרִים לַעֲנוֹת בְּעֵדוּתֶךָ

תִּרְדֹּף צֶדֶק בְּכָל אֹרְחֹתֶיךָ

לֹא תַחְמֹד יְפִי צַחוּת קִנְיַן עֲמִיתֶךָ

בִּנְוֵה מִשְׁכְּנוֹת הַשָּׁלוֹם תִּשְׁכַּב וְעָרְבָה שְׁנָתֶךָ.

בָּרוּךְ אַתָּה יְהוה

הַפּוֹרֵשׂ סֻכַּת שָׁלוֹם עָלֵינוּ וְעַל כָּל עַמּוֹ יִשְׂרָאֵל

וְעַל יְרוּשָׁלָיִם.

Continue with "וַיְדַבֵּר מֹשֶׁה" on page 61.

Kiddush for Shabbat Evening

BLESSING THE CHILDREN

On the evening of Shabbat, many have the custom to bless their children.

To sons, say:

יְשִׂמְךָ May God make you like Ephraim and Manasseh.

To daughters, say:

יְשִׂימֵךְ May God make you like Sarah, Rebecca, Rachel and Leah.

Gen. 48

יְבָרֶכְךָ May the LORD bless you and protect you.
May the LORD make His face shine on you and be gracious to you.
May the LORD turn His face toward you and grant you peace.

Num. 6

Many people sing each of the four verses of the following song three times:

שָׁלוֹם עֲלֵיכֶם Welcome,
ministering angels, angels of the Most High,
from the Supreme King of kings,
the Holy One, blessed be He.

Enter in peace,
angels of peace, angels of the Most High,
from the Supreme King of kings,
the Holy One, blessed be He.

Bless me with peace,
angels of peace, angels of the Most High,
from the Supreme King of kings,
the Holy One, blessed be He.

Go in peace,
angels of peace, angels of the Most High,
from the Supreme King of kings,
the Holy One, blessed be He.

כִּי מַלְאָכָיו He will command His angels about you,
to guard you in all your ways.
May the LORD guard your going out and your return,
from now and for all time.

Ps. 91

Ps. 121

קידוש לליל שבת

ברכת הבנים

On ליל שבת, *many have the custom to bless their children.*

<table>
<tr><td align="right">To daughters, say:</td><td align="right">To sons, say:</td></tr>
</table>

בראשית מח

יְשִׂמֵךְ אֱלֹהִים   יְשִׂמְךָ אֱלֹהִים

כְּשָׂרָה רִבְקָה רָחֵל וְלֵאָה: כְּאֶפְרַיִם וְכִמְנַשֶּׁה:

במדבר ו

יְבָרֶכְךָ יהוה וְיִשְׁמְרֶךָ:

יָאֵר יהוה פָּנָיו אֵלֶיךָ וִיחֻנֶּךָּ:

יִשָּׂא יהוה פָּנָיו אֵלֶיךָ וְיָשֵׂם לְךָ שָׁלוֹם:

Many people sing each of the four verses of the following song three times:

שָׁלוֹם עֲלֵיכֶם

מַלְאֲכֵי הַשָּׁרֵת, מַלְאֲכֵי עֶלְיוֹן

מִמֶּלֶךְ מַלְכֵי הַמְּלָכִים, הַקָּדוֹשׁ בָּרוּךְ הוּא.

בּוֹאֲכֶם לְשָׁלוֹם

מַלְאֲכֵי הַשָּׁלוֹם, מַלְאֲכֵי עֶלְיוֹן

מִמֶּלֶךְ מַלְכֵי הַמְּלָכִים, הַקָּדוֹשׁ בָּרוּךְ הוּא.

בָּרְכוּנִי לְשָׁלוֹם

מַלְאֲכֵי הַשָּׁלוֹם, מַלְאֲכֵי עֶלְיוֹן

מִמֶּלֶךְ מַלְכֵי הַמְּלָכִים, הַקָּדוֹשׁ בָּרוּךְ הוּא.

צֵאתְכֶם לְשָׁלוֹם

מַלְאֲכֵי הַשָּׁלוֹם, מַלְאֲכֵי עֶלְיוֹן

מִמֶּלֶךְ מַלְכֵי הַמְּלָכִים, הַקָּדוֹשׁ בָּרוּךְ הוּא.

תהלים צא

כִּי מַלְאָכָיו יְצַוֶּה-לָּךְ, לִשְׁמָרְךָ בְּכָל-דְּרָכֶיךָ:

תהלים קכא

יהוה יִשְׁמָר-צֵאתְךָ וּבוֹאֶךָ, מֵעַתָּה וְעַד-עוֹלָם:

Some say:

רִבּוֹן כָּל הָעוֹלָמִים Master of all worlds, LORD of all souls, LORD of peace, mighty, blessed and great King, King who speaks peace, King who is glorious, enduring and pure, King who gives life to worlds, King who is good and does good, King alone and unique, great King who robes Himself in compassion, King who reigns over all kings, who is exalted and supports those who fall, King who is Author of creation, who redeems and rescues, who is radiant and ruddy, King who is holy, high and exalted, King who hears prayer, King whose way is just: I thank You, LORD my God and God of my ancestors, for all the loving-kindness You have done and will do for me, and all the members of my household and all my fellow creatures. Blessed are Your angels, holy and pure, who do Your will. LORD of peace, King to whom peace belongs, bless me with peace, and grant me and the members of my household, and all Your people the house of Israel, a good and peaceful life. King exalted over all the heavenly array, who formed me and who formed creation, I entreat Your radiant presence, that You find me and all the members of my household worthy of grace and good favor in Your eyes and the eyes of all people and all who see us, that we may serve You. May we be worthy to receive Sabbaths amidst great joy, wealth and honor, and few sins. May You remove from me and all the members of my household and all Your people the house of Israel all sickness and disease, all poverty, hardship and destitution. Grant us a virtuous desire to serve You in truth, awe and love. May we find honor in Your eyes and the eyes of all who see us, for You are the King of honor: to You it belongs, to You it accords. Please, King who reigns over all kings, command Your angels, ministering angels who minister to the Most High, to act compassionately toward me when they enter my house on our holy day, for I have lit my lights, spread my couch and changed my clothes in honor of the Sabbath; I have come to Your House to lay my pleas before You that You remove my sighs; I have testified that in six days You created all things, and said it a second time, and will testify to it a third time over my cup, in joy, as You commanded me to remember it, delighting in the extra soul You have given me. On it [the Sabbath] I shall rest as You have commanded me, thereby to serve You. So too I will declare Your greatness in joyful song, for I have set the LORD before me, that You may have compassion upon me in my exile, redeeming me and awakening my heart to Your love. Then I will keep Your commands and statutes without sadness, praying correctly as is right and fitting. Angels of peace, come in peace and bless me with peace; declare blessed the table I have prepared, and go in peace, now and forever. Amen, Selah.

Some say:

רִבּוֹן כָּל הָעוֹלָמִים, אֲדוֹן כָּל הַנְּשָׁמוֹת, אֲדוֹן הַשָּׁלוֹם. מֶלֶךְ אַבִּיר, מֶלֶךְ
בָּרוּךְ, מֶלֶךְ גָּדוֹל, מֶלֶךְ דּוֹבֵר שָׁלוֹם, מֶלֶךְ הָדוּר, מֶלֶךְ וָתִיק, מֶלֶךְ זַךְ, מֶלֶךְ
חֵי הָעוֹלָמִים, מֶלֶךְ טוֹב וּמֵטִיב, מֶלֶךְ יָחִיד וּמְיֻחָד, מֶלֶךְ כַּבִּיר, מֶלֶךְ לוֹבֵשׁ
רַחֲמִים, מֶלֶךְ מַלְכֵי הַמְּלָכִים, מֶלֶךְ נִשְׂגָּב, מֶלֶךְ סוֹמֵךְ נוֹפְלִים, מֶלֶךְ עֹשֶׂה
מַעֲשֵׂה בְרֵאשִׁית, מֶלֶךְ פּוֹדֶה וּמַצִּיל, מֶלֶךְ צַח וְאָדֹם, מֶלֶךְ קָדוֹשׁ, מֶלֶךְ רָם
וְנִשָּׂא, מֶלֶךְ שׁוֹמֵעַ תְּפִלָּה, מֶלֶךְ תָּמִים דַּרְכּוֹ. מוֹדֶה אֲנִי לְפָנֶיךָ, יהוה אֱלֹהַי
וֵאלֹהֵי אֲבוֹתַי, עַל כָּל הַחֶסֶד אֲשֶׁר עָשִׂיתָ עִמָּדִי וַאֲשֶׁר אַתָּה עָתִיד לַעֲשׂוֹת
עִמִּי וְעִם כָּל בְּנֵי בֵיתִי וְעִם כָּל בְּרִיּוֹתֶיךָ, בְּנֵי בְרִיתִי. וּבְרוּכִים הֵם מַלְאָכֶיךָ
הַקְּדוֹשִׁים וְהַטְּהוֹרִים שֶׁעוֹשִׂים רְצוֹנָךְ. אֲדוֹן הַשָּׁלוֹם, מֶלֶךְ שֶׁהַשָּׁלוֹם שֶׁלּוֹ,
בָּרְכֵנִי בַשָּׁלוֹם, וְתִפְקֹד אוֹתִי וְאֶת כָּל בְּנֵי בֵיתִי וְכָל עַמְּךָ בֵּית יִשְׂרָאֵל לְחַיִּים
טוֹבִים וּלְשָׁלוֹם. מֶלֶךְ עֶלְיוֹן עַל כָּל צְבָא מָרוֹם, יוֹצְרֵנוּ, יוֹצֵר בְּרֵאשִׁית,
אֲחַלֶּה פָנֶיךָ הַמְּאִירִים, שֶׁתְּזַכֶּה אוֹתִי וְאֶת כָּל בְּנֵי בֵיתִי לִמְצֹא חֵן וְשֵׂכֶל
טוֹב בְּעֵינֶיךָ וּבְעֵינֵי כָל בְּנֵי אָדָם וּבְעֵינֵי כָל רוֹאֵינוּ לַעֲבוֹדָתֶךָ. וְזַכֵּנוּ לְקַבֵּל
שַׁבָּתוֹת מִתּוֹךְ רֹב שִׂמְחָה וּמִתּוֹךְ עֹשֶׁר וְכָבוֹד וּמִתּוֹךְ מְעוּט עֲוֹנוֹת. וְהָסֵר
מִמֶּנִּי וּמִכָּל בְּנֵי בֵיתִי וּמִכָּל עַמְּךָ בֵּית יִשְׂרָאֵל כָּל מִינֵי חֹלִי וְכָל מִינֵי מַדְוֶה
וְכָל מִינֵי דַלּוּת וַעֲנִיּוּת וְאֶבְיוֹנוּת. וְתֶן בָּנוּ יֵצֶר טוֹב לְעָבְדְּךָ בֶּאֱמֶת וּבְיִרְאָה
וּבְאַהֲבָה. וְנִהְיֶה מְכֻבָּדִים בְּעֵינֶיךָ וּבְעֵינֵי כָל רוֹאֵינוּ, כִּי אַתָּה הוּא מֶלֶךְ
הַכָּבוֹד, כִּי לְךָ נָאֶה, כִּי לְךָ יָאֶה. אָנָּא, מֶלֶךְ מַלְכֵי הַמְּלָכִים, צַוֵּה לְמַלְאָכֶיךָ,
מַלְאֲכֵי הַשָּׁרֵת, מְשָׁרְתֵי עֶלְיוֹן, שֶׁיִּפְקְדוּנִי בְּרַחֲמִים וִיבָרְכוּנִי בְּבוֹאָם לְבֵיתִי
בְּיוֹם קָדְשֵׁנוּ, כִּי הִדְלַקְתִּי נֵרוֹתַי וְהִצַּעְתִּי מִטָּתִי וְהֶחֱלַפְתִּי שִׂמְלוֹתַי לִכְבוֹד
יוֹם הַשַּׁבָּת וּבָאתִי לְבֵיתְךָ לְהַפִּיל תְּחִנָּתִי לְפָנֶיךָ, שֶׁתַּעֲבִיר אַנְחָתִי, וְאָעִיד
אֲשֶׁר בָּרֵאתָ בְּשִׁשָּׁה יָמִים כָּל הַיְצוּר, וְאֶשְׁנֶה וַאֲשַׁלֵּשׁ עוֹד לְהָעִיד עַל כּוֹסִי
בְּתוֹךְ שִׂמְחָתִי, כַּאֲשֶׁר צִוִּיתַנִי לְזָכְרוֹ וּלְהִתְעַנֵּג בְּיֶתֶר נִשְׁמָתִי אֲשֶׁר נָתַתָּ בִּי.
בּוֹ אֶשְׁבַּת כַּאֲשֶׁר צִוִּיתַנִי לְשָׁרְתֶךָ, וְכֵן אַגִּיד גְּדֻלָּתְךָ בְּרִנָּה, וְשִׁוִּיתִי יהוה
לְקִרְאָתִי שֶׁתְּרַחֲמֵנִי עוֹד בְּגָלוּתִי לְגָאֳלֵנִי לְעוֹרֵר לִבִּי לְאַהֲבָתֶךָ. וְאָז אֶשְׁמֹר
פִּקּוּדֶיךָ וְחֻקֶּיךָ בְּלִי עֶצֶב, וְאֶתְפַּלֵּל כַּדָּת כָּרָאוּי וְכַנָּכוֹן. מַלְאֲכֵי הַשָּׁלוֹם,
בּוֹאֲכֶם לְשָׁלוֹם, בָּרְכוּנִי לְשָׁלוֹם, וְאִמְרוּ בָּרוּךְ לְשֻׁלְחָנִי הֶעָרוּךְ, וְצֵאתְכֶם
לְשָׁלוֹם מֵעַתָּה וְעַד עוֹלָם, אָמֵן סֶלָה.

אֵשֶׁת־חַיִל A woman of strength, who can find? *Prov. 31*
> Her worth is far beyond pearls.

Her husband's heart trusts in her, and he has no lack of gain.

She brings him good, not harm, all the days of her life.

She seeks wool and linen, and works with willing hands.

She is like a ship laden with merchandise, bringing her food from afar.

She rises while it is still night, providing food for her household,
> portions for her maids.

She considers a field and buys it;
> from her earnings she plants a vineyard.

She girds herself with strength, and braces her arms for her tasks.

She sees that her business goes well; her lamp does not go out at night.

She holds the distaff in her hand,
> and grasps the spindle with her palms.

She reaches out her palm to the poor,
> and extends her hand to the needy.

She has no fear for her family when it snows,
> for all her household is clothed in crimson wool.

She makes elegant coverings;
> her clothing is fine linen and purple wool.

Her husband is well known in the gates,
> where he sits with the elders of the land.

She makes linen garments and sells them,
> and supplies merchants with sashes.

She is clothed with strength and dignity;
> she can laugh at the days to come.

She opens her mouth with wisdom,
> and the law of kindness is on her tongue.

She watches over the ways of her household,
> and never eats the bread of idleness.

Her children rise and call her happy; her husband also praises her:

"Many women have excelled, but you surpass them all."

Charm is deceptive and beauty vain:
> it is the God-fearing woman who deserves praise.

Give her the reward she has earned;
> let her deeds bring her praise in the gates.

אֵֽשֶׁת־חַֽיִל מִי יִמְצָא, וְרָחֹק מִפְּנִינִים מִכְרָהּ:

בָּֽטַח בָּהּ לֵב בַּעְלָהּ, וְשָׁלָל לֹא יֶחְסָר:

גְּמָלַֽתְהוּ טוֹב וְלֹא־רָע, כֹּל יְמֵי חַיֶּֽיהָ:

דָּֽרְשָׁה צֶֽמֶר וּפִשְׁתִּים, וַתַּֽעַשׂ בְּחֵֽפֶץ כַּפֶּֽיהָ:

הָֽיְתָה כָּאֳנִיּוֹת סוֹחֵר, מִמֶּרְחָק תָּבִיא לַחְמָהּ:

וַתָּֽקָם בְּעוֹד לַֽיְלָה, וַתִּתֵּן טֶֽרֶף לְבֵיתָהּ, וְחֹק לְנַעֲרֹתֶֽיהָ:

זָֽמְמָה שָׂדֶה וַתִּקָּחֵֽהוּ, מִפְּרִי כַפֶּֽיהָ נָֽטְעָה כָּֽרֶם:

חָֽגְרָה בְעוֹז מָתְנֶֽיהָ, וַתְּאַמֵּץ זְרוֹעֹתֶֽיהָ:

טָֽעֲמָה כִּי־טוֹב סַחְרָהּ, לֹא־יִכְבֶּה בַלַּֽיְלָה נֵרָהּ:

יָדֶֽיהָ שִׁלְּחָה בַכִּישׁוֹר, וְכַפֶּֽיהָ תָּֽמְכוּ פָֽלֶךְ:

כַּפָּהּ פָּֽרְשָׂה לֶעָנִי, וְיָדֶֽיהָ שִׁלְּחָה לָאֶבְיוֹן:

לֹא־תִירָא לְבֵיתָהּ מִשָּֽׁלֶג, כִּי כָל־בֵּיתָהּ לָבֻשׁ שָׁנִים:

מַרְבַדִּים עָֽשְׂתָה־לָּהּ, שֵׁשׁ וְאַרְגָּמָן לְבוּשָׁהּ:

נוֹדָע בַּשְּׁעָרִים בַּעְלָהּ, בְּשִׁבְתּוֹ עִם־זִקְנֵי־אָֽרֶץ:

סָדִין עָֽשְׂתָה וַתִּמְכֹּר, וַחֲגוֹר נָֽתְנָה לַכְּנַעֲנִי:

עוֹז־וְהָדָר לְבוּשָׁהּ, וַתִּשְׂחַק לְיוֹם אַחֲרוֹן:

פִּֽיהָ פָּֽתְחָה בְחָכְמָה, וְתֽוֹרַת־חֶֽסֶד עַל־לְשׁוֹנָהּ:

צוֹפִיָּה הֲלִיכוֹת בֵּיתָהּ, וְלֶֽחֶם עַצְלוּת לֹא תֹאכֵל:

קָֽמוּ בָנֶֽיהָ וַיְאַשְּׁרֽוּהָ, בַּעְלָהּ וַֽיְהַלְלָהּ:

רַבּוֹת בָּנוֹת עָֽשׂוּ חָֽיִל, וְאַתְּ עָלִית עַל־כֻּלָּֽנָה:

שֶֽׁקֶר הַחֵן וְהֶֽבֶל הַיֹּֽפִי, אִשָּׁה יִרְאַת־יהוה הִיא תִתְהַלָּל:

תְּנוּ־לָהּ מִפְּרִי יָדֶֽיהָ, וִיהַלְלֽוּהָ בַשְּׁעָרִים מַעֲשֶֽׂיהָ:

Some say:

Prepare the feast of perfect faith, joy of the holy King.
Prepare the royal feast.

This is the feast [mystically known as] 'the Field of Holy Apples' –
and 'the Small Face' and 'the Holy Ancient One'
[mystical terms for aspects of the Divine] come to partake in the feast with it.

With songs of praise I will cut away [evil forces],
    to enter the holy gates of 'the Field of Apples.'
We now invite Her [the Divine Presence] with a newly prepared table
    and a fine candelabrum spreading light upon our heads.
Between right and left is the bride, decked with jewelry, adorned and robed.
Her husband embraces her, and in the joy of their togetherness
    [evil forces] are crushed.
Cries and suffering stop and cease; a new face comes upon spirits and souls.
She will have great and doubled joy; light will come, and bounteous blessing.
Come near, dear friends, and prepare delicacies of many kinds, and fish and fowl.
Renewing souls and spirits through the thirty-two [paths of wisdom]
    and the three branches [of Scripture].
She [the Divine Presence] has seventy crowns, and above,
    the King is crowned with all in the Holy of Holies.
Engraved and hidden with her are all worlds,
    but the pestle of the Ancient of Days releases all that is hidden.
May it be His will that the Divine Presence rest on His people who,
    for His name's sake, delight in sweet foods and honey.
To the south, I will arrange the candelabrum of hidden [wisdom],
    to the north I will set the table with bread.
With wine in the cup, and myrtle clusters for bridegroom and bride,
    the weak will be given strength.
Let us make them crowns of precious words, seventy crowns beyond the fifty.
May the Divine Presence be crowned with six loaves on each side, like
    the two sets of six loaves [of showbread] and other articles [in the Temple].
[On the Sabbath] impure powers and afflicting angels cease and desist; and
    those who are confined have respite.
To break bread the size of an olive or an egg, for there are two ways of inter-
    preting the *Yod* [of the Divine name], restrictively or expansively.
It is like pure olive oil, pressed in a mill, flowing like rivers, whispering secrets.
Let us speak of mysteries, secrets unrevealed, hidden and concealed.
To crown the bride with mysteries above, at this,
    the holy angels' wedding celebration.

Some say:

אַתְקִינוּ סְעוּדָתָא דִּמְהֵימְנוּתָא שְׁלֵימָתָא
חֶדְוָתָא דְּמַלְכָּא קַדִּישָׁא.
אַתְקִינוּ סְעוּדָתָא דְּמַלְכָּא.

דָּא הִיא סְעוּדָתָא דַּחֲקַל תַּפּוּחִין קַדִּישִׁין
וּזְעֵיר אַנְפִּין וְעַתִּיקָא קַדִּישָׁא אָתְיָן לְסַעֲדָה בַּהֲדַהּ.

אֲזַמֵּר בִּשְׁבָחִין / לְמֵעַל גּוֹ פִתְחִין / דְּבַחֲקַל תַּפּוּחִין / דְּאִנּוּן קַדִּישִׁין.

נְזַמֵּן לַהּ הַשְׁתָּא / בִּפְתוֹרָא חַדְתָּא / וּבִמְנַרְתָּא טָבְתָּא / דְּנָהֲרָה עַל רֵישִׁין.

יְמִינָא וּשְׂמָאלָא / וּבֵינַיְהוּ כַלָּה / בְּקִשּׁוּטִין אָזְלָא / וּמָנִין וּלְבוּשִׁין.

יְחַבֵּק לַהּ בַּעְלָהּ / וּבִיסוֹדָא דִי לַהּ / דְּעָבֵד נַיְחָא לַהּ / יְהֵא כָּתֵשׁ כְּתִישִׁין.

צְוָחִין אוּף עָקְתִין / בְּטִילִין וּשְׁבִיתִין / בְּרַם אַנְפִּין חַדְתִּין / וְרוּחִין עִם נַפְשִׁין.

חֲדוּ סַגִּי יֵיתֵי / וְעַל חֲדָה תַּרְתֵּי / נְהוֹרָא לַהּ יַמְטֵי / וּבִרְכָן דִּנְפִישִׁין.

קְרִיבוּ שׁוֹשְׁבִינִין / עֲבִידוּ תִקּוּנִין / לְאַפָּשָׁה זֵינִין / וְנוּנִין עִם רַחְשִׁין.

לְמֶעְבַּד נִשְׁמָתִין / וְרוּחִין חַדְתִּין / בְּתַרְתֵּי וּתְלָתִין / וּבִתְלָתָא שְׁבְשִׁין.

וְעִטְרִין שַׁבְעִין לַהּ / וּמַלְכָּא דִּלְעֵלָּא / דְּיִתְעַטַּר כֹּלָּא / בְּקַדִּישׁ קַדִּישִׁין.

רְשִׁימִין וּסְתִימִין / בְּגַוֵּהּ כָּל עָלְמִין / בְּרַם עַתִּיק יוֹמִין / הֲלָא בָטֵשׁ בְּטִישִׁין.

יְהֵא רַעֲוָה קַמֵּהּ / דְּתִשְׁרֵי עַל עַמֵּהּ / דְּיִתְעַנַּג לִשְׁמֵהּ / בְּמִתְקִין וְדֻבְשִׁין.

אֲסַדֵּר לִדְרוֹמָא / מְנַרְתָּא דִסְתִימָא / וְשֻׁלְחָן עִם נַהֲמָא / בְּצִפוּנָא אַדְשִׁין.

בְּחַמְרָא גּוֹ כָסָא / וּמַדָּנֵי אָסָא / לְאָרוּס וַאֲרוּסָה / לְאַתְקָפָא חֲלָשִׁין.

נַעֲבֵד לוֹן כִּתְרִין / בְּמִלִּין יַקִּירִין / בְּשַׁבְעִין עִטּוּרִין / דְּעַל גַּבֵּי חַמְשִׁין.

שְׁכִינְתָּא תִתְעַטַּר / בְּשִׁית נַהֲמֵי לִסְטַר / בְּוָוִין תִּתְקַטַּר / וְזַיְנִין דִּכְנִישִׁין.

(שְׁבִיתִין וּשְׁבִיקִין / מְסָאֲבִין דְּדָחֲקִין / חֲבִילִין דִּמְעִיקִין / וְכָל זֵינֵי חַרְשִׁין.)

לְמִבְצַע עַל רִיפְתָּא / כְּזֵיתָא וּכְבֵיעֲתָא / תְּרֵין יוּדִין נָקְטָא / סְתִימִין וּפְרִישִׁין.

מְשַׁח זֵיתָא דַכְיָא / דְּטַחֲנִין רֵיחַיָּא / וְנָגְדִין נַחֲלַיָּא / בְּגַוֵּהּ בִּלְחִישִׁין.

הֲלָא נֵימָא רָזִין / וּמִלִּין דִּגְנִיזִין / דְּלֵיתֵיהוֹן מִתְחַזְיָן / טְמִירִין וּכְבִישִׁין.

לְאַעְטָרָה כַלָּה / בְּרָזִין דִּלְעֵלָּא / בְּגוֹ הַאי הִלּוּלָה / דְּעִירִין קַדִּישִׁין.

Kiddush for Yom Tov Evening

On Shabbat add:

quietly: And it was evening, and it was morning – Gen. 1

יוֹם הַשִּׁשִּׁי the sixth day.

Then the heavens and the earth were completed, and all their array. Gen. 2
With the seventh day, God completed the work He had done.
He ceased on the seventh day from all the work He had done.
God blessed the seventh day and declared it holy,
because on it He ceased from all His work He had created to do.

On other evenings Kiddush starts here:

When saying Kiddush for others, add:

Please pay attention, my masters.

Blessed are You, Lord our God, King of the Universe,
who creates the fruit of the vine.

On Shabbat, add the words in parentheses.

בָּרוּךְ Blessed are You, Lord our God, King of the Universe,
who has chosen us from among all peoples,
raised us above all tongues,
and made us holy through His commandments.
You have given us, Lord our God, in love
(Sabbaths for rest), festivals for rejoicing,
holy days and seasons for joy, (this Sabbath day and)
this day of the festival of Shavuot,
the time of the giving of our Torah
(with love), a holy assembly in memory of the exodus from Egypt.
For You have chosen us and sanctified us above all peoples,
and given us as our heritage

---

which we proclaim the holiness of the day. We do this in two ways, first by
declaring the holiness of the day in the central blessing of the evening Amida,
then at home by making a similar declaration over a cup of wine. Holiness
in Judaism lives in these two environments: the community and the family.

קידוש לליל יום טוב

On שבת add:

בראשית א

quietly וַיְהִי־עֶרֶב וַיְהִי־בְקֶר

יוֹם הַשִּׁשִּׁי:

בראשית ב

וַיְכֻלּוּ הַשָּׁמַיִם וְהָאָרֶץ וְכָל־צְבָאָם:

וַיְכַל אֱלֹהִים בַּיּוֹם הַשְּׁבִיעִי מְלַאכְתּוֹ אֲשֶׁר עָשָׂה

וַיִּשְׁבֹּת בַּיּוֹם הַשְּׁבִיעִי מִכָּל־מְלַאכְתּוֹ אֲשֶׁר עָשָׂה:

וַיְבָרֶךְ אֱלֹהִים אֶת־יוֹם הַשְּׁבִיעִי, וַיְקַדֵּשׁ אֹתוֹ

כִּי בוֹ שָׁבַת מִכָּל־מְלַאכְתּוֹ, אֲשֶׁר־בָּרָא אֱלֹהִים, לַעֲשׂוֹת:

On other evenings the קידוש starts here:

When saying קידוש for others, add:

סַבְרִי מָרָנָן

בָּרוּךְ אַתָּה יהוה אֱלֹהֵינוּ מֶלֶךְ הָעוֹלָם, בּוֹרֵא פְּרִי הַגָּפֶן.

On שבת, add the words in parentheses.

בָּרוּךְ אַתָּה יהוה אֱלֹהֵינוּ מֶלֶךְ הָעוֹלָם

אֲשֶׁר בָּחַר בָּנוּ מִכָּל עָם

וְרוֹמְמָנוּ מִכָּל לָשׁוֹן, וְקִדְּשָׁנוּ בְּמִצְוֹתָיו

וַתִּתֶּן לָנוּ יהוה אֱלֹהֵינוּ בְּאַהֲבָה

(שַׁבָּתוֹת לִמְנוּחָה וּ)מוֹעֲדִים לְשִׂמְחָה

חַגִּים וּזְמַנִּים לְשָׂשׂוֹן אֶת יוֹם (הַשַּׁבָּת הַזֶּה וְאֶת יוֹם)

חַג הַשָּׁבוּעוֹת הַזֶּה, זְמַן מַתַּן תּוֹרָתֵנוּ

(בְּאַהֲבָה) מִקְרָא קֹדֶשׁ, זֵכֶר לִיצִיאַת מִצְרָיִם

כִּי בָנוּ בָחַרְתָּ וְאוֹתָנוּ קִדַּשְׁתָּ מִכָּל הָעַמִּים

KIDDUSH

The first thing declared holy in the Torah is not a place but a time. God "blessed the seventh day and made it holy." Kiddush is a performative act in

(Your holy Sabbath in love and favor and)
Your holy festivals for joy and gladness.
Blessed are you, LORD,
who sanctifies (the Sabbath,) Israel and the festivals.

> On Motza'ei Shabbat, the following Havdala is added.
> Lift the hands toward the flame of the Havdala candle and say:
>
> בָּרוּךְ Blessed are You, LORD our God, King of the Universe,
> who creates the lights of fire.
>
> Blessed are You, LORD our God, King of the Universe, who distinguishes
> between sacred and secular, between light and darkness, between Israel
> and the nations, between the seventh day and the six days of work. You
> have made a distinction between the holiness of the Sabbath and the
> holiness of festivals, and have sanctified the seventh day above the six
> days of work. You have distinguished and sanctified Your people Israel
> with Your holiness. Blessed are You, LORD, who distinguishes between
> sacred and sacred.

בָּרוּךְ Blessed are You, LORD our God, King of the Universe,
who has given us life, sustained us, and brought us to this time.

> It is customary for all present to drink of the wine.

> On washing hands before eating the Ḥalla:
> Blessed are You, LORD our God, King of the Universe,
> who has made us holy through His commandments,
> and has commanded us about washing hands.

> Before eating the Ḥalla:
> Blessed are You, LORD our God, King of the Universe,
> who brings forth bread from the earth.

---

structure of the passage as a whole. On Shabbat, Kiddush begins with the
sanctity of the day and only then speaks of Israel as the chosen people. On
festivals, Kiddush begins with God's choice of Israel and only then speaks of
the holiness of the day.

שֶׁהֶחֱיָנוּ וְקִיְּמָנוּ *Who has given us life.* A blessing over the passage of time, made
at moments when we are specifically aware of the passage of time, like festivals, or memorable events like buying a new house. It is at such moments that

(וְשַׁבָּת) וּמוֹעֲדֵי קָדְשֶׁךָ (בְּאַהֲבָה וּבְרָצוֹן)
בְּשִׂמְחָה וּבְשָׂשׂוֹן הִנְחַלְתָּנוּ.
בָּרוּךְ אַתָּה יהוה, מְקַדֵּשׁ (הַשַּׁבָּת וְ) יִשְׂרָאֵל וְהַזְּמַנִּים.

On מוצאי שבת, *the following* הבדלה *is added.*
Lift the hands toward the flame of the הבדלה *candle and say:*

בָּרוּךְ אַתָּה יהוה אֱלֹהֵינוּ מֶלֶךְ הָעוֹלָם, בּוֹרֵא מְאוֹרֵי הָאֵשׁ.

בָּרוּךְ אַתָּה יהוה אֱלֹהֵינוּ מֶלֶךְ הָעוֹלָם, הַמַּבְדִּיל בֵּין קֹדֶשׁ לְחֹל,
בֵּין אוֹר לְחְשֶׁךְ, בֵּין יִשְׂרָאֵל לָעַמִּים, בֵּין יוֹם הַשְּׁבִיעִי לְשֵׁשֶׁת יְמֵי
הַמַּעֲשֶׂה. בֵּין קְדֻשַּׁת שַׁבָּת לִקְדֻשַּׁת יוֹם טוֹב הִבְדַּלְתָּ, וְאֶת יוֹם
הַשְּׁבִיעִי מִשֵּׁשֶׁת יְמֵי הַמַּעֲשֶׂה קִדַּשְׁתָּ, הִבְדַּלְתָּ וְקִדַּשְׁתָּ אֶת עַמְּךָ
יִשְׂרָאֵל בִּקְדֻשָּׁתֶךָ. בָּרוּךְ אַתָּה יהוה, הַמַּבְדִּיל בֵּין קֹדֶשׁ לְקֹדֶשׁ.

בָּרוּךְ אַתָּה יהוה אֱלֹהֵינוּ מֶלֶךְ הָעוֹלָם
שֶׁהֶחֱיָנוּ וְקִיְּמָנוּ, וְהִגִּיעָנוּ לַזְּמַן הַזֶּה.

It is customary for all present to drink of the wine.

On washing hands before eating the חלה:
בָּרוּךְ אַתָּה יהוה אֱלֹהֵינוּ מֶלֶךְ הָעוֹלָם
אֲשֶׁר קִדְּשָׁנוּ בְּמִצְוֹתָיו וְצִוָּנוּ עַל נְטִילַת יָדָיִם.

Before eating the חלה:
בָּרוּךְ אַתָּה יהוה אֱלֹהֵינוּ מֶלֶךְ הָעוֹלָם
הַמּוֹצִיא לֶחֶם מִן הָאָרֶץ.

מְקַדֵּשׁ יִשְׂרָאֵל וְהַזְּמַנִּים *Who sanctifies Israel and the festivals.* The order here is precise. It was God who sanctified the Sabbath, but the Israelites who were charged – in the first mitzva given to them while they were still in Egypt – to sanctify the months, regulate the calendar and thus determine on which day the festival would fall. Hence the sanctity of the people of Israel takes precedence over the sanctity of the day, but the sanctity of the Sabbath precedes both. This is evident in both the concluding blessing and in the

Birkat HaMazon / Grace after Meals

שִׁיר הַמַּעֲלוֹת A song of ascents.   *Ps. 126*
When the LORD brought back the exiles of Zion
we were like people who dream.
Then were our mouths filled with laughter,
 and our tongues with songs of joy.
Then was it said among the nations,
"The LORD has done great things for them."
The LORD did do great things for us and we rejoiced.
Bring back our exiles, LORD, like streams in a dry land.
May those who sowed in tears, reap in joy.
May one who goes out weeping, carrying a bag of seed,
come back with songs of joy, carrying his sheaves.

Some say:
תְּהִלַּת My mouth shall speak the praise of God,   *Ps. 145*
and all creatures shall bless His holy name for ever and all time.
We will bless God now and for ever. Halleluya!   *Ps. 115*
Thank the LORD for He is good;   *Ps. 136*
His loving-kindness is for ever.
Who can tell of the LORD's mighty acts   *Ps. 106*
and make all His praise be heard?

---

wealth for me'" (ibid, vv. 14–17). Bereft of a sense of gratitude and of a power
higher than humans, nations, like individuals, eventually decay.

The original form of Grace consisted of three blessings, which move
sequentially from the universal to the particular. In the first, we thank God
for sustaining the world and all that lives. The second is national: we thank
God for the land of Israel as well as for the other blessings of Jewish life:
the covenant and its sign, circumcision, and the Torah. The third turns to
Jerusalem. The fourth paragraph is a later addition: according to the Talmud
(*Berakhot* 48b), it was added after the Bar Kokhba rebellion, c. 135 CE. Over
the course of time, it has expanded considerably.

ברכת המזון

תהלים קכו

שִׁיר הַמַּעֲלוֹת, בְּשׁוּב יהוה אֶת־שִׁיבַת צִיּוֹן
הָיִינוּ כְּחֹלְמִים:
אָז יִמָּלֵא שְׂחוֹק פִּינוּ וּלְשׁוֹנֵנוּ רִנָּה
אָז יֹאמְרוּ בַגּוֹיִם הִגְדִּיל יהוה לַעֲשׂוֹת עִם־אֵלֶּה:
הִגְדִּיל יהוה לַעֲשׂוֹת עִמָּנוּ, הָיִינוּ שְׂמֵחִים:
שׁוּבָה יהוה אֶת־שְׁבִיתֵנוּ, כַּאֲפִיקִים בַּנֶּגֶב:
הַזֹּרְעִים בְּדִמְעָה בְּרִנָּה יִקְצֹרוּ:
הָלוֹךְ יֵלֵךְ וּבָכֹה נֹשֵׂא מֶשֶׁךְ־הַזָּרַע
בֹּא־יָבֹא בְרִנָּה נֹשֵׂא אֲלֻמֹּתָיו:

Some say:

תהלים קמה

תְּהִלַּת יהוה יְדַבֶּר פִּי
וִיבָרֵךְ כָּל־בָּשָׂר שֵׁם קָדְשׁוֹ לְעוֹלָם וָעֶד:

תהלים קטו
וַאֲנַחְנוּ נְבָרֵךְ יָהּ מֵעַתָּה וְעַד־עוֹלָם, הַלְלוּיָהּ:

תהלים קלו
הוֹדוּ לַיהוה כִּי־טוֹב, כִּי לְעוֹלָם חַסְדּוֹ:

תהלים קו
מִי יְמַלֵּל גְּבוּרוֹת יהוה, יַשְׁמִיעַ כָּל־תְּהִלָּתוֹ:

---

we cease merely to exist. We feel vividly alive. We are aware of the power of
now. Life is God's gift. The breath we breathe is His. To be a Jew is to make
a blessing over life.

BIRKAT HAMAZON / GRACE AFTER MEALS

Grace after Meals is specifically mandated by the Torah itself: "You shall
eat and be satisfied, then you shall bless the LORD your God" (Deut. 8:10).
Thanksgiving, Moses taught the Israelites, is central to Jewish life, "lest your
heart grow haughty and you forget the LORD your God... and you say to
yourselves, 'My own power and the might of my own hand have won this

ZIMMUN / INVITATION

When three or more men say Birkat HaMazon together, the following zimmun is said.
When three or more women say Birkat HaMazon, substitute "Friends" for "Gentlemen."
The leader should ask permission from those with precedence to lead the Birkat HaMazon.

Leader   Gentlemen, let us say grace.

Others   May the name of the LORD be blessed   *Ps. 113*
from now and for ever.

Leader   May the name of the LORD be blessed
from now and for ever.
With your permission,
(my father and teacher / my mother and
teacher / the Kohanim present / our teacher
the Rabbi / the master of this house /
the mistress of this house)
my masters and teachers,
let us bless (*in a minyan:* our God,)
the One from whose food we have eaten.

Others   Blessed be (*in a minyan:* our God,) the One from whose food
we have eaten, and by whose goodness we live.

   *People present who have not taken part in the meal say:
   *Blessed be (*in a minyan:* our God,) the One whose name
   is continually blessed for ever and all time.

Leader   Blessed be (*in a minyan:* our God,) the One from whose food
we have eaten, and by whose goodness we live.
Blessed be He, and blessed be His name.

"Bless the LORD," with which morning and evening services begin. It emphasizes the essentially communal nature of prayer in Judaism. In addition
to the regular *zimmun* here, there are special forms of *zimmun* for (1) a
wedding meal, (2) a meal after a circumcision, and (3) a meal in a house
of mourning.

סדר הזימון

When three or more men say ברכת המזון together, the following זימון is said.
When three or more women say ברכת המזון, substitute חֲבֵרוֹתַי for רַבּוֹתַי.
The leader should ask permission from those with precedence to lead the ברכת המזון.

רַבּוֹתַי, נְבָרֵךְ. *Leader*

תהלים קיג

יְהִי שֵׁם יהוה מְבֹרָךְ מֵעַתָּה וְעַד־עוֹלָם: *Others*

יְהִי שֵׁם יהוה מְבֹרָךְ מֵעַתָּה וְעַד־עוֹלָם: *Leader*
בִּרְשׁוּת (אָבִי מוֹרִי / אִמִּי מוֹרָתִי /
כֹּהֲנִים / מוֹרֵנוּ הָרַב /
בַּעַל הַבַּיִת הַזֶּה / בַּעֲלַת הַבַּיִת הַזֶּה)
מָרָנָן וְרַבָּנָן וְרַבּוֹתַי
נְבָרֵךְ (במנין: אֱלֹהֵינוּ) שֶׁאָכַלְנוּ מִשֶּׁלּוֹ.

בָּרוּךְ (במנין: אֱלֹהֵינוּ) שֶׁאָכַלְנוּ מִשֶּׁלּוֹ וּבְטוּבוֹ חָיִינוּ. *Others*

*People present who have not taken part in the meal say:
*בָּרוּךְ (במנין: אֱלֹהֵינוּ) וּמְבֹרָךְ שְׁמוֹ תָּמִיד לְעוֹלָם וָעֶד.

בָּרוּךְ (במנין: אֱלֹהֵינוּ) שֶׁאָכַלְנוּ מִשֶּׁלּוֹ וּבְטוּבוֹ חָיִינוּ. *Leader*
בָּרוּךְ הוּא וּבָרוּךְ שְׁמוֹ.

ZIMMUN

A meal at which there are three adult males requires a formal invitation, *zimmun*, to say Grace. The Talmud derives this from the verse, "Magnify the LORD with me; let us exalt His name together" (Psalm 34:4). A slightly longer version is used when at least ten are present. The act of inviting those present to join in the act of praise is similar to the recitation of *Barekhu*,

BLESSING OF NOURISHMENT

בָּרוּךְ Blessed are You, LORD our God, King of the Universe,
who in His goodness feeds the whole world
with grace, kindness and compassion.
He gives food to all living things,
for His kindness is for ever.
Because of His continual great goodness,
we have never lacked food,
nor may we ever lack it,
for the sake of His great name.
For He is God who feeds and sustains all,
does good to all,
and prepares food for all creatures He has created.
Blessed are You, LORD,
who feeds all.

BLESSING OF LAND

נוֹדֶה We thank You, LORD our God,
for having granted as a heritage to our ancestors
a desirable, good and spacious land;
for bringing us out, LORD our God,
from the land of Egypt,
freeing us from the house of slavery;
for Your covenant which You sealed in our flesh;
for Your Torah which You taught us;
for Your laws which You made known to us;
for the life, grace and kindness You have bestowed on us;
and for the food
by which You continually feed and sustain us,
every day, every season, every hour.

---

the covenant and its sign, circumcision, the giving of the Torah and the
commandments.

ברכת הזן

בָּרוּךְ אַתָּה יהוה אֱלֹהֵינוּ מֶלֶךְ הָעוֹלָם
הַזָּן אֶת הָעוֹלָם כֻּלּוֹ בְּטוּבוֹ, בְּחֵן בְּחֶסֶד וּבְרַחֲמִים
הוּא נוֹתֵן לֶחֶם לְכָל בָּשָׂר
כִּי לְעוֹלָם חַסְדּוֹ.
וּבְטוּבוֹ הַגָּדוֹל, תָּמִיד לֹא חָסַר לָנוּ
וְאַל יֶחְסַר לָנוּ מָזוֹן לְעוֹלָם וָעֶד
בַּעֲבוּר שְׁמוֹ הַגָּדוֹל.
כִּי הוּא אֵל זָן וּמְפַרְנֵס לַכֹּל וּמֵטִיב לַכֹּל
וּמֵכִין מָזוֹן לְכָל בְּרִיּוֹתָיו אֲשֶׁר בָּרָא.
בָּרוּךְ אַתָּה יהוה, הַזָּן אֶת הַכֹּל.

ברכת הארץ

נוֹדֶה לְךָ, יהוה אֱלֹהֵינוּ
עַל שֶׁהִנְחַלְתָּ לַאֲבוֹתֵינוּ אֶרֶץ חֶמְדָּה טוֹבָה וּרְחָבָה
וְעַל שֶׁהוֹצֵאתָנוּ יהוה אֱלֹהֵינוּ מֵאֶרֶץ מִצְרַיִם
וּפְדִיתָנוּ מִבֵּית עֲבָדִים
וְעַל בְּרִיתְךָ שֶׁחָתַמְתָּ בִּבְשָׂרֵנוּ
וְעַל תּוֹרָתְךָ שֶׁלִּמַּדְתָּנוּ
וְעַל חֻקֶּיךָ שֶׁהוֹדַעְתָּנוּ
וְעַל חַיִּים חֵן וָחֶסֶד שֶׁחוֹנַנְתָּנוּ
וְעַל אֲכִילַת מָזוֹן שָׁאַתָּה זָן וּמְפַרְנֵס אוֹתָנוּ תָּמִיד
בְּכָל יוֹם וּבְכָל עֵת וּבְכָל שָׁעָה.

נוֹדֶה *We thank.* After thanking God for the land, the paragraph goes on to
add thanks for God's other kindnesses to Israel: the exodus from Egypt,

וְעַל הַכֹּל For all this, LORD our God,
we thank and bless You.
May Your name be blessed continually
by the mouth of all that lives, for ever and all time –
for so it is written:
"You will eat and be satisfied,   *Deut. 8*
then you shall bless the LORD your God
for the good land He has given you."
Blessed are You, LORD,
for the land and for the food.

BLESSING FOR JERUSALEM

רַחֵם נָא Have compassion, please,
LORD our God,
on Israel Your people,
on Jerusalem Your city,
on Zion the dwelling place of Your glory,
on the royal house of David Your anointed,
and on the great and holy House that bears Your name.
Our God, our Father,
tend us, feed us,
sustain us and support us,
relieve us and send us relief,
LORD our God,
swiftly from all our troubles.
Please, LORD our God,
do not make us dependent
on the gifts or loans of other people,
but only on Your full, open, holy and generous hand
so that we may suffer neither shame nor humiliation
for ever and all time.

וְעַל הַכֹּל, יהוה אֱלֹהֵינוּ
אֲנַחְנוּ מוֹדִים לָךְ וּמְבָרְכִים אוֹתָךְ
יִתְבָּרַךְ שִׁמְךָ בְּפִי כָל חַי תָּמִיד לְעוֹלָם וָעֶד
כַּכָּתוּב:

דברים ח

וְאָכַלְתָּ וְשָׂבָעְתָּ, וּבֵרַכְתָּ אֶת־יהוה אֱלֹהֶיךָ
עַל־הָאָרֶץ הַטֹּבָה אֲשֶׁר נָתַן־לָךְ:
בָּרוּךְ אַתָּה יהוה
עַל הָאָרֶץ וְעַל הַמָּזוֹן.

ברכת ירושלים

רַחֵם נָא, יהוה אֱלֹהֵינוּ
עַל יִשְׂרָאֵל עַמֶּךָ
וְעַל יְרוּשָׁלַיִם עִירֶךָ
וְעַל צִיּוֹן מִשְׁכַּן כְּבוֹדֶךָ
וְעַל מַלְכוּת בֵּית דָּוִד מְשִׁיחֶךָ
וְעַל הַבַּיִת הַגָּדוֹל וְהַקָּדוֹשׁ שֶׁנִּקְרָא שִׁמְךָ עָלָיו.
אֱלֹהֵינוּ, אָבִינוּ
רְעֵנוּ, זוּנֵנוּ, פַּרְנְסֵנוּ וְכַלְכְּלֵנוּ
וְהַרְוִיחֵנוּ, וְהַרְוַח לָנוּ יהוה אֱלֹהֵינוּ מְהֵרָה מִכָּל צָרוֹתֵינוּ.
וְנָא אַל תַּצְרִיכֵנוּ, יהוה אֱלֹהֵינוּ
לֹא לִידֵי מַתְּנַת בָּשָׂר וָדָם
וְלֹא לִידֵי הַלְוָאָתָם
כִּי אִם לְיָדְךָ הַמְּלֵאָה, הַפְּתוּחָה, הַקְּדוֹשָׁה וְהָרְחָבָה
שֶׁלֹּא נֵבוֹשׁ וְלֹא נִכָּלֵם לְעוֹלָם וָעֶד.

On Shabbat, say:

רְצֵה Favor and strengthen us, LORD our God,
through Your commandments,
especially through the commandment of the seventh day,
this great and holy Sabbath.
For it is, for You, a great and holy day.
On it we cease work and rest in love
in accord with Your will's commandment.
May it be Your will, LORD our God,
to grant us rest without distress,
grief, or lament on our day of rest.
May You show us the consolation of Zion Your city,
and the rebuilding of Jerusalem Your holy city,
for You are the Master of salvation and consolation.

אֱלֹהֵֽינוּ Our God and God of our ancestors,
may there rise, come, reach, appear, be favored, heard, regarded
and remembered before You,
our recollection and remembrance,
as well as the remembrance of our ancestors,
and of the Messiah son of David Your servant,
and of Jerusalem Your holy city,
and of all Your people the house of Israel –
for deliverance and well-being,
grace, loving-kindness and compassion,
life and peace, on this day of
the Festival of Shavuot.
On it remember us, LORD our God, for good;
recollect us for blessing,
and deliver us for life.
In accord with Your promise of salvation and compassion,
spare us and be gracious to us;
have compassion on us and deliver us,
for our eyes are turned to You because You are God,
gracious and compassionate.

On שבת, say:

רְצֵה וְהַחֲלִיצֵנוּ, יהוה אֱלֹהֵינוּ, בְּמִצְוֹתֶיךָ
וּבְמִצְוַת יוֹם הַשְּׁבִיעִי הַשַּׁבָּת הַגָּדוֹל וְהַקָּדוֹשׁ הַזֶּה
כִּי יוֹם זֶה גָּדוֹל וְקָדוֹשׁ הוּא לְפָנֶיךָ
לִשְׁבָּת בּוֹ, וְלָנוּחַ בּוֹ בְּאַהֲבָה כְּמִצְוַת רְצוֹנֶךָ
וּבִרְצוֹנְךָ הָנִיחַ לָנוּ, יהוה אֱלֹהֵינוּ
שֶׁלֹּא תְהֵא צָרָה וְיָגוֹן וַאֲנָחָה בְּיוֹם מְנוּחָתֵנוּ
וְהַרְאֵנוּ, יהוה אֱלֹהֵינוּ, בְּנֶחָמַת צִיּוֹן עִירֶךָ
וּבְבִנְיַן יְרוּשָׁלַיִם עִיר קָדְשֶׁךָ
כִּי אַתָּה הוּא בַּעַל הַיְשׁוּעוֹת וּבַעַל הַנֶּחָמוֹת.

אֱלֹהֵינוּ וֵאלֹהֵי אֲבוֹתֵינוּ
יַעֲלֶה וְיָבוֹא וְיַגִּיעַ, וְיֵרָאֶה וְיֵרָצֶה וְיִשָּׁמַע
וְיִפָּקֵד וְיִזָּכֵר זִכְרוֹנֵנוּ וּפִקְדוֹנֵנוּ
וְזִכְרוֹן אֲבוֹתֵינוּ
וְזִכְרוֹן מָשִׁיחַ בֶּן דָּוִד עַבְדֶּךָ
וְזִכְרוֹן יְרוּשָׁלַיִם עִיר קָדְשֶׁךָ
וְזִכְרוֹן כָּל עַמְּךָ בֵּית יִשְׂרָאֵל
לְפָנֶיךָ, לִפְלֵיטָה לְטוֹבָה, לְחֵן וּלְחֶסֶד וּלְרַחֲמִים
לְחַיִּים וּלְשָׁלוֹם
בְּיוֹם חַג הַשָּׁבוּעוֹת הַזֶּה.
זָכְרֵנוּ יהוה אֱלֹהֵינוּ בּוֹ לְטוֹבָה
וּפָקְדֵנוּ בוֹ לִבְרָכָה
וְהוֹשִׁיעֵנוּ בוֹ לְחַיִּים.
וּבִדְבַר יְשׁוּעָה וְרַחֲמִים, חוּס וְחָנֵּנוּ וְרַחֵם עָלֵינוּ, וְהוֹשִׁיעֵנוּ
כִּי אֵלֶיךָ עֵינֵינוּ, כִּי אֵל חַנּוּן וְרַחוּם אָתָּה.

וּבְנֵה And may Jerusalem the holy city be rebuilt soon, in our time.
Blessed are You, LORD, who in His compassion
will rebuild Jerusalem. Amen.

BLESSING OF GOD'S GOODNESS

בָּרוּךְ Blessed are You, LORD our God, King of the Universe –
God our Father, our King, our Sovereign,
our Creator, our Redeemer, our Maker,
our Holy One, the Holy One of Jacob.
He is our Shepherd, Israel's Shepherd,
the good King who does good to all.
Every day He has done, is doing, and will do good to us.
He has acted, is acting,
and will always act kindly toward us for ever,
granting us grace, kindness and compassion,
relief and rescue,
prosperity, blessing, redemption and comfort,
sustenance and support, compassion, life,
peace and all good things,
and of all good things may He never let us lack.

בָּרוּךְ *Blessed.* A later addition, dated by the Talmud (*Berakhot* 48b) to
the period following the Bar Kokhba rebellion when, after a long delay,
the Romans gave permission to the Jews to bury their dead. The failure
of the Bar Kokhba rebellion was one of the low points of Jewish history.
According to the Roman historian Dio, 580,000 Jews died in the fighting
and many others by starvation. Nine hundred and eighty-five towns, villages and settlements were destroyed. Jerusalem was leveled to the ground
and rebuilt as a Roman city, Aelia Capitolina. The fact that the sages were
able to salvage a fragment of consolation from the fact that the dead were
not denied the dignity of burial is testimony to an extraordinary ability to
survive catastrophe and preserve the lineaments of hope. The passage is
built around threefold references to God's kingship, goodness and bestowal
of kindness.

וּבְנֵה יְרוּשָׁלַיִם עִיר הַקֹּדֶשׁ בִּמְהֵרָה בְיָמֵינוּ.
בָּרוּךְ אַתָּה יהוה, בּוֹנֵה בְרַחֲמָיו יְרוּשָׁלָיִם, אָמֵן.

ברכת הטוב והמטיב

בָּרוּךְ אַתָּה יהוה אֱלֹהֵינוּ מֶלֶךְ הָעוֹלָם
הָאֵל אָבִינוּ, מַלְכֵּנוּ, אַדִּירֵנוּ
בּוֹרְאֵנוּ, גּוֹאֲלֵנוּ, יוֹצְרֵנוּ, קְדוֹשֵׁנוּ, קְדוֹשׁ יַעֲקֹב
רוֹעֵנוּ, רוֹעֵה יִשְׂרָאֵל, הַמֶּלֶךְ הַטּוֹב וְהַמֵּטִיב לַכֹּל
שֶׁבְּכָל יוֹם וָיוֹם
הוּא הֵיטִיב, הוּא מֵיטִיב, הוּא יֵיטִיב לָנוּ
הוּא גְמָלָנוּ, הוּא גוֹמְלֵנוּ, הוּא יִגְמְלֵנוּ לָעַד
לְחֵן וּלְחֶסֶד וּלְרַחֲמִים, וּלְרֶוַח, הַצָּלָה וְהַצְלָחָה
בְּרָכָה וִישׁוּעָה, נֶחָמָה, פַּרְנָסָה וְכַלְכָּלָה
וְרַחֲמִים וְחַיִּים וְשָׁלוֹם וְכָל טוֹב
וּמִכָּל טוּב לְעוֹלָם אַל יְחַסְּרֵנוּ.

וּבְנֵה יְרוּשָׁלַיִם *And may Jerusalem.* The third blessing speaks of Jerusalem, home of God's glory, as well as the Davidic monarchy and the Temple, for the restoration of which we pray. As is often the case in the siddur, Jerusalem is associated with the divine attribute of compassion, reflecting the words of Zechariah: "Therefore, this is what the LORD says: I will return to Jerusalem with compassion, and there My House will be rebuilt" (1:16). According to tradition, the Divine Presence never left Jerusalem, even when the city lay in ruins (*Shemot Raba* 2:2).

בּוֹנֵה בְרַחֲמָיו יְרוּשָׁלָיִם, אָמֵן *Who in His compassion will rebuild Jerusalem. Amen.* the unusual appearance of the word *Amen* in this passage (normally we do not say it after our own blessings) signals that this was originally the end of Grace.

ADDITIONAL REQUESTS

הָרַחֲמָן May the Compassionate One reign over us
    for ever and all time.

May the Compassionate One be blessed
    in heaven and on earth.

May the Compassionate One be praised
    from generation to generation,
    be glorified by us to all eternity,
    and honored among us for ever and all time.

May the Compassionate One
    grant us an honorable livelihood.

May the Compassionate One break the yoke from our neck
    and lead us upright to our land.

May the Compassionate One send us many blessings to this house
    and this table at which we have eaten.

May the Compassionate One send us Elijah the prophet –
    may he be remembered for good –
    to bring us good tidings of salvation and consolation.

May the Compassionate One bless the State of Israel,
    first flowering of our redemption.

May the Compassionate One bless
    the members of Israel's Defense Forces,
    who stand guard over our land.

A guest says:

יְהִי רָצוֹן May it be Your will that the master of this house shall not suffer shame in this world, nor humiliation in the World to Come. May all he owns prosper greatly, and may his and our possessions be successful and close to hand. Let not the Accuser hold sway over his deeds or ours, and may no thought of sin, iniquity or transgression enter him or us from now and for evermore.

_____

on the hosts and their family. This is immediately preceded by a prayer that Elijah may come and announce the coming of the Messiah. The juxtaposition

בקשות נוספות

הָרַחֲמָן הוּא יִמְלֹךְ עָלֵינוּ לְעוֹלָם וָעֶד.

הָרַחֲמָן הוּא יִתְבָּרַךְ בַּשָּׁמַיִם וּבָאָרֶץ.

הָרַחֲמָן הוּא יִשְׁתַּבַּח לְדוֹר דּוֹרִים

וְיִתְפָּאַר בָּנוּ לָעַד וּלְנֵצַח נְצָחִים

וְיִתְהַדַּר בָּנוּ לָעַד וּלְעוֹלְמֵי עוֹלָמִים.

הָרַחֲמָן הוּא יְפַרְנְסֵנוּ בְּכָבוֹד.

הָרַחֲמָן הוּא יִשְׁבֹּר עֻלֵּנוּ מֵעַל צַוָּארֵנוּ

וְהוּא יוֹלִיכֵנוּ קוֹמְמִיּוּת לְאַרְצֵנוּ.

הָרַחֲמָן הוּא יִשְׁלַח לָנוּ בְּרָכָה מְרֻבָּה בַּבַּיִת הַזֶּה

וְעַל שֻׁלְחָן זֶה שֶׁאָכַלְנוּ עָלָיו.

הָרַחֲמָן הוּא יִשְׁלַח לָנוּ אֶת אֵלִיָּהוּ הַנָּבִיא זָכוּר לַטּוֹב

וִיבַשֶּׂר לָנוּ בְּשׂוֹרוֹת טוֹבוֹת יְשׁוּעוֹת וְנֶחָמוֹת.

הָרַחֲמָן הוּא יְבָרֵךְ אֶת מְדִינַת יִשְׂרָאֵל

רֵאשִׁית צְמִיחַת גְּאֻלָּתֵנוּ.

הָרַחֲמָן הוּא יְבָרֵךְ אֶת חַיָּלֵי צְבָא הַהֲגַנָּה לְיִשְׂרָאֵל

הָעוֹמְדִים עַל מִשְׁמַר אַרְצֵנוּ.

A guest says:

יְהִי רָצוֹן שֶׁלֹּא יֵבוֹשׁ בַּעַל הַבַּיִת בָּעוֹלָם הַזֶּה, וְלֹא יִכָּלֵם לְעוֹלָם
הַבָּא, וְיִצְלַח מְאֹד בְּכָל נְכָסָיו, וְיִהְיוּ נְכָסָיו וּנְכָסֵינוּ מֻצְלָחִים וּקְרוֹבִים
לָעִיר, וְאַל יִשְׁלֹט שָׂטָן שַׁטָן לֹא בְּמַעֲשֵׂה יָדָיו וְלֹא בְּמַעֲשֵׂה יָדֵינוּ. וְאַל
יִזְדַּקֵּר לֹא לְפָנָיו וְלֹא לְפָנֵינוּ שׁוּם דְּבַר הִרְהוּר חֵטְא, עֲבֵרָה וְעָוֹן,
מֵעַתָּה וְעַד עוֹלָם.

הָרַחֲמָן *May the Compassionate One.* A series of additional prayers, dating from
the Geonic period. The oldest is the one in which a guest invokes blessings

הָרַחֲמָן May the Compassionate One bless –

> *When eating at one's own table, say (include the words in parentheses that apply):*
> me, (my wife/husband, / my father, my teacher / my mother,
> my teacher/ my children,) and all that is mine,

> *A guest at someone else's table says (include the words in parentheses that apply):*
> the master of this house, him (and his wife,
> the mistress of this house / and his children,) and all that is his,

> *Children at their parents' table say (include the words in parentheses that apply):*
> my father, my teacher, (master of this house,) and my mother,
> my teacher, (mistress of this house,) them, their household,
> their children, and all that is theirs.

> *For all other guests, add:*
> and all the diners here,

together with us and all that is ours.
Just as our forefathers
Abraham, Isaac and Jacob were blessed in all, from all, with all,
so may He bless all of us together with a complete blessing,
and let us say: Amen.

בַּמָּרוֹם On high, may grace be invoked for them and for us,
as a safeguard of peace.
May we receive a blessing from the Lord
and a just reward from the God of our salvation,
and may we find grace
and good favor in the eyes of God and man.

On Shabbat: May the Compassionate One let us inherit the time,
  that will be entirely Shabbat and rest for life everlasting.

May the Compassionate One let us inherit the day,
that is all good.

_____

guests would begin to thank them, Abraham would reply, "Thank the One
from whom all we have enjoyed has come" (*Sota* 10b).

הָרַחֲמָן הוּא יְבָרֵךְ

When eating at one's own table, say (include the words in parentheses that apply):

אוֹתִי (וְאֶת אִשְׁתִּי / וְאֶת בַּעְלִי / וְאֶת אָבִי מוֹרִי / וְאֶת אִמִּי מוֹרָתִי / וְאֶת זַרְעִי) וְאֶת כָּל אֲשֶׁר לִי.

A guest at someone else's table says (include the words in parentheses that apply):

אֶת בַּעַל הַבַּיִת הַזֶּה, אוֹתוֹ (וְאֶת אִשְׁתּוֹ בַּעֲלַת הַבַּיִת הַזֶּה / וְאֶת זַרְעוֹ) וְאֶת כָּל אֲשֶׁר לוֹ.

Children at their parents' table say (include the words in parentheses that apply):

אֶת אָבִי מוֹרִי (בַּעַל הַבַּיִת הַזֶּה), וְאֶת אִמִּי מוֹרָתִי (בַּעֲלַת הַבַּיִת הַזֶּה), אוֹתָם וְאֶת בֵּיתָם וְאֶת זַרְעָם וְאֶת כָּל אֲשֶׁר לָהֶם

For all other guests, add:

וְאֶת כָּל הַמְסֻבִּין כָּאן

אוֹתָנוּ וְאֶת כָּל אֲשֶׁר לָנוּ, כְּמוֹ שֶׁנִּתְבָּרְכוּ אֲבוֹתֵינוּ אַבְרָהָם יִצְחָק וְיַעֲקֹב, בַּכֹּל, מִכֹּל, כֹּל, כֵּן יְבָרֵךְ אוֹתָנוּ כֻּלָּנוּ יַחַד בִּבְרָכָה שְׁלֵמָה, וְנֹאמַר אָמֵן.

בַּמָּרוֹם יְלַמְּדוּ עֲלֵיהֶם וְעָלֵינוּ זְכוּת שֶׁתְּהֵא לְמִשְׁמֶרֶת שָׁלוֹם וְנִשָּׂא בְרָכָה מֵאֵת יהוה וּצְדָקָה מֵאֱלֹהֵי יִשְׁעֵנוּ וְנִמְצָא חֵן וְשֵׂכֶל טוֹב בְּעֵינֵי אֱלֹהִים וְאָדָם.

בשבת: הָרַחֲמָן הוּא יַנְחִילֵנוּ יוֹם שֶׁכֻּלּוֹ שַׁבָּת וּמְנוּחָה לְחַיֵּי הָעוֹלָמִים.

הָרַחֲמָן הוּא יַנְחִילֵנוּ יוֹם שֶׁכֻּלּוֹ טוֹב.

is striking: we bring redemption by acts of hospitality. This, according to the sages, is how Abraham and Sarah brought monotheism to the world. They would provide hospitality to strangers. When the meal was over, and the

הָרַחֲמָן May the Compassionate One make us worthy
of the Messianic Age and life in the World to Come.
He is a tower of salvation to His king,   *II Sam. 22*
showing kindness to His anointed,
to David and his descendants for ever.
He who makes peace in His high places,
may He make peace for us and all Israel,
and let us say: Amen.

יִרְאוּ Fear the Lord, you His holy ones;   *Ps. 34*
those who fear Him lack nothing.
Young lions may grow weak and hungry,
but those who seek the Lord lack no good thing.
Thank the Lord for He is good;   *Ps. 118*
His loving-kindness is for ever.
You open Your hand,   *Ps. 145*
and satisfy every living thing with favor.
Blessed is the person who trusts in the Lord,   *Jer. 17*
whose trust is in the Lord alone.
Once I was young, and now I am old,   *Ps. 37*
yet I have never watched a righteous man forsaken
or his children begging for bread.
The Lord will give His people strength.   *Ps. 29*
The Lord will bless His people with peace.

---

forsaken or his children forced to search for bread, I never merely stood and
watched." Understood thus, it is a warning against being a mere bystander
while other people suffer. It thus brings the Grace to a symmetrical close:
It began by speaking of God's goodness in feeding the hungry and ends
with an injunction for us to do likewise. This too is part of "walking in
God's ways."

הָרַחֲמָן הוּא יְזַכֵּנוּ לִימוֹת הַמָּשִׁיחַ וּלְחַיֵּי הָעוֹלָם הַבָּא

שמואל ב׳ כב

מִגְדּוֹל יְשׁוּעוֹת מַלְכּוֹ

וְעֹשֶׂה־חֶסֶד לִמְשִׁיחוֹ, לְדָוִד וּלְזַרְעוֹ עַד־עוֹלָם:

עֹשֶׂה שָׁלוֹם בִּמְרוֹמָיו

הוּא יַעֲשֶׂה שָׁלוֹם עָלֵינוּ וְעַל כָּל יִשְׂרָאֵל

וְאִמְרוּ אָמֵן.

תהלים לד

יְראוּ אֶת־יהוה קְדֹשָׁיו, כִּי־אֵין מַחְסוֹר לִירֵאָיו:

כְּפִירִים רָשׁוּ וְרָעֵבוּ, וְדֹרְשֵׁי יהוה לֹא־יַחְסְרוּ כָל־טוֹב:

תהלים קיח

הוֹדוּ לַיהוה כִּי־טוֹב, כִּי לְעוֹלָם חַסְדּוֹ:

תהלים קמה

פּוֹתֵחַ אֶת־יָדֶךָ, וּמַשְׂבִּיעַ לְכָל־חַי רָצוֹן:

ירמיה יז

בָּרוּךְ הַגֶּבֶר אֲשֶׁר יִבְטַח בַּיהוה, וְהָיָה יהוה מִבְטַחוֹ:

תהלים לו

נַעַר הָיִיתִי גַּם־זָקַנְתִּי

וְלֹא־רָאִיתִי צַדִּיק נֶעֱזָב וְזַרְעוֹ מְבַקֶּשׁ־לָחֶם:

תהלים כט

יהוה עֹז לְעַמּוֹ יִתֵּן, יהוה יְבָרֵךְ אֶת־עַמּוֹ בַשָּׁלוֹם:

נַעַר הָיִיתִי *Once I was young.* The standard translation of this verse (Psalm 37:25) is "I was young and now am old and I have not seen the righteous forsaken or his children searching for bread." I have translated it here according to a fine insight, author unknown, suggesting that the verb *ra'iti* should be understood in the sense in which it appears in the book of Esther, when Esther, pleading on behalf of Jewry, says: "For how can I watch the evil that shall come unto my people? Or how can I watch the destruction of my kindred?" (8:6). The verb there means "stand as a passive witness to." Taken in this sense, Psalm 37:25 should be understood as, "When the righteous was

BLESSING AFTER FOOD – AL HAMIḤYA

Grace after eating from the "seven species" of produce with which Israel is blessed:
food made from the five grains (but not bread); wine or grape
juice; grapes, figs, pomegranates, olives, or dates.

בָּרוּךְ Blessed are You, LORD our God, King of the Universe,

After grain products *(but not bread):*	*After wine or grape juice:*	*After grapes, figs, olives,* *pomegranates or dates:*
for the nourishment and sustenance,	for the vine and the fruit of the vine,	for the tree and the fruit of the tree,

After grain products (but not bread), and wine or grape juice:
for the nourishment and sustenance
and for the vine and the fruit of the vine,

and for the produce of the field;
for the desirable, good and spacious land
that You willingly gave as heritage to our ancestors,
that they might eat of its fruit
and be satisfied with its goodness.
Have compassion, please, LORD our God,
on Israel Your people,
on Jerusalem, Your city,
on Zion the home of Your glory,
on Your altar and Your Temple.
May You rebuild Jerusalem, the holy city swiftly in our time,
and may You bring us back there, rejoicing in its rebuilding,
eating from its fruit, satisfied by its goodness,
and blessing You for it in holiness and purity.

On Shabbat: Be pleased to refresh us on this Sabbath Day.

Israel is praised in the Torah (Deut. 8:8) other than bread or matza, namely:
(1) food made from wheat, barley, rye, oats or spelt; (2) grape wine or juice;
or (3) grapes, figs, pomegranates, olives or dates.

ברכה מעין שלוש

Grace after eating from the "seven species" of produce with which Israel is blessed:
food made from the five grains (but not bread); wine or grape
juice; grapes, figs, pomegranates, olives, or dates.

בָּרוּךְ אַתָּה יהוה אֱלֹהֵינוּ מֶלֶךְ הָעוֹלָם, עַל

After grapes, figs, olives,		
pomegranates or dates:	*After wine or grape juice:*	*After grain products*
		(but not bread):
הָעֵץ וְעַל פְּרִי הָעֵץ	הַגֶּפֶן וְעַל פְּרִי הַגֶּפֶן	הַמִּחְיָה וְעַל הַכַּלְכָּלָה

After grain products (but not bread), and wine or grape juice:

הַמִּחְיָה וְעַל הַכַּלְכָּלָה וְעַל הַגֶּפֶן וְעַל פְּרִי הַגֶּפֶן

וְעַל תְּנוּבַת הַשָּׂדֶה וְעַל אֶרֶץ חֶמְדָּה טוֹבָה וּרְחָבָה
שֶׁרָצִיתָ וְהִנְחַלְתָּ לַאֲבוֹתֵינוּ
לֶאֱכֹל מִפִּרְיָהּ וְלִשְׂבֹּעַ מִטּוּבָהּ.
רַחֶם נָא יהוה אֱלֹהֵינוּ
עַל יִשְׂרָאֵל עַמֶּךָ וְעַל יְרוּשָׁלַיִם עִירֶךָ
וְעַל צִיּוֹן מִשְׁכַּן כְּבוֹדֶךָ וְעַל מִזְבַּחֶךָ וְעַל הֵיכָלֶךָ.
וּבְנֵה יְרוּשָׁלַיִם עִיר הַקֹּדֶשׁ בִּמְהֵרָה בְיָמֵינוּ
וְהַעֲלֵנוּ לְתוֹכָהּ וְשַׂמְּחֵנוּ בְּבִנְיָנָהּ
וְנֹאכַל מִפִּרְיָהּ וְנִשְׂבַּע מִטּוּבָהּ
וּנְבָרֶכְךָ עָלֶיהָ בִּקְדֻשָּׁה וּבְטָהֳרָה.

בשבת: וּרְצֵה וְהַחֲלִיצֵנוּ בְּיוֹם הַשַּׁבָּת הַזֶּה

עַל הַמִּחְיָה *A blessing after other food or drink.* Known as the "three-in-one" blessing, this prayer summarizes the first three paragraphs of the Grace after Meals. It is said after consuming any of the "seven kinds" of produce for which

Grant us joy on this Festival of Shavuot.
For You, God, are good and do good to all
and we thank You for the land

After grain products (but not bread):	*After wine or grape juice:*	*After grapes, figs, olives, pomegranates or dates:*
and for the nourishment. Blessed are You, LORD, for the land and for the nourishment.	and for the fruit of the vine.* Blessed are You, LORD, for the land and for the fruit of the vine.*	and for the fruit.** Blessed are You, LORD, for the land and for the fruit.**

After grain products (but not bread), and wine or grape juice:
and for the nourishment and for the fruit of the vine.*
Blessed are You, LORD, for the land and for the nourishment
and the fruit of the vine.*

* If the wine is from Israel, then substitute "her vine" for "the vine."
** If the fruit is from Israel, then substitute "her fruit" for "the fruit."

BLESSING AFTER FOOD – BOREH NEFASHOT

*After food or drink that does not require Birkat HaMazon or
Al HaMiḥya – such as meat, fish, dairy products, vegetables, beverages,
or fruit other than grapes, figs, pomegranates, olives or dates – say:*

בָּרוּךְ Blessed are You, LORD our God, King of the Universe,
who creates the many forms of life and their needs.
For all You have created
to sustain the life of all that lives,
blessed be He, Giver of life to the worlds.

וְשַׂמְּחֵנוּ בְּיוֹם חַג הַשָּׁבוּעוֹת הַזֶּה.
כִּי אַתָּה יהוה טוֹב וּמֵטִיב לַכֹּל, וְנוֹדֶה לְךָ עַל הָאָרֶץ

After grapes, figs, olives, pomegranates or dates:	After wine or grape juice:	After grain products (but not bread):
*וְעַל הַפֵּרוֹת.**	*וְעַל פְּרִי הַגָּפֶן.*	וְעַל הַמִּחְיָה.
בָּרוּךְ אַתָּה יהוה עַל הָאָרֶץ וְעַל הַפֵּרוֹת.**	בָּרוּךְ אַתָּה יהוה עַל הָאָרֶץ וְעַל פְּרִי הַגָּפֶן.*	בָּרוּךְ אַתָּה יהוה עַל הָאָרֶץ וְעַל הַמִּחְיָה.

After grain products (but not bread), and wine or grape juice:

וְעַל הַמִּחְיָה וְעַל פְּרִי הַגָּפֶן.*
בָּרוּךְ אַתָּה יהוה, עַל הָאָרֶץ וְעַל הַמִּחְיָה וְעַל פְּרִי הַגָּפֶן.*

*If the wine is from ארץ ישראל, then substitute גְפֶנָהּ for הַגָּפֶן.
**If the fruit is from ארץ ישראל, then substitute פֵּרוֹתֶיהָ for הַפֵּרוֹת.

בורא נפשות

or ברכת המזון — After food or drink that does not require
מעין שלוש – such as meat, fish, dairy products, vegetables, beverages,
or fruit other than grapes, figs, pomegranates, olives or dates – say:

בָּרוּךְ אַתָּה יהוה אֱלֹהֵינוּ מֶלֶךְ הָעוֹלָם
בּוֹרֵא נְפָשׁוֹת רַבּוֹת וְחֶסְרוֹנָן
עַל כָּל מַה שֶּׁבָּרָאתָ
לְהַחֲיוֹת בָּהֶם נֶפֶשׁ כָּל חָי.
בָּרוּךְ חֵי הָעוֹלָמִים.

תיקון ליל שבועות

TIKKUN LEIL SHAVUOT

•

מעמד הר סיני לפי מסכת שבת

THE REVELATION AT MOUNT SINAI
TRACTATE SHABBAT

TIKKUN LEIL SHAVUOT

The first reference to a *Tikkun Leil Shavuot*, the custom of staying awake all night on Shavuot, studying or reciting passages from the Torah, is found in the *Zohar*, one of the foundational texts of Jewish mysticism. The *Zohar* sees the revelation at Mount Sinai as the marriage between God and His people. The Counting of the Omer, the seven weeks between Pesaḥ and Shavuot, were thus, for the nation as a whole, like the seven "clean days" a woman must count before immersion in the *mikveh*. The people, defiled by their experiences in Egypt, had to undergo seven-times-seven days of purification before they could be united with God. The evening of Shavuot is thus like the night before the wedding, and the friends of the bride stay with her all night to make sure that she is fully adorned and ready for the momentous day (*Zohar, Emor*, 97b–98a).

R. Moses de Leon (c.1250–1305) writes that it was the custom of pious individuals to spend the entire night reading from the Torah, the Prophets and the Writings, and from there to move on to passages from the Talmud and Midrash and the mystical literature until the light of day (*Sod Ḥag HaShavuot*). A later kabbalist, R. Isaac HaAzovi, laid special emphasis on spending the night studying the Oral Torah, "and in the daytime will come the acceptance of the Written Torah, so that he is then crowned with both" (*Agudat Ezov*).

The most dramatic account of a study session on the night of Shavuot was given by R. Shlomo Alkabetz, a sixteenth-century mystic and composer of the poem we sing on Friday night, *Lekha Dodi*. In Adrianople, around 1530, on the first night of Shavuot, he was studying through the night with R. Joseph Karo, author of the *Shulḥan Arukh*, when he heard a divine voice, identifying itself as the spirit of the Mishna, coming from Karo's mouth. Karo was known to have intense mystical experiences during which he felt himself addressed by a celestial spirit that he called the *Maggid*. He noted down these experiences, extending over fifty years, in a book called *Maggid Meisharim* (Preacher of Uprightness). On this night the spirit, speaking through Karo, commended the two men on their study, and then urged them to make *aliya* to the land of Israel, which they both eventually did, settling in Safed, at that time the center of Jewish mysticism.

◄ Once

Once Karo and Alkabetz had arrived in the town and news of their mystical encounter spread, the custom was taken up throughout Safed, by then a major focus of Jewish life in the Holy Land. R. Abraham Galanti records that all the congregations would gather on the night of Shavuot and study Torah until dawn when they would go to the *mikveh* and then pray. One significant factor was the endorsement of the custom by the leader of the Safed mystics, R. Isaac Luria, who wrote that whoever stays up on the night of Shavuot, studying Torah without a moment's sleep, will live out the rest of the year without harm (*The Gate of Intentions*, Shavuot, ch. 1, 89a).

Around 1620, R. Isaiah Horowitz, in his *Shenei Luḥot HaBerit*, could write that the custom had been adopted "in all of the land of Israel; in the entire kingdom, no one is left out from the great to the small," adding that "on this night of Shavuot, sleep should be denied from anyone who wants to cling to holiness." From Israel it spread to Europe, so that several decades later, in Poland, R. Abraham Gombiner (*Magen Avraham*) could report that scholars did so, and by the beginning of the eighteenth century, according to R. Yaakov Reischer, it had been adopted by the general community.

The early accounts of the practice were deeply mystical, based on the idea central to Jewish mysticism of the union of God-as-He-is-in-Himself and the *Shekhina*, the Divine Presence that lives in the midst of the Jewish people. *Tikkun* in this sense means healing the spiritual rift between these two aspects of the Divine Being. R. Gombiner, however, added a different kind of explanation. There is a midrash, based on a phrase in Isaiah (50:2), "When I came, why was there no one?" that suggests that when God came on the morning of Shavuot to give the Torah to the Israelites, He found them asleep! That is why the Torah states that "On the morning of the third day there was thunder and lightning... and a very loud trumpet blast" – to wake the people who had overslept. Only then did Moses "lead the people out of the camp to meet with God" (Ex. 19:16–17; *Shir HaShirim Raba*, 1; *Magen Avraham* 494:1). In this sense, *Tikkun* means putting right a wrong in the past, an act of moral reparation.

R. Gombiner's explanation, critical as it was of the Israelites' behavior on the great day, was not universally accepted. R. Levi Yitzḥak of Berdichev, known as one of the most passionate defenders of the Jewish

◄ people

people, argued that the Israelites slept that night for the best possible reason. Exhausted after several days of preparation, they wanted to be in a state of maximum alertness the next day to receive the divine word (cited by R. Israel Hopstein, the Maggid of Koznitz, in his *Avodat Yisrael*). R. Pinhas HaLevi Horowitz (in *Panim Yafot*) added a further ingenious defense. The Israelites had been commanded to "be ready the next morning" (Ex. 19:16). Until the giving of the Torah, morning had been defined as sunrise. Only with the giving of the Torah and the accompanying Oral Tradition did the Israelites learn that it began at dawn. They were late not through any fault of their own but because they did not yet know the Torah's definition of times.

Rabbi Yerahmiel Danziger, the Rebbe of Aleksander, in his *Yismah Yisrael*, offered a quite different line of interpretation. It was God Himself who caused the people to fall into a sleep. Had they remained awake the whole of the previous night, they might have thought that they were being given the Torah because of their exhaustive preparations: their seven-week purification and their all-night vigil. Instead God wanted the people to receive the Torah unprepared, so that they would know that He had given it as an act of pure divine grace. All the preparations in the world are insufficient to merit God's greatest gift. Instead we must have the humility to see it as a gift.

R. Hayyim Palachi, in his *Mo'ed leKhol Hai*, argued that the *Tikkun* was not an act of atonement for the past but rather an admission that we have not reached the spiritual heights of our ancestors. They did not need an all-night preparation; we do.

Interestingly, already in the twelfth century Ibn Ezra had argued in his Torah commentary (to Ex. 19:11), that the Israelites were in fact told by Moses to stay awake all night. That is what God meant when He said to Moses, "Be sure they are ready for the third day." Ibn Ezra relates this to the rule that, on Yom Kippur the High Priest stayed up all night (Mishna, *Yoma* 1:7). Indeed this may well be one of the subterranean streams of influence on the custom of the Shavuot *Tikkun*. Prior to the revelation at Mount Sinai, God told Moses to tell the people the terms of the covenant He was proposing, which would charge them with the mission of becoming "a kingdom of priests and a holy nation" (Ex. 19:6). If the High Priest stayed awake throughout his holiest night, should not each of us

◀ see ourselves

see ourselves as summoned to this height, on the anniversary of our birth as a kingdom of priests?

So there were many tributaries that fed into the river of custom that led to the *Tikkun*, and there were surely others. Unlike Pesaḥ and Sukkot, Shavuot lacks a distinctive mitzva related to the historical experience it commemorates. The *Tikkun* filled that void. Besides, the custom of staying up all night was known on these other festivals also. On Pesaḥ, as we say in the Haggada, there were rabbis who stayed up all night telling the story of the exodus until a student came to tell them it was time for the morning prayers. On Sukkot when the Temple stood there were all-night celebrations – the *Simḥat Beit HaSho'eva* – until the time came to draw water the next morning. The Talmud records the remark that when the Temple stood "we did not see any sleep for our eyes" throughout the festivities (*Sukka* 53a). So the idea of spending the night of the festival dedicated to the primary theme of the festival – on Pesaḥ, telling the exodus story, and on Sukkot, rejoicing – naturally leads to the conclusion that the night of Shavuot should be dedicated to Torah.

What was studied varied from community to community. Many followed fixed texts: the beginning and end of the year's Torah portions, the opening and closing of the Prophetic books and the Writings, passages from the Mishna and Talmud, and from other more mystical texts. Some communities recited *Azharot*, literally "Warnings," summary statements of the 613 commands (see page 731; 768). In some places the emphasis was on communal recitation, in others, private study. In recent years the custom has developed to engage in group study sessions. One of the unforgettable sights of Jerusalem is to see, as the festival night draws to a close, crowds streaming into the courtyard in front of the Western Wall from all parts of the city, to say the morning prayers as the sky is slowly lit by the light of the rising sun, an extraordinary demonstration of a people reborn after the Holocaust.

At the heart of the concept of the *Tikkun* is the tension between two radically opposed Talmudic accounts of the Israelites at the time of the Giving of the Torah. One states that God offered the Torah to all the nations, and none except Israel accepted it (*Avoda Zara* 2b). The other says that at Sinai God lifted the mountain and suspended it over the heads of the people like an inverted barrel, saying, "If you accept the Torah,

◄ excellent

excellent, and if not, there will be your burial" (*Shabbat* 88b). Did Israel choose to be chosen? Or was it chosen almost against its will? If the former, the *Tikkun* celebrates and reenacts. If the latter, the *Tikkun* atones and makes amends.

Both have been true at different times in Jewish history. There were long periods in biblical and post-biblical history when Jews seemed to want to escape from particularity and to be instead "like all the nations." At such times they often neglected or abandoned their religious heritage. Yet for the most part Jews saw the Torah as God's most precious gift, their written constitution as a nation, their intimation of eternity, their marriage contract with Heaven itself. The Torah was at once God's law of life and His letter of love.

To paraphrase Aḥad HaAm, more than the Jewish people kept the Torah, the Torah kept the Jewish people. They carried it, and it carried them. No people has loved or lived a book more. It was and is our life and the length of our days. And on the night before the day on which God embraced a people and betrothed them in a covenant of love, the people themselves declared their love for God and His sacred word, written, as the sages said, in letters of black fire on white fire, inscribed before the universe existed, the deep structure of Creation, the roadmap of Redemption, and the text and subtext of Revelation. When a people's love of God meets God's love of a people, a great *Tikkun* takes place: a healing of the wounds of a fractured world. Such is the faith that still inspires us on the night of Shavuot, for the Torah was given once, but it is received whenever we open our hearts and minds to it, allowing it to speak to us in "the great voice that never ceased" (Deut. 5:19) and that summons us still.

JS

Note to the reader:
The text of tractate *Shabbat* is based upon *The Koren Talmud Bavli*, with commentary by Rabbi Adin Steinsaltz (Even Israel). The direct translation of the Talmudic text appears in bold, while the elucidation and explanatory text by Rabbi Steinsaltz is in the lighter font.

The Revelation at Mount Sinai

In Tractate Shabbat (Perek 9, 86b–89b) the sages have a disscussion relating to the Revelation at Sinai on Shavuot night.

The Sages taught: On the sixth day of the month of Sivan, the Ten Commandments were given to the Jewish people. Rabbi Yose says: On the seventh day of the month. Rava said: Everyone agrees that the Jews came to the Sinai desert on the New Moon, as it is written here: "In the third month after the children of Israel were gone forth out of the land of Egypt, the same day came they into the wilderness of Sinai" (Exodus 19:1), without elaborating what day it was. And it is written there: "This month shall be to you the beginning of months; it shall be the first month of the year to you" (Exodus 12:2). Just as there, the term "this" is referring to the New Moon, so too, here the term is referring to the New Moon. And similarly, everyone agrees that the Torah was given to the Jewish people on Shabbat, as it is written here in the Ten Commandments: "Remember the Shabbat day to keep it holy" (Exodus 20:8), and it is written there: "And Moses said to the people: Remember this day, in which you came out from Egypt, out of the house of bondage, for by strength of hand the LORD brought you out from this place; there shall be no leaven eaten" (Exodus 13:3). Just as there, the mitzva of remembrance was commanded on the very day of the Exodus, so too, here the mitzva of remembrance was commanded on the very day of Shabbat. Where Rabbi Yose and the Sages disagree is with regard to the determination of the month, meaning which day of the week was established as the New Moon. Rabbi Yose held: The New Moon was established on the first day of the week, and on the first day of the week He did not say anything to them due to the weariness caused by the journey. On the second day of the week, He said to them: "And you shall be to Me a kingdom of priests and a holy nation; these are the words that you shall speak to the children of Israel" (Exodus 19:6).

Shabbat 86b

---

refers to the month or the New Moon. It states: "In the third ḥodesh after the children of Israel went forth out of the land of Egypt" (Exodus 19:1). The

מעמד הר סיני

In מסכת שבת (Perek 9, 86b–89b) the sages have a disscussion
relating to the Revelation at Sinai on שבועות night.

שבת פו:

תָּנוּ רַבָּנָן: בְּשִׁשִּׁי בַּחֹדֶשׁ נִיתְּנוּ עֲשֶׂרֶת הַדִּבְּרוֹת לְיִשְׂרָאֵל.
רַבִּי יוֹסֵי אוֹמֵר: בְּשִׁבְעָה בּוֹ.

אָמַר רָבָא: דְּכוּלֵי עָלְמָא – בְּרֹאשׁ חֹדֶשׁ אָתוּ לְמִדְבַּר סִינַי
כְּתִיב הָכָא: "בַּיּוֹם הַזֶּה בָּאוּ מִדְבַּר סִינָי"
וּכְתִיב הָתָם: "הַחֹדֶשׁ הַזֶּה לָכֶם רֹאשׁ חֳדָשִׁים"
מַה לְּהַלָּן – רֹאשׁ חֹדֶשׁ, אַף כָּאן – רֹאשׁ חֹדֶשׁ.
וּדְכוּלֵי עָלְמָא – בְּשַׁבָּת נִיתְּנָה תוֹרָה לְיִשְׂרָאֵל
כְּתִיב הָכָא: "זָכוֹר אֶת יוֹם הַשַּׁבָּת לְקַדְּשׁוֹ"
וּכְתִיב הָתָם: "וַיֹּאמֶר מֹשֶׁה אֶל הָעָם זָכוֹר אֶת הַיּוֹם הַזֶּה"
מַה לְּהַלָּן – בְּעַצּוּמוֹ שֶׁל יוֹם, אַף כָּאן – בְּעַצּוּמוֹ שֶׁל יוֹם.
כִּי פְּלִיגִי – בִּקְבִיעָא דְּיַרְחָא;
רַבִּי יוֹסֵי סָבַר: בְּחַד בְּשַׁבָּא אִיקְּבַע יַרְחָא
וּבְחַד בְּשַׁבָּא לָא אֲמַר לְהוּ וְלָא מִידֵּי –
מִשּׁוּם חוּלְשָׁא דְּאוֹרְחָא.
בִּתְרֵי בְּשַׁבָּא אֲמַר לְהוּ: "וְאַתֶּם תִּהְיוּ לִי מַמְלֶכֶת כֹּהֲנִים"

בַּיּוֹם הַזֶּה *The same day.* The word ḥodesh is understood throughout the Bible to mean month. Occasionally, it is a reference to the New Moon. Examples include: "Tomorrow is the ḥodesh" (I Samuel 20:18); "Its holiday, its ḥodesh, its Shabbat" (Hosea 2:13); and "The burnt-offering of the ḥodesh and its meal-offering" (Numbers 29:6). Therefore, the verse: "This ḥodesh shall be unto you the beginning of months" is understood as indicating that this New Moon is the first New Moon that the Jewish people are celebrating. In the verse describing their arrival in the desert, it is unclear whether ḥodesh

On the third day of the week, God **said to them the mitzva of** *Shabbat*
setting boundaries around Mount Sinai. **On the fourth** day of the *87a*
week, the husbands and wives **separated** from one another. **And the**
Rabbis hold: On the second day **of the week** the **New Moon was**
established, and **on the second** day **of the week** God **did not say**
anything to them due to the weariness caused by **their journey. On**
the third day of the week, God **said to them:** "And you shall be to
Me a kingdom of priests and a holy nation; these are the words that
you shall speak to the children of Israel" (Exodus 19:6). **On the fourth**
day of the week, God **said to them the mitzva of setting boundaries**
around Mount Sinai. **On the fifth** day of the week, the husbands and
wives **separated** from one another. **The Gemara raises an objection:**
Doesn't the verse state: "And the LORD said to Moses: Go to the
people **and sanctify them today and tomorrow** and let them wash
their garments" (Exodus 19:10), indicating that the husbands and
wives were separated for only two days? This is **difficult** according **to**
the opinion of **Rabbi Yose,** who said earlier that the separation was
for three days.

Thursday	5		4	Moses ascended and descended the mountain and commanded the men to separate from their wives
Friday	6		5	
Shabbat	7	Revelation at Sinai	6	Revelation at Sinai

With regard to the command to the men to separate from their wives in
preparation for the revelation, it is written: "And the LORD said to Moses:
Go to the people, and sanctify them today and tomorrow, and let them wash
their garments, and be ready against the third day; for the third day the LORD
will come down in the sight of all the people upon Mount Sinai" (Exodus
19:10–11).According to Rabbi Yose, Moses added an extra day of separation
to the two mentioned in the verse.

בִּתְלָתָא אֲמַר לְהוּ מִצְוַת הַגְבָּלָה
בְּאַרְבָּעָה עֲבוּד פְּרִישָׁה.
וְרַבָּנַן סָבְרִי: בִּתְרֵי בְּשַׁבָּא אִיקְבַּע יַרְחָא
בִּתְרֵי בְּשַׁבָּא לָא אֲמַר לְהוּ וְלָא מִידֵּי –
מִשּׁוּם חוּלְשָׁא דְּאוֹרְחָא
בִּתְלָתָא אֲמַר לְהוּ "וְאַתֶּם תִּהְיוּ לִי".
בְּאַרְבָּעָה אֲמַר לְהוּ מִצְוַת הַגְבָּלָה
בַּחֲמִישִׁי עֲבוּד פְּרִישָׁה.
מֵיתִיבִי: "וְקִדַּשְׁתָּם הַיּוֹם וּמָחָר"
קַשְׁיָא לְרַבִּי יוֹסֵי!

emphasis on the words at the end of the verse, "on this day," proves that it is referring to the day of the New Moon.

THE OPINIONS OF RABBI YOSE AND THE RABBIS
WITH REGARD TO THE REVELATION AT SINAI:

Day of the Week	Date in Sivan: Rabbi Yose		Date in Sivan: The Rabbis
Sunday	1	The New Moon; the nation arrives in Sinai	
Monday	2	Moses ascended and descended the mountain and said: "And you shall be to Me, etc."	1 The New Moon; the nation arrives in Sinai
Tuesday	3	Moses ascended and descended the mountain and commanded the mitzva of setting boundaries	2 Moses ascended and descended the mountain and said: "And you shall be to Me, etc."
Wednesday	4	Moses ascended and descended the mountain and commanded the men to separate from their wives	3 Moses ascended and descended the mountain and commanded the mitzva of setting boundaries

The Gemara answers: **Rabbi Yose** could have **said to you: Moses added one day** to the number of days that God commanded based **on his** own **perception, as it was taught** in a *baraita*: **Moses did three things** based **on his** own **perception, and the Holy One, Blessed be He, agreed with him.** He added one day to the days of separation before the revelation at Sinai based **on his** own **perception. And he** totally **separated from** his **wife** after the revelation at Sinai. **And he broke the tablets** following the sin of the Golden Calf.

The Gemara discusses these cases: **He added one day** based **on his** own **perception. What** source **did he interpret** that led him to do so? He reasoned that since the Holy One, Blessed be He, said: "Sanctify them **today and tomorrow,**" the juxtaposition of the two days teaches that **today** is **like tomorrow; just as tomorrow** the men and women will separate for that day **and** the **night** preceding **it, so too, today** requires separation for the day **and** the **night** preceding **it.** Since God spoke to him in the morning, **and the night of that day** already **passed,** Moses concluded: **Derive from it** that separation must be in effect for **two days besides that day.** Therefore, he extended the mitzva of separation by one day. **And from where do we** derive that **the Holy One, Blessed be He, agreed with his** interpretation? It is derived from the fact that the **Divine Presence did not rest** upon Mount Sinai **until Shabbat morning,** as Moses had determined.

And he totally **separated from** his **wife** after the revelation at Sinai. **What** source **did he interpret** that led him to do so? **He reasoned an** *a fortiori* **inference by himself** and **said: If Israel, with whom**

Divine Presence rested upon him at all times. It is prohibited for others to do so.

הוֹסִיף יוֹם אֶחָד **He added one day.** The question can be raised: If he arrived at this conclusion by expounding upon the command of God, and if all of God's statements were given to Israel for the purpose of expounding upon them, why is this considered to have been based on his own perception? Although God was aware that Moses could arrive at this conclusion and he gave him

אָמַר לְךָ רַבִּי יוֹסֵי: יוֹם אֶחָד הוֹסִיף מֹשֶׁה מִדַּעְתּוֹ

דְּתַנְיָא: שְׁלֹשָׁה דְּבָרִים עָשָׂה מֹשֶׁה מִדַּעְתּוֹ

וְהִסְכִּים הַקָּדוֹשׁ בָּרוּךְ הוּא עִמּוֹ:

הוֹסִיף יוֹם אֶחָד מִדַּעְתּוֹ, וּפֵרֵשׁ מִן הָאִשָּׁה, וְשָׁבַר אֶת הַלּוּחוֹת.

הוֹסִיף יוֹם אֶחָד מִדַּעְתּוֹ.

מַאי דָּרֵישׁ?

"הַיּוֹם וּמָחָר" – הַיּוֹם כְּמָחָר

מַה לְמָחָר – לֵילוֹ עִמּוֹ, אַף הַיּוֹם – לֵילוֹ עִמּוֹ.

וְלֵילָה דְּהָאִידְנָא נָפְקָא לֵיהּ.

שְׁמַע מִינַהּ – תְּרֵי יוֹמֵי לְבַר מֵהָאִידְנָא.

וּמְנָלָן דְּהִסְכִּים הַקָּדוֹשׁ בָּרוּךְ הוּא עַל יָדוֹ –

דְּלָא שָׁרְיָא שְׁכִינָה עַד צַפְרָא דְּשַׁבַּתָּא.

וּפֵרֵשׁ מִן הָאִשָּׁה.

מַאי דָּרֵישׁ?

נָשָׂא קַל וָחוֹמֶר בְּעַצְמוֹ

שְׁלֹשָׁה דְּבָרִים עָשָׂה מֹשֶׁה מִדַּעְתּוֹ Moses did three things based on his own perception. This statement was explained in different ways. Some commentaries suggest that God did not command Moses with regard to these three matters because it was revealed before Him that it was unnecessary. Clearly, a woman will not be impure when discharging semen on the third day, God would not communicate with Moses when he was impure, and the children of Israel would repent. Nevertheless, since it is beyond the purview of man to know the precise parameters of these matters, Moses instituted additional stringencies to ensure that no prohibitions would be violated. He received divine approval for those stringencies (Rabbi Elazar Moshe Horowitz). Rashi explains that Moses was able to take the initiative on these matters only because the

the Divine Presence spoke only one time and God set a specific time for them when the Divine Presence would be revealed, and yet the Torah stated: "Prepare yourselves for three days, do not approach a woman" (Exodus 19:15); I, with whom the Divine Presence speaks all the time and God does not set a specific time for me, all the more so that I must separate from my wife. And from where do we derive that the Holy One, Blessed be He, agreed with him? As it is written after the revelation at Sinai: "Go say to them: Return to your tents" (Deuteronomy 5:26), meaning to your homes and wives. And afterward it is written that God told Moses: "And you, stand here with Me" (Deuteronomy 5:27), indicating that Moses was not allowed to return home, as he must constantly be prepared to receive the word of God. And some say a different source indicating that God agreed with his reasoning. When Aaron and Miriam criticized Moses' separation from his wife, God said: "With him do I speak mouth to mouth, even manifestly, and not in dark speeches; and the similitude of the LORD does he behold; why then were you not afraid to speak against My servant, against Moses?" (Numbers 12:8). This indicates that God agreed with his reasoning.

And he broke the tablets following the sin of the Golden Calf. What source did he interpret that led him to do so? Moses said: With regard to the Paschal lamb, which is only one of six hundred and thirteen mitzvot, the Torah stated: "And the LORD said unto Moses and Aaron: This is the ordinance of the Paschal offering; no alien shall eat of it" (Exodus 12:43), referring not only to gentiles, but to apostate Jews as well. Regarding the tablets, which represented the entire Torah, and Israel at that moment were apostates, as they were worshipping the calf, all the more so are they not worthy of receiving the Torah. And from where do we derive that the Holy One, Blessed be He, agreed with his reasoning? As it is stated: "The first tablets which you broke [asher shibarta]" (Exodus 34:1), and Reish Lakish said: The word asher is an allusion to the phrase: May your strength be true [yishar koḥakha] due to the fact that you broke the tablets.

אָמַר:

וּמַה יִשְׂרָאֵל שֶׁלֹּא דִּבְּרָה שְׁכִינָה עִמָּהֶן אֶלָּא שָׁעָה אַחַת
וְקָבַע לָהֶן זְמַן

אָמְרָה תוֹרָה: "וְהָיוּ נְכֹנִים וְגוֹ' אַל תִּגְּשׁוּ"
אֲנִי שֶׁכָּל שָׁעָה וְשָׁעָה שְׁכִינָה מְדַבֶּרֶת עִמִּי
וְאֵינוּ קוֹבֵעַ לִי זְמַן – עַל אַחַת כַּמָּה וְכַמָּה!
וּמִנַּיִן דְּהִסְכִּים הַקָּדוֹשׁ בָּרוּךְ הוּא עַל יָדוֹ –
דִּכְתִיב: "לֵךְ אֱמֹר לָהֶם שׁוּבוּ לָכֶם לְאָהֳלֵיכֶם"
וּכְתִיב בַּתְרֵיהּ: "וְאַתָּה פֹּה עֲמֹד עִמָּדִי".
וְאִית דְּאָמְרִי: "פֶּה אֶל פֶּה אֲדַבֶּר בּוֹ".

שָׁבַּר אֶת הַלּוּחוֹת.

מַאי דָרֵישׁ?

אָמַר: וּמַה פֶּסַח שֶׁהוּא אֶחָד מִתַּרְיַ"ג מִצְוֹת
אָמְרָה תוֹרָה: "וְכָל בֶּן נֵכָר לֹא יֹאכַל בּוֹ"
הַתּוֹרָה כּוּלָהּ [כָּאן]
וְיִשְׂרָאֵל מְשֻׁמָּדִים – עַל אַחַת כַּמָּה וְכַמָּה!
וּמִנַּיִן דְּהִסְכִּים הַקָּדוֹשׁ בָּרוּךְ הוּא עַל יָדוֹ –
שֶׁנֶּאֱמַר: "אֲשֶׁר שִׁבַּרְתָּ"
וְאָמַר רֵישׁ לָקִישׁ: יַשֵׁר כֹּחֲךָ שֶׁשִּׁבַּרְתָּ.

_____

leeway to do so, he was in no way required to do so, and he could have concluded that an additional day was unnecessary (Ramban).

אֲשֶׁר שִׁבַּרְתָּ *Which you broke [asher shibarta].* The proof from the words,
"which you broke" is merely a support for the conclusion but not an absolute proof. There are several instances in the Bible where the word *asher* is

Come and **hear** an additional difficulty from the verse: **"And be prepared for the third day,** for on the third day God will descend onto Mount Sinai before the eyes of the entire nation" (Exodus 19:11). This indicates that God said that the Torah would be given on the third day after two days of separation. This is **difficult** according **to** the opinion of **Rabbi Yose.** The Gemara answers: **Didn't we say** that **Moses added one day** based **on his** own **perception? Come** and **hear** a proof against this from what was taught in a *baraita.* That which is stated in the Torah: "For on the **third** day," means **the third** day **of the month and the third** day **of the week.** Apparently, the New Moon was on Sunday. This is **difficult** according **to** the opinion of **the Rabbis.** The Gemara answers: **The Rabbis** could have **said to you: Whose** is the opinion in **this** *baraita*? It is the opinion of **Rabbi Yose.** Therefore, this *baraita* poses no difficulty to the opinion of the Rabbis.

According to the opinion of the Rabbis, that day was the **third** day of **what** reckoning? **As it was taught** in a *baraita*: It is written: **"And Moses reported the words of the people to the Lord"** (Exodus 19:8). **And it is written** immediately thereafter: "And God said to Moses: Behold I will come to you in a thick cloud so that the people will hear when I speak with you, and they will also believe in you forever. **And Moses told the words of the people to the Lord"** (Exodus 19:9).

The Gemara asks: **What did the Holy One, Blessed be He, say to Moses, and what did Moses say to Israel, and what did Israel say to Moses, and what did Moses report to the Almighty?** The verses do not elaborate on the content of God's command to Moses, which Moses then told the people and which they accepted. It must be that **this** refers to **the mitzva of setting boundaries,** which Moses told the people and which they accepted. He then went back and reported to God that the people accepted the mitzva; this is **the statement of Rabbi Yose bar Yehuda. Rabbi** Yehuda HaNasi **says: At first, he explained** the **punishment** and the hardship involved in receiving the Torah, **as it is written: "And Moses reported** [*vayashev*]," which is interpreted homiletically as: **Matters that shatter** [*meshabbevin*] (Rav

תָּא שְׁמַע:

"וְהָיוּ נְכֹנִים לַיּוֹם הַשְּׁלִישִׁי"

קַשְׁיָא לְרַבִּי יוֹסֵי!

הָא אָמְרִינַן: יוֹם אֶחָד הוֹסִיף מֹשֶׁה מִדַּעְתּוֹ.

תָּא שְׁמַע: 'שְׁלִישִׁי' – שְׁלִישִׁי בַּחֹדֶשׁ, וּשְׁלִישִׁי בַּשַּׁבָּת

קַשְׁיָא לְרַבָּנַן!

אָמְרִי לָךְ רַבָּנַן: הָא מַנִּי – רַבִּי יוֹסֵי הִיא.

'שְׁלִישִׁי' לְמַאי – לְכִדְתַנְיָא:

"וַיָּשֶׁב מֹשֶׁה אֶת דִּבְרֵי הָעָם אֶל ה'"

וּכְתִיב: "וַיַּגֵּד מֹשֶׁה אֶת דִּבְרֵי הָעָם אֶל ה'".

מָה אָמַר לוֹ הַקָּדוֹשׁ בָּרוּךְ הוּא לְמֹשֶׁה

וּמָה אָמַר לָהֶם מֹשֶׁה לְיִשְׂרָאֵל

וּמָה אָמְרוּ יִשְׂרָאֵל לְמֹשֶׁה

וּמָה הֵשִׁיב מֹשֶׁה לִפְנֵי הַגְּבוּרָה?

זוֹ מִצְוַת הַגְבָּלָה, דִּבְרֵי רַבִּי יוֹסֵי בַּר יְהוּדָה.

רַבִּי אוֹמֵר: בַּתְּחִילָּה פֵּירֵשׁ עוֹנְשָׁהּ

דִּכְתִיב: "וַיָּשֶׁב מֹשֶׁה" – דְּבָרִים שֶׁמְּשַׁבְּבִין דַּעְתּוֹ שֶׁל אָדָם

---

not interpreted as approval. Some commentaries explain that the conclusion that God agreed with Moses is drawn from the fact that God mentioned the breaking of the tablets without anger (Rashi). Alternatively, God's agreement can be ascertained from His later command that Moses store the broken tablets in the Ark. He would not have commanded Moses to do so had they been associated with an infraction that incurred God's disapproval (Rashbam).

Hai Gaon) **a person's mind; and, ultimately, he explained its reward, as it is written: "And Moses told** [*vayagged*]**,"** which is interpreted homiletically as: **Matters that draw a person's heart like** *aggada*. **And some say** that **at first, he explained its reward, as it is written: "And Moses reported,"** which is interpreted homiletically as: **Matters that restore** [*meshivin*] **and calm a person's mind; and ultimately, he explained its punishment, as it is written: "And Moses told,"** matters that are as difficult for a person as wormwood [*gidin*].

Come and **hear** a proof from that which was taught in a *baraita*: The **sixth** was **the sixth** day **of the month** and **the sixth** day **of the week.** This is also **difficult** according to the opinion of **the Rabbis.** The Gemara answers: **This** *baraita* is **also** according to the opinion of **Rabbi Yose.** But if so, according to the opinion of the Rabbis, that day was the **sixth** day of **what** reckoning? **Rava said:** the sixth day **from their encampment. Rav Aḥa bar Ya'akov said:** The sixth day **from** the start of **their journey.** They left Refidim and arrived and camped in the desert on the same Shabbat. **And** Rava and Rav Aḥa bar Ya'akov **disagree** with regard to the mitzva of **Shabbat** commanded to the Jewish people at **Mara, as it is written** in the fourth commandment: "Observe the Shabbat day to keep it holy **as the LORD your God commanded you"** (Deuteronomy 5:11). **And Rav Yehuda said** that **Rav said: As He commanded you in Mara,** as it is stated: "There He made for him a statute and an ordinance, and there He proved him" (Exodus 15:25). Their dispute was: One **Master held: They were commanded** about **Shabbat, but they were not commanded** about Shabbat **boundaries.** Therefore, it was permitted to travel from Refidim on Shabbat, because the restriction of Shabbat boundaries was not yet in effect. **And** one **Master held: They were also commanded** about the **boundaries,** and therefore, it was prohibited to leave Refidim on Shabbat.

The translation continues on page 183.

Shabbat 87b

in the Bible. However, clearly its taste is extremely bitter and it may even be poisonous. Some identify it as the *Securigera coronilla*.

וּלְבַסּוֹף פֵּירֵשׁ מַתַּן שְׂכָרָהּ –

דִּכְתִיב: "וַיַּגֵּד מֹשֶׁה" –

דְּבָרִים שֶׁמּוֹשְׁכִין לִבּוֹ שֶׁל אָדָם כְּאַגָּדָה.

וְאִיכָּא דְּאָמְרִי: בַּתְּחִילָּה פֵּירֵשׁ מַתַּן שְׂכָרָהּ

דִּכְתִיב "וַיָּשֶׁב מֹשֶׁה" –

דְּבָרִים שֶׁמְּשִׁיבִין דַּעְתּוֹ שֶׁל אָדָם

וּלְבַסּוֹף פֵּירֵשׁ עוֹנְשָׁהּ –

דִּכְתִיב "וַיַּגֵּד מֹשֶׁה" –

דְּבָרִים שֶׁקָּשִׁין לָאָדָם כְּגִידִין.

תָּא שְׁמַע 'שִׁשִּׁי' –

שִׁשִּׁי בַּחוֹדֶשׁ, שִׁשִּׁי בַּשַּׁבָּת

קַשְׁיָא לְרַבָּנַן!

הָא נַמִי רַבִּי יוֹסֵי הִיא.

'שִׁשִּׁי' לְמַאי?

שבת פו:

רָבָא אָמַר: לַחֲנָיָיתָן.

רַב אַחָא בַּר יַעֲקֹב אָמַר: לְמַסָּעָן.

וְקָמִיפַּלְגִי בְּשַׁבָּת דִּמְרָה

דִּכְתִיב: "כַּאֲשֶׁר צִוְּךָ ה' אֱלֹהֶיךָ"

וְאָמַר רַב יְהוּדָה אָמַר רַב: 'כַּאֲשֶׁר צִוְּךָ' – בְּמָרָה.

מָר סָבַר: אַשַּׁבָּת אִיפְּקוּד, אַתְּחוּמִין לָא אִיפְּקוּד.

וּמָר סָבַר: אַתְּחוּמִין נַמִי אִיפְּקוּד.

גִּידִין *Wormwood [gidin].* According to the translations, apparently *gida* or *gidra* is wormwood. There is no certainty regarding the identity of this plant

שְׁנַת יְצִיאַת מִצְרַיִם *The year of the Exodus:*

Nisan			Iyyar			Sivan		
Mekhilta Seder Olam			*Mekhilta Seder Olam*			*Mekhilta Seder Olam*		
1	Thurs	Fri	1	Shabbat	Sun	1	Sun	Mon
2	Fri	Shabbat	2	Sun	Mon	2	Mon	Tues
3	Shabbat	Sun	3	Mon	Tues	3	Tues	Wed
4	Sun	Mon	4	Tues	Wed	4	Wed	Thurs
5	Mon	Tues	5	Wed	Thurs	5	Thurs	Fri
6	Tues	Wed	6	Thurs	Fri	6	Fri	Shabbat
7	Wed	Thurs	7	Fri	Shabbat	7	Shabbat	
8	Thurs	Fri	8	Shabbat	Sun			
9	Fri	Shabbat	9	Sun	Mon			
10	Shabbat	Sun	10	Mon	Tues			
11	Sun	Mon	11	Tues	Wed			
12	Mon	Tues	12	Wed	Thurs			
13	Tues	Wed	13	Thurs	Fri			
14	Wed	Thurs	14	Fri	Shabbat			
15	Thurs	Fri	15	Shabbat	Sun			
16	Fri	Shabbat	16	Sun	Mon			
17	Shabbat	Sun	17	Mon	Tues			
18	Sun	Mon	18	Tues	Wed			
19	Mon	Tues	19	Wed	Thurs			
20	Tues	Wed	20	Thurs	Fri			
21	Wed	Thurs	21	Fri	Shabbat			
22	Thurs	Fri	22	Shabbat	Sun			
23	Fri	Shabbat	23	Sun	Mon			
24	Shabbat	Sun	24	Mon	Tues			
25	Sun	Mon	25	Tues	Wed			
26	Mon	Tues	26	Wed	Thurs			
27	Tues	Wed	27	Thurs	Fri			
28	Wed	Thurs	28	Fri	Shabbat			
29	Thurs	Fri	29	Shabbat	Sun			
30	Fri	Shabbat	30	Sun	Mon			

תָּא שְׁמַע: נִיסָן שֶׁבּוֹ יָצְאוּ יִשְׂרָאֵל מִמִּצְרַיִם
בְּאַרְבָּעָה עָשָׂר שָׁחֲטוּ פִּסְחֵיהֶם
וּבַחֲמִשָּׁה עָשָׂר יָצְאוּ
וְלָעֶרֶב לָקוּ בְּכוֹרוֹת.
'לָעֶרֶב' סָלְקָא דַּעְתָּךְ?!
אֶלָּא: 'מִבְּעֶרֶב' לָקוּ בְּכוֹרוֹת.
וְאוֹתוֹ הַיּוֹם חֲמִישִׁי בְּשַׁבָּת הָיָה.
מִדַּחֲמֵיסַר בְּנִיסָן חֲמִשָּׁה בְּשַׁבָּת –
רֵישׁ יַרְחָא דְּאִיָּיר שַׁבְּתָא

Come and **hear** an additional proof with regard to the day of the revelation at Sinai from what was taught in a *baraita*: In the month of **Nisan during which** the **Jewish people left Egypt, on the fourteenth, they slaughtered their Paschal** lambs; **on the fifteenth, they left** Egypt; **and in the evening,** the **firstborn were stricken.** The Gemara asks: **Does it enter your mind** to say that they were stricken **in the evening?** Was the Plague of the Firstborn after the Jews left Egypt? **Rather, say** that **the evening before, the firstborn were stricken. And that day was** the **fifth** day **of the week. From** the fact **that** the **fifteenth of Nisan** was a **Thursday,** the **New Moon** of **Iyyar** was **Shabbat,** as Nisan is typically thirty days long. **And** the **New Moon** of **Sivan** was on the **first** day **of the week,** as Iyyar is typically twenty-nine days long.

The translation continues on the next page.

This table on the right illustrates the opinion of the *baraita* in *Seder Olam*, which is in accordance with the opinion of the Rabbis. If the months are calculated in their typical configuration, the day of the Revelation at Sinai would fall out on the sixth of Sivan. Even assuming that the Exodus was on Thursday, the New Moon of Sivan could still have been on Monday and the Revelation at Sinai on Shabbat, the sixth of Sivan, if one asserts that Iyyar that year was a thirty-day month.

This is **difficult** according **to** the opinion of **the Rabbis,** who hold that the New Moon of Sivan that year was on Monday.

The Gemara answers: **The Rabbis** could have **said to you** that **a day was added to Iyyar that year** and it was thirty days long. The New Moon was determined by testimony of witnesses who saw the new moon, together with astronomical calculations that the testimony was feasible. Therefore, Iyyar could be thirty days long. If that was the case, the New Moon of Sivan was on Monday. **Come** and **hear** an objection from what was taught in a different *baraita* that **they did not add a day** to Iyyar that year, as the Sages taught: In the month of **Nisan during which** the **Jewish people left Egypt, on the fourteenth, they slaughtered their Paschal** lambs; **on the fifteenth, they left** Egypt; **and in the evening,** the **firstborn were stricken.** The Gemara asks: **Does it enter your mind** to say that they were stricken **in the evening?** Was the Plague of the Firstborn after the Jews left Egypt? **Rather, say** that **the evening before, the firstborn were stricken. And that day was** the **fifth** day **of the week. Nisan was complete,** i.e., it was thirty days long, **and** the New Moon of **Iyyar occurred on** a **Shabbat.**

Iyyar was lacking, i.e., it was twenty-nine days long, **and** the New Moon of **Sivan occurred** on the **first** day **of the week.** This is **difficult** according **to** the opinion of **the Rabbis.** The Gemara answers: **Whose** is the opinion in **this** *baraita*? **It is** the opinion of **Rabbi Yose.** Therefore, this *baraita* poses no difficulty to the opinion of the Rabbis.

Rav Pappa said: Come and **hear** a different proof from another verse, as it is stated: **"And they took their journey from Elim, and all the congregation of the children of Israel** came unto the wilderness of Sin, which is between Elim and Sinai, **on the fifteenth day of the second month** after their departing out of the land of Egypt" (Exodus 16:1). **And that day was Shabbat, as it is written: "And in the morning, then you shall see the glory of the LORD;** for He has heard your murmurings against the LORD; and what are we, that you murmur against us?" (Exodus 16:7). The next day the glory of God was revealed, and He told them that in the afternoon the manna and quail would begin to fall, **and it is written: "Six days you shall gather it;**

וְרֵישׁ יַרְחָא דְּסִיוָן – חַד בְּשַׁבָּת
קַשְׁיָא לְרַבָּנָן!

אָמְרִי לָךְ רַבָּנָן: אִיָּיר דְּהַהִיא שַׁתָּא – עַבּוּרֵי עַבְּרוּהּ.

תָּא שְׁמַע דְּלָא עַבְּרוּהּ:

נִיסָן שֶׁבּוֹ יָצְאוּ יִשְׂרָאֵל מִמִּצְרַיִם
בְּאַרְבָּעָה עָשָׂר שָׁחֲטוּ פִּסְחֵיהֶם

בַּחֲמִשָּׁה עָשָׂר שֶׁ יָצְאוּ
וְלָעֶרֶב לָקוּ בְּכוֹרוֹת.

'לָעֶרֶב' סַלְקָא דַעְתָּךְ?!

אֶלָּא אֵימָא: 'מִבְּעֶרֶב' לָקוּ בְּכוֹרוֹת.

וְאוֹתוֹ הַיּוֹם חֲמִישִׁי בְּשַׁבָּת הָיָה, הַשְׁלִים נִיסָן
וְאֵירַע אִיָּיר לִהְיוֹת בְּשַׁבָּת.

חָסֵר אִיָּיר
וְאֵירַע סִיוָן לִהְיוֹת בְּאֶחָד בְּשַׁבָּת
קַשְׁיָא לְרַבָּנָן!

הָא מַנִּי רַבִּי יוֹסֵי הִיא.

אָמַר רַב פָּפָּא, תָּא שְׁמַע:
"וַיִּסְעוּ מֵאֵלִים וַיָּבֹאוּ כָּל עֲדַת בְּנֵי יִשְׂרָאֵל וְגוֹ'
בַּחֲמִשָּׁה עָשָׂר יוֹם לַחֹדֶשׁ הַשֵּׁנִי"

וְאוֹתוֹ הַיּוֹם שַׁבָּת הָיָה
דִּכְתִיב: "וּבֹקֶר וּרְאִיתֶם אֶת כְּבוֹד ה'"
וּכְתִיב: "שֵׁשֶׁת יָמִים תִּלְקְטֻהוּ".

but on the seventh day is Sabbath, there shall be none in it" (Exodus 16:26). Apparently, the first six days after this command were weekdays on which the manna fell, and the fifteenth of Iyyar was Shabbat. **And from** the fact **that** the **fifteenth of Iyyar** was **Shabbat,** the **New Moon** of **Sivan** was on the **first** day **of the week.** This is **difficult** according to the opinion of **the Rabbis.** The Gemara answers: According to the Rabbis, **a day was added to Iyyar that year** and it was thirty days long. Therefore, the New Moon of Sivan was on Monday.

Rav Ḥavivi from Ḥozena'a said to Rav Ashi: Come and **hear** a different proof from the following verse: **"And it came to pass in the first month in the second year, on the first day of the month, that the tabernacle was erected"** (Exodus 40:17). It **was taught: That day took ten crowns.** It was **the first** day **of Creation,** meaning Sunday, **the first** day **of** the offerings brought by the **princes, the first** day **of the priesthood, the first** day **of service** in the Temple, **the first** time **for the descent of fire** onto the altar, **the first** time that **consecrated** foods **were eaten, the first** day of **the resting of the Divine Presence** upon the Jewish people, **the first** day that **the Jewish people were blessed** by the priests, and **the first** day **of the prohibition** to bring offerings on **improvised altars.** Once the Tabernacle was erected, it was prohibited to offer sacrifices elsewhere. And it was the **first of the months. And from** the fact **that** the **New Moon** of **Nisan** of **that year** was on **the first** day **of the week,** in **the previous year,** it was on **the fourth** day **of the week.**

---

notably with the sacrifices of Cain and Abel and continuing throughout the generations. However, the eating of consecrated items was introduced to the Jewish people with the command of the peace-offerings that coincided with the dedication of the Tabernacle. In addition, although priests were eating their portions from the sacrifices of the most sacred order, the sin-offerings from their inauguration prior to the dedication, the eighth day of the inauguration was the first day when portions of sacrifices of lesser sanctity were eaten.

וּמִדְּחֲמֵיסַר בְּאִיָּיר שַׁבַּתָּא –
רֵישׁ יַרְחָא דְּסִיוָן חַד בְּשַׁבַּת
קַשְׁיָא לְרַבָּנַן!
אָמְרִי לָךְ רַבָּנַן: אִיָּיר דְּהַהִיא שַׁתָּא עַבּוּרֵי עַבְּרוּהּ.

אָמַר לֵיהּ רַב חֲבִיבִי מֵחוֹזְנָאָה לְרַב אַשִׁי:
תָּא שְׁמַע
"וַיְהִי בַּחֹדֶשׁ הָרִאשׁוֹן בַּשָּׁנָה הַשֵּׁנִית בְּאֶחָד לַחֹדֶשׁ
הוּקַם הַמִּשְׁכָּן"
תָּנָא: אוֹתוֹ יוֹם נָטַל עֶשֶׂר עֲטָרוֹת;
רִאשׁוֹן לְמַעֲשֵׂה בְרֵאשִׁית, רִאשׁוֹן לִנְשִׂיאִים, רִאשׁוֹן לִכְהוּנָּה,
רִאשׁוֹן לַעֲבוֹדָה, רִאשׁוֹן לִירִידַת הָאֵשׁ, רִאשׁוֹן לַאֲכִילַת קָדָשִׁים,
רִאשׁוֹן לִשְׁכּוֹן שְׁכִינָה, רִאשׁוֹן לְבָרֵךְ אֶת יִשְׂרָאֵל, רִאשׁוֹן לְאִיסּוּר
הַבָּמוֹת, רִאשׁוֹן לָחֳדָשִׁים.
וּמִדְּרֵישׁ יַרְחָא דְּנִיסָן דְּהַאי שַׁתָּא חַד בְּשַׁבַּת –
דְּאֶשְׁתְּקַד [בָּרְבִיעִי] בְּשַׁבַּת;

קְבִיעַת הֶחֳדָשִׁים *Establishing the months.* On the calendar used by the *amora'im*, the spring and summer months had fixed numbers of days. Nisan had thirty days, Iyyar had twenty-nine. In earlier generations, until the fourth century, the New Moon was established based on the testimony of witnesses who saw the new moon, and the number of days in each month was not fixed. Therefore, it was possible for the month of Iyyar to be a month of thirty days.

רִאשׁוֹן לַאֲכִילַת קָדָשִׁים *The first time that consecrated foods were eaten.* The eating of consecrated items is underscored here because the offering of sacrifices predated the dedication of the Sanctuary by thousands of years, beginning

As it was taught in a *baraita, Aḥerim* **say: Between** the festival of **Assembly,** i.e., *Shavuot,* of one year and the festival of **Assembly** of the following year, **and** similarly, **between Rosh HaShana** of one year and **Rosh HaShana** of the following year, **there is only** a difference of **four days** of the week. **And if it was a leap year,** there is a difference of **five** days between them. There are three hundred and fifty four days in a year, which are divided into twelve months, six months that are thirty days long and six months that are twenty-nine days long. If the New Moon of Nisan was on Wednesday, the **New Moon** of **Iyyar was on Shabbat eve, and** the **New Moon** of **Sivan** was on **Shabbat.** This is **difficult both** according **to Rabbi Yose,** who holds that the New Moon of Sivan was on Sunday, and according **to the Rabbis,** who hold it was on Monday. The Gemara answers: Both Rabbi Yose and the Rabbis disagree with *Aḥerim.* According **to Rabbi Yose, they established seven** months that were **lacking** in the first year, i.e., seven months that were twenty-nine days long, and according **to the Rabbis, they established eight** months that were **lacking.**

Shabbat
88a

The Gemara cites another objection. **Come** and **hear** that **which was taught** in a *baraita* in the anthology called *Seder Olam:* In the month of **Nisan during which** the **Jewish people left Egypt, on the**

---

with the opinion of *Aḥerim.* Practically speaking, the calculations are made based on the seasons and the vernal and autumnal equinoxes, which determine the dates on the solar calendar and influence when the festivals occur. In addition, there are halakhic and other reasons for adjusting the calendar, and Rosh HaShana is sometimes postponed so that it falls a day or two after the moon becomes visible in the sky. There is no set number of days in each month, and consequently, there is no set number of days of the year. The months during which changes may be introduced are Marḥeshvan and Kislev. Sometimes they are both twenty-nine days long, while other times they are both thirty days long; and sometimes, one is twenty-nine days long and the other is thirty days long. In non-leap years, the Jewish calendar year can be 353, 354, or 355 days. When the months were sanctified based on the testimony of eyewitnesses, even larger fluctuations were possible, as any of the months could be twenty-nine or thirty days long.

דְּתַנְיָא, אֲחֵרִים אוֹמְרִים:

אֵין בֵּין עֲצֶרֶת לַעֲצֶרֶת, וְאֵין בֵּין רֹאשׁ הַשָּׁנָה לְרֹאשׁ הַשָּׁנָה

אֶלָּא אַרְבָּעָה יָמִים בִּלְבַד

וְאִם הָיְתָה שָׁנָה מְעוּבֶּרֶת – חֲמִשָּׁה.

הֲוָה לֵיהּ רֵישׁ יַרְחָא דְּאִיָּיר – מַעֲלֵי שַׁבְּתָא

וְרֵישׁ יַרְחָא דְּסִיוָן – שַׁבְּתָא

קַשְׁיָא בֵּין לְרַבִּי יוֹסֵי בֵּין לְרַבָּנַן!

לְרַבִּי יוֹסֵי – שִׁבְעָה חֲסֵרִין עֲבוּד

לְרַבָּנַן – שְׁמוֹנָה חֲסֵרִים עֲבוּד.

תָּא שְׁמַע, דְּתַנְיָא בְּסֵדֶר עוֹלָם:

נִיסָן שֶׁבּוֹ יָצְאוּ יִשְׂרָאֵל מִמִּצְרַיִם

שבת פח.

שִׁיטַת אֲחֵרִים **The opinion of Aḥerim.** According to the opinion of Aḥerim, the number of days in each month is fixed, with thirty-day months alternating with twenty-nine-day months. The New Moon following each twenty-nine-day month is one weekday later than the previous New Moon, and the New Moon following each thirty-day month is two weekdays later. Since, in a typical year, there are six twenty-nine-day months and six thirty-day months, the days of the New Moon advance a total of eighteen days, which are two weeks and four days. In a leap year, the additional Adar is twenty-nine days, bringing the total to nineteen days, or two weeks and five days. As a result, in a leap year, Rosh HaShana falls five weekdays later than it did the previous year.

סֵדֶר הֶחֳדָשִׁים **The order of the months.** The halakha was not ruled in accordance with the opinion of Aḥerim, and the months of the year follow a fixed order, alternating between thirty-day and twenty-nine-day months, beginning only in Tevet. A year may have as many as seven twenty-nine-day months, if Kislev is lacking, or as few as five incomplete months, if Marḥeshvan is full (Tur, Oraḥ Ḥayyim 428).

יְמֵי הַשָּׁנָה **The days of the year.** Our calendar is not calculated in accordance

fourteenth they slaughtered their Paschal lambs, **on the fifteenth** they **left** Egypt, **and that day was Shabbat eve. From** the fact **that the New Moon** of **Nisan** was on **Shabbat eve,** we can infer that the **New Moon** of **Iyyar** was on the **first** day **of the week, and** the New Moon of **Sivan** was **on** the **second** day **of the week. This is difficult** according **to** the opinion of **Rabbi Yose,** who holds that the New Moon of Sivan was on Sunday. The Gemara answers that **Rabbi Yose** could have **said to you: Whose** is the opinion in **this** *baraita*? **It is** the opinion of the **Rabbis.** Therefore, this *baraita* poses no difficulty to the opinion of the Rabbi Yose.

The Gemara cites another objection: **Come** and **hear** from that which was taught, that **Rabbi Yose says: On the second** day of Sivan, **Moses ascended** Mount Sinai **and descended. On the third** day, **he ascended and descended. On the fourth** day, **he descended and did not ascend** Mount Sinai **again** until he was commanded along with all of the Jewish people. **And** the Gemara asks: How is it possible that he descended on the fourth day? **Since he did not ascend, from where did he descend? Rather,** this must be emended: **On the fourth** day, **he ascended and descended. On the fifth** day, **he built an altar and sacrificed an offering. On the sixth** day, **he had no time.** The Gemara asks: **Is that not because** he received the **Torah** on the sixth day of the month? Apparently, this *baraita* supports the opinion of the Rabbis.

The Gemara rejects this: **No,** he had no time **due to the burden of** preparing for **Shabbat.** The Gemara adds: **A Galilean taught,** while standing **above Rav Ḥisda: Blessed is the all-Merciful One, Who gave the three-fold Torah:** Torah, Prophets, and Writings, **to the three-fold nation:** Priests, Levites, and Israelites, **by means of a third-**born: Moses, who followed Aaron and Miriam in birth order, **on the third day** of the separation of men and women, **in the third month:** Sivan. On **whose** opinion is this homily based? It is based on the opinion of **the Rabbis,** who hold that the Torah was given on the third day of separation and not on the fourth day.

בְּאַרְבָּעָה עָשָׂר שָׁחֲטוּ פִּסְחֵיהֶן
בַּחֲמִשָּׁה עָשָׂר יָצְאוּ, וְאוֹתוֹ הַיּוֹם עֶרֶב שַׁבָּת הָיָה.
וּמִדְרֵישׁ יַרְחָא דְּנִיסָן עֶרֶב שַׁבָּת
רֵישׁ יַרְחָא דְּאִיָּיר חַד בְּשַׁבָּא
וְסִיוָן בִּתְרֵי בְּשַׁבָּא
קַשְׁיָא לְרַבִּי יוֹסֵי!
אָמַר לָךְ רַבִּי יוֹסֵי: הָא מַנִּי – רַבָּנַן הִיא.

תָּא שְׁמַע, רַבִּי יוֹסֵי אוֹמֵר:
בַּשֵּׁנִי עָלָה מֹשֶׁה וְיָרַד
בַּשְּׁלִישִׁי עָלָה וְיָרַד
בָּרְבִיעִי יָרַד וְשׁוּב לֹא עָלָה.
וּמֵאַחַר שֶׁלֹּא עָלָה מֵהֵיכָן יָרַד?!
אֶלָּא: בָּרְבִיעִי עָלָה וְיָרַד
בַּחֲמִישִׁי בָּנָה מִזְבֵּחַ וְהִקְרִיב עָלָיו קָרְבָּן
בַּשִּׁשִּׁי לֹא הָיָה לוֹ פְּנַאי.
מַאי לָאו – מִשּׁוּם תּוֹרָה?

לֹא, מִשּׁוּם טוֹרַח שַׁבָּת.
דָּרַשׁ הַהוּא גְּלִילָאָה עֲלֵיהּ דְּרַב חִסְדָּא:
בְּרִיךְ רַחֲמָנָא דִּיהַב אוֹרְיָאן תְּלִיתָאי לְעַם תְּלִיתָאי
עַל יְדֵי תְּלִיתָאי, בְּיוֹם תְּלִיתָאי, בְּיַרְחָא תְּלִיתָאי
כְּמַאן – כְּרַבָּנַן.

אוֹרְיָאן תְּלִיתָאי *Three-fold Torah.* Different theories have been offered regarding the significance of the number three. One opinion says that it is an allusion

The Gemara cites additional homiletic interpretations on the topic of the revelation at Sinai. The Torah says, "And Moses brought forth the people out of the camp to meet God; **and they stood at the lowermost part of the mount**" (Exodus 19:17). **Rabbi Avdimi bar Ḥama bar Ḥasa said:** the Jewish people actually stood beneath the mountain, and the verse **teaches that the Holy One, Blessed be He, overturned the mountain above** the Jews **like a tub, and said to them: If you accept the Torah, excellent, and if not, there will be your burial. Rav Aḥa bar Ya'akov said: From here** there is **a substantial caveat to** the obligation to fulfill the **Torah.** The Jewish people can claim that they were coerced into accepting the Torah, and it is therefore not binding. **Rava said: Even so, they again accepted it** willingly **in the time of Ahasuerus, as it is written:** "The Jews **ordained, and took upon them,** and upon their seed, and upon all such as joined themselves unto them" (Esther 9:27), and he taught: The Jews **ordained what they had already taken upon themselves** through coercion at Sinai.

Ḥizkiya said: What is the meaning of that **which is written: "You caused sentence to be heard from heaven; the earth feared, and was silent"** (Psalms 76:9)? **If it was afraid, why was it silent; and if it was silent, why was it afraid? Rather,** the meaning is: **At first, it was afraid, and in the end, it was silent.** "You caused sentence to be heard from

---

Rashba challenges this argument. If this is the case, why were the Jewish people punished and exiled from their land for having violated the Torah (see *Tosafot*)? He explains that certainly the Jews' continued existence in Eretz Yisrael is contingent on their fulfillment of the Torah's commandments. In other words, it is explained that holding the uprooted mountain like a tub over their heads alludes to the abundance of love that God bestowed upon the Jewish people during the Exodus, in giving them the manna, etc. In response, the people said: "We will do, and we will hear." Still, in their hearts the people did not accept the Torah on behalf of later generations, for whom life would proceed naturally, without the revelation of constant miracles.

"וַיִּתְיַצְּבוּ בְּתַחְתִּית הָהָר"

אָמַר רַב אַבְדִּימִי בַּר חָמָא בַּר חָסָא:

מְלַמֵּד שֶׁכָּפָה הַקָּדוֹשׁ בָּרוּךְ הוּא עֲלֵיהֶם אֶת הָהָר כְּגִיגִית

וְאָמַר לָהֶם:

אִם אַתֶּם מְקַבְּלִים הַתּוֹרָה – מוּטָב

וְאִם לָאו – שָׁם תְּהֵא קְבוּרַתְכֶם.

אָמַר רַב אַחָא בַּר יַעֲקֹב:

מִכָּאן מוֹדָעָא רַבָּה לְאוֹרַיְתָא.

אָמַר רָבָא:

אַף עַל פִּי כֵן, הֲדוּר קַבְּלוּהָ בִּימֵי אֲחַשְׁוֵרוֹשׁ.

דִּכְתִיב: "קִיְּמוּ וְקִבְּלוּ הַיְּהוּדִים"

קִיְּמוּ מַה שֶּׁקִּבְּלוּ כְּבָר.

אָמַר חִזְקִיָּה, מַאי דִכְתִיב:

"מִשָּׁמַיִם הִשְׁמַעְתָּ דִּין אֶרֶץ יָרְאָה וְשָׁקָטָה"

אִם יָרְאָה לָמָּה שָׁקָטָה, וְאִם שָׁקְטָה לָמָּה יָרְאָה?

אֶלָּא: בַּתְּחִלָּה – יָרְאָה, וּלְבַסּוֹף – שָׁקָטָה.

---

to the verse: "A three-fold thread is not easily broken" (Ecclesiastes 4:12; *Yefe Toar*). The midrash adds other sets of three to this list: Moses' name has three letters, and Moses' tribe is Levi, which also has three letters. With regard to the three-fold Torah, beyond the simple meaning of the text, some commentaries explained that there are three additional manners in which the Torah may be interpreted: Homiletic interpretation, allusion, and esoterica (*Divrei Shaul*). Additionally, the passage might be an allusion to the Written Torah, the Oral Torah, and the Esoteric Torah (*Ein Ya'akov*).

מוֹדָעָא רַבָּה לְאוֹרַיְתָא *A substantial caveat to the obligation to fulfill the Torah.*

heaven" refers to the revelation at Sinai. **And why was** the earth **afraid? It is in accordance with** the statement of **Reish Lakish, as Reish Lakish said: What is** the meaning of that **which is written: "And there was evening and there was morning, the sixth day"** (Genesis 1:31)? **Why do I require the superfluous** letter *heh,* the definite article, which does not appear on any of the other days? It **teaches that the Holy One, Blessed be He, established a condition with the act of Creation, and said to them: If Israel accepts the Torah** on the sixth day of Sivan, **you will exist; and if** they do **not** accept it, **I will return you to** the primordial state of **chaos and disorder.** Therefore, the earth was afraid until the Torah was given to Israel, lest it be returned to a state of chaos. Once the Jewish people accepted the Torah, the earth was calmed.

Rabbi Simai taught: When Israel accorded precedence to the declaration **"We will do"** over the declaration **"We will hear," 600,000 ministering angels came** and **tied two crowns to each and every member of the Jewish people, one corresponding to "We will do" and one corresponding to "We will hear." And when the people sinned** with the Golden Calf, **120,000 angels of destruction descended and removed them** from the people, **as it is stated** in the wake of the sin of the Golden Calf: **"And the children of Israel stripped themselves of their ornaments from Mount Horeb onward"** (Exodus 33:6). **Rabbi Ḥama, son of Rabbi Ḥanina, said: At Horeb they put on** their ornaments, **and at Horeb they removed** them. The source for this is: **At Horeb they put them on, as we have said; at Horeb they removed them, as it is written: "And the children of Israel stripped themselves** of their ornaments from Mount Horeb." **Rabbi Yoḥanan said: And Moses merited all** of these crowns **and took** them. What is the source for this? **Because juxtaposed to this** verse, it is stated: **"And Moses would take the tent [*ohel*]"** (Exodus 33:7). The word *ohel* is interpreted homiletically as an allusion to an aura or illumination [*hila*]. **Reish Lakish said: In the future, the Holy One, Blessed be He, will return them to us, as it is stated: "And the ransomed of the LORD shall return, and come with singing unto Zion, and everlasting joy shall be upon their heads"** (Isaiah 35:10). **The joy that** they **once** had will once again be **upon their heads.**

וְלָמָּה יָרְאָה – כִּדְרֵישׁ לָקִישׁ
דְּאָמַר רֵישׁ לָקִישׁ, מַאי דִּכְתִיב:
"וַיְהִי עֶרֶב וַיְהִי בֹקֶר יוֹם הַשִּׁשִּׁי", ה' יְתֵירָה לָמָּה לִי?
מְלַמֵּד שֶׁהִתְנָה הַקָּדוֹשׁ בָּרוּךְ הוּא עִם מַעֲשֵׂה בְרֵאשִׁית
וְאָמַר לָהֶם:
אִם יִשְׂרָאֵל מְקַבְּלִים הַתּוֹרָה – אַתֶּם מִתְקַיְימִין
וְאִם לָאו – אֲנִי מַחֲזִיר אֶתְכֶם לְתוֹהוּ וָבוֹהוּ.

דָּרַשׁ רַבִּי סִימַאי:
בְּשָׁעָה שֶׁהִקְדִּימוּ יִשְׂרָאֵל 'נַעֲשֶׂה' לְ'נִשְׁמַע'
בָּאוּ שִׁשִּׁים רִיבּוֹא שֶׁל מַלְאֲכֵי הַשָּׁרֵת
לְכָל אֶחָד וְאֶחָד מִיִּשְׂרָאֵל קָשְׁרוּ לוֹ שְׁנֵי כְתָרִים
אֶחָד כְּנֶגֶד 'נַעֲשֶׂה' וְאֶחָד כְּנֶגֶד 'נִשְׁמַע'.
וְכֵיוָן שֶׁחָטְאוּ יִשְׂרָאֵל
יָרְדוּ מֵאָה וְעֶשְׂרִים רִיבּוֹא מַלְאֲכֵי חַבָּלָה, וּפֵירְקוּם.
שֶׁנֶּאֱמַר: "וַיִּתְנַצְּלוּ בְנֵי יִשְׂרָאֵל אֶת עֶדְיָם מֵהַר חוֹרֵב".
אָמַר רַבִּי חָמָא בְּרַבִּי חֲנִינָא:
בְּחוֹרֵב טָעֲנוּ, בְּחוֹרֵב פֵּרְקוּ.
בְּחוֹרֵב טָעֲנוּ – כִּדְאָמְרַן, בְּחוֹרֵב פֵּרְקוּ –
דִּכְתִיב: "וַיִּתְנַצְּלוּ בְנֵי יִשְׂרָאֵל וְגוֹ'".
אָמַר רַבִּי יוֹחָנָן: וְכוּלָּן זָכָה מֹשֶׁה וּנְטָלָן
דִּסְמִיךְ לֵיהּ: "וּמֹשֶׁה יִקַּח אֶת הָאֹהֶל".
אָמַר רֵישׁ לָקִישׁ: עָתִיד הַקָּדוֹשׁ בָּרוּךְ הוּא לְהַחֲזִירָן לָנוּ
שֶׁנֶּאֱמַר:
"וּפְדוּיֵי ה' יְשֻׁבוּן וּבָאוּ צִיּוֹן בְּרִנָּה וְשִׂמְחַת עוֹלָם עַל רֹאשָׁם" –
שִׂמְחָה שֶׁמֵּעוֹלָם עַל רֹאשָׁם.

Rabbi Elazar said: When the Jewish people accorded precedence to the declaration "We will do" over "We will hear," a Divine Voice emerged and said to them: Who revealed to my children this secret that the ministering angels use? As it is written: "Bless the LORD, you angels of His, you mighty in strength, that fulfill His word, hearkening unto the voice of His word" (Psalms 103:20). At first, the angels fulfill His word, and then afterward they hearken. Rabbi Ḥama, son of Rabbi Ḥanina, said: What is the meaning of that which is written: "As an apple tree among the trees of the wood, so is my beloved among the sons. Under its shadow I delighted to sit and its fruit was sweet to my taste" (Song of Songs 2:3)? Why were the Jewish people likened to an apple tree? It is to tell you that just as this apple tree, its fruit grows before its leaves, so too, the Jewish people accorded precedence to "We will do" over "We will hear."

The Gemara relates that a heretic saw that Rava was immersed in studying *halakha*, and his fingers were beneath his leg and he was squeezing them, and his fingers were spurting blood. Rava did not notice that he was bleeding because he was engrossed in study. The heretic said to Rava: You impulsive nation, who accorded precedence to your mouths over your ears. You still bear your impulsiveness, as you act without thinking. You should listen first. Then, if you are capable of fulfilling the commands, accept them. And if not, do not

---

among the sons"? The allusion in the verse is to God. Some commentaries explain that the verse praises the Jewish people for choosing God even though the other nations rejected Him.

הַתַּפּוּחַ וּפִרְיוֹ *The apple tree and its fruit.* Most native species of apple trees blossom before the leaves sprout, or at least before the entire tree is covered with leaves. The Sages referred to this phenomenon when they said that the beginning of the tree's fruit, meaning the blossoms, precedes its leaves. Different versions of this Gemara state explicitly that its blossoming precedes its leaves.

אָמַר רַבִּי אֶלְעָזָר:

בְּשָׁעָה שֶׁהִקְדִּימוּ יִשְׂרָאֵל 'נַעֲשֶׂה' לְ'נִשְׁמַע'

יָצְתָה בַּת קוֹל וְאָמְרָה לָהֶן:

מִי גִּלָּה לְבָנַי רָז זֶה שֶׁמַּלְאֲכֵי הַשָּׁרֵת מִשְׁתַּמְּשִׁין בּוֹ?

דִּכְתִיב:

"בָּרְכוּ ה' מַלְאָכָיו גִּבֹּרֵי כֹחַ עֹשֵׂי דְבָרוֹ לִשְׁמֹעַ בְּקוֹל דְּבָרוֹ"

בְּרֵישָׁא 'עֹשֵׂי', וַהֲדַר 'לִשְׁמֹעַ'.

אָמַר רַבִּי חָמָא בְּרַבִּי חֲנִינָא.

מַאי דִּכְתִיב: "כְּתַפּוּחַ בַּעֲצֵי הַיַּעַר וְגוֹ'"

לָמָּה נִמְשְׁלוּ יִשְׂרָאֵל לְתַפּוּחַ –

לוֹמַר לָךְ:

מַה תַּפּוּחַ זֶה פִּרְיוֹ קוֹדֵם לְעָלָיו

אַף יִשְׂרָאֵל – הִקְדִּימוּ נַעֲשֶׂה לְנִשְׁמַע.

הַהוּא מִינָא דְּחַזְיֵיהּ לְרָבָא דְּקָא מְעַיֵּין בִּשְׁמַעְתָא

וְיָתְבָה אֶצְבְּעָתָא דִּידֵיהּ תּוֹתֵי כַּרְעָא

וְקָא מָיֵיץ בְּהוּ, וְקָא מַבְּעָן אֶצְבְּעָתֵיהּ דְּמָא

אָמַר לֵיהּ: עַמָּא פְּזִיזָא דְּקַדְּמִיתוּ פּוּמַיְיכוּ לְאוּדְנַיְיכוּ

אַכַּתִּי בִּפְחִזוּתַיְיכוּ קַיְּימִיתוּ!

בְּרֵישָׁא אִיבַּעֲיָא לְכוּ לְמִשְׁמַע

אִי מָצִיתוּ – קַבְּלִיתוּ, וְאִי לָא – לָא קַבְּלִיתוּ.

כְּתַפּוּחַ בַּעֲצֵי הַיַּעַר As an apple tree among the trees of the wood. Tosafot asked: What proof with regard to the children of Israel does the Gemara cite from the verse: "As an apple tree among the trees of the wood, so is my beloved

accept them. He **said to him:** About **us, who proceed wholeheartedly** and with integrity, **it is written: "The integrity of the upright will guide them"** (Proverbs 11:3), whereas **about those people who walk in deceit, it is written** at the end of the same verse: **"And the perverseness of the faithless will destroy them."** *Shabbat 88b*

Rabbi Shmuel bar Naḥamani said that **Rabbi Yonatan said: What is** the meaning of that **which is written: "You have ravished my heart, my sister, my bride; you have ravished my heart with one of your eyes,** with one bead of your necklace" (Song of Songs 4:9)? **At first** when you, the Jewish people, merely accepted the Torah upon yourselves it was **with one of your eyes;** however, **when you** actually **perform** the mitzvot it will be **with both of your eyes. Ulla said** with regard to the sin of the Golden Calf: **Insolent is the bride who is promiscuous under her wedding canopy. Rav Mari, son of the daughter of Shmuel, said: What verse** alludes to this? **"While the king was still at his table my spikenard** gave off its fragrance" (Song of Songs 1:12). Its pleasant odor dissipated, leaving only an offensive odor. **Rav said:** Nevertheless, it is apparent from the verse that **the affection** of the Holy One, Blessed be He, **is still upon us, as it is written** euphemistically as "gave off its fragrance," **and** the verse **did not write, it reeked.** And **the Sages taught: About** those who **are insulted and do not insult, who hear their shame and do not respond, who act out of love and are joyful in suffering, the verse says: "And they that love Him are as the sun going forth in its might"** (Judges 5:31).

With regard to the revelation at Sinai, **Rabbi Yoḥanan said: What is** the meaning of that **which is written: "The LORD gives the word; the women that proclaim the tidings are a great host"** (Psalms 68:12)? It means that **each and every utterance that emerged from the mouth of the Almighty divided into seventy languages,** a great

---

My servant Israel, in whom I will be glorified" (Isaiah 49:3; Rambam *Sefer HaMadda, Hilkhot Deot* 5:13).

נֶחֱלַק לְשִׁבְעִים לְשׁוֹנוֹת *Divided into seventy languages.* This was done so the

אָמַר לֵיהּ: אֲנַן דְּסַגְיֵין בִּשְׁלֵימוּתָא –

כְּתִיב בָּן: "תֻּמַּת יְשָׁרִים תַּנְחֵם"

הָנָךְ אֱינָשֵׁי דְּסַגָּן בַּעֲלִילוּתָא –

כְּתִיב בְּהוּ: "וְסֶלֶף בּוֹגְדִים יְשָׁדֵּם".

אָמַר רַבִּי שְׁמוּאֵל בַּר נַחֲמָנִי אָמַר רַבִּי יוֹנָתָן

מַאי דִּכְתִיב: "לִבַּבְתִּנִי אֲחוֹתִי כַלָּה לִבַּבְתִּנִי בְּאַחַת מֵעֵינַיִךְ"

בַּתְּחִילָה – "בְּאַחַת מֵעֵינַיִךְ"

לִכְשֶׁתַּעֲשִׂי – בִּשְׁתֵּי עֵינַיִךְ.

אָמַר עוּלָּא: עֲלוּבָה כַּלָּה מְזַנָּה בְּתוֹךְ חוּפָּתָהּ.

אָמַר רַב מָרִי בְּרָה דְּבַת שְׁמוּאֵל:

מַאי קְרָא – "עַד שֶׁהַמֶּלֶךְ בִּמְסִבּוֹ נִרְדִּי וְגו'".

אָמַר רַב: וַעֲדַיִין חֲבִיבוּתָא הִיא גַּבָּן

דִּכְתִיב: 'נָתַן' וְלֹא כָּתַב 'הִסְרִיחַ'.

תָּנוּ רַבָּנַן: עֲלוּבִין וְאֵינָן עוֹלְבִין, שׁוֹמְעִין חֶרְפָּתָן וְאֵינָן מְשִׁיבִין

עוֹשִׂין מֵאַהֲבָה וּשְׂמֵחִין בְּיִסּוּרִין –

עֲלֵיהֶן הַכָּתוּב אוֹמֵר: "וְאֹהֲבָיו כְּצֵאת הַשֶּׁמֶשׁ בִּגְבֻרָתוֹ".

אָמַר רַבִּי יוֹחָנָן, מַאי דִּכְתִיב:

"ה' יִתֶּן אֹמֶר הַמְבַשְּׂרוֹת צָבָא רָב" –

כָּל דִּבּוּר וְדִבּוּר שֶׁיָּצָא מִפִּי הַגְּבוּרָה נֶחֱלַק לְשִׁבְעִים לְשׁוֹנוֹת.

עֲלוּבִין וְאֵינָן עוֹלְבִין *Those who are insulted and do not insult.* A Torah scholar, as well as anyone who seeks to follow a righteous path, should be among those who are persecuted and not among those who persecute others; among those who are insulted, and not among those who insult. With regard to one who conducts himself in that manner, the verse says: "And He said to me, you are

host. And, similarly, **the school of Rabbi Yishmael taught** with regard to the verse: "Behold, is My word not like fire, declares the LORD, **and like a hammer that shatters a rock?**" (Jeremiah 23:29). **Just as this hammer breaks** a stone **into several fragments, so too, each and every utterance that emerged from the mouth of the Holy One, Blessed be He, divided into seventy languages.** The Gemara continues in praise of the Torah. **Rav Ḥananel bar Pappa said: What is** the meaning of that **which is written: "Listen, for I will speak royal things,** and my lips will open with upright statements" (Proverbs 8:6)? **Why are matters of Torah likened to a king? To teach you** that **just as this king has** the power **to kill and to grant life, so too, matters of Torah have** the power **to kill and to grant life.**

And **that is** what **Rava said: To those who are right-handed in** their approach to Torah, and engage in its study with strength, good will, and sanctity, Torah is **a drug of life,** and **to those who are left-handed in** their approach to Torah, it is **a drug of death. Alternatively,** why are matters of Torah referred to as **royal?** Because **to each and every utterance that emerged from the mouth of the Holy One, Blessed be He, two crowns are tied. Rabbi Yehoshua ben Levi said: What is** the meaning of that **which is written: "My beloved is to me like a bundle of myrrh that lies between my breasts"** (Song of Songs 1:13)? **The Congregation of Israel said before the Holy One, Blessed be He: Master of the Universe, even though my beloved,** God, **causes me suffering and bitterness, He** still **lies between my breasts.** And Rabbi Yehoshua ben Levi interpreted the verse: **"My beloved is to me like a cluster** [*eshkol*] **of henna** [*hakofer*] **in the vineyards of** [*karmei*] **Ein Gedi"** (Song of Songs 1:14). **He, Whom everything** [*shehakol*] **is His, forgives** [*mekhapper*] **me for the sin of the kid** [*gedi*], i.e., the calf, **that I collected** [*shekaramti*] **for myself.** The

---

עַל עֲוֹן גְּדִי *For the sin of the kid.* According to the commentaries on the Torah, the word *gedi* means any young offspring of a kosher animal, including a calf and a lamb. Therefore, the Torah does not use the term *gedi* on its own.

תָּנֵי דְּבֵי רַבִּי יִשְׁמָעֵאל: "וּכְפַטִּישׁ יְפוֹצֵץ סָלַע"

מַה פַּטִּישׁ זֶה נֶחֱלָק לְכַמָּה נִיצוֹצוֹת –

אַף כָּל דִּיבּוּר וְדִיבּוּר שֶׁיָּצָא מִפִּי הַקָּדוֹשׁ בָּרוּךְ

הוּא נֶחֱלָק לְשִׁבְעִים לְשׁוֹנוֹת.

אָמַר רַב חֲנַנְאֵל בַּר פָּפָּא

מַאי דִּכְתִיב: "שִׁמְעוּ כִּי נְגִידִים אֲדַבֵּר"

לָמָה נִמְשְׁלוּ דִּבְרֵי תוֹרָה כְּנָגִיד –

לוֹמַר לְךָ: מַה נָּגִיד זֶה יֵשׁ בּוֹ לְהָמִית וּלְהַחֲיוֹת –

אַף דִּבְרֵי תוֹרָה יֵשׁ בָּם לְהָמִית וּלְהַחֲיוֹת.

הַיְינוּ דְּאָמַר רָבָא:

לְמַיְימִינִין בָּהּ – סַמָּא דְחַיֵּי, לְמַשְׂמְאִילִים בָּהּ – סַמָּא דְמוֹתָא.

דָּבָר אַחֵר: 'נְגִידִים' –

כָּל דִּיבּוּר וְדִיבּוּר שֶׁיָּצָא מִפִּי הַקָּדוֹשׁ בָּרוּךְ הוּא

קוֹשְׁרִים לוֹ שְׁנֵי כְתָרִים.

אָמַר רַבִּי יְהוֹשֻׁעַ בֶּן לֵוִי

מַאי דִּכְתִיב: "צְרוֹר הַמּוֹר דּוֹדִי לִי בֵּין שָׁדַי יָלִין" –

אָמְרָה כְּנֶסֶת יִשְׂרָאֵל לִפְנֵי הַקָּדוֹשׁ בָּרוּךְ הוּא:

רִבּוֹנוֹ שֶׁל עוֹלָם, אַף עַל פִּי שֶׁמֵּיצֵר וּמֵימֵר לִי דּוֹדִי –

"בֵּין שָׁדַי יָלִין".

"אֶשְׁכּוֹל הַכּוֹפֶר דּוֹדִי לִי בְּכַרְמֵי עֵין גֶּדִי" –

מִי שֶׁהַכּוֹל שֶׁלּוֹ מְכַפֵּר לִי עַל עֲוֹן גְּדִי שֶׁכְּרַמְתִּי לִי.

nations of the world could not claim that the reason they did not accept the Torah was because it was not written in their language (Maharsha).

Gemara explains: **From where** is it **inferred that** the word in **this** verse, *karmei*, **is a term of gathering? Mar Zutra, son of Rav Naḥman, said** that it is **as we learned** in a mishna: **A launderer's chair upon which one gathers** [*koremim*] **the garments.**

And Rabbi Yehoshua ben Levi said: What is the meaning of that **which is written: "His cheeks are as a bed of spices,** as banks of sweet herbs, his lips are lilies dripping with flowing myrrh" (Song of Songs 5:13)? It is interpreted homiletically: From **each and every utterance that emerged from** His cheeks, i.e., **the mouth of the Holy One, Blessed be He, the entire world was filled with fragrant spices. And since** the world **was** already **filled by the first utterance, where** was there room for the spices of **the second utterance** to go? The Holy One, Blessed be He, **brought forth wind from His treasuries and made the** spices **pass one at a time,** leaving room for the consequences of the next utterance. **As it is stated: "His lips are lilies** [*shoshanim*] **dripping with flowing myrrh."** Each and every utterance resulted in flowing myrrh. **Do not read** the word in the verse as *shoshanim*; **rather,** read it as *sheshonim*, meaning repeat. Each repeat utterance produced its own fragrance.

And Rabbi Yehoshua ben Levi said: From each and every utterance that emerged from the mouth of the Holy One, Blessed be He, the souls of the Jewish people left their bodies, **as it is stated: "My soul departed when he spoke"** (Song of Songs 5:6). **And since their souls left** their bodies **from the first utterance, how did they receive the second utterance?** Rather, God **rained the dew** upon them **that, in the future, will revive the dead, and He revived them, as it is stated: "You, God, poured down a bountiful rain; when Your inheritance was weary You sustained it"** (Psalms 68:10).

Rather, it uses the seemingly redundant phrase, a *gedi* of goats [*gedi izim*]. Based on this understanding, the verse: "Do not cook a *gedi* in its mother's milk" (Exodus 23:19, 34:26; Deuteronomy 14:21) is interpreted as prohibiting all kosher animals (Maharsha).

מַאי מַשְׁמַע דְּהַאי 'כַּרְמֵי' לִישָׁנָא דְּמַכְנִישׁ הוּא?

אָמַר מָר זוּטְרָא בְּרֵיהּ דְּרַב נַחְמָן

כִּדְתָנַן: "כִּסֵּא שֶׁל כּוֹבֵס שֶׁכּוֹרְמִים עָלָיו אֶת הַכֵּלִים".

וְאָמַר רַבִּי יְהוֹשֻׁעַ בֶּן לֵוִי

מַאי דִּכְתִיב: "לְחָיָו כַּעֲרוּגַת הַבֹּשֶׂם" –

כָּל דִּבּוּר וְדִבּוּר שֶׁיָּצָא מִפִּי הַקָּדוֹשׁ בָּרוּךְ הוּא

נִתְמַלֵּא כָל הָעוֹלָם כּוּלוֹ בְּשָׂמִים.

וְכֵיוָן שֶׁמִּדִּיבּוּר רִאשׁוֹן נִתְמַלֵּא

דִּיבּוּר שֵׁנִי לְהֵיכָן הָלַךְ?

הוֹצִיא הַקָּדוֹשׁ בָּרוּךְ הוּא הָרוּחַ מֵאוֹצְרוֹתָיו

וְהָיָה מַעֲבִיר רִאשׁוֹן רִאשׁוֹן

שֶׁנֶּאֱמַר:

"שִׂפְתוֹתָיו שׁוֹשַׁנִּים נֹטְפוֹת מוֹר עֹבֵר"

אַל תִּקְרֵי 'שׁוֹשַׁנִּים' אֶלָּא 'שֶׁשּׁוֹנִים'.

וְאָמַר רַבִּי יְהוֹשֻׁעַ בֶּן לֵוִי:

כָּל דִּבּוּר וְדִבּוּר שֶׁיָּצָא מִפִּי הַקָּדוֹשׁ בָּרוּךְ הוּא

יָצְתָה נִשְׁמָתָן שֶׁל יִשְׂרָאֵל

שֶׁנֶּאֱמַר: "נַפְשִׁי יָצְאָה בְדַבְּרוֹ".

וּמֵאַחַר שֶׁמִּדִּיבּוּר רִאשׁוֹן יָצְתָה נִשְׁמָתָן

דִּיבּוּר שֵׁנִי הֵיאַךְ קִיבְּלוּ?

הוֹרִיד טַל שֶׁעָתִיד לְהַחֲיוֹת בּוֹ מֵתִים, וְהֶחֱיָה אוֹתָם

שֶׁנֶּאֱמַר:

"גֶּשֶׁם נְדָבוֹת תָּנִיף אֱלֹהִים נַחֲלָתְךָ וְנִלְאָה אַתָּה כוֹנַנְתָּהּ".

And Rabbi Yehoshua ben Levi said: With **each and every utterance that emerged from the mouth of the Holy One, Blessed be He, the Jewish people retreated** in fear **twelve** *mil*, **and the ministering angels walked them** back toward the mountain, **as it is stated: "The hosts of angels will scatter [*yidodun*]"** (Psalms 68:13). **Do not read** the word as *yidodun*, meaning scattered; **rather,** read it as *yedadun*, they walked them.

And Rabbi Yehoshua ben Levi said: **When Moses ascended on High** to receive the Torah, **the ministering angels said before the Holy One, Blessed be He: Master of the Universe, what is one born of a woman** doing here **among us?** The Holy One, Blessed be He, said to them: **He came to receive the Torah.** The angels **said before Him:** The Torah is a **hidden treasure that was concealed by you 974 generations before the creation of the world,** and **you seek to give it to flesh and blood?** As it is stated: "The word which He commanded to a thousand generations" (Psalms 105:8). Since the Torah, the word of God, was given to the twenty-sixth generation after Adam, the first man, the remaining 974 generations must have preceded the creation of the world. **"What is man that You are mindful of him and the son of man that You think of him?"** (Psalms 8:5). Rather, **"God our LORD, how glorious is Your name in all the earth that Your majesty is placed above the heavens"** (Psalms 8:2). The rightful place of God's majesty, the Torah, is in the heavens.

The Holy One, Blessed be He, said to Moses: Provide them with **an answer** as to why the Torah should be given to the people. Moses

---

תְּשַׁע מֵאוֹת וְשִׁבְעִים וְאַרְבָּעָה דּוֹרוֹת *Nine hundred and seventy-four generations.* This idea has been presented elsewhere as: The Torah preceded creation of the world by 2,000 years. Some claim that the two calculations are equal (*Ba'al Halakhot Gedolot*). The calculation is based on the following: There were ten generations from Adam to Noah, and ten from Noah to Abraham. Abraham, Isaac, Jacob, Levi, Kehat, and Amram are six additional generations. The last twenty-six of 1,000 generations began with the Creation.

וְאָמַר רַבִּי יְהוֹשֻׁעַ בֶּן לֵוִי:
כָּל דִּיבּוּר וְדִיבּוּר שֶׁיָּצָא מִפִּי הַקָּדוֹשׁ בָּרוּךְ הוּא
חָזְרוּ יִשְׂרָאֵל לַאֲחוֹרֵיהֶן שְׁנֵים עָשָׂר מִיל
וְהָיוּ מַלְאֲכֵי הַשָּׁרֵת מְדַדִּין אוֹתָן
שֶׁנֶּאֱמַר: "מַלְאֲכֵי צְבָאוֹת יִדֹּדוּן יִדֹּדוּן"
אַל תִּיקְרֵי 'יִדֹּדוּן' אֶלָּא 'יְדַדּוּן'.

וְאָמַר רַבִּי יְהוֹשֻׁעַ בֶּן לֵוִי:
בְּשָׁעָה שֶׁעָלָה מֹשֶׁה לַמָּרוֹם
אָמְרוּ מַלְאֲכֵי הַשָּׁרֵת לִפְנֵי הַקָּדוֹשׁ בָּרוּךְ הוּא:
רִבּוֹנוֹ שֶׁל עוֹלָם, מַה לִּילוּד אִשָּׁה בֵּינֵינוּ?
אָמַר לָהֶן: לְקַבֵּל תּוֹרָה בָּא.
אָמְרוּ לְפָנָיו:
חֲמוּדָה גְּנוּזָה שֶׁגְּנוּזָה לָךְ
תְּשַׁע מֵאוֹת וְשִׁבְעִים וְאַרְבָּעָה דּוֹרוֹת קוֹדֶם שֶׁנִּבְרָא הָעוֹלָם
אַתָּה מְבַקֵּשׁ לִיתְּנָהּ לְבָשָׂר וָדָם?
"מָה אֱנוֹשׁ כִּי תִזְכְּרֶנּוּ וּבֶן אָדָם כִּי תִפְקְדֶנּוּ
ה' אֲדֹנֵינוּ מָה אַדִּיר שִׁמְךָ בְּכָל הָאָרֶץ
אֲשֶׁר תְּנָה הוֹדְךָ עַל הַשָּׁמָיִם"!
אָמַר לוֹ הַקָּדוֹשׁ בָּרוּךְ הוּא לְמֹשֶׁה:
הַחֲזִיר לָהֶן תְּשׁוּבָה!

חָזְרוּ יִשְׂרָאֵל לַאֲחוֹרֵיהֶן *The Jewish people retreated.* According to some commentaries, after each utterance, the Jewish people felt that they had to again draw near to God (*Beit Ya'akov*).

said before Him: Master of the Universe, I am afraid lest they burn me with the breath of their mouths. God said to him: Grasp My throne of glory for strength and protection, and provide them with an answer. And from where is this derived? As it is stated: "He causes him to grasp the front of the throne, and spreads His cloud over it" (Job 26:9), and Rabbi Naḥum said: This verse teaches that God spread the radiance of His presence and His cloud over Moses. Moses said before Him: Master of the Universe, the Torah that You are giving me, what is written in it? God said to him: "I am the LORD your God Who brought you out of Egypt from the house of bondage" (Exodus 20:2). Moses said to the angels: Did you descend to Egypt? Were you enslaved to Pharaoh? Why should the Torah be yours? Again Moses asked: What else is written in it? God said to him: "You shall have no other gods before Me" (Exodus 20:3). Moses said to the angels: Do you dwell among the nations who worship idols that you require this special warning? Again Moses asked: What else is written in it? The Holy One, Blessed be He, said to him: "Remember the Shabbat day to sanctify it" (Exodus 20:8). Moses asked the angels: Do you perform labor that you require rest from it? Again Moses asked: What else is written in it? "Do not take the name of the LORD your God in vain" (Exodus 20:7), meaning that it is prohibited to swear falsely. Moses asked the angels: Do you conduct business with one another that may lead you to swear falsely? Again Moses asked: What else is written in it? The Holy One, Blessed be He, said to him: "Honor your father and your mother" (Exodus 20:12). Moses asked the angels: Do you have a father or a mother that would render the commandment to honor them relevant to you? Again Moses asked: What else is written in it? God said to him: "You shall not murder, you shall not commit adultery, you shall not steal." Moses asked the angels: Is there jealousy among you, or is there an evil inclination within you that would render these

Shabbat 89a

---

the influence of the evil inclination, nevertheless, he overcomes his inclination and honors God (Ḥoshev Maḥshavot, Bina Le'Itim).

אָמַר לְפָנָיו:

רִבּוֹנוֹ שֶׁל עוֹלָם, מִתְיָרֵא אֲנִי שֶׁמָּא יִשְׂרְפוּנִי בַּהֶבֶל שֶׁבְּפִיהֶם.

אָמַר לוֹ: אֱחֹז בְּכִסֵּא כְבוֹדִי, וַחֲזוֹר לָהֶן תְּשׁוּבָה

שֶׁנֶּאֱמַר: "מְאַחֵז פְּנֵי כִסֵּא פַּרְשֵׁז עָלָיו עֲנָנוֹ".

וְאָמַר רַבִּי נַחוּם: מְלַמֵּד שֶׁפֵּירֵשׁ שַׁדַּי מִזִּיו שְׁכִינָתוֹ וַעֲנָנוֹ עָלָיו.

אָמַר לְפָנָיו:

רִבּוֹנוֹ שֶׁל עוֹלָם, תּוֹרָה שֶׁאַתָּה נוֹתֵן לִי מַה כְּתִיב בָּהּ –

"אָנֹכִי ה' אֱלֹהֶיךָ אֲשֶׁר הוֹצֵאתִיךָ מֵאֶרֶץ מִצְרַיִם".

אָמַר לָהֶן: לְמִצְרַיִם יְרַדְתֶּם, לְפַרְעֹה הִשְׁתַּעְבַּדְתֶּם

תּוֹרָה לָמָּה תְּהֵא לָכֶם?

שׁוּב מַה כְּתִיב בָּהּ – "לֹא יִהְיֶה לְךָ אֱלֹהִים אֲחֵרִים"

בֵּין הַגּוֹיִם אַתֶּם שְׁרוּיִין שֶׁעוֹבְדִין עֲבוֹדַת גְּלוּלִים?

שׁוּב מַה כְּתִיב בָּהּ – "זָכוֹר אֶת יוֹם הַשַּׁבָּת לְקַדְּשׁוֹ"

כְּלוּם אַתֶּם עוֹשִׂים מְלָאכָה שֶׁאַתֶּם צְרִיכִין שְׁבוּת?

שׁוּב מַה כְּתִיב בָּהּ – "לֹא תִשָּׂא"

מַשָּׂא וּמַתָּן יֵשׁ בֵּינֵיכֶם?

שׁוּב מַה כְּתִיב בָּהּ – "כַּבֵּד אֶת אָבִיךָ וְאֶת אִמֶּךָ"

אָב וָאֵם יֵשׁ לָכֶם?

שׁוּב מַה כְּתִיב בָּהּ "לֹא תִּרְצַח" "לֹא תִּנְאָף" "לֹא תִּגְנֹב"

קִנְאָה יֵשׁ בֵּינֵיכֶם, יֵצֶר הָרַע יֵשׁ בֵּינֵיכֶם?

שבת פט.

מִתְיָרֵא אֲנִי שֶׁמָּא *I am afraid lest they burn me with the breath of their mouths.*
Moses feared the breath of the angels because angels do not sin and, therefore,
their breath is without sin. God told him to grasp the throne of glory, because
God's glory comes from man. Although man is flesh and blood and subject to

commandments relevant? **Immediately they agreed with the Holy One, Blessed be He,** that He made the right decision to give the Torah to the people, and **as it is stated: "God our LORD, how glorious is Your name in all the earth"** (Psalms 8:10), **while "that Your majesty is placed above the heavens" is not written** because the angels agreed with God that it is appropriate to give the Torah to the people on earth.

Immediately, each and every one of the angels **became an admirer** of Moses **and passed something to him, as it is stated: "You ascended on high, you took a captive, you took gifts on account of man,** and even among the rebellious also that the LORD God might dwell there" (Psalms 68:19). The meaning of the verse is: **In reward for** the fact **that they called you man,** you are not an angel and the Torah is applicable to you, **you took gifts** from the angels. And **even the Angel of Death gave him something,** as Moses told Aaron how to stop the plague, **as it is stated: "And he placed the incense, and he atoned for the people"** (Numbers 17:12). **And** the verse **says: "And he stood between the dead and the living,** and the plague was stopped" (Numbers 17:13). **If** it were **not that** the Angel of Death **told him** this remedy, **would he have known** it?

And Rabbi Yehoshua ben Levi said: When Moses descended from standing **before the Holy One, Blessed be He,** with the Torah, **Satan came and said before Him: Master of the Universe, where is the Torah?**

He said to him: I have given it to the earth. He went to the earth, and **said to it: Where is the Torah? It said to him:** I do not know, as only: **"God understands its way,** and He knows its place" (Job 28:23).

---

enough to contain the Torah. Moses humbles himself and says that even though he received the Torah, he is nevertheless not worthy of it. Therefore, he was privileged to have the Torah called: The Torah of Moses (*Kur LeZahav*).

מִיָּד הוֹדוּ לוֹ לְהַקָּדוֹשׁ בָּרוּךְ הוּא

שֶׁנֶּאֱמַר: "ה' אֲדֹנֵינוּ מָה אַדִּיר שִׁמְךָ וְגוֹ'"

וְאִילּוּ "תְּנָה הוֹדְךָ עַל הַשָּׁמַיִם" – לָא כְּתִיב.

מִיָּד כָּל אֶחָד וְאֶחָד נַעֲשָׂה לוֹ אוֹהֵב, וּמָסַר לוֹ דָּבָר

שֶׁנֶּאֱמַר: "עָלִיתָ לַמָּרוֹם שָׁבִיתָ שֶּׁבִי לָקַחְתָּ מַתָּנוֹת בָּאָדָם"

בִּשְׂכַר שֶׁקְּרָאוּךָ אָדָם לָקַחְתָּ מַתָּנוֹת.

אַף מַלְאַךְ הַמָּוֶת מָסַר לוֹ דָּבָר

שֶׁנֶּאֱמַר: "וַיִּתֵּן אֶת הַקְּטֹרֶת וַיְכַפֵּר עַל הָעָם"

וְאוֹמֵר: "וַיַּעֲמֹד בֵּין הַמֵּתִים וּבֵין הַחַיִּים וְגוֹ'"

אִי לָאו דַּאֲמַר לֵיהּ – מִי הֲוָה יָדַע?

וְאָמַר רַבִּי יְהוֹשֻׁעַ בֶּן לֵוִי:

בְּשָׁעָה שֶׁיָּרַד מֹשֶׁה מִלִּפְנֵי הַקָּדוֹשׁ בָּרוּךְ הוּא

בָּא שָׂטָן וְאָמַר לְפָנָיו:

רִבּוֹנוֹ שֶׁל עוֹלָם, תּוֹרָה הֵיכָן הִיא?

אָמַר לוֹ: נְתַתִּיהָ לָאָרֶץ.

הָלַךְ אֵצֶל אֶרֶץ

אָמַר לָהּ: תּוֹרָה הֵיכָן הִיא?

אָמְרָה לוֹ: "אֱלֹהִים הֵבִין דַּרְכָּהּ וְגוֹ'".

בָּא שָׂטָן וְאָמַר לְפָנָיו *Satan came and said before Him.* Satan is the perpetual prosecutor, constantly seeking to diminish the merit of the inhabitants of the world. The Gemara relates that Satan opposed giving the Torah to this world, because no one in the world deserves it. Therefore, he travels from place to place and is unsuccessful in finding an area large

He went to the sea and asked: Where is the Torah? **And** the sea **said to him: "It is not with me."**

He went to the depths and asked: Where is the Torah? And the depths **said to him: "It is not within me."** And from where is it derived that the sea and the depths answered him this way? **As it is stated: "The depth said: It is not within me, and the sea said: It is not with me"** (Job 28:14). **"Destruction and death said: We heard a rumor of it with our ears"** (Job 28:22).

Satan **returned and said before the Holy One, Blessed be He: Master of the Universe, I searched** for the Torah **throughout all the earth and did not find it.** He **said to him: Go to** Moses, **son of Amram.**

He went to Moses and **said to him: The Torah that the Holy One, Blessed be He, gave you, where is it?** Moses evaded the question and **said to him: And what am I that the Holy One, Blessed be He, would have given me the Torah?** I am unworthy. **The Holy One, Blessed be He, said to Moses: Moses, are you a fabricator?** Moses **said before Him: Master of the Universe, You have a hidden treasure in which You delight every day,** as it is stated: "And I was His delight every day, playing before Him at every moment" (Proverbs 8:30). **Should I take credit for myself** and say that You gave it to me? **The Holy One, Blessed be He, said to Moses: Since you belittled yourself,** the Torah **will be called by your name, as it is stated: "Remember the Torah of Moses My servant** to whom I commanded at Horeb laws and statutes for all of Israel" (Malachi 3:22).

And Rabbi Yehoshua ben Levi said: When Moses ascended on High, he found the Holy One, Blessed be He, tying crowns to letters. On the tops of certain letters there are ornamental crownlets. Moses said

---

toiling to complete the writing of the Torah with those crowns. Incidentally, the Gemara mentions an additional lesson: One should conduct himself respectfully in every circumstance (*Adderet Eliyahu*).

הָלַךְ אֵצֶל יָם וְאָמַר לוֹ: "אֵין עִמָּדִי".

הָלַךְ אֵצֶל תְּהוֹם, אָמַר לוֹ: "אֵין בִּי"

שֶׁנֶּאֱמַר: "תְּהוֹם אָמַר לֹא בִי הִיא וְיָם אָמַר אֵין עִמָּדִי

אֲבַדּוֹן וָמָוֶת אָמְרוּ בְּאָזְנֵינוּ שָׁמַעְנוּ שִׁמְעָהּ".

חָזַר וְאָמַר לִפְנֵי הַקָּדוֹשׁ בָּרוּךְ הוּא:

רִבּוֹנוֹ שֶׁל עוֹלָם, חִפַּשְׂתִּי בְּכָל הָאָרֶץ וְלֹא מְצָאתִיהָ.

אָמַר לוֹ: לֵךְ אֵצֶל בֶּן עַמְרָם.

הָלַךְ אֵצֶל מֹשֶׁה

אָמַר לוֹ: תּוֹרָה שֶׁנָּתַן לְךָ הַקָּדוֹשׁ בָּרוּךְ הוּא הֵיכָן הִיא?

אָמַר לוֹ: וְכִי מָה אֲנִי שֶׁנָּתַן לִי הַקָּדוֹשׁ בָּרוּךְ הוּא תּוֹרָה?!

אָמַר לוֹ הַקָּדוֹשׁ בָּרוּךְ הוּא לְמֹשֶׁה: מֹשֶׁה, בַּדַּאי אַתָּה?!

אָמַר לְפָנָיו: רִבּוֹנוֹ שֶׁל עוֹלָם

חֲמוּדָה גְנוּזָה יֵשׁ לְךָ שֶׁאַתָּה מִשְׁתַּעֲשֵׁעַ בָּהּ בְּכָל יוֹם.

אֲנִי אַחֲזִיק טוֹבָה לְעַצְמִי?!

אָמַר לוֹ הַקָּדוֹשׁ בָּרוּךְ הוּא לְמֹשֶׁה:

הוֹאִיל וּמִיעַטְתָּ עַצְמְךָ – תִּקָּרֵא עַל שִׁמְךָ

שֶׁנֶּאֱמַר: "זִכְרוּ תּוֹרַת מֹשֶׁה עַבְדִּי וְגו'".

וְאָמַר רַבִּי יְהוֹשֻׁעַ בֶּן לֵוִי:

בְּשָׁעָה שֶׁעָלָה מֹשֶׁה לַמָּרוֹם

מְצָאוֹ לְהַקָּדוֹשׁ בָּרוּךְ הוּא שֶׁהָיָה קוֹשֵׁר כְּתָרִים לָאוֹתִיּוֹת.

קוֹשֵׁר כְּתָרִים לָאוֹתִיּוֹת *Tying crowns to letters.* Elsewhere, the Gemara reports that Rabbi Akiva interpreted each and every point on the crowns above the Torah's letters. This midrash relates that the Holy One, Blessed be He, was

nothing, and God **said to him: Moses, is there no greeting in your city?** Do people not greet each other in your city? He **said before Him: Does a servant greet his master?** That would be disrespectful. He **said to him:** At least **you should have assisted Me** and wished Me success in My work. **Immediately** he **said to Him: "And now, may the power of the LORD be great as you have spoken"** (Numbers 14:17).

And **Rabbi Yehoshua ben Levi said: What** is the meaning of that which is written: **"And the people saw that Moses delayed [*boshesh*] to come down from the mount"** (Exodus 32:1)? **Do not read** the word in the verse as *boshesh*; **rather,** read it as *ba'u shesh*, **six** hours **have arrived. When Moses ascended on High, he told** the **the Jewish people: In forty days, at the beginning of six** hours, **I will come. After forty days, Satan came and brought confusion to the world** by means of a storm, and it was impossible to ascertain the time. Satan **said to** the Jews: **Where is your teacher Moses?** They **said to him: He ascended on High.** He **said to them: Six** hours **have arrived** and he has not yet come. Surely he won't. **And they paid him no attention.** Satan said to them: Moses **died. And they paid him no attention.** Ultimately, **he showed them an image of his** death-**bed** and an image of Moses' corpse in a cloud. **And that is what** the Jewish people **said to Aaron: "For this Moses, the man** who brought us up out of the land of Egypt, we know not what has become of him" (Exodus 32:1).

One of the Sages said to Rav Kahana: Did you hear what is the reason that the mountain was called **Mount Sinai?** Rav Kahana **said to him:** It is because it is **a mountain upon which miracles [*nissim*] were performed for the Jewish people.** The Sage said to him: If so, **it should have been** called **Mount Nisai,** the mountain of miracles. **Rather,** Rav Kahana said to him: It is **a mountain that was a good omen [*siman*] for the Jewish people.** The Sage said to him: If so, **it should have been** called **Har Simanai,** the mountain of omens.

אָמַר לוֹ: מֹשֶׁה, אֵין שָׁלוֹם בְּעִירְךָ?

אָמַר לְפָנָיו: כְּלוּם יֵשׁ עֶבֶד שֶׁנּוֹתֵן שָׁלוֹם לְרַבּוֹ?

אָמַר לוֹ: הָיָה לְךָ לְעָזְרֵנִי.

מִיָּד אָמַר לוֹ: "וְעַתָּה יִגְדַּל נָא כֹּחַ ה' כַּאֲשֶׁר דִּבַּרְתָּ".

(אָמַר) רַבִּי יְהוֹשֻׁעַ בֶּן לֵוִי, מַאי דִכְתִיב:

"וַיַּרְא הָעָם כִּי בֹשֵׁשׁ מֹשֶׁה"

אַל תִּקְרֵי 'בוֹשֵׁשׁ' אֶלָּא 'בָּאוּ שֵׁשׁ'.

בְּשָׁעָה שֶׁעָלָה מֹשֶׁה לַמָּרוֹם אָמַר לָהֶן לְיִשְׂרָאֵל:

לְסוֹף אַרְבָּעִים יוֹם, בִּתְחִלַּת שֵׁשׁ, אֲנִי בָא.

לְסוֹף אַרְבָּעִים יוֹם בָּא שָׂטָן וְעִרְבֵּב אֶת הָעוֹלָם.

אָמַר לָהֶן: מֹשֶׁה רַבְּכֶם הֵיכָן הוּא?

אָמְרוּ לוֹ: עָלָה לַמָּרוֹם.

אָמַר לָהֶן: "בָּאוּ שֵׁשׁ" – וְלֹא הִשְׁגִּיחוּ עָלָיו.

"מֵת" – וְלֹא הִשְׁגִּיחוּ עָלָיו.

הֶרְאָה לָהֶן דְּמוּת מִטָּתוֹ.

וְהַיְינוּ דְּקָאָמְרִי לֵיהּ לְאַהֲרֹן: "כִּי זֶה מֹשֶׁה הָאִישׁ וְגו'".

אָמַר לֵיהּ הַהוּא מֵרַבָּנָן לְרַב כַּהֲנָא:

מִי שָׁמִיעַ לָךְ מַאי הַר סִינַי?

אָמַר לֵיהּ: הַר שֶׁנַּעֲשׂוּ בּוֹ נִסִּים לְיִשְׂרָאֵל.

הַר נִסַּאי מִיבָּעֵי לֵיהּ!

אֶלָּא: הַר שֶׁנַּעֲשָׂה סִימָן טוֹב לְיִשְׂרָאֵל.

הַר סִימָנַאי מִיבָּעֵי לֵיהּ!

Rav Kahana **said to him: What is the reason** that **you do not frequent** the school where you can study **before Rav Pappa and Rav Huna, son** of **Rav Yehoshua, who study** *aggada*? **As Rav Ḥisda and Rabba, son of Rav Huna, both said: What** is the reason it is called **Mount Sinai?** It is because it is **a mountain upon which hatred** [*sina*] **for the nations of the world descended** because they did not accept the Torah. **And that is what Rabbi Yose, son of Rabbi Ḥanina, said:** The desert in which Israel remained for forty years **has five names.** Each name has a source and a rationale: **The Zin Desert,** because **the Jewish people were commanded** [*nitztavu*] **in it; the Kadesh Desert,** because **the Jewish people were sanctified** [*nitkadshu*] **in it.** **The Kedemot Desert,** because the **ancient** [*keduma*] Torah, which preceded the world, **was given in it. The Paran Desert,** because **the Jewish people were fruitful** [*paru*] **and multiplied in it; the Sinai Desert,** because **hatred descended upon the nations of the world on it,** on the mountain on which the Jewish people received the Torah. **And what is** the mountain's true **name? Horeb is its name. And** that **disputes** the opinion of **Rabbi Abbahu, as Rabbi Abbahu said: Mount Sinai is its name. And why is it called Mount Horeb?** It is because **destruction** [*ḥurba*] **of the nations of the world descended upon it.**

Shabbat 89b

שֶׁיָּרְדָה שִׂנְאָה לְאֻמּוֹת הָעוֹלָם עָלָיו *Upon which hatred for the nations of the world descended.* Some commentaries explain that the nations of the world began hating the Jewish people when the Torah was given at Sinai. A different version of this statement, which appears in some collections of the midrash, supports this explanation. From the moment they received the Torah, the Jewish people became isolated. Still, most sources explain this differently, as indicating that hatred descended among the nations of the world. The revelation at Sinai introduced compulsory faith to the world, as well as the concept of a correct and incorrect way to worship God. This became a bone of contention between the nations of the world.

אֲמַר לֵיהּ:

מַאי טַעְמָא לָא שְׁכִיחַת קַמֵּיהּ

דְּרַב פַּפָּא וְרַב הוּנָא בְּרֵיהּ דְּרַב יְהוֹשֻׁעַ, דִּמְעַיְּינֵי בְּאַגַּדְתָּא.

דְּרַב חִסְדָּא וְרַבָּה בְּרֵיהּ דְּרַב הוּנָא דְּאָמְרִי תַּרְוַויְיהוּ:

מַאי הַר סִינַי – הַר שֶׁיָּרְדָה שִׂנְאָה לְאֻמּוֹת הָעוֹלָם עָלָיו.

וְהַיְינוּ דְּאָמַר רַבִּי יוֹסֵי בְּרַבִּי חֲנִינָא:

חֲמִשָּׁה שֵׁמוֹת יֵשׁ לוֹ:

מִדְבַּר צִין – שֶׁנִּצְטַוּוּ יִשְׂרָאֵל עָלָיו

מִדְבַּר קָדֵשׁ – שֶׁנִּתְקַדְּשׁוּ יִשְׂרָאֵל עָלָיו

מִדְבַּר קְדֵמוֹת – שֶׁנִּתְּנָה קְדוּמָה עָלָיו

מִדְבַּר פָּארָן – שֶׁפָּרוּ וְרָבוּ עָלֶיהָ יִשְׂרָאֵל

מִדְבַּר סִינַי – שֶׁיָּרְדָה שִׂנְאָה לְאוּמּוֹת הָעוֹלָם עָלָיו

וּמַה שְּׁמוֹ – חוֹרֵב שְׁמוֹ.

וּפְלִיגָא דְּרַבִּי אַבָּהוּ

דְּאָמַר רַבִּי אַבָּהוּ: הַר סִינַי שְׁמוֹ

וְלָמָּה נִקְרָא הַר חוֹרֵב –

שֶׁיָּרְדָה חוּרְבָּה לְאוּמּוֹת הָעוֹלָם עָלָיו.

שבת פט:

מַאי טַעְמָא לָא שְׁכִיחַת קַמֵּיהּ *What is the reason that you do not frequent the school where you can study before them.* Some commentaries interpret this differently, saying that it was the questioner who asked Rav Kahana why he doesn't go study *aggada* with Rav Pappa and Rav Huna, son of Rav Yehoshua. They are very precise in their statements, even when discussing *aggada*, while Rav Kahana is not.

Shaḥarit

The following order of prayers and blessings, which departs from that of most prayer books,
is based on the consensus of recent halakhic authorities.

ON WAKING

On waking, our first thought should be that we are in the presence of God. Since
we are forbidden to speak God's name until we have washed our hands, the
following prayer is said, which, without mentioning God's name, acknowledges
His presence and gives thanks for a new day and for the gift of life.

מוֹדֶה I thank You, living and eternal King,
for giving me back my soul in mercy.
Great is Your faithfulness.

Wash hands and say the following blessings.
Some have the custom to say "Wisdom begins" on page 222 at this point.

בָּרוּךְ Blessed are You, Lord our God, King of the Universe,
who has made us holy through His commandments,
and has commanded us about washing hands.

בָּרוּךְ Blessed are You, Lord our God, King of the Universe,
who formed man in wisdom
and created in him many orifices and cavities.
It is revealed and known before the throne of Your glory
that were one of them to be ruptured or blocked,
it would be impossible to survive and stand before You.
Blessed are You, Lord,
Healer of all flesh who does wondrous deeds.

---

not contain God's name so that it may be said immediately on waking, even
prior to washing hands.

אֲשֶׁר יָצַר אֶת הָאָדָם בְּחָכְמָה *Who formed man in wisdom.* There are a hundred
trillion cells in the human body. Within each cell is a nucleus and within
each nucleus a double copy of the human genome. Each genome consists
of 3.1 billion letters of genetic code, sufficient if transcribed to fill a library of
five thousand volumes. Even this is only the beginning of the miracle, for the
development of the body is not a matter of simple genetic determinism. It is

שחרית

The following order of prayers and blessings, which departs from that of most prayer books,
is based on the consensus of recent halakhic authorities.

השכמת הבוקר

On waking, our first thought should be that we are in the presence of God. Since
we are forbidden to speak God's name until we have washed our hands, the
following prayer is said, which, without mentioning God's name, acknowledges
His presence and gives thanks for a new day and for the gift of life.

מוֹדֶה/ *women* מוֹדָה/ אֲנִי לְפָנֶיךָ מֶלֶךְ חַי וְקַיָּם
שֶׁהֶחֱזַרְתָּ בִּי נִשְׁמָתִי בְּחֶמְלָה
רַבָּה אֱמוּנָתֶךָ.

Wash hands and say the following blessings.
Some have the custom to say רֵאשִׁית חָכְמָה *on page 223 at this point.*

בָּרוּךְ אַתָּה יהוה אֱלֹהֵינוּ מֶלֶךְ הָעוֹלָם
אֲשֶׁר קִדְּשָׁנוּ בְּמִצְוֺתָיו וְצִוָּנוּ עַל נְטִילַת יָדָיִם.

בָּרוּךְ אַתָּה יהוה אֱלֹהֵינוּ מֶלֶךְ הָעוֹלָם
אֲשֶׁר יָצַר אֶת הָאָדָם בְּחָכְמָה
וּבָרָא בוֹ נְקָבִים נְקָבִים, חֲלוּלִים חֲלוּלִים.
גָּלוּי וְיָדוּעַ לִפְנֵי כִסֵּא כְבוֹדֶךָ
שֶׁאִם יִפָּתֵחַ אֶחָד מֵהֶם אוֹ יִסָּתֵם אֶחָד מֵהֶם
אִי אֶפְשָׁר לְהִתְקַיֵּם וְלַעֲמֹד לְפָנֶיךָ.
בָּרוּךְ אַתָּה יהוה, רוֹפֵא כָל בָּשָׂר וּמַפְלִיא לַעֲשׂוֹת.

מוֹדֶה אֲנִי *I thank You.* Sleep, said the sages, is a sixtieth, a foretaste, of death
(*Berakhot* 57b). Waking each morning is therefore a miniature resurrection.
We are new, the universe is new (we say later in our prayers, "who renews
every day the work of creation"), and before us lies an open page of possibili-
ties. In this simple prayer we thank God for giving us back our life. It does

אֱלֹהַי My God,
the soul You placed within me is pure.
You created it, You formed it, You breathed it into me,
and You guard it while it is within me.
One day You will take it from me,
and restore it to me in the time to come.
As long as the soul is within me,
I will thank You,
LORD my God and God of my ancestors,
Master of all works, LORD of all souls.
Blessed are You, LORD,
who restores souls to lifeless bodies.

TZITZIT

*The following blessing is said before putting on tzitzit. Neither it nor the subsequent prayer
is said by those who wear a tallit. The blessing over the latter exempts the former.*

בָּרוּךְ Blessed are You, LORD our God, King of the Universe,
who has made us holy through His commandments,
and has commanded us about the command of tasseled garments.

After putting on tzitzit, say:

יְהִי רָצוֹן May it be Your will, LORD my God and God of my ancestors, that
the commandment of the tasseled garment be considered before You as if
I had fulfilled it in all its specifics, details and intentions, as well as the 613
commandments dependent on it, Amen, Selah.

נְשָׁמָה שֶׁנָּתַתָּ בִּי טְהוֹרָה הִיא *The soul You placed within me is pure.* Despite the
fact that we have genetically encoded instincts and desires, there is nothing
predetermined about whether we use them for good or bad.

הַמַּחֲזִיר נְשָׁמוֹת לִפְגָרִים מֵתִים *Who restores souls to lifeless bodies.* Since waking
each morning is like a resurrection, it is an intimation of the fact that the dead
can be restored to life, as we believe they will be at the end of days. This prayer
is a simple, subtle way of making us daily aware of the interplay between
mortality and immortality in the human condition. It opens our eyes to the
wonder of being, the miracle that we are here at all.

אֱלֹהַי
נְשָׁמָה שֶׁנָּתַתָּ בִּי טְהוֹרָה הִיא.
אַתָּה בְרָאתָהּ, אַתָּה יְצַרְתָּהּ, אַתָּה נְפַחְתָּהּ בִּי
וְאַתָּה מְשַׁמְּרָהּ בְּקִרְבִּי, וְאַתָּה עָתִיד לִטְּלָהּ מִמֶּנִּי
וּלְהַחֲזִירָהּ בִּי לֶעָתִיד לָבוֹא.
כָּל זְמַן שֶׁהַנְּשָׁמָה בְקִרְבִּי, מוֹדֶה/ women/מוֹדָה/ אֲנִי לְפָנֶיךָ
יהוה אֱלֹהַי וֵאלֹהֵי אֲבוֹתַי
רִבּוֹן כָּל הַמַּעֲשִׂים, אֲדוֹן כָּל הַנְּשָׁמוֹת.
בָּרוּךְ אַתָּה יהוה, הַמַּחֲזִיר נְשָׁמוֹת לִפְגָרִים מֵתִים.

לביישת ציצית

The following blessing is said before putting on a טלית קטן. *Neither it nor* יְהִי רָצוֹן *is said by those who wear a* טלית. *The blessing over the latter exempts the former.*

בָּרוּךְ אַתָּה יהוה אֱלֹהֵינוּ מֶלֶךְ הָעוֹלָם
אֲשֶׁר קִדְּשָׁנוּ בְּמִצְוֹתָיו וְצִוָּנוּ עַל מִצְוַת צִיצִית.

After putting on the טלית קטן, *say:*

יְהִי רָצוֹן מִלְּפָנֶיךָ, יהוה אֱלֹהַי וֵאלֹהֵי אֲבוֹתַי, שֶׁתְּהֵא חֲשׁוּבָה מִצְוַת
צִיצִית לְפָנֶיךָ כְּאִלּוּ קִיַּמְתִּיהָ בְּכָל פְּרָטֶיהָ וְדִקְדּוּקֶיהָ וְכַוָּנוֹתֶיהָ, וְתַרְיַ"ג
מִצְוֹת הַתְּלוּיוֹת בָּהּ, אָמֵן סֶלָה.

an elaborate process of interaction between genes and environment, nature and nurture, genetic and epigenetic influences. Faith is not opposed to science, nor is science incompatible with faith. Faith is wonder and gratitude. Therefore, said Maimonides, natural science is one of the paths to the love and awe of God, as we realize the vastness of the universe and the complexity of life (Laws of the Foundations of the Torah 2:2). Each new scientific discovery gives added resonance to the words of the psalm: "How numerous are Your works, LORD; You made them all in wisdom; the earth is full of Your creations" (Ps. 104:24).

BLESSINGS OVER THE TORAH

In Judaism, study is greater even than prayer. So, before beginning to pray, we engage in a miniature act of study, preceded by the appropriate blessings. The blessings are followed by brief selections from Scripture, Mishna and Gemara, the three foundational texts of Judaism.

בָּרוּךְ Blessed are You, Lord our God, King of the Universe,
who has made us holy through His commandments,
and has commanded us to engage in study
of the words of Torah.
Please, Lord our God, make the words of Your Torah
sweet in our mouths and in the mouths of Your people,
the house of Israel,
so that we, our descendants (and their descendants)
and the descendants of Your people,
the house of Israel,
may all know Your name and study Your Torah for its own sake.
Blessed are You, Lord,
who teaches Torah to His people Israel.

בָּרוּךְ Blessed are You, Lord our God, King of the Universe,
who has chosen us from all the peoples and given us His Torah.
Blessed are You, Lord,
Giver of the Torah.

בְּמִצְוֹתָיו *Through His commandments.* This blessing, said over commands between us and God, represents the intention to fulfill an act as a command, thus endowing it with holiness. Only commands between us and God require a blessing beforehand. Commands between us and our fellow humans – such as giving charity, visiting the sick, comforting mourners and so on – do not require a blessing beforehand, since in these cases the command has to do with its effect (*nifal*), rather than the act itself (*pe'ula*) or its agent (*po'el*). Since the effect of acts of kindness is independent of the intention of the agent, no preliminary declaration of intent – that is, a blessing – is necessary.

בָּרוּךְ אַתָּה...אֲשֶׁר בָּחַר בָּנוּ *Blessed are You... who has chosen us.* Unlike the previous blessing, which is one of the *birkot hamitzvot*, blessings over a command, this is a *birkat hoda'a*, a blessing of thanks and acknowledgment.

ברכות התורה

In Judaism, study is greater even than prayer. So, before beginning to pray, we engage in a miniature act of study, preceded by the appropriate blessings. The blessings are followed by brief selections from משנה, תנ"ך *and* גמרא, *the three foundational texts of Judaism.*

בָּרוּךְ אַתָּה יהוה אֱלֹהֵינוּ מֶלֶךְ הָעוֹלָם
אֲשֶׁר קִדְּשָׁנוּ בְּמִצְוֹתָיו, וְצִוָּנוּ לַעֲסֹק בְּדִבְרֵי תוֹרָה.

וְהַעֲרֶב נָא יהוה אֱלֹהֵינוּ אֶת דִּבְרֵי תוֹרָתְךָ
בְּפִינוּ וּבְפִי עַמְּךָ בֵּית יִשְׂרָאֵל
וְנִהְיֶה אֲנַחְנוּ וְצֶאֱצָאֵינוּ (וְצֶאֱצָאֵי צֶאֱצָאֵינוּ)
וְצֶאֱצָאֵי עַמְּךָ בֵּית יִשְׂרָאֵל
כֻּלָּנוּ יוֹדְעֵי שְׁמֶךָ וְלוֹמְדֵי תוֹרָתֶךָ לִשְׁמָהּ.
בָּרוּךְ אַתָּה יהוה, הַמְלַמֵּד תּוֹרָה לְעַמּוֹ יִשְׂרָאֵל.

בָּרוּךְ אַתָּה יהוה אֱלֹהֵינוּ מֶלֶךְ הָעוֹלָם
אֲשֶׁר בָּחַר בָּנוּ מִכָּל הָעַמִּים, וְנָתַן לָנוּ אֶת תּוֹרָתוֹ.
בָּרוּךְ אַתָּה יהוה, נוֹתֵן הַתּוֹרָה.

BLESSINGS OVER THE TORAH

In Judaism, Torah study is the highest of all spiritual engagements, higher even than prayer (*Shabbat* 10a), for in prayer we speak to God but in Torah study we listen to God speaking to us, through the sacred texts of our tradition. Judaism is supremely a religion of study. Hence we preface prayer with an act of Torah study.

There are three types of Torah study: (1) study in order to know what to do, (2) study as a substitute for rituals that we are unable to perform, most notably the sacrifices, and (3) study as a religious act for its own sake, an aligning of our intellect with the mind of God.

אֲשֶׁר קִדְּשָׁנוּ *Who has made us holy.* Holiness is not a given of birth, a genetic endowment. It is what we become when we submit our will to that of God. We become holy by what we do. The word "holy" means distinctive, set apart. Just as God is holy because He transcends the physical universe, so we become holy by transcending natural impulses and instincts.

יְבָרֶכְךָ May the LORD bless you and protect you.
May the LORD make His face shine on you
and be gracious to you.
May the LORD turn His face toward you
and grant you peace.

Num. 6

אֵלּוּ These are the things for which there is no fixed measure:
the corner of the field, first fruits,
appearances before the LORD [on festivals, with offerings],
acts of kindness and the study of Torah.

Mishna
Pe'ah 1:1

אֵלּוּ These are the things whose fruits we eat in this world
but whose full reward awaits us in the World to Come:
honoring parents; acts of kindness;
arriving early at the house of study morning and evening;
hospitality to strangers; visiting the sick;
helping the needy bride; attending to the dead;
devotion in prayer;
and bringing peace between people –
but the study of Torah is equal to them all.

Shabbat
127a

Some say:

רֵאשִׁית חָכְמָה Wisdom begins in awe of the LORD;
all who fulfill [His commandments] gain good understanding;
His praise is ever-lasting.
The Torah Moses commanded us is the heritage of the congregation of Jacob.
Listen, my son, to your father's instruction,
and do not forsake your mother's teaching.
May the Torah be my faith and Almighty God my help.
Blessed be the name of His glorious kingdom for ever and all time.

Ps. 111

Deut. 33

Prov. 1

So here, "May the LORD bless you" is a passage from the Torah (Num. 6:24–26), "These are the things for which there is no fixed measure" is a passage from the Mishna (*Pe'ah* 1:1), and "These are the things of which a man enjoys the fruits in this life" is a teaching from the Talmud (*Shabbat* 127a).

וְתַלְמוּד תּוֹרָה כְּנֶגֶד כֻּלָּם *The study of the Torah is equal to them all.* There was a debate among the sages as to which is greater, learning or doing? The conclusion was that "Great is learning, for it leads to doing" (*Kiddushin* 40b).

במדבר ו

יְבָרֶכְךָ יהוה וְיִשְׁמְרֶךָ:
יָאֵר יהוה פָּנָיו אֵלֶיךָ וִיחֻנֶּךָּ:
יִשָּׂא יהוה פָּנָיו אֵלֶיךָ וְיָשֵׂם לְךָ שָׁלוֹם:

משנה,
פאה א: א

אֵלּוּ דְבָרִים שֶׁאֵין לָהֶם שִׁעוּר
הַפֵּאָה וְהַבִּכּוּרִים וְהָרֵאָיוֹן
וּגְמִילוּת חֲסָדִים וְתַלְמוּד תּוֹרָה.

שבת קכז.

אֵלּוּ דְבָרִים שֶׁאָדָם אוֹכֵל פֵּרוֹתֵיהֶם בָּעוֹלָם הַזֶּה
וְהַקֶּרֶן קַיֶּמֶת לוֹ לָעוֹלָם הַבָּא, וְאֵלּוּ הֵן
כִּבּוּד אָב וָאֵם, וּגְמִילוּת חֲסָדִים
וְהַשְׁכָּמַת בֵּית הַמִּדְרָשׁ שַׁחֲרִית וְעַרְבִית
וְהַכְנָסַת אוֹרְחִים, וּבִקּוּר חוֹלִים
וְהַכְנָסַת כַּלָּה, וּלְוָיַת הַמֵּת
וְעִיּוּן תְּפִלָּה
וַהֲבָאַת שָׁלוֹם בֵּין אָדָם לַחֲבֵרוֹ
וְתַלְמוּד תּוֹרָה כְּנֶגֶד כֻּלָּם.

Some say:

תהלים קיא
דברים לג
משלי א

רֵאשִׁית חָכְמָה יִרְאַת יהוה, שֵׂכֶל טוֹב לְכָל־עֹשֵׂיהֶם, תְּהִלָּתוֹ עֹמֶדֶת לָעַד:
תּוֹרָה צִוָּה־לָנוּ מֹשֶׁה, מוֹרָשָׁה קְהִלַּת יַעֲקֹב:
שְׁמַע בְּנִי מוּסַר אָבִיךָ וְאַל־תִּטֹּשׁ תּוֹרַת אִמֶּךָ:
תּוֹרָה תְּהֵא אֱמוּנָתִי, וְאֵל שַׁדַּי בְּעֶזְרָתִי.
בָּרוּךְ שֵׁם כְּבוֹד מַלְכוּתוֹ לְעוֹלָם וָעֶד.

יְבָרֶכְךָ יהוה *May the* LORD *bless you.* According to the sages (*Kiddushin* 30a), one should divide one's study time into three: (1) *Mikra*, study of the written Torah; (2) *Mishna*, study of the Mishna, primary text of the Oral Torah; (3) *Talmud*, that is, either the Babylonian or Jerusalem Talmud or other parts of the rabbinic literature dedicated to explaining the logic of the Oral Law (Maimonides, Laws of Torah Study 1:11).

TALLIT

*Say the following meditation before putting on the tallit. Meditations before
the fulfillment of mitzvot are to ensure that we do so with the requisite intention
(kavana). This particularly applies to mitzvot whose purpose is to induce in
us certain states of mind, as is the case with tallit and tefillin, both of which are
external symbols of inward commitment to the life of observance of the mitzvot.*

בָּרְכִי נַפְשִׁי Bless the LORD, my soul. LORD, my God, You are very great, *Ps. 104*
clothed in majesty and splendor, wrapped in a robe of light, spreading
out the heavens like a tent.

Some say:

For the sake of the unification of the Holy One, blessed be He, and His Divine Presence,
in reverence and love, to unify the name *Yod-Heh* with *Vav-Heh* in perfect unity in the
name of all Israel.

I am about to wrap myself in this tasseled garment (tallit). So may my soul, my 248
limbs and 365 sinews be wrapped in the light of the tassel (*hatzitzit*) which amounts to
613 [commandments]. And just as I cover myself with a tasseled garment in this world,
so may I be worthy of rabbinical dress and a fine garment in the World to Come in the
Garden of Eden. Through the commandment of tassels may my life's-breath, spirit, soul
and prayer be delivered from external impediments, and may the tallit spread its wings
over them like an eagle stirring up its nest, hovering over its young. May the command- *Deut. 32*
ment of the tasseled garment be considered before the Holy One, blessed be He, as if I
had fulfilled it in all its specifics, details and intentions, as well as the 613 commandments
dependent on it, Amen, Selah.

Before wrapping oneself in the tallit, say:

בָּרוּךְ Blessed are You, LORD our God, King of the Universe,
who has made us holy through His commandments,
and has commanded us to wrap ourselves in the tasseled garment.

*According to the Shela (R. Isaiah Horowitz), one should say
these verses after wrapping oneself in the tallit:*

מַה־יָּקָר How precious is Your loving-kindness, O God, and the children of men find refuge *Ps. 36*
under the shadow of Your wings. They are filled with the rich plenty of Your House. You give
them drink from Your river of delights. For with You is the fountain of life; in Your light, we
see light. Continue Your loving-kindness to those who know You, and Your righteousness
to the upright in heart.

Wrapping oneself in a tallit to pray is already mentioned in the Talmud
(*Rosh HaShana* 17b). It symbolizes the idea of being enveloped by holiness.
It is said that God "wraps Himself in light as with a garment" (Ps. 104:2). To
be wrapped and robed in holiness as we begin to pray is a momentous way of
sensing the closeness of God, who bathes the universe in light if we have eyes
to see it or a heart to feel it.

עֲטִיפַת טַלִּית

Say the following meditation before putting on the טלית. Meditations before
the fulfillment of מצוות are to ensure that we do so with the requisite intention
(כוונה). This particularly applies to מצוות whose purpose is to induce in us certain
states of mind, as is the case with טלית and תפילין, both of which are external
symbols of inward commitment to the life of observance of the מצוות.

תהלים קד

בָּרְכִי נַפְשִׁי אֶת־יהוה, יהוה אֱלֹהַי גָּדַלְתָּ מְּאֹד, הוֹד וְהָדָר לָבָשְׁתָּ: עֹטֶה־אוֹר כַּשַּׂלְמָה, נוֹטֶה שָׁמַיִם כַּיְרִיעָה:

Some say:

לְשֵׁם יִחוּד קֻדְשָׁא בְּרִיךְ הוּא וּשְׁכִינְתֵּהּ בִּדְחִילוּ וּרְחִימוּ, לְיַחֵד שֵׁם י"ה בו"ה בְּיִחוּדָא שְׁלִים בְּשֵׁם כָּל יִשְׂרָאֵל.

הֲרֵינִי מִתְעַטֵּף בַּצִּיצִית. כֵּן תִּתְעַטֵּף נִשְׁמָתִי וּרְמַ"ח אֵבָרַי וּשְׁסַ"ה גִידַי בְּאוֹר הַצִּיצִית הָעוֹלָה תַּרְיַ"ג. וּכְשֵׁם שֶׁאֲנִי מִתְכַּסֶּה בְּטַלִית בָּעוֹלָם הַזֶּה, כָּךְ אֶזְכֶּה לַחֲלוּקָא דְרַבָּנָן וּלְטַלִית נָאָה לָעוֹלָם הַבָּא בְּגַן עֵדֶן. וְעַל יְדֵי מִצְוַת צִיצִית תִּנָּצֵל נַפְשִׁי רוּחִי וְנִשְׁמָתִי

דברים לב

וּתְפִלָּתִי מִן הַחִיצוֹנִים. וְהַטַּלִית תִּפְרֹשׂ כְּנָפֶיהָ עֲלֵיהֶם וְתַצִּילֵם, כְּנֶשֶׁר יָעִיר קִנּוֹ, עַל גּוֹזָלָיו יְרַחֵף. וּתְהֵא חֲשׁוּבָה מִצְוַת צִיצִית לִפְנֵי הַקָּדוֹשׁ בָּרוּךְ הוּא, כְּאִלּוּ קִיַּמְתִּיהָ בְּכָל פְּרָטֶיהָ וְדִקְדּוּקֶיהָ וְכַוָּנוֹתֶיהָ וְתַרְיַ"ג מִצְוֹת הַתְּלוּיוֹת בָּהּ, אָמֵן סֶלָה.

Before wrapping oneself in the טלית, say:

בָּרוּךְ אַתָּה יהוה אֱלֹהֵינוּ מֶלֶךְ הָעוֹלָם אֲשֶׁר קִדְּשָׁנוּ בְּמִצְוֹתָיו וְצִוָּנוּ לְהִתְעַטֵּף בַּצִּיצִית.

According to the Shela (R. Isaiah Horowitz), one should say
these verses after wrapping oneself in the טלית:

תהלים לו

מַה־יָּקָר חַסְדְּךָ אֱלֹהִים, וּבְנֵי אָדָם בְּצֵל כְּנָפֶיךָ יֶחֱסָיוּן: יִרְוְיֻן מִדֶּשֶׁן בֵּיתֶךָ, וְנַחַל עֲדָנֶיךָ תַשְׁקֵם: כִּי־עִמְּךָ מְקוֹר חַיִּים, בְּאוֹרְךָ נִרְאֶה־אוֹר: מְשֹׁךְ חַסְדְּךָ לְיֹדְעֶיךָ, וְצִדְקָתְךָ לְיִשְׁרֵי־לֵב:

TALLIT

Tallit, which means a cloak or gown, is one of the ways in which we fulfill the mitzva of *tzitzit*, placing tassels on the corners of our garments to recall us constantly to our vocation: "Thus you will be reminded to keep all My commands, and be holy to your God" (Num. 15:39). In the course of time two different fringed garments were worn: the *tallit*, worn as a mantle during prayer, *over* our clothes; and the *tallit katan*, worn as an undergarment *beneath* our outer clothes.

PREPARATION FOR PRAYER

On entering the synagogue:

HOW GOODLY

Num. 24

are your tents, Jacob, your dwelling places, Israel.
As for me,

Ps. 5

in Your great loving-kindness,
I will come into Your House.
I will bow down to Your holy Temple
in awe of You.
Lord, I love the habitation of Your House,

Ps. 26

the place where Your glory dwells.

As for me,
I will bow in worship;

> I will bend the knee
> before the Lord my Maker.

As for me,
may my prayer come to You, Lord,

Ps. 69

> at a time of favor.
> God, in Your great loving-kindness,
> answer me with Your faithful salvation.

הכנה לתפילה

On entering the בֵּית כְּנֶסֶת:

במדבר כד

מַה־טֹּבוּ

אֹהָלֶיךָ יַעֲקֹב, מִשְׁכְּנֹתֶיךָ יִשְׂרָאֵל:

תהלים ה

וַאֲנִי בְּרֹב חַסְדְּךָ אָבוֹא בֵיתֶךָ
אֶשְׁתַּחֲוֶה אֶל־הֵיכַל־קָדְשְׁךָ
בְּיִרְאָתֶךָ:

תהלים כו

יהוה אָהַבְתִּי מְעוֹן בֵּיתֶךָ
וּמְקוֹם מִשְׁכַּן כְּבוֹדֶךָ:

וַאֲנִי אֶשְׁתַּחֲוֶה

וְאֶכְרָעָה
אֲבָרְכָה לִפְנֵי יהוה עֹשִׂי.

תהלים סט

וַאֲנִי תְפִלָּתִי־לְךָ יהוה

עֵת רָצוֹן
אֱלֹהִים בְּרָב־חַסְדֶּךָ
עֲנֵנִי בֶּאֱמֶת יִשְׁעֶךָ:

*The following poems, on this page and the next, both from the Middle Ages,
are summary statements of Jewish faith, orienting us to the spiritual contours
of the world that we actualize in the mind by the act of prayer.*

LORD OF THE UNIVERSE,
who reigned before the birth of any thing –

When by His will all things were made
then was His name proclaimed King.

And when all things shall cease to be
He alone will reign in awe.

He was, He is, and He shall be
glorious for evermore.

He is One, there is none else,
alone, unique, beyond compare;

Without beginning, without end,
His might, His rule are everywhere.

He is my God; my Redeemer lives.
He is the Rock on whom I rely –

My banner and my safe retreat,
my cup, my portion when I cry.

Into His hand my soul I place,
when I awake and when I sleep.

The LORD is with me, I shall not fear;
body and soul from harm will He keep.

The following poems, on this page and the next, both from the Middle Ages,
are summary statements of Jewish faith, orienting us to the spiritual contours
of the world that we actualize in the mind by the act of prayer.

אֲדוֹן עוֹלָם

אֲשֶׁר מָלַךְ בְּטֶרֶם כָּל־יְצִיר נִבְרָא.

לְעֵת נַעֲשָׂה בְחֶפְצוֹ כֹּל אֲזַי מֶלֶךְ שְׁמוֹ נִקְרָא.

וְאַחֲרֵי כִּכְלוֹת הַכֹּל לְבַדּוֹ יִמְלֹךְ נוֹרָא.

וְהוּא הָיָה וְהוּא הֹוֶה וְהוּא יִהְיֶה בְּתִפְאָרָה.

וְהוּא אֶחָד וְאֵין שֵׁנִי לְהַמְשִׁיל לוֹ לְהַחְבִּירָה.

בְּלִי רֵאשִׁית בְּלִי תַכְלִית וְלוֹ הָעֹז וְהַמִּשְׂרָה.

וְהוּא אֵלִי וְחַי גּוֹאֲלִי וְצוּר חֶבְלִי בְּעֵת צָרָה.

וְהוּא נִסִּי וּמָנוֹס לִי מְנָת כּוֹסִי בְּיוֹם אֶקְרָא.

בְּיָדוֹ אַפְקִיד רוּחִי בְּעֵת אִישָׁן וְאָעִירָה.

וְעִם רוּחִי גְּוִיָּתִי יהוה לִי וְלֹא אִירָא.

GREAT

is the living God and praised.
He exists, and His existence is beyond time.

He is One, and there is no unity like His.
Unfathomable, His Oneness is infinite.

He has neither bodily form nor substance;
His holiness is beyond compare.

He preceded all that was created.
He was first: there was no beginning to His beginning.

Behold He is Master of the Universe; and every creature
shows His greatness and majesty.

The rich flow of His prophecy He gave
to His treasured people in whom He gloried.

Never in Israel has there arisen another like Moses,
a prophet who beheld God's image.

God gave His people a Torah of truth
by the hand of His prophet, most faithful of His House.

God will not alter or change His law
for any other, for eternity.

He sees and knows our secret thoughts;
as soon as something is begun, He foresees its end.

He rewards people with loving-kindness according to their deeds;
He punishes the wicked according to his wickedness.

At the end of days He will send our Messiah
to redeem those who await His final salvation.

God will revive the dead in His great loving-kindness.
Blessed for evermore is His glorious name!

יִגְדַּל

אֱלֹהִים חַי וְיִשְׁתַּבַּח, נִמְצָא וְאֵין עֵת אֶל מְצִיאוּתוֹ.

אֶחָד וְאֵין יָחִיד כְּיִחוּדוֹ, נֶעְלָם וְגַם אֵין סוֹף לְאַחְדּוּתוֹ.

אֵין לוֹ דְּמוּת הַגּוּף וְאֵינוֹ גוּף, לֹא נַעֲרֹךְ אֵלָיו קְדֻשָּׁתוֹ.

קַדְמוֹן לְכָל דָּבָר אֲשֶׁר נִבְרָא, רִאשׁוֹן וְאֵין רֵאשִׁית לְרֵאשִׁיתוֹ.

הִנּוֹ אֲדוֹן עוֹלָם, וְכָל נוֹצָר יוֹרֶה גְדֻלָּתוֹ וּמַלְכוּתוֹ.

שֶׁפַע נְבוּאָתוֹ נְתָנוֹ אֶל־אַנְשֵׁי סְגֻלָּתוֹ וְתִפְאַרְתּוֹ.

לֹא קָם בְּיִשְׂרָאֵל כְּמֹשֶׁה עוֹד נָבִיא וּמַבִּיט אֶת תְּמוּנָתוֹ.

תּוֹרַת אֱמֶת נָתַן לְעַמּוֹ אֵל עַל יַד נְבִיאוֹ נֶאֱמַן בֵּיתוֹ.

לֹא יַחֲלִיף הָאֵל וְלֹא יָמִיר דָּתוֹ לְעוֹלָמִים לְזוּלָתוֹ.

צוֹפֶה וְיוֹדֵעַ סְתָרֵינוּ, מַבִּיט לְסוֹף דָּבָר בְּקַדְמָתוֹ.

גּוֹמֵל לְאִישׁ חֶסֶד כְּמִפְעָלוֹ, נוֹתֵן לְרָשָׁע רָע כְּרִשְׁעָתוֹ.

יִשְׁלַח לְקֵץ יָמִין מְשִׁיחֵנוּ לִפְדּוֹת מְחַכֵּי קֵץ יְשׁוּעָתוֹ.

מֵתִים יְחַיֶּה אֵל בְּרֹב חַסְדּוֹ, בָּרוּךְ עֲדֵי עַד שֵׁם תְּהִלָּתוֹ.

MORNING BLESSINGS

The following blessings are said aloud by the Leader, but each individual should say them quietly as well. It is our custom to say them standing.

בָּרוּךְ Blessed are You, LORD our God,
King of the Universe,
who gives the heart understanding
to distinguish day from night.

Blessed are You, LORD our God,
King of the Universe,
who has not made me a heathen.

Blessed are You, LORD our God,
King of the Universe,
who has not made me a slave.

Blessed are You, LORD our God,
King of the Universe,
men: who has not made me a woman.
women: who has made me according to His will.

Blessed are You, LORD our God,
King of the Universe,
who gives sight to the blind.

שֶׁלֹּא עָשַׂנִי גּוֹי...עֶבֶד *Who has not made me a heathen… a slave.* We each have our part to play in the divine economy. We thank God for ours, for the privilege of being part of "a kingdom of priests and a holy nation" (Ex. 19:6).

פּוֹקֵחַ עִוְרִים *Gives sight to the blind… etc.* A series of blessings originally said at home, later made part of the synagogue service. They were initially said to accompany the various actions involved in waking and getting up – opening our eyes, putting on clothes, stretching our limbs, setting foot on the ground and so on. Descartes said: I *think* therefore I am. A Jew says: I *thank*

ברכות השחר

The following blessings are said aloud by the שליח ציבור, but each individual should say them quietly as well. It is our custom to say them standing.

בָּרוּךְ אַתָּה יהוה אֱלֹהֵינוּ מֶלֶךְ הָעוֹלָם
אֲשֶׁר נָתַן לַשֶּׂכְוִי בִינָה
לְהַבְחִין בֵּין יוֹם וּבֵין לָיְלָה.

בָּרוּךְ אַתָּה יהוה אֱלֹהֵינוּ מֶלֶךְ הָעוֹלָם
שֶׁלֹּא עָשַׂנִי גּוֹי.

בָּרוּךְ אַתָּה יהוה אֱלֹהֵינוּ מֶלֶךְ הָעוֹלָם
שֶׁלֹּא עָשַׂנִי עָבֶד.

בָּרוּךְ אַתָּה יהוה אֱלֹהֵינוּ מֶלֶךְ הָעוֹלָם
men שֶׁלֹּא עָשַׂנִי אִשָּׁה. / *women* שֶׁעָשַׂנִי כִּרְצוֹנוֹ.

בָּרוּךְ אַתָּה יהוה אֱלֹהֵינוּ מֶלֶךְ הָעוֹלָם
פּוֹקֵחַ עִוְרִים.

MORNING BLESSINGS

A series of thanksgivings, designed to open our eyes to the wonders of the world and of existence. The religious sense is not so much a matter of seeing new things but of seeing things anew.

אֲשֶׁר נָתַן לַשֶּׂכְוִי בִינָה *Who gives the heart understanding.* The translation follows the view of Rabbeinu Asher (Rosh). Rashi and Abudarham translate it as "Who gives the cockerel understanding." The blessing, which tells us that understanding begins in the ability to make distinctions, refers to the first distinction mentioned in the Torah, when God divided darkness from light, creating night and day.

Blessed are You, LORD our God,
    King of the Universe,
    who clothes the naked.

Blessed are You, LORD our God,
    King of the Universe,
    who sets captives free.

Blessed are You, LORD our God,
    King of the Universe,
    who raises those bowed down.

Blessed are You, LORD our God,
    King of the Universe,
    who spreads the earth above the waters.

Blessed are You, LORD our God,
    King of the Universe,
    who has provided me with all I need.

Blessed are You, LORD our God,
    King of the Universe,
    who makes firm the steps of man.

Blessed are You, LORD our God,
    King of the Universe,
    who girds Israel with strength.

Blessed are You, LORD our God,
    King of the Universe,
    who crowns Israel with glory.

Blessed are You, LORD our God,
    King of the Universe,
    who gives strength to the weary.

בָּרוּךְ אַתָּה יהוה אֱלֹהֵינוּ מֶלֶךְ הָעוֹלָם
מַלְבִּישׁ עֲרֻמִּים.

בָּרוּךְ אַתָּה יהוה אֱלֹהֵינוּ מֶלֶךְ הָעוֹלָם
מַתִּיר אֲסוּרִים.

בָּרוּךְ אַתָּה יהוה אֱלֹהֵינוּ מֶלֶךְ הָעוֹלָם
זוֹקֵף כְּפוּפִים.

בָּרוּךְ אַתָּה יהוה אֱלֹהֵינוּ מֶלֶךְ הָעוֹלָם
רוֹקַע הָאָרֶץ עַל הַמָּיִם.

בָּרוּךְ אַתָּה יהוה אֱלֹהֵינוּ מֶלֶךְ הָעוֹלָם
שֶׁעָשָׂה לִי כָּל צָרְכִּי.

בָּרוּךְ אַתָּה יהוה אֱלֹהֵינוּ מֶלֶךְ הָעוֹלָם
הַמֵּכִין מִצְעֲדֵי גָבֶר.

בָּרוּךְ אַתָּה יהוה אֱלֹהֵינוּ מֶלֶךְ הָעוֹלָם
אוֹזֵר יִשְׂרָאֵל בִּגְבוּרָה.

בָּרוּךְ אַתָּה יהוה אֱלֹהֵינוּ מֶלֶךְ הָעוֹלָם
עוֹטֵר יִשְׂרָאֵל בְּתִפְאָרָה.

בָּרוּךְ אַתָּה יהוה אֱלֹהֵינוּ מֶלֶךְ הָעוֹלָם
הַנּוֹתֵן לַיָּעֵף כֹּחַ.

---

therefore I am. To stand consciously in the presence of God involves an attitude of gratitude.

בָּרוּךְ Blessed are You, LORD our God, King of the Universe,
who removes sleep from my eyes
and slumber from my eyelids.
And may it be Your will, LORD our God
and God of our ancestors,
to accustom us to Your Torah,
and make us attached to Your commandments.
Lead us not into error, transgression,
iniquity, temptation or disgrace.
Do not let the evil instinct dominate us.
Keep us far from a bad man and a bad companion.
Help us attach ourselves
to the good instinct and to good deeds
and bend our instincts to be subservient to You.
Grant us, this day and every day,
grace, loving-kindness and compassion in Your eyes
and in the eyes of all who see us,
and bestow loving-kindness upon us.
Blessed are You, LORD,
who bestows loving-kindness on His people Israel.

יְהִי רָצוֹן May it be Your will, LORD my God and God of my ancestors, to
save me today and every day, from the arrogant and from arrogance itself, *Berakhot*
from a bad man, a bad friend, a bad neighbor, a bad mishap, a destructive *16b*
adversary, a harsh trial and a harsh opponent, whether or not he is a son
of the covenant.

---

to act badly if we do so without deliberation and foresight, in the heat of
the moment. We are also social animals. Therefore we are influenced by
our environment. So we pray to be protected from bad social influences:
not only from bad companions but also, in a secular age, from the ambient
culture.

בָּרוּךְ אַתָּה יהוה אֱלֹהֵינוּ מֶלֶךְ הָעוֹלָם

הַמַּעֲבִיר שֵׁנָה מֵעֵינַי וּתְנוּמָה מֵעַפְעַפָּי.

וִיהִי רָצוֹן מִלְּפָנֶיךָ יהוה אֱלֹהֵינוּ וֵאלֹהֵי אֲבוֹתֵינוּ

שֶׁתַּרְגִּילֵנוּ בְּתוֹרָתֶךָ

וְדַבְּקֵנוּ בְּמִצְוֹתֶיךָ

וְאַל תְּבִיאֵנוּ לֹא לִידֵי חֵטְא

וְלֹא לִידֵי עֲבֵרָה וְעָוֹן

וְלֹא לִידֵי נִסָּיוֹן וְלֹא לִידֵי בִזָּיוֹן

וְאַל תַּשְׁלֶט בָּנוּ יֵצֶר הָרָע

וְהַרְחִיקֵנוּ מֵאָדָם רָע וּמֵחָבֵר רָע

וְדַבְּקֵנוּ בְּיֵצֶר הַטּוֹב וּבְמַעֲשִׂים טוֹבִים

וְכֹף אֶת יִצְרֵנוּ לְהִשְׁתַּעְבֶּד לָךְ

וּתְנֵנוּ הַיּוֹם וּבְכָל יוֹם לְחֵן וּלְחֶסֶד וּלְרַחֲמִים

בְּעֵינֶיךָ, וּבְעֵינֵי כָל רוֹאֵינוּ

וְתִגְמְלֵנוּ חֲסָדִים טוֹבִים.

בָּרוּךְ אַתָּה יהוה

גּוֹמֵל חֲסָדִים טוֹבִים לְעַמּוֹ יִשְׂרָאֵל.

ברכות טז:

יְהִי רָצוֹן מִלְּפָנֶיךָ יהוה אֱלֹהַי וֵאלֹהֵי אֲבוֹתַי, שֶׁתַּצִּילֵנִי הַיּוֹם וּבְכָל יוֹם מֵעַזֵּי פָנִים וּמֵעַזּוּת פָּנִים, מֵאָדָם רָע, וּמֵחָבֵר רָע, וּמִשָּׁכֵן רָע, וּמִפֶּגַע רָע, וּמִשָּׂטָן הַמַּשְׁחִית, מִדִּין קָשֶׁה, וּמִבַּעַל דִּין קָשֶׁה, בֵּין שֶׁהוּא בֶן בְּרִית וּבֵין שֶׁאֵינוֹ בֶן בְּרִית.

וִיהִי רָצוֹן *May it be Your will.* We ask for God's help in leading a holy and moral life. We need that help. We have primal instincts that can lead us

THE BINDING OF ISAAC

On the basis of Jewish mystical tradition, some have the custom of saying daily the biblical passage recounting the Binding of Isaac, the supreme trial of faith in which Abraham demonstrated his love of God above all other loves. On Shabbat and Yom Tov, most omit the introductory and concluding prayers, "Our God and God of our ancestors" and "Master of the Universe." Others skip to "A person should" on page 242.

Our God and God of our ancestors, remember us with a favorable memory, and recall us with a remembrance of salvation and compassion from the highest of high heavens. Remember, LORD our God, on our behalf, the love of the ancients, Abraham, Isaac and Yisrael Your servants; the covenant, the loving-kindness, and the oath You swore to Abraham our father on Mount Moriah, and the Binding, when he bound Isaac his son on the altar, as is written in Your Torah:

It happened after these things that God tested Abraham. He *Gen. 22* said to him, "Abraham!" "Here I am," he replied. He said, "Take your son, your only son, Isaac, whom you love, and go to the land of Moriah and offer him there as a burnt-offering on one of the mountains which I shall say to you." Early the next morning Abraham rose and saddled his donkey and took his two lads with him, and Isaac his son, and he cut wood for the burnt-offering, and he set out for the place of which God had told him. On the third day Abraham looked up and saw the place from afar. Abraham said to his lads, "Stay here with the donkey while I and the boy go on ahead. We will worship and we will return to you." Abraham took the wood for the burnt-offering and placed it on Isaac his son, and he took in his hand the fire and the knife, and the two of them went together. Isaac said to Abraham his father, "Father?" and he said "Here I am, my son." And he said, "Here are the fire and the wood, but where is the sheep for the burnt-offering?" Abraham said, "God will see to the sheep for the burnt-offering, my son." And the two

contradiction. On the one hand God had told him that it would be Isaac and Isaac's children through whom the covenant would continue and become eternal (Gen. 17:19). On the other, God had now commanded him to take

פרשת העקדה

On the basis of Jewish mystical tradition, some have the custom of saying daily
the biblical passage recounting the Binding of Isaac, the supreme trial of faith in
which Abraham demonstrated his love of God above all other loves. On שבת *and*
יום טוב, *most omit the introductory and concluding prayers,* אֱלֹהֵינוּ וֵאלֹהֵי אֲבוֹתֵינוּ
and רִבּוֹנוֹ שֶׁל עוֹלָם. *Others skip to* לְעוֹלָם יְהֵא אָדָם *on page 243.*

אֱלֹהֵינוּ וֵאלֹהֵי אֲבוֹתֵינוּ, זָכְרֵנוּ בְּזִכָּרוֹן טוֹב לְפָנֶיךָ, וּפָקְדֵנוּ בִּפְקֻדַּת יְשׁוּעָה
וְרַחֲמִים מִשְּׁמֵי שְׁמֵי קֶדֶם, וּזְכָר לָנוּ יהוה אֱלֹהֵינוּ, אַהֲבַת הַקַּדְמוֹנִים אַבְרָהָם
יִצְחָק וְיִשְׂרָאֵל עֲבָדֶיךָ, אֶת הַבְּרִית וְאֶת הַחֶסֶד וְאֶת הַשְּׁבוּעָה שֶׁנִּשְׁבַּעְתָּ
לְאַבְרָהָם אָבִינוּ בְּהַר הַמּוֹרִיָּה, וְאֶת הָעֲקֵדָה שֶׁעָקַד אֶת יִצְחָק בְּנוֹ עַל גַּבֵּי
הַמִּזְבֵּחַ, כַּכָּתוּב בְּתוֹרָתֶךָ:

בראשית כב

וַיְהִי אַחַר הַדְּבָרִים הָאֵלֶּה, וְהָאֱלֹהִים נִסָּה אֶת־אַבְרָהָם, וַיֹּאמֶר
אֵלָיו אַבְרָהָם, וַיֹּאמֶר הִנֵּנִי: וַיֹּאמֶר קַח־נָא אֶת־בִּנְךָ אֶת־יְחִידְךָ
אֲשֶׁר־אָהַבְתָּ, אֶת־יִצְחָק, וְלֶךְ־לְךָ אֶל־אֶרֶץ הַמֹּרִיָּה, וְהַעֲלֵהוּ
שָׁם לְעֹלָה עַל אַחַד הֶהָרִים אֲשֶׁר אֹמַר אֵלֶיךָ: וַיַּשְׁכֵּם אַבְרָהָם
בַּבֹּקֶר, וַיַּחֲבֹשׁ אֶת־חֲמֹרוֹ, וַיִּקַּח אֶת־שְׁנֵי נְעָרָיו אִתּוֹ וְאֵת יִצְחָק בְּנוֹ,
וַיְבַקַּע עֲצֵי עֹלָה, וַיָּקָם וַיֵּלֶךְ אֶל־הַמָּקוֹם אֲשֶׁר־אָמַר־לוֹ הָאֱלֹהִים:
בַּיּוֹם הַשְּׁלִישִׁי וַיִּשָּׂא אַבְרָהָם אֶת־עֵינָיו וַיַּרְא אֶת־הַמָּקוֹם מֵרָחֹק:
וַיֹּאמֶר אַבְרָהָם אֶל־נְעָרָיו, שְׁבוּ־לָכֶם פֹּה עִם־הַחֲמוֹר, וַאֲנִי וְהַנַּעַר
נֵלְכָה עַד־כֹּה, וְנִשְׁתַּחֲוֶה וְנָשׁוּבָה אֲלֵיכֶם: וַיִּקַּח אַבְרָהָם אֶת־עֲצֵי
הָעֹלָה וַיָּשֶׂם עַל־יִצְחָק בְּנוֹ, וַיִּקַּח בְּיָדוֹ אֶת־הָאֵשׁ וְאֶת־הַמַּאֲכֶלֶת,
וַיֵּלְכוּ שְׁנֵיהֶם יַחְדָּו: וַיֹּאמֶר יִצְחָק אֶל־אַבְרָהָם אָבִיו, וַיֹּאמֶר אָבִי,
וַיֹּאמֶר הִנֶּנִּי בְנִי, וַיֹּאמֶר, הִנֵּה הָאֵשׁ וְהָעֵצִים, וְאַיֵּה הַשֶּׂה לְעֹלָה:
וַיֹּאמֶר אַבְרָהָם, אֱלֹהִים יִרְאֶה־לּוֹ הַשֶּׂה לְעֹלָה, בְּנִי, וַיֵּלְכוּ שְׁנֵיהֶם

THE BINDING OF ISAAC

This passage, said daily by those whose liturgy follows the Jewish mystical
tradition, evokes the supreme moment of sacrifice by the grandfather of
Jewish faith, Abraham. Abraham found himself caught within a seeming

of them went together. They came to the place God had told him about, and Abraham built there an altar and arranged the wood and bound Isaac his son and laid him on the altar on top of the wood. He reached out his hand and took the knife to slay his son. Then an angel of the LORD called out to him from heaven, "Abraham! Abraham!" He said, "Here I am." He said, "Do not reach out your hand against the boy; do not do anything to him, for now I know that you fear God, because you have not held back your son, your only son, from Me." Abraham looked up and there he saw a ram caught in a thicket by its horns, and Abraham went and took the ram and offered it as a burnt-offering instead of his son. Abraham called that place "The LORD will see," as is said to this day, "On the mountain of the LORD He will be seen." The angel of the LORD called to Abraham a second time from heaven, and said, "By Myself I swear, declares the LORD, that because you have done this and have not held back your son, your only son, I will greatly bless you and greatly multiply your descendants, as the stars of heaven and the sand of the seashore, and your descendants shall take possession of the gates of their enemies. Through your descendants, all the nations of the earth will be blessed, because you have heeded My voice." Then Abraham returned to his lads, and they rose and went together to Beersheba, and Abraham stayed in Beersheba.

Most omit this passage on Shabbat and Yom Tov.

Master of the Universe, just as Abraham our father suppressed his compassion to do Your will wholeheartedly, so may Your compassion suppress Your anger from us and may Your compassion prevail over Your other attributes. Deal with us, LORD our God, with the attributes of loving-kindness and compassion, and in Your great goodness may Your anger be turned away from Your people, Your city, Your land and Your inheritance. Fulfill in us, LORD our God, the promise You made in Your Torah through the hand of Moses Your servant, as it is said: "I will remember My covenant with Jacob, and also My *Lev. 26* covenant with Isaac, and also My covenant with Abraham I will remember, and the land I will remember."

יַחְדָּו: וַיָּבֹאוּ אֶל־הַמָּקוֹם אֲשֶׁר אָמַר־לוֹ הָאֱלֹהִים, וַיִּבֶן שָׁם אַבְרָהָם
אֶת־הַמִּזְבֵּחַ וַיַּעֲרֹךְ אֶת־הָעֵצִים, וַיַּעֲקֹד אֶת־יִצְחָק בְּנוֹ, וַיָּשֶׂם אֹתוֹ
עַל־הַמִּזְבֵּחַ מִמַּעַל לָעֵצִים: וַיִּשְׁלַח אַבְרָהָם אֶת־יָדוֹ, וַיִּקַּח אֶת־
הַמַּאֲכֶלֶת, לִשְׁחֹט אֶת־בְּנוֹ: וַיִּקְרָא אֵלָיו מַלְאַךְ יהוה מִן־הַשָּׁמַיִם,
וַיֹּאמֶר אַבְרָהָם אַבְרָהָם, וַיֹּאמֶר הִנֵּנִי: וַיֹּאמֶר אַל־תִּשְׁלַח יָדְךָ אֶל־
הַנַּעַר, וְאַל־תַּעַשׂ לוֹ מְאוּמָה, כִּי עַתָּה יָדַעְתִּי כִּי־יְרֵא אֱלֹהִים אַתָּה,
וְלֹא חָשַׂכְתָּ אֶת־בִּנְךָ אֶת־יְחִידְךָ מִמֶּנִּי: וַיִּשָּׂא אַבְרָהָם אֶת־עֵינָיו,
וַיַּרְא וְהִנֵּה־אַיִל, אַחַר נֶאֱחַז בַּסְּבַךְ בְּקַרְנָיו, וַיֵּלֶךְ אַבְרָהָם וַיִּקַּח אֶת־
הָאַיִל, וַיַּעֲלֵהוּ לְעֹלָה תַּחַת בְּנוֹ: וַיִּקְרָא אַבְרָהָם שֵׁם־הַמָּקוֹם הַהוּא
יהוה יִרְאֶה, אֲשֶׁר יֵאָמֵר הַיּוֹם בְּהַר יהוה יֵרָאֶה: וַיִּקְרָא מַלְאַךְ יהוה
אֶל־אַבְרָהָם שֵׁנִית מִן־הַשָּׁמַיִם: וַיֹּאמֶר, בִּי נִשְׁבַּעְתִּי נְאֻם־יהוה, כִּי
יַעַן אֲשֶׁר עָשִׂיתָ אֶת־הַדָּבָר הַזֶּה, וְלֹא חָשַׂכְתָּ אֶת־בִּנְךָ אֶת־יְחִידֶךָ:
כִּי־בָרֵךְ אֲבָרֶכְךָ, וְהַרְבָּה אַרְבֶּה אֶת־זַרְעֲךָ כְּכוֹכְבֵי הַשָּׁמַיִם, וְכַחוֹל
אֲשֶׁר עַל־שְׂפַת הַיָּם, וְיִרַשׁ זַרְעֲךָ אֵת שַׁעַר אֹיְבָיו: וְהִתְבָּרְכוּ בְזַרְעֲךָ
כֹּל גּוֹיֵי הָאָרֶץ, עֵקֶב אֲשֶׁר שָׁמַעְתָּ בְּקֹלִי: וַיָּשָׁב אַבְרָהָם אֶל־נְעָרָיו,
וַיָּקֻמוּ וַיֵּלְכוּ יַחְדָּו אֶל־בְּאֵר שָׁבַע, וַיֵּשֶׁב אַבְרָהָם בִּבְאֵר שָׁבַע:

Most omit this passage on שבת *and* יום טוב.

רִבּוֹנוֹ שֶׁל עוֹלָם, כְּמוֹ שֶׁכָּבַשׁ אַבְרָהָם אָבִינוּ אֶת רַחֲמָיו לַעֲשׂוֹת רְצוֹנְךָ בְּלֵבָב
שָׁלֵם, כֵּן יִכְבְּשׁוּ רַחֲמֶיךָ אֶת כַּעַסְךָ מֵעָלֵינוּ וְיִגֹּלּוּ רַחֲמֶיךָ עַל מִדּוֹתֶיךָ. וְתִתְנַהֵג
עִמָּנוּ יהוה אֱלֹהֵינוּ בְּמִדַּת הַחֶסֶד וּבְמִדַּת הָרַחֲמִים, וּבְטוּבְךָ הַגָּדוֹל יָשׁוּב
חֲרוֹן אַפְּךָ מֵעַמְּךָ וּמֵעִירְךָ וּמֵאַרְצְךָ וּמִנַּחֲלָתֶךָ. וְקַיֶּם לָנוּ יהוה אֱלֹהֵינוּ אֶת
הַדָּבָר שֶׁהִבְטַחְתָּנוּ בְּתוֹרָתֶךָ עַל יְדֵי מֹשֶׁה עַבְדֶּךָ, כָּאָמוּר: וְזָכַרְתִּי אֶת־בְּרִיתִי וַיִּקְרָא כו
יַעֲקוֹב וְאַף אֶת־בְּרִיתִי יִצְחָק, וְאַף אֶת־בְּרִיתִי אַבְרָהָם אֶזְכֹּר, וְהָאָרֶץ אֶזְכֹּר:

_____

Isaac and offer him as a sacrifice (Gen. 22:2). It was Abraham's willingness,
not merely to sacrifice that which was most precious to him, but to live with
the contradiction, in the faith that God would resolve it in the course of time,
that made him the hero of faith and its role model through the centuries.

ACCEPTING THE SOVEREIGNTY OF HEAVEN

לְעוֹלָם A person should always be God-fearing, privately and publicly, *Tanna*
acknowledging the truth and speaking it in his heart. *DeVei*
He should rise early and say: *Eliyahu,*
ch. 21

> Master of all worlds,
> not because of our righteousness *Dan. 9*
> do we lay our pleas before You,
> but because of Your great compassion.

What are we? What are our lives?
What is our loving-kindness? What is our righteousness?
What is our salvation? What is our strength?
What is our might? What shall we say before You,
Lord our God and God of our ancestors?
Are not all the mighty like nothing before You,
the men of renown as if they had never been,
the wise as if they know nothing,
and the understanding as if they lack intelligence?
For their many works are in vain,
and the days of their lives like a fleeting breath before You.
The pre-eminence of man over the animals is nothing, *Eccl. 3*
for all is but a fleeting breath.

---

among the multitudes," refers to the martyrdom of those who went to their
deaths rather than renounce their faith. Martyrdom is called *Kiddush HaShem*,
"sanctifying [God's] name."

רִבּוֹן כָּל הָעוֹלָמִים *Master of all worlds.* This passage expresses the paradox of
the human condition in the presence of God. We know how small we are
and how brief our lives.

הֶבֶל *Fleeting breath.* The Hebrew word *hevel* – the key word of the opening
chapters of Ecclesiastes, from which this line is taken – has been translated as
"vain, meaningless, empty, futile." However, it literally means "a short breath."
It conveys a sense of the brevity and insubstantiality of life as a physical phenomenon. All that lives soon dies, and is as if it had never been.

קבלת עול מלכות שמים

תנא דבי
אליהו,
פרק כא

לְעוֹלָם יְהֵא אָדָם יְרֵא שָׁמַיִם בְּסֵתֶר וּבְגָלוּי
וּמוֹדֶה עַל הָאֱמֶת, וְדוֹבֵר אֱמֶת בִּלְבָבוֹ
וְיַשְׁכֵּם וְיֹאמַר

רִבּוֹן כָּל הָעוֹלָמִים
דניאל ט לֹא עַל־צִדְקוֹתֵינוּ אֲנַחְנוּ מַפִּילִים תַּחֲנוּנֵינוּ לְפָנֶיךָ
כִּי עַל־רַחֲמֶיךָ הָרַבִּים:

מָה אָנוּ, מֶה חַיֵּינוּ, מֶה חַסְדֵּנוּ, מַה צִּדְקוֹתֵינוּ
מַה יְשׁוּעָתֵנוּ, מַה כֹּחֵנוּ, מַה גְּבוּרָתֵנוּ
מַה נֹּאמַר לְפָנֶיךָ, יהוה אֱלֹהֵינוּ וֵאלֹהֵי אֲבוֹתֵינוּ
הֲלֹא כָּל הַגִּבּוֹרִים כְּאַיִן לְפָנֶיךָ
וְאַנְשֵׁי הַשֵּׁם כְּלֹא הָיוּ
וַחֲכָמִים כִּבְלִי מַדָּע, וּנְבוֹנִים כִּבְלִי הַשְׂכֵּל
כִּי רֹב מַעֲשֵׂיהֶם תֹּהוּ, וִימֵי חַיֵּיהֶם הֶבֶל לְפָנֶיךָ
קהלת ג וּמוֹתַר הָאָדָם מִן־הַבְּהֵמָה אָיִן
כִּי הַכֹּל הָבֶל:

ACCEPTING THE SOVEREIGNTY OF HEAVEN

לְעוֹלָם יְהֵא אָדָם *A person should always.* This whole section until "Who sancti-fies His name among the multitudes" appears in the ninth-century Midrash, *Tanna DeVei Eliyahu* (ch. 21). Some believe that it dates from a period of persecution under the Persian ruler Yazdegerd II who, in 456 CE, forbade the observance of Shabbat and the reading of the Torah. Jews continued to practice their faith in secret, saying prayers at times and in ways that would not be detected by their persecutors. This explains the reference to fearing God "privately" and "speaking truth in the heart" (that is, the secret practice of Judaism) and the recitation here of the first lines of the *Shema*, which could not be said at the normal time. The final blessing, "Who sanctifies His name

אֲבָל Yet we are Your people, the children of Your covenant,
the children of Abraham, Your beloved,
to whom You made a promise on Mount Moriah;
the offspring of Isaac his only one who was bound on the altar;
the congregation of Jacob Your firstborn son
whom – because of the love with which You loved him
and the joy with which You rejoiced in him –
You called Yisrael and Yeshurun.

לְפִיכָךְ Therefore it is our duty
to thank You, and to praise, glorify, bless, sanctify
and give praise and thanks to Your name.
Happy are we, how good is our portion,
how lovely our fate, how beautiful our heritage.

▸ Happy are we who, early and late, evening and morning,
say twice each day –

Listen, Israel: the LORD is our God, the LORD is One.   *Deut. 6*

Quietly: Blessed be the name of His glorious kingdom for ever and all time.

*Some congregations say the entire first paragraph of the Shema (below) at this point.
If there is a concern that the Shema will not be recited within the
prescribed time, then all three paragraphs should be said.*

Love the LORD your God with all your heart, with all your soul, and with all your
might. These words which I command you today shall be on your heart. Teach
them repeatedly to your children, speaking of them when you sit at home and
when you travel on the way, when you lie down and when you rise. Bind them as
a sign on your hand, and they shall be an emblem between your eyes. Write them
on the doorposts of your house and gates.

---

descendants of those You singled out to be witnesses to the world of Your
existence and majesty.

יַעֲקֹב בִּנְךָ בְכוֹרֶךָ *Jacob your firstborn son.* Though Jacob was not the biological
firstborn of Isaac and Rebecca, God subsequently declared, "My child, My
firstborn, Israel" (Ex. 4:22).

אֲבָל אֲנַחְנוּ עַמְּךָ בְּנֵי בְרִיתֶךָ

בְּנֵי אַבְרָהָם אֹהַבְךָ שֶׁנִּשְׁבַּעְתָּ לּוֹ בְּהַר הַמּוֹרִיָּה

זֶרַע יִצְחָק יְחִידוֹ שֶׁנֶּעֱקַד עַל גַּבֵּי הַמִּזְבֵּחַ

עֲדַת יַעֲקֹב בִּנְךָ בְּכוֹרֶךָ

שֶׁמֵאַהֲבָתְךָ שֶׁאָהַבְתָּ אוֹתוֹ, וּמִשִּׂמְחָתְךָ שֶׁשָּׂמַחְתָּ בּוֹ

קָרָאתָ אֶת שְׁמוֹ יִשְׂרָאֵל וִישֻׁרוּן.

לְפִיכָךְ אֲנַחְנוּ חַיָּבִים

לְהוֹדוֹת לְךָ וּלְשַׁבֵּחֲךָ וּלְפָאֶרְךָ

וּלְבָרֵךְ וּלְקַדֵּשׁ וְלָתֵת שֶׁבַח וְהוֹדָיָה לִשְׁמֶךָ.

אַשְׁרֵינוּ, מַה טּוֹב חֶלְקֵנוּ

וּמַה נָּעִים גּוֹרָלֵנוּ, וּמַה יָּפָה יְרֻשָּׁתֵנוּ.

◀ אַשְׁרֵינוּ, שֶׁאֲנַחְנוּ מַשְׁכִּימִים וּמַעֲרִיבִים עֶרֶב וָבֹקֶר

וְאוֹמְרִים פַּעֲמַיִם בְּכָל יוֹם

דברים ו

שְׁמַע יִשְׂרָאֵל, יהוה אֱלֹהֵינוּ, יהוה אֶחָד:

Quietly בָּרוּךְ שֵׁם כְּבוֹד מַלְכוּתוֹ לְעוֹלָם וָעֶד.

Some congregations say the entire first paragraph of the שמע (below) at this point.
If there is a concern that the שמע will not be recited within the
prescribed time, then all three paragraphs should be said.

וְאָהַבְתָּ אֵת יהוה אֱלֹהֶיךָ, בְּכָל-לְבָבְךָ, וּבְכָל-נַפְשְׁךָ, וּבְכָל-מְאֹדֶךָ: וְהָיוּ הַדְּבָרִים
הָאֵלֶּה, אֲשֶׁר אָנֹכִי מְצַוְּךָ הַיּוֹם, עַל-לְבָבֶךָ: וְשִׁנַּנְתָּם לְבָנֶיךָ, וְדִבַּרְתָּ בָּם, בְּשִׁבְתְּךָ
בְּבֵיתֶךָ, וּבְלֶכְתְּךָ בַדֶּרֶךְ, וּבְשָׁכְבְּךָ וּבְקוּמֶךָ: וּקְשַׁרְתָּם לְאוֹת עַל-יָדֶךָ וְהָיוּ
לְטֹטָפֹת בֵּין עֵינֶיךָ: וּכְתַבְתָּם עַל-מְזֻזוֹת בֵּיתֶךָ וּבִשְׁעָרֶיךָ:

‗‗‗

אֲבָל *Yet.* Though we may be insignificant as individuals, we are part of something momentous, for "we are Your people, the children of Your covenant,"

אַתָּה הוּא It was You who existed before the world was created,
it is You now that the world has been created.
It is You in this world and You in the World to Come.
▸ Sanctify Your name through those who sanctify Your name,
and sanctify Your name throughout Your world.
By Your salvation may our pride be exalted;
raise high our pride.
Blessed are You, LORD,
who sanctifies His name among the multitudes.

אַתָּה הוּא You are the LORD our God
in heaven and on earth, and in the highest heaven of heavens.
Truly, You are the first and You are the last,
and besides You there is no god.
Gather those who hope in You from the four quarters of the earth.
May all mankind recognize and know
that You alone are God over all the kingdoms on earth.

You made the heavens and the earth, the sea and all they contain.
Who among all the works of Your hands, above and below,
can tell You what to do?

Heavenly Father,
deal kindly with us
for the sake of Your great name by which we are called,
and fulfill for us, LORD our God, that which is written:

> "At that time I will bring you home, and at that time I will *Zeph. 3*
> gather you, for I will give you renown and praise among all
> the peoples of the earth when I bring back your exiles before
> your eyes, says the LORD."

His covenant; therefore, we may not renounce our religion or identity: "I,
God, do not change; so you, children of Jacob, are not destroyed" (Mal. 3:6).

אַתָּה הוּא יהוה אֱלֹהֵינוּ *You are the LORD our God.* A prayer for the end of exile,
culminating with the verse from Zephaniah (3:20) which speaks of the
ingathering of Jews and of a time when "I will give you renown and praise

אַתָּה הוּא עַד שֶׁלֹּא נִבְרָא הָעוֹלָם, אַתָּה הוּא מִשֶּׁנִּבְרָא הָעוֹלָם.
אַתָּה הוּא בָּעוֹלָם הַזֶּה, וְאַתָּה הוּא לָעוֹלָם הַבָּא.
◂ קַדֵּשׁ אֶת שִׁמְךָ עַל מַקְדִּישֵׁי שְׁמֶךָ, וְקַדֵּשׁ אֶת שִׁמְךָ בְּעוֹלָמֶךָ,
וּבִישׁוּעָתְךָ תָּרוּם וְתַגְבִּיהַּ קַרְנֵנוּ.
בָּרוּךְ אַתָּה יהוה, הַמְקַדֵּשׁ אֶת שְׁמוֹ בָּרַבִּים.

אַתָּה הוּא יהוה אֱלֹהֵינוּ
בַּשָּׁמַיִם וּבָאָרֶץ, וּבִשְׁמֵי הַשָּׁמַיִם הָעֶלְיוֹנִים.
אֱמֶת, אַתָּה הוּא רִאשׁוֹן, וְאַתָּה הוּא אַחֲרוֹן
וּמִבַּלְעָדֶיךָ אֵין אֱלֹהִים.
קַבֵּץ קֹוֶיךָ מֵאַרְבַּע כַּנְפוֹת הָאָרֶץ.
יַכִּירוּ וְיֵדְעוּ כָּל בָּאֵי עוֹלָם
כִּי אַתָּה הוּא הָאֱלֹהִים לְבַדְּךָ לְכֹל מַמְלְכוֹת הָאָרֶץ.

אַתָּה עָשִׂיתָ אֶת הַשָּׁמַיִם וְאֶת הָאָרֶץ
אֶת הַיָּם וְאֶת כָּל אֲשֶׁר בָּם
וּמִי בְּכָל מַעֲשֵׂי יָדֶיךָ בָּעֶלְיוֹנִים אוֹ בַתַּחְתּוֹנִים
שֶׁיֹּאמַר לְךָ מַה תַּעֲשֶׂה.

אָבִינוּ שֶׁבַּשָּׁמַיִם
עֲשֵׂה עִמָּנוּ חֶסֶד בַּעֲבוּר שִׁמְךָ הַגָּדוֹל שֶׁנִּקְרָא עָלֵינוּ
וְקַיֶּם לָנוּ יהוה אֱלֹהֵינוּ מַה שֶׁכָּתוּב:
בָּעֵת הַהִיא אָבִיא אֶתְכֶם, וּבָעֵת קַבְּצִי אֶתְכֶם
כִּי־אֶתֵּן אֶתְכֶם לְשֵׁם וְלִתְהִלָּה בְּכֹל עַמֵּי הָאָרֶץ
בְּשׁוּבִי אֶת־שְׁבוּתֵיכֶם לְעֵינֵיכֶם, אָמַר יהוה:

צפניה ג

אַתָּה הוּא *It was You who existed.* This prayer, with its emphasis on the change-lessness of God, may have been incorporated at a time of persecution, expressing the refusal of Jews to abandon their faith. God does not alter or revoke

OFFERINGS

The sages held that, in the absence of the Temple, studying the laws of sacrifices is the equivalent of offering them. Hence the following texts. There are different customs as to how many passages are to be said, and one should follow the custom of one's congregation. The minimum requirement is to say the verses relating to The Daily Sacrifice on the next page.

THE BASIN

The LORD spoke to Moses, saying: Make a bronze basin, with its bronze *Ex. 30* stand for washing, and place it between the Tent of Meeting and the altar, and put water in it. From it, Aaron and his sons are to wash their hands and feet. When they enter the Tent of Meeting, they shall wash with water so that they will not die; likewise when they approach the altar to minister, presenting a fire-offering to the LORD. They must wash their hands and feet so that they will not die. This shall be an everlasting ordinance for Aaron and his descendants throughout their generations.

TAKING OF THE ASHES

The LORD spoke to Moses, saying: Instruct Aaron and his sons, saying, *Lev. 6* This is the law of the burnt-offering. The burnt-offering shall remain on the altar hearth throughout the night until morning, and the altar fire shall be kept burning on it. The priest shall then put on his linen garments, and linen breeches next to his body, and shall remove the ashes of the burnt-offering that the fire has consumed on the altar and place them beside the altar. Then he shall take off these clothes and put on others, and carry the ashes outside the camp to a clean place. The fire on the altar must be kept burning; it must not go out. Each morning the priest shall burn wood on it, and prepare on it the burnt-offering and burn the fat of the peace-offerings. A perpetual fire must be kept burning on the altar; it must not go out.

---

that study of the laws about sacrifice was a substitute for sacrifice itself (*Ta'anit* 27b). The passage from the Mishna (*Zevaḥim* 5) is also about sacrifices, and was chosen because it does not contain any disagreement between the sages, and thus accords with the rule that one should pray "after a decided *halakha*" (*Berakhot* 31a), that is, an item of Jewish law about which there is no debate.

There are different customs about how many and which passages are to be said. The passages in large type represent the text as it exists in the earliest Siddurim, those of Rabbi Amram Gaon and Rabbi Sa'adia Gaon.

סדר הקרבנות

חז"ל *held that, in the absence of the Temple, studying the laws of sacrifices is the equivalent of offering them. Hence the following texts. There are different customs as to how many passages are to be said, and one should follow the custom of one's congregation. The minimum requirement is to say the verses relating to the* קרבן תמיד *on the next page.*

פרשת הכיור

שמות ל

וַיְדַבֵּר יהוה אֶל־מֹשֶׁה לֵּאמֹר: וְעָשִׂיתָ כִּיּוֹר נְחֹשֶׁת וְכַנּוֹ נְחֹשֶׁת לְרָחְצָה, וְנָתַתָּ אֹתוֹ בֵּין־אֹהֶל מוֹעֵד וּבֵין הַמִּזְבֵּחַ, וְנָתַתָּ שָׁמָּה מָיִם: וְרָחֲצוּ אַהֲרֹן וּבָנָיו מִמֶּנּוּ אֶת־יְדֵיהֶם וְאֶת־רַגְלֵיהֶם: בְּבֹאָם אֶל־אֹהֶל מוֹעֵד יִרְחֲצוּ־מַיִם, וְלֹא יָמֻתוּ, אוֹ בְגִשְׁתָּם אֶל־הַמִּזְבֵּחַ לְשָׁרֵת, לְהַקְטִיר אִשֶּׁה לַיהוה: וְרָחֲצוּ יְדֵיהֶם וְרַגְלֵיהֶם וְלֹא יָמֻתוּ, וְהָיְתָה לָהֶם חָק־עוֹלָם, לוֹ וּלְזַרְעוֹ לְדֹרֹתָם:

פרשת תרומת הדשן

ויקרא ו

וַיְדַבֵּר יהוה אֶל־מֹשֶׁה לֵּאמֹר: צַו אֶת־אַהֲרֹן וְאֶת־בָּנָיו לֵאמֹר, זֹאת תּוֹרַת הָעֹלָה, הִוא הָעֹלָה עַל מוֹקְדָה עַל־הַמִּזְבֵּחַ כָּל־הַלַּיְלָה עַד־הַבֹּקֶר, וְאֵשׁ הַמִּזְבֵּחַ תּוּקַד בּוֹ: וְלָבַשׁ הַכֹּהֵן מִדּוֹ בַד, וּמִכְנְסֵי־בַד יִלְבַּשׁ עַל־בְּשָׂרוֹ, וְהֵרִים אֶת־הַדֶּשֶׁן אֲשֶׁר תֹּאכַל הָאֵשׁ אֶת־הָעֹלָה, עַל־הַמִּזְבֵּחַ, וְשָׂמוֹ אֵצֶל הַמִּזְבֵּחַ: וּפָשַׁט אֶת־בְּגָדָיו, וְלָבַשׁ בְּגָדִים אֲחֵרִים, וְהוֹצִיא אֶת־הַדֶּשֶׁן אֶל־מִחוּץ לַמַּחֲנֶה, אֶל־מָקוֹם טָהוֹר: וְהָאֵשׁ עַל־הַמִּזְבֵּחַ תּוּקַד־בּוֹ, לֹא תִכְבֶּה, וּבִעֵר עָלֶיהָ הַכֹּהֵן עֵצִים בַּבֹּקֶר בַּבֹּקֶר, וְעָרַךְ עָלֶיהָ הָעֹלָה, וְהִקְטִיר עָלֶיהָ חֶלְבֵי הַשְּׁלָמִים: אֵשׁ, תָּמִיד תּוּקַד עַל־הַמִּזְבֵּחַ, לֹא תִכְבֶּה:

---

among all the peoples of the earth." This entire sequence of prayers is eloquent testimony to how Jews sustained faith and hope, dignity and pride, during some of the most prolonged periods of persecution in history.

OFFERINGS

There now follows a second cycle of study, with the same structure as the first, with passages from: (1) the Torah, (2) the Mishna, and (3) the Talmud (see below). The passages from the Torah relate to the daily, weekly and monthly sacrifices because, in the absence of the Temple, the sages held

May it be Your will, LORD our God and God of our ancestors, that You have compassion on us and pardon us all our sins, grant atonement for all our iniquities and forgive all our transgressions. May You rebuild the Temple swiftly in our days so that we may offer You the continual-offering that it may atone for us as You have prescribed for us in Your Torah through Moses Your servant, from the mouthpiece of Your glory, as it is said:

THE DAILY SACRIFICE

וַיְדַבֵּר The LORD said to Moses, "Command the Israelites and *Num. 28* tell them: 'Be careful to offer to Me at the appointed time My food-offering consumed by fire, as an aroma pleasing to Me.' Tell them: 'This is the fire-offering you shall offer to the LORD – two lambs a year old without blemish, as a regular burnt-offering each day. Prepare one lamb in the morning and the other toward evening, together with a meal-offering of a tenth of an ephah of fine flour mixed with a quarter of a hin of oil from pressed olives. This is the regular burnt-offering instituted at Mount Sinai as a pleasing aroma, a fire-offering made to the LORD. Its libation is to be a quarter of a hin [of wine] with each lamb, poured in the Sanctuary as a libation of strong drink to the LORD. Prepare the second lamb in the afternoon, along with the same meal-offering and libation as in the morning. This is a fire-offering, an aroma pleasing to the LORD.'"

וְשָׁחַט He shall slaughter it at the north side of the altar before *Lev. 1* the LORD, and Aaron's sons the priests shall sprinkle its blood against the altar on all sides.

May it be Your will, LORD our God and God of our ancestors, that this recitation be considered accepted and favored before You as if we had offered the daily sacrifice at its appointed time and place, according to its laws.

It is You, LORD our God, to whom our ancestors offered fragrant incense when the Temple stood, as You commanded them through Moses Your prophet, as is written in Your Torah:

THE INCENSE

The LORD said to Moses: Take fragrant spices – balsam, onycha, galba- *Ex. 30* num and pure frankincense, all in equal amounts – and make a fragrant blend of incense, the work of a perfumer, well mixed, pure and holy. Grind it very finely and place it in front of the [Ark of] Testimony in the Tent of Meeting, where I will meet with you. It shall be most holy to you.

יְהִי רָצוֹן מִלְּפָנֶיךָ יהוה אֱלֹהֵינוּ וֵאלֹהֵי אֲבוֹתֵינוּ, שֶׁתְּרַחֵם עָלֵינוּ, וְתִמְחָל לָנוּ עַל כָּל חַטֹּאתֵינוּ וּתְכַפֶּר לָנוּ עַל כָּל עֲוֹנוֹתֵינוּ וְתִסְלַח לָנוּ עַל כָּל פְּשָׁעֵינוּ, וְתִבְנֶה בֵּית הַמִּקְדָּשׁ בִּמְהֵרָה בְיָמֵינוּ, וְנַקְרִיב לְפָנֶיךָ קָרְבַּן הַתָּמִיד שֶׁיְּכַפֵּר בַּעֲדֵנוּ, כְּמוֹ שֶׁכָּתַבְתָּ עָלֵינוּ בְּתוֹרָתֶךָ עַל יְדֵי מֹשֶׁה עַבְדֶּךָ מִפִּי כְבוֹדֶךָ, כָּאָמוּר:

פרשת קרבן התמיד

במדבר כח

וַיְדַבֵּר יהוה אֶל־מֹשֶׁה לֵּאמֹר: צַו אֶת־בְּנֵי יִשְׂרָאֵל וְאָמַרְתָּ אֲלֵהֶם, אֶת־קָרְבָּנִי לַחְמִי לְאִשַּׁי, רֵיחַ נִיחֹחִי, תִּשְׁמְרוּ לְהַקְרִיב לִי בְּמוֹעֲדוֹ: וְאָמַרְתָּ לָהֶם, זֶה הָאִשֶּׁה אֲשֶׁר תַּקְרִיבוּ לַיהוה, כְּבָשִׂים בְּנֵי־שָׁנָה תְמִימִם שְׁנַיִם לַיּוֹם, עֹלָה תָמִיד: אֶת־הַכֶּבֶשׂ אֶחָד תַּעֲשֶׂה בַבֹּקֶר, וְאֵת הַכֶּבֶשׂ הַשֵּׁנִי תַּעֲשֶׂה בֵּין הָעַרְבָּיִם: וַעֲשִׂירִית הָאֵיפָה סֹלֶת לְמִנְחָה, בְּלוּלָה בְּשֶׁמֶן כָּתִית רְבִיעִת הַהִין: עֹלַת תָּמִיד, הָעֲשֻׂיָה בְּהַר סִינַי, לְרֵיחַ נִיחֹחַ אִשֶּׁה לַיהוה: וְנִסְכּוֹ רְבִיעִת הַהִין לַכֶּבֶשׂ הָאֶחָד, בַּקֹּדֶשׁ הַסֵּךְ נֶסֶךְ שֵׁכָר לַיהוה: וְאֵת הַכֶּבֶשׂ הַשֵּׁנִי תַּעֲשֶׂה בֵּין הָעַרְבָּיִם, כְּמִנְחַת הַבֹּקֶר וּכְנִסְכּוֹ תַּעֲשֶׂה, אִשֵּׁה רֵיחַ נִיחֹחַ לַיהוה:

ויקרא א

וְשָׁחַט אֹתוֹ עַל יֶרֶךְ הַמִּזְבֵּחַ צָפֹנָה לִפְנֵי יהוה, וְזָרְקוּ בְּנֵי אַהֲרֹן הַכֹּהֲנִים אֶת־דָּמוֹ עַל־הַמִּזְבֵּחַ, סָבִיב:

יְהִי רָצוֹן מִלְּפָנֶיךָ, יהוה אֱלֹהֵינוּ וֵאלֹהֵי אֲבוֹתֵינוּ, שֶׁתְּהֵא אֲמִירָה זוֹ חֲשׁוּבָה וּמְקֻבֶּלֶת וּמְרֻצָּה לְפָנֶיךָ, כְּאִלּוּ הִקְרַבְנוּ קָרְבַּן הַתָּמִיד בְּמוֹעֲדוֹ וּבִמְקוֹמוֹ וּכְהִלְכָתוֹ.

אַתָּה הוּא יהוה אֱלֹהֵינוּ שֶׁהִקְטִירוּ אֲבוֹתֵינוּ לְפָנֶיךָ אֶת קְטֹרֶת הַסַּמִּים בִּזְמַן שֶׁבֵּית הַמִּקְדָּשׁ הָיָה קַיָּם, כַּאֲשֶׁר צִוִּיתָ אוֹתָם עַל יְדֵי מֹשֶׁה נְבִיאֶךָ, כַּכָּתוּב בְּתוֹרָתֶךָ:

פרשת הקטורת

שמות ל

וַיֹּאמֶר יהוה אֶל־מֹשֶׁה, קַח־לְךָ סַמִּים נָטָף וּשְׁחֵלֶת וְחֶלְבְּנָה, סַמִּים וּלְבֹנָה זַכָּה, בַּד בְּבַד יִהְיֶה: וְעָשִׂיתָ אֹתָהּ קְטֹרֶת, רֹקַח מַעֲשֵׂה רוֹקֵחַ, מְמֻלָּח, טָהוֹר קֹדֶשׁ: וְשָׁחַקְתָּ מִמֶּנָּה הָדֵק, וְנָתַתָּה מִמֶּנָּה לִפְנֵי הָעֵדֻת בְּאֹהֶל מוֹעֵד אֲשֶׁר אִוָּעֵד לְךָ שָׁמָּה, קֹדֶשׁ קָדָשִׁים תִּהְיֶה לָכֶם:

And it is said:

> Aaron shall burn fragrant incense on the altar every morning when he cleans the lamps. He shall burn incense again when he lights the lamps toward evening so that there will be incense before the LORD at all times, throughout your generations.

The rabbis taught: How was the incense prepared? It weighed 368 manehs, 365 corresponding to the number of days in a solar year, a maneh for each day, half to be offered in the morning and half in the afternoon, and three additional manehs from which the High Priest took two handfuls on Yom Kippur. These were put back into the mortar on the day before Yom Kippur and ground again very thoroughly so as to be extremely fine. The incense contained eleven kinds of spices: balsam, onycha, galbanum and frankincense, each weighing seventy manehs; myrrh, cassia, spikenard and saffron, each weighing sixteen manehs; twelve manehs of costus, three of aromatic bark; nine of cinnamon; nine kabs of Carsina lye; three seahs and three kabs of Cyprus wine. If Cyprus wine was not available, old white wine might be used. A quarter of a kab of Sodom salt, and a minute amount of a smoke-raising herb. Rabbi Nathan the Babylonian says: also a minute amount of Jordan amber. If one added honey to the mixture, he rendered it unfit for sacred use. If he omitted any one of its ingredients, he is guilty of a capital offense. *Keritot 6a*

Rabban Shimon ben Gamliel says: "Balsam" refers to the sap that drips from the balsam tree. The Carsina lye was used for bleaching the onycha to improve it. The Cyprus wine was used to soak the onycha in it to make it pungent. Though urine is suitable for this purpose, it is not brought into the Temple out of respect.

It was taught, Rabbi Nathan says: While it was being ground, another would say, "Grind well, well grind," because the [rhythmic] sound is good for spices. If it was mixed in half-quantities, it is fit for use, but we have not heard whether this applies to a third or a quarter. Rabbi Judah said: The general rule is that if it was made in the correct proportions, it is fit for use even if made in half-quantity, but if he omitted any one of its ingredients, he is guilty of a capital offense.

It was taught, Bar Kappara says: Once every sixty or seventy years, the accumulated surpluses amounted to half the yearly quantity. Bar Kappara also taught: If a minute quantity of honey had been mixed into the incense, no one could have resisted the scent. Why did they not put honey into it? Because the Torah says, "For you are not to burn any leaven or honey in a fire-offering made to the LORD." *JT Yoma 4:5* *Lev. 2*

וְנֶאֱמַר

וְהִקְטִיר עָלָיו אַהֲרֹן קְטֹרֶת סַמִּים, בַּבֹּקֶר בַּבֹּקֶר בְּהֵיטִיבוֹ אֶת־הַנֵּרֹת
יַקְטִירֶנָּה: וּבְהַעֲלֹת אַהֲרֹן אֶת־הַנֵּרֹת בֵּין הָעַרְבַּיִם יַקְטִירֶנָּה, קְטֹרֶת
תָּמִיד לִפְנֵי יהוה לְדֹרֹתֵיכֶם:

כריתות ו

תָּנוּ רַבָּנָן: פִּטּוּם הַקְּטֹרֶת כֵּיצַד, שְׁלֹשׁ מֵאוֹת וְשִׁשִּׁים וּשְׁמוֹנָה מָנִים הָיוּ
בָהּ. שְׁלֹשׁ מֵאוֹת וְשִׁשִּׁים וַחֲמִשָּׁה כְּמִנְיַן יְמוֹת הַחַמָּה, מָנֶה לְכָל יוֹם, פְּרָס
בְּשַׁחֲרִית וּפְרָס בֵּין הָעַרְבַּיִם, וּשְׁלֹשָׁה מָנִים יְתֵרִים שֶׁמֵּהֶם מַכְנִיס כֹּהֵן גָּדוֹל
מְלֹא חָפְנָיו בְּיוֹם הַכִּפּוּרִים, וּמַחֲזִירָן לְמַכְתֶּשֶׁת בְּעֶרֶב יוֹם הַכִּפּוּרִים וְשׁוֹחֲקָן
יָפֶה יָפֶה, כְּדֵי שֶׁתְּהֵא דַקָּה מִן הַדַּקָּה. וְאַחַד עָשָׂר סַמָּנִים הָיוּ בָהּ, וְאֵלּוּ הֵן:
הַצֳּרִי, וְהַצִּפֹּרֶן, וְהַחֶלְבְּנָה, וְהַלְּבוֹנָה מִשְׁקַל שִׁבְעִים שִׁבְעִים מָנֶה, מֹר, וּקְצִיעָה,
שִׁבֹּלֶת נֵרְדְּ, וְכַרְכֹּם מִשְׁקַל שִׁשָּׁה עָשָׂר שִׁשָּׁה עָשָׂר מָנֶה, הַקֹּשְׁטְ שְׁנֵים עָשָׂר,
קִלּוּפָה שְׁלֹשָׁה, קִנָּמוֹן תִּשְׁעָה, בֹּרִית כַּרְשִׁינָה תִּשְׁעָה קַבִּין, יֵין קַפְרִיסִין סְאִין
תְּלָת וְקַבִּין תְּלָתָא, וְאִם לֹא מָצָא יֵין קַפְרִיסִין, מֵבִיא חֲמַר חִוַּרְיָן עַתִּיק.
מֶלַח סְדוֹמִית רֹבַע, מַעֲלֶה עָשָׁן כָּל שֶׁהוּא. רַבִּי נָתָן הַבַּבְלִי אוֹמֵר: אַף כִּפַּת
הַיַּרְדֵּן כָּל שֶׁהוּא, וְאִם נָתַן בָּהּ דְּבַשׁ פְּסָלָהּ, וְאִם חִסֵּר אֶחָד מִכָּל סַמָּנֶיהָ,
חַיָּב מִיתָה.

רַבָּן שִׁמְעוֹן בֶּן גַּמְלִיאֵל אוֹמֵר: הַצֳּרִי אֵינוֹ אֶלָּא שְׂרָף הַנּוֹטֵף מֵעֲצֵי הַקְּטָף.
בֹּרִית כַּרְשִׁינָה שֶׁשָּׁפִין בָּהּ אֶת הַצִּפֹּרֶן כְּדֵי שֶׁתְּהֵא נָאָה, יֵין קַפְרִיסִין שֶׁשּׁוֹרִין
בּוֹ אֶת הַצִּפֹּרֶן כְּדֵי שֶׁתְּהֵא עַזָּה, וַהֲלֹא מֵי רַגְלַיִם יָפִין לָהּ, אֶלָּא שֶׁאֵין מַכְנִיסִין
מֵי רַגְלַיִם בַּמִּקְדָּשׁ מִפְּנֵי הַכָּבוֹד:

תַּנְיָא, רַבִּי נָתָן אוֹמֵר: כְּשֶׁהוּא שׁוֹחֵק אוֹמֵר, הָדֵק הֵיטֵב הֵיטֵב הָדֵק, מִפְּנֵי
שֶׁהַקּוֹל יָפֶה לַבְּשָׂמִים. פִּטְּמָהּ לַחֲצָאִין כְּשֵׁרָה, לִשְׁלִישׁ וְלִרְבִיעַ לֹא שָׁמַעְנוּ.
אָמַר רַבִּי יְהוּדָה: זֶה הַכְּלָל, אִם כְּמִדָּתָהּ כְּשֵׁרָה לַחֲצָאִין, וְאִם חִסֵּר אֶחָד
מִכָּל סַמָּנֶיהָ חַיָּב מִיתָה.

ירושלמי
יומא ד,
הלכה ה

תַּנְיָא, בַּר קַפָּרָא אוֹמֵר: אַחַת לְשִׁשִּׁים אוֹ לְשִׁבְעִים שָׁנָה הָיְתָה בָאָה שֶׁל שִׁירַיִם
לַחֲצָאִין. וְעוֹד תָּנֵי בַּר קַפָּרָא: אִלּוּ הָיָה נוֹתֵן בָּהּ קוֹרְטוֹב שֶׁל דְּבַשׁ אֵין אָדָם
יָכוֹל לַעֲמֹד מִפְּנֵי רֵיחָהּ, וְלָמָּה אֵין מְעָרְבִין בָּהּ דְּבַשׁ, מִפְּנֵי שֶׁהַתּוֹרָה אָמְרָה:

ויקרא ב

כִּי כָל־שְׂאֹר וְכָל־דְּבַשׁ לֹא־תַקְטִירוּ מִמֶּנּוּ אִשֶּׁה לַיהוה:

The following three verses are each said three times:

The LORD of hosts is with us; the God of Jacob is our stronghold, Selah. *Ps. 46*

LORD of hosts, happy is the one who trusts in You. *Ps. 84*

LORD, save! May the King answer us on the day we call. *Ps. 20*

You are my hiding place; You will protect me from distress and surround *Ps. 32*
me with songs of salvation, Selah.

Then the offering of Judah and Jerusalem will be pleasing to the LORD *Mal. 3*
as in the days of old and as in former years.

THE ORDER OF THE PRIESTLY FUNCTIONS

Abaye related the order of the daily priestly functions in the name of tradi- *Yoma 33a*
tion and in accordance with Abba Shaul: The large pile [of wood] comes
before the second pile for the incense; the second pile for the incense
precedes the laying in order of the two logs of wood; the laying in order of
the two logs of wood comes before the removing of ashes from the inner
altar; the removing of ashes from the inner altar precedes the cleaning of
the five lamps; the cleaning of the five lamps comes before the blood of
the daily offering; the blood of the daily offering precedes the cleaning
of the [other] two lamps; the cleaning of the two lamps comes before the
incense-offering; the incense-offering precedes the burning of the limbs;
the burning of the limbs comes before the meal-offering; the meal-offering
precedes the pancakes; the pancakes come before the wine-libations; the
wine-libations precede the additional offerings; the additional offerings
come before the [frankincense] censers; the censers precede the daily
afternoon offering; as it is said, "On it he shall arrange burnt-offerings, and *Lev. 6*
on it he shall burn the fat of the peace-offerings" – "on it" [the daily offering]
all the offerings were completed.

> Please, by the power of Your great right hand, set the captive nation free.
> Accept Your people's prayer. Strengthen us, purify us, You who are revered.
> Please, Mighty One, guard like the pupil of the eye those who seek Your unity.
> Bless them, cleanse them, have compassion on them,
> grant them Your righteousness always.
> Mighty One, Holy One, in Your great goodness guide Your congregation.
> Only One, Exalted One, turn to Your people, who proclaim Your holiness.
> Accept our plea and heed our cry, You who know all secret thoughts.
>   Blessed be the name of His glorious kingdom for ever and all time.

Master of the Universe, You have commanded us to offer the daily sacrifice at its
appointed time with the priests at their service, the Levites on their platform, and
the Israelites at their post. Now, because of our sins, the Temple is destroyed and
the daily sacrifice discontinued, and we have no priest at his service, no Levite

The following three verses are each said three times:

תהלים מו

יהוה צְבָאוֹת עִמָּנוּ, מִשְׂגָּב לָנוּ אֱלֹהֵי יַעֲקֹב סֶלָה:

תהלים פד

יהוה צְבָאוֹת, אַשְׁרֵי אָדָם בֹּטֵחַ בָּךְ:

תהלים כ

יהוה הוֹשִׁיעָה, הַמֶּלֶךְ יַעֲנֵנוּ בְיוֹם־קָרְאֵנוּ:

תהלים לב

אַתָּה סֵתֶר לִי, מִצַּר תִּצְּרֵנִי, רָנֵּי פַלֵּט תְּסוֹבְבֵנִי סֶלָה:

מלאכי ג

וְעָרְבָה לַיהוה מִנְחַת יְהוּדָה וִירוּשָׁלָ͏ִם

כִּימֵי עוֹלָם וּכְשָׁנִים קַדְמֹנִיּוֹת:

סדר המערכה

יומא לג.

אַבַּיֵּי הֲוָה מְסַדֵּר סֵדֶר הַמַּעֲרָכָה מִשְּׁמָא דִגְמָרָא, וְאַלִּבָּא דְאַבָּא שָׁאוּל: מַעֲרָכָה גְדוֹלָה קוֹדֶמֶת לְמַעֲרָכָה שְׁנִיָּה שֶׁל קְטֹרֶת, וּמַעֲרָכָה שְׁנִיָּה שֶׁל קְטֹרֶת קוֹדֶמֶת לְסִדּוּר שְׁנֵי גִזְרֵי עֵצִים, וְסִדּוּר שְׁנֵי גִזְרֵי עֵצִים קוֹדֵם לְדִשּׁוּן מִזְבֵּחַ הַפְּנִימִי, וְדִשּׁוּן מִזְבֵּחַ הַפְּנִימִי קוֹדֵם לַהֲטָבַת חָמֵשׁ נֵרוֹת, וַהֲטָבַת חָמֵשׁ נֵרוֹת קוֹדֶמֶת לְדַם הַתָּמִיד, וְדַם הַתָּמִיד קוֹדֵם לַהֲטָבַת שְׁתֵּי נֵרוֹת, וַהֲטָבַת שְׁתֵּי נֵרוֹת קוֹדֶמֶת לִקְטֹרֶת, וּקְטֹרֶת קוֹדֶמֶת לְאֵבָרִים, וְאֵבָרִים לְמִנְחָה, וּמִנְחָה לַחֲבִתִּין, וַחֲבִתִּין לִנְסָכִין, וּנְסָכִין לְמוּסָפִין, וּמוּסָפִין

ויקרא ו

לְבָזִיכִין, וּבָזִיכִין קוֹדְמִין לְתָמִיד שֶׁל בֵּין הָעַרְבָּיִם. שֶׁנֶּאֱמַר: וְעָרַךְ עָלֶיהָ הָעֹלָה, וְהִקְטִיר עָלֶיהָ חֶלְבֵי הַשְּׁלָמִים: עָלֶיהָ הַשְׁלֵם כָּל הַקָּרְבָּנוֹת כֻּלָּם.

אָנָּא, בְּכֹחַ גְּדֻלַּת יְמִינְךָ, תַּתִּיר צְרוּרָה.

קַבֵּל רִנַּת עַמְּךָ, שַׂגְּבֵנוּ, טַהֲרֵנוּ, נוֹרָא.

נָא גִבּוֹר, דּוֹרְשֵׁי יִחוּדְךָ כְּבָבַת שָׁמְרֵם.

בָּרְכֵם, טַהֲרֵם, רַחֲמֵם, צִדְקָתְךָ תָּמִיד גָּמְלֵם.

חֲסִין קָדוֹשׁ, בְּרֹב טוּבְךָ נַהֵל עֲדָתֶךָ.

יָחִיד גֵּאֶה, לְעַמְּךָ פְּנֵה, זוֹכְרֵי קְדֻשָּׁתֶךָ.

שַׁוְעָתֵנוּ קַבֵּל וּשְׁמַע צַעֲקָתֵנוּ, יוֹדֵעַ תַּעֲלוּמוֹת.

בָּרוּךְ שֵׁם כְּבוֹד מַלְכוּתוֹ לְעוֹלָם וָעֶד.

רִבּוֹן הָעוֹלָמִים, אַתָּה צִוִּיתָנוּ לְהַקְרִיב קָרְבַּן הַתָּמִיד בְּמוֹעֲדוֹ וְלִהְיוֹת כֹּהֲנִים בַּעֲבוֹדָתָם וּלְוִיִּם בְּדוּכָנָם וְיִשְׂרָאֵל בְּמַעֲמָדָם, וְעַתָּה בַּעֲוֹנוֹתֵינוּ חָרַב בֵּית הַמִּקְדָּשׁ וּבָטֵל הַתָּמִיד וְאֵין לָנוּ לֹא כֹהֵן בַּעֲבוֹדָתוֹ וְלֹא לֵוִי בְּדוּכָנוֹ וְלֹא יִשְׂרָאֵל

on his platform, no Israelite at his post. But You said: "We will offer in place of *Hos. 14* bullocks [the prayer of] our lips." Therefore may it be Your will, LORD our God and God of our ancestors, that the prayer of our lips be considered, accepted and favored before You as if we had offered the daily sacrifice at its appointed time and place, according to its laws.

On Shabbat: וּבְיוֹם הַשַּׁבָּת On the Shabbat day,   *Num. 28*
          make an offering of two lambs a year old, without blemish,
          together with two-tenths of an ephah of fine flour
          mixed with oil as a meal-offering, and its appropriate libation.
          This is the burnt-offering for every Shabbat,
          in addition to the regular daily burnt-offering and its libation.

LAWS OF OFFERINGS, MISHNA ZEVAHIM

אֵיזֶהוּ מְקוֹמָן What is the location for sacrifices? The holiest offerings were slaugh- *Zevahim* tered on the north side. The bull and he-goat of Yom Kippur were slaughtered *Ch. 5* on the north side. Their blood was received in a sacred vessel on the north side, and had to be sprinkled between the poles [of the Ark], toward the veil [screening the Holy of Holies], and on the golden altar. [The omission of] one of these sprinklings invalidated [the atonement ceremony]. The leftover blood was to be poured onto the western base of the outer altar. If this was not done, however, the omission did not invalidate [the ceremony].

The bulls and he-goats that were completely burnt were slaughtered on the north side, their blood was received in a sacred vessel on the north side, and had to be sprinkled toward the veil and on the golden altar. [The omission of] one of these sprinklings invalidated [the ceremony]. The leftover blood was to be poured onto the western base of the outer altar. If this was not done, however, the omission did not invalidate [the ceremony]. All these offerings were burnt where the altar ashes were deposited.

The communal and individual sin-offerings – these are the communal sin-offerings: the he-goats offered on Rosh Ḥodesh and Festivals were slaughtered on the north side, their blood was received in a sacred vessel on the north side, and required four sprinklings, one on each of the four corners of the altar. How was this done? The priest ascended the ramp and turned [right] onto the surrounding ledge. He came to the southeast corner, then went to the northeast, then to the northwest, then to the southwest. The leftover blood he poured onto the southern base. [The meat of these offerings], prepared in any manner, was eaten within the [courtyard] curtains, by males of the priest-hood, on that day and the following night, until midnight.

בְּמַעֲמָדוֹ, וְאַתָּה אָמַרְתָּ: וּנְשַׁלְּמָה פָרִים שְׂפָתֵינוּ: לָכֵן יְהִי רָצוֹן מִלְּפָנֶיךָ יהוה הושע יד
אֱלֹהֵינוּ וֵאלֹהֵי אֲבוֹתֵינוּ, שֶׁיְּהֵא שִׂיחַ שִׂפְתוֹתֵינוּ חָשׁוּב וּמְקֻבָּל וּמְרֻצֶּה לְפָנֶיךָ,
כְּאִלּוּ הִקְרַבְנוּ קָרְבַּן הַתָּמִיד בְּמוֹעֲדוֹ וּבִמְקוֹמוֹ וּכְהִלְכָתוֹ.

במדבר כח

בְּשַׁבָּת: וּבְיוֹם הַשַּׁבָּת שְׁנֵי־כְבָשִׂים בְּנֵי־שָׁנָה תְּמִימִם
וּשְׁנֵי עֶשְׂרֹנִים סֹלֶת מִנְחָה בְּלוּלָה בַשֶּׁמֶן, וְנִסְכּוֹ:
עֹלַת שַׁבַּת בְּשַׁבַּתּוֹ, עַל־עֹלַת הַתָּמִיד וְנִסְכָּהּ:

דיני זבחים

זבחים
פרק ה

אֵיזֶהוּ מְקוֹמָן שֶׁל זְבָחִים. קָדְשֵׁי קָדָשִׁים שְׁחִיטָתָן בַּצָּפוֹן. פַּר וְשָׂעִיר
שֶׁל יוֹם הַכִּפּוּרִים, שְׁחִיטָתָן בַּצָּפוֹן, וְקִבּוּל דָּמָן בִּכְלִי שָׁרֵת בַּצָּפוֹן,
וְדָמָן טָעוּן הַזָּיָה עַל בֵּין הַבַּדִּים, וְעַל הַפָּרֹכֶת, וְעַל מִזְבַּח הַזָּהָב.
מַתָּנָה אַחַת מֵהֶן מְעַכֶּבֶת. שְׁיָרֵי הַדָּם הָיָה שׁוֹפֵךְ עַל יְסוֹד מַעֲרָבִי
שֶׁל מִזְבֵּחַ הַחִיצוֹן, אִם לֹא נָתַן לֹא עִכֵּב.

פָּרִים הַנִּשְׂרָפִים וּשְׂעִירִים הַנִּשְׂרָפִים, שְׁחִיטָתָן בַּצָּפוֹן, וְקִבּוּל דָּמָן
בִּכְלִי שָׁרֵת בַּצָּפוֹן, וְדָמָן טָעוּן הַזָּיָה עַל הַפָּרֹכֶת וְעַל מִזְבַּח הַזָּהָב.
מַתָּנָה אַחַת מֵהֶן מְעַכֶּבֶת. שְׁיָרֵי הַדָּם הָיָה שׁוֹפֵךְ עַל יְסוֹד מַעֲרָבִי
שֶׁל מִזְבֵּחַ הַחִיצוֹן, אִם לֹא נָתַן לֹא עִכֵּב. אֵלּוּ וָאֵלּוּ נִשְׂרָפִין בְּבֵית
הַדֶּשֶׁן.

חַטֹּאת הַצִּבּוּר וְהַיָּחִיד. אֵלּוּ הֵן חַטֹּאת הַצִּבּוּר: שְׂעִירֵי רָאשֵׁי חֳדָשִׁים
וְשֶׁל מוֹעֲדוֹת. שְׁחִיטָתָן בַּצָּפוֹן, וְקִבּוּל דָּמָן בִּכְלִי שָׁרֵת בַּצָּפוֹן,
וְדָמָן טָעוּן אַרְבַּע מַתָּנוֹת עַל אַרְבַּע קְרָנוֹת. כֵּיצַד, עָלָה בַכֶּבֶשׁ,
וּפָנָה לַסּוֹבֵב, וּבָא לוֹ לְקֶרֶן דְּרוֹמִית מִזְרָחִית, מִזְרָחִית צְפוֹנִית,
צְפוֹנִית מַעֲרָבִית, מַעֲרָבִית דְּרוֹמִית. שְׁיָרֵי הַדָּם הָיָה שׁוֹפֵךְ עַל יְסוֹד
דְּרוֹמִי. וְנֶאֱכָלִין לִפְנִים מִן הַקְּלָעִים, לְזִכְרֵי כְהֻנָּה, בְּכָל מַאֲכָל, לְיוֹם
וָלַיְלָה עַד חֲצוֹת.

The burnt-offering was among the holiest of sacrifices. It was slaughtered on the north side, its blood was received in a sacred vessel on the north side, and required two sprinklings [at opposite corners of the altar], making four in all. The offering had to be flayed, dismembered and wholly consumed by fire.

The communal peace-offerings and the guilt-offerings – these are the guilt-offerings: the guilt-offering for robbery; the guilt-offering for profane use of a sacred object; the guilt-offering [for violating] a betrothed maidservant; the guilt-offering of a Nazirite [who had become defiled by a corpse]; the guilt-offering of a leper [at his cleansing]; and the guilt-offering in case of doubt. All these were slaughtered on the north side, their blood was received in a sacred vessel on the north side, and required two sprinklings [at opposite corners of the altar], making four in all. [The meat of these offerings], prepared in any manner, was eaten within the [courtyard] curtains, by males of the priesthood, on that day and the following night, until midnight.

The thanksgiving-offering and the ram of a Nazirite were offerings of lesser holiness. They could be slaughtered anywhere in the Temple court, and their blood required two sprinklings [at opposite corners of the altar], making four in all. The meat of these offerings, prepared in any manner, was eaten anywhere within the city [Jerusalem], by anyone during that day and the following night until midnight. This also applied to the portion of these sacrifices [given to the priests], except that the priests' portion was only to be eaten by the priests, their wives, children and servants.

Peace-offerings were [also] of lesser holiness. They could be slaughtered anywhere in the Temple court, and their blood required two sprinklings [at opposite corners of the altar], making four in all. The meat of these offerings, prepared in any manner, was eaten anywhere within the city [Jerusalem], by anyone, for two days and one night. This also applied to the portion of these sacrifices [given to the priests], except that the priests' portion was only to be eaten by the priests, their wives, children and servants.

The firstborn and tithe of cattle and the Pesaḥ lamb were sacrifices of lesser holiness. They could be slaughtered anywhere in the Temple court, and their blood required only one sprinkling, which had to be done at the base of the altar. They differed in their consumption: the firstborn was eaten only by priests, while the tithe could be eaten by anyone. Both could be eaten anywhere within the city, prepared in any manner, during two days and one night. The Pesaḥ lamb had to be eaten that night until midnight. It could only be eaten by those who had been numbered for it, and eaten only roasted.

הָעוֹלָה קֹדֶשׁ קָדָשִׁים. שְׁחִיטָתָהּ בַּצָּפוֹן, וְקִבּוּל דָּמָהּ בִּכְלִי שָׁרֵת בַּצָּפוֹן, וְדָמָהּ טָעוּן שְׁתֵּי מַתָּנוֹת שֶׁהֵן אַרְבַּע, וּטְעוּנָה הֶפְשֵׁט וְנִתּוּחַ, וְכָלִיל לָאִשִּׁים.

זִבְחֵי שַׁלְמֵי צִבּוּר וַאֲשָׁמוֹת. אֵלּוּ הֵן אֲשָׁמוֹת: אֲשַׁם גְּזֵלוֹת, אֲשַׁם מְעִילוֹת, אֲשַׁם שִׁפְחָה חֲרוּפָה, אֲשַׁם נָזִיר, אֲשַׁם מְצֹרָע, אָשָׁם תָּלוּי. שְׁחִיטָתָן בַּצָּפוֹן, וְקִבּוּל דָּמָן בִּכְלִי שָׁרֵת בַּצָּפוֹן, וְדָמָן טָעוּן שְׁתֵּי מַתָּנוֹת שֶׁהֵן אַרְבַּע. וְנֶאֱכָלִין לִפְנִים מִן הַקְּלָעִים, לְזִכְרֵי כְהֻנָּה, בְּכָל מַאֲכָל, לְיוֹם וָלַיְלָה עַד חֲצוֹת.

הַתּוֹדָה וְאֵיל נָזִיר קָדָשִׁים קַלִּים. שְׁחִיטָתָן בְּכָל מָקוֹם בָּעֲזָרָה, וְדָמָן טָעוּן שְׁתֵּי מַתָּנוֹת שֶׁהֵן אַרְבַּע, וְנֶאֱכָלִין בְּכָל הָעִיר, לְכָל אָדָם, בְּכָל מַאֲכָל, לְיוֹם וָלַיְלָה עַד חֲצוֹת. הַמּוּרָם מֵהֶם כַּיּוֹצֵא בָהֶם, אֶלָּא שֶׁהַמּוּרָם נֶאֱכָל לַכֹּהֲנִים, לִנְשֵׁיהֶם, וְלִבְנֵיהֶם וּלְעַבְדֵּיהֶם.

שְׁלָמִים קָדָשִׁים קַלִּים. שְׁחִיטָתָן בְּכָל מָקוֹם בָּעֲזָרָה, וְדָמָן טָעוּן שְׁתֵּי מַתָּנוֹת שֶׁהֵן אַרְבַּע, וְנֶאֱכָלִין בְּכָל הָעִיר, לְכָל אָדָם, בְּכָל מַאֲכָל, לִשְׁנֵי יָמִים וְלַיְלָה אֶחָד. הַמּוּרָם מֵהֶם כַּיּוֹצֵא בָהֶם, אֶלָּא שֶׁהַמּוּרָם נֶאֱכָל לַכֹּהֲנִים, לִנְשֵׁיהֶם, וְלִבְנֵיהֶם וּלְעַבְדֵּיהֶם.

הַבְּכוֹר וְהַמַּעֲשֵׂר וְהַפֶּסַח קָדָשִׁים קַלִּים. שְׁחִיטָתָן בְּכָל מָקוֹם בָּעֲזָרָה, וְדָמָן טָעוּן מַתָּנָה אֶחָת, וּבִלְבַד שֶׁיִּתֵּן כְּנֶגֶד הַיְסוֹד. שִׁנָּה בַאֲכִילָתָן, הַבְּכוֹר נֶאֱכָל לַכֹּהֲנִים וְהַמַּעֲשֵׂר לְכָל אָדָם, וְנֶאֱכָלִין בְּכָל הָעִיר, בְּכָל מַאֲכָל, לִשְׁנֵי יָמִים וְלַיְלָה אֶחָד. הַפֶּסַח אֵינוֹ נֶאֱכָל אֶלָּא בַלַּיְלָה, וְאֵינוֹ נֶאֱכָל אֶלָּא עַד חֲצוֹת, וְאֵינוֹ נֶאֱכָל אֶלָּא לִמְנוּיָיו, וְאֵינוֹ נֶאֱכָל אֶלָּא צָלִי.

THE INTERPRETIVE PRINCIPLES OF RABBI YISHMAEL

רַבִּי יִשְׁמָעֵאל Rabbi Yishmael says:

The Torah is expounded by thirteen principles:

1. An inference from a lenient law to a strict one, and vice versa.
2. An inference drawn from identical words in two passages.
3. A general principle derived from one text or two related texts.
4. A general law followed by specific examples
   [where the law applies exclusively to those examples].
5. A specific example followed by a general law
   [where the law applies to everything implied in the general statement].
6. A general law followed by specific examples and concluding with a general law: here you may infer only cases similar to the examples.
7. When a general statement requires clarification by a specific example, or a specific example requires clarification by a general statement
   [then rules 4 and 5 do not apply].
8. When a particular case, already included in the general statement, is expressly mentioned to teach something new, that special provision applies to all other cases included in the general statement.
9. When a particular case, though included in the general statement, is expressly mentioned with a provision similar to the general law, such a case is singled out to lessen the severity of the law, not to increase it.
10. When a particular case, though included in the general statement, is explicitly mentioned with a provision differing from the general law, it is singled out to lessen in some respects, and in others to increase, the severity of the law.
11. When a particular case, though included in the general statement, is explicitly mentioned with a new provision, the terms of the general statement no longer apply to it, unless Scripture indicates explicitly that they do apply.
12. A matter elucidated from its context, or from the following passage.
‣ 13. Also, when two passages [seem to] contradict each other, [they are to be elucidated by] a third passage that reconciles them.

May it be Your will, LORD our God and God of our ancestors, that the Temple be speedily rebuilt in our days, and grant us our share in Your Torah. And may we serve You there in reverence, as in the days of old and as in former years.

Torah is interpreted" (Maimonides, *Laws of Torah Study* 1:11). It was chosen because it appears at the beginning of the *Sifra*, the halakhic commentary to Leviticus, which is the source of most of the laws of offerings. It also reminds us of the indissoluble connection between the Written Law (the Mosaic books) and the Oral Law (Mishna, Midrash and Talmud). Rabbi Yishmael's principles show how the latter can be derived from the former.

בָּרַיְתָא דְרַבִּי יִשְׁמָעֵאל

רַבִּי יִשְׁמָעֵאל אוֹמֵר: בִּשְׁלֹשׁ עֶשְׂרֵה מִדּוֹת הַתּוֹרָה נִדְרֶשֶׁת

א מִקַּל וָחֹמֶר

ב וּמִגְּזֵרָה שָׁוָה

ג מִבִּנְיַן אָב מִכָּתוּב אֶחָד, וּמִבִּנְיַן אָב מִשְּׁנֵי כְתוּבִים

ד מִכְּלָל וּפְרָט

ה מִפְּרָט וּכְלָל

ו כְּלָל וּפְרָט וּכְלָל, אִי אַתָּה דָן אֶלָּא כְּעֵין הַפְּרָט

ז מִכְּלָל שֶׁהוּא צָרִיךְ לִפְרָט, וּמִפְּרָט שֶׁהוּא צָרִיךְ לִכְלָל

ח כָּל דָּבָר שֶׁהָיָה בִּכְלָל, וְיָצָא מִן הַכְּלָל לְלַמֵּד
לֹא לְלַמֵּד עַל עַצְמוֹ יָצָא, אֶלָּא לְלַמֵּד עַל הַכְּלָל כֻּלּוֹ יָצָא

ט כָּל דָּבָר שֶׁהָיָה בִּכְלָל, וְיָצָא לִטְעֹן טְעַן אֶחָד שֶׁהוּא כְעִנְיָנוֹ
יָצָא לְהָקֵל וְלֹא לְהַחֲמִיר

י כָּל דָּבָר שֶׁהָיָה בִּכְלָל, וְיָצָא לִטְעֹן טְעַן אַחֵר שֶׁלֹּא כְעִנְיָנוֹ
יָצָא לְהָקֵל וּלְהַחֲמִיר

יא כָּל דָּבָר שֶׁהָיָה בִּכְלָל, וְיָצָא לִדּוֹן בַּדָּבָר הֶחָדָשׁ
אִי אַתָּה יָכוֹל לְהַחֲזִירוֹ לִכְלָלוֹ
עַד שֶׁיַּחֲזִירֶנּוּ הַכָּתוּב לִכְלָלוֹ בְּפֵרוּשׁ

יב דָּבָר הַלָּמֵד מֵעִנְיָנוֹ, וְדָבָר הַלָּמֵד מִסּוֹפוֹ

‹ יג וְכֵן שְׁנֵי כְתוּבִים הַמַּכְחִישִׁים זֶה אֶת זֶה
עַד שֶׁיָּבוֹא הַכָּתוּב הַשְּׁלִישִׁי וְיַכְרִיעַ בֵּינֵיהֶם.

יְהִי רָצוֹן מִלְּפָנֶיךָ, יהוה אֱלֹהֵינוּ וֵאלֹהֵי אֲבוֹתֵינוּ, שֶׁיִּבָּנֶה בֵּית הַמִּקְדָּשׁ
בִּמְהֵרָה בְיָמֵינוּ, וְתֵן חֶלְקֵנוּ בְּתוֹרָתֶךָ, וְשָׁם נַעֲבָדְךָ בְּיִרְאָה כִּימֵי עוֹלָם
וּכְשָׁנִים קַדְמוֹנִיּוֹת.

THE INTERPRETIVE PRINCIPLES OF RABBI YISHMAEL

This passage is included as an item of Talmud, defined in its broadest sense as
"deducing conclusions from premises, developing implications of statements,
comparing dicta, and studying the hermeneutical principles by which the

THE RABBIS' KADDISH

The following prayer, said by mourners, requires the presence of a minyan.
A transliteration can be found on page 778.

Mourner: יִתְגַּדַּל **Magnified and sanctified**
may His great name be,
in the world He created by His will.
May He establish His kingdom in your lifetime
and in your days,
and in the lifetime of all the house of Israel,
swiftly and soon – and say: Amen.

All: May His great name be blessed for ever and all time.

Mourner: Blessed and praised, glorified and exalted,
raised and honored, uplifted and lauded
be the name of the Holy One,
blessed be He,
beyond any blessing,
song, praise and consolation
uttered in the world – and say: Amen.

To Israel, to the teachers,
their disciples and their disciples' disciples,
and to all who engage in the study of Torah,
in this (*in Israel add:* holy) place or elsewhere,
may there come to them and you great peace,
grace, kindness and compassion,
long life, ample sustenance and deliverance,
from their Father in Heaven – and say: Amen.

May there be great peace from heaven,
and (good) life for us and all Israel – and say: Amen.

Bow, take three steps back, as if taking leave of the Divine Presence,
then bow, first left, then right, then center, while saying:
May He who makes peace in His high places,
in His compassion make peace
for us and all Israel – and say: Amen.

קדיש דרבנן

The following prayer, said by mourners, requires the presence of a מנין.
A transliteration can be found on page 778.

אבל: יִתְגַּדַּל וְיִתְקַדַּשׁ שְׁמֵהּ רַבָּא (קהל: אָמֵן)

בְּעָלְמָא דִּי בְרָא כִרְעוּתֵהּ, וְיַמְלִיךְ מַלְכוּתֵהּ

בְּחַיֵּיכוֹן וּבְיוֹמֵיכוֹן וּבְחַיֵּי דְכָל בֵּית יִשְׂרָאֵל

בַּעֲגָלָא וּבִזְמַן קָרִיב, וְאִמְרוּ אָמֵן. (קהל: אָמֵן)

קהל
ואבל: יְהֵא שְׁמֵהּ רַבָּא מְבָרַךְ לְעָלַם וּלְעָלְמֵי עָלְמַיָּא.

אבל: יִתְבָּרַךְ וְיִשְׁתַּבַּח וְיִתְפָּאַר וְיִתְרוֹמַם וְיִתְנַשֵּׂא

וְיִתְהַדָּר וְיִתְעַלֶּה וְיִתְהַלָּל

שְׁמֵהּ דְּקֻדְשָׁא בְּרִיךְ הוּא (קהל: בְּרִיךְ הוּא)

לְעֵלָּא מִן כָּל בִּרְכָתָא וְשִׁירָתָא, תֻּשְׁבְּחָתָא וְנֶחֱמָתָא

דַּאֲמִירָן בְּעָלְמָא, וְאִמְרוּ אָמֵן. (קהל: אָמֵן)

עַל יִשְׂרָאֵל וְעַל רַבָּנָן

וְעַל תַּלְמִידֵיהוֹן וְעַל כָּל תַּלְמִידֵי תַלְמִידֵיהוֹן

וְעַל כָּל מָאן דְּעָסְקִין בְּאוֹרַיְתָא

דִּי בְאַתְרָא (בארץ ישראל: קַדִּישָׁא) הָדֵין, וְדִי בְּכָל אֲתַר וַאֲתַר

יְהֵא לְהוֹן וּלְכוֹן שְׁלָמָא רַבָּא

חִנָּא וְחִסְדָּא, וְרַחֲמֵי, וְחַיֵּי אֲרִיכֵי, וּמְזוֹנֵי רְוִיחֵי

וּפֻרְקָנָא מִן קֳדָם אֲבוּהוֹן דִּי בִשְׁמַיָּא, וְאִמְרוּ אָמֵן. (קהל: אָמֵן)

יְהֵא שְׁלָמָא רַבָּא מִן שְׁמַיָּא

וְחַיִּים (טוֹבִים) עָלֵינוּ וְעַל כָּל יִשְׂרָאֵל, וְאִמְרוּ אָמֵן. (קהל: אָמֵן)

Bow, take three steps back, as if taking leave of the Divine Presence,
then bow, first left, then right, then center, while saying:

עֹשֶׂה שָׁלוֹם בִּמְרוֹמָיו

הוּא יַעֲשֶׂה בְרַחֲמָיו שָׁלוֹם

עָלֵינוּ וְעַל כָּל יִשְׂרָאֵל, וְאִמְרוּ אָמֵן. (קהל: אָמֵן)

Shaḥarit for Shabbat and Yom Tov

A PSALM BEFORE VERSES OF PRAISE

מִזְמוֹר שִׁיר A psalm of David. *Ps. 30*
A song for the dedication of the House.
I will exalt You, Lᴏʀᴅ, for You have lifted me up,
and not let my enemies rejoice over me.
Lᴏʀᴅ, my God, I cried to You for help and You healed me.
Lᴏʀᴅ, You lifted my soul from the grave;
You spared me from going down to the pit.
Sing to the Lᴏʀᴅ, you His devoted ones,
and give thanks to His holy name.
For His anger is for a moment, but His favor for a lifetime.
At night there may be weeping, but in the morning there is joy.
When I felt secure, I said, "I shall never be shaken."
Lᴏʀᴅ, when You favored me,
You made me stand firm as a mountain,
but when You hid Your face, I was terrified.
To You, Lᴏʀᴅ, I called; I pleaded with my Lᴏʀᴅ:
"What gain would there be if I died and went down to the grave?
Can dust thank You? Can it declare Your truth?
Hear, Lᴏʀᴅ, and be gracious to me; Lᴏʀᴅ, be my help."
You have turned my sorrow into dancing.
▸ You have removed my sackcloth and clothed me with joy,
so that my soul may sing to You and not be silent.
Lᴏʀᴅ my God, for ever will I thank You.

---

to be sung on that occasion (Rashi). In it David relates how, when his life was
in danger, God delivered him to safety. Set here, it beautifully connects the
dawn blessings (waking from sleep as a miniature experience of being saved
from death to life) with the Verses of Praise that are about to follow ("So that
my soul may sing to You").

שחרית לשבת וליום טוב

מזמור לפני פסוקי דזמרה

מִזְמוֹר שִׁיר־חֲנֻכַּת הַבַּיִת לְדָוִד:

אֲרוֹמִמְךָ יהוה כִּי דִלִּיתָנִי, וְלֹא־שִׂמַּחְתָּ אֹיְבַי לִי:

יהוה אֱלֹהָי, שִׁוַּעְתִּי אֵלֶיךָ וַתִּרְפָּאֵנִי:

יהוה, הֶעֱלִיתָ מִן־שְׁאוֹל נַפְשִׁי, חִיִּיתַנִי מִיָּרְדִי־בוֹר:

זַמְּרוּ לַיהוה חֲסִידָיו, וְהוֹדוּ לְזֵכֶר קָדְשׁוֹ:

כִּי רֶגַע בְּאַפּוֹ, חַיִּים בִּרְצוֹנוֹ, בָּעֶרֶב יָלִין בֶּכִי וְלַבֹּקֶר רִנָּה:

וַאֲנִי אָמַרְתִּי בְשַׁלְוִי, בַּל־אֶמּוֹט לְעוֹלָם:

יהוה, בִּרְצוֹנְךָ הֶעֱמַדְתָּה לְהַרְרִי עֹז

הִסְתַּרְתָּ פָנֶיךָ הָיִיתִי נִבְהָל:

אֵלֶיךָ יהוה אֶקְרָא, וְאֶל־אֲדֹנָי אֶתְחַנָּן:

מַה־בֶּצַע בְּדָמִי, בְּרִדְתִּי אֶל שָׁחַת, הֲיוֹדְךָ עָפָר, הֲיַגִּיד אֲמִתֶּךָ:

שְׁמַע־יהוה וְחָנֵּנִי, יהוה הֱיֵה־עֹזֵר לִי:

‹ הָפַכְתָּ מִסְפְּדִי לְמָחוֹל לִי, פִּתַּחְתָּ שַׂקִּי, וַתְּאַזְּרֵנִי שִׂמְחָה:

לְמַעַן יְזַמֶּרְךָ כָבוֹד וְלֹא יִדֹּם, יהוה אֱלֹהָי, לְעוֹלָם אוֹדֶךָּ:

מִזְמוֹר שִׁיר *Psalm 30.* This psalm was a late addition to the morning prayers, appearing for the first time in the seventeenth century. Although entitled "A psalm of David. A song for the dedication of the House," we know that the Temple was not built in his lifetime. As a soldier and military leader he was deemed not to be privileged to build a Temple that symbolized peace (1 Chr. 22:8). Hence it was built by his son King Solomon, whose name means peace and whose reign was marked by peace. Nonetheless, since it was David who conceived the plan to build the Temple, he wrote this psalm

MOURNER'S KADDISH

The following prayer, said by mourners, requires the presence of a minyan.
A transliteration can be found on page 779.

Mourner: **יִתְגַּדַּל** Magnified and sanctified
may His great name be,
in the world He created by His will.
May He establish His kingdom
in your lifetime and in your days,
and in the lifetime
of all the house of Israel,
swiftly and soon –
and say: Amen.

All: May His great name be blessed
for ever and all time.

Mourner: Blessed and praised, glorified and exalted,
raised and honored,
uplifted and lauded
be the name of the Holy One,
blessed be He,
beyond any blessing,
song, praise and consolation
uttered in the world –
and say: Amen.

May there be great peace from heaven,
and life for us and all Israel –
and say: Amen.

Bow, take three steps back, as if taking leave of the Divine Presence,
then bow, first left, then right, then center, while saying:
May He who makes peace in His high places,
make peace for us and all Israel –
and say: Amen.

קדיש יתום

The following prayer, said by mourners, requires the presence of a מנין.
A transliteration can be found on page 779.

אבל: יִתְגַּדַּל וְיִתְקַדַּשׁ שְׁמֵהּ רַבָּא (קהל: אָמֵן)
בְּעָלְמָא דִּי בְרָא כִרְעוּתֵהּ
וְיַמְלִיךְ מַלְכוּתֵהּ
בְּחַיֵּיכוֹן וּבְיוֹמֵיכוֹן וּבְחַיֵּי דְכָל בֵּית יִשְׂרָאֵל
בַּעֲגָלָא וּבִזְמַן קָרִיב
וְאִמְרוּ אָמֵן. (קהל: אָמֵן)

קהל
ואבל: יְהֵא שְׁמֵהּ רַבָּא מְבָרַךְ לְעָלַם וּלְעָלְמֵי עָלְמַיָּא.

אבל: יִתְבָּרַךְ וְיִשְׁתַּבַּח וְיִתְפָּאַר
וְיִתְרוֹמַם וְיִתְנַשֵּׂא וְיִתְהַדָּר וְיִתְעַלֶּה וְיִתְהַלָּל
שְׁמֵהּ דְּקֻדְשָׁא בְּרִיךְ הוּא (קהל: בְּרִיךְ הוּא)
לְעֵלָּא מִן כָּל בִּרְכָתָא וְשִׁירָתָא, תֻּשְׁבְּחָתָא וְנֶחֱמָתָא
דַּאֲמִירָן בְּעָלְמָא
וְאִמְרוּ אָמֵן. (קהל: אָמֵן)

יְהֵא שְׁלָמָא רַבָּא מִן שְׁמַיָּא
וְחַיִּים, עָלֵינוּ וְעַל כָּל יִשְׂרָאֵל
וְאִמְרוּ אָמֵן. (קהל: אָמֵן)

Bow, take three steps back, as if taking leave of the Divine Presence,
then bow, first left, then right, then center, while saying:

עֹשֶׂה שָׁלוֹם בִּמְרוֹמָיו
הוּא יַעֲשֶׂה שָׁלוֹם עָלֵינוּ
וְעַל כָּל יִשְׂרָאֵל
וְאִמְרוּ אָמֵן. (קהל: אָמֵן)

PESUKEI DEZIMRA

*The following introductory blessing to the Pesukei DeZimra (Verses of Praise) is
said standing, while holding the two front tzitziot of the tallit. They are kissed and
released at the end of the blessing at "songs of praise" (on the next page). From the
beginning of this prayer to the end of the Amida, conversation is forbidden.*

Some say:

I hereby prepare my mouth to thank, praise and laud my Creator, for the sake of the
unification of the Holy One, blessed be He, and His Divine Presence, through that
which is hidden and concealed, in the name of all Israel.

BLESSED IS HE
WHO SPOKE

and the world came into being, blessed is He.

> Blessed is He who creates the universe.
> Blessed is He who speaks and acts.
> Blessed is He who decrees and fulfills.
> Blessed is He who shows compassion to the earth.
> Blessed is He who shows compassion to all creatures.
> Blessed is He who gives a good reward
> > to those who fear Him.
> Blessed is He who lives for ever and exists to eternity.
> Blessed is He who redeems and saves.
> Blessed is His name.

145–150, of the book of Psalms, which correspond to the six days of creation in
Genesis 1.

בָּרוּךְ שֶׁאָמַר וְהָיָה הָעוֹלָם **Blessed is He who spoke and the world came into being.** In
the sharpest possible contrast to the mythology of the pagan world, creation
unfolds in Genesis 1 without clash or conflict between the elements. God said,
"Let there be" and there was. There is an essential underlying harmony in the
universe. All that exists is the result of a single creative will. The world is fundamentally good – the word "good" appears seven times in the opening chapter.
The opening section of this two-part blessing is a ten-line litany of blessings,
corresponding to the ten times in Genesis 1 in which the phrase, "And God
said" appears: the "ten utterances" by which the world was made (*Avot* 5:1).

פסוקי דזמרה

The following introductory blessing to the פסוקי דזמרה is said standing, while holding the two front ציצית of the טלית. They are kissed and released at the end of the blessing at בְּתִשְׁבָּחוֹת (on the next page). From the beginning of this prayer to the end of the עמידה, conversation is forbidden.

Some say:

הֲרֵינִי מְזַמֵּן אֶת פִּי לְהוֹדוֹת וּלְהַלֵּל וּלְשַׁבֵּחַ אֶת בּוֹרְאִי, לְשֵׁם יִחוּד קֻדְשָׁא בְּרִיךְ הוּא וּשְׁכִינְתֵּהּ עַל יְדֵי הַהוּא טָמִיר וְנֶעְלָם בְּשֵׁם כָּל יִשְׂרָאֵל.

בָּרוּךְ
שֶׁאָמַר
וְהָיָה הָעוֹלָם, בָּרוּךְ הוּא.
בָּרוּךְ עוֹשֶׂה בְרֵאשִׁית
בָּרוּךְ אוֹמֵר וְעוֹשֶׂה
בָּרוּךְ גּוֹזֵר וּמְקַיֵּם
בָּרוּךְ מְרַחֵם עַל הָאָרֶץ
בָּרוּךְ מְרַחֵם עַל הַבְּרִיּוֹת
בָּרוּךְ מְשַׁלֵּם שָׂכָר טוֹב לִירֵאָיו
בָּרוּךְ חַי לָעַד וְקַיָּם לָנֶצַח
בָּרוּךְ פּוֹדֶה וּמַצִּיל
בָּרוּךְ שְׁמוֹ

בָּרוּךְ שֶׁאָמַר **Blessed is He who spoke.** An introductory blessing to the Verses of Praise that follow, mainly taken from the Psalms. Their essential theme is God as He exists in Creation, designing and sustaining the universe in wisdom, justice and compassion. At their core are the last six psalms,

Blessed are You, LORD our God, King of the Universe,
God, compassionate Father, extolled by the mouth of His people,
praised and glorified by the tongue of His devoted ones
and those who serve Him.
With the songs of Your servant David
we will praise You, O LORD our God.
With praises and psalms we will magnify and praise You, glorify You,
Speak Your name and proclaim Your kingship,
our King, our God, ‣ the only One, Giver of life to the worlds
the King whose great name is praised and glorified to all eternity.
Blessed are You, LORD,
the King extolled with songs of praise.

הוֹדוּ Thank the LORD, call on His name, make His acts known   *1 Chr. 16*
among the peoples. Sing to Him, make music to Him, tell of all
His wonders. Glory in His holy name; let the hearts of those who
seek the LORD rejoice. Search out the LORD and His strength; seek
His presence at all times. Remember the wonders He has done,
His miracles, and the judgments He pronounced. Descendants of
Yisrael His servant, sons of Jacob His chosen ones: He is the LORD
our God. His judgments are throughout the earth. Remember His
covenant for ever, the word He commanded for a thousand generations. He made it with Abraham, vowed it to Isaac, and confirmed it
to Jacob as a statute and to Israel as an everlasting covenant, saying,

---

מְבַקְשֵׁי יהוה *Those who seek the LORD.* including those of other nations (Radak).

בַּקְּשׁוּ פָנָיו *Seek His presence.* in prayer (Radak), or contemplation (Malbim;
see commentary on Psalms 105:4).

וּמִשְׁפְּטֵי־פִיהוּ *The judgments He pronounced.* the warnings God sends in
advance through His prophets, as Moses warned Pharaoh of the impending
plagues (Radak, Ps. 105:5).

לְאֶלֶף דּוֹר *For a thousand generations.* a poetic way of saying "forever."

אַבְרָהָם, יִצְחָק, יַעֲקֹב *Abraham, Isaac, Jacob.* God made a promise to each of the
three patriarchs that their descendants would inherit the land.

בָּרוּךְ אַתָּה יהוה אֱלֹהֵינוּ מֶלֶךְ הָעוֹלָם
הָאֵל הָאָב הָרַחֲמָן הַמְהֻלָּל בְּפִי עַמּוֹ
מְשֻׁבָּח וּמְפֹאָר בִּלְשׁוֹן חֲסִידָיו וַעֲבָדָיו
וּבְשִׁירֵי דָוִד עַבְדֶּךָ, נְהַלֶּלְךָ יהוה אֱלֹהֵינוּ.
בִּשְׁבָחוֹת וּבִזְמִירוֹת
נְגַדֶּלְךָ וּנְשַׁבֵּחֲךָ וּנְפָאֶרְךָ, וְנַזְכִּיר שִׁמְךָ וְנַמְלִיכְךָ
מַלְכֵּנוּ אֱלֹהֵינוּ, ◂ יָחִיד חֵי הָעוֹלָמִים
מֶלֶךְ, מְשֻׁבָּח וּמְפֹאָר עֲדֵי עַד שְׁמוֹ הַגָּדוֹל
בָּרוּךְ אַתָּה יהוה, מֶלֶךְ מְהֻלָּל בַּתִּשְׁבָּחוֹת.

הוֹדוּ לַיהוה קִרְאוּ בִשְׁמוֹ, הוֹדִיעוּ בָעַמִּים עֲלִילֹתָיו: שִׁירוּ לוֹ, ‹דברי הימים א׳ טז›
זַמְּרוּ־לוֹ, שִׂיחוּ בְּכָל־נִפְלְאוֹתָיו: הִתְהַלְלוּ בְּשֵׁם קָדְשׁוֹ, יִשְׂמַח לֵב
מְבַקְשֵׁי יהוה: דִּרְשׁוּ יהוה וְעֻזּוֹ, בַּקְּשׁוּ פָנָיו תָּמִיד: זִכְרוּ נִפְלְאוֹתָיו
אֲשֶׁר עָשָׂה, מֹפְתָיו וּמִשְׁפְּטֵי־פִיהוּ: זֶרַע יִשְׂרָאֵל עַבְדּוֹ, בְּנֵי יַעֲקֹב
בְּחִירָיו: הוּא יהוה אֱלֹהֵינוּ בְּכָל־הָאָרֶץ מִשְׁפָּטָיו: זִכְרוּ לְעוֹלָם
בְּרִיתוֹ, דָּבָר צִוָּה לְאֶלֶף דּוֹר: אֲשֶׁר כָּרַת אֶת־אַבְרָהָם, וּשְׁבוּעָתוֹ
לְיִצְחָק: וַיַּעֲמִידֶהָ לְיַעֲקֹב לְחֹק, לְיִשְׂרָאֵל בְּרִית עוֹלָם: לֵאמֹר, לְךָ

בָּרוּךְ אַתָּה *Blessed are You.* The second part of this two-part blessing is an introduction to the biblical passages that follow.

וּבְשִׁירֵי דָוִד עַבְדֶּךָ *With the songs of Your servant David.* A reference to the psalms that form the core of the Verses of Praise.

הוֹדוּ לַיהוה *Thank the LORD.* A joyous celebration of Jewish history, this is the song David composed for the day the Ark was brought, in joy and dance, to Jerusalem.

הוֹדִיעוּ בָעַמִּים עֲלִילֹתָיו *Make His acts known among the peoples.* According to Radak this is a reference to the miraculous afflictions that struck the Philistines when they captured the Ark (1 Sam. 5).

"To you I will give the land of Canaan as your allotted heritage." You were then small in number, few, strangers there, wandering from nation to nation, from one kingdom to another, but He let no man oppress them, and for their sake He rebuked kings: "Do not touch My anointed ones, and do My prophets no harm." Sing to the Lord, all the earth; proclaim His salvation daily. Declare His glory among the nations, His marvels among all the peoples. For great is the Lord and greatly to be praised; He is awesome beyond all heavenly powers. ▸ For all the gods of the peoples are mere idols; it was the Lord who made the heavens.

Before Him are majesty and splendor; there is strength and beauty in His holy place. Render to the Lord, families of the peoples, render to the Lord honor and might. Render to the Lord the glory due to His name; bring an offering and come before Him; bow down to the Lord in the splendor of holiness. Tremble before Him, all the earth; the world stands firm, it will not be shaken. Let the heavens rejoice and the earth be glad; let them declare among the nations, "The Lord is King." Let the sea roar, and all that is in it; let the fields be jubilant, and all they contain. Then the trees of the forest will sing for joy before the Lord, for He is coming to judge the earth. Thank the Lord for He is good; His loving-kindness is for ever. Say: "Save us, God of our salvation; gather us and rescue us from the nations, to acknowledge Your holy name and glory in Your praise. Blessed is the Lord, God of Israel, from this world to eternity." And let all the people say "Amen" and "Praise the Lord."

---

pagans worshiped the sun, moon and stars as gods, not realizing that none was an independent power. Each had been made by the One God.

יִשְׂמְחוּ הַשָּׁמַיִם *Let the heavens rejoice.* A sentiment typical of the radiant vision of the Psalms: the universe moves in accordance with both the natural and moral laws that ensure its order and stability. Nature is not something to fear, but to celebrate.

וַיֹּאמְרוּ כָל־הָעָם *And let all the people say.* This was their response to the song sung the day the Ark was brought to Jerusalem (Ralbag).

אֶתֵּן אֶרֶץ־כְּנָעַן, חֶבֶל נַחֲלַתְכֶם: בִּהְיוֹתְכֶם מְתֵי מִסְפָּר, כִּמְעַט
וְגָרִים בָּהּ: וַיִּתְהַלְּכוּ מִגּוֹי אֶל־גּוֹי, וּמִמַּמְלָכָה אֶל־עַם אַחֵר: לֹא־
הִנִּיחַ לְאִישׁ לְעָשְׁקָם, וַיּוֹכַח עֲלֵיהֶם מְלָכִים: אַל־תִּגְּעוּ בִּמְשִׁיחָי,
וּבִנְבִיאַי אַל־תָּרֵעוּ: שִׁירוּ לַיהוה כָּל־הָאָרֶץ, בַּשְּׂרוּ מִיּוֹם־אֶל־
יוֹם יְשׁוּעָתוֹ: סַפְּרוּ בַגּוֹיִם אֶת־כְּבוֹדוֹ, בְּכָל־הָעַמִּים נִפְלְאֹתָיו:
כִּי גָדוֹל יהוה וּמְהֻלָּל מְאֹד, וְנוֹרָא הוּא עַל־כָּל־אֱלֹהִים: • כִּי
כָּל־אֱלֹהֵי הָעַמִּים אֱלִילִים, וַיהוה שָׁמַיִם עָשָׂה:

הוֹד וְהָדָר לְפָנָיו, עֹז וְחֶדְוָה בִּמְקֹמוֹ: הָבוּ לַיהוה מִשְׁפְּחוֹת
עַמִּים, הָבוּ לַיהוה כָּבוֹד וָעֹז: הָבוּ לַיהוה כְּבוֹד שְׁמוֹ, שְׂאוּ מִנְחָה
וּבֹאוּ לְפָנָיו, הִשְׁתַּחֲווּ לַיהוה בְּהַדְרַת־קֹדֶשׁ: חִילוּ מִלְּפָנָיו כָּל־
הָאָרֶץ, אַף־תִּכּוֹן תֵּבֵל בַּל־תִּמּוֹט: יִשְׂמְחוּ הַשָּׁמַיִם וְתָגֵל הָאָרֶץ,
וְיֹאמְרוּ בַגּוֹיִם יהוה מָלָךְ: יִרְעַם הַיָּם וּמְלֹאוֹ, יַעֲלֹץ הַשָּׂדֶה
וְכָל־אֲשֶׁר־בּוֹ: אָז יְרַנְּנוּ עֲצֵי הַיָּעַר, מִלִּפְנֵי יהוה, כִּי־בָא לִשְׁפּוֹט
אֶת־הָאָרֶץ: הוֹדוּ לַיהוה כִּי טוֹב, כִּי לְעוֹלָם חַסְדּוֹ: וְאִמְרוּ,
הוֹשִׁיעֵנוּ אֱלֹהֵי יִשְׁעֵנוּ, וְקַבְּצֵנוּ וְהַצִּילֵנוּ מִן־הַגּוֹיִם, לְהֹדוֹת
לְשֵׁם קָדְשֶׁךָ, לְהִשְׁתַּבֵּחַ בִּתְהִלָּתֶךָ: בָּרוּךְ יהוה אֱלֹהֵי יִשְׂרָאֵל
מִן־הָעוֹלָם וְעַד־הָעֹלָם, וַיֹּאמְרוּ כָל־הָעָם אָמֵן, וְהַלֵּל לַיהוה:

וַיִּתְהַלְּכוּ *Wandering.* Each of the patriarchs was forced to leave the land because of famine.

וַיּוֹכַח עֲלֵיהֶם מְלָכִים *For their sake He rebuked kings.* A reference to God's affliction of Pharaoh (Gen. 12:17) and Abimelech, King of Gerar (Gen. 20:18) for taking Sarah; and Laban when he was pursuing Jacob (Gen. 31:24, 29).

מְשִׁיחָי *My anointed ones.* Although only kings and high priests were anointed, here the phrase is used as a metaphor meaning "chosen ones."

אֱלִילִים, וַיהוה שָׁמַיִם עָשָׂה *Mere idols; it was the* Lord *who made the heavens.* The

‣ Exalt the Lord our God and bow before His footstool: He is *Ps. 99*
holy. Exalt the Lord our God and bow at His holy mountain; for
holy is the Lord our God.

He is compassionate. He forgives iniquity and does not destroy. *Ps. 78*
Repeatedly He suppresses His anger, not rousing His full wrath.
You, Lord: do not withhold Your compassion from me. May Your *Ps. 40*
loving-kindness and truth always guard me. Remember, Lord, *Ps. 25*
Your acts of compassion and love, for they have existed for ever.
Ascribe power to God, whose majesty is over Israel and whose *Ps. 68*
might is in the skies. You are awesome, God, in Your holy places.
It is the God of Israel who gives might and strength to the people,
may God be blessed. God of retribution, Lord, God of retribu- *Ps. 94*
tion, appear. Arise, Judge of the earth, to repay the arrogant their
just deserts. Salvation belongs to the Lord; may Your blessing *Ps. 3*
rest upon Your people, Selah! ‣ The Lord of hosts is with us, the *Ps. 46*
God of Jacob is our stronghold, Selah! Lord of hosts, happy is *Ps. 84*
the one who trusts in You. Lord, save! May the King answer us *Ps. 20*
on the day we call.

Save Your people and bless Your heritage; tend them and carry *Ps. 28*
them for ever. Our soul longs for the Lord; He is our Help and *Ps. 33*
Shield. For in Him our hearts rejoice, for in His holy name we
have trusted. May Your loving-kindness, Lord, be upon us, as we
have put our hope in You. Show us, Lord, Your loving-kindness *Ps. 85*
and grant us Your salvation. Arise, help us and redeem us for the *Ps. 44*
sake of Your love. I am the Lord your God who brought you *Ps. 81*
up from the land of Egypt: open your mouth wide and I will fill
it. Happy is the people for whom this is so; happy is the people *Ps. 144*
whose God the Lord. ‣ As for me, I trust in Your loving-kindness; *Ps. 13*
my heart rejoices in Your salvation. I will sing to the Lord for He
has been good to me.

---

divine justice and compassion, moving seamlessly from national to individual
thanksgiving.

‹ רוֹמְמוּ יהוה אֱלֹהֵינוּ וְהִשְׁתַּחֲווּ לַהֲדֹם רַגְלָיו, קָדוֹשׁ הוּא: תהלים צט
רוֹמְמוּ יהוה אֱלֹהֵינוּ וְהִשְׁתַּחֲווּ לְהַר קָדְשׁוֹ, כִּי־קָדוֹשׁ יהוה
אֱלֹהֵינוּ:

וְהוּא רַחוּם, יְכַפֵּר עָוֹן וְלֹא־יַשְׁחִית, וְהִרְבָּה לְהָשִׁיב אַפּוֹ, תהלים עח
וְלֹא־יָעִיר כָּל־חֲמָתוֹ: אַתָּה יהוה לֹא־תִכְלָא רַחֲמֶיךָ מִמֶּנִּי, תהלים מ
חַסְדְּךָ וַאֲמִתְּךָ תָּמִיד יִצְּרוּנִי: זְכֹר־רַחֲמֶיךָ יהוה וַחֲסָדֶיךָ, כִּי תהלים כה
מֵעוֹלָם הֵמָּה: תְּנוּ עֹז לֵאלֹהִים, עַל־יִשְׂרָאֵל גַּאֲוָתוֹ, וְעֻזּוֹ תהלים סח
בַּשְּׁחָקִים: נוֹרָא אֱלֹהִים מִמִּקְדָּשֶׁיךָ, אֵל יִשְׂרָאֵל הוּא נֹתֵן עֹז
וְתַעֲצֻמוֹת לָעָם, בָּרוּךְ אֱלֹהִים: אֵל־נְקָמוֹת יהוה, אֵל נְקָמוֹת תהלים צד
הוֹפִיעַ: הִנָּשֵׂא שֹׁפֵט הָאָרֶץ, הָשֵׁב גְּמוּל עַל־גֵּאִים: לַיהוה תהלים ג
הַיְשׁוּעָה, עַל־עַמְּךָ בִרְכָתֶךָ סֶּלָה: ‹ יהוה צְבָאוֹת עִמָּנוּ, מִשְׂגָּב תהלים מו
לָנוּ אֱלֹהֵי יַעֲקֹב סֶלָה: יהוה צְבָאוֹת, אַשְׁרֵי אָדָם בֹּטֵחַ בָּךְ: תהלים פד
יהוה הוֹשִׁיעָה, הַמֶּלֶךְ יַעֲנֵנוּ בְיוֹם־קָרְאֵנוּ: תהלים כ

הוֹשִׁיעָה אֶת־עַמֶּךָ, וּבָרֵךְ אֶת־נַחֲלָתֶךָ, וּרְעֵם וְנַשְּׂאֵם תהלים כח
עַד־הָעוֹלָם: נַפְשֵׁנוּ חִכְּתָה לַיהוה, עֶזְרֵנוּ וּמָגִנֵּנוּ הוּא: כִּי־בוֹ תהלים לג
יִשְׂמַח לִבֵּנוּ, כִּי בְשֵׁם קָדְשׁוֹ בָטָחְנוּ: יְהִי־חַסְדְּךָ יהוה עָלֵינוּ,
כַּאֲשֶׁר יִחַלְנוּ לָךְ: הַרְאֵנוּ יהוה חַסְדֶּךָ, וְיֶשְׁעֲךָ תִּתֶּן־לָנוּ: קוּמָה תהלים פה
עֶזְרָתָה לָּנוּ, וּפְדֵנוּ לְמַעַן חַסְדֶּךָ: אָנֹכִי יהוה אֱלֹהֶיךָ הַמַּעַלְךָ תהלים מד
מֵאֶרֶץ מִצְרָיִם, הַרְחֶב־פִּיךָ וַאֲמַלְאֵהוּ: אַשְׁרֵי הָעָם שֶׁכָּכָה תהלים פא
לּוֹ, אַשְׁרֵי הָעָם שֶׁיהוה אֱלֹהָיו: ‹ וַאֲנִי בְּחַסְדְּךָ בָטַחְתִּי, יָגֵל תהלים קמד
לִבִּי בִּישׁוּעָתֶךָ, אָשִׁירָה לַיהוה, כִּי גָמַל עָלָי: תהלים יג

───────────────────────

רוֹמְמוּ *Exalt.* A selection of verses from the book of Psalms, on the themes of

לַמְנַצֵּחַ For the conductor of music. A psalm of David. *Ps. 19*

The heavens declare the glory of God;
    the skies proclaim the work of His hands.
Day to day they pour forth speech;
    night to night they communicate knowledge.
There is no speech, there are no words,
    their voice is not heard.
Yet their music carries throughout the earth,
    their words to the end of the world.
    In them He has set a tent for the sun.
It emerges like a groom from his marriage chamber,
    rejoicing like a champion about to run a race.
It rises at one end of the heaven
    and makes its circuit to the other:
    nothing is hidden from its heat.
The LORD's Torah is perfect, refreshing the soul.
    The LORD's testimony is faithful, making the simple wise.
The LORD's precepts are just, gladdening the heart.
    The LORD's commandment is radiant, giving light to the eyes.
The fear of the LORD is pure, enduring for ever.
    The LORD's judgments are true, altogether righteous.
More precious than gold, than much fine gold.
    They are sweeter than honey, than honey from the comb.
Your servant, too, is careful of them,
    for in observing them there is great reward.
Yet who can discern his errors?
    Cleanse me of hidden faults.

Torah to transform those who open themselves to its radiance. In Creation we encounter the world that is, but in Revelation we catch a glimpse of the world that ought to be, and will come to be when we align our will with the will of God. Finally comes the speech of humanity to God ("the words of my mouth and the meditation of my heart") in the form of prayer.

שְׁגִיאוֹת מִי־יָבִין *Yet who can discern his errors?* The Psalmist notes the fundamental difference between humans and inanimate nature: the latter automatically

לַמְנַצֵּחַ מִזְמוֹר לְדָוִד:

הַשָּׁמַיִם מְסַפְּרִים כְּבוֹד־אֵל, וּמַעֲשֵׂה יָדָיו מַגִּיד הָרָקִיעַ:

יוֹם לְיוֹם יַבִּיעַ אְׂמֶר, וְלַיְלָה לְּלַיְלָה יְחַוֶּה־דָּעַת:

אֵין־אְׂמֶר וְאֵין דְּבָרִים, בְּלִי נִשְׁמָע קוֹלָם:

בְּכָל־הָאָרֶץ יָצָא קַוָּם, וּבִקְצֵה תֵבֵל מִלֵּיהֶם
לַשֶּׁמֶשׁ שָׂם־אְׂהֶל בָּהֶם:

וְהוּא כְּחָתָן יֹצֵא מֵחֻפָּתוֹ, יָשִׂישׂ כְּגִבּוֹר לָרוּץ אְׂרַח:

מִקְצֵה הַשָּׁמַיִם מוֹצָאוֹ, וּתְקוּפָתוֹ עַל־קְצוֹתָם
וְאֵין נִסְתָּר מֵחַמָּתוֹ:

תּוֹרַת יהוה תְּמִימָה, מְשִׁיבַת נָפֶשׁ

עֵדוּת יהוה נֶאֱמָנָה, מַחְכִּימַת פֶּתִי:

פִּקּוּדֵי יהוה יְשָׁרִים, מְשַׂמְּחֵי־לֵב

מִצְוַת יהוה בָּרָה, מְאִירַת עֵינָיִם:

יִרְאַת יהוה טְהוֹרָה, עוֹמֶדֶת לָעַד

מִשְׁפְּטֵי־יהוה אֱמֶת, צָדְקוּ יַחְדָּו:

הַנֶּחֱמָדִים מִזָּהָב וּמִפַּז רָב, וּמְתוּקִים מִדְּבַשׁ וְנֹפֶת צוּפִים:

גַּם־עַבְדְּךָ נִזְהָר בָּהֶם, בְּשָׁמְרָם עֵקֶב רָב:

שְׁגִיאוֹת מִי־יָבִין, מִנִּסְתָּרוֹת נַקֵּנִי:

לַמְנַצֵּחַ *Psalm 19.* A magnificent psalm in three parts, corresponding to the basic tripartite structure of Jewish belief: Creation, Revelation and Redemption. The first seven verses are a hymn about Creation as God's work. The second section (verses 8–11) is about Revelation – Torah – as God's word. The third is a prayer for forgiveness, ending with the word "Redeemer." What connects them is the idea of speech. First is the silent speech of the universe, the "music of the spheres," that the universe continually utters to its Creator. Then comes the audible speech of God to humankind, the revelation of His will in the form of the Torah. The Psalmist speaks ecstatically about the power of

Keep Your servant also from willful sins;
>   let them not have dominion over me.
Then shall I be blameless,
>   and innocent of grave sin.
▸ May the words of my mouth and the meditation of my heart
find favor before You, LORD, my Rock and my Redeemer.

לְדָוִד Of David. When he pretended to be insane before Abimelech,   *Ps. 34*
who drove him away, and he left.
I will bless the LORD at all times;
>   His praise will be always on my lips.
My soul will glory in the LORD;
>   let the lowly hear this and rejoice.
Magnify the LORD with me;
>   let us exalt His name together.
I sought the LORD, and He answered me;
>   He saved me from all my fears.
Those who look to Him are radiant;
>   Their faces are never downcast.
This poor man called, and the LORD heard;
>   He saved him from all his troubles.
The LORD's angel encamps around those who fear Him,
>   and He rescues them.
Taste and see that the LORD is good;
>   happy is the man who takes refuge in Him.
Fear the LORD, you His holy ones,
>   for those who fear Him lack nothing.
Young lions may grow weak and hungry,
>   but those who seek the LORD lack no good thing.
Come, my children, listen to me;
>   I will teach you the fear of the LORD.

---

in Him shall be condemned." God is not on the side of those who embody
the arrogance of power: "The LORD is close to the brokenhearted, and saves
those who are crushed in spirit."

גַּם מִזֵּדִים חֲשֹׂךְ עַבְדֶּךָ, אַל־יִמְשְׁלוּ־בִי אָז אֵיתָם
וְנִקֵּיתִי מִפֶּשַׁע רָב:

‹ יִהְיוּ לְרָצוֹן אִמְרֵי־פִי וְהֶגְיוֹן לִבִּי לְפָנֶיךָ, יהוה, צוּרִי וְגֹאֲלִי:

תהלים לד

לְדָוִד, בְּשַׁנּוֹתוֹ אֶת־טַעְמוֹ לִפְנֵי אֲבִימֶלֶךְ, וַיְגָרְשֵׁהוּ וַיֵּלַךְ:
אֲבָרְכָה אֶת־יהוה בְּכָל־עֵת, תָּמִיד תְּהִלָּתוֹ בְּפִי:
בַּיהוה תִּתְהַלֵּל נַפְשִׁי, יִשְׁמְעוּ עֲנָוִים וְיִשְׂמָחוּ:
גַּדְּלוּ לַיהוה אִתִּי, וּנְרוֹמְמָה שְׁמוֹ יַחְדָּו:
דָּרַשְׁתִּי אֶת־יהוה וְעָנָנִי, וּמִכָּל־מְגוּרוֹתַי הִצִּילָנִי:
הִבִּיטוּ אֵלָיו וְנָהָרוּ, וּפְנֵיהֶם אַל־יֶחְפָּרוּ:
זֶה עָנִי קָרָא, וַיהוה שָׁמֵעַ, וּמִכָּל־צָרוֹתָיו הוֹשִׁיעוֹ:
חֹנֶה מַלְאַךְ־יהוה סָבִיב לִירֵאָיו, וַיְחַלְּצֵם:
טַעֲמוּ וּרְאוּ כִּי־טוֹב יהוה, אַשְׁרֵי הַגֶּבֶר יֶחֱסֶה־בּוֹ:
יְראוּ אֶת־יהוה קְדֹשָׁיו, כִּי־אֵין מַחְסוֹר לִירֵאָיו:
כְּפִירִים רָשׁוּ וְרָעֵבוּ, וְדֹרְשֵׁי יהוה לֹא־יַחְסְרוּ כָל־טוֹב:
לְכוּ־בָנִים שִׁמְעוּ־לִי, יִרְאַת יהוה אֲלַמֶּדְכֶם:

conforms to the will of its Creator, but mankind does not. He therefore prays
to be protected from sin, deliberate or unwitting.

יִהְיוּ לְרָצוֹן אִמְרֵי־פִי *May the words of my mouth.* A beautiful prayer we say at the
end of every Amida.

לְדָוִד *Psalm 34.* David, fleeing from Saul, took refuge in the Philistine city
of Gath. There he was recognized, and knew that his life was in danger. He
decided to pretend to be insane, "making marks on the doors of the gate and
letting saliva run down his beard." The Philistine king, dismissing him as a
madman, told his servants to remove him. Thus David was able to make good
his escape (1 Sam. 21:11–16). He composed this psalm as a song of thanksgiving: "This poor man called, and the LORD heard…None who take refuge

Who desires life, loving each day to see good?
Then guard your tongue from evil
and your lips from speaking deceit.
Turn from evil and do good;
seek peace and pursue it.
The eyes of the Lord are on the righteous
and His ears attentive to their cry;
The Lord's face is set against those who do evil,
to erase their memory from the earth.
The righteous cry out, and the Lord hears them;
delivering them from all their troubles.
The Lord is close to the brokenhearted,
and saves those who are crushed in spirit.
Many troubles may befall the righteous,
but the Lord delivers him from them all;
He protects all his bones,
so that none of them will be broken.
Evil will slay the wicked;
the enemies of the righteous will be condemned.
► The Lord redeems His servants;
none who take refuge in Him shall be condemned.

תְּפִלָּה לְמֹשֶׁה A prayer of Moses, the man of God. Lord, You have *Ps. 90*
been our shelter in every generation. Before the mountains were born,
before You brought forth the earth and the world, from everlasting to
everlasting You are God. You turn men back to dust, saying, "Return,
you children of men." For a thousand years in Your sight are like yesterday when it has passed, like a watch in the night. You sweep men
away; they sleep. In the morning they are like grass newly grown: in the
morning it flourishes and is new, but by evening it withers and dries up.

אֶלֶף שָׁנִים... וְאַשְׁמוּרָה בַלַּיְלָה *A thousand years... a watch in the night.* A dramatic
contrast between God's time-scale and ours. Note the succession of poetic
images conveying the brevity of human life: it flows as fast as a swollen river,

מִי־הָאִישׁ הֶחָפֵץ חַיִּים, אֹהֵב יָמִים לִרְאוֹת טוֹב:

נְצֹר לְשׁוֹנְךָ מֵרָע, וּשְׂפָתֶיךָ מִדַּבֵּר מִרְמָה:

סוּר מֵרָע וַעֲשֵׂה־טוֹב, בַּקֵּשׁ שָׁלוֹם וְרָדְפֵהוּ:

עֵינֵי יהוה אֶל־צַדִּיקִים, וְאָזְנָיו אֶל־שַׁוְעָתָם:

פְּנֵי יהוה בְּעֹשֵׂי רָע, לְהַכְרִית מֵאֶרֶץ זִכְרָם:

צָעֲקוּ וַיהוה שָׁמֵעַ, וּמִכָּל־צָרוֹתָם הִצִּילָם:

קָרוֹב יהוה לְנִשְׁבְּרֵי־לֵב, וְאֶת־דַּכְּאֵי־רוּחַ יוֹשִׁיעַ:

רַבּוֹת רָעוֹת צַדִּיק, וּמִכֻּלָּם יַצִּילֶנּוּ יהוה:

שֹׁמֵר כָּל־עַצְמוֹתָיו, אַחַת מֵהֵנָּה לֹא נִשְׁבָּרָה:

תְּמוֹתֵת רָשָׁע רָעָה, וְשֹׂנְאֵי צַדִּיק יֶאְשָׁמוּ:

◂ פּוֹדֶה יהוה נֶפֶשׁ עֲבָדָיו, וְלֹא יֶאְשְׁמוּ כָּל־הַחֹסִים בּוֹ:

תהלים צ

תְּפִלָּה לְמֹשֶׁה אִישׁ־הָאֱלֹהִים, אֲדֹנָי, מָעוֹן אַתָּה הָיִיתָ לָּנוּ בְּדֹר וָדֹר: בְּטֶרֶם הָרִים יֻלָּדוּ, וַתְּחוֹלֵל אֶרֶץ וְתֵבֵל, וּמֵעוֹלָם עַד־עוֹלָם אַתָּה אֵל: תָּשֵׁב אֱנוֹשׁ עַד־דַּכָּא, וַתֹּאמֶר שׁוּבוּ בְנֵי־אָדָם: כִּי אֶלֶף שָׁנִים בְּעֵינֶיךָ, כְּיוֹם אֶתְמוֹל כִּי יַעֲבֹר, וְאַשְׁמוּרָה בַלָּיְלָה: זְרַמְתָּם, שֵׁנָה יִהְיוּ, בַּבֹּקֶר כֶּחָצִיר יַחֲלֹף: בַּבֹּקֶר יָצִיץ וְחָלָף, לָעֶרֶב

תְּפִלָּה לְמֹשֶׁה *Psalm 90.* A magnificent poem, the only psalm attributed to Moses, on God's eternity and our mortality. However long we live, our lives are a mere microsecond in the history of the cosmos. Wisdom consists in knowing how brief is our stay on earth, and in the determination to use every day in service of the right, the just and the holy. The good we do lives after us; the rest is oft interred with our bones.

אִישׁ הָאֱלֹהִים *The man of God.* This description also occurs in Deuteronomy 33:1, prefacing Moses' final blessing to the people. In the Torah only Moses is given this description. Elsewhere in Tanakh it is used as a synonym for a prophet.

For we are consumed by Your anger, terrified by Your fury. You have set our iniquities before You, our secret sins in the light of Your presence. All our days pass away in Your wrath, we spend our years like a sigh. The span of our life is seventy years, or if we are strong, eighty years; but the best of them is trouble and sorrow, for they quickly pass, and we fly away. Who can know the force of Your anger? Your wrath matches the fear due to You. Teach us rightly to number our days, that we may gain a heart of wisdom. Relent, O LORD! How much longer? Be sorry for Your servants. Satisfy us in the morning with Your loving-kindness, that we may sing and rejoice all our days. Grant us joy for as many days as You have afflicted us, for as many years as we saw trouble. Let Your deeds be seen by Your servants, and Your glory by their children. ‣ May the pleasantness of the LORD our God be upon us. Establish for us the work of our hands, O establish the work of our hands.

יֹשֵׁב בְּסֵתֶר He who lives in the shelter of the Most High dwells in the *Ps. 91* shadow of the Almighty. I say of the LORD, my Refuge and Stronghold, my God in whom I trust, that He will save you from the fowler's snare and the deadly pestilence. With His pinions He will cover you, and beneath His wings you will find shelter; His faithfulness is an encircling shield. You need not fear terror by night, nor the arrow that flies by day; not the pestilence that stalks in darkness, nor the plague that ravages at noon. A thousand may fall at your side, ten thousand at your right hand, but it will not come near you. You will only look with your eyes and see the punishment of the wicked. Because you said "The LORD is my Refuge," taking the Most High as your shelter, no harm will befall you, no plague will come near your tent, for He will command His angels about you, to guard you in all your ways. They will lift you in their hands, lest your foot stumble on a stone.

יֹשֵׁב בְּסֵתֶר *Psalm 91*. A psalm for protection at a time of danger. There is no life without risk, and courage does not mean having no fear; it means feeling it yet overcoming it in the knowledge that we are not alone. "We have nothing to fear but fear itself," and faith is the antidote to fear. The psalm radiates a sense of confidence and trust even in a world full of hazards.

יִמּוֹלֵל וְיָבֵשׁ: כִּי־כָלִינוּ בְאַפֶּךָ, וּבַחֲמָתְךָ נִבְהָלְנוּ: שַׁתָּ עֲוֹנֹתֵינוּ
לְנֶגְדֶּךָ, עֲלֻמֵנוּ לִמְאוֹר פָּנֶיךָ: כִּי כָל־יָמֵינוּ פָּנוּ בְעֶבְרָתֶךָ, כִּלִּינוּ
שָׁנֵינוּ כְמוֹ־הֶגֶה: יְמֵי־שְׁנוֹתֵינוּ בָהֶם שִׁבְעִים שָׁנָה, וְאִם בִּגְבוּרֹת
שְׁמוֹנִים שָׁנָה, וְרָהְבָּם עָמָל וָאָוֶן, כִּי־גָז חִישׁ וַנָּעֻפָה: מִי־יוֹדֵעַ
עֹז אַפֶּךָ, וּכְיִרְאָתְךָ עֶבְרָתֶךָ, לִמְנוֹת יָמֵינוּ כֵּן הוֹדַע, וְנָבִא לְבַב
חָכְמָה: שׁוּבָה יהוה עַד־מָתָי, וְהִנָּחֵם עַל־עֲבָדֶיךָ: שַׂבְּעֵנוּ בַבֹּקֶר
חַסְדֶּךָ, וּנְרַנְּנָה וְנִשְׂמְחָה בְּכָל־יָמֵינוּ: שַׂמְּחֵנוּ כִּימוֹת עִנִּיתָנוּ, שְׁנוֹת
רָאִינוּ רָעָה: יֵרָאֶה אֶל־עֲבָדֶיךָ פָעֳלֶךָ, וַהֲדָרְךָ עַל־בְּנֵיהֶם: ◂ וִיהִי
נֹעַם אֲדֹנָי אֱלֹהֵינוּ עָלֵינוּ, וּמַעֲשֵׂה יָדֵינוּ כּוֹנְנָה עָלֵינוּ, וּמַעֲשֵׂה
יָדֵינוּ כּוֹנְנֵהוּ:

תהלים צא

יֹשֵׁב בְּסֵתֶר עֶלְיוֹן, בְּצֵל שַׁדַּי יִתְלוֹנָן: אֹמַר לַיהוה מַחְסִי וּמְצוּדָתִי,
אֱלֹהַי אֶבְטַח־בּוֹ: כִּי הוּא יַצִּילְךָ מִפַּח יָקוּשׁ, מִדֶּבֶר הַוּוֹת:
בְּאֶבְרָתוֹ יָסֶךְ לָךְ, וְתַחַת־כְּנָפָיו תֶּחְסֶה, צִנָּה וְסֹחֵרָה אֲמִתּוֹ:
לֹא־תִירָא מִפַּחַד לָיְלָה, מֵחֵץ יָעוּף יוֹמָם: מִדֶּבֶר בָּאֹפֶל יַהֲלֹךְ,
מִקֶּטֶב יָשׁוּד צָהֳרָיִם: יִפֹּל מִצִּדְּךָ אֶלֶף, וּרְבָבָה מִימִינֶךָ, אֵלֶיךָ
לֹא יִגָּשׁ: רַק בְּעֵינֶיךָ תַבִּיט, וְשִׁלֻּמַת רְשָׁעִים תִּרְאֶה: כִּי־אַתָּה
יהוה מַחְסִי, עֶלְיוֹן שַׂמְתָּ מְעוֹנֶךָ: לֹא־תְאֻנֶּה אֵלֶיךָ רָעָה, וְנֶגַע
לֹא־יִקְרַב בְּאָהֳלֶךָ: כִּי מַלְאָכָיו יְצַוֶּה־לָּךְ, לִשְׁמָרְךָ בְּכָל־דְּרָכֶיךָ:
עַל־כַּפַּיִם יִשָּׂאוּנְךָ, פֶּן־תִּגֹּף בָּאֶבֶן רַגְלֶךָ: עַל־שַׁחַל וָפֶתֶן תִּדְרֹךְ,

---

as quickly as a sleep or a dream, it is like grass in a parched land that soon withers, it is like a sigh, a mere breath, like a bird that briefly lands then flies away.

וּמַעֲשֵׂה יָדֵינוּ כּוֹנְנָה עָלֵינוּ *Establish for us the work of our hands.* Help us create
achievements that last. According to the sages, this is the blessing Moses gave
the Israelites when they completed the building of the Tabernacle.

You will tread on lions and vipers, you will trample on young lions and snakes. [God says] "Because he loves Me, I will rescue him; I will protect him, because he acknowledges My name. When he calls on Me, I will answer him, I will be with him in distress, I will deliver him and bring him honor. ▸ With long life I will satisfy him, and show him My salvation. With long life I will satisfy him, and show him My salvation."

הַלְלוּיָהּ **Halleluya!** Praise the name of the LORD. Praise Him, you ser- Ps. 135 vants of the LORD who stand in the LORD's House, in the courtyards of the House of our God. Praise the LORD, for the LORD is good; sing praises to His name, for it is lovely. For the LORD has chosen Jacob as His own, Israel as his treasure. For I know that the LORD is great, that our LORD is above all heavenly powers. Whatever pleases the LORD, He does, in heaven and on earth, in the seas and all the depths. He raises clouds from the ends of the earth; He sends lightning with the rain; He brings out the wind from His storehouses. He struck down the firstborn of Egypt, of both man and animals. He sent signs and wonders into your midst, Egypt – against Pharaoh and all his servants. He struck down many nations and slew mighty kings: Siḥon, King of the Amorites, Og, King of Bashan, and all the kingdoms of Canaan, giving their land as a heritage, a heritage for His people Israel. Your name, LORD, endures for ever; Your renown, LORD, for all generations. For the LORD will bring justice to His people, and have compassion on His servants. The idols of the nations are silver and gold, the work of human hands. They have mouths, but cannot speak; eyes, but cannot see; ears, but cannot hear; there is no breath in their mouths. Those who make them will become like them: so will all who trust in them. ▸ House of Israel, bless the LORD. House of Aaron, bless the LORD. House of Levi, bless the LORD. You who fear the LORD, bless the

---

פֶּה־לָהֶם וְלֹא יְדַבֵּרוּ *They have mouths, but cannot speak.* Those who put their faith in forces that are less than human, themselves become less than human. Many have been the idols of history: power, wealth, status, the nation, the race, the state, the ideology, the system. None has lasted, for each has crushed the human spirit. None has given rise to stable systems of liberty and dignity.

תִּרְהְבֵנִי בְנַפְשִׁי עֹז:

תַּרְמֵם כְּפִיר וְתַנִּין: כִּי בִי חָשַׁק וַאֲפַלְּטֵהוּ, אֲשַׂגְּבֵהוּ כִּי־יָדַע

שְׁמִי: יִקְרָאֵנִי וְאֶעֱנֵהוּ, עִמּוֹ אָנֹכִי בְצָרָה, אֲחַלְּצֵהוּ וַאֲכַבְּדֵהוּ:

‹ אֹרֶךְ יָמִים אַשְׂבִּיעֵהוּ, וְאַרְאֵהוּ בִּישׁוּעָתִי:

אֹרֶךְ יָמִים אַשְׂבִּיעֵהוּ, וְאַרְאֵהוּ בִּישׁוּעָתִי:

תהלים קלה

הַלְלוּיָהּ, הַלְלוּ אֶת־שֵׁם יהוה, הַלְלוּ עַבְדֵי יהוה: שֶׁעֹמְדִים בְּבֵית

יהוה, בְּחַצְרוֹת בֵּית אֱלֹהֵינוּ: הַלְלוּיָהּ כִּי־טוֹב יהוה, זַמְּרוּ לִשְׁמוֹ

כִּי נָעִים: כִּי־יַעֲקֹב בָּחַר לוֹ יָהּ, יִשְׂרָאֵל לִסְגֻלָּתוֹ: כִּי אֲנִי יָדַעְתִּי

כִּי־גָדוֹל יהוה, וַאֲדֹנֵינוּ מִכָּל־אֱלֹהִים: כֹּל אֲשֶׁר־חָפֵץ יהוה עָשָׂה,

בַּשָּׁמַיִם וּבָאָרֶץ, בַּיַּמִּים וְכָל־תְּהֹמוֹת: מַעֲלֶה נְשִׂאִים מִקְצֵה

הָאָרֶץ, בְּרָקִים לַמָּטָר עָשָׂה, מוֹצֵא־רוּחַ מֵאוֹצְרוֹתָיו: שֶׁהִכָּה בְּכוֹרֵי

מִצְרָיִם, מֵאָדָם עַד־בְּהֵמָה: שָׁלַח אוֹתֹת וּמֹפְתִים בְּתוֹכֵכִי מִצְרָיִם,

בְּפַרְעֹה וּבְכָל־עֲבָדָיו: שֶׁהִכָּה גּוֹיִם רַבִּים, וְהָרַג מְלָכִים עֲצוּמִים:

לְסִיחוֹן מֶלֶךְ הָאֱמֹרִי, וּלְעוֹג מֶלֶךְ הַבָּשָׁן, וּלְכֹל מַמְלְכוֹת כְּנָעַן:

וְנָתַן אַרְצָם נַחֲלָה, נַחֲלָה לְיִשְׂרָאֵל עַמּוֹ: יהוה שִׁמְךָ לְעוֹלָם,

יהוה זִכְרְךָ לְדֹר־וָדֹר: כִּי־יָדִין יהוה עַמּוֹ, וְעַל־עֲבָדָיו יִתְנֶחָם:

עֲצַבֵּי הַגּוֹיִם כֶּסֶף וְזָהָב, מַעֲשֵׂה יְדֵי אָדָם: פֶּה־לָהֶם וְלֹא יְדַבֵּרוּ,

עֵינַיִם לָהֶם וְלֹא יִרְאוּ: אָזְנַיִם לָהֶם וְלֹא יַאֲזִינוּ, אַף אֵין־יֶשׁ־רוּחַ

בְּפִיהֶם: כְּמוֹהֶם יִהְיוּ עֹשֵׂיהֶם, כֹּל אֲשֶׁר־בֹּטֵחַ בָּהֶם: ‹ בֵּית יִשְׂרָאֵל

בָּרְכוּ אֶת־יהוה, בֵּית אַהֲרֹן בָּרְכוּ אֶת־יהוה: בֵּית הַלֵּוִי בָּרְכוּ

הַלְלוּיָהּ *Psalm 135.* Psalms 135 and 136 are a matched pair, describing the same events: the exodus from Egypt and the battles prior to the Israelites' entry into the Promised Land. What Psalm 135 says in prose, Psalm 136 says in poetry. Both are joyous celebrations of the redeeming power of God in history. Blaise Pascal thought that the history of the Jews was proof of the existence of God. Israel are the people who, in themselves, testify to something greater than themselves. Their miraculous survival is a signal of transcendence.

LORD. Blessed is the LORD from Zion, He who dwells in Jerusalem. Halleluya!

The custom is to stand for the following psalm.

הוֹדוּ Thank the LORD for He is good;   His loving-kindness is for ever. *Ps. 136*

Thank the God of gods,   His loving-kindness is for ever.

Thank the LORD of Lords,   His loving-kindness is for ever.

To the One who alone

    works great wonders,   His loving-kindness is for ever.

Who made the heavens with wisdom,   His loving-kindness is for ever.

Who spread the earth upon the waters,   His loving-kindness is for ever.

Who made the great lights,   His loving-kindness is for ever.

The sun to rule by day,   His loving-kindness is for ever.

The moon and the stars to rule by night;   His loving-kindness is for ever.

Who struck Egypt

    through their firstborn,   His loving-kindness is for ever.

And brought out Israel from their midst,   His loving-kindness is for ever.

With a strong hand

    and outstretched arm,   His loving-kindness is for ever.

Who split the Reed Sea into parts,   His loving-kindness is for ever.

And made Israel pass through it,   His loving-kindness is for ever.

Casting Pharaoh and his army

    into the Reed Sea;   His loving-kindness is for ever.

Who led His people

    through the wilderness;   His loving-kindness is for ever.

Who struck down great kings,   His loving-kindness is for ever.

And slew mighty kings,   His loving-kindness is for ever.

כִּי־טוֹב *For He is good.* The phrase *ki tov* occurs repeatedly in Genesis 1: "And God said, Let there be … and there was … and God saw that it was good [*ki tov*]." Rabbi Yaakov Tzvi Mecklenburg suggested that the phrase be translated, as here, "and God saw, *because* He is good." The phrase does not mean merely that what God created was good. It means that He created because of His goodness. One who is good seeks to share good with others. It was God's desire to share the blessing of existence with others that led Him to create the universe.

אֶת־יהוה, יְרְאֵי יהוה בָּרְכוּ אֶת־יהוה: בָּרוּךְ יהוה מִצִּיּוֹן, שֹׁכֵן יְרוּשָׁלֶָם, הַלְלוּיָהּ:

The custom is to stand for the following psalm.

כִּי לְעוֹלָם חַסְדּוֹ:	הוֹדוּ לַיהוה כִּי־טוֹב
כִּי לְעוֹלָם חַסְדּוֹ:	הוֹדוּ לֵאלֹהֵי הָאֱלֹהִים
כִּי לְעוֹלָם חַסְדּוֹ:	הוֹדוּ לַאֲדֹנֵי הָאֲדֹנִים
כִּי לְעוֹלָם חַסְדּוֹ:	לְעֹשֵׂה נִפְלָאוֹת גְּדֹלוֹת לְבַדּוֹ
כִּי לְעוֹלָם חַסְדּוֹ:	לְעֹשֵׂה הַשָּׁמַיִם בִּתְבוּנָה
כִּי לְעוֹלָם חַסְדּוֹ:	לְרֹקַע הָאָרֶץ עַל־הַמָּיִם
כִּי לְעוֹלָם חַסְדּוֹ:	לְעֹשֵׂה אוֹרִים גְּדֹלִים
כִּי לְעוֹלָם חַסְדּוֹ:	אֶת־הַשֶּׁמֶשׁ לְמֶמְשֶׁלֶת בַּיּוֹם
כִּי לְעוֹלָם חַסְדּוֹ:	אֶת־הַיָּרֵחַ וְכוֹכָבִים לְמֶמְשְׁלוֹת בַּלָּיְלָה
כִּי לְעוֹלָם חַסְדּוֹ:	לְמַכֵּה מִצְרַיִם בִּבְכוֹרֵיהֶם
כִּי לְעוֹלָם חַסְדּוֹ:	וַיּוֹצֵא יִשְׂרָאֵל מִתּוֹכָם
כִּי לְעוֹלָם חַסְדּוֹ:	בְּיָד חֲזָקָה וּבִזְרוֹעַ נְטוּיָה
כִּי לְעוֹלָם חַסְדּוֹ:	לְגֹזֵר יַם־סוּף לִגְזָרִים
כִּי לְעוֹלָם חַסְדּוֹ:	וְהֶעֱבִיר יִשְׂרָאֵל בְּתוֹכוֹ
כִּי לְעוֹלָם חַסְדּוֹ:	וְנִעֵר פַּרְעֹה וְחֵילוֹ בְיַם־סוּף
כִּי לְעוֹלָם חַסְדּוֹ:	לְמוֹלִיךְ עַמּוֹ בַּמִּדְבָּר
כִּי לְעוֹלָם חַסְדּוֹ:	לְמַכֵּה מְלָכִים גְּדֹלִים

תהלים קלו

הודו *Psalm 136.* This psalm, known as *Hallel HaGadol,* "the Great Hallel," is one of the earliest forms of a litany, a prayer in which the leader utters a series of praises to which the congregation responds with a set reply. Jewish prayer contains many litanies, most notably during *Seliḥot,* the penitential prayers prior to and during Yom Kippur, and the *Hoshanot* said on Sukkot and Hoshana Raba.

Siḥon, King of the Amorites,	His loving-kindness is for ever.
And Og, King of Bashan,	His loving-kindness is for ever.
And gave their land as a heritage,	His loving-kindness is for ever.
A heritage for His servant Israel;	His loving-kindness is for ever.
Who remembered us in our lowly state,	His loving-kindness is for ever.
And rescued us from our tormentors,	His loving-kindness is for ever.
▸ Who gives food to all flesh,	His loving-kindness is for ever.
Give thanks to the God of heaven.	His loving-kindness is for ever.

רַנְּנוּ Sing joyfully to the Lord, you righteous, for praise from the *Ps. 33* upright is seemly. Give thanks to the Lord with the harp; make music to Him on the ten-stringed lute. Sing Him a new song, play skillfully with shouts of joy. For the Lord's word is right, and all His deeds are done in faith. He loves righteousness and justice; the earth is full of the Lord's loving-kindness. By the Lord's word the heavens were made, and all their starry host by the breath of His mouth. He gathers the sea waters as a heap, and places the deep in storehouses. Let all the earth fear the Lord, and all the world's inhabitants stand in awe of Him. For He spoke, and it was; He commanded, and it stood firm. The Lord foils the plans of nations; He thwarts the intentions of peoples. The Lord's plans stand for ever, His heart's intents for all generations. Happy is the nation whose God is the Lord, the people He has chosen as His own. From heaven the Lord looks down and sees all mankind; from His dwelling place He oversees all who live on earth. He forms the hearts of all, and discerns all their deeds. No king is saved by the size of his army; no warrior is delivered by great strength. A horse is a vain hope for deliverance; despite its great strength, it cannot save. The eye of the Lord is on those who fear Him, on those who place their hope in His unfailing

---

the universe has a moral as well as physical beauty: "The earth is full of the Lord's loving-kindness." Love and justice prevail in the end, not power and aggression. "No king is saved by the size of his army," and tyrannical regimes eventually fall.

וַיַּהֲרֹג מְלָכִים אַדִּירִים   כִּי לְעוֹלָם חַסְדּוֹ:

לְסִיחוֹן מֶלֶךְ הָאֱמֹרִי   כִּי לְעוֹלָם חַסְדּוֹ:

וּלְעוֹג מֶלֶךְ הַבָּשָׁן   כִּי לְעוֹלָם חַסְדּוֹ:

וְנָתַן אַרְצָם לְנַחֲלָה   כִּי לְעוֹלָם חַסְדּוֹ:

נַחֲלָה לְיִשְׂרָאֵל עַבְדּוֹ   כִּי לְעוֹלָם חַסְדּוֹ:

שֶׁבְּשִׁפְלֵנוּ זָכַר לָנוּ   כִּי לְעוֹלָם חַסְדּוֹ:

וַיִּפְרְקֵנוּ מִצָּרֵינוּ   כִּי לְעוֹלָם חַסְדּוֹ:

◄ נֹתֵן לֶחֶם לְכָל־בָּשָׂר   כִּי לְעוֹלָם חַסְדּוֹ:

הוֹדוּ לְאֵל הַשָּׁמָיִם   כִּי לְעוֹלָם חַסְדּוֹ:

תהלים לג

רַנְּנוּ צַדִּיקִים בַּיהוה, לַיְשָׁרִים נָאוָה תְהִלָּה: הוֹדוּ לַיהוה בְּכִנּוֹר,

בְּנֵבֶל עָשׂוֹר זַמְּרוּ־לוֹ: שִׁירוּ־לוֹ שִׁיר חָדָשׁ, הֵיטִיבוּ נַגֵּן בִּתְרוּעָה:

כִּי־יָשָׁר דְּבַר־יהוה, וְכָל־מַעֲשֵׂהוּ בֶּאֱמוּנָה: אֹהֵב צְדָקָה וּמִשְׁפָּט,

חֶסֶד יהוה מָלְאָה הָאָרֶץ: בִּדְבַר יהוה שָׁמַיִם נַעֲשׂוּ, וּבְרוּחַ פִּיו

כָּל־צְבָאָם: כֹּנֵס כַּנֵּד מֵי הַיָּם, נֹתֵן בְּאוֹצָרוֹת תְּהוֹמוֹת: יִירְאוּ

מֵיהוה כָּל־הָאָרֶץ, מִמֶּנּוּ יָגוּרוּ כָּל־יֹשְׁבֵי תֵבֵל: כִּי הוּא אָמַר וַיֶּהִי,

הוּא־צִוָּה וַיַּעֲמֹד: יהוה הֵפִיר עֲצַת־גּוֹיִם, הֵנִיא מַחְשְׁבוֹת עַמִּים:

עֲצַת יהוה לְעוֹלָם תַּעֲמֹד, מַחְשְׁבוֹת לִבּוֹ לְדֹר וָדֹר: אַשְׁרֵי הַגּוֹי

אֲשֶׁר־יהוה אֱלֹהָיו, הָעָם בָּחַר לְנַחֲלָה לוֹ: מִשָּׁמַיִם הִבִּיט יהוה,

רָאָה אֶת־כָּל־בְּנֵי הָאָדָם: מִמְּכוֹן־שִׁבְתּוֹ הִשְׁגִּיחַ, אֶל כָּל־יֹשְׁבֵי

הָאָרֶץ: הַיֹּצֵר יַחַד לִבָּם, הַמֵּבִין אֶל־כָּל־מַעֲשֵׂיהֶם: אֵין־הַמֶּלֶךְ

נוֹשָׁע בְּרָב־חָיִל, גִּבּוֹר לֹא־יִנָּצֵל בְּרָב־כֹּחַ: שֶׁקֶר הַסּוּס לִתְשׁוּעָה,

וּבְרֹב חֵילוֹ לֹא יְמַלֵּט: הִנֵּה עֵין יהוה אֶל־יְרֵאָיו, לַמְיַחֲלִים לְחַסְדּוֹ:

רַנְּנוּ *Psalm* 33. A joyous creation psalm inviting us to sing God's praises on the earth He created and in the midst of the history He guides. To the Psalmist

love, to rescue their soul from death, and keep them alive in famine. Our soul waits for the LORD; He is our Help and Shield. ‣ In Him our hearts rejoice, for we trust in His holy name. Let Your unfailing love be upon us, LORD, as we have put our hope in You.

מִזְמוֹר שִׁיר A psalm. A song for the Sabbath day. It is good to thank *Ps. 92* the LORD and sing psalms to Your name, Most High – to tell of Your loving-kindness in the morning and Your faithfulness at night, to the music of the ten-stringed lyre and the melody of the harp. For You have made me rejoice by Your work, O LORD; I sing for joy at the deeds of Your hands. How great are Your deeds, LORD, and how very deep Your thoughts. A boor cannot know, nor can a fool understand, that though the wicked spring up like grass and all evildoers flourish, it is only that they may be destroyed for ever. But You, LORD, are eternally exalted. For behold Your enemies, LORD, behold Your enemies will perish; all evildoers will be scattered. You have raised my pride like that of a wild ox; I am anointed with fresh oil. My eyes shall look in triumph on my adversaries, my ears shall hear the downfall of the wicked who rise against me. ‣ The righteous will flourish like a palm tree and grow tall like a cedar in Lebanon. Planted in the LORD's House, blossoming in our God's courtyards, they will still bear fruit in old age, and stay vigorous and fresh, proclaiming that the LORD is upright: He is my Rock, in whom there is no wrong.

---

the guilty escape punishment? The psalm tells us that our time-horizon is too constricted. We look at the short term, not the long. Evil may win temporary victories but in the long run, right, justice and liberty prevail. Tyrants may seem impregnable in their day, but evil empires crumble, and are condemned by the full perspective of history. That is what "a fool cannot understand" but the wise know. The Sabbath of the psalm is thus not the Sabbath of past or present but of the future, the Messianic age, the "day that is entirely Shabbat," when there will be neither master nor slave, oppressor and oppressed, when hierarchies of power are abandoned and humanity finally recognizes the universe as God's work, and the human person as God's image. That is the ultimate Shabbat to which all our current Sabbaths are a prelude and preparation.

לְהַצִּיל מִמָּוֶת נַפְשָׁם, וּלְחַיּוֹתָם בָּרָעָב: נַפְשֵׁנוּ חִכְּתָה לַיהוה,
עֶזְרֵנוּ וּמָגִנֵּנוּ הוּא: ◦ כִּי־בוֹ יִשְׂמַח לִבֵּנוּ, כִּי בְשֵׁם קָדְשׁוֹ בָטָחְנוּ:
יְהִי־חַסְדְּךָ יהוה עָלֵינוּ, כַּאֲשֶׁר יִחַלְנוּ לָךְ:

תהלים צב

מִזְמוֹר שִׁיר לְיוֹם הַשַּׁבָּת: טוֹב לְהֹדוֹת לַיהוה, וּלְזַמֵּר לְשִׁמְךָ
עֶלְיוֹן: לְהַגִּיד בַּבֹּקֶר חַסְדֶּךָ, וֶאֱמוּנָתְךָ בַּלֵּילוֹת: עֲלֵי־עָשׂוֹר וַעֲלֵי־
נָבֶל, עֲלֵי הִגָּיוֹן בְּכִנּוֹר: כִּי שִׂמַּחְתַּנִי יהוה בְּפָעֳלֶךָ, בְּמַעֲשֵׂי יָדֶיךָ
אֲרַנֵּן: מַה־גָּדְלוּ מַעֲשֶׂיךָ יהוה, מְאֹד עָמְקוּ מַחְשְׁבֹתֶיךָ: אִישׁ־בַּעַר
לֹא יֵדָע, וּכְסִיל לֹא־יָבִין אֶת־זֹאת: בִּפְרֹחַ רְשָׁעִים כְּמוֹ עֵשֶׂב,
וַיָּצִיצוּ כָּל־פֹּעֲלֵי אָוֶן, לְהִשָּׁמְדָם עֲדֵי־עַד: וְאַתָּה מָרוֹם לְעֹלָם
יהוה: כִּי הִנֵּה אֹיְבֶיךָ יהוה, כִּי־הִנֵּה אֹיְבֶיךָ יֹאבֵדוּ, יִתְפָּרְדוּ כָּל־
פֹּעֲלֵי אָוֶן: וַתָּרֶם כִּרְאֵים קַרְנִי, בַּלֹּתִי בְּשֶׁמֶן רַעֲנָן: וַתַּבֵּט עֵינִי
בְּשׁוּרָי, בַּקָּמִים עָלַי מְרֵעִים תִּשְׁמַעְנָה אָזְנָי: ◦ צַדִּיק כַּתָּמָר יִפְרָח,
כְּאֶרֶז בַּלְּבָנוֹן יִשְׂגֶּה: שְׁתוּלִים בְּבֵית יהוה, בְּחַצְרוֹת אֱלֹהֵינוּ
יַפְרִיחוּ: עוֹד יְנוּבוּן בְּשֵׂיבָה, דְּשֵׁנִים וְרַעֲנַנִּים יִהְיוּ: לְהַגִּיד כִּי־יָשָׁר
יהוה, צוּרִי, וְלֹא־עַוְלָתָה בּוֹ:

מִזְמוֹר שִׁיר *Psalm 92.* The sages interpreted the opening of this psalm as meaning not just "a song *for* the Sabbath day" but also "a song sung *by* the Sabbath
day" (see page 566), as if the day itself gave testimony to the Creator, which
in effect it does. By being the day on which we do no creative work, time
itself makes us aware that we are not just creators; we are also creations. The
more we understand about the nature of the universe, its vast complexity, and
the way it is finely tuned for the emergence of life, the more we sense a vast
intelligence at work, framing its "fearful symmetry."

Yet the psalm speaks not about creation but about justice. The universe is
not simply matter and anti-matter governed by certain scientific laws. It is also –
as Genesis 1 tells us seven times – "good." But how can we consider it good if,
all too often, evildoers seize power, injustice prevails, the innocent suffer and

יהוה מָלָךְ The LORD reigns. He is robed in majesty. The LORD is robed, *Ps. 93*
girded with strength. The world is firmly established; it cannot be
moved. Your throne stands firm as of old; You are eternal. Rivers lift
up, LORD, rivers lift up their voice, rivers lift up their Crashing waves.
‣ Mightier than the noise of many waters, than the mighty waves of
the sea is the LORD on high. Your testimonies are very sure; holiness
adorns Your House, LORD, for evermore.

יְהִי כְבוֹד May the LORD's glory be for ever; may the LORD rejoice in *Ps. 104*
His works. May the LORD's name be blessed, now and for ever. From *Ps. 113*
the rising of the sun to its setting, may the LORD's name be praised.
The LORD is high above all nations; His glory is above the heavens.
LORD, Your name is for ever. Your renown, LORD, is for all generations. *Ps. 135*
The LORD has established His throne in heaven; His kingdom rules *Ps. 103*
all. Let the heavens rejoice and the earth be glad. Let them say among *1 Chr. 16*
the nations, "The LORD is King." The LORD is King, the LORD was
King, the LORD will be King for ever and all time. The LORD is King *Ps. 10*
for ever and all time; nations will perish from His land. The LORD foils *Ps. 33*
the plans of nations; He frustrates the intentions of peoples. Many are *Prov. 19*
the intentions in a person's mind, but the LORD's plan prevails. The *Ps. 33*
LORD's plan shall stand for ever, His mind's intent for all generations.
For He spoke and it was; He commanded and it stood firm. For the *Ps. 132*
LORD has chosen Zion; He desired it for His dwelling. For the LORD *Ps. 135*
has chosen Jacob, Israel as His special treasure. For the LORD will not *Ps. 94*
abandon His people; nor will He forsake His heritage. ‣ He is com- *Ps. 78*
passionate. He forgives iniquity and does not destroy. Repeatedly He
suppresses His anger, not rousing His full wrath. LORD, save! May the *Ps. 20*
King answer us on the day we call.

---

beautifully expressed in this psalm which sees the roar of the oceans as part of
creation paying homage to its Creator. God is beyond – not within – nature,
time and space.

יְהִי כְבוֹד *May the LORD's glory.* An anthology of verses, mainly from the books
of Psalms, Proverbs, and Chronicles. God created the universe; therefore He

תהלים צג

יהוה מָלָךְ, גֵּאוּת לָבֵשׁ, לָבֵשׁ יהוה עֹז הִתְאַזָּר, אַף־תִּכּוֹן תֵּבֵל בַּל־תִּמּוֹט: נָכוֹן כִּסְאֲךָ מֵאָז, מֵעוֹלָם אָתָּה: נָשְׂאוּ נְהָרוֹת יהוה, נָשְׂאוּ נְהָרוֹת קוֹלָם, יִשְׂאוּ נְהָרוֹת דָּכְיָם: ‹ מִקֹּלוֹת מַיִם רַבִּים, אַדִּירִים מִשְׁבְּרֵי־יָם, אַדִּיר בַּמָּרוֹם יהוה: עֵדֹתֶיךָ נֶאֶמְנוּ מְאֹד לְבֵיתְךָ נַאֲוָה־קֹדֶשׁ, יהוה לְאֹרֶךְ יָמִים:

תהלים קד
תהלים קיג

יְהִי כְבוֹד יהוה לְעוֹלָם, יִשְׂמַח יהוה בְּמַעֲשָׂיו: יְהִי שֵׁם יהוה מְבֹרָךְ, מֵעַתָּה וְעַד־עוֹלָם: מִמִּזְרַח־שֶׁמֶשׁ עַד־מְבוֹאוֹ, מְהֻלָּל שֵׁם יהוה:

תהלים קלה

רָם עַל־כָּל־גּוֹיִם יהוה, עַל הַשָּׁמַיִם כְּבוֹדוֹ: יהוה שִׁמְךָ לְעוֹלָם,

תהלים קג

יהוה זִכְרְךָ לְדֹר־וָדֹר: יהוה בַּשָּׁמַיִם הֵכִין כִּסְאוֹ, וּמַלְכוּתוֹ בַּכֹּל

דברי הימים א' טז

מָשָׁלָה: יִשְׂמְחוּ הַשָּׁמַיִם וְתָגֵל הָאָרֶץ, וְיֹאמְרוּ בַגּוֹיִם יהוה מָלָךְ:

תהלים י

יהוה מֶלֶךְ, יהוה מָלָךְ, יהוה יִמְלֹךְ לְעוֹלָם וָעֶד. יהוה מֶלֶךְ עוֹלָם

תהלים לג

וָעֶד, אָבְדוּ גוֹיִם מֵאַרְצוֹ: יהוה הֵפִיר עֲצַת־גּוֹיִם, הֵנִיא מַחְשְׁבוֹת

משלי יט

עַמִּים: רַבּוֹת מַחֲשָׁבוֹת בְּלֶב־אִישׁ, וַעֲצַת יהוה הִיא תָקוּם:

תהלים לג

עֲצַת יהוה לְעוֹלָם תַּעֲמֹד, מַחְשְׁבוֹת לִבּוֹ לְדֹר וָדֹר: כִּי הוּא אָמַר

תהלים קלב

וַיֶּהִי, הוּא־צִוָּה וַיַּעֲמֹד: כִּי־בָחַר יהוה בְּצִיּוֹן, אִוָּהּ לְמוֹשָׁב לוֹ:

תהלים קלה
תהלים צד

כִּי־יַעֲקֹב בָּחַר לוֹ יָהּ, יִשְׂרָאֵל לִסְגֻלָּתוֹ: כִּי לֹא־יִטֹּשׁ יהוה עַמּוֹ,

תהלים עח

וְנַחֲלָתוֹ לֹא יַעֲזֹב: ‹ וְהוּא רַחוּם, יְכַפֵּר עָוֹן וְלֹא־יַשְׁחִית, וְהִרְבָּה

תהלים כ

לְהָשִׁיב אַפּוֹ, וְלֹא־יָעִיר כָּל־חֲמָתוֹ: יהוה הוֹשִׁיעָה, הַמֶּלֶךְ יַעֲנֵנוּ בְיוֹם־קָרְאֵנוּ:

יהוה מָלָךְ *Psalm 93.* Almost all ancient polytheistic myths saw the sea as an independent force of chaos against which the gods were forced to do battle. The great revolution of monotheism was to insist that there is only one creative power, that the universe is fundamentally good, and that chaos is merely order of a complexity we can neither understand nor predict. This is

The line beginning with "You open Your hand" should be said with special
concentration, representing as it does the key idea of this psalm, and of
Pesukei DeZimra as a whole, that God is the creator and sustainer of all.

אַשְׁרֵי Happy are those who dwell in Your House;   *Ps. 84*
they shall continue to praise You, Selah!
Happy are the people for whom this is so;   *Ps. 144*
happy are the people whose God is the Lord.
A song of praise by David.   *Ps. 145*

I will exalt You, my God, the King, and bless Your name for ever
and all time. Every day I will bless You, and praise Your name for
ever and all time. Great is the Lord and greatly to be praised; His
greatness is unfathomable. One generation will praise Your works
to the next, and tell of Your mighty deeds. On the glorious splendor
of Your majesty I will meditate, and on the acts of Your wonders.
They shall talk of the power of Your awesome deeds, and I will tell
of Your greatness. They shall recite the record of Your great goodness, and sing with joy of Your righteousness. The Lord is gracious
and compassionate, slow to anger and great in loving-kindness. The
Lord is good to all, and His compassion extends to all His works.
All Your works shall thank You, Lord, and Your devoted ones shall
bless You. They shall talk of the glory of Your kingship, and speak
of Your might. To make known to mankind His mighty deeds and
the glorious majesty of His kingship. Your kingdom is an everlasting
kingdom, and Your reign is for all generations. The Lord supports
all who fall, and raises all who are bowed down. All raise their eyes to

---

אַשְׁרֵי *Happy are those.* Psalm 145 was seen by the sages as the quintessential
expression of the book of Psalms, especially the creation psalms that dominate
the Verses of Praise, because (a) it is an alphabetic acrostic, praising God with
each letter of the alphabet (with the exception of *nun*, a letter omitted lest it
recall *nefila*, the fall of ancient Israel), and (b) because it contains the line, "You
open Your hand, and satisfy every living thing with favor." It is also (c) the only
poem to be explicitly called *tehilla*, "a psalm" (the book of Psalms is called, in
Hebrew, *Sefer Tehillim*). To it have been added two verses at the beginning and
one at the end, so that the psalm begins with the word *Ashrei*, the first word in
the book of Psalms, and ends with *Halleluya*, the book's last word.

The line beginning with פּוֹתֵחַ אֶת יָדֶךָ *should be said with special concentration, representing as it does the key idea of this psalm, and of* פסוקי דזמרה *as a whole, that God is the creator and sustainer of all.*

תהלים פד

תהלים קמד

תהלים קמה

אַשְׁרֵי יוֹשְׁבֵי בֵיתֶךָ, עוֹד יְהַלְלוּךָ סֶּלָה:

אַשְׁרֵי הָעָם שֶׁכָּכָה לּוֹ, אַשְׁרֵי הָעָם שֶׁיהוה אֱלֹהָיו:

תְּהִלָּה לְדָוִד

אֲרוֹמִמְךָ אֱלוֹהַי הַמֶּלֶךְ, וַאֲבָרְכָה שִׁמְךָ לְעוֹלָם וָעֶד:

בְּכָל־יוֹם אֲבָרְכֶךָּ, וַאֲהַלְלָה שִׁמְךָ לְעוֹלָם וָעֶד:

גָּדוֹל יהוה וּמְהֻלָּל מְאֹד, וְלִגְדֻלָּתוֹ אֵין חֵקֶר:

דּוֹר לְדוֹר יְשַׁבַּח מַעֲשֶׂיךָ, וּגְבוּרֹתֶיךָ יַגִּידוּ:

הֲדַר כְּבוֹד הוֹדֶךָ, וְדִבְרֵי נִפְלְאֹתֶיךָ אָשִׂיחָה:

וֶעֱזוּז נוֹרְאֹתֶיךָ יֹאמֵרוּ, וּגְדוּלָּתְךָ אֲסַפְּרֶנָּה:

זֵכֶר רַב־טוּבְךָ יַבִּיעוּ, וְצִדְקָתְךָ יְרַנֵּנוּ:

חַנּוּן וְרַחוּם יהוה, אֶרֶךְ אַפַּיִם וּגְדָל־חָסֶד:

טוֹב־יהוה לַכֹּל, וְרַחֲמָיו עַל־כָּל־מַעֲשָׂיו:

יוֹדוּךָ יהוה כָּל־מַעֲשֶׂיךָ, וַחֲסִידֶיךָ יְבָרְכוּכָה:

כְּבוֹד מַלְכוּתְךָ יֹאמֵרוּ, וּגְבוּרָתְךָ יְדַבֵּרוּ:

לְהוֹדִיעַ לִבְנֵי הָאָדָם גְּבוּרֹתָיו, וּכְבוֹד הֲדַר מַלְכוּתוֹ:

מַלְכוּתְךָ מַלְכוּת כָּל־עֹלָמִים, וּמֶמְשַׁלְתְּךָ בְּכָל־דּוֹר וָדֹר:

סוֹמֵךְ יהוה לְכָל־הַנֹּפְלִים, וְזוֹקֵף לְכָל־הַכְּפוּפִים:

is sole Sovereign of the universe, ruling nature through scientific law, and history through the moral law. Those who pit themselves against God are destined to fail: "Many are the intentions in a person's mind, but the LORD's plan prevails." Israel, as the people of the eternal God, is itself eternal, and though it often suffers persecution, it will never be destroyed, for divine compassion ultimately prevails over divine anger: "The LORD will not abandon His people."

You in hope, and You give them their food in due season. You open Your hand, and satisfy every living thing with favor. The LORD is righteous in all His ways, and kind in all He does. The LORD is close to all who call on Him, to all who call on Him in truth. He fulfills the will of those who revere Him; He hears their cry and saves them. The LORD guards all who love Him, but all the wicked He will destroy.
‣ My mouth shall speak the praise of the LORD, and all creatures shall bless His holy name for ever and all time.
We will bless the LORD now and for ever. Halleluya!   Ps. 115

הַלְלוּיָהּ Halleluya! Praise the LORD, my soul. I will praise the LORD Ps. 146 all my life; I will sing to my God as long as I live. Put not your trust in princes, or in mortal man who cannot save. His breath expires, he returns to the earth; on that day his plans come to an end. Happy is he whose help is the God of Jacob, whose hope is in the LORD his God who made heaven and earth, the sea and all they contain; He who keeps faith for ever. He secures justice for the oppressed. He gives food to the hungry. The LORD sets captives free. The LORD gives sight to the blind. The LORD raises those bowed down. The LORD loves the righteous. The LORD protects the stranger. He gives courage to the orphan and widow. He thwarts the way of the wicked.
‣ The LORD shall reign for ever. He is your God, Zion, for all generations. Halleluya!

הַלְלוּיָהּ Halleluya! How good it is to sing songs to our God; how pleas- Ps. 147 ant and fitting to praise Him. The LORD rebuilds Jerusalem. He gathers the scattered exiles of Israel. He heals the brokenhearted and binds up their wounds. He counts the number of the stars, calling each by name. Great is our LORD and mighty in power; His understanding has no limit. The LORD gives courage to the humble, but casts the wicked

---

the victims of injustice, and those who have no one else to care for them. The supreme Power supremely cares for the powerless.

הַלְלוּיָהּ *Psalm 147.* God, the Shaper of history ("gathers the scattered exiles") and Architect of the cosmos ("counts the number of the stars"), is nonetheless

עֵינֵי־כֹל אֵלֶיךָ יְשַׂבֵּרוּ, וְאַתָּה נוֹתֵן־לָהֶם אֶת־אָכְלָם בְּעִתּוֹ:

פּוֹתֵחַ אֶת־יָדֶךָ, וּמַשְׂבִּיעַ לְכָל־חַי רָצוֹן:

צַדִּיק יהוה בְּכָל־דְּרָכָיו, וְחָסִיד בְּכָל־מַעֲשָׂיו:

קָרוֹב יהוה לְכָל־קֹרְאָיו, לְכֹל אֲשֶׁר יִקְרָאֻהוּ בֶאֱמֶת:

רְצוֹן־יְרֵאָיו יַעֲשֶׂה, וְאֶת־שַׁוְעָתָם יִשְׁמַע, וְיוֹשִׁיעֵם:

שׁוֹמֵר יהוה אֶת־כָּל־אֹהֲבָיו, וְאֵת כָּל־הָרְשָׁעִים יַשְׁמִיד:

◂ תְּהִלַּת יהוה יְדַבֶּר־פִּי, וִיבָרֵךְ כָּל־בָּשָׂר שֵׁם קָדְשׁוֹ לְעוֹלָם וָעֶד:

וַאֲנַחְנוּ נְבָרֵךְ יָהּ מֵעַתָּה וְעַד־עוֹלָם, הַלְלוּיָהּ:

תהלים קטו

הַלְלוּיָהּ, הַלְלִי נַפְשִׁי אֶת־יהוה: אֲהַלְלָה יהוה בְּחַיָּי, אֲזַמְּרָה

לֵאלֹהַי בְּעוֹדִי: אַל־תִּבְטְחוּ בִנְדִיבִים, בְּבֶן־אָדָם שֶׁאֵין לוֹ

תְשׁוּעָה: תֵּצֵא רוּחוֹ, יָשֻׁב לְאַדְמָתוֹ, בַּיּוֹם הַהוּא אָבְדוּ עֶשְׁתֹּנֹתָיו:

אַשְׁרֵי שֶׁאֵל יַעֲקֹב בְּעֶזְרוֹ, שִׂבְרוֹ עַל־יהוה אֱלֹהָיו: עֹשֶׂה שָׁמַיִם

וָאָרֶץ, אֶת־הַיָּם וְאֶת־כָּל־אֲשֶׁר־בָּם, הַשֹּׁמֵר אֱמֶת לְעוֹלָם: עֹשֶׂה

מִשְׁפָּט לַעֲשׁוּקִים, נֹתֵן לֶחֶם לָרְעֵבִים, יהוה מַתִּיר אֲסוּרִים:

יהוה פֹּקֵחַ עִוְרִים, יהוה זֹקֵף כְּפוּפִים, יהוה אֹהֵב צַדִּיקִים: יהוה

שֹׁמֵר אֶת־גֵּרִים, יָתוֹם וְאַלְמָנָה יְעוֹדֵד, וְדֶרֶךְ רְשָׁעִים יְעַוֵּת:

◂ יִמְלֹךְ יהוה לְעוֹלָם, אֱלֹהַיִךְ צִיּוֹן לְדֹר וָדֹר, הַלְלוּיָהּ:

תהלים קמו

הַלְלוּיָהּ, כִּי־טוֹב זַמְּרָה אֱלֹהֵינוּ, כִּי־נָעִים נָאוָה תְהִלָּה: בּוֹנֵה

יְרוּשָׁלַםִ יהוה, נִדְחֵי יִשְׂרָאֵל יְכַנֵּס: הָרֹפֵא לִשְׁבוּרֵי לֵב, וּמְחַבֵּשׁ

לְעַצְּבוֹתָם: מוֹנֶה מִסְפָּר לַכּוֹכָבִים, לְכֻלָּם שֵׁמוֹת יִקְרָא: גָּדוֹל

אֲדוֹנֵינוּ וְרַב־כֹּחַ, לִתְבוּנָתוֹ אֵין מִסְפָּר: מְעוֹדֵד עֲנָוִים יהוה,

תהלים קמז

‗‗

הַלְלוּיָהּ *Psalm 146.* A hymn of praise to God's justice and compassion. Put not your faith in mortals but in God, who cares for the oppressed, the hungry,

to the ground. Sing to the LORD in thanks; make music to our God on the harp. He covers the sky with clouds. He provides the earth with rain and makes grass grow on the hills. He gives food to the cattle and to the ravens when they cry. He does not take delight in the strength of horses nor pleasure in the fleetness of man. The LORD takes pleasure in those who fear Him, who put their hope in His loving care. Praise the LORD, Jerusalem; sing to your God, Zion, for He has strengthened the bars of your gates and blessed your children in your midst. He has brought peace to your borders, and satisfied you with the finest wheat. He sends His commandment to earth; swiftly runs His word. He spreads snow like fleece, sprinkles frost like ashes, scatters hail like crumbs. Who can stand His cold? He sends His word and melts them; He makes the wind blow and the waters flow. ‣ He has declared His words to Jacob, His statutes and laws to Israel. He has done this for no other nation; such laws they do not know. Halleluya!

הַלְלוּיָהּ Halleluya! Praise the LORD from the heavens, praise Him *Ps. 148* in the heights. Praise Him, all His angels; praise Him, all His hosts. Praise Him, sun and moon; praise Him, all shining stars. Praise Him, highest heavens and the waters above the heavens. Let them praise the name of the LORD, for He commanded and they were created. He established them for ever and all time, issuing a decree that will never change. Praise the LORD from the earth: sea monsters and all the deep seas; fire and hail, snow and mist, storm winds that obey His word; mountains and all hills, fruit trees and all cedars; wild animals and all cattle, creeping things and winged birds; kings of the earth and all nations, princes and all judges on earth; youths and maidens, old and young. ‣ Let them praise the name of the LORD, for His name alone is sublime; His majesty is above earth and heaven. He has raised the

a society under the sovereignty of God, dedicated to justice, holiness and respect for human dignity.

הַלְלוּיָהּ *Psalm 148.* A cosmic psalm of praise, beginning with the heavens, sun, moon and stars; then moving to earth and all living things, culminating with humanity.

מַשְׁפִּיל רְשָׁעִים עֲדֵי־אָרֶץ: עֱנוּ לַיהוה בְּתוֹדָה, זַמְּרוּ לֵאלֹהֵינוּ בְכִנּוֹר: הַמְכַסֶּה שָׁמַיִם בְּעָבִים, הַמֵּכִין לָאָרֶץ מָטָר, הַמַּצְמִיחַ הָרִים חָצִיר: נוֹתֵן לִבְהֵמָה לַחְמָהּ, לִבְנֵי עֹרֵב אֲשֶׁר יִקְרָאוּ: לֹא בִגְבוּרַת הַסּוּס יֶחְפָּץ, לֹא־בְשׁוֹקֵי הָאִישׁ יִרְצֶה: רוֹצֶה יהוה אֶת־יְרֵאָיו, אֶת־הַמְיַחֲלִים לְחַסְדּוֹ: שַׁבְּחִי יְרוּשָׁלַֽם אֶת־יהוה, הַלְלִי אֱלֹהַֽיִךְ צִיּוֹן: כִּי־חִזַּק בְּרִיחֵי שְׁעָרָֽיִךְ, בֵּרַךְ בָּנַֽיִךְ בְּקִרְבֵּךְ: הַשָּׂם־ גְּבוּלֵךְ שָׁלוֹם, חֵֽלֶב חִטִּים יַשְׂבִּיעֵךְ: הַשֹּׁלֵחַ אִמְרָתוֹ אָֽרֶץ, עַד־ מְהֵרָה יָרוּץ דְּבָרוֹ: הַנֹּתֵן שֶֽׁלֶג כַּצָּֽמֶר, כְּפוֹר כָּאֵֽפֶר יְפַזֵּר: מַשְׁלִיךְ קַרְחוֹ כְפִתִּים, לִפְנֵי קָרָתוֹ מִי יַעֲמֹד: יִשְׁלַח דְּבָרוֹ וְיַמְסֵם, יַשֵּׁב רוּחוֹ יִזְּלוּ־מָֽיִם: ‹ מַגִּיד דְּבָרָו לְיַעֲקֹב, חֻקָּיו וּמִשְׁפָּטָיו לְיִשְׂרָאֵל: לֹא עָֽשָׂה כֵן לְכָל־גּוֹי, וּמִשְׁפָּטִים בַּל־יְדָעוּם, הַלְלוּיָהּ:

תהלים קמח

הַלְלוּיָהּ, הַלְלוּ אֶת־יהוה מִן־הַשָּׁמַֽיִם, הַלְלֽוּהוּ בַּמְּרוֹמִים: הַלְלֽוּהוּ כָל־מַלְאָכָיו, הַלְלֽוּהוּ כָּל־צְבָאָו: הַלְלֽוּהוּ שֶֽׁמֶשׁ וְיָרֵֽחַ, הַלְלֽוּהוּ כָּל־ כּֽוֹכְבֵי אוֹר: הַלְלֽוּהוּ שְׁמֵי הַשָּׁמָֽיִם, וְהַמַּֽיִם אֲשֶׁר מֵעַל הַשָּׁמָֽיִם: יְהַלְלוּ אֶת־שֵׁם יהוה, כִּי הוּא צִוָּה וְנִבְרָֽאוּ: וַיַּעֲמִידֵם לָעַד לְעוֹלָם, חָק־נָתַן וְלֹא יַעֲבוֹר: הַלְלוּ אֶת־יהוה מִן־הָאָֽרֶץ, תַּנִּינִים וְכָל־ תְּהֹמוֹת: אֵשׁ וּבָרָד שֶֽׁלֶג וְקִיטוֹר, רֽוּחַ סְעָרָה עֹשָׂה דְבָרוֹ: הֶהָרִים וְכָל־גְּבָעוֹת, עֵץ פְּרִי וְכָל־אֲרָזִים: הַחַיָּה וְכָל־בְּהֵמָה, רֶֽמֶשׂ וְצִפּוֹר כָּנָף: מַלְכֵי־אֶֽרֶץ וְכָל־לְאֻמִּים, שָׂרִים וְכָל־שֹֽׁפְטֵי אָֽרֶץ: בַּחוּרִים וְגַם־בְּתוּלוֹת, זְקֵנִים עִם־נְעָרִים: ‹ יְהַלְלוּ אֶת־שֵׁם יהוה, כִּי־נִשְׂגָּב

---

close to us, healing the broken heart and ministering to our emotional wounds.

לֹא עָֽשָׂה כֵן לְכָל־גּוֹי *He has done this for no other nation.* Although there has been a covenant between God and all humanity since the days of Noah, only to Israel did He reveal an entire body of laws, the detailed architectonics of

pride of His people, for the glory of all His devoted ones, the children of Israel, the people close to Him. Halleluya!

הַלְלוּיָהּ Halleluya! Sing to the LORD a new song, His praise in the *Ps. 149* assembly of the devoted. Let Israel rejoice in its Maker; let the children of Zion exult in their King. Let them praise His name with dancing; sing praises to Him with timbrel and harp. For the LORD delights in His people; He adorns the humble with salvation. Let the devoted revel in glory; let them sing for joy on their beds. Let high praises of God be in their throats, and a two-edged sword in their hand: to impose retribution on the nations, punishment on the peoples, ‣ binde ing their kings with chains, their nobles with iron fetters, carrying out the judgment written against them. This is the glory of all His devoted ones. Halleluya!

הַלְלוּיָהּ Halleluya! *Ps. 150*
Praise God in His holy place;
　　praise Him in the heavens of His power.
Praise Him for His mighty deeds;
　　praise Him for His surpassing greatness.
Praise Him with blasts of the shofar;
　　praise Him with the harp and lyre.
Praise Him with timbrel and dance;
　　praise Him with strings and flute.
‣ Praise Him with clashing cymbals;
　　praise Him with resounding cymbals.
Let all that breathes praise the LORD. Halleluya!
Let all that breathes praise the LORD. Halleluya!

כֹּל הַנְּשָׁמָה *Let all that breathes.* The psalm mentions nine musical and creative expressions of praise, culminating in the tenth, the breath of all that lives – echoing the tenfold blessing with which the Verses of Praise begin, itself an echo of the ten creative utterances with which God created the universe (the ten times the phrase "God said" appears in Genesis 1). Note the difference between a scientific and a religious way of describing the universe. "Not *how* the world is but *that* it is, is the mystical" (Wittgenstein).

שְׁמוֹ לְבַדּוֹ, הוֹדוֹ עַל־אֶרֶץ וְשָׁמָיִם: וַיָּרֶם קֶרֶן לְעַמּוֹ, תְּהִלָּה לְכָל־
חֲסִידָיו, לִבְנֵי יִשְׂרָאֵל עַם קְרֹבוֹ, הַלְלוּיָהּ:

תהלים קמט

הַלְלוּיָהּ, שִׁירוּ לַיהוה שִׁיר חָדָשׁ, תְּהִלָּתוֹ בִּקְהַל חֲסִידִים: יִשְׂמַח
יִשְׂרָאֵל בְּעֹשָׂיו, בְּנֵי־צִיּוֹן יָגִילוּ בְמַלְכָּם: יְהַלְלוּ שְׁמוֹ בְמָחוֹל, בְּתֹף
וְכִנּוֹר יְזַמְּרוּ־לוֹ: כִּי־רוֹצֶה יהוה בְּעַמּוֹ, יְפָאֵר עֲנָוִים בִּישׁוּעָה:
יַעְלְזוּ חֲסִידִים בְּכָבוֹד, יְרַנְּנוּ עַל־מִשְׁכְּבוֹתָם: רוֹמְמוֹת אֵל בִּגְרוֹנָם,
וְחֶרֶב פִּיפִיּוֹת בְּיָדָם: לַעֲשׂוֹת נְקָמָה בַּגּוֹיִם, תּוֹכֵחוֹת בַּלְאֻמִּים:
‹ לֶאְסֹר מַלְכֵיהֶם בְּזִקִּים, וְנִכְבְּדֵיהֶם בְּכַבְלֵי בַרְזֶל: לַעֲשׂוֹת בָּהֶם
מִשְׁפָּט כָּתוּב, הָדָר הוּא לְכָל־חֲסִידָיו, הַלְלוּיָהּ:

תהלים קנ

הַלְלוּיָהּ
הַלְלוּ־אֵל בְּקָדְשׁוֹ, הַלְלוּהוּ בִּרְקִיעַ עֻזּוֹ:
הַלְלוּהוּ בִגְבוּרֹתָיו, הַלְלוּהוּ כְּרֹב גֻּדְלוֹ:
הַלְלוּהוּ בְּתֵקַע שׁוֹפָר, הַלְלוּהוּ בְּנֵבֶל וְכִנּוֹר:
הַלְלוּהוּ בְתֹף וּמָחוֹל, הַלְלוּהוּ בְּמִנִּים וְעֻגָב:
‹ הַלְלוּהוּ בְצִלְצְלֵי־שָׁמַע, הַלְלוּהוּ בְּצִלְצְלֵי תְרוּעָה:
כֹּל הַנְּשָׁמָה תְּהַלֵּל יָהּ, הַלְלוּיָהּ:
כֹּל הַנְּשָׁמָה תְּהַלֵּל יָהּ, הַלְלוּיָהּ:

הַלְלוּיָהּ *Psalm 149.* A song of victory. Israel emerges triumphant over those who seek to destroy it, not because of its strength but because of its faith.

חֶרֶב פִּיפִיּוֹת *A two-edged sword.* Literally, "a sword of mouths." Israel does not live by the physical sword but by words: the power of prayer. Thus the "sword of mouths" echoes the previous phrase, "praises of God be in their throats" (*Or Penei Moshe*).

הַלְלוּיָהּ *Psalm 150.* The last psalm in the book of Psalms, gathering all previous praise into a majestic choral finale. More than a third of the words consist of various forms of the verb "to praise."

בָּרוּךְ Blessed be the LORD for ever. Amen and Amen. *Ps. 89*

Blessed from Zion be the LORD *Ps. 135*

who dwells in Jerusalem. Halleluya!

Blessed be the LORD, God of Israel, *Ps. 72*

who alone does wonders.

▸ Blessed be His glorious name for ever,

and may all the earth be filled with His glory.

Amen and Amen.

Stand until "The soul" on page 310.

וַיְבָרֶךְ David blessed the LORD in front of the entire assembly. David *1 Chr. 29*
said, "Blessed are You, LORD, God of our father Yisrael, for ever
and ever. Yours, LORD, are the greatness and the power, the glory,
majesty and splendor, for everything in heaven and earth is Yours.
Yours, LORD, is the kingdom; You are exalted as Head over all. Both
riches and honor are in Your gift and You reign over all things. In
Your hand are strength and might. It is in Your power to make great
and give strength to all. Therefore, our God, we thank You and
praise Your glorious name."   You alone are the LORD. You *Neh. 9*
made the heavens, even the highest heavens, and all their hosts,
the earth and all that is on it, the seas and all they contain. You
give life to them all, and the hosts of heaven worship You. ▸ You are
the LORD God who chose Abram and brought him out of Ur of
the Chaldees, changing his name to Abraham. You found his heart
faithful toward You, ◂ and You made a covenant with him to give
to his descendants the land of the Canaanites, Hittites, Amorites,
Perizzites, Jebusites and Girgashites. You fulfilled Your promise for

---

וַיְבָרֶךְ דָּוִיד *David blessed.* There now follow three biblical passages that strictly
speaking do not belong to the Verses of Praise, either in source or subject
matter. The Verses of Praise are "songs of Your servant David" – that is,
passages from the book of Psalms – and they are about "He who spoke and
the world came into being," about God as Creator and Sovereign of the

תהלים פט
בָּרוּךְ יהוה לְעוֹלָם, אָמֵן וְאָמֵן:

תהלים קלה
בָּרוּךְ יהוה מִצִּיּוֹן, שֹׁכֵן יְרוּשָׁלָ͏ִם, הַלְלוּיָהּ:

תהלים עב
בָּרוּךְ יהוה אֱלֹהִים אֱלֹהֵי יִשְׂרָאֵל, עֹשֵׂה נִפְלָאוֹת לְבַדּוֹ:

‹ וּבָרוּךְ שֵׁם כְּבוֹדוֹ לְעוֹלָם

וְיִמָּלֵא כְבוֹדוֹ אֶת־כָּל־הָאָרֶץ

אָמֵן וְאָמֵן:

Stand until נִשְׁמַת *on page 311.*

דברי
הימים א'
כט
וַיְבָרֶךְ דָּוִיד אֶת־יהוה לְעֵינֵי כָּל־הַקָּהָל, וַיֹּאמֶר דָּוִיד, בָּרוּךְ
אַתָּה יהוה, אֱלֹהֵי יִשְׂרָאֵל אָבִינוּ, מֵעוֹלָם וְעַד־עוֹלָם: לְךָ יהוה
הַגְּדֻלָּה וְהַגְּבוּרָה וְהַתִּפְאֶרֶת וְהַנֵּצַח וְהַהוֹד, כִּי־כֹל בַּשָּׁמַיִם
וּבָאָרֶץ, לְךָ יהוה הַמַּמְלָכָה וְהַמִּתְנַשֵּׂא לְכֹל לְרֹאשׁ: וְהָעֹשֶׁר
וְהַכָּבוֹד מִלְּפָנֶיךָ, וְאַתָּה מוֹשֵׁל בַּכֹּל, וּבְיָדְךָ כֹּחַ וּגְבוּרָה, וּבְיָדְךָ
לְגַדֵּל וּלְחַזֵּק לַכֹּל: וְעַתָּה אֱלֹהֵינוּ מוֹדִים אֲנַחְנוּ לָךְ, וּמְהַלְלִים
לְשֵׁם תִּפְאַרְתֶּךָ:   אַתָּה־הוּא יהוה לְבַדֶּךָ, אַתָּ עָשִׂיתָ
נחמיה ט
אֶת־הַשָּׁמַיִם, שְׁמֵי הַשָּׁמַיִם וְכָל־צְבָאָם, הָאָרֶץ וְכָל־אֲשֶׁר
עָלֶיהָ, הַיַּמִּים וְכָל־אֲשֶׁר בָּהֶם, וְאַתָּה מְחַיֶּה אֶת־כֻּלָּם, וּצְבָא
הַשָּׁמַיִם לְךָ מִשְׁתַּחֲוִים: ‹ אַתָּה הוּא יהוה הָאֱלֹהִים אֲשֶׁר בָּחַרְתָּ
בְּאַבְרָם, וְהוֹצֵאתוֹ מֵאוּר כַּשְׂדִּים, וְשַׂמְתָּ שְּׁמוֹ אַבְרָהָם: וּמָצָאתָ
אֶת־לְבָבוֹ נֶאֱמָן לְפָנֶיךָ, ‹ וְכָרוֹת עִמּוֹ הַבְּרִית לָתֵת אֶת־אֶרֶץ
הַכְּנַעֲנִי הַחִתִּי הָאֱמֹרִי וְהַפְּרִזִּי וְהַיְבוּסִי וְהַגִּרְגָּשִׁי, לָתֵת לְזַרְעוֹ,

---

בָּרוּךְ יהוה לְעוֹלָם *Blessed be the* LORD *for ever.* A passage marking the end of the
Verses of Praise, consisting of four verses from Psalms, each opening with the
word "Blessed," thus echoing the opening paragraph, "Blessed is He who spoke."

You are righteous. You saw the suffering of our ancestors in Egypt. You heard their cry at the Sea of Reeds. You sent signs and wonders against Pharaoh, all his servants and all the people of his land, because You knew how arrogantly the Egyptians treated them. You created for Yourself renown that remains to this day. ▸ You divided the sea before them, so that they passed through the sea on dry land, but You cast their pursuers into the depths, like a stone into mighty waters.

וַיּוֹשַׁע That day the LORD saved Israel from the hands of the Egyptians, and Israel saw the Egyptians lying dead on the seashore. ▸ When Israel saw the great power the LORD had displayed against the Egyptians, the people feared the LORD, and believed in the LORD and in His servant, Moses. *Ex. 14*

אָז יָשִׁיר־מֹשֶׁה Then Moses and the Israelites sang this song to the LORD, saying: *Ex. 15*
   I will sing to the LORD, for He has triumphed gloriously;
   horse and rider He has hurled into the sea.
The LORD is my strength and song; He has become my salvation.
   This is my God, and I will beautify Him,
   my father's God, and I will exalt Him.

---

as the human body is more than a collection of cells. It is an emergent phenomenon, a higher order of being. The *tzibbur* that prays is a microcosm of the Jewish people. At this moment of transition, therefore, we undergo a metamorphosis, and we do so by a historical reenactment, retracing the steps of our ancestors as they cast off their private concerns as individuals to become a community of faith dedicated to the collective worship of God.

THE SONG AT THE SEA

Rashi, explaining the Talmudic view (*Sota* 30b) that at the Sea of Reeds Moses and the Israelites spontaneously sang the song together, says that

וַתָּקֶם אֶת־דְּבָרֶיךָ, כִּי צַדִּיק אָתָּה: וַתֵּרֶא אֶת־עֳנִי אֲבֹתֵינוּ בְּמִצְרָיִם, וְאֶת־זַעֲקָתָם שָׁמַעְתָּ עַל־יַם־סוּף: וַתִּתֵּן אֹתֹת וּמֹפְתִים בְּפַרְעֹה וּבְכָל־עֲבָדָיו וּבְכָל־עַם אַרְצוֹ, כִּי יָדַעְתָּ כִּי הֵזִידוּ עֲלֵיהֶם, וַתַּעַשׂ־לְךָ שֵׁם כְּהַיּוֹם הַזֶּה: › וְהַיָּם בָּקַעְתָּ לִפְנֵיהֶם, וַיַּעַבְרוּ בְתוֹךְ־הַיָּם בַּיַּבָּשָׁה, וְאֶת־רֹדְפֵיהֶם הִשְׁלַכְתָּ בִמְצוֹלֹת כְּמוֹ־אֶבֶן, בְּמַיִם עַזִּים:

שמות יד

וַיּוֹשַׁע יהוה בַּיּוֹם הַהוּא אֶת־יִשְׂרָאֵל מִיַּד מִצְרָיִם, וַיַּרְא יִשְׂרָאֵל אֶת־מִצְרַיִם מֵת עַל־שְׂפַת הַיָּם: › וַיַּרְא יִשְׂרָאֵל אֶת־הַיָּד הַגְּדֹלָה אֲשֶׁר עָשָׂה יהוה בְּמִצְרַיִם, וַיִּירְאוּ הָעָם אֶת־יהוה, וַיַּאֲמִינוּ בַּיהוה וּבְמֹשֶׁה עַבְדּוֹ:

שמות טו

אָז יָשִׁיר־מֹשֶׁה וּבְנֵי יִשְׂרָאֵל אֶת־הַשִּׁירָה הַזֹּאת לַיהוה, וַיֹּאמְרוּ לֵאמֹר, אָשִׁירָה לַיהוה כִּי־גָאֹה גָּאָה, סוּס וְרֹכְבוֹ רָמָה בַיָּם: עָזִּי וְזִמְרָת יָהּ וַיְהִי־לִי לִישׁוּעָה, זֶה אֵלִי וְאַנְוֵהוּ, אֱלֹהֵי

---

universe. None of the following passages belongs to either category. They are (1) the national assembly convened by David shortly before his death to initiate the building of the Temple under the aegis of his son and successor Solomon; (2) the national assembly gathered by Ezra and Nehemiah to renew the covenant between Israel and God; and (3) the song sung by the Israelites after they had crossed the Sea of Reeds and become "the people You acquired." These were key historic moments when the Jewish people came together as a collective body to praise God and pledge their loyalty to Him. Their presence here marks the transition from private to public prayer, which is about to begin.

A *tzibbur*, a public, is more than a mere assemblage of individuals, just

The LORD is a Master of war; LORD is His name.
Pharaoh's chariots and army He cast into the sea;
    the best of his officers drowned in the Sea of Reeds.
The deep waters covered them;
    they went down to the depths like a stone.
Your right hand, LORD, is majestic in power.
    Your right hand, LORD, shatters the enemy.
In the greatness of Your majesty, You overthrew those who rose
    against You.
    You sent out Your fury; it consumed them like stubble.
By the blast of Your nostrils the waters piled up.
    The surging waters stood straight like a wall;
    the deeps congealed in the heart of the sea.
The enemy said, "I will pursue. I will overtake. I will divide the spoil.
    My desire shall have its fill of them.
    I will draw my sword. My hand will destroy them."
You blew with Your wind; the sea covered them.
    They sank in the mighty waters like lead.
Who is like You, LORD, among the mighty?
    Who is like You – majestic in holiness, awesome in glory,
    working wonders?
You stretched out Your right hand,
    the earth swallowed them.
In Your loving-kindness, You led the people You redeemed.
    In Your strength, You guided them to Your holy abode.
Nations heard and trembled;
    terror gripped Philistia's inhabitants.

---

marvel." Words are the language of the mind. Music is the language of the
soul.

Faith is the ability to hear the music beneath the noise. Philosopher Roger
Scruton calls music "an encounter with the pure subject, released from the

אָבִי וַאֲרֹמְמֶנְהוּ: יְהוה אִישׁ מִלְחָמָה, יְהוה

שְׁמוֹ: מַרְכְּבֹת פַּרְעֹה וְחֵילוֹ יָרָה בַיָּם, וּמִבְחַר

שָׁלִשָׁיו טֻבְּעוּ בְיַם־סוּף: תְּהֹמֹת יְכַסְיֻמוּ, יָרְדוּ בִמְצוֹלֹת כְּמוֹ־

אָבֶן: יְמִינְךָ יהוה נֶאְדָּרִי בַּכֹּחַ, יְמִינְךָ

יְהוה תִּרְעַץ אוֹיֵב: וּבְרֹב גְּאוֹנְךָ תַּהֲרֹס

קָמֶיךָ, תְּשַׁלַּח חֲרֹנְךָ יֹאכְלֵמוֹ כַּקַּשׁ: וּבְרוּחַ

אַפֶּיךָ נֶעֶרְמוּ מַיִם, נִצְּבוּ כְמוֹ־נֵד

נֹזְלִים, קָפְאוּ תְהֹמֹת בְּלֶב־יָם: אָמַר

אוֹיֵב אֶרְדֹּף, אַשִּׂיג, אֲחַלֵּק שָׁלָל, תִּמְלָאֵמוֹ

נַפְשִׁי, אָרִיק חַרְבִּי תּוֹרִישֵׁמוֹ יָדִי: נָשַׁפְתָּ

בְרוּחֲךָ כִּסָּמוֹ יָם, צָלֲלוּ כַּעוֹפֶרֶת בְּמַיִם

אַדִּירִים: מִי־כָמֹכָה בָּאֵלִם יְהוה, מִי

כָּמֹכָה נֶאְדָּר בַּקֹּדֶשׁ, נוֹרָא תְהִלֹּת עֹשֵׂה

פֶלֶא: נָטִיתָ יְמִינְךָ תִּבְלָעֵמוֹ אָרֶץ: נָחִיתָ

בְחַסְדְּךָ עַם־זוּ גָּאָלְתָּ, נֵהַלְתָּ בְעָזְּךָ אֶל־נְוֵה

קָדְשֶׁךָ: שָׁמְעוּ עַמִּים יִרְגָּזוּן, חִיל

אָחַז יֹשְׁבֵי פְּלָשֶׁת: אָז נִבְהֲלוּ אַלּוּפֵי

---

the holy spirit rested on them and miraculously the same words came into their minds at the same time. It was a moment of collective epiphany, and it expressed itself as song.

When language aspires to the transcendent and the soul longs to break free of the gravitational pull of the earth, it modulates into song. Richter called music "the poetry of the air." Tolstoy called it "the shorthand of emotion." Goethe said, "Religious worship cannot do without music. It is one of the foremost means to work upon man with an effect of

The chiefs of Edom were dismayed,
>Moab's leaders were seized with trembling,
>the people of Canaan melted away.
Fear and dread fell upon them.
>By the power of Your arm, they were still as stone –
>until Your people crossed, LORD,
>until the people You acquired crossed over.
You will bring them and plant them
>on the mountain of Your heritage –
>the place, LORD, You made for Your dwelling,
>the Sanctuary, LORD, Your hands established.
>The LORD will reign for ever and all time.

The LORD will reign for ever and all time.
The LORD's kingship is established for ever and to all eternity.

When Pharaoh's horses, chariots and riders went into the sea,
>the LORD brought the waters of the sea back over them,
>but the Israelites walked on dry land through the sea.

▸ For kingship is the LORD's   *Ps. 22*
>and He rules over the nations.
>Saviors shall go up to Mount Zion   *Ob. 1*
>to judge Mount Esau,
>and the LORD's shall be the kingdom.

>Then the LORD shall be King over all the earth;   *Zech. 14*
>on that day the LORD shall be One and His name One,

>(as it is written in Your Torah, saying:
>Listen, Israel: the LORD is our God, the LORD is One.) *Deut. 6*

---

music, always new, from palpitating stones / Builds in useless space its godly home." The history of the Jewish spirit is written in its songs.

אֱדוֹם, אֵילֵי מוֹאָב יֹאחֲזֵמוֹ רָעַד, נָמֹגוּ

כֹּל יֹשְׁבֵי כְנָעַן: תִּפֹּל עֲלֵיהֶם אֵימָתָה

וָפַחַד, בִּגְדֹל זְרוֹעֲךָ יִדְּמוּ כָּאָבֶן, עַד־

יַעֲבֹר עַמְּךָ יְהוָה, עַד־יַעֲבֹר עַם־זוּ

קָנִיתָ: תְּבִאֵמוֹ וְתִטָּעֵמוֹ בְּהַר נַחֲלָתְךָ, מָכוֹן

לְשִׁבְתְּךָ פָּעַלְתָּ יְהוָה, מִקְּדָשׁ אֲדֹנָי כּוֹנֲנוּ

יָדֶיךָ: יְהוָה יִמְלֹךְ לְעֹלָם וָעֶד:

יְהוָה יִמְלֹךְ לְעֹלָם וָעֶד.

יְהוָה מַלְכוּתֵהּ קָאֵם לְעָלַם וּלְעָלְמֵי עָלְמַיָּא.

כִּי

בָא סוּס פַּרְעֹה בְּרִכְבּוֹ וּבְפָרָשָׁיו בַּיָּם, וַיָּשֶׁב יְהוָה עֲלֵהֶם אֶת־מֵי

הַיָּם, וּבְנֵי יִשְׂרָאֵל הָלְכוּ בַיַּבָּשָׁה בְּתוֹךְ הַיָּם:

‹ כִּי לַיהוָה הַמְּלוּכָה וּמֹשֵׁל בַּגּוֹיִם: תהלים כב

וְעָלוּ מוֹשִׁעִים בְּהַר צִיּוֹן עובדיה א

לִשְׁפֹּט אֶת־הַר עֵשָׂו

וְהָיְתָה לַיהוָה הַמְּלוּכָה:

וְהָיָה יְהוָה לְמֶלֶךְ עַל־כָּל־הָאָרֶץ זכריה יד

בַּיּוֹם הַהוּא יִהְיֶה יְהוָה אֶחָד וּשְׁמוֹ אֶחָד:

(וּבְתוֹרָתְךָ כָּתוּב לֵאמֹר, שְׁמַע יִשְׂרָאֵל, יְהוָה אֱלֹהֵינוּ יְהוָה אֶחָד:) דברים ו

world of objects, and moving in obedience to the laws of freedom alone."
He quotes Rilke: "Words still go softly forth towards the unsayable. / And

THE SOUL

of all that lives shall bless Your name, LORD our God,
and the spirit of all flesh shall always glorify
and exalt Your remembrance, our King.
From eternity to eternity You are God.
Without You, we have no king, redeemer or savior,
who liberates, rescues, sustains
and shows compassion in every time of trouble and distress.
We have no king but You, God of the first and last,
God of all creatures, Master of all ages,
extolled by a multitude of praises,
who guides His world with loving-kindness
and His creatures with compassion.
The LORD neither slumbers nor sleeps.
He rouses the sleepers and wakens the slumberers.
He makes the dumb speak, sets the bound free,
supports the fallen, and raises those bowed down.
To You alone we give thanks:
If our mouths were as full of song as the sea,
and our tongue with jubilation as its myriad waves,
if our lips were full of praise like the spacious heavens,
and our eyes shone like the sun and moon,
if our hands were outstretched like eagles of the sky,
and our feet as swift as hinds –

Mishna as a conclusion to Hallel in the Pesaḥ Seder service (*Pesaḥim* 118a).
Just as there, so here, it stands as a conclusion to the recitation of Psalms.
The second part, beginning "To You alone we give thanks," is mentioned in
the Talmud (*Berakhot* 59b) as a thanksgiving prayer for rain.

The first section is an extended meditation on the last words of the book of
Psalms: "Let all that breathes praise the LORD." Hebrew has many words for
soul, all deriving from verbs related to breathing. *Neshama* – the word linking
this passage to the end of Psalms, means to breathe deeply, as we are able to
do in a state of rest. Hence the sages said that on Shabbat we have "an extra

The commentary continues on page 315.

נִשְׁמַת

כָּל חַי תְּבָרֵךְ אֶת שִׁמְךָ, יהוה אֱלֹהֵינוּ

וְרוּחַ כָּל בָּשָׂר תְּפָאֵר וּתְרוֹמֵם זִכְרְךָ מַלְכֵּנוּ תָּמִיד.

מִן הָעוֹלָם וְעַד הָעוֹלָם אַתָּה אֵל

וּמִבַּלְעָדֶיךָ אֵין לָנוּ מֶלֶךְ גּוֹאֵל וּמוֹשִׁיעַ

פּוֹדֶה וּמַצִּיל וּמְפַרְנֵס וּמְרַחֵם

בְּכָל עֵת צָרָה וְצוּקָה אֵין לָנוּ מֶלֶךְ אֶלָּא אָתָּה.

אֱלֹהֵי הָרִאשׁוֹנִים וְהָאַחֲרוֹנִים, אֱלוֹהַּ כָּל בְּרִיּוֹת

אֲדוֹן כָּל תּוֹלָדוֹת, הַמְהֻלָּל בְּרֹב הַתִּשְׁבָּחוֹת

הַמְנַהֵג עוֹלָמוֹ בְּחֶסֶד וּבְרִיּוֹתָיו בְּרַחֲמִים.

וַיהוה לֹא יָנוּם וְלֹא יִישָׁן

הַמְעוֹרֵר יְשֵׁנִים וְהַמֵּקִיץ נִרְדָּמִים

וְהַמֵּשִׂיחַ אִלְּמִים וְהַמַּתִּיר אֲסוּרִים

וְהַסּוֹמֵךְ נוֹפְלִים וְהַזּוֹקֵף כְּפוּפִים.

לְךָ לְבַדְּךָ אֲנַחְנוּ מוֹדִים.

אִלּוּ פִינוּ מָלֵא שִׁירָה כַּיָּם

וּלְשׁוֹנֵנוּ רִנָּה כַּהֲמוֹן גַּלָּיו

וְשִׂפְתוֹתֵינוּ שֶׁבַח כְּמֶרְחֲבֵי רָקִיעַ

וְעֵינֵינוּ מְאִירוֹת כַּשֶּׁמֶשׁ וְכַיָּרֵחַ

וְיָדֵינוּ פְרוּשׂוֹת כְּנִשְׁרֵי שָׁמָיִם

וְרַגְלֵינוּ קַלּוֹת כָּאַיָּלוֹת

נִשְׁמַת *The soul.* This magnificent poem is composed of two parts. The first, according to Rabbi Yoḥanan, is the "blessing of the song" mentioned in the

still we could not thank You enough,
LORD our God and God of our ancestors,
or bless Your name
for even one of the thousand thousands
and myriad myriads of favors
You did for our ancestors and for us.
You redeemed us from Egypt, LORD our God,
and freed us from the house of bondage.
In famine You nourished us; in times of plenty You sustained us.
You delivered us from the sword, saved us from the plague,
and spared us from serious and lasting illness.
Until now Your mercies have helped us.
Your love has not forsaken us.
May You, LORD our God, never abandon us.
Therefore the limbs You formed within us,
the spirit and soul You breathed into our nostrils,
and the tongue You placed in our mouth –
they will thank and bless, praise and glorify, exalt and esteem,
hallow and do homage to Your name, O our King.
For every mouth shall give thanks to You,
every tongue vow allegiance to You, every knee shall bend to You,
every upright body shall bow to You, all hearts shall fear You,
and our innermost being sing praises to Your name,
as is written:

> "All my bones shall say: LORD, who is like You?   *Ps. 35*
> You save the poor from one stronger than him,
> the poor and needy from one who would rob him."

Who is like You? Who is equal to You?
Who can be compared to You?
O great, mighty and awesome God, God Most High,
Maker of heaven and earth.
▸ We will laud, praise and glorify You and bless Your holy name,
as it is said:

> "Of David. Bless the LORD, O my soul,   *Ps. 103*
> and all that is within me bless His holy name."

אֵין אֲנַחְנוּ מַסְפִּיקִים לְהוֹדוֹת לָךְ

יהוה אֱלֹהֵינוּ וֵאלֹהֵי אֲבוֹתֵינוּ

וּלְבָרֵךְ אֶת שְׁמֶךָ

עַל אַחַת מֵאֶלֶף אֶלֶף אַלְפֵי אֲלָפִים

וְרִבֵּי רְבָבוֹת פְּעָמִים הַטּוֹבוֹת שֶׁעָשִׂיתָ עִם אֲבוֹתֵינוּ וְעִמָּנוּ.

מִמִּצְרַיִם גְּאַלְתָּנוּ, יהוה אֱלֹהֵינוּ, וּמִבֵּית עֲבָדִים פְּדִיתָנוּ

בְּרָעָב זַנְתָּנוּ וּבְשָׂבָע כִּלְכַּלְתָּנוּ

מֵחֶרֶב הִצַּלְתָּנוּ וּמִדֶּבֶר מִלַּטְתָּנוּ

וּמֵחֳלָיִים רָעִים וְנֶאֱמָנִים דִּלִּיתָנוּ.

עַד הֵנָּה עֲזָרוּנוּ רַחֲמֶיךָ, וְלֹא עֲזָבוּנוּ חֲסָדֶיךָ

וְאַל תִּטְּשֵׁנוּ, יהוה אֱלֹהֵינוּ, לָנֶצַח.

עַל כֵּן אֵבָרִים שֶׁפִּלַּגְתָּ בָּנוּ

וְרוּחַ וּנְשָׁמָה שֶׁנָּפַחְתָּ בְּאַפֵּינוּ, וְלָשׁוֹן אֲשֶׁר שַׂמְתָּ בְּפִינוּ

הֵן הֵם יוֹדוּ וִיבָרְכוּ וִישַׁבְּחוּ וִיפָאֲרוּ

וִירוֹמְמוּ וְיַעֲרִיצוּ וְיַקְדִּישׁוּ וְיַמְלִיכוּ אֶת שִׁמְךָ מַלְכֵּנוּ

כִּי כָל פֶּה לְךָ יוֹדֶה וְכָל לָשׁוֹן לְךָ תִשָּׁבַע

וְכָל בֶּרֶךְ לְךָ תִכְרַע וְכָל קוֹמָה לְפָנֶיךָ תִשְׁתַּחֲוֶה

וְכָל לְבָבוֹת יִירָאוּךָ וְכָל קֶרֶב וּכְלָיוֹת יְזַמְּרוּ לִשְׁמֶךָ

כַּדָּבָר שֶׁכָּתוּב

תהלים לה

כָּל עַצְמֹתַי תֹּאמַרְנָה יהוה מִי כָמוֹךָ

מַצִּיל עָנִי מֵחָזָק מִמֶּנּוּ, וְעָנִי וְאֶבְיוֹן מִגֹּזְלוֹ:

מִי יִדְמֶה לָּךְ וּמִי יִשְׁוֶה לָּךְ וּמִי יַעֲרָךְ לָךְ

הָאֵל הַגָּדוֹל, הַגִּבּוֹר וְהַנּוֹרָא, אֵל עֶלְיוֹן, קֹנֵה שָׁמַיִם וָאָרֶץ.

◂ נְהַלֶּלְךָ וּנְשַׁבֵּחֲךָ וּנְפָאֶרְךָ וּנְבָרֵךְ אֶת שֵׁם קָדְשֶׁךָ

כָּאָמוּר

תהלים קג

לְדָוִד, בָּרְכִי נַפְשִׁי אֶת־יהוה, וְכָל־קְרָבַי אֶת־שֵׁם קָדְשׁוֹ:

The Leader begins:

הָאֵל GOD –
in Your absolute power,
Great – in the glory of Your name,
Mighty – for ever,
Awesome – in Your awe-inspiring deeds,
The King – who sits on a throne.
High and lofty

He inhabits eternity;
exalted and holy is His name.
And it is written:

Sing joyfully to the LORD, you righteous,   *Ps. 33*
for praise from the upright is seemly

‣ By the mouth	of the upright	You shall be praised.
By the words	of the righteous	You shall be blessed.
By the tongue	of the devout	You shall be extolled,
And in the midst	of the holy	You shall be sanctified.

On Shabbat and festivals it is often the custom to change prayer leaders between the Verses of Praise, essentially a preparation for public prayer, and public prayer itself, beginning with *Barekhu.* The dividing point varies according to the day and its central theme. On Shabbat the division occurs at "He inhabits eternity," emphasizing creation. On Rosh HaShana and Yom Kippur, it is at "The King," highlighting the ideas of justice and judgment. On festivals, it is at "God – in Your absolute power," evoking God as He acts in history, for the festivals are commemorations of the formative events of Jewish history.

יְשָׁרִים, צַדִּיקִים, חֲסִידִים, קְדוֹשִׁים *Upright, righteous, devout, holy.* A fourfold classification of the types of human excellence, from the most people-centered to the most God-centered. Upright means dealing honestly and with integrity. Righteous means one who practices equity and justice. Devout, says Maimonides, means going beyond the letter of the law, doing more than is

The שליח ציבור *begins:*

הָאֵל

בְּתַעֲצֻמוֹת עֻזֶּךָ

הַגָּדוֹל בִּכְבוֹד שְׁמֶךָ

הַגִּבּוֹר לָנֶצַח וְהַנּוֹרָא בְּנוֹרְאוֹתֶיךָ

הַמֶּלֶךְ הַיּוֹשֵׁב עַל כִּסֵּא

רָם וְנִשָּׂא

שׁוֹכֵן עַד מָרוֹם וְקָדוֹשׁ שְׁמוֹ

וְכָתוּב

תהלים לג

רַנְּנוּ צַדִּיקִים בַּיהוה, לַיְשָׁרִים נָאוָה תְהִלָּה:

‹ בְּפִי	יְשָׁרִים	תִּתְהַלָּל
וּבְדִבְרֵי	צַדִּיקִים	תִּתְבָּרַךְ
וּבִלְשׁוֹן	חֲסִידִים	תִּתְרוֹמָם
וּבְקֶרֶב	קְדוֹשִׁים	תִּתְקַדָּשׁ

---

soul." In the still silence of the turning world, it is as if we hear all that lives sing a song of praise to God who brought the universe into being, sustains it, and guides the destinies of all things.

The second section is composed around a phrase from Psalms: "All my bones shall say, LORD, who is like You?" – thus ingeniously linking the Psalms of praise with the Song at the Sea, which contains the same phrase "Who is like You?" Through a fine series of images, the poet expresses the human inadequacy in thanking God, itemizing how the various limbs ("All my bones") may praise Him, yet "still we could not thank You enough."

הָאֵל בְּתַעֲצֻמוֹת עֻזֶּךָ *God – in Your absolute power.* A word-by-word explication of the four terms above: "O great, mighty and awesome God," a phrase used by Moses (Deut. 10:17).

וּבְמַקְהֲלוֹת And in the assemblies
of tens of thousands of Your people, the house of Israel,
with joyous song shall Your name, our King,
be glorified in every generation.
▸ For this is the duty of all creatures before You,
LORD our God and God of our ancestors:
to thank, praise, laud, glorify, exalt,
honor, bless, raise high and acclaim –
even beyond all the words of song and praise
of David, son of Jesse, Your servant, Your anointed.

Stand until after "Barekhu" on page 320.

יִשְׁתַּבַּח May Your name be praised forever, our King,
the great and holy God, King in heaven and on earth.
For to You, LORD our God and God of our ancestors,
it is right to offer song and praise,
hymn and psalm,
strength and dominion,
eternity, greatness and power,
song of praise and glory,
holiness and kingship,
▸ blessings and thanks, from now and for ever.

---

based on the prayers of the patriarchs or is it a reminder of the service in the Temple? Ultimately, of course, it is both, but as we approach the start of communal prayers, for which we require a *minyan*, we emphasize the public dimension, the thronged assemblies such as gathered in the Temple. "In the multitude of people is the glory of the King" (Prov. 14:28).

יִשְׁתַּבַּח שִׁמְךָ לָעַד *May Your name be praised for ever.* The concluding blessing over the Verses of Praise which, like the introductory blessing, is said standing. The fifteen terms of glorification equal the number of psalms in the Verses of Praise on Sabbaths and festivals, as well as the number of "Songs of Ascents."

וּבְמַקְהֲלוֹת רִבְבוֹת עַמְּךָ בֵּית יִשְׂרָאֵל

בְּרִנָּה יִתְפָּאַר שִׁמְךָ מַלְכֵּנוּ בְּכָל דּוֹר וָדוֹר

‹ שֶׁכֵּן חוֹבַת כָּל הַיְצוּרִים

לְפָנֶיךָ יהוה אֱלֹהֵינוּ וֵאלֹהֵי אֲבוֹתֵינוּ

לְהוֹדוֹת, לְהַלֵּל, לְשַׁבֵּחַ, לְפָאֵר, לְרוֹמֵם

לְהַדֵּר, לְבָרֵךְ, לְעַלֵּה וּלְקַלֵּס

עַל כָּל דִּבְרֵי שִׁירוֹת וְתִשְׁבְּחוֹת

דָּוִד בֶּן יִשַׁי, עַבְדְּךָ מְשִׁיחֶךָ.

Stand until after בָּרְכוּ *on page 321.*

יִשְׁתַּבַּח שִׁמְךָ לָעַד, מַלְכֵּנוּ

הָאֵל הַמֶּלֶךְ הַגָּדוֹל וְהַקָּדוֹשׁ בַּשָּׁמַיִם וּבָאָרֶץ

כִּי לְךָ נָאֶה, יהוה אֱלֹהֵינוּ וֵאלֹהֵי אֲבוֹתֵינוּ

שִׁיר וּשְׁבָחָה, הַלֵּל וְזִמְרָה

עֹז וּמֶמְשָׁלָה, נֶצַח, גְּדֻלָּה וּגְבוּרָה

תְּהִלָּה וְתִפְאֶרֶת, קְדֻשָּׁה וּמַלְכוּת

‹ בְּרָכוֹת וְהוֹדָאוֹת, מֵעַתָּה וְעַד עוֹלָם.

---

required (*Laws of the Murderer and the Protection of Life* 13:4). Holy means dedicated to God, unconcerned with worldly goods or values. The initial letters of the second word in each phrase spell the name Yitzḥak, probably the name of the composer of this prayer.

וּבְמַקְהֲלוֹת *And in the assemblies.* There is a difference of opinion between Maimonides and Nahmanides as to whether prayer in origin is private or public – the inner conversation between the soul and God, or the public celebration of His presence in the midst of nation and community (see Maimonides, Laws of Prayer 1:1, Laws of Kings 9:1; Nahmanides on Exodus 13:16). Is it

Blessed are You, LORD,
God and King, exalted in praises,
God of thanksgivings,
Master of wonders,
who delights in hymns of song,
King, God, Giver of life to the worlds.

HALF KADDISH

Leader: יִתְגַּדַּל Magnified and sanctified
may His great name be,
in the world He created by His will.
May He establish His kingdom
in your lifetime and in your days,
and in the lifetime of all the house of Israel,
swiftly and soon –
and say: Amen.

All: May His great name be blessed
for ever and all time.

Leader: Blessed and praised, glorified and exalted,
raised and honored, uplifted and lauded
be the name of the Holy One,
blessed be He,
beyond any blessing,
song, praise and consolation uttered in the world –
and say: Amen.

---

different movements of a symphony rather than the beginning of a new piece, the Half Kaddish denotes an internal break between two connected sections of prayer. Like all other versions of Kaddish it requires a quorum of ten men, the smallest number that constitutes a community as opposed to a group of individuals.

בָּרוּךְ אַתָּה יהוה
אֵל מֶלֶךְ גָּדוֹל בַּתִּשְׁבָּחוֹת
אֵל הַהוֹדָאוֹת
אֲדוֹן הַנִּפְלָאוֹת
הַבּוֹחֵר בְּשִׁירֵי זִמְרָה
מֶלֶךְ, אֵל, חֵי הָעוֹלָמִים.

חצי קדיש

ש״ץ: יִתְגַּדַּל וְיִתְקַדַּשׁ שְׁמֵהּ רַבָּא (קהל: אָמֵן)
בְּעָלְמָא דִּי בְרָא כִרְעוּתֵהּ
וְיַמְלִיךְ מַלְכוּתֵהּ
בְּחַיֵּיכוֹן וּבְיוֹמֵיכוֹן וּבְחַיֵּי דְּכָל בֵּית יִשְׂרָאֵל
בַּעֲגָלָא וּבִזְמַן קָרִיב, וְאִמְרוּ אָמֵן. (קהל: אָמֵן)

קהל וש״ץ: יְהֵא שְׁמֵהּ רַבָּא מְבָרַךְ לְעָלַם וּלְעָלְמֵי עָלְמַיָּא.

ש״ץ: יִתְבָּרַךְ וְיִשְׁתַּבַּח וְיִתְפָּאַר וְיִתְרוֹמַם וְיִתְנַשֵּׂא
וְיִתְהַדָּר וְיִתְעַלֶּה וְיִתְהַלָּל
שְׁמֵהּ דְּקֻדְשָׁא בְּרִיךְ הוּא (קהל: בְּרִיךְ הוּא)
לְעֵלָּא מִן כָּל בִּרְכָתָא וְשִׁירָתָא
תֻּשְׁבְּחָתָא וְנֶחֱמָתָא
דַּאֲמִירָן בְּעָלְמָא, וְאִמְרוּ אָמֵן. (קהל: אָמֵן)

HALF KADDISH
This, the shortest of the five forms of Kaddish, marks the end of one section of the prayers. More like a semicolon than a period, or a pause between the

BLESSINGS OF THE SHEMA

The following blessing and response are said only in the presence of a minyan.
They represent a formal summons to the congregation to engage in an act of collective prayer.
The custom of bowing at this point is based on 1 Chronicles 29:20, "David said to
the whole assembly, 'Now bless the Lᴏʀᴅ your God.' All the assembly blessed
the Lᴏʀᴅ God of their fathers and bowed their heads low to the Lᴏʀᴅ and the King."
The Leader says the following, bowing at "Bless," standing straight at "the Lᴏʀᴅ." The congregation,
followed by the Leader, responds, bowing at "Bless," standing straight at "the Lᴏʀᴅ."

Leader: # BLESS
the Lᴏʀᴅ, the blessed One.

Congregation: Bless the Lᴏʀᴅ, the blessed One,
for ever and all time.

Leader: Bless the Lᴏʀᴅ, the blessed One,
for ever and all time.

The custom is to sit from this point until the Amida, since the predominant
emotion of this section of the prayers is love rather than awe.
Conversation is forbidden until after the Amida.

Some congregations interweave piyutim (known as Yotzerot) within the blessings of the Shema.
For Yotzerot for the first day, turn to page 700;
for the second day, turn to page 745.

בָּרוּךְ Blessed are You, Lᴏʀᴅ our God, King of the Universe,
who forms light and creates darkness,
makes peace and creates all.

יוֹצֵר אוֹר וּבוֹרֵא חֹשֶׁךְ *Who forms light and creates darkness.* This affirmation,
based on a verse in Isaiah (45:7), is an emphatic denial of dualism, the idea,
whose origin lay in Greek Gnosticism, that there are two supreme and contending forces at work in the universe, one of good, the other of evil – known
variously as the demiurge, the devil, Satan, Belial, Lucifer or the prince of
darkness. Dualism arises as an attempt to explain the prevalence of evil in
the world by attributing it to a malign power, the enemy of God and the
good. Such a view is radically incompatible with monotheism. It is also

קריאת שמע וברכותיה

The following blessing and response are said only in the presence of a מנין.
They represent a formal summons to the קהל *to engage in an act of collective prayer.*
The custom of bowing at this point is based on דברי הימים א׳ כט, כ, *"David said to
the whole assembly, 'Now bless the* Lord *your God.' All the assembly blessed
the* Lord *God of their fathers and bowed their heads low to the* Lord *and the King."*
The שליח ציבור *says the following, bowing at* בָּרְכוּ, *standing straight at* ה׳.
The קהל, *followed by the* שליח ציבור, *responds, bowing at* בָּרוּךְ, *standing straight at* ה׳.

ש״ץ:

בָּרְכוּ

אֶת יהוה הַמְבֹרָךְ.

קהל: **בָּרוּךְ יהוה הַמְבֹרָךְ לְעוֹלָם וָעֶד.**

ש״ץ: בָּרוּךְ יהוה הַמְבֹרָךְ לְעוֹלָם וָעֶד.

The custom is to sit from this point until the עמידה, *since the predominant
emotion of this section of the prayers is love rather than awe.
Conversation is forbidden until after the* עמידה.

Some congregations interweave piyutim (known as יוצרות) *within the blessings of the* שמע.
For יוצרות *for the first day, turn to page 700;
for the second day, turn to page 745.*

בָּרוּךְ אַתָּה יהוה אֱלֹהֵינוּ מֶלֶךְ הָעוֹלָם
יוֹצֵר אוֹר וּבוֹרֵא חֹשֶׁךְ
עֹשֶׂה שָׁלוֹם וּבוֹרֵא אֶת הַכֹּל.

בָּרְכוּ *Bless the* Lord. The formal start of communal prayer, to which the Verses
of Praise have been a prelude and preparation. *Barekhu,* like the *zimmun*
said before the Grace after Meals, is an invitation to others to join in an act
of praise, based on the verse, "Magnify the Lord with me, let us exalt His
name together" (Ps. 34:4).

On the second day of Shavuot, if also Shabbat, continue with "All will thank You" on the next page.
On a weekday continue here:

הַמֵּאִיר In compassion He gives light to the earth and its inhabitants,
and in His goodness continually renews the work of creation,
day after day.

How numerous are Your works, LORD;   *Ps. 104*
You made them all in wisdom;
the earth is full of Your creations.

He is the King exalted alone since the beginning of time –
praised, glorified and elevated since the world began.
Eternal God,

> in Your great compassion, have compassion on us,
> LORD of our strength, Rock of our refuge,
> Shield of our salvation, Stronghold of our safety.

The blessed God, great in knowledge,
prepared and made the rays of the sun.
He who is good formed glory for His name,
surrounding His power with radiant stars.
The leaders of His hosts, the holy ones, exalt the Almighty,
constantly proclaiming God's glory and holiness.

▸ Be blessed, LORD our God, for the magnificence of Your handiwork
and for the radiant lights You have made.
May they glorify You, Selah!

Continue with "May You be blessed, our Rock" on page 328.

———————————————————————————————

and then finding a smoother pebble or a prettier shell than ordinary, whilst
the great ocean of truth lay all undiscovered before me." The more we discover
about the universe, the greater its mystery and majesty inspire awe.

אֵל בָּרוּךְ *The blessed God.* An alphabetical acrostic of twenty-two words.
Although this, the first blessing before the Shema, is about creation as a
whole, the morning prayer emphasizes the element of which we are most
conscious at the start of the day: the creation of light. Of this, there are two
forms: the physical light of the sun, moon and stars, made on the fourth day of
creation, and the spiritual light created on the first day ("Let there be light").
The prayer modulates from the first to the second, from the universe as we
see it, to the mystical vision of God enthroned in glory, surrounded by angels.

On the second day of שבועות, if also שבת, continue with הַכֹּל יוֹדוּךָ on the next page.
On a weekday continue here:

הַמֵּאִיר לָאָרֶץ וְלַדָּרִים עָלֶיהָ בְּרַחֲמִים

וּבְטוּבוֹ מְחַדֵּשׁ בְּכָל יוֹם תָּמִיד מַעֲשֵׂה בְרֵאשִׁית.

תהלים קד

מָה רַבּוּ מַעֲשֶׂיךָ יהוה, כֻּלָּם בְּחָכְמָה עָשִׂיתָ

מָלְאָה הָאָרֶץ קִנְיָנֶךָ:

הַמֶּלֶךְ הַמְרוֹמָם לְבַדּוֹ מֵאָז

הַמְשֻׁבָּח וְהַמְפֹאָר וְהַמִּתְנַשֵּׂא מִימוֹת עוֹלָם.

אֱלֹהֵי עוֹלָם

בְּרַחֲמֶיךָ הָרַבִּים רַחֵם עָלֵינוּ

אֲדוֹן עֻזֵּנוּ, צוּר מִשְׂגַּבֵּנוּ

מָגֵן יִשְׁעֵנוּ, מִשְׂגָּב בַּעֲדֵנוּ.

אֵל בָּרוּךְ גְּדוֹל דֵּעָה

הֵכִין וּפָעַל זָהֳרֵי חַמָּה

טוֹב יָצַר כָּבוֹד לִשְׁמוֹ

מְאוֹרוֹת נָתַן סְבִיבוֹת עֻזּוֹ

פִּנּוֹת צְבָאָיו קְדוֹשִׁים, רוֹמְמֵי שַׁדַּי

תָּמִיד מְסַפְּרִים כְּבוֹד אֵל וּקְדֻשָּׁתוֹ.

‹ תִּתְבָּרַךְ יהוה אֱלֹהֵינוּ, עַל שֶׁבַח מַעֲשֵׂה יָדֶיךָ

וְעַל מְאוֹרֵי אוֹר שֶׁעָשִׂיתָ, יְפָאֲרוּךָ סֶּלָה.

Continue with תִּתְבָּרַךְ, צוּרֵנוּ on page 329.

---

exceptionally dangerous: it has led some groups to see others as the personi-
fication of evil. Nonetheless, there is evidence that such views were held by
some sectarian groups of Jews in the late Second Temple period; hence the
need to discountenance it at the very start of communal prayer.

Isaac Newton, the greatest scientist of the seventeenth century, once said:
"I do not know what I may appear to the world, but to myself I seem to have
been only like a boy playing on the sea-shore, and diverting myself in now

On Shabbat continue here:

All will thank You. All will praise You.
All will declare: Nothing is as holy as the LORD.
All will exalt You, Selah, You who form all –
the God who daily opens the doors of the gates of the East
and cleaves the windows of the sky,
who brings out the sun from its place and the moon from its abode,
giving light to the whole world and its inhabitants
whom He created by the attribute of compassion.
In compassion He gives light to the earth and its inhabitants,
and in His goodness daily, continually, renews the work of creation.
He is the King who alone was exalted since time began,
praised, glorified and raised high from days of old.
Eternal God, in Your great compassion, have compassion on us,
LORD of our strength, Rock of our refuge,
Shield of our salvation, Stronghold of our safety.

אֵין כְּעֶרְכְּךָ None can be compared to You, there is none besides You;
 None without You. Who is like You?

▸ None can be compared to You, LORD our God –
 in this world.
 There is none besides You, our King –
 in the life of the World to Come.
 There is none but You, our Redeemer –
 in the days of the Messiah.
 There is none like You, our Savior –
 at the resurrection of the dead.

---

joined the attribute of compassion (*Bereshit Raba* 8:5). One of the supreme
ironies of literature is that Portia's speech in Shakespeare's *The Merchant of
Venice*, framed in opposition to Jewish ethics, is in fact a precise statement of it:

 The quality of mercy is not strained. It droppeth as the gentle rain from
  heaven
 Upon the place beneath […] / It is an attribute to God himself
 And earthly power doth then show likest God's
 Where mercy seasons justice. (IV, i)

On שבת *continue here:*

הַכֹּל יוֹדוּךָ וְהַכֹּל יְשַׁבְּחוּךָ

וְהַכֹּל יֹאמְרוּ אֵין קָדוֹשׁ כַּיהוה

הַכֹּל יְרוֹמְמוּךָ סֶּלָה, יוֹצֵר הַכֹּל.

הָאֵל הַפּוֹתֵחַ בְּכָל יוֹם דַּלְתוֹת שַׁעֲרֵי מִזְרָח

וּבוֹקֵעַ חַלּוֹנֵי רָקִיעַ

מוֹצִיא חַמָּה מִמְּקוֹמָהּ וּלְבָנָה מִמְּכוֹן שִׁבְתָּהּ

וּמֵאִיר לָעוֹלָם כֻּלּוֹ וּלְיוֹשְׁבָיו, שֶׁבָּרָא בְּמִדַּת הָרַחֲמִים.

הַמֵּאִיר לָאָרֶץ וְלַדָּרִים עָלֶיהָ בְּרַחֲמִים

וּבְטוּבוֹ מְחַדֵּשׁ בְּכָל יוֹם תָּמִיד מַעֲשֵׂה בְרֵאשִׁית.

הַמֶּלֶךְ הַמְרוֹמָם לְבַדּוֹ מֵאָז

הַמְשֻׁבָּח וְהַמְפֹאָר וְהַמִּתְנַשֵּׂא מִימוֹת עוֹלָם.

אֱלֹהֵי עוֹלָם, בְּרַחֲמֶיךָ הָרַבִּים רַחֵם עָלֵינוּ

אֲדוֹן עֻזֵּנוּ, צוּר מִשְׂגַּבֵּנוּ, מָגֵן יִשְׁעֵנוּ, מִשְׂגָּב בַּעֲדֵנוּ.

אֵין כְּעֶרְכְּךָ, וְאֵין זוּלָתֶךָ

אֶפֶס בִּלְתֶּךָ, וּמִי דּוֹמֶה לָּךְ.

‹ אֵין כְּעֶרְכְּךָ, יהוה אֱלֹהֵינוּ, בָּעוֹלָם הַזֶּה

וְאֵין זוּלָתְךָ, מַלְכֵּנוּ, לְחַיֵּי הָעוֹלָם הַבָּא

אֶפֶס בִּלְתְּךָ, גּוֹאֲלֵנוּ, לִימוֹת הַמָּשִׁיחַ

וְאֵין דּוֹמֶה לְךָ, מוֹשִׁיעֵנוּ, לִתְחִיַּת הַמֵּתִים.

הַכֹּל יוֹדוּךָ *All will thank You.* This passage, said on Shabbat, is longer than its weekday equivalent since Shabbat is a memorial of creation (*Roke'aḥ*).

שֶׁבָּרָא בְּמִדַּת הָרַחֲמִים *Whom He created by the attribute of compassion.* According to tradition, God initially sought to create the world under the attribute of strict justice, but saw that it could not survive. What did He do? To justice He

אֵל אָדוֹן God, LORD of all creation,
the Blessed, is blessed by every soul.
His greatness and goodness fill the world;
knowledge and wisdom surround Him.

> Exalted above the holy Ḥayyot,
> adorned in glory on the Chariot;
> merit and right are before His throne,
> kindness and compassion before His glory.

Good are the radiant stars our God created;
He formed them with knowledge,
understanding and deliberation.
He gave them strength and might
to rule throughout the world.

> Full of splendor, radiating light,
> beautiful is their splendor throughout the world.
> Glad as they go forth, joyous as they return,
> they fulfill with awe their Creator's will.

Glory and honor they give to His name,
jubilation and song at the mention of His majesty.
He called the sun into being and it shone with light.
He looked and fashioned the form of the moon.

> All the hosts on high give Him praise;
> the Seraphim, Ophanim and holy Ḥayyot
> ascribe glory and greatness –

אֵל אָדוֹן עַל כָּל הַמַּעֲשִׂים *God, LORD of all creation.* An ancient prayer, influenced by *Merkava* mysticism, envisioning God surrounded by the angels and the myriad stars. *Merkava* or "Chariot" mysticism was based on the vision seen by Ezekiel and described by him in the first chapter of the book that bears his name.

כָּל צְבָא מָרוֹם *All the hosts on high.* Having mentioned the sun and moon, the Hebrew hints at the other planets of the Ptolemaic system: שֶׁבַח נוֹתְנִים לוֹ כָּל צְבָא מָרוֹם – the שׁ of *shevaḥ* signaling Saturn (*Shabbetai*), and so on for Venus (נ for *Noga*), Mercury (כ for *Kokhav*), Jupiter (צ for *Tzedek*), and Mars (מ for *Maadim*).

אֵל אָדוֹן עַל כָּל הַמַּעֲשִׂים
בָּרוּךְ וּמְבֹרָךְ בְּפִי כָּל נְשָׁמָה
גָּדְלוֹ וְטוּבוֹ מָלֵא עוֹלָם
דַּעַת וּתְבוּנָה סוֹבְבִים אוֹתוֹ.

הַמִּתְגָּאֶה עַל חַיּוֹת הַקֹּדֶשׁ
וְנֶהְדָּר בְּכָבוֹד עַל הַמֶּרְכָּבָה
זְכוּת וּמִישׁוֹר לִפְנֵי כִסְאוֹ
חֶסֶד וְרַחֲמִים לִפְנֵי כְבוֹדוֹ.

טוֹבִים מְאוֹרוֹת שֶׁבָּרָא אֱלֹהֵינוּ
יְצָרָם בְּדַעַת בְּבִינָה וּבְהַשְׂכֵּל
כֹּחַ וּגְבוּרָה נָתַן בָּהֶם
לִהְיוֹת מוֹשְׁלִים בְּקֶרֶב תֵּבֵל.

מְלֵאִים זִיו וּמְפִיקִים נֹגַהּ
נָאֶה זִיוָם בְּכָל הָעוֹלָם
שְׂמֵחִים בְּצֵאתָם וְשָׂשִׂים בְּבוֹאָם
עוֹשִׂים בְּאֵימָה רְצוֹן קוֹנָם.

פְּאֵר וְכָבוֹד נוֹתְנִים לִשְׁמוֹ
צָהֳלָה וְרִנָּה לְזֵכֶר מַלְכוּתוֹ
קָרָא לַשֶּׁמֶשׁ וַיִּזְרַח אוֹר
רָאָה וְהִתְקִין צוּרַת הַלְּבָנָה.

שֶׁבַח נוֹתְנִים לוֹ כָּל צְבָא מָרוֹם
תִּפְאֶרֶת וּגְדֻלָּה, שְׂרָפִים וְאוֹפַנִּים וְחַיּוֹת הַקֹּדֶשׁ.

לָאֵל To God who rested from all works, and on the seventh day
ascended and sat on His throne of glory.
He robed the day of rest in glory and called the Sabbath day a delight.
This is the praise of the seventh day,
that on it God rested from all His work.
The seventh day itself gives praise, saying,
"A psalm, a song for the Sabbath day.   *Ps. 92*
It is good to give thanks to the LORD."
Therefore let all He has formed glorify and bless God.
Let them give praise, honor and grandeur to God,
the King, who formed all things,
and in His holiness gave a heritage of rest
to His people Israel on the holy Sabbath day.
May Your name, O LORD our God, be sanctified,
and Your renown, O our King, be glorified
in the heavens above and on earth below.
May You be blessed, our Deliverer,
by the praises of Your handiwork,
and by the radiant lights You have made:
may they glorify You. Selah!

On both days continue here:

תִּתְבָּרַךְ May You be blessed,
our Rock, King and Redeemer,
Creator of holy beings.
May Your name be praised for ever,
our King, Creator of the ministering angels,
all of whom stand in the universe's heights,
proclaiming together, in awe, aloud,
the words of the living God, the eternal King.

---

understood not as a song *for* the Sabbath, but *by* the Sabbath. It is as if, in the
silence of Shabbat, we hear the song creation sings to its Creator, the "music
of the spheres."

תִּתְבָּרַךְ *May You be blessed.* Two prophets, Isaiah and Ezekiel, saw mystical
visions of God enthroned among His heavenly host, the choir of angels.

לָאֵל אֲשֶׁר שָׁבַת מִכָּל הַמַּעֲשִׂים

בַּיּוֹם הַשְּׁבִיעִי נִתְעַלָּה וְיָשַׁב עַל כִּסֵּא כְּבוֹדוֹ.

תִּפְאֶרֶת עָטָה לְיוֹם הַמְּנוּחָה

עֹנֶג קָרָא לְיוֹם הַשַּׁבָּת.

זֶה שֶׁבַח שֶׁל יוֹם הַשְּׁבִיעִי

שֶׁבּוֹ שָׁבַת אֵל מִכָּל מְלַאכְתּוֹ

וְיוֹם הַשְּׁבִיעִי מְשַׁבֵּחַ וְאוֹמֵר

תהלים צב

מִזְמוֹר שִׁיר לְיוֹם הַשַּׁבָּת, טוֹב לְהֹדוֹת לַיהוה:

לְפִיכָךְ יְפָאֲרוּ וִיבָרְכוּ לָאֵל כָּל יְצוּרָיו

שֶׁבַח יְקָר וּגְדֻלָּה יִתְּנוּ לָאֵל מֶלֶךְ יוֹצֵר כֹּל

הַמַּנְחִיל מְנוּחָה לְעַמּוֹ יִשְׂרָאֵל בִּקְדֻשָּׁתוֹ בְּיוֹם שַׁבַּת קֹדֶשׁ.

שִׁמְךָ יהוה אֱלֹהֵינוּ יִתְקַדַּשׁ, וְזִכְרְךָ מַלְכֵּנוּ יִתְפָּאַר

בַּשָּׁמַיִם מִמַּעַל וְעַל הָאָרֶץ מִתָּחַת.

תִּתְבָּרַךְ מוֹשִׁיעֵנוּ עַל שֶׁבַח מַעֲשֵׂה יָדֶיךָ

וְעַל מְאוֹרֵי אוֹר שֶׁעָשִׂיתָ, יְפָאֲרוּךָ סֶּלָה.

On both days continue here:

תִּתְבָּרַךְ

צוּרֵנוּ מַלְכֵּנוּ וְגוֹאֲלֵנוּ, בּוֹרֵא קְדוֹשִׁים

יִשְׁתַּבַּח שִׁמְךָ לָעַד

מַלְכֵּנוּ, יוֹצֵר מְשָׁרְתִים

וַאֲשֶׁר מְשָׁרְתָיו כֻּלָּם עוֹמְדִים בְּרוּם עוֹלָם

וּמַשְׁמִיעִים בְּיִרְאָה יַחַד בְּקוֹל

דִּבְרֵי אֱלֹהִים חַיִּים וּמֶלֶךְ עוֹלָם.

וְיוֹם הַשְּׁבִיעִי מְשַׁבֵּחַ *The seventh day itself gives praise.* A midrashic idea, based on the phrase that opens Psalm 92: "A psalm, a song of the Sabbath day," here

They are all beloved, all pure, all mighty,
and all perform in awe and reverence
the will of their Maker.
▸ All open their mouths
in holiness and purity,
with song and psalm,
and bless, praise, glorify,
revere, sanctify and declare the sovereignty of – ◂
the name of the great, mighty
and awesome God and King,
holy is He.
▸ All accept on themselves, one from another,
the yoke of the kingdom of heaven,
granting permission to one another
to sanctify the One who formed them,
in serene spirit,
pure speech and sweet melody.
All, as one, proclaim His holiness,
saying in awe:

> *All say aloud:*
> Holy, holy, holy is the Lᴏʀᴅ of hosts;   *Is. 6*
> the whole world is filled with His glory.

Some congregations say here a piyut (known as an Ophan).
For the Ophan, turn to page 703.

---

prayer, except on Shabbat and festivals, when the third is transferred to the afternoon.

This section of the prayers – the vision of the heavenly throne and the angels – is part of the mystical tradition in Judaism. Prayer is Jacob's ladder, stretching from earth to heaven, with "angels of the Lᴏʀᴅ" ascending and descending (*Zohar*). The three *kedushot* represent, respectively, the ascent, the summit, and the descent: the journey of the soul from earth to heaven and back again, transformed by our experience of the Divine.

כֻּלָּם אֲהוּבִים, כֻּלָּם בְּרוּרִים, כֻּלָּם גִּבּוֹרִים

וְכֻלָּם עוֹשִׂים בְּאֵימָה וּבְיִרְאָה רְצוֹן קוֹנָם

‹ וְכֻלָּם פּוֹתְחִים אֶת פִּיהֶם

בִּקְדֻשָּׁה וּבְטׇהֳרָה

בְּשִׁירָה וּבְזִמְרָה

וּמְבָרְכִים וּמְשַׁבְּחִים וּמְפָאֲרִים

‹ וּמַעֲרִיצִים וּמַקְדִּישִׁים וּמַמְלִיכִים

אֶת שֵׁם הָאֵל הַמֶּלֶךְ הַגָּדוֹל, הַגִּבּוֹר וְהַנּוֹרָא

קָדוֹשׁ הוּא.

‹ וְכֻלָּם מְקַבְּלִים עֲלֵיהֶם עֹל מַלְכוּת שָׁמַיִם זֶה מִזֶּה

וְנוֹתְנִים רְשׁוּת זֶה לָזֶה

לְהַקְדִּישׁ לְיוֹצְרָם בְּנַחַת רוּחַ

בְּשָׂפָה בְרוּרָה וּבִנְעִימָה

קְדֻשָּׁה כֻּלָּם כְּאֶחָד

עוֹנִים וְאוֹמְרִים בְּיִרְאָה

All say aloud:

ישעיהו

קָדוֹשׁ, קָדוֹשׁ, קָדוֹשׁ יהוה צְבָאוֹת

מְלֹא כׇל־הָאָרֶץ כְּבוֹדוֹ:

Some congregations say here a piyut (known as an אוֹפָן).
For the אוֹפָן, turn to page 703.

These visions, together with the words the prophets heard the angels sing
("Holy, holy, holy" in Isaiah's vision, "Blessed be the LORD's glory from
His place" in Ezekiel's), form the heart of *Kedusha*, the "Holiness" prayer.
This is recited three times in the morning prayers – (1) before the Shema,
(2) during the Leader's Repetition of the Amida, and (3) toward the end of

▸ Then the Ophanim and the Holy Ḥayyot,
with a roar of noise,
raise themselves toward the Seraphim and,
facing them, give praise, saying:

> *All say aloud:*
> Blessed is the LORD's glory from His place.   *Ezek. 3*

לָאֵל To the blessed God they offer melodies.
To the King, living and eternal God,
they say psalms and proclaim praises.

> For it is He alone
> who does mighty deeds and creates new things,
> who is Master of battles and sows righteousness,
> who makes salvation grow and creates cures,
> who is is revered in praises, the LORD of wonders,
who in His goodness, continually renews the work of creation,
day after day,
as it is said:
> "[Praise] Him who made the great lights,   *Ps. 136*
> for His love endures for ever."

▸ May You make a new light shine over Zion,
and may we all soon be worthy of its light.
Blessed are You, LORD,
who forms the radiant lights.

אַהֲבָה You have loved us with great love, LORD our God,
and with surpassing compassion
have You had compassion on us.
Our Father, our King,
for the sake of our ancestors who trusted in You,
and to whom You taught the laws of life,
be gracious also to us and teach us.

אַהֲבָה רַבָּה אֲהַבְתָּנוּ *You have loved us with great love.* Even before reciting the
Shema with its command, "Love the LORD your God with all your heart,

◄ וְהָאוֹפַנִּים וְחַיּוֹת הַקֹּֽדֶשׁ
בְּרַֽעַשׁ גָּדוֹל מִתְנַשְּׂאִים לְעֻמַּת שְׂרָפִים
לְעֻמָּתָם מְשַׁבְּחִים וְאוֹמְרִים

All say aloud:

יחזקאל ג

בָּרוּךְ כְּבוֹד־יהוה מִמְּקוֹמוֹ:

לְאֵל בָּרוּךְ נְעִימוֹת יִתֵּֽנוּ
לְמֶֽלֶךְ אֵל חַי וְקַיָּם
זְמִירוֹת יֹאמֵֽרוּ וְתִשְׁבָּחוֹת יַשְׁמִֽיעוּ
כִּי הוּא לְבַדּוֹ
פּוֹעֵל גְּבוּרוֹת, עוֹשֶׂה חֲדָשׁוֹת
בַּֽעַל מִלְחָמוֹת, זוֹרֵֽעַ צְדָקוֹת
מַצְמִֽיחַ יְשׁוּעוֹת, בּוֹרֵא רְפוּאוֹת
נוֹרָא תְהִלּוֹת, אֲדוֹן הַנִּפְלָאוֹת
הַמְחַדֵּשׁ בְּטוּבוֹ בְּכָל יוֹם תָּמִיד מַעֲשֵׂה בְרֵאשִׁית
כָּאָמוּר

תהלים קלו

לְעֹשֵׂה אוֹרִים גְּדֹלִים, כִּי לְעוֹלָם חַסְדּוֹ:

◄ אוֹר חָדָשׁ עַל צִיּוֹן תָּאִיר
וְנִזְכֶּה כֻלָּֽנוּ מְהֵרָה לְאוֹרוֹ.
בָּרוּךְ אַתָּה יהוה, יוֹצֵר הַמְּאוֹרוֹת.

אַהֲבָה רַבָּה אֲהַבְתָּֽנוּ, יהוה אֱלֹהֵֽינוּ
חֶמְלָה גְדוֹלָה וִיתֵרָה חָמַֽלְתָּ עָלֵֽינוּ.
אָבִֽינוּ מַלְכֵּֽנוּ
בַּעֲבוּר אֲבוֹתֵֽינוּ שֶׁבָּטְחוּ בְךָ, וַתְּלַמְּדֵם חֻקֵּי חַיִּים
כֵּן תְּחָנֵּֽנוּ וּתְלַמְּדֵֽנוּ.

Our Father, compassionate Father, ever compassionate,
have compassion on us.
Instill in our hearts the desire to understand and discern,
to listen, learn and teach, to observe, perform and fulfill
all the teachings of Your Torah in love.
Enlighten our eyes in Your Torah
and let our hearts cling to Your commandments.
Unite our hearts to love and revere Your name,
so that we may never be ashamed.
And because we have trusted
in Your holy, great and revered name,
may we be glad and rejoice in Your salvation.

At this point, gather the four tzitziot of the tallit, holding them in the left hand.

Bring us back in peace from the four quarters of the earth
and lead us upright to our land.

▸ For You are a God who performs acts of salvation,
and You chose us from all peoples and tongues,
bringing us close to Your great name for ever in truth,
that we may thank You
and proclaim Your Oneness in love.
Blessed are You, LORD,
who chooses His people Israel in love.

---

centrality of law in Judaism: "…the law of millennia, studied and lived, ana-
lyzed and rhapsodized, the law of everyday and of the day of death, petty and
yet sublime, sober and yet woven in legend; a law which knows both the fire
of the Sabbath candle and that of the martyr's stake" (Franz Rosenzweig,
On Jewish Learning, 77). The law, through which Israel is charged with bringing the Divine Presence into the shared spaces of our common life, is itself
based on a threefold love: for God, the neighbor, and the stranger. Through
law – the choreography of grace in relationship – we redeem our finitude,
turning the prose of daily life into religious poetry and making gentle the
life of this world.

אָבִינוּ, הָאָב הָרַחֲמָן, הַמְרַחֵם

רַחֵם עָלֵינוּ

וְתֵן בְּלִבֵּנוּ לְהָבִין וּלְהַשְׂכִּיל

לִשְׁמֹעַ, לִלְמֹד וּלְלַמֵּד, לִשְׁמֹר וְלַעֲשׂוֹת, וּלְקַיֵּם

אֶת כָּל דִּבְרֵי תַלְמוּד תּוֹרָתֶךָ בְּאַהֲבָה.

וְהָאֵר עֵינֵינוּ בְּתוֹרָתֶךָ

וְדַבֵּק לִבֵּנוּ בְּמִצְוֹתֶיךָ

וְיַחֵד לְבָבֵנוּ לְאַהֲבָה וּלְיִרְאָה אֶת שְׁמֶךָ

וְלֹא נֵבוֹשׁ לְעוֹלָם וָעֶד.

כִּי בְשֵׁם קָדְשְׁךָ הַגָּדוֹל וְהַנּוֹרָא בָּטָחְנוּ

נָגִילָה וְנִשְׂמְחָה בִּישׁוּעָתֶךָ.

At this point, gather the four ציציות *of the* טלית, *holding them in the left hand.*

וַהֲבִיאֵנוּ לְשָׁלוֹם מֵאַרְבַּע כַּנְפוֹת הָאָרֶץ

וְתוֹלִיכֵנוּ קוֹמְמִיּוּת לְאַרְצֵנוּ.

‹ כִּי אֵל פּוֹעֵל יְשׁוּעוֹת אָתָּה

וּבָנוּ בָחַרְתָּ מִכָּל עַם וְלָשׁוֹן

וְקֵרַבְתָּנוּ לְשִׁמְךָ הַגָּדוֹל סֶלָה, בֶּאֱמֶת

לְהוֹדוֹת לְךָ וּלְיַחֶדְךָ בְּאַהֲבָה.

בָּרוּךְ אַתָּה יהוה, הַבּוֹחֵר בְּעַמּוֹ יִשְׂרָאֵל בְּאַהֲבָה.

---

with all your soul, and with all your might," we speak of God's love for us. Note how that love is expressed: in the fact that God taught us "the laws of life." Christianity at times contrasted law and love as if they were opposed. In Judaism law *is* love: the expression of God's love for us and ours for Him.

Franz Rosenzweig criticized Martin Buber for failing to understand the

The Shema must be said with intense concentration. In the first
paragraph one should accept, with love, the sovereignty of God; in the second, the
mitzvot as the will of God. The end of the third paragraph constitutes fulfillment
of the mitzva to remember, morning and evening, the exodus from Egypt.
When not praying with a minyan, say:

God, faithful King!

The following verse should be said aloud, while covering the eyes with the right hand:

Listen, Israel: the LORD is our God, the LORD is One.

Deut. 6

Quietly: Blessed be the name of His glorious kingdom for ever and all time.

וְאָהַבְתָּ Love the LORD your God with all your heart, with all your soul, and with all your might. These words which I command you today shall be on your heart. Teach them repeatedly to your children, speaking of them when you sit at home and when you travel on the way, when you lie down and when you rise. Bind them as a sign on your hand, and they shall be an emblem between your eyes. Write them on the doorposts of your house and gates. *Deut. 6*

וְהָיָה If you indeed heed My commandments with which I charge you today, to love the LORD your God and worship Him with all your heart and with all your soul, I will give rain in your land in its season, the early and late rain; and you shall gather in your grain, wine and oil. I will give grass in your field for your cattle, and you shall eat and be satisfied. Be careful lest your heart be tempted and *Deut. 11*

וְאָהַבְתָּ אֵת יהוה אֱלֹהֶיךָ *Love the LORD your God.* "What is the love of God that is befitting? It is to love God with a great and exceeding love, so strong that one's soul shall be knit up with the love of God, such that it is continually enraptured by it, like a lovesick individual whose mind is at no time free from passion for a particular woman and is enraptured by her at all times... Even more intense should be the love of God in the hearts of those who love Him; they should be enraptured by this love at all times" (Maimonides, Laws of Repentance, 10:3).

The שמע must be said with intense concentration. In the first paragraph one should accept,
with love, the sovereignty of God; in the second, the מצוות as the will of God.
The end of the third paragraph constitutes fulfillment of the מצוה to
remember, morning and evening, the exodus from Egypt.
When not praying with a מנין, say:

אֵל מֶלֶךְ נֶאֱמָן

The following verse should be said aloud, while covering the eyes with the right hand:

דברים ו

שְׁמַע יִשְׂרָאֵל, יהוה אֱלֹהֵינוּ, יהוה ׀ אֶחָד:

Quietly בָּרוּךְ שֵׁם כְּבוֹד מַלְכוּתוֹ לְעוֹלָם וָעֶד.

דברים ו

וְאָהַבְתָּ אֵת יהוה אֱלֹהֶיךָ, בְּכָל־לְבָבְךָ וּבְכָל־נַפְשְׁךָ וּבְכָל־מְאֹדֶךָ: וְהָיוּ הַדְּבָרִים הָאֵלֶּה, אֲשֶׁר אָנֹכִי מְצַוְּךָ הַיּוֹם, עַל־לְבָבֶךָ: וְשִׁנַּנְתָּם לְבָנֶיךָ וְדִבַּרְתָּ בָּם, בְּשִׁבְתְּךָ בְּבֵיתֶךָ, וּבְלֶכְתְּךָ בַדֶּרֶךְ, וּבְשָׁכְבְּךָ וּבְקוּמֶךָ: וּקְשַׁרְתָּם לְאוֹת עַל־יָדֶךָ וְהָיוּ לְטֹטָפֹת בֵּין עֵינֶיךָ: וּכְתַבְתָּם עַל־מְזֻזוֹת בֵּיתֶךָ וּבִשְׁעָרֶיךָ:

דברים יא

וְהָיָה אִם־שָׁמֹעַ תִּשְׁמְעוּ אֶל־מִצְוֹתַי אֲשֶׁר אָנֹכִי מְצַוֶּה אֶתְכֶם הַיּוֹם, לְאַהֲבָה אֶת־יהוה אֱלֹהֵיכֶם וּלְעָבְדוֹ, בְּכָל־לְבַבְכֶם וּבְכָל־נַפְשְׁכֶם: וְנָתַתִּי מְטַר־אַרְצְכֶם בְּעִתּוֹ, יוֹרֶה וּמַלְקוֹשׁ, וְאָסַפְתָּ דְגָנֶךָ וְתִירֹשְׁךָ וְיִצְהָרֶךָ: וְנָתַתִּי עֵשֶׂב בְּשָׂדְךָ לִבְהֶמְתֶּךָ, וְאָכַלְתָּ וְשָׂבָעְתָּ: הִשָּׁמְרוּ לָכֶם פֶּן־יִפְתֶּה לְבַבְכֶם, וְסַרְתֶּם וַעֲבַדְתֶּם

שְׁמַע יִשְׂרָאֵל *Listen, Israel.* Most of the ancient civilizations, from Mesopotamia and Egypt to Greece and Rome, were predominantly visual, with monumental architecture and iconic use of art. Judaism with its faith in the invisible God emphasized hearing over seeing, and listening over looking. Hence the verb "Listen" in this key text, as well as our custom, when saying it, to cover our eyes, shutting out the visible world to concentrate on the commanding Voice.

you go astray and worship other gods, bowing down to them. Then the LORD's anger will flare against you and He will close the heavens so that there will be no rain. The land will not yield its crops, and you will perish swiftly from the good land that the LORD is giving you. Therefore, set these, My words, on your heart and soul. Bind them as a sign on your hand, and they shall be an emblem between your eyes. Teach them to your children, speaking of them when you sit at home and when you travel on the way, when you lie down and when you rise. Write them on the doorposts of your house and gates, so that you and your children may live long in the land that the LORD swore to your ancestors to give them, for as long as the heavens are above the earth.

Hold the tzitziot in the right hand also (some transfer to the right hand) kissing them at °.

וַיֹּאמֶר The LORD spoke to Moses, saying: Speak to the Israelites   *Num. 15* and tell them to make °tassels on the corners of their garments for all generations. They shall attach to the °tassel at each corner a thread of blue. This shall be your °tassel, and you shall see it and remember all of the LORD's commandments and keep them, not straying after your heart and after your eyes, following your own sinful desires. Thus you will be reminded to keep all My

---

cues to remind us of fundamental propositions: who we are and what we are called on to do. The Shema speaks of three such symbols: tefillin, mezuza and tzitzit. The first relates to who we are, the second to where we live, the third to how we dress and appear to the world and to ourselves.

וְלֹא תָתוּרוּ אַחֲרֵי לְבַבְכֶם וְאַחֲרֵי עֵינֵיכֶם *Not straying after your heart and after your eyes.* Note the unexpected order of the phrases. We would have thought that seeing gives rise to desiring rather than the other way around (see Rashi to Numbers 15:39). In fact, however, the story of the spies that precedes the command of tzitzit in the Torah (Num. 13–14) shows that the reverse is frequently the case. Our perception is framed and often distorted by our emotions. The spies were afraid: therefore they saw their enemies as giants and themselves as grasshoppers. They did not realize that the reverse was the case (see Joshua 2:9–11).

אֱלֹהִים אֲחֵרִים וְהִשְׁתַּחֲוִיתֶם לָהֶם: וְחָרָה אַף־יהוה בָּכֶם, וְעָצַר
אֶת־הַשָּׁמַיִם וְלֹא־יִהְיֶה מָטָר, וְהָאֲדָמָה לֹא תִתֵּן אֶת־יְבוּלָהּ,
וַאֲבַדְתֶּם מְהֵרָה מֵעַל הָאָרֶץ הַטֹּבָה אֲשֶׁר יהוה נֹתֵן לָכֶם:
וְשַׂמְתֶּם אֶת־דְּבָרַי אֵלֶּה עַל־לְבַבְכֶם וְעַל־נַפְשְׁכֶם, וּקְשַׁרְתֶּם
אֹתָם לְאוֹת עַל־יֶדְכֶם, וְהָיוּ לְטוֹטָפֹת בֵּין עֵינֵיכֶם: וְלִמַּדְתֶּם
אֹתָם אֶת־בְּנֵיכֶם לְדַבֵּר בָּם, בְּשִׁבְתְּךָ בְּבֵיתֶךָ וּבְלֶכְתְּךָ בַדֶּרֶךְ,
וּבְשָׁכְבְּךָ וּבְקוּמֶךָ: וּכְתַבְתָּם עַל־מְזוּזוֹת בֵּיתֶךָ וּבִשְׁעָרֶיךָ: לְמַעַן
יִרְבּוּ יְמֵיכֶם וִימֵי בְנֵיכֶם עַל הָאֲדָמָה אֲשֶׁר נִשְׁבַּע יהוה לַאֲבֹתֵיכֶם
לָתֵת לָהֶם, כִּימֵי הַשָּׁמַיִם עַל־הָאָרֶץ:

Hold the ציצית *in the right hand also (some transfer to the right hand) kissing them at °.*

במדבר טו

וַיֹּאמֶר יהוה אֶל־מֹשֶׁה לֵּאמֹר: דַּבֵּר אֶל־בְּנֵי יִשְׂרָאֵל וְאָמַרְתָּ
אֲלֵהֶם, וְעָשׂוּ לָהֶם °צִיצִת עַל־כַּנְפֵי בִגְדֵיהֶם לְדֹרֹתָם, וְנָתְנוּ
°עַל־צִיצִת הַכָּנָף פְּתִיל תְּכֵלֶת: וְהָיָה לָכֶם °לְצִיצִת, וּרְאִיתֶם
אֹתוֹ וּזְכַרְתֶּם אֶת־כָּל־מִצְוֺת יהוה וַעֲשִׂיתֶם אֹתָם, וְלֹא תָתוּרוּ
אַחֲרֵי לְבַבְכֶם וְאַחֲרֵי עֵינֵיכֶם, אֲשֶׁר־אַתֶּם זֹנִים אַחֲרֵיהֶם: לְמַעַן

וְלִמַּדְתֶּם אֹתָם אֶת־בְּנֵיכֶם *Teach them to your children.* Jews are the only people to
have predicated their very survival on education. The Mesopotamians built
ziggurats, the Egyptians built pyramids, the Athenians the Parthenon and the
Romans the Colosseum. Jews built schools and houses of study. Those other
civilizations died and disappeared; Jews and Judaism survived.

לְמַעַן יִרְבּוּ יְמֵיכֶם וִימֵי בְנֵיכֶם *So that you and your children may live long.* Strong
nations are impossible without strong families dedicated to passing on their
heritage across the generations. Those who plan for one year plant crops.
Those who plan for ten years plant trees. Those who plan for centuries educate children.

וּרְאִיתֶם אֹתוֹ, וּזְכַרְתֶּם *And you shall see it and remember.* Though Judaism is primarily a religion of hearing rather than seeing, we nonetheless need visual

commandments, and be holy to your God. I am the LORD your God, who brought you out of the land of Egypt to be your God. I am the LORD your God.

°True –

The Leader repeats:

► The LORD your God is true –

וְיַצִּיב And firm, established and enduring, right, faithful,
beloved, cherished, delightful, pleasant,
awesome, mighty, perfect, accepted,
good and beautiful
is this faith for us for ever.

True is the eternal God, our King, Rock of Jacob,
Shield of our salvation.
He exists and His name exists through all generations.
His throne is established,
His kingship and faithfulness endure for ever.

At °, kiss the tzitziot and release them.

His words live and persist, faithful and desirable
°for ever and all time.
► So they were for our ancestors, so they are for us,
and so they will be for our children
and all our generations and for all future generations
of the seed of Israel, Your servants.

---

your promises, being true to your word, doing what you said you would do. According to Rashi (to Exodus 6:3), the holiest name of God means "the One who is true to His word." This concept of truth serves as the bridge between the end of the Shema, with its reference to the exodus from Egypt, and the quintessential prayer, the Amida, that we are now approaching. The fact that God redeemed His people in the past is the basis of our prayer for redemption in the future. Just as God was true to His word then, so we pray He will be now. The sixfold repetition of *emet* acts as a reminder of the six steps we have

תִּזְכְּרוּ וַעֲשִׂיתֶם אֶת־כָּל־מִצְוֺתָי, וִהְיִיתֶם קְדֹשִׁים לֵאלֹהֵיכֶם: אֲנִי
יהוה אֱלֹהֵיכֶם, אֲשֶׁר הוֹצֵאתִי אֶתְכֶם מֵאֶרֶץ מִצְרַיִם, לִהְיוֹת לָכֶם
לֵאלֹהִים, אֲנִי יהוה אֱלֹהֵיכֶם:

אֱמֶת°

The שליח ציבור repeats:

‹ יהוה אֱלֹהֵיכֶם אֱמֶת

וְיַצִּיב, וְנָכוֹן וְקַיָּם, וְיָשָׁר וְנֶאֱמָן
וְאָהוּב וְחָבִיב, וְנֶחְמָד וְנָעִים
וְנוֹרָא וְאַדִּיר, וּמְתֻקָּן וּמְקֻבָּל, וְטוֹב וְיָפֶה
הַדָּבָר הַזֶּה עָלֵינוּ לְעוֹלָם וָעֶד.

אֱמֶת אֱלֹהֵי עוֹלָם מַלְכֵּנוּ
צוּר יַעֲקֹב מָגֵן יִשְׁעֵנוּ
לְדוֹר וָדוֹר הוּא קַיָּם וּשְׁמוֹ קַיָּם
וְכִסְאוֹ נָכוֹן
וּמַלְכוּתוֹ וֶאֱמוּנָתוֹ לָעַד קַיֶּמֶת.

At °, kiss the ציציות and release them.

וּדְבָרָיו חָיִים וְקַיָּמִים
נֶאֱמָנִים וְנֶחֱמָדִים
°לָעַד וּלְעוֹלְמֵי עוֹלָמִים
‹ עַל אֲבוֹתֵינוּ וְעָלֵינוּ
עַל בָּנֵינוּ וְעַל דּוֹרוֹתֵינוּ
וְעַל כָּל דּוֹרוֹת זֶרַע יִשְׂרָאֵל עֲבָדֶיךָ.

אֱמֶת *True.* The word *emet* does not just mean "true" in the narrow Western sense of something that corresponds to reality. In Hebrew it means honoring

For the early and the later generations
this faith has proved good and enduring for ever –
True   and faithful, an irrevocable law.
True   You are the LORD: our God and God of our ancestors,
   ▸ our King and King of our ancestors,
     our Redeemer and Redeemer of our ancestors,
     our Maker, Rock of our salvation,
     our Deliverer and Rescuer: this has ever been Your name.
     There is no God but You.

*Some congregations say here a piyut (known as a Zulat).
For the Zulat, turn to page 705.*

עֶזְרַת You have always been the help of our ancestors,
Shield and Savior of their children
after them in every generation.
Your dwelling is in the heights of the universe,
and Your judgments and righteousness
reach to the ends of the earth.
Happy is the one who obeys Your commandments
and takes to heart Your teaching and Your word.
True   You are the Master of Your people
and a mighty King who pleads their cause.
True   You are the first and You are the last.
Besides You, we have no king, redeemer or savior.
From Egypt You redeemed us, LORD our God,
and from the slave-house You delivered us.
All their firstborn You killed,
but Your firstborn You redeemed.
You split the Sea of Reeds and drowned the arrogant.
You brought Your beloved ones across.
The water covered their foes; not one of them was left.   *Ps. 106*

taken – the three blessings surrounding the Shema and the three paragraphs
of the Shema itself – toward the ultimate destination of prayer, the act of

עַל הָרִאשׁוֹנִים וְעַל הָאַחֲרוֹנִים

דָּבָר טוֹב וְקַיָּם לְעוֹלָם וָעֶד

אֱמֶת וֶאֱמוּנָה, חֹק וְלֹא יַעֲבֹר.

אֱמֶת שָׁאַתָּה הוּא יהוה אֱלֹהֵינוּ וֵאלֹהֵי אֲבוֹתֵינוּ

◂ מַלְכֵּנוּ מֶלֶךְ אֲבוֹתֵינוּ

גּוֹאֲלֵנוּ גּוֹאֵל אֲבוֹתֵינוּ, יוֹצְרֵנוּ צוּר יְשׁוּעָתֵנוּ

פּוֹדֵנוּ וּמַצִּילֵנוּ מֵעוֹלָם שְׁמֶךָ

אֵין אֱלֹהִים זוּלָתֶךָ.

Some congregations say here a piyut (known as a זולת).
For the זולת, turn to page 705.

עֶזְרַת אֲבוֹתֵינוּ אַתָּה הוּא מֵעוֹלָם

מָגֵן וּמוֹשִׁיעַ לִבְנֵיהֶם אַחֲרֵיהֶם בְּכָל דּוֹר וָדוֹר.

בְּרוּם עוֹלָם מוֹשָׁבֶךָ, וּמִשְׁפָּטֶיךָ וְצִדְקָתְךָ עַד אַפְסֵי אָרֶץ.

אַשְׁרֵי אִישׁ שֶׁיִּשְׁמַע לְמִצְוֹתֶיךָ

וְתוֹרָתְךָ וּדְבָרְךָ יָשִׂים עַל לִבּוֹ.

אֱמֶת אַתָּה הוּא אָדוֹן לְעַמֶּךָ

וּמֶלֶךְ גִּבּוֹר לָרִיב רִיבָם.

אֱמֶת אַתָּה הוּא רִאשׁוֹן וְאַתָּה הוּא אַחֲרוֹן

וּמִבַּלְעָדֶיךָ אֵין לָנוּ מֶלֶךְ גּוֹאֵל וּמוֹשִׁיעַ.

מִמִּצְרַיִם גְּאַלְתָּנוּ, יהוה אֱלֹהֵינוּ

וּמִבֵּית עֲבָדִים פְּדִיתָנוּ

כָּל בְּכוֹרֵיהֶם הָרַגְתָּ, וּבְכוֹרְךָ גָּאָלְתָּ

וְיַם סוּף בָּקַעְתָּ, וְזֵדִים טִבַּעְתָּ, וִידִידִים הֶעֱבַרְתָּ

וַיְכַסּוּ־מַיִם צָרֵיהֶם, אֶחָד מֵהֶם לֹא נוֹתָר:

תהלים קו

For this, the beloved ones praised and exalted God,
the cherished ones sang psalms, songs and praises,
blessings and thanksgivings to the King,
the living and enduring God.
High and exalted, great and awesome,
He humbles the haughty and raises the lowly,
freeing captives and redeeming those in need, helping the poor
and answering His people when they cry out to Him.

Stand in preparation for the Amida. Take three steps back before beginning the Amida.

‣ Praises to God Most High,
the Blessed One who is blessed.
Moses and the children of Israel
recited to You a song with great joy,
and they all exclaimed:

"Who is like You, LORD, among the mighty? *Ex. 15*
Who is like You, majestic in holiness,
awesome in praises, doing wonders?"

‣ With a new song, the redeemed people praised
Your name at the seashore.
Together they all gave thanks,
proclaimed Your kingship, and declared:

"The LORD shall reign for ever and ever." *Ibid.*

Congregants should end the following blessing together with the Leader so as to be able to move directly from the words "redeemed Israel" to the Amida, without the interruption of saying Amen.

‣ צוּר יִשְׂרָאֵל Rock of Israel! Arise to the help of Israel.
Deliver, as You promised, Judah and Israel.

Our Redeemer, the LORD of hosts is His name, *Is. 47*
the Holy One of Israel.

Blessed are You, LORD, who redeemed Israel.

---

standing directly before God in the Amida. This is the seventh step, and in
Judaism seven is the sign of the Holy.

עַל זֹאת שִׁבְּחוּ אֲהוּבִים, וְרוֹמְמוּ אֵל

וְנָתְנוּ יְדִידִים זְמִירוֹת, שִׁירוֹת וְתִשְׁבָּחוֹת

בְּרָכוֹת וְהוֹדָאוֹת לְמֶלֶךְ אֵל חַי וְקַיָּם

רָם וְנִשָּׂא, גָּדוֹל וְנוֹרָא

מַשְׁפִּיל גֵּאִים וּמַגְבִּיהַּ שְׁפָלִים

מוֹצִיא אֲסִירִים, וּפוֹדֶה עֲנָוִים וְעוֹזֵר דַּלִּים

וְעוֹנֶה לְעַמּוֹ בְּעֵת שַׁוְּעָם אֵלָיו.

Stand in preparation for the עמידה. Take three steps back before beginning the עמידה.

‹ תְּהִלּוֹת לְאֵל עֶלְיוֹן, בָּרוּךְ הוּא וּמְבֹרָךְ

מֹשֶׁה וּבְנֵי יִשְׂרָאֵל

לְךָ עָנוּ שִׁירָה בְּשִׂמְחָה רַבָּה

וְאָמְרוּ כֻלָּם

שמות טו
מִי־כָמֹכָה בָּאֵלִם, יְהוה

מִי כָּמֹכָה נֶאְדָּר בַּקֹּדֶשׁ, נוֹרָא תְהִלֹּת, עֹשֵׂה פֶלֶא:

‹ שִׁירָה חֲדָשָׁה שִׁבְּחוּ גְאוּלִים

לְשִׁמְךָ עַל שְׂפַת הַיָּם

יַחַד כֻּלָּם הוֹדוּ וְהִמְלִיכוּ

וְאָמְרוּ

שם
יְהוה יִמְלֹךְ לְעֹלָם וָעֶד:

The קהל should end the following blessing together with the שליח ציבור so as to be able to move directly from the words גָּאַל יִשְׂרָאֵל to the עמידה, without the interruption of saying אמן.

‹ צוּר יִשְׂרָאֵל, קוּמָה בְּעֶזְרַת יִשְׂרָאֵל

וּפְדֵה כִנְאֻמֶךָ יְהוּדָה וְיִשְׂרָאֵל.

ישעיה מז
גֹּאֲלֵנוּ יְהוה צְבָאוֹת שְׁמוֹ, קְדוֹשׁ יִשְׂרָאֵל:

בָּרוּךְ אַתָּה יְהוה, גָּאַל יִשְׂרָאֵל.

THE AMIDA

The following prayer, until "in former years" on page 358, is said silently, standing with feet together. If there is a minyan, the Amida is repeated aloud by the Leader. Take three steps forward and at the points indicated by ˒, bend the knees at the first word, bow at the second, and stand straight before saying God's name.

O LORD, open my lips, so that my mouth may declare Your praise. *Ps. 51*

PATRIARCHS

˒בָּרוּךְ Blessed are You, LORD our God and God of our fathers,
God of Abraham, God of Isaac and God of Jacob;
the great, mighty and awesome God, God Most High,
who bestows acts of loving-kindness and creates all,
who remembers the loving-kindness of the fathers
and will bring a Redeemer to their children's children
for the sake of His name, in love.
King, Helper, Savior, Shield:
˒Blessed are You, LORD,
Shield of Abraham.

DIVINE MIGHT

אַתָּה גִּבּוֹר You are eternally mighty, LORD.
You give life to the dead
and have great power to save.

> *In Israel:*
> He causes the dew to fall.

He sustains the living with loving-kindness,
and with great compassion revives the dead.

---

when you were a bride; how you walked after Me in the desert, through a land not sown." The patriarchs and matriarchs were willing to undertake a physical and spiritual journey, fraught with risk, in response to the call of God. They listened to God. Therefore in their merit we ask God to listen to us. That is the historical basis on which we pray.

עמידה

The following prayer, until קַדְמֹנִיּוֹת *on page 359, is said silently, standing with feet together. If there is a* מנין, *the* עמידה *is repeated aloud by the* שליח ציבור. *Take three steps forward and at the points indicated by* ΄, *bend the knees at the first word, bow at the second, and stand straight before saying God's name.*

תהלים נא

אֲדֹנָי, שְׂפָתַי תִּפְתָּח, וּפִי יַגִּיד תְּהִלָּתֶךָ:

אבות

יּבָּרוּךְ אַתָּה יהוה, אֱלֹהֵינוּ וֵאלֹהֵי אֲבוֹתֵינוּ

אֱלֹהֵי אַבְרָהָם, אֱלֹהֵי יִצְחָק, וֵאלֹהֵי יַעֲקֹב

הָאֵל הַגָּדוֹל הַגִּבּוֹר וְהַנּוֹרָא, אֵל עֶלְיוֹן

גּוֹמֵל חֲסָדִים טוֹבִים, וְקֹנֵה הַכֹּל, וְזוֹכֵר חַסְדֵי אָבוֹת

וּמֵבִיא גוֹאֵל לִבְנֵי בְנֵיהֶם לְמַעַן שְׁמוֹ בְּאַהֲבָה.

מֶלֶךְ עוֹזֵר וּמוֹשִׁיעַ וּמָגֵן.

יּבָּרוּךְ אַתָּה יהוה, מָגֵן אַבְרָהָם.

גבורות

אַתָּה גִּבּוֹר לְעוֹלָם, אֲדֹנָי

מְחַיֵּה מֵתִים אַתָּה, רַב לְהוֹשִׁיעַ

In ארץ ישראל:

מוֹרִיד הַטָּל

מְכַלְכֵּל חַיִּים בְּחֶסֶד, מְחַיֵּה מֵתִים בְּרַחֲמִים רַבִּים

וְזוֹכֵר חַסְדֵי אָבוֹת *Remembers the loving-kindness of the fathers.* The reference is not just to obvious acts of kindness like Abraham offering hospitality to passersby, or Rebecca bringing water for a stranger and his camels – though these acts were essential in establishing a template of Jewish character, in seeking to be a blessing to others. There is also, in this phrase, an echo of Jeremiah (2:2): "I remember of you the kindness of your youth, your love

He supports the fallen, heals the sick, sets captives free,
and keeps His faith with those who sleep in the dust.
Who is like You, Master of might,
and who can compare to You,
O King who brings death and gives life,
and makes salvation grow?
Faithful are You to revive the dead.
Blessed are You, LORD, who revives the dead.

When saying the Amida silently, continue with "You are holy" on the next page.

KEDUSHA
*During the Leader's Repetition, the following is said standing
with feet together, rising on the toes at the words indicated by ˄.*

*Cong. then
Leader:* נְקַדֵּשׁ We will sanctify Your name on earth, as they sanctify it in
the highest heavens, as is written by Your prophet, "And they [the
angels] call to one another saying:
Is. 6

*Cong. then
Leader:* ˄Holy, ˄holy, ˄holy is the LORD of hosts; the whole world is filled
with His glory."

Then with a sound of mighty noise, majestic and strong, they make
their voice heard, raising themselves toward the Seraphim, and facing them say: "Blessed –"

*Cong. then
Leader:* "˄Blessed is the LORD's glory from His place."
Ezek. 3

Reveal Yourself from Your place, O our King, and reign over us, for
we are waiting for You. When will You reign in Zion? May it be soon
in our days, and may You dwell there for ever and all time. May
You be exalted and sanctified in the midst of Jerusalem, Your city,
from generation to generation for evermore. May our eyes see Your
kingdom, as is said in the songs of Your splendor, written by David
Your righteous anointed one:

*Cong. then
Leader:* "˄The LORD shall reign for ever. He is your God, Zion, from genera-
tion to generation, Halleluya!"
Ps. 146

Leader: From generation to generation we will declare Your greatness, and
we will proclaim Your holiness for evermore. Your praise, our God,
shall not leave our mouth forever, for You, God, are a great and holy
King. Blessed are You, LORD, the holy God.

The Leader continues with "You have chosen us" on the next page.

סוֹמֵךְ נוֹפְלִים, וְרוֹפֵא חוֹלִים, וּמַתִּיר אֲסוּרִים

וּמְקַיֵּם אֱמוּנָתוֹ לִישֵׁנֵי עָפָר.

מִי כָמוֹךָ, בַּעַל גְּבוּרוֹת, וּמִי דּוֹמֶה לָּךְ

מֶלֶךְ, מֵמִית וּמְחַיֶּה וּמַצְמִיחַ יְשׁוּעָה.

וְנֶאֱמָן אַתָּה לְהַחֲיוֹת מֵתִים.

בָּרוּךְ אַתָּה יהוה, מְחַיֵּה הַמֵּתִים.

When saying the עמידה silently, continue with אַתָּה קָדוֹשׁ on the next page.

קְדוּשָּׁה

*During the חזרת הש״ץ, the following is said standing
with feet together, rising on the toes at the words indicated by ٨.*

קהל ש״ץ then	נְקַדֵּשׁ אֶת שִׁמְךָ בָּעוֹלָם, כְּשֵׁם שֶׁמַּקְדִּישִׁים אוֹתוֹ בִּשְׁמֵי מָרוֹם
ישעיה ו	כַּכָּתוּב עַל יַד נְבִיאֶךָ: וְקָרָא זֶה אֶל־זֶה וְאָמַר

קהל ש״ץ then	٨קָדוֹשׁ, ٨קָדוֹשׁ, ٨קָדוֹשׁ, יהוה צְבָאוֹת, מְלֹא כָל־הָאָרֶץ כְּבוֹדוֹ:
	אָז בְּקוֹל רַעַשׁ גָּדוֹל אַדִּיר וְחָזָק, מַשְׁמִיעִים קוֹל
	מִתְנַשְּׂאִים לְעֻמַּת שְׂרָפִים, לְעֻמָּתָם בָּרוּךְ יֹאמֵרוּ

יחזקאל ג	קהל ש״ץ then ٨בָּרוּךְ כְּבוֹד־יהוה מִמְּקוֹמוֹ:
	מִמְּקוֹמְךָ מַלְכֵּנוּ תוֹפִיעַ וְתִמְלֹךְ עָלֵינוּ, כִּי מְחַכִּים אֲנַחְנוּ לָךְ
	מָתַי תִּמְלֹךְ בְּצִיּוֹן, בְּקָרוֹב בְּיָמֵינוּ לְעוֹלָם וָעֶד תִּשְׁכֹּן
	תִּתְגַּדַּל וְתִתְקַדַּשׁ בְּתוֹךְ יְרוּשָׁלַיִם עִירְךָ לְדוֹר וָדוֹר וּלְנֵצַח נְצָחִים.
	וְעֵינֵינוּ תִרְאֶינָה מַלְכוּתֶךָ
	כַּדָּבָר הָאָמוּר בְּשִׁירֵי עֻזֶּךָ עַל יְדֵי דָוִד מְשִׁיחַ צִדְקֶךָ

תהלים קמו	קהל ש״ץ then יִמְלֹךְ יהוה לְעוֹלָם, אֱלֹהַיִךְ צִיּוֹן לְדֹר וָדֹר, הַלְלוּיָהּ:

ש״ץ	לְדוֹר וָדוֹר נַגִּיד גָּדְלֶךָ, וּלְנֵצַח נְצָחִים קְדֻשָּׁתְךָ נַקְדִּישׁ
	וְשִׁבְחֲךָ אֱלֹהֵינוּ מִפִּינוּ לֹא יָמוּשׁ לְעוֹלָם וָעֶד
	כִּי אֵל מֶלֶךְ גָּדוֹל וְקָדוֹשׁ אָתָּה.
	בָּרוּךְ אַתָּה יהוה, הָאֵל הַקָּדוֹשׁ.

The שליח ציבור continues with אַתָּה בְחַרְתָּנוּ on the next page.

When saying the Amida silently, continue here:

HOLINESS

אַתָּה קָדוֹשׁ You are holy and Your name is holy,
and holy ones praise You daily, Selah!
Blessed are You, LORD, the holy God.

HOLINESS OF THE DAY

אַתָּה בְחַרְתָּנוּ You have chosen us from among all peoples.
You have loved and favored us.
You have raised us above all tongues.
You have made us holy through Your commandments.
You have brought us near, our King, to Your service,
and have called us by Your great and holy name.

On Shabbat, add the words in parentheses:

וַתִּתֶּן לָנוּ And You, LORD our God, have given us in love
(Sabbaths for rest and) festivals for rejoicing,
holy days and seasons for joy, (this Sabbath day and)
this day of the festival of Shavuot,
the time of the giving of our Torah
(with love), a holy assembly in memory of the exodus from Egypt.

אֱלֹהֵינוּ Our God and God of our ancestors,
may there rise, come, reach, appear, be favored, heard,
regarded and remembered before You,
our recollection and remembrance,
as well as the remembrance of our ancestors,
and of the Messiah son of David Your servant,
and of Jerusalem Your holy city,
and of all Your people the house of Israel –

---

story of the survival of the nation against all odds lies the most obvious outward sign of the Jewish mission, to be God's witnesses to the world.

זִכְרוֹנֵנוּ וּפִקְדוֹנֵנוּ *Our recollection and remembrance.* According to Malbim (Gen. 21:1), the verb ז-כ-ר, "remember," means the opposite of "forget." It is cognitive.

When saying the עמידה *silently, continue here:*

קדושת השם

אַתָּה קָדוֹשׁ וְשִׁמְךָ קָדוֹשׁ, וּקְדוֹשִׁים בְּכָל יוֹם יְהַלְלוּךָ סֶּלָה.
בָּרוּךְ אַתָּה יהוה, הָאֵל הַקָּדוֹשׁ.

קדושת היום

אַתָּה בְחַרְתָּנוּ מִכָּל הָעַמִּים
אָהַבְתָּ אוֹתָנוּ וְרָצִיתָ בָּנוּ, וְרוֹמַמְתָּנוּ מִכָּל הַלְּשׁוֹנוֹת
וְקִדַּשְׁתָּנוּ בְּמִצְוֹתֶיךָ, וְקֵרַבְתָּנוּ מַלְכֵּנוּ לַעֲבוֹדָתֶךָ
וְשִׁמְךָ הַגָּדוֹל וְהַקָּדוֹשׁ עָלֵינוּ קָרָאתָ.

On שבת, *add the words in parentheses:*

וַתִּתֶּן לָנוּ יהוה אֱלֹהֵינוּ בְּאַהֲבָה
(שַׁבָּתוֹת לִמְנוּחָה וּ)מוֹעֲדִים לְשִׂמְחָה, חַגִּים וּזְמַנִּים לְשָׂשׂוֹן
אֶת יוֹם (הַשַּׁבָּת הַזֶּה וְאֶת יוֹם)
חַג הַשָּׁבוּעוֹת הַזֶּה, זְמַן מַתַּן תּוֹרָתֵנוּ
(בְּאַהֲבָה) מִקְרָא קֹדֶשׁ, זֵכֶר לִיצִיאַת מִצְרָיִם.

אֱלֹהֵינוּ וֵאלֹהֵי אֲבוֹתֵינוּ
יַעֲלֶה וְיָבוֹא וְיַגִּיעַ וְיֵרָאֶה וְיֵרָצֶה וְיִשָּׁמַע
וְיִפָּקֵד וְיִזָּכֵר זִכְרוֹנֵנוּ וּפִקְדוֹנֵנוּ וְזִכְרוֹן אֲבוֹתֵינוּ
וְזִכְרוֹן מָשִׁיחַ בֶּן דָּוִד עַבְדֶּךָ
וְזִכְרוֹן יְרוּשָׁלַיִם עִיר קָדְשֶׁךָ
וְזִכְרוֹן כָּל עַמְּךָ בֵּית יִשְׂרָאֵל, לְפָנֶיךָ

אַתָּה בְחַרְתָּנוּ *You have chosen us.* The three pilgrimage festivals, Pesah, Shavuot and Sukkot are festivals of history. Therefore the Amida on these days emphasizes the uniqueness of Jewish history, for in and through the extraordinary

for deliverance and well-being,
grace, loving-kindness and compassion,
life and peace,

on this day of the festival of Shavuot.
On it remember us, LORD our God, for good;
recollect us for blessing, and deliver us for life.
In accord with Your promise of salvation and compassion,
spare us and be gracious to us;
have compassion on us and deliver us,
for our eyes are turned to You
because You, God, are a gracious and compassionate King.

On Shabbat, add the words in parentheses:

וְהַשִּׂיאֵנוּ Bestow on us, LORD our God,
the blessings of Your festivals
for good life and peace, joy and gladness,
as You desired and promised to bless us.
(Our God and God of our fathers, find favor in our rest.)
Make us holy through Your commandments
and grant us a share in Your Torah.
Satisfy us with Your goodness,
gladden us with Your salvation,
and purify our hearts to serve You in truth.
Grant us as our heritage, LORD our God (with love and favor,)
with joy and gladness, Your holy (Sabbath and) festivals,
and may Israel, who sanctify Your name, rejoice in You.
Blessed are You, LORD,
who sanctifies (the Sabbath and) Israel and the festive seasons.

---

(4) lifting, raising; and many others. The richness of resonances of the verb
may reflect the multidimensional nature of the experience of the pilgrimage
festivals: reliving history, celebrating the season and its harvest, together with
the joy of journeying to Jerusalem, being in the Temple and being part of a
thronged national celebration.

לִפְלֵיטָה, לְטוֹבָה, לְחֵן וּלְחֶסֶד וּלְרַחֲמִים
לְחַיִּים וּלְשָׁלוֹם
בְּיוֹם חַג הַשָּׁבוּעוֹת הַזֶּה.
זׇכְרֵנוּ יהוה אֱלֹהֵינוּ בּוֹ לְטוֹבָה
וּפׇקְדֵנוּ בוֹ לִבְרָכָה, וְהוֹשִׁיעֵנוּ בוֹ לְחַיִּים.
וּבִדְבַר יְשׁוּעָה וְרַחֲמִים, חוּס וְחׇנֵּנוּ
וְרַחֵם עָלֵינוּ וְהוֹשִׁיעֵנוּ
כִּי אֵלֶיךָ עֵינֵינוּ, כִּי אֵל מֶלֶךְ חַנּוּן וְרַחוּם אָתָּה.

On שבת, add the words in parentheses:

וְהַשִּׂיאֵנוּ יהוה אֱלֹהֵינוּ אֶת בִּרְכַּת מוֹעֲדֶיךָ
לְחַיִּים וּלְשָׁלוֹם, לְשִׂמְחָה וּלְשָׂשׂוֹן
כַּאֲשֶׁר רָצִיתָ וְאָמַרְתָּ לְבָרְכֵנוּ.
(אֱלֹהֵינוּ וֵאלֹהֵי אֲבוֹתֵינוּ, רְצֵה בִמְנוּחָתֵנוּ)
קַדְּשֵׁנוּ בְּמִצְוֹתֶיךָ, וְתֵן חֶלְקֵנוּ בְּתוֹרָתֶךָ
שַׂבְּעֵנוּ מִטּוּבֶךָ, וְשַׂמְּחֵנוּ בִּישׁוּעָתֶךָ
וְטַהֵר לִבֵּנוּ לְעׇבְדְּךָ בֶּאֱמֶת.
וְהַנְחִילֵנוּ יהוה אֱלֹהֵינוּ (בְּאַהֲבָה וּבְרָצוֹן)
בְּשִׂמְחָה וּבְשָׂשׂוֹן (שַׁבָּת וּ)מוֹעֲדֵי קׇדְשֶׁךָ
וְיִשְׂמְחוּ בְךָ יִשְׂרָאֵל מְקַדְּשֵׁי שְׁמֶךָ.
בָּרוּךְ אַתָּה יהוה, מְקַדֵּשׁ (הַשַּׁבָּת וְ)יִשְׂרָאֵל וְהַזְּמַנִּים.

The verb פ-ק-ד, "to recollect," refers to an act of focused attention and may also involve the emotions and the will.

וְהַשִּׂיאֵנוּ *Bestow on us.* A verb that has a multiplicity of meanings, among them: (1) giving a gift, (2) loading, (3) causing someone to receive a blessing,

TEMPLE SERVICE

רְצֵה Find favor, LORD our God,
in Your people Israel and their prayer.
Restore the service to Your most holy House,
and accept in love and favor
the fire-offerings of Israel and their prayer.
May the service of Your people Israel always find favor with You.
And may our eyes witness Your return to Zion in compassion.
Blessed are You, LORD, who restores His Presence to Zion.

THANKSGIVING

Bow at the first nine words.

מוֹדִים We give thanks to You,
for You are the LORD our God
and God of our ancestors
for ever and all time.
You are the Rock of our lives,
Shield of our salvation
from generation to generation.
We will thank You and
declare Your praise for our lives,
which are entrusted into Your hand;
for our souls,
which are placed in Your charge;
for Your miracles
which are with us every day;
and for Your wonders and favors
at all times, evening,
morning and midday.
You are good –
for Your compassion never fails.
You are compassionate –
for Your loving-kindnesses never cease.
We have always placed our hope in You.

*During the Leader's Repetition,
the congregation says quietly:*

מוֹדִים We give thanks to You,
for You are the LORD our God
and God of our ancestors,
God of all flesh,
who formed us
and formed the universe.
Blessings and thanks
are due to Your great
and holy name for giving us
life and sustaining us.
May You continue
to give us life and sustain us;
and may You gather our
exiles to Your holy courts,
to keep Your decrees,
do Your will and serve You
with a perfect heart,
for it is for us
to give You thanks.
Blessed be God to whom
thanksgiving is due.

עבודה

רְצֵה יהוה אֱלֹהֵינוּ בְּעַמְּךָ יִשְׂרָאֵל, וּבִתְפִלָּתָם

וְהָשֵׁב אֶת הָעֲבוֹדָה לִדְבִיר בֵּיתֶךָ

וְאִשֵּׁי יִשְׂרָאֵל וּתְפִלָּתָם בְּאַהֲבָה תְקַבֵּל בְּרָצוֹן

וּתְהִי לְרָצוֹן תָּמִיד עֲבוֹדַת יִשְׂרָאֵל עַמֶּךָ.

וְתֶחֱזֶינָה עֵינֵינוּ בְּשׁוּבְךָ לְצִיּוֹן בְּרַחֲמִים.

בָּרוּךְ אַתָּה יהוה, הַמַּחֲזִיר שְׁכִינָתוֹ לְצִיּוֹן.

הודאה

Bow at the first five words.

יּמוֹדִים אֲנַחְנוּ לָךְ

שָׁאַתָּה הוּא יהוה אֱלֹהֵינוּ

וֵאלֹהֵי אֲבוֹתֵינוּ לְעוֹלָם וָעֶד.

צוּר חַיֵּינוּ, מָגֵן יִשְׁעֵנוּ

אַתָּה הוּא לְדוֹר וָדוֹר.

נוֹדֶה לְּךָ וּנְסַפֵּר תְּהִלָּתֶךָ

עַל חַיֵּינוּ הַמְּסוּרִים בְּיָדֶךָ

וְעַל נִשְׁמוֹתֵינוּ הַפְּקוּדוֹת לָךְ

וְעַל נִסֶּיךָ שֶׁבְּכָל יוֹם עִמָּנוּ

וְעַל נִפְלְאוֹתֶיךָ וְטוֹבוֹתֶיךָ

שֶׁבְּכָל עֵת

עֶרֶב וָבֹקֶר וְצָהֳרָיִם.

הַטּוֹב, כִּי לֹא כָלוּ רַחֲמֶיךָ

וְהַמְרַחֵם, כִּי לֹא תַמּוּ חֲסָדֶיךָ

מֵעוֹלָם קִוִּינוּ לָךְ.

During the חזרת הש״ץ,
the קהל *says quietly:*

יּמוֹדִים אֲנַחְנוּ לָךְ

שָׁאַתָּה הוּא יהוה אֱלֹהֵינוּ

וֵאלֹהֵי אֲבוֹתֵינוּ

אֱלֹהֵי כָל בָּשָׂר

יוֹצְרֵנוּ, יוֹצֵר בְּרֵאשִׁית

בְּרָכוֹת וְהוֹדָאוֹת

לְשִׁמְךָ הַגָּדוֹל וְהַקָּדוֹשׁ

עַל שֶׁהֶחֱיִיתָנוּ וְקִיַּמְתָּנוּ.

כֵּן תְּחַיֵּנוּ וּתְקַיְּמֵנוּ

וְתֶאֱסֹף גָּלֻיּוֹתֵינוּ

לְחַצְרוֹת קָדְשֶׁךָ

לִשְׁמֹר חֻקֶּיךָ

וְלַעֲשׂוֹת רְצוֹנֶךָ וּלְעָבְדְּךָ

בְּלֵבָב שָׁלֵם

עַל שֶׁאֲנַחְנוּ מוֹדִים לָךְ.

בָּרוּךְ אֵל הַהוֹדָאוֹת.

וְעַל כֻּלָּם For all these things
may Your name be blessed and exalted, our King,
continually, for ever and all time.
Let all that lives thank You, Selah!
and praise Your name in truth, God, our Savior and Help, Selah!
▾Blessed are You, LORD,
whose name is "the Good" and to whom thanks are due.

For the blessing of the Kohanim in Israel, see page 696.
The Leader says the following during the Repetition of the Shaharit Amida.
It is also said in Israel when no Kohanim bless the congregation.

Our God and God of our fathers, bless us with the threefold blessing in the Torah,
written by the hand of Moses Your servant and pronounced by Aaron and his
sons the priests, Your holy people, as it is said:

> May the LORD bless you and protect you.   *Num. 6*
>> *Cong:* May it be Your will.
> May the LORD make His face shine on you and be gracious to you.
>> *Cong:* May it be Your will.
> May the LORD turn His face toward you, and grant you peace.
>> *Cong:* May it be Your will.

PEACE
שִׂים שָׁלוֹם Grant peace, goodness and blessing,
grace, loving-kindness and compassion
to us and all Israel Your people.
Bless us, our Father, all as one, with the light of Your face,
for by the light of Your face You have given us, LORD our God,
the Torah of life and love of kindness,
righteousness, blessing, compassion, life and peace.
May it be good in Your eyes to bless Your people Israel
at every time, in every hour, with Your peace.
Blessed are You, LORD,
who blesses His people Israel with peace.

The following verse concludes the Leader's Repetition of the Amida.
Some also say it here as part of the silent Amida.

May the words of my mouth and the meditation of my heart   *Ps. 19*
find favor before You, LORD, my Rock and Redeemer.

וְעַל כֻּלָּם יִתְבָּרַךְ וְיִתְרוֹמַם שִׁמְךָ מַלְכֵּנוּ תָּמִיד לְעוֹלָם וָעֶד.

וְכֹל הַחַיִּים יוֹדוּךָ סֶּלָה, וִיהַלְלוּ אֶת שִׁמְךָ בֶּאֱמֶת

הָאֵל יְשׁוּעָתֵנוּ וְעֶזְרָתֵנוּ סֶלָה.

יָּבָרוּךְ אַתָּה יהוה, הַטּוֹב שִׁמְךָ וּלְךָ נָאֶה לְהוֹדוֹת.

For the blessing of the כהנים *in* ארץ ישראל *see page 697.*
The שליח ציבור *of* חזרת הש״ץ *says the following during the* שחרית.
It is also said in ארץ ישראל *when no* כהנים *bless the congregation.*

אֱלֹהֵינוּ וֵאלֹהֵי אֲבוֹתֵינוּ, בָּרְכֵנוּ בַּבְּרָכָה הַמְשֻׁלֶּשֶׁת בַּתּוֹרָה, הַכְּתוּבָה עַל

במדברו יְדֵי מֹשֶׁה עַבְדֶּךָ, הָאֲמוּרָה מִפִּי אַהֲרֹן וּבָנָיו כֹּהֲנִים עַם קְדוֹשֶׁיךָ, כָּאָמוּר

יְבָרֶכְךָ יהוה וְיִשְׁמְרֶךָ: קהל: כֵּן יְהִי רָצוֹן

יָאֵר יהוה פָּנָיו אֵלֶיךָ וִיחֻנֶּךָּ: קהל: כֵּן יְהִי רָצוֹן

יִשָּׂא יהוה פָּנָיו אֵלֶיךָ וְיָשֵׂם לְךָ שָׁלוֹם: קהל: כֵּן יְהִי רָצוֹן

בַּרְכַּת שָׁלוֹם

שִׂים שָׁלוֹם טוֹבָה וּבְרָכָה

חֵן וָחֶסֶד וְרַחֲמִים עָלֵינוּ וְעַל כָּל יִשְׂרָאֵל עַמֶּךָ.

בָּרְכֵנוּ אָבִינוּ כֻּלָּנוּ כְּאֶחָד בְּאוֹר פָּנֶיךָ

כִּי בְאוֹר פָּנֶיךָ נָתַתָּ לָּנוּ יהוה אֱלֹהֵינוּ

תּוֹרַת חַיִּים וְאַהֲבַת חֶסֶד

וּצְדָקָה וּבְרָכָה וְרַחֲמִים וְחַיִּים וְשָׁלוֹם.

וְטוֹב בְּעֵינֶיךָ לְבָרֵךְ אֶת עַמְּךָ יִשְׂרָאֵל

בְּכָל עֵת וּבְכָל שָׁעָה בִּשְׁלוֹמֶךָ.

בָּרוּךְ אַתָּה יהוה, הַמְבָרֵךְ אֶת עַמּוֹ יִשְׂרָאֵל בַּשָּׁלוֹם.

The following verse concludes the חזרת הש״ץ.
Some also say it here as part of the silent עמידה.

תהלים יט יִהְיוּ לְרָצוֹן אִמְרֵי־פִי וְהֶגְיוֹן לִבִּי לְפָנֶיךָ, יהוה צוּרִי וְגֹאֲלִי:

אֱלֹהַי My God, Berakhot 17a
guard my tongue from evil and my lips from deceitful speech.
To those who curse me, let my soul be silent;
may my soul be to all like the dust.
Open my heart to Your Torah
and let my soul pursue Your commandments.
As for all who plan evil against me,
swiftly thwart their counsel and frustrate their plans.

> Act for the sake of Your name;
> act for the sake of Your right hand;
> act for the sake of Your holiness;
> act for the sake of Your Torah.

That Your beloved ones may be delivered, Ps. 60
save with Your right hand and answer me.

May the words of my mouth and the meditation of my heart Ps. 19
find favor before You, LORD, my Rock and Redeemer.

Bow, take three steps back, then bow, first left, then right, then center, while saying:

May He who makes peace in His high places,
make peace for us and all Israel – and say: Amen.

יְהִי רָצוֹן May it be Your will, LORD our God and God of our ancestors,
that the Temple be rebuilt speedily in our days,
and grant us a share in Your Torah.
And there we will serve You with reverence,
as in the days of old and as in former years.
Then the offering of Judah and Jerusalem Mal. 3
will be pleasing to the LORD as in the days of old and as in former years.

The Leader repeats the Amida (page 346).

*In congregations that recite piyutim, the Repetition
for the first day begins on page 707;
for the second day on page 747.*

ברכות יז.

אֱלֹהַי

נְצֹר לְשׁוֹנִי מֵרָע וּשְׂפָתַי מִדַּבֵּר מִרְמָה

וְלִמְקַלְלַי נַפְשִׁי תִדֹּם, וְנַפְשִׁי כֶּעָפָר לַכֹּל תִּהְיֶה.

פְּתַח לִבִּי בְּתוֹרָתֶךָ, וּבְמִצְוֹתֶיךָ תִּרְדֹּף נַפְשִׁי.

וְכָל הַחוֹשְׁבִים עָלַי רָעָה

מְהֵרָה הָפֵר עֲצָתָם וְקַלְקֵל מַחֲשַׁבְתָּם.

עֲשֵׂה לְמַעַן שְׁמֶךָ, עֲשֵׂה לְמַעַן יְמִינֶךָ

עֲשֵׂה לְמַעַן קְדָשָּׁתֶךָ, עֲשֵׂה לְמַעַן תּוֹרָתֶךָ.

תהלים ס

לְמַעַן יֵחָלְצוּן יְדִידֶיךָ, הוֹשִׁיעָה יְמִינְךָ וַעֲנֵנִי:

תהלים יט

יִהְיוּ לְרָצוֹן אִמְרֵי־פִי וְהֶגְיוֹן לִבִּי לְפָנֶיךָ, יהוה צוּרִי וְגֹאֲלִי:

Bow, take three steps back, then bow, first left, then right, then center, while saying:

עֹשֶׂה שָׁלוֹם בִּמְרוֹמָיו

הוּא יַעֲשֶׂה שָׁלוֹם עָלֵינוּ וְעַל כָּל יִשְׂרָאֵל, וְאִמְרוּ אָמֵן.

יְהִי רָצוֹן מִלְּפָנֶיךָ יהוה אֱלֹהֵינוּ וֵאלֹהֵי אֲבוֹתֵינוּ

שֶׁיִּבָּנֶה בֵּית הַמִּקְדָּשׁ בִּמְהֵרָה בְיָמֵינוּ

וְתֵן חֶלְקֵנוּ בְּתוֹרָתֶךָ

וְשָׁם נַעֲבָדְךָ בְּיִרְאָה כִּימֵי עוֹלָם וּכְשָׁנִים קַדְמֹנִיּוֹת.

מלאכי ג

וְעָרְבָה לַיהוה מִנְחַת יְהוּדָה וִירוּשָׁלָם כִּימֵי עוֹלָם וּכְשָׁנִים קַדְמֹנִיּוֹת:

The שליח ציבור repeats the עמידה (page 347).

*In congregations that recite piyutim, the חזרת הש"ץ
for the first day begins on page 707;
for the second day on page 747.*

Hallel

בָּרוּךְ Blessed are You, LORD our God, King of the Universe,
who has made us holy through His commandments
and has commanded us to recite the Hallel.

הַלְלוּיָהּ Halleluya! Servants of the LORD, give praise; praise the name   *Ps. 113*
of the LORD. Blessed be the name of the LORD now and for ever-
more. From the rising of the sun to its setting, may the LORD's name
be praised. High is the LORD above all nations; His glory is above

---

after they had defeated Sisera; Hezekiah and the people who survived
the siege of Sennacherib; Hananiah, Mishael and Azariah after surviving
Nebuchadnezzar's fiery furnace; and Mordekhai and Esther after their deliverance from Haman (*Pesaḥim* 119a). The saying of Hallel was also ordained
after the victory of the Maccabees against the Seleucid Greeks.

Hallel is said during Pesaḥ, Shavuot, Sukkot, Shemini Atzeret, Simḥat
Torah and Ḥanukka – and in modern times, also on Yom HaAtzma'ut and
Yom Yerushalayim. It is a feature of the Pesaḥ Seder service (some also say
it in the synagogue at the end of Ma'ariv). On Rosh Ḥodesh and the last
days of Pesaḥ, the custom arose to say an abridged form (known as "Half
Hallel").

Hallel is supremely the poetry of the three pilgrimage festivals, as Jews
remember the deliverances of the past, give thanks for the present, and pray
for a safe future. It is constructed in three movements: (1) Psalms 113–115
are songs of collective gratitude and indebtedness to God, (2) Psalm 116 is a
song sung over a thanksgiving-offering (*korban toda*), and (3) Psalms 117–118
reflect the joy of the pilgrims as they celebrate in the Temple.

הַלְלוּיָהּ *Psalm 113. Halleluya!* A prelude to the praises that follow. The verb
ה-ל-ל, "to praise in joyous song" – from which come the words *Tehillim*, the
generic name for the psalms, and *Halleluya*, "Praise God" – appears three
times in the first verse, setting the mood of elation. It appears five times in
the psalm, and ten times in Hallel as a whole.

מֵעַתָּה וְעַד־עוֹלָם: מִמִּזְרַח־שֶׁמֶשׁ *Now and for evermore. From the rising of the sun.*
God's praises echo through all time and space.

סדר הלל

בָּרוּךְ אַתָּה יהוה אֱלֹהֵינוּ מֶלֶךְ הָעוֹלָם
אֲשֶׁר קִדְּשָׁנוּ בְּמִצְוֹתָיו וְצִוָּנוּ לִקְרֹא אֶת הַהַלֵּל.

הַלְלוּיָהּ, הַלְלוּ עַבְדֵי יהוה, הַלְלוּ אֶת־שֵׁם יהוה: יְהִי שֵׁם יהוה __ תהלים קיג
מְבֹרָךְ, מֵעַתָּה וְעַד־עוֹלָם: מִמִּזְרַח־שֶׁמֶשׁ עַד־מְבוֹאוֹ, מְהֻלָּל שֵׁם
יהוה: רָם עַל־כָּל־גּוֹיִם יהוה, עַל הַשָּׁמַיִם כְּבוֹדוֹ: מִי כַּיהוה אֱלֹהֵינוּ,

---

HALLEL

The six psalms, 113–118, known as Hallel, form a distinct unit that was sung on festivals in the Second Temple. It is sometimes known as the Egyptian Hallel (because of the reference to the exodus from Egypt in the second paragraph) to distinguish it from the daily Hallel (Psalms 145–150) and the "Great Hallel," Psalms 135 and 136, sung on Shabbat.

To get a sense of what Hallel in the Temple was like, we have to imagine the throng of pilgrims who have come to Jerusalem from all over Israel to "be seen by the LORD your God, three times each year" (Ex. 34:24). Eyewitness testimony tells us that on one Pesaḥ when the worshipers were counted, there were found to be 1.2 million people, "twice the number of those who came out of Egypt" (*Pesaḥim* 64b). Jerusalem was packed, the roads leading up to it often blocked by the sheer number of pilgrims, and the Temple courtyard so full that it was considered a miracle that "though people stood crowded together, there was room enough for them to prostrate themselves."

The Levites sang, musical instruments played (something not permitted on holy days outside the Temple), and as the leader sang the verses, the crowd responded with refrains: "Halleluya," "His loving-kindness is for ever," "LORD, please, save us," and other responses. It was colorful, atmospheric, joyous: a people coming to pay homage to God who had brought it to freedom, watched over its destinies and saved it from its enemies.

Hallel is the oldest extended sequence of prayer that has been preserved in its entirety. The sages sensed in it echoes of ancient songs of deliverance: Moses and the Israelites after they had crossed the Sea of Reeds; Joshua and the Israelites after their battles of conquest; Deborah and Barak

the heavens. Who is like the LORD our God, who sits enthroned so high, yet turns so low to see the heavens and the earth? ▸ He raises the poor from the dust and the needy from the refuse heap, giving them a place alongside princes, the princes of His people. He makes the woman in a childless house a happy mother of children. Halleluya!

בְּצֵאת When Israel came out of Egypt, the house of Jacob from a *Ps. 114* people of foreign tongue, Judah became His sanctuary, Israel His dominion. The sea saw and fled; the Jordan turned back. The mountains skipped like rams, the hills like lambs. ▸ Why was it, sea, that you fled? Jordan, why did you turn back? Why, mountains, did you skip like rams, and you, hills, like lambs? It was at the presence of the LORD, Creator of the earth, at the presence of the God of Jacob, who turned the rock into a pool of water, flint into a flowing spring.

הַיָּם רָאָה וַיָּנֹס *The sea saw and fled.* An elision of two separate events: the division of the Sea of Reeds in the days of Moses, and the parting of the Jordan in the days of Joshua.

הֶהָרִים רָקְדוּ *The mountains skipped.* A description, echoing Psalm 29, of how the earth moved when the Torah was given at Sinai.

מַה־לְּךָ *Why was it.* An unusual recasting of the previous two lines in the form of a series of rhetorical questions, heightening the tension before the triumphant declaration of the name of God.

הַהֹפְכִי הַצּוּר *Who turned the rock.* A reference to the occasions (Ex. 17; Num. 20) when God, through Moses, brought water from the rocks so that a parched and thirsty people could drink.

Rabbi Joseph Soloveitchik has an insightful comment on this passage. There are two types of personal and political change, one brought about by physical force (conquest), the other by spiritual transformation (sanctity). Conquest involves a change of masters, but slaves remain slaves. Sanctity involves a change in the person him- or herself. The slave, achieving inner freedom, is no longer existentially a slave. Thus in Jewish law a slave whose master puts tefillin on him goes free (*Gittin* 40a), and a slave from outside

הַמַּגְבִּיהִי לָשֶׁבֶת: הַמַּשְׁפִּילִי לִרְאוֹת, בַּשָּׁמַיִם וּבָאָרֶץ: ‹ מְקִימִי
מֵעָפָר דָּל, מֵאַשְׁפֹּת יָרִים אֶבְיוֹן: לְהוֹשִׁיבִי עִם־נְדִיבִים, עִם נְדִיבֵי
עַמּוֹ: מוֹשִׁיבִי עֲקֶרֶת הַבַּיִת, אֵם־הַבָּנִים שְׂמֵחָה, הַלְלוּיָהּ:

תהלים קיד

בְּצֵאת יִשְׂרָאֵל מִמִּצְרָיִם, בֵּית יַעֲקֹב מֵעַם לֹעֵז: הָיְתָה יְהוּדָה
לְקָדְשׁוֹ, יִשְׂרָאֵל מַמְשְׁלוֹתָיו: הַיָּם רָאָה וַיָּנֹס, הַיַּרְדֵּן יִסֹּב לְאָחוֹר:
הֶהָרִים רָקְדוּ כְאֵילִים, גְּבָעוֹת כִּבְנֵי־צֹאן: ‹ מַה־לְּךָ הַיָּם כִּי תָנוּס,
הַיַּרְדֵּן תִּסֹּב לְאָחוֹר: הֶהָרִים תִּרְקְדוּ כְאֵילִים, גְּבָעוֹת כִּבְנֵי־צֹאן:
מִלִּפְנֵי אָדוֹן חֽוּלִי אָרֶץ, מִלִּפְנֵי אֱלֽוֹהַּ יַעֲקֹב: הַהֹפְכִי הַצּוּר אֲגַם־
מָיִם, חַלָּמִישׁ לְמַעְיְנוֹ־מָיִם:

הַמַּגְבִּיהִי לָשֶׁבֶת: הַמַּשְׁפִּילִי לִרְאוֹת *Who sits enthroned so high, yet turns so low to see.* Though God is beyond the heavens, He sees all that happens on earth. God is close to all who seek to be close to Him, and He is never far from those who need His help.

מְקִימִי מֵעָפָר דָּל *He raises the poor from the dust.* This section is strikingly reminiscent of Hannah's song of thanksgiving after God answered her prayers for a child. She sang: "He lifts the poor out of the dust and rasises abject men from the dunghills, to seat them up there with princes, to bequeath them chairs of honor" (I Sam. 2:6–7). God cares for great and small alike; in His eyes there are no distinctions of class or caste. God humbles the arrogant and lifts the humble. The deep underlying egalitarianism of the Hebrew Bible – that we are all equal in dignity under the sovereignty of God – was a revolutionary idea in the ancient world and remains so today.

בְּצֵאת יִשְׂרָאֵל מִמִּצְרָיִם *Psalm 114. When Israel came out of Egypt.* The psalm starts slowly, opening with a subordinate clause and delaying explicit mention of God's name until the penultimate verse. It builds to a tremendous climax, bringing together a series of miracles that happened to the Israelites in the days of Moses and Joshua. Inanimate nature – sea, river, mountains, hills, rock, flint – come alive, trembling and retreating at the approach of God.

לֹא לָנוּ Not to us, Lᴏʀᴅ, not to us, but to Your name give glory, for Your   *Ps. 115*
love, for Your faithfulness. Why should the nations say, "Where now is
their God?" Our God is in heaven; whatever He wills He does. Their
idols are silver and gold, made by human hands. They have mouths
but cannot speak; eyes but cannot see. They have ears but cannot
hear; noses but cannot smell. They have hands but cannot feel; feet
but cannot walk. No sound comes from their throat. Those who make
them become like them; so will all who trust in them. ▸ Israel, trust in
the Lᴏʀᴅ – He is their Help and their Shield. House of Aaron, trust in
the Lᴏʀᴅ – He is their Help and their Shield. You who fear the Lᴏʀᴅ,
trust in the Lᴏʀᴅ – He is their Help and their Shield.

---

idolatry. The contrast between God and the idols is brought out by the words
asa, "Whatever He wills He does," and *ma'aseh*, "made by human hands."
God *makes*; idols are *made*. God makes man in His image; man makes idols
in his. Hence, "Those who make them become like them." We are shaped by
what we worship. Those who worship lifeless icons become lifeless. Only by
worshiping the God of life do we truly live.

יִשְׂרָאֵל בְּטַח בַּיהוה *Israel, trust in the Lᴏʀᴅ.* The Psalmist turns to three groups
of people worshiping in the Temple: *Israel*, the Jewish worshipers, *House of
Aaron*, the officiating priests and Levites, and *You who fear the* Lᴏʀᴅ, meaning
converts (Rashi) or righteous gentiles of all nations (Ibn Ezra). In his song
at the dedication of the Temple, Solomon foresaw that gentiles, not just
Jews, would come to the Temple to pray (1 Kings 8:41–43). Isaiah envisions
the day when "My House shall be called a house of prayer for all peoples"
(Is. 56:7). The sharp opposition to idolatry in this psalm does not preclude a
universalistic openness to humanity as a whole.

עֶזְרָם וּמָגִנָּם הוּא *He is their Help and their Shield.* This thrice-repeated phrase
may originally have been a congregational response.

יהוה זְכָרָנוּ *The* Lᴏʀᴅ *remembers us.* Still part of Psalm 115, the Psalmist asks
God to bless the same three groups as above: Israel, the House of Aaron and
those who fear the Lᴏʀᴅ among the nations.

הַשָּׁמַיִם שָׁמַיִם לַיהוה, וְהָאָרֶץ נָתַן לִבְנֵי־אָדָם *The heavens are the* Lᴏʀᴅ*'s, but the earth
He has given over to mankind.* When God is God, humanity can be humane,

לֹא לָנוּ יהוה לֹא לָנוּ, כִּי־לְשִׁמְךָ תֵּן כָּבוֹד, עַל־חַסְדְּךָ עַל־אֲמִתֶּךָ: לָמָּה יֹאמְרוּ הַגּוֹיִם אַיֵּה־נָא אֱלֹהֵיהֶם: וֵאלֹהֵינוּ בַשָּׁמָיִם, כֹּל אֲשֶׁר־ חָפֵץ עָשָׂה: עֲצַבֵּיהֶם כֶּסֶף וְזָהָב, מַעֲשֵׂה יְדֵי אָדָם: פֶּה־לָהֶם וְלֹא יְדַבֵּרוּ, עֵינַיִם לָהֶם וְלֹא יִרְאוּ: אָזְנַיִם לָהֶם וְלֹא יִשְׁמָעוּ, אַף לָהֶם וְלֹא יְרִיחוּן: יְדֵיהֶם וְלֹא יְמִישׁוּן, רַגְלֵיהֶם וְלֹא יְהַלֵּכוּ, לֹא־יֶהְגּוּ בִּגְרוֹנָם: כְּמוֹהֶם יִהְיוּ עֹשֵׂיהֶם, כֹּל אֲשֶׁר־בֹּטֵחַ בָּהֶם: ‹ יִשְׂרָאֵל בְּטַח בַּיהוה, עֶזְרָם וּמָגִנָּם הוּא: בֵּית אַהֲרֹן בִּטְחוּ בַיהוה, עֶזְרָם וּמָגִנָּם הוּא: יִרְאֵי יהוה בִּטְחוּ בַיהוה, עֶזְרָם וּמָגִנָּם הוּא:

Israel who escapes to Israel is not returned to his master (*Gittin* 45a). Sanctity liberates from within.

That is why the Israelites had to celebrate the first Passover while they were still in Egypt. "Had the Jews not first redeemed themselves by self-sanctification on that night-of-watching in Egypt, the redemption through conquest [the signs and wonders of the exodus] would not have been complete." Hence *When Israel came out of Egypt ... Judah became His sanctuary, Israel His dominion.* Only after that, *the sea saw and fled.* The inner liberation had to precede the outer redemption (Rabbi J. Soloveitchik, *Festival of Freedom*).

לֹא לָנוּ *Psalm 115. Not to us.* According to some, this psalm is a continuation of the previous one. Recalling its past, Israel pledges itself to faith in God in the future (Radak). In the first three verses, the Psalmist pleads with God to protect His people, for His sake not ours.

לָמָּה יֹאמְרוּ הַגּוֹיִם אַיֵּה־נָא אֱלֹהֵיהֶם *Why should the nations say, "Where now is their God?"* The idea that Israel's sufferings constitute a desecration of God's name is first heard in Moses' plea after the sin of the golden calf: "Why should Egypt speak, and say, 'In an evil hour did He bring them out'" (Ex. 32:12). It is repeated in Moses' song at the end of his life, "I dreaded the taunt of the enemy, lest the adversary misunderstand and say, 'Our hand has triumphed; the Lord has not done all this'" (Deut. 32:27), and developed at length in Ezekiel 20. Israel are God's witnesses (Is. 43; 44). Therefore their fate affects how people think of God.

עֲצַבֵּיהֶם כֶּסֶף וְזָהָב *Their idols are silver and gold.* An extended polemic against

יהוה זְכָרָנוּ **The** Lord **remembers us and will bless us.** He will bless the house of Israel. He will bless the house of Aaron. He will bless those who fear the Lord, small and great alike. May the Lord give you increase: you and your children. May you be blessed by the Lord, Maker of heaven and earth. ‣ The heavens are the Lord's, but the earth He has given over to mankind. It is not the dead who praise the Lord, nor those who go down to the silent grave. But we will bless the Lord, now and for ever. Halleluya!

אָהַבְתִּי **I love the** Lord, **for He hears my voice, my pleas.** He turns His ear   Ps. 116
to me whenever I call. The bonds of death encompassed me, the anguish of the grave came upon me, I was overcome by trouble and sorrow. Then I called on the name of the Lord: "Lord, I pray, save my life." Gracious is the Lord, and righteous; our God is full of compassion. The Lord protects the simple hearted. When I was brought low, He saved me. My soul, be at peace once more, for the Lord has been good to you. For You have rescued me from death, my eyes from weeping, my feet from stumbling. ‣ I shall walk in the presence of the Lord in the land of the living. I had faith, even when I said, "I am greatly afflicted," even when I said rashly, "All men are liars."

─────────────────────────────────────

preceding it. It is deeply personal; it consistently uses the first person singular, "I" and "my." It tells of how the speaker turned to God in deep distress, close to death. God answered his prayer and saved him. Therefore he is bringing a thanksgiving-offering to fulfill the vow he made then. Several of the words have unusual, antiquated and poeticized endings which further slow the pace. At the end the poet turns to address Jerusalem in the second person ("in your midst, Jerusalem") as if it were an intimate friend.

שֹׁמֵר פְּתָאִים יהוה... שׁוּבִי נַפְשִׁי לִמְנוּחָיְכִי *The* Lord *protects the simple hearted…* *My soul, be at peace once more.* It is simple trust that has brought God's healing; therefore the poet urges himself not to be anxious but to trust and stay calm.

כִּי חִלַּצְתָּ נַפְשִׁי *For You have rescued me.* Now, becalmed, the poet turns directly to God, thanking Him for His deliverance.

בְּאַרְצוֹת הַחַיִּים *In the land of the living.* As was said in the previous psalm, "It is

יהוה זְכָרָנוּ יְבָרֵךְ, יְבָרֵךְ אֶת־בֵּית יִשְׂרָאֵל, יְבָרֵךְ אֶת־בֵּית אַהֲרֹן: יְבָרֵךְ יִרְאֵי יהוה, הַקְּטַנִּים עִם־הַגְּדֹלִים: יֹסֵף יהוה עֲלֵיכֶם, עֲלֵיכֶם וְעַל־בְּנֵיכֶם: בְּרוּכִים אַתֶּם לַיהוה, עֹשֵׂה שָׁמַיִם וָאָרֶץ: ‹ הַשָּׁמַיִם שָׁמַיִם לַיהוה, וְהָאָרֶץ נָתַן לִבְנֵי־אָדָם: לֹא הַמֵּתִים יְהַלְלוּ־יָהּ, וְלֹא כָּל־יֹרְדֵי דוּמָה: וַאֲנַחְנוּ נְבָרֵךְ יָהּ, מֵעַתָּה וְעַד־עוֹלָם, הַלְלוּיָהּ:

תהלים קטז

אָהַבְתִּי, כִּי־יִשְׁמַע יהוה, אֶת־קוֹלִי תַּחֲנוּנָי: כִּי־הִטָּה אָזְנוֹ לִי, וּבְיָמַי אֶקְרָא: אֲפָפוּנִי חֶבְלֵי־מָוֶת, וּמְצָרֵי שְׁאוֹל מְצָאוּנִי, צָרָה וְיָגוֹן אֶמְצָא: וּבְשֵׁם־יהוה אֶקְרָא, אָנָּה יהוה מַלְּטָה נַפְשִׁי: חַנּוּן יהוה וְצַדִּיק, וֵאלֹהֵינוּ מְרַחֵם: שֹׁמֵר פְּתָאִים יהוה, דַּלּוֹתִי וְלִי יְהוֹשִׁיעַ: שׁוּבִי נַפְשִׁי לִמְנוּחָיְכִי, כִּי־יהוה גָּמַל עָלָיְכִי: כִּי חִלַּצְתָּ נַפְשִׁי מִמָּוֶת, אֶת־עֵינִי מִן־דִּמְעָה, אֶת־רַגְלִי מִדֶּחִי: ‹ אֶתְהַלֵּךְ לִפְנֵי יהוה, בְּאַרְצוֹת הַחַיִּים: הֶאֱמַנְתִּי כִּי אֲדַבֵּר, אֲנִי עָנִיתִי מְאֹד: אֲנִי אָמַרְתִּי בְחָפְזִי, כָּל־הָאָדָם כֹּזֵב:

---

but when man tries to be like God he becomes inhumane. It was the attempt to build "a tower that reaches to the heavens" that was the sin of the builders of Babel (Gen. 11:4). God has given us the earth, but He reigns supreme; and we must have humility, knowing the proper limits of our striving. When humans have worshiped other humans as gods, the result has been hubris followed by nemesis, often involving tyranny and bloodshed on a massive scale.

לֹא הַמֵּתִים יְהַלְלוּ־יָהּ *It is not the dead who praise the LORD.* A theme sounded often in the book of Psalms. The God of life is to be found in life.

וַאֲנַחְנוּ נְבָרֵךְ יָהּ *But we will bless the LORD.* One of the best-known lines of Psalms, having been added as a conclusion to *Ashrei* and thus said three times daily.

אָהַבְתִּי *Psalm 116. I love the LORD.* The second section of Hallel is the slow movement in the symphony, significantly different in tone from those

מֶה־אָשִׁיב How can I repay the Lᴏʀᴅ for all His goodness to me? I will lift the cup of salvation and call on the name of the Lᴏʀᴅ. I will fulfill my vows to the Lᴏʀᴅ in the presence of all His people. Grievous in the Lᴏʀᴅ's sight is the death of His devoted ones. Truly, Lᴏʀᴅ, I am Your servant; I am Your servant, the son of Your maidservant. You set me free from my chains. ‣ To You I shall bring a thanksgiving-offering and call on the Lᴏʀᴅ by name. I will fulfill my vows to the Lᴏʀᴅ in the presence of all His people, in the courts of the House of the Lᴏʀᴅ, in your midst, Jerusalem. Halleluya.

הַלְלוּ Praise the Lᴏʀᴅ, all nations; acclaim Him, all you peoples;　　*Ps. 117*
　　　　for His loving-kindness to us is strong,
　　　　　　and the Lᴏʀᴅ's faithfulness is everlasting.
　　　　　　　　Halleluya.

נְדָרַי לַיהוה אֲשַׁלֵּם *I will fulfill my vows to the Lᴏʀᴅ.* This sentence appears twice in the psalm, which contains a number of other repetitions (such as "I am Your servant") for poetic effect.

הַלְלוּ *Psalm 117. Praise.* The briefest of psalms, the shortest chapter in Tanakh, this psalm fulfills three functions. First, it reestablishes the mood of public worship after the introspective and private nature of the previous psalm. Second, it serves as a prelude to the great psalm that follows. Third, it is a call, a summons to the crowd inviting them to take part in what is about to follow: an act of praise and thanks that will involve their active participation.

At one level the leader is inviting the entire crowd, both Jews and gentiles (the "God-fearers" of the previous psalms) to join in an act of praise. At a deeper level he is articulating a belief that runs through Jewish history, beginning with God's first call to Abraham: "Through you all the nations of the earth shall be blessed." Jewish history is of significance not just to Jews but to humanity. Jews are God's witnesses to the world. Those who try to destroy people's belief in God – the God who stands above all nations and powers – try to destroy the Jewish people. Those who respect God tend to respect the Jewish people. The Jews are God's question mark over all attempts to rule by power and persuade by force.

חַסְדּוֹ, וֶאֱמֶת *His loving-kindness… faithfulness.* Ḥesed and *emet,* the two words

מָה־אָשִׁיב לַיהוה, כָּל־תַּגְמוּלְוֹהִי עָלָי: כּוֹס־יְשׁוּעוֹת אֶשָּׂא, וּבְשֵׁם
יהוה אֶקְרָא: נְדָרַי לַיהוה אֲשַׁלֵּם, נֶגְדָה־נָּא לְכָל־עַמּוֹ: יָקָר בְּעֵינֵי
יהוה, הַמָּוְתָה לַחֲסִידָיו: אָנָּה יהוה כִּי־אֲנִי עַבְדֶּךָ, אֲנִי־עַבְדְּךָ
בֶּן־אֲמָתֶךָ, פִּתַּחְתָּ לְמוֹסֵרָי: ◀ לְךָ־אֶזְבַּח זֶבַח תּוֹדָה, וּבְשֵׁם יהוה
אֶקְרָא: נְדָרַי לַיהוה אֲשַׁלֵּם, נֶגְדָה־נָּא לְכָל־עַמּוֹ: בְּחַצְרוֹת בֵּית
יהוה, בְּתוֹכֵכִי יְרוּשָׁלָיִם, הַלְלוּיָהּ:

תהלים קיז

הַלְלוּ אֶת־יהוה כָּל־גּוֹיִם, שַׁבְּחוּהוּ כָּל־הָאֻמִּים:
כִּי גָבַר עָלֵינוּ חַסְדּוֹ, וֶאֱמֶת־יהוה לְעוֹלָם
הַלְלוּיָהּ:

---

not the dead who praise the Lᴏʀᴅ." The poet is thanking God for the physical gift of life and the spiritual gift of being able to "walk in the presence of the Lᴏʀᴅ."

הֶאֱמַנְתִּי...אֲנִי אָמַרְתִּי בְחָפְזִי, כָּל־הָאָדָם כֹּזֵב *I had faith … even when I said rashly, "All men are liars" (previous page)*. The commentators relate this to King David who, when forced to flee from Saul, felt betrayed by everyone. Alternatively, "Even when I was fleeing for my life, I knew that those [who preached despair] were false" (Radak).

מָה־אָשִׁיב לַיהוה *How can I repay the Lᴏʀᴅ*. A rhetorical question. We cannot repay God for what He has given us. Faith is, among other things, gratitude – the sense of life-as-a-gift that we often only have when we have come close to losing it.

כּוֹס־יְשׁוּעוֹת אֶשָּׂא *I will lift the cup of salvation*. A reference to the wine libation that accompanied a thanksgiving-offering (Rashi).

יָקָר בְּעֵינֵי יהוה, הַמָּוְתָה לַחֲסִידָיו *Grievous in the Lᴏʀᴅ's sight is the death of His devoted ones*. A reference back to the deliverance from death, to the memory of which this psalm is dedicated.

אָנָּה יהוה כִּי־אֲנִי עַבְדֶּךָ *Truly, Lᴏʀᴅ, I am Your servant*. The poet speaks of himself during his crisis, feeling as if he were a slave enchained by an angry master. Now, healed, he feels both forgiven and released.

The following verses are chanted by the Leader.
At the end of each verse, the congregation responds, "Thank the Lord
for He is good; His loving-kindness is for ever."

הוֹדוּ Thank the Lord for He is good;   His loving-kindness is for ever. *Ps. 118*

Let Israel say   His loving-kindness is for ever.

Let the house of Aaron say   His loving-kindness is for ever.

Let those who fear the Lord say   His loving-kindness is for ever.

מִן־הַמֵּצַר In my distress I called on the Lord. The Lord answered me and set me free. The Lord is with me; I will not be afraid. What can man do to me? The Lord is with me. He is my Helper. I will see the downfall of my enemies. It is better to take refuge in the Lord than to trust in man. It is better to take refuge in the Lord than to trust in princes. The nations all surrounded me, but in the Lord's name I drove

---

מִן־הַמֵּצַר *In my distress.* Here, personal and national sentiments merge. At one level the Psalmist is speaking of an individual deliverance, at another he is speaking of the rescue of the nation from its foes. Note how, throughout this section of the psalm, phrases repeat themselves ("the Lord is with me," "It is better to take refuge," "they surrounded me," "right hand") two or three times. This may be because different lines were sung by different choirs, or alternately by leader, Levites and congregation. The effect in any case is choral.

מִן־הַמֵּצַר...בַּמֶּרְחָב *In my distress… set me free.* The Hebrew words carry the literal meanings of narrow straits and wide open spaces, conveying an almost physical sense of confinement and release.

טוֹב לַחֲסוֹת בַּיהוה *It is better to take refuge in the Lord.* A sentiment found repeatedly in Psalms. People disappoint, betray, fail to keep their promises, prove untrustworthy. Former allies become enemies. People in pursuit of wealth or power often let advantage override principle and loyalty. Hence the loneliness of public life. Trust in God is ultimately the only reliable source of strength.

כָּל־גּוֹיִם סְבָבוּנִי *The nations all surrounded me.* The geographical position of Israel meant that in both ancient and modern times it was peculiarly vulnerable to attack, bordering as it did on several states and within the reach of larger imperial powers.

The following verses are chanted by the שליח ציבור.
At the end of each verse, the קהל responds: הוֹדוּ לַיהוה כִּי־טוֹב, כִּי לְעוֹלָם חַסְדּוֹ.

תהלים קיח

כִּי לְעוֹלָם חַסְדּוֹ:	הוֹדוּ לַיהוה כִּי־טוֹב
כִּי לְעוֹלָם חַסְדּוֹ:	יֹאמַר־נָא יִשְׂרָאֵל
כִּי לְעוֹלָם חַסְדּוֹ:	יֹאמְרוּ־נָא בֵית־אַהֲרֹן
כִּי לְעוֹלָם חַסְדּוֹ:	יֹאמְרוּ־נָא יִרְאֵי יהוה

מִן־הַמֵּצַר קָרָאתִי יָּהּ, עָנָנִי בַמֶּרְחָב יָהּ: יהוה לִי לֹא אִירָא, מַה־
יַּעֲשֶׂה לִי אָדָם: יהוה לִי בְּעֹזְרָי, וַאֲנִי אֶרְאֶה בְשֹׂנְאָי: טוֹב לַחֲסוֹת
בַּיהוה, מִבְּטֹחַ בָּאָדָם: טוֹב לַחֲסוֹת בַּיהוה, מִבְּטֹחַ בִּנְדִיבִים:
כָּל־גּוֹיִם סְבָבוּנִי, בְּשֵׁם יהוה כִּי אֲמִילַם: סַבּוּנִי גַם־סְבָבוּנִי, בְּשֵׁם

___

used here, often appear together in Tanakh. They are the central covenantal virtues. Often translated as "kindness" and "truth," they have a highly specific meaning in the context of Judaism. *Hesed* is love-as-loyalty and loyalty-as-love. It means love not as an emotion but as a moral commitment, as in marriage. *Emet* means being true to your word, keeping your promises, honoring your pledge. It is not a cognitive term but a moral one, so it is best translated as "faithfulness." The Psalmist is calling on the world to witness and celebrate the special covenantal bond between God and His people.

הוֹדוּ *Psalm 118. Thank.* This extended psalm, written in four or five movements, is written to be sung antiphonally, the leader singing a line or half-line, with the congregation then responding. We do not know exactly how the psalm was sung in Temple times, and there are differences of custom even today, but this was the moment of maximum participation by the pilgrims, many of whom had traveled long distances to be there. It was a high point in the Temple service: a nation celebrating its past and praying for the future.

הוֹדוּ לַיהוה כִּי־טוֹב *Thank the* Lord *for He is good.* This verse was first recited by King David when he brought the ark to Jerusalem (1 Chron. 16:34).

יֹאמַר־נָא יִשְׂרָאֵל *Let Israel say.* The Psalmist turns to the same three groups – Israel, the House of Aaron, and God-fearers – as he has done in previous psalms.

them off. They surrounded me on every side, but in the LORD's name
I drove them off. They surrounded me like bees, they attacked me as
fire attacks brushwood, but in the LORD's name I drove them off. They
thrust so hard against me, I nearly fell, but the LORD came to my help.
The LORD is my strength and my song; He has become my salvation.
Sounds of song and salvation resound in the tents of the righteous:
"The LORD's right hand has done mighty deeds. The LORD's right hand
is lifted high. The LORD's right hand has done mighty deeds." I will not
die but live, and tell what the LORD has done. The LORD has chastened
me severely, but He has not given me over to death. ‣ Open for me the
gates of righteousness that I may enter them and thank the LORD. This
is the gateway to the LORD; through it, the righteous shall enter.

אוֹדְךָ I will thank You, for You answered me,
and became my salvation.

I will thank You, for You answered me, and became my salvation.

The stone the builders rejected
has become the main cornerstone.

The stone the builders rejected has become the main cornerstone.

This is the LORD's doing.
It is wondrous in our eyes.

This is the LORD's doing. It is wondrous in our eyes.

This is the day the LORD has made.
Let us rejoice and be glad in it.

This is the day the LORD has made. Let us rejoice and be glad in it.

─────────────────────────────────

זֶה־הַשַּׁעַר *This is the gateway.* A response to the pilgrims by the gatekeepers.

אוֹדְךָ *I will thank You.* From here to the end of the psalm the lines are repeated,
in memory of the way they were sung responsively in the Temple.

אֶבֶן מָאֲסוּ הַבּוֹנִים *The stone the builders rejected.* This is a reference to the people
of Israel. Two of the first references to Israel in non-Jewish sources – the
Merneptah stele (Egypt, thirteenth century BCE) and the Mesha stele (Moab,
ninth century BCE) – both declare that Israel has been destroyed. Israel is the
people that outlives its obituaries.

יהוה כִּי אֲמִילַם: סַבּוּנִי כִדְבֹרִים, דֹּעֲכוּ כְּאֵשׁ קוֹצִים, בְּשֵׁם יהוה
כִּי אֲמִילַם: דָּחֹה דְחִיתַנִי לִנְפֹּל, וַיהוה עֲזָרָנִי: עָזִּי וְזִמְרָת יָהּ,
וַיְהִי־לִי לִישׁוּעָה: קוֹל רִנָּה וִישׁוּעָה בְּאָהֳלֵי צַדִּיקִים, יְמִין יהוה
עֹשָׂה חָיִל: יְמִין יהוה רוֹמֵמָה, יְמִין יהוה עֹשָׂה חָיִל: לֹא־אָמוּת
כִּי־אֶחְיֶה, וַאֲסַפֵּר מַעֲשֵׂי יָהּ: יַסֹּר יִסְּרַנִּי יָּהּ, וְלַמָּוֶת לֹא נְתָנָנִי:
‣ פִּתְחוּ־לִי שַׁעֲרֵי־צֶדֶק, אָבֹא־בָם אוֹדֶה יָהּ: זֶה־הַשַּׁעַר לַיהוה,
צַדִּיקִים יָבֹאוּ בוֹ:

אוֹדְךָ כִּי עֲנִיתָנִי, וַתְּהִי־לִי לִישׁוּעָה:
אוֹדְךָ כִּי עֲנִיתָנִי, וַתְּהִי־לִי לִישׁוּעָה:

אֶבֶן מָאֲסוּ הַבּוֹנִים, הָיְתָה לְרֹאשׁ פִּנָּה:
אֶבֶן מָאֲסוּ הַבּוֹנִים, הָיְתָה לְרֹאשׁ פִּנָּה:

מֵאֵת יהוה הָיְתָה זֹּאת, הִיא נִפְלָאת בְּעֵינֵינוּ:
מֵאֵת יהוה הָיְתָה זֹּאת, הִיא נִפְלָאת בְּעֵינֵינוּ:

זֶה־הַיּוֹם עָשָׂה יהוה, נָגִילָה וְנִשְׂמְחָה בוֹ:
זֶה־הַיּוֹם עָשָׂה יהוה, נָגִילָה וְנִשְׂמְחָה בוֹ:

כְּאֵשׁ קוֹצִים *As fire attacks brushwood.* Flaring up dramatically but quickly
burning itself out.

קוֹל רִנָּה *Sounds of song.* A prelude to the dramatic choral piece that follows,
three phrases each beginning, "The Lord's right hand."

לֹא־אָמוּת כִּי־אֶחְיֶה, וַאֲסַפֵּר *I will not die but live, and tell.* A quintessential expression of the Jewish instinct for survival, itself intimately connected to the role
of Jews as witnesses. A witness must survive if truth is not to be buried.

פִּתְחוּ־לִי שַׁעֲרֵי־צֶדֶק *Open for me the gates of righteousness.* In Temple times this
referred literally to the gates of the city, and would have resonated with the
pilgrims as they entered Jerusalem.

Leader followed by congregation:

אָנָּא LORD, please, save us.
LORD, please, save us.
LORD, please, grant us success.
LORD, please, grant us success.

בָּרוּךְ Blessed is one who comes in the name of the LORD;
we bless you from the House of the LORD.

Blessed is one who comes in the name of the LORD;
we bless you from the House of the LORD.

The LORD is God; He has given us light. Bind the festival offering
with thick cords [and bring it] to the horns of the altar.

The LORD is God; He has given us light. Bind the festival offering
with thick cords [and bring it] to the horns of the altar.

You are my God and I will thank You; You are my God, I will exalt You.

You are my God and I will thank You; You are my God, I will exalt You.

Thank the LORD for He is good; His loving-kindness is for ever.

Thank the LORD for He is good; His loving-kindness is for ever.

יְהַלְלוּךָ All Your works will praise You, LORD our God, and Your
devoted ones – the righteous who do Your will, together with all
Your people the house of Israel – will joyously thank, bless, praise,

---

bring to the altar a festival offering: *ḥag* in biblical Hebrew, *ḥagiga* in rabbinic
Hebrew.

אֵלִי אַתָּה *You are my God.* Said by the offerer at the time of the offering.

הוֹדוּ לַיהוה כִּי־טוֹב *Thank the LORD for He is good.* The psalm ends with the same
verse with which it began. Note the difference between praise (*hallel, shevaḥ*)
and thanks (*hoda'a*). Worship, both in the Temple and the synagogue, in both
Hallel and the Amida, begins with praise and ends with thanks. Praise is more
external and formal, thanks more inward and deeply felt.

יְהַלְלוּךָ...כָּל מַעֲשֶׂיךָ *All Your works will praise You.* Not part of Hallel itself, this

שליח ציבור followed by קהל:

אָנָּא יהוה הוֹשִׁיעָה נָּא:

אָנָּא יהוה הוֹשִׁיעָה נָּא:

אָנָּא יהוה הַצְלִיחָה נָּא:

אָנָּא יהוה הַצְלִיחָה נָּא:

בָּרוּךְ הַבָּא בְּשֵׁם יהוה, בֵּרַכְנוּכֶם מִבֵּית יהוה:

בָּרוּךְ הַבָּא בְּשֵׁם יהוה, בֵּרַכְנוּכֶם מִבֵּית יהוה:

אֵל יהוה וַיָּאֶר לָנוּ, אִסְרוּ־חַג בַּעֲבֹתִים עַד־קַרְנוֹת הַמִּזְבֵּחַ:

אֵל יהוה וַיָּאֶר לָנוּ, אִסְרוּ־חַג בַּעֲבֹתִים עַד־קַרְנוֹת הַמִּזְבֵּחַ:

אֵלִי אַתָּה וְאוֹדֶךָּ, אֱלֹהַי אֲרוֹמְמֶךָּ:

אֵלִי אַתָּה וְאוֹדֶךָּ, אֱלֹהַי אֲרוֹמְמֶךָּ:

הוֹדוּ לַיהוה כִּי־טוֹב, כִּי לְעוֹלָם חַסְדּוֹ:

הוֹדוּ לַיהוה כִּי־טוֹב, כִּי לְעוֹלָם חַסְדּוֹ:

יְהַלְלוּךָ יהוה אֱלֹהֵינוּ כָּל מַעֲשֶׂיךָ, וַחֲסִידֶיךָ צַדִּיקִים עוֹשֵׂי
רְצוֹנֶךָ, וְכָל עַמְּךָ בֵּית יִשְׂרָאֵל בְּרִנָּה יוֹדוּ וִיבָרְכוּ וִישַׁבְּחוּ וִיפָאֲרוּ

אָנָּא יהוה הוֹשִׁיעָה נָּא LORD, *please, save us.* A dramatic sequence in which leader and congregation turn directly in plea to God. It became the basis of the extended litanies said on Sukkot during *Hakafot,* the procession around the altar in the Temple and the *bima* in the synagogue, as well as the source of the English word "hosanna" (=*hosha na*).

בָּרוּךְ הַבָּא *Blessed is one who comes.* A greeting by the priests to the pilgrims (Rashi, Radak).

אֵל יהוה *The* LORD *is God.* A response by the pilgrims, declaring their intent to glorify, exalt, revere, sanctify, and proclaim the sovereignty of Your name, our King. ‣ For it is good to thank You and fitting to sing psalms to Your name, for from eternity to eternity You are God. Blessed are You, LORD, King who is extolled with praises.

FULL KADDISH

Leader: יִתְגַּדַּל Magnified and sanctified may His great name be,
in the world He created by His will.
May He establish His kingdom
in your lifetime and in your days,
and in the lifetime of all the house of Israel,
swiftly and soon – and say: Amen.

All: May His great name be blessed for ever and all time.

Leader: Blessed and praised, glorified and exalted,
raised and honored, uplifted and lauded be
the name of the Holy One,
blessed be He,
beyond any blessing,
song, praise and consolation
uttered in the world – and say: Amen.

May the prayers and pleas of all Israel
be accepted by their Father in heaven – and say: Amen.

May there be great peace from heaven,
and life for us and all Israel – and say: Amen.

*Bow, take three steps back, as if taking leave of the Divine Presence,
then bow, first left, then right, then center, while saying:*

May He who makes peace in His high places,
make peace for us and all Israel – and say: Amen.

*On the first day of Shavuot continue with Removing the Torah on the next page
(in Israel turn to Megillat Rut on page 438). On the second day of Shavuot
continue with Megillat Rut on page 438.*

is a concluding blessing, similar to the one said after the Verses of Praise in the morning service.

וִירוֹמְמוּ וְיַעֲרִיצוּ וְיַקְדִּישׁוּ וְיַמְלִיכוּ אֶת שִׁמְךָ מַלְכֵּנוּ, ◀ כִּי לְךָ
טוֹב לְהוֹדוֹת וּלְשִׁמְךָ נָאֶה לְזַמֵּר, כִּי מֵעוֹלָם וְעַד עוֹלָם אַתָּה אֵל.
בָּרוּךְ אַתָּה יהוה, מֶלֶךְ מְהֻלָּל בַּתִּשְׁבָּחוֹת.

קדיש שלם

שׁ״ץ: יִתְגַּדַּל וְיִתְקַדַּשׁ שְׁמֵהּ רַבָּא (קהל: אָמֵן)
בְּעָלְמָא דִּי בְרָא כִרְעוּתֵהּ, וְיַמְלִיךְ מַלְכוּתֵהּ
בְּחַיֵּיכוֹן וּבְיוֹמֵיכוֹן וּבְחַיֵּי דְכָל בֵּית יִשְׂרָאֵל
בַּעֲגָלָא וּבִזְמַן קָרִיב, וְאִמְרוּ אָמֵן. (קהל: אָמֵן)

קהל ושׁ״ץ: יְהֵא שְׁמֵהּ רַבָּא מְבָרַךְ לְעָלַם וּלְעָלְמֵי עָלְמַיָּא.

שׁ״ץ: יִתְבָּרַךְ וְיִשְׁתַּבַּח וְיִתְפָּאַר
וְיִתְרוֹמַם וְיִתְנַשֵּׂא וְיִתְהַדָּר וְיִתְעַלֶּה וְיִתְהַלָּל
שְׁמֵהּ דְּקֻדְשָׁא בְּרִיךְ הוּא (קהל: בְּרִיךְ הוּא)
לְעֵלָּא מִן כָּל בִּרְכָתָא וְשִׁירָתָא, תֻּשְׁבְּחָתָא וְנֶחֱמָתָא
דַּאֲמִירָן בְּעָלְמָא, וְאִמְרוּ אָמֵן. (קהל: אָמֵן)

תִּתְקַבַּל צְלוֹתְהוֹן וּבָעוּתְהוֹן דְּכָל יִשְׂרָאֵל
קֳדָם אֲבוּהוֹן דִּי בִשְׁמַיָּא, וְאִמְרוּ אָמֵן. (קהל: אָמֵן)

יְהֵא שְׁלָמָא רַבָּא מִן שְׁמַיָּא
וְחַיִּים, עָלֵינוּ וְעַל כָּל יִשְׂרָאֵל, וְאִמְרוּ אָמֵן. (קהל: אָמֵן)

Bow, take three steps back, as if taking leave of the Divine Presence,
then bow, first left, then right, then center, while saying:

עֹשֶׂה שָׁלוֹם בִּמְרוֹמָיו
הוּא יַעֲשֶׂה שָׁלוֹם
עָלֵינוּ וְעַל כָּל יִשְׂרָאֵל, וְאִמְרוּ אָמֵן. (קהל: אָמֵן)

On the first day of שבועות continue with הוצאת ספר תורה on the next page (in ארץ ישראל turn
to מגילת רות on page 439). *On the second day of שבועות continue with מגילת רות on page 439.*

REMOVING THE TORAH FROM THE ARK

אֵין־כָּמוֹךָ There is none like You among the heavenly powers, *Ps. 86*
LORD, and there are no works like Yours.
Your kingdom is an eternal kingdom, *Ps. 145*
and Your dominion is for all generations.

The LORD is King, the LORD was King,
the LORD shall be King for ever and all time.
The LORD will give strength to His people; *Ps. 29*
the LORD will bless His people with peace.

Father of compassion,
favor Zion with Your goodness; rebuild the walls of Jerusalem. *Ps. 51*
For we trust in You alone, King, God, high and exalted, Master of worlds.

The Ark is opened and the congregation stands. All say:

וַיְהִי בִּנְסֹעַ Whenever the Ark set out, Moses would say, *Num. 10*
"Arise, LORD, and may Your enemies be scattered.
May those who hate You flee before You."
For the Torah shall come forth from Zion, *Is. 2*
and the word of the LORD from Jerusalem.
Blessed is He who in His Holiness
gave the Torah to His people Israel.

Thus from its earliest days the synagogue was a place of study as well as prayer. In Second Temple and later eras, the reading was accompanied by verse-by-verse translation into the vernacular, mainly Aramaic. In the course of time the act of taking the Torah from, and returning it to, the Ark became ceremonial moments in their own right.

אֵין־כָּמוֹךָ בָאֱלֹהִים *There is none like You among the heavenly powers.* A collection of verses and phrases from the book of Psalms, focusing on God's sovereignty.

וַיְהִי בִּנְסֹעַ הָאָרֹן *Whenever the Ark set out.* A description of the Ark during the journeys of the Israelites in the wilderness. The parallel verse, "When the Ark came to rest," is recited when the Torah is returned to the Ark. Thus the taking of the *Sefer Torah* from the Ark and its return, recall the Ark of the Covenant which accompanied the Israelites in the days of Moses.

כִּי מִצִּיּוֹן תֵּצֵא תוֹרָה *For the Torah shall come forth from Zion.* Part of Isaiah's famous vision (2:2–4) of the end of days.

הוצאת ספר תורה

תהילים פו

אֵין־כָּמוֹךָ בָאֱלֹהִים, אֲדֹנָי, וְאֵין כְּמַעֲשֶׂיךָ:

תהילים קמה

מַלְכוּתְךָ מַלְכוּת כָּל־עֹלָמִים, וּמֶמְשַׁלְתְּךָ בְּכָל־דּוֹר וָדֹר:

יהוה מֶלֶךְ, יהוה מָלָךְ, יהוה יִמְלֹךְ לְעֹלָם וָעֶד.

תהילים כט

יהוה עֹז לְעַמּוֹ יִתֵּן, יהוה יְבָרֵךְ אֶת־עַמּוֹ בַשָּׁלוֹם:

תהילים נא

אַב הָרַחֲמִים, הֵיטִיבָה בִרְצוֹנְךָ אֶת־צִיּוֹן תִּבְנֶה חוֹמוֹת יְרוּשָׁלָֽיִם:

כִּי בְךָ לְבַד בָּטָחְנוּ, מֶלֶךְ אֵל רָם וְנִשָּׂא, אֲדוֹן עוֹלָמִים.

The ארון קודש *is opened and the* קהל *stands. All say:*

במדבר י

וַיְהִי בִּנְסֹעַ הָאָרֹן וַיֹּאמֶר מֹשֶׁה

קוּמָה יהוה וְיָפֻצוּ אֹיְבֶיךָ וְיָנֻסוּ מְשַׂנְאֶיךָ מִפָּנֶיךָ:

ישעיה ב

כִּי מִצִּיּוֹן תֵּצֵא תוֹרָה וּדְבַר־יהוה מִירוּשָׁלָֽיִם:

בָּרוּךְ שֶׁנָּתַן תּוֹרָה לְעַמּוֹ יִשְׂרָאֵל בִּקְדֻשָּׁתוֹ.

READING OF THE TORAH

Since the revelation at Mount Sinai, the Jewish people has been a nation defined by a book: the Torah. The Mosaic books are more than sacred literature. They are the written constitution of the house of Israel as a nation under the sovereignty of God, the basis of its collective memory, the record of its covenant with God, the template of its existence as "a kingdom of priests and a holy nation" (Ex. 19:6), and the detailed specification of the task it is called on to perform – to construct a society on the basis of justice and compassion and the inalienable dignity of the human person as the image of God. Just as the Torah is central to Jewish life, so the reading of the Torah is central to the synagogue service.

The penultimate command Moses gave to the Israelites was the institution of a national assembly once every seven years when the king would read the Torah to the people (Deut. 31:10–13). The Tanakh records several key moments in Jewish history when national rededication was accompanied by a public reading of the Torah, most famously in the days of king Josiah (ii Kings 23) and Ezra (Neh. 8). According to tradition, Moses ordained that the Torah be read regularly and publicly; a long reading on Shabbat morning and shorter readings on Mondays and Thursdays. Ezra, reinstituting this practice, added the reading on Shabbat afternoon.

The following (The Thirteen Attributes of Mercy) is said three times:

יהוה The LORD, the LORD, compassionate and gracious God,   *Ex. 34*
slow to anger, abounding in loving-kindness and truth,
extending loving-kindness to a thousand generations,
forgiving iniquity, rebellion and sin,
and absolving [the guilty who repent].

Each individual says silently, inserting appropriate phrase/s in parentheses:

רבונו Master of the Universe, fulfill my heart's requests for good. Satisfy my desire, grant my request, and enable me (*name*, son/daughter of *father's name*), (and my wife/ husband, and my sons/daughters) and all the members of my household to do Your will with a perfect heart. Deliver us from the evil impulse, grant us our share in Your Torah, and make us worthy that Your Presence may rest upon us. Confer on us a spirit of wisdom and understanding, and may there be fulfilled in us the verse: "The spirit of the LORD *Is. 11* will rest upon him – a spirit of wisdom and understanding, a spirit of counsel and strength, a spirit of knowledge and reverence for the LORD." So too may it be Your will, LORD our God and God of our ancestors, that we be worthy to do deeds that are good in Your sight, and to walk before You in the ways of the upright. Make us holy through Your holiness, so that we may be worthy of a good and long life, and of the World to Come. Guard us from evil deeds and bad times that threaten to bring turmoil to the world. May *Ps. 32* loving-kindness surround one who trusts in the LORD. Amen.

יהי May the words of my mouth and the meditation of my   *Ps. 19*
heart find favor before You, LORD, my Rock and Redeemer.

Say the following verse three times:

ואני As for me, may my prayer come to You, LORD,   *Ps. 69*
at a time of favor. O God, in Your great love,
answer me with Your faithful salvation.

רבונו של עולם *Master of the Universe.* The festivals are heightened times of holiness, and the opening of the Ark is a moment when we most intensely feel the transformative energy of the Divine Presence. Thus, when these two sacred moments coincide, we say a personal prayer for God's blessing in our lives and the lives of our family, that we may have a material and spiritual environment that will allow us to serve God without distraction or hindrance.

שמות לד

The following (י״ג מידות הרחמים) *is said three times:*

יהוה, יהוה, אֵל רַחוּם וְחַנּוּן, אֶרֶךְ אַפַּיִם וְרַב־חֶסֶד וֶאֱמֶת:
נֹצֵר חֶסֶד לָאֲלָפִים, נֹשֵׂא עָוֹן וָפֶשַׁע וְחַטָּאָה, וְנַקֵּה:

Each individual says silently, inserting appropriate phrase/s in parentheses:

רִבּוֹנוֹ שֶׁל עוֹלָם, מַלֵּא מִשְׁאֲלוֹת לִבִּי לְטוֹבָה, וְהָפֵק רְצוֹנִי וְתֵן שְׁאֵלָתִי, וְזַכֵּה
לִי (פלוני(ת) בֶּן/בַּת פלוני) (וְאִשְׁתִּי/בַּעֲלִי וּבָנַי וּבְנוֹתַי) וְכָל בְּנֵי בֵיתִי, לַעֲשׂוֹת
רְצוֹנְךָ בְּלֵבָב שָׁלֵם, וּמַלְּטֵנוּ מִיֵּצֶר הָרָע, וְתֵן חֶלְקֵנוּ בְּתוֹרָתֶךָ, וְזַכֵּנוּ שֶׁתִּשְׁרֶה
שְׁכִינָתְךָ עָלֵינוּ, וְהוֹפַע עָלֵינוּ רוּחַ חָכְמָה וּבִינָה. וְיִתְקַיֶּם בָּנוּ מִקְרָא שֶׁכָּתוּב:

ישעיה יא

וְנָחָה עָלָיו רוּחַ יהוה, רוּחַ חָכְמָה וּבִינָה, רוּחַ עֵצָה וּגְבוּרָה, רוּחַ דַּעַת וְיִרְאַת
יהוה: וּבְכֵן יְהִי רָצוֹן מִלְּפָנֶיךָ יהוה אֱלֹהֵינוּ וֵאלֹהֵי אֲבוֹתֵינוּ, שֶׁתְּזַכֵּנוּ לַעֲשׂוֹת
מַעֲשִׂים טוֹבִים בְּעֵינֶיךָ וְלָלֶכֶת בְּדַרְכֵי יְשָׁרִים לְפָנֶיךָ, וְקַדְּשֵׁנוּ בִּקְדֻשָּׁתֶךָ
כְּדֵי שֶׁנִּזְכֶּה לְחַיִּים טוֹבִים וַאֲרוּכִים וּלְחַיֵּי הָעוֹלָם הַבָּא, וְתִשְׁמְרֵנוּ מִמַּעֲשִׂים
רָעִים וּמִשָּׁעוֹת רָעוֹת הַמִּתְרַגְּשׁוֹת לָבוֹא לָעוֹלָם, וְהַבּוֹטֵחַ בַּיהוה חֶסֶד

תהלים לב

יְסוֹבְבֶנּוּ: אָמֵן.

תהלים יט

יִהְיוּ לְרָצוֹן אִמְרֵי־פִי וְהֶגְיוֹן לִבִּי לְפָנֶיךָ, יהוה צוּרִי וְגֹאֲלִי:

Say the following verse three times:

תהלים סט

וַאֲנִי תְפִלָּתִי־לְךָ יהוה, עֵת רָצוֹן, אֱלֹהִים בְּרָב־חַסְדֶּךָ
עֲנֵנִי בֶּאֱמֶת יִשְׁעֶךָ:

THE THIRTEEN ATTRIBUTES OF MERCY

The "Thirteen attributes of compassion" is the name given by the sages to
God's declaration to Moses when he prayed on the people's behalf after the
golden calf. They constitute God's Self-definition as the source of compassion and pardon that frames the moral life. According to the Talmud (*Rosh
HaShana* 17b), God made a covenant that no prayer for forgiveness accompanied by these words would go unanswered. This and the following prayer
are not said on Shabbat since we do not make personal requests of God on
that day.

בְּרִיךְ Blessed is the name of the Master of the Universe. Blessed is Your crown *Zohar,*
and Your place. May Your favor always be with Your people Israel. Show Your *Vayak'hel*
people the salvation of Your right hand in Your Temple. Grant us the gift
of Your good light, and accept our prayers in mercy. May it be Your will to
prolong our life in goodness. May I be counted among the righteous, so that
You will have compassion on me and protect me and all that is mine and all
that is Your people Israel's. You feed all; You sustain all; You rule over all;
You rule over kings, for sovereignty is Yours. I am a servant of the Holy One,
blessed be He, before whom and before whose glorious Torah I bow at all
times. Not in man do I trust, nor on any angel do I rely, but on the God of
heaven who is the God of truth, whose Torah is truth, whose prophets speak
truth, and who abounds in acts of love and truth. ▸ In Him I trust, and to
His holy and glorious name I offer praises. May it be Your will to open my
heart to the Torah, and to fulfill the wishes of my heart and of the hearts of
all Your people Israel for good, for life, and for peace.

Two Torah scrolls are removed from the Ark. The Leader takes one
in his right arm and, followed by the congregation, says:

Listen, Israel: the LORD is our God, the LORD is One. *Deut. 6*

Leader then congregation:

One is our God; great is our Master;
holy is His name.

The Leader turns to face the Ark, bows and says:

Magnify the LORD with me,
and let us exalt His name together. *Ps. 34*

The Ark is closed. The Leader carries the Torah scroll to the bima and the congregation says:

לְךָ Yours, LORD, are the greatness and the power, the glory and the *1 Chr. 29*
majesty and splendor, for everything in heaven and earth is Yours.
Yours, LORD, is the kingdom; You are exalted as Head over all.

---

of reciting it has its origins in the circle of mystics in Safed associated with
Rabbi Isaac Luria. It is a beautiful prayer in which we yearn to be open to
the Torah and faithful to our vocation as a servant of the Holy One, for the
highest privilege is to serve the Author of all. As the doors of the Ark open,
so we open our hearts.

זוהר ויקהל

בְּרִיךְ שְׁמֵהּ דְּמָרֵא עָלְמָא, בְּרִיךְ כִּתְרָךְ וְאַתְרָךְ. יְהֵא רְעוּתָךְ עִם עַמָּךְ יִשְׂרָאֵל לְעָלַם, וּפֻרְקַן יְמִינָךְ אַחֲזֵי לְעַמָּךְ בְּבֵית מַקְדְּשָׁךְ, וּלְאַמְטוֹיֵי לָנָא מִטּוּב נְהוֹרָךְ, וּלְקַבֵּל צְלוֹתָנָא בְּרַחֲמִין. יְהֵא רַעֲוָא קֳדָמָךְ דְּתוֹרִיךְ לַן חַיִּין בְּטִיבוּ, וְלֶהֱוֵי אֲנָא פְקִידָא בְּגוֹ צַדִּיקַיָּא, לְמִרְחַם עֲלַי וּלְמִנְטַר יָתִי וְיָת כָּל דִּי לִי וְדִי לְעַמָּךְ יִשְׂרָאֵל. אַנְתְּ הוּא זָן לְכֹלָּא וּמְפַרְנֵס לְכֹלָּא, אַנְתְּ הוּא שַׁלִּיט עַל כֹּלָּא, אַנְתְּ הוּא דְּשַׁלִּיט עַל מַלְכַיָּא, וּמַלְכוּתָא דִּילָךְ הִיא. אֲנָא עַבְדָּא דְקֻדְשָׁא בְּרִיךְ הוּא, דְּסָגִדְנָא קַמֵּהּ וּמִקַּמֵּי דִיקַר אוֹרַיְתֵהּ בְּכָל עִדָּן וְעִדָּן. לָא עַל אֱנָשׁ רְחִיצְנָא וְלָא עַל בַּר אֱלָהִין סְמֵיכְנָא, אֶלָּא בֵּאלָהָא דִשְׁמַיָּא, דְּהוּא אֱלָהָא קְשׁוֹט, וְאוֹרַיְתֵהּ קְשׁוֹט, וּנְבִיאוֹהִי קְשׁוֹט, וּמַסְגֵּא לְמֶעְבַּד טָבְוָן וּקְשׁוֹט. ‹ בֵּהּ אֲנָא רְחִיץ, וְלִשְׁמֵהּ קַדִּישָׁא יַקִּירָא אֲנָא אֵמַר תֻּשְׁבְּחָן. יְהֵא רַעֲוָא קֳדָמָךְ דְּתִפְתַּח לִבַּאי בְּאוֹרַיְתָא, וְתַשְׁלִים מִשְׁאֲלִין דְּלִבַּאי וְלִבָּא דְכָל עַמָּךְ יִשְׂרָאֵל לְטַב וּלְחַיִּין וְלִשְׁלָם.

Two ספרי תורה are removed from the ארון קודש. The שליח צבור takes
one in his right arm, and, followed by the קהל, says:

דברים ו

שְׁמַע יִשְׂרָאֵל, יהוה אֱלֹהֵינוּ, יהוה אֶחָד:

קהל then שליח ציבור:

אֶחָד אֱלֹהֵינוּ, גָּדוֹל אֲדוֹנֵינוּ, קָדוֹשׁ שְׁמוֹ.

The שליח ציבור turns to face the ארון קודש, bows and says:

תהלים לד

גַּדְּלוּ לַיהוה אִתִּי וּנְרוֹמְמָה שְׁמוֹ יַחְדָּו:

The ארון קודש is closed. The שליח ציבור carries the ספר תורה to the בימה and the קהל says:

דברי הימים א׳ כט

לְךָ יהוה הַגְּדֻלָּה וְהַגְּבוּרָה וְהַתִּפְאֶרֶת וְהַנֵּצַח וְהַהוֹד, כִּי־כֹל בַּשָּׁמַיִם וּבָאָרֶץ, לְךָ יהוה הַמַּמְלָכָה וְהַמִּתְנַשֵּׂא לְכֹל לְרֹאשׁ:

בְּרִיךְ שְׁמֵהּ *Blessed is the name.* This passage, from the mystical text, the *Zohar*, is prefaced in its original context with the words: "Rabbi Shimon said: When the scroll of the Torah is taken out to be read in public, the Gates of Compassion are opened, and love is aroused on high. Therefore one should say [at this time] …" The words "Blessed is the name" then follow. The custom

רוֹמְמוּ Exalt the Lord our God and bow to His footstool; He is holy. *Ps. 99*
Exalt the Lord our God, and bow at His holy mountain, for holy is
the Lord our God.

Over all may the name of the Supreme King of kings, the Holy One blessed be
He, be magnified and sanctified, praised and glorified, exalted and extolled, in the
worlds that He has created – this world and the World to Come – in accordance
with His will, and the will of those who fear Him, and the will of the whole house
of Israel. He is the Rock of worlds, Lord of all creatures, God of all souls, who
dwells in the spacious heights and inhabits the high heavens of old. His holiness is
over the Ḥayyot and over the throne of glory. Therefore may Your name, Lord our
God, be sanctified among us in the sight of all that lives. Let us sing before Him a
new song, as it is written: "Sing to God, make music for His name, extol Him who *Ps. 68*
rides the clouds – the Lord is His name – and exult before Him." And may we
see Him eye to eye when He returns to His abode as it is written: "For they shall *Is. 52*
see eye to eye when the Lord returns to Zion." And it is said: "Then will the glory *Is. 40*
of the Lord be revealed, and all mankind together shall see that the mouth of the
Lord has spoken."

Father of mercy, have compassion on the people borne by Him. May He remember
the covenant with the mighty (patriarchs), and deliver us from evil times. May He
reproach the evil instinct in the people by Him, and graciously grant that we be
an eternal remnant. May He fulfill in good measure our requests for salvation and
compassion.

The Torah scroll is placed on the bima and the Gabbai calls a Kohen to the Torah.
וְיַעֲזֹר May He help, shield and save all who seek refuge in Him, and let us say:
Amen. Let us all render greatness to our God and give honor to the Torah.
*Let the Kohen come forward. Arise (*name* son of *father's name*), the Kohen.

*If no Kohen is present, a Levi or Yisrael is called up as follows:
/As there is no Kohen, arise (*name* son of *father's name*) in place of a Kohen./
Blessed is He who, in His holiness, gave the Torah to His people Israel.

The congregation followed by the Gabbai:
You who cling to the Lord your God are all alive today.   *Deut. 4*

---

cally, known as the *ba'al koreh*), "so as not to shame those who do not know
how to read" their own portions (see *Beit Yosef, Oraḥ Ḥayyim* 141). Instead,
the *oleh* says the blessings before and after the portion, and recites the text
silently along with the reader.

רוֹמְמוּ יהוה אֱלֹהֵינוּ וְהִשְׁתַּחֲווּ לַהֲדֹם רַגְלָיו, קָדוֹשׁ הוּא: רוֹמְמוּ
יהוה אֱלֹהֵינוּ וְהִשְׁתַּחֲווּ לְהַר קָדְשׁוֹ, כִּי־קָדוֹשׁ יהוה אֱלֹהֵינוּ:

עַל הַכֹּל יִתְגַּדַּל וְיִתְקַדַּשׁ וְיִשְׁתַּבַּח וְיִתְפָּאַר וְיִתְרוֹמַם וְיִתְנַשֵּׂא שְׁמוֹ שֶׁל מֶלֶךְ
מַלְכֵי הַמְּלָכִים הַקָּדוֹשׁ בָּרוּךְ הוּא בָּעוֹלָמוֹת שֶׁבָּרָא, הָעוֹלָם הַזֶּה וְהָעוֹלָם הַבָּא,
כִּרְצוֹנוֹ וְכִרְצוֹן יְרֵאָיו וְכִרְצוֹן כָּל בֵּית יִשְׂרָאֵל. צוּר הָעוֹלָמִים, אֲדוֹן כָּל הַבְּרִיּוֹת,
אֱלוֹהַּ כָּל הַנְּפָשׁוֹת, הַיּוֹשֵׁב בְּמֶרְחֲבֵי מָרוֹם, הַשּׁוֹכֵן בִּשְׁמֵי שְׁמֵי קֶדֶם, קְדֻשָּׁתוֹ
עַל הַחַיּוֹת, וּקְדֻשָּׁתוֹ עַל כִּסֵּא הַכָּבוֹד. וּבְכֵן יִתְקַדַּשׁ שִׁמְךָ בָּנוּ יהוה אֱלֹהֵינוּ
לְעֵינֵי כָּל חָי, וְנֹאמַר לְפָנָיו שִׁיר חָדָשׁ, כַּכָּתוּב: שִׁירוּ לֵאלֹהִים זַמְּרוּ שְׁמוֹ, סֹלּוּ
לָרֹכֵב בָּעֲרָבוֹת, בְּיָהּ שְׁמוֹ, וְעִלְזוּ לְפָנָיו: וְנִרְאֵהוּ עַיִן בְּעַיִן בְּשׁוּבוֹ אֶל נָוֵהוּ,
כַּכָּתוּב: כִּי עַיִן בְּעַיִן יִרְאוּ בְּשׁוּב יהוה צִיּוֹן: וְנֶאֱמַר: וְנִגְלָה כְּבוֹד יהוה, וְרָאוּ
כָל־בָּשָׂר יַחְדָּו כִּי פִּי יהוה דִּבֵּר:

אַב הָרַחֲמִים הוּא יְרַחֵם עַם עֲמוּסִים, וְיִזְכֹּר בְּרִית אֵיתָנִים, וְיַצִּיל נַפְשׁוֹתֵינוּ מִן
הַשָּׁעוֹת הָרָעוֹת, וְיִגְעַר בְּיֵצֶר הָרָע מִן הַנְּשׂוּאִים, וְיָחֹן אוֹתָנוּ לִפְלֵיטַת עוֹלָמִים,
וִימַלֵּא מִשְׁאֲלוֹתֵינוּ בְּמִדָּה טוֹבָה יְשׁוּעָה וְרַחֲמִים.

The ספר תורה *is placed on the* שולחן *and the* גבאי *calls a* כהן *to the* תורה.

וְיַעֲזֹר וְיָגֵן וְיוֹשִׁיעַ לְכָל הַחוֹסִים בּוֹ, וְנֹאמַר אָמֵן. הַכֹּל הָבוּ גֹדֶל לֵאלֹהֵינוּ
וּתְנוּ כָבוֹד לַתּוֹרָה. *כֹּהֵן קְרַב, יַעֲמֹד (פלוני בֶּן פלוני) הַכֹּהֵן.

**If no* כהן *is present, a* לוי *or* ישראל *is called up as follows:*

/אֵין כָּאן כֹּהֵן, יַעֲמֹד (פלוני בֶּן פלוני) בִּמְקוֹם כֹּהֵן./

בָּרוּךְ שֶׁנָּתַן תּוֹרָה לְעַמּוֹ יִשְׂרָאֵל בִּקְדֻשָּׁתוֹ.

The קהל *followed by the* גבאי:

וְאַתֶּם הַדְּבֵקִים בַּיהוה אֱלֹהֵיכֶם חַיִּים כֻּלְּכֶם הַיּוֹם:

ASCENT TO THE TORAH

The original custom was that each of those called to the Torah read his own
portion. Not everyone was able to do this, so the practice developed of en-
trusting the reading to one with expertise (commonly, though ungrammati-

The Reader shows the oleh the section to be read. The oleh touches the scroll at that place with the tzitzit of his tallit, which he then kisses. Holding the handles of the scroll, he says:

Oleh: Bless the LORD, the blessed One.

Cong: Bless the LORD, the blessed One, for ever and all time.

Oleh: Bless the LORD, the blessed One, for ever and all time.
   Blessed are You, LORD our God, King of the Universe,
   who has chosen us from all peoples
   and has given us His Torah.
   Blessed are You, LORD, Giver of the Torah.

After the reading, the oleh says:

Oleh: Blessed are You, LORD our God, King of the Universe,
   who has given us the Torah of truth,
   planting everlasting life in our midst.
   Blessed are You, LORD, Giver of the Torah.

One who has survived a situation of danger, says:

Blessed are You, LORD our God, King of the Universe, who bestows good
on the unworthy, who has bestowed on me much good.

The congregation responds:

Amen. May He who bestowed much good on you
continue to bestow on you much good, Selah.

After a Bar Mitzva boy has finished the Torah blessing, his father says aloud:

Blessed is He who has released me from the responsibility
for this child.

אֲשֶׁר נָתַן לָנוּ תּוֹרַת אֱמֶת *Who has given us the Torah of truth.* An act of affirmation following the reading. There is truth that is thought and there is truth
that is lived. Judaism is about the transformative truths that we enact when
we align our will with that of God.

וְחַיֵּי עוֹלָם *Everlasting life.* Immortality lies not in how long we live but in how
we live. Reaching out to the Eternal and finding Him reaching out to us, we
touch eternity.

The קורא *shows the* עולה *the section to be read. The* עולה *touches the scroll at that place with the* ציצית *of his* טלית, *which he then kisses. Holding the handles of the scroll, he says:*

עולה: בָּרְכוּ אֶת יהוה הַמְבֹרָךְ.

קהל: בָּרוּךְ יהוה הַמְבֹרָךְ לְעוֹלָם וָעֶד.

עולה: בָּרוּךְ יהוה הַמְבֹרָךְ לְעוֹלָם וָעֶד.

בָּרוּךְ אַתָּה יהוה, אֱלֹהֵינוּ מֶלֶךְ הָעוֹלָם

אֲשֶׁר בָּחַר בָּנוּ מִכָּל הָעַמִּים וְנָתַן לָנוּ אֶת תּוֹרָתוֹ.

בָּרוּךְ אַתָּה יהוה, נוֹתֵן הַתּוֹרָה.

After the קריאת התורה, *the* עולה *says:*

עולה: בָּרוּךְ אַתָּה יהוה אֱלֹהֵינוּ מֶלֶךְ הָעוֹלָם

אֲשֶׁר נָתַן לָנוּ תּוֹרַת אֱמֶת וְחַיֵּי עוֹלָם נָטַע בְּתוֹכֵנוּ.

בָּרוּךְ אַתָּה יהוה, נוֹתֵן הַתּוֹרָה.

One who has survived a situation of danger, says:

בָּרוּךְ אַתָּה יהוה אֱלֹהֵינוּ מֶלֶךְ הָעוֹלָם

הַגּוֹמֵל לְחַיָּבִים טוֹבוֹת, שֶׁגְּמָלַנִי כָּל טוֹב.

The קהל *responds:*

אָמֵן. מִי שֶׁגְּמָלְךָ כָּל טוֹב הוּא יִגְמָלְךָ כָּל טוֹב, סֶלָה.

After a בר מצווה *has finished the* תורה *blessing, his father says aloud:*

בָּרוּךְ שֶׁפְּטָרַנִי מֵעָנְשׁוֹ שֶׁלָּזֶה.

בָּרוּךְ יהוה *Bless the Lord.* An invitation to the congregation to join in blessing God, similar to the one that precedes communal prayer in the morning and evening services.

אֲשֶׁר בָּחַר בָּנוּ מִכָּל הָעַמִּים *Who has chosen us from all peoples.* This ancient blessing, to be said before Torah study as well as before the public reading of the Torah, makes it clear that chosenness is not a right but a responsibility.

FOR AN OLEH

May He who blessed our fathers, Abraham, Isaac and Jacob, bless (*name*, son of *father's name*) who has been called up in honor of the All-Present, in honor of the Torah, and in honor of the festival. As a reward for this, may the Holy One, blessed be He, protect and deliver him from all trouble and distress, all infection and illness, and send blessing and success to all the work of his hands, and may he merit to go up to Jerusalem for the festivals, together with all Israel, his brethren, and let us say: Amen.

FOR A SICK MAN

May He who blessed our fathers, Abraham, Isaac and Jacob, Moses and Aaron, David and Solomon, bless and heal one who is ill, (*sick person's name*, son of *mother's name*), on whose behalf (*name of the one making the offering*) is making a contribution to charity. As a reward for this, may the Holy One, blessed be He, be filled with compassion for him, to restore his health, cure him, strengthen and revive him, sending him a swift and full recovery from heaven to all his 248 organs and 365 sinews, amongst the other sick ones in Israel, a healing of the spirit and a healing of the body – though on festivals it is forbidden to cry out, may healing be quick to come – now, swiftly and soon, and let us say: Amen.

FOR A SICK WOMAN

May He who blessed our fathers, Abraham, Isaac and Jacob, Moses and Aaron, David and Solomon, bless and heal one who is ill, (*sick person's name*, daughter of *mother's name*), on whose behalf (*name of the one making the offering*) is making a contribution to charity. As a reward for this, may the Holy One, blessed be He, be filled with compassion for her, to restore her health, cure her, strengthen and revive her, sending her a swift and full recovery from heaven to all her organs and sinews, amongst the other sick ones in Israel, a healing of the spirit and a healing of the body – though on festivals it is forbidden to cry out, may healing be quick to come – now, swiftly and soon, and let us say: Amen.

מי שבירך לעולה לתורה

מִי שֶׁבֵּרַךְ אֲבוֹתֵינוּ אַבְרָהָם יִצְחָק וְיַעֲקֹב, הוּא יְבָרֵךְ אֶת (פלוני בֶּן
פלוני), בַּעֲבוּר שֶׁעָלָה לִכְבוֹד הַמָּקוֹם וְלִכְבוֹד הַתּוֹרָה וְלִכְבוֹד הָרֶגֶל.
בִּשְׂכַר זֶה הַקָּדוֹשׁ בָּרוּךְ הוּא יִשְׁמְרֵהוּ וְיַצִּילֵהוּ מִכָּל צָרָה וְצוּקָה
וּמִכָּל נֶגַע וּמַחֲלָה, וְיִשְׁלַח בְּרָכָה וְהַצְלָחָה בְּכָל מַעֲשֵׂה יָדָיו, וְיִזְכֶּה
לַעֲלוֹת לָרֶגֶל עִם כָּל יִשְׂרָאֵל אֶחָיו, וְנֹאמַר אָמֵן.

מי שבירך לחולה

מִי שֶׁבֵּרַךְ אֲבוֹתֵינוּ אַבְרָהָם יִצְחָק וְיַעֲקֹב, מֹשֶׁה וְאַהֲרֹן דָּוִד וּשְׁלֹמֹה
הוּא יְבָרֵךְ וִירַפֵּא אֶת הַחוֹלֶה (פלוני בֶּן פלונית) בַּעֲבוּר שֶׁ(פלוני בֶּן פלוני)
נוֹדֵר צְדָקָה בַּעֲבוּרוֹ. בִּשְׂכַר זֶה הַקָּדוֹשׁ בָּרוּךְ הוּא יִמָּלֵא רַחֲמִים
עָלָיו לְהַחֲלִימוֹ וּלְרַפֹּאתוֹ וּלְהַחֲזִיקוֹ וּלְהַחֲיוֹתוֹ וְיִשְׁלַח לוֹ מְהֵרָה
רְפוּאָה שְׁלֵמָה מִן הַשָּׁמַיִם לִרְמַ״ח אֵבָרָיו וּשְׁסַ״ה גִּידָיו בְּתוֹךְ שְׁאָר
חוֹלֵי יִשְׂרָאֵל, רְפוּאַת הַנֶּפֶשׁ וּרְפוּאַת הַגּוּף. יוֹם טוֹב הוּא מִלִּזְעֹק
וּרְפוּאָה קְרוֹבָה לָבוֹא, הַשְׁתָּא בַּעֲגָלָא וּבִזְמַן קָרִיב, וְנֹאמַר אָמֵן.

מי שבירך לחולה

מִי שֶׁבֵּרַךְ אֲבוֹתֵינוּ אַבְרָהָם יִצְחָק וְיַעֲקֹב, מֹשֶׁה וְאַהֲרֹן דָּוִד וּשְׁלֹמֹה
הוּא יְבָרֵךְ וִירַפֵּא אֶת הַחוֹלָה (פלונית בַּת פלונית) בַּעֲבוּר שֶׁ(פלוני בֶּן
פלוני) נוֹדֵר צְדָקָה בַּעֲבוּרָהּ. בִּשְׂכַר זֶה הַקָּדוֹשׁ בָּרוּךְ הוּא יִמָּלֵא
רַחֲמִים עָלֶיהָ לְהַחֲלִימָהּ וּלְרַפֹּאתָהּ וּלְהַחֲזִיקָהּ וּלְהַחֲיוֹתָהּ וְיִשְׁלַח
לָהּ מְהֵרָה רְפוּאָה שְׁלֵמָה מִן הַשָּׁמַיִם לְכָל אֵבָרֶיהָ וּלְכָל גִּידֶיהָ
בְּתוֹךְ שְׁאָר חוֹלֵי יִשְׂרָאֵל, רְפוּאַת הַנֶּפֶשׁ וּרְפוּאַת הַגּוּף. יוֹם טוֹב
הוּא מִלִּזְעֹק וּרְפוּאָה קְרוֹבָה לָבוֹא, הַשְׁתָּא בַּעֲגָלָא וּבִזְמַן קָרִיב,
וְנֹאמַר אָמֵן.

ON THE BIRTH OF A SON

May He who blessed our fathers, Abraham, Isaac and Jacob, Moses and Aaron, David and Solomon, Sarah, Rebecca, Rachel and Leah, bless the woman (*name*, daughter of *father's name*) who has given birth, and her son who has been born to her as an auspicious sign. Her husband, the child's father, is making a contribution to charity. As a reward for this, may father and mother merit to bring the child into the covenant of Abraham and to a life of Torah, to the marriage canopy and to good deeds, and let us say: Amen.

ON THE BIRTH OF A DAUGHTER

May He who blessed our fathers, Abraham, Isaac and Jacob, Moses and Aaron, David and Solomon, Sarah, Rebecca, Rachel and Leah, bless the woman (*name*, daughter of *father's name*) who has given birth, and her daughter who has been born to her as an auspicious sign; and may her name be called in Israel (*baby's name*, daughter of *father's name*). Her husband, the child's father, is making a contribution to charity. As a reward for this, may father and mother merit to raise her to a life of Torah, to the marriage canopy, and to good deeds, and let us say: Amen.

FOR A BAR MITZVA

May He who blessed our fathers, Abraham, Isaac and Jacob, bless (*name*, son of *father's name*) who has completed thirteen years and attained the age of the commandments, who has been called to the Torah to give praise and thanks to God, may His name be blessed, for all the good He has bestowed on him. May the Holy One, blessed be He, protect and sustain him and direct his heart to be perfect with God, to walk in His ways and keep the commandments all the days of his life, and let us say: Amen.

FOR A BAT MITZVA

May He who blessed our fathers, Abraham, Isaac and Jacob, Sarah, Rebecca, Rachel and Leah, bless (*name*, daughter of *father's name*) who has completed twelve years and attained the age of the commandments, and gives praise and thanks to God, may His name be blessed, for all the good He has bestowed on her. May the Holy One, blessed be He, protect and sustain her and direct her heart to be perfect with God, to walk in His ways and keep the commandments all the days of her life, and let us say: Amen.

מי שבירך ליולדת בן

מִי שֶׁבֵּרַךְ אֲבוֹתֵינוּ אַבְרָהָם יִצְחָק וְיַעֲקֹב, מֹשֶׁה וְאַהֲרֹן דָּוִד וּשְׁלֹמֹה,
שָׂרָה רִבְקָה רָחֵל וְלֵאָה הוּא יְבָרֵךְ אֶת הָאִשָּׁה הַיּוֹלֶדֶת (פלונית בת פלוני)
וְאֶת בְּנָהּ שֶׁנּוֹלַד לָהּ לְמַזָּל טוֹב בַּעֲבוּר שֶׁבַּעְלָהּ וְאָבִיו נוֹדֵר צְדָקָה
בַּעֲדָם. בִּשְׂכַר זֶה יִזְכּוּ אָבִיו וְאִמּוֹ לְהַכְנִיסוֹ בִּבְרִיתוֹ שֶׁל אַבְרָהָם אָבִינוּ
וּלְגַדְּלוֹ לְתוֹרָה וּלְחֻפָּה וּלְמַעֲשִׂים טוֹבִים, וְנֹאמַר אָמֵן.

מי שבירך ליולדת בת

מִי שֶׁבֵּרַךְ אֲבוֹתֵינוּ אַבְרָהָם יִצְחָק וְיַעֲקֹב, מֹשֶׁה וְאַהֲרֹן דָּוִד וּשְׁלֹמֹה,
שָׂרָה רִבְקָה רָחֵל וְלֵאָה הוּא יְבָרֵךְ אֶת הָאִשָּׁה הַיּוֹלֶדֶת (פלונית בת פלוני)
וְאֶת בִּתָּהּ שֶׁנּוֹלְדָה לָהּ לְמַזָּל טוֹב וְיִקָּרֵא שְׁמָהּ בְּיִשְׂרָאֵל (פלונית בת פלוני),
בַּעֲבוּר שֶׁבַּעְלָהּ וְאָבֶיהָ נוֹדֵר צְדָקָה בַּעֲדָן. בִּשְׂכַר זֶה יִזְכּוּ אָבֶיהָ וְאִמָּהּ
לְגַדְּלָהּ לְתוֹרָה וּלְחֻפָּה וּלְמַעֲשִׂים טוֹבִים, וְנֹאמַר אָמֵן.

מי שבירך לבר מצווה

מִי שֶׁבֵּרַךְ אֲבוֹתֵינוּ אַבְרָהָם יִצְחָק וְיַעֲקֹב הוּא יְבָרֵךְ אֶת (פלוני בן פלוני)
שֶׁמָּלְאוּ לוֹ שְׁלֹשׁ עֶשְׂרֵה שָׁנָה וְהִגִּיעַ לְמִצְוֹת, וְעָלָה לַתּוֹרָה, לָתֵת שֶׁבַח
וְהוֹדָיָה לְהַשֵּׁם יִתְבָּרַךְ עַל כָּל הַטּוֹבָה שֶׁגָּמַל אִתּוֹ. יִשְׁמְרֵהוּ הַקָּדוֹשׁ
בָּרוּךְ הוּא וִיחַיֵּהוּ, וִיכוֹנֵן אֶת לִבּוֹ לִהְיוֹת שָׁלֵם עִם יהוה וְלָלֶכֶת בִּדְרָכָיו
וְלִשְׁמֹר מִצְוֹתָיו כָּל הַיָּמִים, וְנֹאמַר אָמֵן.

מי שבירך לבת מצווה

מִי שֶׁבֵּרַךְ אֲבוֹתֵינוּ אַבְרָהָם יִצְחָק וְיַעֲקֹב, שָׂרָה רִבְקָה רָחֵל וְלֵאָה,
הוּא יְבָרֵךְ אֶת (פלונית בת פלוני) שֶׁמָּלְאוּ לָהּ שְׁתֵּים עֶשְׂרֵה שָׁנָה וְהִגִּיעָה
לְמִצְוֹת, וְנוֹתֶנֶת שֶׁבַח וְהוֹדָיָה לְהַשֵּׁם יִתְבָּרַךְ עַל כָּל הַטּוֹבָה שֶׁגָּמַל
אִתָּהּ. יִשְׁמְרָהּ הַקָּדוֹשׁ בָּרוּךְ הוּא וִיחַיֶּהָ, וִיכוֹנֵן אֶת לִבָּהּ לִהְיוֹת שָׁלֵם
עִם יהוה וְלָלֶכֶת בִּדְרָכָיו וְלִשְׁמֹר מִצְוֹתָיו כָּל הַיָּמִים, וְנֹאמַר אָמֵן.

TORAH READING FOR THE FIRST DAY OF SHAVUOT

On Shavuot, after the Kohen is called up to the Torah and before he makes the blessing,
the following is said responsively by the Reader and the congregation.

AKDAMUT

Leader: The beginning of words – the opening of speech:
   I shall ask permission and leave to begin.

Cong: Trembling I open my mouth with two matters and three,
   by leave of the One who bears us through to old age.

Leader: His are eternal mighty acts,
    which could not be laid out in words,
   even were all the skies parchment, and all the forests reeds;

Cong: if all the seas were ink, and all the lakes,
   and the all people, scribes and clerks.

Leader: The glorious Master of Heaven, Ruler of the land,
   founded His world alone, and took control of it.

Cong: Without weariness He perfected it, without tiring at all;
   by the lightest of letters, something without substance.

It is about Torah as it stands *outside* history, from the beginning of time to
the end of days.

These features differentiate it from other liturgical poems, but what is most
unusual and eventually gave rise to controversy was the point of the service
at which it was said, namely after the first verse of the reading of the Torah.
As authorities (among them the *Taz*, Rabbi David HaLevi Segal, 1586–1667)
pointed out, this is a seemingly forbidden interruption. Eventually, under
cumulative opposition, many communities moved it to immediately *be-*
fore the reading and its blessing. Yet for several centuries, beginning with
R. Jacob Moelin (Maharil, 1365–1427), great authorities had sanctioned its

קְרִיאָה לְיוֹם טוֹב רִאשׁוֹן שֶׁל שָׁבוּעוֹת

On שבועות, after the כהן is called up to the תורה and before he makes the ברכה,
the following is said responsively by the שליח ציבור and the קהל.

אַקְדָּמוּת

ש״ץ: אַקְדָּמוּת מִלִּין וְשָׁרָיוּת שׁוּתָא
אַוְלָא שָׁקֵלְנָא הַרְמָן וּרְשׁוּתָא.

קהל: בְּבָבֵי תְּרֵי וּתְלַת דְּאֶפְתַּח בְּנַקְשׁוּתָא
בְּבָרֵי דְּבָרֵי וְטָרֵי עֲדֵי לְקַשִּׁישׁוּתָא.

ש״ץ: גְּבוּרָן עָלְמִין לֵהּ, וְלָא סְפֵק פְּרִישׁוּתָא
גְּוִיל אִלּוּ רְקִיעֵי, קְנֵי כָּל חֻרְשָׁתָא.

קהל: דְּיוֹ אִלּוּ יַמֵּי וְכָל מֵי כְנִישׁוּתָא
דָּיְרֵי אַרְעָא סָפְרֵי וְרָשְׁמֵי רַשְׁוָתָא.

ש״ץ: הֲדַר מָרֵי שְׁמַיָּא וְשַׁלִּיט בְּיַבֶּשְׁתָּא
הֲקֵים עָלְמָא יְחִידַאי, וְכַבְּשֵׁהּ בְּכַבְּשׁוּתָא.

קהל: וּבְלָא לֵאוּ שַׁכְלְלֵהּ, וּבְלָא תְשָׁשׁוּתָא
וּבְאָתָא קַלִּילָא דְּלֵית בַּהּ מְשָׁשׁוּתָא.

AKDAMUT

Akdamut – meaning, "preface, prologue, introduction" – is one of the best known of all *piyutim*. In several respects, though, it stands outside the standard conventions of liturgical poetry. First, it is not written as an addition to prayer. It is about a different feature of the synagogue service, namely, the reading of the Torah. Second, *piyut* is normally written in Hebrew, whereas *Akdamut* is written in Aramaic. Third, the poetry of prayer is usually about the specific day on which it is said, but *Akdamut* is not, except in its very last line, about Shavuot and the giving of the Torah at a specific time and place.

Leader: He summoned forth all creation in those six days;
and then His shining glory rose, to sit upon His throne of fire.

Cong: A heavenly host of a thousand thousands
and myriads serve Him –
created each morning anew, so great is His faithfulness.

Leader: Seraphim, covered with six wings, bow many times over,
and stand in utter silence until they have leave.

Cong: They receive leave from each other –
and at once, without pause,
His glory fills all the world, at their threefold sanctifying.

Leader: Like a voice from the Almighty, like the noise of many waters –
Cherubim raise themselves towards the Ophanim
in a roar of noise,

Cong: to see face to face what looks like sparks of the rainbow flying,
and wherever they are sent, they arrive in a flash of motion.

Leader: They bless His glory in every secret term,
from the place of the home of His Presence,
which cannot even be sought.

---

language of Ashdod or the language of one of the other peoples, and did not know how to speak the language of Judah" (Neh. 13:24). At the great public Torah reading in Jerusalem convened by Ezra, learned Levites were stationed throughout the crowd to explain what was being read, "making it clear and giving the meaning so that the people understood what was being read" (Neh. 8:8). The Talmud (*Megilla* 3a) explains that "making it clear" means "*Targum,*" that is, providing a translation.

Eventually in Europe the custom of line-by-line translation during the Torah reading lapsed, since Aramaic was no longer the everyday language of Jews (Yemenite Jews, however, still continue the practice). There were, though, two exceptions: the reading on the seventh day of Pesaḥ (the Song at the Sea), and the first day of Shavuot (the Ten Commandments). This explains *Akdamut.* It is a *reshut* – a request for permission from the

ש״ץ: זְמֵן כָּל עֲבִידְתֵּהּ בְּהַךְ יוֹמֵי שִׁתָּא
זְהוֹר יְקָרֵהּ עֲלֵי, עֲלֵי כָּרְסְיֵהּ דְּאֶשְׁתָּא.

קהל: חֵיַל אֶלֶף אַלְפִּין וְרִבּוֹא לְשַׁמְּשׁוּתָא
חַדְתִּין נְבוֹט לְצַפְרִין, סַגִּיאָה טְרָשׁוּתָא.

ש״ץ: טְפֵי יְקִידִין שְׂרָפִין, כְּלוּל גַּפֵּי שִׁתָּא
טְעֵם עַד יִתְיְהֵב לְהוֹן, שְׁתִיקִין בְּאַדִּישְׁתָּא.

קהל: יְקַבְּלוּן דֵּין מִן דֵּין שָׁוֵי דְּלָא בְּשַׁשְׁתָּא
יְקָר מְלֵי כָל אַרְעָא לְתַלּוֹתֵי קְדֻשְׁתָּא.

ש״ץ: כְּקָל מִן קֳדָם שַׁדַּי, כְּקָל מֵי נְפִישׁוּתָא
כְּרוּבִין קָבֵל גַּלְגַּלִּין מְרוֹמְמִין בְּאוּשַׁשְׁתָּא.

קהל: לְמֶחֱזֵי בְּאַנְפָּא עֵין כְּוָת גִּירֵי קַשְׁתָּא
לְכָל אֲתַר דְּמִשְׁתַּלְּחִין, זְרִיזִין בְּאַשְׁוָתָא.

ש״ץ: מְבָרְכִין בְּרִיךְ יְקָרֵהּ בְּכָל לְשַׁן לְחִישׁוּתָא
מֵאֲתַר בֵּית שְׁכִינְתֵּהּ, דְּלָא צְרִיךְ בְּחִישׁוּתָא.

recitation *during* the reading. To understand all this requires a historical context.

During the period of the Second Temple, as the institution of the synagogue gradually spread, it became the custom during the reading of the Torah for a member of the community to translate it line by line into Aramaic, the spoken language of Jews at the time. This was known as the *Targum* (translation), and it was done purely orally, without reference to a written text, by a member of the congregation known as the *Meturgeman* (translator). Eventually a normative translation was recorded in written form in several versions, best known of which was that of Onkelos in the first century.

Maimonides (Laws of Prayer, 12:10–11) dates the practice to the days of Ezra in the fifth century BCE. The book of Nehemiah tells us that this was a time when Jews in the land of Israel had become so assimilated that they no longer knew how to speak Hebrew: "Half of their children spoke the

Cong: And all the hosts of heaven give praises in great fear,
    of the sovereignty that will last through all ages, forever.

Leader: They each lay out His holiness in praise,
        and when their moment has passed
    it is gone forever; seven years will go by and it will not return.

Cong: His precious estate, Israel – they are more fortunate, for always
    may they praise Him, dawn and dusk.

Leader: They are set apart, His portion, to perform His will,
    and they will tell the wonders of His praise in speech.

Cong: He desires and values and yearns for them
        to labor for Him to weariness,
    and so He accepts their prayers; it is their pleas that are fulfilled.

Leader: And those pleas are joined, with a crown and an oath,
    to the One who lives forever,
        and worn with the phylacteries He binds to Himself always,

Cong: which are inscribed inside with wisdom and with insight,
    with the greatness of Israel, who read the Shema.

Sephardi Jews came together in a single synagogue. The Sephardim, who came from Spain and Portugal, had never said *Akdamut*, a composition that came from the world of Ashkenaz in Germany and France. Not knowing its history, they were amazed that a poem was allowed to interrupt the Torah reading. The halakhic authorities were themselves torn. On the one hand they knew that *Akdamut*, said at that point, had long been approved of, and one should not change existing custom. On the other, its original context, the public recitation of the *Targum*, beginning after the first line of the Torah reading, no longer applied. Eventually a compromise was reached, whereby *Akdamut* was said *prior* to the Torah reading and its blessing.

The poem continued to be read, even without its original context, because it had become well-loved by Ashkenazi communities, it was an established part of the Shavuot service and its traditional melody was part of the music of the day. Besides, it still had a bearing on the theme of the day itself, namely

קהל: נְהֵם כָּל חֵיל מְרוֹמָא, מְקַלְּסִין בַּחֲשַׁשְׁתָּא
נְהִירָא מַלְכוּתֵהּ לְדָר וְדָר לְאַפְרַשְׁתָּא.

ש"ץ: סְדִירָא בְּהוֹן קְדֻשְׁתָּא, וְכַד חָלְפָא שַׁעְתָּא
סִיּוּמָא דִּלְעָלַם, וְאוֹף לָא לִשְׁבוּעֲתָא.

קהל: עֲדַב יְקָר אַחְסַנְתֵּהּ חֲבִיבִין, דִּבְקַבְעָתָא
עֲבִידִין לֵהּ חֲטִיבָא בְּדְנַח וּשְׁקַעְתָּא.

ש"ץ: פְּרִישָׁן לְמָנָתֵהּ לְמֶעְבַּד לֵהּ רְעוּתָא
פְּרִישָׁתֵי שְׁבָחֵהּ יְחַוּוֹן בִּשְׁעוּתָא.

קהל: צְבִי וְחָמֵד וְרָגֵג דְּיִלְאוֹן בְּלָעוּתָא
צְלוֹתְהוֹן בְּכֵן מְקַבֵּל, וְהַנְיָא בָעוּתָא.

ש"ץ: קְטִירָא לְחַי עָלְמָא בְּתָגָא בִּשְׁבוּעֲתָא
קָבֵל יְקָר טוֹטֶפְתָּא יְתִיבָא בִּקְבִיעֲתָא.

קהל: רְשִׁימָא הִיא גוּפָא בְּחָכְמְתָא וּבְדַעְתָּא
וּרְבוּתְהוֹן דְּיִשְׂרָאֵל, קְרָאֵי בִּשְׁמַעְתָּא.

---

congregation – to engage in this verse-by-verse translation. That is why it is
written in Aramaic, and why it was said after the first verse of the Hebrew
reading, immediately before the first line of the Aramaic translation. It is also
why it was said on Shavuot, one of only two occasions in which the *Targum*
was still incorporated into the public Torah reading.

It was written in the late eleventh century by Rabbi Meir bar Yitzhak
Nehorai of Orléans, one of the great sages of his generation, cited approv-
ingly by Rashi and the Tosafists. At the time and for several centuries later,
everyone understood why the poem was said at that point. Eventually, though,
the public recitation on the *Targum* was discontinued even on these two days,
yet the poem remained – now, without a context. That is why, having been
accepted without demur for several centuries, in the seventeenth century
Akdamut occasioned controversy.

It began in Venice where, in the seventeenth century, Ashkenazi and

Leader: And I, in the same way, praise the Master of the Universe,
and it befits me to speak of Him to those of other nations,

Cong: who come and form crowds, like waves all around,
doubting, asking about Him, about the signs He performs –

Leader: "Where is your Beloved from, yes who is He, who is so beautiful,
that you let yourselves be killed for Him in the lions' den?

Cong: "You would be more respected, lovelier,
if you bent yourselves to our rule:
your will would be done then wherever you would be."

Leader: With wisdom I reply to them, telling them of the end –
"If you only knew, if you only truly knew Him,

Cong: "and what your greatness is worth when compared to that glory,
or the greatness
I will be granted when my salvation comes...

Leader: "When light comes to me, and shame covers you over;
when His presence is revealed to me in might and in great pride."

Cong: He shall pay His enemies back in kind, the aggressors
of the distant isles,
and perform justice for the beloved people, rich in merit,

Jewish people, composed by R. Israel Najara in Safed in the late sixteenth century.

The poem, ninety lines long, is constructed in the form of two-line verses said responsively by the leader of prayer and the congregation. The first 44 lines form a double alphabetical acrostic, while the remainder spell out the words, "Meir, son of Rabbi Isaac, may he grow in strength and good deeds, Amen. Be strong and of good courage." Each line ends with the letters תא, the last and first letters of the Hebrew alphabet, suggesting the idea of uninterrupted study of the Torah: no sooner have we reached the last letter than we begin again.

The overarching theme of *Akdamut* is the Torah itself, not as it was given at

ש"ץ: שְׁבַח רִבּוֹן עָלְמָא, אֲמִירָא דְּכַוָּתָא
שְׁפַר עֲלַי לְחַוּוֵיהּ בְּאַפֵּי מַלְכּוּתָא.

קהל: תָּאִין וּמִתְכַּנְּשִׁין כְּחֵזוּ אַדְוָתָא
תְּמֵהִין וְשָׁיְלִין לֵהּ בְּעֵסֶק אָתְוָתָא.

ש"ץ: מְנָן וּמַאן הוּא רְחִימָךְ, שַׁפִּירָא בְּרֵוָתָא
אֲרוּם בְּגִינֵהּ סָפֵית מְדוֹר אַרְיְוָתָא.

קהל: יְקָרָא וְיָאָה אַתְּ, אִין תְּעָרְבִי לְמָרְוָתָא
רְעוּתֵךְ נַעֲבֵד לִיךְ בְּכָל אַתְרְוָתָא.

ש"ץ: בְּחָכְמְתָא מְתִיבְתָּא לְהוֹן, קְצָת לְהוֹדָעוּתָא
יְדַעְתּוּן חַכְּמִין לֵהּ בְּאִשְׁתְּמוֹדָעוּתָא.

קהל: רְבוּתְכוֹן מֶה חֲשִׁיבָא קֳבֵל הַהִיא שְׁבַחְתָּא
רְבוּתָא דְּיַעֲבֵד לִי, כַּד מָטְיָא יְשׁוּעָתָא.

ש"ץ: בְּמֵיתֵי לִי נְהוֹרָא, וְתַחֲפֵי לְכוֹן בַּהֲתָא
יְקָרֵהּ כַּד אִתְגְּלֵי בְּתָקְפָּא וּבְגֵיוָתָא.

קהל: יְשַׁלֵּם גְּמֻלַיָּא לְשָׂנְאַי וְנַגְוָתָא
צִדְקָתָא לְעַם חָבִיב וְסַגִּי זַכְוָתָא.

_____

the giving of the Torah. R. Yitzḥak Hadari (*Shana BeShana*, 1987) has suggested a further reason. The two occasions on which the *Targum* was recited in the days of R. Meir recalled the two greatest miracles in Jewish history: the division of the Reed Sea on the seventh day of Pesaḥ and the giving of the Torah on Shavuot. At the Sea the people sang a song, but at Mount Sinai after the giving of the Torah they were too terrified to do so (they "trembled with fear and stood at a distance," Ex. 20:18). *Akdamut* fills that gap: it is the song the Israelites might have sung had they not been paralyzed by fear. Supporting this hypothesis is the fact that Sephardi communities have their own song, written as a *ketuba*, a marriage contract, between God and the

Leader: when He brings perfect happiness, and us as pure vessels;
when He brings the exiles back into the city of Jerusalem.

Cong: He shall cast His glory over them day and night,
as a canopy where they shall voice the splendor in
joyful songs,

Leader: for the shining of those clouds will make each canopy fine
as the actions of the one who sits in it; so will each shelter
be made.

Cong: On seats of finest gold, in seven tiers, sit the righteous
in their places before the One whose acts are manifold.

Leader: And they appear as seven tiers of joy,
like the dome of the sky in its brilliance, like stars of light.

Cong: This is a glory no mouth can express,
glory that the prophets never heard or saw in their visions.

Leader: For no eye has ever overseen the Garden of Eden,
where the righteous circle the place of the dance, and the holy
Presence among them.

Cong: And they point to Him, saying with awe, "It is He!
"The One for whom we longed when we were captives, in our
powerful faith.

From here the poet moves to his second theme. Rabbi Meir was writing
in the late eleventh century. At that time, while Spanish Jewry was enjoy-
ing its golden age, the condition of Jews in Northern Europe was palpably
worsening. The First Crusade, with its massacre of Jews in Speyer, Worms
and Mainz (1096) had not yet happened. R. Meir died in 1095. But there
were already ominous signs of what a historian has called "the formation of
a persecuting society."

Christians were calling on Jews to convert, arguing that their lowly condition showed that God had abandoned them: "Where is your Beloved … that
you let yourselves be killed for Him in the lion's den?" If only they would

ש״ץ: חֲדוּ שְׁלֵמָא בְּמֵיתֵי, וּמָנָא דְכָוָתָא
קִרְיָתָא דִירוּשְׁלֵם כַּד יְכַנֵּשׁ גַּלְוָתָא.

קהל: יְקָרֵהּ מַטֵּל עֲלַהּ בְּיוֹמֵי וְלֵילְוָתָא
גְנוּנֵהּ לְמֶעְבַּד בַּהּ בְּתִשְׁבְּחָן כְּלִילָתָא.

ש״ץ: דְּזֵהוֹר עֲנָנָא לְמִשְׁפַּר כִּילָתָא
לְפֻמֵּהּ דַּעֲבִידְתָּא עֲבִידָן מְטַלַּלְתָּא.

קהל: בְּתַכְתְּקֵי דְּהַב פְּזָא, וְשֶׁבַע מַעֲלָתָא
תְּחִימִין צַדִּיקֵי קֳדָם רַב פָּעֳלָתָא.

ש״ץ: וְרֵיוֵיהוֹן דָּמֵי לְשָׁבְעָא חֶדְוָתָא
רְקִיעָא בְּזֵהוֹרֵהּ וְכוֹכְבֵי זִיוָתָא.

קהל: הֲדָרָא דְּלָא אֶפְשַׁר לְמִפְרַט שְׂפְוָתָא
וְלָא אִשְׁתְּמַע וַחֲמֵי נְבִיאָן חֲזָוָתָא.

ש״ץ: בְּלָא שָׁלְטָא בֵהּ עֵין, בְּגוֹ עֵדֶן גִּנְּתָא
מְטַיְּלֵי בֵהּ חִנְגָּא לְבַהֲדֵי דִשְׁכִינְתָּא.

קהל: עֲלַהּ רָמְזֵי דֵּין הוּא, בְּרַם בְּאֵימְתָנוּתָא
שְׁבָרְנָא לֵהּ בְּשִׁבְיַן, תְּקוֹף הֵמָנוּתָא.

Mount Sinai but as it existed in the mind of God prior to the creation of the universe. In sharp contrast to ancient myth in which the universe was thought to have achieved order only after an epic battle between contending forces, the poet emphasizes how God brought the world into being without effort and "by the lightest of letters." God is worshiped in the heavens by myriads of angels, yet more valued by Him than this is the praise of "his precious estate, Israel." The poet invokes the ancient rabbinic image (*Berakhot* 6a) that just as Israel binds itself to God by wearing tefillin, so God binds Himself to Israel by wearing tefillin in which are written the words, "And who is like Your people Israel – one nation on earth?" (1 Chr. 17:21).

Leader: "And He will lead us in both worlds; and He will lead us dancing,
      as if we were young again;
    lead us to our land, set aside from the beginning of the world
      for us."

Cong: He plays with the Leviathan, with the Behemoth of the
      high mountain,
    and when they wrestle one another in their great duel,

Leader: the horns of the great Behemoth will gore,
    and the mighty Leviathan will leap out at him with his fins,

Cong: and finally, his Creator will step forward with His great sword,
    and prepare a meal, a feast, of that meat, for all the righteous.

Leader: And they shall sit at tables of rubies and gems,
    with rivers of balsam flowing before them,

Cong: and quench their thirst in luxury with overflowing cups
    of the wondrous wine stored up for them since the first days
      of creation.

Leader: My righteous listeners, as you have heard the praises in this song,
    so may you be promised a place in those joyous circles.

Cong: And may you merit to sit in those heavenly rows,
    for heeding God's words, which come forth in splendor.

Leader: Our God is in the highest heights, the first and the last,
    desiring us and cherishing us, and giving us the Torah.

---

faithful where they will drink from "the wondrous wine stored up for them since the first days of creation."

This is a dignified, even joyous, affirmation of Judaism at the beginning of one of its darkest nights, and a refusal to accept the definition their enemies gave of Jews as a pariah people rejected by God. *Akdamut* is the joyous declaration of a God-intoxicated people who know that no earthly honor is equal to the spiritual greatness that has been thrust on them by the God of love

ש״ץ: יְדַבֵּר לַן עָלְמִין, עָלְמִין מְדַמּוּתָא
מְנָת דִּילַן דְּמִלְּקַדְמִין פְּרֵשׁ בַּאֲרָמוּתָא.

קהל: טְלוּלָא דִלְוַיָתָן וְתוֹר טוּר רָמוּתָא
וְחַד בְּחַד כִּי סָבֵךְ וְעָבֵד קְרָבוּתָא.

ש״ץ: בְּקַרְנוֹהִי מְנַגַּח בְּהֵמוֹת בְּרַבוּתָא
יְקַרְטַע נוּן לְקָבְלֵהּ בְּצִיצוֹי בִּגְבוּרְתָּא.

קהל: מְקָרֵב לֵהּ בָּרְיֵהּ בְּחַרְבֵּהּ בְּרַבְרְבוּתָא
אֲרִסְטוֹן לְצַדִּיקֵי יְתַקֵּן, וְשֵׁרוּתָא.

ש״ץ: מְסַחֲרִין עֲלֵי תַבֵּי דְכַדְכֹד וְגוּמַרְתָּא
נְגִידִין קָמֵיהוֹן אֲפַרְסְמוֹן נַהֲרָתָא.

קהל: וּמִתְפַּנְּקִין וְרַוּוֹ בְּכָסֵי רְוָיָתָא
חֲמַר מְרַת דְּמִבְּרֵאשִׁית נְטִיר בֵּי נַעֲוָתָא.

ש״ץ: זַכָּאִין, כַּד שְׁמַעְתּוּן שְׁבַח דָּא שִׁירָתָא
קְבִיעִין כֵּן תֶּהֱווֹן בְּהַנְהוּ חֲבוּרָתָא.

קהל: וְתִזְכּוּן דִּי תֵיתְבוּן בְּעֵלָּא דָרָתָא
אֲרֵי תְצִיתוּן לְמִלּוֹי, דְּנָפְקִין בְּהַדְרָתָא.

ש״ץ: מְרוֹמַם הוּא אֱלָהִין בְּקַדְמְתָא וּבַתְרַיְתָא
צְבִי וְאִתְרְעִי בַן, וּמְסַר לַן אוֹרַיְתָא.

_____

abandon their faith, "You would be more respected, lovelier." Rabbi Meir
rejects this utterly. God has given Israel His most precious gift, the Torah.
And though Jews are being persecuted in exile, they will one day return to
their land and to Jerusalem. God will "cast His glory over them day and night."
And in the End of Days, the righteous will dance around the Divine Presence,
saying, "It is He – the One for whom we longed when we were captives." God
will slay the legendary Leviathan and Behemoth, and prepare a meal for His

On the third new moon after the people of Israel had left the land   *Ex.*
of Egypt, on that first day, they arrived at the wilderness of Sinai.   *19:1–20:23*
They had traveled from Refidim and they arrived in the wilderness
of Sinai, and encamped there in the desert; there, in view of the
mountain, Israel laid out its camp. And there Moses ascended to
God; and the LORD called out to him from the mountain, telling
him, "This you must say to the house of Jacob, must tell the children
of Israel: You have seen what I did in Egypt; and how I lifted you
high, on the wings of eagles, and brought you to Me. And now – if
you will listen to My voice, if you will guard close My covenant,
you shall be My treasure among all the peoples – for all the earth

---

phrase meant the women, the second, the men (*Mekhilta*). God spoke to
the women before the men because (1) they were more religiously dedicated
than the men, and (2) because they were the most significant influence on
the people's future: they would ensure that their children were educated in
the Torah (*Shemot Raba* 28:2).

אַתֶּם רְאִיתֶם *You have seen.* The emphasis is on the immediacy of the experience. The people had witnessed a divine intervention into history. They had
been redeemed from slavery under Pharaoh. God was now proposing that
they become a nation under His own direct sovereignty in fulfillment of
what He had earlier told Moses: "I will take you as My people, and I will be
your God" (Ex. 6:7). This would mark the culmination of their seven-week
journey from servitude to law-governed liberty.

עַל־כַּנְפֵי נְשָׁרִים *On the wings of eagles.* An expression of parental concern. Just
as the eagle protects its young, so God protected the Israelites, surrounding
them with clouds of glory (Ex. 14:19–20). The phrase was used in modern
Jewish history to describe the airlifting of 49,000 Jews from Yemen to Israel
in 1949–50.

סְגֻלָּה מִכָּל־הָעַמִּים *My treasure among all the peoples.* God is the Creator of
the universe and the God of all humanity, but through the covenant, Israel
would have a special closeness to Him in virtue of the role and responsibility
they would thereby be undertaking, to be His emissaries and exemplars, His
ambassadors to humanity.

שמות
יט:א-כ:כג

בַּחֹ֙דֶשׁ֙ הַשְּׁלִישִׁ֔י לְצֵ֥את בְּנֵֽי־יִשְׂרָאֵ֖ל מֵאֶ֣רֶץ מִצְרָ֑יִם בַּיּ֣וֹם הַזֶּ֔ה
בָּ֖אוּ מִדְבַּ֥ר סִינָֽי: וַיִּסְע֣וּ מֵרְפִידִ֗ים וַיָּבֹ֙אוּ֙ מִדְבַּ֣ר סִינַ֔י וַֽיַּחֲנ֖וּ בַּמִּדְבָּ֑ר
וַיִּֽחַן־שָׁ֥ם יִשְׂרָאֵ֖ל נֶ֥גֶד הָהָֽר: וּמֹשֶׁ֥ה עָלָ֖ה אֶל־הָֽאֱלֹהִ֑ים וַיִּקְרָ֙א
אֵלָ֤יו יהוה֙ מִן־הָהָ֣ר לֵאמֹ֔ר כֹּ֤ה תֹאמַר֙ לְבֵ֣ית יַֽעֲקֹ֔ב וְתַגֵּ֖יד לִבְנֵ֥י
יִשְׂרָאֵֽל: אַתֶּ֣ם רְאִיתֶ֔ם אֲשֶׁ֥ר עָשִׂ֖יתִי לְמִצְרָ֑יִם וָֽאֶשָּׂ֤א אֶתְכֶם֙ עַל־
כַּנְפֵ֣י נְשָׁרִ֔ים וָֽאָבִ֥א אֶתְכֶ֖ם אֵלָֽי: וְעַתָּ֗ה אִם־שָׁמֹ֤עַ תִּשְׁמְעוּ֙ בְּקֹלִ֔י
וּשְׁמַרְתֶּ֖ם אֶת־בְּרִיתִ֑י וִֽהְיִ֨יתֶם לִ֤י סְגֻלָּה֙ מִכָּל־הָ֣עַמִּ֔ים כִּי־לִ֖י כָּל־

---

whom they serve in love and whose living expression is the Torah: God's law of life, His constitution of liberty for the people He rescued from slavery and chose to become His emissaries to the world.

READING OF THE TORAH: FIRST DAY

The reading for the first day describes the revelation at Mount Sinai, the event commemorated by Shavuot and the defining moment of Jewish history. It was then that, uniquely, God revealed Himself to an entire people, making a covenant with them that would charge them with the mission of becoming a holy nation, dedicated to God and an inspiration to the world. It was also the occasion on which God spoke the Ten Commandments or "Utterances" that eventually became the world's most famous moral code.

בַּיּוֹם הַזֶּה *On that first day.* The first day of the month of Sivan.

מִדְבַּר סִינַי *The wilderness of Sinai.* The plain at the foot of the mountain where God had first appeared to Moses at the burning bush, and where He had told Moses that He would eventually bring the people after their liberation (Ex. 3:12).

וַיִּחַן־שָׁם *Israel laid out its camp.* The unusual use of the singular verb suggested to the sages that the people were united "like one person with one heart" (*Mekhilta*, Rashi). The text throughout emphasizes the unity of the people in accepting the covenant: they did so "as one" (Ex. 19:7), "with one voice" (Ex. 24:3).

בֵית יַעֲקֹב ... בְּנֵי יִשְׂרָאֵל *The house of Jacob... the children of Israel.* Explaining the apparent redundancy of these two descriptions, the sages said that the first

is Mine; but you shall be a kingdom of priests to Me, a holy nation. These are the words you must say to the children of Israel."

So Moses came back, and called together the elders of the people, LEVI and laid out before them all these words with which the LORD had charged him. And all the people responded as one: "All that the LORD has spoken, we shall perform." And Moses brought the words of the people back to the LORD.

The LORD said to Moses, "I shall come to you in the thick of the cloud, that the people may hear as I speak to you, that they should believe in you also, forever," and Moses told the LORD what the people had said. "Go to the people," said the LORD to Moses, "And have them consecrate themselves today and tomorrow, and wash their clothes. Be sure they are ready for the third day, for on the third day the LORD shall descend to Mount Sinai, in the sight of all the people. Mark a boundary for the people around, and tell them:

---

made with humans in the Mosaic books that was conditional on their consent. Those with Noah (Gen. 9:1–11) and Abraham (Gen. 17:1–14) were not. Despite the abyss between the infinite power of God and the finitude of humankind, at the heart of the Sinai covenant is the idea of reciprocity and mutuality. It is God's call to human responsibility. The Israelites were called on to create a society that, by its justice and compassion, would become a home for the Divine Presence and a source of blessing to humanity as a whole.

וְגַם־בְּךָ יַאֲמִינוּ לְעוֹלָם *That they should believe in you also, forever.* The fact that the entire nation heard God speaking to Moses is, according to Judah HaLevi (*Kuzari* I: 88–89) and Maimonides (*Hilkhot Yesodei HaTorah* 8:1), the basis of our faith in Moses as the supreme prophet. God spoke *to* the other prophets; He spoke *through* Moses. Moses was "not a man of words ... slow of speech and slow of tongue" (Ex. 4:10). One of the reasons God chose a man who could not speak in public was so that people would know that the words he spoke were not his own but God's. In Judaism, God is the sole ultimate legislator. All man-made rules are secondary and subsidiary.

וְהָיוּ נְכֹנִים לַיּוֹם הַשְּׁלִישִׁי *Be sure that they are ready for the third day.* That is, the sixth of Sivan. Moses told this to the people on the fourth day (*Mekhilta*).

הָאָרֶץ: וְאַתֶּם תִּהְיוּ־לִי מַמְלֶכֶת כֹּהֲנִים וְגוֹי קָדוֹשׁ אֵלֶּה הַדְּבָרִים

אֲשֶׁר תְּדַבֵּר אֶל־בְּנֵי יִשְׂרָאֵל: *וַיָּבֹא מֹשֶׁה וַיִּקְרָא לְזִקְנֵי הָעָם לוי

וַיָּשֶׂם לִפְנֵיהֶם אֵת כָּל־הַדְּבָרִים הָאֵלֶּה אֲשֶׁר צִוָּהוּ יהוה: וַיַּעֲנוּ

כָל־הָעָם יַחְדָּו וַיֹּאמְרוּ כֹּל אֲשֶׁר־דִּבֶּר יהוה נַעֲשֶׂה וַיָּשֶׁב מֹשֶׁה

אֶת־דִּבְרֵי הָעָם אֶל־יהוה: וַיֹּאמֶר יהוה אֶל־מֹשֶׁה הִנֵּה אָנֹכִי

בָּא אֵלֶיךָ בְּעַב הֶעָנָן בַּעֲבוּר יִשְׁמַע הָעָם בְּדַבְּרִי עִמָּךְ וְגַם־בְּךָ

יַאֲמִינוּ לְעוֹלָם וַיַּגֵּד מֹשֶׁה אֶת־דִּבְרֵי הָעָם אֶל־יהוה: וַיֹּאמֶר יהוה

אֶל־מֹשֶׁה לֵךְ אֶל־הָעָם וְקִדַּשְׁתָּם הַיּוֹם וּמָחָר וְכִבְּסוּ שִׂמְלֹתָם:

וְהָיוּ נְכֹנִים לַיּוֹם הַשְּׁלִישִׁי כִּי בַּיּוֹם הַשְּׁלִשִׁי יֵרֵד יהוה לְעֵינֵי כָל־

הָעָם עַל־הַר סִינָי: וְהִגְבַּלְתָּ אֶת־הָעָם סָבִיב לֵאמֹר הִשָּׁמְרוּ לָכֶם

מַמְלֶכֶת כֹּהֲנִים *A kingdom of priests.* Interpreted to mean servants (Ibn Ezra, Ramban), or princes (Rashi, Rashbam). A nation charged with being a source of instruction and inspiration to the nations of the world (Seforno; see Is. 61:6).

וְגוֹי קָדוֹשׁ *A holy nation.* The word "holy" in biblical Hebrew means "set apart," designated for a sacred purpose. All nations contain individuals seen by others as holy. In the case of Israel, the whole nation would have this responsibility (see Lev. 19:2 and Rashi ad. loc.). This verse is thus the mission statement of the Jewish people as a nation under the sovereignty of God.

וַיָּבֹא מֹשֶׁה *So Moses came back.* Only when the people had signaled their consent, did God proceed with the covenant and the accompanying revelation. This is the first instance in history of the idea that government derives its authority from the consent of the governed, and it applies even when the Governor is Creator of heaven and earth. God does not act tyrannically toward His creatures (*Avoda Zara* 3a). The free God seeks the worship of free human beings. God rules by right, not merely by might.

וַיַּעֲנוּ כָל־הָעָם *And all the people responded.* They responded before they had heard the specific terms of the covenant. They subsequently ratified it twice (Ex. 24:3; 7). Note that this is the only one of the three covenants God

Take care not to climb the mountain, or even to touch its edge, for anyone who touches the mountain shall die. Let no hand touch it, for that person will be stoned or shot down; man or beast, he shall not live. Only when the horn sounds a long blast, may you ascend the mountain again."

Moses descended the mountain to the people, and he consecrated SHELISHI them, and they washed their clothes. "Be ready," he told the people, "for three days' time; let no man come close to a woman."

On the third day, in the early morning – thunder and lightning; heavy cloud covered the mountain, there was a very loud sound of the shofar, and all of the people in the camp quaked. And Moses went apart from the people, to meet God, leaving the camp behind, and the people came to stand at the foot of the mountain. And Mount Sinai was all enveloped in smoke, for the LORD had descended upon it in fire, and its smoke rose up like the smoke of a furnace, and all the mountain shook. And the sound of the shofar grew ever louder – Moses spoke, and God answered him with a voice.

The LORD descended to Mount Sinai, to the mountain top – and REVI'I the LORD called Moses forth to the top of the mountain, and Moses ascended. "Now go down," said the LORD to Moses, "and warn the people, lest they break away to come to see the LORD, and fall in their great numbers. Even the priests who draw near the LORD – let them, too, set themselves apart, lest the LORD bursts in among them." But Moses told the LORD, "The people cannot ascend to Mount Sinai, for You have already warned us, 'Mark a boundary

---

the sound of the shofar but the voice of God could be heard by all (Rashbam). R. Elie Munk, citing the *Zohar* (*VaYikra* 7a), suggests a larger idea, that God would confirm what Moses said, even when he spoke on his own initiative. Likewise God ratifies the decisions of the sages in each generation when they apply the principles of the Oral Law.

רֵד *Now go down.* God wanted Moses to be at the foot of the mountain not at the top, so that he would be among the people, not apart from them, when the revelation took place.

עֲלוֹת בָּהָר וְנָגַע בְּקָצֵהוּ כָּל־הַנֹּגֵעַ בָּהָר מוֹת יוּמָת: לֹא־תִגַּע בּוֹ

יָד כִּי־סָקוֹל יִסָּקֵל אוֹ־יָרֹה יִיָּרֶה אִם־בְּהֵמָה אִם־אִישׁ לֹא יִחְיֶה

בִּמְשֹׁךְ הַיֹּבֵל הֵמָּה יַעֲלוּ בָהָר: *וַיֵּרֶד מֹשֶׁה מִן־הָהָר אֶל־הָעָם

וַיְקַדֵּשׁ אֶת־הָעָם וַיְכַבְּסוּ שִׂמְלֹתָם: וַיֹּאמֶר אֶל־הָעָם הֱיוּ נְכֹנִים

לִשְׁלֹשֶׁת יָמִים אַל־תִּגְּשׁוּ אֶל־אִשָּׁה: וַיְהִי בַיּוֹם הַשְּׁלִישִׁי בִּהְיֹת

הַבֹּקֶר וַיְהִי קֹלֹת וּבְרָקִים וְעָנָן כָּבֵד עַל־הָהָר וְקֹל שֹׁפָר חָזָק מְאֹד

וַיֶּחֱרַד כָּל־הָעָם אֲשֶׁר בַּמַּחֲנֶה: וַיּוֹצֵא מֹשֶׁה אֶת־הָעָם לִקְרַאת

הָאֱלֹהִים מִן־הַמַּחֲנֶה וַיִּתְיַצְּבוּ בְּתַחְתִּית הָהָר: וְהַר סִינַי עָשַׁן

כֻּלּוֹ מִפְּנֵי אֲשֶׁר יָרַד עָלָיו יְהוָה בָּאֵשׁ וַיַּעַל עֲשָׁנוֹ כְּעֶשֶׁן הַכִּבְשָׁן

וַיֶּחֱרַד כָּל־הָהָר מְאֹד: וַיְהִי קוֹל הַשֹּׁפָר הוֹלֵךְ וְחָזֵק מְאֹד מֹשֶׁה

יְדַבֵּר וְהָאֱלֹהִים יַעֲנֶנּוּ בְקוֹל: *וַיֵּרֶד יְהוָה עַל־הַר סִינַי אֶל־רֹאשׁ

הָהָר וַיִּקְרָא יְהוָה לְמֹשֶׁה אֶל־רֹאשׁ הָהָר וַיַּעַל מֹשֶׁה: וַיֹּאמֶר

יְהוָה אֶל־מֹשֶׁה רֵד הָעֵד בָּעָם פֶּן־יֶהֶרְסוּ אֶל־יְהוָה לִרְאוֹת וְנָפַל

מִמֶּנּוּ רָב: וְגַם הַכֹּהֲנִים הַנִּגָּשִׁים אֶל־יְהוָה יִתְקַדָּשׁוּ פֶּן־יִפְרֹץ בָּהֶם

יְהוָה: וַיֹּאמֶר מֹשֶׁה אֶל־יְהוָה לֹא־יוּכַל הָעָם לַעֲלֹת אֶל־הַר סִינָי

כִּי־אַתָּה הַעֵדֹתָה בָּנוּ לֵאמֹר הַגְבֵּל אֶת־הָהָר וְקִדַּשְׁתּוֹ: וַיֹּאמֶר

שְׁלִישִׁי

רְבִיעִי

כָּל־הַנֹּגֵעַ בָּהָר *Anyone who touches the mountain.* The mountain became holy
in preparation for the revelation, which temporarily made it sacred space
like the Sanctuary (see Num. 3:10). There must be a boundary between the
sacred and the secular. Transgression of that boundary is fraught with danger.

קֹלֹת וּבְרָקִים וְעָנָן כָּבֵד *Thunder, lightning, heavy cloud.* Auguries of the approach
of the Divine Presence; likewise the sound of the shofar, a clarion announcing
the imminent arrival of the King. Later accounts of the revelation at Mount
Sinai (Judges 5: 4–5; Ps. 29:5–9; Ps. 68:8–9) all emphasize the stormy skies,
the violent thunder and the shaking of the earth.

מֹשֶׁה יְדַבֵּר וְהָאֱלֹהִים יַעֲנֶנּוּ בְקוֹל *Moses spoke, and God answered him with a voice.*
This refers not to the Ten Commandments but to the conversation about
preparations for that event (Ramban). Moses' words were inaudible against

to the mountain around and consecrate it.'" So the LORD said to him, "Go down and ascend again, together with Aaron, but let the priests and the people not break away to ascend to the LORD, lest disaster burst out upon them." So Moses descended to the people and told them.

In some congregations the piyut אַרְכִין *(on page 730) is added here.*

And God spoke all these words, saying:

I am the LORD your God who brought you out of the land of Egypt, from the slave-house. Have no other gods besides Me. Do not make a sculptured image for yourself, or any likeness of what is in the heavens above, or on the earth below, or in the waters under the earth. Do not bow down to them or worship them, for I am the LORD your God, a zealous God, visiting the guilt of the parents on the children to the third and fourth generation, if they also reject Me; but showing kindness to thousands of generations of those who love Me and keep My commandments.

Do not take the name of the LORD your God in vain. The LORD will not leave unpunished one who utters His name in vain.

---

now giving them their constitution of liberty as a law-governed society under the sovereignty of God.

לֹא־יִהְיֶה לְךָ אֱלֹהִים אֲחֵרִים *Have no other gods.* Monotheism is more than belief in one God. It is also undivided loyalty to the one God, involving a moral bond, not just an intellectual one. It was this exclusivity of worship that was unique in the ancient world, making faith in Judaism akin to faithfulness in marriage.

עַל־שִׁלֵּשִׁים וְעַל־רִבֵּעִים לְשׂנְאָי *To the third and fourth generation, if they also reject Me.* Deuteronomy 24:16, Jeremiah 31:28–29 and Ezekiel 18:2–4 all make clear that there is no intergenerational transfer of guilt. Children are only punished for the sins of their parents if they themselves commit those sins. The phrase is therefore a warning to parents not to have a negative influence on their children, not a statement of vicarious guilt or punishment.

לֹא תִשָּׂא אֶת־שֵׁם־יהוה אֱלֹהֶיךָ לַשָּׁוְא *Do not take the name of the LORD your God*

אֵלָיו יהוה לֶךְ־רֵד וְעָלִיתָ אַתָּה וְאַהֲרֹן עִמָּךְ וְהַכֹּהֲנִים וְהָעָם
אַל־יֶהֶרְסוּ לַעֲלֹת אֶל־יהוה פֶּן־יִפְרָץ־בָּם: וַיֵּרֶד מֹשֶׁה אֶל־הָעָם

In some congregations the piyut אַרְכִין (on page 730) is added here.

וַיֹּאמֶר אֲלֵהֶם:* וַיְדַבֵּר אֱלֹהִים אֵת כָּל־הַדְּבָרִים
הָאֵלֶּה לֵאמֹר: אָנֹכִי יהוה אֱלֹהֶיךָ אֲשֶׁר הוֹצֵאתִיךָ
מֵאֶרֶץ מִצְרַיִם מִבֵּית עֲבָדִים: לֹא־יִהְיֶה לְךָ אֱלֹהִים אֲחֵרִים עַל־
פָּנָי לֹא תַעֲשֶׂה־לְךָ פֶסֶל ׀ וְכָל־תְּמוּנָה אֲשֶׁר בַּשָּׁמַיִם ׀ מִמַּעַל
וַאֲשֶׁר בָּאָרֶץ מִתָּחַת וַאֲשֶׁר בַּמַּיִם ׀ מִתַּחַת לָאָרֶץ לֹא־תִשְׁתַּחְוֶה
לָהֶם וְלֹא תָעָבְדֵם כִּי אָנֹכִי יהוה אֱלֹהֶיךָ אֵל קַנָּא פֹּקֵד עֲוֹן
אָבֹת עַל־בָּנִים עַל־שִׁלֵּשִׁים וְעַל־רִבֵּעִים לְשֹׂנְאָי וְעֹשֶׂה חֶסֶד
לַאֲלָפִים לְאֹהֲבַי וּלְשֹׁמְרֵי מִצְוֹתָי: לֹא תִשָּׂא אֶת־שֵׁם־
יהוה אֱלֹהֶיךָ לַשָּׁוְא כִּי לֹא יְנַקֶּה יהוה אֵת אֲשֶׁר־יִשָּׂא אֶת־שְׁמוֹ
לַשָּׁוְא:

THE TEN COMMANDMENTS

For an essay on the Ten Commandments, see Introduction, page xlix.

וַיְדַבֵּר אֱלֹהִים אֵת כָּל־הַדְּבָרִים הָאֵלֶּה לֵאמֹר *And God spoke all these words, saying.*
The emphasis here is on the direct speech of God. There is a difference of
opinion in the Talmud and among the commentators as to how many of the
commands the people heard directly from God. Some held that they heard
all ten, others that they heard only the first two, after which they came to
Moses saying they were unable to endure this direct revelation. Thus the last
eight they heard from Moses.

אָנֹכִי יהוה אֱלֹהֶיךָ *I am the Lord your God.* According to Maimonides, this is the
first command: to believe in God. According to Nahmanides, it is a prelude
and prologue to the commands. Judah HaLevi in the *Kuzari* (1:11–25) notes
that God does not identify himself as Creator of heaven and earth, but as
He who brought the people out of slavery. God as Creator of the universe is
the God of all humankind, but He is also, especially in His relationship with
Israel, the God of history. Having freed the people from enslavement, He is

Remember the Sabbath day and keep it holy. Six days you shall labor and do all your work, but the seventh day is a Sabbath of the LORD your God; on it you shall not do any work – you, your son or daughter, your male or female slaves, your cattle, or the stranger within your gates. For in six days the LORD made heaven and earth and sea, and all that is in them, and rested on the seventh day; therefore the LORD blessed the Sabbath day and made it holy.

Honor your father and your mother, so that you may live long in the land that the LORD your God is giving you.

Do not murder.

Do not commit adultery.

Do not steal.

---

private; a holy day is public. We take a vacation as individuals choosing to do so for our own enjoyment. By contrast, a holy day is not something we choose. It is part of public time, the way a park is part of public space. It and the freedom it represents belong to everyone equally. Thus it is essential that on Shabbat no one – not slaves, servants, employees, even farm animals – can be made to work against their will.

כַּבֵּד אֶת־אָבִיךָ וְאֶת־אִמֶּךָ *Honor your father and mother.* The first five commands are generally considered to be about our relationship with God, the second five about our relationships with our human fellows. The command to honor parents, the fifth command, belongs to the first group because it is about the duties we owe to those who brought us into being. Collectively, they represent ontological gratitude, an attitude of thankfulness and respect to those to whom we owe the gift of life itself.

לְמַעַן יַאֲרִכוּן יָמֶיךָ עַל הָאֲדָמָה *So that you may live long in the land.* "People will not look forward to posterity who never look backward to their ancestors" (Edmund Burke).

לֹא תִּגְנֹב *Do not steal.* The sages interpreted this as primarily applying to kidnapping (*Sanhedrin* 86a), though it includes other forms of wrongful appropriation.

זָכוֹר אֶת־יוֹם הַשַּׁבָּת לְקַדְּשׁוֹ שֵׁשֶׁת יָמִים תַּעֲבֹד וְעָשִׂיתָ כָּל־
מְלַאכְתֶּךָ וְיוֹם הַשְּׁבִיעִי שַׁבָּת ׀ לַיהוה אֱלֹהֶיךָ לֹא תַעֲשֶׂה כָל־
מְלָאכָה אַתָּה ׀ וּבִנְךָ וּבִתֶּךָ עַבְדְּךָ וַאֲמָתְךָ וּבְהֶמְתֶּךָ וְגֵרְךָ אֲשֶׁר
בִּשְׁעָרֶיךָ כִּי שֵׁשֶׁת־יָמִים עָשָׂה יהוה אֶת־הַשָּׁמַיִם וְאֶת־הָאָרֶץ
אֶת־הַיָּם וְאֶת־כָּל־אֲשֶׁר־בָּם וַיָּנַח בַּיּוֹם הַשְּׁבִיעִי עַל־כֵּן בֵּרַךְ
יהוה אֶת־יוֹם הַשַּׁבָּת וַיְקַדְּשֵׁהוּ׃   כַּבֵּד אֶת־אָבִיךָ
וְאֶת־אִמֶּךָ לְמַעַן יַאֲרִכוּן יָמֶיךָ עַל הָאֲדָמָה אֲשֶׁר־יהוה אֱלֹהֶיךָ
נֹתֵן לָךְ׃   לֹא תִּרְצָח׃   לֹא
תִּנְאָף׃   לֹא תִּגְנֹב׃   לֹא־

---

in vain. A prohibition against false or unnecessary oaths, and more generally against unnecessary use of the divine name in secular contexts. Note that the commands from here on are in the third person, while the first two are in the first person. Some (Rashi, Rambam) take this as evidence that the Israelites heard only the first two commands directly from God. Ramban says that the people did not fully understand the last eight and Moses had to explain them. Ibn Ezra holds that change of person is common in biblical prose and has no special significance.

יוֹם הַשַּׁבָּת *The Sabbath day.* There are differences between the fourth command as reported here and in Deuteronomy (5:12–15). Here the verb is "remember," there "observe." Here Shabbat is a memorial of creation, there of the exodus from Egypt. The sages said that both versions were uttered simultaneously (*Rosh HaShana* 27a; *Shevuot* 20b). At the simplest level, this means that the Torah says sequentially what is true simultaneously, namely that the God of creation is also the God of redemption. The freedom represented by the day of rest is, on the one hand, the ability to rise beyond nature (creation), and on the other, a respite from human forms of oppression (redemption). Shabbat is a sustained tutorial in the exercise and experience of both forms of liberty.

אַתָּה וּבִנְךָ וּבִתֶּךָ עַבְדְּךָ ... וּבְהֶמְתֶּךָ וְגֵרְךָ *You, your son or daughter... slaves... cattle... stranger.* The difference between a holiday and a holy day is that a holiday is

Do not testify as a false witness against your neighbor.

Do not be envious of your neighbor's house.

Do not be envious of your neighbor's wife, his male or female slave, his ox, his ass, or anything else that is your neighbor's.

And all the people saw the thunder and the flames, and the sound HAMISHI of the shofar, and the mountain asmoke; the people saw and they staggered, and stood far back. They called out to Moses, "You speak to us and we shall listen, but let God not speak to us, lest we die." "Do not be afraid," said Moses, "For it is to test you that God comes so, and that His awe may be upon you, that you should not sin." The people stood at a distance, and Moses approached the mist, in which God was.

The LORD said to Moses, "Say this to the people of Israel: You have seen now that I have spoken to you from the heavens. Make yourself no silver gods or golden gods alongside Me. Make Me an earthen altar, and sacrifice your burnt offerings and your peace offerings on that, of your flock and of your herd. In those places where I shall recall My name, there I shall come to you and bless you. And if you should build Me an altar of stone, let it not be of stone that is hewn – for if you pass your sword-blade over it, it will be desecrated. And do not ascend My altar by steps, for over it you may not expose your naked flesh."

וְכָל־הָעָם רֹאִים אֶת־הַקּוֹלֹת *And all the people saw the thunder.* Literally, "they saw the sounds." According to some, this means they experienced synesthesia: they saw what is normally only heard. An auditory experience became a visual one (*Mekhilta*, Rashi). Moses emphasized later how it was the sound that was the essential element of revelation: "Then God spoke to you out of the fire. You heard the sound of words, but saw no image; there was only a voice" (Deut. 4:12).

לֹא־תִבְנֶה אֶתְהֶן גָּזִית *Let it not be of stone that is hewn.* The sword shortens life;

תַעֲנֶה בְרֵעֲךָ עֵד שָׁקֶר:

לֹא

תַחְמֹד בֵּית רֵעֶךָ

לֹא

לֹא־

תַחְמֹד אֵשֶׁת רֵעֶךָ וְעַבְדּוֹ וַאֲמָתוֹ וְשׁוֹרוֹ וַחֲמֹרוֹ וְכֹל אֲשֶׁר לְרֵעֶךָ:

חמישי וְכָל־הָעָם רֹאִים אֶת־הַקּוֹלֹת וְאֶת־הַלַּפִּידִם וְאֵת קוֹל הַשֹּׁפָר וְאֶת־הָהָר עָשֵׁן וַיַּרְא הָעָם וַיָּנֻעוּ וַיַּעַמְדוּ מֵרָחֹק: וַיֹּאמְרוּ אֶל־מֹשֶׁה דַּבֵּר־אַתָּה עִמָּנוּ וְנִשְׁמָעָה וְאַל־יְדַבֵּר עִמָּנוּ אֱלֹהִים פֶּן־נָמוּת: וַיֹּאמֶר מֹשֶׁה אֶל־הָעָם אַל־תִּירָאוּ כִּי לְבַעֲבוּר נַסּוֹת אֶתְכֶם בָּא הָאֱלֹהִים וּבַעֲבוּר תִּהְיֶה יִרְאָתוֹ עַל־פְּנֵיכֶם לְבִלְתִּי תֶחֱטָאוּ: וַיַּעֲמֹד הָעָם מֵרָחֹק וּמֹשֶׁה נִגַּשׁ אֶל־הָעֲרָפֶל אֲשֶׁר־שָׁם הָאֱלֹהִים: וַיֹּאמֶר יהוה אֶל־מֹשֶׁה כֹּה תֹאמַר אֶל־בְּנֵי יִשְׂרָאֵל אַתֶּם רְאִיתֶם כִּי מִן־הַשָּׁמַיִם דִּבַּרְתִּי עִמָּכֶם: לֹא תַעֲשׂוּן אִתִּי אֱלֹהֵי כֶסֶף וֵאלֹהֵי זָהָב לֹא תַעֲשׂוּ לָכֶם: מִזְבַּח אֲדָמָה תַּעֲשֶׂה־לִּי וְזָבַחְתָּ עָלָיו אֶת־עֹלֹתֶיךָ וְאֶת־שְׁלָמֶיךָ אֶת־צֹאנְךָ וְאֶת־בְּקָרֶךָ בְּכָל־הַמָּקוֹם אֲשֶׁר אַזְכִּיר אֶת־שְׁמִי אָבוֹא אֵלֶיךָ וּבֵרַכְתִּיךָ: וְאִם־מִזְבַּח אֲבָנִים תַּעֲשֶׂה־לִּי לֹא־תִבְנֶה אֶתְהֶן גָּזִית כִּי חַרְבְּךָ הֵנַפְתָּ עָלֶיהָ וַתְּחַלְלֶהָ: וְלֹא־תַעֲלֶה בְמַעֲלֹת עַל־מִזְבְּחִי אֲשֶׁר לֹא־תִגָּלֶה עֶרְוָתְךָ עָלָיו:

לֹא תַחְמֹד *Do not be envious.* Envy, the desire to have what is not ours, is the most destructive of social emotions, and one of the most irrational: it involves letting someone else's happiness diminish your own. It can lead a person to break the prohibitions against stealing and adultery. In extremis, it can lead to false testimony and even murder. The best cure for envy is to acknowledge that everything we have is the gift of God: "Who is rich? One who rejoices in his portion" (*Avot* 4:1).

HALF KADDISH

*Before Maftir is read, the second Sefer Torah is placed on
the bima and the Reader says Half Kaddish:*

Reader: יִתְגַּדֵּל Magnified and sanctified may His great name be,
in the world He created by His will.
May He establish His kingdom
in your lifetime and in your days,
and in the lifetime of all the house of Israel,
swiftly and soon – and say: Amen.

All: May His great name be blessed for ever and all time.

Reader: Blessed and praised, glorified and exalted,
raised and honored, uplifted and lauded
be the name of the Holy One, blessed be He,
beyond any blessing,
song, praise and consolation
uttered in the world – and say: Amen.

HAGBAHA AND GELILA

The first Torah scroll is lifted and the congregation says:

וְזֹאת הַתּוֹרָה This is the Torah   *Deut. 4*
that Moses placed before the children of Israel,
at the Lord's commandment, by the hand of Moses.   *Num. 9*

Some add: It is a tree of life to those who grasp it,   *Prov. 3*
and those who uphold it are happy.
Its ways are ways of pleasantness, and all its paths are peace.
Long life is in its right hand; in its left, riches and honor.
It pleased the Lord for the sake of [Israel's] righteousness,   *Is. 42*
to make the Torah great and glorious.

*The first Torah scroll is bound and covered and the oleh
for Maftir is called to the second Torah scroll.*

---

the altar prolongs it. The sword symbolizes strife; the altar is a symbol of
peace. That is why the sword, and metal instruments generally, were not to
be used to hew stones for the altar (Mishna, *Midot* 3:4).

חצי קדיש

Before מפטיר is read, the second ספר תורה is placed
on the שולחן and the קורא says חצי קדיש:

קורא: יִתְגַּדַּל וְיִתְקַדַּשׁ שְׁמֵהּ רַבָּא (קהל: אָמֵן)

בְּעָלְמָא דִּי בְרָא כִרְעוּתֵהּ

וְיַמְלִיךְ מַלְכוּתֵהּ

בְּחַיֵּיכוֹן וּבְיוֹמֵיכוֹן וּבְחַיֵּי דְכָל בֵּית יִשְׂרָאֵל

בַּעֲגָלָא וּבִזְמַן קָרִיב

וְאִמְרוּ אָמֵן. (קהל: אָמֵן)

קהל ויהֵא שְׁמֵהּ רַבָּא מְבָרַךְ לְעָלַם וּלְעָלְמֵי עָלְמַיָּא.
וקורא:

קורא: יִתְבָּרַךְ וְיִשְׁתַּבַּח וְיִתְפָּאַר וְיִתְרוֹמַם וְיִתְנַשֵּׂא

וְיִתְהַדָּר וְיִתְעַלֶּה וְיִתְהַלָּל

שְׁמֵהּ דְּקֻדְשָׁא בְּרִיךְ הוּא (קהל: בְּרִיךְ הוּא)

לְעֵלָּא מִן כָּל בִּרְכָתָא וְשִׁירָתָא

תֻּשְׁבְּחָתָא וְנֶחֱמָתָא

דַּאֲמִירָן בְּעָלְמָא

וְאִמְרוּ אָמֵן. (קהל: אָמֵן)

הגבהה וגלילה

The first ספר תורה is lifted and the קהל says:

וְזֹאת הַתּוֹרָה אֲשֶׁר־שָׂם מֹשֶׁה לִפְנֵי בְּנֵי יִשְׂרָאֵל: דברים ד

עַל־פִּי יהוה בְּיַד מֹשֶׁה: במדבר ט

Some add עֵץ־חַיִּים הִיא לַמַּחֲזִיקִים בָּהּ וְתֹמְכֶיהָ מְאֻשָּׁר: משלי ג

דְּרָכֶיהָ דַרְכֵי־נֹעַם וְכָל־נְתִיבֹתֶיהָ שָׁלוֹם:

אֹרֶךְ יָמִים בִּימִינָהּ, בִּשְׂמֹאולָהּ עֹשֶׁר וְכָבוֹד:

יהוה חָפֵץ לְמַעַן צִדְקוֹ יַגְדִּיל תּוֹרָה וְיַאְדִּיר: ישעיה מב

The first ספר תורה is bound and covered and the עולה
for מפטיר is called to the second ספר תורה.

MAFTIR

On the day of the first fruits, when you bring an offering of new *Num.* *28: 26–31*
grain to the LORD, on your Festival of Weeks, there shall be a
sacred assembly: you shall do no laborious work. You shall offer a
burnt-offering of pleasing aroma to the LORD: two young bullocks,
one ram, and seven yearling male lambs. And also their meal-
offerings, fine flour mixed with oil, three-tenths of an ephah for
each of the bulls, two-tenths of an ephah for the ram, and one tenth
of an ephah each for every one of the seven lambs. And one male
goat as a sin-offering, as well as the regular daily sacrifice with its
meal-offering; and they shall all be perfect for you, they and their
libations.

HAGBAHA AND GELILA

The second Torah scroll is lifted and the congregation says:

וְזֹאת הַתּוֹרָה This is the Torah *Deut. 4*
that Moses placed before the children of Israel,
at the LORD's commandment, by the hand of Moses. *Num. 9*

Some add: It is a tree of life to those who grasp it, *Prov. 3*
and those who uphold it are happy.
Its ways are ways of pleasantness, and all its paths are peace.
Long life is in its right hand; in its left, riches and honor.
It pleased the LORD for the sake of [Israel's] righteousness, *Is. 42*
to make the Torah great and glorious.

*The second Torah scroll is bound and covered and the oleh
for Maftir reads the Haftara.*

BLESSING BEFORE READING THE HAFTARA

Before reading the Haftara, the person called up for Maftir says:

בָּרוּךְ Blessed are You, LORD our God, King of the Universe, who chose
good prophets and was pleased with their words, spoken in truth.
Blessed are You, LORD, who chose the Torah, His servant Moses, His
people Israel, and the prophets of truth and righteousness.

מפטיר

במדבר
כח:כו-לא

וּבְיוֹם הַבִּכּוּרִים בְּהַקְרִיבְכֶם מִנְחָה חֲדָשָׁה לַיהוה בְּשָׁבֻעֹתֵיכֶם מִקְרָא־קֹדֶשׁ יִהְיֶה לָכֶם כָּל־מְלֶאכֶת עֲבֹדָה לֹא תַעֲשׂוּ: וְהִקְרַבְתֶּם עוֹלָה לְרֵיחַ נִיחֹחַ לַיהוה פָּרִים בְּנֵי־בָקָר שְׁנַיִם אַיִל אֶחָד שִׁבְעָה כְבָשִׂים בְּנֵי שָׁנָה: וּמִנְחָתָם סֹלֶת בְּלוּלָה בַשֶּׁמֶן שְׁלֹשָׁה עֶשְׂרֹנִים לַפָּר הָאֶחָד שְׁנֵי עֶשְׂרֹנִים לָאַיִל הָאֶחָד: עִשָּׂרוֹן עִשָּׂרוֹן לַכֶּבֶשׂ הָאֶחָד לְשִׁבְעַת הַכְּבָשִׂים: שְׂעִיר עִזִּים אֶחָד לְכַפֵּר עֲלֵיכֶם: מִלְּבַד עֹלַת הַתָּמִיד וּמִנְחָתוֹ תַּעֲשׂוּ תְּמִימִם יִהְיוּ־לָכֶם וְנִסְכֵּיהֶם:

הגבהה וגלילה

The second ספר תורה is lifted and the קהל says:

דברים ד

וְזֹאת הַתּוֹרָה אֲשֶׁר־שָׂם מֹשֶׁה לִפְנֵי בְּנֵי יִשְׂרָאֵל:

במדבר ט

עַל־פִּי יהוה בְּיַד מֹשֶׁה:

משלי ג

Some add עֵץ־חַיִּים הִיא לַמַּחֲזִיקִים בָּהּ וְתֹמְכֶיהָ מְאֻשָּׁר:
דְּרָכֶיהָ דַרְכֵי־נֹעַם וְכָל־נְתִיבֹתֶיהָ שָׁלוֹם:
אֹרֶךְ יָמִים בִּימִינָהּ בִּשְׂמֹאולָהּ עֹשֶׁר וְכָבוֹד:

ישעיה מב

יהוה חָפֵץ לְמַעַן צִדְקוֹ יַגְדִּיל תּוֹרָה וְיַאְדִּיר:

The second ספר תורה is bound and covered and the עולה
reads the הפטרה for מפטיר.

ברכה קודם ההפטרה

Before reading the הפטרה, the person called up for מפטיר says:

בָּרוּךְ אַתָּה יהוה אֱלֹהֵינוּ מֶלֶךְ הָעוֹלָם אֲשֶׁר בָּחַר בִּנְבִיאִים טוֹבִים, וְרָצָה בְדִבְרֵיהֶם הַנֶּאֱמָרִים בֶּאֱמֶת. בָּרוּךְ אַתָּה יהוה, הַבּוֹחֵר בַּתּוֹרָה וּבְמֹשֶׁה עַבְדּוֹ וּבְיִשְׂרָאֵל עַמּוֹ וּבִנְבִיאֵי הָאֱמֶת וָצֶדֶק.

HAFTARA FOR FIRST DAY OF SHAVUOT

And it was in the thirtieth year, in the fourth month on the fifth day of the month: I was out in the exile, by the river Kevar, and the heavens opened up and I saw visions of God; on the fifth day of the month – it was the fifth year of the exile of king Jehoiachin. *Ezek. 1:1–28*

And so it was: the word of the LORD came to Ezekiel, the son of Buzi, the priest, in the land of Kasdim, by the river Kevar; the hand of the LORD was upon him there.

And I saw: behold, a storm-wind came from the north, a great cloud and a flaring fire with a bright glow about it, and inside it, within the fire, a semblance of amber; and within that was the form of four living beings – this was their appearance: they had the form of a man, and each one had four faces, and each of these had four wings; and their legs were straight-standing, and their feet were like a calf's hoof, and they gleamed with a semblance of burnished copper; they had man's hands beneath their wings, on their four sides, and the four of them had wings and faces.

Ezekiel lived through one of the great crises of Jewish history. After the death of Solomon, the kingdom had split in two. The northern kingdom, Israel, had been defeated by the Assyrians in 722 BCE. Its population was transported, and mostly assimilated and disappeared, becoming known to history as the Lost Ten Tribes. The southern kingdom, Judah, was conquered by the Babylonians under Nebuchadnezzar in 597 BCE. The king, Jehoiakim, was taken captive to Babylon, together with the elite of the population, Ezekiel among them. Some years later, those who remained rose in rebellion and were defeated a second time. Jerusalem fell in 586 BCE, and the Temple was destroyed. The book of Lamentations conveys a vivid sense of the trauma and tragedy Judeans felt, seeing their world in ruins.

The Haftara opens by locating itself in time. "In the thirtieth year" is taken by many commentators to refer to the religious reforms of King Josiah (II Kings 22). "The fifth year of the exile" dates the vision to 593 BCE. "The river Kevar" is probably the canal, fed by water from the Euphrates, known in Akkadian as *nar Kabari*. The Temple was still standing in Jerusalem. The revolt that would

הפטרה ליום טוב ראשון של שבועות

יחזקאל
א:א–כח

וַיְהִ֣י ׀ בִּשְׁלֹשִׁ֣ים שָׁנָ֗ה בָּרְבִיעִי֙ בַּחֲמִשָּׁ֣ה לַחֹ֔דֶשׁ וַאֲנִ֖י בְתֽוֹךְ־
הַגּוֹלָ֖ה עַל־נְהַר־כְּבָ֑ר נִפְתְּחוּ֙ הַשָּׁמַ֔יִם וָאֶרְאֶ֖ה מַרְא֥וֹת אֱלֹהִֽים:
בַּחֲמִשָּׁ֣ה לַחֹ֔דֶשׁ הִ֚יא הַשָּׁנָ֣ה הַחֲמִישִׁ֔ית לְגָל֖וּת הַמֶּ֥לֶךְ יוֹיָכִֽין:
הָיֹ֣ה הָיָ֣ה דְבַר־יהו֡ה אֶל־יְחֶזְקֵ֣אל בֶּן־בּוּזִ֣י הַכֹּהֵ֗ן בְּאֶ֤רֶץ כַּשְׂדִּים֙
עַל־נְהַר־כְּבָ֔ר וַתְּהִ֥י עָלָ֛יו שָׁ֖ם יַד־יהֽוה: וָאֵ֡רֶא וְהִנֵּה֩ ר֨וּחַ סְעָרָ֜ה
בָּאָ֣ה מִן־הַצָּפ֗וֹן עָנָ֤ן גָּדוֹל֙ וְאֵ֣שׁ מִתְלַקַּ֔חַת וְנֹ֥גַהּ ל֖וֹ סָבִ֑יב וּמִ֨תּוֹכָ֔הּ
כְּעֵ֥ין הַחַשְׁמַ֖ל מִתּ֥וֹךְ הָאֵֽשׁ: וּמִ֨תּוֹכָ֔הּ דְּמ֖וּת אַרְבַּ֣ע חַיּ֑וֹת וְזֶה֙
מַרְאֵֽיהֶ֔ן דְּמ֥וּת אָדָ֖ם לָהֵֽנָּה: וְאַרְבָּעָ֥ה פָנִ֖ים לְאֶחָ֑ת וְאַרְבַּ֥ע
כְּנָפַ֖יִם לְאַחַ֥ת לָהֶֽם: וְרַגְלֵיהֶ֖ם רֶ֣גֶל יְשָׁרָ֑ה וְכַ֣ף רַגְלֵיהֶ֗ם כְּכַף֙
רֶ֣גֶל עֵ֔גֶל וְנֹ֣צְצִ֔ים כְּעֵ֖ין נְחֹ֥שֶׁת קָלָֽל: וְיָדוֹ אָדָ֗ם מִתַּ֨חַת֙ כַּנְפֵיהֶ֔ם
עַ֖ל אַרְבַּ֣עַת רִבְעֵיהֶ֑ם וּפְנֵיהֶ֥ם וְכַנְפֵיהֶ֖ם לְאַרְבַּעְתָּֽם: חֹֽבְרֹ֛ת

HAFTARA: FIRST DAY

The Haftara for the first day is taken from the opening of the book of Ezekiel. The connection between it and the Torah reading is Revelation: the direct unmediated encounter with the transcendental God. It was this that, in the days of Moses, transformed the Israelites into "a kingdom of priests and a holy nation," and it was this that turned Ezekiel, a priest, into the great prophet of exile, bringing hope to his contemporaries who, like him, had been carried captive to Babylon.

There are, though, marked differences between the two revelations. At Sinai, God revealed Himself to an entire nation; by the waters of Babylon He revealed Himself to an individual, a prophet. At Sinai, as Moses said, "You saw no image: there was only a voice" (Deut. 4:12). Ezekiel's experience, by contrast, was intensely visual. There is only one other vision like it, that of Isaiah who saw God enthroned, surrounded by angels (Is. ch. 6). What Isaiah and Ezekiel heard the angels singing – "Holy, holy, holy is the LORD of Hosts, the whole earth is full of His glory" and "Blessed is the LORD's glory from His place" – became the basis of *Kedusha,* the supreme point of daily prayer.

Their wings were joined to each other; they did not turn when they moved: each one moved in the direction of its face. And their faces were in the form of the face of a man, with the face of a lion on the right of the four, the face of an ox on the left of the four, and the face of an eagle. Their faces, and their wings were separate above: each one had two joining it to the other, and two covering its body; each one moved in the direction of its face – wherever the spirit wished to move, they moved – they did not turn when they moved; and the form of the living beings, their appearance, was like coals burning, like the appearance of torch-flames, it passed among the living beings; the fire had a bright glow, and lightning flashed out from the fire. And the living beings ran forward and back, like the appearance of darting-flames.

And I saw the living beings – and behold, a wheel was on the ground with the living beings with the four faces. And the appearance of the wheels and their action had a semblance of topaz, and there was one form to each of the four; their appearance and their actions were as though one wheel were inside the other. When they moved, they moved on each of their four sides; they did not turn as they moved. Their rims were high, fearful; and the rims of all four of them were covered with eyes, all around. And when the living beings moved, the wheels moved with them; and when the living beings rose up above the ground, the wheels also rose up;

---

eyes." The beating of their wings makes a noise like rushing water, or the camp of an army, or the voice of God Himself. Above them is a dome as if of ice, and above that a throne of sapphire, and a being of human form surrounded by fire and the radiance of a rainbow. Terrified, the prophet falls on his face and hears a voice speak. The Haftara then moves to the close of the vision, in which Ezekiel, lifted by a wind, hears a great voice saying, "Blessed is the LORD's glory from His place."

Much of this is deeply obscure, and became the basis of an esoteric tradition known as *Merkava*, or "chariot," mysticism (a trace of this can be found in the poem, "God, LORD of all creation," said on Shabbat morning). The

אִשָּׁה אֶל־אֲחוֹתָהּ כַּנְפֵיהֶם לֹא־יִסַּבּוּ בְלֶכְתָּ֔ן אִ֛ישׁ אֶל־עֵ֥בֶר פָּנָ֖יו
יֵלֵֽכוּ: וּדְמ֣וּת פְּנֵיהֶם֮ פְּנֵ֣י אָדָם֒ וּפְנֵ֨י אַרְיֵ֤ה אֶל־הַיָּמִין֙ לְאַרְבַּעְתָּ֔ם
וּפְנֵי־שׁ֥וֹר מֵֽהַשְּׂמֹ֖אול לְאַרְבַּעְתָּ֑ן וּפְנֵי־נֶ֖שֶׁר לְאַרְבַּעְתָּֽן: וּפְנֵיהֶ֣ם
וְכַנְפֵיהֶ֣ם פְּרֻד֖וֹת מִלְמָ֑עְלָה לְאִ֗ישׁ שְׁתַּ֨יִם֙ חֹבְר֣וֹת אִ֔ישׁ וּשְׁתַּ֣יִם
מְכַסּ֔וֹת אֵ֖ת גְּוִיֹּתֵיהֶֽנָה: וְאִ֛ישׁ אֶל־עֵ֥בֶר פָּנָ֖יו יֵלֵ֑כוּ אֶ֣ל אֲשֶׁר֩
יִֽהְיֶה־שָּׁ֨מָּה הָר֤וּחַ לָלֶ֙כֶת֙ יֵלֵ֔כוּ לֹ֥א יִסַּ֖בּוּ בְּלֶכְתָּֽן: וּדְמ֣וּת הַֽחַיּ֗וֹת
מַרְאֵיהֶם֙ כְּגַֽחֲלֵי־אֵשׁ֙ בֹּֽעֲר֔וֹת כְּמַרְאֵ֖ה הַלַּפִּדִ֑ים הִ֚יא מִתְהַלֶּ֣כֶת
בֵּ֣ין הַֽחַיּ֔וֹת וְנֹ֣גַהּ לָאֵ֔שׁ וּמִן־הָאֵ֖שׁ יוֹצֵ֥א בָרָֽק: וְהַֽחַיּ֖וֹת רָצ֣וֹא
וָשׁ֑וֹב כְּמַרְאֵ֖ה הַבָּזָֽק: וָאֵ֖רֶא הַֽחַיּ֑וֹת וְהִנֵּה֩ אוֹפַ֨ן אֶחָ֥ד בָּאָ֛רֶץ
אֵ֥צֶל הַֽחַיּ֖וֹת לְאַרְבַּ֥עַת פָּנָֽיו: מַרְאֵ֨ה הָאֽוֹפַנִּ֤ים וּמַֽעֲשֵׂיהֶם֙
כְּעֵ֣ין תַּרְשִׁ֔ישׁ וּדְמ֥וּת אֶחָ֖ד לְאַרְבַּעְתָּ֑ן וּמַרְאֵיהֶם֙ וּמַ֣עֲשֵׂיהֶ֔ם
כַּֽאֲשֶׁ֛ר יִֽהְיֶ֥ה הָאוֹפַ֖ן בְּת֥וֹךְ הָאוֹפָֽן: עַל־אַרְבַּ֤עַת רִבְעֵיהֶן֙ בְּלֶכְתָּ֣ם
יֵלֵ֔כוּ לֹ֥א יִסַּ֖בּוּ בְּלֶכְתָּֽן: וְגַ֨בֵּיהֶ֔ן וְגֹ֥בַהּ לָהֶ֖ם וְיִרְאָ֣ה לָהֶ֑ם וְגַבֹּתָ֗ם
מְלֵאֹ֥ת עֵינַ֛יִם סָבִ֖יב לְאַרְבַּעְתָּֽן: וּבְלֶ֙כֶת֙ הַֽחַיּ֔וֹת יֵלְכ֥וּ הָאוֹפַנִּ֖ים
אֶצְלָ֑ם וּבְהִנָּשֵׂ֤א הַֽחַיּוֹת֙ מֵעַ֣ל הָאָ֔רֶץ יִנָּשְׂא֖וּ הָאוֹפַנִּֽים: עַ֣ל אֲשֶׁר֩

---

lead to its destruction had not yet taken place. But Ezekiel, like his older contemporary Jeremiah, believed that disaster was imminent. Both prophets were
charged by God to warn the people of the coming catastrophe, to urge them to
repent, and to provide a compelling narrative of hope. If the people returned
to God, God would return to them and bring them home.

Ezekiel's prophetic mission began with the dazzling vision set out in the
Haftara, the most vivid of its kind anywhere in Tanakh. He sees a storm, a
great cloud lit from within by fire and a radiance like ḥashmal, a word that
appears only in Ezekiel and was adopted in Modern Hebrew to mean "elec-
tricity." He discerns four creatures, each with four wings and four faces, those
of a man, a lion, a bull and an eagle (probably symbolizing, respectively, intelligence, sovereignty, strength and swiftness). They blaze with light, they have
strange wheels-within-wheels that shine like topaz, and rims "covered with

wherever the spirit wished to move, they moved, there where the spirit moved, the wheels rose up with them, for the spirit of the living being was also in the wheels: when they moved, they too moved, and when they stood, they too stood, and when they rose up from the ground, the wheels too rose up with them, because the spirit of the living being was in the wheels.

And above the heads of the living beings there was the form of a dome, with a semblance of the terrible ice, suspended over their heads from above; and beneath the dome, their wings were straightened out towards each other, a pair covering them here, and another pair covering them there, over their bodies. And I heard the sound of their wings and it was like the sound of a mass of waters, like the voice of the Almighty, when they moved; the sound of roaring, like the sound of an encampment. Standing still, they lowered their wings; a voice came from upon the dome which was over their heads – standing still, they lowered their wings.

And above the dome which was over their heads, with the appearance of a sapphire, was the form of a throne; and on the form of the throne there was a form with the appearance of a man, upon it, from above. And I saw: a semblance of amber, the appearance of fire encasing it, from what appeared to be his waist and above; and from what appeared to be his waist and below, I saw an appearance like fire with a brightness around it – it was like the appearance of the rainbow in the clouds on a rainy day, the brightness around it had that appearance. This was the appearance of the form of the glory of God – and I saw it, and I fell upon my face, and I heard a voice speak.

Then a wind lifted me up and I heard behind me the sound of a great noise, saying, "Blessed is the LORD's glory from His place." *Ezek. 3:12*

---

permanent, that the covenant was still in place, and that when the spirit lifts us, as the wind lifted Ezekiel, we can still sense the glory of God, however opaque, for though we may seem far from Him, He is never far from us.

יִהְיֶה־שָּׁם הָרֹ֙וּחַ֙ לָלֶ֣כֶת יֵלֵ֔כוּ שָׁ֛מָּה הָר֖וּחַ לָלֶ֑כֶת וְהָאוֹפַנִּ֗ים
יִנָּשְׂאוּ֙ לְעֻמָּתָ֔ם כִּ֛י ר֥וּחַ הַחַיָּ֖ה בָּאוֹפַנִּֽים: בְּלֶכְתָּ֣ם יֵלֵ֔כוּ וּבְעָמְדָ֖ם
יַֽעֲמֹ֑דוּ וּֽבְהִנָּֽשְׂאָ֞ם מֵעַ֣ל הָאָ֗רֶץ יִנָּשְׂא֤וּ הָאֽוֹפַנִּים֙ לְעֻמָּתָ֔ם כִּ֛י
ר֥וּחַ הַחַיָּ֖ה בָּאוֹפַנִּֽים: וּדְמ֞וּת עַל־רָאשֵׁ֤י הַֽחַיָּה֙ רָקִ֔יעַ כְּעֵ֖ין
הַקֶּ֣רַח הַנּוֹרָ֑א נָט֛וּי עַל־רָאשֵׁיהֶ֖ם מִלְמָֽעְלָה: וְתַ֙חַת֙ הָֽרָקִ֔יעַ
כַּנְפֵיהֶ֣ם יְשָׁר֔וֹת אִשָּׁ֖ה אֶל־אֲחוֹתָ֑הּ לְאִ֗ישׁ שְׁתַּ֤יִם מְכַסּוֹת֙ לָהֵ֔נָּה
וּלְאִ֗ישׁ שְׁתַּ֤יִם מְכַסּוֹת֙ לָהֵ֔נָּה אֵ֖ת גְּוִֽיֹּתֵיהֶֽם: וָאֶשְׁמַ֣ע אֶת־ק֣וֹל
כַּנְפֵיהֶ֡ם כְּקוֹל֩ מַ֙יִם רַבִּ֤ים כְּקוֹל־שַׁדַּי֙ בְּלֶכְתָּ֔ם ק֥וֹל הֲמֻלָּ֖ה כְּק֣וֹל
מַחֲנֶ֑ה בְּעָמְדָ֖ם תְּרַפֶּ֥ינָה כַנְפֵיהֶֽן: וַֽיְהִי־ק֕וֹל מֵעַ֕ל לָרָקִ֖יעַ אֲשֶׁ֣ר
עַל־רֹאשָׁ֑ם בְּעָמְדָ֖ם תְּרַפֶּ֥ינָה כַנְפֵיהֶֽן: וּמִמַּ֗עַל לָרָקִ֙יעַ֙ אֲשֶׁ֣ר
עַל־רֹאשָׁ֔ם כְּמַרְאֵ֥ה אֶֽבֶן־סַפִּ֖יר דְּמ֣וּת כִּסֵּ֑א וְעַל֙ דְּמ֣וּת הַכִּסֵּ֔א
דְּמ֞וּת כְּמַרְאֵ֥ה אָדָ֛ם עָלָ֖יו מִלְמָֽעְלָה: וָאֵ֣רֶא ׀ כְּעֵ֣ין חַשְׁמַ֗ל
כְּמַרְאֵה־אֵ֤שׁ בֵּֽית־לָהּ֙ סָבִ֔יב מִמַּרְאֵ֥ה מָתְנָ֖יו וּלְמָ֑עְלָה וּמִמַּרְאֵ֤ה
מָתְנָיו֙ וּלְמַ֔טָּה רָאִ֙יתִי֙ כְּמַרְאֵה־אֵ֔שׁ וְנֹ֥גַֽהּ ל֖וֹ סָבִֽיב: כְּמַרְאֵ֣ה
הַקֶּ֡שֶׁת אֲשֶׁר֩ יִֽהְיֶ֙ה בֶֽעָנָ֜ן בְּי֣וֹם הַגֶּ֗שֶׁם כֵּ֣ן מַרְאֵ֤ה הַנֹּ֙גַהּ֙ סָבִ֔יב
ה֕וּא מַרְאֵ֖ה דְּמ֣וּת כְּבוֹד־יְהֹוָ֑ה וָֽאֶרְאֶה֙ וָֽאֶפֹּ֣ל עַל־פָּנַ֔י וָֽאֶשְׁמַ֖ע
ק֥וֹל מְדַבֵּֽר:

יחזקאל ג:יב

וַתִּשָּׂאֵ֣נִי ר֔וּחַ וָֽאֶשְׁמַ֣ע אַֽחֲרַ֔י ק֖וֹל רַ֣עַשׁ גָּד֑וֹל בָּר֥וּךְ כְּבֽוֹד־יְהֹוָ֖ה
מִמְּקוֹמֽוֹ:

Mishna (Ḥaggiga 2:1), aware of the dangers of unguided mysticism, rules that
this passage should not be expounded in public or even studied in private
except by a sage with a deep understanding of such matters. What we can
say, however, is that this vision, mysteriously transmitted as it were from the
Temple in Jerusalem to the prophet in exile, carried with it the assurance
that God was still with His people, that their defeat and dispersion were not

BLESSINGS AFTER THE HAFTARA

After the Haftara, the person called up for Maftir says the following blessings:

בָּרוּךְ Blessed are You, LORD our God, King of the Universe, Rock of all worlds, righteous for all generations, the faithful God who says and does, speaks and fulfills, all of whose words are truth and righteousness. You are faithful, LORD our God, and faithful are Your words, not one of which returns unfulfilled, for You, God, are a faithful (and compassionate) King. Blessed are You, LORD, faithful in all His words.

רַחֵם Have compassion on Zion for it is the source of our life, and save the one grieved in spirit swiftly in our days. Blessed are You, LORD, who makes Zion rejoice in her children.

שַׂמְּחֵנוּ Grant us joy, LORD our God, through Elijah the prophet Your servant, and through the kingdom of the house of David Your anointed – may he soon come and make our hearts glad. May no stranger sit on his throne, and may others not continue to inherit his glory, for You promised him by Your holy name that his light would never be extinguished. Blessed are You, LORD, Shield of David.

עַל הַתּוֹרָה For the Torah, for Divine worship, for the prophets, and for this day of the festival of Shavuot which You, LORD our God, have given us for gladness and joy, for honor and glory – for all these we thank and bless You, LORD our God, and may Your name be blessed by the mouth of all that lives, continually, for ever and all time. Blessed are You, LORD, who sanctifies Israel and the festive seasons.

רַחֵם עַל צִיּוֹן *Have compassion on Zion.* Zion is a synonym for Jerusalem. There is, in this brief blessing, a piercing note of love for the holy city ("the source of our life") as well as sadness for its ruined state ("grieved in spirit"). Jerusalem is the home of the Jewish heart, the place from which the Divine Presence was never exiled (Maimonides, Laws of the Chosen House 6:16).

עַל כִּסְאוֹ לֹא יֵשֵׁב זָר *May no stranger sit on his throne.* A prayer for the return of the Davidic monarchy and the restoration of Jewish sovereignty over the land of Israel. There may be the hint here of a polemic against rival claims to sovereignty such as that of the Hasmonean kings of the Second Temple period who were not from the house of David.

עַל הַתּוֹרָה *For the Torah.* A prayer specific to the day, be it Shabbat, festival or both.

ברכות לאחר ההפטרה

After the הפטרה, *the person called up for* מפטיר *says the following blessings:*

בָּרוּךְ אַתָּה יהוה אֱלֹהֵינוּ מֶלֶךְ הָעוֹלָם, צוּר כָּל הָעוֹלָמִים, צַדִּיק בְּכָל הַדּוֹרוֹת, הָאֵל הַנֶּאֱמָן, הָאוֹמֵר וְעוֹשֶׂה, הַמְדַבֵּר וּמְקַיֵּם, שֶׁכָּל דְּבָרָיו אֱמֶת וָצֶדֶק. נֶאֱמָן אַתָּה הוּא יהוה אֱלֹהֵינוּ וְנֶאֱמָנִים דְּבָרֶיךָ, וְדָבָר אֶחָד מִדְּבָרֶיךָ אָחוֹר לֹא יָשׁוּב רֵיקָם, כִּי אֵל מֶלֶךְ נֶאֱמָן (וְרַחֲמָן) אָתָּה. בָּרוּךְ אַתָּה יהוה, הָאֵל הַנֶּאֱמָן בְּכָל דְּבָרָיו.

רַחֵם עַל צִיּוֹן כִּי הִיא בֵּית חַיֵּינוּ, וְלַעֲלוּבַת נֶפֶשׁ תּוֹשִׁיעַ בִּמְהֵרָה בְיָמֵינוּ. בָּרוּךְ אַתָּה יהוה, מְשַׂמֵּחַ צִיּוֹן בְּבָנֶיהָ.

שַׂמְּחֵנוּ יהוה אֱלֹהֵינוּ בְּאֵלִיָּהוּ הַנָּבִיא עַבְדֶּךָ, וּבְמַלְכוּת בֵּית דָּוִד מְשִׁיחֶךָ, בִּמְהֵרָה יָבוֹא וְיָגֵל לִבֵּנוּ. עַל כִּסְאוֹ לֹא יֵשֶׁב זָר, וְלֹא יִנְחֲלוּ עוֹד אֲחֵרִים אֶת כְּבוֹדוֹ, כִּי בְשֵׁם קָדְשְׁךָ נִשְׁבַּעְתָּ לּוֹ שֶׁלֹּא יִכְבֶּה נֵרוֹ לְעוֹלָם וָעֶד. בָּרוּךְ אַתָּה יהוה, מָגֵן דָּוִד.

עַל הַתּוֹרָה וְעַל הָעֲבוֹדָה וְעַל הַנְּבִיאִים, וְעַל יוֹם חַג הַשָּׁבוּעוֹת הַזֶּה שֶׁנָּתַתָּ לָּנוּ יהוה אֱלֹהֵינוּ לְשָׂשׂוֹן וּלְשִׂמְחָה, לְכָבוֹד וּלְתִפְאָרֶת. עַל הַכֹּל יהוה אֱלֹהֵינוּ אֲנַחְנוּ מוֹדִים לָךְ וּמְבָרְכִים אוֹתָךְ, יִתְבָּרַךְ שִׁמְךָ בְּפִי כָּל חַי תָּמִיד לְעוֹלָם וָעֶד. בָּרוּךְ אַתָּה יהוה, מְקַדֵּשׁ יִשְׂרָאֵל וְהַזְּמַנִּים.

The Prayer for the Welfare of the Canadian Government is on the next page.

BLESSINGS AFTER THE HAFTARA

There are three blessings after each Haftara; a fourth is added on Shabbat and festivals.

בָּרוּךְ אַתָּה *Blessed are You.* The first of a sequence of blessings begins with this formula, but not the subsequent ones. The key word of this first paragraph is *ne'eman,* "faithful," meaning: God keeps His word. Many of the haftarot are prophetic visions of the future, communicated to the prophet by God Himself. Historically these have formed the basis of Jewish hope. Hence we affirm our faith that the visions will come true. What God has promised, He will fulfill.

The Prayer for the Welfare of the Canadian Government is on the next page.

PRAYER FOR THE WELFARE OF THE AMERICAN GOVERNMENT

The Leader says the following:

הַנּוֹתֵן תְּשׁוּעָה May He who gives salvation to kings and dominion to princes, whose kingdom is an everlasting kingdom, who delivers His servant David from the evil sword, who makes a way in the sea and a path through the mighty waters, bless and protect, guard and help, exalt, magnify and uplift the President, Vice President and all officials of this land. May the Supreme King of kings in His mercy put into their hearts and the hearts of all their counselors and officials, to deal kindly with us and all Israel. In their days and in ours, may Judah be saved and Israel dwell in safety, and may the Redeemer come to Zion. May this be His will, and let us say: Amen.

PRAYER FOR THE SAFETY OF THE AMERICAN MILITARY FORCES

The Leader says the following:

אַדִּיר בַּמָּרוֹם God on high who dwells in might, the King to whom peace belongs, look down from Your holy habitation and bless the soldiers of the American military forces who risk their lives for the sake of peace on earth. Be their shelter and stronghold, and let them not falter. Give them the strength and courage to thwart the plans of the enemy and end the rule of evil. May their enemies be scattered and their foes flee before them, and may they rejoice in Your salvation. Bring them back safely to their homes, as is written: "The Lord *Ps. 121* will guard you from all harm, He will guard your life. The Lord will guard your going and coming, now and for evermore." And may there be fulfilled for us the verse: "Nation shall not lift up sword against *Is. 2* nation, nor shall they learn war any more." Let all the inhabitants on earth know that sovereignty is Yours and Your name inspires awe over all You have created – and let us say: Amen.

---

city to which I have carried you in exile. Pray to the Lord for it, because in its peace, you shall find peace." This is the first statement in history of what it is to be a creative minority, integrating without assimilating, maintaining

The Prayer for the Welfare of the Canadian Government is on the next page.

תפילה לשלום המלכות

The שליח ציבור *says the following:*

הַנּוֹתֵן תְּשׁוּעָה לַמְּלָכִים וּמֶמְשָׁלָה לַנְּסִיכִים, מַלְכוּתוֹ מַלְכוּת כָּל
עוֹלָמִים, הַפּוֹצֶה אֶת דָּוִד עַבְדּוֹ מֵחֶרֶב רָעָה, הַנּוֹתֵן בַּיָּם דֶּרֶךְ וּבְמַיִם
עַזִּים נְתִיבָה, הוּא יְבָרֵךְ וְיִשְׁמֹר וְיִנְצֹר וְיַעֲזֹר וִירוֹמֵם וִיגַדֵּל וִינַשֵּׂא
לְמַעְלָה אֶת הַנָּשִׂיא וְאֶת מִשְׁנֵהוּ וְאֶת כָּל שָׂרֵי הָאָרֶץ הַזֹּאת. מֶלֶךְ
מַלְכֵי הַמְּלָכִים, בְּרַחֲמָיו יִתֵּן בְּלִבָּם וּבְלֵב כָּל יוֹעֲצֵיהֶם וְשָׂרֵיהֶם
לַעֲשׂוֹת טוֹבָה עִמָּנוּ וְעִם כָּל יִשְׂרָאֵל. בִּימֵיהֶם וּבְיָמֵינוּ תִּוָּשַׁע יְהוּדָה,
וְיִשְׂרָאֵל יִשְׁכֹּן לָבֶטַח, וּבָא לְצִיּוֹן גּוֹאֵל. וְכֵן יְהִי רָצוֹן, וְנֹאמַר אָמֵן.

תפילה לשלום חיילי צבא ארצות הברית

The שליח ציבור *says the following:*

אַדִּיר בַּמָּרוֹם שׁוֹכֵן בִּגְבוּרָה, מֶלֶךְ שֶׁהַשָּׁלוֹם שֶׁלּוֹ, הַשְׁקִיפָה מִמְּעוֹן
קָדְשְׁךָ, וּבָרֵךְ אֶת חַיָּלֵי צְבָא אַרְצוֹת הַבְּרִית, הַמְחָרְפִים נַפְשָׁם
בְּלֶכְתָּם לָשִׂים שָׁלוֹם בָּאָרֶץ. הֱיֵה נָא לָהֶם מַחֲסֶה וּמָעוֹז, וְאַל תִּתֵּן
לַמּוֹט רַגְלָם, חַזֵּק יְדֵיהֶם וְאַמֵּץ רוּחָם לְהָפֵר עֲצַת אוֹיֵב וּלְהַעֲבִיר
מֶמְשֶׁלֶת זָדוֹן, יָפוּצוּ אוֹיְבֵיהֶם וְיָנוּסוּ מְשַׂנְאֵיהֶם מִפְּנֵיהֶם, וְיִשְׂמְחוּ
בִישׁוּעָתֶךָ. הֲשִׁיבֵם בְּשָׁלוֹם אֶל בֵּיתָם, כַּכָּתוּב בְּדִבְרֵי קָדְשֶׁךָ: יהוה
יִשְׁמָרְךָ מִכָּל־רָע, יִשְׁמֹר אֶת־נַפְשֶׁךָ: יהוה יִשְׁמָר־צֵאתְךָ וּבוֹאֶךָ,
מֵעַתָּה וְעַד־עוֹלָם: וְקַיֵּם בָּנוּ מִקְרָא שֶׁכָּתוּב: לֹא־יִשָּׂא גוֹי אֶל־גּוֹי
חֶרֶב, וְלֹא־יִלְמְדוּ עוֹד מִלְחָמָה: וְיֵדְעוּ כָּל יוֹשְׁבֵי תֵבֵל כִּי לְךָ מְלוּכָה
יָאָתָה, וְשִׁמְךָ נוֹרָא עַל כָּל מַה שֶּׁבָּרָאתָ. וְנֹאמַר אָמֵן.

תהלים קכא

ישעיה ב

PRAYER FOR THE WELFARE OF THE GOVERNMENT

This prayer echoes the instruction of Jeremiah (29:7) to those dispersed at
the time of the Babylonian exile (sixth century BCE): "Seek the peace of the

PRAYER FOR THE WELFARE OF THE CANADIAN GOVERNMENT

The Leader says the following:

הַנּוֹתֵן תְּשׁוּעָה May He who gives salvation to kings and dominion to princes, whose kingdom is an everlasting kingdom, who delivers His servant David from the evil sword, who makes a way in the sea and a path through the mighty waters, bless and protect, guard and help, exalt, magnify and uplift the Prime Minister and all the elected and appointed officials of Canada. May the Supreme King of kings in His mercy put into their hearts and the hearts of all their counselors and officials, to deal kindly with us and all Israel. In their days and in ours, may Judah be saved and Israel dwell in safety, and may the Redeemer come to Zion. May this be His will, and let us say: Amen.

PRAYER FOR THE SAFETY OF THE CANADIAN FORCES

The Leader says the following:

אַדִּיר בַּמָּרוֹם God on high who dwells in might, the King to whom peace belongs, look down from Your holy habitation and bless the soldiers of the Canadian Forces who risk their lives for the sake of peace on earth. Be their shelter and stronghold, and let them not falter. Give them the strength and courage to thwart the plans of the enemy and end the rule of evil. May their enemies be scattered and their foes flee before them, and may they rejoice in Your salvation. Bring them back safely to their homes, as is written: "The LORD will *Ps. 121* guard you from all harm, He will guard your life. The LORD will guard your going and coming, now and for evermore." And may there be fulfilled for us the verse: "Nation shall not lift up sword *Is. 2* against nation, nor shall they learn war any more." Let all the inhabitants on earth know that sovereignty is Yours and Your name inspires awe over all You have created – and let us say: Amen.

---

another alive" (*Avot* 3:2). To be a Jew is to be loyal to the country in which we live, to work for the common good and for the good of all humankind, to care for the welfare of others, and to work for good relations between different groups.

תפילה לשלום המלכות

The שליח ציבור *says the following:*

הַנּוֹתֵן תְּשׁוּעָה לַמְּלָכִים וּמֶמְשָׁלָה לַנְּסִיכִים, מַלְכוּתוֹ מַלְכוּת כָּל
עוֹלָמִים, הַפּוֹצֶה אֶת דָּוִד עַבְדּוֹ מֵחֶרֶב רָעָה, הַנּוֹתֵן בַּיָּם דֶּרֶךְ וּבְמַיִם
עַזִּים נְתִיבָה, הוּא יְבָרֵךְ וְיִשְׁמֹר וְיִנְצֹר וְיַעֲזֹר וִירוֹמֵם וִיגַדֵּל וִינַשֵּׂא
לְמַעְלָה אֶת רֹאשׁ הַמֶּמְשָׁלָה וְאֶת כָּל שָׂרֵי הָאָרֶץ הַזֹּאת. מֶלֶךְ מַלְכֵי
הַמְּלָכִים, בְּרַחֲמָיו יִתֵּן בְּלִבָּם וּבְלֵב כָּל יוֹעֲצֵיהֶם וְשָׂרֵיהֶם לַעֲשׂוֹת
טוֹבָה עִמָּנוּ וְעִם כָּל יִשְׂרָאֵל. בִּימֵיהֶם וּבְיָמֵינוּ תִּוָּשַׁע יְהוּדָה, וְיִשְׂרָאֵל
יִשְׁכֹּן לָבֶטַח, וּבָא לְצִיּוֹן גּוֹאֵל. וְכֵן יְהִי רָצוֹן, וְנֹאמַר אָמֵן.

תפילה לשלום חיילי צבא קנדה

The שליח ציבור *says the following:*

אַדִּיר בַּמָּרוֹם שׁוֹכֵן בִּגְבוּרָה, מֶלֶךְ שֶׁהַשָּׁלוֹם שֶׁלּוֹ, הַשְׁקִיפָה מִמְּעוֹן
קָדְשֶׁךָ, וּבָרֵךְ אֶת חַיָּלֵי צְבָא קָנָדָה, הַמְחָרְפִים נַפְשָׁם בְּלֶכְתָּם לָשִׂים
שָׁלוֹם בָּאָרֶץ. הֱיֵה נָא לָהֶם מַחֲסֶה וּמָעוֹז, וְאַל תִּתֵּן לַמּוֹט רַגְלָם, חַזֵּק
יְדֵיהֶם וְאַמֵּץ רוּחָם לְהָפֵר עֲצַת אוֹיֵב וּלְהַעֲבִיר מֶמְשֶׁלֶת זָדוֹן, יָפוּצוּ
אוֹיְבֵיהֶם וְיָנוּסוּ מְשַׂנְאֵיהֶם מִפְּנֵיהֶם, וְיִשְׂמְחוּ בִּישׁוּעָתֶךָ. הֲשִׁיבֵם
תהלים קכא בְּשָׁלוֹם אֶל בֵּיתָם, כַּכָּתוּב בְּדִבְרֵי קָדְשֶׁךָ: יהוה יִשְׁמָרְךָ מִכָּל־רָע,
יִשְׁמֹר אֶת־נַפְשֶׁךָ: יהוה יִשְׁמָר־צֵאתְךָ וּבוֹאֶךָ, מֵעַתָּה וְעַד־עוֹלָם:
ישעיה ב וְקַיֵּם בָּנוּ מִקְרָא שֶׁכָּתוּב: לֹא־יִשָּׂא גוֹי אֶל־גּוֹי חֶרֶב, וְלֹא־יִלְמְדוּ עוֹד
מִלְחָמָה: וְיֵדְעוּ כָּל יוֹשְׁבֵי תֵבֵל כִּי לְךָ מְלוּכָה יָאָתָה, וְשִׁמְךָ נוֹרָא
עַל כָּל מַה שֶּׁבָּרָאתָ. וְנֹאמַר אָמֵן.

one's identity while contributing to society as a whole. Similar guidance
was given at a later period (first century CE) after the Roman conquest of
Jerusalem: "Rabbi Ḥanina, the deputy High Priest, said: Pray for the welfare
of the government, for were it not for fear of it, people would swallow one

PRAYER FOR THE STATE OF ISRAEL

The Leader says the following prayer:

אָבִינוּ שֶׁבַּשָּׁמַיִם Heavenly Father, Israel's Rock and Redeemer, bless the State of Israel, the first flowering of our redemption. Shield it under the wings of Your loving-kindness and spread over it the Tabernacle of Your peace. Send Your light and truth to its leaders, ministers and counselors, and direct them with good counsel before You.

Strengthen the hands of the defenders of our Holy Land; grant them deliverance, our God, and crown them with the crown of victory. Grant peace in the land and everlasting joy to its inhabitants.

As for our brothers, the whole house of Israel, remember them in all the lands of our (*In Israel say:* their) dispersion, and swiftly lead us (*In Israel say:* them) upright to Zion Your city, and Jerusalem Your dwelling place, as is written in the Torah of Moses Your servant: "Even if *Deut. 30* you are scattered to the furthermost lands under the heavens, from there the LORD your God will gather you and take you back. The LORD your God will bring you to the land your ancestors possessed and you will possess it; and He will make you more prosperous and numerous than your ancestors. Then the LORD your God will open up your heart and the heart of your descendants, to love the LORD your God with all your heart and with all your soul, that you may live."

Unite our hearts to love and revere Your name and observe all the words of Your Torah, and swiftly send us Your righteous anointed one of the house of David, to redeem those who long for Your salvation.

Appear in Your glorious majesty over all the dwellers on earth, and let all who breathe declare: The LORD God of Israel is King and His kingship has dominion over all. Amen, Selah.

---

powerlessness. It is hard not to see in this event the fulfillment of the vision of Moses at the end of his life: "Even if you are scattered to the furthermost lands under the heavens, from there the LORD your God will gather you and take you back" (Deut. 30:4).

תפילה לשלום מדינת ישראל

The שליח ציבור *says the following prayer:*

אָבִינוּ שֶׁבַּשָּׁמַיִם, צוּר יִשְׂרָאֵל וְגוֹאֲלוֹ, בָּרֵךְ אֶת מְדִינַת יִשְׂרָאֵל,
רֵאשִׁית צְמִיחַת גְּאֻלָּתֵנוּ. הָגֵן עָלֶיהָ בְּאֶבְרַת חַסְדֶּךָ וּפְרֹשׂ עָלֶיהָ
סֻכַּת שְׁלוֹמֶךָ, וּשְׁלַח אוֹרְךָ וַאֲמִתְּךָ לְרָאשֶׁיהָ, שָׂרֶיהָ וְיוֹעֲצֶיהָ,
וְתַקְּנֵם בְּעֵצָה טוֹבָה מִלְּפָנֶיךָ.

חַזֵּק אֶת יְדֵי מְגִנֵּי אֶרֶץ קָדְשֵׁנוּ, וְהַנְחִילֵם אֱלֹהֵינוּ יְשׁוּעָה וַעֲטֶרֶת
נִצָּחוֹן תְּעַטְּרֵם, וְנָתַתָּ שָׁלוֹם בָּאָרֶץ וְשִׂמְחַת עוֹלָם לְיוֹשְׁבֶיהָ.

וְאֶת אַחֵינוּ כָּל בֵּית יִשְׂרָאֵל, פְּקָד נָא בְּכָל אַרְצוֹת פְּזוּרֵינוּ, וְתוֹלִיכֵנוּ
/בְּאֶרֶץ יִשְׂרָאֵל פְּזוּרֵיהֶם, וְתוֹלִיכֵם/ מְהֵרָה קוֹמְמִיּוּת לְצִיּוֹן עִירְךָ וְלִירוּשָׁלַיִם
דברים ל מִשְׁכַּן שְׁמֶךָ, כַּכָּתוּב בְּתוֹרַת מֹשֶׁה עַבְדֶּךָ: אִם־יִהְיֶה נִדַּחֲךָ בִּקְצֵה
הַשָּׁמָיִם, מִשָּׁם יְקַבֶּצְךָ יהוה אֱלֹהֶיךָ וּמִשָּׁם יִקָּחֶךָ: וֶהֱבִיאֲךָ יהוה
אֱלֹהֶיךָ אֶל־הָאָרֶץ אֲשֶׁר־יָרְשׁוּ אֲבֹתֶיךָ וִירִשְׁתָּהּ, וְהֵיטִבְךָ וְהִרְבְּךָ
מֵאֲבֹתֶיךָ: וּמָל יהוה אֱלֹהֶיךָ אֶת־לְבָבְךָ וְאֶת־לְבַב זַרְעֶךָ, לְאַהֲבָה
אֶת־יהוה אֱלֹהֶיךָ בְּכָל־לְבָבְךָ וּבְכָל־נַפְשְׁךָ, לְמַעַן חַיֶּיךָ:

וְיַחֵד לְבָבֵנוּ לְאַהֲבָה וּלְיִרְאָה אֶת שְׁמֶךָ, וְלִשְׁמֹר אֶת כָּל דִּבְרֵי
תוֹרָתֶךָ, וּשְׁלַח לָנוּ מְהֵרָה בֶן דָּוִד מְשִׁיחַ צִדְקֶךָ, לִפְדּוֹת מְחַכֵּי
קֵץ יְשׁוּעָתֶךָ.

וְהוֹפַע בַּהֲדַר גְּאוֹן עֻזֶּךָ עַל כָּל יוֹשְׁבֵי תֵבֵל אַרְצֶךָ וְיֹאמַר כֹּל אֲשֶׁר
נְשָׁמָה בְאַפּוֹ, יהוה אֱלֹהֵי יִשְׂרָאֵל מֶלֶךְ וּמַלְכוּתוֹ בַּכֹּל מָשָׁלָה,
אָמֵן סֶלָה.

PRAYER FOR THE STATE OF ISRAEL

Introduced after the birth of the modern State of Israel in 1948 and the restoration of Jewish sovereignty after almost two millennia of homelessness and

PRAYER FOR ISRAEL'S DEFENSE FORCES

The Leader says the following prayer:

מִי שֶׁבֵּרַךְ May He who blessed our ancestors, Abraham, Isaac and Jacob, bless the members of Israel's Defense Forces and its security services who stand guard over our land and the cities of our God from the Lebanese border to the Egyptian desert, from the Mediterranean sea to the approach of the Aravah, and wherever else they are, on land, in air and at sea. May the LORD make the enemies who rise against us be struck down before them. May the Holy One, blessed be He, protect and deliver them from all trouble and distress, affliction and illness, and send blessing and success to all the work of their hands. May He subdue our enemies under them and crown them with deliverance and victory. And may there be fulfilled in them the verse, "It is the LORD your God who goes with you to *Deut. 20* fight for you against your enemies, to deliver you." And let us say: Amen.

PRAYER FOR THOSE BEING HELD IN CAPTIVITY

If Israeli soldiers or civilians are being held in captivity, the Leader says the following:

מִי שֶׁבֵּרַךְ May He who blessed our ancestors, Abraham, Isaac and Jacob, Joseph, Moses and Aaron, David and Solomon, bless, protect and guard the members of Israel's Defense Forces missing in action or held captive, and other captives among our brethren, the whole house of Israel, who are in distress or captivity, as we, the members of this holy congregation, pray on their behalf. May the Holy One, blessed be He, have compassion on them and bring them out from darkness and the shadow of death; may He break their bonds, deliver them from their distress, and bring them swiftly back to their families' embrace. Give thanks to the LORD for His *Ps. 107* loving-kindness and for the wonders He does for the children of men; and may there be fulfilled in them the verse: "Those redeemed by the *Is. 35* LORD will return; they will enter Zion with singing, and everlasting joy will crown their heads. Gladness and joy will overtake them, and sorrow and sighing will flee away." And let us say: Amen.

In Israel, Yizkor is said at this point (page 502).

---

neighbors, places its faith in God and the justice of its cause, not on military might alone.

מי שבירך לחיילי צה״ל

The שליח ציבור says the following prayer:

מִי שֶׁבֵּרֵךְ אֲבוֹתֵינוּ אַבְרָהָם יִצְחָק וְיַעֲקֹב הוּא יְבָרֵךְ אֶת חַיָּלֵי צְבָא
הַהֲגָנָה לְיִשְׂרָאֵל וְאַנְשֵׁי כֹּחוֹת הַבִּטָּחוֹן, הָעוֹמְדִים עַל מִשְׁמַר אַרְצֵנוּ
וְעָרֵי אֱלֹהֵינוּ, מִגְּבוּל הַלְּבָנוֹן וְעַד מִדְבַּר מִצְרַיִם וּמִן הַיָּם הַגָּדוֹל עַד
לְבוֹא הָעֲרָבָה וּבְכָל מָקוֹם שֶׁהֵם, בַּיַּבָּשָׁה, בָּאֲוִיר וּבַיָּם. יִתֵּן יהוה אֶת
אוֹיְבֵינוּ הַקָּמִים עָלֵינוּ נִגָּפִים לִפְנֵיהֶם. הַקָּדוֹשׁ בָּרוּךְ הוּא יִשְׁמֹר וְיַצִּיל
אֶת חַיָּלֵינוּ מִכָּל צָרָה וְצוּקָה וּמִכָּל נֶגַע וּמַחֲלָה, וְיִשְׁלַח בְּרָכָה וְהַצְלָחָה
בְּכָל מַעֲשֵׂי יְדֵיהֶם. יַדְבֵּר שׂוֹנְאֵינוּ תַּחְתֵּיהֶם וִיעַטְּרֵם בְּכֶתֶר יְשׁוּעָה
וּבַעֲטֶרֶת נִצָּחוֹן. וִיקֻיַּם בָּהֶם הַכָּתוּב: כִּי יהוה אֱלֹהֵיכֶם הַהֹלֵךְ עִמָּכֶם   דברים כ
לְהִלָּחֵם לָכֶם עִם־אֹיְבֵיכֶם לְהוֹשִׁיעַ אֶתְכֶם: וְנֹאמַר אָמֵן.

מי שבירך לשבויים

If Israeli soldiers or civilians are being held in captivity, the שליח ציבור says the following:

מִי שֶׁבֵּרֵךְ אֲבוֹתֵינוּ אַבְרָהָם יִצְחָק וְיַעֲקֹב, יוֹסֵף מֹשֶׁה וְאַהֲרֹן, דָּוִד
וּשְׁלֹמֹה, הוּא יְבָרֵךְ וְיִשְׁמֹר וְיִנְצֹר אֶת נֶעְדְּרֵי צְבָא הַהֲגָנָה לְיִשְׂרָאֵל
וּשְׁבוּיָיו, וְאֶת כָּל אַחֵינוּ הַנְּתוּנִים בְּצָרָה וּבְשִׁבְיָה, בַּעֲבוּר שֶׁכָּל הַקָּהָל
הַקָּדוֹשׁ הַזֶּה מִתְפַּלֵּל בַּעֲבוּרָם. הַקָּדוֹשׁ בָּרוּךְ הוּא יִמָּלֵא רַחֲמִים
עֲלֵיהֶם, וְיוֹצִיאֵם מֵחֹשֶׁךְ וְצַלְמָוֶת, וּמוֹסְרוֹתֵיהֶם יְנַתֵּק, וּמִמְּצוּקוֹתֵיהֶם
יוֹשִׁיעֵם, וִישִׁיבֵם מְהֵרָה לְחֵיק מִשְׁפְּחוֹתֵיהֶם. יוֹדוּ לַיהוה חַסְדּוֹ   תהלים קז
וְנִפְלְאוֹתָיו לִבְנֵי אָדָם: וִיקֻיַּם בָּהֶם מִקְרָא שֶׁכָּתוּב: וּפְדוּיֵי יהוה יְשֻׁבוּן,   ישעיה לה
וּבָאוּ צִיּוֹן בְּרִנָּה, וְשִׂמְחַת עוֹלָם עַל־רֹאשָׁם, שָׂשׂוֹן וְשִׂמְחָה יַשִּׂיגוּ, וְנָסוּ
יָגוֹן וַאֲנָחָה: וְנֹאמַר אָמֵן.

In ארץ ישראל, יזכור is said at this point (page 503).

PRAYER FOR ISRAEL'S DEFENSE FORCES

The verse with which the prayer ends is taken from the speech that the "priest anointed for war" spoke to the Israelites before they went into battle in biblical times (Deut. 20:4). Israel, always small and outnumbered by its

יָהּ אֵלִי LORD my God and Redeemer, I will stand to greet You;
[God] who was and will be, was and is,
the land of every nation is Yours.

The thanksgiving-offering, burnt-offering, meal-offering, sin-offering,
guilt-offering, peace-offering and inauguration-offering are all offerings to You.
Remember the weary nation that has borne much, and bring it back to Your
land. I will always praise You with "Happy are those who dwell in Your House."

Fine beyond fine, undecipherable, His understanding is unfathomable,
Awesome God who distinguishes between
good and evil with a single glance.

The thanksgiving-offering, burnt-offering, meal-offering, sin-offering,
guilt-offering, peace-offering and inauguration-offering are all offerings to You.
Remember the weary nation that has borne much, and bring it back to Your
land. I will always praise You with "Happy are those who dwell in Your House."

LORD of hosts, with many wonders, He joined all His tent,
making all blossom in the ways of the heart:
the Rock, perfect is His work.

The thanksgiving-offering, burnt-offering, meal-offering, sin-offering,
guilt-offering, peace-offering and inauguration-offering are all offerings to You.
Remember the weary nation that has borne much, and bring it back to Your
land. I will always praise You with "Happy are those who dwell in Your House." *Ps. 84*

The service continues with "Happy are those" on page 510.

the holiest name of God is that He is past, present and future, both in and
beyond time.

דַּק עַל דַּק *Fine beyond fine.* The universe is finely tuned for the emergence of
life, its delicately balanced mechanisms beyond the reach of human senses
and understanding.

בְּאַחַת סְקִירָה *With a single glance.* There is no time-lag between an event and
God's knowledge and judgment of it.

כָּל אָהֳלוֹ *All His tent.* A metaphor for the universe as a whole.

בִּנְתִיבוֹת לֵב *In the ways of the heart.* A mystical reference to thirty-two (the numerical value of *lev,* "heart") paths of wisdom with which the universe was created (*Sefer Yetzira*). God's name "*Elohim*" appears thirty-two times in Genesis 1.

יָהּ אֵלִי וְגוֹאֲלִי, אֶתְיַצְּבָה לִקְרָאתֶךְ
הָיָה וְיִהְיֶה, הָיָה וְהֹוֶה, כָּל גּוֹי אַדְמָתֶךְ.

וְתוֹדָה וְלָעוֹלָה וְלַמִּנְחָה וְלַחַטָּאת וְלָאָשָׁם
וְלַשְּׁלָמִים וְלַמִּלּוּאִים כָּל קָרְבָּנֶךְ.
זְכֹר נִלְאָה אֲשֶׁר נָשָׂאָה וְהָשִׁיבָה לְאַדְמָתֶךְ
סֶלָה אֲהַלֶּלְךָ בְּאַשְׁרֵי יוֹשְׁבֵי בֵיתֶךְ.

דַּק עַל דַּק, עַד אֵין נִבְדַּק, וְלִתְבוּנָתוֹ אֵין חֵקֶר
הָאֵל נוֹרָא, בְּאַחַת סְקִירָה, בֵּין טוֹב לְרַע יְבַקֵּר.

וְתוֹדָה וְלָעוֹלָה וְלַמִּנְחָה וְלַחַטָּאת וְלָאָשָׁם
וְלַשְּׁלָמִים וְלַמִּלּוּאִים כָּל קָרְבָּנֶךְ.
זְכֹר נִלְאָה אֲשֶׁר נָשָׂאָה וְהָשִׁיבָה לְאַדְמָתֶךְ
סֶלָה אֲהַלֶּלְךָ בְּאַשְׁרֵי יוֹשְׁבֵי בֵיתֶךְ.

אֲדוֹן צְבָאוֹת, בְּרֹב פְּלָאוֹת, חִבֵּר כָּל אָהֳלוֹ
בִּנְתִיבוֹת לֵב לְבָלֵב, הַצּוּר תָּמִים פָּעֳלוֹ.

וְתוֹדָה וְלָעוֹלָה וְלַמִּנְחָה וְלַחַטָּאת וְלָאָשָׁם
וְלַשְּׁלָמִים וְלַמִּלּוּאִים כָּל קָרְבָּנֶךְ.
זְכֹר נִלְאָה אֲשֶׁר נָשָׂאָה וְהָשִׁיבָה לְאַדְמָתֶךְ
סֶלָה אֲהַלֶּלְךָ בְּאַשְׁרֵי יוֹשְׁבֵי בֵיתֶךְ.

The service continues with אַשְׁרֵי *on page 511.*

יָהּ אֵלִי LORD *my God.* A poem that originated in mystical circles, appearing for the first time in the Siddur of Rabbi Isaiah Horowitz (c. 1565–1630; known as *Shela*). It is a prelude, specific to the three pilgrimage festivals, to *Ashrei*, the first three words of which form its refrain. It expresses the sadness that we can no longer be present at the Temple bringing our offerings and rejoicing as our ancestors once did on these days when the nation came together in celebration. Some do not say it on Shabbat; some omit it on days when *Yizkor* is said, when our grief is specifically focused remembering the deceased.

הָיָה וְיִהְיֶה, הָיָה וְהֹוֶה *Who was and will be, was and is.* One of the senses of

RUTH

In Israel, the book of Ruth is read on the first day of Shavuot.

1 Once, in the days when the Judges judged, there was a famine in the land. And one man set out from Bethlehem of Judah and journeyed to live for a while in the land of Moab, and his wife and two sons came with him. This man's name was Elimelekh, his wife's was Naomi, and his two sons' names were Maḥlon and Kilyon, all Efratites from Bethlehem of Judah. They duly arrived in the land of Moab, and there they stayed.

---

ancestry that led eventually to national greatness under his leadership. The sages pointed out that the opening phrase could be read as "Once, when the people judged the judges," that is, when the leaders had lost the respect of the people (*Bereshit Raba* 42:3).

וַיֵּלֶךְ אִישׁ *And one man set out.* This anonymous opening recalls the only other time this phrase appears in Tanakh, in Exodus 2:1, describing the father of Moses – a hint that the story we are about to read ends with the birth of a great leader.

מִבֵּית לֶחֶם יְהוּדָה *From Bethlehem of Judah.* As opposed to the Bethlehem in the territory of Zevulun. The name means "House of Bread," a reference to the fertility of the area and its rich produce. Hence the short-sightedness of the decision to leave the area in search of food elsewhere.

וְשֵׁם הָאִישׁ *This man's name.* The threefold repetition of the word "name" in this verse draws our attention to the names themselves, each of which has significance. Naomi, meaning "pleasant," will prove ironic by the end of this chapter when she says to the townswomen, "Call me not Naomi. Call me Bitter." The two sons have ill-fated names. Maḥlon suggests "illness" or "profanation" (see *Bava Batra* 91b), though it may also mean "forgiven." Kilyon means "destruction." The name Elimelekh is ambiguous. It may mean, "My God is the king," or "Kingship is mine" (*Rut Raba* 2:5). Subsequent names are equally emblematic. Orpah means "back of the neck," which she will eventually show to Naomi as she returns to her land and family. Ruth means "saturated" (*Berakhot* 7b) or "friend". Coincidentally, Ruth in English means "kind, compassionate" – no longer in common use, though its opposite, "ruthless," still is – but its source is not biblical Hebrew but Old Norse. Boaz means "in him is strength."

וַיִּהְיוּ־שָׁם *And there they stayed.* The implication is that the deaths were a

רות

In ארץ ישראל, מגילת רות is read on the first day of שבועות.

א וַיְהִי בִּימֵי שְׁפֹט הַשֹּׁפְטִים וַיְהִי רָעָב בָּאָרֶץ וַיֵּלֶךְ אִישׁ מִבֵּית לֶחֶם
יְהוּדָה לָגוּר בִּשְׂדֵי מוֹאָב הוּא וְאִשְׁתּוֹ וּשְׁנֵי בָנָיו: וְשֵׁם הָאִישׁ
אֱלִימֶלֶךְ וְשֵׁם אִשְׁתּוֹ נָעֳמִי וְשֵׁם שְׁנֵי־בָנָיו ׀ מַחְלוֹן וְכִלְיוֹן אֶפְרָתִים
מִבֵּית לֶחֶם יְהוּדָה וַיָּבֹאוּ שְׂדֵי־מוֹאָב וַיִּהְיוּ־שָׁם: וַיָּמָת אֱלִימֶלֶךְ

THE BOOK OF RUTH

For essays on the book of Ruth, see Introduction, page lii.

The book of Ruth is read on Shavuot for seasonal and substantive reasons.
The main events of the book take place at the time of the barley and wheat
harvests, the period that begins with the seven-week Counting of the Omer
initiated by a barley offering, and culminates in Shavuot and its offering of
two loaves of wheat. Second, Ruth's entry into the faith and way of life of
Israel recalls the entry of the Israelites into the covenant and its commands
at Mount Sinai, commemorated on Shavuot. The book of Ruth thus portrays
in narrative form the two dimensions of Shavuot: the festival of the grain
harvest and of the Sinai covenant.

No less significantly, the book paints a series of vignettes of the kind of
society the Torah was meant to give rise to. In it, more vividly than any
other book of Tanakh, we see Jewish law in action: the parts of the harvest
left for the poor, the redemption of ancestral land and the care to be shown
to childless widows. It is a book of ḥesed – love as deed. It is also about the
meaning of faith in Judaism, which is less cognitive than it is moral: a matter
of faithfulness, loyalty, a refusal to walk away from people who need our help.
This is the human dimension of Torah.

CHAPTER 1

וַיְהִי בִּימֵי שְׁפֹט הַשֹּׁפְטִים Once, in the days when the Judges judged. The book
begins by locating the narrative in the days of the Judges. It ends with an
announcement of the birth of David, Israel's greatest king. It thus stands
historically as a link between the books of Judges and Samuel. The period of
the Judges ended in division, dissension and decline: "In those days there was
no king in Israel: everyone did what was right in his own eyes" (Judges 17:6;
21:25). The book of Ruth tells us about the qualities of character in David's

But then Elimelekh, Naomi's husband, died, and she was left there with her two sons. Both of them married Moabite women – the first was called Orpah, and the second was called Ruth – and they lived on there for some ten years. And after that, the two of them – Maḥlon and Kilyon – died as well, and the woman was left bereaved of both her children and of her husband. And she got up, her daughters-in-law with her, to return from the land of Moab; for word had reached her in the land of Moab, that the LORD had brought His people to mind, and granted them bread.

So she left the place where she had been, both of her daughters-in-law with her, and set off back to the land of Judah. But to her two daughters-in-law she said, "Go on now, please, turn back, each to your own mother's house, and may the LORD show you that same kindness that you have shown the dead, and me. May the LORD grant that you find your resting place, each in her husband's home –" and as she kissed them, they wept aloud. And they said to her, "No. We are returning with you to your people."

Said Naomi, "Turn back, daughters, why would you come with me? Have I still sons in my womb who could be husbands to you? Turn back, my daughters, go; I am too old to be with a man. Even were I to say, 'there is hope for me still'; were I even this night to be married, even if I could bear sons again – are you to wait for them as they grow? Would you be chained to them, never to be another man's? No, daughters, your presence is very bitter to me now, for the hand of the LORD has beaten me."

Aloud they wept, still more, and then Orpah kissed her mother-in-law – but Ruth clung to her.

And Naomi said, "Your sister-in-law has turned back, to her people, to her gods. Turn back after your sister-in-law."

---

page). The action of Providence beneath the surface of events is apparent throughout the narrative.

יַעַשׂ יהוה עִמָּכֶם *May the LORD show you.* Acts in which people bless one another form one of the connecting motifs of the book. There are seven such acts in all, each occurring at a key juncture in the narrative: (1) Here, Naomi blesses her two daughters-in-law; (2) Boaz and the harvesters bless one another (2:4); (3) Boaz blesses Ruth (2:12); (4) Naomi blesses Boaz (2:20); (5) Boaz again blesses Ruth (3:10); (6) the townspeople bless Boaz and Ruth (4:11); (7) the women of the town bless Naomi (4:14). These blessings reflect

אִישׁ נָעֳמִי וַתִּשָּׁאֵר הִיא וּשְׁנֵי בָנֶיהָ: וַיִּשְׂאוּ לָהֶם נָשִׁים מֹאֲבִיּוֹת שֵׁם הָאַחַת עָרְפָּה וְשֵׁם הַשֵּׁנִית רוּת וַיֵּשְׁבוּ שָׁם כְּעֶשֶׂר שָׁנִים: וַיָּמֻתוּ גַם־שְׁנֵיהֶם מַחְלוֹן וְכִלְיוֹן וַתִּשָּׁאֵר הָאִשָּׁה מִשְּׁנֵי יְלָדֶיהָ וּמֵאִישָׁהּ: וַתָּקָם הִיא וְכַלֹּתֶיהָ וַתָּשָׁב מִשְּׂדֵי מוֹאָב כִּי שָׁמְעָה בִּשְׂדֵה מוֹאָב כִּי־פָקַד יְהוָה אֶת־עַמּוֹ לָתֵת לָהֶם לָחֶם: וַתֵּצֵא מִן־הַמָּקוֹם אֲשֶׁר הָיְתָה־שָּׁמָּה וּשְׁתֵּי כַלֹּתֶיהָ עִמָּהּ וַתֵּלַכְנָה בַדֶּרֶךְ לָשׁוּב אֶל־אֶרֶץ יְהוּדָה: וַתֹּאמֶר נָעֳמִי לִשְׁתֵּי כַלֹּתֶיהָ לֵכְנָה שֹּׁבְנָה אִשָּׁה לְבֵית אִמָּהּ יַעֲשֶׂה יְהוָה עִמָּכֶם חֶסֶד כַּאֲשֶׁר עֲשִׂיתֶם עִם־הַמֵּתִים וְעִמָּדִי: יִתֵּן יְהוָה לָכֶם וּמְצֶאןָ מְנוּחָה אִשָּׁה בֵּית אִישָׁהּ וַתִּשַּׁק לָהֶן וַתִּשֶּׂאנָה קוֹלָן וַתִּבְכֶּינָה: וַתֹּאמַרְנָה־לָּהּ כִּי־אִתָּךְ נָשׁוּב לְעַמֵּךְ: וַתֹּאמֶר נָעֳמִי שֹׁבְנָה בְנֹתַי לָמָּה תֵלַכְנָה עִמִּי הַעוֹד־לִי בָנִים בְּמֵעַי וְהָיוּ לָכֶם לַאֲנָשִׁים: שֹׁבְנָה בְנֹתַי לֵכְןָ כִּי זָקַנְתִּי מִהְיוֹת לְאִישׁ כִּי אָמַרְתִּי יֶשׁ־לִי תִקְוָה גַּם הָיִיתִי הַלַּיְלָה לְאִישׁ וְגַם יָלַדְתִּי בָנִים: הֲלָהֵן ׀ תְּשַׂבֵּרְנָה עַד אֲשֶׁר יִגְדָּלוּ הֲלָהֵן תֵּעָגֵנָה לְבִלְתִּי הֱיוֹת לְאִישׁ אַל בְּנֹתַי כִּי־מַר־לִי מְאֹד מִכֶּם כִּי־יָצְאָה בִי יַד־יְהוָה: וַתִּשֶּׂנָה קוֹלָן וַתִּבְכֶּינָה עוֹד וַתִּשַּׁק עָרְפָּה לַחֲמוֹתָהּ וְרוּת דָּבְקָה בָּהּ: וַתֹּאמֶר הִנֵּה שָׁבָה יְבִמְתֵּךְ אֶל־עַמָּהּ וְאֶל־אֱלֹהֶיהָ שׁוּבִי אַחֲרֵי יְבִמְתֵּךְ: וַתֹּאמֶר רוּת אַל־תִּפְגְּעִי־

punishment, though it is not clear what the sin was. Elimelekh may have done wrong in leaving the land, lacking faith that God would provide food (*Bava Batra* 91a). As a prominent citizen, his departure for the land of Israel's enemies would have been demoralizing for his fellow countrymen. The sages said that, as a man of substance, he was reluctant to provide support to those who would come seeking it at a time of distress (*Rut Raba, Petiḥta* 6). Implicit in this midrash is the idea that the cause of the family's misfortunes was a lack of *ḥesed*, loving-kindness, a willingness to make sacrifices for the sake of others, and it was the presence of this quality in Ruth and Boaz that restored the family's fortunes. Naomi was convinced that her tragedies were the result of divine judgment (see commentary on "Call me not Naomi," on the next

But Ruth replied, "Do not entreat me to leave you, to turn back and not to go after you. Wherever you walk, I shall walk; wherever you lie down, there shall I lie. Your people is my people; your God is my God. Wherever you die, there I die, and there shall I be buried. All of this may the Lᴏʀᴅ show me, and more, for death alone will part me from you."

Naomi saw that Ruth was determined to come with her, and she spoke to her no more. The two of them walked on until they came to Bethlehem; and when they arrived at Bethlehem the whole town crowded round, the women saying, "Can this be Naomi?"

She said, "Call me not Naomi. Call me Bitter, for the Almighty has made my life bitter beyond words. I was full when I left this place, and empty has the Lᴏʀᴅ returned me. Why call me, 'Naomi'? The Lᴏʀᴅ has spoken up against me, the Almighty, and ruined me."

This is how Naomi, returning from the land of Moab, and, with her, her daughter-in-law, Ruth the Moabitess, returned. And they arrived at Bethlehem just as the barley harvest began.

2 Naomi had a relation from her husband Elimelekh's family: a man of substance and great strength; his name was Boaz. Ruth the Moabitess said to Naomi, "I shall go and gather the fallen grains among the barley-stalks – go

---

בִּתְחִלַּת קְצִיר שְׂעֹרִים *Just as the barley harvest began.* Note how each chapter of the book ends by setting the scene for the next, while the last sets the scene for a new chapter in Israel's history, as a tribal confederation is about to become a kingdom.

CHAPTER 2

Chapters two and three both begin and end with conversations between Naomi and Ruth, while the center point of each is an encounter between Ruth and Boaz. The book as a whole is tightly structured in the form of mirror-image symmetry (chiasmus), in which the beginning and end are mirror-images of one another and the dramatic climax is in the center.

אִישׁ גִּבּוֹר חַיִל *A man of great strength and substance.* Mirroring Boaz's later description of Ruth as a woman of strength (3:11). David, their great-grandson will eventually himself be so described (1 Sam. 16:18).

אֵלְכָה-נָּא הַשָּׂדֶה וַאֲלַקֳטָה בַשִׁבֳּלִים *I shall go and gather the fallen grains.* The law that parts of the harvest are to be left for the poor is itself stated in the

בִּי לְעָזְבֵךְ לָשׁוּב מֵאַחֲרָיִךְ כִּי אֶל־אֲשֶׁר תֵּלְכִי אֵלֵךְ וּבַאֲשֶׁר תָּלִינִי
אָלִין עַמֵּךְ עַמִּי וֵאלֹהַיִךְ אֱלֹהָי: בַּאֲשֶׁר תָּמוּתִי אָמוּת וְשָׁם אֶקָּבֵר
כֹּה יַעֲשֶׂה יהוה לִי וְכֹה יוֹסִיף כִּי הַמָּוֶת יַפְרִיד בֵּינִי וּבֵינֵךְ: וַתֵּרֶא
כִּי־מִתְאַמֶּצֶת הִיא לָלֶכֶת אִתָּהּ וַתֶּחְדַּל לְדַבֵּר אֵלֶיהָ: וַתֵּלַכְנָה
שְׁתֵּיהֶם עַד־בּוֹאֲנָה בֵּית לָחֶם וַיְהִי כְּבוֹאֲנָה בֵּית לֶחֶם וַתֵּהֹם כָּל־
הָעִיר עֲלֵיהֶן וַתֹּאמַרְנָה הֲזֹאת נָעֳמִי: וַתֹּאמֶר אֲלֵיהֶן אַל־תִּקְרֶאנָה
לִי נָעֳמִי קְרֶאןָ לִי מָרָא כִּי־הֵמַר שַׁדַּי לִי מְאֹד: אֲנִי מְלֵאָה הָלַכְתִּי
וְרֵיקָם הֱשִׁיבַנִי יהוה לָמָּה תִקְרֶאנָה לִי נָעֳמִי וַיהוה עָנָה בִי וְשַׁדַּי
הֵרַע־לִי: וַתָּשָׁב נָעֳמִי וְרוּת הַמּוֹאֲבִיָּה כַלָּתָהּ עִמָּהּ הַשָּׁבָה מִשְּׂדֵי
מוֹאָב וְהֵמָּה בָּאוּ בֵּית לֶחֶם בִּתְחִלַּת קְצִיר שְׂעֹרִים: וּלְנָעֳמִי מוֹדַע   ב
לְאִישָׁהּ אִישׁ גִּבּוֹר חַיִל מִמִּשְׁפַּחַת אֱלִימֶלֶךְ וּשְׁמוֹ בֹּעַז: וַתֹּאמֶר
רוּת הַמּוֹאֲבִיָּה אֶל־נָעֳמִי אֵלְכָה־נָּא הַשָּׂדֶה וַאֲלַקֳטָה בַשִּׁבֳּלִים אַחַר

---

a society in which, by acknowledging and invoking the presence of God in
their lives, people seek one another's good and rejoice in one another's good
fortune.

עַמֵּךְ עַמִּי וֵאלֹהַיִךְ אֱלֹהָי *Your people is my people; your God is my God.* This simple,
moving pledge of loyalty became the rabbinic paradigm of an act of conversion to Judaism (*Yevamot* 47b). The double affirmation represents two
distinct aspects of conversion: first, joining a people and sharing its fate; and
second, entering the covenant and its divinely ordained way of life based on
the Torah's 613 commands. Rabbi Joseph Soloveitchik called these two dimensions respectively the covenants of fate (*berit goral*) and faith (*berit ye'ud*).

אַל־תִּקְרֶאנָה לִי נָעֳמִי *"Call me not Naomi."* This scene between Naomi and the
townswomen defines the theme of the story as a whole. She had left full,
she returns empty. She had left "pleasant," she returns bitter. She left with a
husband and two sons; she has now lost them all. All this followed from the
initial act of Elimelekh's disloyalty toward his people and his land. The story
that now follows tells of how these reversals were themselves reversed by a
series of acts of loyalty, Ruth's to Naomi and Boaz's to them both. The last
scene again takes place between Naomi and the women of the town, but now
with life and blessing restored.

after anyone who should show me favor." Naomi said, "Go then, my daughter." And so she went, to gather in the field after the harvestmen. And it was the field-plot of Boaz she chanced to come to; that man of Elimelekh's family.

And there, indeed, came Boaz, arriving from Bethlehem, and saying to the harvestmen, "The LORD be with you." "May the LORD bless you," they replied.

"Whose is that young woman over there?" asked Boaz of his servant, who was in charge of the harvestmen. "That is some Moabite girl," replied the servant in charge of the harvestmen, "the one who came back with Naomi from the land of Moab. She said, 'Let me come gleaning, gathering the fallen grains from among the bundles, where the harvestmen have been'; and so she came, and has been standing out here from early morning until now, and hardly sat at all in the shelter."

Boaz went to Ruth and said, "Daughter, take heed. Do not go gleaning in any other field, and do not leave this one; cling close by my young women. Keep your eyes on the field they are harvesting from and follow after them. I have instructed the young men, of course, not to touch you. When you are thirsty, go to the jugs and drink of the water the young men have drawn."

Ruth bowed down low, to the ground, and she asked him, "Why is it that I have found favor in your eyes, that you give me recognition such as this, when I am a foreigner?"

Boaz said, "I have heard what you have done for your mother-in-law, since your husband died; of how you left your father, your mother, the land of your birth, and came to a people you knew not the day before. May the

---

it for the stranger, the orphan and the widow, *so that the LORD your God may bless you* in all the work of your hands." Those who do well, fare well. Moral good is blessed by material good.

שָׁמַעַתְּ בִּתִּי *Daughter, take heed.* Boaz's affectionate greeting contrasts sharply with the cold remark of the servant: "That is some Moabite girl." He senses and seeks to ease her emotional vulnerability.

לְהַכִּירֵנִי *That you give me recognition such as this.* On this verse, see Introduction, pages lxvii–lxviii.

וַתַּעַזְבִי אָבִיךְ וְאִמֵּךְ *How you left your father, your mother.* A phrase that evokes God's first words to Abraham, "Leave your land, your birthplace and your father's house" (Gen. 12:2). See Introduction, pages lvi–lvii.

אֲשֶׁר אֶמְצָא־חֵן בְּעֵינָיו וַתֹּאמֶר לָהּ לְכִי בִתִּי: וַתֵּלֶךְ וַתָּבוֹא וַתְּלַקֵּט
בַּשָּׂדֶה אַחֲרֵי הַקֹּצְרִים וַיִּקֶר מִקְרֶהָ חֶלְקַת הַשָּׂדֶה לְבֹעַז אֲשֶׁר
מִמִּשְׁפַּחַת אֱלִימֶלֶךְ: וְהִנֵּה־בֹעַז בָּא מִבֵּית לֶחֶם וַיֹּאמֶר לַקּוֹצְרִים
יהוה עִמָּכֶם וַיֹּאמְרוּ לוֹ יְבָרֶכְךָ יהוה: וַיֹּאמֶר בֹּעַז לְנַעֲרוֹ הַנִּצָּב עַל־
הַקּוֹצְרִים לְמִי הַנַּעֲרָה הַזֹּאת: וַיַּעַן הַנַּעַר הַנִּצָּב עַל־הַקּוֹצְרִים
וַיֹּאמַר נַעֲרָה מוֹאֲבִיָּה הִיא הַשָּׁבָה עִם־נָעֳמִי מִשְּׂדֵי מוֹאָב: וַתֹּאמֶר
אֲלַקֳטָה־נָּא וְאָסַפְתִּי בָעֳמָרִים אַחֲרֵי הַקּוֹצְרִים וַתָּבוֹא וַתַּעֲמוֹד
מֵאָז הַבֹּקֶר וְעַד־עַתָּה זֶה שִׁבְתָּהּ הַבַּיִת מְעָט: וַיֹּאמֶר בֹּעַז אֶל־רוּת
הֲלֹא שָׁמַעַתְּ בִּתִּי אַל־תֵּלְכִי לִלְקֹט בְּשָׂדֶה אַחֵר וְגַם לֹא תַעֲבוּרִי
מִזֶּה וְכֹה תִדְבָּקִין עִם־נַעֲרֹתָי: עֵינַיִךְ בַּשָּׂדֶה אֲשֶׁר־יִקְצֹרוּן וְהָלַכְתְּ
אַחֲרֵיהֶן הֲלֹא צִוִּיתִי אֶת־הַנְּעָרִים לְבִלְתִּי נָגְעֵךְ וְצָמִת וְהָלַכְתְּ אֶל־
הַכֵּלִים וְשָׁתִית מֵאֲשֶׁר יִשְׁאֲבוּן הַנְּעָרִים: וַתִּפֹּל עַל־פָּנֶיהָ וַתִּשְׁתַּחוּ
אַרְצָה וַתֹּאמֶר אֵלָיו מַדּוּעַ מָצָאתִי חֵן בְּעֵינֶיךָ לְהַכִּירֵנִי וְאָנֹכִי נָכְרִיָּה:
וַיַּעַן בֹּעַז וַיֹּאמֶר לָהּ הֻגֵּד הֻגַּד לִי כֹּל אֲשֶׁר־עָשִׂית אֶת־חֲמוֹתֵךְ אַחֲרֵי
מוֹת אִישֵׁךְ וַתַּעַזְבִי אָבִיךְ וְאִמֵּךְ וְאֶרֶץ מוֹלַדְתֵּךְ וַתֵּלְכִי אֶל־עַם אֲשֶׁר

Torah immediately after the laws of Shavuot (Lev. 23:22), making a further connection between the book and the festival. Note that Ruth volunteers to do the gathering, to spare her mother-in-law not only the labor but also the shame (Malbim).

וַיִּקֶר מִקְרֶהָ *She chanced to come.* There is deliberate irony in this phrase. Ruth's encounter with Boaz may have seemed from her perspective to be mere chance but we the readers sense the underlying action of Divine Providence that is the background to the story as a whole. Nothing in the book happens by chance.

יְבָרֶכְךָ יהוה *May the LORD bless you.* The use of the divine name in greeting was, according to the sages (*Rut Raba*) instituted at that time. There is also an intertextual echo of the law in Deuteronomy (19:24), "When you are harvesting in your field and you overlook a sheaf, do not go back to get it. Leave

LORD repay your labors; may your reward be full, at the hand of the LORD, the God of Israel, under whose mantle you come to take shelter."

"Sir," she said, "I hope to find favor in your eyes, for you give me solace. For you have spoken to your servant's heart, though I am not like your servants."

When the time came for eating, Boaz said to her, "Come here, eat of this food, and dip your bread in the vinegar." She sat down beside the harvestmen and he served her roasted grains, and she ate, and had her fill, and more left over. And when she stood up to begin gleaning again, Boaz instructed his workers, "Let her glean among the sheaves as well, do not disgrace her. And drop some ears from the bunches as well; leave them, let her glean them and do not reproach her."

Ruth carried on gleaning in the field until evening and then threshed what she had gleaned; it was almost an ephah of barley. She picked it up and came into the city; her mother-in-law saw what she had gleaned; and she produced all that was left beyond her fill, and gave it to her.

"Where did you gather today," she asked, "where were you? Bless whoever gave you this recognition." So Ruth told her mother-in-law under whose patronage she had worked: "The man's name is Boaz, with whom I worked today." Said Naomi to her daughter-in-law, "The LORD bless him; for he has not left behind his kindness for the living or the dead –" and Naomi told her, "The man is our relative; one of our redeemers."

"He said to me, as well," said Ruth the Moabitess: "'Cling by my young men, until they finish all my harvest,'" and Naomi told her daughter-in-law Ruth, "That is well, my daughter. Go out with his young women; do not go and come to harm in other fields."

חַסְדּוֹ אֶת־הַחַיִּים וְאֶת־הַמֵּתִים *His kindness for the living and the dead.* The Hebrew is ambiguous as to whether Naomi is referring here to God or to Boaz. She may mean both. The reference to the dead suggests that Naomi has already conceived the idea that Boaz may be persuaded to marry Ruth "to rebuild the name of the dead (Maḥlon, Ruth's husband) on his estate" (4:10).

מִגֹּאֲלֵנוּ הוּא *One of our redeemers.* The first instance of the word "redeemer" that is a key-term of the narrative, occurring seven times in the next chapter and sixteen in chapter 4. Redemption is both a legal as well as theological term. Legally it refers to the right and responsibility of a relative to buy back

לֹא־יָדַעַתְּ תְּמוֹל שִׁלְשׁוֹם: יְשַׁלֵּם יהוה פָּעֳלֵךְ וּתְהִי מַשְׂכֻּרְתֵּךְ שְׁלֵמָה
מֵעִם יהוה אֱלֹהֵי יִשְׂרָאֵל אֲשֶׁר־בָּאת לַחֲסוֹת תַּחַת־כְּנָפָיו: וַתֹּאמֶר
אֶמְצָא־חֵן בְּעֵינֶיךָ אֲדֹנִי כִּי נִחַמְתָּנִי וְכִי דִבַּרְתָּ עַל־לֵב שִׁפְחָתֶךָ
וְאָנֹכִי לֹא אֶהְיֶה כְּאַחַת שִׁפְחֹתֶיךָ: וַיֹּאמֶר לָה בֹעַז לְעֵת הָאֹכֶל גֹּשִׁי
הֲלֹם וְאָכַלְתְּ מִן־הַלֶּחֶם וְטָבַלְתְּ פִּתֵּךְ בַּחֹמֶץ וַתֵּשֶׁב מִצַּד הַקֹּצְרִים
וַיִּצְבָּט־לָהּ קָלִי וַתֹּאכַל וַתִּשְׂבַּע וַתֹּתַר: וַתָּקָם לְלַקֵּט וַיְצַו בֹּעַז אֶת־
נְעָרָיו לֵאמֹר גַּם בֵּין הָעֳמָרִים תְּלַקֵּט וְלֹא תַכְלִימוּהָ: וְגַם שֹׁל־תָּשֹׁלּוּ
לָהּ מִן־הַצְּבָתִים וַעֲזַבְתֶּם וְלִקְּטָה וְלֹא תִגְעֲרוּ־בָהּ: וַתְּלַקֵּט בַּשָּׂדֶה
עַד־הָעָרֶב וַתַּחְבֹּט אֵת אֲשֶׁר־לִקֵּטָה וַיְהִי כְּאֵיפָה שְׂעֹרִים: וַתִּשָּׂא
וַתָּבוֹא הָעִיר וַתֵּרֶא חֲמוֹתָהּ אֵת אֲשֶׁר־לִקֵּטָה וַתּוֹצֵא וַתִּתֶּן־לָהּ
אֵת אֲשֶׁר־הוֹתִרָה מִשָּׂבְעָהּ: וַתֹּאמֶר לָהּ חֲמוֹתָהּ אֵיפֹה לִקַּטְתְּ הַיּוֹם
וְאָנָה עָשִׂית יְהִי מַכִּירֵךְ בָּרוּךְ וַתַּגֵּד לַחֲמוֹתָהּ אֵת אֲשֶׁר־עָשְׂתָה
עִמּוֹ וַתֹּאמֶר שֵׁם הָאִישׁ אֲשֶׁר עָשִׂיתִי עִמּוֹ הַיּוֹם בֹּעַז: וַתֹּאמֶר נָעֳמִי
לְכַלָּתָהּ בָּרוּךְ הוּא לַיהוה אֲשֶׁר לֹא־עָזַב חַסְדּוֹ אֶת־הַחַיִּים וְאֶת־
הַמֵּתִים וַתֹּאמֶר לָהּ נָעֳמִי קָרוֹב לָנוּ הָאִישׁ מִגֹּאֲלֵנוּ הוּא: וַתֹּאמֶר
רוּת הַמּוֹאֲבִיָּה גַּם | כִּי־אָמַר אֵלַי עִם־הַנְּעָרִים אֲשֶׁר־לִי תִּדְבָּקִין
עַד אִם־כִּלּוּ אֵת כָּל־הַקָּצִיר אֲשֶׁר־לִי: וַתֹּאמֶר נָעֳמִי אֶל־רוּת כַּלָּתָהּ
טוֹב בִּתִּי כִּי תֵצְאִי עִם־נַעֲרוֹתָיו וְלֹא יִפְגְּעוּ־בָךְ בְּשָׂדֶה אַחֵר: וַתִּדְבַּק

אֲשֶׁר־בָּאת לַחֲסוֹת תַּחַת־כְּנָפָיו *Under whose mantle you come to take shelter.* Literally, "under whose wings," an expression of tender divine protection that appears several times in the book of Psalms (see for example, 36:8, 57:2, 61:5, 91:4). Ruth herself uses the same term in the next chapter when she asks Boaz to "spread your mantle over your maidservant."

וַיְהִי כְּאֵיפָה שְׂעֹרִים *It was almost an ephah of barley.* A substantial amount. An omer-measure, sufficient for one meal, is one-tenth of an ephah (Ex. 16:36). Thus she had collected sufficient for ten meals.

And so it was that she clung by Boaz's young women to glean, until the barley harvest was over, and then the wheat; and after that she sat at home with her mother-in-law.

3 One day her mother-in-law Naomi said to her, "Daughter, do I not wish I could find you a resting place that would be good for you? Now there is Boaz, our relative, whose young women you were with – and he will be doing his winnowing in the barley shed tonight. And you are going to wash yourself and anoint yourself and put on your dress, and go down to that shed. Do not let the man know that you are there until he has finished eating and drinking. And when he lies down, take note of the place where he lies, and afterwards go there, uncover his feet and lie down also – and he will tell you what to do next."

"I shall do," said Ruth, "all that you tell me to do."

She went down to the shed and did exactly as her mother-in-law had instructed her. Boaz ate, and drank, and was happy, and he went and lay down at the edge of the heap of grain; and then she came to him silently, uncovered his feet and lay herself down.

At midnight the man started and turned over – there was a woman lying at his feet. "Who are you?" he said, and she answered, "I am your servant Ruth – spread your mantle over your maidservant, for you are a redeemer." And he replied,

"God bless you, daughter, for this last kindness is yet greater than your first, for you have not gone after the young men, poor or rich. Now, daughter, do

---

a covenant with you, declares the Sovereign LORD, and you became Mine" (Ezek. 16:8). The act symbolizes betrothal.

הֵיטַבְתְּ חַסְדֵּךְ *This last kindness is yet greater.* We now understand why Boaz has not made a proposal of marriage thus far. He fears himself too old for Ruth. Boaz immediately understands that a double proposal is being suggested, whose nature becomes clear in the next chapter: first that he redeem a field belonging to Elimelekh that Naomi will be forced to sell; second that he marry Ruth in order to perpetuate the memory of her late husband, Naomi's son. He realizes that her motives are loyalty to Naomi and to the laws and customs of the people she has come to join. When he calls her "a woman of great strength" he means a figure of moral courage, determination and principle. It is dark; he cannot see her. This is important: unlike the lovers in

בִּנְעָרוֹת בֹּעַז לְלַקֵּט עַד־כְּלוֹת קְצִיר־הַשְּׂעֹרִים וּקְצִיר הַחִטִּים

ג וַתֵּשֶׁב אֶת־חֲמוֹתָהּ: וַתֹּאמֶר לָהּ נָעֳמִי חֲמוֹתָהּ בִּתִּי הֲלֹא אֲבַקֶּשׁ־
לָךְ מָנוֹחַ אֲשֶׁר יִיטַב־לָךְ: וְעַתָּה הֲלֹא בֹעַז מֹדַעְתָּנוּ אֲשֶׁר הָיִית
אֶת־נַעֲרוֹתָיו הִנֵּה־הוּא זֹרֶה אֶת־גֹּרֶן הַשְּׂעֹרִים הַלָּיְלָה: וְרָחַצְתְּ ׀

שִׂמְלֹתַיִךְ
וְיָרַדְתְּ

וָסַכְתְּ וְשַׂמְתְּ שִׂמְלֹתֵךְ עָלַיִךְ וְיָרַדְתִּי הַגֹּרֶן אַל־תִּוָּדְעִי לָאִישׁ עַד
כַּלֹּתוֹ לֶאֱכֹל וְלִשְׁתּוֹת: וִיהִי בְשָׁכְבוֹ וְיָדַעַתְּ אֶת־הַמָּקוֹם אֲשֶׁר

וְשָׁכַבְתִּ
אֵלַי

יִשְׁכַּב־שָׁם וּבָאת וְגִלִּית מַרְגְּלֹתָיו ושכבתי וְהוּא יַגִּיד לָךְ אֵת אֲשֶׁר
תַּעֲשִׂין: וַתֹּאמֶר אֵלֶיהָ כֹּל אֲשֶׁר־תֹּאמְרִי   אֶעֱשֶׂה: וַתֵּרֶד הַגֹּרֶן
וַתַּעַשׂ כְּכֹל אֲשֶׁר־צִוַּתָּה חֲמוֹתָהּ: וַיֹּאכַל בֹּעַז וַיֵּשְׁתְּ וַיִּיטַב לִבּוֹ וַיָּבֹא
לִשְׁכַּב בִּקְצֵה הָעֲרֵמָה וַתָּבֹא בַלָּט וַתְּגַל מַרְגְּלֹתָיו וַתִּשְׁכָּב: וַיְהִי
בַּחֲצִי הַלַּיְלָה וַיֶּחֱרַד הָאִישׁ וַיִּלָּפֵת וְהִנֵּה אִשָּׁה שֹׁכֶבֶת מַרְגְּלֹתָיו:
וַיֹּאמֶר מִי־אָתְּ וַתֹּאמֶר אָנֹכִי רוּת אֲמָתֶךָ וּפָרַשְׂתָּ כְנָפֶךָ עַל־אֲמָתְךָ
כִּי גֹאֵל אָתָּה: וַיֹּאמֶר בְּרוּכָה אַתְּ לַיהוה בִּתִּי הֵיטַבְתְּ חַסְדֵּךְ הָאַחֲרוֹן
מִן־הָרִאשׁוֹן לְבִלְתִּי־לֶכֶת אַחֲרֵי הַבַּחוּרִים אִם־דַּל וְאִם־עָשִׁיר:

---

land that poverty has forced a member of the family to sell, or to pay to restore
an impoverished relative to freedom (Lev. 25:25, 49). Theologically, it refers
to God's actions in rescuing His people from slavery in Egypt, and in general
to divine deliverance from harm.

CHAPTER 3

At this point Naomi proposes audacious action on the part of Ruth. The grain
harvest is over. Boaz has not made any proposal about their situation. This
may be the last moment of opportunity for some time. She suggests a nighttime encounter, a stratagem fraught with risks, evidently relying on Boaz's
strength of character not to misconstrue or take advantage of the situation.

וּפָרַשְׂתָּ כְנָפֶךָ עַל־אֲמָתְךָ *Spread your mantle over your maidservant.* This phrase,
together with much of the language of this section of the story, is echoed in
Ezekiel's vision of how God redeemed Israel from Egypt: "I spread the corner of My garment over you… I gave you my solemn oath and entered into

not be afraid. I shall do all that you ask, for all within my people's gate know well, that you are a woman of great strength. And I am indeed a redeemer to you, but there is a redeemer still closer than me. Carry on lying here tonight, and in the morning if he would redeem you, good: let him redeem. And if he cares not to redeem you, I shall redeem you myself, as the LORD lives – lie on here until morning."

And so she lay at his feet until morning, and left before one man could recognize another. "Let not a soul know there was a woman in the shed," said he. And then, "Give me the wrap that you are wearing, hold it out –" and he measured six measures of barley into it; he gave them to her, and she went out into the city.

She came to her mother-in-law; "Who are you, my daughter?" she said. And Ruth told her all that the man had done for her. "He gave me these six measures of barley," she said, "saying, 'Do not go back to your mother-in-law empty-handed.'" Said Naomi, "Sit down now, daughter, until you find out how the matter will fall. For that man will not rest today until it is settled."

4 Boaz went up to the City Gate and sat down. And the very redeemer of whom he had spoken passed by: "Such-and-such," said Boaz, "come here and be seated," and he came and sat down. Then Boaz took ten men from among the elders of the city; "Be seated here," he said, and they too sat. And

---

putes resolved (see Deut. 16:18). The presence of a court in the gate made justice accessible; it also helped ensure that the people of the town would know what had been transacted, thus minimizing the temptation subsequently to deny that a transaction had taken place or a commitment made.

פְּלֹנִי אַלְמֹנִי *Such-and-such.* "*Peloni Almoni,*" an unnamed individual (similarly in I Sam. 21:3; II Kings 6:8). The man's name is not mentioned, either because it is not relevant to the story or perhaps to suggest a moral: because he was not willing to "restore" his relative's "name," his own name was not immortalized in the narrative. The unnamed redeemer functions within the narrative as a contrast to Boaz, as does Ruth's sister-in-law Orpah to her. Neither the anonymous relative nor Orpah do anything wrong, but neither is prepared to go *lifnim mishurat hadin,* beyond the line of duty. They are good but not great, and the book of Ruth is ultimately about the source of moral greatness that eventually found expression in the life of King David, Boaz and Ruth's great-grandson.

וְעַתָּה בִּתִּי אַל־תִּירְאִי כָּל אֲשֶׁר־תֹּאמְרִי אֶעֱשֶׂה־לָּךְ כִּי יוֹדֵעַ כָּל־
שַׁעַר עַמִּי כִּי אֵשֶׁת חַיִל אָתְּ: וְעַתָּה כִּי אָמְנָם כִּי אִם גֹּאֵל אָנֹכִי וְגַם
יֵשׁ גֹּאֵל קָרוֹב מִמֶּנִּי ׀ לִינִי ׀ הַלַּיְלָה וְהָיָה בַבֹּקֶר אִם־יִגְאָלֵךְ טוֹב
יִגְאָל וְאִם־לֹא יַחְפֹּץ לְגָאֳלֵךְ וּגְאַלְתִּיךְ אָנֹכִי חַי־יהוה שִׁכְבִי עַד־
בְּטֶרֶם הַבֹּקֶר: וַתִּשְׁכַּב מַרְגְּלוֹתָו עַד־הַבֹּקֶר וַתָּקָם בטרום יַכִּיר אִישׁ אֶת־
רֵעֵהוּ וַיֹּאמֶר אַל־יִוָּדַע כִּי־בָאָה הָאִשָּׁה הַגֹּרֶן: וַיֹּאמֶר הָבִי הַמִּטְפַּחַת
אֲשֶׁר־עָלַיִךְ וְאֶחֳזִי־בָהּ וַתֹּאחֶז בָּהּ וַיָּמָד שֵׁשׁ־שְׂעֹרִים וַיָּשֶׁת עָלֶיהָ
וַיָּבֹא הָעִיר: וַתָּבוֹא אֶל־חֲמוֹתָהּ וַתֹּאמֶר מִי־אַתְּ בִּתִּי וַתַּגֶּד־לָהּ
אֵת כָּל־אֲשֶׁר עָשָׂה־לָהּ הָאִישׁ: וַתֹּאמֶר שֵׁשׁ־הַשְּׂעֹרִים הָאֵלֶּה נָתַן
אֵלָי לִי כִּי אָמַר אַל־תָּבוֹאִי רֵיקָם אֶל־חֲמוֹתֵךְ: וַתֹּאמֶר שְׁבִי בִתִּי
עַד אֲשֶׁר תֵּדְעִין אֵיךְ יִפֹּל דָּבָר כִּי לֹא יִשְׁקֹט הָאִישׁ כִּי אִם־כִּלָּה
ד הַדָּבָר הַיּוֹם: וּבֹעַז עָלָה הַשַּׁעַר וַיֵּשֶׁב שָׁם וְהִנֵּה הַגֹּאֵל עֹבֵר אֲשֶׁר
דִּבֶּר־בֹּעַז וַיֹּאמֶר סוּרָה שְׁבָה־פֹּה פְּלֹנִי אַלְמֹנִי וַיָּסַר וַיֵּשֵׁב: וַיִּקַּח
עֲשָׂרָה אֲנָשִׁים מִזִּקְנֵי הָעִיר וַיֹּאמֶר שְׁבוּ־פֹה וַיֵּשֵׁבוּ: וַיֹּאמֶר לַגֹּאֵל

---

the Song of Songs, who rhapsodize about one another's appearance, here it is Ruth's moral, not physical, beauty that Boaz admires.

וַתָּקָם בְּטֶרֶם יַכִּיר אִישׁ אֶת־רֵעֵהוּ *And left before one man could recognize another.* Ruth and Boaz were both concerned to avoid any suspicion: "One should always keep oneself far from anything unseemly, or even resembling it" (*Tosefta Ḥullin* 2:6).

שֵׁשׁ־שְׂעֹרִים *Six measures of barley.* A significant amount. Note again that in the midst of the many deliberations that must have been going through Boaz's mind in relation to the redemption and despite the haste brought on by the approach of daylight, he does not forget to stay sensitive to the material and emotional needs of Naomi.

CHAPTER 4

הַשַּׁעַר *The City Gate.* The place where legal matters were transacted and disthen he said to the redeemer, "Naomi, coming back from the land of Moab, must sell the field-plot of our kinsman Elimelekh. And I told her I would let you know of it, inviting you to buy it, in front of those sitting here, in front of the elders of this city. If you would like to redeem this: redeem; and if you will not redeem it, tell me: let me know, for there is none but you to redeem, and I am next in line to you." "I shall redeem," he said.

"On the day you buy that field from Naomi," said Boaz, "and from Ruth the Moabitess – you will have bought the wife of a dead man with it, to restore the dead man's name on his estate."

Said the redeemer: "Such a redemption I could not perform; it would be the ruin of my own estate. You redeem in my place, I cannot redeem."

In those long-ago days in Israel, a redemption or exchange – anything to be officially enacted – was completed as follows. One man would take off his shoe, and would hand it to the other: that was the bond then recognized among Israel. And now this redeemer said to Boaz, "Take possession." And he took off his shoe.

"You bear witness on this day," said Boaz to the elders and to all the people present, "that I take possession of all that was Elimelekh's, and all that was Kilyon's and Maḥlon's, from Naomi's hand. And with it I take Ruth the Moabitess, Maḥlon's wife, to be mine, to rebuild the name of the dead on his estate. And the dead man's name will not be cut off from among his brothers, from the gate of his home town – you are my witnesses this day."

And all the people at the gate, and the elders, said, "We bear witness. May

---

Ramban (Commentary to Gen. 38:8) explains that there was nonetheless an established custom that any relative who was able to redeem the property of one who left a childless widow should, if possible, marry her, and this was called redemption. Alternatively, Rashi suggests that Boaz was simply imply-ing that Naomi was only willing to sell the land if the buyer was also willing to take Ruth as a wife.

לְפָנִים *In those long ago days.* An excursus, not part of the main narrative, to indicate that this was once a legally binding gesture of acquisition (the equivalent of a *kinyan sudar,* the handing over of a symbolic object, in rab-binic law). It should not be confused with a similar ceremony, specified by biblical law, performed when a brother-in-law was unwilling to undertake

חֶלְקַת הַשָּׂדֶה אֲשֶׁר לְאָחִינוּ לֶאֱלִימֶלֶךְ מָכְרָה נָעֳמִי הַשָּׁבָה מִשְּׂדֵה
מוֹאָב: וַאֲנִי אָמַרְתִּי אֶגְלֶה אָזְנְךָ לֵאמֹר קְנֵה נֶגֶד הַיֹּשְׁבִים וְנֶגֶד
זִקְנֵי עַמִּי אִם־תִּגְאַל גְּאָל וְאִם־לֹא יִגְאַל הַגִּידָה לִּי וְאֵדְעָ כִּי אֵין
זוּלָתְךָ לִגְאוֹל וְאָנֹכִי אַחֲרֶיךָ וַיֹּאמֶר אָנֹכִי אֶגְאָל: וַיֹּאמֶר בֹּעַז בְּיוֹם־ קָנִיתְ
קְנוֹתְךָ הַשָּׂדֶה מִיַּד נָעֳמִי וּמֵאֵת רוּת הַמּוֹאֲבִיָּה אֵשֶׁת־הַמֵּת קָנִיתִי לִגְאָל־
לְהָקִים שֵׁם־הַמֵּת עַל־נַחֲלָתוֹ: וַיֹּאמֶר הַגֹּאֵל לֹא אוּכַל לִגְאָול־לִי
פֶּן־אַשְׁחִית אֶת־נַחֲלָתִי גְּאַל־לְךָ אַתָּה אֶת־גְּאֻלָּתִי כִּי לֹא־אוּכַל
לִגְאָל: וְזֹאת לְפָנִים בְּיִשְׂרָאֵל עַל־הַגְּאוּלָּה וְעַל־הַתְּמוּרָה לְקַיֵּם
כָּל־דָּבָר שָׁלַף אִישׁ נַעֲלוֹ וְנָתַן לְרֵעֵהוּ וְזֹאת הַתְּעוּדָה בְּיִשְׂרָאֵל:
וַיֹּאמֶר הַגֹּאֵל לְבֹעַז קְנֵה־לָךְ וַיִּשְׁלֹף נַעֲלוֹ: וַיֹּאמֶר בֹּעַז לַזְּקֵנִים וְכָל־
הָעָם עֵדִים אַתֶּם הַיּוֹם כִּי קָנִיתִי אֶת־כָּל־אֲשֶׁר לֶאֱלִימֶלֶךְ וְאֵת
כָּל־אֲשֶׁר לְכִלְיוֹן וּמַחְלוֹן מִיַּד נָעֳמִי: וְגַם אֶת־רוּת הַמֹּאֲבִיָּה אֵשֶׁת
מַחְלוֹן קָנִיתִי לִי לְאִשָּׁה לְהָקִים שֵׁם־הַמֵּת עַל־נַחֲלָתוֹ וְלֹא־יִכָּרֵת
שֵׁם־הַמֵּת מֵעִם אֶחָיו וּמִשַּׁעַר מְקוֹמוֹ עֵדִים אַתֶּם הַיּוֹם: וַיֹּאמְרוּ
כָּל־הָעָם אֲשֶׁר־בַּשַּׁעַר וְהַזְּקֵנִים עֵדִים יִתֵּן יהוה אֶת־הָאִשָּׁה הַבָּאָה

אִם־תִּגְאַל *If you would like to redeem this.* The legislative principles of the redemption of family landholdings are set out in Leviticus 25. In general, close relatives were not merely permitted but encouraged to redeem, that is, buy back, land that an impoverished relative was forced to sell, the principle being that land in Israel is an ancestral inheritance since the days of Moses and Joshua, and it should if possible stay within the family as its patrimony.

אֵשֶׁת־הַמֵּת קָנִית *You will have bought the wife of a dead man.* There is no connection in biblical law between *geula*, the duty of a relative to redeem the land of an impoverished family member, and *yibum*, levirate marriage, the duty of a brother-in-law to marry his brother's childless widow to "perpetuate the name of the dead" (Deut. 25:5–6). Besides, Boaz cannot be referring to the biblical institution of levirate marriage which applies only to a brother-in-law.

the LORD make the woman who is joining your house like Rachel and like Leah, who together built the house of Israel; may you go from strength to strength in Efrata, and your name be ever spoken in Bethlehem. And may your house be as the house of Peretz, whom Tamar bore to Judah, growing from the seed that the LORD will give you from this young woman."

And so it was that Boaz took Ruth, and she became his wife, and he came to her; the LORD granted her conception, and she bore a son. And the women said to Naomi, "Blessed be the LORD, who has not withheld your redeemer on this day – may the child's name be spoken in all Israel. And may he restore your spirit, and sustain your old age, for your daughter-in-law, who loves you, she has borne him: she who is better to you than seven sons could be."

Naomi took the child and fed him in her bosom, and became his nurse. And her neighbors named him, saying, "A son is born for Naomi!" They called him Oved. And that was Oved the father of Jesse, the father of David.

This is the line of Peretz: Ḥetzron was born to Peretz. Ram was born to Ḥetzron; Aminadav was born to Ram. Naḥshon was born to Aminadav; Salma was born to Naḥshon. Boaz was born to Salma; Oved was born to Boaz. And Jesse was born to Oved – and to Jesse, David was born.

וַתִּקְרֶאנָה לוֹ הַשְּׁכֵנוֹת שֵׁם *And her neighbors named him.* The text seems to suggest that it was the neighbors who gave the child the name Oved, but this is unlikely and there is no other such instance in Tanakh. More likely, the meaning is that they spoke of him often, recognizing the appropriateness of the name his parents had given him. It means, "One who serves" (as in Obadiah, "One who serves God"). The townswomen recognized that the greatness of Ruth and Boaz was *avoda*, the service to others that is a mark of true service to God. The highest accolade given to David in Tanakh, as it was to Moses, was that he was called God's servant (II Sam. 3:18). Evidently the townspeople saw this attribute in Ruth and Boaz's son as it was in them. At a crucial stage in the subsequent history of Israel, David's grandson Rehoboam would ignore the advice of his father's counselors ("If today you will be a *servant* to these people and *serve* them … they will always be your *servants*," [I Kings 12:7]). The result was the division of the kingdom, from which it never fully recovered. As a prelude to the Davidic monarchy, the book of Ruth makes this point to emphasize that to lead is to serve, and the mark of a king is humility (see Rambam, *Hilkhot Melakhim* 2:6). The king serves the people; the people do not serve the king.

אֶל־בֵּיתֶ֔ךָ כְּרָחֵ֤ל ׀ וּכְלֵאָה֙ אֲשֶׁ֨ר בָּנ֤וּ שְׁתֵּיהֶם֙ אֶת־בֵּ֣ית יִשְׂרָאֵ֔ל
וַעֲשֵׂה־חַ֣יִל בְּאֶפְרָ֔תָה וּקְרָא־שֵׁ֖ם בְּבֵ֥ית לָֽחֶם: וִיהִ֤י בֵֽיתְךָ֙ כְּבֵ֣ית פֶּ֔רֶץ
אֲשֶׁר־יֽלְדָ֥ה תָמָ֖ר לִֽיהוּדָ֑ה מִן־הַזֶּ֗רַע אֲשֶׁ֨ר יִתֵּ֤ן יהוה֙ לְךָ֔ מִן־הַנַּֽעֲרָ֖ה
הַזֹּֽאת: וַיִּקַּ֨ח בֹּ֤עַז אֶת־רוּת֙ וַתְּהִי־ל֣וֹ לְאִשָּׁ֔ה וַיָּבֹ֖א אֵלֶ֑יהָ וַיִּתֵּ֨ן יהוֹה֥
לָ֛הּ הֵרָי֖וֹן וַתֵּ֥לֶד בֵּֽן: וַתֹּאמַ֤רְנָה הַנָּשִׁים֙ אֶֽל־נָֽעֳמִ֔י בָּר֣וּךְ יהוֹ֗ה אֲשֶׁ֨ר
לֹ֣א הִשְׁבִּ֥ית לָ֛ךְ גֹּאֵ֖ל הַיּ֑וֹם וְיִקָּרֵ֥א שְׁמ֖וֹ בְּיִשְׂרָאֵֽל: וְהָ֤יָה לָךְ֙ לְמֵשִׁ֣יב
נֶ֔פֶשׁ וּלְכַלְכֵּ֖ל אֶת־שֵׂיבָתֵ֑ךְ כִּ֣י כַלָּתֵ֤ךְ אֲשֶׁר־אֲהֵבַ֨תֶךְ֙ יְלָדַ֔תּוּ אֲשֶׁר־
הִיא֙ ט֣וֹבָה לָ֔ךְ מִשִּׁבְעָ֖ה בָּנִֽים: וַתִּקַּ֨ח נָֽעֳמִ֤י אֶת־הַיֶּ֨לֶד֙ וַתְּשִׁתֵ֣הוּ
בְחֵיקָ֔הּ וַתְּהִי־ל֖וֹ לְאֹמֶֽנֶת: וַתִּקְרֶ֩אנָה֩ ל֨וֹ הַשְּׁכֵנ֥וֹת שֵׁם֙ לֵאמֹ֔ר יֻלַּד־
בֵּ֖ן לְנָֽעֳמִ֑י וַתִּקְרֶ֤אנָֽה שְׁמוֹ֙ עוֹבֵ֔ד ה֥וּא אֲבִי־יִשַׁ֖י אֲבִ֥י דָוִֽד:
וְאֵ֨לֶּה֙ תּֽוֹלְד֣וֹת פָּ֔רֶץ פֶּ֖רֶץ הוֹלִ֥יד אֶת־חֶצְרֽוֹן: וְחֶצְרוֹן֙ הוֹלִ֣יד אֶת־
רָ֔ם וְרָ֖ם הוֹלִ֥יד אֶת־עַמִּֽינָדָֽב: וְעַמִּינָדָב֙ הוֹלִ֣יד אֶת־נַחְשׁ֔וֹן וְנַחְשׁ֖וֹן
הוֹלִ֥יד אֶת־שַׂלְמָֽה: וְשַׂלְמוֹן֙ הוֹלִ֣יד אֶת־בֹּ֔עַז וּבֹ֖עַז הוֹלִ֥יד אֶת־עוֹבֵֽד:
וְעֹבֵד֙ הוֹלִ֣יד אֶת־יִשַׁ֔י וְיִשַׁ֖י הוֹלִ֥יד אֶת־דָּוִֽד:

___

levirate marriage. The woman would then remove the man's shoe as part of a stigmatizing ceremony designed to express disapproval (Deut. 25:9).

כְּרָחֵל וּכְלֵאָה **Like Rachel and like Leah.** Probably a conventional wedding blessing. Possibly also a hint that it would be David who would unite the tribes, descendants of Leah, Rachel and their handmaids, into a single nation.

כְּבֵית פֶּרֶץ **As the house of Peretz.** See Introduction, page lviii.

וַתֹּאמַרְנָה הַנָּשִׁים אֶל־נָעֳמִי **And the women said to Naomi.** A scene parallel to that of the first chapter, between the women of the town and Naomi, for whom misfortune has been transformed to blessing, grief to joy and bereavement to new life. The neighbors say, "A son is born for Naomi" because the grandson has, as it were, taken the place of her lost son. The missing link in the chain of the generations has been restored. The transformation has been the result of ḥesed: love, kindness, loyalty, and a willingness to ensure that the most marginal in society are not left without those who will love and "redeem" them. Ultimately the book is about the redemptive power of love.

MOURNER'S KADDISH

The following prayer, said by mourners, requires the presence of a minyan.
A transliteration can be found on page 779.

Mourner: יִתְגַּדַּל Magnified and sanctified
may His great name be,
in the world He created by His will.
May He establish His kingdom
in your lifetime and in your days,
and in the lifetime of all the house of Israel,
swiftly and soon –
and say: Amen.

All: May His great name be blessed
for ever and all time.

Mourner: Blessed and praised, glorified and exalted,
raised and honored,
uplifted and lauded
be the name of the Holy One,
blessed be He,
beyond any blessing,
song, praise and consolation
uttered in the world –
and say: Amen.

May there be great peace from heaven,
and life for us and all Israel –
and say: Amen.

Bow, take three steps back, as if taking leave of the Divine Presence,
then bow, first left, then right, then center, while saying:

May He who makes peace in His high places,
make peace for us and all Israel –
and say: Amen.

In Israel continue with Removing the Torah on page 378.

קדיש יתום

The following prayer, said by mourners, requires the presence of a מנין.
A transliteration can be found on page 779.

אבל: יִתְגַּדַּל וְיִתְקַדַּשׁ שְׁמֵהּ רַבָּא (קהל: אָמֵן)

בְּעָלְמָא דִּי בְרָא כִרְעוּתֵהּ

וְיַמְלִיךְ מַלְכוּתֵהּ

בְּחַיֵּיכוֹן וּבְיוֹמֵיכוֹן וּבְחַיֵּי דְּכָל בֵּית יִשְׂרָאֵל

בַּעֲגָלָא וּבִזְמַן קָרִיב

וְאִמְרוּ אָמֵן. (קהל: אָמֵן)

קהל ואבל: יְהֵא שְׁמֵהּ רַבָּא מְבָרַךְ לְעָלַם וּלְעָלְמֵי עָלְמַיָּא.

אבל: יִתְבָּרַךְ וְיִשְׁתַּבַּח וְיִתְפָּאַר

וְיִתְרוֹמַם וְיִתְנַשֵּׂא וְיִתְהַדָּר וְיִתְעַלֶּה וְיִתְהַלָּל

שְׁמֵהּ דְּקֻדְשָׁא בְּרִיךְ הוּא (קהל: בְּרִיךְ הוּא)

לְעֵלָּא מִן כָּל בִּרְכָתָא וְשִׁירָתָא, תֻּשְׁבְּחָתָא וְנֶחֱמָתָא

דַּאֲמִירָן בְּעָלְמָא

וְאִמְרוּ אָמֵן. (קהל: אָמֵן)

יְהֵא שְׁלָמָא רַבָּא מִן שְׁמַיָּא

וְחַיִּים, עָלֵינוּ וְעַל כָּל יִשְׂרָאֵל

וְאִמְרוּ אָמֵן. (קהל: אָמֵן)

Bow, take three steps back, as if taking leave of the Divine Presence,
then bow, first left, then right, then center, while saying:

עֹשֶׂה שָׁלוֹם בִּמְרוֹמָיו

הוּא יַעֲשֶׂה שָׁלוֹם עָלֵינוּ וְעַל כָּל יִשְׂרָאֵל

וְאִמְרוּ אָמֵן. (קהל: אָמֵן)

In ארץ ישראל *continue with* הוצאת ספר תורה *on page 379.*

REMOVING THE TORAH FROM THE ARK

אֵין־כָּמֽוֹךָ There is none like You among the heavenly powers,   *Ps. 86*
LORD, and there are no works like Yours.
Your kingdom is an eternal kingdom,   *Ps. 145*
and Your dominion is for all generations.

The LORD is King, the LORD was King,
the LORD shall be King for ever and all time.
The LORD will give strength to His people;   *Ps. 29*
the LORD will bless His people with peace.

Father of compassion,
favor Zion with Your goodness; rebuild the walls of Jerusalem.   *Ps. 51*
For we trust in You alone, King, God, high and exalted, Master of worlds.

The Ark is opened and the congregation stands. All say:
וַיְהִי בִּנְסֹעַ Whenever the Ark set out, Moses would say,   *Num. 10*
"Arise, LORD, and may Your enemies be scattered.
May those who hate You flee before You."
For the Torah shall come forth from Zion,   *Is. 2*
and the word of the LORD from Jerusalem.
Blessed is He who in His Holiness gave the Torah to His people Israel.

On Shabbat, continue with "Blessed is the name" on the next page.

The following (The Thirteen Attributes of Mercy) is said three times:
יהוה The LORD, the LORD, compassionate and gracious God,   *Ex. 34*
slow to anger, abounding in loving-kindness and truth,
extending loving-kindness to a thousand generations,
forgiving iniquity, rebellion and sin,
and absolving [the guilty who repent].

Each individual says silently, inserting appropriate phrase/s in parentheses:
רִבּוֹנוֹ Master of the Universe, fulfill my heart's requests for good. Satisfy my desire,
grant my request, and enable me (*name*, son/daughter of *father's name*), (and my
wife/ husband, and my sons/daughters) and all the members of my household
to do Your will with a perfect heart. Deliver us from the evil impulse, grant us our
share in Your Torah, and make us worthy that Your Presence may rest upon us.
Confer on us a spirit of wisdom and understanding, and may there be fulfilled
in us the verse: "The spirit of the LORD will rest upon him – a spirit of wisdom   *Is. 11*
and understanding, a spirit of counsel and strength, a spirit of knowledge and

הוצאת ספר תורה

תהלים פו

אֵין־כָּמְוֹךָ בָאֱלֹהִים, אֲדֹנָי, וְאֵין כְּמַעֲשֶׂיךָ:

תהלים קמה

מַלְכוּתְךָ מַלְכוּת כָּל־עֹלָמִים, וּמֶמְשַׁלְתְּךָ בְּכָל־דּוֹר וָדֹר:

יהוה מֶלֶךְ, יהוה מָלָךְ, יהוה יִמְלֹךְ לְעֹלָם וָעֶד.

תהלים כט

יהוה עֹז לְעַמּוֹ יִתֵּן, יהוה יְבָרֵךְ אֶת־עַמּוֹ בַשָּׁלוֹם:

תהלים נא

אַב הָרַחֲמִים, הֵיטִיבָה בִרְצוֹנְךָ אֶת־צִיּוֹן תִּבְנֶה חוֹמוֹת יְרוּשָׁלָֽיִם:

כִּי בְךָ לְבַד בָּטָחְנוּ, מֶלֶךְ אֵל רָם וְנִשָּׂא, אֲדוֹן עוֹלָמִים.

The ארון קודש *is opened and the* קהל *stands. All say:*

במדבר י

וַיְהִי בִּנְסֹעַ הָאָרֹן וַיֹּאמֶר מֹשֶׁה

קוּמָה יהוה וְיָפֻצוּ אֹיְבֶֽיךָ וְיָנֻסוּ מְשַׂנְאֶֽיךָ מִפָּנֶֽיךָ:

ישעיה ב

כִּי מִצִּיּוֹן תֵּצֵא תוֹרָה וּדְבַר־יהוה מִירוּשָׁלָֽיִם:

בָּרוּךְ שֶׁנָּתַן תּוֹרָה לְעַמּוֹ יִשְׂרָאֵל בִּקְדֻשָּׁתוֹ.

On שבת, *continue with* בְּרִיךְ שְׁמֵהּ *on the next page.*

The following (י"ג מידות הרחמים) *is said three times:*

שמות לד

יהוה, יהוה, אֵל רַחוּם וְחַנּוּן, אֶֽרֶךְ אַפַּֽיִם וְרַב־חֶֽסֶד וֶאֱמֶת:

נֹצֵר חֶֽסֶד לָאֲלָפִים, נֹשֵׂא עָוֹן וָפֶֽשַׁע וְחַטָּאָה, וְנַקֵּה:

Each individual says silently, inserting appropriate phrase/s in parentheses:

רִבּוֹנוֹ שֶׁל עוֹלָם, מַלֵּא מִשְׁאֲלוֹת לִבִּי לְטוֹבָה, וְהָפֵק רְצוֹנִי וְתֵן שְׁאֵלָתִי, וְזַכֵּה לִי (פלוני/ת בֶּן/בַּת פלוני) (וְאִשְׁתִּי/בַּעֲלִי וּבָנַי וּבְנוֹתַי) וְכָל בְּנֵי בֵיתִי, לַעֲשׂוֹת רְצוֹנְךָ בְּלֵבָב שָׁלֵם, וּמַלְּטֵֽנוּ מִיֵּֽצֶר הָרָע, וְתֵן חֶלְקֵֽנוּ בְּתוֹרָתֶֽךָ, וְזַכֵּֽנוּ שֶׁתִּשְׁרֶה שְׁכִינָתְךָ עָלֵֽינוּ, וְהוֹפַע עָלֵֽינוּ רֽוּחַ חָכְמָה וּבִינָה. וִיְקֻיַּם בָּֽנוּ מִקְרָא שֶׁכָּתוּב:

ישעיה יא

וְנָחָה עָלָיו רֽוּחַ יהוה, רֽוּחַ חָכְמָה וּבִינָה, רֽוּחַ עֵצָה וּגְבוּרָה, רֽוּחַ דַּֽעַת וְיִרְאַת יהוה: וּבְכֵן יְהִי רָצוֹן מִלְּפָנֶֽיךָ יהוה אֱלֹהֵֽינוּ וֵאלֹהֵי אֲבוֹתֵֽינוּ, שֶׁתְּזַכֵּֽנוּ לַעֲשׂוֹת

For commentary on the Reading of the Torah, see page 379.

reverence for the LORD." So too may it be Your will, LORD our God and God of our ancestors, that we be worthy to do deeds that are good in Your sight, and to walk before You in the ways of the upright. Make us holy through Your holiness, so that we may be worthy of a good and long life, and of the World to Come. Guard us from evil deeds and bad times that threaten to bring turmoil to the world. May loving-kindness surround one who trusts in the LORD. Amen. *Ps. 32*

יִהְיוּ May the words of my mouth and the meditation of my *Ps. 19* heart find favor before You, LORD, my Rock and Redeemer.

Say the following verse three times:

וַאֲנִי As for me, may my prayer come to You, LORD, *Ps. 69* at a time of favor. O God, in Your great love, answer me with Your faithful salvation.

On all days continue:

בְּרִיךְ Blessed is the name of the Master of the Universe. Blessed is Your crown *Zohar,* and Your place. May Your favor always be with Your people Israel. Show Your *Vayak'hel* people the salvation of Your right hand in Your Temple. Grant us the gift of Your good light, and accept our prayers in mercy. May it be Your will to prolong our life in goodness. May I be counted among the righteous, so that You will have compassion on me and protect me and all that is mine and all that is Your people Israel's. You feed all; You sustain all; You rule over all; You rule over kings, for sovereignty is Yours. I am a servant of the Holy One, blessed be He, before whom and before whose glorious Torah I bow at all times. Not in man do I trust, nor on any angel do I rely, but on the God of heaven who is the God of truth, whose Torah is truth, whose prophets speak truth, and who abounds in acts of love and truth. ‣ In Him I trust, and to His holy and glorious name I offer praises. May it be Your will to open my heart to the Torah, and to fulfill the wishes of my heart and of the hearts of all Your people Israel for good, for life, and for peace.

Two Torah scrolls are removed from the Ark. The Leader takes one in his right arm and, followed by the congregation, says:

Listen, Israel: the LORD is our God, the LORD is One. *Deut. 6*

Leader then congregation:

One is our God; great is our Master; holy is His name.

The Leader turns to face the Ark, bows and says:

Magnify the LORD with me, and let us exalt His name together. *Ps. 34*

מַעֲשִׂים טוֹבִים בְּעֵינֶיךָ וְלָלֶכֶת בְּדַרְכֵי יְשָׁרִים לְפָנֶיךָ, וְקַדְּשֵׁנוּ בִּקְדֻשָּׁתֶךָ
כְּדֵי שֶׁנִּזְכֶּה לְחַיִּים טוֹבִים וַאֲרוּכִים וּלְחַיֵּי הָעוֹלָם הַבָּא, וְתִשְׁמְרֵנוּ מִמַּעֲשִׂים
רָעִים וּמִשָּׁעוֹת רָעוֹת הַמִּתְרַגְּשׁוֹת לָבוֹא לָעוֹלָם, וְהַבּוֹטֵחַ בַּיהוה חֶסֶד

תהלים לב
יְסוֹבְבֶנּוּ: אָמֵן.

תהלים יט
יִהְיוּ לְרָצוֹן אִמְרֵי־פִי וְהֶגְיוֹן לִבִּי לְפָנֶיךָ, יהוה צוּרִי וְגֹאֲלִי:

Say the following verse three times:

תהלים סט
וַאֲנִי תְפִלָּתִי־לְךָ יהוה, עֵת רָצוֹן, אֱלֹהִים בְּרָב־חַסְדֶּךָ
עֲנֵנִי בֶּאֱמֶת יִשְׁעֶךָ:

On all days continue:

זוהר ויקהל
בְּרִיךְ שְׁמֵהּ דְּמָרֵא עָלְמָא, בְּרִיךְ כִּתְרָךְ וְאַתְרָךְ. יְהֵא רְעוּתָךְ עִם עַמָּךְ יִשְׂרָאֵל
לְעָלַם, וּפֻרְקָן יְמִינָךְ אַחֲזֵי לְעַמָּךְ בְּבֵית מַקְדְּשָׁךְ, וּלְאַמְטוֹיֵי לָנָא מִטּוּב נְהוֹרָךְ,
וּלְקַבֵּל צְלוֹתָנָא בְּרַחֲמִין. יְהֵא רַעֲוָא קֳדָמָךְ דְּתוֹרִיךְ לָן חַיִּין בְּטִיבוּ, וְלֶהֱוֵי
אֲנָא פְּקִידָא בְּגוֹ צַדִּיקַיָּא, לְמִרְחַם עֲלַי וּלְמִנְטַר יָתִי וְיָת כָּל דִּי לִי וְדִי לְעַמָּךְ
יִשְׂרָאֵל. אַנְתְּ הוּא זָן לְכֹלָּא וּמְפַרְנֵס לְכֹלָּא, אַנְתְּ הוּא שַׁלִּיט עַל כֹּלָּא, אַנְתְּ
הוּא דְּשַׁלִּיט עַל מַלְכַיָּא, וּמַלְכוּתָא דִּילָךְ הִיא. אֲנָא עַבְדָּא דְּקֻדְשָׁא בְּרִיךְ
הוּא, דְּסָגֵדְנָא קַמֵּהּ וּמִקַּמֵּי דִּיקַר אוֹרַיְתֵהּ בְּכָל עִדָּן וְעִדָּן. לָא עַל אֱנָשׁ רְחִיצְנָא
וְלָא עַל בַּר אֱלָהִין סְמִיכְנָא, אֶלָּא בֶּאֱלָהָא דִשְׁמַיָּא, דְּהוּא אֱלָהָא קְשׁוֹט,
וְאוֹרַיְתֵהּ קְשׁוֹט, וּנְבִיאוֹהִי קְשׁוֹט, וּמַסְגֵּא לְמֶעְבַּד טָבְוָן וּקְשׁוֹט. ◂ בֵּהּ אֲנָא
רְחִיץ, וְלִשְׁמֵהּ קַדִּישָׁא יַקִּירָא אֲנָא אֵמַר תֻּשְׁבְּחָן. יְהֵא רַעֲוָא קֳדָמָךְ דְּתִפְתַּח
לִבַּאי בְּאוֹרַיְתָא, וְתַשְׁלִים מִשְׁאֲלִין דְּלִבַּאי וְלִבָּא דְכָל עַמָּךְ יִשְׂרָאֵל לְטַב
וּלְחַיִּין וְלִשְׁלָם.

Two ספרי תורה *are removed from the* ארון הקודש. The שליח צבור *takes*
one in his right arm, and, followed by the קהל, *says:*

דברים ו
שְׁמַע יִשְׂרָאֵל, יהוה אֱלֹהֵינוּ, יהוה אֶחָד:

קהל *then* שליח ציבור:
אֶחָד אֱלֹהֵינוּ, גָּדוֹל אֲדוֹנֵינוּ, קָדוֹשׁ שְׁמוֹ.

The שליח ציבור *turns to face the* ארון קודש, *bows and says:*

תהלים לד
גַּדְּלוּ לַיהוה אִתִּי וּנְרוֹמְמָה שְׁמוֹ יַחְדָּו:

The Ark is closed. The Leader carries the Torah scroll to the bima and the congregation says:

לְךָ Yours, LORD, are the greatness and the power, the glory and the   *1 Chr. 29* majesty and splendor, for everything in heaven and earth is Yours. Yours, LORD, is the kingdom; You are exalted as Head over all.

רוֹמְמוּ Exalt the LORD our God and bow to His footstool; He is holy.   *Ps. 99* Exalt the LORD our God, and bow at His holy mountain, for holy is the LORD our God.

Over all may the name of the Supreme King of kings, the Holy One blessed be He, be magnified and sanctified, praised and glorified, exalted and extolled, in the worlds that He has created – this world and the World to Come – in accordance with His will, and the will of those who fear Him, and the will of the whole house of Israel. He is the Rock of worlds, LORD of all creatures, God of all souls, who dwells in the spacious heights and inhabits the high heavens of old. His holiness is over the Ḥayyot and over the throne of glory. Therefore may Your name, LORD our God, be sanctified among us in the sight of all that lives. Let us sing before Him a new song, as it is written: "Sing to God, make music for His name, extol Him who   *Ps. 68* rides the clouds – the LORD is His name – and exult before Him." And may we see Him eye to eye when He returns to His abode as it is written: "For they shall   *Is. 52* see eye to eye when the LORD returns to Zion." And it is said: "Then will the glory   *Is. 40* of the LORD be revealed, and all mankind together shall see that the mouth of the LORD has spoken."

Father of mercy, have compassion on the people borne by Him. May He remember the covenant with the mighty (patriarchs), and deliver us from evil times. May He reproach the evil instinct in the people by Him, and graciously grant that we be an eternal remnant. May He fulfill in good measure our requests for salvation and compassion.

The Torah scroll is placed on the bima and the Gabbai calls a Kohen to the Torah.

וְיַעֲזוֹר May He help, shield and save all who seek refuge in Him, and let us say: Amen. Let us all render greatness to our God and give honor to the Torah. *Let the Kohen come forward. Arise (*name son of father's name*), the Kohen.

If no Kohen is present, a Levi or Yisrael is called up as follows:

/As there is no Kohen, arise (*name son of father's name*) in place of a Kohen./

Blessed is He who, in His holiness, gave the Torah to His people Israel.

The congregation followed by the Gabbai:

You who cling to the LORD your God are all alive today.   *Deut. 4*

The קהל ארון קודש is closed. The שליח ציבור carries the ספר תורה to the בימה and the קהל says:

דברי
הימים א'
כט

לְךָ יהוה הַגְּדֻלָּה וְהַגְּבוּרָה וְהַתִּפְאֶרֶת וְהַנֵּצַח וְהַהוֹד, כִּי־כֹל
בַּשָּׁמַיִם וּבָאָרֶץ, לְךָ יהוה הַמַּמְלָכָה וְהַמִּתְנַשֵּׂא לְכֹל לְרֹאשׁ:

תהלים צט

רוֹמְמוּ יהוה אֱלֹהֵינוּ וְהִשְׁתַּחֲווּ לַהֲדֹם רַגְלָיו, קָדוֹשׁ הוּא: רוֹמְמוּ
יהוה אֱלֹהֵינוּ וְהִשְׁתַּחֲווּ לְהַר קָדְשׁוֹ, כִּי־קָדוֹשׁ יהוה אֱלֹהֵינוּ:

עַל הַכֹּל יִתְגַּדַּל וְיִתְקַדַּשׁ וְיִשְׁתַּבַּח וְיִתְפָּאַר וְיִתְרוֹמַם וְיִתְנַשֵּׂא שְׁמוֹ שֶׁל מֶלֶךְ
מַלְכֵי הַמְּלָכִים הַקָּדוֹשׁ בָּרוּךְ הוּא בָּעוֹלָמוֹת שֶׁבָּרָא, הָעוֹלָם הַזֶּה וְהָעוֹלָם
הַבָּא, כִּרְצוֹנוֹ וְכִרְצוֹן יְרֵאָיו וְכִרְצוֹן כָּל בֵּית יִשְׂרָאֵל. צוּר הָעוֹלָמִים, אֲדוֹן כָּל
הַבְּרִיּוֹת, אֱלוֹהַּ כָּל הַנְּפָשׁוֹת, הַיּוֹשֵׁב בְּמֶרְחֲבֵי מָרוֹם, הַשּׁוֹכֵן בִּשְׁמֵי שְׁמֵי קֶדֶם,
קְדֻשָּׁתוֹ עַל הַחַיּוֹת, וּקְדֻשָּׁתוֹ עַל כִּסֵּא הַכָּבוֹד. וּבְכֵן יִתְקַדַּשׁ שִׁמְךָ בָּנוּ יהוה

תהלים סח

אֱלֹהֵינוּ לְעֵינֵי כָּל חָי, וְנֹאמַר לְפָנָיו שִׁיר חָדָשׁ, כַּכָּתוּב: שִׁירוּ לֵאלֹהִים זַמְּרוּ
שְׁמוֹ, סֹלּוּ לָרֹכֵב בָּעֲרָבוֹת, בְּיָהּ שְׁמוֹ, וְעִלְזוּ לְפָנָיו: וְנֵרָאֵהוּ עַיִן בְּעַיִן בְּשׁוּבוֹ

ישעיה נב
ישעיה מ

אֶל נָוֵהוּ, כַּכָּתוּב: כִּי עַיִן בְּעַיִן יִרְאוּ בְּשׁוּב יהוה צִיּוֹן: וְנֶאֱמַר: וְנִגְלָה כְּבוֹד
יהוה, וְרָאוּ כָל־בָּשָׂר יַחְדָּו כִּי פִּי יהוה דִּבֵּר:

אַב הָרַחֲמִים הוּא יְרַחֵם עַם עֲמוּסִים, וְיִזְכֹּר בְּרִית אֵיתָנִים, וְיַצִּיל נַפְשׁוֹתֵינוּ
מִן הַשָּׁעוֹת הָרָעוֹת, וְיִגְעַר בְּיֵצֶר הָרָע מִן הַנְּשׂוּאִים, וְיָחָן אוֹתָנוּ לִפְלֵיטַת
עוֹלָמִים, וִימַלֵּא מִשְׁאֲלוֹתֵינוּ בְּמִדָּה טוֹבָה יְשׁוּעָה וְרַחֲמִים.

The ספר תורה is placed on the שולחן and the גבאי calls a כהן to the תורה.

וְיַעֲזֹר וְיָגֵן וְיוֹשִׁיעַ לְכָל הַחוֹסִים בּוֹ, וְנֹאמַר אָמֵן. הַכֹּל הָבוּ גֹדֶל לֵאלֹהֵינוּ
וּתְנוּ כָבוֹד לַתּוֹרָה. *כֹּהֵן קְרָב, יַעֲמֹד (פלוני בֶּן פלוני) הַכֹּהֵן.

*If no כהן is present, a לוי or ישראל is called up as follows:

/אֵין כָּאן כֹּהֵן, יַעֲמֹד (פלוני בֶּן פלוני) בִּמְקוֹם כֹּהֵן./

בָּרוּךְ שֶׁנָּתַן תּוֹרָה לְעַמּוֹ יִשְׂרָאֵל בִּקְדֻשָּׁתוֹ.

The קהל followed by the גבאי:

דברים ד

וְאַתֶּם הַדְּבֵקִים בַּיהוה אֱלֹהֵיכֶם חַיִּים כֻּלְּכֶם הַיּוֹם:

The Reader shows the oleh the section to be read.
The oleh touches the scroll at that place with the tzitzit of his tallit,
which he then kisses. Holding the handles of the scroll, he says:

Oleh: Bless the LORD, the blessed One.

Cong: Bless the LORD, the blessed One,
for ever and all time.

Oleh: Bless the LORD, the blessed One,
for ever and all time.
Blessed are You, LORD our God,
King of the Universe,
who has chosen us from all peoples
and has given us His Torah.
Blessed are You, LORD,
Giver of the Torah.

After the reading, the oleh says:

Oleh: Blessed are You, LORD our God,
King of the Universe,
who has given us the Torah of truth,
planting everlasting life in our midst.
Blessed are You, LORD,
Giver of the Torah.

One who has survived a situation of danger, says:
Blessed are You, LORD our God, King of the Universe,
who bestows good on the unworthy,
who has bestowed on me much good.

The congregation responds:
Amen. May He who bestowed much good on you
continue to bestow on you much good, Selah.

After a Bar Mitzva boy has finished the Torah blessing, his father says aloud:
Blessed is He who has released me from the responsibility
for this child.

The קורא *shows the* עולה *the section to be read.*
The עולה *touches the scroll at that place with the* ציצית *of his* טלית,
which he then kisses. Holding the handles of the scroll, he says:

עולה: בָּרְכוּ אֶת יהוה הַמְבֹרָךְ.

קהל: בָּרוּךְ יהוה הַמְבֹרָךְ לְעוֹלָם וָעֶד.

עולה: בָּרוּךְ יהוה הַמְבֹרָךְ לְעוֹלָם וָעֶד.

בָּרוּךְ אַתָּה יהוה, אֱלֹהֵינוּ מֶלֶךְ הָעוֹלָם
אֲשֶׁר בָּחַר בָּנוּ מִכָּל הָעַמִּים
וְנָתַן לָנוּ אֶת תּוֹרָתוֹ.
בָּרוּךְ אַתָּה יהוה, נוֹתֵן הַתּוֹרָה.

After the קריאת התורה, *the* עולה *says:*

עולה: בָּרוּךְ אַתָּה יהוה אֱלֹהֵינוּ מֶלֶךְ הָעוֹלָם
אֲשֶׁר נָתַן לָנוּ תּוֹרַת אֱמֶת
וְחַיֵּי עוֹלָם נָטַע בְּתוֹכֵנוּ.
בָּרוּךְ אַתָּה יהוה, נוֹתֵן הַתּוֹרָה.

One who has survived a situation of danger, says:

בָּרוּךְ אַתָּה יהוה אֱלֹהֵינוּ מֶלֶךְ הָעוֹלָם
הַגּוֹמֵל לְחַיָּבִים טוֹבוֹת, שֶׁגְּמָלַנִי כָּל טוֹב.

The קהל *responds:*

אָמֵן. מִי שֶׁגְּמָלְךָ כָּל טוֹב
הוּא יִגְמָלְךָ כָּל טוֹב, סֶלָה.

After a בר מצווה *has finished the* תורה *blessing, his father says aloud:*

בָּרוּךְ שֶׁפְּטָרַנִי מֵעָנְשׁוֹ שֶׁלָּזֶה.

FOR AN OLEH

May He who blessed our fathers, Abraham, Isaac and Jacob, bless (*name, son of father's name*) who has been called up in honor of the All-Present, in honor of the Torah, and in honor of (*On Shabbat:* the Sabbath and in honor of) the festival. As a reward for this, may the Holy One, blessed be He, protect and deliver him from all trouble and distress, all infection and illness, and send blessing and success to all the work of his hands, and may he merit to go up to Jerusalem for the festivals, together with all Israel, his brethren, and let us say: Amen.

FOR A SICK MAN

May He who blessed our fathers, Abraham, Isaac and Jacob, Moses and Aaron, David and Solomon, bless and heal one who is ill, (*sick person's name, son of mother's name*), on whose behalf (*name of the one making the offering*) is making a contribution to charity. As a reward for this, may the Holy One, blessed be He, be filled with compassion for him, to restore his health, cure him, strengthen and revive him, sending him a swift and full recovery from heaven to all his 248 organs and 365 sinews, amongst the other sick ones in Israel, a healing of the spirit and a healing of the body – though on (*On Shabbat:* the Sabbath and) festivals it is forbidden to cry out, may healing be quick to come – now, swiftly and soon, and let us say: Amen.

FOR A SICK WOMAN

May He who blessed our fathers, Abraham, Isaac and Jacob, Moses and Aaron, David and Solomon, bless and heal one who is ill, (*sick person's name, daughter of mother's name*), on whose behalf (*name of the one making the offering*) is making a contribution to charity. As a reward for this, may the Holy One, blessed be He, be filled with compassion for her, to restore her health, cure her, strengthen and revive her, sending her a swift and full recovery from heaven to all her organs and sinews, amongst the other sick ones in Israel, a healing of the spirit and a healing of the body – though on (*On Shabbat:* the Sabbath and) festivals it is forbidden to cry out, may healing be quick to come – now, swiftly and soon, and let us say: Amen.

מי שבירך לעולה לתורה

מִי שֶׁבֵּרַךְ אֲבוֹתֵינוּ אַבְרָהָם יִצְחָק וְיַעֲקֹב, הוּא יְבָרֵךְ אֶת (פלוני בֶּן פלוני),
בַּעֲבוּר שֶׁעָלָה לִכְבוֹד הַמָּקוֹם וְלִכְבוֹד הַתּוֹרָה (בשבת: וְלִכְבוֹד הַשַּׁבָּת)
וְלִכְבוֹד הָרֶגֶל. בִּשְׂכַר זֶה הַקָּדוֹשׁ בָּרוּךְ הוּא יִשְׁמְרֵהוּ וְיַצִּילֵהוּ מִכָּל
צָרָה וְצוּקָה וּמִכָּל נֶגַע וּמַחֲלָה, וְיִשְׁלַח בְּרָכָה וְהַצְלָחָה בְּכָל מַעֲשֵׂה
יָדָיו, וְיִזְכֶּה לַעֲלוֹת לָרֶגֶל עִם כָּל יִשְׂרָאֵל אֶחָיו, וְנֹאמַר אָמֵן.

מי שבירך לחולה

מִי שֶׁבֵּרַךְ אֲבוֹתֵינוּ אַבְרָהָם יִצְחָק וְיַעֲקֹב, מֹשֶׁה וְאַהֲרֹן דָּוִד וּשְׁלֹמֹה
הוּא יְבָרֵךְ וִירַפֵּא אֶת הַחוֹלֶה (פלוני בֶּן פלונית) בַּעֲבוּר שֶׁ(פלוני בֶּן פלוני) נוֹדֵר
צְדָקָה בַּעֲבוּרוֹ. בִּשְׂכַר זֶה הַקָּדוֹשׁ בָּרוּךְ הוּא יִמָּלֵא רַחֲמִים עָלָיו
לְהַחֲלִימוֹ וּלְרַפֹּאתוֹ וּלְהַחֲזִיקוֹ וּלְהַחֲיוֹתוֹ וְיִשְׁלַח לוֹ מְהֵרָה רְפוּאָה
שְׁלֵמָה מִן הַשָּׁמַיִם לִרְמַ"ח אֵבָרָיו וּשְׁסַ"ה גִידָיו בְּתוֹךְ שְׁאָר חוֹלֵי יִשְׂרָאֵל,
רְפוּאַת הַנֶּפֶשׁ וּרְפוּאַת הַגּוּף. יוֹם טוֹב הוּא /בשבת: שַׁבָּת וְיוֹם טוֹב הֵם/
מִלִּזְעֹק וּרְפוּאָה קְרוֹבָה לָבוֹא, הַשְׁתָּא בַּעֲגָלָא וּבִזְמַן קָרִיב, וְנֹאמַר
אָמֵן.

מי שבירך לחולה

מִי שֶׁבֵּרַךְ אֲבוֹתֵינוּ אַבְרָהָם יִצְחָק וְיַעֲקֹב, מֹשֶׁה וְאַהֲרֹן דָּוִד וּשְׁלֹמֹה
הוּא יְבָרֵךְ וִירַפֵּא אֶת הַחוֹלָה (פלונית בַּת פלונית) בַּעֲבוּר שֶׁ(פלוני בֶּן פלוני)
נוֹדֵר צְדָקָה בַּעֲבוּרָהּ. בִּשְׂכַר זֶה הַקָּדוֹשׁ בָּרוּךְ הוּא יִמָּלֵא רַחֲמִים
עָלֶיהָ לְהַחֲלִימָהּ וּלְרַפֹּאתָהּ וּלְהַחֲזִיקָהּ וּלְהַחֲיוֹתָהּ וְיִשְׁלַח לָהּ מְהֵרָה
רְפוּאָה שְׁלֵמָה מִן הַשָּׁמַיִם לְכָל אֵבָרֶיהָ וּלְכָל גִּידֶיהָ בְּתוֹךְ שְׁאָר חוֹלֵי
יִשְׂרָאֵל, רְפוּאַת הַנֶּפֶשׁ וּרְפוּאַת הַגּוּף. יוֹם טוֹב הוּא /בשבת: שַׁבָּת וְיוֹם
טוֹב הֵם/ מִלִּזְעֹק וּרְפוּאָה קְרוֹבָה לָבוֹא, הַשְׁתָּא בַּעֲגָלָא וּבִזְמַן קָרִיב,
וְנֹאמַר אָמֵן.

ON THE BIRTH OF A SON

May He who blessed our fathers, Abraham, Isaac and Jacob, Moses and Aaron, David and Solomon, Sarah, Rebecca, Rachel and Leah, bless the woman (*name*, daughter of *father's name*) who has given birth, and her son who has been born to her as an auspicious sign. Her husband, the child's father, is making a contribution to charity. As a reward for this, may father and mother merit to bring the child into the covenant of Abraham and to a life of Torah, to the marriage canopy and to good deeds, and let us say: Amen.

ON THE BIRTH OF A DAUGHTER

May He who blessed our fathers, Abraham, Isaac and Jacob, Moses and Aaron, David and Solomon, Sarah, Rebecca, Rachel and Leah, bless the woman (*name*, daughter of *father's name*) who has given birth, and her daughter who has been born to her as an auspicious sign; and may her name be called in Israel (*baby's name*, daughter of *father's name*). Her husband, the child's father, is making a contribution to charity. As a reward for this, may father and mother merit to raise her to a life of Torah, to the marriage canopy, and to good deeds, and let us say: Amen.

FOR A BAR MITZVA

May He who blessed our fathers, Abraham, Isaac and Jacob, bless (*name*, son of *father's name*) who has completed thirteen years and attained the age of the commandments, who has been called to the Torah to give praise and thanks to God, may His name be blessed, for all the good He has bestowed on him. May the Holy One, blessed be He, protect and sustain him and direct his heart to be perfect with God, to walk in His ways and keep the commandments all the days of his life, and let us say: Amen.

FOR A BAT MITZVA

May He who blessed our fathers, Abraham, Isaac and Jacob, Sarah, Rebecca, Rachel and Leah, bless (*name*, daughter of *father's name*) who has completed twelve years and attained the age of the commandments, and gives praise and thanks to God, may His name be blessed, for all the good He has bestowed on her. May the Holy One, blessed be He, protect and sustain her and direct her heart to be perfect with God, to walk in His ways and keep the commandments all the days of her life, and let us say: Amen.

מי שברך ליולדת בן

מִי שֶׁבֵּרַךְ אֲבוֹתֵינוּ אַבְרָהָם יִצְחָק וְיַעֲקֹב, מֹשֶׁה וְאַהֲרֹן דָּוִד וּשְׁלֹמֹה, שָׂרָה רִבְקָה רָחֵל וְלֵאָה הוּא יְבָרֵךְ אֶת הָאִשָּׁה הַיּוֹלֶדֶת (פלונית בת פלוני) וְאֶת בְּנָהּ שֶׁנּוֹלַד לָהּ לְמַזָּל טוֹב בַּעֲבוּר שֶׁבַּעְלָהּ וְאָבִיו נוֹדֵר צְדָקָה בַּעֲדָם. בִּשְׂכַר זֶה יִזְכּוּ אָבִיו וְאִמּוֹ לְהַכְנִיסוֹ בִּבְרִיתוֹ שֶׁל אַבְרָהָם אָבִינוּ וּלְגַדְּלוֹ לְתוֹרָה וּלְחֻפָּה וּלְמַעֲשִׂים טוֹבִים, וְנֹאמַר אָמֵן.

מי שברך ליולדת בת

מִי שֶׁבֵּרַךְ אֲבוֹתֵינוּ אַבְרָהָם יִצְחָק וְיַעֲקֹב, מֹשֶׁה וְאַהֲרֹן דָּוִד וּשְׁלֹמֹה, שָׂרָה רִבְקָה רָחֵל וְלֵאָה הוּא יְבָרֵךְ אֶת הָאִשָּׁה הַיּוֹלֶדֶת (פלונית בת פלוני) וְאֶת בִּתָּהּ שֶׁנּוֹלְדָה לָהּ לְמַזָּל טוֹב וְיִקָּרֵא שְׁמָהּ בְּיִשְׂרָאֵל (פלונית בת פלוני), בַּעֲבוּר שֶׁבַּעְלָהּ וְאָבִיהָ נוֹדֵר צְדָקָה בַּעֲדָן. בִּשְׂכַר זֶה יִזְכּוּ אָבִיהָ וְאִמָּהּ לְגַדְּלָהּ לְתוֹרָה וּלְחֻפָּה וּלְמַעֲשִׂים טוֹבִים, וְנֹאמַר אָמֵן.

מי שברך לבר מצווה

מִי שֶׁבֵּרַךְ אֲבוֹתֵינוּ אַבְרָהָם יִצְחָק וְיַעֲקֹב הוּא יְבָרֵךְ אֶת (פלוני בן פלוני) שֶׁמָּלְאוּ לוֹ שְׁלֹשׁ עֶשְׂרֵה שָׁנָה וְהִגִּיעַ לְמִצְוֹת, וְעָלָה לַתּוֹרָה, לָתֵת שֶׁבַח וְהוֹדָיָה לְהַשֵּׁם יִתְבָּרַךְ עַל כָּל הַטּוֹבָה שֶׁגְּמַל אִתּוֹ. יִשְׁמְרֵהוּ הַקָּדוֹשׁ בָּרוּךְ הוּא וִיחַיֵּהוּ, וִיכוֹנֵן אֶת לִבּוֹ לִהְיוֹת שָׁלֵם עִם יהוה וְלָלֶכֶת בִּדְרָכָיו וְלִשְׁמֹר מִצְוֹתָיו כָּל הַיָּמִים, וְנֹאמַר אָמֵן.

מי שברך לבת מצווה

מִי שֶׁבֵּרַךְ אֲבוֹתֵינוּ אַבְרָהָם יִצְחָק וְיַעֲקֹב, שָׂרָה רִבְקָה רָחֵל וְלֵאָה, הוּא יְבָרֵךְ אֶת (פלונית בת פלוני) שֶׁמָּלְאוּ לָהּ שְׁתֵּים עֶשְׂרֵה שָׁנָה וְהִגִּיעָה לְמִצְוֹת, וְנוֹתֶנֶת שֶׁבַח וְהוֹדָיָה לְהַשֵּׁם יִתְבָּרַךְ עַל כָּל הַטּוֹבָה שֶׁגְּמַל אִתָּהּ. יִשְׁמְרֶהָ הַקָּדוֹשׁ בָּרוּךְ הוּא וִיחַיֶּהָ, וִיכוֹנֵן אֶת לִבָּהּ לִהְיוֹת שָׁלֵם עִם יהוה וְלָלֶכֶת בִּדְרָכָיו וְלִשְׁמֹר מִצְוֹתָיו כָּל הַיָּמִים, וְנֹאמַר אָמֵן.

TORAH READING FOR THE SECOND DAY OF SHAVUOT

*If the second day of Shavuot falls on Shabbat, start here. If it falls on
a weekday, start with "Every male firstborn" on page 476.*

You must tithe all the produce of your grain, that which grows in *Deut.
14:22–16:17* the field, each year. You shall then eat it in the presence of the Lord your God, at the place He will choose as a dwelling place for His name; the tithes of your grain, wine and oil as well as the firstborn of your herd and flock, so that you might learn to hold the Lord your God in awe as long as you live. If the distance is very great for you, so that you cannot carry it all; if the place the Lord your God chooses as a dwelling place for His name is far away from you, and the Lord your God blesses you with plenty, then you may sell your produce for money and, holding that money in your hand, go to the place which the Lord your God will choose. You may purchase with that money anything you may wish for of the herd or flock, of wine or intoxicating drinks: anything your heart desires; and you shall eat there, in the presence of the Lord your God, and you and your household shall rejoice. As for the Levite who dwells within

---

Moses also emphasizes the important dimension of social inclusion. They are times when people are to invite those at the margins of society: the widow, the orphan, the Levites who have no land of their own, the temporary residents, as well as slaves. No one is to be left out.

The preceding passages are also included when the second day of Shavuot falls on Shabbat, to extend the reading because of the two extra people called to the Torah on that day.

עַשֵּׂר תְּעַשֵּׂר *You must tithe.* This is the law of the second tithe. Unlike the first that was given to the Levites, this was taken by its owners to Jerusalem and eaten there, either in the form of the produce itself or money for which it had been exchanged. This reminded the nation that its wealth came from God who was a constant presence in its midst. Maimonides adds that since people could not eat all the food themselves they would naturally give part of it to others as charity. This strengthened the bond of love and brotherhood among the people as a whole: it reinforced civil society and the sense of national unity (*The Guide for the Perplexed* III: 39).

קריאה ליום שני של שבועות

If the second day of שבועות *falls on* שבת, *start here.*
If it falls on a weekday, start with כָּל־הַבְּכוֹר *on page 477.*

דברים
יד,כב-טז,יז

עַשֵּׂר תְּעַשֵּׂר אֵת כָּל־תְּבוּאַת זַרְעֶךָ הַיֹּצֵא הַשָּׂדֶה שָׁנָה שָׁנָה: וְאָכַלְתָּ לִפְנֵי ׀ יהוה אֱלֹהֶיךָ בַּמָּקוֹם אֲשֶׁר־יִבְחַר לְשַׁכֵּן שְׁמוֹ שָׁם מַעְשַׂר דְּגָנְךָ תִּירְשְׁךָ וְיִצְהָרֶךָ וּבְכֹרֹת בְּקָרְךָ וְצֹאנֶךָ לְמַעַן תִּלְמַד לְיִרְאָה אֶת־יהוה אֱלֹהֶיךָ כָּל־הַיָּמִים: וְכִי־יִרְבֶּה מִמְּךָ הַדֶּרֶךְ כִּי לֹא תוּכַל שְׂאֵתוֹ כִּי־יִרְחַק מִמְּךָ הַמָּקוֹם אֲשֶׁר יִבְחַר יהוה אֱלֹהֶיךָ לָשׂוּם שְׁמוֹ שָׁם כִּי יְבָרֶכְךָ יהוה אֱלֹהֶיךָ: וְנָתַתָּה בַּכָּסֶף וְצַרְתָּ הַכֶּסֶף בְּיָדְךָ וְהָלַכְתָּ אֶל־הַמָּקוֹם אֲשֶׁר יִבְחַר יהוה אֱלֹהֶיךָ בּוֹ: וְנָתַתָּה הַכֶּסֶף בְּכֹל אֲשֶׁר־תְּאַוֶּה נַפְשְׁךָ בַּבָּקָר וּבַצֹּאן וּבַיַּיִן וּבַשֵּׁכָר וּבְכֹל אֲשֶׁר תִּשְׁאָלְךָ נַפְשֶׁךָ וְאָכַלְתָּ שָּׁם לִפְנֵי יהוה אֱלֹהֶיךָ וְשָׂמַחְתָּ אַתָּה וּבֵיתֶךָ: וְהַלֵּוִי אֲשֶׁר־בִּשְׁעָרֶיךָ

READING OF THE TORAH: SECOND DAY

The core of the reading for the second day is the passage dealing with the festivals in the book of Deuteronomy. The festivals are extensively described in three places in the Torah, in Leviticus (23), in Numbers (28–29), and here (Deut. 16). The sages explained that the first is to establish their order, the second to prescribe their sacrifices, and the third to explain them to the public (Sifrei).

Throughout Deuteronomy, Moses explains the laws to the people as a whole, reminding them of the historical background against which they are set, and the future of which they are the parameters. In the case of the festivals, Moses' presentation here has a strong emphasis on the seasons of the agricultural year: Pesaḥ is the festival of spring, the countdown to Shavuot begins from "when the sickle begins to cut the standing grain," and Sukkot is celebrated at the time when "when you gather into your granary and wine-vat." These are dimensions of the festivals the people have not yet experienced as desert nomads but which they will once they enter and make their home in the land which the LORD has blessed.

your gates – you shall not forsake him, for he does not have a portion or an inheritance among you.

At the end of every third year, you must take out all the tithes of your harvest from that year, and set them down within your gates. Then the Levite, who does not have a portion or an inheritance among you, along with the stranger and orphan and widow within your gates, shall come and eat and be satisfied; do this, so that the LORD your God might bless you in all that you do.

At the end of every seven years, you shall institute a release. And LEVI this is the manner of the release: every creditor shall let go of what he is entitled to from his debtor; he may not demand payment from his fellow or his kinsman, for a release has been proclaimed for [the honor of] the LORD. You may ask payment of a gentile, but any claim you hold against your kinsmen must be released. Nevertheless, you will not have paupers among you, for the LORD shall surely bless you in the land that He is giving you as a portion, to inherit it – but only if you heed the voice of the LORD your God, safeguarding and keeping all of the commandments I am commanding you today. For the LORD your God will bless you as He has promised you: you shall lend to many nations and you shall not borrow; you shall rule over many nations and shall not be ruled by others.

If there should be a poor person among you, one of your kinsmen

---

than they need share their blessings with those who have less. In particular, we should ensure that no one in the nation God liberated from slavery is permanently enslaved, either by debt or poverty (the usual reason people sold themselves as slaves).

כִּי־יִהְיֶה בְךָ אֶבְיוֹן *If there should be a poor person among you.* This passage became, in the Talmud, the basis of the elaborate laws of *tzedaka*, one of the pillars of Jewish life, especially outside Israel where the agricultural laws that formed the basis of the Torah's welfare legislation were less applicable.

לֹא תַעַזְבֶנּוּ כִּי אֵין לוֹ חֵלֶק וְנַחֲלָה עִמָּךְ: מִקְצֵה |

שָׁלֹשׁ שָׁנִים תּוֹצִיא אֶת־כָּל־מַעְשַׂר תְּבוּאָתְךָ֫ בַּשָּׁנָה הַהִוא

וְהִנַּחְתָּ בִּשְׁעָרֶיךָ: וּבָא הַלֵּוִי כִּי אֵין־לוֹ חֵלֶק וְנַחֲלָה עִמָּךְ וְהַגֵּר

וְהַיָּתוֹם וְהָאַלְמָנָה֙ אֲשֶׁר בִּשְׁעָרֶיךָ וְאָכְלוּ וְשָׂבֵעוּ לְמַעַן יְבָרֶכְךָ֫

יהוה אֱלֹהֶ֫יךָ בְּכָל־מַעֲשֵׂה יָדְךָ אֲשֶׁר תַּעֲשֶׂה: מִקֵּץ ⟨לוי⟩

שֶׁבַע־שָׁנִים תַּעֲשֶׂה שְׁמִטָּה: וְזֶה דְּבַר הַשְּׁמִטָּה שָׁמוֹט כָּל־בַּעַל

מַשֵּׁה יָדוֹ אֲשֶׁר יַשֶּׁה בְּרֵעֵהוּ לֹא־יִגֹּשׂ אֶת־רֵעֵ֫הוּ וְאֶת־אָחִיו

כִּי־קָרָא שְׁמִטָּה לַיהוה: אֶת־הַנָּכְרִי תִּגֹּשׂ וַאֲשֶׁר יִהְיֶה לְךָ֫ אֶת־

אָחִ֫יךָ תַּשְׁמֵט יָדֶךָ: אֶפֶס כִּי לֹא יִהְיֶה־בְּךָ אֶבְיוֹן כִּי־בָרֵךְ יְבָרֶכְךָ֫

יהוה בָּאָ֫רֶץ אֲשֶׁר יהוה אֱלֹהֶ֫יךָ נֹתֵן־לְךָ֫ נַחֲלָה לְרִשְׁתָּהּ: רַק

אִם־שָׁמוֹעַ תִּשְׁמַע בְּקוֹל יהוה אֱלֹהֶ֫יךָ לִשְׁמֹר לַעֲשׂוֹת אֶת־

כָּל־הַמִּצְוָה הַזֹּאת אֲשֶׁר אָנֹכִי מְצַוְּךָ הַיּוֹם: כִּי־יהוה אֱלֹהֶ֫יךָ

בֵּרַכְךָ֫ כַּאֲשֶׁר דִּבֶּר־לָךְ וְהַעֲבַטְתָּ֫ גּוֹיִם רַבִּים וְאַתָּה לֹא תַעֲבֹט

וּמָשַׁלְתָּ֫ בְּגוֹיִם רַבִּים וּבְךָ לֹא יִמְשֹׁלוּ:   כִּי־יִהְיֶה

בְךָ אֶבְיוֹן מֵאַחַד אַחֶ֫יךָ בְּאַחַד שְׁעָרֶ֫יךָ בְּאַרְצְךָ אֲשֶׁר־יהוה

מִקְצֵה שָׁלֹשׁ שָׁנִים *At the end of every third year.* On the third and sixth year of each septennial cycle, the second tithe, instead of being consumed by its owners in Jerusalem, is given locally to the poor. This, the *ma'aser oni,* "poor person's tithe," is part of the Torah's elaborate welfare system, designed to ensure that no one is left destitute or without the means of a dignified existence.

לְמַעַן יְבָרֶכְךָ יהוה אֱלֹהֶ֫יךָ *So that the LORD your God might bless you.* God blesses those who are a source of blessing to others.

מִקֵּץ שֶׁבַע־שָׁנִים *At the end of every seven years.* The sequence here – second and poor person's tithe, and the release of debts and slaves in the seventh year – are ways in which we serve God *bekhol me'odekha,* "with all your wealth." We use our wealth to serve God when we ensure that those who have more

in one of the cities in your land, which the LORD your God has given to you, you must not harden your heart and you must not close your hand to your impoverished kinsman. Rather, you must open your hand to him, making him a loan to tide him over his lack. Take care, lest evil thoughts enter your heart, saying: "The seventh year, the year of release draws near," causing you to treat your impoverished kinsman meanly, withholding loans from him; he might then call out to God because of you and it will be held against you as a sin. You must certainly give to him, and let your heart not be grudging when you give, for because of this deed, the LORD your God shall bless you in all that you do and in all of your endeavors. For there will never cease to be poor people in the land; and so I am commanding you: you must open your hand to your kinsman, to the poor and destitute in your land.

If your Hebrew kinsman or kinswoman is sold to you, he shall work for you for six years, and in the seventh year, you must release him from your service, free. When you set him free from your service you must not send him away empty-handed. You must give generously to him of your flock, your granary and your wine-vat with which the LORD your God has blessed you; so you shall give him. And you shall remember that you were once a slave in the land of Egypt and the LORD your God redeemed you; this is why, today, I command you thus. Should [the slave] say: "I would not leave your home;" because he is fond of you and of your household, and is happy living with you, then you shall take an awl and pierce his ear upon the door with it, and he shall then be your slave forever; the same should be done with your female slave. Do not feel it a hardship when you release him from your service, free; for he has served you for six years – twice a hired hand's work, and now the LORD your God will bless you in all that you do.

---

dehumanizing about servitude, for servant and master alike. The gift is a humanizing gesture that marks a benign end to a less-than-benign episode.

אֱלֹהֶיךָ נֹתֵן לָךְ לֹא תְאַמֵּץ אֶת־לְבָבְךָ וְלֹא תִקְפֹּץ אֶת־יָדְךָ
מֵאָחִיךָ הָאֶבְיוֹן: כִּי־פָתֹחַ תִּפְתַּח אֶת־יָדְךָ לוֹ וְהַעֲבֵט תַּעֲבִיטֶנּוּ
דֵּי מַחְסֹרוֹ אֲשֶׁר יֶחְסַר לוֹ: הִשָּׁמֶר לְךָ פֶּן־יִהְיֶה דָבָר עִם־
לְבָבְךָ בְלִיַּעַל לֵאמֹר קָרְבָה שְׁנַת־הַשֶּׁבַע שְׁנַת הַשְּׁמִטָּה וְרָעָה
עֵינְךָ בְּאָחִיךָ הָאֶבְיוֹן וְלֹא תִתֵּן לוֹ וְקָרָא עָלֶיךָ אֶל־יהוה
וְהָיָה בְךָ חֵטְא: נָתוֹן תִּתֵּן לוֹ וְלֹא־יֵרַע לְבָבְךָ בְּתִתְּךָ לוֹ כִּי
בִּגְלַל ׀ הַדָּבָר הַזֶּה יְבָרֶכְךָ יהוה אֱלֹהֶיךָ בְּכָל־מַעֲשֶׂךָ וּבְכֹל
מִשְׁלַח יָדֶךָ: כִּי לֹא־יֶחְדַּל אֶבְיוֹן מִקֶּרֶב הָאָרֶץ עַל־כֵּן אָנֹכִי
מְצַוְּךָ לֵאמֹר פָּתֹחַ תִּפְתַּח אֶת־יָדְךָ לְאָחִיךָ לַעֲנִיֶּךָ וּלְאֶבְיֹנְךָ
בְּאַרְצֶךָ:   כִּי־יִמָּכֵר לְךָ אָחִיךָ הָעִבְרִי אוֹ הָעִבְרִיָּה
וַעֲבָדְךָ שֵׁשׁ שָׁנִים וּבַשָּׁנָה הַשְּׁבִיעִת תְּשַׁלְּחֶנּוּ חָפְשִׁי מֵעִמָּךְ:
וְכִי־תְשַׁלְּחֶנּוּ חָפְשִׁי מֵעִמָּךְ לֹא תְשַׁלְּחֶנּוּ רֵיקָם: הַעֲנֵיק תַּעֲנִיק
לוֹ מִצֹּאנְךָ וּמִגָּרְנְךָ וּמִיִּקְבֶךָ אֲשֶׁר בֵּרַכְךָ יהוה אֱלֹהֶיךָ תִּתֶּן־לוֹ:
וְזָכַרְתָּ כִּי עֶבֶד הָיִיתָ בְּאֶרֶץ מִצְרַיִם וַיִּפְדְּךָ יהוה אֱלֹהֶיךָ עַל־כֵּן
אָנֹכִי מְצַוְּךָ אֶת־הַדָּבָר הַזֶּה הַיּוֹם: וְהָיָה כִּי־יֹאמַר אֵלֶיךָ לֹא
אֵצֵא מֵעִמָּךְ כִּי אֲהֵבְךָ וְאֶת־בֵּיתֶךָ כִּי־טוֹב לוֹ עִמָּךְ: וְלָקַחְתָּ
אֶת־הַמַּרְצֵעַ וְנָתַתָּה בְאָזְנוֹ וּבַדֶּלֶת וְהָיָה לְךָ עֶבֶד עוֹלָם וְאַף
לַאֲמָתְךָ תַּעֲשֶׂה־כֵּן: לֹא־יִקְשֶׁה בְעֵינֶךָ בְּשַׁלֵּחֲךָ אֹתוֹ חָפְשִׁי
מֵעִמָּךְ כִּי מִשְׁנֶה שְׂכַר שָׂכִיר עֲבָדְךָ שֵׁשׁ שָׁנִים וּבֵרַכְךָ יהוה
אֱלֹהֶיךָ בְּכֹל אֲשֶׁר תַּעֲשֶׂה:

הַעֲנֵיק תַּעֲנִיק לוֹ *You must give generously to him.* There are three reasons for
this law: first, to give the released slave the means to make a fresh start;
second, to demonstrate your gratitude for the service he has given you; and
third to establish closure with goodwill. There is something profoundly

If the second day of Shavuot falls on a weekday, start here:

Every male firstborn that is delivered among your herd and your flock, you shall consecrate to the Lord your God: you may not perform work with the male firstborn of your oxen, nor shear the male firstborn of your sheep. You shall eat them in the presence of the Lord your God each year, you and your household, in the place which the Lord will choose. If it is blemished: lame or blind, or with any other serious blemish, you may not offer it to the Lord your God. Eat it within your gates; [it may be eaten by] pure and impure alike, as the gazelle and as the hart. But its blood you may not eat; you must spill it on the ground like water.

(Shabbat: SHELISHI)

Remember the month of Spring: bring a Pesaḥ offering to the Lord your God, for in the month of Spring, the Lord your God took you out of Egypt at night. You shall bring a Pesaḥ offering to the Lord your God, sheep and cattle, at the place the Lord shall choose as a dwelling place for His name. You may not eat leaven with it; you must eat matzot, the bread of oppression, with it for seven days – for you left Egypt in great haste – so that you remember the day of your exodus from Egypt all the days of your life. *And no leaven shall be seen by you within all your borders for seven days, and none of the meat which you offer in the evening of the first day shall be allowed to remain until morning. You may not sacrifice the Pesaḥ offering in any one of your cities, which the Lord your God gives you. Only at the place which the Lord your God shall choose as a dwelling place for His name – that is where you should sacrifice the Pesaḥ offering in the evening, before sunset, in the season of your exodus from Egypt. You shall cook it and eat it in the place the Lord your

LEVI
(Shabbat: REVI'I)

SHELISHI
(Shabbat: ḤAMISHI)

לֶחֶם עֹנִי *Bread of oppression.* It is this phrase that defines matza as the taste of servitude, either because they were given it to eat in Egypt (being harder to digest than ordinary bread, it staved off hunger longer), or because, eating it on their escape from Egypt, it served as a reminder of the slavery they were escaping from.

If the second day of שבועות falls on a weekday, start here:

כָּל־הַבְּכוֹר אֲשֶׁר יִוָּלֵד בִּבְקָרְךָ וּבְצֹאנְךָ הַזָּכָר תַּקְדִּישׁ לַיהוָה (בשבת
שלישי)
אֱלֹהֶיךָ לֹא תַעֲבֹד בִּבְכֹר שׁוֹרֶךָ וְלֹא תָגֹז בְּכוֹר צֹאנֶךָ: לִפְנֵי

יְהוָה אֱלֹהֶיךָ תֹאכְלֶנּוּ שָׁנָה בְשָׁנָה בַּמָּקוֹם אֲשֶׁר־יִבְחַר יְהוָה

אַתָּה וּבֵיתֶךָ: וְכִי־יִהְיֶה בוֹ מוּם פִּסֵּחַ אוֹ עִוֵּר כֹּל מוּם רָע לֹא

תִזְבָּחֶנּוּ לַיהוָה אֱלֹהֶיךָ: בִּשְׁעָרֶיךָ תֹּאכְלֶנּוּ הַטָּמֵא וְהַטָּהוֹר

יַחְדָּו כַּצְּבִי וְכָאַיָּל: רַק אֶת־דָּמוֹ לֹא תֹאכֵל עַל־הָאָרֶץ תִּשְׁפְּכֶנּוּ
כַּמָּיִם:

שָׁמוֹר אֶת־חֹדֶשׁ הָאָבִיב וְעָשִׂיתָ פֶּסַח לַיהוָה אֱלֹהֶיךָ כִּי בְּחֹדֶשׁ (לוי
בשבת)
רביעי)
הָאָבִיב הוֹצִיאֲךָ יְהוָה אֱלֹהֶיךָ מִמִּצְרַיִם לָיְלָה: וְזָבַחְתָּ פֶּסַח

לַיהוָה אֱלֹהֶיךָ צֹאן וּבָקָר בַּמָּקוֹם אֲשֶׁר יִבְחַר יְהוָה לְשַׁכֵּן שְׁמוֹ

שָׁם: לֹא־תֹאכַל עָלָיו חָמֵץ שִׁבְעַת יָמִים תֹּאכַל־עָלָיו מַצּוֹת

לֶחֶם עֹנִי כִּי בְחִפָּזוֹן יָצָאתָ מֵאֶרֶץ מִצְרַיִם לְמַעַן תִּזְכֹּר אֶת־יוֹם

צֵאתְךָ מֵאֶרֶץ מִצְרַיִם כֹּל יְמֵי חַיֶּיךָ: וְלֹא־יֵרָאֶה לְךָ שְׂאֹר בְּכָל־ (שלישי
בשבת)
חמישי)
גְּבֻלְךָ שִׁבְעַת יָמִים וְלֹא־יָלִין מִן־הַבָּשָׂר אֲשֶׁר תִּזְבַּח בָּעֶרֶב בַּיּוֹם

הָרִאשׁוֹן לַבֹּקֶר: לֹא תוּכַל לִזְבֹּחַ אֶת־הַפָּסַח בְּאַחַד שְׁעָרֶיךָ

אֲשֶׁר־יְהוָה אֱלֹהֶיךָ נֹתֵן לָךְ: כִּי אִם־אֶל־הַמָּקוֹם אֲשֶׁר־יִבְחַר

יְהוָה אֱלֹהֶיךָ לְשַׁכֵּן שְׁמוֹ שָׁם תִּזְבַּח אֶת־הַפֶּסַח בָּעֶרֶב כְּבוֹא

הַשֶּׁמֶשׁ מוֹעֵד צֵאתְךָ מִמִּצְרָיִם: וּבִשַּׁלְתָּ וְאָכַלְתָּ בַּמָּקוֹם אֲשֶׁר

חֹדֶשׁ הָאָבִיב *The month of Spring.* It is this requirement that Pesaḥ be celebrated in spring that necessitates the complex system by which the lunar calendar
of Judaism is coordinated with the solar cycle of the seasons, by means of
adding an extra month (a second Adar) from time to time. Originally this
was done by decision of the Beit Din. Only a court in Israel has this power.
So from the fourth century onward, when the center of Jewish life had moved
from Israel to Babylon, a fixed calendar was adopted on the authority of Israel,
by which seven leap years are observed in the course of nineteen years.

God will choose, and in the morning you shall turn back and go to your abode. For six days, you shall eat matzot; the seventh day is a day of assembly for the LORD your God: on it, you may not perform work.

Count for yourselves seven weeks; when the sickle begins to cut the standing grain, then shall you begin to count the seven weeks. And you shall celebrate a Festival of Weeks [Shavuot] for the LORD your God, bringing a free-will offering, as much as you can afford, according to the blessing the LORD your God has given you. And you shall rejoice in the presence of the LORD your God: you and your sons and daughters, your male and female slaves, and the Levite who dwells within your gates, along with the stranger and orphan and widow that are among you, at the place that the LORD your God shall choose as a dwelling place for His name. And you shall remember that you were once a slave in Egypt; keep and fulfill all of these statutes. REVI'I (*Shabbat:* SHISHI)

You shall celebrate a Festival of Booths [Sukkot] for yourselves for seven days, when you gather [your produce] into your granary and wine-vat. And you shall rejoice on your festival: you and your sons and daughters, your male and female slaves, and the Levite, the stranger and orphan and widow that dwell within your gates. You shall celebrate for seven days for the LORD your God in the place which the LORD shall choose, for the LORD your God shall bless you in all of your produce and all that you do; and you will be truly joyful. Three times in the year, all your males shall appear before the LORD your God at the place He will choose: on Pesaḥ, Shavuot and Sukkot. They shall not appear before the LORD empty-handed. Each shall bring such a gift as he can, in proportion to the blessing the LORD your God grants you. ḤAMISHI (*Shabbat:* SHEVI'I)

---

as a holy nation in a holy land, keeping God's law, sensing His presence and celebrating His blessings. Note, however, that the word "rejoice" does not appear in the context of Pesaḥ, for it recalls two periods of suffering, the suffering inflicted on the Israelites by the Egyptians, and the subsequent

יִבְחַר יהוה אֱלֹהֶיךָ בּוֹ וּפָנִיתָ בַבֹּקֶר וְהָלַכְתָּ לְאֹהָלֶיךָ: שֵׁשֶׁת

יָמִים תֹּאכַל מַצּוֹת וּבַיּוֹם הַשְּׁבִיעִי עֲצֶרֶת לַיהוה אֱלֹהֶיךָ לֹא

רביעי
(בשבת
ששי)

תַעֲשֶׂה מְלָאכָה: שִׁבְעָה שָׁבֻעֹת תִּסְפָּר־לָךְ מֵהָחֵל

חֶרְמֵשׁ בַּקָּמָה תָּחֵל לִסְפֹּר שִׁבְעָה שָׁבֻעוֹת: וְעָשִׂיתָ חַג שָׁבֻעוֹת

לַיהוה אֱלֹהֶיךָ מִסַּת נִדְבַת יָדְךָ אֲשֶׁר תִּתֵּן כַּאֲשֶׁר יְבָרֶכְךָ יהוה

אֱלֹהֶיךָ: וְשָׂמַחְתָּ לִפְנֵי ׀ יהוה אֱלֹהֶיךָ אַתָּה וּבִנְךָ וּבִתֶּךָ וְעַבְדְּךָ

וַאֲמָתֶךָ וְהַלֵּוִי אֲשֶׁר בִּשְׁעָרֶיךָ וְהַגֵּר וְהַיָּתוֹם וְהָאַלְמָנָה אֲשֶׁר

בְּקִרְבֶּךָ בַּמָּקוֹם אֲשֶׁר יִבְחַר יהוה אֱלֹהֶיךָ לְשַׁכֵּן שְׁמוֹ שָׁם:

וְזָכַרְתָּ כִּי־עֶבֶד הָיִיתָ בְּמִצְרָיִם וְשָׁמַרְתָּ וְעָשִׂיתָ אֶת־הַחֻקִּים

הָאֵלֶּה:

חמישי
(בשבת
שביעי)

חַג הַסֻּכֹּת תַּעֲשֶׂה לְךָ שִׁבְעַת יָמִים בְּאָסְפְּךָ מִגָּרְנְךָ וּמִיִּקְבֶךָ:

וְשָׂמַחְתָּ בְּחַגֶּךָ אַתָּה וּבִנְךָ וּבִתֶּךָ וְעַבְדְּךָ וַאֲמָתֶךָ וְהַלֵּוִי וְהַגֵּר

וְהַיָּתוֹם וְהָאַלְמָנָה אֲשֶׁר בִּשְׁעָרֶיךָ: שִׁבְעַת יָמִים תָּחֹג לַיהוה

אֱלֹהֶיךָ בַּמָּקוֹם אֲשֶׁר־יִבְחַר יהוה כִּי יְבָרֶכְךָ יהוה אֱלֹהֶיךָ בְּכֹל־

תְּבוּאָתְךָ וּבְכֹל מַעֲשֵׂה יָדֶיךָ וְהָיִיתָ אַךְ שָׂמֵחַ: שָׁלוֹשׁ פְּעָמִים ׀

בַּשָּׁנָה יֵרָאֶה כָל־זְכוּרְךָ אֶת־פְּנֵי ׀ יהוה אֱלֹהֶיךָ בַּמָּקוֹם אֲשֶׁר

יִבְחָר בְּחַג הַמַּצּוֹת וּבְחַג הַשָּׁבֻעוֹת וּבְחַג הַסֻּכּוֹת וְלֹא יֵרָאֶה

אֶת־פְּנֵי יהוה רֵיקָם: אִישׁ כְּמַתְּנַת יָדוֹ כְּבִרְכַּת יהוה אֱלֹהֶיךָ

אֲשֶׁר נָתַן־לָךְ:

וְשָׂמַחְתָּ *You shall rejoice.* There is greater emphasis on rejoicing in Deuteronomy than elsewhere in the Torah. The root שׂ-מ-ח, "to rejoice," appears
only once in each of the books of Genesis, Exodus, Leviticus and Numbers,
but twelve times in Deuteronomy as a whole. The previous books have been
about the long journey, begun by Abraham, toward the fulfillment of the divine promises of children and a land. Deuteronomy is about the destination:
a land where the people of the covenant can be free to pursue their vocation

HALF KADDISH

*Before Maftir is read, the second Sefer Torah is placed on
the bima and the Reader says Half Kaddish:*

Reader: יִתְגַּדַּל Magnified and sanctified may His great name be,
in the world He created by His will.
May He establish His kingdom
in your lifetime and in your days,
and in the lifetime of all the house of Israel,
swiftly and soon – and say: Amen.

All: May His great name be blessed for ever and all time.

Reader: Blessed and praised, glorified and exalted,
raised and honored, uplifted and lauded
be the name of the Holy One, blessed be He,
beyond any blessing,
song, praise and consolation
uttered in the world – and say: Amen.

HAGBAHA AND GELILA

The first Torah scroll is lifted and the congregation says:

וְזֹאת הַתּוֹרָה This is the Torah   *Deut. 4*
that Moses placed before the children of Israel,
at the LORD's commandment, by the hand of Moses.   *Num. 9*

Some add: It is a tree of life to those who grasp it,   *Prov. 3*
and those who uphold it are happy.
Its ways are ways of pleasantness, and all its paths are peace.
Long life is in its right hand; in its left, riches and honor.
It pleased the LORD for the sake of [Israel's] righteousness,   *Is. 42*
to make the Torah great and glorious.

*The first Torah scroll is bound and covered and the oleh
for Maftir is called to the second Torah scroll.*

---

and bitterness (matza and maror) and on the last with the memory of the
Egyptians who died at the Reed Sea, and as Proverbs 24:17 states, "Do not
rejoice when your enemy falls" (*Yalkut Shimoni, Emor*, 654).

חצי קדיש

Before מפטיר is read, the second ספר תורה is placed
on the שולחן and the קורא says חצי קדיש:

קורא: יִתְגַּדַּל וְיִתְקַדַּשׁ שְׁמֵהּ רַבָּא (קהל: אָמֵן)
בְּעָלְמָא דִּי בְרָא כִרְעוּתֵהּ
וְיַמְלִיךְ מַלְכוּתֵהּ
בְּחַיֵּיכוֹן וּבְיוֹמֵיכוֹן וּבְחַיֵּי דְּכָל בֵּית יִשְׂרָאֵל
בַּעֲגָלָא וּבִזְמַן קָרִיב, וְאִמְרוּ אָמֵן. (קהל: אָמֵן)

קהל
וקורא: יְהֵא שְׁמֵהּ רַבָּא מְבָרַךְ לְעָלַם וּלְעָלְמֵי עָלְמַיָּא.

קורא: יִתְבָּרַךְ וְיִשְׁתַּבַּח וְיִתְפָּאַר וְיִתְרוֹמַם וְיִתְנַשֵּׂא
וְיִתְהַדָּר וְיִתְעַלֶּה וְיִתְהַלָּל
שְׁמֵהּ דְּקֻדְשָׁא בְּרִיךְ הוּא (קהל: בְּרִיךְ הוּא)
לְעֵלָּא מִן כָּל בִּרְכָתָא וְשִׁירָתָא, תֻּשְׁבְּחָתָא וְנֶחֱמָתָא
דַּאֲמִירָן בְּעָלְמָא, וְאִמְרוּ אָמֵן. (קהל: אָמֵן)

הגבהה וגלילה

The first ספר תורה is lifted and the קהל says:

דברים ד   וְזֹאת הַתּוֹרָה אֲשֶׁר־שָׂם מֹשֶׁה לִפְנֵי בְּנֵי יִשְׂרָאֵל:
במדבר ט   עַל־פִּי יהוה בְּיַד מֹשֶׁה:

משלי ג   *Some add*   עֵץ־חַיִּים הִיא לַמַּחֲזִיקִים בָּהּ וְתֹמְכֶיהָ מְאֻשָּׁר:
דְּרָכֶיהָ דַרְכֵי־נֹעַם וְכָל־נְתִיבֹתֶיהָ שָׁלוֹם:
אֹרֶךְ יָמִים בִּימִינָהּ, בִּשְׂמֹאולָהּ עֹשֶׁר וְכָבוֹד:

ישעיה מב   יהוה חָפֵץ לְמַעַן צִדְקוֹ יַגְדִּיל תּוֹרָה וְיַאְדִּיר:

The first ספר תורה is bound and covered and the עולה
for מפטיר is called to the second ספר תורה.

---

suffering of the Egyptians themselves. Halakhically there is a mitzva of *simḥa* on Pesaḥ, but it comes on the first day(s) mixed with the taste of oppression

MAFTIR

On the day of the first fruits, when you bring an offering of new grain to the LORD, on your Festival of Weeks, there shall be a sacred assembly: you shall do no laborious work. You shall offer a burnt-offering of pleasing aroma to the LORD: two young bullocks, one ram, and seven yearling male lambs. And also their meal-offerings, fine flour mixed with oil, three-tenths of an ephah for each of the bulls, two-tenths of an ephah for the ram, and one tenth of an ephah each for every one of the seven lambs. And one male goat as a sin-offering, as well as the regular daily sacrifice with its meal-offering; and they shall all be perfect for you, they and their libations.

Num. 28: 26–31

HAGBAHA AND GELILA

The second Torah scroll is lifted and the congregation says:

וְזֹאת הַתּוֹרָה This is the Torah *Deut. 4*
that Moses placed before the children of Israel,
at the LORD's commandment, by the hand of Moses. *Num. 9*

Some add: It is a tree of life to those who grasp it, *Prov. 3*
and those who uphold it are happy.
Its ways are ways of pleasantness, and all its paths are peace.
Long life is in its right hand; in its left, riches and honor.
It pleased the LORD for the sake of [Israel's] righteousness, *Is. 42*
to make the Torah great and glorious.

*The second Torah scroll is bound and covered and the oleh
for Maftir reads the Haftara.*

BLESSING BEFORE READING THE HAFTARA

Before reading the Haftara, the person called up for Maftir says:

בָּרוּךְ Blessed are You, LORD our God, King of the Universe, who chose good prophets and was pleased with their words, spoken in truth. Blessed are You, LORD, who chose the Torah, His servant Moses, His people Israel, and the prophets of truth and righteousness.

מפטיר

במדבר
כח:כו-לא

וּבְיוֹם הַבִּכּוּרִים בְּהַקְרִיבְכֶם מִנְחָה חֲדָשָׁה לַיהוה בְּשָׁבֻעֹתֵיכֶם מִקְרָא־קֹדֶשׁ יִהְיֶה לָכֶם כָּל־מְלֶאכֶת עֲבֹדָה לֹא תַעֲשׂוּ: וְהִקְרַבְתֶּם עוֹלָה לְרֵיחַ נִיחֹחַ לַיהוה פָּרִים בְּנֵי־בָקָר שְׁנַיִם אַיִל אֶחָד שִׁבְעָה כְבָשִׂים בְּנֵי שָׁנָה: וּמִנְחָתָם סֹלֶת בְּלוּלָה בַשָּׁמֶן שְׁלֹשָׁה עֶשְׂרֹנִים לַפָּר הָאֶחָד שְׁנֵי עֶשְׂרֹנִים לָאַיִל הָאֶחָד: עִשָּׂרוֹן עִשָּׂרוֹן לַכֶּבֶשׂ הָאֶחָד לְשִׁבְעַת הַכְּבָשִׂים: שְׂעִיר עִזִּים אֶחָד לְכַפֵּר עֲלֵיכֶם: מִלְּבַד עֹלַת הַתָּמִיד וּמִנְחָתוֹ תַּעֲשׂוּ תְּמִימִם יִהְיוּ־לָכֶם וְנִסְכֵּיהֶם:

הגבהה וגלילה

The second ספר תורה is lifted and the קהל says:

דברים ד

וְזֹאת הַתּוֹרָה אֲשֶׁר־שָׂם מֹשֶׁה לִפְנֵי בְּנֵי יִשְׂרָאֵל:

במדבר ט

עַל־פִּי יהוה בְּיַד מֹשֶׁה:

משלי ג

Some add עֵץ־חַיִּים הִיא לַמַּחֲזִיקִים בָּהּ וְתֹמְכֶיהָ מְאֻשָּׁר:

דְּרָכֶיהָ דַרְכֵי־נֹעַם וְכָל־נְתִיבֹתֶיהָ שָׁלוֹם:

אֹרֶךְ יָמִים בִּימִינָהּ בִּשְׂמֹאולָהּ עֹשֶׁר וְכָבוֹד:

ישעיה מב

יהוה חָפֵץ לְמַעַן צִדְקוֹ יַגְדִּיל תּוֹרָה וְיַאְדִּיר:

The second ספר תורה is bound and covered and the עולה for מפטיר reads the הפטרה.

ברכה קודם ההפטרה

Before reading the הפטרה, the person called up for מפטיר says:

בָּרוּךְ אַתָּה יהוה אֱלֹהֵינוּ מֶלֶךְ הָעוֹלָם אֲשֶׁר בָּחַר בִּנְבִיאִים טוֹבִים, וְרָצָה בְדִבְרֵיהֶם הַנֶּאֱמָרִים בֶּאֱמֶת. בָּרוּךְ אַתָּה יהוה, הַבּוֹחֵר בַּתּוֹרָה וּבְמֹשֶׁה עַבְדּוֹ וּבְיִשְׂרָאֵל עַמּוֹ וּבִנְבִיאֵי הָאֱמֶת וָצֶדֶק.

HAFTARA FOR THE SECOND DAY OF SHAVUOT

The LORD is in His holy Sanctuary: hush before Him, all the earth! *Habakkuk* *2:30–3:19*
A prayer of Habakkuk the prophet, upon Shigyonot:

Many say the following in the Haftara.

יָצִיב פִּתְגָם May this praise be desired, for God, Sign and Witness,
    alone among myriad myriad angels.
Where is it that He dwells, among that company of angels who
    dismissed the four great mountains [and chose Sinai].
Out before Him springs and flows, into His wells, a river of fire.
In a mountain of snow bright light shines out, and sparks and
    brands of fire,
and He creates and sees all that lies in darkness, for present with Him
    is all light.
He oversees all distances, judging without hastiness, and to Him
    are revealed all the world's secrets.
From Him will I ask permission to read; and afterwards also from
    the people before me,
who know the Law the Mishna, Tosefta, Sifra and Sifrei.
The King who lives for evermore will destroy the people that sub-
    jugates them.
For they have been told that they will be like sand, too many to be
    counted, like dust of the earth.
Make their valleys white today, with produce, their vats flowing
    over with wine.
Bring what they wish for, make their faces shine – let them shine
    out like morning light.
Grant me strength, and lift Your eyes to see Your enemies, those
    who deny You,
and make them like straw within the bricks; like stones, silent and
    ashamed.
As I stand here, translating the words of the most superior of books,
the LORD has given [Torah] through the humble [Moses], and so to
    Him – our gracious thanks.

Middle Ages, and Aramaic ceased to be the language of everyday speech,
but, as with *Akdamut*, the introductory poem remained. The text spells out

הפטרה ליום טוב השני של שבועות

תְּפִלָּה חֲבַקּוּק
ב:כ-ג:יט

וַיהוה בְּהֵיכַל קָדְשׁוֹ הַס מִפָּנָיו כָּל־הָאָרֶץ:
לַחֲבַקּוּק הַנָּבִיא עַל שִׁגְיֹנוֹת:

Many say the following in the הפטרה.

יַצִּיב פִּתְגָם, לְאָת וּדְגַם, בְּרִבּוֹ רִבְבָן עִירִין.

עֲנֵה אֲנָא, בְּמִנְיָנָא, דְּפָסְלִין אַרְבְּעָה טוּרִין.

קַדְמוֹהִי, לְגוֹ מוֹהִי, נְגִיד וּנְפִיק נְהַר דִּי נוּרִין.

בְּטוּר תַּלְגָא, נְהוֹר שְׁרָגָא, וְזִיקִין דִּי נוּר וּבַעֲוֹרִין.

בְּרָא וּסְכָא, מַה בַּחֲשׁוֹכָא, וְעִמֵּהּ שָׁרְיָן נְהוֹרִין.

רְחִיקִין צָפָא, בְּלָא שְׁטָפָא, וּגְלֵין לֵהּ דִּמְטַמְּרִין.

בְּעֵית מִנֵּהּ, יָת הַרְמְנֵהּ, וּבְתַרְוֹהִי עֲדֵי גִבְרִין.

יָדְעֵי הִלְכָתָא, וּמַתְנִיתָא, וְתוֹסֶפְתָּא סִפְרָא וְסִפְרִין.

מֶלֶךְ חַיָּא, לְעָלְמַיָּא, יְמַגַּר עִם לְהוֹן מְשַׁחֲרִין.

אֲמִיר עֲלֵיהוֹן, כְּחַלָּא יְהוֹן, וְלָא יִתְמְנוֹן הֵיךְ עַפְרִין.

יְחַוְּרוּן כְּעַן, לְהוֹן בִּקְעָן, יְטוּפוּן נַעֲוֵי חַמְרִין.

רְעוּתְהוֹן הַב, וְאַפֵּיהוֹן צָהַב, יְנַהֲרוּן כִּנְהוֹר צַפְרִין.

לִי הַב תְּקֹף, וְעֵינָךְ זְקֹף, חֲזִי עָרָךְ דְּבָךְ כָּפְרִין.

יְהוֹן כְּתַבְנָא, בְּגוֹ לִבְנָא, כְּאַבְנָא יִשְׁתְּקוּן חָפְרִין.

כְּקָאֲמְנָא, וְתַרְגְּמְנָא, בְּמִלּוֹי דִּבְחִיר סָפְרִין.

יְהוֹנָתָן, גְּבַר עִנְוְתָן, בְּכֵן נַמְטִין אַפְרִין.

YATZIV PITGAM: MAY THIS PRAISE BE DESIRED

This poem, like *Akdamut* said on the first day, is a *reshut*, a request for permission to recite the Aramaic translation of the text about to be read, in this case the Haftara from Habakkuk. The reason it is not said on the first day is that the passage read then – the vision of Ezekiel – was considered too mystical and open to misinterpretation to be translated into the vernacular. The custom of verse-by-verse translation of the biblical Hebrew into Aramaic lapsed as the center of Jewish life moved from Babylon to Europe in the

LORD, I heard tell of You, and I feared; LORD, in these years, revive Your work, in these years, make it known; in wrath, remember mercy. God is coming, from Teiman, the Holy One, from Mount Paran, Selah. His glory covers the heavens, His praise fills the earth, its brilliance like light, beams, from His hand, from the hidden place of His might. Plague will go before Him, fire following His feet; He stands, and measures up the land, He looks, and the nations tremble; ancient mountains shatter, age-old hills collapse – the world's ways are His. I saw the tents of Kushan distressed, the curtains of the land of Midian quivering. Is the LORD angry at the rivers – is Your fury against the rivers, Your wrath, against the sea, that You ride upon Your horses, upon Your chariot of deliverance? Your bow is bared, uncovered, according to the promise said to the tribes, Selah. You slice the land into rivers; seeing You, the mountains quake, rushing waters flow past, the deep raises its voice, lifts its

---

The text opens and closes with musical instructions, "Upon Shigyonot," – thought by some to mean a passionate song with rapid changes of rhythm – and "To the conductor, to be sung with my instruments," together with other expressions like the threefold Selah, that appear elsewhere only in the book of Psalms, suggesting that it was written to be sung as a psalm-like prayer for the overthrow of the nation's enemy, the Chaldeans, that is, Babylonia. A phrase near the opening, "In wrath, remember mercy," became a key-text in later penitential prayer.

The passage culminates in one of the most beautiful sentiments in the entire prophetic literature. Habakkuk declares that though the fig tree does not blossom and there are no grapes on the vines, though there is no grain in the fields and the flocks and herds have gone, still "I will rejoice in the LORD, will exult in the God who delivers me." This is faith at its most sublime. Though everything else were to be taken from me, I would still have God, and it would be more than enough. To live in the presence of God, knowing that He is with us whatever fate brings, is to experience ultimate existential joy: joy in the simple fact that He is and we are, that we are *because* He is. Nothing can separate us from the Source of our being. We live in the light of His presence, and thus in hope and joy.

יְהוֹה שָׁמַעְתִּי שִׁמְעֲךָ יָרֵאתִי יהוה פָּעָלְךָ בְּקֶרֶב שָׁנִים חַיֵּיהוּ
בְּקֶרֶב שָׁנִים תּוֹדִיעַ בְּרֹגֶז רַחֵם תִּזְכּוֹר: אֱלוֹהַ מִתֵּימָן יָבוֹא וְקָדוֹשׁ
מֵהַר־פָּארָן סֶלָה כִּסָּה שָׁמַיִם הוֹדוֹ וּתְהִלָּתוֹ מָלְאָה הָאָרֶץ: וְנֹגַהּ
כָּאוֹר תִּהְיֶה קַרְנַיִם מִיָּדוֹ לוֹ וְשָׁם חֶבְיוֹן עֻזֹּה: לְפָנָיו יֵלֶךְ דָּבֶר
וְיֵצֵא רֶשֶׁף לְרַגְלָיו: עָמַד ׀ וַיְמֹדֶד אֶרֶץ רָאָה וַיַּתֵּר גּוֹיִם וַיִּתְפֹּצְצוּ
הַרְרֵי־עַד שַׁחוּ גִּבְעוֹת עוֹלָם הֲלִיכוֹת עוֹלָם לוֹ: תַּחַת אָוֶן רָאִיתִי
אָהֳלֵי כוּשָׁן יִרְגְּזוּן יְרִיעוֹת אֶרֶץ מִדְיָן: הַבִּנְהָרִים חָרָה
יְהוֹה אִם בַּנְּהָרִים אַפֶּךָ אִם בַּיָּם עֶבְרָתֶךָ כִּי תִרְכַּב עַל־סוּסֶיךָ
מַרְכְּבֹתֶיךָ יְשׁוּעָה: עֶרְיָה תֵעוֹר קַשְׁתֶּךָ שְׁבֻעוֹת מַטּוֹת אֹמֶר
סֶלָה נְהָרוֹת תְּבַקַּע־אָרֶץ: רָאוּךָ יָחִילוּ הָרִים זֶרֶם מַיִם עָבָר נָתַן

---

in acrostic the name of the author, Yaakov beRebbi Meir Levi. It begins
with a dazzling description of the light that streams from the Divine. The
poet asks permission to recite the translation, first from God, then from
the learned members of the congregation, masters of the early rabbinic
literature (Mishna, *Tosefta*, *Sifra* and *Sifrei*, the four main documents from
the Mishnaic age). He expresses his faith that justice will prevail in history and Israel will be free of persecution. The last line, beginning "The
LORD has given through the humble," can also be translated as "Jonathan
the humble," a reference to the Aramaic translation of the prophetic books
attributed to Jonathan ben Uziel, said to have been Hillel's most brilliant
disciple (*Sukka* 28a).

HAFTARA: SECOND DAY

The Haftara, taken from the conclusion of the short prophetic book of
Habakkuk, was chosen because it describes a future revelation similar, at least
in externals, to the one that took place on Mount Sinai on the first Shavuot.
As then, so in the future, God will make an appearance in history, shaking
the earth to its foundations. Ancient mountains will shatter, age-old hills
will collapse – language reminiscent of the theophany at Sinai as described
in Deuteronomy 33:2–5, Judges 5:4, and Psalms 68:8–9.

hands skyward. The sun, the moon, stand still, in their place – by the light of Your arrows the world goes on, in the brilliance from Your shining spear. In rage, You walk over the land, in fury, You trample nations: You come forth, to deliver Your people, to deliver Your anointed. You crush the head of the house of the wicked, baring the foundation up to its neck, Selah. You pierce with his own sticks the head of his leaders – who come like a storm to scatter me, exultant as though secretly devouring the poor. You drive Your horses through the sea, the mass of raging waters. I hear and my stomach churns, at the sound my lips stutter, a rot enters my bones, I quiver where I stand yet I calmly wait for the day of trouble, when he comes up against the people to attack them. The fig tree does not blossom, and there is no yield from the vines; the olive grows gaunt, and the grain fields grow no food; the sheep are gone from the pens, and there are no cattle in the sheds. But I – I will rejoice in the LORD, will exult in the God who delivers me: God, my LORD, my Strength, who makes my feet like the deer's, who leads me to my highest places.

To the conductor: to be sung with my instruments.

BLESSINGS AFTER THE HAFTARA

After the Haftara, the person called up for Maftir says the following blessings:

בָּרוּךְ Blessed are You, LORD our God, King of the Universe, Rock of all worlds, righteous for all generations, the faithful God who says and does, speaks and fulfills, all of whose words are truth and righteousness. You are faithful, LORD our God, and faithful are Your words, not one of which returns unfulfilled, for You, God, are a faithful (and compassionate) King. Blessed are You, LORD, faithful in all His words.

רַחֵם Have compassion on Zion for it is the source of our life, and save the one grieved in spirit swiftly in our days. Blessed are You, LORD, who makes Zion rejoice in her children.

תְּהוֹם קוֹלוֹ רוֹם יָדֵיהוּ נָשָׂא: שֶׁמֶשׁ יָרֵחַ עָמַד זְבֻלָה לְאוֹר חִצֶּיךָ
יְהַלֵּכוּ לְנֹגַהּ בְּרַק חֲנִיתֶךָ: בְּזַעַם תִּצְעַד־אָרֶץ בְּאַף תָּדוּשׁ גּוֹיִם:
יָצָאתָ לְיֵשַׁע עַמֶּךָ לְיֵשַׁע אֶת־מְשִׁיחֶךָ מָחַצְתָּ רֹּאשׁ מִבֵּית רָשָׁע
עָרוֹת יְסוֹד עַד־צַוָּאר סֶלָה: נָקַבְתָּ בְמַטָּיו רֹאשׁ
פְּרָזָו יִסְעֲרוּ לַהֲפִיצֵנִי עֲלִיצֻתָם כְּמוֹ־לֶאֱכֹל עָנִי בַּמִּסְתָּר: דָּרַכְתָּ
בַיָּם סוּסֶיךָ חֹמֶר מַיִם רַבִּים: שָׁמַעְתִּי וַתִּרְגַּז בִּטְנִי לְקוֹל צָלְלוּ
שְׂפָתַי יָבוֹא רָקָב בַּעֲצָמַי וְתַחְתַּי אֶרְגָּז אֲשֶׁר אָנוּחַ לְיוֹם צָרָה
לַעֲלוֹת לְעַם יְגוּדֶנּוּ: כִּי־תְאֵנָה לֹא־תִפְרָח וְאֵין יְבוּל בַּגְּפָנִים
כִּחֵשׁ מַעֲשֵׂה־זַיִת וּשְׁדֵמוֹת לֹא־עָשָׂה אֹכֶל גָּזַר מִמִּכְלָה צֹאן
וְאֵין בָּקָר בָּרְפָתִים: וַאֲנִי בַּיהוה אֶעְלוֹזָה אָגִילָה בֵּאלֹהֵי יִשְׁעִי:
יהוה אֲדֹנָי חֵילִי וַיָּשֶׂם רַגְלַי כָּאַיָּלוֹת וְעַל־בָּמוֹתַי יַדְרִכֵנִי לַמְנַצֵּחַ
בִּנְגִינוֹתָי:

ברכות לאחר ההפטרה

After the הפטרה, *the person called up for* מפטיר *says the following blessings:*

בָּרוּךְ אַתָּה יהוה אֱלֹהֵינוּ מֶלֶךְ הָעוֹלָם, צוּר כָּל הָעוֹלָמִים,
צַדִּיק בְּכָל הַדּוֹרוֹת, הָאֵל הַנֶּאֱמָן, הָאוֹמֵר וְעוֹשֶׂה, הַמְדַבֵּר
וּמְקַיֵּם, שֶׁכָּל דְּבָרָיו אֱמֶת וָצֶדֶק. נֶאֱמָן אַתָּה הוּא יהוה אֱלֹהֵינוּ
וְנֶאֱמָנִים דְּבָרֶיךָ, וְדָבָר אֶחָד מִדְּבָרֶיךָ אָחוֹר לֹא יָשׁוּב רֵיקָם, כִּי
אֵל מֶלֶךְ נֶאֱמָן (וְרַחֲמָן) אָתָּה. בָּרוּךְ אַתָּה יהוה, הָאֵל הַנֶּאֱמָן
בְּכָל דְּבָרָיו.

רַחֵם עַל צִיּוֹן כִּי הִיא בֵּית חַיֵּינוּ, וְלַעֲלוּבַת נֶפֶשׁ תּוֹשִׁיעַ בִּמְהֵרָה
בְיָמֵינוּ. בָּרוּךְ אַתָּה יהוה, מְשַׂמֵּחַ צִיּוֹן בְּבָנֶיהָ.

שַׂמְּחֵנוּ Grant us joy, LORD our God, through Elijah the prophet Your servant, and through the kingdom of the house of David Your anointed – may he soon come and make our hearts glad. May no stranger sit on his throne, and may others not continue to inherit his glory, for You promised him by Your holy name that his light would never be extinguished. Blessed are You, LORD, Shield of David.

On Shabbat, add the words in parentheses:

עַל הַתּוֹרָה For the Torah, for Divine worship, for the prophets (and for this Sabbath day), and for this day of the festival of Shavuot which You, LORD our God, have given us (for holiness and rest) for gladness and joy, for honor and glory – for all these we thank and bless You, LORD our God, and may Your name be blessed by the mouth of all that lives, continually, for ever and all time. Blessed are You, LORD, who sanctifies (the Sabbath and) Israel and the festive seasons.

On a weekday, the service continues with the various prayers for government on page 494.

On the second day of Shavuot, if also Shabbat, continue:

יְקוּם פֻּרְקָן May deliverance arise from heaven, bringing grace, love and compassion, long life, ample sustenance and heavenly help, physical health and enlightenment of mind, living and thriving children who will neither interrupt nor cease from the words of the Torah – to our masters and teachers of the holy communities in the land of Israel and Babylon; to the leaders of assemblies and the leaders of communities in exile; to the heads of academies and to the judges in the gates; to all their disciples and their disciples' disciples, and to all who occupy themselves in study of the Torah. May the King of the Universe bless them, prolonging their lives, increasing their days, and adding to their years. May they be redeemed and

---

for the welfare of the leaders of the Jewish community. The "leaders of assemblies" were scholars who taught the public on Sabbaths and festivals.

שַׂמְּחֵנוּ יהוה אֱלֹהֵינוּ בְּאֵלִיָּהוּ הַנָּבִיא עַבְדֶּךָ, וּבְמַלְכוּת בֵּית
דָּוִד מְשִׁיחֶךָ, בִּמְהֵרָה יָבוֹא וְיָגֵל לִבֵּנוּ. עַל כִּסְאוֹ לֹא יֵשֵׁב זָר,
וְלֹא יִנְחֲלוּ עוֹד אֲחֵרִים אֶת כְּבוֹדוֹ, כִּי בְשֵׁם קָדְשְׁךָ נִשְׁבַּעְתָּ
לּוֹ שֶׁלֹּא יִכְבֶּה נֵרוֹ לְעוֹלָם וָעֶד. בָּרוּךְ אַתָּה יהוה, מָגֵן דָּוִד.

On שבת, add the words in parentheses:

עַל הַתּוֹרָה וְעַל הָעֲבוֹדָה וְעַל הַנְּבִיאִים (וְעַל יוֹם הַשַּׁבָּת הַזֶּה),
וְעַל יוֹם חַג הַשָּׁבוּעוֹת הַזֶּה שֶׁנָּתַתָּ לָּנוּ יהוה אֱלֹהֵינוּ (לִקְדֻשָּׁה
וְלִמְנוּחָה) לְשָׂשׂוֹן וּלְשִׂמְחָה, לְכָבוֹד וּלְתִפְאָרֶת. עַל הַכֹּל יהוה
אֱלֹהֵינוּ אֲנַחְנוּ מוֹדִים לָךְ וּמְבָרְכִים אוֹתָךְ, יִתְבָּרַךְ שִׁמְךָ בְּפִי
כָּל חַי תָּמִיד לְעוֹלָם וָעֶד. בָּרוּךְ אַתָּה יהוה, מְקַדֵּשׁ (הַשַּׁבָּת
וְ)יִשְׂרָאֵל וְהַזְּמַנִּים.

On a weekday, the service continues with the various prayers for government on page 495.

On the second day of שבועות, if also שבת, continue:

יְקוּם פֻּרְקָן מִן שְׁמַיָּא, חִנָּא וְחִסְדָּא וְרַחֲמֵי וְחַיֵּי אֲרִיכֵי וּמְזוֹנֵי
רְוִיחֵי, וְסִיַּעְתָּא דִשְׁמַיָּא, וּבַרְיוּת גּוּפָא וּנְהוֹרָא מְעַלְּיָא, זַרְעָא
חַיָּא וְקַיָּמָא, זַרְעָא דִּי לָא יִפְסֹק וְדִי לָא יִבְטַל מִפִּתְגָמֵי אוֹרַיְתָא,
לְמָרָנָן וְרַבָּנָן חֲבוּרָתָא קַדִּישָׁתָא דִּי בְאַרְעָא דְיִשְׂרָאֵל וְדִי בְבָבֶל,
לְרֵישֵׁי כַלָּה, וּלְרֵישֵׁי גָלְוָתָא, וּלְרֵישֵׁי מְתִיבָתָא, וּלְדַיָּנֵי דְבָבָא,
לְכָל תַּלְמִידֵיהוֹן, וּלְכָל תַּלְמִידֵי תַלְמִידֵיהוֹן, וּלְכָל מָאן דְּעָסְקִין
בְּאוֹרַיְתָא. מַלְכָּא דְעָלְמָא יְבָרֵךְ יָתְהוֹן, יַפֵּשׁ חַיֵּיהוֹן וְיַסְגֵּא
יוֹמֵיהוֹן, וְיִתֵּן אַרְכָא לִשְׁנֵיהוֹן, וְיִתְפָּרְקוּן וְיִשְׁתֵּיזְבוּן מִן כָּל עָקָא

יְקוּם פֻּרְקָן *May deliverance arise.* Two Aramaic prayers originating in
Babylon in the age of the Geonim (late sixth to early eleventh century)

delivered from all distress and illness. May our Master in heaven be their help at all times and seasons; and let us say: Amen.

יְקוּם פֻּרְקָן May deliverance arise from heaven, bringing grace, love and compassion, long life, ample sustenance and heavenly help, physical health and enlightenment of mind, living and thriving children who will neither interrupt nor cease from the words of the Torah – to all this holy congregation, great and small, women and children. May the King of the Universe bless you, prolonging your lives, increasing your days, and adding to your years. May you be redeemed and delivered from all distress and illness. May our Master in heaven be your help at all times and seasons; and let us say: Amen.

מִי שֶׁבֵּרַךְ May He who blessed our fathers, Abraham, Isaac and Jacob, bless all this holy congregation, together with all other holy congregations: them, their wives, their sons and daughters, and all that is theirs. May He bless those who unite to form synagogues for prayer and those who come there to pray; those who provide lamps for light and wine for Kiddush and Havdala, food for visitors and charity for the poor, and all who faithfully occupy themselves with the needs of the community. May the Holy One, blessed be He, give them their reward; may He remove from them all illness, grant them complete healing, and forgive all their sins. May He send blessing and success to all the work of their hands, together with all Israel their brethren; and let us say: Amen.

---

especially those who contribute by time or money to its upkeep. Just as the Tabernacle – the first collective house of worship of the Jewish people – was made from voluntary contributions, so Jewish communities and their religious, educational and welfare institutions have been sustained ever since by offerings "from everyone whose heart prompts them to give" (Ex. 25:2). These three prayers were instituted to be said on the Sabbath and are usually not said at other times.

וּמִן כָּל מַרְעִין בִּישִׁין. מָרַן דִּי בִשְׁמַיָּא יְהֵא בְסַעְדְּהוֹן כָּל זְמַן וְעִדָּן, וְנֹאמַר אָמֵן.

יְקוּם פֻּרְקָן מִן שְׁמַיָּא, חִנָּא וְחִסְדָּא וְרַחֲמֵי וְחַיֵּי אֲרִיכֵי וּמְזוֹנֵי רְוִיחֵי, וְסִיַּעְתָּא דִשְׁמַיָּא, וּבַרְיוּת גּוּפָא וּנְהוֹרָא מְעַלְיָא, זַרְעָא חַיָּא וְקַיָּמָא, זַרְעָא דִּי לָא יִפְסֹק וְדִי לָא יִבְטֻל מִפִּתְגָּמֵי אוֹרַיְתָא, לְכָל קְהָלָא קַדִּישָׁא הָדֵין, רַבְרְבַיָּא עִם זְעֵרַיָּא, טַפְלָא וּנְשַׁיָּא. מַלְכָּא דְעָלְמָא יְבָרֵךְ יָתְכוֹן, יַפֵּשׁ חַיֵּיכוֹן וְיַסְגֵּא יוֹמֵיכוֹן, וְיִתֵּן אַרְכָא לִשְׁנֵיכוֹן, וְתִתְפָּרְקוּן וְתִשְׁתֵּיזְבוּן מִן כָּל עָקָא וּמִן כָּל מַרְעִין בִּישִׁין. מָרַן דִּי בִשְׁמַיָּא יְהֵא בְסַעְדְּכוֹן כָּל זְמַן וְעִדָּן, וְנֹאמַר אָמֵן.

מִי שֶׁבֵּרַךְ אֲבוֹתֵינוּ אַבְרָהָם יִצְחָק וְיַעֲקֹב, הוּא יְבָרֵךְ אֶת כָּל הַקָּהָל הַקָּדוֹשׁ הַזֶּה עִם כָּל קְהִלּוֹת הַקֹּדֶשׁ, הֵם וּנְשֵׁיהֶם וּבְנֵיהֶם וּבְנוֹתֵיהֶם וְכֹל אֲשֶׁר לָהֶם, וּמִי שֶׁמְּיַחֲדִים בָּתֵּי כְנֵסִיּוֹת לִתְפִלָּה, וּמִי שֶׁבָּאִים בְּתוֹכָם לְהִתְפַּלֵּל, וּמִי שֶׁנּוֹתְנִים נֵר לַמָּאוֹר וְיַיִן לְקִדּוּשׁ וּלְהַבְדָּלָה וּפַת לְאוֹרְחִים וּצְדָקָה לַעֲנִיִּים, וְכָל מִי שֶׁעוֹסְקִים בְּצָרְכֵי צִבּוּר בֶּאֱמוּנָה. הַקָּדוֹשׁ בָּרוּךְ הוּא יְשַׁלֵּם שְׂכָרָם, וְיָסִיר מֵהֶם כָּל מַחֲלָה, וְיִרְפָּא לְכָל גּוּפָם, וְיִסְלַח לְכָל עֲוֹנָם, וְיִשְׁלַח בְּרָכָה וְהַצְלָחָה בְּכָל מַעֲשֵׂי יְדֵיהֶם עִם כָּל יִשְׂרָאֵל אֲחֵיהֶם, וְנֹאמַר אָמֵן.

"Leaders of communities in exile" were the lay-leaders, headed in Babylon by the Exilarch. The second prayer is for the welfare of the members of the congregation.

מִי שֶׁבֵּרַךְ *May He who blessed.* This third prayer, a Hebrew equivalent and expansion of the previous one, is for the members of the congregation,

The Prayer for the Welfare of the Canadian Government is on the next page.

PRAYER FOR THE WELFARE OF THE AMERICAN GOVERNMENT

The Leader says the following:

הַנּוֹתֵן תְּשׁוּעָה May He who gives salvation to kings and dominion to princes, whose kingdom is an everlasting kingdom, who delivers His servant David from the evil sword, who makes a way in the sea and a path through the mighty waters, bless and protect, guard and help, exalt, magnify and uplift the President, Vice President and all officials of this land. May the Supreme King of kings in His mercy put into their hearts and the hearts of all their counselors and officials, to deal kindly with us and all Israel. In their days and in ours, may Judah be saved and Israel dwell in safety, and may the Redeemer come to Zion. May this be His will, and let us say: Amen.

PRAYER FOR THE SAFETY OF THE AMERICAN MILITARY FORCES

The Leader says the following:

אַדִּיר בַּמָּרוֹם God on high who dwells in might, the King to whom peace belongs, look down from Your holy habitation and bless the soldiers of the American military forces who risk their lives for the sake of peace on earth. Be their shelter and stronghold, and let them not falter. Give them the strength and courage to thwart the plans of the enemy and end the rule of evil. May their enemies be scattered and their foes flee before them, and may they rejoice in Your salvation. Bring them back safely to their homes, as is written: "The LORD will guard you from all harm, He will guard your life. *Ps. 121* The LORD will guard your going and coming, now and for evermore." And may there be fulfilled for us the verse: "Nation shall *Is. 2* not lift up sword against nation, nor shall they learn war any more." Let all the inhabitants on earth know that sovereignty is Yours and Your name inspires awe over all You have created – and let us say: Amen.

The Prayer for the Welfare of the Canadian Government is on the next page.

תפילה לשלום המלכות

The שליח ציבור *says the following:*

הַנּוֹתֵן תְּשׁוּעָה לַמְּלָכִים וּמֶמְשָׁלָה לַנְּסִיכִים, מַלְכוּתוֹ מַלְכוּת כָּל עוֹלָמִים, הַפּוֹצֶה אֶת דָּוִד עַבְדּוֹ מֵחֶרֶב רָעָה, הַנּוֹתֵן בַּיָּם דֶּרֶךְ וּבְמַיִם עַזִּים נְתִיבָה, הוּא יְבָרֵךְ וְיִשְׁמֹר וְיִנְצֹר וְיַעֲזֹר וִירוֹמֵם וִיגַדֵּל וִינַשֵּׂא לְמַעְלָה אֶת הַנָּשִׂיא וְאֶת מִשְׁנֵהוּ וְאֶת כָּל שָׂרֵי הָאָרֶץ הַזֹּאת. מֶלֶךְ מַלְכֵי הַמְּלָכִים, בְּרַחֲמָיו יִתֵּן בְּלִבָּם וּבְלֵב כָּל יוֹעֲצֵיהֶם וְשָׂרֵיהֶם לַעֲשׂוֹת טוֹבָה עִמָּנוּ וְעִם כָּל יִשְׂרָאֵל. בִּימֵיהֶם וּבְיָמֵינוּ תִּוָּשַׁע יְהוּדָה, וְיִשְׂרָאֵל יִשְׁכֹּן לָבֶטַח, וּבָא לְצִיּוֹן גּוֹאֵל. וְכֵן יְהִי רָצוֹן, וְנֹאמַר אָמֵן.

תפילה לשלום חיילי צבא ארצות הברית

The שליח ציבור *says the following:*

אַדִּיר בַּמָּרוֹם שׁוֹכֵן בִּגְבוּרָה, מֶלֶךְ שֶׁהַשָּׁלוֹם שֶׁלּוֹ, הַשְׁקִיפָה מִמְּעוֹן קָדְשֶׁךָ, וּבָרֵךְ אֶת חַיָּלֵי צְבָא אַרְצוֹת הַבְּרִית, הַמְחָרְפִים נַפְשָׁם בְּלֶכְתָּם לָשִׂים שָׁלוֹם בָּאָרֶץ. הֱיֵה נָא לָהֶם מַחֲסֶה וּמָעוֹז, וְאַל תִּתֵּן לַמּוֹט רַגְלָם, חַזֵּק יְדֵיהֶם וְאַמֵּץ רוּחָם לְהָפֵר עֲצַת אוֹיֵב וּלְהַעֲבִיר מֶמְשֶׁלֶת זָדוֹן, יָפוּצוּ אוֹיְבֵיהֶם וְיָנוּסוּ מְשַׂנְאֵיהֶם מִפְּנֵיהֶם, וְיִשְׂמְחוּ בִּישׁוּעָתֶךָ. הֲשִׁיבֵם בְּשָׁלוֹם אֶל בֵּיתָם, כַּכָּתוּב בְּדִבְרֵי קָדְשֶׁךָ: יהוה יִשְׁמָרְךָ מִכָּל־רָע, יִשְׁמֹר אֶת־נַפְשֶׁךָ: יהוה יִשְׁמָר־צֵאתְךָ וּבוֹאֶךָ, מֵעַתָּה וְעַד־עוֹלָם: וְקַיֵּם בָּנוּ מִקְרָא שֶׁכָּתוּב: לֹא־יִשָּׂא גוֹי אֶל־גּוֹי חֶרֶב, וְלֹא־יִלְמְדוּ עוֹד מִלְחָמָה: וְיֵדְעוּ כָּל יוֹשְׁבֵי תֵבֵל כִּי לְךָ מְלוּכָה יָאָתָה, וְשִׁמְךָ נוֹרָא עַל כָּל מַה שֶּׁבָּרָאתָ. וְנֹאמַר אָמֵן.

תהלים קכא

ישעיה ב

PRAYER FOR THE WELFARE OF THE CANADIAN GOVERNMENT

The Leader says the following:

הַנּוֹתֵן תְּשׁוּעָה May He who gives salvation to kings and dominion to princes, whose kingdom is an everlasting kingdom, who delivers His servant David from the evil sword, who makes a way in the sea and a path through the mighty waters, bless and protect, guard and help, exalt, magnify and uplift the Prime Minister and all the elected and appointed officials of Canada. May the Supreme King of kings in His mercy put into their hearts and the hearts of all their counselors and officials, to deal kindly with us and all Israel. In their days and in ours, may Judah be saved and Israel dwell in safety, and may the Redeemer come to Zion. May this be His will, and let us say: Amen.

PRAYER FOR THE SAFETY OF THE CANADIAN FORCES

The Leader says the following:

אַדִּיר בַּמָּרוֹם God on high who dwells in might, the King to whom peace belongs, look down from Your holy habitation and bless the soldiers of the Canadian Forces who risk their lives for the sake of peace on earth. Be their shelter and stronghold, and let them not falter. Give them the strength and courage to thwart the plans of the enemy and end the rule of evil. May their enemies be scattered and their foes flee before them, and may they rejoice in Your salvation. Bring them back safely to their homes, as is written: "The LORD will guard you from all harm, He will guard *Ps. 121* your life. The LORD will guard your going and coming, now and for evermore." And may there be fulfilled for us the verse: "Nation *Is. 2* shall not lift up sword against nation, nor shall they learn war any more." Let all the inhabitants on earth know that sovereignty is Yours and Your name inspires awe over all You have created – and let us say: Amen.

תפילה לשלום המלכות

The *שליח ציבור* says the following:

הַנּוֹתֵן תְּשׁוּעָה לַמְּלָכִים וּמֶמְשָׁלָה לַנְּסִיכִים, מַלְכוּתוֹ מַלְכוּת כָּל
עוֹלָמִים, הַפּוֹצֶה אֶת דָּוִד עַבְדּוֹ מֵחֶרֶב רָעָה, הַנּוֹתֵן בַּיָּם דֶּרֶךְ
וּבְמַיִם עַזִּים נְתִיבָה, הוּא יְבָרֵךְ וְיִשְׁמֹר וְיִנְצֹר וְיַעֲזֹר וִירוֹמֵם וִיגַדֵּל
וִינַשֵּׂא לְמַעְלָה אֶת רֹאשׁ הַמֶּמְשָׁלָה וְאֶת כָּל שָׂרֵי הָאָרֶץ הַזֹּאת.
מֶלֶךְ מַלְכֵי הַמְּלָכִים, בְּרַחֲמָיו יִתֵּן בְּלִבָּם וּבְלֵב כָּל יוֹעֲצֵיהֶם
וְשָׂרֵיהֶם לַעֲשׂוֹת טוֹבָה עִמָּנוּ וְעִם כָּל יִשְׂרָאֵל. בִּימֵיהֶם וּבְיָמֵינוּ
תִּוָּשַׁע יְהוּדָה, וְיִשְׂרָאֵל יִשְׁכֹּן לָבֶטַח, וּבָא לְצִיּוֹן גּוֹאֵל. וְכֵן יְהִי
רָצוֹן, וְנֹאמַר אָמֵן.

תפילה לשלום חיילי צבא קנדה

The *שליח ציבור* says the following:

אַדִּיר בַּמָּרוֹם שׁוֹכֵן בִּגְבוּרָה, מֶלֶךְ שֶׁהַשָּׁלוֹם שֶׁלּוֹ, הַשְׁקִיפָה
מִמְּעוֹן קָדְשֶׁךָ, וּבָרֵךְ אֶת חַיְלֵי צְבָא קָנָדָה, הַמְחָרְפִים נַפְשָׁם
בְּלֶכְתָּם לָשִׂים שָׁלוֹם בָּאָרֶץ. הֱיֵה נָא לָהֶם מַחֲסֶה וּמָעוֹז, וְאַל
תִּתֵּן לַמּוֹט רַגְלָם, חַזֵּק יְדֵיהֶם וְאַמֵּץ רוּחָם לְהָפֵר עֲצַת אוֹיֵב
וּלְהַעֲבִיר מֶמְשֶׁלֶת זָדוֹן, יָפוּצוּ אוֹיְבֵיהֶם וְיָנוּסוּ מְשַׂנְאֵיהֶם
מִפְּנֵיהֶם, וְיִשְׂמְחוּ בִישׁוּעָתֶךָ. הֲשִׁיבֵם בְּשָׁלוֹם אֶל בֵּיתָם, כַּכָּתוּב
בְּדִבְרֵי קָדְשֶׁךָ: יהוה יִשְׁמָרְךָ מִכָּל־רָע, יִשְׁמֹר אֶת־נַפְשֶׁךָ: יהוה
יִשְׁמָר־צֵאתְךָ וּבוֹאֶךָ, מֵעַתָּה וְעַד־עוֹלָם: וְקַיֵּם בָּנוּ מִקְרָא
שֶׁכָּתוּב: לֹא־יִשָּׂא גוֹי אֶל־גּוֹי חֶרֶב, וְלֹא־יִלְמְדוּ עוֹד מִלְחָמָה:
וְיֵדְעוּ כָּל יוֹשְׁבֵי תֵבֵל כִּי לְךָ מְלוּכָה יָאָתָה, וְשִׁמְךָ נוֹרָא עַל כָּל
מַה שֶּׁבָּרָאתָ. וְנֹאמַר אָמֵן.

תהלים קכא

ישעיה ב

PRAYER FOR THE STATE OF ISRAEL

The Leader says the following prayer:

אָבִינוּ שֶׁבַּשָּׁמַיִם Heavenly Father, Israel's Rock and Redeemer, bless the State of Israel, the first flowering of our redemption. Shield it under the wings of Your loving-kindness and spread over it the Tabernacle of Your peace. Send Your light and truth to its leaders, ministers and counselors, and direct them with good counsel before You.

Strengthen the hands of the defenders of our Holy Land; grant them deliverance, our God, and crown them with the crown of victory. Grant peace in the land and everlasting joy to its inhabitants.

As for our brothers, the whole house of Israel, remember them in all the lands of our (*In Israel say:* their) dispersion, and swiftly lead us (*In Israel say:* them) upright to Zion Your city, and Jerusalem Your dwelling place, as is written in the Torah of Moses Your servant: "Even if you are scattered to the furthermost lands under the heavens, from there the LORD your God will gather you and take you back. The LORD your God will bring you to the land your ancestors possessed and you will possess it; and He will make you more prosperous and numerous than your ancestors. Then the LORD your God will open up your heart and the heart of your descendants, to love the LORD your God with all your heart and with all your soul, that you may live." *Deut. 30*

Unite our hearts to love and revere Your name and observe all the words of Your Torah, and swiftly send us Your righteous anointed one of the house of David, to redeem those who long for Your salvation.

Appear in Your glorious majesty over all the dwellers on earth, and let all who breathe declare: The LORD God of Israel is King and His kingship has dominion over all. Amen, Selah.

תפילה לשלום מדינת ישראל

The שליח ציבור *says the following prayer:*

אָבִינוּ שֶׁבַּשָּׁמַיִם, צוּר יִשְׂרָאֵל וְגוֹאֲלוֹ, בָּרֵךְ אֶת מְדִינַת יִשְׂרָאֵל,
רֵאשִׁית צְמִיחַת גְּאֻלָּתֵנוּ. הָגֵן עָלֶיהָ בְּאֶבְרַת חַסְדֶּךָ וּפְרֹשׂ עָלֶיהָ
סֻכַּת שְׁלוֹמֶךָ, וּשְׁלַח אוֹרְךָ וַאֲמִתְּךָ לְרָאשֶׁיהָ, שָׂרֶיהָ וְיוֹעֲצֶיהָ,
וְתַקְּנֵם בְּעֵצָה טוֹבָה מִלְּפָנֶיךָ.

חַזֵּק אֶת יְדֵי מְגִנֵּי אֶרֶץ קָדְשֵׁנוּ, וְהַנְחִילֵם אֱלֹהֵינוּ יְשׁוּעָה וַעֲטֶרֶת
נִצָּחוֹן תְּעַטְּרֵם, וְנָתַתָּ שָׁלוֹם בָּאָרֶץ וְשִׂמְחַת עוֹלָם לְיוֹשְׁבֶיהָ.

וְאֶת אַחֵינוּ כָּל בֵּית יִשְׂרָאֵל, פְּקָד נָא בְּכָל אַרְצוֹת פְּזוּרֵינוּ,
וְתוֹלִיכֵנוּ / בארץ ישראל: פְּזוּרֵיהֶם, וְתוֹלִיכֵם/ מְהֵרָה קוֹמְמִיּוּת לְצִיּוֹן
עִירֶךָ וְלִירוּשָׁלַיִם מִשְׁכַּן שְׁמֶךָ, כַּכָּתוּב בְּתוֹרַת מֹשֶׁה עַבְדֶּךָ:
אִם־יִהְיֶה נִדַּחֲךָ בִּקְצֵה הַשָּׁמָיִם, מִשָּׁם יְקַבֶּצְךָ יהוה אֱלֹהֶיךָ
וּמִשָּׁם יִקָּחֶךָ: וֶהֱבִיאֲךָ יהוה אֱלֹהֶיךָ אֶל־הָאָרֶץ אֲשֶׁר־יָרְשׁוּ
אֲבֹתֶיךָ וִירִשְׁתָּהּ, וְהֵיטִבְךָ וְהִרְבְּךָ מֵאֲבֹתֶיךָ: וּמָל יהוה אֱלֹהֶיךָ
אֶת־לְבָבְךָ וְאֶת־לְבַב זַרְעֶךָ, לְאַהֲבָה אֶת־יהוה אֱלֹהֶיךָ בְּכָל־
לְבָבְךָ וּבְכָל־נַפְשְׁךָ, לְמַעַן חַיֶּיךָ:

דברים ל

וְיַחֵד לְבָבֵנוּ לְאַהֲבָה וּלְיִרְאָה אֶת שְׁמֶךָ, וְלִשְׁמֹר אֶת כָּל דִּבְרֵי
תוֹרָתֶךָ, וּשְׁלַח לָנוּ מְהֵרָה בֶּן דָּוִד מְשִׁיחַ צִדְקֶךָ, לִפְדּוֹת מְחַכֵּי
קֵץ יְשׁוּעָתֶךָ.

וְהוֹפַע בַּהֲדַר גְּאוֹן עֻזֶּךָ עַל כָּל יוֹשְׁבֵי תֵבֵל אַרְצֶךָ וְיֹאמַר כֹּל
אֲשֶׁר נְשָׁמָה בְאַפּוֹ, יהוה אֱלֹהֵי יִשְׂרָאֵל מֶלֶךְ וּמַלְכוּתוֹ בַּכֹּל
מָשָׁלָה, אָמֵן סֶלָה.

PRAYER FOR ISRAEL'S DEFENSE FORCES

The Leader says the following prayer:

מִי שֶׁבֵּרַךְ May He who blessed our ancestors, Abraham, Isaac and Jacob, bless the members of Israel's Defense Forces and its security services who stand guard over our land and the cities of our God from the Lebanese border to the Egyptian desert, from the Mediterranean sea to the approach of the Aravah, and wherever else they are, on land, in air and at sea. May the LORD make the enemies who rise against us be struck down before them. May the Holy One, blessed be He, protect and deliver them from all trouble and distress, affliction and illness, and send blessing and success to all the work of their hands. May He subdue our enemies under them and crown them with deliverance and victory. And may there be fulfilled in them the verse, "It is   *Deut. 20* the LORD your God who goes with you to fight for you against your enemies, to deliver you." And let us say: Amen.

PRAYER FOR THOSE BEING HELD IN CAPTIVITY

If Israeli soldiers or civilians are being held in captivity, the Leader says the following:

מִי שֶׁבֵּרַךְ May He who blessed our ancestors, Abraham, Isaac and Jacob, Joseph, Moses and Aaron, David and Solomon, bless, protect and guard the members of Israel's Defense Forces missing in action or held captive, and other captives among our brethren, the whole house of Israel, who are in distress or captivity, as we, the members of this holy congregation, pray on their behalf. May the Holy One, blessed be He, have compassion on them and bring them out from darkness and the shadow of death; may He break their bonds, deliver them from their distress, and bring them swiftly back to their families' embrace. Give   *Ps. 107* thanks to the LORD for His loving-kindness and for the wonders He does for the children of men; and may there be fulfilled in them the verse: "Those redeemed by the LORD will return; they will enter Zion   *Is. 35* with singing, and everlasting joy will crown their heads. Gladness and joy will overtake them, and sorrow and sighing will flee away." And let us say: Amen.

מִי שֶׁבֵּרַךְ לְחַיָּלֵי צָהַ"ל

The שליח ציבור says the following prayer:

מִי שֶׁבֵּרַךְ אֲבוֹתֵינוּ אַבְרָהָם יִצְחָק וְיַעֲקֹב הוּא יְבָרֵךְ אֶת חַיָּלֵי
צְבָא הַהֲגָנָּה לְיִשְׂרָאֵל וְאַנְשֵׁי כֹּחוֹת הַבִּטָּחוֹן, הָעוֹמְדִים עַל
מִשְׁמַר אַרְצֵנוּ וְעָרֵי אֱלֹהֵינוּ, מִגְּבוּל הַלְּבָנוֹן וְעַד מִדְבַּר מִצְרַיִם
וּמִן הַיָּם הַגָּדוֹל עַד לְבוֹא הָעֲרָבָה וּבְכָל מָקוֹם שֶׁהֵם, בַּיַּבָּשָׁה,
בָּאֲוִיר וּבַיָּם. יִתֵּן יהוה אֶת אוֹיְבֵינוּ הַקָּמִים עָלֵינוּ נִגָּפִים לִפְנֵיהֶם.
הַקָּדוֹשׁ בָּרוּךְ הוּא יִשְׁמֹר וְיַצִּיל אֶת חַיָּלֵינוּ מִכָּל צָרָה וְצוּקָה
וּמִכָּל נֶגַע וּמַחֲלָה, וְיִשְׁלַח בְּרָכָה וְהַצְלָחָה בְּכָל מַעֲשֵׂי יְדֵיהֶם.
יַדְבֵּר שׂוֹנְאֵינוּ תַּחְתֵּיהֶם וִיעַטְּרֵם בְּכֶתֶר יְשׁוּעָה וּבַעֲטֶרֶת נִצָּחוֹן.
וִיקֻיַּם בָּהֶם הַכָּתוּב: כִּי יהוה אֱלֹהֵיכֶם הַהֹלֵךְ עִמָּכֶם לְהִלָּחֵם
לָכֶם עִם־אֹיְבֵיכֶם לְהוֹשִׁיעַ אֶתְכֶם: וְנֹאמַר אָמֵן.

דברים כ

מִי שֶׁבֵּרַךְ לַשְּׁבוּיִים

If Israeli soldiers or civilians are being held in captivity, the שליח ציבור says the following:

מִי שֶׁבֵּרַךְ אֲבוֹתֵינוּ אַבְרָהָם יִצְחָק וְיַעֲקֹב, יוֹסֵף מֹשֶׁה וְאַהֲרֹן,
דָּוִד וּשְׁלֹמֹה, הוּא יְבָרֵךְ וְיִשְׁמֹר וְיִנְצֹר אֶת נְעֻדְרֵי צְבָא הַהֲגָנָּה
לְיִשְׂרָאֵל וּשְׁבוּיָיו, וְאֶת כָּל אַחֵינוּ הַנְּתוּנִים בְּצָרָה וּבְשִׁבְיָה,
בַּעֲבוּר שֶׁכָּל הַקָּהָל הַקָּדוֹשׁ הַזֶּה מִתְפַּלֵּל בַּעֲבוּרָם. הַקָּדוֹשׁ
בָּרוּךְ הוּא יִמָּלֵא רַחֲמִים עֲלֵיהֶם, וְיוֹצִיאֵם מֵחֹשֶׁךְ וְצַלְמָוֶת,
וּמוֹסְרוֹתֵיהֶם יְנַתֵּק, וּמִמְּצוּקוֹתֵיהֶם יוֹשִׁיעֵם, וִישִׁיבֵם מְהֵרָה
לְחֵיק מִשְׁפְּחוֹתֵיהֶם. יוֹדוּ לַיהוה חַסְדּוֹ וְנִפְלְאוֹתָיו לִבְנֵי אָדָם:
וִיקֻיַּם בָּהֶם מִקְרָא שֶׁכָּתוּב: וּפְדוּיֵי יהוה יְשֻׁבוּן, וּבָאוּ צִיּוֹן
בְּרִנָּה, וְשִׂמְחַת עוֹלָם עַל־רֹאשָׁם, שָׂשׂוֹן וְשִׂמְחָה יַשִּׂיגוּ, וְנָסוּ יָגוֹן
וַאֲנָחָה: וְנֹאמַר אָמֵן.

תהלים קז

ישעיה לה

YIZKOR

On the second day of Shavuot (in Israel on the first), the Yizkor (memorial) service is said.
In some communities, those who have not been bereaved of a parent or
close relative do not participate in the service, but leave the synagogue
and return for "Father of compassion" on page 508.

יהוה LORD, what is man that You care for him, a mortal that You notice him?   *Ps. 144*
Man is like a fleeting breath, his days like a passing shadow.

In the morning he flourishes and grows;   *Ps. 90*
   in the evening he withers and dries up.
Teach us to number our days, that we may get a heart of wisdom.
Mark the blameless, note the upright, for the end of such a person is peace.   *Ps. 37*
God will redeem my soul from the grave, for He will receive me, Selah.   *Ps. 49*
My flesh and my heart may fail,   *Ps. 73*
   but God is the strength of my heart and my portion for ever.
The dust returns to the earth as it was,   *Eccl. 12*
   but the spirit returns to God who gave it.

---

for the sake of the future. This can be seen in the three cases in which the word *Yizkor* appears in connection with God in Genesis. God "remembered Noah" (8:1) and brought him out onto dry land. God "remembered Abraham" (19:29) and rescued his nephew Lot from the destruction of Sodom. God "remembered Rachel" (30:22) and gave her a child. In each case the act of remembering was for the sake of the future and of life.

Judaism gave two majestic ideas their greatest religious expression: *memory* and *hope*. Memory is our living connection to those who came before us. Hope is what we hand on to the generations yet to come. Those we remember live on in us: in words, gestures, a smile here, an act of kindness there, that we would not have done had that person not left their mark on our lives. That is what *Yizkor* is: memory as a religious act of thanksgiving for a life that was, and that still sends its echoes and reverberations into the life that is. For when Jews remember, they do so for the future, the place where, if we are faithful to it, the past never dies.

PRAYER FOR LIVING RELATIVES
Our Father in heaven: On this holy day, I give You thanks for my [father / mother / husband / wife / brother(s) / sister(s) / son(s) / daughter(s) / grandchild(ren)] who are with me in life, and for whose continued health and blessing I pray. Be with them, I pray You, in the days and months to come. Protect them from harm and distress, sickness and affliction, trouble

סדר הזכרת נשמות

On the second day of שבועות *(in* ארץ ישראל *on the first), the* יזכור *(memorial) service is said.*
In some communities, those who have not been bereaved of a parent or close relative do not
participate in the service, but leave the בית כנסת *and return for* אב הרחמים *on page 509.*

תהלים קמד

יהוה מָה־אָדָם וַתֵּדָעֵהוּ, בֶּן־אֱנוֹשׁ וַתְּחַשְּׁבֵהוּ:

אָדָם לַהֶבֶל דָּמָה, יָמָיו כְּצֵל עוֹבֵר:

תהלים צ

בַּבְּקֶר יָצִיץ וְחָלָף, לָעֶרֶב יְמוֹלֵל וְיָבֵשׁ:

לִמְנוֹת יָמֵינוּ כֵּן הוֹדַע, וְנָבִא לְבַב חָכְמָה:

תהלים לז

שְׁמָר־תָּם וּרְאֵה יָשָׁר, כִּי־אַחֲרִית לְאִישׁ שָׁלוֹם:

תהלים מט

אַךְ־אֱלֹהִים יִפְדֶּה נַפְשִׁי מִיַּד שְׁאוֹל, כִּי יִקָּחֵנִי סֶלָה:

תהלים עג

פָּלָה שְׁאֵרִי וּלְבָבִי, צוּר־לְבָבִי וְחֶלְקִי אֱלֹהִים לְעוֹלָם:

קהלת יב

וְיָשֹׁב הֶעָפָר עַל־הָאָרֶץ כְּשֶׁהָיָה, וְהָרוּחַ תָּשׁוּב אֶל־הָאֱלֹהִים אֲשֶׁר נְתָנָהּ:

YIZKOR

From the eleventh century onward it has become customary to pray, at key moments in the year, for the souls of the departed. At first, this prayer was said only on Yom Kippur, but it was soon extended to the last days of the other festivals.

The formal name for this prayer is *Hazkarat Neshamot*, "the Remembrance of Souls," but it became popularly known as *Yizkor* because of the first word of the memorial prayer. Remembrance holds a special place in the Jewish soul. Jews were the first people to regard remembering as a religious duty. The verb "to remember" in one or other of its forms occurs 169 times in Tanakh.

At *Yizkor*, our memory reaches out to that of God. We ask Him to remember those of our family who are no longer here. We ask Him to look on the good we do, for it is because of their influence on us that we are in the synagogue; that we pray, and that we try to do good in this life. Hence it is a custom to donate a sum to charity at this time and dedicate it to the memory and merit of the departed ones. Nowadays, we also add prayers for the Jewish martyrs of the past and for the victims of the Holocaust, as well as those who went to their deaths defending the State of Israel, for we collectively are the guardians of their memory. A connection is thus made between the dead and the living. We remember them, and with God's help, their virtues live on in us. That is as much of immortality as we can know in the land of the living.

In Judaism we remember not just for the past but also, and especially,

יָשַׁב He who lives in the shelter of the Most High dwells in the shadow of the *Ps. 91*
Almighty. I say of the LORD, my Refuge and Stronghold, my God in whom I
trust, that He will save you from the fowler's snare and the deadly pestilence.
With His pinions He will cover you, and beneath His wings you will find shelter; His faithfulness is an encircling shield. You need not fear terror by night,
nor the arrow that flies by day; not the pestilence that stalks in darkness, nor
the plague that ravages at noon. A thousand may fall at your side, ten thousand
at your right hand, but it will not come near you. You will only look with your
eyes and see the punishment of the wicked. Because you said, "the LORD is
my Refuge," taking the Most High as your shelter, no harm will befall you,
no plague will come near your tent, for He will command His angels about
you, to guard you in all your ways. They will lift you in their hands, lest your
foot stumble on a stone. You will tread on lions and vipers; you will trample
on young lions and snakes. [God says:] "Because he loves Me, I will rescue
him; I will protect him, because he acknowledges My name. When he calls
on Me, I will answer him; I will be with him in distress, I will deliver him and
bring him honor. With long life I will satisfy him and show him My salvation.
With long life I will satisfy him and show him My salvation.

For one's father:

יִזְכּוֹר May God remember the soul of my father, my teacher (*name* son
of *father's name*) who has gone to his eternal home, and to this I pledge
(without formal vow) to give charity on his behalf, that his soul may be
bound in the bond of everlasting life together with the souls of Abraham,
Isaac and Jacob, Sarah, Rebecca, Rachel and Leah, and all the other
righteous men and women in the Garden of Eden, and let us say: Amen.

For one's mother:

יִזְכּוֹר May God remember the soul of my mother, my teacher (*name*
daughter of *father's name*) who has gone to her eternal home, and to
this I pledge (without formal vow) to give charity on her behalf, that
her soul may be bound in the bond of everlasting life together with the
souls of Abraham, Isaac and Jacob, Sarah, Rebecca, Rachel and Leah,
and all the other righteous men and women in the Garden of Eden, and
let us say: Amen.

the words of my mouth and the meditation of my heart find favor before You,
my Rock and Redeemer.

יֹשֵׁב בְּסֵתֶר עֶלְיוֹן, בְּצֵל שַׁדַּי יִתְלוֹנָן: אֹמַר לַיהוה מַחְסִי וּמְצוּדָתִי, אֱלֹהַי אֶבְטַח־בּוֹ: כִּי הוּא יַצִּילְךָ מִפַּח יָקוּשׁ, מִדֶּבֶר הַוּוֹת: בְּאֶבְרָתוֹ יָסֶךְ לָךְ, וְתַחַת־כְּנָפָיו תֶּחְסֶה, צִנָּה וְסֹחֵרָה אֲמִתּוֹ: לֹא־תִירָא מִפַּחַד לָיְלָה, מֵחֵץ יָעוּף יוֹמָם: מִדֶּבֶר בָּאֹפֶל יַהֲלֹךְ, מִקֶּטֶב יָשׁוּד צָהֳרָיִם: יִפֹּל מִצִּדְּךָ אֶלֶף, וּרְבָבָה מִימִינֶךָ, אֵלֶיךָ לֹא יִגָּשׁ: רַק בְּעֵינֶיךָ תַבִּיט, וְשִׁלֻּמַת רְשָׁעִים תִּרְאֶה: כִּי־אַתָּה יהוה מַחְסִי, עֶלְיוֹן שַׂמְתָּ מְעוֹנֶךָ: לֹא־תְאֻנֶּה אֵלֶיךָ רָעָה, וְנֶגַע לֹא־יִקְרַב בְּאָהֳלֶךָ: כִּי מַלְאָכָיו יְצַוֶּה־לָּךְ, לִשְׁמָרְךָ בְּכָל־דְּרָכֶיךָ: עַל־כַּפַּיִם יִשָּׂאוּנְךָ, פֶּן־תִּגֹּף בָּאֶבֶן רַגְלֶךָ: עַל־שַׁחַל וָפֶתֶן תִּדְרֹךְ, תִּרְמֹס כְּפִיר וְתַנִּין: כִּי בִי חָשַׁק וַאֲפַלְּטֵהוּ, אֲשַׂגְּבֵהוּ כִּי־יָדַע שְׁמִי: יִקְרָאֵנִי וְאֶעֱנֵהוּ, עִמּוֹ־אָנֹכִי בְצָרָה, אֲחַלְּצֵהוּ וַאֲכַבְּדֵהוּ: אֹרֶךְ יָמִים אַשְׂבִּיעֵהוּ, וְאַרְאֵהוּ בִּישׁוּעָתִי: אֹרֶךְ יָמִים אַשְׂבִּיעֵהוּ, וְאַרְאֵהוּ בִּישׁוּעָתִי:

For one's father:

יִזְכֹּר אֱלֹהִים נִשְׁמַת אָבִי מוֹרִי (פלוני בֶּן פלוני) שֶׁהָלַךְ לְעוֹלָמוֹ, בַּעֲבוּר שֶׁבְּלִי נֶדֶר אֶתֵּן צְדָקָה בַּעֲדוֹ. בִּשְׂכַר זֶה תְּהֵא נַפְשׁוֹ צְרוּרָה בִּצְרוֹר הַחַיִּים עִם נִשְׁמוֹת אַבְרָהָם יִצְחָק וְיַעֲקֹב, שָׂרָה רִבְקָה רָחֵל וְלֵאָה, וְעִם שְׁאָר צַדִּיקִים וְצִדְקָנִיּוֹת שֶׁבְּגַן עֵדֶן, וְנֹאמַר אָמֵן.

For one's mother:

יִזְכֹּר אֱלֹהִים נִשְׁמַת אִמִּי מוֹרָתִי (פלונית בַּת פלוני) שֶׁהָלְכָה לְעוֹלָמָהּ, בַּעֲבוּר שֶׁבְּלִי נֶדֶר אֶתֵּן צְדָקָה בַּעֲדָהּ. בִּשְׂכַר זֶה תְּהֵא נַפְשָׁהּ צְרוּרָה בִּצְרוֹר הַחַיִּים עִם נִשְׁמוֹת אַבְרָהָם יִצְחָק וְיַעֲקֹב, שָׂרָה רִבְקָה רָחֵל וְלֵאָה, וְעִם שְׁאָר צַדִּיקִים וְצִדְקָנִיּוֹת שֶׁבְּגַן עֵדֶן, וְנֹאמַר אָמֵן.

and misfortune. Spread over them Your canopy of peace and may Your spirit live in the work of their hands. Prolong their days in goodness and happiness and may they and we have the privilege of seeing children and grandchildren occupying themselves with Torah and the life of the commandments. May

For martyrs:

יִזְכּוֹר May God remember the soul of (*name, son/daughter of father's name*), and the souls of all my relatives, on my father's or mother's side, who were killed, murdered, slaughtered, burned, drowned or strangled for the sanctification of God's name, and to this I pledge (without formal vow) to give charity in their memory. May their souls be bound in the bond of everlasting life together with the souls of Abraham, Isaac and Jacob, Sarah, Rebecca, Rachel and Leah, and all the other righteous men and women in the Garden of Eden, and let us say: Amen.

For a male close relative:

אֵל מָלֵא רַחֲמִים God, full of mercy, who dwells on high, grant fitting rest on the wings of the Divine Presence, in the heights of the holy and the pure who shine like the radiance of heaven, to the soul of (*name son of father's name*) who has gone to his eternal home, and to this I pledge (without formal vow) to give charity in his memory, may his resting place be in the Garden of Eden. Therefore, Master of compassion, shelter him in the shadow of Your wings forever and bind his soul in the bond of everlasting life. The LORD is his heritage; may he rest in peace, and let us say: Amen.

For a female close relative:

אֵל מָלֵא רַחֲמִים God, full of mercy, who dwells on high, grant fitting rest on the wings of the Divine Presence, in the heights of the holy and the pure who shine like the radiance of heaven, to the soul of (*name daughter of father's name*) who has gone to her eternal home, and to this I pledge (without formal vow) to give charity in her memory, may her resting place be in the Garden of Eden. Therefore, Master of compassion, shelter her in the shadow of Your wings forever and bind her soul in the bond of everlasting life. The LORD is her heritage; may she rest in peace, and let us say: Amen.

For the Israeli soldiers:

אֵל מָלֵא רַחֲמִים God, full of mercy, who dwells on high, grant fitting rest on the wings of the Divine Presence, in the heights of the holy, the pure and the brave, who shine like the radiance of heaven, to the souls of the holy ones who fought in any of Israel's battles, in clandestine operations and in Israel's Defense Forces, who fell in battle and sacrificed their lives for the consecration of God's name, for the people and the land, and for this we pray for the ascent of their souls. Therefore, Master of compassion, shelter them in the shadow of Your wings forever, and bind their souls in the bond

For martyrs:

יִזְכֹּר אֱלֹהִים נִשְׁמַת (male פלוני בֶּן פלוני / female פלונית בַּת פלוני) וְנִשְׁמוֹת כָּל קְרוֹבַי
וּקְרוֹבוֹתַי, הֵן מִצַּד אָבִי הֵן מִצַּד אִמִּי, שֶׁהוּמְתוּ וְשֶׁנֶּהֶרְגוּ וְשֶׁנִּשְׁחֲטוּ
וְשֶׁנִּשְׂרְפוּ וְשֶׁנִּטְבְּעוּ וְשֶׁנֶּחְנְקוּ עַל קִדּוּשׁ הַשֵּׁם, בַּעֲבוּר שֶׁבְּלִי נֶדֶר אֶתֵּן
צְדָקָה בְּעַד הַזְכָּרַת נִשְׁמוֹתֵיהֶם. בִּשְׂכַר זֶה תִּהְיֶינָה נַפְשׁוֹתֵיהֶם צְרוּרוֹת
בִּצְרוֹר הַחַיִּים עִם נִשְׁמוֹת אַבְרָהָם יִצְחָק וְיַעֲקֹב, שָׂרָה רִבְקָה רָחֵל
וְלֵאָה, וְעִם שְׁאָר צַדִּיקִים וְצִדְקָנִיּוֹת שֶׁבְּגַן עֵדֶן, וְנֹאמַר אָמֵן.

For a male close relative:

אֵל מָלֵא רַחֲמִים, שׁוֹכֵן בַּמְּרוֹמִים, הַמְצֵא מְנוּחָה נְכוֹנָה עַל כַּנְפֵי
הַשְּׁכִינָה, בְּמַעֲלוֹת קְדוֹשִׁים וּטְהוֹרִים, כְּזֹהַר הָרָקִיעַ מַזְהִירִים, לְנִשְׁמַת
(פלוני בֶּן פלוני) שֶׁהָלַךְ לְעוֹלָמוֹ, בַּעֲבוּר שֶׁבְּלִי נֶדֶר אֶתֵּן צְדָקָה בְּעַד הַזְכָּרַת
נִשְׁמָתוֹ, בְּגַן עֵדֶן תְּהֵא מְנוּחָתוֹ. לָכֵן, בַּעַל הָרַחֲמִים יַסְתִּירֵהוּ בְּסֵתֶר
כְּנָפָיו לְעוֹלָמִים, וְיִצְרוֹר בִּצְרוֹר הַחַיִּים אֶת נִשְׁמָתוֹ, יהוה הוּא נַחֲלָתוֹ,
וְיָנוּחַ בְּשָׁלוֹם עַל מִשְׁכָּבוֹ, וְנֹאמַר אָמֵן.

For a female close relative:

אֵל מָלֵא רַחֲמִים, שׁוֹכֵן בַּמְּרוֹמִים, הַמְצֵא מְנוּחָה נְכוֹנָה עַל כַּנְפֵי
הַשְּׁכִינָה, בְּמַעֲלוֹת קְדוֹשִׁים וּטְהוֹרִים, כְּזֹהַר הָרָקִיעַ מַזְהִירִים, לְנִשְׁמַת
(פלונית בַּת פלוני) שֶׁהָלְכָה לְעוֹלָמָהּ, בַּעֲבוּר שֶׁבְּלִי נֶדֶר אֶתֵּן צְדָקָה בְּעַד
הַזְכָּרַת נִשְׁמָתָהּ, בְּגַן עֵדֶן תְּהֵא מְנוּחָתָהּ. לָכֵן, בַּעַל הָרַחֲמִים יַסְתִּירָהּ
בְּסֵתֶר כְּנָפָיו לְעוֹלָמִים, וְיִצְרוֹר בִּצְרוֹר הַחַיִּים אֶת נִשְׁמָתָהּ, יהוה הוּא
נַחֲלָתָהּ, וְתָנוּחַ בְּשָׁלוֹם עַל מִשְׁכָּבָהּ, וְנֹאמַר אָמֵן.

For the Israeli soldiers:

אֵל מָלֵא רַחֲמִים, שׁוֹכֵן בַּמְּרוֹמִים, הַמְצֵא מְנוּחָה נְכוֹנָה עַל כַּנְפֵי
הַשְּׁכִינָה, בְּמַעֲלוֹת קְדוֹשִׁים טְהוֹרִים וְגִבּוֹרִים, כְּזֹהַר הָרָקִיעַ מַזְהִירִים,
לְנִשְׁמוֹת הַקְּדוֹשִׁים שֶׁנִּלְחֲמוּ בְּכָל מַעַרְכוֹת יִשְׂרָאֵל, בַּמַּחְתֶּרֶת וּבִצְבָא
הַהֲגָנָה לְיִשְׂרָאֵל, וְשֶׁנָּפְלוּ בְּמִלְחַמְתָּם וּמָסְרוּ נַפְשָׁם עַל קְדֻשַּׁת הַשֵּׁם,
הָעָם וְהָאָרֶץ, בַּעֲבוּר שֶׁאָנוּ מִתְפַּלְּלִים לְעִלּוּי נִשְׁמוֹתֵיהֶם. לָכֵן, בַּעַל

of everlasting life. The LORD is their heritage; may the Garden of Eden be their resting place, may they rest in peace, may their merit stand for all Israel, and may they receive their reward at the End of Days, and let us say: Amen.

For the Holocaust victims:

אֵל מָלֵא רַחֲמִים God, full of mercy, Justice of widows and Father of orphans, please do not be silent and hold Your peace for the blood of Israel that was shed like water. Grant fitting rest on the wings of the Divine Presence, in the heights of the holy and the pure who shine and radiate light like the radiance of heaven, to the souls of the millions of Jews, men, women and children, who were murdered, slaughtered, burned, strangled, and buried alive, in the lands touched by the German enemy and its followers. They were all holy and pure; among them were great scholars and righteous individuals, cedars of Lebanon and noble masters of Torah, may the Garden of Eden be their resting place. Therefore, Master of compassion, shelter them in the shadow of Your wings forever, and bind their souls in the bond of everlasting life. The LORD is their heritage; may they rest in peace, and let us say: Amen.

Congregation and Leader:

אַב הָרַחֲמִים Father of compassion, who dwells on high: may He remember in His compassion the pious, the upright and the blameless – holy communities who sacrificed their lives for the sanctification of God's name. Lovely and pleasant in their lives, in death they were not parted. They were swifter than eagles and stronger than lions to do the will of their Maker and the desire of their Creator. O our God, remember them for good with the other righteous of the world, and may He exact retribution for the shed blood of His servants, as it is written in the Torah of Moses, the man of God: "O nations, acclaim *Deut. 32* His people, for He will avenge the blood of His servants, wreak vengeance on His foes, and make clean His people's land." And by Your servants, the prophets, it is written: "I shall cleanse their blood which I have not yet *Joel 4* cleansed, says the LORD who dwells in Zion." And in the holy Writings it says: "Why should the nations say: Where is their God? Before our eyes, may *Ps. 79* those nations know that You avenge the shed blood of Your servants." And it also says: "For the Avenger of blood remembers them and does not forget the *Ps. 9* cry of the afflicted." And it further says: "He will execute judgment among *Ps. 110* the nations, filled with the dead, crushing rulers far and wide. From the brook by the wayside he will drink, then he will hold his head high."

הָרַחֲמִים יַסְתִּירֵם בְּסֵתֶר כְּנָפָיו לְעוֹלָמִים, וְיִצְרֹר בִּצְרוֹר הַחַיִּים אֶת
נִשְׁמוֹתֵיהֶם, יהוה הוּא נַחֲלָתָם, בְּגַן עֵדֶן תְּהֵא מְנוּחָתָם, וְיָנוּחוּ בְשָׁלוֹם
עַל מִשְׁכְּבוֹתֵיהֶם וְתַעֲמֹד לְכָל יִשְׂרָאֵל זְכוּתָם, וְיַעַמְדוּ לְגוֹרָלָם לְקֵץ
הַיָּמִין, וְנֹאמַר אָמֵן.

For the Holocaust victims:

אֵל מָלֵא רַחֲמִים, דִּין אַלְמָנוֹת וַאֲבִי יְתוֹמִים, אַל נָא תֶחֱשֶׁה וְתִתְאַפַּק
לְדַם יִשְׂרָאֵל שֶׁנִּשְׁפַּךְ כַּמָּיִם. הַמְצֵא מְנוּחָה נְכוֹנָה עַל כַּנְפֵי הַשְּׁכִינָה,
בְּמַעֲלוֹת קְדוֹשִׁים וּטְהוֹרִים, כְּזֹהַר הָרָקִיעַ מְאִירִים וּמַזְהִירִים,
לְנִשְׁמוֹתֵיהֶם שֶׁל רִבְבוֹת אַלְפֵי יִשְׂרָאֵל, אֲנָשִׁים וְנָשִׁים, יְלָדִים וִילָדוֹת,
שֶׁנֶּהֶרְגוּ וְנִשְׁחֲטוּ וְנִשְׂרְפוּ וְנֶחְנְקוּ וְנִקְבְּרוּ חַיִּים, בָּאֲרָצוֹת אֲשֶׁר נָגְעָה
בָהֶן יַד הַצּוֹרֵר הַגֶּרְמָנִי וּגְרוּרָיו. כֻּלָּם קְדוֹשִׁים וּטְהוֹרִים, וּבָהֶם גְּאוֹנִים
וְצַדִּיקִים, אַרְזֵי הַלְּבָנוֹן אַדִּירֵי הַתּוֹרָה. בְּגַן עֵדֶן תְּהֵא מְנוּחָתָם. לָכֵן,
בַּעַל הָרַחֲמִים יַסְתִּירֵם בְּסֵתֶר כְּנָפָיו לְעוֹלָמִים, וְיִצְרֹר בִּצְרוֹר הַחַיִּים אֶת
נִשְׁמָתָם, יהוה הוּא נַחֲלָתָם, וְיָנוּחוּ בְשָׁלוֹם עַל מִשְׁכָּבָם, וְנֹאמַר אָמֵן.

The קהל *and the* שליח ציבור:

אַב הָרַחֲמִים שׁוֹכֵן מְרוֹמִים, בְּרַחֲמָיו הָעֲצוּמִים הוּא יִפְקֹד בְּרַחֲמִים
הַחֲסִידִים וְהַיְשָׁרִים וְהַתְּמִימִים, קְהִלּוֹת הַקֹּדֶשׁ שֶׁמָּסְרוּ נַפְשָׁם עַל קְדֻשַּׁת
הַשֵּׁם, הַנֶּאֱהָבִים וְהַנְּעִימִים בְּחַיֵּיהֶם, וּבְמוֹתָם לֹא נִפְרָדוּ, מִנְּשָׁרִים קַלּוּ
וּמֵאֲרָיוֹת גָּבֵרוּ לַעֲשׂוֹת רְצוֹן קוֹנָם וְחֵפֶץ צוּרָם. יִזְכְּרֵם אֱלֹהֵינוּ לְטוֹבָה
עִם שְׁאָר צַדִּיקֵי עוֹלָם, וְיִנְקֹם לְעֵינֵינוּ נִקְמַת דַּם עֲבָדָיו הַשָּׁפוּךְ, כַּכָּתוּב
דברים לב בְּתוֹרַת מֹשֶׁה אִישׁ הָאֱלֹהִים, הַרְנִינוּ גוֹיִם עַמּוֹ, כִּי דַם־עֲבָדָיו יִקּוֹם,
וְנָקָם יָשִׁיב לְצָרָיו, וְכִפֶּר אַדְמָתוֹ עַמּוֹ: וְעַל יְדֵי עֲבָדֶיךָ הַנְּבִיאִים כָּתוּב
יואל ד לֵאמֹר, וְנִקֵּיתִי, דָּמָם לֹא־נִקֵּיתִי, וַיהוה שֹׁכֵן בְּצִיּוֹן: וּבְכִתְבֵי הַקֹּדֶשׁ
תהלים עט נֶאֱמַר, לָמָּה יֹאמְרוּ הַגּוֹיִם אַיֵּה אֱלֹהֵיהֶם, יִוָּדַע בַּגּוֹיִם לְעֵינֵינוּ נִקְמַת
תהלים ט דַּם־עֲבָדֶיךָ הַשָּׁפוּךְ: וְאוֹמֵר, כִּי־דֹרֵשׁ דָּמִים אוֹתָם זָכָר, לֹא־שָׁכַח צַעֲקַת
תהלים קי עֲנָוִים: וְאוֹמֵר, יָדִין בַּגּוֹיִם מָלֵא גְוִיּוֹת, מָחַץ רֹאשׁ עַל־אֶרֶץ רַבָּה: מִנַּחַל
בַּדֶּרֶךְ יִשְׁתֶּה, עַל־כֵּן יָרִים רֹאשׁ:

אַשְׁרֵי Happy are those who dwell in Your House; *Ps. 84*
they shall continue to praise You, Selah!
Happy are the people for whom this is so; *Ps. 144*
happy are the people whose God is the Lord.
A song of praise by David. *Ps. 145*

I will exalt You, my God, the King, and bless Your name for
ever and all time. Every day I will bless You, and praise Your
name for ever and all time. Great is the Lord and greatly to be
praised; His greatness is unfathomable. One generation will
praise Your works to the next, and tell of Your mighty deeds.
On the glorious splendor of Your majesty I will meditate, and
on the acts of Your wonders. They shall talk of the power of
Your awesome deeds, and I will tell of Your greatness. They
shall recite the record of Your great goodness, and sing with
joy of Your righteousness. The Lord is gracious and compassionate, slow to anger and great in loving-kindness. The Lord
is good to all, and His compassion extends to all His works. All
Your works shall thank You, Lord, and Your devoted ones shall
bless You. They shall talk of the glory of Your kingship, and
speak of Your might. To make known to mankind His mighty
deeds and the glorious majesty of His kingship. Your kingdom
is an everlasting kingdom, and Your reign is for all generations.
The Lord supports all who fall, and raises all who are bowed
down. All raise their eyes to You in hope, and You give them
their food in due season. You open Your hand, and satisfy every
living thing with favor. The Lord is righteous in all His ways,
and kind in all He does. The Lord is close to all who call on
Him, to all who call on Him in truth. He fulfills the will of those
who revere Him; He hears their cry and saves them. The Lord
guards all who love Him, but all the wicked He will destroy.
▸ My mouth shall speak the praise of the Lord, and all creatures shall bless His holy name for ever and all time.

We will bless the Lord now and for ever. Halleluya! *Ps. 115*

תהלים פד
תהלים קמד
תהלים קמה

אַשְׁרֵי יוֹשְׁבֵי בֵיתֶךָ, עוֹד יְהַלְלוּךָ סֶּלָה:

אַשְׁרֵי הָעָם שֶׁכָּכָה לּוֹ, אַשְׁרֵי הָעָם שֶׁיהוה אֱלֹהָיו:

תְּהִלָּה לְדָוִד

אֲרוֹמִמְךָ אֱלוֹהַי הַמֶּלֶךְ, וַאֲבָרְכָה שִׁמְךָ לְעוֹלָם וָעֶד:

בְּכָל־יוֹם אֲבָרְכֶךָּ, וַאֲהַלְלָה שִׁמְךָ לְעוֹלָם וָעֶד:

גָּדוֹל יהוה וּמְהֻלָּל מְאֹד, וְלִגְדֻלָּתוֹ אֵין חֵקֶר:

דּוֹר לְדוֹר יְשַׁבַּח מַעֲשֶׂיךָ, וּגְבוּרֹתֶיךָ יַגִּידוּ:

הֲדַר כְּבוֹד הוֹדֶךָ, וְדִבְרֵי נִפְלְאֹתֶיךָ אָשִׂיחָה:

וֶעֱזוּז נוֹרְאֹתֶיךָ יֹאמֵרוּ, וּגְדוּלָּתְךָ אֲסַפְּרֶנָּה:

זֵכֶר רַב־טוּבְךָ יַבִּיעוּ, וְצִדְקָתְךָ יְרַנֵּנוּ:

חַנּוּן וְרַחוּם יהוה, אֶרֶךְ אַפַּיִם וּגְדָל־חָסֶד:

טוֹב־יהוה לַכֹּל, וְרַחֲמָיו עַל־כָּל־מַעֲשָׂיו:

יוֹדוּךָ יהוה כָּל־מַעֲשֶׂיךָ, וַחֲסִידֶיךָ יְבָרְכוּכָה:

כְּבוֹד מַלְכוּתְךָ יֹאמֵרוּ, וּגְבוּרָתְךָ יְדַבֵּרוּ:

לְהוֹדִיעַ לִבְנֵי הָאָדָם גְּבוּרֹתָיו, וּכְבוֹד הֲדַר מַלְכוּתוֹ:

מַלְכוּתְךָ מַלְכוּת כָּל־עֹלָמִים, וּמֶמְשַׁלְתְּךָ בְּכָל־דּוֹר וָדֹר:

סוֹמֵךְ יהוה לְכָל־הַנֹּפְלִים, וְזוֹקֵף לְכָל־הַכְּפוּפִים:

עֵינֵי־כֹל אֵלֶיךָ יְשַׂבֵּרוּ, וְאַתָּה נוֹתֵן־לָהֶם אֶת־אָכְלָם בְּעִתּוֹ:

פּוֹתֵחַ אֶת־יָדֶךָ, וּמַשְׂבִּיעַ לְכָל־חַי רָצוֹן:

צַדִּיק יהוה בְּכָל־דְּרָכָיו, וְחָסִיד בְּכָל־מַעֲשָׂיו:

קָרוֹב יהוה לְכָל־קֹרְאָיו, לְכֹל אֲשֶׁר יִקְרָאֻהוּ בֶאֱמֶת:

רְצוֹן־יְרֵאָיו יַעֲשֶׂה, וְאֶת־שַׁוְעָתָם יִשְׁמַע, וְיוֹשִׁיעֵם:

שׁוֹמֵר יהוה אֶת־כָּל־אֹהֲבָיו, וְאֵת כָּל־הָרְשָׁעִים יַשְׁמִיד:

‹ תְּהִלַּת יהוה יְדַבֶּר פִּי, וִיבָרֵךְ כָּל־בָּשָׂר שֵׁם קָדְשׁוֹ לְעוֹלָם וָעֶד:

וַאֲנַחְנוּ נְבָרֵךְ יָהּ מֵעַתָּה וְעַד־עוֹלָם, הַלְלוּיָהּ:

תהלים קטו

RETURNING THE TORAH TO THE ARK

The Ark is opened. All stand.
The Leader takes one of the Torah scrolls and says:

יְהַלְלוּ Let them praise the name of the LORD,   *Ps. 148*
for His name alone is sublime.

The congregation responds:

הוֹדוֹ His majesty is above earth and heaven.
He has raised the horn of His people,
for the glory of all His devoted ones,
the children of Israel, the people close to Him.
Halleluya!

While the Torah scrolls are being returned to the Ark, on a weekday the
following is said. On Shabbat, Psalm 29, on the next page, is said.

לְדָוִד מִזְמוֹר A psalm of David. The earth is the LORD's and all it   *Ps. 24*
contains, the world and all who live in it. For He founded it on the
seas and established it on the streams. Who may climb the mountain of the LORD? Who may stand in His holy place? He who has
clean hands and a pure heart, who has not taken My name in vain,
or sworn deceitfully. He shall receive blessing from the LORD, and
just reward from God, his salvation. This is a generation of those
who seek Him, the descendants of Jacob who seek Your presence,
Selah! Lift up your heads, O gates; be uplifted, eternal doors, so
that the King of glory may enter. Who is the King of glory? It is the
LORD, strong and mighty, the LORD mighty in battle. Lift up your
heads, O gates; be uplifted, eternal doors, so that the King of glory
may enter. ▸ Who is He, the King of glory? The LORD of hosts, He
is the King of glory, Selah!

"Lift up your heads, O gates" – makes this an appropriate psalm to say as we
open the doors of the Ark to receive the Torah scrolls.

הכנסת ספר תורה

The ארון קודש *is opened. All stand.*
The שליח ציבור *takes one of the* ספרי תורה *and says:*

יְהַלְלוּ אֶת־שֵׁם יהוה, כִּי־נִשְׂגָּב שְׁמוֹ, לְבַדּוֹ

The קהל *responds:*

הוֹדוֹ עַל־אֶרֶץ וְשָׁמָיִם:
וַיָּרֶם קֶרֶן לְעַמּוֹ
תְּהִלָּה לְכָל־חֲסִידָיו
לִבְנֵי יִשְׂרָאֵל עַם קְרֹבוֹ
הַלְלוּיָהּ:

While the ספרי תורה *are being returned to the* ארון קודש*, on a weekday*
the following is said. On שבת*, Psalm 29, on the next page, is said.*

לְדָוִד מִזְמוֹר, לַיהוה הָאָרֶץ וּמְלוֹאָהּ, תֵּבֵל וְיֹשְׁבֵי בָהּ: כִּי־הוּא
עַל־יַמִּים יְסָדָהּ, וְעַל־נְהָרוֹת יְכוֹנְנֶהָ: מִי־יַעֲלֶה בְהַר־יהוה,
וּמִי־יָקוּם בִּמְקוֹם קָדְשׁוֹ: נְקִי כַפַּיִם וּבַר־לֵבָב, אֲשֶׁר לֹא־נָשָׂא
לַשָּׁוְא נַפְשִׁי וְלֹא נִשְׁבַּע לְמִרְמָה: יִשָּׂא בְרָכָה מֵאֵת יהוה, וּצְדָקָה
מֵאֱלֹהֵי יִשְׁעוֹ: זֶה דּוֹר דֹּרְשָׁו, מְבַקְשֵׁי פָנֶיךָ, יַעֲקֹב, סֶלָה: שְׂאוּ
שְׁעָרִים רָאשֵׁיכֶם, וְהִנָּשְׂאוּ פִּתְחֵי עוֹלָם, וְיָבוֹא מֶלֶךְ הַכָּבוֹד:
מִי זֶה מֶלֶךְ הַכָּבוֹד, יהוה עִזּוּז וְגִבּוֹר, יהוה גִּבּוֹר מִלְחָמָה: שְׂאוּ
שְׁעָרִים רָאשֵׁיכֶם, וּשְׂאוּ פִּתְחֵי עוֹלָם, וְיָבֹא מֶלֶךְ הַכָּבוֹד: ‹ מִי
הוּא זֶה מֶלֶךְ הַכָּבוֹד, יהוה צְבָאוֹת הוּא מֶלֶךְ הַכָּבוֹד, סֶלָה:

לְדָוִד מִזְמוֹר *Psalm 24.* Associated with the occasion on which Solomon
brought the Ark into the Temple. The reference to the opening of the gates –

On Shabbat the following is said:

מִזְמוֹר לְדָוִד A psalm of David. Render to the Lord, you angelic *Ps. 29* powers, render to the Lord glory and might. Render to the Lord the glory due to His name. Bow to the Lord in the beauty of holiness. The Lord's voice echoes over the waters; the God of glory thunders; the Lord is over the mighty waters. The Lord's voice in power, the Lord's voice in beauty, the Lord's voice breaks cedars, the Lord shatters the cedars of Lebanon. He makes Lebanon skip like a calf, Sirion like a young wild ox. The Lord's voice cleaves flames of fire. The Lord's voice makes the desert quake, the Lord shakes the desert of Kadesh. The Lord's voice makes hinds calve and strips the forests bare, and in His temple all say: "Glory!" ▸ The Lord sat enthroned at the Flood, the Lord sits enthroned as King for ever. The Lord will give strength to His people; the Lord will bless His people with peace.

As the Torah scrolls are placed into the Ark, all say:

וּבְנֻחֹה יֹאמַר When the Ark came to rest, Moses would say:
"Return, O Lord, to the myriad thousands of Israel." *Num. 10*
Advance, Lord, to Your resting place, *Ps. 132*
You and Your mighty Ark.
Your priests are clothed in righteousness,
and Your devoted ones sing in joy.
For the sake of Your servant David,
do not reject Your anointed one.
For I give you good instruction; *Prov. 4*
do not forsake My Torah.
It is a tree of life to those who grasp it, *Prov. 3*
and those who uphold it are happy.

---

were forbidden to eat from the Tree of Life "lest they live forever" (Gen. 3:22). In this fine instance of intertextuality the book of Proverbs tells us that

On שבת *the following is said:*

תהלים כט

מִזְמוֹר לְדָוִד, הָבוּ לַיהוה בְּנֵי אֵלִים, הָבוּ לַיהוה כָּבוֹד וָעֹז:
הָבוּ לַיהוה כְּבוֹד שְׁמוֹ, הִשְׁתַּחֲווּ לַיהוה בְּהַדְרַת־קֹדֶשׁ: קוֹל
יהוה עַל־הַמַּיִם, אֵל־הַכָּבוֹד הִרְעִים, יהוה עַל־מַיִם רַבִּים:
קוֹל־יהוה בַּכֹּחַ, קוֹל יהוה בֶּהָדָר: קוֹל יהוה שֹׁבֵר אֲרָזִים,
וַיְשַׁבֵּר יהוה אֶת־אַרְזֵי הַלְּבָנוֹן: וַיַּרְקִידֵם כְּמוֹ־עֵגֶל, לְבָנוֹן
וְשִׂרְיֹן כְּמוֹ בֶן־רְאֵמִים: קוֹל־יהוה חֹצֵב לַהֲבוֹת אֵשׁ: קוֹל
יהוה יָחִיל מִדְבָּר, יָחִיל יהוה מִדְבַּר קָדֵשׁ: קוֹל יהוה יְחוֹלֵל
אַיָּלוֹת וַיֶּחֱשֹׂף יְעָרוֹת, וּבְהֵיכָלוֹ, כֻּלּוֹ אֹמֵר כָּבוֹד: ‹ יהוה לַמַּבּוּל
יָשָׁב, וַיֵּשֶׁב יהוה מֶלֶךְ לְעוֹלָם: יהוה עֹז לְעַמּוֹ יִתֵּן, יהוה יְבָרֵךְ
אֶת־עַמּוֹ בַשָּׁלוֹם:

As the ספרי תורה *are placed into the* ארון קודש, *all say:*

במדבר י

וּבְנֻחֹה יֹאמַר, שׁוּבָה יהוה רִבְבוֹת אַלְפֵי יִשְׂרָאֵל:

תהלים קלב

קוּמָה יהוה לִמְנוּחָתֶךָ, אַתָּה וַאֲרוֹן עֻזֶּךָ:
כֹּהֲנֶיךָ יִלְבְּשׁוּ־צֶדֶק, וַחֲסִידֶיךָ יְרַנֵּנוּ:
בַּעֲבוּר דָּוִד עַבְדֶּךָ אַל־תָּשֵׁב פְּנֵי מְשִׁיחֶךָ:

משלי ד

כִּי לֶקַח טוֹב נָתַתִּי לָכֶם, תּוֹרָתִי אַל־תַּעֲזֹבוּ:

משלי ג

עֵץ־חַיִּים הִיא לַמַּחֲזִיקִים בָּהּ, וְתֹמְכֶיהָ מְאֻשָּׁר:

מִזְמוֹר לְדָוִד *Psalm 29.* A psalm whose sevenfold reference to the "voice" of God shaking the earth and making the wilderness tremble is taken as an allusion to the giving of the Torah at Mount Sinai accompanied by thunder and lightning, when the mountain "trembled violently" (Exodus 19:18).

עֵץ־חַיִּים הִיא לַמַּחֲזִיקִים בָּהּ *It is a tree of life to those who grasp it.* The first humans

Its ways are ways of pleasantness, and all its paths are peace.
▸ Turn us back, O LORD, to You, and we will return.   *Lam. 5*
Renew our days as of old.

The Ark is closed.

HALF KADDISH

Leader: יִתְגַּדַּל Magnified and sanctified
may His great name be,
in the world He created by His will.
May He establish His kingdom
in your lifetime and in your days,
and in the lifetime of all the house of Israel,
swiftly and soon –
and say: Amen.

All: May His great name be blessed
for ever and all time.

Leader: Blessed and praised,
glorified and exalted,
raised and honored,
uplifted and lauded
be the name of the Holy One,
blessed be He,
beyond any blessing,
song, praise and consolation
uttered in the world –
and say: Amen.

חַדֵּשׁ יָמֵינוּ כְּקֶדֶם *Renew our days as of old.* A poignant verse taken from the book of Lamentations. In Judaism – the world's oldest monotheistic faith – the new is old, and the old remains new. The symbol of this constant renewal is the Torah, the word of the One beyond time.

דְּרָכֶיהָ דַרְכֵי־נֹעַם וְכָל־נְתִיבֹתֶיהָ שָׁלוֹם:

‹ הֲשִׁיבֵנוּ יהוה אֵלֶיךָ וְנָשׁוּבָה, חַדֵּשׁ יָמֵינוּ כְּקֶדֶם:

איכה ה

The ארון קודש is closed.

חצי קדיש

שׁ״ץ: יִתְגַּדַּל וְיִתְקַדַּשׁ שְׁמֵהּ רַבָּא (קהל: אָמֵן)

בְּעָלְמָא דִּי בְרָא כִרְעוּתֵהּ

וְיַמְלִיךְ מַלְכוּתֵהּ

בְּחַיֵּיכוֹן וּבְיוֹמֵיכוֹן וּבְחַיֵּי דְּכָל בֵּית יִשְׂרָאֵל

בַּעֲגָלָא וּבִזְמַן קָרִיב

וְאִמְרוּ אָמֵן. (קהל: אָמֵן)

קהל
ושׁ״ץ: יְהֵא שְׁמֵהּ רַבָּא מְבָרַךְ לְעָלַם וּלְעָלְמֵי עָלְמַיָּא.

שׁ״ץ: יִתְבָּרַךְ וְיִשְׁתַּבַּח וְיִתְפָּאַר וְיִתְרוֹמַם וְיִתְנַשֵּׂא

וְיִתְהַדָּר וְיִתְעַלֶּה וְיִתְהַלָּל

שְׁמֵהּ דְּקֻדְשָׁא בְּרִיךְ הוּא (קהל: בְּרִיךְ הוּא)

לְעֵלָּא מִן כָּל בִּרְכָתָא וְשִׁירָתָא

תֻּשְׁבְּחָתָא וְנֶחֱמָתָא

דַּאֲמִירָן בְּעָלְמָא

וְאִמְרוּ אָמֵן. (קהל: אָמֵן)

---

immortality is to be found in how we live, not how long. In the union of divine word and human mind we become part of something beyond time, chance and change. The first humans may have lost paradise, but by giving us the Torah, God has given us access to it again.

Musaf for Shavuot

The following prayer, until "in former years" on page 534, is said silently, standing with
feet together. Take three steps forward and at the points indicated by ˈ, bend the knees
at the first word, bow at the second, and stand straight before saying God's name.

When I proclaim the LORD's name, give glory to our God. *Deut. 32*
O LORD, open my lips, so that my mouth may declare Your praise. *Ps. 51*

PATRIARCHS

בָּרוּךְˈ Blessed are You, LORD our God and God of our fathers,
God of Abraham, God of Isaac and God of Jacob;
the great, mighty and awesome God, God Most High,
who bestows acts of loving-kindness and creates all,
who remembers the loving-kindness of the fathers
and will bring a Redeemer to their children's children
for the sake of His name, in love.
King, Helper, Savior, Shield:
ˈBlessed are You, LORD, Shield of Abraham.

DIVINE MIGHT

אַתָּה גִבּוֹר You are eternally mighty, LORD.
You give life to the dead and have great power to save.

> *In Israel:*
> He causes the dew to fall.

---

for a sacrifice. As our ancestors brought offerings in the Temple so we bring
an offering of words.

אֱלֹהֵינוּ וֵאלֹהֵי אֲבוֹתֵינוּ *Our God and God of our fathers.* This is the same sequence as in the Song at the Sea: "This is my God, and I will beautify Him,
my father's God, and I will exalt Him" (Ex. 15:2). There are two kinds of
inheritance. If I inherit gold, I need do nothing to maintain its value: it will
happen inevitably. But if I inherit a business and do not work to maintain it,
it will eventually be valueless. Faith is less like gold than like a business. I have
to work to sustain its value if I am truly to inherit it. We have to make God
our God if we are truly to honor the God of our ancestors.

אַתָּה גִבּוֹר *You are eternally mighty.* This paragraph, with its fivefold reference
to the resurrection of the dead, reflects one of the major areas of contention

מוסף לשבועות

The following prayer, until קְדֻמְנִיּוֹת *on page 535, is said silently, standing with feet together.*
Take three steps forward and at the points indicated by ׳, *bend the knees at the first word,*
bow at the second, and stand straight before saying God's name.

דברים לב

תהלים נא

כִּי שֵׁם יהוה אֶקְרָא, הָבוּ גֹדֶל לֵאלֹהֵינוּ:

אֲדֹנָי, שְׂפָתַי תִּפְתָּח, וּפִי יַגִּיד תְּהִלָּתֶךָ:

אבות

יּבָּרוּךְ אַתָּה יהוה, אֱלֹהֵינוּ וֵאלֹהֵי אֲבוֹתֵינוּ

אֱלֹהֵי אַבְרָהָם, אֱלֹהֵי יִצְחָק, וֵאלֹהֵי יַעֲקֹב

הָאֵל הַגָּדוֹל הַגִּבּוֹר וְהַנּוֹרָא, אֵל עֶלְיוֹן

גּוֹמֵל חֲסָדִים טוֹבִים, וְקֹנֵה הַכֹּל, וְזוֹכֵר חַסְדֵי אָבוֹת

וּמֵבִיא גוֹאֵל לִבְנֵי בְנֵיהֶם לְמַעַן שְׁמוֹ בְּאַהֲבָה.

מֶלֶךְ עוֹזֵר וּמוֹשִׁיעַ וּמָגֵן.

יּבָּרוּךְ אַתָּה יהוה, מָגֵן אַבְרָהָם.

גבורות

אַתָּה גִבּוֹר לְעוֹלָם, אֲדֹנָי

מְחַיֵּה מֵתִים אַתָּה, רַב לְהוֹשִׁיעַ

ארץ ישראל *In*

מוֹרִיד הַטָּל

MUSAF

The Musaf service corresponds to the additional sacrifice that was offered in Temple times on Shabbat and festivals. The sacrificial element is more pronounced in Musaf than in other services, since the other services have a double aspect. On the one hand, they too represent sacrifice (except Ma'ariv, the evening service, because no sacrifices were offered at night). But they also represent the prayers of the patriarchs: the morning service is associated with Abraham, the afternoon service with Isaac, and the evening service with Jacob. Musaf has no such additional dimension. It is, simply, the substitute

He sustains the living with loving-kindness,
and with great compassion revives the dead.
He supports the fallen, heals the sick, sets captives free,
and keeps His faith with those who sleep in the dust.
Who is like You, Master of might,
and who can compare to You,
O King who brings death and gives life,
and makes salvation grow?
Faithful are You to revive the dead.
Blessed are You, Lord, who revives the dead.

HOLINESS

אַתָּה קָדוֹשׁ You are holy and Your name is holy,
and holy ones praise You daily, Selah!
Blessed are You, Lord, the holy God.

HOLINESS OF THE DAY

אַתָּה בְחַרְתָּנוּ You have chosen us from among all peoples.
You have loved and favored us.
You have raised us above all tongues.
You have made us holy through Your commandments.
You have brought us near, our King, to Your service,
and have called us by Your great and holy name.

אַתָּה קָדוֹשׁ *You are holy.* The infinite light of God is hidden in the finite spaces
of the physical universe. Indeed the word *olam*, universe, is semantically
linked to the word *ne'elam*, hidden. "Holy" is the name we give to those special times, places, people and deeds that are signals of transcendence, points
at which the infinity of God becomes manifest within the finite world. The
holiness of God therefore refers to divine transcendence: God beyond, not
within, the world. The holiness of Israel ("Be holy, for I the Lord your God
am holy" [Lev. 19:2]) refers to the points within our life where we efface
ourselves in order to become a vehicle through which God's light flows into
the world.

אַתָּה בְחַרְתָּנוּ *You have chosen us.* The form of sacrifice in Judaism is different

מְכַלְכֵּל חַיִּים בְּחֶסֶד, מְחַיֵּה מֵתִים בְּרַחֲמִים רַבִּים

סוֹמֵךְ נוֹפְלִים, וְרוֹפֵא חוֹלִים, וּמַתִּיר אֲסוּרִים

וּמְקַיֵּם אֱמוּנָתוֹ לִישֵׁנֵי עָפָר.

מִי כָמוֹךָ, בַּעַל גְּבוּרוֹת, וּמִי דוֹמֶה לָּךְ

מֶלֶךְ, מֵמִית וּמְחַיֶּה וּמַצְמִיחַ יְשׁוּעָה.

וְנֶאֱמָן אַתָּה לְהַחֲיוֹת מֵתִים.

בָּרוּךְ אַתָּה יהוה, מְחַיֵּה הַמֵּתִים.

קדושת השם

אַתָּה קָדוֹשׁ וְשִׁמְךָ קָדוֹשׁ

וּקְדוֹשִׁים בְּכָל יוֹם יְהַלְלוּךָ סֶּלָה.

בָּרוּךְ אַתָּה יהוה, הָאֵל הַקָּדוֹשׁ.

קדושת היום

אַתָּה בְחַרְתָּנוּ מִכָּל הָעַמִּים, אָהַבְתָּ אוֹתָנוּ וְרָצִיתָ בָּנוּ

וְרוֹמַמְתָּנוּ מִכָּל הַלְּשׁוֹנוֹת, וְקִדַּשְׁתָּנוּ בְּמִצְוֹתֶיךָ

וְקֵרַבְתָּנוּ מַלְכֵּנוּ לַעֲבוֹדָתֶךָ

וְשִׁמְךָ הַגָּדוֹל וְהַקָּדוֹשׁ עָלֵינוּ קָרָאתָ.

___

between the Pharisees and Sadducees in Second Temple times. The Sadducees, influenced by the Greeks, believed that the true home of the soul is in heaven, not on earth. Therefore the highest state is *Olam HaBa*, the World to Come, life after death. That anyone, having experienced such serenity and closeness to God, might wish to return to bodily life on earth was as unintelligible to them as it would have been to Plato. The Pharisees believed otherwise, that justice belongs on earth not only in heaven, and that those who died – including those who died unjustly or before their time – will one day live again, not just immortally in heaven but physically on earth. There is a World to Come, life after death, but there will also be in the future a resurrection of those who died. This is a deep and fundamental statement of Jewish faith.

On Shabbat, add the words in parentheses:

וַתִּתֶּן־לֶֽנוּ And You, LORD our God, have given us in love
(Sabbaths for rest and) festivals for rejoicing,
holy days and seasons for joy,
(this Sabbath day and) this day of
the festival of Shavuot, the time of the giving of our Torah
(with love), a holy assembly
in memory of the exodus from Egypt.

וּמִפְּנֵי חֲטָאֵֽינוּ But because of our sins we were exiled from our land
and driven far from our country.
We cannot go up to appear and bow before You,
and to perform our duties in Your chosen House,
the great and holy Temple that was called by Your name,
because of the hand that was stretched out against Your Sanctuary.
May it be Your will, LORD our God and God of our ancestors,
merciful King,

God we are a mere concatenation of chemicals that will one day turn to dust.
Only by the gift of self to the eternal God do we touch – and are touched by –
eternity.

וּמִפְּנֵי חֲטָאֵֽינוּ גָּלִֽינוּ מֵאַרְצֵֽנוּ *But because of our sins we were exiled from our land.*
An explanation of why we are no longer able to offer sacrifices in the Temple.
The word *ḥet,* "sin," also means to miss a target. *Avera,* like the English
word "transgression," means to cross a boundary into forbidden territory.
Thus a sin is an act in the wrong place, one that disturbs the moral order
of the universe. Its punishment, measure for measure, is that the sinner
is sent to the wrong place, that is, into exile. For their sin, Adam and Eve
were exiled from Eden. For our ancestors' sins they were exiled from their
land. The Hebrew word *teshuva,* the proper response to sin, thus has the
double sense of spiritual *repentance* for wrongdoing and physical *return* to
the land.

וַתִּתֶּן־לֶֽנוּ...וּמִפְּנֵי חֲטָאֵֽינוּ...אֱלֹהֵֽינוּ וֵאלֹהֵי אֲבוֹתֵֽינוּ *And You* [LORD *our God*] *have
given us… But because of our sins… Our God and God of our ancestors.* Rabbi

On שבת, add the words in parentheses:

וַתִּתֶּן לָנוּ יהוה אֱלֹהֵינוּ בְּאַהֲבָה

(שַׁבָּתוֹת לִמְנוּחָה וּ)מוֹעֲדִים לְשִׂמְחָה, חַגִּים וּזְמַנִּים לְשָׂשׂוֹן

אֶת יוֹם (הַשַּׁבָּת הַזֶּה וְאֶת יוֹם)

חַג הַשָּׁבוּעוֹת הַזֶּה, זְמַן מַתַּן תּוֹרָתֵנוּ

(בְּאַהֲבָה) מִקְרָא קֹדֶשׁ, זֵכֶר לִיצִיאַת מִצְרָיִם.

וּמִפְּנֵי חֲטָאֵינוּ גָּלִינוּ מֵאַרְצֵנוּ, וְנִתְרַחַקְנוּ מֵעַל אַדְמָתֵנוּ

וְאֵין אֲנַחְנוּ יְכוֹלִים לַעֲלוֹת וְלֵרָאוֹת וּלְהִשְׁתַּחֲווֹת לְפָנֶיךָ

וְלַעֲשׂוֹת חוֹבוֹתֵינוּ בְּבֵית בְּחִירָתֶךָ

בַּבַּיִת הַגָּדוֹל וְהַקָּדוֹשׁ שֶׁנִּקְרָא שִׁמְךָ עָלָיו

מִפְּנֵי הַיָּד שֶׁנִּשְׁתַּלְּחָה בְּמִקְדָּשֶׁךָ.

יְהִי רָצוֹן מִלְּפָנֶיךָ יהוה אֱלֹהֵינוּ וֵאלֹהֵי אֲבוֹתֵינוּ

מֶלֶךְ רַחֲמָן

with and without a Temple, but its centrality remains. Where once our ancestors offered animals, now, lacking a Temple, we offer words. Yet the essential act is the same in both cases: a giving of self to God. In Judaism, to love is to give. Jewish marriage is consecrated by the gift of a ring. It is not that the recipient needs to receive. It is that love is emotion turned outward. Love is the sacrifice of self to other, and the result is ק-ר-ב, the "coming close" that is the root of the word *korban*, "sacrifice." At the beginning of Leviticus, the book containing many of the details of the sacrifices, the Torah states, "When a person offers *of you* an offering to the LORD" (Lev. 1:2). The order of the words is unexpected: it would be more natural to say, "When one of you brings an offering." From this, the Jewish mystics concluded that the real offering is "of you," that is, of self. The animals were the outer form of the command, but its essential core is the inward act of self-sacrificing love. That is why, after the destruction of the Temple, prayer could substitute for sacrifice, for true prayer *is* the giving of self, the acknowledgment that without

that You in Your abounding compassion may once more
have mercy on us and on Your Sanctuary,
rebuilding it swiftly and adding to its glory.
Our Father, our King,
reveal the glory of Your kingdom to us swiftly.
Appear and be exalted over us in the sight of all that lives.
Bring back our scattered ones from among the nations,
and gather our dispersed people from the ends of the earth.
Lead us to Zion, Your city, in jubilation,
and to Jerusalem, home of Your Temple, with everlasting joy.
There we will prepare for You our obligatory offerings:
the regular daily offerings in their order
and the additional offerings according to their law.
And the additional offering(s of this Sabbath day and)
of this day of the festival of Shavuot.
we will prepare and offer before You in love,
in accord with Your will's commandment,
as You wrote for us in Your Torah
through Your servant Moses,
by Your own word, as it is said:

On Shabbat:
וּבְיוֹם הַשַּׁבָּת On the Sabbath day, make an offering   *Num. 28*
of two lambs a year old, without blemish,
together with two-tenths of an ephah of fine flour
mixed with oil as a meal-offering,
and its appropriate libation.
This is the burnt-offering for every Sabbath,
in addition to the regular daily burnt-offering and its libation.

---

of the festivals. The second corresponds to Numbers 28–29, which speci-
fies the sacrifices offered on each holy day. The third, with its reference to
a reinstatement of pilgrimage to a rebuilt Temple, echoes a key theme of
Deuteronomy 16.

שֶׁתָּשׁוּב וּתְרַחֵם עָלֵינוּ וְעַל מִקְדָּשְׁךָ בְּרַחֲמֶיךָ הָרַבִּים

וְתִבְנֵהוּ מְהֵרָה וּתְגַדֵּל כְּבוֹדוֹ.

אָבִינוּ מַלְכֵּנוּ, גַּלֵּה כְּבוֹד מַלְכוּתְךָ עָלֵינוּ מְהֵרָה

וְהוֹפַע וְהִנָּשֵׂא עָלֵינוּ לְעֵינֵי כָּל חָי

וְקָרֵב פְּזוּרֵינוּ מִבֵּין הַגּוֹיִם

וּנְפוּצוֹתֵינוּ כַּנֵּס מִיַּרְכְּתֵי אָרֶץ.

וַהֲבִיאֵנוּ לְצִיּוֹן עִירְךָ בְּרִנָּה

וְלִירוּשָׁלַיִם בֵּית מִקְדָּשְׁךָ בְּשִׂמְחַת עוֹלָם

וְשָׁם נַעֲשֶׂה לְפָנֶיךָ אֶת קָרְבְּנוֹת חוֹבוֹתֵינוּ

תְּמִידִים כְּסִדְרָם וּמוּסָפִים כְּהִלְכָתָם

וְאֶת מוּסַף יוֹם / שבת: וְאֶת מוּסְפֵי יוֹם הַשַּׁבָּת הַזֶּה וְיוֹם/

חַג הַשָּׁבוּעוֹת הַזֶּה.

נַעֲשֶׂה וְנַקְרִיב לְפָנֶיךָ בְּאַהֲבָה כְּמִצְוַת רְצוֹנֶךָ

כְּמוֹ שֶׁכָּתַבְתָּ עָלֵינוּ בְּתוֹרָתֶךָ

עַל יְדֵי מֹשֶׁה עַבְדֶּךָ

מִפִּי כְבוֹדֶךָ, כָּאָמוּר.

On שבת:

במדבר כח

וּבְיוֹם הַשַּׁבָּת, שְׁנֵי־כְבָשִׂים בְּנֵי־שָׁנָה תְּמִימִם

וּשְׁנֵי עֶשְׂרֹנִים סֹלֶת מִנְחָה בְּלוּלָה בַשֶּׁמֶן וְנִסְכּוֹ:

עֹלַת שַׁבַּת בְּשַׁבַּתּוֹ, עַל־עֹלַת הַתָּמִיד וְנִסְכָּהּ:

Joseph Soloveitchik suggests that this three-paragraph structure of the middle section of Musaf corresponds to the three passages in the Torah dealing with the festivals. The first paragraph, which identifies the theme of the festival, corresponds to Leviticus 23, which sets out the character and dates

וּבְיוֹם הַבִּכּוּרִים On the day of the first fruits, *Num. 28*
when you bring an offering of new grain to the Lᴏʀᴅ,
on your Festival of Weeks, there shall be a sacred assembly:
you shall do no laborious work.
You shall offer a burnt-offering of pleasing aroma to the Lᴏʀᴅ:
two young bullocks, one ram, and seven yearling male lambs.

And their meal-offerings and wine-libations as ordained:
three-tenths of an ephah for each bull,
two-tenths of an ephah for the ram,
one-tenth of an ephah for each lamb,
wine for the libations,
a male goat for atonement,
and two regular daily offerings according to their law.

> *On Shabbat:*
> יִשְׂמְחוּ Those who keep the Sabbath and call it a delight
> shall rejoice in Your kingship.
> The people who sanctify the seventh day shall all be satisfied
> and take delight in Your goodness,
> for You favored the seventh day and declared it holy.
> You called it "most desirable of days" in remembrance of Creation.

אֱלֹהֵינוּ Our God and God of our ancestors,
merciful King, have compassion upon us.
You who are good and do good, respond to our call.
Return to us in Your abounding mercy
for the sake of our fathers who did Your will.
Rebuild Your Temple as at the beginning,
and establish Your Sanctuary on its site.
Let us witness its rebuilding and gladden us by its restoration.
Bring the priests back to their service,
the Levites to their song and music,
and the Israelites to their homes.

וּבְיוֹם הַבִּכּוּרִים, בְּהַקְרִיבְכֶם מִנְחָה חֲדָשָׁה לַיהוה בְּשָׁבֻעֹתֵיכֶם במדבר כח

מִקְרָא־קֹדֶשׁ יִהְיֶה לָכֶם, כָּל־מְלֶאכֶת עֲבֹדָה לֹא תַעֲשׂוּ:

וְהִקְרַבְתֶּם עוֹלָה לְרֵיחַ נִיחֹחַ לַיהוה

פָּרִים בְּנֵי־בָקָר שְׁנַיִם, אַיִל אֶחָד

שִׁבְעָה כְבָשִׂים בְּנֵי שָׁנָה:

וּמִנְחָתָם וְנִסְכֵּיהֶם כִּמְדֻבָּר

שְׁלֹשָׁה עֶשְׂרֹנִים לַפָּר וּשְׁנֵי עֶשְׂרֹנִים לָאַיִל

וְעִשָּׂרוֹן לַכֶּבֶשׂ, וְיַיִן כְּנִסְכּוֹ, וְשָׂעִיר לְכַפֵּר

וּשְׁנֵי תְמִידִים כְּהִלְכָתָם.

שבת *On*:

יִשְׂמְחוּ בְמַלְכוּתְךָ שׁוֹמְרֵי שַׁבָּת וְקוֹרְאֵי עֹנֶג.

עַם מְקַדְּשֵׁי שְׁבִיעִי כֻּלָּם יִשְׂבְּעוּ וְיִתְעַנְּגוּ מִטּוּבֶךָ

וּבַשְּׁבִיעִי רָצִיתָ בּוֹ וְקִדַּשְׁתּוֹ

חֶמְדַּת יָמִים אוֹתוֹ קָרָאתָ, זֵכֶר לְמַעֲשֵׂה בְרֵאשִׁית.

אֱלֹהֵינוּ וֵאלֹהֵי אֲבוֹתֵינוּ

מֶלֶךְ רַחֲמָן רַחֵם עָלֵינוּ, טוֹב וּמֵטִיב הִדָּרֶשׁ לָנוּ

שׁוּבָה אֵלֵינוּ בַּהֲמוֹן רַחֲמֶיךָ

בִּגְלַל אָבוֹת שֶׁעָשׂוּ רְצוֹנֶךָ.

בְּנֵה בֵיתְךָ כְּבַתְּחִלָּה, וְכוֹנֵן מִקְדָּשְׁךָ עַל מְכוֹנוֹ

וְהַרְאֵנוּ בְּבִנְיָנוֹ, וְשַׂמְּחֵנוּ בְּתִקּוּנוֹ

וְהָשֵׁב כֹּהֲנִים לַעֲבוֹדָתָם

וּלְוִיִּם לְשִׁירָם וּלְזִמְרָם

וְהָשֵׁב יִשְׂרָאֵל לִנְוֵיהֶם.

וְשָׁם נַעֲלֶה There we will go up and appear and bow before You
on the three pilgrimage festivals,
as is written in Your Torah:

> "Three times in the year all your males shall appear   *Deut. 16*
> before the LORD your God
> at the place He will choose:
> on Pesaḥ, Shavuot and Sukkot.
> They shall not appear before the LORD empty-handed.
> Each shall bring such a gift as he can,
> in proportion to the blessing
> that the LORD your God grants you."

On Shabbat add the words in parentheses:

וְהַשִּׂיאֵנוּ Bestow on us, LORD our God,
the blessing of Your festivals
for life and peace, joy and gladness,
as You desired and promised to bless us.
(Our God and God of our fathers, find favor in our rest.)
Make us holy through Your commandments
and grant us a share in Your Torah;
satisfy us with Your goodness,
gladden us with Your salvation,
and purify our hearts to serve You in truth.
And grant us a heritage, LORD our God,
(with love and favor,) with joy and gladness,
Your holy (Sabbath and) festivals.
May Israel, who sanctify Your name, rejoice in You.
Blessed are You, LORD,
who sanctifies (the Sabbath and) Israel and the festive seasons.

---

the other. A person can be inwardly joyful without showing it, or be dressed
in festive clothes while feeling inwardly sad. Festivals are a time for both.
They are or should be times of inward joy: that is why in Jewish law a festival

וְשָׁם נַעֲלֶה וְנֵרָאֶה וְנִשְׁתַּחֲוֶה לְפָנֶיךָ בְּשָׁלֹשׁ פַּעֲמֵי רְגָלֵינוּ
כַּכָּתוּב בְּתוֹרָתֶךָ

דברים טז

שָׁלֹשׁ פְּעָמִים בַּשָּׁנָה יֵרָאֶה כָל־זְכוּרְךָ
אֶת־פְּנֵי יהוה אֱלֹהֶיךָ
בַּמָּקוֹם אֲשֶׁר יִבְחָר
בְּחַג הַמַּצּוֹת, וּבְחַג הַשָּׁבֻעוֹת, וּבְחַג הַסֻּכּוֹת
וְלֹא יֵרָאֶה אֶת־פְּנֵי יהוה רֵיקָם:
אִישׁ כְּמַתְּנַת יָדוֹ, כְּבִרְכַּת יהוה אֱלֹהֶיךָ אֲשֶׁר נָתַן־לָךְ:

On שבת add the words in parentheses:

וְהַשִּׂיאֵנוּ יהוה אֱלֹהֵינוּ אֶת בִּרְכַּת מוֹעֲדֶיךָ
לְחַיִּים וּלְשָׁלוֹם, לְשִׂמְחָה וּלְשָׂשׂוֹן
כַּאֲשֶׁר רָצִיתָ וְאָמַרְתָּ לְבָרְכֵנוּ.
(אֱלֹהֵינוּ וֵאלֹהֵי אֲבוֹתֵינוּ, רְצֵה בִמְנוּחָתֵנוּ)
קַדְּשֵׁנוּ בְּמִצְוֹתֶיךָ, וְתֵן חֶלְקֵנוּ בְּתוֹרָתֶךָ
שַׂבְּעֵנוּ מִטּוּבֶךָ, וְשַׂמְּחֵנוּ בִּישׁוּעָתֶךָ
וְטַהֵר לִבֵּנוּ לְעָבְדְּךָ בֶּאֱמֶת
וְהַנְחִילֵנוּ יהוה אֱלֹהֵינוּ (בְּאַהֲבָה וּבְרָצוֹן)
בְּשִׂמְחָה וּבְשָׂשׂוֹן (שַׁבָּת וּ) מוֹעֲדֵי קָדְשֶׁךָ
וְיִשְׂמְחוּ בְךָ יִשְׂרָאֵל מְקַדְּשֵׁי שְׁמֶךָ.
בָּרוּךְ אַתָּה יהוה, מְקַדֵּשׁ (הַשַּׁבָּת וְ) יִשְׂרָאֵל וְהַזְּמַנִּים.

לְשִׂמְחָה וּלְשָׂשׂוֹן *Joy and gladness.* The difference between these two terms, according to Malbim, is that *simḥa*, joy, refers to inward emotion. *Sasson*, gladness, refers to the outward signs of celebration. One can exist without

TEMPLE SERVICE

רְצֵה Find favor, LORD our God,
in Your people Israel and their prayer.
Restore the service to Your most holy House,
and accept in love and favor
the fire-offerings of Israel and their prayer.
May the service of Your people Israel
always find favor with You.
And may our eyes witness Your return to Zion in compassion.
Blessed are You, LORD,
who restores His Presence to Zion.

THANKSGIVING

Bow at the first nine words.

מוֹדִים We give thanks to You,
for You are the LORD our God and God of our ancestors
for ever and all time.
You are the Rock of our lives,
Shield of our salvation from generation to generation.
We will thank You and declare Your praise for our lives,
which are entrusted into Your hand;
for our souls, which are placed in Your charge;
for Your miracles which are with us every day;
and for Your wonders and favors
at all times, evening, morning and midday.
You are good – for Your compassion never fails.
You are compassionate –
for Your loving-kindnesses never cease.
We have always placed our hope in You.

מוֹדִים אֲנַחְנוּ לָךְ *We give thanks to You.* This, the middle of the closing three
blessings, mirrors the middle of the first three blessings, with this difference –
that where that paragraph spoke of God who restores life to the dead, here

עבודה

רְצֵה יהוה אֱלֹהֵינוּ בְּעַמְּךָ יִשְׂרָאֵל, וּבִתְפִלָּתָם
וְהָשֵׁב אֶת הָעֲבוֹדָה לִדְבִיר בֵּיתֶךָ
וְאִשֵּׁי יִשְׂרָאֵל וּתְפִלָּתָם בְּאַהֲבָה תְקַבֵּל בְּרָצוֹן
וּתְהִי לְרָצוֹן תָּמִיד עֲבוֹדַת יִשְׂרָאֵל עַמֶּךָ.
וְתֶחֱזֶינָה עֵינֵינוּ בְּשׁוּבְךָ לְצִיּוֹן בְּרַחֲמִים.
בָּרוּךְ אַתָּה יהוה, הַמַּחֲזִיר שְׁכִינָתוֹ לְצִיּוֹן.

הודאה

Bow at the first five words.

ʾמוֹדִים אֲנַחְנוּ לָךְ
שָׁאַתָּה הוּא יהוה אֱלֹהֵינוּ וֵאלֹהֵי אֲבוֹתֵינוּ לְעוֹלָם וָעֶד.
צוּר חַיֵּינוּ, מָגֵן יִשְׁעֵנוּ, אַתָּה הוּא לְדוֹר וָדוֹר.
נוֹדֶה לְּךָ וּנְסַפֵּר תְּהִלָּתֶךָ
עַל חַיֵּינוּ הַמְּסוּרִים בְּיָדֶךָ
וְעַל נִשְׁמוֹתֵינוּ הַפְּקוּדוֹת לָךְ
וְעַל נִסֶּיךָ שֶׁבְּכָל יוֹם עִמָּנוּ
וְעַל נִפְלְאוֹתֶיךָ וְטוֹבוֹתֶיךָ
שֶׁבְּכָל עֵת, עֶרֶב וָבֹקֶר וְצָהֳרָיִם.
הַטּוֹב, כִּי לֹא כָלוּ רַחֲמֶיךָ
וְהַמְרַחֵם, כִּי לֹא תַמּוּ חֲסָדֶיךָ
מֵעוֹלָם קִוִּינוּ לָךְ.

brings to an end a time of mourning. They are also times of public gladness where we celebrate together by the way we dress, eat and sing.

For all these things may Your name be blessed and exalted,
our King, continually, for ever and all time.
Let all that lives thank You, Selah!
and praise Your name in truth,
God, our Savior and Help, Selah!
˒Blessed are You, LORD,
whose name is "the Good"
and to whom thanks are due.

PEACE

שִׂים שָׁלוֹם Grant peace, goodness and blessing,
grace, loving-kindness and compassion to us
and all Israel Your people.
Bless us, our Father, all as one,
with the light of Your face,
for by the light of Your face You have given us,
LORD our God,
the Torah of life and love of kindness,
righteousness, blessing, compassion, life and peace.
May it be good in Your eyes to bless Your people Israel
at every time, in every hour, with Your peace.
Blessed are You, LORD,
who blesses His people Israel with peace.

Some say the following verse:

May the words of my mouth and the meditation of my heart   Ps. 19
find favor before You, LORD, my Rock and Redeemer.

---

the more we recognize all the "wonders" that are with us at every moment.
If we would only open our eyes to the sheer improbability of existence we
would realize that we are surrounded by the astonishing, intricate beauty of
God's constant creativity: "Lift up your eyes on high, and see who has created
these things" (Is. 40:26).

וְעַל כֻּלָּם יִתְבָּרַךְ וְיִתְרוֹמַם שִׁמְךָ מַלְכֵּנוּ תָּמִיד לְעוֹלָם וָעֶד.

וְכֹל הַחַיִּים יוֹדִוּךָ סֶּלָה, וִיהַלְלוּ אֶת שִׁמְךָ בֶּאֱמֶת הָאֵל יְשׁוּעָתֵנוּ וְעֶזְרָתֵנוּ סֶלָה.

יּבָּרוּךְ אַתָּה יהוה, הַטּוֹב שִׁמְךָ וּלְךָ נָאֶה לְהוֹדוֹת.

שלום

שִׂים שָׁלוֹם טוֹבָה וּבְרָכָה חֵן וָחֶסֶד וְרַחֲמִים עָלֵינוּ וְעַל כָּל יִשְׂרָאֵל עַמֶּךָ.

בָּרְכֵנוּ אָבִינוּ כֻּלָּנוּ כְּאֶחָד בְּאוֹר פָּנֶיךָ כִּי בְאוֹר פָּנֶיךָ נָתַתָּ לָּנוּ, יהוה אֱלֹהֵינוּ תּוֹרַת חַיִּים וְאַהֲבַת חֶסֶד

וּצְדָקָה וּבְרָכָה וְרַחֲמִים וְחַיִּים וְשָׁלוֹם.

וְטוֹב בְּעֵינֶיךָ לְבָרֵךְ אֶת עַמְּךָ יִשְׂרָאֵל בְּכָל עֵת וּבְכָל שָׁעָה בִּשְׁלוֹמֶךָ.

בָּרוּךְ אַתָּה יהוה, הַמְבָרֵךְ אֶת עַמּוֹ יִשְׂרָאֵל בַּשָּׁלוֹם.

Some say the following verse:

תהלים יט

יִהְיוּ לְרָצוֹן אִמְרֵי־פִי וְהֶגְיוֹן לִבִּי לְפָנֶיךָ, יהוה צוּרִי וְגֹאֲלִי:

---

we speak of the no less miraculous fact that God gives life to the living. The fact that increasingly we can give scientific explanations for the *how* of life, does not diminish – indeed should intensify – our sense of wonder and gratitude at the *gift* of life. There is nothing "mere" about the fact that we are here. The more we learn about cosmology (the birth of the physical universe), life (the emergence of forms of self-organizing complexity), sentience (the fact that we can feel) and self-consciousness (the fact that we can stand outside our feelings, exercising freedom and asking the question, Why?) –

אֱלֹהַי My God, *Berakhot 17a*
guard my tongue from evil and my lips from deceitful speech.
To those who curse me, let my soul be silent;
may my soul be to all like the dust.
Open my heart to Your Torah
and let my soul pursue Your commandments.
As for all who plan evil against me,
swiftly thwart their counsel and frustrate their plans.

    Act for the sake of Your name;
     act for the sake of Your right hand;
     act for the sake of Your holiness;
     act for the sake of Your Torah.

That Your beloved ones may be delivered, *Ps. 60*
save with Your right hand and answer me.
May the words of my mouth *Ps. 19*
and the meditation of my heart find favor before You,
LORD, my Rock and Redeemer.

Bow, take three steps back, then bow, first left, then right, then center, while saying:
May He who makes peace in His high places,
make peace for us and all Israel –
and say: Amen.

יְהִי רָצוֹן May it be Your will, LORD our God and God of our ancestors,
that the Temple be rebuilt speedily in our days,
and grant us a share in Your Torah.
And there we will serve You with reverence,
as in the days of old and as in former years.
Then the offering of Judah and Jerusalem *Mal. 3*
will be pleasing to the LORD as in the days of old and as in former years.

נַפְשִׁי תִדֹּם *Let my soul be silent.* "The way of the just is to be insulted but not
to insult; to hear yourself reviled but not to reply; to act out of love and to
rejoice even in affliction" (Maimonides, Laws of Ethical Character 2:3, based
on *Yoma* 23a).

ברכות יז.

אֱלֹהַי

נְצֹר לְשׁוֹנִי מֵרָע וּשְׂפָתַי מִדַּבֵּר מִרְמָה

וְלִמְקַלְלַי נַפְשִׁי תִדֹּם, וְנַפְשִׁי כֶּעָפָר לַכֹּל תִּהְיֶה.

פְּתַח לִבִּי בְּתוֹרָתֶךָ, וּבְמִצְוֹתֶיךָ תִּרְדֹּף נַפְשִׁי.

וְכָל הַחוֹשְׁבִים עָלַי רָעָה

מְהֵרָה הָפֵר עֲצָתָם וְקַלְקֵל מַחֲשַׁבְתָּם.

עֲשֵׂה לְמַעַן שְׁמֶךָ

עֲשֵׂה לְמַעַן יְמִינֶךָ

עֲשֵׂה לְמַעַן קְדֻשָּׁתֶךָ

עֲשֵׂה לְמַעַן תּוֹרָתֶךָ.

תהלים ס

לְמַעַן יֵחָלְצוּן יְדִידֶיךָ, הוֹשִׁיעָה יְמִינְךָ וַעֲנֵנִי:

תהלים יט

יִהְיוּ לְרָצוֹן אִמְרֵי־פִי וְהֶגְיוֹן לִבִּי לְפָנֶיךָ, יהוה צוּרִי וְגֹאֲלִי:

Bow, take three steps back, then bow, first left, then right, then center, while saying:

עֹשֶׂה שָׁלוֹם בִּמְרוֹמָיו

הוּא יַעֲשֶׂה שָׁלוֹם עָלֵינוּ וְעַל כָּל יִשְׂרָאֵל, וְאִמְרוּ אָמֵן.

יְהִי רָצוֹן מִלְּפָנֶיךָ יהוה אֱלֹהֵינוּ וֵאלֹהֵי אֲבוֹתֵינוּ

שֶׁיִּבָּנֶה בֵּית הַמִּקְדָּשׁ בִּמְהֵרָה בְיָמֵינוּ, וְתֵן חֶלְקֵנוּ בְּתוֹרָתֶךָ

וְשָׁם נַעֲבָדְךָ בְּיִרְאָה כִּימֵי עוֹלָם וּכְשָׁנִים קַדְמֹנִיּוֹת.

מלאכי ג

וְעָרְבָה לַיהוה מִנְחַת יְהוּדָה וִירוּשָׁלָ͏ִם כִּימֵי עוֹלָם וּכְשָׁנִים קַדְמֹנִיּוֹת:

אֱלֹהַי, נְצֹר לְשׁוֹנִי *My God, guard my tongue.* Having asked God at the beginning of the Amida to "Open my lips, so that my mouth may declare Your praise," we now, at the end, ask God to help us close our lips from speaking harshly or deceitfully to others. Evil speech is one of the worst of all sins. It is especially wrong to pass from speaking well to God to speaking badly to our fellow humans, as if the one compensated for the other.

Leader's Repetition for Musaf

The Leader takes three steps forward and at the points indicated by ˎ, bends the knees at the first word, bows at the second, and stands straight before saying God's name.

When I proclaim the LORD's name, give glory to our God.   *Deut. 32*

O LORD, open my lips, so that my mouth may declare Your praise.   *Ps. 51*

PATRIARCHS

ˎבָּרוּךְ Blessed are You, LORD our God and God of our fathers,
God of Abraham, God of Isaac and God of Jacob;
the great, mighty and awesome God, God Most High,
who bestows acts of loving-kindness and creates all,
who remembers the loving-kindness of the fathers
and will bring a Redeemer
to their children's children
for the sake of His name, in love.
King, Helper, Savior, Shield:
ˎBlessed are You, LORD, Shield of Abraham.

DIVINE MIGHT

אַתָּה גִּבּוֹר You are eternally mighty, LORD.
You give life to the dead and have great power to save.

> *In Israel:*
> He causes the dew to fall.

He sustains the living with loving-kindness,
and with great compassion revives the dead.
He supports the fallen, heals the sick, sets captives free,
and keeps His faith with those who sleep in the dust.
Who is like You, Master of might,
and who can compare to You,
O King who brings death and gives life,
and makes salvation grow?
Faithful are You to revive the dead.
Blessed are You, LORD, who revives the dead.

חזרת הש״ץ למוסף

The שליח ציבור *takes three steps forward and at the points indicated by* ˚, *bends the knees at the first word, bows at the second, and stands straight before saying God's name.*

דברים לב
תהלים נא

כִּי שֵׁם יהוה אֶקְרָא, הָבוּ גֹדֶל לֵאלֹהֵינוּ:

אֲדֹנָי, שְׂפָתַי תִּפְתָּח, וּפִי יַגִּיד תְּהִלָּתֶךָ:

אבות

˚בָּרוּךְ אַתָּה יהוה, אֱלֹהֵינוּ וֵאלֹהֵי אֲבוֹתֵינוּ
אֱלֹהֵי אַבְרָהָם, אֱלֹהֵי יִצְחָק, וֵאלֹהֵי יַעֲקֹב
הָאֵל הַגָּדוֹל הַגִּבּוֹר וְהַנּוֹרָא, אֵל עֶלְיוֹן
גּוֹמֵל חֲסָדִים טוֹבִים, וְקֹנֵה הַכֹּל, וְזוֹכֵר חַסְדֵי אָבוֹת
וּמֵבִיא גוֹאֵל לִבְנֵי בְנֵיהֶם לְמַעַן שְׁמוֹ בְּאַהֲבָה.
מֶלֶךְ עוֹזֵר וּמוֹשִׁיעַ וּמָגֵן.
˚בָּרוּךְ אַתָּה יהוה, מָגֵן אַבְרָהָם.

גבורות

אַתָּה גִּבּוֹר לְעוֹלָם אֲדֹנָי
מְחַיֵּה מֵתִים אַתָּה, רַב לְהוֹשִׁיעַ

In ארץ ישראל:

מוֹרִיד הַטָּל

מְכַלְכֵּל חַיִּים בְּחֶסֶד, מְחַיֵּה מֵתִים בְּרַחֲמִים רַבִּים
סוֹמֵךְ נוֹפְלִים, וְרוֹפֵא חוֹלִים, וּמַתִּיר אֲסוּרִים
וּמְקַיֵּם אֱמוּנָתוֹ לִישֵׁנֵי עָפָר.
מִי כָמוֹךָ, בַּעַל גְּבוּרוֹת, וּמִי דּוֹמֶה לָּךְ
מֶלֶךְ, מֵמִית וּמְחַיֶּה וּמַצְמִיחַ יְשׁוּעָה.
וְנֶאֱמָן אַתָּה לְהַחֲיוֹת מֵתִים.
בָּרוּךְ אַתָּה יהוה, מְחַיֵּה הַמֵּתִים.

KEDUSHA

*The following is said standing with feet together,
rising on the toes at the words indicated by ˄.*

*Cong. then
Leader:* נַעֲרִיצְךָ We will revere and sanctify You
with the words uttered by the holy Seraphim
who sanctify Your name in the Sanctuary;
as is written by Your prophet:
"They call out to one another, saying: Is. 6

*Cong. then
Leader:* ˄Holy, ˄holy, ˄holy is the Lᴏʀᴅ of hosts;
the whole world is filled with His glory."
His glory fills the universe.
His ministering angels ask each other,
"Where is the place of His glory?"
Those facing them say "Blessed –"

*Cong. then
Leader:* "˄Blessed is the Lᴏʀᴅ's glory from His place."   Ezek. 3
From His place may He turn with compassion
and be gracious to the people who proclaim the unity
of His name, morning and evening, every day, continually,
twice each day reciting in love the Shema:

*Cong. then
Leader:* "Listen, Israel, the Lᴏʀᴅ is our God, the Lᴏʀᴅ is One."   Deut. 6
He is our God, He is our Father, He is our King,
He is our Savior – and He, in His compassion,
will let us hear a second time in the presence of all that lives,
His promise "to be your God.   Num. 15
I am the Lᴏʀᴅ your God."

───────────────────────────────────────

still turn their thoughts and hearts to the creative Source of the universe
and the redeeming Presence of history, the Infinite before whom we stand,
to whom we offer praise.

שְׁמַע יִשְׂרָאֵל *Listen, Israel.* With the exception of Yom Kippur, the Musaf
Kedusha is the only one to contain the first verse of the Shema. According
to a Geonic tradition (cited in *Or Zarua* 2:50), the custom to so include it
originated at a time of persecution when Jews were forbidden publicly to
declare their faith by saying the Shema in the synagogue. To circumvent this
they incorporated its first line into the Musaf *Kedusha,* where it remains to
this day.

קדושה

The following is said standing with feet together,
rising on the toes at the words indicated by ▲.

קהל
then
ש״ץ
נַעֲרִיצְךָ וְנַקְדִּישְׁךָ כְּסוֹד שִׂיחַ שַׂרְפֵי קֹדֶשׁ, הַמַּקְדִּישִׁים שִׁמְךָ

ישעיהו ו
בַּקֹּדֶשׁ, כַּכָּתוּב עַל יַד נְבִיאֶךָ: וְקָרָא זֶה אֶל־זֶה וְאָמַר

קהל
then
ש״ץ
▲קָדוֹשׁ, ▲קָדוֹשׁ, ▲קָדוֹשׁ, יהוה צְבָאוֹת, מְלֹא כָל־הָאָרֶץ כְּבוֹדוֹ:

כְּבוֹדוֹ מָלֵא עוֹלָם, מְשָׁרְתָיו שׁוֹאֲלִים זֶה לָזֶה, אַיֵּה מְקוֹם

כְּבוֹדוֹ לְעֻמָּתָם בָּרוּךְ יֹאמֵרוּ

קהל
then
ש״ץ
יחזקאל ג
▲בָּרוּךְ כְּבוֹד־יהוה מִמְּקוֹמוֹ:

מִמְּקוֹמוֹ הוּא יִפֶן בְּרַחֲמִים, וְיָחֹן עַם הַמְיַחֲדִים שְׁמוֹ

עֶרֶב וָבֹקֶר בְּכָל יוֹם תָּמִיד, פַּעֲמַיִם בְּאַהֲבָה שְׁמַע אוֹמְרִים

קהל
then
ש״ץ
דברים ו
שְׁמַע יִשְׂרָאֵל, יהוה אֱלֹהֵינוּ, יהוה אֶחָד:

הוּא אֱלֹהֵינוּ, הוּא אָבִינוּ, הוּא מַלְכֵּנוּ, הוּא מוֹשִׁיעֵנוּ

וְהוּא יַשְׁמִיעֵנוּ בְּרַחֲמָיו שֵׁנִית לְעֵינֵי כָּל חַי

במדבר טו
לִהְיוֹת לָכֶם לֵאלֹהִים

אֲנִי יהוה אֱלֹהֵיכֶם:

KEDUSHA

Kedusha is the Everest of prayer, the summit of the spiritual life. It is based
on the two mystical visions in which Isaiah and Ezekiel saw God in heaven,
enthroned in glory and surrounded by a chorus of angels singing His praises.
Isaiah heard them say "Holy, holy, holy…the whole world is filled with His
glory" (Is. 6:3). Ezekiel heard them say, "Blessed is the LORD's glory from
His place" (Ezek. 3:12). By saying *Kedusha* we join the angelic chorus, singing God's praises on earth as they do in heaven. What empowers us to do
so is the declaration of Psalm 8:5–6, "What is man, that You are mindful of
him, the son of man, that You think of him? Yet You have made him but little
lower than the angels, and crowned him with glory and honor." The paradox
is that though God is surrounded by angels singing His praises, what He
seeks is *our* praise – the praise of free, fallible, finite agents for whom God is
often hidden, who sometimes sin and despair and lose their faith, but who

Cong. then Glorious is our Glorious One, LORD our Master,   *Ps. 8*
   Leader: and glorious is Your name throughout the earth.
               Then the LORD shall be King over all the earth;   *Zech. 14*
               on that day the LORD shall be One and His name One.

   Leader: And in Your holy Writings it is written:

Cong. then "The LORD shall reign for ever.   *Ps. 146*
   Leader: He is your God, Zion, from generation to generation,
               Halleluya!"

   Leader: לְדוֹר וָדוֹר From generation to generation
               we will declare Your greatness,
               and we will proclaim Your holiness for evermore.
               Your praise, our God, shall not leave our mouth forever,
               for You, God, are a great and holy King.
               Blessed are You, LORD,
               the holy God.

HOLINESS OF THE DAY

אַתָּה בְחַרְתָּנוּ You have chosen us
from among all peoples.
You have loved and favored us.
You have raised us above all tongues.
You have made us holy through Your commandments.
You have brought us near, our King, to Your service,
and have called us by Your great and holy name.

On Shabbat, add the words in parentheses:

וַתִּתֶּן לָנוּ And You, LORD our God, have given us in love
(Sabbaths for rest and) festivals for rejoicing,
holy days and seasons for joy, (this Sabbath day and)
this day of the festival of Shavuot,
the time of the giving of our Torah
(with love), a holy assembly
in memory of the exodus from Egypt.

קהל then
אַדִּיר אַדִּירֵנוּ, יהוה אֲדֹנֵינוּ, מָה־אַדִּיר שִׁמְךָ בְּכָל־הָאָרֶץ: תהלים ח
ש״ץ

וְהָיָה יהוה לְמֶלֶךְ עַל־כָּל־הָאָרֶץ זכריה יד
בַּיּוֹם הַהוּא יִהְיֶה יהוה אֶחָד וּשְׁמוֹ אֶחָד:

ש״ץ וּבְדִבְרֵי קָדְשְׁךָ כָּתוּב לֵאמֹר:

קהל then
יִמְלֹךְ יהוה לְעוֹלָם, אֱלֹהַיִךְ צִיּוֹן לְדֹר וָדֹר, הַלְלוּיָהּ: תהלים קמו
ש״ץ

ש״ץ לְדוֹר וָדוֹר נַגִּיד גָּדְלֶךָ, וּלְנֵצַח נְצָחִים קְדֻשָּׁתְךָ נַקְדִּישׁ
וְשִׁבְחֲךָ אֱלֹהֵינוּ מִפִּינוּ לֹא יָמוּשׁ לְעוֹלָם וָעֶד
כִּי אֵל מֶלֶךְ גָּדוֹל וְקָדוֹשׁ אָתָּה.
בָּרוּךְ אַתָּה יהוה, הָאֵל הַקָּדוֹשׁ.

קְדֻשַּׁת הַיּוֹם
אַתָּה בְחַרְתָּנוּ מִכָּל הָעַמִּים
אָהַבְתָּ אוֹתָנוּ וְרָצִיתָ בָּנוּ
וְרוֹמַמְתָּנוּ מִכָּל הַלְּשׁוֹנוֹת
וְקִדַּשְׁתָּנוּ בְּמִצְוֹתֶיךָ
וְקֵרַבְתָּנוּ מַלְכֵּנוּ לַעֲבוֹדָתֶךָ
וְשִׁמְךָ הַגָּדוֹל וְהַקָּדוֹשׁ עָלֵינוּ קָרָאתָ.

On שבת, add the words in parentheses:

וַתִּתֶּן לָנוּ יהוה אֱלֹהֵינוּ בְּאַהֲבָה
(שַׁבָּתוֹת לִמְנוּחָה וּ)מוֹעֲדִים לְשִׂמְחָה
חַגִּים וּזְמַנִּים לְשָׂשׂוֹן
אֶת יוֹם (הַשַּׁבָּת הַזֶּה וְאֶת יוֹם) חַג הַשָּׁבוּעוֹת הַזֶּה
זְמַן מַתַּן תּוֹרָתֵנוּ
(בְּאַהֲבָה) מִקְרָא קֹדֶשׁ, זֵכֶר לִיצִיאַת מִצְרָיִם.

וּמִפְּנֵי חֲטָאֵינוּ But because of our sins we were exiled from our land
and driven far from our country.
We cannot go up to appear and bow before You,
and to perform our duties in Your chosen House,
the great and holy Temple that was called by Your name,
because of the hand that was stretched out against Your Sanctuary.
May it be Your will, LORD our God and God of our ancestors,
merciful King,
that You in Your abounding compassion may once more
have mercy on us and on Your Sanctuary,
rebuilding it swiftly and adding to its glory.
Our Father, our King, reveal the glory of Your kingdom to us swiftly.
Appear and be exalted over us in the sight of all that lives.
Bring back our scattered ones from among the nations,
and gather our dispersed people from the ends of the earth.

Lead us to Zion, Your city, in jubilation,
and to Jerusalem, home of Your Temple, with everlasting joy.
There we will prepare for You our obligatory offerings:
the regular daily offerings in their order
and the additional offerings according to their law.
And the additional offering(s of this Sabbath day and)
of this day of the festival of Shavuot.
we will prepare and offer before You in love,
in accord with Your will's commandment,
as You wrote for us in Your Torah
through Your servant Moses, by Your own word, as it is said:

On Shabbat:
    וּבְיוֹם הַשַּׁבָּת On the Sabbath day,   *Num. 28*
    make an offering of two lambs a year old, without blemish,
    together with two-tenths of an ephah of fine flour mixed
    with oil as a meal-offering, and its appropriate libation.
    This is the burnt-offering for every Sabbath,
    in addition to the regular daily burnt-offering and its libation.

וּמִפְּנֵי חֲטָאֵינוּ גָּלִינוּ מֵאַרְצֵנוּ, וְנִתְרַחַקְנוּ מֵעַל אַדְמָתֵנוּ

וְאֵין אֲנַחְנוּ יְכוֹלִים לַעֲלוֹת וְלֵרָאוֹת וּלְהִשְׁתַּחֲווֹת לְפָנֶיךָ

וְלַעֲשׂוֹת חוֹבוֹתֵינוּ בְּבֵית בְּחִירָתֶךָ

בַּבַּיִת הַגָּדוֹל וְהַקָּדוֹשׁ שֶׁנִּקְרָא שִׁמְךָ עָלָיו

מִפְּנֵי הַיָּד שֶׁנִּשְׁתַּלְּחָה בְּמִקְדָּשֶׁךָ.

יְהִי רָצוֹן מִלְּפָנֶיךָ יהוה אֱלֹהֵינוּ וֵאלֹהֵי אֲבוֹתֵינוּ, מֶלֶךְ רַחֲמָן

שֶׁתָּשׁוּב וּתְרַחֵם עָלֵינוּ וְעַל מִקְדָּשְׁךָ בְּרַחֲמֶיךָ הָרַבִּים

וְתִבְנֵהוּ מְהֵרָה וּתְגַדֵּל כְּבוֹדוֹ.

אָבִינוּ מַלְכֵּנוּ, גַּלֵּה כְּבוֹד מַלְכוּתְךָ עָלֵינוּ מְהֵרָה

וְהוֹפַע וְהִנָּשֵׂא עָלֵינוּ לְעֵינֵי כָּל חָי

וְקָרֵב פְּזוּרֵינוּ מִבֵּין הַגּוֹיִם, וּנְפוּצוֹתֵינוּ כַּנֵּס מִיַּרְכְּתֵי אָרֶץ.

וַהֲבִיאֵנוּ לְצִיּוֹן עִירְךָ בְּרִנָּה

וְלִירוּשָׁלַיִם בֵּית מִקְדָּשְׁךָ בְּשִׂמְחַת עוֹלָם

וְשָׁם נַעֲשֶׂה לְפָנֶיךָ אֶת קָרְבְּנוֹת חוֹבוֹתֵינוּ

תְּמִידִים כְּסִדְרָם וּמוּסָפִים כְּהִלְכָתָם

וְאֶת מוּסַף יוֹם / שבת: וְאֶת מוּסְפֵי יוֹם הַשַּׁבָּת הַזֶּה וְיוֹם/

חַג הַשָּׁבוּעוֹת הַזֶּה

נַעֲשֶׂה וְנַקְרִיב לְפָנֶיךָ בְּאַהֲבָה כְּמִצְוַת רְצוֹנֶךָ

כְּמוֹ שֶׁכָּתַבְתָּ עָלֵינוּ בְּתוֹרָתֶךָ

עַל יְדֵי מֹשֶׁה עַבְדֶּךָ מִפִּי כְבוֹדֶךָ, כָּאָמוּר

שבת: *On*

וּבְיוֹם הַשַּׁבָּת, שְׁנֵי־כְבָשִׂים בְּנֵי־שָׁנָה תְּמִימִם

וּשְׁנֵי עֶשְׂרֹנִים סֹלֶת מִנְחָה בְּלוּלָה בַשֶּׁמֶן וְנִסְכּוֹ:

עֹלַת שַׁבַּת בְּשַׁבַּתּוֹ, עַל־עֹלַת הַתָּמִיד וְנִסְכָּהּ:

במדבר כח

וּבְיוֹם הַבִּכּוּרִים On the day of the first fruits, *Num. 28*
when you bring an offering of new grain to the LORD,
on your Festival of Weeks, there shall be a sacred assembly:
you shall do no laborious work.
You shall offer a burnt-offering of pleasing aroma to the LORD:
two young bullocks, one ram,
and seven yearling male lambs.

And their meal-offerings and wine-libations as ordained:
three-tenths of an ephah for each bull,
two-tenths of an ephah for the ram,
one-tenth of an ephah for each lamb,
wine for the libations,
a male goat for atonement,
and two regular daily offerings according to their law.

Some congregations add the piyut אַתָּה הִנְחַלְתָּ (page 731) on the
first day of Shavuot and the piyut אַזְהָרַת רֹאשִׁית on the second day
(page 768) at this point. Many recite the following piyut:

אָז שֵׁשׁ מֵאוֹת Then, six hundred and thirteen mitzvot,
their punishments and rewards –
pure sayings, / rarified sevenfold,
refined like silver, / choice as gold;
already then, the beloved ones kept them,
those borne by God studied them,
guarded them with all their hearts,
and sought them with all their wisdom:
remember these for us, / God our Stronghold,
and favor us also, / and grant us what we ask.

The angels rejoiced, / and those on earth were jubilant,
when the bride received / her groom's ketuba.
And the bride's face / grew radiant, exalted,
when, on this day, she received / the Ten Commandments.

וּבְיוֹם הַבִּכּוּרִים, בְּהַקְרִיבְכֶם מִנְחָה חֲדָשָׁה לַיהוה בְּשָׁבֻעֹתֵיכֶם במדבר כח

מִקְרָא־קֹדֶשׁ יִהְיֶה לָכֶם

כָּל־מְלֶאכֶת עֲבֹדָה לֹא תַעֲשׂוּ:

וְהִקְרַבְתֶּם עוֹלָה לְרֵיחַ נִיחֹחַ לַיהוה

פָּרִים בְּנֵי־בָקָר שְׁנַיִם, אַיִל אֶחָד

שִׁבְעָה כְבָשִׂים בְּנֵי שָׁנָה:

וּמִנְחָתָם וְנִסְכֵּיהֶם כִּמְדֻבָּר

שְׁלֹשָׁה עֶשְׂרֹנִים לַפָּר וּשְׁנֵי עֶשְׂרֹנִים לָאַיִל

וְעִשָּׂרוֹן לַכֶּבֶשׂ, וְיַיִן כְּנִסְכּוֹ, וְשָׂעִיר לְכַפֵּר

וּשְׁנֵי תְמִידִים כְּהִלְכָתָם.

Some congregations add the piyut אַתָּה הִנְחַלְתָּ *(page 731) on the
first day of* שבועות *and the piyut* אַזְהָרַת רֵאשִׁית *on the second day
(page 768) at this point. Many recite the following piyut:*

אָז שֵׁשׁ מֵאוֹת וְשָׁלֹשׁ עֶשְׂרֵה מִצְוֹת / פֵּרוּשׁ עָנְשָׁן וּמַתַּן שְׂכָרַן

אֲמָרוֹת טְהֹרוֹת / מְזֻקָּקוֹת שִׁבְעָתַיִם

צְרוּפוֹת כַּכֶּסֶף / וּבְחוּנוֹת כַּזָּהָב

אֲהוּבִים שְׁמָרוּם / עֲמוּסִים חֲקָרוּם

בְּכָל לֵב נְצָרוּם / בְּחָכְמָה דְּרָשׁוּם

אֶת אֵלֶּה תִּזְכָּר לָנוּ / אֱלוֹהַּ מְעוּזֵּנוּ

וְתִרְצֶה לָנוּ / וּתְמַלֵּא מִשְׁאֲלוֹתֵינוּ.

עֶלְיוֹנִים שָׂשׂוּ / וְתַחְתּוֹנִים עָלְזוּ

בְּקַבָּלַת כַּלָּה / כְּתֻבַּת חָתָן.

תֹּאַר כַּלָּה / מְאֹד נִתְעַלָּה

בְּקַבָּלַת יוֹם זֶה / עֲשֶׂרֶת הַדִּבְּרוֹת.

On Shabbat:

יִשְׂמְחוּ Those who keep the Sabbath and call it a delight
shall rejoice in Your kingship.
The people who sanctify the seventh day shall all be satisfied
and take delight in Your goodness,
for You favored the seventh day and declared it holy.
You called it "most desirable of days"
in remembrance of Creation.

אֱלֹהֵינוּ Our God and God of our ancestors,
merciful King, have compassion upon us.
You who are good and do good,
respond to our call.
Return to us in Your abounding mercy
for the sake of our fathers who did Your will.
Rebuild Your Temple as at the beginning,
and establish Your Sanctuary on its site.
Let us witness its rebuilding
and gladden us by its restoration.
Bring the priests back to their service,
the Levites to their song and music,
and the Israelites to their homes.

וְשָׁם נַעֲלֶה There we will go up and appear and bow before You
on the three pilgrimage festivals,
as is written in Your Torah:

> "Three times in the year all your males shall appear   *Deut. 16*
> before the Lᴏʀᴅ your God
> at the place He will choose:
> on Pesaḥ, Shavuot and Sukkot.
> They shall not appear before the Lᴏʀᴅ empty-handed.
> Each shall bring such a gift as he can,
> in proportion to the blessing
> that the Lᴏʀᴅ your God grants you."

שבת :On

יִשְׂמְחוּ בְמַלְכוּתְךָ שׁוֹמְרֵי שַׁבָּת וְקוֹרְאֵי עְנֶג.
עַם מְקַדְּשֵׁי שְׁבִיעִי
כֻּלָּם יִשְׂבְּעוּ וְיִתְעַנְּגוּ מִטּוּבֶךָ
וּבַשְּׁבִיעִי רָצִיתָ בּוֹ וְקִדַּשְׁתּוֹ
חֶמְדַּת יָמִים אוֹתוֹ קָרֵאתָ
זֵכֶר לְמַעֲשֵׂה בְרֵאשִׁית.

אֱלֹהֵינוּ וֵאלֹהֵי אֲבוֹתֵינוּ, מֶלֶךְ רַחֲמָן רַחֵם עָלֵינוּ
טוֹב וּמֵטִיב הִדָּרֶשׁ לָנוּ
שׁוּבָה אֵלֵינוּ בַּהֲמוֹן רַחֲמֶיךָ
בִּגְלַל אָבוֹת שֶׁעָשׂוּ רְצוֹנֶךָ.
בְּנֵה בֵיתְךָ כְּבַתְּחִלָּה וְכוֹנֵן מִקְדָּשְׁךָ עַל מְכוֹנוֹ
וְהַרְאֵנוּ בְּבִנְיָנוֹ, וְשַׂמְּחֵנוּ בְּתִקּוּנוֹ
וְהָשֵׁב כֹּהֲנִים לַעֲבוֹדָתָם
וּלְוִיִּם לְשִׁירָם וּלְזִמְרָם
וְהָשֵׁב יִשְׂרָאֵל לִנְוֵיהֶם.

וְשָׁם נַעֲלֶה וְנֵרָאֶה וְנִשְׁתַּחֲוֶה לְפָנֶיךָ בְּשָׁלֹשׁ פַּעֲמֵי רְגָלֵינוּ
כַּכָּתוּב בְּתוֹרָתֶךָ
שָׁלוֹשׁ פְּעָמִים בַּשָּׁנָה יֵרָאֶה כָל־זְכוּרְךָ אֶת־פְּנֵי יהוה אֱלֹהֶיךָ   דברים טז
בַּמָּקוֹם אֲשֶׁר יִבְחָר
בְּחַג הַמַּצּוֹת, וּבְחַג הַשָּׁבֻעוֹת, וּבְחַג הַסֻּכּוֹת
וְלֹא יֵרָאֶה אֶת־פְּנֵי יהוה רֵיקָם:
אִישׁ כְּמַתְּנַת יָדוֹ, כְּבִרְכַּת יהוה אֱלֹהֶיךָ אֲשֶׁר נָתַן־לָךְ:

On Shabbat add the words in parentheses:

וְהַשִּׂיאֵנוּ Bestow on us, LORD our God,
the blessing of Your festivals
for life and peace, joy and gladness,
as You desired and promised to bless us.
(Our God and God of our fathers, find favor in our rest.)
Make us holy through Your commandments
and grant us a share in Your Torah;
satisfy us with Your goodness, gladden us with Your salvation,
and purify our hearts to serve You in truth.
And grant us a heritage, LORD our God, (with love and favor,)
with joy and gladness, Your holy (Sabbath and) festivals.
May Israel, who sanctify Your name, rejoice in You.
Blessed are You, LORD,
who sanctifies (the Sabbath and) Israel and the festive seasons.

TEMPLE SERVICE

רְצֵה Find favor, LORD our God, in Your people Israel
and their prayer.
Restore the service to Your most holy House,
and accept in love and favor the fire-offerings of Israel
and their prayer.
May the service of Your people Israel always find favor with You.

*If Kohanim say the Priestly Blessing during the Leader's Repetition,
the following is said (In Israel the formula on the next page is said);
otherwise the Leader continues with "And may our eyes" on the next page.*

All: וְתֶעֱרַב May our entreaty be as pleasing to You as a burnt-offering and sacrifice. Please, Compassionate One, in Your abounding mercy restore Your Presence to Zion, Your city, and the order of the Temple service to Jerusalem. And may our eyes witness Your return to Zion in compassion, there we may serve You with reverence as in the days of old and as in former years.

Leader: Blessed are You, LORD, for You alone do we serve with reverence.

The service continues with "We give thanks" on the next page.

On שבת *add the words in parentheses:*

וְהַשִּׂיאֵנוּ יהוה אֱלֹהֵינוּ אֶת בִּרְכַּת מוֹעֲדֶיךָ

לְחַיִּים וּלְשָׁלוֹם, לְשִׂמְחָה וּלְשָׂשׂוֹן

כַּאֲשֶׁר רָצִיתָ וְאָמַרְתָּ לְבָרְכֵנוּ.

(אֱלֹהֵינוּ וֵאלֹהֵי אֲבוֹתֵינוּ, רְצֵה בִמְנוּחָתֵנוּ)

קַדְּשֵׁנוּ בְּמִצְוֺתֶיךָ, וְתֵן חֶלְקֵנוּ בְּתוֹרָתֶךָ

שַׂבְּעֵנוּ מִטּוּבֶךָ, וְשַׂמְּחֵנוּ בִּישׁוּעָתֶךָ

וְטַהֵר לִבֵּנוּ לְעָבְדְּךָ בֶּאֱמֶת

וְהַנְחִילֵנוּ יהוה אֱלֹהֵינוּ (בְּאַהֲבָה וּבְרָצוֹן) בְּשִׂמְחָה וּבְשָׂשׂוֹן

(שַׁבָּת וּ)מוֹעֲדֵי קָדְשֶׁךָ וְיִשְׂמְחוּ בְךָ יִשְׂרָאֵל מְקַדְּשֵׁי שְׁמֶךָ.

בָּרוּךְ אַתָּה יהוה, מְקַדֵּשׁ (הַשַּׁבָּת וְ)יִשְׂרָאֵל וְהַזְּמַנִּים.

עבודה

רְצֵה יהוה אֱלֹהֵינוּ בְּעַמְּךָ יִשְׂרָאֵל, וּבִתְפִלָּתָם

וְהָשֵׁב אֶת הָעֲבוֹדָה לִדְבִיר בֵּיתֶךָ

וְאִשֵּׁי יִשְׂרָאֵל וּתְפִלָּתָם בְּאַהֲבָה תְקַבֵּל בְּרָצוֹן

וּתְהִי לְרָצוֹן תָּמִיד עֲבוֹדַת יִשְׂרָאֵל עַמֶּךָ.

If כהנים *say* ברכת כהנים *during* חזרת הש״ץ,
the following is said (In ארץ ישראל *the formula on the next page is said);*
otherwise the שליח ציבור *continues with* וְתֶחֱזֶינָה *on the next page.*

קהל
וש״ץ:
וְתֶעֱרַב עָלֶיךָ עֲתִירָתֵנוּ כְּעוֹלָה וּכְקָרְבָּן. אָנָּא רַחוּם, בְּרַחֲמֶיךָ הָרַבִּים
הָשֵׁב שְׁכִינָתְךָ לְצִיּוֹן עִירֶךָ, וְסֵדֶר הָעֲבוֹדָה לִירוּשָׁלָיִם. וְתֶחֱזֶינָה
עֵינֵינוּ בְּשׁוּבְךָ לְצִיּוֹן בְּרַחֲמִים. וְשָׁם נַעֲבָדְךָ בְּיִרְאָה כִּימֵי עוֹלָם
וּכְשָׁנִים קַדְמוֹנִיּוֹת.

ש״ץ:
בָּרוּךְ אַתָּה יהוה שֶׁאוֹתְךָ לְבַדְּךָ בְּיִרְאָה נַעֲבֹד.

The service continues with מודים *on the next page.*

In Israel the following formula is used instead:

All: וְתֶעֱרַב May our entreaty be as pleasing to You as a burnt-offering and sacrifice. Please, Compassionate One, in Your abounding mercy restore Your Presence to Zion, Your city, and the order of the Temple service to Jerusalem. That there we may serve You with reverence as in the days of old and as in former years.

When the Priestly Blessing is not said, and also in Israel, the Leader continues:

And may our eyes witness Your return to Zion in compassion. Blessed are You, LORD, who restores His Presence to Zion.

THANKSGIVING

Bow at the first nine words.

מוֹדִים We give thanks to You, for You are the LORD our God and God of our ancestors for ever and all time. You are the Rock of our lives, Shield of our salvation from generation to generation. We will thank You and declare Your praise for our lives, which are entrusted into Your hand; for our souls, which are placed in Your charge; for Your miracles which are with us every day; and for Your wonders and favors at all times, evening, morning and midday. You are good – for Your compassion never fails. You are compassionate – for Your loving-kindnesses never cease. We have always placed our hope in You.

As the Leader recites Modim, the congregation says quietly:

מוֹדִים We give thanks to You, for You are the LORD our God and God of our ancestors, God of all flesh, who formed us and formed the universe. Blessings and thanks are due to Your great and holy name for giving us life and sustaining us. May You continue to give us life and sustain us; and may You gather our exiles to Your holy courts, to keep Your decrees, do Your will and serve You with a perfect heart, for it is for us to give You thanks. Blessed be God to whom thanksgiving is due.

In ארץ ישראל *the following formula is used instead:*

קהל
ושץ:
וְתֶעֱרַב עָלֶיךָ עֲתִירָתֵנוּ כְּעוֹלָה וּכְקָרְבָּן. אָנָּא רַחוּם, בְּרַחֲמֶיךָ הָרַבִּים
הָשֵׁב שְׁכִינָתְךָ לְצִיּוֹן עִירָךְ, וְסֵדֶר הָעֲבוֹדָה לִירוּשָׁלָיִם. וְשָׁם נַעֲבָדְךָ
בְּיִרְאָה כִּימֵי עוֹלָם וּכְשָׁנִים קַדְמוֹנִיּוֹת.

When ארץ ישראל, *the* שליח ציבור *is not said, and also in* ברכת כהנים *continues:*

וְתֶחֱזֶינָה עֵינֵינוּ בְּשׁוּבְךָ לְצִיּוֹן בְּרַחֲמִים.
בָּרוּךְ אַתָּה יהוה, הַמַּחֲזִיר שְׁכִינָתוֹ לְצִיּוֹן.

הודאה

Bow at the first five words.

As the שליח ציבור *recites* מודים,
the קהל *says quietly:*

מוֹדִים אֲנַחְנוּ לָךְ
שָׁאַתָּה הוּא יהוה אֱלֹהֵינוּ
וֵאלֹהֵי אֲבוֹתֵינוּ
אֱלֹהֵי כָל בָּשָׂר,
יוֹצְרֵנוּ, יוֹצֵר בְּרֵאשִׁית.
בְּרָכוֹת וְהוֹדָאוֹת
לְשִׁמְךָ הַגָּדוֹל וְהַקָּדוֹשׁ
עַל שֶׁהֶחֱיִיתָנוּ וְקִיַּמְתָּנוּ.
כֵּן תְּחַיֵּנוּ וּתְקַיְּמֵנוּ
וְתֶאֱסֹף גָּלֻיּוֹתֵינוּ
לְחַצְרוֹת קָדְשֶׁךָ
לִשְׁמֹר חֻקֶּיךָ
וְלַעֲשׂוֹת רְצוֹנֶךָ וּלְעָבְדְּךָ
בְּלֵבָב שָׁלֵם
עַל שֶׁאֲנַחְנוּ מוֹדִים לָךְ.
בָּרוּךְ אֵל הַהוֹדָאוֹת.

מוֹדִים אֲנַחְנוּ לָךְ
שָׁאַתָּה הוּא יהוה אֱלֹהֵינוּ
וֵאלֹהֵי אֲבוֹתֵינוּ לְעוֹלָם וָעֶד.
צוּר חַיֵּינוּ, מָגֵן יִשְׁעֵנוּ
אַתָּה הוּא לְדוֹר וָדוֹר.
נוֹדֶה לְּךָ וּנְסַפֵּר תְּהִלָּתֶךָ
עַל חַיֵּינוּ הַמְּסוּרִים בְּיָדֶךָ
וְעַל נִשְׁמוֹתֵינוּ הַפְּקוּדוֹת לָךְ
וְעַל נִסֶּיךָ שֶׁבְּכָל יוֹם עִמָּנוּ
וְעַל נִפְלְאוֹתֶיךָ וְטוֹבוֹתֶיךָ
שֶׁבְּכָל עֵת
עֶרֶב וָבֹקֶר וְצָהֳרָיִם.
הַטּוֹב, כִּי לֹא כָלוּ רַחֲמֶיךָ
וְהַמְרַחֵם, כִּי לֹא תַמּוּ חֲסָדֶיךָ
מֵעוֹלָם קִוִּינוּ לָךְ.

וְעַל כֻּלָּם For all these things may Your name be
blessed and exalted, our King, continually, for ever and all time.
Let all that lives thank You, Selah! and praise Your name in truth,
God, our Savior and Help, Selah!
′Blessed are You, LORD, whose name is "the Good"
and to whom thanks are due.

BIRKAT KOHANIM

For the blessing of the Kohanim in Israel, see page 696.
When the Priestly Blessing is not said, the Leader says the formula on page 560.
The following supplication is recited quietly while the Leader says "Let all that lives" above.

In some communities, the congregation says:	*The Kohanim say:*
יְהִי רָצוֹן May it be Your will, LORD our God and God of our ancestors, that this blessing with which You have commanded to bless Your people Israel should be a complete blessing, with neither hindrance nor sin, now and forever.	יְהִי רָצוֹן May it be Your will, LORD our God and God of our ancestors, that this blessing with which You have commanded us to bless Your people Israel should be a complete blessing, with neither hindrance nor sin, now and forever.

The following is recited quietly by the Leader:
אֱלֹהֵינוּ Our God and God of our fathers,
bless us with the threefold blessing in the Torah,
written by the hand of Moses Your servant
and pronounced by Aaron and his sons:

---

in Israel. Outside Israel, our custom is that the priestly blessings are said
only on festivals, for only then do we experience the joy that those who live
in God's land feel every day.

During the Leader's Repetition of the Amida, and prior to the Priestly
Blessings, the Kohanim remove their shoes and wash their hands in water
poured from a special vessel by the Levites. When the Leader reaches "Find
favor," they ascend to stand in front of the Ark. They cover the head and up-
per body with the tallit.

When blessing the people, the Kohanim raise their arms and hands as
Aaron did when he first blessed the people (Lev. 9:22). Their fingers are
spread apart, as a symbol of generosity of spirit (the closed hand symbolizes
possessiveness [Deut. 15:7]) and of the Divine Presence that shines through
the spaces like the beloved in the Song of Songs who "peers through the

וְעַל כֻּלָּם יִתְבָּרַךְ וְיִתְרוֹמַם שִׁמְךָ מַלְכֵּנוּ תָּמִיד לְעוֹלָם וָעֶד.
וְכֹל הַחַיִּים יוֹדוּךָ סֶּלָה, וִיהַלְלוּ אֶת שִׁמְךָ בֶּאֱמֶת
הָאֵל יְשׁוּעָתֵנוּ וְעֶזְרָתֵנוּ סֶלָה.
בָּרוּךְ אַתָּה יהוה, הַטּוֹב שִׁמְךָ וּלְךָ נָאֶה לְהוֹדוֹת.

ברכת כוהנים

For the blessing of the כהנים *in* ארץ ישראל *see page 697.*
When ברכת כהנים *is not said, the* שליח ציבור *says the formula on page 561.*
The following supplication is recited quietly while the שליח ציבור *says* וְכֹל הַחַיִּים *above.*

The כהנים *say:*	*In some communities, the* קהל *says:*
יְהִי רָצוֹן מִלְּפָנֶיךָ, יהוה אֱלֹהֵינוּ וֵאלֹהֵי	יְהִי רָצוֹן מִלְּפָנֶיךָ, יהוה אֱלֹהֵינוּ וֵאלֹהֵי
אֲבוֹתֵינוּ, שֶׁתְּהֵא הַבְּרָכָה הַזֹּאת שֶׁצִּוִּיתָנוּ	אֲבוֹתֵינוּ, שֶׁתְּהֵא הַבְּרָכָה הַזֹּאת שֶׁצִּוִּיתָ
לְבָרֵךְ אֶת עַמְּךָ יִשְׂרָאֵל בְּרָכָה שְׁלֵמָה,	לְבָרֵךְ אֶת עַמְּךָ יִשְׂרָאֵל בְּרָכָה שְׁלֵמָה,
וְלֹא יִהְיֶה בָּהּ שׁוּם מִכְשׁוֹל וְעָוֹן מֵעַתָּה	וְלֹא יִהְיֶה בָּהּ שׁוּם מִכְשׁוֹל וְעָוֹן מֵעַתָּה
וְעַד עוֹלָם.	וְעַד עוֹלָם.

The following is recited quietly by the שליח ציבור:
אֱלֹהֵינוּ וֵאלֹהֵי אֲבוֹתֵינוּ, בָּרְכֵנוּ בַבְּרָכָה הַמְשֻׁלֶּשֶׁת בַּתּוֹרָה
הַכְּתוּבָה עַל יְדֵי מֹשֶׁה עַבְדֶּךָ, הָאֲמוּרָה מִפִּי אַהֲרֹן וּבָנָיו

BIRKAT KOHANIM

The Priestly Blessings are unique among our prayers: not only are they ordained by the Torah itself, but so is their precise wording (Num. 6:24–26).
They are therefore our most ancient prayer. Beautifully constructed, the
blessings grow in length – the first line has three words; the second, five; the
third, seven – and in each, God's holiest name is the second word of the blessing. They ascend thematically: the first is for material blessing, the second
for spiritual blessing, and the third for peace, without which no blessings
can be enjoyed.

The Torah is careful to state: "So they (the priests) shall place My name on
the Israelites and I will bless them" (Num. 6:27). Thus it is not the priests who
bless the people, but God. The priests – whose entire lives were dedicated to
divine service – were holy vehicles through which divine blessing flowed. In
Temple times, the priests blessed the people daily. That remains the custom

The Leader says aloud:

Kohanim!

In most places, the congregation responds:
Your holy people, as it said:

The Kohanim say the following blessing in unison:

בָּרוּךְ Blessed are You, LORD our God, King of the Universe, who has made us holy with the holiness of Aaron, and has commanded us to bless His people Israel with love.

The first word in each sentence is said by the Leader, followed by the Kohanim. Some read silently the accompanying verses. One should remain silent and not look at the Kohanim while the blessings are being said.

May [He] bless you	May the LORD, Maker of heaven and earth, bless you from Zion.	Ps. 134
The LORD	LORD our Master, how majestic is Your name throughout the earth.	Ps. 8
And protect you.	Protect me, God, for in You I take refuge.	Ps. 16

Read the following silently while the Kohanim chant. Omit on Shabbat.

Master of the Universe, I am Yours and my dreams are Yours. I have dreamt a dream and I do not know what it means. May it be Your will, LORD my God and God of my fathers, that all my dreams be, for me and all Israel, for good, whether I have

———————————————

וְצִוָּנוּ לְבָרֵךְ אֶת עַמּוֹ יִשְׂרָאֵל בְּאַהֲבָה *And has commended us to bless His people Israel with love.* A unique stipulation ("with love") which we do not find in connection with any other command. According to Rashi (to Numbers 6:23), God told Moses to instruct the priests that they should make the blessing "with concentration and a full heart." Hillel suggested that it was Aaron's gift for love and peace that made him and his children the conduit for divine blessings: "Be among the disciples of Aaron, loving peace and pursuing peace, loving people and drawing them close to Torah" (*Avot* 1:12). Love is the conduit through which divine energy flows into the world.

יְבָרֶכְךָ *May the LORD bless you* with your material needs and good health and *protect you* from harm. *May the LORD make His face shine on you,* granting you spiritual growth, especially through Torah study (*Targum Yonatan*), *and be gracious to you,* so that you find favor in the eyes of God and your

The שליח ציבור *says aloud:*

כֹּהֲנִים

In most places, the קהל *responds:*

עַם קְדוֹשֶׁךָ, כָּאָמוּר:

The כהנים *say the following blessing in unison:*

בָּרוּךְ אַתָּה יהוה אֱלֹהֵינוּ מֶלֶךְ הָעוֹלָם, אֲשֶׁר קִדְּשָׁנוּ בִּקְדֻשָּׁתוֹ שֶׁל אַהֲרֹן,
וְצִוָּנוּ לְבָרֵךְ אֶת עַמּוֹ יִשְׂרָאֵל בְּאַהֲבָה.

The first word in each sentence is said by the שליח ציבור, *followed by the*
כהנים. *Some read silently the accompanying verses. One should remain*
silent and not look at the כהנים *while the blessings are being said.*

תהלים קלד

יְבָרֶכְךָ **יְבָרֶכְךָ** יהוה מִצִּיּוֹן, עֹשֵׂה שָׁמַיִם וָאָרֶץ:

תהלים ח

יהוה **יהוה** אֲדֹנֵינוּ, מָה־אַדִּיר שִׁמְךָ בְּכָל־הָאָרֶץ:

תהלים טז

וְיִשְׁמְרֶךָ **שָׁמְרֵנִי** אֵל, כִּי־חָסִיתִי בָךְ:

Read the following silently while the כהנים *chant. Omit on* שבת.

רִבּוֹנוֹ שֶׁל עוֹלָם, אֲנִי שֶׁלָּךְ וַחֲלוֹמוֹתַי שֶׁלָּךְ. חֲלוֹם חָלַמְתִּי וְאֵינִי יוֹדֵעַ מַה הוּא. יְהִי
רָצוֹן מִלְּפָנֶיךָ, יהוה אֱלֹהַי וֵאלֹהֵי אֲבוֹתַי, שֶׁיִּהְיוּ כָּל חֲלוֹמוֹתַי עָלַי וְעַל כָּל יִשְׂרָאֵל

---

lattices" (Song. 2:9; *Bemidbar Raba* 11:2). The priests cover their hands and
faces with the tallit in memory of the Holy of Holies that was screened from
public gaze by a curtain (*Beit Yosef*, OḤ 128).

The biblical command is preceded by the words, "The LORD said to Moses,
'Tell Aaron and his sons: This is how you are to bless the Israelites. *Say to
them …*" (Num. 6:22–23). In memory of Moses instructing the priests, the
custom is that the Leader recites each word, followed by the Kohanim (Maimonides, Laws of Prayer 14:3; others argue that the custom is merely to avoid
error on the part of the priests).

During the blessings, the members of the congregation should be in front
of the Kohanim. Those sitting behind should move forward at this time.
Their faces should be turned toward the Kohanim, but they should not look
directly at them while the blessings are being said (Rema, OḤ 128:23, following the Yerushalmi).

dreamt about myself, or about others, or others have dreamt about me. If they are good, strengthen and reinforce them, and may they be fulfilled in me and them like the dreams of the righteous Joseph. If, though, they need healing, heal them as You healed Hezekiah King of Judah from his illness, like Miriam the prophetess from her leprosy, like Na'aman from his leprosy, like the waters of Mara by Moses our teacher, and like the waters of Jericho by Elisha. And just as You turned the curses of Balaam the wicked from curse to blessing, so turn all my dreams about me and all Israel to good; protect me, be gracious to me and accept me. Amen.

May [He] make shine	May God be gracious to us and bless us; may He make His face shine upon us, Selah.	Ps. 67
The LORD	The LORD, the LORD, compassionate and gracious God, slow to anger, abounding in kindness and truth.	Ex. 34
His face	Turn to me and be gracious to me, for I am alone and afflicted.	Ps. 25
On you	To You, LORD, I lift up my soul.	Ps. 25
And be gracious to you.	As the eyes of slaves turn to their master's hand, or the eyes of a slave-girl to the hand of her mistress, so our eyes are turned to the LORD our God, awaiting His favor.	Ps. 123

Read the following silently while the Kohanim chant. Omit on Shabbat.

Master of the Universe, I am Yours and my dreams are Yours. I have dreamt a dream and I do not know what it means. May it be Your will, LORD my God and God of my fathers, that all my dreams be, for me and all Israel, for good, whether I have dreamt about myself, or about others, or others have dreamt about me. If they are good, strengthen and reinforce them, and may they be fulfilled in me and them like the dreams of the righteous Joseph. If, though, they need healing, heal them as You healed Hezekiah King of Judah from his illness, like Miriam the prophetess from her leprosy, like Na'aman from his leprosy, like the waters of Mara by Moses our teacher, and like the waters of Jericho by Elisha. And just as You turned the curses of Balaam the wicked from curse to blessing, so turn all my dreams about me and all Israel to good; protect me, be gracious to me and accept me. Amen.

(Sforno), *and grant you peace,* external and internal, harmony with the world and with yourself.

לְטוֹבָה, בֵּין שֶׁחָלַמְתִּי עַל עַצְמִי, וּבֵין שֶׁחָלַמְתִּי עַל אֲחֵרִים, וּבֵין שֶׁחָלְמוּ אֲחֵרִים עָלָי. אִם טוֹבִים הֵם, חַזְּקֵם וְאַמְּצֵם, וְיִתְקַיְּמוּ בִי וּבָהֶם, כַּחֲלוֹמוֹתָיו שֶׁל יוֹסֵף הַצַּדִּיק. וְאִם צְרִיכִים רְפוּאָה, רְפָאֵם כְּחִזְקִיָּהוּ מֶלֶךְ יְהוּדָה מֵחָלְיוֹ, וּכְמִרְיָם הַנְּבִיאָה מִצָּרַעְתָּהּ, וּכְנַעֲמָן מִצָּרַעְתּוֹ, וּכְמֵי מָרָה עַל יְדֵי מֹשֶׁה רַבֵּנוּ, וּכְמֵי יְרִיחוֹ עַל יְדֵי אֱלִישָׁע. וּכְשֵׁם שֶׁהָפַכְתָּ אֶת קִלְלַת בִּלְעָם הָרָשָׁע מִקְּלָלָה לִבְרָכָה, כֵּן תַּהֲפֹךְ כָּל חֲלוֹמוֹתַי עָלַי וְעַל כָּל יִשְׂרָאֵל לְטוֹבָה, וְתִשְׁמְרֵנִי וּתְחָנֵּנִי וְתִרְצֵנִי. אָמֵן.

תהלים סז	**יָאֵר** אֱלֹהִים יְחָנֵּנוּ וִיבָרְכֵנוּ, יָאֵר פָּנָיו אִתָּנוּ סֶלָה:	
שמות לד	**יהוה** יְהוָה, יְהוָה, אֵל רַחוּם וְחַנּוּן אֶרֶךְ אַפַּיִם וְרַב־חֶסֶד וֶאֱמֶת:	
תהלים כה	**פָּנָיו** פְּנֵה־אֵלַי וְחָנֵּנִי, כִּי־יָחִיד וְעָנִי אָנִי:	
תהלים כה	**אֵלֶיךָ** אֵלֶיךָ יְהוָה נַפְשִׁי אֶשָּׂא:	
תהלים קכג	**וִיחֻנֶּךָּ:** הִנֵּה כְעֵינֵי עֲבָדִים אֶל־יַד אֲדוֹנֵיהֶם כְּעֵינֵי שִׁפְחָה אֶל־יַד גְּבִרְתָּהּ, כֵּן עֵינֵינוּ אֶל־יְהוָה אֱלֹהֵינוּ עַד שֶׁיְּחָנֵּנוּ:	

Read the following silently while the כהנים chant. Omit on שבת.

רִבּוֹנוֹ שֶׁל עוֹלָם, אֲנִי שֶׁלָּךְ וַחֲלוֹמוֹתַי שֶׁלָּךְ. חֲלוֹם חָלַמְתִּי וְאֵינִי יוֹדֵעַ מַה הוּא. יְהִי רָצוֹן מִלְּפָנֶיךָ, יְהוָה אֱלֹהַי וֵאלֹהֵי אֲבוֹתַי, שֶׁיִּהְיוּ כָּל חֲלוֹמוֹתַי עָלַי וְעַל כָּל יִשְׂרָאֵל לְטוֹבָה, בֵּין שֶׁחָלַמְתִּי עַל עַצְמִי, וּבֵין שֶׁחָלַמְתִּי עַל אֲחֵרִים, וּבֵין שֶׁחָלְמוּ אֲחֵרִים עָלָי. אִם טוֹבִים הֵם, חַזְּקֵם וְאַמְּצֵם, וְיִתְקַיְּמוּ בִי וּבָהֶם, כַּחֲלוֹמוֹתָיו שֶׁל יוֹסֵף הַצַּדִּיק. וְאִם צְרִיכִים רְפוּאָה, רְפָאֵם כְּחִזְקִיָּהוּ מֶלֶךְ יְהוּדָה מֵחָלְיוֹ, וּכְמִרְיָם הַנְּבִיאָה מִצָּרַעְתָּהּ, וּכְנַעֲמָן מִצָּרַעְתּוֹ, וּכְמֵי מָרָה עַל יְדֵי מֹשֶׁה רַבֵּנוּ, וּכְמֵי יְרִיחוֹ עַל יְדֵי אֱלִישָׁע. וּכְשֵׁם שֶׁהָפַכְתָּ אֶת קִלְלַת בִּלְעָם הָרָשָׁע מִקְּלָלָה לִבְרָכָה, כֵּן תַּהֲפֹךְ כָּל חֲלוֹמוֹתַי עָלַי וְעַל כָּל יִשְׂרָאֵל לְטוֹבָה, וְתִשְׁמְרֵנִי וּתְחָנֵּנִי וְתִרְצֵנִי. אָמֵן.

fellow humans. *May the LORD turn His face toward you,* bestowing on you His providential care (Rashbam, Ibn Ezra), or, may He grant you eternal life

May [He] turn	May he receive a blessing from the LORD and a just reward from the God of his salvation. And he will win grace and good favor in the eyes of God and man.	*Ps. 24* *Prov. 3*
The LORD	LORD, be gracious to us; we yearn for You. Be their strength every morning, our salvation in time of distress.	*Is. 33*
His face	Do not hide Your face from me in the day of my distress. Turn Your ear to me; on the day I call, swiftly answer me.	*Ps. 102*
Toward you	To You, enthroned in heaven, I lift my eyes.	*Ps. 123*
And give	They shall place My name on the children of Israel, and I will bless them.	*Num. 6*
You	Yours, LORD, are the greatness and the power, the glory, majesty and splendor, for everything in heaven and earth is Yours. Yours, LORD, is the kingdom; You are exalted as Head over all.	*1 Chr. 29*
Peace.	"Peace, peace, to those far and near," says the LORD, "and I will heal him."	*Is. 57*

Read the following silently while the Kohanim chant. Omit on Shabbat.

May it be Your will, LORD my God and God of my fathers, that You act for the sake of Your simple, sacred kindness and great compassion, and for the purity of Your great, mighty and awesome name of twenty-two letters derived from the verses of the priestly blessing spoken by Aaron and his sons, Your holy people. May You be close to me when I call to You. May You hear my prayer, plea and cry as You did the cry of Jacob Your perfect one who was called "a plain man." May You grant me and all the members of my household our food and sustenance, generously not meagerly, honestly not otherwise, with satisfaction not pain, from Your generous hand, just as You gave a portion of bread to eat and clothes to wear to Jacob our father who was called "a plain man." May we find love, grace, kindness and compassion in Your sight and in the eyes of all who see us. May my words in service to You be heard, as You granted Joseph Your righteous one, at the time when he was robed by his father in a cloak of fine wool, that he find grace, kindness and compassion in Your sight and in the eyes of all who saw him. May You do wonders and miracles with me, and a sign for good. Grant me success in my paths, and set in my heart understanding that I may understand, discern and fulfill all the words of Your Torah's teachings and mysteries. Save me from errors and purify my thoughts and my heart to serve You and be in awe of You. Prolong my days (*add, where appropriate:* and those of my father, mother, wife, husband, son/s, and daughter/s) in joy and happiness, with much strength and peace. Amen, Selah.

The Leader continues with "Grant peace" on the next page.

| תהלים כד | **יִשָּׂא** יִשָּׂא בְרָכָה מֵאֵת יהוה, וּצְדָקָה מֵאֱלֹהֵי יִשְׁעוֹ: |
| משלי ג | וּמְצָא־חֵן וְשֵׂכֶל־טוֹב בְּעֵינֵי אֱלֹהִים וְאָדָם: |

| ישעיה לג | **יהוה** יהוה חָנֵּנוּ, לְךָ קִוִּינוּ, הֱיֵה זְרֹעָם לַבְּקָרִים |
| | אַף־יְשׁוּעָתֵנוּ בְּעֵת צָרָה: |

| תהלים קב | **פָּנָיו** אַל־תַּסְתֵּר פָּנֶיךָ מִמֶּנִּי בְּיוֹם צַר לִי, הַטֵּה־אֵלַי אָזְנֶךָ |
| | בְּיוֹם אֶקְרָא מַהֵר עֲנֵנִי: |

| תהלים קכג | **אֵלֶיךָ** אֵלֶיךָ נָשָׂאתִי אֶת־עֵינַי, הַיֹּשְׁבִי בַּשָּׁמָיִם: |

| במדבר ו | **וְיָשֵׂם** וְשָׂמוּ אֶת־שְׁמִי עַל־בְּנֵי יִשְׂרָאֵל, וַאֲנִי אֲבָרְכֵם: |

דברי הימים א' כט	**לְךָ** לְךָ יהוה הַגְּדֻלָּה וְהַגְּבוּרָה וְהַתִּפְאֶרֶת וְהַנֵּצַח וְהַהוֹד
	כִּי־כֹל בַּשָּׁמַיִם וּבָאָרֶץ, לְךָ יהוה הַמַּמְלָכָה
	וְהַמִּתְנַשֵּׂא לְכֹל לְרֹאשׁ:

| ישעיה נו | **שָׁלוֹם:** שָׁלוֹם שָׁלוֹם לָרָחוֹק וְלַקָּרוֹב, אָמַר יהוה, וּרְפָאתִיו: |

Read the following silently while the כהנים chant. Omit on שבת.

יְהִי רָצוֹן מִלְּפָנֶיךָ, יהוה אֱלֹהֵי וֵאלֹהֵי אֲבוֹתַי, שֶׁתַּעֲשֶׂה לְמַעַן קְדֻשַּׁת חֲסָדֶיךָ וְגֹדֶל
רַחֲמֶיךָ הַפְּשׁוּטִים, וּלְמַעַן טָהֳרַת שִׁמְךָ הַגָּדוֹל הַגִּבּוֹר וְהַנּוֹרָא, בֶּן עֶשְׂרִים וּשְׁתַּיִם
אוֹתִיּוֹת הַיּוֹצֵא מִפְּסוּקִים שֶׁל בִּרְכַּת כֹּהֲנִים הָאֲמוּרָה מִפִּי אַהֲרֹן וּבָנָיו עַם קְדוֹשֶׁךָ,
שֶׁתִּהְיֶה קָרוֹב לִי בְּקָרְאִי לָךְ, וְתִשְׁמַע תְּפִלָּתִי נַאֲקָתִי וְאֶנְקָתִי תָּמִיד, כְּשֵׁם שֶׁשָּׁמַעְתָּ
אֶנְקַת יַעֲקֹב תְּמִימֶךָ הַנִּקְרָא אִישׁ תָּם. וְתִתֶּן לִי וּלְכָל נַפְשׁוֹת בֵּיתִי מְזוֹנוֹתֵינוּ וּפַרְנָסָתֵנוּ
בְּרֶוַח וְלֹא בְצִמְצוּם, בְּהֶתֵּר וְלֹא בְאִסּוּר, בְּנַחַת וְלֹא בְצַעַר, מִתַּחַת יָדְךָ הָרְחָבָה,
כְּשֵׁם שֶׁנָּתַתָּ פִּסַּת לֶחֶם לֶאֱכֹל וּבֶגֶד לִלְבּוֹשׁ לְיַעֲקֹב אָבִינוּ הַנִּקְרָא אִישׁ תָּם. וְתִתְּנֵנוּ
לְאַהֲבָה, לְחֵן וּלְחֶסֶד וּלְרַחֲמִים בְּעֵינֶיךָ וּבְעֵינֵי כָל רוֹאֵינוּ, וְיִהְיוּ דְבָרַי נִשְׁמָעִים
לַעֲבוֹדָתֶךָ, כְּשֵׁם שֶׁנָּתַתָּ אֶת יוֹסֵף צַדִּיקֶךָ בְּשָׁעָה שֶׁהִלְבִּישׁוֹ אָבִיו כְּתֹנֶת פַּסִּים לְחֵן
וּלְחֶסֶד וּלְרַחֲמִים בְּעֵינֶיךָ וּבְעֵינֵי כָל רוֹאָיו. וְתַעֲשֶׂה עִמִּי נִפְלָאוֹת וְנִסִּים, וּלְטוֹבָה אוֹת,
וְתַצְלִיחֵנִי בִּדְרָכַי, וְתֵן בְּלִבִּי בִּינָה לְהָבִין וּלְהַשְׂכִּיל וּלְקַיֵּם אֶת כָּל דִּבְרֵי תַלְמוּד תּוֹרָתֶךָ
וְסוֹדוֹתֶיהָ, וְתַצִּילֵנִי מִשְּׁגִיאוֹת, וּתְטַהֵר רַעְיוֹנַי וְלִבִּי לַעֲבוֹדָתֶךָ, וְתַאֲרִיךְ יָמַי (וִימֵי אָבִי
וְאִמִּי / וְאִשְׁתִּי / וּבַעְלִי / וּבָנַי וּבְנוֹתַי) בְּטוֹב וּבִנְעִימוּת, בְּרֹב עֹז וְשָׁלוֹם, אָמֵן סֶלָה.

The שליח ציבור continues with שִׂים שָׁלוֹם on the next page.

The congregation says:

אַדִּיר Majestic One on high who dwells in power: You are peace and Your name is peace. May it be Your will to bestow on us and on Your people the house of Israel, life and blessing as a safeguard for peace.

The Kohanim say:

רִבּוֹנוֹ Master of the Universe: we have done what You have decreed for us. So too may You deal with us as You have promised us. Look down from Your holy dwelling place, from heaven, and bless Your people Israel and the land You have given us as You promised on oath to our ancestors, a land flowing with milk and honey.

Deut. 26

If the Priestly Blessing is not said, the following is said by the Leader:

Our God and God of our fathers, bless us with the threefold blessing in the Torah, written by the hand of Moses Your servant and pronounced by Aaron and his sons the priests, Your holy people, as it is said:

> May the LORD bless you and protect you.
> > *Cong:* May it be Your will.
> May the LORD make His face shine on you and be gracious to you.
> > *Cong:* May it be Your will.
> May the LORD turn His face toward you, and grant you peace.
> > *Cong:* May it be Your will.

Num. 6

PEACE

שִׂים שָׁלוֹם Grant peace, goodness and blessing,
grace, loving-kindness and compassion to us
and all Israel Your people.
Bless us, our Father, all as one,
with the light of Your face,
for by the light of Your face You have given us, LORD our God,
the Torah of life and love of kindness,
righteousness, blessing, compassion, life and peace.
May it be good in Your eyes to bless Your people Israel
at every time, in every hour, with Your peace.
Blessed are You, LORD,
who blesses His people Israel with peace.

The following verse concludes the Leader's Repetition of the Amida.

May the words of my mouth and the meditation of my heart
find favor before You, LORD, my Rock and Redeemer.

Ps. 19

The קהל says:

אַדִּיר בַּמָּרוֹם שׁוֹכֵן בִּגְבוּרָה,
אַתָּה שָׁלוֹם וְשִׁמְךָ שָׁלוֹם.
יְהִי רָצוֹן שֶׁתָּשִׂים עָלֵינוּ וְעַל
כָּל עַמְּךָ בֵּית יִשְׂרָאֵל חַיִּים
וּבְרָכָה לְמִשְׁמֶרֶת שָׁלוֹם.

The כהנים say:

רִבּוֹנוֹ שֶׁל עוֹלָם, עָשִׂינוּ מַה שֶׁגָּזַרְתָּ עָלֵינוּ, אַף אַתָּה
עֲשֵׂה עִמָּנוּ כְּמוֹ שֶׁהִבְטַחְתָּנוּ. הַשְׁקִיפָה מִמְּעוֹן
קָדְשְׁךָ מִן־הַשָּׁמַיִם, וּבָרֵךְ אֶת־עַמְּךָ אֶת־יִשְׂרָאֵל,
וְאֵת הָאֲדָמָה אֲשֶׁר נָתַתָּה לָנוּ, כַּאֲשֶׁר נִשְׁבַּעְתָּ
לַאֲבֹתֵינוּ, אֶרֶץ זָבַת חָלָב וּדְבָשׁ:

דברים כו

If בִּרְכַּת כֹּהֲנִים is not said, the following is said by the שְׁלִיחַ צִבּוּר:

אֱלֹהֵינוּ וֵאלֹהֵי אֲבוֹתֵינוּ, בָּרְכֵנוּ בַּבְּרָכָה הַמְשֻׁלֶּשֶׁת בַּתּוֹרָה, הַכְּתוּבָה עַל יְדֵי
מֹשֶׁה עַבְדֶּךָ, הָאֲמוּרָה מִפִּי אַהֲרֹן וּבָנָיו כֹּהֲנִים עַם קְדוֹשֶׁךָ, כָּאָמוּר

יְבָרֶכְךָ יהוה וְיִשְׁמְרֶךָ: קהל: כֵּן יְהִי רָצוֹן

יָאֵר יהוה פָּנָיו אֵלֶיךָ וִיחֻנֶּךָּ: קהל: כֵּן יְהִי רָצוֹן

יִשָּׂא יהוה פָּנָיו אֵלֶיךָ וְיָשֵׂם לְךָ שָׁלוֹם: קהל: כֵּן יְהִי רָצוֹן

במדבר ו

שָׁלוֹם

שִׂים שָׁלוֹם טוֹבָה וּבְרָכָה, חֵן וָחֶסֶד וְרַחֲמִים
עָלֵינוּ וְעַל כָּל יִשְׂרָאֵל עַמֶּךָ.
בָּרְכֵנוּ אָבִינוּ כֻּלָּנוּ כְּאֶחָד בְּאוֹר פָּנֶיךָ
כִּי בְאוֹר פָּנֶיךָ נָתַתָּ לָנוּ, יהוה אֱלֹהֵינוּ
תּוֹרַת חַיִּים וְאַהֲבַת חֶסֶד
וּצְדָקָה וּבְרָכָה וְרַחֲמִים וְחַיִּים וְשָׁלוֹם.
וְטוֹב בְּעֵינֶיךָ לְבָרֵךְ אֶת עַמְּךָ יִשְׂרָאֵל
בְּכָל עֵת וּבְכָל שָׁעָה בִּשְׁלוֹמֶךָ.
בָּרוּךְ אַתָּה יהוה, הַמְבָרֵךְ אֶת עַמּוֹ יִשְׂרָאֵל בַּשָּׁלוֹם.

The following verse concludes the חֲזָרַת הַשַּׁץ.

יִהְיוּ לְרָצוֹן אִמְרֵי־פִי וְהֶגְיוֹן לִבִּי לְפָנֶיךָ, יהוה צוּרִי וְגֹאֲלִי:

תהלים יט

אַדִּיר בַּמָּרוֹם *Majestic One on high.* A prayer by the congregation, echoing three
times the last word of the priestly blessing: peace.

FULL KADDISH

Leader: יִתְגַּדַּל Magnified and sanctified
may His great name be,
in the world He created by His will.
May He establish His kingdom
in your lifetime and in your days,
and in the lifetime of all the house of Israel,
swiftly and soon –
and say: Amen.

All: May His great name be blessed
for ever and all time.

Leader: Blessed and praised,
glorified and exalted,
raised and honored,
uplifted and lauded be the name of the Holy One,
blessed be He, beyond any blessing,
song, praise and consolation
uttered in the world –
and say: Amen.

May the prayers and pleas of all Israel
be accepted by their Father in heaven –
and say: Amen.

May there be great peace from heaven,
and life for us and all Israel –
and say: Amen.

*Bow, take three steps back, as if taking leave of the Divine Presence,
then bow, first left, then right, then center, while saying:*
May He who makes peace in His high places,
make peace for us and all Israel –
and say: Amen.

קדיש שלם

ש״ץ יִתְגַּדַּל וְיִתְקַדַּשׁ שְׁמֵהּ רַבָּא (קהל: אָמֵן)
בְּעָלְמָא דִּי בְרָא כִרְעוּתֵהּ
וְיַמְלִיךְ מַלְכוּתֵהּ
בְּחַיֵּיכוֹן וּבְיוֹמֵיכוֹן וּבְחַיֵּי דְּכָל בֵּית יִשְׂרָאֵל
בַּעֲגָלָא וּבִזְמַן קָרִיב
וְאִמְרוּ אָמֵן. (קהל: אָמֵן)

קהל
ושׁ״ץ יְהֵא שְׁמֵהּ רַבָּא מְבָרַךְ לְעָלַם וּלְעָלְמֵי עָלְמַיָּא.

ש״ץ יִתְבָּרַךְ וְיִשְׁתַּבַּח וְיִתְפָּאַר
וְיִתְרוֹמַם וְיִתְנַשֵּׂא וְיִתְהַדָּר וְיִתְעַלֶּה וְיִתְהַלָּל
שְׁמֵהּ דְּקֻדְשָׁא בְּרִיךְ הוּא (קהל: בְּרִיךְ הוּא)
לְעֵלָּא מִן כָּל בִּרְכָתָא וְשִׁירָתָא, תֻּשְׁבְּחָתָא וְנֶחֱמָתָא
דַּאֲמִירָן בְּעָלְמָא
וְאִמְרוּ אָמֵן. (קהל: אָמֵן)

תִּתְקַבַּל צְלוֹתְהוֹן וּבָעוּתְהוֹן דְּכָל יִשְׂרָאֵל
קֳדָם אֲבוּהוֹן דִּי בִשְׁמַיָּא
וְאִמְרוּ אָמֵן. (קהל: אָמֵן)

יְהֵא שְׁלָמָא רַבָּא מִן שְׁמַיָּא
וְחַיִּים, עָלֵינוּ וְעַל כָּל יִשְׂרָאֵל
וְאִמְרוּ אָמֵן. (קהל: אָמֵן)

Bow, take three steps back, as if taking leave of the Divine Presence,
then bow, first left, then right, then center, while saying:

עֹשֶׂה שָׁלוֹם בִּמְרוֹמָיו
הוּא יַעֲשֶׂה שָׁלוֹם עָלֵינוּ וְעַל כָּל יִשְׂרָאֵל
וְאִמְרוּ אָמֵן. (קהל: אָמֵן)

אֵין כֵּאלֹהֵינוּ There is none like our God, none like our Lord,
     none like our King, none like our Savior.
Who is like our God? Who is like our Lord?
Who is like our King? Who is like our Savior?
We will thank our God, we will thank our Lord,
we will thank our King, we will thank our Savior.
Blessed is our God, blessed is our Lord,
blessed is our King, blessed is our Savior.
You are our God, You are our Lord,
You are our King, You are our Savior.
You are He to whom our ancestors offered the fragrant incense.

פִּטּוּם הַקְּטֹרֶת The incense mixture consisted of balsam, onycha, galbanum and *Keritot 6a*
frankincense, each weighing seventy manehs; myrrh, cassia, spikenard and saffron, each weighing sixteen manehs; twelve manehs of costus, three of aromatic
bark; nine of cinnamon; nine kabs of Carsina lye; three seahs and three kabs of
Cyprus wine. If Cyprus wine was not available, old white wine might be used.
A quarter of a kab of Sodom salt, and a minute amount of a smoke-raising herb.
Rabbi Nathan says: Also a minute amount of Jordan amber. If one added honey
to the mixture, he rendered it unfit for sacred use. If he omitted any one of its
ingredients, he is guilty of a capital offense.

Rabban Shimon ben Gamliel says: "Balsam" refers to the sap that drips from the
balsam tree. The Carsina lye was used for bleaching the onycha to improve it.
The Cyprus wine was used to soak the onycha in it to make it pungent. Though
urine is suitable for this purpose, it is not brought into the Temple out of respect.

These were the psalms which the Levites used to recite in the Temple: *Mishna,*
On the first day of the week they used to say: *Tamid 7*
  "The earth is the Lord's and all it contains, *Ps. 24*
  the world and all who live in it."

פִּטּוּם הַקְּטֹרֶת *The incense mixture.* A Talmudic passage (*Keritot* 6a) describing
the composition of the incense, burned in the Temple every morning and
evening (Ex. 30:7–9).

הַשִּׁיר שֶׁהַלְוִיִּם הָיוּ אוֹמְרִים *These were the psalms which the Levites used to recite.*
Each day of the week, after the regular offerings in the Temple, the Levites

אֵין כֵּאלֹהֵינוּ, אֵין כַּאדוֹנֵינוּ, אֵין כְּמַלְכֵּנוּ, אֵין כְּמוֹשִׁיעֵנוּ.

מִי כֵאלֹהֵינוּ, מִי כַאדוֹנֵינוּ, מִי כְמַלְכֵּנוּ, מִי כְמוֹשִׁיעֵנוּ.

נוֹדֶה לֵאלֹהֵינוּ, נוֹדֶה לַאדוֹנֵינוּ, נוֹדֶה לְמַלְכֵּנוּ, נוֹדֶה לְמוֹשִׁיעֵנוּ.

בָּרוּךְ אֱלֹהֵינוּ, בָּרוּךְ אֲדוֹנֵינוּ, בָּרוּךְ מַלְכֵּנוּ, בָּרוּךְ מוֹשִׁיעֵנוּ.

אַתָּה הוּא אֱלֹהֵינוּ, אַתָּה הוּא אֲדוֹנֵינוּ,

אַתָּה הוּא מַלְכֵּנוּ, אַתָּה הוּא מוֹשִׁיעֵנוּ.

אַתָּה הוּא שֶׁהִקְטִירוּ אֲבוֹתֵינוּ לְפָנֶיךָ אֶת קְטֹרֶת הַסַּמִּים.

כריתות ו
פִּטּוּם הַקְּטֹרֶת. הַצֳּרִי, וְהַצִּפֹּרֶן, וְהַחֶלְבְּנָה, וְהַלְּבוֹנָה מִשְׁקָל שִׁבְעִים שִׁבְעִים מָנֶה. מֹר, וּקְצִיעָה, שִׁבֹּלֶת נֵרְדְּ, וְכַרְכֹּם מִשְׁקָל שִׁשָּׁה עָשָׂר שִׁשָּׁה עָשָׂר מָנֶה, הַקֹּשְׁטְ שְׁנֵים עָשָׂר, קִלּוּפָה שְׁלֹשָׁה, וְקִנָּמוֹן תִּשְׁעָה, בֹּרִית כַּרְשִׁינָה תִּשְׁעָה קַבִּין, יֵין קַפְרִיסִין סְאִין תְּלָת וְקַבִּין תְּלָתָא, וְאִם אֵין לוֹ יֵין קַפְרִיסִין, מֵבִיא חֲמַר חִוַּרְיָן עַתִּיק. מֶלַח סְדוֹמִית רֹבַע, מַעֲלֶה עָשָׁן כָּל שֶׁהוּא. רַבִּי נָתָן הַבַּבְלִי אוֹמֵר: אַף כִּפַּת הַיַּרְדֵּן כָּל שֶׁהוּא, וְאִם נָתַן בָּהּ דְּבַשׁ פְּסָלָהּ, וְאִם חִסַּר אֶחָד מִכָּל סַמָּנֶיהָ, חַיָּב מִיתָה.

רַבָּן שִׁמְעוֹן בֶּן גַּמְלִיאֵל אוֹמֵר: הַצֳּרִי אֵינוֹ אֶלָּא שְׂרָף הַנּוֹטֵף מֵעֲצֵי הַקְּטָף. בֹּרִית כַּרְשִׁינָה שֶׁשָּׁפִין בָּהּ אֶת הַצִּפֹּרֶן כְּדֵי שֶׁתְּהֵא נָאָה, יֵין קַפְרִיסִין שֶׁשּׁוֹרִין בּוֹ אֶת הַצִּפֹּרֶן כְּדֵי שֶׁתְּהֵא עַזָּה, וַהֲלֹא מֵי רַגְלַיִם יָפִין לָהּ, אֶלָּא שֶׁאֵין מַכְנִיסִין מֵי רַגְלַיִם בַּמִּקְדָּשׁ מִפְּנֵי הַכָּבוֹד.

משנה
תמיד ז
הַשִּׁיר שֶׁהַלְוִיִּם הָיוּ אוֹמְרִים בְּבֵית הַמִּקְדָּשׁ:
בַּיּוֹם הָרִאשׁוֹן הָיוּ אוֹמְרִים

תהלים כד
לַיהוה הָאָרֶץ וּמְלוֹאָהּ, תֵּבֵל וְיֹשְׁבֵי בָהּ:

אֵין כֵּאלֹהֵינוּ *There is none like our God.* A poetic introduction to the reading of the passage about the incense offering in the Temple. The initial letters of the first three lines spell Amen, followed by several phrases beginning with "Blessed." Thus the poem is also a way of reaffirming the preceding prayers, a coded coda to the service as a whole.

On the second day they used to say:

"Great is the LORD and greatly to be praised *Ps. 48*
in the city of God, on His holy mountain."

On the third day they used to say:

"God stands in the divine assembly. *Ps. 82*
Among the judges He delivers judgment."

On the fourth day they used to say:

"God of retribution, LORD, God of retribution, appear." *Ps. 94*

On the fifth day they used to say:

"Sing for joy to God, our strength. *Ps. 81*
Shout aloud to the God of Jacob."

On the sixth day they used to say:

"The LORD reigns: He is robed in majesty; *Ps. 93*
the LORD is robed, girded with strength;
the world is firmly established; it cannot be moved."

On the Sabbath they used to say:

"A psalm, a song for the Sabbath day" – *Ps. 92*
[meaning] a psalm and song for the time to come,
for the day which will be entirely Sabbath and rest for life everlasting.

It was taught in the Academy of Elijah: Whoever studies [Torah] laws every day *Megilla 28b*
is assured that he will be destined for the World to Come, as it is said, "The ways *Hab. 3*
of the world are His" – read not, "ways" [*halikhot*] but "laws" [*halakhot*].

Rabbi Elazar said in the name of Rabbi Ḥanina: The disciples of the sages *Berakhot 64a*
increase peace in the world, as it is said, "And all your children shall be taught *Is. 54*
of the LORD, and great shall be the peace of your children [*banayikh*]." Read
not *banayikh*, "your children," but *bonayikh*, "your builders." Those who love *Ps. 119*
Your Torah have great peace; there is no stumbling block for them. May there *Ps. 122*
be peace within your ramparts, prosperity in your palaces. For the sake of my
brothers and friends, I shall say, "Peace be within you." For the sake of the
House of the LORD our God, I will seek your good. ‣ May the LORD grant *Ps. 29*
strength to His people; may the LORD bless His people with peace.

---

banayikh, 'your children' but *bonayikh* 'your builders.'" When scholars are
also builders, they create peace. At many stages during their wanderings in
the desert, there was dissension among the Israelites, but when they were
building the Tabernacle there was harmony. The best way to bring peace to
any fractured group is to build something together.

בַּשֵּׁנִי הָיוּ אוֹמְרִים

גָּדוֹל יהוה וּמְהֻלָּל מְאֹד, בְּעִיר אֱלֹהֵינוּ הַר־קָדְשׁוֹ: תהלים מח

בַּשְּׁלִישִׁי הָיוּ אוֹמְרִים

אֱלֹהִים נִצָּב בַּעֲדַת־אֵל, בְּקֶרֶב אֱלֹהִים יִשְׁפֹּט: תהלים פב

בָּרְבִיעִי הָיוּ אוֹמְרִים

אֵל־נְקָמוֹת יהוה, אֵל נְקָמוֹת הוֹפִיעַ: תהלים צד

בַּחֲמִישִׁי הָיוּ אוֹמְרִים

הַרְנִינוּ לֵאלֹהִים עוּזֵּנוּ, הָרִיעוּ לֵאלֹהֵי יַעֲקֹב: תהלים פא

בַּשִּׁשִּׁי הָיוּ אוֹמְרִים

יהוה מָלָךְ גֵּאוּת לָבֵשׁ לָבֵשׁ יהוה עֹז הִתְאַזָּר תהלים צג
אַף־תִּכּוֹן תֵּבֵל בַּל־תִּמּוֹט:

בַּשַּׁבָּת הָיוּ אוֹמְרִים

מִזְמוֹר שִׁיר לְיוֹם הַשַּׁבָּת: תהלים צב
מִזְמוֹר שִׁיר לֶעָתִיד לָבוֹא
לְיוֹם שֶׁכֻּלּוֹ שַׁבָּת וּמְנוּחָה לְחַיֵּי הָעוֹלָמִים.

תָּנָא דְבֵי אֵלִיָּהוּ: כָּל הַשּׁוֹנֶה הֲלָכוֹת בְּכָל יוֹם, מֻבְטָח לוֹ שֶׁהוּא בֶּן עוֹלָם מגילה כח:
הַבָּא, שֶׁנֶּאֱמַר, הֲלִיכוֹת עוֹלָם לוֹ: אַל תִּקְרֵי הֲלִיכוֹת אֶלָּא הֲלָכוֹת. חבקוק ג

אָמַר רַבִּי אֶלְעָזָר, אָמַר רַבִּי חֲנִינָא: תַּלְמִידֵי חֲכָמִים מַרְבִּים שָׁלוֹם בָּעוֹלָם, ברכות סד.
שֶׁנֶּאֱמַר, וְכָל־בָּנַיִךְ לִמּוּדֵי יהוה, וְרַב שְׁלוֹם בָּנָיִךְ: אַל תִּקְרֵי בָּנָיִךְ, אֶלָּא ישעיה נד
בּוֹנָיִךְ. שָׁלוֹם רָב לְאֹהֲבֵי תוֹרָתֶךָ, וְאֵין־לָמוֹ מִכְשׁוֹל: יְהִי־שָׁלוֹם בְּחֵילֵךְ, תהלים קיט
תהלים קכב
שַׁלְוָה בְּאַרְמְנוֹתָיִךְ: לְמַעַן אַחַי וְרֵעָי אֲדַבְּרָה־נָּא שָׁלוֹם בָּךְ: לְמַעַן בֵּית־יהוה
אֱלֹהֵינוּ אֲבַקְשָׁה טוֹב לָךְ: ‹ יהוה עֹז לְעַמּוֹ יִתֵּן, יהוה יְבָרֵךְ אֶת־עַמּוֹ בַשָּׁלוֹם: תהלים כט

---

would sing a particular psalm. We still say these psalms, usually at the end of
the service. In this way, a further connection is made between our prayers
and the Temple service.

תַּלְמִידֵי חֲכָמִים מַרְבִּים שָׁלוֹם בָּעוֹלָם *The disciples of the sages increase peace in the
world.* The full meaning of this statement is clear only at the end: "Read not

THE RABBIS' KADDISH

The following prayer, said by mourners, requires the presence of a minyan.
A transliteration can be found on page 778.

Mourner: יִתְגַּדַּל **Magnified and sanctified**
may His great name be,
in the world He created by His will.
May He establish His kingdom in your lifetime
and in your days,
and in the lifetime of all the house of Israel,
swiftly and soon –
and say: Amen.

All: May His great name be blessed for ever and all time.

Mourner: Blessed and praised, glorified and exalted,
raised and honored, uplifted and lauded
be the name of the Holy One, blessed be He,
beyond any blessing,
song, praise and consolation uttered in the world –
and say: Amen.

To Israel, to the teachers,
their disciples and their disciples' disciples,
and to all who engage in the study of Torah,
in this (*in Israel add:* holy) place or elsewhere,
may there come to them and you great peace,
grace, kindness and compassion, long life, ample sustenance
and deliverance, from their Father in Heaven –
and say: Amen.

May there be great peace from heaven,
and (good) life for us and all Israel –
and say: Amen.

Bow, take three steps back, as if taking leave of the Divine Presence,
then bow, first left, then right, then center, while saying:

May He who makes peace in His high places,
in His compassion make peace for us and all Israel –
and say: Amen.

קדיש דרבנן

The following prayer, said by mourners, requires the presence of a מנין.
A transliteration can be found on page 778.

אבל: יִתְגַּדַּל וְיִתְקַדַּשׁ שְׁמֵהּ רַבָּא (קהל: אָמֵן)

בְּעָלְמָא דִּי בְרָא כִרְעוּתֵהּ

וְיַמְלִיךְ מַלְכוּתֵהּ

בְּחַיֵּיכוֹן וּבְיוֹמֵיכוֹן וּבְחַיֵּי דְכָל בֵּית יִשְׂרָאֵל

בַּעֲגָלָא וּבִזְמַן קָרִיב, וְאִמְרוּ אָמֵן. (קהל: אָמֵן)

קהל ואבל: יְהֵא שְׁמֵהּ רַבָּא מְבָרַךְ לְעָלַם וּלְעָלְמֵי עָלְמַיָּא.

אבל: יִתְבָּרַךְ וְיִשְׁתַּבַּח וְיִתְפָּאַר וְיִתְרוֹמַם וְיִתְנַשֵּׂא

וְיִתְהַדָּר וְיִתְעַלֶּה וְיִתְהַלָּל

שְׁמֵהּ דְּקֻדְשָׁא בְּרִיךְ הוּא (קהל: בְּרִיךְ הוּא)

לְעֵלָּא מִן כָּל בִּרְכָתָא וְשִׁירָתָא, תֻּשְׁבְּחָתָא וְנֶחֱמָתָא

דַּאֲמִירָן בְּעָלְמָא, וְאִמְרוּ אָמֵן. (קהל: אָמֵן)

עַל יִשְׂרָאֵל וְעַל רַבָּנָן

וְעַל תַּלְמִידֵיהוֹן וְעַל כָּל תַּלְמִידֵי תַלְמִידֵיהוֹן

וְעַל כָּל מָאן דְּעָסְקִין בְּאוֹרַיְתָא

דִּי בְאַתְרָא (בארץ ישראל: קַדִּישָׁא) הָדֵין, וְדִי בְּכָל אֲתַר וַאֲתַר

יְהֵא לְהוֹן וּלְכוֹן שְׁלָמָא רַבָּא

חִנָּא וְחִסְדָּא, וְרַחֲמֵי, וְחַיֵּי אֲרִיכֵי, וּמְזוֹנֵי רְוִיחֵי

וּפֻרְקָנָא מִן קֳדָם אֲבוּהוֹן דִּי בִשְׁמַיָּא, וְאִמְרוּ אָמֵן. (קהל: אָמֵן)

יְהֵא שְׁלָמָא רַבָּא מִן שְׁמַיָּא

וְחַיִּים (טוֹבִים) עָלֵינוּ וְעַל כָּל יִשְׂרָאֵל, וְאִמְרוּ אָמֵן. (קהל: אָמֵן)

Bow, take three steps back, as if taking leave of the Divine Presence,
then bow, first left, then right, then center, while saying:

עֹשֶׂה שָׁלוֹם בִּמְרוֹמָיו

הוּא יַעֲשֶׂה בְרַחֲמָיו שָׁלוֹם

עָלֵינוּ וְעַל כָּל יִשְׂרָאֵל, וְאִמְרוּ אָמֵן. (קהל: אָמֵן)

Stand while saying Aleinu. Bow at ˈ.

עָלֵינוּ It is our duty to praise the Master of all,
and ascribe greatness to the Author of creation,
who has not made us like the nations of the lands
nor placed us like the families of the earth;
who has not made our portion like theirs,
nor our destiny like all their multitudes.
(For they worship vanity and emptiness,
and pray to a god who cannot save.)
ˈBut we bow in worship
and thank the Supreme King of kings, the Holy One, blessed be He,
who extends the heavens and establishes the earth,
whose throne of glory is in the heavens above,
and whose power's Presence is in the highest of heights.
He is our God; there is no other.
Truly He is our King, there is none else,
as it is written in His Torah:
"You shall know and take to heart this day that the LORD is God,   *Deut. 4*
in heaven above and on earth below.
There is no other."

Therefore, we place our hope in You, LORD our God,
that we may soon see the glory of Your power,
when You will remove abominations from the earth,
and idols will be utterly destroyed,
when the world will be perfected
under the sovereignty of the Almighty,
when all humanity will call on Your name,
to turn all the earth's wicked toward You.
All the world's inhabitants will realize and know
that to You every knee must bow and every tongue swear loyalty.
Before You, LORD our God, they will kneel and bow down
and give honor to Your glorious name.
They will all accept the yoke of Your kingdom,
and You will reign over them soon and for ever.
For the kingdom is Yours, and to all eternity You will reign in glory,
as it is written in Your Torah: "The LORD will reign for ever and ever."   *Ex. 15*

Stand while saying עָלֵינוּ. *Bow at* יְ.

עָלֵינוּ לְשַׁבֵּחַ לַאֲדוֹן הַכֹּל, לָתֵת גְּדֻלָּה לְיוֹצֵר בְּרֵאשִׁית
שֶׁלֹּא עָשָׂנוּ כְּגוֹיֵי הָאֲרָצוֹת, וְלֹא שָׂמָנוּ כְּמִשְׁפְּחוֹת הָאֲדָמָה
שֶׁלֹּא שָׂם חֶלְקֵנוּ כָּהֶם וְגוֹרָלֵנוּ כְּכָל הֲמוֹנָם.
(שֶׁהֵם מִשְׁתַּחֲוִים לְהֶבֶל וָרִיק וּמִתְפַּלְלִים אֶל אֵל לֹא יוֹשִׁיעַ.)
וַאֲנַחְנוּ כּוֹרְעִים וּמִשְׁתַּחֲוִים וּמוֹדִים
לִפְנֵי מֶלֶךְ מַלְכֵי הַמְּלָכִים, הַקָּדוֹשׁ בָּרוּךְ הוּא
שֶׁהוּא נוֹטֶה שָׁמַיִם וְיוֹסֵד אָרֶץ
וּמוֹשַׁב יְקָרוֹ בַּשָּׁמַיִם מִמַּעַל
וּשְׁכִינַת עֻזּוֹ בְּגָבְהֵי מְרוֹמִים.
הוּא אֱלֹהֵינוּ, אֵין עוֹד.
אֱמֶת מַלְכֵּנוּ, אֶפֶס זוּלָתוֹ, כַּכָּתוּב בְּתוֹרָתוֹ
וְיָדַעְתָּ הַיּוֹם וַהֲשֵׁבֹתָ אֶל־לְבָבֶךָ

דברים ד

כִּי יהוה הוּא הָאֱלֹהִים בַּשָּׁמַיִם מִמַּעַל וְעַל־הָאָרֶץ מִתָּחַת
אֵין עוֹד:

עַל כֵּן נְקַוֶּה לְּךָ יהוה אֱלֹהֵינוּ, לִרְאוֹת מְהֵרָה בְּתִפְאֶרֶת עֻזֶּךָ
לְהַעֲבִיר גִּלּוּלִים מִן הָאָרֶץ, וְהָאֱלִילִים כָּרוֹת יִכָּרֵתוּן
לְתַקֵּן עוֹלָם בְּמַלְכוּת שַׁדַּי.
וְכָל בְּנֵי בָשָׂר יִקְרְאוּ בִשְׁמֶךָ לְהַפְנוֹת אֵלֶיךָ כָּל רִשְׁעֵי אָרֶץ.
יַכִּירוּ וְיֵדְעוּ כָּל יוֹשְׁבֵי תֵבֵל
כִּי לְךָ תִּכְרַע כָּל בֶּרֶךְ, תִּשָּׁבַע כָּל לָשׁוֹן.
לְפָנֶיךָ יהוה אֱלֹהֵינוּ יִכְרְעוּ וְיִפֹּלוּ, וְלִכְבוֹד שִׁמְךָ יְקָר יִתֵּנוּ
וִיקַבְּלוּ כֻלָּם אֶת עֹל מַלְכוּתֶךָ
וְתִמְלֹךְ עֲלֵיהֶם מְהֵרָה לְעוֹלָם וָעֶד.
כִּי הַמַּלְכוּת שֶׁלְּךָ הִיא וּלְעוֹלְמֵי עַד תִּמְלֹךְ בְּכָבוֹד
כַּכָּתוּב בְּתוֹרָתֶךָ, יהוה יִמְלֹךְ לְעֹלָם וָעֶד:

שמות טו

▸ And it is said: "Then the Lᴏʀᴅ shall be King over all the earth; on that day the Lᴏʀᴅ shall be One and His name One."

Zech. 14

Some add:

Have no fear of sudden terror or of the ruin when it overtakes the wicked.

Prov. 3

Devise your strategy, but it will be thwarted; propose your plan, but it will not stand, for God is with us.

Is. 8

When you grow old, I will still be the same. When your hair turns gray, I will still carry you. I made you, I will bear you, I will carry you, and I will rescue you.

Is. 46

MOURNER'S KADDISH

The following prayer, said by mourners, requires the presence of a minyan. A transliteration can be found on page 779.

Mourner: יִתְגַּדֵּל Magnified and sanctified
may His great name be,
in the world He created by His will.
May He establish His kingdom
in your lifetime and in your days,
and in the lifetime of all the house of Israel,
swiftly and soon –
and say: Amen.

All: May His great name be blessed for ever and all time.

Mourner: Blessed and praised, glorified and exalted,
raised and honored, uplifted and lauded
be the name of the Holy One, blessed be He,
beyond any blessing, song, praise and consolation
uttered in the world –
and say: Amen.

May there be great peace from heaven,
and life for us and all Israel –
and say: Amen.

Bow, take three steps back, as if taking leave of the Divine Presence, then bow, first left, then right, then center, while saying:

May He who makes peace in His high places,
make peace for us and all Israel –
and say: Amen.

זכריה יד

‹ וְנֶאֱמַר, וְהָיָה יהוה לְמֶלֶךְ עַל־כָּל־הָאָרֶץ
בַּיּוֹם הַהוּא יִהְיֶה יהוה אֶחָד וּשְׁמוֹ אֶחָד:

Some add:

משלי ג

אַל־תִּירָא מִפַּחַד פִּתְאֹם וּמִשֹּׁאַת רְשָׁעִים כִּי תָבֹא:

ישעיה ח

עֻצוּ עֵצָה וְתֻפָר, דַּבְּרוּ דָבָר וְלֹא יָקוּם, כִּי עִמָּנוּ אֵל:

ישעיה מו

וְעַד־זִקְנָה אֲנִי הוּא, וְעַד־שֵׂיבָה אֲנִי אֶסְבֹּל, אֲנִי עָשִׂיתִי וַאֲנִי אֶשָּׂא וַאֲנִי אֶסְבֹּל וַאֲמַלֵּט:

קדיש יתום

The following prayer, said by mourners, requires the presence of a מִנְיָן.
A transliteration can be found on page 779.

אבל: יִתְגַּדַּל וְיִתְקַדַּשׁ שְׁמֵהּ רַבָּא (קהל: אָמֵן)
בְּעָלְמָא דִּי בְרָא כִרְעוּתֵהּ
וְיַמְלִיךְ מַלְכוּתֵהּ
בְּחַיֵּיכוֹן וּבְיוֹמֵיכוֹן וּבְחַיֵּי דְכָל בֵּית יִשְׂרָאֵל
בַּעֲגָלָא וּבִזְמַן קָרִיב, וְאִמְרוּ אָמֵן. (קהל: אָמֵן)

קהל ואבל: יְהֵא שְׁמֵהּ רַבָּא מְבָרַךְ לְעָלַם וּלְעָלְמֵי עָלְמַיָּא.

אבל: יִתְבָּרַךְ וְיִשְׁתַּבַּח וְיִתְפָּאַר
וְיִתְרוֹמַם וְיִתְנַשֵּׂא וְיִתְהַדָּר וְיִתְעַלֶּה וְיִתְהַלָּל
שְׁמֵהּ דְּקֻדְשָׁא בְּרִיךְ הוּא (קהל: בְּרִיךְ הוּא)
לְעֵלָּא מִן כָּל בִּרְכָתָא וְשִׁירָתָא, תֻּשְׁבְּחָתָא וְנֶחֱמָתָא
דַּאֲמִירָן בְּעָלְמָא, וְאִמְרוּ אָמֵן. (קהל: אָמֵן)

יְהֵא שְׁלָמָא רַבָּא מִן שְׁמַיָּא
וְחַיִּים, עָלֵינוּ וְעַל כָּל יִשְׂרָאֵל, וְאִמְרוּ אָמֵן. (קהל: אָמֵן)

Bow, take three steps back, as if taking leave of the Divine Presence,
then bow, first left, then right, then center, while saying:

עֹשֶׂה שָׁלוֹם בִּמְרוֹמָיו
הוּא יַעֲשֶׂה שָׁלוֹם עָלֵינוּ וְעַל כָּל יִשְׂרָאֵל
וְאִמְרוּ אָמֵן. (קהל: אָמֵן)

THE DAILY PSALM

One of the following psalms is said on the appropriate day of the week as indicated.
After the psalm, the Mourner's Kaddish is said.
Many congregations say the Daily Psalm after the Song of Glory, page 586.

Sunday: הַיּוֹם Today is the first day of the week,
on which the Levites used to say this psalm in the Temple:

לְדָוִד מִזְמוֹר A psalm of David. The earth is the Lord's and all it contains, *Ps. 24*
the world and all who live in it. For He founded it on the seas and established it on the streams. Who may climb the mountain of the Lord? Who may stand in His holy place? He who has clean hands and a pure heart, who has not taken My name in vain or sworn deceitfully. He shall receive a blessing from the Lord, and just reward from the God of his salvation. This is a generation of those who seek Him, the descendants of Jacob who seek Your presence, Selah! Lift up your heads, O gates; be uplifted, eternal doors, so that the King of glory may enter. Who is the King of glory? It is the Lord, strong and mighty, the Lord mighty in battle. Lift up your heads, O gates; be uplifted, eternal doors, that the King of glory may enter. ‣ Who is He, the King of glory? The Lord of hosts, He is the King of glory, Selah!

Mourner's Kaddish (page 584)

Monday: הַיּוֹם Today is the second day of the week,
on which the Levites used to say this psalm in the Temple:

שִׁיר מִזְמוֹר A song. A psalm of the sons of Koraḥ. Great is the Lord and *Ps. 48*
greatly to be praised in the city of God, on His holy mountain – beautiful in its heights, joy of all the earth, Mount Zion on its northern side, city of the great King. In its citadels God is known as a stronghold.

---

psalm also alludes to the Temple, built on "the mountain of the Lord." The connection between the two is based on the idea that the Temple was a microcosm of the universe, and its construction a human counterpart to the divine creation of the cosmos.

שִׁיר מִזְמוֹר לִבְנֵי־קֹרַח *Monday: Psalm 48.* A hymn of praise to the beauty and

שיר של יום

One of the following psalms is said on the appropriate day of the week as indicated.
After the psalm, קדיש יתום is said.
Many congregations say the שיר של יום after the שיר הכבוד, page 587.

Sunday הַיּוֹם יוֹם רִאשׁוֹן בְּשַׁבָּת, שֶׁבּוֹ הָיוּ הַלְוִיִּם אוֹמְרִים בְּבֵית הַמִּקְדָּשׁ:

תהלים כד לְדָוִד מִזְמוֹר, לַיהוה הָאָרֶץ וּמְלוֹאָהּ, תֵּבֵל וְיֹשְׁבֵי בָהּ: כִּי־הוּא עַל־יַמִּים יְסָדָהּ, וְעַל־נְהָרוֹת יְכוֹנְנֶהָ: מִי־יַעֲלֶה בְהַר־יהוה, וּמִי־ יָקוּם בִּמְקוֹם קָדְשׁוֹ: נְקִי כַפַּיִם וּבַר־לֵבָב, אֲשֶׁר לֹא־נָשָׂא לַשָּׁוְא נַפְשִׁי, וְלֹא נִשְׁבַּע לְמִרְמָה: יִשָּׂא בְרָכָה מֵאֵת יהוה, וּצְדָקָה מֵאֱלֹהֵי יִשְׁעוֹ: זֶה דּוֹר דֹּרְשָׁו, מְבַקְשֵׁי פָנֶיךָ יַעֲקֹב סֶלָה: שְׂאוּ שְׁעָרִים רָאשֵׁיכֶם, וְהִנָּשְׂאוּ פִּתְחֵי עוֹלָם, וְיָבוֹא מֶלֶךְ הַכָּבוֹד: מִי זֶה מֶלֶךְ הַכָּבוֹד, יהוה עִזּוּז וְגִבּוֹר, יהוה גִּבּוֹר מִלְחָמָה: שְׂאוּ שְׁעָרִים רָאשֵׁיכֶם, וּשְׂאוּ פִּתְחֵי עוֹלָם, וְיָבֹא מֶלֶךְ הַכָּבוֹד: ‹ מִי הוּא זֶה מֶלֶךְ הַכָּבוֹד, יהוה צְבָאוֹת הוּא מֶלֶךְ הַכָּבוֹד סֶלָה:

קדיש יתום *(page 585)*

Monday הַיּוֹם יוֹם שֵׁנִי בְּשַׁבָּת, שֶׁבּוֹ הָיוּ הַלְוִיִּם אוֹמְרִים בְּבֵית הַמִּקְדָּשׁ:

תהלים מח שִׁיר מִזְמוֹר לִבְנֵי־קֹרַח: גָּדוֹל יהוה וּמְהֻלָּל מְאֹד, בְּעִיר אֱלֹהֵינוּ, הַר־קָדְשׁוֹ: יְפֵה נוֹף מְשׂוֹשׂ כָּל־הָאָרֶץ, הַר־צִיּוֹן יַרְכְּתֵי צָפוֹן, קִרְיַת מֶלֶךְ רָב: אֱלֹהִים בְּאַרְמְנוֹתֶיהָ נוֹדַע לְמִשְׂגָּב: כִּי־הִנֵּה הַמְּלָכִים

THE DAILY PSALM

A special psalm was said in the Temple on each of the seven days of the week. We say them still, in memory of those days and in hope of future restoration.

לְדָוִד מִזְמוֹר *Sunday: Psalm 24.* The opening verses mirror the act of creation, reminding us that each week mirrors the seven days of creation itself. The

See how the kings joined forces, advancing together. They saw, they were astounded, they panicked, they fled. There fear seized them, like the pains of a woman giving birth, like ships of Tarshish wrecked by an eastern wind. What we had heard, now we have seen, in the city of the LORD of hosts, in the city of our God. May God preserve it for ever, Selah! In the midst of Your Temple, God, we meditate on Your love. As is Your name, God, so is Your praise: it reaches to the ends of the earth. Your right hand is filled with righteousness. Let Mount Zion rejoice, let the towns of Judah be glad, because of Your judgments. Walk around Zion and encircle it. Count its towers, note its strong walls, view its citadels, so that you may tell a future genera-tion ▸ that this is God, our God, for ever and ever. He will guide us for evermore.

Mourner's Kaddish (page 584)

Tuesday: **הַיּוֹם** Today is the third day of the week,
on which the Levites used to say this psalm in the Temple:

מִזְמוֹר לְאָסָף A psalm of Asaph. God stands in the Divine assembly. *Ps. 82* Among the judges He delivers judgment. How long will you judge unjustly, showing favor to the wicked? Selah. Do justice to the weak and the orphaned. Vindicate the poor and destitute. Rescue the weak and needy. Save them from the hand of the wicked. They do not know nor do they understand. They walk about in darkness while all the earth's foundations shake. I once said, "You are like gods, all of you are sons of the Most High." But you shall die like mere men, you will fall like any prince. ▸ Arise, O LORD, judge the earth, for all the nations are Your possession.

Mourner's Kaddish (page 584)

Capitolina, and prohibited any Jew from entering its precincts on pain of death. Persians and Arabs, Barbarians and Crusaders and Turks took it and retook it, ravaged it and burnt it; and yet, marvellous to relate, it ever rises from its ashes to renewed life and glory. It is the Eternal City of the Eternal People. (Rabbi J.H. Hertz)

מִזְמוֹר לְאָסָף *Tuesday: Psalm 82.* A psalm about judges and justice. Justice, the

נוֹעֲדוּ, עָבְרוּ יַחְדָּו: הֵמָּה רָאוּ כֵּן תָּמָהוּ, נִבְהֲלוּ נֶחְפָּזוּ: רְעָדָה
אֲחָזָתַם שָׁם, חִיל כַּיּוֹלֵדָה: בְּרוּחַ קָדִים תְּשַׁבֵּר אֳנִיּוֹת תַּרְשִׁישׁ:
כַּאֲשֶׁר שָׁמַעְנוּ כֵּן רָאִינוּ, בְּעִיר־יהוה צְבָאוֹת, בְּעִיר אֱלֹהֵינוּ,
אֱלֹהִים יְכוֹנְנֶהָ עַד־עוֹלָם סֶלָה: דִּמִּינוּ אֱלֹהִים חַסְדֶּךָ, בְּקֶרֶב
הֵיכָלֶךָ: כְּשִׁמְךָ אֱלֹהִים כֵּן תְּהִלָּתְךָ עַל־קַצְוֵי־אֶרֶץ, צֶדֶק מָלְאָה
יְמִינֶךָ: יִשְׂמַח הַר־צִיּוֹן, תָּגֵלְנָה בְּנוֹת יְהוּדָה, לְמַעַן מִשְׁפָּטֶיךָ:
סֹבּוּ צִיּוֹן וְהַקִּיפוּהָ, סִפְרוּ מִגְדָּלֶיהָ: שִׁיתוּ לִבְּכֶם לְחֵילָה, פַּסְּגוּ
אַרְמְנוֹתֶיהָ, לְמַעַן תְּסַפְּרוּ לְדוֹר אַחֲרוֹן: ‹ כִּי זֶה אֱלֹהִים אֱלֹהֵינוּ
עוֹלָם וָעֶד, הוּא יְנַהֲגֵנוּ עַל־מוּת:

קדיש יתום *(page 585)*

תהלים פב

Tuesday הַיּוֹם יוֹם שְׁלִישִׁי בְּשַׁבָּת, שֶׁבּוֹ הָיוּ הַלְוִיִּם אוֹמְרִים בְּבֵית הַמִּקְדָּשׁ:

מִזְמוֹר לְאָסָף, אֱלֹהִים נִצָּב בַּעֲדַת־אֵל, בְּקֶרֶב אֱלֹהִים יִשְׁפֹּט:
עַד־מָתַי תִּשְׁפְּטוּ־עָוֶל, וּפְנֵי רְשָׁעִים תִּשְׂאוּ־סֶלָה: שִׁפְטוּ־דָל
וְיָתוֹם, עָנִי וָרָשׁ הַצְדִּיקוּ: פַּלְּטוּ־דַל וְאֶבְיוֹן, מִיַּד רְשָׁעִים הַצִּילוּ:
לֹא יָדְעוּ וְלֹא יָבִינוּ, בַּחֲשֵׁכָה יִתְהַלָּכוּ, יִמּוֹטוּ כָּל־מוֹסְדֵי אָרֶץ:
אֲנִי־אָמַרְתִּי אֱלֹהִים אַתֶּם, וּבְנֵי עֶלְיוֹן כֻּלְּכֶם: אָכֵן כְּאָדָם תְּמוּתוּן,
וּכְאַחַד הַשָּׂרִים תִּפֹּלוּ: ‹ קוּמָה אֱלֹהִים שָׁפְטָה הָאָרֶץ, כִּי־אַתָּה
תִנְחַל בְּכָל־הַגּוֹיִם:

קדיש יתום *(page 585)*

---

endurance of Jerusalem, the city that outlived all those who sought to conquer it.

A score of conquerors have held it as their choicest prize; and more than a dozen times has it been utterly destroyed. The Babylonians burnt it, and deported its population; the Romans slew a million of its inhabitants, razed it to the ground, passed the ploughshare over it, and strewed its furrows with salt; Hadrian banished its very name from the lips of men, changed it to *Aelia*

Wednesday: הַיּוֹם Today is the fourth day of the week,
on which the Levites used to say this psalm in the Temple:

אֵל־נְקָמוֹת God of retribution, LORD, God of retribution, appear! Rise *Ps. 94* up, Judge of the earth. Repay to the arrogant what they deserve. How long shall the wicked, LORD, how long shall the wicked triumph? They pour out insolent words. All the evildoers are full of boasting. They crush Your people, LORD, and oppress Your inheritance. They kill the widow and the stranger. They murder the orphaned. They say, "The LORD does not see. The God of Jacob pays no heed." Take heed, you most brutish people. You fools, when will you grow wise? Will He who implants the ear not hear? Will He who formed the eye not see? Will He who disciplines nations – He who teaches man knowledge – not punish? The LORD knows that the thoughts of man are a mere fleeting breath. Happy is the man whom You discipline, LORD, the one You instruct in Your Torah, giving him tranquility in days of trouble, until a pit is dug for the wicked. For the LORD will not forsake His people, nor abandon His heritage. Judgment shall again accord with justice, and all the upright in heart will follow it. Who will rise up for me against the wicked? Who will stand up for me against wrongdoers? Had the LORD not been my help, I would soon have dwelt in death's silence. When I thought my foot was slipping, Your loving-kindness, LORD, gave me support. When I was filled with anxiety, Your consolations soothed my soul. Can a corrupt throne be allied with You? Can injustice be framed into law? They join forces against the life of the righteous, and condemn the innocent to death. But the LORD is my stronghold, my God is the Rock of my refuge. He will bring back on them their wickedness, and destroy them for their evil deeds. The LORD our God will destroy them.

אֵל־נְקָמוֹת יהוה *Wednesday: Psalm 94.* A psalm of intense power about the connection between religious faith and ethical conduct and their opposite: lack of faith and a failure of humanity. When man begins to worship himself, he dreams of becoming a god but ends by becoming lower than the beasts.

תהלים צד

אֵל־נְקָמוֹת יהוה, אֵל נְקָמוֹת הוֹפִיעַ: הִנָּשֵׂא שֹׁפֵט הָאָרֶץ, הָשֵׁב גְּמוּל עַל־גֵּאִים: עַד־מָתַי רְשָׁעִים, יהוה, עַד־מָתַי רְשָׁעִים יַעֲלֹזוּ: יַבִּיעוּ יְדַבְּרוּ עָתָק, יִתְאַמְּרוּ כָּל־פֹּעֲלֵי אָוֶן: עַמְּךָ יהוה יְדַכְּאוּ, וְנַחֲלָתְךָ יְעַנּוּ: אַלְמָנָה וְגֵר יַהֲרֹגוּ, וִיתוֹמִים יְרַצֵּחוּ: וַיֹּאמְרוּ לֹא יִרְאֶה־יָּהּ, וְלֹא־יָבִין אֱלֹהֵי יַעֲקֹב: בִּינוּ בֹּעֲרִים בָּעָם, וּכְסִילִים מָתַי תַּשְׂכִּילוּ: הֲנֹטַע אֹזֶן הֲלֹא יִשְׁמָע, אִם־יֹצֵר עַיִן הֲלֹא יַבִּיט: הֲיֹסֵר גּוֹיִם הֲלֹא יוֹכִיחַ, הַמְלַמֵּד אָדָם דָּעַת: יהוה יֹדֵעַ מַחְשְׁבוֹת אָדָם, כִּי־הֵמָּה הָבֶל: אַשְׁרֵי הַגֶּבֶר אֲשֶׁר־תְּיַסְּרֶנּוּ יָּהּ, וּמִתּוֹרָתְךָ תְלַמְּדֶנּוּ: לְהַשְׁקִיט לוֹ מִימֵי רָע, עַד יִכָּרֶה לָרָשָׁע שָׁחַת: כִּי לֹא־יִטֹּשׁ יהוה עַמּוֹ, וְנַחֲלָתוֹ לֹא יַעֲזֹב: כִּי־עַד־צֶדֶק יָשׁוּב מִשְׁפָּט, וְאַחֲרָיו כָּל־יִשְׁרֵי־לֵב: מִי־יָקוּם לִי עִם־מְרֵעִים, מִי־יִתְיַצֵּב לִי עִם־פֹּעֲלֵי אָוֶן: לוּלֵי יהוה עֶזְרָתָה לִּי, כִּמְעַט שָׁכְנָה דוּמָה נַפְשִׁי: אִם־אָמַרְתִּי מָטָה רַגְלִי, חַסְדְּךָ יהוה יִסְעָדֵנִי: בְּרֹב שַׂרְעַפַּי בְּקִרְבִּי, תַּנְחוּמֶיךָ יְשַׁעַשְׁעוּ נַפְשִׁי: הַיְחָבְרְךָ כִּסֵּא הַוּוֹת, יֹצֵר עָמָל עֲלֵי־חֹק: יָגוֹדּוּ עַל־נֶפֶשׁ צַדִּיק, וְדָם נָקִי יַרְשִׁיעוּ: וַיְהִי יהוה לִי לְמִשְׂגָּב, וֵאלֹהַי לְצוּר מַחְסִי: וַיָּשֶׁב עֲלֵיהֶם אֶת־אוֹנָם, וּבְרָעָתָם יַצְמִיתֵם, יַצְמִיתֵם יהוה אֱלֹהֵינוּ:

application of law, brings order to society as scientific law brings order to the cosmos. Justice ultimately belongs to God. A judge must therefore act with humility and integrity, bringing divine order to human chaos. "A judge who delivers a true judgment becomes a partner of the Holy One, blessed be He, in the work of creation" (*Shabbat* 10a).

▸ Come, let us sing for joy to the LORD; let us shout aloud to the Rock   *Ps. 95*
of our salvation. Let us greet Him with thanksgiving, shout aloud to
Him with songs of praise. For the LORD is the great God, the King
great above all powers.

                                                      Mourner's Kaddish (page 584)

Thursday: הַיּוֹם Today is the fifth day of the week,
              on which the Levites used to say this psalm in the Temple:

לַמְנַצֵּחַ For the conductor of music. On the Gittit. By Asaph. Sing for   *Ps. 81*
joy to God, our strength. Shout aloud to the God of Jacob. Raise a
song, beat the drum, play the sweet harp and lyre. Sound the shofar
on the new moon, on our feast day when the moon is hidden. For it is
a statute for Israel, an ordinance of the God of Jacob. He established
it as a testimony for Joseph when He went forth against the land of
Egypt, where I heard a language that I did not know. I relieved his
shoulder of the burden. His hands were freed from the builder's basket. In distress you called and I rescued you. I answered you from the
secret place of thunder; I tested you at the waters of Meribah, Selah!
Hear, My people, and I will warn you. Israel, if you would only listen
to Me! Let there be no strange god among you. Do not bow down to
an alien god. I am the LORD your God who brought you out of the
land of Egypt. Open your mouth wide and I will fill it. But My people
would not listen to Me. Israel would have none of Me. So I left them
to their stubborn hearts, letting them follow their own devices. If
only My people would listen to Me, if Israel would walk in My ways, I
would soon subdue their enemies, and turn My hand against their foes.
Those who hate the LORD would cower before Him and their doom
would last for ever. ▸ He would feed Israel with the finest wheat – with
honey from the rock I would satisfy you.

                                                      Mourner's Kaddish (page 584)

---

love for, but exasperation with, His children. "If only My people would listen
to Me."

תהלים צה

‹ לְכוּ נְרַנְּנָה לַיהוה, נָרְיעָה לְצוּר יִשְׁעֵנוּ: נְקַדְּמָה פָנָיו בְּתוֹדָה,
בִּזְמִרוֹת נָרִיעַ לוֹ: כִּי אֵל גָּדוֹל יהוה, וּמֶלֶךְ גָּדוֹל עַל־כָּל־אֱלֹהִים:

קדיש יתום (page 585)

Thursday הַיּוֹם יוֹם חֲמִישִׁי בְּשַׁבָּת, שֶׁבּוֹ הָיוּ הַלְוִיִּם אוֹמְרִים בְּבֵית הַמִּקְדָּשׁ:

תהלים פא

לַמְנַצֵּחַ עַל־הַגִּתִּית לְאָסָף: הַרְנִינוּ לֵאלֹהִים עוּזֵּנוּ, הָרְיעוּ לֵאלֹהֵי
יַעֲקֹב: שְׂאוּ־זִמְרָה וּתְנוּ־תֹף, כִּנּוֹר נָעִים עִם־נָבֶל: תִּקְעוּ בַחְדֶשׁ
שׁוֹפָר, בַּכֵּסֶה לְיוֹם חַגֵּנוּ: כִּי חֹק לְיִשְׂרָאֵל הוּא, מִשְׁפָּט לֵאלֹהֵי
יַעֲקֹב: עֵדוּת בִּיהוֹסֵף שָׂמוֹ, בְּצֵאתוֹ עַל־אֶרֶץ מִצְרָיִם, שְׂפַת לֹא־
יָדַעְתִּי אֶשְׁמָע: הֲסִירוֹתִי מִסֵּבֶל שִׁכְמוֹ, כַּפָּיו מִדּוּד תַּעֲבֹרְנָה:
בַּצָּרָה קָרָאתָ וָאֲחַלְּצֶךָּ, אֶעֶנְךָ בְּסֵתֶר רַעַם, אֶבְחָנְךָ עַל־מֵי
מְרִיבָה סֶלָה: שְׁמַע עַמִּי וְאָעִידָה בָּךְ, יִשְׂרָאֵל אִם־תִּשְׁמַע־לִי:
לֹא־יִהְיֶה בְךָ אֵל זָר, וְלֹא תִשְׁתַּחֲוֶה לְאֵל נֵכָר: אָנֹכִי יהוה אֱלֹהֶיךָ,
הַמַּעַלְךָ מֵאֶרֶץ מִצְרָיִם, הַרְחֶב־פִּיךָ וַאֲמַלְאֵהוּ: וְלֹא־שָׁמַע עַמִּי
לְקוֹלִי, וְיִשְׂרָאֵל לֹא־אָבָה לִי: וָאֲשַׁלְּחֵהוּ בִּשְׁרִירוּת לִבָּם, יֵלְכוּ
בְּמוֹעֲצוֹתֵיהֶם: לוּ עַמִּי שֹׁמֵעַ לִי, יִשְׂרָאֵל בִּדְרָכַי יְהַלֵּכוּ: כִּמְעַט
אוֹיְבֵיהֶם אַכְנִיעַ, וְעַל־צָרֵיהֶם אָשִׁיב יָדִי: מְשַׂנְאֵי יהוה יְכַחֲשׁוּ־
לוֹ, וִיהִי עִתָּם לְעוֹלָם: ‹ וַיַּאֲכִילֵהוּ מֵחֵלֶב חִטָּה, וּמִצּוּר, דְּבַשׁ
אַשְׂבִּיעֶךָ:

קדיש יתום (on the next 585)

Appropriately, some communities recite this psalm on Yom HaSho'a, Holocaust Memorial Day (27 Nisan).

לַמְנַצֵּחַ Thursday: Psalm 81. God pleads with His people: a classic expression of
one of the great themes of the prophetic literature, the divine pathos – God's

Friday: הַיּוֹם Today is the sixth day of the week,
on which the Levites used to say this psalm in the Temple:

יהוה מָלָךְ The Lord reigns. He is robed in majesty. The Lord is robed, *Ps. 93*
girded with strength. The world is firmly established; it cannot be
moved. Your throne stands firm as of old; You are eternal. Rivers lift
up, Lord, rivers lift up their voice, rivers lift up their crashing waves.
Mightier than the noise of many waters, than the mighty waves of the
sea is the Lord on high. ‣ Your testimonies are very sure; holiness
adorns Your House, Lord, for evermore.

Mourner's Kaddish (on the next page)

Shabbat: הַיּוֹם Today is the holy Sabbath,
on which the Levites used to say this psalm in the Temple:

מִזְמוֹר A psalm. A song for the Sabbath day. It is good to thank the Lord *Ps. 92*
and sing psalms to Your name, Most High – to tell of Your loving-
kindness in the morning and Your faithfulness at night, to the music of
the ten-stringed lyre and the melody of the harp. For You have made me
rejoice by Your work, O Lord; I sing for joy at the deeds of Your hands.
How great are Your deeds, Lord, and how very deep Your thoughts. A
boor cannot know, nor can a fool understand, that though the wicked
spring up like grass and all evildoers flourish, it is only that they may
be destroyed for ever. But You, Lord, are eternally exalted. For behold
Your enemies, Lord, behold Your enemies will perish; all evildoers
will be scattered. You have raised my pride like that of a wild ox; I am
anointed with fresh oil. My eyes shall look in triumph on my adversaries; my ears shall hear the downfall of the wicked who rise against me.
The righteous will flourish like a palm tree and grow tall like a cedar in
Lebanon. Planted in the Lord's House, blossoming in our God's courtyards, ‣ they will still bear fruit in old age, and stay vigorous and fresh,
proclaiming that the Lord is upright: He is my Rock, in whom there is
no wrong.

מִזְמוֹר *The Sabbath: Psalm 92.* A psalm about the Sabbath of the end of days
when the world will be restored to its primal harmony, violence will cease,
lives will not be cut short by war or terror, and each being will recognize its

Friday הַיּוֹם יוֹם שִׁשִּׁי בְּשַׁבָּת, שֶׁבּוֹ הָיוּ הַלְוִיִּם אוֹמְרִים בְּבֵית הַמִּקְדָּשׁ:

תהלים צג

יְהוה מָלָךְ, גֵּאוּת לָבֵשׁ, לָבֵשׁ יְהוה עֹז הִתְאַזָּר, אַף־תִּכּוֹן תֵּבֵל בַּל־תִּמּוֹט: נָכוֹן כִּסְאֲךָ מֵאָז, מֵעוֹלָם אָתָּה: נָשְׂאוּ נְהָרוֹת יְהוה, נָשְׂאוּ נְהָרוֹת קוֹלָם, יִשְׂאוּ נְהָרוֹת דָּכְיָם: מִקֹּלוֹת מַיִם רַבִּים, אַדִּירִים מִשְׁבְּרֵי־יָם, אַדִּיר בַּמָּרוֹם יְהוה: ◂ עֵדֹתֶיךָ נֶאֶמְנוּ מְאֹד, לְבֵיתְךָ נַאֲוָה־קֹּדֶשׁ, יְהוה לְאֹרֶךְ יָמִים:

קדיש יתום (on the next page)

שבת הַיּוֹם יוֹם שַׁבַּת קֹדֶשׁ, שֶׁבּוֹ הָיוּ הַלְוִיִּם אוֹמְרִים בְּבֵית הַמִּקְדָּשׁ:

תהלים צב

מִזְמוֹר שִׁיר לְיוֹם הַשַּׁבָּת: טוֹב לְהֹדוֹת לַיהוה, וּלְזַמֵּר לְשִׁמְךָ עֶלְיוֹן: לְהַגִּיד בַּבֹּקֶר חַסְדֶּךָ, וֶאֱמוּנָתְךָ בַּלֵּילוֹת: עֲלֵי־עָשׂוֹר וַעֲלֵי־נָבֶל, עֲלֵי הִגָּיוֹן בְּכִנּוֹר: כִּי שִׂמַּחְתַּנִי יְהוה בְּפָעֳלֶךָ, בְּמַעֲשֵׂי יָדֶיךָ אֲרַנֵּן: מַה־גָּדְלוּ מַעֲשֶׂיךָ יְהוה, מְאֹד עָמְקוּ מַחְשְׁבֹתֶיךָ: אִישׁ־בַּעַר לֹא יֵדָע, וּכְסִיל לֹא־יָבִין אֶת־זֹאת: בִּפְרֹחַ רְשָׁעִים כְּמוֹ־עֵשֶׂב, וַיָּצִיצוּ כָּל־פֹּעֲלֵי אָוֶן, לְהִשָּׁמְדָם עֲדֵי־עַד: וְאַתָּה מָרוֹם לְעֹלָם יְהוה: כִּי הִנֵּה אֹיְבֶיךָ יְהוה, כִּי־הִנֵּה אֹיְבֶיךָ יֹאבֵדוּ, יִתְפָּרְדוּ כָּל־פֹּעֲלֵי אָוֶן: וַתָּרֶם כִּרְאֵים קַרְנִי, בַּלֹּתִי בְּשֶׁמֶן רַעֲנָן: וַתַּבֵּט עֵינִי בְּשׁוּרָי, בַּקָּמִים עָלַי מְרֵעִים תִּשְׁמַעְנָה אָזְנָי: צַדִּיק כַּתָּמָר יִפְרָח, כְּאֶרֶז בַּלְּבָנוֹן יִשְׂגֶּה: שְׁתוּלִים בְּבֵית יְהוה, בְּחַצְרוֹת אֱלֹהֵינוּ יַפְרִיחוּ: ◂ עוֹד יְנוּבוּן בְּשֵׂיבָה, דְּשֵׁנִים וְרַעֲנַנִּים יִהְיוּ: לְהַגִּיד כִּי־יָשָׁר יְהוה, צוּרִי, וְלֹא־עַוְלָתָה בּוֹ:

יהוה מָלָךְ *Friday: Psalm 93.* Speaking as it does of the completion of creation ("the world is firmly established"), this psalm is appropriate for the sixth day, when "the heavens and the earth were completed, and all their array" (Gen. 2:1).

MOURNER'S KADDISH

The following prayer, said by mourners, requires the presence of a minyan.
A transliteration can be found on page 779.

Mourner: יִתְגַּדַּל Magnified and sanctified
may His great name be,
in the world He created by His will.
May He establish His kingdom
in your lifetime and in your days,
and in the lifetime of all the house of Israel,
swiftly and soon –
and say: Amen.

All: May His great name be blessed for ever and all time.

Mourner: Blessed and praised, glorified and exalted,
raised and honored,
uplifted and lauded
be the name of the Holy One,
blessed be He,
beyond any blessing,
song, praise and consolation
uttered in the world –
and say: Amen.

May there be great peace from heaven,
and life for us and all Israel –
and say: Amen.

Bow, take three steps back, as if taking leave of the Divine Presence,
then bow, first left, then right, then center, while saying:

May He who makes peace in His high places,
make peace for us and all Israel –
and say: Amen.

---

integrity in the scheme of creation. It is, said the sages, a "song for the time to come, for the day which will be entirely Sabbath and rest for life everlasting" (Mishna, *Tamid* 7:4).

קדיש יתום

The following prayer, said by mourners, requires the presence of a מנין.
A transliteration can be found on page 779.

אבל: יִתְגַּדַּל וְיִתְקַדַּשׁ שְׁמֵהּ רַבָּא (קהל: אָמֵן)

בְּעָלְמָא דִּי בְרָא כִרְעוּתֵהּ

וְיַמְלִיךְ מַלְכוּתֵהּ

בְּחַיֵּיכוֹן וּבְיוֹמֵיכוֹן וּבְחַיֵּי דְּכָל בֵּית יִשְׂרָאֵל

בַּעֲגָלָא וּבִזְמַן קָרִיב

וְאִמְרוּ אָמֵן. (קהל: אָמֵן)

קהל
ואבל: יְהֵא שְׁמֵהּ רַבָּא מְבָרַךְ לְעָלַם וּלְעָלְמֵי עָלְמַיָּא.

אבל: יִתְבָּרַךְ וְיִשְׁתַּבַּח וְיִתְפָּאַר

וְיִתְרוֹמַם וְיִתְנַשֵּׂא וְיִתְהַדָּר וְיִתְעַלֶּה וְיִתְהַלָּל

שְׁמֵהּ דְּקֻדְשָׁא בְּרִיךְ הוּא (קהל: בְּרִיךְ הוּא)

לְעֵלָּא מִן כָּל בִּרְכָתָא וְשִׁירָתָא

תֻּשְׁבְּחָתָא וְנֶחֱמָתָא

דַּאֲמִירָן בְּעָלְמָא

וְאִמְרוּ אָמֵן. (קהל: אָמֵן)

יְהֵא שְׁלָמָא רַבָּא מִן שְׁמַיָּא

וְחַיִּים, עָלֵינוּ וְעַל כָּל יִשְׂרָאֵל

וְאִמְרוּ אָמֵן. (קהל: אָמֵן)

Bow, take three steps back, as if taking leave of the Divine Presence,
then bow, first left, then right, then center, while saying:

עֹשֶׂה שָׁלוֹם בִּמְרוֹמָיו

הוּא יַעֲשֶׂה שָׁלוֹם עָלֵינוּ וְעַל כָּל יִשְׂרָאֵל

וְאִמְרוּ אָמֵן. (קהל: אָמֵן)

SONG OF GLORY

The Ark is opened and all stand.

Leader: I will sing sweet psalms and I will weave songs,
to You for whom my soul longs.

Cong: My soul yearns for the shelter of Your hand,
that all Your mystic secrets I might understand.

Leader: Whenever I speak of Your glory above,
my heart is yearning for Your love.

Cong: So Your glories I will proclaim,
and in songs of love give honor to Your name.

Leader: I will tell of Your glory though I have not seen You,
imagine and describe You, though I have not known You.

Cong: By the hand of Your prophets, through Your servants' mystery,
You gave a glimpse of Your wondrous majesty.

Leader: Recounting Your grandeur and Your glory,
of Your great deeds they told the story.

Cong: They depicted You, though not as You are,
but as You do: Your acts, Your power.

Leader: They represented You in many visions;
through them all You are One without divisions.

Cong: They saw You, now old, then young,
Your head with gray, with black hair hung.

Leader: Aged on the day of judgment, yet on the day of war,
a young warrior with mighty hands they saw.

Cong: Triumph like a helmet He wore on his head;
His right hand and holy arm to victory have led.

הָגֶּךְ אֶחָד בְּכָל דְּמִיוֹנוֹת *Through them all, You are One without divisions.* Literally, "You are One through all the images," a preface to the following verses which give examples of this theme.

וְזָקֵן בְּיוֹם דִּין *Aged on the day of judgment.* A reference to the mystical vision in Daniel (7:9) of God sitting on the throne of judgment: "The hair of His head was white as wool."

בְּיוֹם קְרָב *Yet on the day of war.* From the vision of Zechariah (14:3).

שיר הכבוד

The ארון קודש *is opened and all stand.*

ש"ץ: אַנְעִים זְמִירוֹת וְשִׁירִים אֶאֱרֹג, כִּי אֵלֶיךָ נַפְשִׁי תַעֲרֹג.

קהל: נַפְשִׁי חִמְּדָה בְּצֵל יָדֶךָ, לָדַעַת כָּל רָז סוֹדֶךָ.

ש"ץ: מִדֵּי דַבְּרִי בִּכְבוֹדֶךָ, הוֹמֶה לִבִּי אֶל דּוֹדֶיךָ.

קהל: עַל כֵּן אֲדַבֵּר בְּךָ נִכְבָּדוֹת, וְשִׁמְךָ אֲכַבֵּד בְּשִׁירֵי יְדִידוֹת.

שׁ"ץ: אֲסַפְּרָה כְבוֹדְךָ וְלֹא רְאִיתִיךָ, אֲדַמְּךָ אֲכַנְּךָ וְלֹא יְדַעְתִּיךָ.

קהל: בְּיַד נְבִיאֶיךָ בְּסוֹד עֲבָדֶיךָ, דִּמִּיתָ הֲדַר כְּבוֹד הוֹדֶךָ.

שׁ"ץ: גְּדֻלָּתְךָ וּגְבוּרָתֶךָ, כִּנּוּ לְתְקֶף פְּעֻלָּתֶךָ.

קהל: דִּמּוּ אוֹתְךָ וְלֹא כְּפִי יֶשְׁךָ, וַיְשַׁוּוּךָ לְפִי מַעֲשֶׂיךָ.

שׁ"ץ: הִמְשִׁילוּךָ בְּרֹב חֶזְיוֹנוֹת, הִנְּךָ אֶחָד בְּכָל דִּמְיוֹנוֹת.

קהל: וַיֶּחֱזוּ בְךָ זִקְנָה וּבַחֲרוּת, וּשְׂעַר רֹאשְׁךָ בְּשֵׂיבָה וְשַׁחֲרוּת.

שׁ"ץ: זִקְנָה בְּיוֹם דִּין וּבַחֲרוּת בְּיוֹם קְרָב, כְּאִישׁ מִלְחָמוֹת יָדָיו לוֹ רָב.

קהל: חָבַשׁ כּוֹבַע יְשׁוּעָה בְּרֹאשׁוֹ, הוֹשִׁיעָה לּוֹ יְמִינוֹ וּזְרוֹעַ קָדְשׁוֹ.

ANIM ZEMIROT – SONG OF GLORY
Attributed to either Rabbi Yehuda HeḤasid (d. 1217) or his father Rabbi Shmuel, a hymn structured as an alphabetical acrostic, with a (non-acrostic) four-line introduction and a three-line conclusion, followed by biblical verses. The poem, with great grace and depth, speaks about the limits of language in describing the experience of God. On the one hand, God – infinite, eternal, invisible – is beyond the reach of language. On the other, we can only address Him in and through language. Hence the various literary forms – metaphor, image, mystic vision – used by the prophets and poets and their successors to indicate, through words, that which lies beyond words. The images are many, but God is One.

בְּצֵל יָדֶךָ *The shelter of Your hand.* An image of intimacy and protection (see Isaiah 49:2, 51:16; Song of Songs 2:3).

אֲדַמְּךָ אֲכַנְּךָ וְלֹא יְדַעְתִּיךָ *Imagine and describe You, though I have not known You.* The finite cannot truly know the Infinite; physical beings cannot fully understand the One who is non-physical.

Leader: His curls are filled with dew drops of light,
His locks with fragments of the night.

Cong: He will glory in me, for He delights in me;
My diadem of beauty He shall be.

Leader: His head is like pure beaten gold;
Engraved on His brow, His sacred name behold.

Cong: For grace and glory, beauty and renown,
His people have adorned Him with a crown.

Leader: Like a youth's, His hair in locks unfurls;
Its black tresses flowing in curls.

Cong: Jerusalem, His splendor, is the dwelling place of right;
may He prize it as His highest delight.

Leader: Like a crown in His hand may His treasured people be,
a turban of beauty and of majesty.

Cong: He bore them, carried them, with a crown He adorned them.
They were precious in His sight, and He honored them.

Leader: His glory is on me; my glory is on Him.
He is near to me when I call to Him.

Cong: He is bright and rosy; red will be His dress,
when He comes from Edom, treading the winepress.

Leader: He showed the tefillin-knot to Moses, humble, wise,
when the Lord's likeness was before his eyes.

Cong: He delights in His people; the humble He does raise –
He glories in them; He sits enthroned upon their praise.

Leader: Your first word, Your call to every age, is true:
O seek the people who seek You.

Cong: My many songs please take and hear
and may my hymn of joy to You come near.

Leader: May my praise be a crown for Your head,
and like incense before You, the prayers I have said.

Cong: May a poor man's song be precious in Your eyes,
like a song sung over sacrifice.

---

days, taken from Isaiah 63:1–3. By invoking some of the most dramatic images of God in the Bible and rabbinic literature, the poet tells us that they are not to be understood literally: poetry, metaphor and imagery are ways in which prophets and mystics intimate what lies beyond the sayable.

ש״ץ: טַלְלֵי אוֹרוֹת רֹאשׁוֹ נִמְלָא, קְוֻצּוֹתָיו רְסִיסֵי לָיְלָה.

קהל: יִתְפָּאֵר בִּי כִּי חָפֵץ בִּי, וְהוּא יִהְיֶה לִי לַעֲטֶרֶת צְבִי.

ש״ץ: כֶּתֶם טָהוֹר פָּז דְּמוּת רֹאשׁוֹ, וְחַק עַל מֵצַח כְּבוֹד שֵׁם קָדְשׁוֹ.

קהל: לְחֵן וּלְכָבוֹד צְבִי תִפְאָרָה, אֻמָּתוֹ לוֹ עִטְּרָה עֲטָרָה.

ש״ץ: מַחְלְפוֹת רֹאשׁוֹ כְּבִימֵי בְחוּרוֹת, קְוֻצּוֹתָיו תַּלְתַּלִּים שְׁחוֹרוֹת.

קהל: נְוֵה הַצֶּדֶק צְבִי תִפְאַרְתּוֹ, יַעֲלֶה נָּא עַל רֹאשׁ שִׂמְחָתוֹ.

ש״ץ: סְגֻלָּתוֹ תְּהִי בְיָדוֹ עֲטֶרֶת, וּצְנִיף מְלוּכָה צְבִי תִפְאָרֶת.

קהל: עֲמוּסִים נְשָׂאָם, עֲטֶרֶת עִנְּדָם, מֵאֲשֶׁר יָקְרוּ בְעֵינָיו כִּבְּדָם.

ש״ץ: פְּאֵרוֹ עָלַי וּפְאֵרִי עָלָיו, וְקָרוֹב אֵלַי בְּקָרְאִי אֵלָיו.

קהל: צַח וְאָדֹם לִלְבוּשׁוֹ אָדֹם, פּוּרָה בְדָרְכוֹ בְּבוֹאוֹ מֵאֱדוֹם.

ש״ץ: קֶשֶׁר תְּפִלִּין הֶרְאָה לֶעָנָו, תְּמוּנַת יהוה לְנֶגֶד עֵינָיו.

קהל: רוֹצֶה בְעַמּוֹ עֲנָוִים יְפָאֵר, יוֹשֵׁב תְּהִלּוֹת בָּם לְהִתְפָּאֵר.

ש״ץ: רֹאשׁ דְּבָרְךָ אֱמֶת קוֹרֵא מֵרֹאשׁ דּוֹר וָדוֹר, עַם דּוֹרֶשְׁךָ דְּרֹשׁ.

קהל: שִׁית הֲמוֹן שִׁירַי נָא עָלֶיךָ, וְרִנָּתִי תִקְרַב אֵלֶיךָ.

ש״ץ: תְּהִלָּתִי תְּהִי לְרֹאשְׁךָ עֲטֶרֶת, וּתְפִלָּתִי תִּכּוֹן קְטֹרֶת.

קהל: תִּיקַר שִׁירַת רָשׁ בְּעֵינֶיךָ, כַּשִּׁיר יוּשַׁר עַל קָרְבָּנֶיךָ.

_____

טַלְלֵי אוֹרוֹת **Dew drops of light**. These and the following images are drawn from Isaiah and the Song of Songs.

פְּאֵרוֹ עָלַי וּפְאֵרִי עָלָיו **His glory is on me; my glory is on Him**. A reference to the daring metaphor of the sages (*Berakhot* 6a), that just as the children of Israel wear tefillin (an emblem of glory) containing the verse *Shema Yisrael*, proclaiming the Oneness of God, so God, as it were, wears tefillin containing the verse, "Who is like Your people Israel, a nation unique on earth?" – proclaiming the uniqueness of Israel. This is reiterated in the phrase of the next stanza, "He showed the tefillin-knot to Moses," a reference to Exodus 33:23, "You will see My back." Tefillin symbolize the bond of love between God and His people.

בְּבוֹאוֹ מֵאֱדוֹם **When He comes from Edom**. An image of judgment at the end of

Leader: To the One who sustains all, may my blessing take flight:
Creator, Life-Giver, God of right and might.

Cong: And when I offer blessing, to me Your head incline:
accepting it as spice, fragrant and fine.

Leader: May my prayer be to You sweet song.
For You my soul will always long.

The Ark is closed.

Yours, Lord, are the greatness and the power, the glory, the majesty and splendor, *1 Chr. 29*
for everything in heaven and earth is Yours. Yours, Lord, is the kingdom; You
are exalted as Head over all. ▸ Who can tell of the mighty acts of the Lord and *Ps. 106*
make all His praise be heard?
Mourner's Kaddish (page 584)

Many congregations sing Adon Olam at this point.

Lord of the universe,
who reigned before the birth of any thing –

When by His will all things were made
then was His name proclaimed King.

And when all things shall cease to be
He alone will reign in awe.

He was, He is, and He shall be
glorious for evermore.

He is One, there is none else,
alone, unique, beyond compare;

Without beginning, without end,
His might, His rule are everywhere.

He is my God; my Redeemer lives.
He is the Rock on whom I rely –

My banner and my safe retreat,
my cup, my portion when I cry.

Into His hand my soul I place,
when I awake and when I sleep.

The Lord is with me, I shall not fear;
body and soul from harm will He keep.

שי״ן: בִּרְכָתִי תַעֲלֶה לְרֹאשׁ מַשְׁבִּיר, מְחוֹלֵל וּמוֹלִיד, צַדִּיק כַּבִּיר.

קהל: וּבְבִרְכָתִי תְנַעֲנַע לִי רֹאשׁ, וְאוֹתָהּ קַח לְךָ כִּבְשָׂמִים רֹאשׁ.

שי״ן: יֶעֱרַב נָא שִׂיחִי עָלֶיךָ, כִּי נַפְשִׁי תַעֲרֹג אֵלֶיךָ.

The ארון קודש *is closed.*

דברי הימים
א׳ כט

לְךָ יהוה הַגְּדֻלָּה וְהַגְּבוּרָה וְהַתִּפְאֶרֶת וְהַנֵּצַח וְהַהוֹד
כִּי־כֹל בַּשָּׁמַיִם וּבָאָרֶץ, לְךָ יהוה הַמַּמְלָכָה וְהַמִּתְנַשֵּׂא לְכֹל לְרֹאשׁ:

תהלים קו

‹ מִי יְמַלֵּל גְּבוּרוֹת יהוה, יַשְׁמִיעַ כָּל־תְּהִלָּתוֹ:

(קדיש יתום) (page 585)

Many congregations sing אֲדוֹן עוֹלָם *at this point.*

אֲדוֹן עוֹלָם

אֲשֶׁר מָלַךְ בְּטֶרֶם כָּל־יְצִיר נִבְרָא.

לְעֵת נַעֲשָׂה בְחֶפְצוֹ כֹּל אֲזַי מֶלֶךְ שְׁמוֹ נִקְרָא.

וְאַחֲרֵי כִּכְלוֹת הַכֹּל לְבַדּוֹ יִמְלֹךְ נוֹרָא.

וְהוּא הָיָה וְהוּא הֹוֶה וְהוּא יִהְיֶה בְּתִפְאָרָה.

וְהוּא אֶחָד וְאֵין שֵׁנִי לְהַמְשִׁיל לוֹ לְהַחְבִּירָה.

בְּלִי רֵאשִׁית בְּלִי תַכְלִית וְלוֹ הָעֹז וְהַמִּשְׂרָה.

וְהוּא אֵלִי וְחַי גּוֹאֲלִי וְצוּר חֶבְלִי בְּעֵת צָרָה.

וְהוּא נִסִּי וּמָנוֹס לִי מְנָת כּוֹסִי בְּיוֹם אֶקְרָא.

בְּיָדוֹ אַפְקִיד רוּחִי בְּעֵת אִישַׁן וְאָעִירָה.

וְעִם רוּחִי גְּוִיָּתִי יהוה לִי וְלֹא אִירָא.

כִּי נַפְשִׁי תַעֲרֹג אֵלֶיךָ *For You my soul will always long.* The poet brings the song to an end by referring back to the line with which it began.

Kiddush for Yom Tov Morning

On Shabbat, start Kiddush here:

וְשָׁמְרוּ The children of Israel must keep the Sabbath, observing the Sab- *Ex. 31*
bath in every generation as an everlasting covenant. It is a sign between
Me and the children of Israel for ever, for in six days the Lord made
the heavens and the earth, but on the seventh day He ceased work and
refreshed Himself.

זָכוֹר Remember the Sabbath day to keep it holy. Six days you shall labor *Ex. 20*
and do all your work, but the seventh day is a Sabbath of the Lord your
God; on it you shall not do any work – you, your son or daughter, your
male or female slave, or your cattle, or the stranger within your gates.
For in six days the Lord made heaven and earth and sea and all that is
in them, and rested on the seventh day;

On Shabbat, some start Kiddush here instead:

Therefore the Lord blessed the Sabbath day and declared it holy.

On a weekday, start here:

אֵלֶּה These are the appointed times of the Lord, *Lev. 23*
sacred assemblies, which you shall announce in their due season.
Thus Moses announced the Lord's appointed seasons
to the children of Israel.

When saying Kiddush for others, add: Please pay attention, my masters.

בָּרוּךְ Blessed are You, Lord our God, King of the Universe,
who creates the fruit of the vine.

---

over wine, preceded by scriptural verses which speak of the honor or joy
of the day. It is called "the great Kiddush" as if not to put it to shame when
compared with its biblically mandated counterpart. There is a moral lesson here. If we institute customs (like covering the ḥalla or matza when
making a declaration over wine) so as not to shame inanimate objects or
abstract entities, how much more so should be careful never to shame a
human being.

קידושא רבה

On שבת, *start* קידוש *here:*

שמות לא

וְשָׁמְרוּ בְנֵי־יִשְׂרָאֵל אֶת־הַשַּׁבָּת, לַעֲשׂוֹת אֶת־הַשַּׁבָּת לְדֹרֹתָם בְּרִית
עוֹלָם: בֵּינִי וּבֵין בְּנֵי יִשְׂרָאֵל אוֹת הִוא לְעֹלָם, כִּי־שֵׁשֶׁת יָמִים עָשָׂה
יהוה אֶת־הַשָּׁמַיִם וְאֶת־הָאָרֶץ וּבַיּוֹם הַשְּׁבִיעִי שָׁבַת וַיִּנָּפַשׁ:

שמות כ

זָכוֹר אֶת־יוֹם הַשַּׁבָּת לְקַדְּשׁוֹ: שֵׁשֶׁת יָמִים תַּעֲבֹד, וְעָשִׂיתָ כָּל־מְלַאכְתֶּךָ:
וְיוֹם הַשְּׁבִיעִי שַׁבָּת לַיהוה אֱלֹהֶיךָ, לֹא־תַעֲשֶׂה כָל־מְלָאכָה אַתָּה וּבִנְךָ
וּבִתֶּךָ, עַבְדְּךָ וַאֲמָתְךָ וּבְהֶמְתֶּךָ, וְגֵרְךָ אֲשֶׁר בִּשְׁעָרֶיךָ: כִּי שֵׁשֶׁת־יָמִים
עָשָׂה יהוה אֶת־הַשָּׁמַיִם וְאֶת־הָאָרֶץ אֶת־הַיָּם וְאֶת־כָּל־אֲשֶׁר־בָּם, וַיָּנַח
בַּיּוֹם הַשְּׁבִיעִי

On שבת, *some start* קידוש *here instead:*

עַל־כֵּן בֵּרַךְ יהוה אֶת־יוֹם הַשַּׁבָּת וַיְקַדְּשֵׁהוּ:

On a weekday, start here:

ויקרא כג

אֵלֶּה מוֹעֲדֵי יהוה מִקְרָאֵי קֹדֶשׁ אֲשֶׁר־תִּקְרְאוּ אֹתָם בְּמוֹעֲדָם:
וַיְדַבֵּר מֹשֶׁה אֶת־מֹעֲדֵי יהוה אֶל־בְּנֵי יִשְׂרָאֵל:

When saying קידוש *for others, add* סַבְרִי מָרָנָן

בָּרוּךְ אַתָּה יהוה אֱלֹהֵינוּ מֶלֶךְ הָעוֹלָם, בּוֹרֵא פְּרִי הַגָּפֶן.

KIDDUSH

Kiddush on Sabbath and festival mornings is halakhically different from
its evening counterpart. In the evening, Kiddush is a biblically ordained
performative utterance, declaring the day holy in fulfillment of the command "Remember the Sabbath day to keep it holy," meaning, declare it holy
by a blessing made, if possible, over wine (Ex. 20:8; *Pesaḥim* 106a). In the
morning, the blessing over wine is a rabbinic command, part of a different mitzva, *kevod Shabbat*, "honoring Shabbat" or *simḥat haregel*, rejoicing
on the festival (*Mishna Berura* 271:2). Hence it consists only of a blessing

Minḥa for Shavuot

אַשְׁרֵי Happy are those who dwell in Your House;   *Ps. 84*
they shall continue to praise You, Selah!
Happy are the people for whom this is so;   *Ps. 144*
happy are the people whose God is the Lord.
A song of praise by David.   *Ps. 145*

I will exalt You, my God, the King, and bless Your name for ever
and all time. Every day I will bless You, and praise Your name for
ever and all time. Great is the Lord and greatly to be praised;
His greatness is unfathomable. One generation will praise Your
works to the next, and tell of Your mighty deeds. On the glorious splendor of Your majesty I will meditate, and on the acts
of Your wonders. They shall talk of the power of Your awesome deeds, and I will tell of Your greatness. They shall recite
the record of Your great goodness, and sing with joy of Your
righteousness. The Lord is gracious and compassionate, slow
to anger and great in loving-kindness. The Lord is good to all,
and His compassion extends to all His works. All Your works
shall thank You, Lord, and Your devoted ones shall bless You.
They shall talk of the glory of Your kingship, and speak of Your
might. To make known to mankind His mighty deeds and the
glorious majesty of His kingship. Your kingdom is an everlasting
kingdom, and Your reign is for all generations. The Lord supports all who fall, and raises all who are bowed down. All raise
their eyes to You in hope, and You give them their food in due
season. You open Your hand, and satisfy every living thing with
favor. The Lord is righteous in all His ways, and kind in all He
does. The Lord is close to all who call on Him, to all who call
on Him in truth. He fulfills the will of those who revere Him;
He hears their cry and saves them. The Lord guards all who
love Him, but all the wicked He will destroy. ‣ My mouth shall
speak the praise of the Lord, and all creatures shall bless His
holy name for ever and all time.

We will bless the Lord now and for ever. Halleluya!   *Ps. 115*

מנחה לשבועות

אַשְׁרֵי יוֹשְׁבֵי בֵיתֶךָ, עוֹד יְהַלְלוּךָ סֶּלָה:

אַשְׁרֵי הָעָם שֶׁכָּכָה לּוֹ, אַשְׁרֵי הָעָם שֶׁיהוה אֱלֹהָיו:

תְּהִלָּה לְדָוִד

אֲרוֹמִמְךָ אֱלוֹהַי הַמֶּלֶךְ, וַאֲבָרְכָה שִׁמְךָ לְעוֹלָם וָעֶד:

בְּכָל־יוֹם אֲבָרְכֶךָּ, וַאֲהַלְלָה שִׁמְךָ לְעוֹלָם וָעֶד:

גָּדוֹל יהוה וּמְהֻלָּל מְאֹד, וְלִגְדֻלָּתוֹ אֵין חֵקֶר:

דּוֹר לְדוֹר יְשַׁבַּח מַעֲשֶׂיךָ, וּגְבוּרֹתֶיךָ יַגִּידוּ:

הֲדַר כְּבוֹד הוֹדֶךָ, וְדִבְרֵי נִפְלְאֹתֶיךָ אָשִׂיחָה:

וֶעֱזוּז נוֹרְאֹתֶיךָ יֹאמֵרוּ, וּגְדוּלָּתְךָ אֲסַפְּרֶנָּה:

זֵכֶר רַב־טוּבְךָ יַבִּיעוּ, וְצִדְקָתְךָ יְרַנֵּנוּ:

חַנּוּן וְרַחוּם יהוה, אֶרֶךְ אַפַּיִם וּגְדָל־חָסֶד:

טוֹב־יהוה לַכֹּל, וְרַחֲמָיו עַל־כָּל־מַעֲשָׂיו:

יוֹדוּךָ יהוה כָּל־מַעֲשֶׂיךָ, וַחֲסִידֶיךָ יְבָרְכוּכָה:

כְּבוֹד מַלְכוּתְךָ יֹאמֵרוּ, וּגְבוּרָתְךָ יְדַבֵּרוּ:

לְהוֹדִיעַ לִבְנֵי הָאָדָם גְּבוּרֹתָיו, וּכְבוֹד הֲדַר מַלְכוּתוֹ:

מַלְכוּתְךָ מַלְכוּת כָּל־עֹלָמִים, וּמֶמְשַׁלְתְּךָ בְּכָל־דּוֹר וָדֹר:

סוֹמֵךְ יהוה לְכָל־הַנֹּפְלִים, וְזוֹקֵף לְכָל־הַכְּפוּפִים:

עֵינֵי־כֹל אֵלֶיךָ יְשַׂבֵּרוּ, וְאַתָּה נוֹתֵן־לָהֶם אֶת־אָכְלָם בְּעִתּוֹ:

פּוֹתֵחַ אֶת־יָדֶךָ, וּמַשְׂבִּיעַ לְכָל־חַי רָצוֹן:

צַדִּיק יהוה בְּכָל־דְּרָכָיו, וְחָסִיד בְּכָל־מַעֲשָׂיו:

קָרוֹב יהוה לְכָל־קֹרְאָיו, לְכֹל אֲשֶׁר יִקְרָאֻהוּ בֶאֱמֶת:

רְצוֹן־יְרֵאָיו יַעֲשֶׂה, וְאֶת־שַׁוְעָתָם יִשְׁמַע, וְיוֹשִׁיעֵם:

שׁוֹמֵר יהוה אֶת־כָּל־אֹהֲבָיו, וְאֵת כָּל־הָרְשָׁעִים יַשְׁמִיד:

‹ תְּהִלַּת יהוה יְדַבֶּר פִּי, וִיבָרֵךְ כָּל־בָּשָׂר שֵׁם קָדְשׁוֹ לְעוֹלָם וָעֶד:

וַאֲנַחְנוּ נְבָרֵךְ יָהּ מֵעַתָּה וְעַד־עוֹלָם, הַלְלוּיָהּ:

וּבָא לְצִיּוֹן גּוֹאֵל "A redeemer will come to Zion,   *Is. 59*
to those of Jacob who repent of their sins," declares the LORD.
"As for Me, this is My covenant with them," says the LORD.
"My spirit, that is on you, and My words I have placed in your
mouth will not depart from your mouth, or from the mouth of your
children, or from the mouth of their descendants from this time on
and for ever," says the LORD.

▸ You are the Holy One, enthroned on the praises of Israel.   *Ps. 22*
And [the angels] call to one another, saying, ◂ "Holy, holy, holy   *Is. 6*
is the LORD of hosts; the whole world is filled with His glory."

And they receive permission from one another, saying: *Targum*
"Holy in the highest heavens, home of His Presence; holy on earth,   *Yonatan*
the work of His strength; holy for ever and all time is the LORD of hosts;   *Is. 6*
the whole earth is full of His radiant glory."

▸ Then a wind lifted me up and I heard behind me the sound of a great   *Ezek. 3*
noise, saying, ◂ "Blessed is the LORD's glory from His place."

Then a wind lifted me up and I heard behind me   *Targum*
the sound of a great tempest of those who uttered praise, saying,   *Yonatan*
"Blessed is the LORD's glory from the place of the home of His Presence."   *Ezek. 3*

The LORD shall reign for ever and all time.   *Ex. 15*
The LORD's kingdom is established for ever and all time.   *Targum*
   Onkelos
   Ex. 15

יהוה LORD, God of Abraham, Isaac and Yisrael, our ancestors, may   *1 Chr. 29*
You keep this for ever so that it forms the thoughts in Your people's
heart, and directs their heart toward You. He is compassionate. He   *Ps. 78*
forgives iniquity and does not destroy. Repeatedly He suppresses His
anger, not rousing His full wrath. For You, my LORD, are good and   *Ps. 86*
forgiving, abundantly kind to all who call on You. Your righteousness   *Ps. 119*
is eternally righteous, and Your Torah is truth. Grant truth to Jacob,   *Mic. 7*
loving-kindness to Abraham, as You promised our ancestors in ancient
times. Blessed is my LORD for day after day He burdens us [with His   *Ps. 68*
blessings]; is our salvation, Selah! The LORD of hosts is with us; the   *Ps. 46*
God of Jacob is our refuge, Selah! LORD of hosts, happy is the one who   *Ps. 84*
trusts in You. LORD, save. May the King answer us on the day we call.   *Ps. 20*

ישעיה נט

וּבָא לְצִיּוֹן גּוֹאֵל, וּלְשָׁבֵי פֶשַׁע בְּיַעֲקֹב, נְאֻם יהוה:
וַאֲנִי זֹאת בְּרִיתִי אוֹתָם, אָמַר יהוה
רוּחִי אֲשֶׁר עָלֶיךָ וּדְבָרַי אֲשֶׁר־שַׂמְתִּי בְּפִיךָ
לֹא־יָמוּשׁוּ מִפִּיךָ וּמִפִּי זַרְעֲךָ וּמִפִּי זֶרַע זַרְעֲךָ
אָמַר יהוה, מֵעַתָּה וְעַד־עוֹלָם:

תהלים כב
ישעיה ו

◂ וְאַתָּה קָדוֹשׁ יוֹשֵׁב תְּהִלּוֹת יִשְׂרָאֵל: וְקָרָא זֶה אֶל־זֶה וְאָמַר ▸
קָדוֹשׁ, קָדוֹשׁ, קָדוֹשׁ, יהוה צְבָאוֹת, מְלֹא כָל־הָאָרֶץ כְּבוֹדוֹ:

תרגום
יונתן
ישעיה ו

וּמְקַבְּלִין דֵּין מִן דֵּין וְאָמְרִין, קַדִּישׁ בִּשְׁמֵי מְרוֹמָא עִלָּאָה בֵּית שְׁכִינְתֵּהּ
קַדִּישׁ עַל אַרְעָא עוֹבַד גְּבוּרְתֵּהּ, קַדִּישׁ לְעָלַם וּלְעָלְמֵי עָלְמַיָּא
יהוה צְבָאוֹת, מַלְיָא כָל אַרְעָא זִיו יְקָרֵהּ.

יחזקאל ג

◂ וַתִּשָּׂאֵנִי רוּחַ, וָאֶשְׁמַע אַחֲרַי קוֹל רַעַשׁ גָּדוֹל ▸
בָּרוּךְ כְּבוֹד־יהוה מִמְּקוֹמוֹ:

תרגום
יונתן
יחזקאל ג

וּנְטָלַתְנִי רוּחָא, וּשְׁמָעִית בַּתְרַי קָל זִיעַ סַגִּיא, דִּמְשַׁבְּחִין וְאָמְרִין
בְּרִיךְ יְקָרָא דַיהוה מֵאֲתַר בֵּית שְׁכִינְתֵּהּ.

שמות טו
תרגום
אונקלוס
שמות טו

יהוה יִמְלֹךְ לְעֹלָם וָעֶד:
יהוה מַלְכוּתֵהּ קָאֵם לְעָלַם וּלְעָלְמֵי עָלְמַיָּא.

דברי הימים
א, כט
תהלים עח
תהלים פו
תהלים קיט
מיכה ז
תהלים סח
תהלים מו
תהלים כ
תהלים פד

יהוה אֱלֹהֵי אַבְרָהָם יִצְחָק וְיִשְׂרָאֵל אֲבֹתֵינוּ, שָׁמְרָה־זֹּאת לְעוֹלָם
לְיֵצֶר מַחְשְׁבוֹת לְבַב עַמֶּךָ, וְהָכֵן לְבָבָם אֵלֶיךָ: וְהוּא רַחוּם יְכַפֵּר עָוֹן
וְלֹא־יַשְׁחִית, וְהִרְבָּה לְהָשִׁיב אַפּוֹ, וְלֹא־יָעִיר כָּל־חֲמָתוֹ: כִּי־אַתָּה אֲדֹנָי
טוֹב וְסַלָּח, וְרַב־חֶסֶד לְכָל־קֹרְאֶיךָ: צִדְקָתְךָ צֶדֶק לְעוֹלָם וְתוֹרָתְךָ
אֱמֶת: תִּתֵּן אֱמֶת לְיַעֲקֹב, חֶסֶד לְאַבְרָהָם, אֲשֶׁר־נִשְׁבַּעְתָּ לַאֲבֹתֵינוּ
מִימֵי קֶדֶם: בָּרוּךְ אֲדֹנָי יוֹם יוֹם יַעֲמָס־לָנוּ, הָאֵל יְשׁוּעָתֵנוּ סֶלָה: יהוה
צְבָאוֹת עִמָּנוּ, מִשְׂגָּב לָנוּ אֱלֹהֵי יַעֲקֹב סֶלָה: יהוה צְבָאוֹת, אַשְׁרֵי
אָדָם בֹּטֵחַ בָּךְ: יהוה הוֹשִׁיעָה, הַמֶּלֶךְ יַעֲנֵנוּ בְיוֹם־קָרְאֵנוּ:

בָּרוּךְ Blessed is He, our God, who created us for His glory, separating us from those who go astray; who gave us the Torah of truth, planting within us eternal life. May He open our heart to His Torah, imbuing our heart with the love and awe of Him, that we may do His will and serve Him with a perfect heart, so that we neither toil in vain nor give birth to confusion.

יְהִי רָצוֹן May it be Your will, O Lᴏʀᴅ our God and God of our ances-tors, that we keep Your laws in this world, and thus be worthy to live, see and inherit goodness and blessing in the Messianic Age and in the life of the World to Come. So that my soul may sing to You and *Ps. 30* not be silent. Lᴏʀᴅ, my God, for ever I will thank You. Blessed is the *Jer. 17* man who trusts in the Lᴏʀᴅ, whose trust is in the Lᴏʀᴅ alone. Trust *Is. 26* in the Lᴏʀᴅ for evermore, for God, the Lᴏʀᴅ, is an everlasting Rock. *Ps. 9*
▸ Those who know Your name trust in You, for You, Lᴏʀᴅ, do not for-sake those who seek You. The Lᴏʀᴅ desired, for the sake of Israel's *Is. 42* merit, to make the Torah great and glorious.

HALF KADDISH

Leader: יִתְגַּדַּל Magnified and sanctified may His great name be,
in the world He created by His will.
May He establish His kingdom
in your lifetime and in your days,
and in the lifetime of all the house of Israel,
swiftly and soon – and say: Amen.

All: May His great name be blessed for ever and all time.

Leader: Blessed and praised, glorified and exalted,
raised and honored,
uplifted and lauded
be the name of the Holy One, blessed be He,
beyond any blessing,
song, praise and consolation
uttered in the world – and say: Amen.

On the second day of Shavuot, if also Shabbat, the Torah is read; continue with "As for me"
on the next page. On a weekday continue with the Amida on page 612.

בָּרוּךְ הוּא אֱלֹהֵינוּ שֶׁבְּרָאָנוּ לִכְבוֹדוֹ, וְהִבְדִּילָנוּ מִן הַתּוֹעִים, וְנָתַן לָנוּ תּוֹרַת אֱמֶת, וְחַיֵּי עוֹלָם נָטַע בְּתוֹכֵנוּ. הוּא יִפְתַּח לִבֵּנוּ בְּתוֹרָתוֹ, וְיָשֵׂם בְּלִבֵּנוּ אַהֲבָתוֹ וְיִרְאָתוֹ וְלַעֲשׂוֹת רְצוֹנוֹ וּלְעָבְדוֹ בְּלֵבָב שָׁלֵם, לְמַעַן לֹא נִיגַע לָרִיק וְלֹא נֵלֵד לַבֶּהָלָה.

יְהִי רָצוֹן מִלְּפָנֶיךָ יהוה אֱלֹהֵינוּ וֵאלֹהֵי אֲבוֹתֵינוּ, שֶׁנִּשְׁמֹר חֻקֶּיךָ בָּעוֹלָם הַזֶּה, וְנִזְכֶּה וְנִחְיֶה וְנִרְאֶה וְנִירַשׁ טוֹבָה וּבְרָכָה, לִשְׁנֵי יְמוֹת הַמָּשִׁיחַ וּלְחַיֵּי הָעוֹלָם הַבָּא. לְמַעַן יְזַמֶּרְךָ כָבוֹד וְלֹא יִדֹּם, יהוה אֱלֹהַי, לְעוֹלָם אוֹדֶךָּ: בָּרוּךְ הַגֶּבֶר אֲשֶׁר יִבְטַח בַּיהוה, וְהָיָה יהוה מִבְטַחוֹ: בִּטְחוּ בַיהוה עֲדֵי־עַד, כִּי בְּיָהּ יהוה צוּר עוֹלָמִים: ‹ וְיִבְטְחוּ בְךָ יוֹדְעֵי שְׁמֶךָ, כִּי לֹא־עָזַבְתָּ דֹרְשֶׁיךָ, יהוה: יהוה חָפֵץ לְמַעַן צִדְקוֹ, יַגְדִּיל תּוֹרָה וְיַאְדִּיר:

תהלים ל
ירמיה יז
ישעיה כו
תהלים ט
ישעיה מב

חֲצִי קַדִּישׁ

ש״ץ: יִתְגַּדַּל וְיִתְקַדַּשׁ שְׁמֵהּ רַבָּא (קהל: אָמֵן)

בְּעָלְמָא דִּי בְרָא כִרְעוּתֵהּ

וְיַמְלִיךְ מַלְכוּתֵהּ

בְּחַיֵּיכוֹן וּבְיוֹמֵיכוֹן וּבְחַיֵּי דְכָל בֵּית יִשְׂרָאֵל

בַּעֲגָלָא וּבִזְמַן קָרִיב, וְאִמְרוּ אָמֵן. (קהל: אָמֵן)

קהל ושׁ״ץ: יְהֵא שְׁמֵהּ רַבָּא מְבָרַךְ לְעָלַם וּלְעָלְמֵי עָלְמַיָּא.

שׁ״ץ: יִתְבָּרַךְ וְיִשְׁתַּבַּח וְיִתְפָּאַר וְיִתְרוֹמַם וְיִתְנַשֵּׂא וְיִתְהַדָּר וְיִתְעַלֶּה וְיִתְהַלָּל שְׁמֵהּ דְּקֻדְשָׁא בְּרִיךְ הוּא (קהל: בְּרִיךְ הוּא)

לְעֵלָּא מִן כָּל בִּרְכָתָא וְשִׁירָתָא, תֻּשְׁבְּחָתָא וְנֶחֱמָתָא

דַּאֲמִירָן בְּעָלְמָא, וְאִמְרוּ אָמֵן. (קהל: אָמֵן)

On the second day of שבועות, if also שבת, the Torah is read; continue with וַאֲנִי תְפִלָּתִי־לְךָ on the next page. On a weekday continue with the עמידה on page 613.

וַאֲנִי As for me, may my prayer come to You, LORD, at a time of favor. *Ps. 69*
O God, in Your great love, answer me with Your faithful salvation.

The Ark is opened and the congregation stands. All say:

וַיְהִי בִּנְסֹעַ Whenever the Ark set out, Moses would say, *Num. 10*
"Arise, LORD, and may Your enemies be scattered.
May those who hate You flee before You."
For the Torah shall come forth from Zion, *Is. 2*
and the word of the LORD from Jerusalem.
Blessed is He who in His Holiness
gave the Torah to His people Israel.

Blessed is the name of the Master of the Universe. Blessed is Your crown and Your *Zohar,*
place. May Your favor always be with Your people Israel. Show Your people the *Vayak'hel*
salvation of Your right hand in Your Temple. Grant us the gift of Your good light,
and accept our prayers in mercy. May it be Your will to prolong our life in goodness.
May I be counted among the righteous, so that You will have compassion on me
and protect me and all that is mine and all that is Your people Israel's. You feed all;
You sustain all; You rule over all; You rule over kings, for sovereignty is Yours. I am
a servant of the Holy One, blessed be He, before whom and before whose glorious
Torah I bow at all times. Not in man do I trust, nor on any angel do I rely, but on the
God of heaven who is the God of truth, whose Torah is truth, whose prophets speak
truth, and who abounds in acts of love and truth. ‣ In Him I trust, and to His holy
and glorious name I offer praises. May it be Your will to open my heart to the Torah,
and to fulfill the wishes of my heart and of the hearts of all Your people Israel for
good, for life, and for peace.

The Leader takes the Torah scroll in his right arm, bows toward the Ark and says:
Magnify the LORD with me, and let us exalt His name together. *Ps. 34*

The Ark is closed. The Leader carries the Torah scroll to the bima and the congregation says:
לְךָ Yours, LORD, are the greatness and the power, the glory and the majesty *1 Chr. 29*
and splendor, for everything in heaven and earth is Yours. Yours, LORD, is
the kingdom; You are exalted as Head over all.

רוֹמְמוּ Exalt the LORD our God and bow to His footstool; He is holy. Exalt the *Ps. 99*
LORD our God, and bow at His holy mountain, for holy is the LORD our God.

אַב הָרַחֲמִים May the Father of compassion have compassion on the people
borne by Him. May He remember the covenant with the mighty [patriarchs],
and deliver us from evil times. May He reproach the evil instinct in the people
carried by Him, and graciously grant that we be an everlasting remnant. May
He fulfill in good measure our requests for salvation and compassion.

תהלים סט

וַאֲנִי תְפִלָּתִי־לְךָ יהוה, עֵת רָצוֹן, אֱלֹהִים בְּרָב־חַסְדֶּךָ
עֲנֵנִי בֶּאֱמֶת יִשְׁעֶךָ:

The ארון קודש *is opened and the* קהל *stands. All say:*

במדברי

וַיְהִי בִּנְסֹעַ הָאָרֹן וַיֹּאמֶר מֹשֶׁה
קוּמָה יהוה וְיָפֻצוּ אֹיְבֶיךָ וְיָנֻסוּ מְשַׂנְאֶיךָ מִפָּנֶיךָ:
כִּי מִצִּיּוֹן תֵּצֵא תוֹרָה וּדְבַר־יהוה מִירוּשָׁלָיִם:
בָּרוּךְ שֶׁנָּתַן תּוֹרָה לְעַמּוֹ יִשְׂרָאֵל בִּקְדֻשָּׁתוֹ.

ישעיה ב

זוהר ויקהל

בְּרִיךְ שְׁמֵהּ דְּמָרֵא עָלְמָא, בְּרִיךְ כִּתְרָךְ וְאַתְרָךְ. יְהֵא רְעוּתָךְ עִם עַמָּךְ יִשְׂרָאֵל לְעָלַם,
וּפֻרְקַן יְמִינָךְ אַחֲזֵי לְעַמָּךְ בְּבֵית מַקְדְּשָׁךְ, וּלְאַמְטוּיֵי לָנָא מִטּוּב נְהוֹרָךְ, וּלְקַבֵּל
צְלוֹתַנָא בְּרַחֲמִין. יְהֵא רַעֲוָא קֳדָמָךְ דְּתוֹרִיךְ לַן חַיִּין בְּטִיבוּ, וְלֶהֱוֵי אֲנָא פְקִידָא
בְּגוֹ צַדִּיקַיָּא, לְמִרְחַם עֲלַי וּלְמִנְטַר יָתִי וְיָת כָּל דִּי לִי וְדִי לְעַמָּךְ יִשְׂרָאֵל. אַנְתְּ הוּא
זָן לְכֹלָּא וּמְפַרְנֵס לְכֹלָּא, אַנְתְּ הוּא שַׁלִּיט עַל כֹּלָּא, אַנְתְּ הוּא דְּשַׁלִּיט עַל מַלְכַיָּא,
וּמַלְכוּתָא דִּילָךְ הִיא. אֲנָא עַבְדָּא דְּקֻדְשָׁא בְּרִיךְ הוּא, דְּסָגֵדְנָא קַמֵּהּ וּמִקַּמֵּי דִּיקַר
אוֹרַיְתֵהּ בְּכָל עִדָּן וְעִדָּן. לָא עַל אֱנָשׁ רְחִיצְנָא וְלָא עַל בַּר אֱלָהִין סָמִיכְנָא, אֶלָּא
בֵּאלָהָא דִּשְׁמַיָּא, דְּהוּא אֱלָהָא קְשׁוֹט, וְאוֹרַיְתֵהּ קְשׁוֹט, וּנְבִיאוֹהִי קְשׁוֹט, וּמַסְגֵּא
לְמֶעְבַּד טָבְוָן וּקְשׁוֹט. ◂ בֵּהּ אֲנָא רְחִיץ, וְלִשְׁמֵהּ קַדִּישָׁא יַקִּירָא אֲנָא אֵמַר תֻּשְׁבְּחָן.
יְהֵא רַעֲוָא קֳדָמָךְ דְּתִפְתַּח לִבַּאי בְּאוֹרַיְתָא, וְתַשְׁלִים מִשְׁאֲלִין דְּלִבַּאי וְלִבָּא דְכָל
עַמָּךְ יִשְׂרָאֵל לְטַב וּלְחַיִּין וְלִשְׁלָם.

The שליח ציבור *takes the* ספר תורה *in his right arm, bows toward the* ארון קודש *and says:*

תהלים לד

גַּדְּלוּ לַיהוה אִתִּי וּנְרוֹמְמָה שְׁמוֹ יַחְדָּו:

The ארון קודש *is closed. The* שליח ציבור *carries the* ספר תורה *to the* בימה *and the* קהל *says:*

דברי הימים א' כט

לְךָ יהוה הַגְּדֻלָּה וְהַגְּבוּרָה וְהַתִּפְאֶרֶת וְהַנֵּצַח וְהַהוֹד, כִּי־כֹל בַּשָּׁמַיִם
וּבָאָרֶץ: לְךָ יהוה הַמַּמְלָכָה וְהַמִּתְנַשֵּׂא לְכֹל לְרֹאשׁ:

תהלים צט

רוֹמְמוּ יהוה אֱלֹהֵינוּ וְהִשְׁתַּחֲווּ לַהֲדֹם רַגְלָיו, קָדוֹשׁ הוּא: רוֹמְמוּ יהוה
אֱלֹהֵינוּ וְהִשְׁתַּחֲווּ לְהַר קָדְשׁוֹ, כִּי־קָדוֹשׁ יהוה אֱלֹהֵינוּ:

אַב הָרַחֲמִים הוּא יְרַחֵם עַם עֲמוּסִים, וְיִזְכֹּר בְּרִית אֵיתָנִים, וְיַצִּיל נַפְשׁוֹתֵינוּ
מִן הַשָּׁעוֹת הָרָעוֹת, וְיִגְעַר בְּיֵצֶר הָרָע מִן הַנְּשׂוּאִים, וְיָחֹן אוֹתָנוּ לִפְלֵיטַת
עוֹלָמִים, וִימַלֵּא מִשְׁאֲלוֹתֵינוּ בְּמִדָּה טוֹבָה יְשׁוּעָה וְרַחֲמִים.

The Torah scroll is placed on the bima and the Gabbai calls a Kohen to the Torah.

וְתִגָּלֶה May His kingship over us be soon revealed and made manifest. May He be gracious to our surviving remnant, the remnant of His people the house of Israel in grace, loving-kindness, compassion and favor, and let us say: Amen. Let us all render greatness to our God and give honor to the Torah. *Let the Kohen come forward. Arise (*name* son of father's *name*), the Kohen.

*If no Kohen is present, a Levi or Yisrael is called up as follows:
/As there is no Kohen, arise (*name* son of father's *name*) in place of a Kohen./

Blessed is He who, in His holiness, gave the Torah to His people Israel.

The congregation followed by the Gabbai:
You who cling to the Lord your God are all alive today.   *Deut. 4*

The Reader shows the oleh the section to be read.
The oleh touches the scroll at that place with the tzitzit
of his tallit or the fabric belt of the Torah scroll,
which he then kisses. Holding the handles of the scroll, he says:

Oleh: Bless the Lord, the blessed One.

Cong: Bless the Lord, the blessed One, for ever and all time.

Oleh: Bless the Lord, the blessed One, for ever and all time.

Blessed are You, Lord our God, King of the Universe,
who has chosen us from all peoples
and has given us His Torah.
Blessed are You, Lord,
Giver of the Torah.

After the reading, the oleh says:

Oleh: Blessed are You, Lord our God, King of the Universe,
who has given us the Torah of truth,
planting everlasting life in our midst.
Blessed are You, Lord,
Giver of the Torah.

The Torah portion for Minḥa is from Naso (on the next
page) or from Beha'alotekha (page 606).

The כהן calls a גבאי and the שולחן is placed on the ספר תורה The.
תורה to the כהן.

וְתִגָּלֶה וְתֵרָאֶה מַלְכוּתוֹ עָלֵינוּ בִּזְמַן קָרוֹב, וְיָחֹן פְּלֵיטָתֵנוּ וּפְלֵיטַת עַמּוֹ בֵּית
יִשְׂרָאֵל לְחֵן וּלְחֶסֶד וּלְרַחֲמִים וּלְרָצוֹן וְנֹאמַר אָמֵן. הַכֹּל הָבוּ גֹדֶל לֵאלֹהֵינוּ וּתְנוּ
כָבוֹד לַתּוֹרָה. *כֹּהֵן קְרָב, יַעֲמֹד (פלוני בֶּן פלוני) הַכֹּהֵן.

*If no כהן is present, a לוי or ישראל is called up as follows:

/אֵין כָּאן כֹּהֵן, יַעֲמֹד (פלוני בֶּן פלוני) בִּמְקוֹם כֹּהֵן./

בָּרוּךְ שֶׁנָּתַן תּוֹרָה לְעַמּוֹ יִשְׂרָאֵל בִּקְדֻשָּׁתוֹ.

The קהל followed by the גבאי:

דברים ד

וְאַתֶּם הַדְּבֵקִים בַּיהוה אֱלֹהֵיכֶם חַיִּים כֻּלְּכֶם הַיּוֹם:

The קורא shows the עולה the section to be read.
The עולה touches the scroll at that place with the ציצית of his טלית
or the gartel of the ספר תורה, which he then kisses.
Holding the handles of the scroll, he says:

עולה: בָּרְכוּ אֶת יהוה הַמְבֹרָךְ.

קהל: בָּרוּךְ יהוה הַמְבֹרָךְ לְעוֹלָם וָעֶד.

עולה: בָּרוּךְ יהוה הַמְבֹרָךְ לְעוֹלָם וָעֶד.

בָּרוּךְ אַתָּה יהוה, אֱלֹהֵינוּ מֶלֶךְ הָעוֹלָם
אֲשֶׁר בָּחַר בָּנוּ מִכָּל הָעַמִּים
וְנָתַן לָנוּ אֶת תּוֹרָתוֹ.
בָּרוּךְ אַתָּה יהוה, נוֹתֵן הַתּוֹרָה.

After the קריאת התורה, the עולה says:

עולה: בָּרוּךְ אַתָּה יהוה אֱלֹהֵינוּ מֶלֶךְ הָעוֹלָם
אֲשֶׁר נָתַן לָנוּ תּוֹרַת אֱמֶת
וְחַיֵּי עוֹלָם נָטַע בְּתוֹכֵנוּ.
בָּרוּךְ אַתָּה יהוה, נוֹתֵן הַתּוֹרָה.

The Torah portion for מנחה is from נשא (on the next page) or from בהעלותך (page 607).

NASO

The LORD spoke to Moses, saying: Count the heads of the sons of *Num.*
Gershon as well, according to their ancestral houses and their families. *4:21–37*
You shall count every man who is over thirty years of age and under the
age of fifty, every man eligible to serve, to perform work in the Tent of
Meeting. These are the duties of the family of Gershon: they shall work
and they shall carry. They shall carry the curtains of the Tabernacle, LEVI
the Tent of Meeting, its cover and the cover of tahash leather that is
spread upon it, and the screen for the entrance of the Tent of Meeting.
And the curtains of the courtyard and the screen for the entrance of
the courtyard gate, which surrounds the Tabernacle and the altar, and
their cords and all of the equipment belonging to their service; they
shall do all they were commanded, and perform their work. All of
the service of the sons of Gershon shall be performed according to
the word of Aaron and his sons, all of their burden-carrying and their
tasks; you shall hold them accountable for all of their charges. This
shall be the task of the family of the sons of Gershon for the Tent of
Meeting and their duties under Itamar son of Aaron the priest.

As for the sons of Merari, you shall count them according to their YISRAEL
families and their ancestral houses. You shall count every man who is
over thirty years of age and under the age of fifty, every man eligible
to serve, to perform work in the Tent of Meeting. And this shall be
their charge, the burden that they shall carry as a service to the Tent of
Meeting: the beams of the Tabernacle, its bars and pillars and sockets.
And the pillars surrounding the courtyard and their sockets and bars
and cords and all of the equipment belonging to their service; you
shall designate men by name to carry each of the vessels they are
charged with. This shall be the duty of the family of the sons of Merari,
their service for the Tent of Meeting under Itamar son of Aaron the
priest.

Some extend the "Yisrael" portion:

And Moses and Aaron and the leaders of the congregation counted the
descendants of Kehat according to their families and their ancestral
houses. Every man over thirty years of age and under the age of fifty,

נשא

במדבר
ד:כא-לו

וַיְדַבֵּ֥ר יְהֹוָ֖ה אֶל־מֹשֶׁ֥ה לֵּאמֹֽר: נָשֹׂ֗א אֶת־רֹ֛אשׁ בְּנֵ֥י גֵרְשׁ֖וֹן גַּם־הֵ֑ם לְבֵ֥ית אֲבֹתָ֖ם לְמִשְׁפְּחֹתָֽם: מִבֶּן֩ שְׁלֹשִׁ֨ים שָׁנָ֜ה וָמַ֗עְלָה עַ֛ד בֶּן־ חֲמִשִּׁ֥ים שָׁנָ֖ה תִּפְקֹ֣ד אוֹתָ֑ם כָּל־הַבָּא֙ לִצְבֹ֣א צָבָ֔א לַעֲבֹ֥ד עֲבֹדָ֖ה בְּאֹ֥הֶל מוֹעֵֽד: זֹ֣את עֲבֹדַ֔ת מִשְׁפְּחֹ֖ת הַגֵּרְשֻׁנִּ֑י לַעֲבֹ֖ד וּלְמַשָּֽׂא:

לוי

*וְנָֽשְׂא֜וּ אֶת־יְרִיעֹ֤ת הַמִּשְׁכָּן֙ וְאֶת־אֹ֣הֶל מוֹעֵ֔ד מִכְסֵ֕הוּ וּמִכְסֵ֛ה הַתַּ֥חַשׁ אֲשֶׁר־עָלָ֖יו מִלְמָ֑עְלָה וְאֶ֨ת־מָסַ֔ךְ פֶּ֖תַח אֹ֥הֶל מוֹעֵֽד: וְאֵת֩ קַלְעֵ֨י הֶחָצֵ֜ר וְאֶת־מָסַ֣ךְ ׀ פֶּ֗תַח ׀ שַׁ֤עַר הֶֽחָצֵר֙ אֲשֶׁר֙ עַל־הַמִּשְׁכָּ֣ן וְעַל־הַמִּזְבֵּ֣חַ סָבִ֔יב וְאֵת֙ מֵֽיתְרֵיהֶ֔ם וְאֶֽת־כָּל־כְּלֵ֖י עֲבֹֽדָתָ֑ם וְאֵ֨ת כָּל־ אֲשֶׁ֧ר יֵעָשֶׂ֛ה לָהֶ֖ם וְעָבָֽדוּ: עַל־פִּי֩ אַהֲרֹ֨ן וּבָנָ֜יו תִּהְיֶ֗ה כָּל־עֲבֹדַת֙ בְּנֵ֣י הַגֵּ֣רְשֻׁנִּ֔י לְכָל־מַשָּׂאָ֔ם וּלְכֹ֖ל עֲבֹֽדָתָ֑ם וּפְקַדְתֶּ֤ם עֲלֵהֶם֙ בְּמִשְׁמֶ֔רֶת אֵ֖ת כָּל־מַשָּׂאָֽם: זֹ֣את עֲבֹדַ֗ת מִשְׁפְּחֹ֛ת בְּנֵ֥י הַגֵּרְשֻׁנִּ֖י בְּאֹ֣הֶל מוֹעֵ֑ד וּמִ֨שְׁמַרְתָּ֔ם בְּיַד֙ אִֽיתָמָ֔ר בֶּֽן־אַהֲרֹ֖ן הַכֹּהֵֽן:

ישראל

*בְּנֵ֤י מְרָרִי֙ לְמִשְׁפְּחֹתָ֔ם לְבֵית־אֲבֹתָ֖ם תִּפְקֹ֣ד אֹתָ֑ם מִבֶּן֩ שְׁלֹשִׁ֨ים שָׁנָ֜ה וָמַ֗עְלָה וְעַ֛ד בֶּן־חֲמִשִּׁ֥ים שָׁנָ֖ה תִּפְקְדֵ֑ם כָּל־הַבָּא֙ לַצָּבָ֔א לַעֲבֹ֕ד אֶת־עֲבֹדַ֖ת אֹ֣הֶל מוֹעֵֽד: וְזֹ֤את מִשְׁמֶ֨רֶת֙ מַשָּׂאָ֔ם לְכָל־עֲבֹֽדָתָ֖ם בְּאֹ֣הֶל מוֹעֵ֑ד קַרְשֵׁי֙ הַמִּשְׁכָּ֔ן וּבְרִיחָ֖יו וְעַמּוּדָ֥יו וַאֲדָנָֽיו: וְעַמּוּדֵ֨י הֶחָצֵ֤ר סָבִיב֙ וְאַדְנֵיהֶ֔ם וִיתֵדֹתָ֖ם וּמֵיתְרֵיהֶ֑ם לְכָל־כְּלֵיהֶ֔ם וּלְכֹ֖ל עֲבֹֽדָתָ֑ם וּבְשֵׁמֹ֣ת תִּפְקְד֔וּ אֶת־כְּלֵ֖י מִשְׁמֶ֥רֶת מַשָּׂאָֽם: זֹ֣את עֲבֹדַ֗ת מִשְׁפְּחֹת֙ בְּנֵ֣י מְרָרִ֔י לְכָל־עֲבֹֽדָתָ֖ם בְּאֹ֣הֶל מוֹעֵ֑ד בְּיַד֙ אִֽיתָמָ֔ר בֶּֽן־ אַהֲרֹ֖ן הַכֹּהֵֽן:

Some extend the ישראל portion:

וַיִּפְקֹ֨ד מֹשֶׁ֧ה וְאַהֲרֹ֛ן וּנְשִׂיאֵ֥י הָעֵדָ֖ה אֶת־בְּנֵ֣י הַקְּהָתִ֑י לְמִשְׁפְּחֹתָ֖ם וּלְבֵ֣ית אֲבֹתָֽם: מִבֶּ֨ן שְׁלֹשִׁ֤ים שָׁנָה֙ וָמַ֔עְלָה וְעַ֖ד בֶּן־חֲמִשִּׁ֥ים שָׁנָ֑ה

every man eligible to serve, to perform worship in the Tent of Meeting. And their number according to their families was two thousand seven hundred and fifty. These were the counted of the families of Kehat, all who served in the Tent of Meeting, according to the orders of Moses and Aaron, following the word of the LORD to Moses.

Continue with Hagbaha and Gelila on the next page.

BEHA'ALOTEKHA

And the LORD spoke to Moses, saying: Speak to Aaron and say to him, *Num.* when you light up the lamps, the seven lamps shall shine before the *8:1–14* Menorah. This is what Aaron did; he lit the lamps of the Menorah facing before it, just as the LORD had commanded Moses. And this is how the Menorah was made – it was beaten of one piece of gold, complete from its base to its flowers, all of one piece. Exactly as it had been in the vision the LORD had shown Moses – just so was the Menorah made.

And the LORD said to Moses: Take the Levites from among the people LEVI of Israel and purify them. This is how you shall purify them: sprinkle the water of purification upon them, and have them shave all their bodies, and wash their clothes and be purified. And take a young bull with its meal-offering of fine flour mixed with oil, and a second young bull for a sin offering. And draw the Levites close before the Tent of Meeting, and gather all the community of Israel together there. Bring YISRAEL the Levites close before the LORD, and have the people of Israel press their hands upon the Levites. And Aaron shall bring the Levites as a wave-offering before the LORD, on behalf of the people of Israel, to be instated in the service of the LORD. The Levites shall press their hands upon the heads of the bulls, and you shall offer one as a sin-offering and one as a burnt-offering to the LORD, to make atonement for the Levites. And you shall have the Levites stand before Aaron and his sons, and you shall offer them – a wave-offering to the LORD. You shall separate the Levites from among the people of Israel, and the Levites shall be mine.

כָּל־הַבָּא לַצָּבָא לַעֲבֹדָה בְּאֹהֶל מוֹעֵד: וַיִּהְיוּ פְקֻדֵיהֶם לְמִשְׁפְּחֹתָם אֲלָפִים שְׁבַע מֵאוֹת וַחֲמִשִּׁים: אֵלֶּה פְקוּדֵי מִשְׁפְּחֹת הַקְּהָתִי כָּל־הָעֹבֵד בְּאֹהֶל מוֹעֵד אֲשֶׁר פָּקַד מֹשֶׁה וְאַהֲרֹן עַל־פִּי יהוה בְּיַד־מֹשֶׁה:

Continue with הגבהה וגלילה on the next page.

בהעלותך

במדבר
ח:א-יד

וַיְדַבֵּר יהוה אֶל־מֹשֶׁה לֵּאמֹר: דַּבֵּר אֶל־אַהֲרֹן וְאָמַרְתָּ אֵלָיו בְּהַעֲלֹתְךָ אֶת־הַנֵּרֹת אֶל־מוּל פְּנֵי הַמְּנוֹרָה יָאִירוּ שִׁבְעַת הַנֵּרוֹת: וַיַּעַשׂ כֵּן אַהֲרֹן אֶל־מוּל פְּנֵי הַמְּנוֹרָה הֶעֱלָה נֵרֹתֶיהָ כַּאֲשֶׁר צִוָּה יהוה אֶת־מֹשֶׁה: וְזֶה מַעֲשֵׂה הַמְּנֹרָה מִקְשָׁה זָהָב עַד־יְרֵכָהּ עַד־פִּרְחָהּ מִקְשָׁה הִוא כַּמַּרְאֶה אֲשֶׁר הֶרְאָה יהוה אֶת־מֹשֶׁה כֵּן עָשָׂה אֶת־הַמְּנֹרָה:

לוי

וַיְדַבֵּר יהוה אֶל־מֹשֶׁה לֵּאמֹר: קַח אֶת־הַלְוִיִּם מִתּוֹךְ בְּנֵי יִשְׂרָאֵל וְטִהַרְתָּ אֹתָם: וְכֹה־תַעֲשֶׂה לָהֶם לְטַהֲרָם הַזֵּה עֲלֵיהֶם מֵי חַטָּאת וְהֶעֱבִירוּ תַעַר עַל־כָּל־בְּשָׂרָם וְכִבְּסוּ בִגְדֵיהֶם וְהִטֶּהָרוּ: וְלָקְחוּ פַּר בֶּן־בָּקָר וּמִנְחָתוֹ סֹלֶת בְּלוּלָה בַשָּׁמֶן וּפַר־שֵׁנִי בֶן־בָּקָר תִּקַּח לְחַטָּאת: וְהִקְרַבְתָּ אֶת־הַלְוִיִּם לִפְנֵי אֹהֶל מוֹעֵד וְהִקְהַלְתָּ אֶת־

ישראל

כָּל־עֲדַת בְּנֵי יִשְׂרָאֵל: *וְהִקְרַבְתָּ אֶת־הַלְוִיִּם לִפְנֵי יהוה וְסָמְכוּ בְנֵי־יִשְׂרָאֵל אֶת־יְדֵיהֶם עַל־הַלְוִיִּם: וְהֵנִיף אַהֲרֹן אֶת־הַלְוִיִּם תְּנוּפָה לִפְנֵי יהוה מֵאֵת בְּנֵי יִשְׂרָאֵל וְהָיוּ לַעֲבֹד אֶת־עֲבֹדַת יהוה: וְהַלְוִיִּם יִסְמְכוּ אֶת־יְדֵיהֶם עַל רֹאשׁ הַפָּרִים וַעֲשֵׂה אֶת־הָאֶחָד חַטָּאת וְאֶת־הָאֶחָד עֹלָה לַיהוה לְכַפֵּר עַל־הַלְוִיִּם: וְהַעֲמַדְתָּ אֶת־הַלְוִיִּם לִפְנֵי אַהֲרֹן וְלִפְנֵי בָנָיו וְהֵנַפְתָּ אֹתָם תְּנוּפָה לַיהוה: וְהִבְדַּלְתָּ אֶת־הַלְוִיִּם מִתּוֹךְ בְּנֵי יִשְׂרָאֵל וְהָיוּ לִי הַלְוִיִּם:

HAGBAHA AND GELILA

The Torah scroll is lifted and the congregation says:

וְזֹאת הַתּוֹרָה This is the Torah that   *Deut. 4*
Moses placed before the children of Israel,
at the LORD's commandment, by the hand of Moses.   *Num. 9*

Some add: It is a tree of life to those who grasp it,   *Prov. 3*
and those who uphold it are happy.
Its ways are ways of pleasantness, and all its paths are peace.
Long life is in its right hand; in its left, riches and honor.
It pleased the LORD for the sake of [Israel's] righteousness,   *Is. 42*
to make the Torah great and glorious.

RETURNING THE TORAH TO THE ARK

The Torah scroll is bound and covered.
The Ark is opened. The Leader takes the Torah scroll and says:

יְהַלְלוּ Let them praise the name of the LORD,   *Ps. 148*
for His name alone is sublime.

The congregation responds:

הוֹדוֹ His majesty is above earth and heaven.
He has raised the horn of His people,
for the glory of all His devoted ones,
the children of Israel, the people close to Him. Halleluya!

As the Torah scroll is returned to the Ark say:

לְדָוִד מִזְמוֹר A psalm of David. The earth is the LORD's and all it contains, the   *Ps. 24*
world and all who live in it. For He founded it on the seas and established
it on the streams. Who may climb the mountain of the LORD? Who may
stand in His holy place? He who has clean hands and a pure heart, who has
not taken My name in vain, or sworn deceitfully. He shall receive blessing
from the LORD, and just reward from God, his salvation. This is a generation
of those who seek Him, the descendants of Jacob who seek Your presence,
Selah! Lift up your heads, O gates; be uplifted, eternal doors, so that the
King of glory may enter. Who is the King of glory? It is the LORD, strong and
mighty, the LORD mighty in battle. Lift up your heads, O gates; be uplifted,
eternal doors, so that the King of glory may enter. Who is He, the King of
glory? The LORD of hosts, He is the King of glory, Selah!

הגבהה וגלילה

The ספר תורה *is lifted and the* קהל *says:*

דברים ד

וְזֹאת הַתּוֹרָה אֲשֶׁר־שָׂם מֹשֶׁה לִפְנֵי בְּנֵי יִשְׂרָאֵל:

במדבר ט

עַל־פִּי יהוה בְּיַד מֹשֶׁה:

משלי ג

Some add עֵץ־חַיִּים הִיא לַמַּחֲזִיקִים בָּהּ וְתֹמְכֶיהָ מְאֻשָּׁר:

דְּרָכֶיהָ דַרְכֵי־נֹעַם וְכָל־נְתִיבֹתֶיהָ שָׁלוֹם:

אֹרֶךְ יָמִים בִּימִינָהּ, בִּשְׂמֹאולָהּ עֹשֶׁר וְכָבוֹד:

ישעיה מב

יהוה חָפֵץ לְמַעַן צִדְקוֹ יַגְדִּיל תּוֹרָה וְיַאְדִּיר:

הכנסת ספר תורה

The ספר תורה *is bound and covered.*
The ארון קודש *is opened. The* שליח ציבור *takes the* ספר תורה *and says:*

תהלים קמח

יְהַלְלוּ אֶת־שֵׁם יהוה, כִּי־נִשְׂגָּב שְׁמוֹ, לְבַדּוֹ

The קהל *responds:*

הוֹדוֹ עַל־אֶרֶץ וְשָׁמָיִם:

וַיָּרֶם קֶרֶן לְעַמּוֹ, תְּהִלָּה לְכָל־חֲסִידָיו

לִבְנֵי יִשְׂרָאֵל עַם קְרֹבוֹ, הַלְלוּיָהּ:

As the ספר תורה *is returned to the* ארון קודש, *say:*

תהלים כד

לְדָוִד מִזְמוֹר, לַיהוה הָאָרֶץ וּמְלוֹאָהּ, תֵּבֵל וְיֹשְׁבֵי בָהּ: כִּי־הוּא עַל־

יַמִּים יְסָדָהּ, וְעַל־נְהָרוֹת יְכוֹנְנֶהָ: מִי־יַעֲלֶה בְהַר־יהוה, וּמִי־יָקוּם

בִּמְקוֹם קָדְשׁוֹ: נְקִי כַפַּיִם וּבַר־לֵבָב, אֲשֶׁר לֹא־נָשָׂא לַשָּׁוְא נַפְשִׁי

וְלֹא נִשְׁבַּע לְמִרְמָה: יִשָּׂא בְרָכָה מֵאֵת יהוה, וּצְדָקָה מֵאֱלֹהֵי יִשְׁעוֹ:

זֶה דּוֹר דֹּרְשָׁו, מְבַקְשֵׁי פָנֶיךָ, יַעֲקֹב, סֶלָה: שְׂאוּ שְׁעָרִים רָאשֵׁיכֶם,

וְהִנָּשְׂאוּ פִּתְחֵי עוֹלָם, וְיָבוֹא מֶלֶךְ הַכָּבוֹד: מִי זֶה מֶלֶךְ הַכָּבוֹד,

יהוה עִזּוּז וְגִבּוֹר, יהוה גִּבּוֹר מִלְחָמָה: שְׂאוּ שְׁעָרִים רָאשֵׁיכֶם,

וּשְׂאוּ פִּתְחֵי עוֹלָם, וְיָבֹא מֶלֶךְ הַכָּבוֹד: מִי הוּא זֶה מֶלֶךְ הַכָּבוֹד,

יהוה צְבָאוֹת הוּא מֶלֶךְ הַכָּבוֹד, סֶלָה:

As the Torah scroll is placed into the Ark, say:

וּבְנֻחֹה יֹאמַר When the Ark came to rest, Moses would say:
"Return, O LORD, to the myriad thousands of Israel." *Num. 10*
Advance, LORD, to Your resting place, You and Your mighty Ark. *Ps. 132*
Your priests are clothed in righteousness,
and Your devoted ones sing in joy.
For the sake of Your servant David,
do not reject Your anointed one.
For I give you good instruction; do not forsake My Torah. *Prov. 4*
It is a tree of life to those who grasp it, *Prov. 3*
and those who uphold it are happy.
Its ways are ways of pleasantness, and all its paths are peace.
▸ Turn us back, O LORD, to You, and we will return. *Lam. 5*
Renew our days as of old.

The Ark is closed.

HALF KADDISH

Leader: יִתְגַּדַּל Magnified and sanctified may His great name be,
in the world He created by His will.
May He establish His kingdom
in your lifetime and in your days,
and in the lifetime of all the house of Israel,
swiftly and soon –
and say: Amen.

All: May His great name be blessed
for ever and all time.

Leader: Blessed and praised, glorified and exalted,
raised and honored, uplifted and lauded
be the name of the Holy One,
blessed be He,
beyond any blessing, song,
praise and consolation
uttered in the world –
and say: Amen.

As the ספר תורה is placed into the ארון קודש, say:

במדברי

וּבְנֻחֹה יֹאמַר, שׁוּבָה יהוה רִבְבוֹת אַלְפֵי יִשְׂרָאֵל:

תהלים קלב

קוּמָה יהוה לִמְנוּחָתֶךָ, אַתָּה וַאֲרוֹן עֻזֶּךָ:

כֹּהֲנֶיךָ יִלְבְּשׁוּ־צֶדֶק, וַחֲסִידֶיךָ יְרַנֵּנוּ:

בַּעֲבוּר דָּוִד עַבְדֶּךָ אַל־תָּשֵׁב פְּנֵי מְשִׁיחֶךָ:

משלי ד

כִּי לֶקַח טוֹב נָתַתִּי לָכֶם, תּוֹרָתִי אַל־תַּעֲזֹבוּ:

משלי ג

עֵץ־חַיִּים הִיא לַמַּחֲזִיקִים בָּהּ, וְתֹמְכֶיהָ מְאֻשָּׁר:

דְּרָכֶיהָ דַרְכֵי־נֹעַם וְכָל־נְתִיבֹתֶיהָ שָׁלוֹם:

איכה ה

◂ הֲשִׁיבֵנוּ יהוה אֵלֶיךָ וְנָשׁוּבָה, חַדֵּשׁ יָמֵינוּ כְּקֶדֶם:

The ארון קודש is closed.

חצי קדיש

ש״ץ: יִתְגַּדַּל וְיִתְקַדַּשׁ שְׁמֵהּ רַבָּא (קהל: אָמֵן)

בְּעָלְמָא דִּי בְרָא כִרְעוּתֵהּ

וְיַמְלִיךְ מַלְכוּתֵהּ

בְּחַיֵּיכוֹן וּבְיוֹמֵיכוֹן, וּבְחַיֵּי דְכָל בֵּית יִשְׂרָאֵל

בַּעֲגָלָא וּבִזְמַן קָרִיב

וְאִמְרוּ אָמֵן. (קהל: אָמֵן)

קהל
 וש״ץ: יְהֵא שְׁמֵהּ רַבָּא מְבָרַךְ לְעָלַם וּלְעָלְמֵי עָלְמַיָּא.

ש״ץ: יִתְבָּרַךְ וְיִשְׁתַּבַּח וְיִתְפָּאַר וְיִתְרוֹמַם וְיִתְנַשֵּׂא

וְיִתְהַדָּר וְיִתְעַלֶּה וְיִתְהַלָּל

שְׁמֵהּ דְּקֻדְשָׁא בְּרִיךְ הוּא (קהל: בְּרִיךְ הוּא)

לְעֵלָּא מִן כָּל בִּרְכָתָא וְשִׁירָתָא, תֻּשְׁבְּחָתָא וְנֶחֱמָתָא

דַּאֲמִירָן בְּעָלְמָא

וְאִמְרוּ אָמֵן. (קהל: אָמֵן)

THE AMIDA

The following prayer, until "in former years" on page 624, is said silently, standing with feet together. If there is a minyan, the Amida is then repeated aloud by the Leader. Take three steps forward and at the points indicated by ˙, bend the knees at the first word, bow at the second, and stand straight before saying God's name.

When I proclaim the Lᴏʀᴅ's name, give glory to our God.   *Deut. 32*

O Lᴏʀᴅ, open my lips, so that my mouth may declare Your praise.   *Ps. 51*

PATRIARCHS

˙בָּרוּךְ Blessed are You, Lᴏʀᴅ our God and God of our fathers,
God of Abraham, God of Isaac and God of Jacob;
the great, mighty and awesome God, God Most High,
who bestows acts of loving-kindness and creates all,
who remembers the loving-kindness of the fathers
and will bring a Redeemer
to their children's children
for the sake of His name, in love.
King, Helper, Savior, Shield:
˙Blessed are You,
Lᴏʀᴅ, Shield of Abraham.

DIVINE MIGHT

אַתָּה גִבּוֹר You are eternally mighty, Lᴏʀᴅ.
You give life to the dead
and have great power to save.

> *In Israel:*
> He causes the dew to fall.

He sustains the living with loving-kindness,
and with great compassion revives the dead.
He supports the fallen, heals the sick,
sets captives free,
and keeps His faith with those who sleep in the dust.

עמידה

The following prayer, until קַדְמֹנִיּוֹת *on page 625, is said silently, standing with feet together. If there is a* מִנְיָן, *the* עמידה *is then repeated aloud by the* שְׁלִיחַ צִבּוּר. *Take three steps forward and at the points indicated by* ׳, *bend the knees at the first word, bow at the second, and stand straight before saying God's name.*

דברים לב
תהלים נא

כִּי שֵׁם יהוה אֶקְרָא, הָבוּ גֹדֶל לֵאלֹהֵינוּ:
אֲדֹנָי, שְׂפָתַי תִּפְתָּח, וּפִי יַגִּיד תְּהִלָּתֶךָ:

אבות

יָּבָרוּךְ אַתָּה יהוה, אֱלֹהֵינוּ וֵאלֹהֵי אֲבוֹתֵינוּ
אֱלֹהֵי אַבְרָהָם, אֱלֹהֵי יִצְחָק, וֵאלֹהֵי יַעֲקֹב
הָאֵל הַגָּדוֹל הַגִּבּוֹר וְהַנּוֹרָא, אֵל עֶלְיוֹן
גּוֹמֵל חֲסָדִים טוֹבִים, וְקֹנֵה הַכֹּל
וְזוֹכֵר חַסְדֵי אָבוֹת
וּמֵבִיא גוֹאֵל לִבְנֵי בְנֵיהֶם לְמַעַן שְׁמוֹ בְּאַהֲבָה.
מֶלֶךְ עוֹזֵר וּמוֹשִׁיעַ וּמָגֵן.
יָּבָרוּךְ אַתָּה יהוה, מָגֵן אַבְרָהָם.

גבורות

אַתָּה גִּבּוֹר לְעוֹלָם, אֲדֹנָי
מְחַיֵּה מֵתִים אַתָּה, רַב לְהוֹשִׁיעַ

In ארץ ישראל:
מוֹרִיד הַטָּל

מְכַלְכֵּל חַיִּים בְּחֶסֶד, מְחַיֵּה מֵתִים בְּרַחֲמִים רַבִּים
סוֹמֵךְ נוֹפְלִים, וְרוֹפֵא חוֹלִים, וּמַתִּיר אֲסוּרִים
וּמְקַיֵּם אֱמוּנָתוֹ לִישֵׁנֵי עָפָר.

Who is like You, Master of might,
and who can compare to You,
O King who brings death and gives life, and makes salvation grow?
Faithful are You to revive the dead.
Blessed are You,
LORD, who revives the dead.

When saying the Amida silently, continue with "You are holy" below.

KEDUSHA
During the Leader's Repetition, the following is said standing
with feet together, rising on the toes at the words indicated by ˄.

Cong. then   נְקַדֵּשׁ We will sanctify Your name on earth,
Leader: as they sanctify it in the highest heavens,
    as is written by Your prophet,
    "And they [the angels] call to one another saying: Is. 6

Cong. then   ˄Holy, ˄holy, ˄holy is the LORD of hosts;
Leader: the whole world is filled with His glory."
    Those facing them say "Blessed –"

Cong. then   ˄"Blessed is the LORD's glory from His place."   Ezek. 3
Leader: And in Your holy Writings it is written thus:

Cong. then   ˄"The LORD shall reign for ever. He is your God, Zion,   Ps. 146
Leader: from generation to generation, Halleluya!"

Leader: From generation to generation we will declare Your greatness,
    and we will proclaim Your holiness for evermore.
    Your praise, our God, shall not leave our mouth forever,
    for You, God, are a great and holy King.
    Blessed are You, LORD, the holy God.

The Leader continues with "You have chosen us" on the next page.

When saying the Amida silently, continue here:

HOLINESS
אַתָּה קָדוֹשׁ You are holy and Your name is holy,
and holy ones praise You daily, Selah!
Blessed are You, LORD,
the holy God.

מִי כָמְוֹךָ, בַּעַל גְּבוּרוֹת, וּמִי דְּוֹמֶה לָּךְ
מֶלֶךְ, מֵמִית וּמְחַיֶּה וּמַצְמִיחַ יְשׁוּעָה.
וְנֶאֱמָן אַתָּה לְהַחֲיוֹת מֵתִים.
בָּרוּךְ אַתָּה יהוה, מְחַיֵּה הַמֵּתִים.

When saying the עמידה silently, continue with אַתָּה קָדוֹשׁ below

---

קדושה

During the חזרת הש״ץ, the following is said standing
with feet together, rising on the toes at the words indicated by ▲.

קהל
then
ש״ץ:
נְקַדֵּשׁ אֶת שִׁמְךָ בָּעוֹלָם, כְּשֵׁם שֶׁמַּקְדִּישִׁים אוֹתוֹ בִּשְׁמֵי מָרוֹם
כַּכָּתוּב עַל יַד נְבִיאֶךָ: וְקָרָא זֶה אֶל־זֶה וְאָמַר   ישעיה ו

קהל
then
ש״ץ:
▲קָדוֹשׁ, ▲קָדוֹשׁ, ▲קָדוֹשׁ, יהוה צְבָאוֹת, מְלֹא כָל־הָאָרֶץ כְּבוֹדוֹ:
לְעֻמָּתָם בָּרוּךְ יֹאמֵרוּ

קהל
then
ש״ץ:
▲בָּרוּךְ כְּבוֹד־יהוה מִמְּקוֹמוֹ:   יחזקאל ג
וּבְדִבְרֵי קָדְשְׁךָ כָּתוּב לֵאמֹר

קהל
then
ש״ץ:
▲יִמְלֹךְ יהוה לְעוֹלָם, אֱלֹהַיִךְ צִיּוֹן לְדֹר וָדֹר, הַלְלוּיָהּ:   תהלים קמו

ש״ץ:
לְדוֹר וָדוֹר נַגִּיד גָּדְלֶךָ, וּלְנֵצַח נְצָחִים קְדֻשָּׁתְךָ נַקְדִּישׁ
וְשִׁבְחֲךָ אֱלֹהֵינוּ מִפִּינוּ לֹא יָמוּשׁ לְעוֹלָם וָעֶד
כִּי אֵל מֶלֶךְ גָּדוֹל וְקָדוֹשׁ אֱתָּה.
בָּרוּךְ אַתָּה יהוה, הָאֵל הַקָּדוֹשׁ.

The שליח ציבור continues with אַתָּה בְחַרְתֶּנוּ on the next page.

When saying the עמידה silently, continue here:

קדושת השם
אַתָּה קָדוֹשׁ וְשִׁמְךָ קָדוֹשׁ
וּקְדוֹשִׁים בְּכָל יוֹם יְהַלְלוּךָ סֶּלָה.
בָּרוּךְ אַתָּה יהוה, הָאֵל הַקָּדוֹשׁ.

HOLINESS OF THE DAY

אַתָּה בְחַרְתָּנוּ You have chosen us
from among all peoples.
You have loved and favored us.
You have raised us above all tongues.
You have made us holy through Your commandments.
You have brought us near, our King, to Your service,
and have called us by Your great and holy name.

On Shabbat, add the words in parentheses:

וַתִּתֶּן לָנוּ And You, Lord our God,
have given us in love
(Sabbaths for rest and) festivals for rejoicing,
holy days and seasons for joy,
(this Sabbath day and) this day of the festival of Shavuot,
the time of the giving of our Torah
(with love), a holy assembly
in memory of the exodus from Egypt.

אֱלֹהֵינוּ Our God and God of our ancestors,
may there rise, come, reach,
appear, be favored, heard,
regarded and remembered before You,
our recollection and remembrance,
as well as the remembrance of our ancestors,
and of the Messiah son of David Your servant,
and of Jerusalem Your holy city,
and of all Your people the house of Israel –
for deliverance and well-being,
grace, loving-kindness and compassion,
life and peace,
on this day of the festival of Shavuot.

קדושת היום

אַתָּה בְחַרְתָּנוּ מִכָּל הָעַמִּים

אָהַבְתָּ אוֹתָנוּ וְרָצִיתָ בָּנוּ

וְרוֹמַמְתָּנוּ מִכָּל הַלְּשׁוֹנוֹת

וְקִדַּשְׁתָּנוּ בְּמִצְוֹתֶיךָ

וְקֵרַבְתָּנוּ מַלְכֵּנוּ לַעֲבוֹדָתֶךָ

וְשִׁמְךָ הַגָּדוֹל וְהַקָּדוֹשׁ עָלֵינוּ קָרָאתָ.

On שבת, add the words in parentheses:

וַתִּתֶּן לָנוּ יהוה אֱלֹהֵינוּ בְּאַהֲבָה

(שַׁבָּתוֹת לִמְנוּחָה וּ)מוֹעֲדִים לְשִׂמְחָה

חַגִּים וּזְמַנִּים לְשָׂשׂוֹן

אֶת יוֹם (הַשַּׁבָּת הַזֶּה וְאֶת יוֹם)

חַג הַשָּׁבוּעוֹת הַזֶּה, זְמַן מַתַּן תּוֹרָתֵנוּ

(בְּאַהֲבָה) מִקְרָא קֹדֶשׁ, זֵכֶר לִיצִיאַת מִצְרָיִם.

אֱלֹהֵינוּ וֵאלֹהֵי אֲבוֹתֵינוּ

יַעֲלֶה וְיָבוֹא וְיַגִּיעַ, וְיֵרָאֶה וְיֵרָצֶה וְיִשָּׁמַע

וְיִפָּקֵד וְיִזָּכֵר זִכְרוֹנֵנוּ וּפִקְדוֹנֵנוּ

וְזִכְרוֹן אֲבוֹתֵינוּ

וְזִכְרוֹן מָשִׁיחַ בֶּן דָּוִד עַבְדֶּךָ

וְזִכְרוֹן יְרוּשָׁלַיִם עִיר קָדְשֶׁךָ

וְזִכְרוֹן כָּל עַמְּךָ בֵּית יִשְׂרָאֵל, לְפָנֶיךָ

לִפְלֵיטָה, לְטוֹבָה, לְחֵן וּלְחֶסֶד וּלְרַחֲמִים, לְחַיִּים וּלְשָׁלוֹם

בְּיוֹם חַג הַשָּׁבוּעוֹת הַזֶּה.

On it remember us, LORD our God, for good;
recollect us for blessing, and deliver us for life.
In accord with Your promise of salvation and compassion,
spare us and be gracious to us;
have compassion on us and deliver us,
for our eyes are turned to You
because You, God, are a gracious and compassionate King.

On Shabbat, add the words in parentheses:
וְהַשִּׂיאֵנוּ Bestow on us, LORD our God,
the blessings of Your festivals
for good life and peace, joy and gladness,
as You desired and promised to bless us.
(Our God and God of our fathers, find favor in our rest.)
Make us holy through Your commandments
and grant us a share in Your Torah.
Satisfy us with Your goodness,
gladden us with Your salvation,
and purify our hearts to serve You in truth.
Grant us as our heritage, LORD our God (with love and favor,)
with joy and gladness, Your holy (Sabbath and) festivals,
and may Israel, who sanctify Your name, rejoice in You.
Blessed are You, LORD,
who sanctifies (the Sabbath and) Israel and the festive seasons.

TEMPLE SERVICE
רְצֵה Find favor, LORD our God,
in Your people Israel and their prayer.
Restore the service to Your most holy House,
and accept in love and favor
the fire-offerings of Israel and their prayer.
May the service of Your people Israel
always find favor with You.

זָכְרֵנוּ יהוה אֱלֹהֵינוּ בּוֹ לְטוֹבָה

וּפָקְדֵנוּ בוֹ לִבְרָכָה, וְהוֹשִׁיעֵנוּ בוֹ לְחַיִּים.

וּבִדְבַר יְשׁוּעָה וְרַחֲמִים, חוּס וְחָנֵּנוּ

וְרַחֵם עָלֵינוּ וְהוֹשִׁיעֵנוּ

כִּי אֵלֶיךָ עֵינֵינוּ

כִּי אֵל מֶלֶךְ חַנּוּן וְרַחוּם אָתָּה.

On שבת, add the words in parentheses:

וְהַשִּׂיאֵנוּ יהוה אֱלֹהֵינוּ אֶת בִּרְכַּת מוֹעֲדֶיךָ

לְחַיִּים וּלְשָׁלוֹם, לְשִׂמְחָה וּלְשָׂשׂוֹן

כַּאֲשֶׁר רָצִיתָ וְאָמַרְתָּ לְבָרְכֵנוּ.

(אֱלֹהֵינוּ וֵאלֹהֵי אֲבוֹתֵינוּ, רְצֵה בִמְנוּחָתֵנוּ)

קַדְּשֵׁנוּ בְּמִצְוֹתֶיךָ וְתֵן חֶלְקֵנוּ בְּתוֹרָתֶךָ

שַׂבְּעֵנוּ מִטּוּבֶךָ, וְשַׂמְּחֵנוּ בִּישׁוּעָתֶךָ

וְטַהֵר לִבֵּנוּ לְעָבְדְּךָ בֶּאֱמֶת.

וְהַנְחִילֵנוּ יהוה אֱלֹהֵינוּ (בְּאַהֲבָה וּבְרָצוֹן)

בְּשִׂמְחָה וּבְשָׂשׂוֹן (שַׁבָּת וּ)מוֹעֲדֵי קָדְשֶׁךָ

וְיִשְׂמְחוּ בְךָ יִשְׂרָאֵל מְקַדְּשֵׁי שְׁמֶךָ.

בָּרוּךְ אַתָּה יהוה, מְקַדֵּשׁ (הַשַּׁבָּת וְ)יִשְׂרָאֵל וְהַזְּמַנִּים.

עבודה

רְצֵה יהוה אֱלֹהֵינוּ בְּעַמְּךָ יִשְׂרָאֵל, וּבִתְפִלָּתָם

וְהָשֵׁב אֶת הָעֲבוֹדָה לִדְבִיר בֵּיתֶךָ

וְאִשֵּׁי יִשְׂרָאֵל וּתְפִלָּתָם בְּאַהֲבָה תְקַבֵּל בְּרָצוֹן

וּתְהִי לְרָצוֹן תָּמִיד עֲבוֹדַת יִשְׂרָאֵל עַמֶּךָ.

And may our eyes witness Your return to Zion in compassion.
Blessed are You, LORD,
who restores His Presence to Zion.

THANKSGIVING   *Bow at the first nine words.*

מוֹדִים We give thanks to You,
for You are the LORD our God
and God of our ancestors
for ever and all time.
You are the Rock of our lives,
Shield of our salvation
from generation to generation.
We will thank You and
declare Your praise for our lives,
which are entrusted into Your hand;
for our souls,
which are placed in Your charge;
for Your miracles
which are with us every day;
and for Your wonders and favors
at all times, evening,
morning and midday.
You are good –
for Your compassion never fails.
You are compassionate –
for Your loving-kindnesses never cease.
We have always placed our hope in You.

During the Leader's Repetition,
the congregation says quietly:
מוֹדִים We give thanks to You,
for You are the LORD our God
and God of our ancestors,
God of all flesh,
who formed us
and formed the universe.
Blessings and thanks
are due to Your great
and holy name for giving us
life and sustaining us.
May You continue
to give us life
and sustain us;
and may You gather our
exiles to Your holy courts,
to keep Your decrees,
do Your will and serve You
with a perfect heart,
for it is for us
to give You thanks.
Blessed be God to whom
thanksgiving is due.

וְעַל כֻּלָּם For all these things
may Your name be blessed and exalted, our King,
continually, for ever and all time.
Let all that lives thank You, Selah!
and praise Your name in truth, God, our Savior and Help, Selah!
▸Blessed are You, LORD,
whose name is "the Good" and to whom thanks are due.

וְתֶחֱזֶינָה עֵינֵינוּ בְּשׁוּבְךָ לְצִיּוֹן בְּרַחֲמִים.

בָּרוּךְ אַתָּה יהוה, הַמַּחֲזִיר שְׁכִינָתוֹ לְצִיּוֹן.

הוֹדָאָה

Bow at the first five words.

יְמוֹדִים אֲנַחְנוּ לָךְ

שָׁאַתָּה הוּא יהוה אֱלֹהֵינוּ

וֵאלֹהֵי אֲבוֹתֵינוּ לְעוֹלָם וָעֶד.

צוּר חַיֵּינוּ, מָגֵן יִשְׁעֵנוּ

אַתָּה הוּא לְדוֹר וָדוֹר.

נוֹדֶה לְּךָ וּנְסַפֵּר תְּהִלָּתֶךָ

עַל חַיֵּינוּ הַמְּסוּרִים בְּיָדֶךָ

וְעַל נִשְׁמוֹתֵינוּ הַפְּקוּדוֹת לָךְ

וְעַל נִסֶּיךָ שֶׁבְּכָל יוֹם עִמָּנוּ

וְעַל נִפְלְאוֹתֶיךָ וְטוֹבוֹתֶיךָ

שֶׁבְּכָל עֵת

עֶרֶב וָבֹקֶר וְצָהֳרָיִם.

הַטּוֹב, כִּי לֹא כָלוּ רַחֲמֶיךָ

וְהַמְרַחֵם, כִּי לֹא תַמּוּ חֲסָדֶיךָ

מֵעוֹלָם קִוִּינוּ לָךְ.

During the חֲזָרַת הש"ץ, *the* קָהָל *says quietly:*

מוֹדִים אֲנַחְנוּ לָךְ

שָׁאַתָּה הוּא יהוה אֱלֹהֵינוּ

וֵאלֹהֵי אֲבוֹתֵינוּ

אֱלֹהֵי כָל בָּשָׂר

יוֹצְרֵנוּ, יוֹצֵר בְּרֵאשִׁית.

בְּרָכוֹת וְהוֹדָאוֹת

לְשִׁמְךָ הַגָּדוֹל וְהַקָּדוֹשׁ

עַל שֶׁהֶחֱיִיתָנוּ וְקִיַּמְתָּנוּ.

כֵּן תְּחַיֵּנוּ וּתְקַיְּמֵנוּ

וְתֶאֱסֹף גָּלֻיּוֹתֵינוּ

לְחַצְרוֹת קָדְשֶׁךָ

לִשְׁמֹר חֻקֶּיךָ

וְלַעֲשׂוֹת רְצוֹנֶךָ

וּלְעָבְדְּךָ בְּלֵבָב שָׁלֵם

עַל שֶׁאֲנַחְנוּ מוֹדִים לָךְ.

בָּרוּךְ אֵל הַהוֹדָאוֹת.

וְעַל כֻּלָּם יִתְבָּרַךְ וְיִתְרוֹמַם שִׁמְךָ מַלְכֵּנוּ תָּמִיד לְעוֹלָם וָעֶד.

וְכֹל הַחַיִּים יוֹדוּךָ סֶּלָה

וִיהַלְלוּ אֶת שִׁמְךָ בֶּאֱמֶת, הָאֵל יְשׁוּעָתֵנוּ וְעֶזְרָתֵנוּ סֶלָה.

בָּרוּךְ אַתָּה יהוה

הַטּוֹב שִׁמְךָ וּלְךָ נָאֶה לְהוֹדוֹת.

PEACE

שָׁלוֹם רָב Grant
great peace
to Your people Israel
for ever,
for You are
the sovereign LORD
of all peace;
and may it be good
in Your eyes to bless
Your people Israel
at every time,
at every hour,
with Your peace.

In Israel on Shabbat:

שִׂים שָׁלוֹם Grant peace, goodness and blessing,
grace, loving-kindness and compassion
to us and all Israel Your people.
Bless us, our Father, all as one,
with the light of Your face,
for by the light of Your face
You have given us, LORD our God,
the Torah of life and love of kindness,
righteousness, blessing, compassion,
life and peace.
May it be good in Your eyes to bless
Your people Israel at every time,
in every hour, with Your peace.

Blessed are You, LORD, who blesses His people Israel with peace.

The following verse concludes the Leader's Repetition of the Amida.
Some also say it here as part of the silent Amida.

May the words of my mouth and the meditation of my heart   Ps. 19
find favor before You, LORD, my Rock and Redeemer.

אֱלֹהַי My God,   Berakhot
guard my tongue from evil and my lips from deceitful speech.   17a
To those who curse me, let my soul be silent;
may my soul be to all like the dust.
Open my heart to Your Torah
and let my soul pursue Your commandments.
As for all who plan evil against me,
swiftly thwart their counsel and frustrate their plans.
    Act for the sake of Your name; act for the sake of Your right hand;
    act for the sake of Your holiness; act for the sake of Your Torah.
That Your beloved ones may be delivered,   Ps. 60
save with Your right hand and answer me.
May the words of my mouth and the meditation of my heart   Ps. 19
find favor before You, LORD, my Rock and Redeemer.

ברכת שלום

שָׁלוֹם רָב

עַל יִשְׂרָאֵל עַמְּךָ

תָּשִׂים לְעוֹלָם

כִּי אַתָּה הוּא מֶלֶךְ אָדוֹן

לְכָל הַשָּׁלוֹם.

וְטוֹב בְּעֵינֶיךָ לְבָרֵךְ

אֶת עַמְּךָ יִשְׂרָאֵל

בְּכָל עֵת וּבְכָל שָׁעָה

בִּשְׁלוֹמֶךָ.

שבת on ארץ ישראל In:

שִׂים שָׁלוֹם טוֹבָה וּבְרָכָה

חֵן וָחֶסֶד וְרַחֲמִים

עָלֵינוּ וְעַל כָּל יִשְׂרָאֵל עַמֶּךָ.

בָּרְכֵנוּ אָבִינוּ כֻּלָּנוּ כְּאֶחָד בְּאוֹר פָּנֶיךָ

כִּי בְאוֹר פָּנֶיךָ נָתַתָּ לָּנוּ יהוה אֱלֹהֵינוּ

תּוֹרַת חַיִּים וְאַהֲבַת חֶסֶד

וּצְדָקָה וּבְרָכָה, וְרַחֲמִים וְחַיִּים וְשָׁלוֹם.

וְטוֹב בְּעֵינֶיךָ לְבָרֵךְ אֶת עַמְּךָ יִשְׂרָאֵל

בְּכָל עֵת וּבְכָל שָׁעָה בִּשְׁלוֹמֶךָ.

בָּרוּךְ אַתָּה יהוה, הַמְבָרֵךְ אֶת עַמּוֹ יִשְׂרָאֵל בַּשָּׁלוֹם.

The following verse concludes the חזרת הש״ץ.
Some also say it here as part of the silent עמידה.

תהלים יט

יִהְיוּ לְרָצוֹן אִמְרֵי־פִי וְהֶגְיוֹן לִבִּי לְפָנֶיךָ, יהוה צוּרִי וְגֹאֲלִי:

ברכות יז.

אֱלֹהַי

נְצֹר לְשׁוֹנִי מֵרָע וּשְׂפָתַי מִדַּבֵּר מִרְמָה

וְלִמְקַלְלַי נַפְשִׁי תִדֹּם, וְנַפְשִׁי כֶּעָפָר לַכֹּל תִּהְיֶה.

פְּתַח לִבִּי בְּתוֹרָתֶךָ, וּבְמִצְוֹתֶיךָ תִּרְדֹּף נַפְשִׁי.

וְכָל הַחוֹשְׁבִים עָלַי רָעָה

מְהֵרָה הָפֵר עֲצָתָם וְקַלְקֵל מַחֲשַׁבְתָּם.

עֲשֵׂה לְמַעַן שְׁמֶךָ, עֲשֵׂה לְמַעַן יְמִינֶךָ

עֲשֵׂה לְמַעַן קְדֻשָּׁתֶךָ, עֲשֵׂה לְמַעַן תּוֹרָתֶךָ.

תהלים ס

לְמַעַן יֵחָלְצוּן יְדִידֶיךָ, הוֹשִׁיעָה יְמִינְךָ וַעֲנֵנִי:

תהלים יט

יִהְיוּ לְרָצוֹן אִמְרֵי־פִי וְהֶגְיוֹן לִבִּי לְפָנֶיךָ, יהוה צוּרִי וְגֹאֲלִי:

Bow, take three steps back, then bow, first left, then right, then center, while saying:

May He who makes peace in His high places,
make peace for us and all Israel –
and say: Amen.

יְהִי רָצוֹן May it be Your will, LORD our God and God of our ancestors,
that the Temple be rebuilt speedily in our days,
and grant us a share in Your Torah.
And there we will serve You with reverence,
as in the days of old and as in former years.
Then the offering of Judah and Jerusalem   *Mal. 3*
will be pleasing to the LORD as in the days of old and as in former years.

FULL KADDISH

Leader: יִתְגַּדַּל Magnified and sanctified may His great name be,
in the world He created by His will.
May He establish His kingdom
in your lifetime and in your days,
and in the lifetime of all the house of Israel,
swiftly and soon – and say: Amen.

All: May His great name be blessed for ever and all time.

Leader: Blessed and praised, glorified and exalted,
raised and honored, uplifted and lauded be
the name of the Holy One,
blessed be He,
beyond any blessing,
song, praise and consolation
uttered in the world – and say: Amen.

May the prayers and pleas of all Israel
be accepted by their Father in heaven – and say: Amen.

May there be great peace from heaven,
and life for us and all Israel – and say: Amen.

*Bow, take three steps back, as if taking leave of the Divine Presence,
then bow, first left, then right, then center, while saying:*

May He who makes peace in His high places,
make peace for us and all Israel – and say: Amen.

Bow, take three steps back, then bow, first left, then right, then center, while saying:

עֹשֶׂה שָׁלוֹם בִּמְרוֹמָיו

הוּא יַעֲשֶׂה שָׁלוֹם עָלֵינוּ וְעַל כָּל יִשְׂרָאֵל, וְאִמְרוּ אָמֵן.

יְהִי רָצוֹן מִלְּפָנֶיךָ יהוה אֱלֹהֵינוּ וֵאלֹהֵי אֲבוֹתֵינוּ
שֶׁיִּבָּנֶה בֵּית הַמִּקְדָּשׁ בִּמְהֵרָה בְיָמֵינוּ, וְתֵן חֶלְקֵנוּ בְּתוֹרָתֶךָ
וְשָׁם נַעֲבָדְךָ בְּיִרְאָה כִּימֵי עוֹלָם וּכְשָׁנִים קַדְמֹנִיּוֹת.
וְעָרְבָה לַיהוה מִנְחַת יְהוּדָה וִירוּשָׁלָםִ כִּימֵי עוֹלָם וּכְשָׁנִים קַדְמֹנִיּוֹת:

מלאכי ג

קדיש שלם

ש״ץ: יִתְגַּדַּל וְיִתְקַדַּשׁ שְׁמֵהּ רַבָּא (קהל: אָמֵן)
בְּעָלְמָא דִּי בְרָא כִרְעוּתֵהּ, וְיַמְלִיךְ מַלְכוּתֵהּ
בְּחַיֵּיכוֹן וּבְיוֹמֵיכוֹן וּבְחַיֵּי דְכָל בֵּית יִשְׂרָאֵל
בַּעֲגָלָא וּבִזְמַן קָרִיב, וְאִמְרוּ אָמֵן. (קהל: אָמֵן)

קהל
 וש״ץ: יְהֵא שְׁמֵהּ רַבָּא מְבָרַךְ לְעָלַם וּלְעָלְמֵי עָלְמַיָּא.

ש״ץ: יִתְבָּרַךְ וְיִשְׁתַּבַּח וְיִתְפָּאַר
וְיִתְרוֹמַם וְיִתְנַשֵּׂא וְיִתְהַדָּר וְיִתְעַלֶּה וְיִתְהַלָּל
שְׁמֵהּ דְּקֻדְשָׁא בְּרִיךְ הוּא (קהל: בְּרִיךְ הוּא)
לְעֵלָּא מִן כָּל בִּרְכָתָא וְשִׁירָתָא, תֻּשְׁבְּחָתָא וְנֶחֱמָתָא
דַּאֲמִירָן בְּעָלְמָא, וְאִמְרוּ אָמֵן. (קהל: אָמֵן)

תִּתְקַבַּל צְלוֹתְהוֹן וּבָעוּתְהוֹן דְּכָל יִשְׂרָאֵל
קֳדָם אֲבוּהוֹן דִּי בִשְׁמַיָּא, וְאִמְרוּ אָמֵן. (קהל: אָמֵן)

יְהֵא שְׁלָמָא רַבָּא מִן שְׁמַיָּא
וְחַיִּים, עָלֵינוּ וְעַל כָּל יִשְׂרָאֵל, וְאִמְרוּ אָמֵן. (קהל: אָמֵן)

Bow, take three steps back, as if taking leave of the Divine Presence,
then bow, first left, then right, then center, while saying:

עֹשֶׂה שָׁלוֹם בִּמְרוֹמָיו
הוּא יַעֲשֶׂה שָׁלוֹם עָלֵינוּ וְעַל כָּל יִשְׂרָאֵל, וְאִמְרוּ אָמֵן. (קהל: אָמֵן)

Stand while saying Aleinu. Bow at ˘.

עָלֵינוּ It is our duty to praise the Master of all,
and ascribe greatness to the Author of creation,
who has not made us like the nations of the lands
nor placed us like the families of the earth;
who has not made our portion like theirs,
nor our destiny like all their multitudes.
(For they worship vanity and emptiness,
and pray to a god who cannot save.)
˘But we bow in worship and thank the Supreme King of kings,
the Holy One, blessed be He,
who extends the heavens and establishes the earth,
whose throne of glory is in the heavens above,
and whose power's Presence is in the highest of heights.
He is our God; there is no other.
Truly He is our King, there is none else,
as it is written in His Torah:
"You shall know and take to heart this day   *Deut. 4*
that the LORD is God, in heaven above and on earth below.
There is no other."

Therefore, we place our hope in You, LORD our God,
that we may soon see the glory of Your power,
when You will remove abominations from the earth,
and idols will be utterly destroyed,
when the world will be perfected under the sovereignty of the Almighty,
when all humanity will call on Your name,
to turn all the earth's wicked toward You.
All the world's inhabitants will realize and know
that to You every knee must bow and every tongue swear loyalty.
Before You, LORD our God, they will kneel and bow down
and give honor to Your glorious name.
They will all accept the yoke of Your kingdom,
and You will reign over them soon and for ever.
For the kingdom is Yours, and to all eternity You will reign in glory,
as it is written in Your Torah: "The LORD will reign for ever and ever."   *Ex. 15*

Stand while saying עָלֵינוּ. Bow at ˇ.

עָלֵינוּ לְשַׁבֵּחַ לַאֲדוֹן הַכֹּל, לָתֵת גְּדֻלָּה לְיוֹצֵר בְּרֵאשִׁית
שֶׁלֹּא עָשָׂנוּ כְּגוֹיֵי הָאֲרָצוֹת, וְלֹא שָׂמָנוּ כְּמִשְׁפְּחוֹת הָאֲדָמָה
שֶׁלֹּא שָׂם חֶלְקֵנוּ כָּהֶם וְגוֹרָלֵנוּ כְּכָל הֲמוֹנָם.
(שֶׁהֵם מִשְׁתַּחֲוִים לְהֶבֶל וָרִיק וּמִתְפַּלְּלִים אֶל אֵל לֹא יוֹשִׁיעַ.)
ˇוַאֲנַחְנוּ כּוֹרְעִים וּמִשְׁתַּחֲוִים וּמוֹדִים
לִפְנֵי מֶלֶךְ מַלְכֵי הַמְּלָכִים, הַקָּדוֹשׁ בָּרוּךְ הוּא
שֶׁהוּא נוֹטֶה שָׁמַיִם וְיוֹסֵד אֶרֶץ
וּמוֹשַׁב יְקָרוֹ בַּשָּׁמַיִם מִמַּעַל, וּשְׁכִינַת עֻזּוֹ בְּגָבְהֵי מְרוֹמִים.
הוּא אֱלֹהֵינוּ, אֵין עוֹד.
אֱמֶת מַלְכֵּנוּ, אֶפֶס זוּלָתוֹ, כַּכָּתוּב בְּתוֹרָתוֹ

דברים ד

וְיָדַעְתָּ הַיּוֹם וַהֲשֵׁבֹתָ אֶל־לְבָבֶךָ
כִּי יהוה הוּא הָאֱלֹהִים בַּשָּׁמַיִם מִמַּעַל וְעַל־הָאָרֶץ מִתָּחַת
אֵין עוֹד:

עַל כֵּן נְקַוֶּה לְךָ יהוה אֱלֹהֵינוּ, לִרְאוֹת מְהֵרָה בְּתִפְאֶרֶת עֻזֶּךָ
לְהַעֲבִיר גִּלּוּלִים מִן הָאָרֶץ, וְהָאֱלִילִים כָּרוֹת יִכָּרֵתוּן
לְתַקֵּן עוֹלָם בְּמַלְכוּת שַׁדַּי.
וְכָל בְּנֵי בָשָׂר יִקְרְאוּ בִשְׁמֶךָ לְהַפְנוֹת אֵלֶיךָ כָּל רִשְׁעֵי אָרֶץ.
יַכִּירוּ וְיֵדְעוּ כָּל יוֹשְׁבֵי תֵבֵל
כִּי לְךָ תִּכְרַע כָּל בֶּרֶךְ, תִּשָּׁבַע כָּל לָשׁוֹן.
לְפָנֶיךָ יהוה אֱלֹהֵינוּ יִכְרְעוּ וְיִפֹּלוּ, וְלִכְבוֹד שִׁמְךָ יְקָר יִתֵּנוּ
וִיקַבְּלוּ כֻלָּם אֶת עֹל מַלְכוּתֶךָ
וְתִמְלֹךְ עֲלֵיהֶם מְהֵרָה לְעוֹלָם וָעֶד.
כִּי הַמַּלְכוּת שֶׁלְּךָ הִיא וּלְעוֹלְמֵי עַד תִּמְלֹךְ בְּכָבוֹד
כַּכָּתוּב בְּתוֹרָתֶךָ, יהוה יִמְלֹךְ לְעֹלָם וָעֶד:

שמות טו

‣ And it is said: "Then the LORD shall be King over all the earth;   *Zech. 14*
on that day the LORD shall be One and His name One."

Some add:
Have no fear of sudden terror or of the ruin when it overtakes the wicked.   *Prov. 3*
Devise your strategy, but it will be thwarted;   *Is. 8*
propose your plan, but it will not stand, for God is with us.
When you grow old, I will still be the same.   *Is. 46*
When your hair turns gray, I will still carry you.
I made you, I will bear you, I will carry you, and I will rescue you.

MOURNER'S KADDISH

The following prayer, said by mourners, requires the presence of a minyan.
A transliteration can be found on page 779.

Mourner: יִתְגַּדַּל Magnified and sanctified
may His great name be,
in the world He created by His will.
May He establish His kingdom in your lifetime
and in your days, and in the lifetime
of all the house of Israel,
swiftly and soon – and say: Amen.

All: May His great name be blessed for ever and all time.

Mourner: Blessed and praised, glorified and exalted,
raised and honored, uplifted and lauded
be the name of the Holy One, blessed be He,
beyond any blessing, song, praise and consolation
uttered in the world – and say: Amen.

May there be great peace from heaven,
and life for us and all Israel – and say: Amen.

Bow, take three steps back, as if taking leave of the Divine Presence,
then bow, first left, then right, then center, while saying:
May He who makes peace in His high places,
make peace for us and all Israel – and say: Amen.

For Ma'ariv of Yom Tov turn to page 46; if Yom Tov falls on Shabbat, turn to page 40.
For Ma'ariv of Motza'ei Yom Tov, turn to the next page.

זכריה יד

‹ וְנֶאֱמַר, וְהָיָה יהוה לְמֶלֶךְ עַל־כָּל־הָאָרֶץ
בַּיּוֹם הַהוּא יִהְיֶה יהוה אֶחָד וּשְׁמוֹ אֶחָד:

Some add:

משלי ג

אַל־תִּירָא מִפַּחַד פִּתְאֹם וּמִשֹּׁאַת רְשָׁעִים כִּי תָבֹא:

ישעיה ח

עֻצוּ עֵצָה וְתֻפָר, דַּבְּרוּ דָבָר וְלֹא יָקוּם, כִּי עִמָּנוּ אֵל:

ישעיה מו

וְעַד־זִקְנָה אֲנִי הוּא, וְעַד־שֵׂיבָה אֲנִי אֶסְבֹּל, אֲנִי עָשִׂיתִי וַאֲנִי אֶשָּׂא וַאֲנִי אֶסְבֹּל וַאֲמַלֵּט:

קדיש יתום

The following prayer, said by mourners, requires the presence of a מנין.
A transliteration can be found on page 779.

אבל׃

יִתְגַּדַּל וְיִתְקַדַּשׁ שְׁמֵהּ רַבָּא (קהל׃ אָמֵן)
בְּעָלְמָא דִּי בְרָא כִרְעוּתֵהּ, וְיַמְלִיךְ מַלְכוּתֵהּ
בְּחַיֵּיכוֹן וּבְיוֹמֵיכוֹן וּבְחַיֵּי דְכָל בֵּית יִשְׂרָאֵל
בַּעֲגָלָא וּבִזְמַן קָרִיב, וְאִמְרוּ אָמֵן. (קהל׃ אָמֵן)

קהל ואבל׃

יְהֵא שְׁמֵהּ רַבָּא מְבָרַךְ לְעָלַם וּלְעָלְמֵי עָלְמַיָּא.

אבל׃

יִתְבָּרַךְ וְיִשְׁתַּבַּח וְיִתְפָּאַר
וְיִתְרוֹמַם וְיִתְנַשֵּׂא וְיִתְהַדָּר וְיִתְעַלֶּה וְיִתְהַלָּל
שְׁמֵהּ דְּקֻדְשָׁא בְּרִיךְ הוּא (קהל׃ בְּרִיךְ הוּא)
לְעֵלָּא מִן כָּל בִּרְכָתָא וְשִׁירָתָא, תֻּשְׁבְּחָתָא וְנֶחֱמָתָא
דַּאֲמִירָן בְּעָלְמָא, וְאִמְרוּ אָמֵן. (קהל׃ אָמֵן)

יְהֵא שְׁלָמָא רַבָּא מִן שְׁמַיָּא
וְחַיִּים, עָלֵינוּ וְעַל כָּל יִשְׂרָאֵל, וְאִמְרוּ אָמֵן. (קהל׃ אָמֵן)

Bow, take three steps back, as if taking leave of the Divine Presence,
then bow, first left, then right, then center, while saying:

עֹשֶׂה שָׁלוֹם בִּמְרוֹמָיו, הוּא יַעֲשֶׂה שָׁלוֹם
עָלֵינוּ וְעַל כָּל יִשְׂרָאֵל, וְאִמְרוּ אָמֵן. (קהל׃ אָמֵן)

For מעריב *of* יום טוב *turn to page 47; if* יום טוב *falls on* שבת, *turn to page 41.*
For מוצאי יום טוב *of* מעריב, *turn to the next page.*

Ma'ariv for Motza'ei Yom Tov

וְהוּא רַחוּם He is compassionate.   *Ps. 78*
He forgives iniquity and does not destroy.
Repeatedly He suppresses His anger,
not rousing His full wrath.
LORD, save! May the King, answer us on the day we call.   *Ps. 20*

BLESSINGS OF THE SHEMA

The Leader says the following, bowing at "Bless," standing straight
at "the LORD"; the congregation, followed by the Leader, responds,
bowing at "Bless," standing straight at "the LORD":

Leader: # BLESS
the LORD, the blessed One.

Congregation: Bless the LORD, the blessed One,
for ever and all time.

Leader: Bless the LORD, the blessed One,
for ever and all time.

בָּרוּךְ Blessed are You, LORD our God,
King of the Universe,
who by His word brings on evenings,
by His wisdom opens the gates of heaven,
with understanding makes time change
and the seasons rotate,
and by His will orders the stars in their constellations in the sky.
He creates day and night, rolling away the light before the darkness,
and darkness before the light.

מעריב למוצאי יום טוב

תהלים עח

וְהוּא רַחוּם, יְכַפֵּר עָוֹן וְלֹא־יַשְׁחִית
וְהִרְבָּה לְהָשִׁיב אַפּוֹ, וְלֹא־יָעִיר כָּל־חֲמָתוֹ:

תהלים כ

יהוה הוֹשִׁיעָה, הַמֶּלֶךְ יַעֲנֵנוּ בְיוֹם־קָרְאֵנוּ:

קריאת שמע וברכותיה

The שְׁלִיחַ צִבּוּר *says the following, bowing at* בָּרְכוּ,
standing straight at ה׳; *the* קָהָל, *followed by the* שְׁלִיחַ צִבּוּר,
responds, bowing at בָּרוּךְ, *standing straight at* ה׳:

ש״ץ: **בָּרְכוּ**

אֶת יהוה הַמְבֹרָךְ.

קהל: בָּרוּךְ יהוה הַמְבֹרָךְ לְעוֹלָם וָעֶד.

ש״ץ: בָּרוּךְ יהוה הַמְבֹרָךְ לְעוֹלָם וָעֶד.

בָּרוּךְ אַתָּה יהוה אֱלֹהֵינוּ מֶלֶךְ הָעוֹלָם
אֲשֶׁר בִּדְבָרוֹ מַעֲרִיב עֲרָבִים
בְּחָכְמָה פּוֹתֵחַ שְׁעָרִים
וּבִתְבוּנָה מְשַׁנֶּה עִתִּים וּמַחֲלִיף אֶת הַזְּמַנִּים
וּמְסַדֵּר אֶת הַכּוֹכָבִים בְּמִשְׁמְרוֹתֵיהֶם בָּרָקִיעַ כִּרְצוֹנוֹ.
בּוֹרֵא יוֹם וָלָיְלָה
גּוֹלֵל אוֹר מִפְּנֵי חֹשֶׁךְ וְחֹשֶׁךְ מִפְּנֵי אוֹר

▸ He makes the day pass and brings on night,
  distinguishing day from night:
  the LORD of hosts is His name.
  May the living and forever enduring God rule over us for all time.
  Blessed are You, LORD, who brings on evenings.

אַהֲבַת עוֹלָם With everlasting love
have You loved Your people, the house of Israel.
You have taught us Torah and commandments,
decrees and laws of justice.
Therefore, LORD our God, when we lie down and when we rise up
we will speak of Your decrees,
rejoicing in the words of Your Torah
and Your commandments for ever.
▸ For they are our life and the length of our days;
  on them will we meditate day and night.
  May You never take away Your love from us.
  Blessed are You, LORD, who loves His people Israel.

The Shema must be said with intense concentration.
When not with a minyan, say:
God, faithful King!

The following verse should be said aloud, while covering the eyes with the right hand:

Listen, Israel: the LORD is our God,
the LORD is One.

Deut. 6

Quietly: Blessed be the name of His glorious kingdom for ever and all time.

וְאָהַבְתָּ Love the LORD your God with all your heart, with all your   *Deut. 6*
soul, and with all your might. These words which I command you
today shall be on your heart. Teach them repeatedly to your children, speaking of them when you sit at home and when you travel
on the way, when you lie down and when you rise. Bind them as a
sign on your hand, and they shall be an emblem between your eyes.
Write them on the doorposts of your house and gates.

‹ וּמַעֲבִיר יוֹם וּמֵבִיא לַיְלָה

וּמַבְדִּיל בֵּין יוֹם וּבֵין לַיְלָה,

יהוה צְבָאוֹת שְׁמוֹ.

אֵל חַי וְקַיָּם תָּמִיד, יִמְלֹךְ עָלֵינוּ לְעוֹלָם וָעֶד.

בָּרוּךְ אַתָּה יהוה, הַמַּעֲרִיב עֲרָבִים.

אַהֲבַת עוֹלָם בֵּית יִשְׂרָאֵל עַמְּךָ אָהַבְתָּ,

תּוֹרָה וּמִצְוֹת, חֻקִּים וּמִשְׁפָּטִים, אוֹתָנוּ לִמַּדְתָּ.

עַל כֵּן יהוה אֱלֹהֵינוּ בְּשָׁכְבֵּנוּ וּבְקוּמֵנוּ נָשִׂיחַ בְּחֻקֶּיךָ,

וְנִשְׂמַח בְּדִבְרֵי תוֹרָתֶךָ וּבְמִצְוֹתֶיךָ לְעוֹלָם וָעֶד.

‹ כִּי הֵם חַיֵּינוּ וְאֹרֶךְ יָמֵינוּ, וּבָהֶם נֶהְגֶּה יוֹמָם וָלַיְלָה.

וְאַהֲבָתְךָ אַל תָּסִיר מִמֶּנּוּ לְעוֹלָמִים.

בָּרוּךְ אַתָּה יהוה, אוֹהֵב עַמּוֹ יִשְׂרָאֵל.

The שמע must be said with intense concentration.

When not with a מנין, say:

אֵל מֶלֶךְ נֶאֱמָן

The following verse should be said aloud, while covering the eyes with the right hand:

דברים

שְׁמַע יִשְׂרָאֵל, יהוה אֱלֹהֵינוּ, יהוה ׀ אֶחָד:

בָּרוּךְ שֵׁם כְּבוֹד מַלְכוּתוֹ לְעוֹלָם וָעֶד. *Quietly*

דברים

וְאָהַבְתָּ אֵת יהוה אֱלֹהֶיךָ, בְּכָל־לְבָבְךָ וּבְכָל־נַפְשְׁךָ וּבְכָל־מְאֹדֶךָ:

וְהָיוּ הַדְּבָרִים הָאֵלֶּה, אֲשֶׁר אָנֹכִי מְצַוְּךָ הַיּוֹם, עַל־לְבָבֶךָ: וְשִׁנַּנְתָּם

לְבָנֶיךָ וְדִבַּרְתָּ בָּם, בְּשִׁבְתְּךָ בְּבֵיתֶךָ וּבְלֶכְתְּךָ בַדֶּרֶךְ, וּבְשָׁכְבְּךָ

וּבְקוּמֶךָ: וּקְשַׁרְתָּם לְאוֹת עַל־יָדֶךָ וְהָיוּ לְטֹטָפֹת בֵּין עֵינֶיךָ:

וּכְתַבְתָּם עַל־מְזֻזוֹת בֵּיתֶךָ וּבִשְׁעָרֶיךָ:

וְהָיָה If you indeed heed My commandments with which I charge   *Deut. 11*
you today, to love the LORD your God and worship Him with
all your heart and with all your soul, I will give rain in your land
in its season, the early and late rain; and you shall gather in your
grain, wine and oil. I will give grass in your field for your cattle,
and you shall eat and be satisfied. Be careful lest your heart be
tempted and you go astray and worship other gods, bowing down
to them. Then the LORD's anger will flare against you and He will
close the heavens so that there will be no rain. The land will not
yield its crops, and you will perish swiftly from the good land
that the LORD is giving you. Therefore, set these, My words, on
your heart and soul. Bind them as a sign on your hand, and they
shall be an emblem between your eyes. Teach them to your children, speaking of them when you sit at home and when you travel
on the way, when you lie down and when you rise. Write them
on the doorposts of your house and gates, so that you and your
children may live long in the land that the LORD swore to your
ancestors to give them, for as long as the heavens are above the
earth.

וַיֹּאמֶר The LORD spoke to Moses, saying: Speak to the Israelites   *Num. 15*
and tell them to make tassels on the corners of their garments
for all generations. They shall attach to the tassel at each corner
a thread of blue. This shall be your tassel, and you shall see it
and remember all of the LORD's commandments and keep them,
not straying after your heart and after your eyes, following your
own sinful desires. Thus you will be reminded to keep all My
commandments, and be holy to your God. I am the LORD your
God, who brought you out of the land of Egypt to be your God.
I am the LORD your God.

True –

The Leader repeats:
▸ The LORD your God is true –

דברים יא

וְהָיָה אִם־שָׁמֹעַ תִּשְׁמְעוּ אֶל־מִצְוֹתַי אֲשֶׁר אָנֹכִי מְצַוֶּה אֶתְכֶם
הַיּוֹם, לְאַהֲבָה אֶת־יהוה אֱלֹהֵיכֶם וּלְעָבְדוֹ, בְּכָל־לְבַבְכֶם וּבְכָל־
נַפְשְׁכֶם: וְנָתַתִּי מְטַר־אַרְצְכֶם בְּעִתּוֹ, יוֹרֶה וּמַלְקוֹשׁ, וְאָסַפְתָּ דְגָנֶךָ
וְתִירֹשְׁךָ וְיִצְהָרֶךָ: וְנָתַתִּי עֵשֶׂב בְּשָׂדְךָ לִבְהֶמְתֶּךָ, וְאָכַלְתָּ וְשָׂבָעְתָּ:
הִשָּׁמְרוּ לָכֶם פֶּן־יִפְתֶּה לְבַבְכֶם, וְסַרְתֶּם וַעֲבַדְתֶּם אֱלֹהִים אֲחֵרִים
וְהִשְׁתַּחֲוִיתֶם לָהֶם: וְחָרָה אַף־יהוה בָּכֶם, וְעָצַר אֶת־הַשָּׁמַיִם
וְלֹא־יִהְיֶה מָטָר, וְהָאֲדָמָה לֹא תִתֵּן אֶת־יְבוּלָהּ, וַאֲבַדְתֶּם מְהֵרָה
מֵעַל הָאָרֶץ הַטֹּבָה אֲשֶׁר יהוה נֹתֵן לָכֶם: וְשַׂמְתֶּם אֶת־דְּבָרַי
אֵלֶּה עַל־לְבַבְכֶם וְעַל־נַפְשְׁכֶם, וּקְשַׁרְתֶּם אֹתָם לְאוֹת עַל־יֶדְכֶם,
וְהָיוּ לְטוֹטָפֹת בֵּין עֵינֵיכֶם: וְלִמַּדְתֶּם אֹתָם אֶת־בְּנֵיכֶם לְדַבֵּר בָּם,
בְּשִׁבְתְּךָ בְּבֵיתֶךָ וּבְלֶכְתְּךָ בַדֶּרֶךְ, וּבְשָׁכְבְּךָ וּבְקוּמֶךָ: וּכְתַבְתָּם
עַל־מְזוּזוֹת בֵּיתֶךָ וּבִשְׁעָרֶיךָ: לְמַעַן יִרְבּוּ יְמֵיכֶם וִימֵי בְנֵיכֶם עַל
הָאֲדָמָה אֲשֶׁר נִשְׁבַּע יהוה לַאֲבֹתֵיכֶם לָתֵת לָהֶם, כִּימֵי הַשָּׁמַיִם
עַל־הָאָרֶץ:

במדבר טו

וַיֹּאמֶר יהוה אֶל־מֹשֶׁה לֵּאמֹר: דַּבֵּר אֶל־בְּנֵי יִשְׂרָאֵל וְאָמַרְתָּ
אֲלֵהֶם, וְעָשׂוּ לָהֶם צִיצִת עַל־כַּנְפֵי בִגְדֵיהֶם לְדֹרֹתָם, וְנָתְנוּ
עַל־צִיצִת הַכָּנָף פְּתִיל תְּכֵלֶת: וְהָיָה לָכֶם לְצִיצִת, וּרְאִיתֶם אֹתוֹ
וּזְכַרְתֶּם אֶת־כָּל־מִצְוֹת יהוה וַעֲשִׂיתֶם אֹתָם, וְלֹא תָתוּרוּ אַחֲרֵי
לְבַבְכֶם וְאַחֲרֵי עֵינֵיכֶם, אֲשֶׁר־אַתֶּם זֹנִים אַחֲרֵיהֶם: לְמַעַן תִּזְכְּרוּ
וַעֲשִׂיתֶם אֶת־כָּל־מִצְוֹתָי, וִהְיִיתֶם קְדֹשִׁים לֵאלֹהֵיכֶם: אֲנִי יהוה
אֱלֹהֵיכֶם, אֲשֶׁר הוֹצֵאתִי אֶתְכֶם מֵאֶרֶץ מִצְרַיִם, לִהְיוֹת לָכֶם
לֵאלֹהִים, אֲנִי יהוה אֱלֹהֵיכֶם:

אֱמֶת

The שליח ציבור *repeats:*

‣ יהוה אֱלֹהֵיכֶם אֱמֶת

וֶאֱמוּנָה – and faithful is all this,
 and firmly established for us
 that He is the LORD our God,
 and there is none beside Him,
 and that we, Israel, are His people.
 He is our King, who redeems us from the hand of kings
 and delivers us from the grasp of all tyrants.
 He is our God, who on our behalf repays our foes
 and brings just retribution on our mortal enemies;
 who performs great deeds beyond understanding
 and wonders beyond number;
 who kept us alive, not letting our foot slip; *Ps. 66*
 who led us on the high places of our enemies,
 raising our pride above all our foes;
 who did miracles for us
 and brought vengeance against Pharaoh;
 who performed signs and wonders
 in the land of Ham's children;
 who smote in His wrath all the firstborn of Egypt,
 and brought out His people Israel from their midst
 into everlasting freedom;
 who led His children through the divided Reed Sea,
 plunging their pursuers and enemies into the depths.
 When His children saw His might,
 they gave praise and thanks to His name,
‣ and willingly accepted His Sovereignty.
 Moses and the children of Israel
 then sang a song to You with great joy,
 and they all exclaimed:

  מִי־כָמֹכָה "Who is like You, LORD, among the mighty? *Ex. 15*
  Who is like You, majestic in holiness,
  awesome in praises, doing wonders?"

וֶאֱמוּנָה כָּל זֹאת וְקַיָּם עָלֵינוּ

כִּי הוּא יהוה אֱלֹהֵינוּ וְאֵין זוּלָתוֹ

וַאֲנַחְנוּ יִשְׂרָאֵל עַמּוֹ.

הַפּוֹדֵנוּ מִיַּד מְלָכִים

מַלְכֵּנוּ הַגּוֹאֲלֵנוּ מִכַּף כָּל הֶעָרִיצִים.

הָאֵל הַנִּפְרָע לָנוּ מִצָּרֵינוּ

וְהַמְשַׁלֵּם גְּמוּל לְכָל אוֹיְבֵי נַפְשֵׁנוּ.

הָעוֹשֶׂה גְדוֹלוֹת עַד אֵין חֵקֶר, וְנִפְלָאוֹת עַד אֵין מִסְפָּר

הַשָּׂם נַפְשֵׁנוּ בַּחַיִּים, וְלֹא־נָתַן לַמּוֹט רַגְלֵנוּ:

תהלים סו

הַמַּדְרִיכֵנוּ עַל בָּמוֹת אוֹיְבֵינוּ

וַיָּרֶם קַרְנֵנוּ עַל כָּל שׂוֹנְאֵינוּ.

הָעוֹשֶׂה לָּנוּ נִסִּים וּנְקָמָה בְּפַרְעֹה

אוֹתוֹת וּמוֹפְתִים בְּאַדְמַת בְּנֵי חָם.

הַמַּכֶּה בְעֶבְרָתוֹ כָּל בְּכוֹרֵי מִצְרָיִם

וַיּוֹצֵא אֶת עַמּוֹ יִשְׂרָאֵל מִתּוֹכָם לְחֵרוּת עוֹלָם.

הַמַּעֲבִיר בָּנָיו בֵּין גִּזְרֵי יַם סוּף

אֶת רוֹדְפֵיהֶם וְאֶת שׂוֹנְאֵיהֶם בִּתְהוֹמוֹת טִבַּע

וְרָאוּ בָנָיו גְּבוּרָתוֹ, שִׁבְּחוּ וְהוֹדוּ לִשְׁמוֹ

‹ וּמַלְכוּתוֹ בְרָצוֹן קִבְּלוּ עֲלֵיהֶם.

מֹשֶׁה וּבְנֵי יִשְׂרָאֵל, לְךָ עָנוּ שִׁירָה בְּשִׂמְחָה רַבָּה

וְאָמְרוּ כֻלָּם

מִי־כָמֹכָה בָּאֵלִם יהוה

מִי כָּמֹכָה נֶאְדָּר בַּקֹּדֶשׁ

נוֹרָא תְהִלֹּת עֹשֵׂה פֶלֶא:

שמות טו

▸ Your children beheld Your majesty
  as You parted the sea before Moses.
"This is my God!" they responded, and then said:
      "The Lord shall reign for ever and ever."   *Ex. 15*

▸ And it is said,
        "For the Lord has redeemed Jacob   *Jer. 31*
        and rescued him from a power stronger than his own."
    Blessed are You, Lord, who redeemed Israel.

הַשְׁכִּיבֵנוּ Help us lie down, O Lord our God, in peace,
and rise up, O our King, to life.
Spread over us Your canopy of peace.
Direct us with Your good counsel,
and save us for the sake of Your name.
Shield us and remove from us every enemy,
plague, sword, famine and sorrow.
Remove the adversary from before and behind us.
Shelter us in the shadow of Your wings,
for You, God, are our Guardian and Deliverer;
You, God, are a gracious and compassionate King.
▸ Guard our going out and our coming in,
  for life and peace, from now and for ever.
  Blessed are You, Lord, who guards His people Israel for ever.

In Israel the service continues with Half Kaddish on page 642.
בָּרוּךְ Blessed be the Lord for ever. Amen and Amen.   *Ps. 89*
Blessed from Zion be the Lord   *Ps. 135*
who dwells in Jerusalem. Halleluya.
Blessed be the Lord, God of Israel,   *Ps. 72*
who alone does wondrous things.
Blessed be His glorious name for ever,
and may the whole earth be filled with His glory.
Amen and Amen.

‹ מַלְכוּתְךָ רָאוּ בָנֶיךָ, בּוֹקֵעַ יָם לִפְנֵי מֹשֶׁה
זֶה אֵלִי עָנוּ, וְאָמְרוּ

שמות טו

יהוה יִמְלֹךְ לְעֹלָם וָעֶד:

‹ וְנֶאֱמַר

ירמיה לא

כִּי־פָדָה יהוה אֶת־יַעֲקֹב
וּגְאָלוֹ מִיַּד חָזָק מִמֶּנּוּ:
בָּרוּךְ אַתָּה יהוה, גָּאַל יִשְׂרָאֵל.

הַשְׁכִּיבֵנוּ יהוה אֱלֹהֵינוּ לְשָׁלוֹם
וְהַעֲמִידֵנוּ מַלְכֵּנוּ לְחַיִּים
וּפְרֹשׂ עָלֵינוּ סֻכַּת שְׁלוֹמֶךָ
וְתַקְּנֵנוּ בְּעֵצָה טוֹבָה מִלְּפָנֶיךָ
וְהוֹשִׁיעֵנוּ לְמַעַן שְׁמֶךָ.
וְהָגֵן בַּעֲדֵנוּ, וְהָסֵר מֵעָלֵינוּ אוֹיֵב, דֶּבֶר וְחֶרֶב וְרָעָב וְיָגוֹן
וְהָסֵר שָׂטָן מִלְּפָנֵינוּ וּמֵאַחֲרֵינוּ, וּבְצֵל כְּנָפֶיךָ תַּסְתִּירֵנוּ
כִּי אֵל שׁוֹמְרֵנוּ וּמַצִּילֵנוּ אָתָּה
כִּי אֵל מֶלֶךְ חַנּוּן וְרַחוּם אָתָּה.
‹ וּשְׁמֹר צֵאתֵנוּ וּבוֹאֵנוּ לְחַיִּים וּלְשָׁלוֹם מֵעַתָּה וְעַד עוֹלָם.
בָּרוּךְ אַתָּה יהוה, שׁוֹמֵר עַמּוֹ יִשְׂרָאֵל לָעַד.

In ארץ ישראל the service continues with חצי קדיש on page 643.

תהלים פט

בָּרוּךְ יהוה לְעוֹלָם, אָמֵן וְאָמֵן:

תהלים קלה

בָּרוּךְ יהוה מִצִּיּוֹן, שֹׁכֵן יְרוּשָׁלָיִם, הַלְלוּיָהּ:

תהלים עב

בָּרוּךְ יהוה אֱלֹהִים אֱלֹהֵי יִשְׂרָאֵל, עֹשֵׂה נִפְלָאוֹת לְבַדּוֹ:
וּבָרוּךְ שֵׁם כְּבוֹדוֹ לְעוֹלָם
וְיִמָּלֵא כְבוֹדוֹ אֶת־כָּל־הָאָרֶץ, אָמֵן וְאָמֵן:

May the glory of the LORD endure for ever;   *Ps. 104*
may the LORD rejoice in His works.
May the name of the LORD be blessed now and for all time.   *Ps. 113*
For the sake of His great name   *1 Sam. 12*
the LORD will not abandon His people,
for the LORD vowed to make you a people of His own.
When all the people saw [God's wonders] they fell on their faces   *1 Kings 18*
and said: "The LORD, He is God; the LORD, He is God."
Then the LORD shall be King over all the earth;   *Zech. 14*
on that day the LORD shall be One and His name One.
May Your love, LORD, be upon us,   *Ps. 33*
as we have put our hope in You.
Save us, LORD our God,   *Ps. 106*
gather us and deliver us from the nations,
to thank Your holy name, and glory in Your praise.
All the nations You made shall come and bow before You, LORD,   *Ps. 86*
and pay honor to Your name,
for You are great and You perform wonders:
You alone are God.
We, Your people, the flock of Your pasture, will praise You for ever.   *Ps. 79*
For all generations we will relate Your praise.

בָּרוּךְ Blessed is the LORD by day,
blessed is the LORD by night.
Blessed is the LORD when we lie down;
blessed is the LORD when we rise.
For in Your hand are the souls of the living and the dead,
[as it is written:] "In His hand is every living soul,   *Job 12*
and the breath of all mankind."
Into Your hand I entrust my spirit: *Ps. 31*
You redeemed me, LORD, God of truth.
Our God in heaven, bring unity to Your name,
establish Your kingdom constantly
and reign over us for ever and all time.

תהלים קד
יְהִי כְבוֹד יהוה לְעוֹלָם, יִשְׂמַח יהוה בְּמַעֲשָׂיו:

תהלים קיג
יְהִי שֵׁם יהוה מְבֹרָךְ מֵעַתָּה וְעַד־עוֹלָם:

שמואל א׳, יב
כִּי לֹא־יִטֹּשׁ יהוה אֶת־עַמּוֹ בַּעֲבוּר שְׁמוֹ הַגָּדוֹל

כִּי הוֹאִיל יהוה לַעֲשׂוֹת אֶתְכֶם לוֹ לְעָם:

מלכים א׳, יח
וַיַּרְא כָּל־הָעָם וַיִּפְּלוּ עַל־פְּנֵיהֶם

וַיֹּאמְרוּ, יהוה הוּא הָאֱלֹהִים, יהוה הוּא הָאֱלֹהִים:

זכריה יד
וְהָיָה יהוה לְמֶלֶךְ עַל־כָּל־הָאָרֶץ

בַּיּוֹם הַהוּא יִהְיֶה יהוה אֶחָד וּשְׁמוֹ אֶחָד:

תהלים לג
יְהִי־חַסְדְּךָ יהוה עָלֵינוּ, כַּאֲשֶׁר יִחַלְנוּ לָךְ:

תהלים קו
הוֹשִׁיעֵנוּ יהוה אֱלֹהֵינוּ, וְקַבְּצֵנוּ מִן־הַגּוֹיִם

לְהֹדוֹת לְשֵׁם קָדְשֶׁךָ, לְהִשְׁתַּבֵּחַ בִּתְהִלָּתֶךָ:

תהלים פו
כָּל־גּוֹיִם אֲשֶׁר עָשִׂיתָ, יָבוֹאוּ וְיִשְׁתַּחֲווּ לְפָנֶיךָ, אֲדֹנָי

וִיכַבְּדוּ לִשְׁמֶךָ:

כִּי־גָדוֹל אַתָּה וְעֹשֵׂה נִפְלָאוֹת, אַתָּה אֱלֹהִים לְבַדֶּךָ:

תהלים עט
וַאֲנַחְנוּ עַמְּךָ וְצֹאן מַרְעִיתֶךָ, נוֹדֶה לְךָ לְעוֹלָם

לְדוֹר וָדֹר נְסַפֵּר תְּהִלָּתֶךָ:

בָּרוּךְ יהוה בַּיּוֹם, בָּרוּךְ יהוה בַּלָּיְלָה

בָּרוּךְ יהוה בְּשָׁכְבֵנוּ, בָּרוּךְ יהוה בְּקוּמֵנוּ.

כִּי בְיָדְךָ נַפְשׁוֹת הַחַיִּים וְהַמֵּתִים.

איוב יב
אֲשֶׁר בְּיָדוֹ נֶפֶשׁ כָּל־חָי, וְרוּחַ כָּל־בְּשַׂר־אִישׁ:

תהלים לא
בְּיָדְךָ אַפְקִיד רוּחִי, פָּדִיתָה אוֹתִי יהוה אֵל אֱמֶת:

אֱלֹהֵינוּ שֶׁבַּשָּׁמַיִם

יַחֵד שִׁמְךָ וְקַיֵּם מַלְכוּתְךָ תָּמִיד

וּמְלֹךְ עָלֵינוּ לְעוֹלָם וָעֶד.

יִרְאוּ May our eyes see, our hearts rejoice,
and our souls be glad in Your true salvation,
when Zion is told, "Your God reigns."
The Lord is King, the Lord was King,
the Lord will be King for ever and all time.
▸ For sovereignty is Yours,
and to all eternity You will reign in glory,
for we have no king but You.
Blessed are You, Lord,
the King who in His constant glory will reign over us
and all His creation for ever and all time.

HALF KADDISH

Leader: יִתְגַּדַּל Magnified and sanctified
may His great name be,
in the world He created by His will.
May He establish His kingdom
in your lifetime and in your days,
and in the lifetime of all the house of Israel,
swiftly and soon –
and say: Amen.

All: May His great name be blessed for ever and all time.

Leader: Blessed and praised, glorified and exalted,
raised and honored,
uplifted and lauded
be the name of the Holy One,
blessed be He,
beyond any blessing,
song, praise and consolation
uttered in the world –
and say: Amen.

יִרְאוּ עֵינֵינוּ וְיִשְׂמַח לִבֵּנוּ

וְתָגֵל נַפְשֵׁנוּ בִּישׁוּעָתְךָ בֶּאֱמֶת

בֶּאֱמֹר לְצִיּוֹן מָלַךְ אֱלֹהָיִךְ.

יהוה מֶלֶךְ, יהוה מָלָךְ, יהוה יִמְלֹךְ לְעֹלָם וָעֶד.

‹ כִּי הַמַּלְכוּת שֶׁלְּךָ הִיא, וּלְעוֹלְמֵי עַד תִּמְלֹךְ בְּכָבוֹד

כִּי אֵין לָנוּ מֶלֶךְ אֶלָּא אָתָּה.

בָּרוּךְ אַתָּה יהוה

הַמֶּלֶךְ בִּכְבוֹדוֹ תָּמִיד, יִמְלֹךְ עָלֵינוּ לְעוֹלָם וָעֶד

וְעַל כָּל מַעֲשָׂיו.

חצי קדיש

שׁ״ץ: יִתְגַּדַּל וְיִתְקַדַּשׁ שְׁמֵהּ רַבָּא (קהל: אָמֵן)

בְּעָלְמָא דִּי בְרָא כִרְעוּתֵהּ

וְיַמְלִיךְ מַלְכוּתֵהּ

בְּחַיֵּיכוֹן וּבְיוֹמֵיכוֹן וּבְחַיֵּי דְּכָל בֵּית יִשְׂרָאֵל

בַּעֲגָלָא וּבִזְמַן קָרִיב

וְאִמְרוּ אָמֵן. (קהל: אָמֵן)

קהל
ושׁ״ץ: יְהֵא שְׁמֵהּ רַבָּא מְבָרַךְ לְעָלַם וּלְעָלְמֵי עָלְמַיָּא.

שׁ״ץ: יִתְבָּרַךְ וְיִשְׁתַּבַּח וְיִתְפָּאַר וְיִתְרוֹמַם וְיִתְנַשֵּׂא

וְיִתְהַדָּר וְיִתְעַלֶּה וְיִתְהַלָּל

שְׁמֵהּ דְּקֻדְשָׁא בְּרִיךְ הוּא (קהל: בְּרִיךְ הוּא)

לְעֵלָּא מִן כָּל בִּרְכָתָא וְשִׁירָתָא, תֻּשְׁבְּחָתָא וְנֶחֱמָתָא

דַּאֲמִירָן בְּעָלְמָא

וְאִמְרוּ אָמֵן. (קהל: אָמֵן)

THE AMIDA

The following prayer, until "in former years" on page 656, is said silently, standing with feet together. Take three steps forward and at the points indicated by ˙, bend the knees at the first word, bow at the second, and stand straight before saying God's name.

O LORD, open my lips,   *Ps. 51*
so that my mouth may declare Your praise.

PATRIARCHS

˙בָּרוּךְ Blessed are You, LORD our God and God of our fathers,
God of Abraham, God of Isaac and God of Jacob;
the great, mighty and awesome God, God Most High,
who bestows acts of loving-kindness and creates all,
who remembers the loving-kindness of the fathers
and will bring a Redeemer to their children's children
for the sake of His name, in love.
King, Helper, Savior, Shield:
˙Blessed are You, LORD, Shield of Abraham.

DIVINE MIGHT

אַתָּה גִּבּוֹר You are eternally mighty, LORD.
You give life to the dead and have great power to save.

> *In Israel:*
> He causes the dew to fall.

He sustains the living with loving-kindness,
and with great compassion revives the dead.
He supports the fallen, heals the sick,
sets captives free,
and keeps His faith with those who sleep in the dust.
Who is like You, Master of might,
and who can compare to You,
O King who brings death and gives life,
and makes salvation grow?
Faithful are You to revive the dead.
Blessed are You, LORD, who revives the dead.

עמידה

The following prayer, until קַדְמֹנִיּוֹת *on page 657, is said silently, standing with feet*
together. Take three steps forward and at the points indicated by '*, bend the knees at*
the first word, bow at the second, and stand straight before saying God's name.

תהלים נא

אֲדֹנָי, שְׂפָתַי תִּפְתָּח, וּפִי יַגִּיד תְּהִלָּתֶךָ:

אבות

יּבָּרוּךְ אַתָּה יהוה, אֱלֹהֵינוּ וֵאלֹהֵי אֲבוֹתֵינוּ
אֱלֹהֵי אַבְרָהָם, אֱלֹהֵי יִצְחָק, וֵאלֹהֵי יַעֲקֹב
הָאֵל הַגָּדוֹל הַגִּבּוֹר וְהַנּוֹרָא, אֵל עֶלְיוֹן
גּוֹמֵל חֲסָדִים טוֹבִים, וְקֹנֵה הַכֹּל, וְזוֹכֵר חַסְדֵי אָבוֹת
וּמֵבִיא גוֹאֵל לִבְנֵי בְנֵיהֶם לְמַעַן שְׁמוֹ בְּאַהֲבָה.
מֶלֶךְ עוֹזֵר וּמוֹשִׁיעַ וּמָגֵן.
יּבָּרוּךְ אַתָּה יהוה, מָגֵן אַבְרָהָם.

גבורות

אַתָּה גִּבּוֹר לְעוֹלָם, אֲדֹנָי
מְחַיֵּה מֵתִים אַתָּה, רַב לְהוֹשִׁיעַ

In אֶרֶץ יִשְׂרָאֵל:

מוֹרִיד הַטָּל

מְכַלְכֵּל חַיִּים בְּחֶסֶד, מְחַיֵּה מֵתִים בְּרַחֲמִים רַבִּים
סוֹמֵךְ נוֹפְלִים, וְרוֹפֵא חוֹלִים, וּמַתִּיר אֲסוּרִים
וּמְקַיֵּם אֱמוּנָתוֹ לִישֵׁנֵי עָפָר.
מִי כָמוֹךָ, בַּעַל גְּבוּרוֹת, וּמִי דּוֹמֶה לָּךְ
מֶלֶךְ, מֵמִית וּמְחַיֶּה וּמַצְמִיחַ יְשׁוּעָה.
וְנֶאֱמָן אַתָּה לְהַחֲיוֹת מֵתִים.
בָּרוּךְ אַתָּה יהוה, מְחַיֵּה הַמֵּתִים.

HOLINESS

אַתָּה קָדוֹשׁ You are holy and Your name is holy,
and holy ones praise You daily, Selah!
Blessed are You, LORD, the holy God.

KNOWLEDGE

אַתָּה חוֹנֵן You grace humanity with knowledge
and teach mortals understanding.
You have graced us with the knowledge of Your Torah,
and taught us to perform the statutes of Your will.
You have distinguished, LORD our God,
between sacred and profane,
light and darkness,
Israel and the nations,
and between the seventh day and the six days of work.
Our Father, our King, may the days approaching us bring peace;
may we be free from all sin, cleansed from all iniquity,
holding fast to our reverence of You.
And grace us with the knowledge, understanding
and discernment that come from You.
Blessed are You, LORD, who graciously grants knowledge.

REPENTANCE

הֲשִׁיבֵנוּ Bring us back, our Father, to Your Torah.
Draw us near, our King, to Your service.
Lead us back to You in perfect repentance.
Blessed are You, LORD, who desires repentance.

FORGIVENESS

Strike the left side of the chest at °.

סְלַח לָנוּ Forgive us, our Father, for we have °sinned.
Pardon us, our King, for we have °transgressed;
for You pardon and forgive.
Blessed are You, LORD, the gracious One who repeatedly forgives.

קדושת השם

אַתָּה קָדוֹשׁ וְשִׁמְךָ קָדוֹשׁ
וּקְדוֹשִׁים בְּכָל יוֹם יְהַלְלוּךָ סֶּלָה.
בָּרוּךְ אַתָּה יהוה, הָאֵל הַקָּדוֹשׁ.

דעת

אַתָּה חוֹנֵן לְאָדָם דַּעַת, וּמְלַמֵּד לֶאֱנוֹשׁ בִּינָה.
אַתָּה חוֹנַנְתָּנוּ לְמַדַּע תּוֹרָתֶךָ, וַתְּלַמְּדֵנוּ לַעֲשׂוֹת חֻקֵּי רְצוֹנֶךָ
וַתַּבְדֵּל יהוה אֱלֹהֵינוּ בֵּין קֹדֶשׁ לְחֹל
בֵּין אוֹר לְחֹשֶׁךְ, בֵּין יִשְׂרָאֵל לָעַמִּים
בֵּין יוֹם הַשְּׁבִיעִי לְשֵׁשֶׁת יְמֵי הַמַּעֲשֶׂה.
אָבִינוּ מַלְכֵּנוּ, הָחֵל עָלֵינוּ הַיָּמִים הַבָּאִים לִקְרָאתֵנוּ לְשָׁלוֹם
חֲשׂוּכִים מִכָּל חֵטְא וּמְנֻקִּים מִכָּל עָוֹן וּמְדֻבָּקִים בְּיִרְאָתֶךָ.
וְחָנֵּנוּ מֵאִתְּךָ דֵּעָה בִּינָה וְהַשְׂכֵּל.
בָּרוּךְ אַתָּה יהוה, חוֹנֵן הַדָּעַת.

תשובה

הֲשִׁיבֵנוּ אָבִינוּ לְתוֹרָתֶךָ, וְקָרְבֵנוּ מַלְכֵּנוּ לַעֲבוֹדָתֶךָ
וְהַחֲזִירֵנוּ בִּתְשׁוּבָה שְׁלֵמָה לְפָנֶיךָ.
בָּרוּךְ אַתָּה יהוה, הָרוֹצֶה בִּתְשׁוּבָה.

סליחה

Strike the left side of the chest at °.

סְלַח לָנוּ אָבִינוּ כִּי °חָטָאנוּ
מְחַל לָנוּ מַלְכֵּנוּ כִּי °פָשָׁעְנוּ
כִּי מוֹחֵל וְסוֹלֵחַ אָתָּה.
בָּרוּךְ אַתָּה יהוה, חַנּוּן הַמַּרְבֶּה לִסְלֹחַ.

REDEMPTION

רְאֵה **Look on our affliction,**
plead our cause,
and redeem us soon for Your name's sake,
for You are a powerful Redeemer.
Blessed are You, LORD,
the Redeemer of Israel.

HEALING

רְפָאֵנוּ **Heal us, LORD, and we shall be healed.**
Save us and we shall be saved,
for You are our praise.
Bring complete recovery for all our ailments,

The following prayer for a sick person may be said here:

May it be Your will, O LORD my God and God of my ancestors, that You
speedily send a complete recovery from heaven, a healing of both soul
and body, to the patient (*name*), son/daughter of (*mother's name*) among
the other afflicted of Israel.

---

for You, God, King, are a faithful and compassionate Healer.
Blessed are You, LORD,
Healer of the sick of His people Israel.

PROSPERITY

בָּרֵךְ **Bless this year for us, LORD our God,**
and all its types of produce for good.
Grant blessing on the face of the earth,
and from its goodness satisfy us,
blessing our year as the best of years.
Blessed are You, LORD,
who blesses the years.

גאולה

רְאֵה בְעָנְיֵנוּ, וְרִיבָה רִיבֵנוּ

וּגְאָלֵנוּ מְהֵרָה לְמַעַן שְׁמֶךָ

כִּי גוֹאֵל חָזָק אָתָּה.

בָּרוּךְ אַתָּה יהוה, גּוֹאֵל יִשְׂרָאֵל.

רפואה

רְפָאֵנוּ יהוה וְנֵרָפֵא

הוֹשִׁיעֵנוּ וְנִוָּשֵׁעָה

כִּי תְהִלָּתֵנוּ אָתָּה

וְהַעֲלֵה רְפוּאָה שְׁלֵמָה לְכָל מַכּוֹתֵינוּ

The following prayer for a sick person may be said here:

יְהִי רָצוֹן מִלְּפָנֶיךָ יהוה אֱלֹהַי וֵאלֹהֵי אֲבוֹתַי, שֶׁתִּשְׁלַח מְהֵרָה רְפוּאָה שְׁלֵמָה
מִן הַשָּׁמַיִם רְפוּאַת הַנֶּפֶשׁ וּרְפוּאַת הַגּוּף לַחוֹלֶה/לַחוֹלָה *name of patient*
בֶּן/בַּת *mother's name* בְּתוֹךְ שְׁאָר חוֹלֵי יִשְׂרָאֵל.

כִּי אֵל מֶלֶךְ רוֹפֵא נֶאֱמָן וְרַחֲמָן אָתָּה.

בָּרוּךְ אַתָּה יהוה, רוֹפֵא חוֹלֵי עַמּוֹ יִשְׂרָאֵל.

ברכת השנים

בָּרֵךְ עָלֵינוּ יהוה אֱלֹהֵינוּ אֶת הַשָּׁנָה הַזֹּאת

וְאֶת כָּל מִינֵי תְבוּאָתָהּ, לְטוֹבָה

וְתֵן בְּרָכָה עַל פְּנֵי הָאֲדָמָה

וְשַׂבְּעֵנוּ מִטּוּבָהּ

וּבָרֵךְ שְׁנָתֵנוּ כַּשָּׁנִים הַטּוֹבוֹת.

בָּרוּךְ אַתָּה יהוה, מְבָרֵךְ הַשָּׁנִים.

INGATHERING OF EXILES

תְּקַע Sound the great shofar for our freedom,
raise high the banner to gather our exiles,
and gather us together from the four quarters of the earth.
Blessed are You, LORD,
who gathers the dispersed of His people Israel.

JUSTICE

הָשִׁיבָה Restore our judges as at first,
and our counselors as at the beginning,
and remove from us sorrow and sighing.
May You alone, LORD, reign over us
with loving-kindness and compassion,
and vindicate us in justice.
Blessed are You, LORD,
the King who loves righteousness and justice.

AGAINST INFORMERS

וְלַמַּלְשִׁינִים For the slanderers
let there be no hope,
and may all wickedness perish in an instant.
May all Your people's enemies swiftly be cut down.
May You swiftly uproot,
crush, cast down and humble the arrogant
swiftly in our days.
Blessed are You, LORD,
who destroys enemies and humbles the arrogant.

THE RIGHTEOUS

עַל הַצַּדִּיקִים To the righteous, the pious,
the elders of Your people the house of Israel,
the remnant of their scholars,
the righteous converts, and to us,
may Your compassion be aroused, LORD our God.

קבוץ גלויות

תְּקַע בְּשׁוֹפָר גָּדוֹל לְחֵרוּתֵנוּ

וְשָׂא נֵס לְקַבֵּץ גָּלֻיּוֹתֵינוּ

וְקַבְּצֵנוּ יַחַד מֵאַרְבַּע כַּנְפוֹת הָאָרֶץ.

בָּרוּךְ אַתָּה יהוה, מְקַבֵּץ נִדְחֵי עַמּוֹ יִשְׂרָאֵל.

השבת המשפט

הָשִׁיבָה שׁוֹפְטֵינוּ כְּבָרִאשׁוֹנָה, וְיוֹעֲצֵינוּ כְּבַתְּחִלָּה

וְהָסֵר מִמֶּנּוּ יָגוֹן וַאֲנָחָה

וּמְלֹךְ עָלֵינוּ אַתָּה יהוה לְבַדְּךָ בְּחֶסֶד וּבְרַחֲמִים

וְצַדְּקֵנוּ בַּמִּשְׁפָּט.

בָּרוּךְ אַתָּה יהוה, מֶלֶךְ אוֹהֵב צְדָקָה וּמִשְׁפָּט.

ברכת המינים

וְלַמַּלְשִׁינִים אַל תְּהִי תִקְוָה, וְכָל הָרִשְׁעָה כְּרֶגַע תֹּאבֵד

וְכָל אוֹיְבֵי עַמְּךָ מְהֵרָה יִכָּרֵתוּ

וְהַזֵּדִים מְהֵרָה

תְעַקֵּר וּתְשַׁבֵּר וּתְמַגֵּר וְתַכְנִיעַ

בִּמְהֵרָה בְיָמֵינוּ.

בָּרוּךְ אַתָּה יהוה, שׁוֹבֵר אוֹיְבִים וּמַכְנִיעַ זֵדִים.

על הצדיקים

עַל הַצַּדִּיקִים וְעַל הַחֲסִידִים

וְעַל זִקְנֵי עַמְּךָ בֵּית יִשְׂרָאֵל, וְעַל פְּלֵיטַת סוֹפְרֵיהֶם

וְעַל גֵּרֵי הַצֶּדֶק, וְעָלֵינוּ

יֶהֱמוּ רַחֲמֶיךָ יהוה אֱלֹהֵינוּ

Grant a good reward to all
who sincerely trust in Your name.
Set our lot with them,
so that we may never be ashamed,
for in You we trust.
Blessed are You, LORD,
who is the support and trust of the righteous.

REBUILDING JERUSALEM
וְלִירוּשָׁלַיִם To Jerusalem, Your city,
may You return in compassion,
and may You dwell in it as You promised.
May You rebuild it rapidly in our days
as an everlasting structure,
and install within it soon the throne of David.
Blessed are You, LORD,
who builds Jerusalem.

KINGDOM OF DAVID
אֶת צֶמַח May the offshoot of Your servant David soon flower,
and may his pride be raised high by Your salvation,
for we wait for Your salvation all day.
Blessed are You, LORD,
who makes the glory of salvation flourish.

RESPONSE TO PRAYER
שְׁמַע קוֹלֵנוּ Listen to our voice, LORD our God.
Spare us and have compassion on us,
and in compassion and favor accept our prayer,
for You, God, listen to prayers and pleas.
Do not turn us away, O our King,
empty-handed from Your presence,
for You listen with compassion to the prayer of Your people Israel.
Blessed are You, LORD, who listens to prayer.

וְתֵן שָׂכָר טוֹב לְכָל הַבּוֹטְחִים בְּשִׁמְךָ בֶּאֱמֶת
וְשִׂים חֶלְקֵנוּ עִמָּהֶם
וּלְעוֹלָם לֹא נֵבוֹשׁ כִּי בְךָ בָּטָחְנוּ.
בָּרוּךְ אַתָּה יהוה, מִשְׁעָן וּמִבְטָח לַצַּדִּיקִים.

בניין ירושלים

וְלִירוּשָׁלַיִם עִירְךָ בְּרַחֲמִים תָּשׁוּב
וְתִשְׁכֹּן בְּתוֹכָהּ כַּאֲשֶׁר דִּבַּרְתָּ
וּבְנֵה אוֹתָהּ בְּקָרוֹב בְּיָמֵינוּ בִּנְיַן עוֹלָם
וְכִסֵּא דָוִד מְהֵרָה לְתוֹכָהּ תָּכִין.
בָּרוּךְ אַתָּה יהוה, בּוֹנֵה יְרוּשָׁלָיִם.

משיח בן דוד

אֶת צֶמַח דָּוִד עַבְדְּךָ מְהֵרָה תַצְמִיחַ
וְקַרְנוֹ תָּרוּם בִּישׁוּעָתֶךָ
כִּי לִישׁוּעָתְךָ קִוִּינוּ כָּל הַיּוֹם.
בָּרוּךְ אַתָּה יהוה, מַצְמִיחַ קֶרֶן יְשׁוּעָה.

שומע תפלה

שְׁמַע קוֹלֵנוּ יהוה אֱלֹהֵינוּ
חוּס וְרַחֵם עָלֵינוּ
וְקַבֵּל בְּרַחֲמִים וּבְרָצוֹן אֶת תְּפִלָּתֵנוּ
כִּי אֵל שׁוֹמֵעַ תְּפִלּוֹת וְתַחֲנוּנִים אָתָּה
וּמִלְּפָנֶיךָ מַלְכֵּנוּ רֵיקָם אַל תְּשִׁיבֵנוּ
כִּי אַתָּה שׁוֹמֵעַ תְּפִלַּת עַמְּךָ יִשְׂרָאֵל בְּרַחֲמִים.
בָּרוּךְ אַתָּה יהוה, שׁוֹמֵעַ תְּפִלָּה.

TEMPLE SERVICE

רְצֵה Find favor, LORD our God,
in Your people Israel and their prayer.
Restore the service to Your most holy House,
and accept in love and favor
the fire-offerings of Israel and their prayer.
May the service of Your people Israel always find favor with You.
And may our eyes witness Your return to Zion in compassion.
Blessed are You, LORD,
who restores His Presence to Zion.

THANKSGIVING

Bow at the first nine words.
מוֹדִים We give thanks to You,
for You are the LORD our God and God of our ancestors
for ever and all time.
You are the Rock of our lives,
Shield of our salvation from generation to generation.
We will thank You and declare Your praise for our lives,
which are entrusted into Your hand;
for our souls, which are placed in Your charge;
for Your miracles which are with us every day;
and for Your wonders and favors at all times,
evening, morning and midday.
You are good – for Your compassion never fails.
You are compassionate – for Your loving-kindnesses never cease.
We have always placed our hope in You.
For all these things may Your name be blessed and exalted,
our King, continually, for ever and all time.
Let all that lives thank You, Selah!
and praise Your name in truth,
God, our Savior and Help, Selah!
▸Blessed are You, LORD, whose name is "the Good"
and to whom thanks are due.

עבודה

רְצֵה יהוה אֱלֹהֵינוּ בְּעַמְּךָ יִשְׂרָאֵל, וּבִתְפִלָּתָם

וְהָשֵׁב אֶת הָעֲבוֹדָה לִדְבִיר בֵּיתֶךָ

וְאִשֵּׁי יִשְׂרָאֵל וּתְפִלָּתָם בְּאַהֲבָה תְקַבֵּל בְּרָצוֹן

וּתְהִי לְרָצוֹן תָּמִיד עֲבוֹדַת יִשְׂרָאֵל עַמֶּךָ.

וְתֶחֱזֶינָה עֵינֵינוּ בְּשׁוּבְךָ לְצִיּוֹן בְּרַחֲמִים.

בָּרוּךְ אַתָּה יהוה, הַמַּחֲזִיר שְׁכִינָתוֹ לְצִיּוֹן.

הודאה

Bow at the first five words.

¹מוֹדִים אֲנַחְנוּ לָךְ

שָׁאַתָּה הוּא יהוה אֱלֹהֵינוּ וֵאלֹהֵי אֲבוֹתֵינוּ לְעוֹלָם וָעֶד.

צוּר חַיֵּינוּ, מָגֵן יִשְׁעֵנוּ אַתָּה הוּא לְדוֹר וָדוֹר.

נוֹדֶה לְּךָ וּנְסַפֵּר תְּהִלָּתֶךָ

עַל חַיֵּינוּ הַמְּסוּרִים בְּיָדֶךָ

וְעַל נִשְׁמוֹתֵינוּ הַפְּקוּדוֹת לָךְ

וְעַל נִסֶּיךָ שֶׁבְּכָל יוֹם עִמָּנוּ

וְעַל נִפְלְאוֹתֶיךָ וְטוֹבוֹתֶיךָ

שֶׁבְּכָל עֵת, עֶרֶב וָבֹקֶר וְצָהֳרָיִם. ²

הַטּוֹב, כִּי לֹא כָלוּ רַחֲמֶיךָ

וְהַמְרַחֵם, כִּי לֹא תַמּוּ חֲסָדֶיךָ מֵעוֹלָם קִוִּינוּ לָךְ.

וְעַל כֻּלָּם יִתְבָּרַךְ וְיִתְרוֹמַם שִׁמְךָ מַלְכֵּנוּ תָּמִיד לְעוֹלָם וָעֶד.

וְכֹל הַחַיִּים יוֹדוּךָ סֶּלָה, וִיהַלְלוּ אֶת שִׁמְךָ בֶּאֱמֶת

הָאֵל יְשׁוּעָתֵנוּ וְעֶזְרָתֵנוּ סֶלָה.

³בָּרוּךְ אַתָּה יהוה, הַטּוֹב שִׁמְךָ וּלְךָ נָאֶה לְהוֹדוֹת.

PEACE

שָׁלוֹם רָב Grant great peace to Your people Israel for ever,
for You are the sovereign LORD of all peace;
and may it be good in Your eyes to bless Your people Israel
at every time, at every hour, with Your peace.
Blessed are You, LORD, who blesses His people Israel with peace.

Some say the following verse:
May the words of my mouth and the meditation of my heart   *Ps. 19*
find favor before You, LORD, my Rock and Redeemer.

אֱלֹהַי My God,   *Berakhot*
                                                                          17a
guard my tongue from evil and my lips from deceitful speech.
To those who curse me, let my soul be silent;
may my soul be to all like the dust.
Open my heart to Your Torah
and let my soul pursue Your commandments.
As for all who plan evil against me,
swiftly thwart their counsel and frustrate their plans.
    Act for the sake of Your name; act for the sake of Your right hand;
     act for the sake of Your holiness; act for the sake of Your Torah.
That Your beloved ones may be delivered,   *Ps. 60*
save with Your right hand and answer me.
May the words of my mouth   *Ps. 19*
and the meditation of my heart find favor before You,
LORD, my Rock and Redeemer.

Bow, take three steps back, then bow, first left, then right, then center, while saying:
May He who makes peace in His high places,
make peace for us and all Israel – and say: Amen.

יְהִי רָצוֹן May it be Your will, LORD our God and God of our ancestors,
that the Temple be rebuilt speedily in our days, and grant us a share in Your Torah.
And there we will serve You with reverence,
as in the days of old and as in former years.
Then the offering of Judah and Jerusalem   *Mal. 3*
will be pleasing to the LORD as in the days of old and as in former years.

If Motza'ei Shavuot falls on Motza'ei Shabbat, the Leader continues with
Half Kaddish and "May the pleasantness" on the next page.
On other evenings the Leader says Full Kaddish on page 662.

ברכת שלום

שָׁלוֹם רָב עַל יִשְׂרָאֵל עַמְּךָ תָּשִׂים לְעוֹלָם
כִּי אַתָּה הוּא מֶלֶךְ אָדוֹן לְכָל הַשָּׁלוֹם.
וְטוֹב בְּעֵינֶיךָ לְבָרֵךְ אֶת עַמְּךָ יִשְׂרָאֵל
בְּכָל עֵת וּבְכָל שָׁעָה בִּשְׁלוֹמֶךָ.
בָּרוּךְ אַתָּה יהוה, הַמְבָרֵךְ אֶת עַמּוֹ יִשְׂרָאֵל בַּשָּׁלוֹם.

Some say the following verse:

תהלים יט

יִהְיוּ לְרָצוֹן אִמְרֵי־פִי וְהֶגְיוֹן לִבִּי לְפָנֶיךָ, יהוה צוּרִי וְגֹאֲלִי:

ברכות יז

אֱלֹהַי

נְצֹר לְשׁוֹנִי מֵרָע וּשְׂפָתַי מִדַּבֵּר מִרְמָה
וְלִמְקַלְלַי נַפְשִׁי תִדֹּם, וְנַפְשִׁי כֶּעָפָר לַכֹּל תִּהְיֶה.
פְּתַח לִבִּי בְּתוֹרָתֶךָ, וּבְמִצְוֹתֶיךָ תִּרְדֹּף נַפְשִׁי.
וְכָל הַחוֹשְׁבִים עָלַי רָעָה, מְהֵרָה הָפֵר עֲצָתָם וְקַלְקֵל מַחֲשַׁבְתָּם.
עֲשֵׂה לְמַעַן שְׁמֶךָ, עֲשֵׂה לְמַעַן יְמִינֶךָ
עֲשֵׂה לְמַעַן קְדֻשָּׁתֶךָ, עֲשֵׂה לְמַעַן תּוֹרָתֶךָ.

תהלים ס
תהלים יט

לְמַעַן יֵחָלְצוּן יְדִידֶיךָ, הוֹשִׁיעָה יְמִינְךָ וַעֲנֵנִי:
יִהְיוּ לְרָצוֹן אִמְרֵי־פִי וְהֶגְיוֹן לִבִּי לְפָנֶיךָ, יהוה צוּרִי וְגֹאֲלִי:

Bow, take three steps back, then bow, first left, then right, then center, while saying:

עֹשֶׂה שָׁלוֹם בִּמְרוֹמָיו
הוּא יַעֲשֶׂה שָׁלוֹם עָלֵינוּ וְעַל כָּל יִשְׂרָאֵל, וְאִמְרוּ אָמֵן.

יְהִי רָצוֹן מִלְּפָנֶיךָ יהוה אֱלֹהֵינוּ וֵאלֹהֵי אֲבוֹתֵינוּ
שֶׁיִּבָּנֶה בֵּית הַמִּקְדָּשׁ בִּמְהֵרָה בְיָמֵינוּ, וְתֵן חֶלְקֵנוּ בְּתוֹרָתֶךָ
וְשָׁם נַעֲבָדְךָ בְּיִרְאָה כִּימֵי עוֹלָם וּכְשָׁנִים קַדְמֹנִיּוֹת.

מלאכי ג

וְעָרְבָה לַיהוה מִנְחַת יְהוּדָה וִירוּשָׁלָיִם כִּימֵי עוֹלָם וּכְשָׁנִים קַדְמֹנִיּוֹת:

שְׁלִיחַ צִבּוּר מוֹצָאֵי שַׁבָּת, the מוֹצָאֵי שְׁבוּעוֹת falls on מוֹצָאֵי שַׁבָּת If
continues with וַיְהִי נֹעַם and חֲצִי קַדִּישׁ on the next page.
On other evenings the שְׁלִיחַ צִבּוּר says קַדִּישׁ שָׁלֵם on page 663.

HALF KADDISH

Leader: יִתְגַּדַּל Magnified and sanctified may His great name be,
in the world He created by His will.
May He establish His kingdom
in your lifetime and in your days,
and in the lifetime of all the house of Israel,
swiftly and soon – and say: Amen.

All: May His great name be blessed for ever and all time.

Leader: Blessed and praised, glorified and exalted,
raised and honored, uplifted and lauded be
the name of the Holy One,
blessed be He, beyond any blessing,
song, praise and consolation
uttered in the world – and say: Amen.

וִיהִי נֹעַם May the pleasantness of the Lord our God be upon us. Establish *Ps. 90*
for us the work of our hands, O establish the work of our hands.

יֹשֵׁב He who lives in the shelter of the Most High dwells in the shadow of *Ps. 91*
the Almighty. I say of the Lord, my Refuge and Stronghold, my God in
whom I trust, that He will save you from the fowler's snare and the deadly
pestilence. With His pinions He will cover you, and beneath His wings
you will find shelter; His faithfulness is an encircling shield. You need not
fear terror by night, nor the arrow that flies by day; not the pestilence that
stalks in darkness, nor the plague that ravages at noon. A thousand may fall
at your side, ten thousand at your right hand, but it will not come near you.
You will only look with your eyes and see the punishment of the wicked.
Because you said, "The Lord is my Refuge," taking the Most High as
your shelter, no harm will befall you, no plague come near your tent, for
He will command His angels about you, to guard you in all your ways.
They will lift you in their hands, lest your foot stumble on a stone. You
will tread on lions and vipers; you will trample on young lions and snakes.
[God says:] "Because he loves Me, I will rescue him; I will protect him,
because he acknowledges My name. When he calls on Me, I will answer
him; I will be with him in distress, I will deliver him and bring him honor.
▸ With long life I will satisfy him and show him My salvation.
With long life I will satisfy him and show him My salvation.

חצי קדיש

ש״ץ: יִתְגַּדַּל וְיִתְקַדַּשׁ שְׁמֵהּ רַבָּא (קהל: אָמֵן)
בְּעָלְמָא דִּי בְרָא כִרְעוּתֵהּ
וְיַמְלִיךְ מַלְכוּתֵהּ
בְּחַיֵּיכוֹן וּבְיוֹמֵיכוֹן וּבְחַיֵּי דְכָל בֵּית יִשְׂרָאֵל
בַּעֲגָלָא וּבִזְמַן קָרִיב, וְאִמְרוּ אָמֵן. (קהל: אָמֵן)

קהל
ושׁ״ץ: יְהֵא שְׁמֵהּ רַבָּא מְבָרַךְ לְעָלַם וּלְעָלְמֵי עָלְמַיָּא.

ש״ץ: יִתְבָּרַךְ וְיִשְׁתַּבַּח וְיִתְפָּאַר וְיִתְרוֹמַם וְיִתְנַשֵּׂא
וְיִתְהַדָּר וְיִתְעַלֶּה וְיִתְהַלָּל
שְׁמֵהּ דְּקֻדְשָׁא בְּרִיךְ הוּא (קהל: בְּרִיךְ הוּא)
לְעֵלָּא מִן כָּל בִּרְכָתָא וְשִׁירָתָא, תֻּשְׁבְּחָתָא וְנֶחָמָתָא
דַּאֲמִירָן בְּעָלְמָא, וְאִמְרוּ אָמֵן. (קהל: אָמֵן)

תהלים צ
וִיהִי נֹעַם אֲדֹנָי אֱלֹהֵינוּ עָלֵינוּ וּמַעֲשֵׂה יָדֵינוּ כּוֹנְנָה עָלֵינוּ וּמַעֲשֵׂה יָדֵינוּ
כּוֹנְנֵהוּ:

תהלים צא
יֹשֵׁב בְּסֵתֶר עֶלְיוֹן, בְּצֵל שַׁדַּי יִתְלוֹנָן: אֹמַר לַיהוה מַחְסִי וּמְצוּדָתִי,
אֱלֹהַי אֶבְטַח־בּוֹ: כִּי הוּא יַצִּילְךָ מִפַּח יָקוּשׁ, מִדֶּבֶר הַוּוֹת: בְּאֶבְרָתוֹ
יָסֶךְ לָךְ, וְתַחַת־כְּנָפָיו תֶּחְסֶה, צִנָּה וְסֹחֵרָה אֲמִתּוֹ: לֹא־תִירָא מִפַּחַד
לָיְלָה, מֵחֵץ יָעוּף יוֹמָם: מִדֶּבֶר בָּאֹפֶל יַהֲלֹךְ, מִקֶּטֶב יָשׁוּד צָהֳרָיִם:
יִפֹּל מִצִּדְּךָ אֶלֶף, וּרְבָבָה מִימִינֶךָ, אֵלֶיךָ לֹא יִגָּשׁ: רַק בְּעֵינֶיךָ תַבִּיט,
וְשִׁלֻּמַת רְשָׁעִים תִּרְאֶה: כִּי־אַתָּה יהוה מַחְסִי, עֶלְיוֹן שַׂמְתָּ מְעוֹנֶךָ:
לֹא־תְאֻנֶּה אֵלֶיךָ רָעָה, וְנֶגַע לֹא־יִקְרַב בְּאָהֳלֶךָ: כִּי מַלְאָכָיו יְצַוֶּה־לָּךְ,
לִשְׁמָרְךָ בְּכָל־דְּרָכֶיךָ: עַל־כַּפַּיִם יִשָּׂאוּנְךָ, פֶּן־תִּגֹּף בָּאֶבֶן רַגְלֶךָ: עַל־
שַׁחַל וָפֶתֶן תִּדְרֹךְ, תִּרְמֹס כְּפִיר וְתַנִּין: כִּי בִי חָשַׁק וַאֲפַלְּטֵהוּ, אֲשַׂגְּבֵהוּ
כִּי־יָדַע שְׁמִי: יִקְרָאֵנִי וְאֶעֱנֵהוּ, עִמּוֹ אָנֹכִי בְצָרָה, אֲחַלְּצֵהוּ וַאֲכַבְּדֵהוּ:
‹ אֹרֶךְ יָמִים אַשְׂבִּיעֵהוּ, וְאַרְאֵהוּ בִּישׁוּעָתִי:
אֹרֶךְ יָמִים אַשְׂבִּיעֵהוּ, וְאַרְאֵהוּ בִּישׁוּעָתִי:

▸ You are the Holy One, enthroned on the praises of Israel. *Ps. 22*

And [the angels] call to one another, saying, "Holy, holy, holy *Is. 6*
is the LORD of hosts; the whole world is filled with His glory."

And they receive permission from one another, saying: "Holy in the highest heavens, *Targum*
home of His Presence; holy on earth, the work of His strength; holy for ever and all *Yonatan*
time is the LORD of hosts; the whole earth is full of His radiant glory." *Is. 6*

▸ Then a wind lifted me up and I heard behind me the sound of a great *Ezek. 3*
noise, saying, "Blessed is the LORD's glory from His place."

Then a wind lifted me up and I heard behind me the sound of a great tempest of *Targum*
those who uttered praise, saying, "Blessed is the LORD's glory from the place of the *Yonatan*
home of His Presence." *Ezek. 3*

The LORD shall reign for ever and all time. *Ex. 15*
The LORD's kingdom is established for ever and all time. *Targum Onkelos Ex. 15*

יהוה LORD, God of Abraham, Isaac and Yisrael, our ancestors, may You *1 Chr. 29*
keep this for ever so that it forms the thoughts in Your people's heart, and
directs their heart toward You. He is compassionate. He forgives iniquity *Ps. 78*
and does not destroy. Repeatedly He suppresses His anger, not rousing
His full wrath. For You, my LORD, are good and forgiving, abundantly *Ps. 86*
kind to all who call on You. Your righteousness is eternally righteous, and *Ps. 119*
Your Torah is truth. Grant truth to Jacob, loving-kindness to Abraham, as *Mic. 7*
You promised our ancestors in ancient times. Blessed is my LORD for day *Ps. 68*
after day He burdens us [with His blessings]; God is our salvation, Selah!
The LORD of hosts is with us; the God of Jacob is our refuge, Selah! LORD *Ps. 46 Ps. 84*
of hosts, happy is the one who trusts in You. LORD, save! May the King *Ps. 20*
answer us on the day we call.

בָּרוּךְ Blessed is He, our God, who created us for His glory, separating us
from those who go astray; who gave us the Torah of truth, planting within
us eternal life. May He open our heart to His Torah, imbuing our heart
with the love and awe of Him, that we may do His will and serve Him with
a perfect heart, so that we neither toil in vain nor give birth to confusion.

יְהִי רָצוֹן May it be Your will, O LORD our God and God of our ancestors,
that we keep Your laws in this world, and thus be worthy to live, see and
inherit goodness and blessing in the Messianic Age and in the life of the
World to Come. So that my soul may sing to You and not be silent. LORD, *Ps. 30*
my God, for ever I will thank You. Blessed is the man who trusts in the *Jer. 17*
LORD, whose trust is in the LORD alone. Trust in the LORD for evermore, *Is. 26*

◀ וְאַתָּה קָדוֹשׁ יוֹשֵׁב תְּהִלּוֹת יִשְׂרָאֵל: וְקָרָא זֶה אֶל־זֶה וְאָמַר קָדוֹשׁ, תהלים כב
ישעיה ו
קָדוֹשׁ, קָדוֹשׁ, יהוה צְבָאוֹת, מְלֹא כָל־הָאָרֶץ כְּבוֹדוֹ:

וּמְקַבְּלִין דֵּין מִן דֵּין וְאָמְרִין, קַדִּישׁ בִּשְׁמֵי מְרוֹמָא עִלָּאָה בֵּית שְׁכִינְתֵּהּ, קַדִּישׁ   תרגום יונתן
ישעיה ו
עַל אַרְעָא עוֹבַד גְּבוּרְתֵּהּ, קַדִּישׁ לְעָלַם וּלְעָלְמֵי עָלְמַיָּא יהוה צְבָאוֹת, מַלְיָא
כָל אַרְעָא זִיו יְקָרֵהּ.

◀ וַתִּשָּׂאֵנִי רוּחַ, וָאֶשְׁמַע אַחֲרַי קוֹל רַעַשׁ גָּדוֹל, בָּרוּךְ כְּבוֹד־יהוה מִמְּקוֹמוֹ:   יחזקאל ג

וּנְטָלַתְנִי רוּחָא, וּשְׁמָעִית בַּתְרַי קָל זִיעַ סַגִּיא, דִּמְשַׁבְּחִין וְאָמְרִין, בְּרִיךְ יְקָרָא   תרגום יונתן
יחזקאל ג
דַּיהוה מֵאֲתַר בֵּית שְׁכִינְתֵּהּ.

יהוה יִמְלֹךְ לְעֹלָם וָעֶד: שמות טו

יהוה מַלְכוּתֵהּ קָאֵם לְעָלַם וּלְעָלְמֵי עָלְמַיָּא.   תרגום
אונקלוס
שמות טו

יהוה אֱלֹהֵי אַבְרָהָם יִצְחָק וְיִשְׂרָאֵל אֲבֹתֵינוּ, שָׁמְרָה־זֹּאת לְעוֹלָם לְיֵצֶר   דברי הימים
א׳ כט
מַחְשְׁבוֹת לְבַב עַמֶּךָ, וְהָכֵן לְבָבָם אֵלֶיךָ: וְהוּא רַחוּם יְכַפֵּר עָוֹן וְלֹא־   תהלים עח
יַשְׁחִית, וְהִרְבָּה לְהָשִׁיב אַפּוֹ, וְלֹא־יָעִיר כָּל־חֲמָתוֹ: כִּי־אַתָּה אֲדֹנָי טוֹב   תהלים פו
וְסַלָּח, וְרַב־חֶסֶד לְכָל־קֹרְאֶיךָ: צִדְקָתְךָ צֶדֶק לְעוֹלָם וְתוֹרָתְךָ אֱמֶת: תהלים קיט
תִּתֵּן אֱמֶת לְיַעֲקֹב, חֶסֶד לְאַבְרָהָם, אֲשֶׁר־נִשְׁבַּעְתָּ לַאֲבֹתֵינוּ מִימֵי קֶדֶם: מיכה ז
בָּרוּךְ אֲדֹנָי יוֹם יוֹם יַעֲמָס־לָנוּ, הָאֵל יְשׁוּעָתֵנוּ סֶלָה: יהוה צְבָאוֹת עִמָּנוּ,   תהלים סח
תהלים מו
מִשְׂגָּב לָנוּ אֱלֹהֵי יַעֲקֹב סֶלָה: יהוה צְבָאוֹת, אַשְׁרֵי אָדָם בֹּטֵחַ בָּךְ: יהוה   תהלים פד
תהלים כ
הוֹשִׁיעָה, הַמֶּלֶךְ יַעֲנֵנוּ בְיוֹם־קָרְאֵנוּ:

בָּרוּךְ הוּא אֱלֹהֵינוּ שֶׁבְּרָאָנוּ לִכְבוֹדוֹ, וְהִבְדִּילָנוּ מִן הַתּוֹעִים, וְנָתַן לָנוּ
תּוֹרַת אֱמֶת, וְחַיֵּי עוֹלָם נָטַע בְּתוֹכֵנוּ. הוּא יִפְתַּח לִבֵּנוּ בְּתוֹרָתוֹ, וְיָשֵׂם
בְּלִבֵּנוּ אַהֲבָתוֹ וְיִרְאָתוֹ וְלַעֲשׂוֹת רְצוֹנוֹ וּלְעָבְדוֹ בְּלֵבָב שָׁלֵם, לְמַעַן לֹא
נִיגַע לָרִיק וְלֹא נֵלֵד לַבֶּהָלָה.

יְהִי רָצוֹן מִלְּפָנֶיךָ יהוה אֱלֹהֵינוּ וֵאלֹהֵי אֲבוֹתֵינוּ, שֶׁנִּשְׁמֹר חֻקֶּיךָ בָּעוֹלָם
הַזֶּה, וְנִזְכֶּה וְנִחְיֶה וְנִרְאֶה וְנִירַשׁ טוֹבָה וּבְרָכָה, לִשְׁנֵי יְמוֹת הַמָּשִׁיחַ וּלְחַיֵּי
הָעוֹלָם הַבָּא. לְמַעַן יְזַמֶּרְךָ כָבוֹד וְלֹא יִדֹּם, יהוה אֱלֹהַי, לְעוֹלָם אוֹדֶךָּ:   תהלים ל
בָּרוּךְ הַגֶּבֶר אֲשֶׁר יִבְטַח בַּיהוה, וְהָיָה יהוה מִבְטַחוֹ: בִּטְחוּ בַיהוה עֲדֵי־   ירמיה יז
ישעיה כו

for God, the LORD, is an everlasting Rock. ▸ Those who know Your name *Ps. 9*
trust in You, for You, LORD, do not forsake those who seek You. The LORD *Is. 42*
desired, for the sake of Israel's merit, to make the Torah great and glorious.

FULL KADDISH

Leader: יִתְגַּדַּל Magnified and sanctified may His great name be,
in the world He created by His will.
May He establish His kingdom in your lifetime
and in your days,
and in the lifetime of all the house of Israel,
swiftly and soon –
and say: Amen.

All: May His great name be blessed for ever and all time.

Leader: Blessed and praised, glorified and exalted,
raised and honored, uplifted and lauded be
the name of the Holy One, blessed be He,
beyond any blessing,
song, praise and consolation
uttered in the world –
and say: Amen.

May the prayers and pleas of all Israel
be accepted by their Father in heaven –
and say: Amen.

May there be great peace from heaven,
and life for us and all Israel –
and say: Amen.

*Bow, take three steps back, as if taking leave of the Divine Presence,
then bow, first left, then right, then center, while saying:*
May He who makes peace in His high places,
make peace for us and all Israel –
and say: Amen.

*On Motza'ei Shavuot which is not Motza'ei Shabbat, continue with Havdala on page 670.
On Motza'ei Shabbat, continue "May God give you" on the next page.*

עַד, כִּי בְּיָה יהוה צוּר עוֹלָמִים: ‹ וְיִבְטְחוּ בְךָ יוֹדְעֵי שְׁמֶךָ, כִּי לֹא־עָזַבְתָּ תהלים ט
דֹרְשֶׁיךָ, יהוה: יהוה חָפֵץ לְמַעַן צִדְקוֹ, יַגְדִּיל תּוֹרָה וְיַאְדִּיר: ישעיה מב

קדיש שלם

ש״ץ: יִתְגַּדַּל וְיִתְקַדַּשׁ שְׁמֵהּ רַבָּא (קהל: אָמֵן)
בְּעָלְמָא דִּי בְרָא כִרְעוּתֵהּ
וְיַמְלִיךְ מַלְכוּתֵהּ
בְּחַיֵּיכוֹן וּבְיוֹמֵיכוֹן וּבְחַיֵּי דְכָל בֵּית יִשְׂרָאֵל
בַּעֲגָלָא וּבִזְמַן קָרִיב, וְאִמְרוּ אָמֵן. (קהל: אָמֵן)

קהל
וש״ץ: יְהֵא שְׁמֵהּ רַבָּא מְבָרַךְ לְעָלַם וּלְעָלְמֵי עָלְמַיָּא.

ש״ץ: יִתְבָּרַךְ וְיִשְׁתַּבַּח וְיִתְפָּאַר
וְיִתְרוֹמַם וְיִתְנַשֵּׂא וְיִתְהַדָּר וְיִתְעַלֶּה וְיִתְהַלָּל
שְׁמֵהּ דְּקֻדְשָׁא בְּרִיךְ הוּא (קהל: בְּרִיךְ הוּא)
לְעֵלָּא מִן כָּל בִּרְכָתָא וְשִׁירָתָא, תֻּשְׁבְּחָתָא וְנֶחֱמָתָא
דַּאֲמִירָן בְּעָלְמָא, וְאִמְרוּ אָמֵן. (קהל: אָמֵן)

תִּתְקַבַּל צְלוֹתְהוֹן וּבָעוּתְהוֹן דְּכָל יִשְׂרָאֵל
קֳדָם אֲבוּהוֹן דִּי בִשְׁמַיָּא, וְאִמְרוּ אָמֵן. (קהל: אָמֵן)

יְהֵא שְׁלָמָא רַבָּא מִן שְׁמַיָּא
וְחַיִּים, עָלֵינוּ וְעַל כָּל יִשְׂרָאֵל, וְאִמְרוּ אָמֵן. (קהל: אָמֵן)

Bow, take three steps back, as if taking leave of the Divine Presence,
then bow, first left, then right, then center, while saying:

עֹשֶׂה שָׁלוֹם בִּמְרוֹמָיו
הוּא יַעֲשֶׂה שָׁלוֹם
עָלֵינוּ וְעַל כָּל יִשְׂרָאֵל, וְאִמְרוּ אָמֵן. (קהל: אָמֵן)

On מוצאי שבועות which is not מוצאי שבת, continue with הבדלה on page 671.
On מוצאי שבת, continue וַיְהִֵן לְךָ on the next page.

BIBLICAL VERSES OF BLESSING

וְיִתֶּן־לְךָ May God give you dew from heaven and the richness of the earth, and *Gen. 27*
corn and wine in plenty. May peoples serve you and nations bow down to you.
Be lord over your brothers, and may your mother's sons bow down to you. A
curse on those who curse you, but a blessing on those who bless you.

וְאֵל שַׁדַּי May God Almighty bless you; may He make you fruitful and numerous *Gen. 28*
until you become an assembly of peoples. May He give you and your descendants
the blessing of Abraham, that you may possess the land where you are now staying,
the land God gave to Abraham. This comes from the God of your father – may *Gen. 49*
He help you – and from the Almighty – may He bless you with blessings of the
heaven above and the blessings of the deep that lies below, the blessings of breast
and womb. The blessings of your father surpass the blessings of my fathers to the
bounds of the endless hills. May they rest on the head of Joseph, on the brow of
the prince among his brothers. He will love you and bless you and increase your *Deut. 7*
numbers. He will bless the fruit of your womb and the fruit of your land: your
corn, your wine and oil, the calves of your herds and the lambs of your flocks,
in the land He swore to your fathers to give you. You will be blessed more than
any other people. None of your men or women will be childless, nor any of your
livestock without young. The LORD will keep you free from any disease. He will
not inflict on you the terrible diseases you knew in Egypt, but He will inflict them
on those who hate you.

הַמַּלְאָךְ May the angel who rescued me from all harm, bless these boys. May *Gen. 48*
they be called by my name and the names of my fathers Abraham and Isaac,
and may they increase greatly on the earth. The LORD your God has increased *Deut. 1*
your numbers so that today you are as many as the stars in the sky. May the
LORD, God of your fathers, increase you a thousand times, and bless you as
He promised you.

בָּרוּךְ You will be blessed in the city, and blessed in the field. You will be blessed *Deut. 28*
when you come in, and blessed when you go out. Your basket and your kneading
trough will be blessed. The fruit of your womb will be blessed, and the crops of
your land, and the young of your livestock, the calves of your herds and the lambs
of your flocks. The LORD will send a blessing on your barns, and on everything
you put your hand to. The LORD your God will bless you in the land He is giving
you. The LORD will open for you the heavens, the storehouse of His bounty, to
send rain on your land in season, and to bless all the work of your hands. You
will lend to many nations but will borrow from none. For the LORD your God *Deut. 15*
will bless you as He has promised: you will lend to many nations but will borrow
from none. You will rule over many nations, but none will rule over you. Happy *Deut. 33*

פסוקי ברכה

בראשית כז
וְיִתֶּן־לְךָ הָאֱלֹהִים מִטַּל הַשָּׁמַיִם וּמִשְׁמַנֵּי הָאָרֶץ, וְרֹב דָּגָן וְתִירֹשׁ: יַעַבְדוּךָ
עַמִּים וְיִשְׁתַּחֲווּ לְךָ לְאֻמִּים, הֱוֵה גְבִיר לְאַחֶיךָ וְיִשְׁתַּחֲווּ לְךָ בְּנֵי אִמֶּךָ,
אֹרְרֶיךָ אָרוּר וּמְבָרְכֶיךָ בָּרוּךְ:

בראשית כח
וְאֵל שַׁדַּי יְבָרֵךְ אֹתְךָ וְיַפְרְךָ וְיַרְבֶּךָ, וְהָיִיתָ לִקְהַל עַמִּים: וְיִתֶּן־לְךָ אֶת־
בִּרְכַּת אַבְרָהָם, לְךָ וּלְזַרְעֲךָ אִתָּךְ, לְרִשְׁתְּךָ אֶת־אֶרֶץ מְגֻרֶיךָ אֲשֶׁר־נָתַן

בראשית מט
אֱלֹהִים לְאַבְרָהָם: מֵאֵל אָבִיךָ וְיַעְזְרֶךָּ וְאֵת שַׁדַּי וִיבָרֲכֶךָּ, בִּרְכֹת שָׁמַיִם
מֵעָל בִּרְכֹת תְּהוֹם רֹבֶצֶת תָּחַת, בִּרְכֹת שָׁדַיִם וָרָחַם: בִּרְכֹת אָבִיךָ גָּבְרוּ
עַל־בִּרְכֹת הוֹרַי עַד־תַּאֲוַת גִּבְעֹת עוֹלָם, תִּהְיֶיןָ לְרֹאשׁ יוֹסֵף וּלְקָדְקֹד

דברים ז
נְזִיר אֶחָיו: וַאֲהֵבְךָ וּבֵרַכְךָ וְהִרְבֶּךָ, וּבֵרַךְ פְּרִי־בִטְנְךָ וּפְרִי־אַדְמָתֶךָ, דְּגָנְךָ
וְתִירֹשְׁךָ וְיִצְהָרֶךָ, שְׁגַר־אֲלָפֶיךָ וְעַשְׁתְּרֹת צֹאנֶךָ, עַל הָאֲדָמָה אֲשֶׁר־נִשְׁבַּע
לַאֲבֹתֶיךָ לָתֶת לָךְ: בָּרוּךְ תִּהְיֶה מִכָּל־הָעַמִּים, לֹא־יִהְיֶה בְךָ עָקָר וַעֲקָרָה
וּבִבְהֶמְתֶּךָ: וְהֵסִיר יְהוָה מִמְּךָ כָּל־חֹלִי, וְכָל־מַדְוֵי מִצְרַיִם הָרָעִים אֲשֶׁר
יָדַעְתָּ, לֹא יְשִׂימָם בָּךְ, וּנְתָנָם בְּכָל־שֹׂנְאֶיךָ:

בראשית מח
הַמַּלְאָךְ הַגֹּאֵל אֹתִי מִכָּל־רָע יְבָרֵךְ אֶת־הַנְּעָרִים, וְיִקָּרֵא בָהֶם שְׁמִי וְשֵׁם

דברים א
אֲבֹתַי אַבְרָהָם וְיִצְחָק, וְיִדְגּוּ לָרֹב בְּקֶרֶב הָאָרֶץ: יְהוָה אֱלֹהֵיכֶם הִרְבָּה
אֶתְכֶם, וְהִנְּכֶם הַיּוֹם כְּכוֹכְבֵי הַשָּׁמַיִם לָרֹב: יְהוָה אֱלֹהֵי אֲבוֹתֵכֶם יֹסֵף
עֲלֵיכֶם כָּכֶם אֶלֶף פְּעָמִים, וִיבָרֵךְ אֶתְכֶם כַּאֲשֶׁר דִּבֶּר לָכֶם:

דברים כח
בָּרוּךְ אַתָּה בָּעִיר, וּבָרוּךְ אַתָּה בַּשָּׂדֶה: בָּרוּךְ אַתָּה בְּבֹאֶךָ, וּבָרוּךְ אַתָּה
בְּצֵאתֶךָ: בָּרוּךְ טַנְאֲךָ וּמִשְׁאַרְתֶּךָ: בָּרוּךְ פְּרִי־בִטְנְךָ וּפְרִי אַדְמָתְךָ וּפְרִי
בְהֶמְתֶּךָ, שְׁגַר אֲלָפֶיךָ וְעַשְׁתְּרוֹת צֹאנֶךָ: יְצַו יְהוָה אִתְּךָ אֶת־הַבְּרָכָה
בַּאֲסָמֶיךָ וּבְכֹל מִשְׁלַח יָדֶךָ, וּבֵרַכְךָ בָּאָרֶץ אֲשֶׁר־יְהוָה אֱלֹהֶיךָ נֹתֵן לָךְ:
יִפְתַּח יְהוָה לְךָ אֶת־אוֹצָרוֹ הַטּוֹב אֶת־הַשָּׁמַיִם, לָתֵת מְטַר־אַרְצְךָ בְּעִתּוֹ,

דברים טו
וּלְבָרֵךְ אֵת כָּל־מַעֲשֵׂה יָדֶךָ, וְהִלְוִיתָ גּוֹיִם רַבִּים וְאַתָּה לֹא תִלְוֶה: כִּי־יְהוָה
אֱלֹהֶיךָ בֵּרַכְךָ כַּאֲשֶׁר דִּבֶּר־לָךְ, וְהַעֲבַטְתָּ גּוֹיִם רַבִּים וְאַתָּה לֹא תַעֲבֹט,

דברים לג
וּמָשַׁלְתָּ בְּגוֹיִם רַבִּים וּבְךָ לֹא יִמְשֹׁלוּ: אַשְׁרֶיךָ יִשְׂרָאֵל, מִי כָמוֹךָ, עַם

are you, Israel! Who is like you, a people saved by the LORD? He is your Shield and Helper and your glorious Sword. Your enemies will cower before you, and you will tread on their high places.

מָחִיתִי I have wiped away your transgressions like a cloud, your sins like the morn- *Is. 44* ing mist. Return to Me for I have redeemed you. Sing for joy, O heavens, for the LORD has done this; shout aloud, you depths of the earth; burst into song, you mountains, you forests and all your trees, for the LORD has redeemed Jacob, and will glory in Israel. Our Redeemer, the LORD of hosts is His name, the Holy One *Is. 47* of Israel.

יִשְׂרָאֵל Israel is saved by the LORD with everlasting salvation. You will never be *Is. 45* ashamed or disgraced to time everlasting. You will eat your fill and praise the *Joel 2* name of the LORD your God, who has worked wonders for you. Never again shall My people be shamed. Then you will know that I am in the midst of Israel, that I am the LORD your God, and there is no other. Never again will My people be shamed. You will go out in joy and be led out in peace. The mountains and *Is. 55* hills will burst into song before you, and all the trees of the field will clap their hands. Behold, God is my salvation, I will trust and not be afraid. The LORD, the *Is. 12* LORD, is my strength and my song. He has become my salvation. With joy you will draw water from the springs of salvation. On that day you will say, "Thank the LORD, proclaim His name, make His deeds known among the nations." Declare that His name is exalted. Sing to the LORD, for He has done glorious things; let this be known throughout the world. Shout aloud and sing for joy, you who dwell in Zion, for great in your midst is the Holy One of Israel. On that *Is. 25* day they will say, "See, this is our God; we set our hope in Him and He saved us. This is the LORD in whom we hoped; let us rejoice and be glad in His salvation."

בֵּית Come, house of Jacob: let us walk in the light of the LORD. He will be the *Is. 2* sure foundation of your times; a rich store of salvation, wisdom and knowl- *Is. 32* edge – the fear of the LORD is a person's treasure. In everything he did, David *1 Sam. 18* was successful, for the LORD was with him.

פָּדָה He redeemed my soul in peace from the battle waged against me, for the *Ps. 55* sake of the many who were with me. The people said to Saul, "Shall Jonathan *1 Sam. 14* die – he who has brought about this great deliverance in Israel? Heaven forbid! As surely as the LORD lives, not a hair of his head shall fall to the ground, for he did this today with God's help." So the people rescued Jonathan and he did not die. Those redeemed by the LORD shall return; they will enter Zion singing; *Is. 35* everlasting joy will crown their heads. Gladness and joy will overtake them, and sorrow and sighing will flee away.

נוֹשַׁע בַּיהוה, מָגֵן עֶזְרֶךָ וַאֲשֶׁר־חֶרֶב גַּאֲוָתֶךָ, וְיִכָּחֲשׁוּ אֹיְבֶיךָ לָךְ, וְאַתָּה עַל־בָּמוֹתֵימוֹ תִדְרֹךְ:

ישעיה מד מָחִיתִי כָעָב פְּשָׁעֶיךָ וְכֶעָנָן חַטֹּאותֶיךָ, שׁוּבָה אֵלַי כִּי גְאַלְתִּיךָ: רָנּוּ שָׁמַיִם כִּי־עָשָׂה יהוה, הָרִיעוּ תַּחְתִּיּוֹת אָרֶץ, פִּצְחוּ הָרִים רִנָּה, יַעַר וְכָל־עֵץ בּוֹ, **ישעיה מו** כִּי־גָאַל יהוה יַעֲקֹב וּבְיִשְׂרָאֵל יִתְפָּאָר: גֹּאֲלֵנוּ, יהוה צְבָאוֹת שְׁמוֹ, קְדוֹשׁ יִשְׂרָאֵל:

ישעיה מה יִשְׂרָאֵל נוֹשַׁע בַּיהוה תְּשׁוּעַת עוֹלָמִים, לֹא־תֵבֹשׁוּ וְלֹא־תִכָּלְמוּ עַד־עוֹלְמֵי **יואל ב** עַד: וַאֲכַלְתֶּם אָכוֹל וְשָׂבוֹעַ, וְהִלַּלְתֶּם אֶת־שֵׁם יהוה אֱלֹהֵיכֶם אֲשֶׁר־עָשָׂה עִמָּכֶם לְהַפְלִיא, וְלֹא־יֵבֹשׁוּ עַמִּי לְעוֹלָם: וִידַעְתֶּם כִּי בְקֶרֶב יִשְׂרָאֵל אָנִי, וַאֲנִי יהוה אֱלֹהֵיכֶם וְאֵין עוֹד, וְלֹא־יֵבֹשׁוּ עַמִּי לְעוֹלָם: כִּי־בְשִׂמְחָה **ישעיה נה** תֵצֵאוּ וּבְשָׁלוֹם תּוּבָלוּן, הֶהָרִים וְהַגְּבָעוֹת יִפְצְחוּ לִפְנֵיכֶם רִנָּה, וְכָל־עֲצֵי הַשָּׂדֶה יִמְחֲאוּ־כָף: הִנֵּה אֵל יְשׁוּעָתִי אֶבְטַח, וְלֹא אֶפְחָד, כִּי־עָזִּי וְזִמְרָת **ישעיה יב** יָהּ יהוה, וַיְהִי־לִי לִישׁוּעָה: וּשְׁאַבְתֶּם־מַיִם בְּשָׂשׂוֹן, מִמַּעַיְנֵי הַיְשׁוּעָה: וַאֲמַרְתֶּם בַּיּוֹם הַהוּא, הוֹדוּ לַיהוה קִרְאוּ בִשְׁמוֹ, הוֹדִיעוּ בָעַמִּים עֲלִילֹתָיו, הַזְכִּירוּ כִּי נִשְׂגָּב שְׁמוֹ: זַמְּרוּ יהוה כִּי גֵאוּת עָשָׂה, מוּדַעַת זֹאת בְּכָל־הָאָרֶץ: צַהֲלִי וָרֹנִּי יוֹשֶׁבֶת צִיּוֹן, כִּי־גָדוֹל בְּקִרְבֵּךְ קְדוֹשׁ יִשְׂרָאֵל: וְאָמַר **ישעיה כה** בַּיּוֹם הַהוּא, הִנֵּה אֱלֹהֵינוּ זֶה קִוִּינוּ לוֹ וְיוֹשִׁיעֵנוּ, זֶה יהוה קִוִּינוּ לוֹ, נָגִילָה וְנִשְׂמְחָה בִּישׁוּעָתוֹ:

ישעיה ב **ישעיה לב** **שמואל א יח** בֵּית יַעֲקֹב לְכוּ וְנֵלְכָה בְּאוֹר יהוה: וְהָיָה אֱמוּנַת עִתֶּךָ, חֹסֶן יְשׁוּעֹת חָכְמַת וָדָעַת, יִרְאַת יהוה הִיא אוֹצָרוֹ: וַיְהִי דָוִד לְכָל־דְּרָכָו מַשְׂכִּיל, וַיהוה עִמּוֹ:

תהלים נה **שמואל א יד** פָּדָה בְשָׁלוֹם נַפְשִׁי מִקְּרָב־לִי, כִּי־בְרַבִּים הָיוּ עִמָּדִי: וַיֹּאמֶר הָעָם אֶל־שָׁאוּל, הֲיוֹנָתָן יָמוּת אֲשֶׁר עָשָׂה הַיְשׁוּעָה הַגְּדוֹלָה הַזֹּאת בְּיִשְׂרָאֵל, חָלִילָה, חַי־יהוה אִם־יִפֹּל מִשַּׂעֲרַת רֹאשׁוֹ אַרְצָה, כִּי־עִם־אֱלֹהִים עָשָׂה הַיּוֹם הַזֶּה, וַיִּפְדּוּ הָעָם אֶת־יוֹנָתָן וְלֹא־מֵת: וּפְדוּיֵי יהוה יְשֻׁבוּן וּבָאוּ צִיּוֹן **ישעיה לה** בְּרִנָּה, וְשִׂמְחַת עוֹלָם עַל־רֹאשָׁם, שָׂשׂוֹן וְשִׂמְחָה יַשִּׂיגוּ, וְנָסוּ יָגוֹן וַאֲנָחָה:

הֲפַכְתָּ You have turned my sorrow into dancing. You have removed my sackcloth *Ps. 30* and clothed me with joy. The LORD your God refused to listen to Balaam; in- *Deut. 23* stead the LORD your God turned the curse into a blessing, for the LORD your God loves you. Then maidens will dance and be glad; so too will young men and *Jer. 31* old together; I will turn their mourning into gladness; I will give them comfort and joy instead of sorrow.

בּוֹרֵא I create the speech of lips: Peace, peace to those far and near, says the LORD, *Is. 57* and I will heal them. Then the spirit came upon Amasai, chief of the captains, *1 Chr. 12* and he said: "We are yours, David! We are with you, son of Jesse! Peace, peace to you, and peace to those who help you; for your God will help you." Then David received them and made them leaders of his troop. And you shall say: "To life! *1 Sam. 25* Peace be to you, peace to your household, and peace to all that is yours!" The *Ps. 29* LORD will give strength to His people; the LORD will bless His people with peace.

אָמַר Rabbi Yoḥanan said: Wherever you find the greatness of the Holy One, *Megilla* blessed be He, there you find His humility. This is written in the Torah, repeated *31a* in the Prophets, and stated a third time in the Writings. It is written in the Torah: "For the LORD your God is God of gods and LORD of lords, the great, *Deut. 10* mighty and awe-inspiring God, who shows no favoritism and accepts no bribe." Immediately afterwards it is written, "He upholds the cause of the orphan and widow, and loves the stranger, giving him food and clothing." It is repeated in the Prophets, as it says: "So says the High and Exalted One, who lives for ever and *Is. 57* whose name is Holy: I live in a high and holy place, but also with the contrite and lowly in spirit, to revive the spirit of the lowly, and to revive the heart of the contrite." It is stated a third time in the Writings: "Sing to God, make music for *Ps. 68* His name, extol Him who rides the clouds – the LORD is His name – and exult before Him." Immediately afterwards it is written: "Father of the orphans and Justice of widows, is God in His holy habitation."

יְהִי May the LORD our God be with us, as He was with our ancestors. May He *1 Kings 8* never abandon us or forsake us. You who cleave to the LORD your God are all alive *Deut. 4* this day. For the LORD will comfort Zion, He will comfort all her ruins; He will *Is. 51* make her wilderness like Eden, and her desert like a garden of the LORD. Joy and gladness will be found there, thanksgiving and the sound of singing. It pleased the *Is. 42* LORD for the sake of [Israel's] righteousness to make the Torah great and glorious.

שִׁיר הַמַּעֲלוֹת A song of ascents. Happy are all who fear the LORD, who walk in His *Ps. 128* ways. When you eat the fruit of your labor, happy and fortunate are you. Your wife shall be like a fruitful vine within your house; your sons like olive saplings around your table. So shall the man who fears the LORD be blessed. May the LORD bless you from Zion; may you see the good of Jerusalem all the days of your life; and may you live to see your children's children. Peace be on Israel!

תהלים ל
דברים כג

הָפַכְתָּ מִסְפְּדִי לְמָחוֹל לִי, פִּתַּחְתָּ שַׂקִּי, וַתְּאַזְּרֵנִי שִׂמְחָה: וְלֹא־אָבָה יהוה אֱלֹהֶיךָ לִשְׁמֹעַ אֶל־בִּלְעָם, וַיַּהֲפֹךְ יהוה אֱלֹהֶיךָ לְךָ אֶת־הַקְּלָלָה לִבְרָכָה,

ירמיה לא

כִּי אֲהֵבְךָ יהוה אֱלֹהֶיךָ: אָז תִּשְׂמַח בְּתוּלָה בְּמָחוֹל, וּבַחֻרִים וּזְקֵנִים יַחְדָּו, וְהָפַכְתִּי אֶבְלָם לְשָׂשׂוֹן, וְנִחַמְתִּים, וְשִׂמַּחְתִּים מִיגוֹנָם:

ישעיה נז

בּוֹרֵא נִיב שְׂפָתָיִם, שָׁלוֹם שָׁלוֹם לָרָחוֹק וְלַקָּרוֹב אָמַר יהוה, וּרְפָאתִיו:

דברי
הימים א'יב

וְרוּחַ לָבְשָׁה אֶת־עֲמָשַׂי רֹאשׁ הַשָּׁלִישִׁים, לְךָ דָוִיד וְעִמְּךָ בֶן־יִשַׁי, שָׁלוֹם שָׁלוֹם לְךָ וְשָׁלוֹם לְעֹזְרֶךָ, כִּי עֲזָרְךָ אֱלֹהֶיךָ, וַיְקַבְּלֵם דָּוִיד וַיִּתְּנֵם בְּרָאשֵׁי

שמואל
א'כה

הַגְּדוּד: וַאֲמַרְתֶּם כֹּה לֶחָי, וְאַתָּה שָׁלוֹם וּבֵיתְךָ שָׁלוֹם וְכֹל אֲשֶׁר־לְךָ שָׁלוֹם:

תהלים כט

יהוה עֹז לְעַמּוֹ יִתֵּן, יהוה יְבָרֵךְ אֶת־עַמּוֹ בַשָּׁלוֹם:

מגילה לא.

אָמַר רַבִּי יוֹחָנָן: בְּכָל מָקוֹם שֶׁאַתָּה מוֹצֵא גְּדֻלָּתוֹ שֶׁל הַקָּדוֹשׁ בָּרוּךְ הוּא, שָׁם אַתָּה מוֹצֵא עַנְוְתָנוּתוֹ. דָּבָר זֶה כָּתוּב בַּתּוֹרָה, וְשָׁנוּי בַּנְּבִיאִים,

דברים י

וּמְשֻׁלָּשׁ בַּכְּתוּבִים. כָּתוּב בַּתּוֹרָה: כִּי יהוה אֱלֹהֵיכֶם הוּא אֱלֹהֵי הָאֱלֹהִים וַאֲדֹנֵי הָאֲדֹנִים, הָאֵל הַגָּדֹל הַגִּבֹּר וְהַנּוֹרָא, אֲשֶׁר לֹא־יִשָּׂא פָנִים וְלֹא יִקַּח שֹׁחַד: וּכְתִיב בָּתְרֵהּ: עֹשֶׂה מִשְׁפַּט יָתוֹם וְאַלְמָנָה, וְאֹהֵב גֵּר לָתֶת לוֹ לֶחֶם

ישעיה נז

וְשִׂמְלָה: שָׁנוּי בַּנְּבִיאִים, דִּכְתִיב: כִּי כֹה אָמַר רָם וְנִשָּׂא שֹׁכֵן עַד וְקָדוֹשׁ שְׁמוֹ, מָרוֹם וְקָדוֹשׁ אֶשְׁכּוֹן, וְאֶת־דַּכָּא וּשְׁפַל־רוּחַ, לְהַחֲיוֹת רוּחַ שְׁפָלִים

תהלים סח

וּלְהַחֲיוֹת לֵב נִדְכָּאִים: מְשֻׁלָּשׁ בַּכְּתוּבִים, דִּכְתִיב: שִׁירוּ לֵאלֹהִים, זַמְּרוּ שְׁמוֹ, סֹלּוּ לָרֹכֵב בָּעֲרָבוֹת בְּיָהּ שְׁמוֹ, וְעִלְזוּ לְפָנָיו: וּכְתִיב בָּתְרֵהּ: אֲבִי יְתוֹמִים וְדַיַּן אַלְמָנוֹת, אֱלֹהִים בִּמְעוֹן קָדְשׁוֹ:

מלכים א' ח
דברים ד
ישעיה נא

יְהִי יהוה אֱלֹהֵינוּ עִמָּנוּ כַּאֲשֶׁר הָיָה עִם־אֲבֹתֵינוּ, אַל־יַעַזְבֵנוּ וְאַל־יִטְּשֵׁנוּ: וְאַתֶּם הַדְּבֵקִים בַּיהוה אֱלֹהֵיכֶם, חַיִּים כֻּלְּכֶם הַיּוֹם: כִּי־נִחַם יהוה צִיּוֹן, נִחַם כָּל־חָרְבֹתֶיהָ, וַיָּשֶׂם מִדְבָּרָהּ כְּעֵדֶן וְעַרְבָתָהּ כְּגַן־יהוה, שָׂשׂוֹן וְשִׂמְחָה יִמָּצֵא

ישעיה מב

בָהּ, תּוֹדָה וְקוֹל זִמְרָה: יהוה חָפֵץ לְמַעַן צִדְקוֹ, יַגְדִּיל תּוֹרָה וְיַאְדִּיר:

תהלים קכח

שִׁיר הַמַּעֲלוֹת, אַשְׁרֵי כָּל־יְרֵא יהוה, הַהֹלֵךְ בִּדְרָכָיו: יְגִיעַ כַּפֶּיךָ כִּי תֹאכֵל, אַשְׁרֶיךָ וְטוֹב לָךְ: אֶשְׁתְּךָ כְּגֶפֶן פֹּרִיָּה בְּיַרְכְּתֵי בֵיתֶךָ, בָּנֶיךָ כִּשְׁתִלֵי זֵיתִים, סָבִיב לְשֻׁלְחָנֶךָ: הִנֵּה כִי־כֵן יְבֹרַךְ גָּבֶר יְרֵא יהוה: יְבָרֶכְךָ יהוה מִצִּיּוֹן, וּרְאֵה בְּטוּב יְרוּשָׁלָ͏ִם, כֹּל יְמֵי חַיֶּיךָ: וּרְאֵה־בָנִים לְבָנֶיךָ, שָׁלוֹם עַל־יִשְׂרָאֵל:

HAVDALA IN THE SYNAGOGUE

Some say the full Havdala on page 686.
On Motza'ei Yom Tov that is not on Motza'ei Shabbat, the
blessings for the spices and flame are omitted.

The Leader takes the cup of wine in his right hand, and says:
Please pay attention, my masters.

Blessed are You, LORD our God, King of the Universe,
who creates the fruit of the vine.

Holding the spice box, the Leader says:
Blessed are You, LORD our God, King of the Universe,
who creates the various spices.

The Leader smells the spices and puts the spice box down.
He lifts his hands toward the flame of the Havdala candle and says:
Blessed are You, LORD our God, King of the Universe,
who creates the lights of fire.

He lifts the cup of wine in his right hand, and says:
Blessed are You, LORD our God, King of the Universe,
who distinguishes between sacred and secular,
between light and darkness,
between Israel and the nations,
between the seventh day and the six days of work.
Blessed are You, LORD,
who distinguishes between sacred and secular.

Stand while saying Aleinu. Bow at ˙.
עָלֵינוּ It is our duty to praise the Master of all,
and ascribe greatness to the Author of creation,
who has not made us like the nations of the lands
nor placed us like the families of the earth;
who has not made our portion like theirs,
nor our destiny like all their multitudes.
(For they worship vanity and emptiness,
and pray to a god who cannot save.)
˙But we bow in worship and thank the Supreme King of kings,
the Holy One, blessed be He,

הבדלה בבית הכנסת

Some say the full הבדלה *on page 687.*

On מוצאי שבת *that is not on* מוצאי יום טוב,
the blessings for the spices and flame are omitted.

The שליח ציבור *takes the cup of wine in his right hand, and says:*

סַבְרִי מָרָנָן

בָּרוּךְ אַתָּה יהוה אֱלֹהֵינוּ מֶלֶךְ הָעוֹלָם, בּוֹרֵא פְּרִי הַגָּפֶן.

Holding the spice box, the שליח ציבור *says:*

בָּרוּךְ אַתָּה יהוה אֱלֹהֵינוּ מֶלֶךְ הָעוֹלָם, בּוֹרֵא מִינֵי בְשָׂמִים.

The שליח ציבור *smells the spices and puts the spice box down.*
He lifts his hands toward the flame of the הבדלה *candle and says:*

בָּרוּךְ אַתָּה יהוה אֱלֹהֵינוּ מֶלֶךְ הָעוֹלָם, בּוֹרֵא מְאוֹרֵי הָאֵשׁ.

He lifts the cup of wine in his right hand, and says:

בָּרוּךְ אַתָּה יהוה אֱלֹהֵינוּ מֶלֶךְ הָעוֹלָם

הַמַּבְדִּיל בֵּין קֹדֶשׁ לְחֹל

בֵּין אוֹר לְחֹשֶׁךְ, בֵּין יִשְׂרָאֵל לָעַמִּים

בֵּין יוֹם הַשְּׁבִיעִי לְשֵׁשֶׁת יְמֵי הַמַּעֲשֶׂה.

בָּרוּךְ אַתָּה יהוה, הַמַּבְדִּיל בֵּין קֹדֶשׁ לְחֹל.

Stand while saying עָלֵינוּ. *Bow at* ˚.

עָלֵינוּ לְשַׁבֵּחַ לַאֲדוֹן הַכֹּל, לָתֵת גְּדֻלָּה לְיוֹצֵר בְּרֵאשִׁית

שֶׁלֹּא עָשָׂנוּ כְּגוֹיֵי הָאֲרָצוֹת, וְלֹא שָׂמָנוּ כְּמִשְׁפְּחוֹת הָאֲדָמָה

שֶׁלֹּא שָׂם חֶלְקֵנוּ כָּהֶם וְגוֹרָלֵנוּ כְּכָל הֲמוֹנָם.

(שֶׁהֵם מִשְׁתַּחֲוִים לְהֶבֶל וָרִיק וּמִתְפַּלְלִים אֶל אֵל לֹא יוֹשִׁיעַ.)

˚וַאֲנַחְנוּ כּוֹרְעִים וּמִשְׁתַּחֲוִים וּמוֹדִים

לִפְנֵי מֶלֶךְ מַלְכֵי הַמְּלָכִים, הַקָּדוֹשׁ בָּרוּךְ הוּא

who extends the heavens and establishes the earth,
whose throne of glory is in the heavens above,
and whose power's Presence is in the highest of heights.
He is our God; there is no other.
Truly He is our King, there is none else, as it is written in His Torah:
"You shall know and take to heart this day that the LORD is God,   *Deut. 4*
in heaven above and on earth below.
There is no other."

Therefore, we place our hope in You, LORD our God,
that we may soon see the glory of Your power,
when You will remove abominations from the earth,
and idols will be utterly destroyed,
when the world will be perfected
under the sovereignty of the Almighty,
when all humanity will call on Your name,
to turn all the earth's wicked toward You.
All the world's inhabitants will realize and know
that to You every knee must bow and every tongue swear loyalty.
Before You, LORD our God, they will kneel and bow down
and give honor to Your glorious name.
They will all accept the yoke of Your kingdom,
and You will reign over them soon and for ever.
For the kingdom is Yours, and to all eternity You will reign in glory,
as it is written in Your Torah:
"The LORD will reign for ever and ever."   *Ex. 15*
▸ And it is said: "Then the LORD shall be King over all the earth;   *Zech. 14*
on that day the LORD shall be One and His name One."

Some add:
Have no fear of sudden terror or of the ruin when it overtakes the wicked.   *Prov. 3*
Devise your strategy, but it will be thwarted; propose your plan,   *Is. 8*
but it will not stand, for God is with us.
When you grow old, I will still be the same.   *Is. 46*
When your hair turns gray, I will still carry you.
I made you, I will bear you,
I will carry you, and I will rescue you.

שֶׁהוּא נוֹטֶה שָׁמַיִם וְיֹסֵד אָרֶץ, וּמוֹשַׁב יְקָרוֹ בַּשָּׁמַיִם מִמַּעַל
וּשְׁכִינַת עֻזּוֹ בְּגָבְהֵי מְרוֹמִים.
הוּא אֱלֹהֵינוּ, אֵין עוֹד.
אֱמֶת מַלְכֵּנוּ, אֶפֶס זוּלָתוֹ
כַּכָּתוּב בְּתוֹרָתוֹ

דברים ד

וְיָדַעְתָּ הַיּוֹם וַהֲשֵׁבֹתָ אֶל־לְבָבֶךָ
כִּי יְהוָה הוּא הָאֱלֹהִים בַּשָּׁמַיִם מִמַּעַל וְעַל־הָאָרֶץ מִתָּחַת
אֵין עוֹד:

עַל כֵּן נְקַוֶּה לְּךָ יְהוָה אֱלֹהֵינוּ, לִרְאוֹת מְהֵרָה בְּתִפְאֶרֶת עֻזֶּךָ
לְהַעֲבִיר גִּלּוּלִים מִן הָאָרֶץ, וְהָאֱלִילִים כָּרוֹת יִכָּרֵתוּן
לְתַקֵּן עוֹלָם בְּמַלְכוּת שַׁדַּי.
וְכָל בְּנֵי בָשָׂר יִקְרְאוּ בִשְׁמֶךָ לְהַפְנוֹת אֵלֶיךָ כָּל רִשְׁעֵי אָרֶץ.
יַכִּירוּ וְיֵדְעוּ כָּל יוֹשְׁבֵי תֵבֵל
כִּי לְךָ תִּכְרַע כָּל בֶּרֶךְ, תִּשָּׁבַע כָּל לָשׁוֹן.
לְפָנֶיךָ יְהוָה אֱלֹהֵינוּ יִכְרְעוּ וְיִפֹּלוּ, וְלִכְבוֹד שִׁמְךָ יְקָר יִתֵּנוּ
וִיקַבְּלוּ כֻלָּם אֶת עֹל מַלְכוּתֶךָ וְתִמְלֹךְ עֲלֵיהֶם מְהֵרָה לְעוֹלָם וָעֶד.
כִּי הַמַּלְכוּת שֶׁלְּךָ הִיא וּלְעוֹלְמֵי עַד תִּמְלֹךְ בְּכָבוֹד

שמות טו

כַּכָּתוּב בְּתוֹרָתֶךָ, יְהוָה יִמְלֹךְ לְעֹלָם וָעֶד:

זכריה יד

‹ וְנֶאֱמַר, וְהָיָה יְהוָה לְמֶלֶךְ עַל־כָּל־הָאָרֶץ
בַּיּוֹם הַהוּא יִהְיֶה יְהוָה אֶחָד וּשְׁמוֹ אֶחָד:

Some add:

משלי ג

אַל־תִּירָא מִפַּחַד פִּתְאֹם וּמִשֹּׁאַת רְשָׁעִים כִּי תָבֹא:

ישעיה ח

עֻצוּ עֵצָה וְתֻפָר, דַּבְּרוּ דָבָר וְלֹא יָקוּם, כִּי עִמָּנוּ אֵל:

ישעיה מו

וְעַד־זִקְנָה אֲנִי הוּא, וְעַד־שֵׂיבָה אֲנִי אֶסְבֹּל
אֲנִי עָשִׂיתִי וַאֲנִי אֶשָּׂא וַאֲנִי אֶסְבֹּל וַאֲמַלֵּט:

MOURNER'S KADDISH

*The following prayer, said by mourners, requires the presence of a minyan.
A transliteration can be found on page 779.*

Mourner: יִתְגַּדַּל Magnified and sanctified
may His great name be,
in the world He created by His will.
May He establish His kingdom
in your lifetime and in your days,
and in the lifetime of all the house of Israel,
swiftly and soon –
and say: Amen.

All: May His great name be blessed
for ever and all time.

Mourner: Blessed and praised,
glorified and exalted,
raised and honored,
uplifted and lauded
be the name of the Holy One,
blessed be He,
beyond any blessing,
song, praise and consolation
uttered in the world –
and say: Amen.

May there be great peace from heaven,
and life for us and all Israel –
and say: Amen.

*Bow, take three steps back, as if taking leave of the Divine Presence,
then bow, first left, then right, then center, while saying:*
May He who makes peace in His high places,
make peace for us and all Israel –
and say: Amen.

קדיש יתום

The following prayer, said by mourners, requires the presence of a מנין.
A transliteration can be found on page 779.

אבל: יִתְגַּדַּל וְיִתְקַדַּשׁ שְׁמֵהּ רַבָּא (קהל: אָמֵן)

בְּעָלְמָא דִּי בְרָא כִרְעוּתֵהּ

וְיַמְלִיךְ מַלְכוּתֵהּ

בְּחַיֵּיכוֹן וּבְיוֹמֵיכוֹן וּבְחַיֵּי דְּכָל בֵּית יִשְׂרָאֵל

בַּעֲגָלָא וּבִזְמַן קָרִיב

וְאִמְרוּ אָמֵן. (קהל: אָמֵן)

קהל
ואבל: יְהֵא שְׁמֵהּ רַבָּא מְבָרַךְ לְעָלַם וּלְעָלְמֵי עָלְמַיָּא.

אבל: יִתְבָּרַךְ וְיִשְׁתַּבַּח וְיִתְפָּאַר

וְיִתְרוֹמַם וְיִתְנַשֵּׂא וְיִתְהַדָּר וְיִתְעַלֶּה וְיִתְהַלָּל

שְׁמֵהּ דְּקֻדְשָׁא בְּרִיךְ הוּא (קהל: בְּרִיךְ הוּא)

לְעֵלָּא מִן כָּל בִּרְכָתָא וְשִׁירָתָא

תֻּשְׁבְּחָתָא וְנֶחֱמָתָא

דַּאֲמִירָן בְּעָלְמָא

וְאִמְרוּ אָמֵן. (קהל: אָמֵן)

יְהֵא שְׁלָמָא רַבָּא מִן שְׁמַיָּא

וְחַיִּים, עָלֵינוּ וְעַל כָּל יִשְׂרָאֵל

וְאִמְרוּ אָמֵן. (קהל: אָמֵן)

Bow, take three steps back, as if taking leave of the Divine Presence,
then bow, first left, then right, then center, while saying:

עֹשֶׂה שָׁלוֹם בִּמְרוֹמָיו

הוּא יַעֲשֶׂה שָׁלוֹם עָלֵינוּ וְעַל כָּל יִשְׂרָאֵל

וְאִמְרוּ אָמֵן. (קהל: אָמֵן)

BLESSING OF THE NEW MOON

*Kiddush Levana, the Blessing of the New Moon, is said between the
third day and the middle day of each month. If possible, it should be
said, under the open sky, and in the presence of a minyan. See law 17.*

הַלְלוּיָהּ Halleluya! Praise the LORD from the heavens, praise Him   *Ps. 148*
in the heights. Praise Him, all His angels; praise Him, all His hosts.
Praise Him, sun and moon; praise Him, all shining stars. Praise
Him, highest heavens and the waters above the heavens. Let them
praise the name of the LORD, for He commanded and they were
created. He established them for ever and all time, issuing a decree
that will never change.

כִּי־אֶרְאֶה When I see Your heavens, the work of Your fingers,   *Ps. 8*
the moon and the stars which You have set in place:
What is man that You are mindful of him,
the son of man that You care for him?

Look at the moon, then say:

בָּרוּךְ Blessed are You, LORD our God, King of the Universe
who by His word created the heavens,
and by His breath all their host.
He set for them laws and times,
so that they should not deviate from their appointed task.
They are joyous and glad
to perform the will of their Owner,
the Worker of truth whose work is truth.
To the moon He said that it should renew itself
as a crown of beauty
for those He carried from the womb [Israel],
for they are destined to be renewed like it,
and to praise their Creator
for the sake of His glorious majesty.
Blessed are You, LORD, who renews the months.

קידוש לבנה

קידוש לבנה, *the Blessing of the New Moon, is said between the third day and the middle day of each month. If possible, it should be said, under the open sky, and in the presence of a* מנין. *See law 17.*

תהלים קמח

הַלְלוּיָהּ, הַלְלוּ אֶת־יהוה מִן־הַשָּׁמַיִם, הַלְלוּהוּ בַּמְּרוֹמִים: הַלְלוּהוּ כָל־מַלְאָכָיו, הַלְלוּהוּ כָּל־צְבָאָו: הַלְלוּהוּ שֶׁמֶשׁ וְיָרֵחַ, הַלְלוּהוּ כָּל־כּוֹכְבֵי אוֹר: הַלְלוּהוּ שְׁמֵי הַשָּׁמָיִם, וְהַמַּיִם אֲשֶׁר מֵעַל הַשָּׁמָיִם: יְהַלְלוּ אֶת־שֵׁם יהוה, כִּי הוּא צִוָּה וְנִבְרָאוּ: וַיַּעֲמִידֵם לָעַד לְעוֹלָם, חָק־נָתַן וְלֹא יַעֲבוֹר:

תהלים ח

כִּי־אֶרְאֶה שָׁמֶיךָ מַעֲשֵׂה אֶצְבְּעֹתֶיךָ יָרֵחַ וְכוֹכָבִים אֲשֶׁר כּוֹנָנְתָּה: מָה־אֱנוֹשׁ כִּי־תִזְכְּרֶנּוּ וּבֶן־אָדָם כִּי תִפְקְדֶנּוּ:

Look at the moon, then say:

בָּרוּךְ אַתָּה יהוה אֱלֹהֵינוּ מֶלֶךְ הָעוֹלָם אֲשֶׁר בְּמַאֲמָרוֹ בָּרָא שְׁחָקִים, וּבְרוּחַ פִּיו כָּל צְבָאָם חֹק וּזְמַן נָתַן לָהֶם שֶׁלֹּא יְשַׁנּוּ אֶת תַּפְקִידָם. שָׂשִׂים וּשְׂמֵחִים לַעֲשׂוֹת רְצוֹן קוֹנָם פּוֹעֵל אֱמֶת שֶׁפְּעֻלָּתוֹ אֱמֶת. וְלַלְּבָנָה אָמַר שֶׁתִּתְחַדֵּשׁ עֲטֶרֶת תִּפְאֶרֶת לַעֲמוּסֵי בָטֶן שֶׁהֵם עֲתִידִים לְהִתְחַדֵּשׁ כְּמוֹתָהּ וּלְפָאֵר לְיוֹצְרָם עַל שֵׁם כְּבוֹד מַלְכוּתוֹ. בָּרוּךְ אַתָּה יהוה, מְחַדֵּשׁ חֳדָשִׁים.

The following five verses are each said three times:
Blessed is He who formed you;
blessed is He who made you;
blessed is He who owns you;
blessed is He who created you.

The following verse is said rising on the toes.
Just as I leap toward you but cannot touch you,
so may none of my enemies be able to touch me
to do me harm.

May fear and dread fall upon them;   *Ex. 15*
by the power of Your arm may they be still as stone.

May they be still as stone through the power of Your arm,
when dread and fear fall upon them.

David, King of Israel, lives and endures.

Turn to three people and say to each:
Peace upon you.

They respond:
Upon you, peace.

Say three times:
May it be a good sign and a good omen
for us and all Israel.
Amen.

קוֹל Hark! My beloved!   *Song. 2*
Here he comes, leaping over the mountains,
bounding over the hills.
My beloved is like a gazelle, like a young deer.
There he stands outside our wall,
peering in through the windows,
gazing through the lattice.

The following five verses are each said three times:

בָּרוּךְ יוֹצְרֵךְ, בָּרוּךְ עוֹשֵׂךְ, בָּרוּךְ קוֹנֵךְ, בָּרוּךְ בּוֹרְאֵךְ.

The following verse is said rising on the toes.

כְּשֵׁם שֶׁאֲנִי רוֹקֵד כְּנֶגְדֵּךְ

וְאֵינִי יָכוֹל לִנְגֹּעַ בָּךְ

כָּךְ לֹא יוּכְלוּ כָּל אוֹיְבַי לִנְגֹּעַ בִּי לְרָעָה.

שמות טו

תִּפֹּל עֲלֵיהֶם אֵימָתָה וָפַחַד

בִּגְדֹל זְרוֹעֲךָ יִדְּמוּ כָּאָבֶן:

כָּאָבֶן יִדְּמוּ זְרוֹעֲךָ בִּגְדֹל

וָפַחַד אֵימָתָה עֲלֵיהֶם תִּפֹּל.

דָּוִד מֶלֶךְ יִשְׂרָאֵל חַי וְקַיָּם.

Turn to three people and say to each:

שָׁלוֹם עֲלֵיכֶם.

They respond:

עֲלֵיכֶם שָׁלוֹם.

Say three times:

סִימָן טוֹב וּמַזָּל טוֹב יְהֵא לָנוּ וּלְכָל יִשְׂרָאֵל, אָמֵן.

שיר השירים ב

קוֹל דּוֹדִי הִנֵּה־זֶה בָּא

מְדַלֵּג עַל־הֶהָרִים, מְקַפֵּץ עַל־הַגְּבָעוֹת:

דּוֹמֶה דוֹדִי לִצְבִי אוֹ לְעֹפֶר הָאַיָּלִים

הִנֵּה־זֶה עוֹמֵד אַחַר כָּתְלֵנוּ

מַשְׁגִּיחַ מִן־הַחַלֹּנוֹת, מֵצִיץ מִן־הַחֲרַכִּים:

שִׁיר לַמַּעֲלוֹת A song of ascents. I lift my eyes up to the hills; from where *Ps. 121* will my help come? My help comes from the LORD, Maker of heaven and earth. He will not let your foot stumble; He who guards you does not slumber. See: the Guardian of Israel neither slumbers nor sleeps. The LORD is your Guardian; the LORD is your Shade at your right hand. The sun will not strike you by day, nor the moon by night. The LORD will guard you from all harm; He will guard your life. The LORD will guard your going and coming, now and for evermore.

הַלְלוּיָהּ Halleluya! Praise God in His holy place; praise Him in the heav- *Ps. 150* ens of His power. Praise Him for His mighty deeds; praise Him for His surpassing greatness. Praise Him with blasts of the ram's horn; praise Him with the harp and lyre. Praise Him with timbrel and dance; praise Him with strings and flute. Praise Him with clashing cymbals; praise Him with resounding cymbals. Let all that breathes praise the LORD. Halleluya! Let all that breathes praise the LORD. Halleluya!

תָּנָא In the academy of Rabbi Yishmael it was taught: Were the people of *Sanhedrin* Israel privileged to greet the presence of their heavenly Father only once *42a* a month, it would have been sufficient for them. Abaye said: Therefore it [the blessing of the moon] should be said standing. Who is this coming *Song. 8* up from the desert, leaning on her beloved?

וִיהִי May it be Your will, LORD my God and God of my ancestors, to make good the deficiency of the moon, so that it is no longer in its diminished state. May the light of the moon be like the light of the sun and like the light of the seven days of creation as it was before it was diminished, as it says, "The two great luminaries." And may there be fulfilled for us the *Gen. 1* verse: "They shall seek the LORD their God, and David their king." Amen. *Hos. 3*

לַמְנַצֵּחַ For the conductor of music. With stringed instruments, a psalm. *Ps. 67* A song. May God be gracious to us and bless us. May He make His face shine on us, Selah. Then will Your way be known on earth, Your salvation among all the nations. Let the peoples praise You, God; let all peoples praise You. Let nations rejoice and sing for joy, for You judge the peoples with equity, and guide the nations of the earth, Selah. Let the peoples praise You, God; let all peoples praise You. The earth has yielded its harvest. May God, our God, bless us. God will bless us, and all the ends of the earth will fear Him.

תהלים קכא

שִׁיר לַמַּעֲלוֹת, אֶשָּׂא עֵינַי אֶל־הֶהָרִים, מֵאַיִן יָבֹא עֶזְרִי: עֶזְרִי מֵעִם יהוה, עֹשֵׂה שָׁמַיִם וָאָרֶץ: אַל־יִתֵּן לַמּוֹט רַגְלֶךָ, אַל־יָנוּם שֹׁמְרֶךָ: הִנֵּה לֹא־יָנוּם וְלֹא יִישָׁן, שׁוֹמֵר יִשְׂרָאֵל: יהוה שֹׁמְרֶךָ, יהוה צִלְּךָ עַל־יַד יְמִינֶךָ: יוֹמָם הַשֶּׁמֶשׁ לֹא־יַכֶּכָּה, וְיָרֵחַ בַּלָּיְלָה: יהוה יִשְׁמָרְךָ מִכָּל־רָע, יִשְׁמֹר אֶת־נַפְשֶׁךָ: יהוה יִשְׁמָר־צֵאתְךָ וּבוֹאֶךָ, מֵעַתָּה וְעַד־עוֹלָם:

תהלים קנ

הַלְלוּיָהּ, הַלְלוּ־אֵל בְּקָדְשׁוֹ, הַלְלוּהוּ בִּרְקִיעַ עֻזּוֹ: הַלְלוּהוּ בִגְבוּרֹתָיו, הַלְלוּהוּ כְּרֹב גֻּדְלוֹ: הַלְלוּהוּ בְּתֵקַע שׁוֹפָר, הַלְלוּהוּ בְּנֵבֶל וְכִנּוֹר: הַלְלוּהוּ בְּתֹף וּמָחוֹל, הַלְלוּהוּ בְּמִנִּים וְעֻגָב: הַלְלוּהוּ בְצִלְצְלֵי־שָׁמַע, הַלְלוּהוּ בְּצִלְצְלֵי תְרוּעָה: כֹּל הַנְּשָׁמָה תְּהַלֵּל יָהּ, הַלְלוּיָהּ:

סנהדרין מב.

תָּנָא דְּבֵי רַבִּי יִשְׁמָעֵאל: אִלְמָלֵי לֹא זָכוּ יִשְׂרָאֵל אֶלָּא לְהַקְבִּיל פְּנֵי אֲבִיהֶם שֶׁבַּשָּׁמַיִם פַּעַם אַחַת בַּחֹדֶשׁ, דַּיָּם. אָמַר אַבַּיֵּי: הִלְכָּךְ צָרִיךְ לְמֵימְרָא מְעֻמָּד. מִי זֹאת עֹלָה מִן־הַמִּדְבָּר, מִתְרַפֶּקֶת עַל־דּוֹדָהּ:

שיר השירים ח

יְהִי רָצוֹן מִלְּפָנֶיךָ יהוה אֱלֹהַי וֵאלֹהֵי אֲבוֹתַי, לְמַלֹּאת פְּגִימַת הַלְּבָנָה וְלֹא יִהְיֶה בָּהּ שׁוּם מִעוּט. וִיהִי אוֹר הַלְּבָנָה כְּאוֹר הַחַמָּה וּכְאוֹר שִׁבְעַת יְמֵי בְרֵאשִׁית, כְּמוֹ שֶׁהָיְתָה קֹדֶם מִעוּטָהּ, שֶׁנֶּאֱמַר:

בראשית א
הושע ג

אֶת־שְׁנֵי הַמְּאֹרֹת הַגְּדֹלִים: וְיִתְקַיֵּם בָּנוּ מִקְרָא שֶׁכָּתוּב: וּבִקְשׁוּ אֶת־יהוה אֱלֹהֵיהֶם וְאֵת דָּוִד מַלְכָּם: אָמֵן:

תהלים סז

לַמְנַצֵּחַ בִּנְגִינֹת, מִזְמוֹר שִׁיר: אֱלֹהִים יְחָנֵּנוּ וִיבָרְכֵנוּ, יָאֵר פָּנָיו אִתָּנוּ סֶלָה: לָדַעַת בָּאָרֶץ דַּרְכֶּךָ, בְּכָל־גּוֹיִם יְשׁוּעָתֶךָ: יוֹדוּךָ עַמִּים אֱלֹהִים, יוֹדוּךָ עַמִּים כֻּלָּם: יִשְׂמְחוּ וִירַנְּנוּ לְאֻמִּים, כִּי־תִשְׁפֹּט עַמִּים מִישֹׁר, וּלְאֻמִּים בָּאָרֶץ תַּנְחֵם סֶלָה: יוֹדוּךָ עַמִּים אֱלֹהִים, יוֹדוּךָ עַמִּים כֻּלָּם: אֶרֶץ נָתְנָה יְבוּלָהּ, יְבָרְכֵנוּ אֱלֹהִים אֱלֹהֵינוּ: יְבָרְכֵנוּ אֱלֹהִים, וְיִירְאוּ אוֹתוֹ כָּל־אַפְסֵי־אָרֶץ:

Stand while saying Aleinu. Bow at ˇ.

עָלֵינוּ It is our duty to praise the Master of all, and ascribe greatness to the Author of creation, who has not made us like the nations of the lands nor placed us like the families of the earth; who has not made our portion like theirs, nor our destiny like all their multitudes. (For they worship vanity and emptiness, and pray to a god who cannot save.) ˇBut we bow in worship and thank the Supreme King of kings, the Holy One, blessed be He, who extends the heavens and establishes the earth, whose throne of glory is in the heavens above, and whose power's Presence is in the highest of heights. He is our God; there is no other. Truly He is our King, there is none else, as it is written in His Torah: "You shall know and take to heart this day that the LORD is God, in heaven above and on earth below. There is no other." *Deut. 4*

Therefore, we place our hope in You, LORD our God, that we may soon see the glory of Your power, when You will remove abominations from the earth, and idols will be utterly destroyed, when the world will be perfected under the sovereignty of the Almighty, when all humanity will call on Your name, to turn all the earth's wicked toward You. All the world's inhabitants will realize and know that to You every knee must bow and every tongue swear loyalty. Before You, LORD our God, they will kneel and bow down and give honor to Your glorious name. They will all accept the yoke of Your kingdom, and You will reign over them soon and for ever. For the kingdom is Yours, and to all eternity You will reign in glory, as it is written in Your Torah: "The LORD will reign for ever and ever." ▸ And it is said: "Then the LORD shall be King over all the earth; on that day the LORD shall be One and His name One." *Ex. 15* *Zech. 14*

Some add:

Have no fear of sudden terror or of the ruin when it overtakes the wicked. Devise your strategy, but it will be thwarted; propose your plan, but it will not stand, for God is with us. When you grow old, I will still be the same. When your hair turns gray, I will still carry you. I made you, I will bear you, I will carry you, and I will rescue you. *Prov. 3* *Is. 8* *Is. 46*

Stand while saying עָלֵינוּ. Bow at ˙.

עָלֵינוּ לְשַׁבֵּחַ לַאֲדוֹן הַכֹּל, לָתֵת גְּדֻלָּה לְיוֹצֵר בְּרֵאשִׁית
שֶׁלֹּא עָשָׂנוּ כְּגוֹיֵי הָאֲרָצוֹת, וְלֹא שָׂמָנוּ כְּמִשְׁפְּחוֹת הָאֲדָמָה
שֶׁלֹּא שָׂם חֶלְקֵנוּ כָּהֶם וְגוֹרָלֵנוּ כְּכָל הֲמוֹנָם.
(שֶׁהֵם מִשְׁתַּחֲוִים לְהֶבֶל וָרִיק וּמִתְפַּלְּלִים אֶל אֵל לֹא יוֹשִׁיעַ.)
וַאֲנַחְנוּ כּוֹרְעִים וּמִשְׁתַּחֲוִים וּמוֹדִים
לִפְנֵי מֶלֶךְ מַלְכֵי הַמְּלָכִים, הַקָּדוֹשׁ בָּרוּךְ הוּא
שֶׁהוּא נוֹטֶה שָׁמַיִם וְיוֹסֵד אָרֶץ, וּמוֹשַׁב יְקָרוֹ בַּשָּׁמַיִם מִמַּעַל
וּשְׁכִינַת עֻזּוֹ בְּגָבְהֵי מְרוֹמִים.
הוּא אֱלֹהֵינוּ, אֵין עוֹד.
אֱמֶת מַלְכֵּנוּ, אֶפֶס זוּלָתוֹ, כַּכָּתוּב בְּתוֹרָתוֹ
וְיָדַעְתָּ הַיּוֹם וַהֲשֵׁבֹתָ אֶל לְבָבֶךָ | דברים ד
כִּי יהוה הוּא הָאֱלֹהִים בַּשָּׁמַיִם מִמַּעַל וְעַל הָאָרֶץ מִתָּחַת אֵין עוֹד:

עַל כֵּן נְקַוֶּה לְּךָ יהוה אֱלֹהֵינוּ, לִרְאוֹת מְהֵרָה בְּתִפְאֶרֶת עֻזֶּךָ
לְהַעֲבִיר גִּלּוּלִים מִן הָאָרֶץ, וְהָאֱלִילִים כָּרוֹת יִכָּרֵתוּן
לְתַקֵּן עוֹלָם בְּמַלְכוּת שַׁדַּי.
וְכָל בְּנֵי בָשָׂר יִקְרְאוּ בִשְׁמֶךָ לְהַפְנוֹת אֵלֶיךָ כָּל רִשְׁעֵי אָרֶץ.
יַכִּירוּ וְיֵדְעוּ כָּל יוֹשְׁבֵי תֵבֵל כִּי לְךָ תִּכְרַע כָּל בֶּרֶךְ, תִּשָּׁבַע כָּל לָשׁוֹן.
לְפָנֶיךָ יהוה אֱלֹהֵינוּ יִכְרְעוּ וְיִפֹּלוּ, וְלִכְבוֹד שִׁמְךָ יְקָר יִתֵּנוּ
וִיקַבְּלוּ כֻלָּם אֶת עֹל מַלְכוּתֶךָ וְתִמְלֹךְ עֲלֵיהֶם מְהֵרָה לְעוֹלָם וָעֶד.
כִּי הַמַּלְכוּת שֶׁלְּךָ הִיא וּלְעוֹלְמֵי עַד תִּמְלֹךְ בְּכָבוֹד
כַּכָּתוּב בְּתוֹרָתֶךָ, יהוה יִמְלֹךְ לְעֹלָם וָעֶד: | שמות טו
‹ וְנֶאֱמַר, וְהָיָה יהוה לְמֶלֶךְ עַל כָּל הָאָרֶץ | זכריה יד
בַּיּוֹם הַהוּא יִהְיֶה יהוה אֶחָד וּשְׁמוֹ אֶחָד:

Some add:

אַל תִּירָא מִפַּחַד פִּתְאֹם וּמִשֹּׁאַת רְשָׁעִים כִּי תָבֹא: | משלי ג
עֻצוּ עֵצָה וְתֻפָר, דַּבְּרוּ דָבָר וְלֹא יָקוּם, כִּי עִמָּנוּ אֵל: | ישעיה ח
וְעַד זִקְנָה אֲנִי הוּא, וְעַד שֵׂיבָה אֲנִי אֶסְבֹּל אֲנִי עָשִׂיתִי וַאֲנִי אֶשָּׂא וַאֲנִי אֶסְבֹּל וַאֲמַלֵּט: | ישעיה מו

MOURNER'S KADDISH

The following prayer, said by mourners, requires the presence of a minyan.
A transliteration can be found on page 779.

Mourner: יִתְגַּדַּל Magnified and sanctified may His great name be,
in the world He created by His will.
May He establish His kingdom
in your lifetime and in your days,
and in the lifetime of all the house of Israel,
swiftly and soon – and say: Amen.

All: May His great name be blessed for ever and all time.

Mourner: Blessed and praised, glorified and exalted,
raised and honored, uplifted and lauded
be the name of the Holy One, blessed be He,
beyond any blessing, song, praise and consolation
uttered in the world – and say: Amen.

May there be great peace from heaven,
and life for us and all Israel – and say: Amen.

Bow, take three steps back, as if taking leave of the Divine Presence,
then bow, first left, then right, then center, while saying:

May He who makes peace in His high places,
make peace for us and all Israel – and say: Amen.

All sing:

טוֹבִים Good are the radiant stars our God created;
He formed them with knowledge,
understanding and deliberation.
He gave them strength and might
to rule throughout the world.

Full of splendor, radiating light,
beautiful is their splendor throughout the world.
Glad as they go forth, joyous as they return,
they fulfill with awe their Creator's will.

Glory and honor they give to His name,
jubilation and song at the mention of His majesty.
He called the sun into being and it shone with light.
He looked and fashioned the form of the moon.

קדיש יתום

The following prayer, said by mourners, requires the presence of a מנין.
A transliteration can be found on page 779.

אבל: יִתְגַּדַּל וְיִתְקַדַּשׁ שְׁמֵהּ רַבָּא (קהל: אָמֵן)
בְּעָלְמָא דִּי בְרָא כִרְעוּתֵהּ
וְיַמְלִיךְ מַלְכוּתֵהּ
בְּחַיֵּיכוֹן וּבְיוֹמֵיכוֹן וּבְחַיֵּי דְכָל בֵּית יִשְׂרָאֵל
בַּעֲגָלָא וּבִזְמַן קָרִיב, וְאִמְרוּ אָמֵן. (קהל: אָמֵן)

קהל
ואבל: יְהֵא שְׁמֵהּ רַבָּא מְבָרַךְ לְעָלַם וּלְעָלְמֵי עָלְמַיָּא.

אבל: יִתְבָּרַךְ וְיִשְׁתַּבַּח וְיִתְפָּאַר
וְיִתְרוֹמַם וְיִתְנַשֵּׂא וְיִתְהַדָּר וְיִתְעַלֶּה וְיִתְהַלָּל
שְׁמֵהּ דְּקֻדְשָׁא בְּרִיךְ הוּא (קהל: בְּרִיךְ הוּא)
לְעֵלָּא מִן כָּל בִּרְכָתָא וְשִׁירָתָא, תֻּשְׁבְּחָתָא וְנֶחֱמָתָא
דַּאֲמִירָן בְּעָלְמָא, וְאִמְרוּ אָמֵן. (קהל: אָמֵן)

יְהֵא שְׁלָמָא רַבָּא מִן שְׁמַיָּא
וְחַיִּים, עָלֵינוּ וְעַל כָּל יִשְׂרָאֵל, וְאִמְרוּ אָמֵן. (קהל: אָמֵן)

Bow, take three steps back, as if taking leave of the Divine Presence,
then bow, first left, then right, then center, while saying:

עֹשֶׂה שָׁלוֹם בִּמְרוֹמָיו
הוּא יַעֲשֶׂה שָׁלוֹם עָלֵינוּ וְעַל כָּל יִשְׂרָאֵל, וְאִמְרוּ אָמֵן. (קהל: אָמֵן)

All sing:

טוֹבִים מְאוֹרוֹת שֶׁבָּרָא אֱלֹהֵינוּ, יְצָרָם בְּדַעַת בְּבִינָה וּבְהַשְׂכֵּל
כֹּחַ וּגְבוּרָה נָתַן בָּהֶם, לִהְיוֹת מוֹשְׁלִים בְּקֶרֶב תֵּבֵל.

מְלֵאִים זִיו וּמְפִיקִים נֹגַהּ, נָאֶה זִיוָם בְּכָל הָעוֹלָם
שְׂמֵחִים בְּצֵאתָם וְשָׂשִׂים בְּבוֹאָם, עוֹשִׂים בְּאֵימָה רְצוֹן קוֹנָם.

פְּאֵר וְכָבוֹד נוֹתְנִים לִשְׁמוֹ, צָהֳלָה וְרִנָּה לְזֵכֶר מַלְכוּתוֹ
קָרָא לַשֶּׁמֶשׁ וַיִּזְרַח אוֹר, רָאָה וְהִתְקִין צוּרַת הַלְּבָנָה.

HAVDALA AT HOME

*On Motza'ei Yom Tov that is not on Motza'ei Shabbat, the first
paragraph and the blessings for the spices and flame are omitted.*

Taking a cup of wine in the right hand, say:

הִנֵּה Behold, God is my salvation. I will trust and not be afraid.　　*Is. 12*
The LORD, the LORD, is my strength and my song.
He has become my salvation.
With joy you will draw water from the springs of salvation.
Salvation is the LORD's; on Your people is Your blessing, Selah.　　*Ps. 3*
The LORD of hosts is with us,　　*Ps. 46*
the God of Jacob is our stronghold, Selah.
LORD of hosts: happy is the one who trusts in You.　　*Ps. 84*
LORD, save! May the King answer us on the day we call.　　*Ps. 20*
For the Jews there was light and gladness, joy and honor –　　*Esther 8*
so may it be for us.
I will lift the cup of salvation and call on the name of the LORD.　　*Ps. 116*

When making Havdala for others, add:
Please pay attention, my masters.

Blessed are You, LORD our God, King of the Universe,
who creates the fruit of the vine.

If Havdala is made on beer, substitute:
Blessed are You, LORD our God, King of the Universe,
by whose word all things came to be.

Hold the spice box and say:
Blessed are You, LORD our God, King of the Universe,
who creates the various spices.

Smell the spices and put the spice box down.
Lift the hands toward the flame of the Havdala candle and say:
Blessed are You, LORD our God, King of the Universe,
who creates the lights of fire.

Holding the cup of wine again in the right hand, say:

בָּרוּךְ Blessed are You, LORD our God, King of the Universe, who
distinguishes between sacred and secular, between light and darkness,
between Israel and the nations, between the seventh day and the six
days of work. Blessed are You, LORD, who distinguishes between
sacred and secular.

סדר הבדלה בבית

On מוצאי יום טוב that is not on מוצאי שבת, the first paragraph
and the blessings for the spices and flame are omitted.

Taking a cup of wine in the right hand, say:

ישעיה יב

הִנֵּה אֵל יְשׁוּעָתִי אֶבְטַח, וְלֹא אֶפְחָד

כִּי־עָזִּי וְזִמְרָת יָהּ יהוה, וַיְהִי־לִי לִישׁוּעָה:

וּשְׁאַבְתֶּם־מַיִם בְּשָׂשׂוֹן, מִמַּעַיְנֵי הַיְשׁוּעָה:

תהלים ג

לַיהוה הַיְשׁוּעָה, עַל־עַמְּךָ בִרְכָתֶךָ סֶּלָה:

תהלים מו

יהוה צְבָאוֹת עִמָּנוּ, מִשְׂגָּב לָנוּ אֱלֹהֵי יַעֲקֹב סֶלָה:

תהלים פד

יהוה צְבָאוֹת, אַשְׁרֵי אָדָם בֹּטֵחַ בָּךְ:

תהלים כ

יהוה הוֹשִׁיעָה, הַמֶּלֶךְ יַעֲנֵנוּ בְיוֹם־קָרְאֵנוּ:

אסתר ח

לַיְּהוּדִים הָיְתָה אוֹרָה וְשִׂמְחָה וְשָׂשֹׂן וִיקָר: כֵּן תִּהְיֶה לָנוּ.

תהלים קטז

כּוֹס־יְשׁוּעוֹת אֶשָּׂא, וּבְשֵׁם יהוה אֶקְרָא:

When making הבדלה for others, add:

סַבְרִי מָרָנָן

בָּרוּךְ אַתָּה יהוה אֱלֹהֵינוּ מֶלֶךְ הָעוֹלָם, בּוֹרֵא פְּרִי הַגָּפֶן.

If הבדלה is made on beer, substitute:

בָּרוּךְ אַתָּה יהוה אֱלֹהֵינוּ מֶלֶךְ הָעוֹלָם, שֶׁהַכֹּל נִהְיָה בִּדְבָרוֹ.

Hold the spice box and say:

בָּרוּךְ אַתָּה יהוה אֱלֹהֵינוּ מֶלֶךְ הָעוֹלָם, בּוֹרֵא מִינֵי בְשָׂמִים.

Smell the spices and put the spice box down.
Lift the hands toward the flame of the הבדלה candle and say:

בָּרוּךְ אַתָּה יהוה אֱלֹהֵינוּ מֶלֶךְ הָעוֹלָם, בּוֹרֵא מְאוֹרֵי הָאֵשׁ.

Holding the cup of wine again in the right hand, say:

בָּרוּךְ אַתָּה יהוה אֱלֹהֵינוּ מֶלֶךְ הָעוֹלָם, הַמַּבְדִּיל בֵּין קֹדֶשׁ לְחֹל,
בֵּין אוֹר לְחֹשֶׁךְ, בֵּין יִשְׂרָאֵל לָעַמִּים, בֵּין יוֹם הַשְּׁבִיעִי לְשֵׁשֶׁת
יְמֵי הַמַּעֲשֶׂה. בָּרוּךְ אַתָּה יהוה, הַמַּבְדִּיל בֵּין קֹדֶשׁ לְחֹל.

הַמַּבְדִּיל He who distinguishes between sacred and secular,
may He forgive our sins.
May He multiply our offspring and wealth like the sand,
and like the stars at night.

The day has passed like a palm tree's shadow;
I call on God to fulfill what the watchman said: *Is. 21*
"Morning comes, though now it is night."

Your righteousness is as high as Mount Tabor.
May You pass high over my sins.
[Let them be] like yesterday when it has passed,   *Ps. 90*
like a watch in the night.

The time of offerings has passed. Would that I might rest.
I am weary with my sighing, every night I drench [with tears].   *Ps. 6*

Hear my voice; let it not be cast aside. Open for me the lofty gate.
My head is filled with the dew of dawn,   *Song. 5*
my hair with raindrops of the night.

Heed my prayer, revered and awesome God.
When I cry, grant me deliverance at twilight,   *Prov. 7*
as the day fades, or in the darkness of the night.

I call to You, LORD: Save me. Make known to me the path of life.
Rescue me from misery before day turns to night.

Cleanse the defilement of my deeds, lest those who torment me say,
"Where is the God who made me,   *Job 35*
who gives cause for songs in the night?"

We are in Your hands like clay:
please forgive our sins, light and grave.
Day to day they pour forth speech,   *Ps. 19*
and night to night [they communicate knowledge].

הַמַּבְדִּיל בֵּין קֹדֶשׁ לְחֹל, חַטֹּאתֵינוּ הוּא יִמְחֹל
זַרְעֵנוּ וְכַסְפֵּנוּ יַרְבֶּה כַחוֹל וְכַכּוֹכָבִים בַּלָּיְלָה.

יוֹם פָּנָה כְּצֵל תֹּמֶר, אֶקְרָא לָאֵל עָלַי גּוֹמֵר
אָמַר שֹׁמֵר, אָתָא בֹקֶר וְגַם־לָיְלָה:

ישעיה כא

צִדְקָתְךָ כְּהַר תָּבוֹר, עַל חֲטָאַי עָבֹר תַּעֲבֹר
כְּיוֹם אֶתְמוֹל כִּי יַעֲבֹר, וְאַשְׁמוּרָה בַלָּיְלָה:

תהלים צ

חָלְפָה עוֹנַת מִנְחָתִי, מִי יִתֵּן מְנוּחָתִי
יָגַעְתִּי בְאַנְחָתִי, אַשְׂחֶה בְכָל־לָיְלָה:

תהלים ו

קוֹלִי בַּל יֻנְטָל, פְּתַח לִי שַׁעַר הַמְנֻטָּל
שֶׁרֹּאשִׁי נִמְלָא טָל, קְוֻצּוֹתַי רְסִיסֵי לָיְלָה:

שיר
השירים ה

הֵעָתֵר נוֹרָא וְאָיֹם, אֲשַׁוֵּעַ תְּנָה פִדְיוֹם
בְּנֶשֶׁף־בְּעֶרֶב יוֹם, בְּאִישׁוֹן לָיְלָה:

משלי ז

קְרָאתִיךָ יָהּ, הוֹשִׁיעֵנִי, אֹרַח חַיִּים תּוֹדִיעֵנִי
מִדַּלָּה תְבַצְּעֵנִי, מִיּוֹם עַד לָיְלָה:

טַהֵר טִנּוּף מַעֲשַׂי, פֶּן יֹאמְרוּ מַכְעִיסַי
אַיֵּה אֱלוֹהַּ עֹשָׂי, נֹתֵן זְמִרוֹת בַּלָּיְלָה:

איוב לה

נַחְנוּ בְיָדְךָ כַּחֹמֶר, סְלַח נָא עַל קַל וָחֹמֶר
יוֹם לְיוֹם יַבִּיעַ אֹמֶר, וְלַיְלָה לְלָיְלָה:

תהלים יט

BRIT MILA

When the baby is brought in, all stand and say:
Blessed is he who comes.

The mohel (in some congregations, all) say (in Israel omit):

וַיְדַבֵּר The LORD spoke to Moses, saying: Pinehas the son of Elazar, the   *Num. 25*
son of Aaron the priest, turned back My rage from the children of Israel,
when he was zealous for Me among them, and I did not annihilate the
children of Israel in My own zeal. And so tell him, that I now give him
My covenant for peace.

The following verses, through "LORD, please, grant us success," are only said in Israel.

Mohel: Happy are those You choose and bring near to dwell in Your courts.   *Ps. 65*

All: May we be sated with the goodness of Your House,
       Your holy Temple.

The father takes the baby in his hands and says quietly:

אִם אֶשְׁכָּחֵךְ If I forget you, Jerusalem, may my right hand forget its skill.   *Ps. 137*
May my tongue cling to the roof of my mouth, if I do not remember you,
if I do not set Jerusalem above my highest joy.

The father says aloud, followed by the congregation:
Listen, Israel: the LORD is our God, the LORD is One.   *Deut. 6*

---

the covenant of Abraham, our father – a separate blessing, referring not to
the circumcision itself, but what it is a sign of – namely entry into the life
of the covenant, under the sheltering wings of the Divine Presence (*Arukh
HaShulḥan, Yoreh De'ah* 365:2); (3) *Who made the beloved one [Isaac] holy
from the womb* – a blessing of acknowledgment. Isaac was the first child to
have a circumcision at the age of eight days. He was consecrated before birth,
Abraham having been told that it would be Isaac who would continue the
covenant (Gen. 17:19–21).

כְּשֵׁם שֶׁנִּכְנַס לַבְּרִית *Just as he has entered into the covenant.* Mentioned already
in early rabbinic sources as the response of those present. The three phrases
refer to the duties of a parent to a child: (1) to teach him Torah; (2) to ensure
that he marries; and (3) to train him to do good deeds, as the Torah says in
the case of Abraham: "For I have singled him out so that he may instruct his
children and his posterity to keep the way of the LORD by doing what is just
and right" (Gen. 18:19).

סדר ברית מילה

When the baby is brought in, all stand and say:

בָּרוּךְ הַבָּא.

The מוהל (in some congregations, all) say (in ארץ ישראל omit):

במדבר כה

וַיְדַבֵּר יהוה אֶל־מֹשֶׁה לֵּאמֹר: פִּינְחָס בֶּן־אֶלְעָזָר בֶּן־אַהֲרֹן הַכֹּהֵן הֵשִׁיב אֶת־חֲמָתִי מֵעַל בְּנֵי־יִשְׂרָאֵל, בְּקַנְאוֹ אֶת־קִנְאָתִי בְּתוֹכָם, וְלֹא־כִלִּיתִי אֶת־בְּנֵי־יִשְׂרָאֵל בְּקִנְאָתִי: לָכֵן אֱמֹר, הִנְנִי נֹתֵן לוֹ אֶת־בְּרִיתִי שָׁלוֹם:

The following verses, through אָנָּא יהוה הַצְלִיחָה נָא are only said in Israel.

תהלים סה

המוהל: אַשְׁרֵי תִּבְחַר וּתְקָרֵב, יִשְׁכֹּן חֲצֵרֶיךָ,

הקהל: נִשְׂבְּעָה בְּטוּב בֵּיתֶךָ, קְדֹשׁ הֵיכָלֶךָ:

The father takes the baby in his hands and says quietly:

תהלים קלז

אִם־אֶשְׁכָּחֵךְ יְרוּשָׁלָ͏ִם, תִּשְׁכַּח יְמִינִי, תִּדְבַּק לְשׁוֹנִי לְחִכִּי אִם־לֹא אֶזְכְּרֵכִי, אִם־לֹא אַעֲלֶה אֶת־יְרוּשָׁלַ͏ִם עַל רֹאשׁ שִׂמְחָתִי:

The father says aloud, followed by the קהל:

דברים ו

שְׁמַע יִשְׂרָאֵל, יהוה אֱלֹהֵינוּ, יהוה אֶחָד:

SERVICE AT A CIRCUMCISION

Since the days of Abraham (Gen. 17:4–14), circumcision has been the sign, for Jewish males, of the covenant between God and His people. Despite the fact that the law was restated by Moses (Lev. 12:3), it remains known as the "Covenant of Abraham." The ceremony – always performed on the eighth day, even on Shabbat, unless there are medical reasons for delay – marks the entry of the child into the covenant of Jewish fate and destiny. The duty of circumcision devolves, in principle, on the father of the child; in practice it is performed only by a qualified *mohel*.

בָּרוּךְ *Blessed are You.* There are three blessings to be said at a circumcision: (1) *And has commanded us concerning circumcision* – a blessing over the commandment itself, the "about" formula signaling that the *mohel* is performing the commandment on behalf of the father; (2) *To bring him [our son] into*

The Mohel, followed by the congregation,
  recites each of the following three phrases twice:

The Lᴏʀᴅ is King, the Lᴏʀᴅ was King,
  the Lᴏʀᴅ shall be King for ever and all time.
Lᴏʀᴅ, please, save us.   *Ps. 118*
Lᴏʀᴅ, please, grant us success.

The baby is placed on Eliyahu's seat, and the Mohel says:
This is the throne of Elijah the prophet,
may he be remembered for good.

The Mohel continues:

לִישׁוּעָתְךָ For Your salvation I wait, O Lᴏʀᴅ. I await Your deliverance,   *Gen. 49*
                                                                           Ps. 119
Lᴏʀᴅ, and I observe Your commandments. Elijah, angel of the covenant,
behold: yours is before you. Stand at my right hand and be close to me.
I await Your deliverance, Lᴏʀᴅ. I rejoice in Your word like one who finds   *Ibid.*
much spoil. Those who love Your Torah have great peace, and there is
no stumbling block before them. Happy are those You choose and bring   *Ps. 65*
near to dwell in Your courts.

All respond:
May we be sated with the goodness of Your House, Your holy Temple.

The baby is placed on the knees of the Sandak, and the Mohel says:
בָּרוּךְ Blessed are You, Lᴏʀᴅ our God, King of the Universe,
who has made us holy through His commandments,
and has commanded us concerning circumcision.

Immediately after the circumcision, the father says:
בָּרוּךְ Blessed are You, Lᴏʀᴅ our God, King of the Universe,
who has made us holy through His commandments,
and has commanded us to bring him [our son]
into the covenant of Abraham, our father.

In Israel the father adds (some outside Israel add it as well):
בָּרוּךְ Blessed are You, Lᴏʀᴅ our God, King of the Universe,
who has given us life, sustained us, and brought us to this time.

All respond:
אָמֵן Amen. Just as he has entered into the covenant,
so may he enter into Torah, marriage and good deeds.

The מוהל repeats each of the following three phrases twice, followed by the קהל:

יהוה מֶלֶךְ, יהוה מָלָךְ, יהוה יִמְלֹךְ לְעוֹלָם וָעֶד.
אָנָּא יהוה הוֹשִׁיעָה נָּא
אָנָּא יהוה הַצְלִיחָה נָּא:

The baby is placed on the כסא של אליהו, and the מוהל says:

זֶה הַכִּסֵּא שֶׁל אֵלִיָּהוּ הַנָּבִיא זָכוּר לַטּוֹב.

The מוהל continues:

לִישׁוּעָתְךָ קִוִּיתִי יהוה: שִׂבַּרְתִּי לִישׁוּעָתְךָ יהוה, וּמִצְוֺתֶיךָ עָשִׂיתִי:
אֵלִיָּהוּ מַלְאַךְ הַבְּרִית, הִנֵּה שֶׁלְּךָ לְפָנֶיךָ, עֲמֹד עַל יְמִינִי וְסָמְכֵנִי:

שִׂבַּרְתִּי לִישׁוּעָתְךָ יהוה: שָׂשׂ אָנֹכִי עַל־אִמְרָתֶךָ, כְּמוֹצֵא שָׁלָל רָב:

שָׁלוֹם רָב לְאֹהֲבֵי תוֹרָתֶךָ, וְאֵין־לָמוֹ מִכְשׁוֹל: אַשְׁרֵי תִּבְחַר וּתְקָרֵב,
יִשְׁכֹּן חֲצֵרֶיךָ:

All respond:

נִשְׂבְּעָה בְּטוּב בֵּיתֶךָ, קְדֹשׁ הֵיכָלֶךָ:

The baby is placed on the knees of the סנדק, and the מוהל says:

בָּרוּךְ אַתָּה יהוה אֱלֹהֵינוּ מֶלֶךְ הָעוֹלָם
אֲשֶׁר קִדְּשָׁנוּ בְּמִצְוֺתָיו, וְצִוָּנוּ עַל הַמִּילָה.

Immediately after the circumcision, the father says:

בָּרוּךְ אַתָּה יהוה אֱלֹהֵינוּ מֶלֶךְ הָעוֹלָם, אֲשֶׁר קִדְּשָׁנוּ
בְּמִצְוֺתָיו, וְצִוָּנוּ לְהַכְנִיסוֹ בִּבְרִיתוֹ שֶׁל אַבְרָהָם אָבִינוּ.

In ארץ ישראל the father adds (some in חוץ לארץ add it as well):

בָּרוּךְ אַתָּה יהוה אֱלֹהֵינוּ מֶלֶךְ הָעוֹלָם
שֶׁהֶחֱיָנוּ וְקִיְּמָנוּ וְהִגִּיעָנוּ לַזְּמַן הַזֶּה.

All respond:

אָמֵן. כְּשֵׁם שֶׁנִּכְנַס לַבְּרִית
כֵּן יִכָּנֵס לְתוֹרָה וּלְחֻפָּה וּלְמַעֲשִׂים טוֹבִים.

After the circumcision has been completed, the Mohel
(or another honoree) takes a cup of wine and says:

בָּרוּךְ Blessed are You, Lᴏʀᴅ our God, King of the Universe, who creates
the fruit of the vine.

בָּרוּךְ Blessed are You, Lᴏʀᴅ our God, King of the Universe, who made the
beloved one [Isaac] holy from the womb, marked the decree of circumcision in his flesh, and gave his descendants the seal and sign of the holy
covenant. As a reward for this, the Living God, our Portion, our Rock,
did order deliverance from destruction for the beloved of our flesh, for
the sake of His covenant that He set in our flesh. Blessed are You, Lᴏʀᴅ,
who establishes the covenant.

אֱלֹהֵינוּ Our God and God of our fathers, preserve this child to his father
and mother, and let his name be called in Israel (*baby's name* son of *father's
name*). May the father rejoice in the issue of his body, and the mother
be glad with the fruit of her womb, as is written, "May your father and   *Prov. 23*
mother rejoice, and she who bore you be glad." And it is said, "Then I
passed by you and saw you downtrodden in your blood, and I said to you: *Ezek. 16*
In your blood, live; and I said to you: In your blood, live."

וְנֶאֱמַר And it is said, "He remembered His covenant for ever; the word   *Ps. 105*
He ordained for a thousand generations; the covenant He made with
Abraham and gave on oath to Isaac, confirming it as a statute for Jacob, an
everlasting covenant for Israel." And it is said, "And Abraham circumcised   *Gen. 21*
his son Isaac at the age of eight days, as God had commanded him." Thank   *Ps. 118*
the Lᴏʀᴅ for He is good; His loning-kindness is for ever.

All respond:

Thank the Lᴏʀᴅ for He is good; His loving-kindness is for ever.

The Mohel (or honoree) continues:

May this child (*baby's name* son of *father's name*) become great. Just as he
has entered into the covenant, so may he enter into Torah, marriage and
good deeds.

The Sandak also drinks some of the wine;
some drops are given to the baby.
The cup is then sent to the mother, who also drinks from it.

All say Aleinu on page 682, and Mourner's Kaddish on page 684 is said.

After the circumcision has been completed, the מוהל
(or another honoree), takes a cup of wine and says:

בָּרוּךְ אַתָּה יהוה אֱלֹהֵינוּ מֶלֶךְ הָעוֹלָם, בּוֹרֵא פְּרִי הַגָּפֶן.

בָּרוּךְ אַתָּה יהוה אֱלֹהֵינוּ מֶלֶךְ הָעוֹלָם, אֲשֶׁר קִדַּשׁ יְדִיד מִבֶּטֶן,
וְחֹק בִּשְׁאֵרוֹ שָׂם, וְצֶאֱצָאָיו חָתַם בְּאוֹת בְּרִית קֹדֶשׁ. עַל כֵּן בִּשְׂכַר
זֹאת, אֵל חַי חֶלְקֵנוּ צוּרֵנוּ צִוָּה לְהַצִּיל יְדִידוּת שְׁאֵרֵנוּ מִשַּׁחַת,
לְמַעַן בְּרִיתוֹ אֲשֶׁר שָׂם בִּבְשָׂרֵנוּ. בָּרוּךְ אַתָּה יהוה, כּוֹרֵת הַבְּרִית.

אֱלֹהֵינוּ וֵאלֹהֵי אֲבוֹתֵינוּ, קַיֵּם אֶת הַיֶּלֶד הַזֶּה לְאָבִיו וּלְאִמּוֹ, וְיִקָּרֵא
שְׁמוֹ בְּיִשְׂרָאֵל (פלוני בֶּן פלוני). יִשְׂמַח הָאָב בְּיוֹצֵא חֲלָצָיו וְתָגֵל אִמּוֹ
בִּפְרִי בִטְנָהּ, כַּכָּתוּב: יִשְׂמַח־אָבִיךָ וְאִמֶּךָ, וְתָגֵל יוֹלַדְתֶּךָ: וְנֶאֱמַר: משלי כג
וָאֶעֱבֹר עָלַיִךְ וָאֶרְאֵךְ מִתְבּוֹסֶסֶת בְּדָמָיִךְ, וָאֹמַר לָךְ בְּדָמַיִךְ חֲיִי, יחזקאל טז
וָאֹמַר לָךְ בְּדָמַיִךְ חֲיִי:

וְנֶאֱמַר: זָכַר לְעוֹלָם בְּרִיתוֹ, דָּבָר צִוָּה לְאֶלֶף דּוֹר: אֲשֶׁר כָּרַת אֶת־ תהלים קה
אַבְרָהָם, וּשְׁבוּעָתוֹ לְיִשְׂחָק: וַיַּעֲמִידֶהָ לְיַעֲקֹב לְחֹק, לְיִשְׂרָאֵל
בְּרִית עוֹלָם: וְנֶאֱמַר: וַיָּמָל אַבְרָהָם אֶת־יִצְחָק בְּנוֹ בֶּן־שְׁמֹנַת יָמִים, בראשית כא
כַּאֲשֶׁר צִוָּה אֹתוֹ אֱלֹהִים: הוֹדוּ לַיהוה כִּי־טוֹב, כִּי לְעוֹלָם חַסְדּוֹ: תהלים קיח

All respond:

הוֹדוּ לַיהוה כִּי־טוֹב, כִּי לְעוֹלָם חַסְדּוֹ:

The מוהל *(or honoree) continues:*

(פלוני בֶּן פלוני) זֶה הַקָּטָן גָּדוֹל יִהְיֶה, כְּשֵׁם שֶׁנִּכְנַס לַבְּרִית, כֵּן יִכָּנֵס
לַתּוֹרָה וּלְחֻפָּה וּלְמַעֲשִׂים טוֹבִים.

The סנדק *also drinks some of the wine;*
some drops are given to the baby.
The cup is then sent to the mother, who also drinks from it.

All say עָלֵינוּ *on page 683, and* קדיש יתום *on page 685 is said.*

BIRKAT KOHANIM IN ISRAEL

In Israel, the following is said by the Leader during the Repetition of the Amida when Kohanim bless the congregation. If there is more than one Kohen, a member of the congregation calls:

Kohanim!

The Kohanim respond:

Blessed are You, LORD our God, King of the Universe, who has made us holy with the holiness of Aaron, and has commanded us to bless His people Israel with love.

The Leader calls word by word, followed by the Kohanim:

יְבָרֶכְךָ May the LORD bless you and protect you. (*Cong:* Amen.)   *Num. 6*

May the LORD make His face shine on you

and be gracious to you. (*Cong:* Amen.)

May the LORD turn His face toward you,

and grant you peace. (*Cong:* Amen.)

The congregation says:

אַדִּיר Majestic One on high who dwells in power: You are peace and Your name is peace. May it be Your will to bestow on us and on Your people the house of Israel, life and blessing as a safeguard for peace.

The Kohanim say:

רִבּוֹנוֹ Master of the Universe: we have done what You have decreed for us. So too may You deal with us as You have promised us. Look down from Your holy dwelling place, from heaven, and bless Your people Israel and the land You have given us as You promised on oath to our ancestors, a land flowing with milk and honey.   *Deut. 26*

The Leader continues:

שִׂים שָׁלוֹם Grant peace, goodness and blessing, grace, loving-kindness and compassion to us and all Israel Your people. Bless us, our Father, all as one, with the light of Your face, for by the light of Your face You have given us, LORD our God, the Torah of life and love of kindness, righteousness, blessing, compassion, life and peace. May it be good in Your eyes to bless Your people Israel at every time, in every hour, with Your peace. Blessed are You, LORD, who blesses His people Israel with peace.

The following verse concludes the Leader's Repetition of the Amida.

May the words of my mouth and the meditation of my heart   *Ps. 19*
find favor before You, LORD, my Rock and Redeemer.

Shaharit continues with Hallel on page 360;
Musaf continues with Full Kaddish on page 562.

ברכת כהנים בארץ ישראל

In ארץ ישראל, *the following is said by the* שליח ציבור *during the* חזרת הש״ץ *when* ברכת כהנים *say* כהנים. *If there is more than one* כהן, *a member of the* קהל *calls:*

כֹּהֲנִים

The כהנים *respond:*

בָּרוּךְ אַתָּה יהוה אֱלֹהֵינוּ מֶלֶךְ הָעוֹלָם, אֲשֶׁר קִדְּשָׁנוּ בִּקְדֻשָּׁתוֹ שֶׁל אַהֲרֹן וְצִוָּנוּ לְבָרֵךְ אֶת עַמּוֹ יִשְׂרָאֵל בְּאַהֲבָה.

The שליח ציבור *calls word by word, followed by the* כהנים:

במדברו

יְבָרֶכְךָ יהוה וְיִשְׁמְרֶךָ: קהל: אָמֵן

יָאֵר יהוה פָּנָיו אֵלֶיךָ וִיחֻנֶּךָּ: קהל: אָמֵן

יִשָּׂא יהוה פָּנָיו אֵלֶיךָ וְיָשֵׂם לְךָ שָׁלוֹם: קהל: אָמֵן

The קהל *says:*

אַדִּיר בַּמָּרוֹם שׁוֹכֵן בִּגְבוּרָה, אַתָּה שָׁלוֹם וְשִׁמְךָ שָׁלוֹם. יְהִי רָצוֹן שֶׁתָּשִׂים עָלֵינוּ וְעַל כָּל עַמְּךָ בֵּית יִשְׂרָאֵל חַיִּים וּבְרָכָה לְמִשְׁמֶרֶת שָׁלוֹם.

The כהנים *say:*

רִבּוֹנוֹ שֶׁל עוֹלָם, עָשִׂינוּ מַה שֶּׁגָּזַרְתָּ עָלֵינוּ, אַף אַתָּה עֲשֵׂה עִמָּנוּ כְּמוֹ שֶׁהִבְטַחְתָּנוּ. הַשְׁקִיפָה מִמְּעוֹן קָדְשְׁךָ מִן הַשָּׁמַיִם, וּבָרֵךְ אֶת עַמְּךָ אֶת יִשְׂרָאֵל, וְאֵת הָאֲדָמָה אֲשֶׁר נָתַתָּה לָּנוּ, כַּאֲשֶׁר נִשְׁבַּעְתָּ לַאֲבֹתֵינוּ, אֶרֶץ זָבַת חָלָב וּדְבָשׁ:

דברים כו

The שליח ציבור *continues:*

שִׂים שָׁלוֹם טוֹבָה וּבְרָכָה, חֵן וָחֶסֶד וְרַחֲמִים עָלֵינוּ וְעַל כָּל יִשְׂרָאֵל עַמֶּךָ. בָּרְכֵנוּ אָבִינוּ כֻּלָּנוּ כְּאֶחָד בְּאוֹר פָּנֶיךָ, כִּי בְאוֹר פָּנֶיךָ נָתַתָּ לָּנוּ יהוה אֱלֹהֵינוּ, תּוֹרַת חַיִּים וְאַהֲבַת חֶסֶד, וּצְדָקָה וּבְרָכָה וְרַחֲמִים וְחַיִּים וְשָׁלוֹם. וְטוֹב בְּעֵינֶיךָ לְבָרֵךְ אֶת עַמְּךָ יִשְׂרָאֵל, בְּכָל עֵת וּבְכָל שָׁעָה בִּשְׁלוֹמֶךָ. בָּרוּךְ אַתָּה יהוה, הַמְבָרֵךְ אֶת עַמּוֹ יִשְׂרָאֵל בַּשָּׁלוֹם.

The following verse concludes the חזרת הש״ץ.

יִהְיוּ לְרָצוֹן אִמְרֵי פִי וְהֶגְיוֹן לִבִּי לְפָנֶיךָ, יהוה צוּרִי וְגֹאֲלִי:

תהלים יט

שחרית *continues with* הלל *on page 361;*
מוסף *continues with* קדיש שלם *on page 563.*

פיוטים נוספים

ADDITIONAL PIYUTIM

יוצר ליום טוב ראשון של שבועות

שחרית is said up to and including בָּרְכוּ (page 321).

בָּרוּךְ אַתָּה יהוה אֱלֹהֵינוּ מֶלֶךְ הָעוֹלָם
יוֹצֵר אוֹר וּבוֹרֵא חְשֶׁךְ
עֹשֶׂה שָׁלוֹם וּבוֹרֵא אֶת הַכֹּל.

אוֹר עוֹלָם בְּאוֹצַר חַיִּים
אוֹרוֹת מֵאֹפֶל אָמַר וַיֶּהִי.

יוצר

The piyutim said by the שליח ציבור in שחרית are commonly called יוצרות.
The יוצר for the first day of שבועות was composed by Rabbi Shimon "the Great" of
Mainz (early eleventh century). Comprising three sections (אופן, גוף היוצר, and זולת), it
alludes to the final verses of Proverbs ch. 8, which the Sages interpreted as referring to
the Torah: "Five possessions did the Holy One, blessed be He, declare as His own in
His world, and they are: the Torah… it is written (Prov. 8:32): 'The Lord created me
at the beginning of His way, as the first of His works in days of old'" (Avot 6:10).

The first piyut, said at the beginning of the first blessing of the שמע,
is sometimes referred to as "גוף היוצר". This one consists of two parts: the
first follows a triple alphabetic acrostic in the first three stichs of each
stanza, and the fourth stichs comprise the text of Proverbs 8:22–29.

All:

אָדוֹן אִמְּנַנִי   אֶצְלוֹ שְׁכַנְנִי
אָדָם הִקְנַנִי   יהוה קָנָנִי.

בִּנְיָן בְּעָרְכוֹ   בִּי עַץ צָרְכוֹ
בְּשַׁעֲשׁוּעַי בִּרְכוֹ   רֵאשִׁית דַּרְכּוֹ.

גַּשְׁתִּי לְרַגְלָיו   גַּרְתִּי בְּצִלָּיו
גַּעְגּוּעַי עָלָיו   קֶדֶם מִפְעָלָיו.

דָּתוֹתֵי עֶלֶם   דּוֹדַי לְהוֹעִילָם
דֵּעַת הַנֶּעְלָם   מֵאָז מֵעוֹלָם.

הֲגִיגִי לָאֶרֶשׁ   הַמְזֻקָּק לִפְרֹשׁ
הַנִּפְלָא לִדְרֹשׁ   נִסַּכְתִּי מֵרֹאשׁ.

וָאֶהְיֶה בְּעֶרֶץ   וְשַׁעֲשׁוּעַי יֶרֶץ
וְקִדְּמַנִי בְּמֶרֶץ   מִקַּדְמֵי־אָרֶץ.

זֹהַר נִכְלַלְתִּי   זְכִיּוֹת נִבְלַלְתִּי
זֹאת נִתְהַלַּלְתִּי   בְּאֵין־תְּהֹמוֹת חוֹלַלְתִּי.

חֵקֶר עוֹנוֹת   חָלָל וּמְעוֹנוֹת
חָק בִּי עִנְיָנוֹת   בְּאֵין מַעְיָנוֹת.

טְפוּחֵי שָׁמַיִם   טִפְסְרֵי אֵשׁ וּמַיִם
טְרָמַנִי יוֹמַיִם   נִכְבַּדֵּי־מָיִם.

יְקָרוֹתַי נִבְעוּ   יְתֵדֹתַי נִקְבְּעוּ
יְרִיעֹתַי רֻבְּעוּ   בְּטֶרֶם הָרִים הָטְבָּעוּ.

כְּלָלוֹת נִכְלַלְתִּי   כֵּן פְּרָט נִבְלַלְתִּי
כְּמַדְתִּי נִגְלַלְתִּי   לִפְנֵי גְבָעוֹת חוֹלָלְתִּי.

לִי שָׁת מוֹעֵצוֹת   לָדוּץ בְּדִיצוֹת
לֹא עָשָׂה קְצוֹת   אֶרֶץ וְחוּצוֹת.

מִצְוֹתַי לְקַבֵּל   מָנָה וְחֵבֶל
מִדְבָּקִים לוֹ גִבֵּל   וְרֹאשׁ עַפְרוֹת תֵּבֵל.

נוֹי שְׁלֹשִׁים וּשְׁתַּיִם   נָעַם נְתִיבוֹתַיִם
נָהַר בִּי שְׂפָתַיִם   בַּהֲכִינוֹ שָׁמָיִם.

סְפוּנוֹת הֱרָאַנִי   סוֹדוֹ קְרָאַנִי
סֶמֶךְ לִגְאוֹנִי   שָׁם אָנִי.

עֲצָתִי תָחוּג   עוֹלָם נָהוּג
עֶנֶד בְּמָחוּג   בְּחֻקּוֹ חוּג.

פְּצוּמָה לֶהוֹם   פֶּקֶד קֹר וָחֹם
פִּלֵּס לַתְּהוֹם.   עַל־פְּנֵי תְהוֹם.

צוֹפִיָּה לְמֶרְחַקִּים   צִפְצוּפֵי מְשַׂחֲקִים
צַעֲדִי לֹא דוֹחֲקִים.   בְּאַמְּצוֹ שְׁחָקִים.

קְבוּעָם מִזּוֹ   קְדִירָתָם לַחֲזוֹ
קְרִישָׁתָם לְפָז   מִמַּעַל בַּעֲזוֹ.

רְגָעִים בִּנְהֹם   רְגָבִים יְגִיחוֹם
רִתֵּק חוֹל לַתְּהוֹם.   עִינוֹת תְּהוֹם.

שָׁוָּה אַרְקוֹ   שִׁפֵּר מְתָקוֹ
שָׁב בְּהִנָּתְקוֹ   בְּשׂוּמוֹ לַיָּם חָקוֹ.

תֵּבֵל בְּשַׁכְלְלוֹ   תּוּשִׁיָּה שָׁת שִׂכְלוֹ
תְּכוּנִים קֶדֶם מְלֹא   וּמַיִם לֹא.

שָׁתוֹת חֻבְּרוּ   מְלוֹאָם הָגְבְּרוּ
עֲבָדְתוֹ יִגְבְּרוּ   פִּיו לֹא יַעֲבֹרוּ.

◄ וְעַל נֶאֱמְנֵי־אֶרֶץ   בְּרִיתוֹ הִתְרֶץ
צִדְקָם חֶשֵׁךְ קָרֶץ   בְּחֻקּוֹ מוֹסְדֵי אָרֶץ.

The second part of the גוף היוצר *continues with the words of Proverbs 8:30–31,
with the biblical words at the beginning of each of the rhyming lines. While the first
part described the Torah in God's keeping before and during the creation of the
world, these verses tell of the day the Torah was given to Israel.* מעמד הר סיני *is often
compared by the sages to a wedding (see Introduction, page xlix); in this daring
piyut, the "wedding day" is described from the point of view of the expectant bride.*

*Some have the custom of saying the first four verses responsively,
with the* שליח ציבור *saying the first two words, and the* קהל *the rest.*

וָאֶהְיֶה   שְׁכוּנָה בְּחֶבְיוֹן עֹז אַרְמוֹן
אֶצְלוֹ   מְיֻחֶדֶת בְּתוֹךְ גִּנְזֵי לִטְמָן
אָמוֹן   עֲמוּסָה מְלוֹי מִצְוֹת כְּרִמּוֹן
וָאֶהְיֶה   וְעוֹדָה לְגִינֵי פִצֵּל לַח וְלוּז וְעַרְמוֹן

All:

שַׁעֲשׁוּעִים	נַחֲלִיאֵל מַתָּנָה מִמִּדְבָּר לִזְמָן
יוֹם	בָּאוּ לְסִינַי נוֹחֲלֵי דַּת אָמוֹן
יוֹם	רָדוּ מַלְאֲכֵי צְבָאוֹת בֶּהָמוֹן
מְשַׂחֶקֶת	יְדִידוּת עַל נִשְׁמַעַת כְּפַעֲמוֹן
לְפָנָיו	צָגוּ מְלָכִים בְּפֶרֶשׁ בָּהּ תַּשְׁלֵג בְּצַלְמוֹן
בְּכָל עֵת	חָשְׁכוּ מֵיָשֶׁר מוֹאָב וְעַמּוֹן
מְשַׂחֶקֶת	קִלְקְלוֹן פָּארָן וּבוּז וְאַדְמוֹן
בְּתֵבֵל	חִמְדּוּנִי קַבְּלוּנִי הֹלְכֵי יֵלֵל יְשִׁמֹן
אַרְצוֹ	זָרַח אוֹרִי וְנָדַף רֵיחִי כְּאַפַּרְסְמוֹן
וְשַׁעֲשֻׁעַי	קִדְּשׁוּ חוֹרֵב וְנָדוּ תָבוֹר וְחֶרְמוֹן
אֶת	אֱלֹהֵי קָדְשָׁה וְכָבוֹד כֹּל יְשִׁימוֹן
בְּנֵי	מַעְלָה מוֹרָאוֹ יַעֲרִיצוּן וְיַעֲצִימוּן
אָדָם	נֵצַח תְּהִלָּתוֹ יַקְדִּישׁוּן וִירוֹמְמוּן.

Continue with "הַמֵּאִיר לָאָרֶץ" on page 323
until "מְלֹא כָל־הָאָרֶץ כְּבוֹדוֹ" on page 331.

אופן לשני ימי שבועות

The following piyut, known as the אופן, comprises the second part
of the יוצר and is said on both days. Its five stanzas begin with the words
of Proverbs 8:32, continuing where the previous piyut left off. The piyut speaks
to the people of Israel (those who stood at Mount Sinai or the congregants
about to receive the Torah today, or both), calling them to sing to God
both as sons (בָּנִים) and as servants (עֲבָדָיו). It is followed by the
stanza וְהַחַיּוֹת יְשׁוֹרֵרוּ, as per the Ashkenazi format of the יוצרות.

All:

וְעַתָּה בָנִים   שִׁירוּ לַמֶּלֶךְ בְּתִפְאֶרֶת מְפֹאָר
בְּרִקְמֵי שִׁיר מְעֻטָּף וּמְעֻטָּר וּמְתֹאָר
בְּהוֹד וְהָדָר וְשֶׁבַח מְבֹאָר
בַּעֲטֶרֶת גֵּאוּת וְכֶתֶר נוֹרָא יִתְפָּאָר.

שִׁמְעוּ לִי   מִלְּלוֹ, עֱזוּז נוֹרָא פִּלְאֵי גָדְלוֹ
שֶׁשָּׁמוֹ עָרֵב לוֹ, וְזִכְרוֹ נָעִים לְהַלְּלוֹ
וְהֵיכָלוֹ נֶחְמָד לוֹ, וּכְבוֹדוֹ נֶהְדָּר לוֹ
וְהוֹדוֹ נָאֶה לוֹ, וּמְשָׁרְתָיו מַנְעִימִים לוֹ.

וְאַשְׁרֵי   עֲבָדָיו הַמַּשְׁמִיעִים בְּקוֹל שִׁבְחוֹ
כִּי עֲרֵבִים לְפָנָיו וּמְקֻבָּלִים נִכְחוֹ
שַׁמְעִיאֵל הַשַּׂר מַשְׁמִיעָם בְּכֹחוֹ
לְשַׁתֵּק הֲמוֹן מַעְלָה בְּרָן בְּנֵי אֶזְרָחוֹ.

דַּרְכֵּי   וְחוֹבֵי תֵת קְדֻשָּׁה לַמְּקֹרֶה אֲוֵירִים
הַמִּשְׂגָּב וּמְכֻתָּר בְּקִשְׁרֵי כְתָרִים
פְּאֵר מְלָכִים תְּהִלָּה לַבְּרוּרִים
מִפַּחְדּוֹ יָחִילוּ אֵתָנִים וְצוּרִים.

שְׁלִיחַ צִבּוּר: *The*

יִשְׁמְרוּ   נִכְסָפִים לְחַצְרוֹת מְעַט מִקְדָּשׁוֹ
בְּפַחַד וְיִרְאָה לְהַעֲרִיצוֹ וּלְהַקְדִּישׁוֹ

All::

אַחַר שְׁתֵּי תֵבוֹת מַזְכִּירִים שֵׁם קָדְשׁוֹ
לְהוֹדִיעַ לַכֹּל כִּי הֵם זֶרַע קְדוֹשׁוֹ.

קהל, *followed by the* שְׁלִיחַ צִבּוּר: *The*

וְהַחַיּוֹת יְשׁוֹרֵרוּ / וּכְרוּבִים יְפָאֵרוּ
וּשְׂרָפִים יָרֹנּוּ / וְאֶרְאֶלִּים יְבָרֵכוּ
פְּנֵי כָל חַיָּה וְאוֹפָן וּכְרוּב לְעֻמַּת שְׂרָפִים
לְעֻמָּתָם מְשַׁבְּחִים וְאוֹמְרִים

All say aloud:

יְחֶזְקֵאל ג   בָּרוּךְ כְּבוֹד־יהוה מִמְּקוֹמוֹ:

Continue with "אֵין אֱלֹהִים זוּלָתֶךָ" *on page 333 to* "לָאֵל בָּרוּךְ" *on page 343.*

זולת לשני ימי שבועות

As with the אופן, the third piyut in the יוצר of the first day
(known as the זולת) is said on the second day as well.
Its theme is the Ten Commandments, and the last stichs
of the stanzas are the words of Proverbs 8:33–9:1.

All:

אָנֹכִי   שְׁמַעְתָּ וְנִתְאַיֵּמוּ / קַבְּלוּ מַלְכוּתִי וְלֹא תֵאָשֵׁמוּ
שִׁמְעוּ מוּסָר וַחֲכָמוּ:

לֹא־יִהְיֶה   מִקְוֵיכֶם זָר וְתָרֵעוּ / מֵעָבְדָתִי בַּל תִּגְרָעוּ
וַחֲכָמוּ וְאַל־תִּפְרָעוּ:

לֹא תִשָּׂא   עֹנֶשׁ לְחַלְּלִי / וְתִנָּצֵל מִמַּכְאוֹב וּמֵחֳלִי
אַשְׁרֵי־אָדָם שֹׁמֵעַ לִי:

זָכוֹר   וְשָׁמוֹר אֶת יוֹם / וְתִמְצָא כֹפֶר וּפִדְיוֹם
לִשְׁקֹד עַל־דַּלְתֹתַי יוֹם יוֹם:

כַּבֵּד   נָא הוֹרֶיךָ בְּמִבְטָחִי / וְתַאֲרִיךְ יָמִים וְתִהְיֶה חָי
לִשְׁמֹר מְזוּזֹת פְּתָחָי:

לֹא תִרְצָח   בְּנֶפֶשׁ מֵחַיִּים / וִיהִי חֶלְקְךָ בַּחַיִּים
כִּי מֹצְאִי מָצָא חַיִּים:

לֹא תִנְאָף   רֶשֶׁף כְּוִּוֹנָי / מֵרְחִיקָהּ יִשְׂבַּע עֶדְנָי
וַיָּפֶק רָצוֹן מֵיהוה:

לֹא תִגְנֹב   יְגִיעַ אִישׁ לְאִישׁוֹ / כִּי עֲמָלוֹ לָרִיק יְחִישׁוֹ
וְחֹטְאִי חֹמֵס נַפְשׁוֹ:

לֹא תַעֲנֶה   צֶדֶק לְעֵוֹת / מַלְשָׁנִי יִירַשׁ צַלְמָוֶת
כָּל־מְשַׂנְאַי אָהֲבוּ מָוֶת:

לֹא תַחְמֹד   חֲפָצִים הַרְבֵּית / תְּעוּדָה קָשֵׁר אַהֲבָתָהּ
חָכְמוֹת בָּנְתָה בֵיתָהּ:

וְכָל   קִנְיָנֶיךָ שִׁבְעָה / יָקָר מְאֹד טִבְעָה
חֻצְבָה עַמּוּדֶיהָ שִׁבְעָה:

The שְׁלִיחַ צִבּוּר:

חֲזַק וֶאֱמָץ בְּנִזְרָה / בִּירְאַת צוּרְךָ לְהִתְאַזְּרָה
וְהוּא יִהְיֶה לְךָ לְעֶזְרָה.

Continue with "עֶזְרַת אֲבוֹתֵינוּ" on page 343.

קרובה ליום טוב ראשון של שבועות

The שליח ציבור takes three steps forward and at the points indicated by ׳,
bends his knees at the first word, bows at the second, and
stands straight before saying God's name.

אֲדֹנָי, שְׂפָתַי תִּפְתָּח, וּפִי יַגִּיד תְּהִלָּתֶךָ:

תהלים נא

אבות

יִּבָּרוּךְ אַתָּה יהוה, אֱלֹהֵינוּ וֵאלֹהֵי אֲבוֹתֵינוּ
אֱלֹהֵי אַבְרָהָם, אֱלֹהֵי יִצְחָק, וֵאלֹהֵי יַעֲקֹב
הָאֵל הַגָּדוֹל הַגִּבּוֹר וְהַנּוֹרָא, אֵל עֶלְיוֹן
גּוֹמֵל חֲסָדִים טוֹבִים, וְקֹנֵה הַכֹּל, וְזוֹכֵר חַסְדֵי אָבוֹת
וּמֵבִיא גוֹאֵל לִבְנֵי בְנֵיהֶם לְמַעַן שְׁמוֹ בְּאַהֲבָה.
מֶלֶךְ עוֹזֵר וּמוֹשִׁיעַ וּמָגֵן.

The רשויות (prefatory prayers, asking permission to commence)
consist only of the standard opening "מְסוֹד חֲכָמִים...".

מְסוֹד חֲכָמִים וּנְבוֹנִים
וּמְלֶמֶד דַּעַת מְבִינִים
אֶפְתְּחָה פִּי בְּשִׁיר וּבְרַנָּנִים
לְהוֹדוֹת וּלְהַלֵּל פְּנֵי שׁוֹכֵן מְעוֹנִים

מגן

The old Ashkenazi custom was to say a cycle of piyutim, called a קרובה,
in the שחרית of חזרת הש״ץ. The קרובה said on the first day, composed
by Rabbi Elazar HaKalir, describes the Giving of the Torah.

The מגן, the first piyut of the קרובה, follows a simple alphabetic acrostic.
The concluding stanza stands apart from the others, and returns to the theme of protection
of the blessing "מָגֵן אַבְרָהָם". As part of the חזרת הש״ץ, all the piyutim should ideally be said by
the שליח ציבור alone. However, the prevailing custom is for the קהל to participate, and some
of the piyutim are said together, with the שליח ציבור raising his voice only toward the end.

All:

בְּסַהַר שְׁלִישִׁי הִתְגַּעֲשָׁה	אֶרֶץ מַטָּה וְרָעֲשָׁה
דּוֹד בְּשׂוֹרָה וַתִּתְרַעֲשָׁה.	גַּרְיָה חַיָּתָם נִרְעֲשָׁה

הוֹד אַפְדְנוּ נָטָה · וְעַל גִּבְנוּן אוֹתוֹ הִטָּה
זֶה סִינַי גֵּאוּת עָטָה · חִידָתוֹ כְּעַל אֶבְרָה הֶעְטָה.
טֹהַר צוּף שְׁלִישִׁי · יְשָׁרִים הֻרְגַּל לְפַלְשִׁי
כָּתַב שְׁלִישִׁים שְׁלִישִׁי · לְעֵת גֵּעָה בַּחֹדֶשׁ הַשְּׁלִישִׁי. ‹

All:

גּוֹרָלִי תִּמְתֹּךְ לְגוֹנְנִי · פָּץ בָּאתִי לְגַנִּי
עֻזְרִי וּמָגִנִּי · בְּמָגִנּוֹ לְגוֹנְנִי. ‹

בָּרוּךְ אַתָּה יהוה, מָגֵן אַבְרָהָם. ‹

גבורות

אַתָּה גִּבּוֹר לְעוֹלָם, אֲדֹנָי
מְחַיֶּה מֵתִים אַתָּה, רַב לְהוֹשִׁיעַ

In ארץ ישראל מוֹרִיד הַטָּל

מְכַלְכֵּל חַיִּים בְּחֶסֶד, מְחַיֶּה מֵתִים בְּרַחֲמִים רַבִּים
סוֹמֵךְ נוֹפְלִים, וְרוֹפֵא חוֹלִים, וּמַתִּיר אֲסוּרִים
וּמְקַיֵּם אֱמוּנָתוֹ לִישֵׁנֵי עָפָר.
מִי כָמוֹךָ, בַּעַל גְּבוּרוֹת, וּמִי דּוֹמֶה לָּךְ
מֶלֶךְ, מֵמִית וּמְחַיֶּה וּמַצְמִיחַ יְשׁוּעָה.
וְנֶאֱמָן אַתָּה לְהַחֲיוֹת מֵתִים.

מחיה

The מחיה, the second piyut of the קרובה, follows a double alphabetic acrostic, continuing from the letter ל where the מגן left off. It describes God calling Moses up to Him.

All:

מִן הָהָר לִמְעוֹנָיו · מִהַר וְקָרָא לְעָנָו
נִקְדַּשׁ שִׁבְעָה בַּעֲנָנָיו · נֶהָגוֹ לְפַגְנֵחַ לוֹ עֲנָנָיו.

שָׁש וְדָץ שְׁלַל נְוַת בַּיִת   שַׁר וְנֶאֱמָן כְּהוּשַׁת לַבָּיִת

עֶלְיוֹנִים נַעֲלוּ בַּעֲדוֹ בָּיִת.   עוֹדוֹ צָג בִּפְרוֹזְדוֹר הַבָּיִת

פְּאֵר מִבְטָחָה לְהוֹרִיד מִמַּעְלָה   פְּצוּ מָה אֱנוֹשׁ לְהַזְכֵּר בְּמַעְלָה

צַוָּה צוּר לַצִּיר עֲלֵה וְגַשׁ וְעָלָה.   ◦ צָעַד וְגָבַר וְעָלָה וְנִתְעַלָּה

All:

כְּטַל אִמְרֵי חֲקִים   אֱלֹהִים הִזִּיל מִשְׁחָקִים

נְקוּקִים יָקִים.   ◦ מִמֶּרְחַקִּים

בָּרוּךְ אַתָּה יהוה, מְחַיֵּה הַמֵּתִים.

משלש

The third piyut of the קרובה, the משלש, completes the acrostic.
It describes God descending upon Mount Sinai.

All:

קָדוֹשׁ הוֹפִיעַ מִפָּארָן בְּאַלְפֵי שִׁנְאָן

סִין הֵשִׁית שַׁאֲנָן, וְדָתוֹ בּוֹ שְׁנָן.

רָם רָד בְּמַרְכְּבוֹת בְּעֶשְׂרִים וּשְׁנַיִם אֶלֶף

לְהַכְתִּיר מַטֶּה סְפוּר בְּעֶשְׂרִים וּשְׁנַיִם אֶלֶף.

שִׁנֵּן בְּפָארָן וְשֵׂעִיר, וְאָתָם הַשֵּׂעִיר

וְאָתָא מֵרִבְבֹת קֹדֶשׁ, סִינַי בַּקֹּדֶשׁ.

תּוֹרָה חִנְּכִי, תּוּשִׁיָּה אָנֹכִי

◦ תַּכְלִית פָּץ אָנֹכִי, לָכֵן פָּתַח בְּאָנֹכִי.

The קהל aloud, followed by the שליח ציבור:

תהלים קמו
יִמְלֹךְ יהוה לְעוֹלָם, אֱלֹהַיִךְ צִיּוֹן לְדֹר וָדֹר, הַלְלוּיָהּ:

תהלים כב
וְאַתָּה קָדוֹשׁ, יוֹשֵׁב תְּהִלּוֹת יִשְׂרָאֵל:

אֵל נָא.

The *קרובה* includes several long piyutim usually said by the *קהל* with the *שליח*
ציבור accompanying in an undertone. It begins with the following, relatively
short, piyut which introduces the theme of the Ten Commandments:

All:

אָנֹכִי בְּשֵׁם אֵל שַׁדַּי

פַּצְתִּי מֵאָז לְעוֹלָמִי דִּי

וּבְבֹשֶׁן בֵּאַרְתִּיו בְּפֵרוּשׁ לִידִידַי

וּכְשֶׁקִּבְּלוּ עֹל מַלְכוּתִי עֲבָדַי

צִוִּיתִי לֹא־יִהְיֶה לְךָ אֵל אַחֵר מִבַּלְעָדַי

לֹא תִשָּׂא שֵׁם לַשָּׁוְא וְתִנָּקֶה עָדַי

זָכוֹר וְשָׁמוֹר כִּי הֵם שְׁנֵי עֵדַי

כַּבֵּד אוֹמְנֶךָ כִּי כְבוּדָם כְּבוּדִי

לֹא תִרְצָח מִתֹּאַר מַעֲשֵׂה יָדַי

לֹא תִנְאַף אַף בְּסָפֵק פֶּן תֵּעָנֵשׁ בְּוַדַּאי

לֹא תִגְנֹב וְתִתְבָּרֵךְ עַד בְּלִי דָי

לֹא תַעֲנֶה שֶׁקֶר בְּעֵדַי

לֹא תַחְמֹד כִּי אִם מַחְמַדַּי

אֵלֶּה הֵם סוֹדֵי מוֹדֵי שְׂרִידַי

פִּקּוּדַי שָׁהֲדֵי עֵדַי מְעִידַי

רְאוּ כִּי אֵין בִּלְעָדַי וַאֲנִי אֵל שַׁדָּי.

קהל *then* שליח ציבור:

חַי וְקַיָּם נוֹרָא וּמָרוֹם וְקָדוֹשׁ.

The following piyut describes the actual letters of the Torah.
Its stanzas begin with the author's signature, אלעזר בירבי קליר:

All:

אָז בִּכְתַב אַשּׁוּרִית / וּבִלְשׁוֹן עִבְרִית

וּבְדִבּוּר מִצְרִית / הִנְחַלְתָּ לְבַת עִבְרִית

לְאֶלֶף הִקְדַּמְתָּ בֵּית בִּיצִירַת בְּרֵאשִׁית

כִּי הוּכַן מֵאָז לְמַתַּן קִנְיַן רֵאשִׁית

עוֹלָם הוּכַן בְּאוֹת שֵׁנִי כִּי יֵשׁ עוֹלָם שֵׁנִי
אָנֹכִי בְּאוֹת רִאשׁוֹן כִּי הוּא אֶחָד וְאֵין שֵׁנִי

זָע אֶלֶף וַיֵּדֶא מוּל כִּסֵּא עֶשְׂרִים וְשִׁשָּׁה דוֹרוֹת
עַד שֶׁנִּתַּן תְּחִלָּה לַדִּבְּרוֹת

רֹן דָּת אָנֹכִי בִּכְתָב נוֹטְרִיקוֹן נֶחְבֵּאת
אָנֹכִי אֲנָא נַפְשִׁי כְּתָבִית יַהֲבִית

בְּאֵרָה לָמוֹ פָּנִים בִּפְנִים
וְעַל כָּל נְקֻדָּה וּנְקֻדָּה תִּשְׁעִים וּשְׁמֹנָה פָּנִים

יָהּ רָאָה וַיְסַפְּרָהּ הַכִּינָהּ וְגַם חֲקָרָהּ
לְאוֹהֲבֶיהָ וּלְשׁוֹמְרֶיהָ וְיִשְׁנֶה וְיִתְמְרָהּ

רָשַׁם לְמַפְרֵעַ אוֹתוֹתֵי מַאֲמָרֶיהָ
יְהִיבָה כְּתִיבָה נְעִימִים אֲמָרֶיהָ

בִּשְׁנַיִם הָרִאשׁוֹנִים חַיָּתָם עֻלְּפָה
כִּי הִסְכִּיתוּם מִפֶּה אֶל פֶּה

יִשָּׁקֵנוּ מִנְּשִׁיקוֹת / וְלֹא כָל נְשִׁיקוֹת
סָחוּ אֶל יֶרֶד אוֹתָם מִיֵּין הָרֶקַח לְהַשְׁקוֹת

קְצוּבוֹת וּנְעִימוֹת / וּפֶתִי מַחְכִּימוֹת
רְשׁוּמוֹת וַחֲתוּמוֹת / פְּתוּחוֹת וּסְתוּמוֹת

לְעַם אֲשֶׁר אָהַב / בְּחִבָּה יָהַב
וְהִנְחִיל נֶחֱמָדִים מִזָּהָב / לְעַם לוֹ מָאֳהָב

יָהּ שׁוֹכֵן עֲרָבוֹת / רָד לְהַנְחִיל רְבָבוֹת
בְּעֶשְׂרִים וּשְׁנַיִם אֶלֶף מַרְכָּבוֹת / אֲשֶׁר מֵאֵשׁ וְשֶׁלֶג חֲצוּבוֹת

רַחוּם הַדָּר בַּשְּׁחָקִים / יִסַּד עֹז מִפִּי יוֹנְקִים
וּבִזְכוּת אַפְסֵי־אֶרֶץ הֵקִים / זֹהַר תּוֹרוֹת וְחֻקִּים.

The following two paragraphs are a common feature in many קרובות, summing
up the simpler piyutim before turning to the longer, more complex ones.
Its second paragraph follows the letters of the alphabet from מ to ת,
possibly because the Name "א־ל" encompasses the other letters:

The קהל and the שליח ציבור:

אֵל נָא, לְעוֹלָם תָּעֲרָץ וּלְעוֹלָם תָּקְדַּשׁ
וּלְעוֹלְמֵי עוֹלָמִים תִּמְלֹךְ וְתִתְנַשֵּׂא
הָאֵל מֶלֶךְ נוֹרָא מָרוֹם וְקָדוֹשׁ
כִּי אַתָּה הוּא מֶלֶךְ מַלְכֵי הַמְּלָכִים.

מַלְכוּתוֹ נֶצַח / נוֹרְאוֹתָיו שִׂיחוּ / סַפְּרוּ עֻזּוֹ / פָּארוּהוּ צְבָאָיו /
קַדְּשׁוּהוּ רוֹמְמוּהוּ / רָן שִׁיר / שֶׁבַח תְּקֹף / תְּהִלּוֹת תִּפְאַרְתּוֹ.

סדר

The following piyut is based on the Midrash, according to which the Torah
preceded Creation. Like the יוצר for the first day (see page 700), it is based on
Proverbs 8:22–29 – each of its first sixteen stanzas begins with half a verse – and
describes the creation of the world. The final six stanzas describe the history of
man, with the Torah choosing the people of Israel, as a bride chooses her husband.
In some versions, short verses describing God creating the world "for the sake of
the Torah" are added after three of the first stanzas, and before the last one:

All:

משלי ח

וּבְכֵן, יהוה קָנָנִי רֵאשִׁית דַּרְכּוֹ:

יהוה קָנָנִי רֵאשִׁית דַּרְכּוֹ:
אַלְפַּיִם שָׁנָה נִמְתַּקְתִּי בְּחֻבּוֹ / עַד לֹא מָדַד עוֹלָם רָחְבּוֹ וְאָרְכּוֹ
טֶרֶם מָתַח רוּם עַד כֹּה וְעַד כֹּה / וְקֹדֶם הֵכִין בָּם רֶכֶב אַרְתְּכּוֹ

אֲנִי הָיִיתִי מִשְׁתַּעֲשַׁעַת עַל בִּרְכּוֹ / מְשַׂחֶקֶת לְפָנָיו לְהַלְלוֹ וּלְבָרְכוֹ
מְשַׂחֶקֶת בְּתֵבֵל אוֹתִי אִם בְּעָרְכוֹ / לְהוֹדִיעַ לַכֹּל כִּי אֵין כְּעֶרְכּוֹ.

וָאֶהְיֶה אָמוֹן אֵצֶל אָדוֹן, וָאֶהְיֶה שַׁעֲשׁוּעִים יוֹם יוֹם
מְשַׂחֶקֶת עַד זֶה הַיּוֹם

משלי ח

קֶדֶם מִפְעָלָיו מֵאָז:

בְּקֶדֶם קַדְמֹנִים קִדַּמְתִּי מֵאָז

קֶדֶם עַמּוּדֵי רוֹם הָיִיתִי עַמּוּד מֵאָז

קֶדֶם פָּעַל יְסוֹד הָיָה יְסוֹדִי מֵאָז

קֶדֶם אֶבֶן פִּנָּה הָיִיתִי אֶבֶן פִּנָּה מֵאָז

קֶדֶם כָּל נְסִיכִים הָיִיתִי נְסוּכָה מֵאָז

וּבִהְיוֹת עוֹלָם מַיִם בַּמַּיִם הָיִיתִי חֲקוּקָה מֵאָז

וּבִהְיוֹת עוֹלָם תֹּהוּ וָבֹהוּ הָיִיתִי כְנֵר מֵאָז

וּבִהְיוֹת חֹשֶׁךְ עַל פְּנֵי תְהוֹם הָיִיתִי כִמְנוֹרָה מֵאָז

קֶדֶם כָּל אֵלֶּה הוּא וַאֲנִי הָיִינוּ מֵאָז.

Some add:

וְהָיָה אָמוֹן מְהֻרְהֵר לְמַעֲנָה

וְאָמַר בְּלִבּוֹ אֶבְרָא עוֹלָם בְּבִינָה בַּעֲבוּר אֱמָנָה.

משלי ח

מֵעוֹלָם נִסַּכְתִּי מֵרֹאשׁ:

גְּזֵרָה שָׁוָה גָּזַר בִּי מֵרֹאשׁ / לַחֲקֹר וְלִדְרֹשׁ

הַכֹּל מֵרֹאשׁ / מִי יַעֲלֶה בְּרֹאשׁ / מִי יִהְיֶה בְּרֹאשׁ

מַה שֶּׁהָיָה מֵרֹאשׁ / הוּא שֶׁיִּהְיֶה בַּסּוֹף לְרֹאשׁ

נְסִיכֵי אָדָם נִסְכוּ בִי מֵרֹאשׁ

וְנָסַכְתִּי לְמַלְכֵי הַמִּתְנַשֵּׂא לְכֹל לְרֹאשׁ.

Some add:

וְהָיָה אֵלָיו בְּדָבְדָּהּ / וְנִשְׁתַּעֲשַׁע בְּדִבּוּרָהּ

וְאָמַר בַּעֲבוּרָהּ / אֶבְרָא עוֹלָם לְהַגְבִּירָה / וְלַדּוֹרוֹת לְהַסְבִּירָה.

משלי ח

מִקַּדְמֵי־אֶרֶץ: / מִקְּדוּמֵי אֶרֶץ

דְּבָרִים שִׁבְעָה קָדְמוּ לָאָרֶץ

כִּסֵּא רָם וְנִשָּׂא קָדַם לִשְׁמֵי אֶרֶץ

כִּסֵּא יִשְׂרָאֵל קָדַם לְמַלְכוּת הָאָרֶץ

אֲבוֹת הָעוֹלָם קָדְמוּ לְמוֹסְדֵי אֶרֶץ
שֵׁם מָשִׁיחַ קָדַם לַשֵּׁמוֹת אֲשֶׁר בָּאָרֶץ
גַּן עֵדֶן קָדְמָה לְעַנְוֵי אֶרֶץ
עָרוּךְ מֵאֶתְמוֹל קָדַם לְרִשְׁעֵי אֶרֶץ
יִשְׂרָאֵל וְהַתְּשׁוּבָה קָדְמוּ לְיוֹשְׁבֵי הָאָרֶץ
וַאֲנִי לָהֶם קָדַמְתִּי מִקַּדְמֵי אָרֶץ.

Some add:

וְהָיָה מֶלֶךְ בִּמְסִבּוֹ / מְהַדֵּר בְּמִדַּת טוּבוֹ
וְאָמַר בְּלִבּוֹ / אֶבְרָא עוֹלָם לְיִשּׁוּבוֹ / בַּעֲבוּר יְשׁוּבוֹ.

בְּאֵין־תְּהֹמוֹת חוֹלָלְתִּי: משלי ח

הָאָרֶץ עַד לֹא נִתְחוֹלְלָה נִתְחוֹלַלְתִּי
וּבְאֵין חֹשֶׁךְ עַל־פְּנֵי תְהוֹם הֶאֱרַתִּי וְהִגַּהְתִּי
וּבְאֵין קוֹרֵא תְהוֹם אֶל תְּהוֹם בְּפִיו נִקְרֵאתִי
וּבָעֵת נִבְקְעוּ בְדַעְתּוֹ נִבְקְעוּ בְדַעְתִּי
וּבַתְּהוֹם רַבָּה מִשְׁפָּטַי מִלֵּאתִי
וַעֲלֵיהֶם חֹק חַגְּתִי וְנִגְבַּלְתִּי
וּבַתַּנִּינִים אֲשֶׁר בַּתְּהֹמוֹת נִתְהַלָּלְתִּי.

בְּאֵין מַעְיָנוֹת נִכְבַּדֵּי־מָיִם: משלי ח

וּבְאֵין מַעְיָנוֹת מַעְיָנֵי נוֹבַעַת מַיִם / וּבְאֵין נְהָרוֹת נְהָרֵי מוֹשֵׁךְ מָיִם
וּבְאֵין בְּאֵרוֹת בְּאֵרֵי נוֹבַעַת מַיִם / וּבְאֵין מְקוֹרוֹת מְקוֹרֵי חַיִּים מָיִם
וּבְאֵין מַיִם הָיִיתִי כִּבְרֵכַת מַיִם / וּבְאֵין מִקְוֶה מִקְוֵה מָיִם
מִקְוֵה יִשְׂרָאֵל יהוה, לְהַזּוֹת מִמִּקְוֵה מָיִם. ירמיה י

בְּטֶרֶם הָרִים הָטְבָּעוּ: משלי ח

זָוִיּוֹת עוֹלָם בִּי נְטָעוּ / הָרֵי יִשְׂרָאֵל בִּי נִתְקָעוּ
הָרֵי אֵל בִּי נִתְוַדָּעוּ / הָרֵי עַד בִּי נִתַּיְדָּעוּ

בְּפֶלֶס וּבְמֹאזְנַיִם בִּי נִשְׁקְלוּ וְנוֹדָעוּ
תוֹעֲפוֹת גָּבְהָם וּמֶחְקְרֵי יְסוֹדָם בִּי נִשְׁתַּמְּעוּ
וּבְהוֹדִיעִי בְסִינַי בִּי נִזְדַּעְזָעוּ / וּלְהַר הַמּוֹרִיָּה כֻּלָּם נִכְרָעוּ

איוב לח

וְעַל־מָה אֲדָנֶיהָ הָטְבָּעוּ: / בְּטַבַּעְתִּי אֶרֶץ וַאֲדָנֶיהָ הָטְבָּעוּ.

משלי ח

וְלִפְנֵי גְבָעוֹת חוֹלָלְתִּי:

חֵקֶר גְּבָעוֹת עוֹלָם נִתְחוֹלָלְתִּי / גִּבְעַת הַלְּבוֹנָה אֲנִי חַלְתִּי
גִּבְעָה נְשָׂאָה אֲנִי הוֹלַדְתִּי / וּגְבָעוֹת כְּנִשְׂאוּ בְצִדְקָה נִתְנַשֵּׂאתִי
וּלְכָל הַר וְגִבְעָה קָדְמָה גִבְעָתִי / וּמִגְּבָעוֹת לְגִבְעוֹת עוֹלָם דָּלַגְתִּי
וּמִגִּבְעוֹת עוֹלָם לְגִבְעַת סִינַי נִגְבַּלְתִּי.

משלי ח

עַד־לֹא עָשָׂה אֶרֶץ וְחוּצוֹת:

טַבּוּר הָאָרֶץ וְטַבּוּר חוּצוֹת
טַבּוּרִי הָיָה מַשְׁתִּית אֶרֶץ וְחוּצוֹת
וּמִשְׁתִּית טַבּוּרִי הוּשְׁתוּ אֶרֶץ וְחוּצוֹת
מֶחְקֵי אֶל חֵיק הָאָרֶץ וּמֶחְקֵי הָאָרֶץ אֶל חֵיק חוּצוֹת
וּמִמַּשְׁתִּיתִי מַשְׁתִּית אֶרֶץ וְחוּצוֹת
כְּפִי תַחְרָא בֵּין אֶרֶץ וְחוּצוֹת.

משלי ח

וְרֹאשׁ עַפְרוֹת תֵּבֵל:

יְצִיר אֲשֶׁר יָצַר רֹאשׁ עַפְרוֹת תֵּבֵל / מִמֶּנּוּ הֻצַּק מְצוּקֵי תֵבֵל
וַיָּשֶׁת עֲלֵיהֶם תֵּבֵל: / כְּתְרוּמָה הוּרַם רֹאשׁ עַפְרוֹת תֵּבֵל

שמואל א' ב

כְּחַלָּה מֵעִסָּה הֻפְרִישָׁם לְתָבֵל / וּמִזְבַּח אֲדָמָה רֹאשׁ עַפְרוֹת תֵּבֵל
מְגּוּשֵׁי הֻשְׁלַךְ עָפָר לְתָבֵל / הוּא הָיָה רֹאשׁ עַפְרוֹת תֵּבֵל.

משלי ח

בַּהֲכִינוֹ שָׁמַיִם שָׁם אָנִי:

כְּאֹהֶל עֵת טֶרֶם מְתָחָם יוֹתֵר מֵהֶם מְתָחָנִי
כַּדֹּק עֵת טֶרֶם נָטָם אֶצְלוֹ נְטָנִי

בְּיָמִין טֶרֶם טִפָּחָם מִימִינוֹ אֵשׁ דָּת טִפְּחַנִי
וּבְזֶרֶת טֶרֶם תִּכְּנָם בָּהּ תִּכְּנַנִי
בְּאֶצְבָּעוֹת טֶרֶם קְבָעָם בְּאֶצְבְּעוֹתָיו קְבָעַנִי
וְעֵת פֵּרְשָׁם כָּאֹהֶל כַּיְרִיעָה פֵּרְשַׁנִי
וְלִירִיעוֹתָם אָמַר דַּי וְלִירִיעָתִי לֹא אָמַר דַּיְנִי.

משלי ח   בְּחֻקוֹ חוּג עַל־פְּנֵי תְהוֹם:
לְמַעֲנִי חַק שְׁלֹשָׁה חֻקִּים עַל רוּם וְעַל תַּחַת וְעַל תְּהוֹם
בְּשׂוּמוֹ לַיָּם חֹק חָג עַל פְּנֵי תְהוֹם
בְּחָקוֹ אֶבֶן שְׁתִיָּה עַל פְּנֵי תְהוֹם
בְּחָקוֹ לְוְיָתָן עַל דַּלְתוֹת תְּהוֹם
בְּחָקוֹ אֶבֶן פִּנָּה שֶׁלֹּא יָצִיף לְעוֹלָם תְּהוֹם
בְּחָקוֹ חוּג חֻקִּי כָּבוּשׁ עַל תְּהוֹם.

משלי ח   בְּאַמְּצוֹ שְׁחָקִים מִמָּעַל:
מִתְאַמֶּצֶת הָיִיתִי בִּמְרוֹמֵי מַעַל
בְּאַמְּצוֹ עֲרָבוֹת לִרְכּוּבוֹ / הָיִיתִי רְכוּבוֹ
בְּאַמְּצוֹ שְׁחָקִים לְעֻזּוֹ / הָיִיתִי מָעֻזּוֹ
בְּאַמְּצוֹ מְעֹנָה בִּזְרוֹעוֹ / הָיִיתִי כְּקָמֵעַ עַל זְרוֹעוֹ
בְּאַמְּצוֹ זְבוּל לְקָדְשׁוֹ / הָיִיתִי זְבוּלָה בְּשֵׁם קָדְשׁוֹ
בְּאַמְּצוֹ עֲרָפֶל תַּחַת רַגְלָיו / הָיִיתִי מִשְׁתַּעֲשַׁעַת עַל אַרְכֻּבּוֹת רַגְלָיו
תהלים קמח   בְּאַמְּצוֹ שָׁמַיִם וּשְׁמֵי הַשָּׁמַיִם / וְהַמַּיִם אֲשֶׁר מֵעַל הַשָּׁמָיִם:
בְּאַמְּצוֹ כָל אֵלֶּה אִמְּצַנִי נוֹטֶה שָׁמָיִם.

משלי ח   בַּעֲזוֹז עִינוֹת תְּהוֹם:
נֶעֶזְזָה מַעְיְנִי מִמַּעְיְנוֹת תְּהוֹם / נֶעֶזְזוּ מֵימַי מִמֵּימֵי תְהוֹם
בְּטֶרֶם נֶעֶזְזוּ עַזִּים עֻזָּה הָיִיתִי עַל תְּהוֹם.

משליח

בְּשׂוּמוֹ לַיָּם חֻקּוֹ:

משליח

שָׁם עֲלֵיהֶם חֻקִּי, וּמַיִם לֹא יַעַבְרוּ־פִּיו: / כֵּן לֹא יַעַבְרוּ עַל פִּי
וְנִשְׁתַּכְלֵל עוֹלָם בְּמַאֲמַר פִּי שֶׁהָיִיתִי בְּפִיו.

משליח

בְּחֻקּוֹ מוֹסְדֵי אָרֶץ:

משליח

סָד בְּמוֹסְדֵי מוֹסְדֵי אָרֶץ דֹּ֫רֶץ / הֵמָּה הַיּוֹצְרִים הַיְצוּרִים אֲשֶׁר בָּאָרֶץ
וְיוֹשְׁבֵי נְטָעִים נְטִיעַת שׂוֹרֵק בָּאָרֶץ / לִנְטֹעַ שָׁמַיִם וְלִיסֹד אָרֶץ
וּגְדֵרָה נַעֲשֵׂיתִי גָדֵר בָּאָרֶץ
עִם הַמֶּלֶךְ בִּמְלַאכְתּוֹ מָלַךְ בִּי מֶלֶךְ עַל כָּל הָאָרֶץ

תהלים נ

הַמְלִיכֵנִי וְהִמְלַכְתִּיו עַד לֹא שָׁמַיִם וָאָרֶץ / וּמִיּוֹם דִּבֵּר וַיִּקְרָא־אָרֶץ:
קָרָא לִי רָאשֵׁי דֹרוֹת הָאָרֶץ / קָרָא לְאָדָם הַנּוֹצָר מֵאָרֶץ

בראשית ו

קָרָא לְנֹחַ, אִישׁ צַדִּיק בָּאָרֶץ: / קָרָא לְאַבְרָהָם מֵאֲצִילֵי אָרֶץ
קָרָא לְיִצְחָק הַזֹּרֵעַ בָּאָרֶץ / קָרָא לְיַעֲקֹב הַנֶּחְתָּם בִּשְׁמֵי עָרֶץ
קָרָא לַשְּׁבָטִים, לִקְדוֹשִׁים אֲשֶׁר־בָּאָרֶץ:

תהלים טז

וְעַל כָּל אֶחָד וְאֶחָד שְׁאֵלַנִי יוֹצֵר הָאָרֶץ.

בראשית ה

עָמַד אָדָם רֹאשׁ לַנְּשָׁמוֹת / זֶה סֵפֶר תּוֹלְדֹת אָדָם, רְשׁוּמוֹת
וְאָמַר אֵלֶיהָ הִנֵּה זֶה חָכָם מָלֵא חָכְמוֹת
בִּדְמוּת וּבְצֶלֶם אוֹתוֹ לְדַמּוֹת / כְּאַחַד מִמֶּנּוּ מַעְלָה בְּאֵימוֹת
וּמוֹרָאוֹ עַל חַיּוֹת וּבְהֵמוֹת / וְכֻלָּם יָצַרְתִּי עֲלֵי אֲדָמוֹת
וּבְדַעְתּוֹ קָרָא לָהֶן שֵׁמוֹת
וְאַחֲרֵי כֵן קָרָא שְׁמִי הַנִּכְבָּד וְהַנּוֹרָא בַּשֵּׁמוֹת.

פֵּרֵשׁ זֶה סֵפֶר תּוֹלְדֹת אָדָם
וְנִמְצָא דּוֹר שְׁלִישִׁי דָּחוּף מִבְּנֵי אָדָם
כְּהוּחַל לִקְרֹא בְּשֵׁם מַעֲשֵׂה יְדֵי אָדָם
וְקָם דּוֹר עֲשִׂירִי מְקֻלְקָל בָּאָדָם

בראשית ו

וַיִּרְאוּ בְנֵי־הָאֱלֹהִים אֶת בְּנוֹת הָאָדָם:

בראשית ו

וַיַּרְא יהוה כִּי רַבָּה רָעַת הָאָדָם:

בראשית ו וַיֹּאמֶר יהוה אֶמְחֶה אֶת־הָאָדָם:
לוּלֵי נוֹלַד אִישׁ צַדִּיק בָּאָדָם

יחזקאל א זֶה יְנַחֲמֵנוּ אוֹמְרִים מִלְמַעְלָה, פְּנֵיהֶם פְּנֵי אָדָם:
וּמִמַּטָּה אוֹמְרִים זֶה יְנַחֲמֵנוּ בְּנֵי אָדָם
וְאָמַר אֵלֶיהָ הִנֵּה אָדָם תַּחַת אָדָם
וּמָצָא חֵן וְשֵׂכֶל טוֹב בְּעֵינֵי אֱלֹהִים וְאָדָם.

צָץ מִמִּזְרָח וְכַשַּׁחַר עָלָה / וְנִקְרָא עַיִט פּוֹרֵחַ עַל פְּנֵי מַעֲלָה
אַב הָמוֹן נִקְרָא וְנִתְעַלָּה / וּבַעֲשָׂרָה נִצְרַף וְלֹא נִמְצָא בּוֹ עַוְלָה
עֲבוֹדָה זָרָה זָדוּ עַל יָדוֹ בָּטָלָה / וְקָרֵב רְחוֹקִים לִזְכוּת מְנֻטָּלָה
הִכִּירַנִי וְהִכַּרְתִּיו בְּאַהֲבָה כְּלוּלָה / כְּדֵי הוּא לְיךְ לְשֵׁם וְלִתְהִלָּה
לִשְׁמֹר מִצְוֹתֶיךָ יוֹמָם וָלָיְלָה / דּוֹרוֹת אֲשֶׁר לְפָנָיו לֹא זָכוּ לַמִּילָה
וּמֵעֵת נִתְחַתְּמָה בּוֹ, נִתְמַנָּה רֹאשׁ לְכָל תְּפִלָּה.

קָרְבָּן שָׁלֵם יְחִידוֹ נִמְצָא / כְּטֶנָא בִכּוּרִים אָז נִרְצָה
כְּשֶׂה לַטֶּבַח רָץ בִּמְרוּצָה / שְׁלֹשָׁה יָמִים טֹרַף וְנַפְשׁוֹ לֹא קָצָה
הִוָּעֵצִי נָא עִמִּי דַת מוֹעֵצָה / וְלִקְחִי אוֹתוֹ לְחֶפֶת עֲלִיצָה
לָשׂוּחַ בַּשָּׂדֶה לִקְרָאתֶךָ יָצָא / וּלְמַעֲנוּ אֶרְאֵלִים מִמְּחִיצָה
צָעֲקוּ חָצָה.

רָחַק אִישׁ שָׂדֶה וְקָרֹב אִישׁ תָּם / יֹשֵׁב אֹהָלִים בְּאָהֳלֵי רוֹם נֶחְתָּם
עֹלִים בְּמַעֲלוֹתָם / וְיוֹרְדִים בִּירִידָתָם
תְּמֵהִים עַל מַרְאֶה זֶה חוֹתָם
וְאָמַר אֵלֶיהָ הִנֵּה זֶה חוֹתָם / יָפֶה מִכָּל חוֹתָם
חוֹתָמוֹת שְׁנַיִם עָשָׂר נֶחְתְּמוּ מִזֶּה חוֹתָם
בְּטַבַּעַת הַמֶּלֶךְ טְבוּעִים אֶחָד חוֹתָם
עַל לֵב וְעַל זְרוֹעַ לְמַעֲנֶךָ חֲתַמְתִּי חוֹתָם.

שָׁלְמוּ כָל אֵלֶּה בְּעָמְדוֹ עִם עוֹלָם
כְּשָׁלְמוּ אֲלָפִים עַד שֶׁלֹּא נִבְרָא עוֹלָם
וַאֲלָפַיִם וְאַרְבַּע מֵאוֹת וְאַרְבָּעִים וּשְׁמֹנֶה שָׁנָה מִשֶּׁנִּבְרָא עוֹלָם

וְאָמְרָה תוֹרָה, זֶה מֹשֶׁה אֲשֶׁר נִכְתַּב עָנוּ מֵעוֹלָם

וַיְדַבֵּר יהוה אֶל מֹשֶׁה נִרְשַׁם מֵעוֹלָם / הוּא יִרְשִׁי מוֹרֶשֶׁת עוֹלָם

וְהוּא יִקְחִי מַתְּנַת עוֹלָם / וְכָל בָּאֵי עוֹלָם יַאֲמִינוּ בִי לְעוֹלָם.

Some add:

וְהָיָה אֵל אֱמוּנָה / מְהַרְהֵר לְמַעֲנָה / וּמֵבִין בַּחֲנִינָה

אֶבְרָא עוֹלָם בְּבִינָה / בַּעֲבוּר אֱמָנָה.

תּוֹלְדוֹת רוֹם וָתַחַת בְּהִזְדַּעְזְעָם / שִׁבְעָה קוֹלוֹת כְּנִרְאוּ בְּנָעַם

שְׁתַּיִם זוּ שָׁמַעְנוּ שְׁמָעָם / וּלְשֵׁתֵּי שְׁמִיעוֹת נֶחֱלַק קוֹל רַעַם

לַגּוֹיִם קוֹל זַעַם / וּלְיִשְׂרָאֵל קוֹל נָעַם

וְאָמְרוּ הַכֹּל מַה זֶּה קוֹל מָרְעָם / הוֹלֵךְ וּמִתְגַּלְגֵּל כְּגַלְגַּלֵּי רַעַם

וְאָמַר לָהֶם יֵשׁ לִי טַעַם בֵּינִי וּבֵין עָם

וְרֶכֶב רִבֹּתַיִם נִתְכּוּנוּ מוּל עָם

וְשִׁבְעָה רְקִיעִים נָטוּ בְּזוּעָם / בַּזֶּרֶת אֲשֶׁר תִּקָּנָם בָּהּ קְרָעָם

וַיִּטֵּם וַיַּסִּיעֵם מִמְּקוֹמָם וּמִמַּסָּעָם / וְהָיוּ נוֹטְפִים בְּשֵׁם מִזֵּעָם

וְאָמְרוּ מַלְאֲכֵי קֹדֶשׁ מַה זֶּה הַטַּעַם

נוֹרָא אֱלֹהִים מִמִּקְדָּשׁוֹ הַמְנֹעָם

אֵל יִשְׂרָאֵל הוּא נֹתֵן עֹז וְתַעֲצֻמוֹת לָעָם: <small>תהלים סח</small>

וּבְכֵן אָמַר לְעָנָו, רֵד הָעֵד בָּעָם: <small>שמות יט</small>

וַיִּשְׂמְחוּ כָל הָעָם / בְּשִׂמְחַת אִמְרֵי נֹעַם / וְנִתְמַנָּה צִיר רוֹעָם

וַיֵּרֶד מֹשֶׁה מִן־הָהָר אֶל־הָעָם: <small>שמות יט</small>

<small>סדר דיברין</small>

The following piyut continues from the point at which the previous one ended.
It consists of twelve alphabetic stanzas (with the acrostic alternating between a
straightforward א״ב and the reverse תשר״ק), and focuses on the Ten Commandments.

קהל *then* שליח ציבור:

וּבְכֵן, וַיֵּרֶד מֹשֶׁה מִן־הָהָר אֶל־הָעָם: <small>שמות יט</small>

All:

אִתּוֹ מִצְוֹת וְחֻקִּים / בָּאֵר הֵיטֵב חֲקוּקִים

גְּמוּלֵי חָלָב מֵינִיקִים / דַּדֵּימוֹ חָכְמָה מְפִיקִים

הַשֶּׁפַע מְקוֹר חַיִּים מְזֻנָּקִים / וּמְנֹפֶת צוּפִים וּמִדְּבַשׁ מְתוּקִים

זֹהַר לָעֵינַיִם מַבְהִיקִים / חֹבֶשׁ לָעֲצָמוֹת מַשִּׁיקִים

טוֹבִים יְשָׁרִים וְצַדִּיקִים / יְקָרִים מִפְּנִינִים וּמִכָּל חֲשׁוּקִים

כָּתַב אֶצְבַּע שׁוֹכֵן שְׁחָקִים / לְנִצְרֵימוֹ מֵחֵטְא מְנַקִּים

מַצְדִּיקִים לְכָל בָּם עוֹסְקִים / נִדְבָּרֵימוֹ בַּסֵּפֶר נֶחְקָקִים

משלי ג סֹפְּרֵימוֹ בְּצֶדֶק מְחֻקָּקִים / עֵץ־חַיִּים הִיא לַמַּחֲזִיקִים:

פְּאֵר לִוְיַת חֵן וַעֲנָקִים / צְדָקוֹת מְלֵאִים וְלֹא רֵקִים

קְדוּמִים טֶרֶם יְסוֹד אֲפִיקִים / רוֹם וָעֹמֶק אֵל בָּם הֵקִים

שְׁמָעָם לְשׁוֹשַׁנַּת עֲמָקִים / תּוֹצְאוֹתָם לְחֵךְ מַמְתַּקִים.

תהלים פו ‹ מַמְתַּקִים דִּבְרֵי אֱלֹהִים / לְאוֹמְרֵי, אֵין־כָּמוֹךָ בָּאֱלֹהִים:

All:

שמות כ וַיְדַבֵּר אֱלֹהִים:

תִּתּוֹ קוֹל עֹז אֵל אֵלִים / שַׁלְהֲבוּ לַפִּידֵי גֶחָלִים

רָצוּ בְרָקִים קַלִּים / קוֹלוֹת הִרְעִימוּ גַלְגַּלִּים

צָרַח שׁוֹפָר מִמְּעָלִים / פְּצָמָה רְקוּעַת שְׁעוּלִים

עַמִּים אָחֲזוּ בֶהָלִים / סַעַר צִירִים וַחֲבָלִים

נְהִי כַּיּוֹלֵדָה חָלִים / מַרְצְדִים הָיוּ מְגֻבָּלִים

לְבָנוֹן וְשִׂרְיוֹן כַּעֲגָלִים / כַּרְמֶל וּבָשָׁן כְּמוֹ אֵילִים

יַחַד תָּבוֹר וְכָל תְּלוּלִים / טֹרְחוּ בְגָבְהָהּ וְנִמְצְאוּ פְסוּלִים

חַי רָם רוֹאֶה שְׁפָלִים / זֶה סִינַי כַּדָּךְ לֹא הִכְלִים

וְהִטָּה אֵלָיו זְבוּלִים / הֶעֱטִירוּ עֲנָנִים וַעֲרָפֶלִים

דָּר בּוֹ בְּשִׁנְאַן אֶרְאֶלִים / גְּאוֹן קוֹלוֹ הִשְׁמִיעַ לַנִּדְגָּלִים

בִּסְבִיב הָהָר נִגְבָּלִים / בְּנַעֲשֶׂה וְנִשְׁמַע דָּת מְקַבְּלִים

אֹזְנָם שָׁם רֹאשׁ מִלִּים / אָנֹכִי שָׁמַע לַכֻּלָּלִים.

‹ לַכֻּלָּלִים הִשְׁמַעְתָּ מְלֶיךָ / מְפוֹצֵץ הָרִים קוֹלֶךָ

All:

שמות כ אָנֹכִי יהוה אֱלֹהֶיךָ:

אֲשֶׁר כָּל פָּעֲלוֹ תָמִים / בּוֹנֶה מַעֲלוֹת בַּמְּרוֹמִים

גּוֹדֵר תַּחְתִּיּוֹת הַדָּמִים / דֶּלֶת סוֹגֵר בְּעַד הוֹמִים

הַמַּזְרִיחַ מְאוֹרוֹת רָמִים / וּמַנְהִיגָם לֵילוֹת וְיָמִים

זְקִים עוֹשֶׂה וּרְעָמִים / חוֹשֵׂר טְלָלִים וּגְשָׁמִים

טִיעוֹת מְגַדֵּל וְצַמְּחֵי תְלָמִים / יוֹצֵר וּבוֹרֵא כָּל הַנְּשָׁמִים

כָּל רוּחוֹתָם בְּיָדֵי שָׁמִים / לַחֲמָם אָכִין בְּמַטְעַמִּים

מֵמִית וּמְחַיֶּה וַאֲנִי חַי לְעוֹלָמִים / נִסַּי גְדֹלִים וַעֲצֻמִים

סֶלָה לְעוֹלָם קַיָּמִים / עֹזֶךְ בִּבְרִית אָבוֹת תְּמִימִים

פּוֹדְךָ מִסִּבְלוֹת עֲנָמִים / צֶלָלָם בְּנִבְכֵי תְהוֹמִים

קוֹרֵעַ לְפָנֶיךָ יַמִּים / רֹעֲךָ בְּמָן מַטְעַמִּים

שָׁקַדְתִּי לְבָחֳרָךְ מֵאֻמִּים / תֵּרַתִּי לְסַגֶּלְךָ לִי מֵעַמִּים.

◂ מֵעַמִּים חַשְׁתִּי לְבַדְּךָ / תְּמוּרִי אֵל לֹא יִהְיֶה לָךְ

All:

שמות כ
לֹא־יִהְיֶה לָךְ:

תָּעוּת זוֹרְחִים וְצוֹלְלִים / שִׁקּוּץ תּוֹעֲבוֹת גִּלּוּלִים

רִיק וָתֹהוּ הֵם הָאֱלִילִים / קֶטֶב שְׂעִירֵי בְעָלִים

צַלְמֵי מַסֵּכוֹת וּפְסִילִים / פְּעֻלַּת תַּבְנִית כָּל סְמָלִים

עֲצַבֵּי הַגּוֹיִם הָעֲרֵלִים / סוּמִים חֵרְשִׁים וְלֹא מְמַלְּלִים

נְשָׂאִים בַּכָּתֵף נִסְבָּלִים / מְאוּמָה לְהוֹעִיל לֹא יְכוֹלִים

לֹא עוֹזְרִים וְלֹא מַצִּילִים / כְּנוֹפְלִים נִשְׁבָּרִים כִּנְבָלִים

יֵבֹשׁוּ כָּל בָּם מִתְהַלְּלִים / טוֹעֵיהֶם בַּחֹשֶׁךְ מוּבָלִים

חַגֵּיהֶם מְאוּסִים וּגְעוּלִים / וְזִבְחֵיהֶם מְרַק פִּגּוּלִים

וְנִסְכֵּיהֶם יֵין תַּרְעֵלִים / הֵיכְלֵיהֶם קִבְרֵי חֲלָלִים

דָּתֵיהֶם חֻקּוֹת הֲבָלִים / גּוֹיִם לְתֹפֶת נִדְגָּלִים

בְּנִי לְבֹדֲאָךְ תְּנָה הִלּוּלִים / אַל תִּתֵּן אֶת שְׁמוֹ לַחֲלוּלִים.

◂ לַחֲלוּלִים אַל תִּתֵּן אֶת שֵׁם / וְסוּר מֵרָע פֶּן תִּכָּשֵׁל וְתֶאְשַׁם

All:

שמות כ
לֹא תִשָּׂא אֶת־שֵׁם:

אֵת שֵׁם אַדִּיר בָּאַדִּירִים / בָּרוּךְ זִכְרוֹ לְדוֹר דּוֹרִים
גַּחֲלֵי אֵשׁ מִמֶּנּוּ בּוֹעֲרִים / דָּתוֹ חֶרֶב לְלָהּ מְפִירִים
הַמַּרְעִישׁ אֶרֶץ וּמַרְגִּיז הָרִים / וְגוֹעֵר בַּיָּם וּמַחֲרִיב קָרִים
זַעֲמוֹ לֹא יָכִילוּ יְצוּרִים / חֲמָתוֹ מְנַתֶּצֶת צוּרִים
טוֹב לַיְשָׁרִים וְנֹקֵם לְצָרִים / יֵחַתּוּ מֶנּוּ אַבִּירִים
כֻּלָּם מִפַּחְדּוֹ נִסְעָרִים / לוֹ מְשָׁרְתִים וְתֹאֲרוֹ לֹא שָׁרִים
מוֹרָא שְׁמוֹ לַשָּׁוְא לֹא תָרִים / נִגְעֲךָ בוֹ יְרַעֲדוּ בְךָ אֵבָרִים
סוּר מִשְּׁבוּעַת שְׁקָרִים / עָרוּךְ בָּהּ אָלוֹת וַאֲרוּרִים
פּוֹרַעַת מְעוֹר וּמִבְּשָׂרִים / צוֹפֶרֶת כָּעוֹף וּבָאָה חֲדָרִים
קִירוֹת הוֹפֶכֶת עִם מְקָרִים / רָחֵק מִמֶּנָּה בְּכָל דְּבָרִים
שְׁמֹר שְׁבוּעַת אִסָּר וּנְדָרִים / תִּירָא אֵל נֹתֵן שַׁבָּת לַשּׁוֹמְרִים.

‹ לַשּׁוֹמְרִים יוֹם שַׁבַּת נְפִישׁוֹ / עֲתִידִים בַּקֹּדֶשׁ לְהַקְדִּישׁוֹ

All:

זָכוֹר אֶת־יוֹם הַשַּׁבָּת לְקַדְּשׁוֹ:

שמות כ

תַּכְלִית כָּל פֹּעַל רוֹם וְתַחְתּוֹנִים / שְׁבִיעִי לַיָּמִים הַנִּמְנִים
רִאשׁוֹן לְמִקְרָאֵי זְמַנִּים / קָדוֹשׁ לַאֲדֹנֵי הָאֲדֹנִים
צְבִי שַׁבָּת שַׁאֲנַנִּים / פְּדָת מִדִּין יְצִיר מִלְּפָנִים
עָנְתָה שִׁירָה וְכִפְּרָה פָנִים / סִימָה לְאוֹת וּלְעַד בֵּין אָב לַבָּנִים
נֵצֹר יְצִיאוֹתֶיהָ כְּהוֹרוּ נְבוֹנִים / מַשָּׂא בְּלִי לְהוֹצִיא מִבִּפְנִים
לְמַחַלְלֶיהָ מִיתוֹת דָּנִים / כָּרֵת וּרְגִימַת אֲבָנִים
יְדוּעָה הִיא לְךָ בְּמִן מִיָּמִים קַדְמוֹנִים / טַעֲמוּ לֹא רַד בָּהּ מִמְּעוֹנִים
חַבְרֵי אוֹב בָּהּ לֹא נַעֲנִים / זְכֹר כִּי בָהּ יִשְׁבֹּת נָהָר צְפוֹנִים
וְנַח בָּהּ מִמְּלֶאכֶת חוּץ וּפְנִים / הֶגֶה בָהּ לָאֵל קָדְשׁוֹת וְרַנְּנִים
דַּשֵּׁן עַל שֻׁלְחָנְךָ מַעֲדַנִּים / גַּם עֶבֶד וְאָמָה אֲשֶׁר לְךָ נִקְנִים
בָּהּ יָנוּחוּ עִמְּךָ בְּכָל פָּנִים / אֵל הוֹרָה לְךָ לְכַבֵּד הוֹרִים וּזְקֵנִים.

‹ וּזְקֵנִים הַנְעִימוּךְ מִיָּמֶיךָ / כַּבְּדֵם סֶלָה וְיִרְבּוּ יָמֶיךָ

All:

כַּבֵּד אֶת־אָבִיךָ וְאֶת־אִמֶּךָ:

שמות כ

אֱזֹן לְהוֹרֶיךָ בְּחִבּוּר אֱמוּנִים / בַּעֲתִירוֹת אוֹתְךָ קוֹנִים
גְּרוֹנְךָ בִּבְרִית אֵיתָנִים / דֵּי חֲלֵב שָׁדַיִם לְךָ מְדַשְּׁנִים
הַמַּלְבִּישׁוּךָ לְבוּשׁ עֲדָנִים / וּמַאֲכָלָם בְּפִיךָ נוֹתְנִים
זוֹעֲקִים בַּעֲדָךָ תַּחֲנוּנִים / חִיּוּתְךָ לְמוֹ דָר עֶלְיוֹנִים
טוֹעֲנֶיךָ עַל שִׁכְמָם כְּאוֹמְנִים / יְגֵעֵי בְךָ שָׁבְעֵי אוֹנִים
כְּאֵב אִם יִקְרָאֶךָ הֵם מִתְעַנִּים / לְיִרְאַת שַׁדַּי אוֹתְךָ מַפְנִים
מִצְוֹת וְדָתוֹ לְךָ מְבוֹנְנִים / נַחֲלַת הוֹן וּבֵית לְךָ מַקְנִים
סוֹמְכִים לְךָ עֵזֶר וּמִתְחַתְּנִים / עֲשֵׂה חֶפְצָם וְאַל תָּעֵז פָּנִים
פֶּן יַעֲמִידוּךָ לִפְנֵי דַיָּנִים / צָפֵה דַּת סוֹרֵר וּמוֹרֶה בַּבָּנִים
קָהָל יִרְגְּמוּךָ בָּאֲבָנִים / רְאֵה פֶּן תַּעֲזְבֵם לְעֵת זְקֵנִים
שָׁרֵתֶם כְּעֶבֶד לַאֲדֹנִים / תְּפַלֵּטָם קַח וְתַאֲרִיךָ יָמִים וְשָׁנִים.

◂ וְשָׁנִים תַּאֲרִיךָ וְתִזְכֶּה פְּנֵי צַח / יְצִיר צֶלֶם אִם לֹא תִרְצָח

All:

לֹא תִרְצָח:

שמות כ

תּוּר וְסוּר מֵאַנְשֵׁי דָמִים / שׁוֹמְרִים בַּלֵּב אֵיבָה וְשׂוֹטְמִים
רִשְׁעַת סוֹד מֵעֲרִימִים / קַחַת נֶפֶשׁ צַדִּיק זוֹמְמִים
צוֹפְנִים וְאוֹרְבִים עַל תְּמִימִים / פַּח טוֹמְנִים לְמִישָׁרֵי פְעָמִים
עַל דַּם רֵעַ בְּזָדוֹן קָמִים / שְׂאֵת כְּלֵי מָוֶת בְּאַף מַזְעִימִים
נָקִי רוֹצְחִים בְּאֵין רַחֲמִים / מְאַבְּדִים מַעֲשׂ הַצּוּר תָּמִים
לַנִּבְרָא בְּצַלְמוֹ לַשַּׁחַת הוֹמִים / כְּרֶגַע נְשָׁמָה מַשִּׁימִים
יִרְאַת אֵל בְּלִבָּם לֹא שָׂמִים / טוֹרְדִים נֶפֶשׁ לָמוּת בְּלֹא יָמִים
חֲדַל מִלְהַחֲנִיף גֵּיא בְדָמִים / זְכֹר כִּי יִזְעַק דָּם לַמְּרוֹמִים
וְשֹׁפֵךְ דַּם הָאָדָם בָּאָדָם נִנְקָמִים / הֵן נֶפֶשׁ בְּנֶפֶשׁ מְשַׁלְּמִים
דִּין הֶרֶג לַנְּפָשָׁם גּוֹרְמִים / גּוּר מִפְּנֵי חֶרֶב זְעָמִים
בְּרַח לְךָ מִגַּחֲלֵי רְתָמִים / אֲשׁוּרֶיךָ תַּצְעִיד בְּתָמִים.

◂ בְּתָמִים תֵּלֵךְ וְתִנָּצֵל מֵאַף / סוֹטָה אִם לֹא תִנְאָף

All:

לֹא תִנְאָף:

שמות כ

אַל תִּתְעָרֵב בִּמְנָאֲפִים / בְּמִגְלֵי עֶרְיוֹת גּוּפִים
גּוֹיִם בְּתוֹעֲבוֹת מְטַנְּפִים / דּוֹרְשֵׁי רָע וּמְבַקְשֵׁי כְשָׁפִים
הַמְטַמְּאִים אֶרֶץ וּמַחֲנִיפִים / וּמַעֲשֵׂה יְדֵי אָמָן מְסַלְּפִים
זַרְעָם לְשֵׁם אַחֵר מַחֲלִיפִים / חֲמַת אֵל וְקִצְפּוֹ מַאֲנִיפִים
טוֹר עַצְמְךָ מִסּוֹטַת נֹאֲפִים / יָפְיָה אַל תַּדִיחֲךָ לִרְשָׁפִים
כָּל נֹגְעֶיהָ בָּאוּר נִשְׂרָפִים / לְחַדְרֵי מָוֶת הֵם נִשְׁאָפִים
מַעַמְקֵי שְׁאוֹל נֶהְדָּפִים / נוֹפְלִים לַשַּׁחַת וְלֹא נִזְקָפִים
שְׂמַח בְּחֶלְקְךָ בְּחַיִּים יָפִים / עִם לְקוּחָה לְךָ וְהַכֹּל צוֹפִים
פּוֹרִיָּה תַּפְרִיחַ לְךָ עֲנָפִים / צְמוּדִים לְשֻׁלְחָנְךָ מַקִּיפִים
קָדְשָׁה לָאֵל מַצְנִיפִים / רִנָּה בְּלִבְּךָ אָז מוֹסִיפִים
שְׁתֵה מִבּוֹרְךָ מַיִם כְּסוּפִים / תַּעֵב גְּנוּבַת מַיִם טְנוּפִים.

‹ טְנוּפִים מַיִם לֹא תִגְנֹב / שְׂמַח בְּחֶלְקְךָ וּבְטוֹב תָּנוֹב

All:
לֹא תִגְנֹב:

שמות כ

תִּרְחַק מֵחֲבוּרַת גַּנָּבִים / שׁוֹדְדִים לְלֹא לָמוֹ אוֹרְבִים
רוֹאִים בְּאֶשְׁנַבֵּי עֲרָבִים / קִירוֹת בַּחֹשֶׁךְ נוֹקְבִים
צוֹדְדִים וּבָאִים בְּאֶשְׁנַבִּים / פְּעֻלַּת יְגִיעַ אֲחֵרִים גּוֹנְבִים
עֲשִׁירִים עֲרֻמִּים מַצִּיבִים / שִׂבְעִים לַלֶּחֶם מַרְעִיבִים
נְפָשׁוֹת מַפִּיחִים וּמַדְאִיבִים / מְאָרְבִים עַל דְּרָכִים יוֹשְׁבִים
לִגְזֹל לְכָל עוֹבְרֵי נְתִיבִים / כְּלֵי זַיִן עָלָיו מַלְהִיבִים
יַחַד גַּם לְהָרְגוּ רוֹהֲבִים / טָעֲנוּ וּבָגְדוּ שׁוֹדְדִים כְּאוֹיְבִים
חוֹטְפִים וְטוֹרְפִים כִּזְאֵבִים / זֶה עֲמָלָם לָרִיק חוֹשְׁבִים
וּמְאֵרָה לְבָתֵּיהֶם שׁוֹאֲבִים / הוֹן בְּרָכָה אַחֲרֵימוֹ לֹא עוֹזְבִים
דִּבְרֵי אָלוֹת עֲלֵיהֶם קוֹבְבִים / גּוֹיִם לְמַהֲלוּמוֹת מְחַיְּבִים
בְּשָׁתָם בִּרְחוֹבוֹת מְסוֹבְבִים / אֵידָם בְּבוֹא יִרְאוּ רַבִּים

אֱסֹף יְגִיעֲךָ הַטּוֹבִים / אֱכֹל וּלְנַפְשְׁךָ יְהוּ עֲרֵבִים
אַל תִּפְנֶה בְּנִי אֶל רְהָבִים / אַל תְּהִי עִם שָׁטֵי כְזָבִים.

‹ כְּזָבִים בְּרֵעֲךָ לֹא־תַעֲנֶה / וְרָעָה אֵלֶיךָ לֹא־תְאֻנֶּה

All:

לֹא־תַעֲנֶה:

אֹטֶם שְׂפָתֶיךָ מִתַּפְלוּצִים / בַּל תִּתְחַבַּר לַלֵּצִים
גּוֹלְשִׁים דְּבָרִים נִמְרָצִים / דַּרְדַּר זוֹרְעִים עִם קוֹצִים
הַשּׁוֹנְנִים לְשׁוֹנָם כַּחֲצִים / וּפִימוֹ יִפוֹצֵץ נִיצוֹצִים
זוֹמְמִים אָוֶן וּמִרְמָה יוֹעֲצִים / חֲנֵפִים וְלִרְכִילוּת אָצִים
טְפֵלוּת עֵדוּת שָׁוְא פוֹצִים / יְהִירִים וְעַיִן קוֹרְצִים
כְּצִפְעוֹנִי נְשִׁיכָה מוֹחֲצִים / לָרַע רָצִים וּלְאֵיד דָּצִים
מְדָנִים בֵּין אַחִים מְנַצִּים / נוֹתְנִים מַחֲלֹקֶת וְגֶדֶר פּוֹרְצִים
שְׂנוּאִים לָאֵל וּמְשָׁקָצִים / עֲתִידִים לְמְדוּרַת אֵשׁ וְעֵצִים
פָּעֳלָם עַל רֹאשָׁם קוֹבְצִים / צָרַעַת בְּעוֹרָם מְנַפְּצִים
קְלָלוֹת בִּבְשָׂרָם רוֹבְצִים / רֹאשׁ וְלַעֲנָה כּוֹסָם מוֹצִים
שָׁמְרוּ לְשׁוֹנְךָ מִנְּאוּצִים / תְּתַעֵב תַּרְמִית שֶׁקֶר שִׁקּוּצִים.

‹ שִׁקּוּצִים וּזְנוּת אַל יְהִי מְרֵעֲךָ / וּבְמַרְעֶה טוֹב הוּא יִרְעֶךָ

All:

לֹא תַחְמֹד בֵּית רֵעֶךָ:

תַּחֲמוּדוֹת בָּתִּים וְאֹהָלִים / שֶׁקֶר הַחֵן וְיֹפִי הֲבָלִים
רֶשַׁע חוֹמְסִים וְגוֹזְלִים / קִנְיָן אֲשֶׁר קָנוּ עֲמֵלִים
צוֹפָה עַיִן תַּאֲוַת שְׁלָלִים / פָּז וָכֶסֶף בֶּצַע גְּעוּלִים
עָשׂ בְּגָדִים וּרְקַב כֵּלִים / שָׂדֶה וָכֶרֶם לָרוּחַ נִנְחָלִים
נֶפֶשׁ וְכָל אֲשֶׁר לָהּ בּוֹעֲלִים / מִלַּחְמֹד אֵלֶּה עַיִן תַּעֲלִים
לָמָּה תִהְיֶה בִּפְלִילִים / כְּסוּת אַלְמָנָה חוֹבְלִים
יְתוֹמִים חוֹמְסִים וְלֹא חוֹמְלִים / טוֹרְחִים לְהַשִּׂיג גְּבוּל עוֹלִים

חוֹטְפִים עֲנִיִּים וְדַלִּים / זֵעַת יְגִיעַ אֲחֵרִים גּוֹזְלִים
וְנֶשֶׁךְ וְתַרְבִּית מַכְפִּילִים / הֲלֹא הֵמָּה לִקְבָרוֹת מוּבָלִים
דְּבַר הוֹן בְּיָדָם לֹא מוֹבִילִים / גֶּחָלִים כְּקַשׁ אוֹתָם אוֹכְלִים
בְּיוֹם עֶבְרָה לֹא מַצִּילִים / אֲנָשִׁים אֲשֶׁר עַוְלָה פוֹעֲלִים
אֵלֶּה הַדְּבָרִים בְּלֹא תַחְמֹד תְּלוּלִים / אִם תִּשְׁמְרֵם וְלֵב לָאֵל תַּשְׁלִים
אָז תַּצְלִיחַ בְּכָל מִפְעָלִים / אוֹרְךָ יַזְהִיר כְּמַשְׂכִּילִים
אֲשֶׁר שְׁנֵי עוֹלָמוֹת נוֹחֲלִים / וִיאַשְּׁרוּךָ קְטַנִּים וּגְדוֹלִים.

‹ גְּדוֹלִים וּקְטַנִּים נָעוּ מִקּוֹלֹת / וּנְשָׁמוֹת עָפוּ מִקּוֹלֵי קוֹלֹת

All:

וְכָל־הָעָם רֹאִים אֶת־הַקּוֹלֹת:

שמות כ

All:

וּבְכֵן לְךָ תַעֲלֶה קְדֻשָּׁה, כִּי אַתָּה קְדוֹשׁ יִשְׂרָאֵל וּמוֹשִׁיעַ.

Some congregations say the piyut אֵלֶּה הָעֵדוֹת before קדושה.
Many congregations omit it, and those who do so
continue with "נְקַדֵּשׁ אֶת שִׁמְךָ" on page 349.

סילוק

אֵלֶּה הָעֵדוֹת וְהַחֻקִּים / אֲשֶׁר נִתְּנוּ לְעַם חֲשׁוּקִים
בְּקוֹלוֹת וְשׁוֹפָרוֹת וְלַפִּידִים וּבְרָקִים / בְּרַעַשׁ וּבְרַעַד בְּאֵימָה וָזֵקִים
בִּנְשִׁיקָה מִפִּי שׁוֹכֵן שְׁחָקִים / מְבֹאָרִים וּמְחֻזָּקִים
מְשׁוּלִים בְּכָל מֶתֶק אוֹכְלִים וּמַשְׁקִים / מִנֹּפֶת צוּפִים וּמִדְּבַשׁ מְתוּקִים
בְּתִשְׁעִים וּשְׁמוֹנָה פָנִים בְּפֵרוּשׁ חֲקוּקִים
בְּאַרְבָּעִים וְתִשְׁעָה פָנִים טָמֵא נֶחְקָקִים
אַרְבָּעִים וְתִשְׁעָה פָנִים טָהוֹר מְחֻשָּׁקִים / מִנְיָן וְדִגְלוֹ נִדְרָשִׁים וְנֶחְקָקִים
בְּשֵׁשׁ מֵאוֹת וּשְׁלֹשׁ עֶשְׂרֵה מִצְוֹת זְקוּקִים
מָאתַיִם וְאַרְבָּעִים וּשְׁמוֹנָה בַּעֲשֵׂה לְהָקִים
וּשְׁלֹשׁ מֵאוֹת וְשִׁשִּׁים וְחָמֵשׁ בְּלֹא תַעֲשֶׂה מִתְחַזְּקִים
בַּעֲלִיל שְׁבָעָתַיִם מְזֻקָּקִים / וְשׁוֹמְרֵימוֹ לָעַד לֹא נְזָקִים
וְלִוְיַת חֵן לְרֹאשָׁם מַעֲנִיקִים / וּלְגַרְגְּרוֹתָם עֲטוּר עֲנָקִים

מְשַׂמְּחִים לֵב וְעֵינַיִם מַבְהִיקִים / מָתוֹק לַנֶּפֶשׁ וּמַרְפֵּא לָעֶצֶם מְפִיקִים
עֵץ־חַיִּים הִיא לַמַּחֲזִיקִים:

משלי ג

וּכְעֶלּוֹתָהּ עַל דַּעְתּוֹ לְתֵן תּוֹרָה לְעַמּוֹ / בָּא מִסִּינַי בִּכְבוֹד נֶאֱמוֹ
וְזָרַח מִשֵּׂעִיר לָמוֹ: / וְעָרְךָ לֹא תִרְצַח לְפָנֵימוֹ

דברים לג

וְעַל כִּי בְחַרְבָּם הֵם חַיֵּימוֹ / לֹא קִבְּלוּ עַל תּוֹרָה עָלֵימוֹ
וּמֵהַר פָּארָן הוֹפִיעַ לָמוֹ / לֹא תִגְנֹב שֵׁן בְּמַחֲנֵימוֹ
וְעַל כִּי בִגְנֵבוֹת וּבִגְזֵלוֹת הֵם מִפְעָלֵימוֹ / לֹא קִבְּלוּ עַל תּוֹרָה עָלֵימוֹ
וְאַתָּה מֵרִבְבוֹת קֹדֶשׁ לָתֵן עֹז לְעַמּוֹ / הֵם קִבְּלוּ עַל תּוֹרָה עָלֵימוֹ
וְנַעֲשֶׂה לְנִשְׁמַע הִקְדִּימוּ / טֶרֶם נִשְׁמַע נַעֲשֶׂה נָמוּ
וּצְדָקָה בָּהּ נֶחְשָׁבָה לָמוֹ / וְלִשְׁנֵי כְתָרִים סִימוּ
לִמְלוּכָה וְלִכְהֻנָּה וְלִלְוִיָּה אִימוּ / וּבַעֲשָׂרָה קְדוּשִׁים קַדְּשָׁם אֵל לִשְׁמוֹ
וּבְשִׁבְעִים שֵׁמוֹת יִחֲסָם לְאֻמּוֹ / וּבִשְׁלֹשׁ עֶשְׂרֵה מִדּוֹת תּוֹצָאוֹתָם בְּקַיְּמוּ
וְכָל שְׁמָם בִּשְׁמוֹ / וְכַאֲזוֹר לַחֵלֶץ הַדְּבֵקִים לְנַעֲמוֹ
וּלְסִינַי הִטָּה שְׁמֵי מְרוֹמוֹ / וַיֵּרֶד הוּא וְכָל קְדוֹשָׁיו עִמּוֹ
וְהִגְעִישׁ וְהִרְעִישׁ וְהִרְעִיד הַדּוֹמוֹ / וְאַחַת בְּדַבְּרוֹ הֶחֱרִיד עוֹלָמוֹ
וְעֶשְׂרִים וְאַרְבָּעָה מִיל מַהֲלָךְ נָעוּ עַמּוֹ / שְׁתַּיִם זוּ בְּהַשְׁמִיעוֹ נֶאֱמוֹ.

וְרָגְזוּ וְחָלוּ כָּל בָּאֵי עוֹלָם / מֵאֵימַת חֵי הָעוֹלָם
בְּרִדְתּוֹ לְדַבֵּר לְעַם עוֹלָם / רָעֲשׁוּ אֻמּוֹת הָעוֹלָם
פַּחַד קְרָאָם וְרַעַד הִזְחִילָם / חִיל כַּיּוֹלֵדָה הִבְהִילָם
נָעוּ וְרָעֲדוּ וְסָר צִלָּם / וְאֵצֶל קְמוּאֵל בָּאוּ כֻלָּם
לְנַחֵשׁ בְּקִסְמֵי קִלְקוּלָם / וְשָׁאֲלוּ לוֹ מַה זֶּה בָּא לָעוֹלָם
שָׁמָּא הַיּוֹם לְמֵימָיו חוֹזֵר עוֹלָם / יהוה לַמַּבּוּל יָשָׁב לָבוֹא לָעוֹלָם
וְהֵשִׁיב אוֹתָם בְּשָׁאֲלָם / יהוה עֹז לְעַמּוֹ יִתֵּן לְהַנְחִילָם

תהלים כט

וּכְשָׁמְעָם כָּךְ נָמוּ כֻלָּם / יהוה יְבָרֵךְ אֶת־עַמּוֹ בַשָּׁלוֹם:
וְדִתּוֹ לְהַשְׂכִּילָם.

וְכָל דּוֹר וָדוֹר וּמַנְהִיגֵיהֶם / אֲשֶׁר עָמְדוּ לִפְנֵיהֶם
וְהָעֲתִידִים לַעֲמֹד אַחֲרֵיהֶם / כֻּלָּם הֶעֱמִידָם בְּסִינַי עִמָּהֶם

לְהוֹדִיעָם כִּי דוֹר דֵּעַ נֶחְשַׁק מִכֻּלָּם / טוּב טַעַם וָדַעַת לְהַשְׂכִּילֵיהֶם
וְכָל מוּם לֹא הָיָה בָּהֶם / כִּי שְׁלֵמִים וּמֻשְׁלָמִים הָיוּ כֻּלָּהֶם
בְּהִגָּלוֹתוֹ בְּסִינַי עֲלֵיהֶם / וּבְפָנִים הַרֻבֵּה נִרְאָה לָהֶם
מְדַבֵּר אָנֹכִי עִם כָּל אֶחָד וְאֶחָד מֵהֶם / פָּנִים בְּפָנִים לְהַרְאוֹתֵיהֶם
פָּנִים בְּאֵימָה לְמִקְרָא לְמוּדֵיהֶם / פָּנִים בֵּינוֹנִיּוֹת לְמִשְׁנַת עֲרֵכֵיהֶם
פָּנִים שׂוֹחֲקוֹת לְתַלְמוּד חֲכָמֵיהֶם / פָּנִים מַסְבִּירוֹת לְאַגָּדוֹת טַעֲמֵיהֶם
כְּעַתִּיק יוֹמִין וְצַח נִדְמָה לָהֶם / נֶחְמָדִים בָּהָר חֶמֶד עָרֵךְ לִפְנֵיהֶם
וְחֻקִּים וּמִצְוֹת טוֹבִים וְשֵׂכֶר אֶתְנַנֵּיהֶם /

ויקרא יח אֲשֶׁר יַעֲשֶׂה אֹתָם הָאָדָם וָחַי בָּהֶם:

משלי ד כִּי־חַיִּים הֵם לְמוֹצְאֵיהֶם: / לְמַעַן יִרְבּוּ יְמֵיהֶם וִימֵי בְנֵיהֶם.

וְדִבּוּר אֶחָד / מִפִּיו בְּמִלְלוֹ
שְׁתַּיִם זוּ בְּהַשְׁמִיעוֹ לַקָּהָל / רָחֲקוּ שְׁנֵים עָשָׂר מִיל מִפַּחַד חֵילוֹ
וּפָרְחָה נַפְשָׁם מִמִּשְׁמַע הוֹד קוֹלוֹ / וְהֶעֱמִיד עֲנָנֵי כְבוֹד גָּדְלוֹ
וְגֶשֶׁם נְדָבוֹת הֵנִיפוֹ וְהִזִּילוֹ / וְחָיוּ וְשָׁבוּ שְׁנֵים עָשָׂר מִיל בְּתֹקֶף חֵילוֹ
וְדִבְּרוּ לְצִיר וְאָמְרוּ לוֹ / קְרַב אַתָּה וּשְׁמַע מִלּוּלוֹ
וְדִבֵּר עִמָּנוּ קְנָן פָּעֳלוֹ / פֶּן נָמוּת מֵאֵימַת קוֹלוֹ
וַיִּשְׁמַע אֶל דִּבְרֵי קָהָלוֹ / וַיִּיטַב לְפָנָיו וְגַם עָרֵב לוֹ
וַיִּקְרָא לְצִיר וְלִמְרוֹמוֹ הֶעֱלוֹ / וּבֵינוֹ לָבֵין עַם שְׁלִישִׁי עָלוֹ
וְהֶעֱמִידוֹ וְנִגַּשׁ אֶל עֲרָפֶלּוֹ / וּפָנִים בְּפָנִים דִּבֶּר לוֹ
וְקַרְנַיִם מִיָּדוֹ לוֹ / יְדֹדוּן יִדֹּדוּן רָעֲשׁוּ לְמוּלוֹ
וְדִבְּרוּ לִפְנֵי צוּר וְאָמְרוּ לוֹ / מָה אֱנוֹשׁ כִּי תְגַדְּלוֹ
וּמָה תְחַשְּׁבֵהוּ לִמְקוֹמֶנּוּ לְהַעֲלוֹ / קִנְיָן שַׁעֲשׁוּעִים לְהַנְחִילוֹ
וְהֵשִׁיבָם אֶל הַנִּיחוּ לוֹ / מֵאָז חֲשַׁקְתִּיו לְהַגְדִּילוֹ
קִנְיָן שַׁעֲשׁוּעִים לְנַחֲלוֹ / וּלְהִכָּנֵס לְפָנַי וְלִפְנִים רְשׁוּת נָתַתִּי לוֹ
שְׁבוּיַת מָרוֹם לָתֵת לוֹ / מְנָת חֶלְקוֹ וְגוֹרָלוֹ
לְלַמֵּד לְבָנַי כָּל אֲשֶׁר יְדַבֵּר לוֹ.

וּמֵהַר סִינַי קִבְּלוּ תוֹרָה / לֹא מִפִּי מַלְאָךְ וְלֹא מִפִּי שָׁלִיחַ אֲמוּרָה
כִּי אִם מִפִּי מֶלֶךְ עוֹטֶה אוֹרָה / טְהוֹר עֵינַיִם וִירֵאָתוֹ טְהוֹרָה

מִפִּי גְבוּרָתוֹ לִבְחִירוֹ הוֹרָה / דָּת בָּאֵר הֵיטֵב מְבֹאָרָה
בְּדִבּוּר בַּאֲמִירָה, בְּצִוּוּי בְּאַזְהָרָה / בְּתַלְמוּד בְּאַגָּדָה בְּמִשְׁנָה בְּמִקְרָא
בְּחֻקָּה בְּמִצְוָה בִּבְרִית גְּמוּרָה / עֲרוּכָה בַּכֹּל וּשְׁמוּרָה
וְכָל מִצְוָה שֶׁבָּהּ כְּעִנְיָן סְדוּרָה /

לְהִתְבָּרֵךְ בְּהוֹגֶיהָ בְּכָל יוֹם בָּרוּךְ יוֹם נוֹתֵן הַתּוֹרָה.

וּבְאָלֶף שֶׁהִיא לְכָל הָאוֹתִיּוֹת רֹאשׁ / פָּתַח בְּאָנֹכִי לַדִּבְּרוֹת רֹאשׁ
לְהוֹדִיעַ שֶׁהוּא אֱלֹהֵי קֶדֶם רֹאשׁ / בְּרֵאשִׁית רֹאשׁ, וּבְאַחֲרִית רֹאשׁ
רִאשׁוֹן וְאַחֲרוֹן בְּסוֹף וּבְרֹאשׁ / צוֹפֶה מַה יִּהְיֶה בְּסוֹף מֵרֹאשׁ
וְלָמָּה בְּאָלֶף פָּתַח בְּרֹאשׁ / כְּנֶגֶד אֶלֶף דּוֹר שֶׁצָּפָה מֵרֹאשׁ
לָתֵן לָהֶם אֱמוּנַת רֹאשׁ / לְצַוּוֹת לָהֶם דָּבָר מֵרֹאשׁ
וְעָבַר מֵהֶם תֵּשַׁע מֵאוֹת וְשִׁבְעִים וְאַרְבָּעָה לִפְרֹשׁ
וּלְסוֹף עֶשְׂרִים וְשִׁשָּׁה דּוֹרוֹת חָשַׁק תְּבוּאַת רֹאשׁ
דָּבָר צִוָּה לְאֶלֶף דּוֹר מֵרֹאשׁ / לְנַחֹל חֹק נְסוּכַת רֹאשׁ
בְּתַעֲצוּמוֹתֶיהָ לַחֲקֹר וְלִדְרֹשׁ / לְהִשְׁתַּחֲווֹת וְלִכְרֹעַ וְלָקֹד רֹאשׁ
לָאֵל חַי וְקַיָּם הַמִּתְנַשֵּׂא לְכֹל לְרֹאשׁ.

וּבְשׂוֹרָם צִבְאוֹת אֵלִים / כִּי לְמַתַּן דָּת זָכוּ סְגוּלִים
וַיְכַבְּדוּ בָהּ נִדְגָּלִים / נָתְנוּ שֶׁבַח וּתְהִלָּה לְאֵל אֵלִים
וַהֲמוֹן גְּדוּדִים וְכִתֵּי אֶרְאֶלִים / שִׁיר וְתִשְׁבָּחוֹת מְפָאֲרִים וּמְהַלְּלִים
וּשְׂרָפִים מִמַּעַל לָהֶם עוֹמְדִים וּמְעַלִּים /

וּלְיוֹשֵׁב עַל כִּסֵּא רָם וְנִשָּׂא מַגְדִּילִים

וְצִבְאוֹת גִּבּוֹרֵי חֲיָלִים / מַנְעִימִים שִׁיר הַלּוּלִים
וּפְאֵר כְּרוּבִים וְרַעַשׁ גַּלְגַּלִּים / בְּמַתַּן אָמוֹן הָיוּ גִילִים
וּמַלְאֲכֵי אֵשׁ וּמַיִם בְּלוּלִים / בְּשִׂמְחַת נְוַת בֵּית מְסֻלָּדִים וּמְחֻלִּים
וְזֶה אֶל זֶה קוֹרְאִים וְשׁוֹאֲלִים / לְקָדוֹשׁ וּבָרוּךְ תִּפְאֶרֶת מְכַלְּלִים
רוֹמְמוֹת לְמַלְכָּם מְמַלְּלִים / וְעֻזּוֹ נוֹרְאוֹתָיו מַגְדִּילִים
וְשִׁלּוּשׁ קְדֻשָּׁה לְקָדוֹשׁ בַּקֹּדֶשׁ מַעֲלִים.

Continue with "כַּכָּתוּב עַל יַד נְבִיאֶךָ" on page 349.

פיוט תרגום

In the Talmudic and Geonic eras, the reading of the Torah was accompanied by תרגום –
translation into Aramiac, a custom which Ashkenazi communities kept on שבועות
long after it was discontinued for other readings (see commentary on page 395).
The תרגום *was interlaced with Aramaic piyutim – in some congregations a*
special piyut was said before each of the Ten Commandments. Today, some say
just the first of those, before narrating God's Revelation on Mount Sinai.

אַרְכִין יהוה שְׁמַיָּא לְסִינַי וַאֲמַר לְמֹשֶׁה מְהֵימְנָא תָּא סוּק.

בְּנֵי פַלָּטִין דִּידִי לָא יְבַהֲלוּנָךְ דְּכָבֵשׁ יָתְהוֹן סָבָךְ מִן רֵישׁ.

גּוּמְרִין דְּאַתּוּן הֲוַת נוּרָה דְּנִמְרוֹד דְּלָא יְכִיל לְמִכְוָא רַגְלוֹי דְּסָבָךְ.

דַּבֵּק לֵית הוּא נוּרָא דְמַלְאֲכֵי בָּךְ דְּעִמָּךְ אֶשָּׁא אָכְלָא אֶשָּׁא.

הָא אֲנָא מַלְבֵּישׁ לָךְ פּוֹרְפִירוֹן דִּידִי דְּאִין קָרִיב מַלְאֲכָא תִּנְגִּשְׁנַּהּ בְּהוֹן.

וּקְבָעִית קַרְנֵי הוֹדָא בְּרֵאשָׁךְ דְּלֵית גְּבַר דְּאִתְקְרֵב לְוָתָךְ.

זֵעְרָא לָא תֶהֱוֵי בְּאַפָּךְ מֹשֶׁה דְּלֵית אַתְּ יָדַע מַה חֲבִבְתָּךְ עֲלַי.

חַי וְקַיָּם אֲנָא דְבָרָאִית אִקּוּנָךְ עַד לָא שַׁכְלֵלִית רוּמָא וּמוּכָא.

טְרוֹנֵי מְרוֹמָא קָמוּ לְהוֹן תְּמֵהִין דֵּין אַכְסַנָאָה הָכָא מָאן הוּא.

יָהּ יְהַב רְשׁוּ לְבִשְׂרָא וּדְמָא לְמִקְרַב הָכָא וּמָאן כַּדּוּ אִנְפְּרַטִין

(נ״א: וּמַן כַּדּוּ אֲנָא אִנְפְּרַטִין).

כַּד חָמוֹן מַלְאֲכַיָּא דְּעָנֵי כְדֵין לְהוֹן דֵּין אַכְסַנָאָה אֲנָא מוֹדַע לְכוֹן.

לְעֵנוּתָנָא דְאִתְקְרֵי מֹשֶׁה רַעְיוֹהֶן דְּבְנֵי מְהֵימְנֵהּ דְּבֵיתִי.

מָכוּ שְׁמַיָּא וְרַמַת אַרְעָא וְאִשְׁתְּכַח דְּקָאִים בֵּין חֲוָאתָא.

נָעוּ מַלְאֲכִין וּדְחִילוּ אוֹפַנֵּי וְגַלְגְּלִין כַּד חָמוֹן מֹשֶׁה דְּקָרֵב לְעַרְפֶּלָא.

שַׁעֲרוֹת רֵישֵׁהּ קָמוּ לְהוֹן כַּחֲדָא דְּאִקּוּנִין דְּיַעֲקֹב חֲזָא מָזְקָף לְקָבְלֵהּ.

עוּל וּקְרַב לָךְ הָכָא רַעְיֵיהוֹן דְּבְנֵי צוּח מִן כֻּרְסְיֵהּ מַלְכָּא רָמָא.

פְּסַל לָךְ תְּרֵין לוּחִין מִן סַנְפִּרְנוֹן דְּתַחוֹת כֻּרְסְיֵהּ דְּמַלְכָּא חַיָּא.

צָהִיל הֲוָה לִבֵּהּ דְּמֹשֶׁה וְחָדֵי דַּהֲוָה אֵל רַחוּם אֶפִּילוֹגוֹס דִּידֵהּ.

קָרִיבוּ מַלְאֲכַיָּא לְוָת כֻּרְסְיֵהּ דְּקָרִיס וְאָמְרִין בְּבָעוּ מִנָּךְ דְּלָא יִשְׁלַט בָּן.

רֵישָׁא דְּכֵפָא בְּחוּטְרֵהּ תְּבַר וַאֲנַן קַשְׁיָן לֵהּ לְמִנְגְּשָׁא.

שַׁדִּי אֲמַר לֵהּ לָא תִדְחַל מֹשֶׁה דְּמֵימְרִי יְהֵוי לָךְ בְּסַעְדָּךְ.

תְּסַב אוֹרָיְתִי וְתֵחוֹת לָךְ דְּלָא אַשְׁכַּחִית בִּנְבִיאַי מְהֵימַן כְּוָתָךְ.

Continue with "וַיְדַבֵּר אֱלֹהִים" *on page 411.*

פיוט לחזרת הש״ץ של מוסף ביום ראשון של שבועות

אזהרות

in מעמד הר סיני *After receiving the Torah, we begin to study it. Following reading about*
שחרית חזרת הש״ץ, *the ancient custom was to recite a long piyut detailing the 613 mitzvot in*
of מוסף, *called* אזהרות (*see page 168*). *Today, in Sephardi communities the* אזהרות *are said*
during מנחה *or before* תיקון ליל שבועות; *in Ashkenazi congregations many omit it altogether.*

The אזהרות *for the first day, by an unknown author, are among the earliest of*
the genre, and the most widely recited. The following piyut does not list all 613
mitzvot, and it does mention some מצוות מדרבנן (*Rabbinic decrees*). *The verses*
are of a double-stich form (except for the last verse), and begin with an alphabetic
acrostic, alternating between a straightforward א״ב *and the reverse* תשר״ק.

All:

אַתָּה הִנְחַלְתָּ תּוֹרָה לְעַמֶּךָ

וּכְאָב אֶת בֵּן אוֹתָם יִסַּרְתָּ

בִּימִינְךָ כָּתַבְתָּ דִּבְּרוֹת חַיִּים

וּבְאֶצְבְּעוֹתֶיךָ חָקַקְתָּ תּוֹכְחוֹת מוּסָר

גֵּדֵל עֳנָשִׁין וְאַזְהָרוֹת הַרְבֵּה

מִצְוֹת עֲשֵׂה וּמִצְוֹת לֹא תַעֲשֶׂה

דִּינֵי מָמוֹנוֹת וְדִינֵי נְפָשׁוֹת

וּנְתִינַת מוּם בְּנוֹתְנֵי מוּמִים

הִזְהַרְתָּ שֹׁפְטִים בַּל שֹׁחַד רֶשַׁע לָמוּת

צֵוָּאת שֹׁטְרִים לְבַל הַכֵּר פָּנִים

וּשְׁבוּעַת הָעֵדוּת וּשְׁבוּעַת הַפִּקָּדוֹן

וּשְׁבוּעַת הָעֶלֶם דָּבָר וְשָׁלוּם גֵּזֶל וְהָשֵׁב אֲבֵדָה

זָקוּק בֵּית דִּין בִּדְרִישָׁה וּבַחֲקִירָה

סַנְהֶדְרֵי גְדוֹלָה וְסַנְהֶדְרֵי קְטַנָּה

חִזּוּק בֵּית דִּין בְּאַרְבַּע מִיתוֹת

עֲבֵרָה וַעֲבֵרָה וְעֹנֶשׁ שֶׁלָּהּ

טְרֵפָה לְהַשְׁלִיךְ וּנְבֵלָה לִמְכֹּר לְנָכְרִי

כָּל חֵלֶב וְכָל דָּם שֶׁלֹּא לֶאֱכֹל

יַיִן לְנַסֵּךְ וְשֶׁמֶן לְהַדְלִיק

עִשָּׂרוֹן וּשְׁתֵּי הַלֶּחֶם גֶּרֶשׂ קָלִי וְכַרְמֶל

כֹּהֲנִים לְשָׁרֵת וּלְוִיִם לְשׁוֹרֵר

תְּרוּמוֹת וּמַעְשְׂרוֹת וְעָרֵי מִגְרָשׁ

לֶחָיַיִם וְהַזְּרוֹעַ וְהַקֵּבָה לָתֵת לַכֹּהֵן מֵאֵת הָעָם וּמֵאֵת זוֹבְחֵי הַזֶּבַח

וְרֵאשִׁית הַגֵּז מִגִּזֵּי צֹאן

מַעְשַׂר בְּהֵמָה וְקִדּוּשׁ בְּכֹרוֹת

וּפִדְיוֹן הַבֵּן וְנֶדֶר וְהֶקְדֵּשׁ

נֶטַע רְבָעִי וִדּוּי מַעֲשֵׂר

מִקְרָא בִּכּוּרִים בְּרָכוֹת וּקְלָלוֹת

שִׂמְחַת בֵּית הַשּׁוֹאֵבָה לִשְׂמֹחַ בֶּחָג

סֻכָּה וְלוּלָב וַעֲרָבָה וְנִסּוּךְ הַמַּיִם

עֲרָיוֹת לְהַפְרִישׁ וְנִדָּה לְהַרְחִיק

חֲלִיצָה וְיִבּוּם וְסֵפֶר כְּרִיתוּת

פָּרָשַׁת סוֹטָה וּפָרָשַׁת עֶגְלָה עֲרוּפָה

תְּפִלִּין וּמְזוּזוֹת וּמִצְוַת צִיצִית

צַוָּאת כֹּהֲנִים לְבָרֵךְ קָהָל וְעֵדָה

וּפְקוּד לְוִיִם לַעֲנוֹת בְּקוֹל רָם

קְרִיאַת מוֹעֲדִים וּזְמַנֵּי רְגָלִים

תְּקִיעָה בְּרֹאשׁ הַשָּׁנָה וְעִנּוּי נֶפֶשׁ בְּיוֹם הַכִּפֻּרִים

רְגָלִים לַעֲלוֹת בְּשָׁלוֹשׁ פַּעֲמֵי שָׁנָה

וּמַתְּנוֹת יָדַיִם מִבִּרְכוֹתֶיךָ

שְׁלָמִים וְעוֹלוֹת זְבָחִים וּנְסָכִים

נְדָרִים וּנְדָבוֹת חַטָּאוֹת וַאֲשָׁמוֹת

◂ תְּמִידִין וּמוּסָפִין לַשַּׁבָּתוֹת לֶחֳדָשִׁים וְלַמּוֹעֲדִים

וּכְלֵי הַקֹּדֶשׁ לְשָׁרֵת לְפָנֶיךָ.

תּוֹדָה וּמִנְחָה כְּשֶׂבָה וּשְׂעִירָה

תּוֹרִים וּבְנֵי יוֹנָה וַעֲשִׂירִית הָאֵיפָה

שְׁמִטִּים וְיוֹבְלוֹת וְחִשּׁוּב תְּקוּפוֹת

וּסְפִירַת הָעֹמֶר שִׁבְעָה שָׁבֻעוֹת

רִבִּית הָאֹכֶל וְנֶשֶׁךְ הַכֶּסֶף

הַשְׁמָטַת מִלְוֶה וּגְאֻלַּת מִמְכָּר

קְרִיאַת דְּרוֹר וְשִׁלּוּחַ חָפְשִׁי

חִפּוּשׁ הַנִּרְצָע בַּיּוֹבֵל וְהָאָמָה בְּסִמָּן

צֶדֶק צֶדֶק לִרְדֹּף אֱמֶת וּמִשְׁפָּט לַעֲשׂוֹת

פְּעֻלַּת שָׂכִיר בַּל תָּלִין עַד בֹּקֶר

פְּלִיאַת הַדִּין לְלַמֵּד בְּלִשְׁכַּת הַגָּזִית

וּמִיתַת חֶנֶק לְעוֹשֶׂה בְזָדוֹן

עֲשִׂיַּת מַעֲקֶה לְבַל יִפֹּל הַנֹּפֵל

וְעָרֵי מִקְלָט לְרוֹצֵחַ בִּבְלִי דָעַת

סִדְרֵי קְרָב וּמְשׁוֹחַ מִלְחָמָה

הַזְהָרַת שׁוֹטְרִים וְשָׂרֵי צְבָאוֹת

נְקִיּוּת לַבַּיִת לָבוֹא לִשְׂמֹחַ בַּכַּלָּה מְאָרֵשׂ וּבוֹנֶה וְנוֹטֵעַ וְרַךְ הַלֵּבָב

וְקִדּוּשׁ מַחֲנֶה מֵעֶרְוַת דָּבָר

מוֹצָא שְׂפָתַיִם בְּדִבֵּר וּשְׁבוּעַת הָאָסָר

וּפִיצַת פֶּה בְּנֶדֶר לְהָפֵר וּלְקַיֵּם

לְבִישַׁת שַׁעַטְנֵז וְכִלְאֵי הַכֶּרֶם

הַרְבָּעַת בְּהֵמָה וְהַרְכָּבַת הָאִילָן

כָּתְנוֹת כָּבוֹד לְהַלְבִּישׁ לַכֹּהֲנִים

הַזְהָרַת עֲבֹדָה לְבַל יִקְרַב כָּל זָר

יִדְּעֹנִים לְהַשְׁמִיד וְאוֹבוֹת לְהַכְרִית

לִהְיוֹת תְּמִימִים לְקַבֵּל תְּמִימָה

טָהֳרָה וּנְקִיּוּת מִלָּבֹא מַמְזֵר בַּקָּהָל

עַמּוֹנִי וּמוֹאָבִי פְּצוּעַ דַּכָּה וּכְרוּת שָׁפְכָה

חֲסִימָה וּפְרִיקָה וְתוֹכַחַת

שִׂנְאָה וְקִלְלַת חֵרֵשׁ וּמִכְשׁוֹל עִוֵּר

זְרִיזוּת לְהַבְדִּיל בֵּין טָמֵא לְטָהוֹר

וְשִׁקּוּץ חַיָּה טְמֵאָה הַמַּבְדֶּלֶת לְטָמֵא

וְאֹתוֹ וְאֶת בְּנוֹ בְּיוֹם אֶחָד וְגִיד הַנָּשֶׁה

וְאֵבֶר מִן הַחַי וּבָשָׂר בְּחָלָב

הַחְיַאת אָח וְהַלְוָאַת אֶבְיוֹן

חֲבִילַת רֵחַיִם וָרֶכֶב וַהֲשָׁבַת הָעֲבוֹט

דִּבְרֵי הוֹדָיַת עָוֹן וְקָרְבַּן חַטָּאת

סְמִיכָה וּתְנוּפָה כַּפָּרָה וּסְלִיחָה

גְּנֵבָה וַאֲבֵדָה טְרֵפָה וּשְׁבוּרָה וּשְׁבוּיָה תַּשְׁלוּמֵי כֶפֶל וְתַשְׁלוּמֵי

אַרְבָּעָה וַחֲמִשָּׁה / שׁוֹמֵר חִנָּם וְהַשּׁוֹאֵל נוֹשֵׂא שָׂכָר וְהַשּׂוֹכֵר

בִּעוּר חָמֵץ וַאֲכִילַת מַצָּה

זִכְרוֹן חֹק לֶחָג כָּל שִׁבְעַת הַיָּמִים

‹ אַף פָּרָשַׁת שְׁקָלִים לְהַזְכִּיר אוֹתָהּ בְּכָל שָׁנָה וְשָׁנָה

שמות יב   וּפָרְעֻנוֹת עֲמָלֵק וּפָרָה אֲדֻמָּה, וְהַחֹדֶשׁ הַזֶּה לָכֶם:

אַבְחָנַת מוּמִים מִלְּהַגִּישׁ בַּעַל מוּם

מוּמֵי אָדָם וּמוּמֵי בְהֵמָה

בְּרִית מֶלַח שֶׁלֹּא לְהַשְׁבִּית

לְהַקְרִיב אוֹתָהּ עַל כָּל קָרְבָּן

גַּם בְּלַיְלָה וּפְתִיתָתָהּ קְמִיצָה וְהַקְטָרָה

הַקְרָבָה וְהַגָּשָׁה קַבָּלָה וְהַזָּיָה

דִּין הַבְּכוֹר לִטּוֹל פִּי שְׁנַיִם

וּמִשְׁפַּט אִישׁ כִּי יָמוּת וּבֵן אֵין לוֹ

הַנִּצִּים יַחַד לָקֹץ כַּף שׁוֹלַחַת יָד בִּמְבוּשָׁיו

מִגְרֶה מָדוֹן כְּלִי גֶבֶר עַל אִשָּׁה וְשִׂמְלַת אִשָּׁה עַל גֶּבֶר

וְהַקְרָבַת גֵּרֵי צֶדֶק לָגוּר יַחַד וּלְקַיֵּם חֻקִּים כְּמַחְפְּשֵׂי מִפֶּרֶךְ צְעָנִים

וְלָחֹן גֵּרֵי שַׁעַר וּלְהַאֲכִילָם נְבֵלוֹת

זְרִיקַת דָּם וְהַקְטֵר חֲלָבִים

לִשְׂרֹף בָּאֵשׁ בַּבֹּקֶר כָּל הַנֶּאֱכָלִים לְיוֹם אֶחָד

חֵרֶם וְחַלָּה וְשֶׁמֶן שְׂרֵפָה לָתֵת לַכֹּהֵן

וְהָאָשָׁם הַמּוּשָׁב מִמִּי שֶׁאֵין לוֹ גֹּאֵל

טְמֵאִים לְנֶפֶשׁ אָדָם לַעֲשׂוֹת פֶּסַח שֵׁנִי

וּבַל הוֹצָאַת בָּשָׂר חוּצָה וּשְׁבִירַת הָעֶצֶם

יְצִיקַת שֶׁמֶן הַמִּשְׁחָה עַל רֹאשׁ כֹּהֵן גָּדוֹל

לְמַלֵּא יָדָיו לְכַהֵן תַּחַת אָבִיו

כָּל מַעֲשֵׂה יוֹם הַכִּפּוּרִים לַעֲשׂוֹתָן כְּתִקְנָן

לְכַפֵּר עַל חַטֹּאתֵינוּ אַחַת בַּשָּׁנָה

לָקוּם מִפְּנֵי שֵׂיבָה וּלְהַדֵּר פְּנֵי זָקֵן

אַזְהָרַת שֶׁלֹּא תֵלֵךְ רָכִיל וְשֶׁלֹּא לַעֲמֹד עַל דַּם רֵעַ

מִצְוַת דִּין הַחוֹבֵל בַּחֲבֵרוֹ לְחַיְּבוֹ בַּחֲמִשָּׁה דְבָרִים בְּנֶזֶק וְצַעַר

וְרִפּוּי וְשֶׁבֶת וּבֹשֶׁת / וְנוֹגֵף אִשָּׁה הָרָה לְשַׁלֵּם דְּמֵי וְלָדוֹת

נְקִימָה וּנְטִירָה לְהַרְחִיק מִלֵּב

וְשׁוֹכֵב עִם נֶחֱרֶפֶת לְהָבִיא אֵיל אָשָׁם

שֶׁרֶט לָנֶפֶשׁ וּכְתֹבֶת קַעֲקַע

קָרְחַת וְהַקָּפַת רֹאשׁ וְהַשְׁחָתַת פְּאַת זָקָן

עֶרֶךְ וּמַפְלִיא בַּנֶּדֶר וּתְמוּרַת בְּהֵמָה בִּבְהֵמָה

אֶתְנַן זוֹנָה וּמְחִיר כֶּלֶב לְתַעֵב מִדִּבִּיר קֹדֶשׁ

פּוֹעֵל הַבָּא בְּקָמַת רֵעַ שֶׁלֹּא לְהָנִיף חֶרְמֵשׁ

וְשָׂכִיר הַבָּא בְכֶרֶם שֶׁלֹּא לָתֵן אֶל כֶּלִי

צִוּאַת בּוֹצֵר הַכֶּרֶם לְהַשְׁאִיר עוֹלֵלוֹת

וְחוֹבֵט זֵיתִים שֶׁלֹּא לְפָאֵר אַחֲרָיו

קָרֹב בַּחֲלַל חֶרֶב וְנֹגֵעַ בְּמֵת אוֹ בְעֶצֶם אָדָם אוֹ בְקֶבֶר יִטְמָא שִׁבְעַת יָמִים

לְהַזּוֹת עָלָיו מֵי הַנִּדָּה בַּיּוֹם הַשְּׁלִישִׁי וּבַיּוֹם הַשְּׁבִיעִי

רְאִיַּת נְגָעִים לְהַחְלִיט וּלְהַסְגִּיר

בַּהֶרֶת וְצָרֶבֶת שְׂאֵת וְסַפַּחַת

שְׁחִין וּמִכְוָה נִתְקֵי רֹאשׁ וְזָקָן

קָרַחַת וְגַבַּחַת וְכָל בֹּהַק לְטַהֵר

◀ תּוֹרַת צֶמֶר וּפִשְׁתִּים בֶּגֶד הַשְּׁתִי וְהָעֵרֶב

לִקְרֹעַ וְלִשְׂרֹף וּלְכַבֵּס שֵׁנִית.

תּוֹצֵאת מְשָׁרֵת אֶל מִחוּץ לַמַּחֲנֶה

לְטַהֵר הַמְצֹרָע בְּעֵץ אֶרֶז וְאֵזוֹב וּבִשְׁנִי תוֹלַעַת

שְׁחִיטַת צִפּוֹר אַחַת וְשִׁלּוּחַ אֶחָת

תִּגְלַחַת שֵׂעַר רֹאשׁוֹ וּזְקָנוֹ וְגַבּוֹת עֵינָיו

רֹאשׁ בְּהוֹנוֹת יָדָיו וְרַגְלָיו לְהַצִּיק מִשְּׁמָנִים

וּתְנוּךְ אָזְנוֹ לְחַטֵּא בְּדָמִים

קִירוֹת בָּתִּים לְטַהֲרָם מִנֶּגַע

וַעֲפַר נְתִיצָה לְהַשְׁלִיךְ אֶל חוּץ

צֵאַת טֻמְאַת הַזָּב וְנִבְלוּת דָּוָה

זָבָה נִדָּה וְיוֹלֶדֶת לְטַהֲרָם בְּקָרְבָּן

פִּתּוּי לֵב אִישׁ אִם יִרְאֶה קֶרִי

יָבוֹא בַּמַּיִם עֵת לִפְנוֹת עֶרֶב

עַל רֹאשׁ כֹּהֲנִים שֶׁלֹּא לְהַעֲלוֹת פֶּרַע

וּבַל יַשְׁכִּירוּ נֶפֶשׁ עֵת יָבוֹאוּ לָאֹהֶל

סְנַפִּיר וְקַשְׂקֶשֶׂת בְּנַפְשׁוֹת הַמַּיִם

וְעוֹף טָמֵא לְשַׁקֵּץ וְלֹא אֵכַל מְנַתֵּר

נְתִיצַת פֶּסֶל וּמַצֵּבָה וֵאלֹהֵי מַסֵּכָה

גִּלּוּלִים וּפְסִילִים בַּל יַעֲלוּ עַל לֵב

מוֹרָא וְכִבּוּד אֶת אָב וָאֵם

הַרְחָקַת חֲמוֹד בָּתִּים וְתַאֲוַת נָשִׁים

לַעֲזֹב שִׁכְחָה וּלְהַנִּיחַ פֵּאָה

לְהַפְקִיר לֶקֶט וּפֶרֶט לֶעָנִי וְלַגֵּר

כָּל חֹבֵר חֶבֶר וְדֹרֵשׁ אֶל הַמֵּתִים

מְעוֹנֵן וּמְנַחֵשׁ וּמְכַשֵּׁף וּמַעֲבִיר לַמֹּלֶךְ

יוֹצֵר שָׂנֵאם וְהֵם תּוֹעֲבַת נַפְשׁוֹ

בַּל תִּדְרֹשׁ מֵהֶם פֶּן לְשַׁחַת תּוּרַשׁ

טֶבֶל וְעׇרְלָה וַדַּאי וּדְמַאי וּמְתֻקָּן וְעֹשֶׁק וּתְשׂוּמֶת יָד

וּבַל תֹּאכְלוּ עַל הַדָּם

חֹק שְׁמִירַת שַׁבָּת וּמוֹרָא מִקְדָּשׁ

וְקִדּוּשׁ הָאָרֶץ פֶּן תִּמָּלֵא זִמָּה

זְכוּת וּמִישׁוֹר לְהִתְהַלֵּךְ בָּמוֹ

וּנְתִיב יִרְאָה לַעֲשׂוֹתוֹ מֵאַהֲבָה

וְאָרְחוֹת יָפוֹת וּמַעֲשִׂים טוֹבִים

בְּלִי לַעֲשׂוֹת עָוֶל בַּמִּדָּה בַּמִּשְׁקָל וּבַמְּשׂוּרָה

הִינִין לְצֶדֶק וּמִדּוֹת לְהַאֲמִין

לְהַרְחִיק אֶבֶן וָאֶבֶן מְכִיס אֵיפָה וְאֵיפָה מִבָּיִת

דִּבַּת לְשׁוֹן הָרָע לְהַרְחִיק מִפֶּה

וְדַבֵּר שָׁלוֹם אִישׁ אֶל רֵעֵהוּ

גְּרוּשָׁה וַחֲלָלָה זֹנָה לְהַבְדִּיל מִשְּׁאָר כֹּהֲנִים:

וְכֹהֵן גָּדוֹל לָתֵת זַרְעוֹ בְּאִשָּׁה בְתוּלָה

בִּשְׁאֵרוֹ לֹא יִטַּמָּא בְּמֵת מִצְוָה יִטַּמָּא

בְּנַפְשׁוֹת אָדָם וְלֹא בְּנַפְשׁוֹת בְּהֵמָה

‹ אָז יְלִידֵי בֵיתוֹ הֵם יֹאכְלוּ בְלַחְמוֹ

אִם יִגַּע בְּטָמֵאָה וְיִגַּע בַּקֹּדֶשׁ הוּא יִכָּרֵת.

אֶת שֵׁם הַמְיֻחָד שֶׁלֹּא לְקַלֵּל

וְשֶׁלֹּא לְהַזְכִּיר בְּשֵׁם אֱלֹהִים אֲחֵרִים

בַּת כֹּהֵן כִּי תִזְנֶה מִיתָתָהּ בִּשְׂרֵפָה

וְאִם תְּחַלֵּל זֶרַע לֹא תֹאכַל בַּקֹּדֶשׁ

גְּרִישַׁת טְמֵאִים אֶל מִחוּץ לַמַּחֲנֶה

וְגוֹזֵל הַגֵּר וְכִחֵשׁ בַּעֲמִיתוֹ מְשַׁלֵּם קֶרֶן וָחֹמֶשׁ וּמְעִילוֹת

דִּבְרֵי נְזִירוּת לְטֻמְאָה וּלְתִגְלַחַת

מִלֶּאֱכֹל כָּל מִשְׁרַת גֶּפֶן מֵחַרְצַנִּים וְעַד זַג

הַעֲבָרַת תַּעַר עַל כָּל בְּשַׂר לְוִים

וְלֶהָרִים תְּרוּמָה מִמַּעֲשַׂר נַחֲלָתָם

וְכִסּוּי הַדָּם וּמַגָּע וּמַשָּׂא וְאֹהֶל וְהֶסֵּט

וְאוֹנֵן וּטְבוּל יוֹם וּמְחֻסַּר כִּפּוּרִים

זְבִיחַת בָּשָׂר לֶאֱכֹל בְּתַאֲוָה

וּנְבִיא הַשֶּׁקֶר שֶׁלֹּא לִשְׁמֹעַ לוֹ

חֲקִירַת עֵדִים וּמֵסִית וּמַדִּיחַ

וְעִיר הַנִּדַּחַת לִשְׂרֵפָה בָּאֵשׁ

טֻמְאַת אַרְבָּעָה סְפֵקוֹת וְסוֹד הַשְּׁסוּעָה

וּמַעֲשֵׂר רִאשׁוֹן וְקָרְבַּן נְשִׂיאִים

יֹפִי חֵלֶק כְּחֵלֶק וּמִמְכַּר אָבוֹת

וּפָרָשַׁת הַמֶּלֶךְ וּמַשִּׂיג גְּבוּל רֵעֵהוּ

כָּל עֵד זוֹמֵם לַעֲנַשׁ וּגְדִילִים לַעֲשׂוֹת

מִשְׁפַּט אֲהוּבָה וּשְׂנוּאָה וּבֵן סוֹרֵר וּמוֹרֶה

לְשַׁלַּח הַקֵּן וְלָהָבִיא יְפַת תֹּאַר

מִצְרִי וַאֲדֹמִי עַד דּוֹר שְׁלִישִׁי

מִילָה וּרְחִיצָה דְּמֵי טֻמְאָה וּדְמֵי טָהֳרָה

וּבַל תַּסְגִּיר עֶבֶד אֶל אֲדֹנָיו

וְקָדֵשׁ וּקְדֵשָׁה וְגֹנֵב נֶפֶשׁ מֵאֶחָיו

נְגִיחָה וּנְגִיפָה נְשִׁיכָה רְבִיצָה וּבְעִיטָה

וְדִין יוֹם אוֹ יוֹמַיִם וְחֹפֶשׁ עֶבֶד כְּנַעֲנִי בְּעֵינוֹ אוֹ בְשִׁנּוֹ

סִפּוּק נוֹפֵל לַמִּשְׁכָּב לְרַפֹּאות שִׁבְרוֹ

וְאִם יִתְהַלֵּךְ בַּחוּץ לָתֵת שִׁבְתּוֹ

עֲבֵרַת דְּלֵקָה וְשִׁלּוּחַ בְּעֵירָה

וְהֶרֶג בְּעָרְמָה וְנִמְצָא בַּמַּחְתֶּרֶת

פּוֹתֵחַ וְכוֹרֶה בּוֹר בִּרְשׁוּת הָרַבִּים לְשַׁלֵּם נִזְקֵי נוֹפֵל

וּמְפַתֶּה אִשָּׁה לִשְׁקֹל מֹהַר וְתוֹפֵס לְשַׁלֵּם קְנָס

צַוְּאַת בַּל קַלְלַת חֵרֵשׁ שׁוֹפֵט וְנָשִׂיא

מִלְאָה וְדִמְעָה שֶׁלֹּא לְאַחֵר

קוֹל לְהָרִיעַ בַּחֲצֹצְרוֹת וּלְהַסִּיעַ מַחֲנוֹת

וּמְשִׂים עֲלִילוֹת לְעָנְשׁוֹ בְּמָמוֹן

רְחָבָה בִּגְבוּלוֹתֶיהָ לְהַנְחִיל לַשְׁבָטִים
וְשֶׁלֹּא תִסֹּב נַחֲלָה מִמַּטֶּה לְמַטֶּה אַחֵר
שְׁבוּעַת שָׁוְא וְחִלּוּל הַשֵּׁם
וְשׁוֹכֵב עִם בְּהֵמָה וְהָאִשָּׁה הַנִּרְבַּעַת לִבְהֵמָה
‹ תּוֹעִים בַּדֶּרֶךְ לְהָשִׁיב לְאָח וְלָאוֹיֵב
וְאִם רָחוֹק מִמֶּנּוּ תְּהֵא עִמּוֹ עַד דְּרִישָׁה.

תּוֹרָה לִשְׁמֹר תְּעוּדָה לִנְצֹר
תִּקְוַת מְכַשֵּׁף לְסָקְלוּ בָּאָבֶן
שֵׁמַע שָׁוְא שֶׁלֹּא לִשָּׂא
וְנָקִי וְצַדִּיק שֶׁלֹּא לַהֲרֹג
רִיב דַּלִּים שֶׁלֹּא לְהַטּוֹת
אַחֲרֵי רַבִּים בַּל תְּהִי לְרָעֹת
קְדוֹשִׁים תִּהְיוּ כִּבְנֵי אֱלֹהִים
לִקְרֹא שָׁלוֹם בַּמִּלְחָמָה וְשֶׁלֹּא לָקֹץ כָּל עֵץ מַאֲכָל
צֹאן פְּסָחִים שֶׁלֹּא לִזְבֹּחַ עַל חָמֵץ
נָא וּבָשֵׁל מְבֻשָּׁל בַּל תֹּאכְלוּ מִמֶּנּוּ
פֶּן יִמְכֹּר אִישׁ אֶת בִּתּוֹ לְאָמָה
כְּצֵאת הָעֲבָדִים בַּל יוֹצִיאֶנָּה
עַם נָכְרִי לֹא יִמְשֹׁל לְמָכְרָהּ בַּכֶּסֶף
אָדוֹן אִם לֹא יְעָדָהּ יִפְדֶּנָּה הָאָב
שָׂמָה צֶלַע לִינוֹ לְבֵית
יְכַבֵּד אוֹתָהּ כְּמִשְׁפַּט הַבָּנוֹת
נַפְשׁוֹ אִם תִּתְאַוֶּה לִשָּׂא אִשָּׁה אַחֶרֶת
שְׁאֵרָהּ כְּסוּתָהּ וְעֹנָתָהּ לֹא יִגְרַע מִמֶּנָּה
מִשְּׁלֹשׁ אֵלֶּה אִם יִמְנָעֶנָּה
תֵּצֵא חִנָּם בְּלֹא מַתַּת כֶּסֶף

לֹא לְהִתְחַתֵּן בְּגוֹיֵי הָאֲרָצוֹת וְלֹא לְחָנְנָם וְלֹא לִכְרֹת בְּרִית עִמָּם

וְנִבְלַת חוֹטֵא נִתְלֶה בַּל תָּלִין עַל עֵץ

כִּנּוּס סַמְמָנִים וְסֵדֶר פִּטּוּמִים

וְשֶׁמֶן מִמְלָח וּקְטֹרֶת הַסַּמִּים

יְרִיעֹת וְלֻלָאֹת קְרָסִים וּקְרָשִׁים

וָוִים בְּרִיחִים וְעַמּוּדִים וַאֲדָנִים וִיתֵדֹת לַמִּשְׁכָּן

טֹהַר מִזְבַּח הַזָּהָב וּמִזְבַּח הַנְּחֹשֶׁת

מִכְבָּר וְכַרְכֹּב וְסִירֹתָיו לְדַשְּׁנוֹ

חִנּוּךְ מְנוֹרָה וְנֵרוֹתֶיהָ קָנֶיהָ גְּבִיעֶיהָ כַּפְתֹּרֶיהָ וּפְרָחֶיהָ

מַלְקָחֶיהָ וּמַחְתֹּתֶיהָ לַעֲשׂוֹת מִכִּכַּר הַזָּהָב

זֶבֶד לֶחֶם הַפָּנִים לַעֲרֹךְ עַל הַשֻּׁלְחָן

וְקִדּוּשׁ יָדַיִם וְרַגְלַיִם מִן הַכִּיּוֹר

וְקַלְעֵי הֶחָצֵר וּשְׁתֵּי כְתֵפֹת

בָּתִּים לַבַּדִּים וְנָבוּב לֻחֹת

הֲבָאַת הַבַּדִּים בְּטַבְּעֹת הָאָרוֹן

מָסָךְ וּמִכְסֶה לָאֹהֶל פָּרֹכֶת וְכַפֹּרֶת וּשְׁנֵי כְרוּבִים

דַּקָּה וְקִדָּה קָנֶה וְקִנְּמוֹן מֹר

נָטָף וּשְׁחֵלֶת וְחֶלְבְּנָה וּלְבֹנָה לִרְקֹחַ בְּשָׂמִים

גַּם בְּיוֹם הַשַּׁבָּת שֶׁלֹּא לְבַעֵר אֵשׁ

לְהַסִּיק עֲצֵי הַמַּעֲרָכָה בַּבֹּקֶר בַּבֹּקֶר

בִּגְדֵי קֹדֶשׁ לְכָבוֹד וּלְתִפְאָרֶת

אוּרִים וְתֻמִּים וְאַרְבָּעָה טוּרִים

‹ אֵפוֹד וָחֹשֶׁן וּמְעִיל וְצִיץ הַזָּהָב וְנֵזֶר הַקֹּדֶשׁ

כֻּתֹּנֶת וּמִכְנָסַיִם וּמִצְנֶפֶת וְאַבְנֵט בַּד וּמִגְבָּעוֹת.

אֹהֶל מוֹעֵד לִנְטוֹתוֹ בְּחֶסֶד

לְחָנְכוֹ בְּאִשִּׁים בְּיוֹם הֲקָמָתוֹ

בְּמַחֲבַת וּבְמַרְחֶשֶׁת בְּחַלּוֹת וּבִרְקִיקִים בְּסֹלֶת בְּשֶׁמֶן וּבִלְבֹנָה

וּבְאַזְכָּרָה / בְּלִי לְהַקְרִיב לַשֵּׁם כָּל שְׂאֹר וְכָל דְּבַשׁ

גַּם נָשִׂיא וּמָשִׁיחַ עֵדָה וְיָחִיד אִם יֶחֶטְאוּ בְּשׁוֹגֵג
בְּקׇרְבָּן יְרַצּוּ לַמֶּלֶךְ

דְּבַר שְׁמִיעַת קוֹל אָלָה אוֹ רָאָה אוֹ יָדַע
אִם לֹא יַגִּיד וְנָשָׂא עֲוֹנוֹ

הוֹרָיַת בֵּית דִּין וּשְׁבוּעַת בִּטּוּי וּפַר הַבָּא עַל כׇּל הַמִּצְוֹת
אָשָׁם וַדַּאי וְאָשָׁם תָּלוּי

וְקׇרְבַּן אַהֲרֹן וּבָנָיו לַחֲצוֹת בַּבֹּקֶר וּבָעֶרֶב
מַרְבֶּכֶת תְּפִינֵי מִנְחַת כֹּהֵן וְכֹהֶנֶת

זֶפֶק מׇרְאָה וְנוֹצָה מְלִיקָה וְהַמְצִיָּה
וְהִפְשֵׁט וְנִתּוּחַ בַּבְּהֵמָה וְשִׁסּוּעַ וּבַל הַבְדָּלָה בָּעוֹף

חֵלֶב וּשְׁתֵּי הַכְּלָיוֹת וְיֹתֶרֶת הַכָּבֵד וְהָעֵצֶה
שְׁחִיטַת צֹאן בַּצָּפוֹן וְהַפְרָשַׁת אֵילֵי קֹדֶשׁ אַלְיָה וְאֵמוּרִים

טְמְאַת שֶׁרֶץ בַּבֶּגֶד וּבָעוֹר אוֹ בְשַׂק אוֹ בְכׇל כְּלִי עֵץ
מַעְיָן וּבוֹר תַּנּוּר וְכִירַיִם וְאֹכֶל וּמַשְׁקֶה וְכׇל זֶרַע זָרוּעַ

יִגַּע בִּבְשַׂר קֹדֶשׁ יִקְדָּשׁ וּמַזֶּה מִדָּמָהּ יְכַבֵּס בְּגָדָיו
שְׁבִירָה בִּכְלִי חֶרֶשׂ מְרִיקָה וּשְׁטִיפָה בִּכְלִי נְחֹשֶׁת

כֹּל הוֹלֵךְ עַל גָּחוֹן וְכֹל הוֹלֵךְ עַל אַרְבַּע
חֲגָבִים טְמֵאִים וַחֲגָבִים טְהוֹרִים

לְהַרְחִיץ קֶרֶב וּכְרָעַיִם וּלְהָנִיף הֶחָזֶה וְשׁוֹק הַיָּמִין
פָּרִים הַנִּשְׂרָפִים וְשָׂעִיר הַמִּשְׁתַּלֵּחַ

מַלְקוּת אַרְבָּעִים כְּדֵי רִשְׁעַת אִישׁ
לְזַכּוֹת אֶת הַזַּכַּאי וּלְחַיֵּב אֶת הַחַיָּב

נַעֲרָה הַמְאֹרָסָה כִּי תֵאָנֵס
בְּעָלָהּ יִסָּקֵל וְהִיא תְנֻקֶּה

סֵדֶר עִבּוּרִים לְהַעֲנִיק לְעֶבֶד וְלֶאָמָה
וְשֶׁלֹּא לְאַמֵּץ לֵב וְשֶׁלֹּא לִקְפֹּץ יָד מֵעָנִי וָדַל

עִם זָכָר שֶׁלֹּא לִשְׁכַּב
וְכׇל שְׁאֵר בָּשָׂר לְהַרְחִיק מִגּוּף

פֶּטֶר חֲמוֹר לִפְדּוֹתוֹ בְשֶׂה
וְהַעֲבָרַת שׁוֹפָר בְּיוֹם הַכִּפֻּרִים

צֵאת עֶבֶד עִבְרִי בַּשָּׁנָה הַשְּׁבִיעִית
וְאִם יֹאהַב אֲדֹנוֹ יִהְיֶה לוֹ עֶבֶד עוֹלָם עַד שְׁנַת הַיּוֹבֵל

קִדּוּשׁ שְׁנַת הַחֲמִשִּׁים בַּיּוֹבֵל לָשׁוּב לַאֲחֻזָּה וְלַמִּשְׁפָּחָה
לָתֵת גְּאֻלָּה לָאָרֶץ שֶׁלֹּא תִמָּכֵר לִצְמִתוּת

רֵאשִׁית דָּגָן תִּירוֹשׁ וְיִצְהָר
עֶשְׂרִים וְאַרְבַּע מַתְּנוֹת כְּהֻנָּה

שׁוֹחֵט וּמַעֲלֶה בַחוּץ לְחַיְּבוֹ כָּרֵת
חָק עוֹלָם שֶׁלֹּא לִזְבֹּחַ לַשְּׂעִירִם

‏־ תֵּעוּב בֶּן נֵכָר שֶׁלֹּא לֶאֱכֹל בַּפֶּסַח
כֹּהֲנִים בְּמוּמִים לִפְסֹל וּלְוִיִּם בַּשָּׁנִים.

תִּשְׂמַח לֵוִי בְּיוֹם שִׂמְחָתֶךָ
וּבַל תּוֹנוּ אִישׁ אֶת עֲמִיתוֹ וְגֵר יָתוֹם וְאַלְמָנָה

שֵׁם מֶלֶךְ לְיַחֵד שַׁחֲרִית וְעַרְבִית
בָּתֵּי הַחֲצֵרִים וּבָתֵּי עָרֵי חוֹמָה

רוֹאֶה עִוֵּר וּמַשְׁגֵּהוּ בַּדֶּרֶךְ
תַּשִּׂיגֵהוּ קְלָלָה הַכְּתוּבָה בַּסֵּפֶר

קוֹלֵעַ וּמַכֶּה רֵעֵהוּ בַּסָּתֶר
שֹׁפֵךְ דַּם הָאָדָם בָּאָדָם דָּמוֹ יִשָּׁפֵךְ

צִוּוּי עַל הַסֵּרוּס שָׁרוּעַ וְקָלוּט וּמָעוּךְ וְכָתוּת וְנָתוּק וְכָרוּת
וְשֶׁלֹּא לַעֲבֹד בִּבְכוֹר שׁוֹר וְשֶׁלֹּא לָגֹז בִּבְכוֹר צֹאן

פִּנּוּי מַעֲשֵׂר רִאשׁוֹן מִתּוֹךְ הַבַּיִת
וּמַעֲשֵׂר שֵׁנִי מִן הָאוֹצָר

עַל אֲזֵנֶךָ תָּכִין יָתֵד
לַחְפֹּר וּלְכַסּוֹת צֵאת מַאֲכָלֶיךָ

סְפִיחֵי שְׁבִיעִית וּפֶרֶט כֶּרֶם זַיִת לְשָׂכִיר וּלְתוֹשָׁב
וְיִתְרָם לַחַיָּה

נֶצַח תִּשְׁבֹּת בַּהֲמִתְּךָ בְּיוֹם מְנוּחָתֶךָ
וְגֵר וְעֶבֶד וְאָמָה כָּמוֹךָ יָנוּחוּ

מִזְבַּח אֲדָמָה לִבְנוֹת בַּאֲבָנִים שְׁלֵמוֹת
וְלַחֲקֹק דָּת עֲלֵיהֶם בָּאֵר הֵיטֵב

לָתֵת לַלְוִיִּם מְנָת חֵלֶק בָּאָרֶץ
כִּי בְיִשְׂרָאֵל לֹא יִנְחֲלוּ נַחֲלָה

כִּי יִרְבֶּה הַדֶּרֶךְ לָשֵׂאת מַעֲשֵׂר שֵׁנִי
יִפְדֵּהוּ בַכֶּסֶף וְיַעֲלֵהוּ לְעִיר הַקֹּדֶשׁ

יִתֵּן הַכֶּסֶף בְּכָל אַוַּת נַפְשׁוֹ
בַּבָּקָר וּבַצֹּאן בַּיַּיִן וּבַשֵּׁכָר

טֶרֶף עָשׂוּר תְּבוּאָה בַּשָּׁנָה הַשְּׁלִישִׁית
לְהוֹצִיא וּלְהָנִיחַ בִּשְׁעָרֶיךָ לְהַשְׂבִּיעַ דַּלִּים

חַלּוֹת פְּנֵי אֵל בְּשִׁבְעַת יְמֵי הֶחָג
בִּפְרִי עֵץ הָדָר וּבְקִלּוּס עַרְבֵי נָחַל

זִמְרָה וְהַלֵּל לָתֵת בַּהֲדַס וְרֹב הוֹדָיוֹת בְּכַפֹּת תְּמָרִים
וְיָמִים שְׁמֹנָה עָשָׂר וְלַיְלָה אֶחָד לִגְמֹר בָּהֶן אֶת הַהַלֵּל
וּבַגּוֹלָה עֶשְׂרִים וְאֶחָד יוֹם וּשְׁנֵי לֵילוֹת

וְנֵר חֲנֻכָּה בְּעֵתָּהּ בַּל תַּשְׁבִּית מֵאֹהָלֶיךָ
בְּרָכָה וְהוֹדָאָה עַל הַמָּזוֹן בְּאָכְלְךָ וּבְשָׂבְעֶךָ

הַמְלִיכֵהוּ עָלֶיךָ בְּיוֹם הַזִּכָּרוֹן אוֹהֵב שָׁלוֹם וְרוֹדֵף שָׁלוֹם וְהַצְנֵעַ
לֶכֶת עִם אֱלֹהֶיךָ / הוֹדַע וְלֹא הוֹדַע שְׂעִירֵי עֲבוֹדָה זָרָה

וּשְׂעִירֵי רְגָלִים וּשְׂעִירֵי רָאשֵׁי חֳדָשִׁים שְׂעִירֵי יוֹם הַכִּפּוּרִים
דַּת הַמִּלֻּאִים וּפְסוּלֵי הַמֻּקְדָּשִׁין שֶׁלֹּא לַחֲרֹשׁ בְּשׁוֹר וּבַחֲמוֹר
יַחְדָּו / שֶׁהָיָה דָּרְסָה חֻלְדָּה הַגַּרְמָה וְעָקוּר

גַּם תְּרוּמַת בָּצֵק לָתֵת לַכֹּהֵן הַפִּגּוּל וְהַלָּן וְהַנּוֹתָר וְהַיּוֹצֵא וְהַטָּמֵא
וְהַנִּשְׁחָט חוּץ לִזְמַנּוֹ וְחוּץ לִמְקוֹמוֹ / נֶזֶק וַחֲצִי נֶזֶק וְעֶשְׂרִים
גֵּרָה וּכְשֶׁקִּבְּלוּ פְּסוּלִין וְזָרְקוּ אֶת דָּמָן הַנִּתָּנִין לְמַעְלָה שֶׁנְּתָנָן
לְמַטָּה וְהַנִּתָּנִין לְמַטָּה שֶׁנְּתָנָן לְמַעְלָה הַנִּתָּנִין בִּפְנִים שֶׁנְּתָנָן
בַּחוּץ וְהַנִּתָּנִין בַּחוּץ שֶׁנְּתָנָן בִּפְנִים הַפֶּסַח וְהַחַטָּאת וְהָאָשָׁם
שֶׁשְּׁחָטָן שֶׁלֹּא לִשְׁמָן אִם עָלוּ לֹא יֵרְדוּ
בְּבִיאָה וּבְכֶסֶף וּבִשְׁטָר לִקְנוֹת בָּהֶם אֶת הָאִשָּׁה
שְׂדֵה אֲחֻזָּה וּשְׂדֵה מִקְנָה / רְשׁוּמוֹת קְמוּצוֹת פְּתוּחוֹת
וּסְתוּמוֹת נוֹטְרֵיקוֹן קַלּוֹת וַחֲמוּרוֹת
‹ אַזְכָּרַת מִקְרָא מְגִלָּה וַעֲצֶרֶת וְיוֹם טָבֵחַ
רְאִיָּה חֲגִיגָה וְשִׂמְחָה וְהַקְהֵל וְתִקּוּן גָּדוֹל.

Continue with "אָז שֵׁשׁ מֵאוֹת" on page 545.

יוצר ליום טוב שני של שבועות

שחרית *is said up to and including* בָּרְכוּ *(page 321).*

בָּרוּךְ אַתָּה יהוה אֱלֹהֵינוּ מֶלֶךְ הָעוֹלָם
יוֹצֵר אוֹר וּבוֹרֵא חְשֶׁךְ
עֹשֶׂה שָׁלוֹם וּבוֹרֵא אֶת הַכֹּל.

אוֹר עוֹלָם בְּאוֹצַר חַיִּים, אוֹרוֹת מֵאֹפֶל אָמַר וַיֶּהִי.

יוצר

The יוצר *said on the second day is a stand-alone piyut, not part of any known* יוצרות *cycle (see page 700). It follows the more classical format of* יוצר *piyutim, with a chorus ending in* "קדוש" *after the first and last stanzas. From the chorus, it seems likely the author's name was Shimon (hinted at in the words* "שָׁמְעוּ נִצָּבִים"). *The rest of the piyut has an alphabetic acrostic and, like most of the piyutim said on Shavuot, describes the giving of the Torah. The* אופן *and* זולת *following it are the same as were said on the first day (pages 703; 705).*

All:

אַיֶּלֶת אֲהָבִים מַתְּנַת סִינָי / אָמוֹן שַׁעֲשׁוּעִים מוֹרָשָׁה מִסִּינַי
בְּאוֹר תּוֹרָה אוֹר קְדֻשַׁת סִינַי / בְּהֶחָרֵד עָם סְבִיבוֹת סִינָי.

The שליח ציבור:

הִשָּׁמְרוּ עָם בְּלִי נְגֹעַ בָּהָר / וְעָנָן כָּבֵד עַל הָהָר
קוֹלוֹת וּבְרָקִים מִן הָהָר / שָׁמְעוּ נִצָּבִים בְּתַחְתִּית הָהָר
יוֹצֵר אוֹר בְּעַמּוֹ יְבְחַר, קָדוֹשׁ.

All:

גֶּבֶר חָכָם עָלָה לְסִינַי /גֵּאֶה בְּרָב כֹּחוֹ שָׁכֵן בְּסִינָי.
דָּת מְשַׂחֶקֶת יוֹם יוֹם לְסִינַי / דַּעַת מְחַוֶּה הֵאִירָה הַר סִינָי.
הִגְבִּיל גּוֹי קָדוֹשׁ תַּחְתִּית סִינָי / הוֹפִיעַ בִּכְבוֹדוֹ וְקִדֵּשׁ סִינָי.
וַיֵּט שָׁמַיִם וַיֵּרֶד לְסִינָי / וְעֻמַּהּ שָׂרֵי נְהוֹרָא הֵאִירָה הַר סִינָי.
זֶעֶף בֶּהָרִים וּבָחַר בְּסִינָי / זֹהַר אוֹר הִזְרִיחַ זֶה סִינָי.
חָשׁוּ גִבְעוֹנִים לְקַדֵּם לְסִינָי / חָמַד אֱלֹהִים לְשִׁבְתּוֹ זֶה סִינָי.

טָהוֹרָה יִרְאָה הִשְׁמִיעַ בְּסִינַי / טוֹב בִּמְאוֹר טוֹב נִגַּשׁ לְסִינַי.
יָרְצֻדוּ הָרִים אֶל מוּל סִינַי / יְקַבְּלוּ הֲלָכָה לְמֹשֶׁה מִסִּינַי.

כַּלַּת לְבָנוֹן הִזְהִיר מֹשֶׁה / כָּתַב שְׁלִישִׁים לִמְדָם מֹשֶׁה.
לָעֲרָפֶל נִגַּשׁ מֹשֶׁה / לְהַשְׁמִיעַ לָעָם וַיֵּרֶד מֹשֶׁה.
מִתּוֹךְ הָאֵשׁ אָמַר אֱלֹהִים / מָתוֹק הָאוֹר בְּתוֹרַת אֱלֹהִים.
נֹפֶת צוּפִים נָתַן אֱלֹהִים / נֶחְמָדִים מִזָּהָב וּמִפָּז וַיְדַבֵּר אֱלֹהִים.

שִׂמַּחְתָּ גּוֹי קָדוֹשׁ בְּמַעֲשֵׂה יָדֶיךָ / סִדַּרְתָּ לְעַנֵּן סוֹד שַׁעֲשׁוּעֶיךָ.
עַל הַר סִינַי נִגְלֵיתָ בְּרִבְבוֹת אַלְפֶּיךָ / עָנִיתָ וְאָמַרְתָּ אָנֹכִי יהוה אֱלֹהֶיךָ.

פּוֹרַרְתָּ יָם בְּעֻזְּךָ וְעָלָיו דַּרְכָּה וְגַלֶּךָ / פָּדִיתָ בְּלַהֲבוֹת אֵשׁ אֲשֶׁר חָצַב קוֹלֶךָ.
צִהַרְתָּ אוֹר מְקַבְלֵי לֹא יִהְיֶה לָךְ /
צִוִּיתָ לֹא תִשָּׂא לַשָּׁוְא כְּבוֹד שְׁמִי בְּמִלּוּלֶךָ.

קַדֵּשׁ זָכוֹר וְקַיֵּם שָׁמוֹר / קְהִלּוֹת יַעֲקֹב יַעֲנוּ מִזְמוֹר.
רוּץ לְמִצְוַת כַּבֵּד וְאוֹר נְתִיבוֹתֶיהָ תִּגְמוֹר /
רְאֵה לֹא תִרְצַח צֶלֶם צוּרְךָ וְעַצְמְךָ תִּשְׁמוֹר.

שֵׁם רַע לֹא תִנְאַף וְנוּגֵי זִמָּה / שָׁמוֹר לֹא תִגְנֹב פֶּן תּוּשַׁת לִכְלִמָּה.
תָּמִיד לֹא תַעֲנֶה בְּרֵעֲךָ עֵדוּת מִזְמָה /

תַּאֲוַת רֵעֲךָ לֹא תַחְמֹד מֵאָדָם וְעַד בְּהֵמָה.

The שליח ציבור:

הִשָּׁמְרוּ עָם בְּלִי נְגֹעַ בָּהָר / וְעָנָן כָּבֵד עַל הָהָר
קוֹלוֹת וּבְרָקִים מִן הָהָר / שָׁמְעוּ נִצָּבִים בְּתַחְתִּית הָהָר
יוֹצֵר אוֹר בְּעַמּוֹ יִבְחָר, קָדוֹשׁ.

Continue with "הַמֵּאִיר לָאָרֶץ" on page 323
(on שבת, with "הַכֹּל יוֹדוּךָ" on page 325)
to "מְלֹא כָל הָאָרֶץ כְּבוֹדוֹ" on page 331.

קרובה ליום טוב שני של שבועות

The שליח ציבור *takes three steps forward and at the points indicated by* ',
*bends his knees at the first word, bows at the second, and
stands straight before saying God's name.*

תהלים נא

אֲדֹנָי, שְׂפָתַי תִּפְתָּח, וּפִי יַגִּיד תְּהִלָּתֶךָ:

אבות

ְבָּרוּךְ אַתָּה יהוה, אֱלֹהֵינוּ וֵאלֹהֵי אֲבוֹתֵינוּ
אֱלֹהֵי אַבְרָהָם, אֱלֹהֵי יִצְחָק, וֵאלֹהֵי יַעֲקֹב
הָאֵל הַגָּדוֹל הַגִּבּוֹר וְהַנּוֹרָא, אֵל עֶלְיוֹן
גּוֹמֵל חֲסָדִים טוֹבִים, וְקֹנֵה הַכֹּל, וְזוֹכֵר חַסְדֵי אָבוֹת
וּמֵבִיא גוֹאֵל לִבְנֵי בְנֵיהֶם לְמַעַן שְׁמוֹ בְּאַהֲבָה.
מֶלֶךְ עוֹזֵר וּמוֹשִׁיעַ וּמָגֵן.

מְסוֹד חֲכָמִים וּנְבוֹנִים
וּמִלֶּמֶד דַּעַת מְבִינִים
אֶפְתְּחָה פִי בְּשִׁיר וּבְרַנָנִים
לְהוֹדוֹת וּלְהַלֵּל פְּנֵי שׁוֹכֵן מְעוֹנִים

מגן

The קרובה *(see page 707) said on the second day was written by
Rabbi Shimon ben Yitzhak ("the Great," see page 700). It follows closely
the* קרובה *for the first day in form and content, but is considerably longer.*

All:

אְֹרַח חַיִּים מוּסַר תּוֹכַחַת / בְּתִתְּךָ לַנּוֹשָׁעִים בְּשׁוּבָה וָנַחַת
גָּעֲשׁוּ עַמּוּדֵי רוֹם וָתַחַת / דְּבֵקֶיךָ בְּבוֹאָם מַתָּנוֹת לָקַחַת.

הִסַּעְתָּ עַם כַּצֹּאן לַנְחוֹת / וְנִהֲגְתָּם כְּעֵדֶר בְּשֶׁבַע שְׂמָחוֹת
זֵבִיתָם לַתּוֹרָה בְּאַהַב לְהֵאָחוֹת / חָדֵשׁ שְׁלִישִׁי בְּצֵאתָם לִרְוָחוֹת.

טֶרֶם נִגְלֵיתָ בְּשֵׂעִיר וּפָארָן / יָדְעְתָּם חֻקֶּיךָ עָנָן וּשְׂכָרָן
כִּרְאוֹתְךָ כִּי מֵאֲנוּ לְשָׁמְרָן / לֹא חֲשַׁבְתָּם וְרָאִיתָ לְהַתִּירָן.

מִמִּדְבָּר נִתְּנָה מָקוֹם הֶפְקֵר / נֶגֶד הַשֶּׁמֶשׁ לְעֵין כָּל סוֹקֵר
סוֹרְרִים שָׁכְנוּ צְחִיחָה לְהִתְעַקֵּר / עֵת יָבוֹאוּ בַמִּשְׁפָּט לְהִתְחַקֵּר.

פִּיךָ לֹא דִבֵּר בַּמִּסְתָּרִים / צֶדֶק דְּבַר מַגִּיד מֵישָׁרִים
קוֹלוֹת וְלַפִּידִים וּבְרָקִים בּוֹעֲרִים / רָאוּ וְתָמְהוּ מְלָכִים וְשָׂרִים.

שְׁלִישִׁים כָּתַבְתָּ לְעַם מְשֻׁלָּשִׁי / שְׁלֹשֶׁת שָׁלִישׁ מִשֵּׁבֶט שְׁלִישִׁי
‹ תְּמִימָה וּבָרָה מְשִׁיבַת נַפְשִׁי / תְּמַכְתָּ לְהַנְחִילִי בְּיֶרַח שְׁלִישִׁי.

All:

מֵישָׁרִים כָּל מַעְגְּלֵי טוּבוֹ / הִשְׁמִיעַ מִפִּיו לְעַם קְרֹבוֹ
‹ לַהֲבוֹת אֵשׁ בְּקוֹל כְּחָצְבוֹ / מָגֵן הוּא לְכָל הַחֹסִים בּוֹ.

‹בָּרוּךְ אַתָּה יהוה, מָגֵן אַבְרָהָם.

גבורות
אַתָּה גִּבּוֹר לְעוֹלָם, אֲדֹנָי
מְחַיֵּה מֵתִים אַתָּה, רַב לְהוֹשִׁיעַ

In ‹בארץ ישראל:
מוֹרִיד הַטָּל

מְכַלְכֵּל חַיִּים בְּחֶסֶד, מְחַיֶּה מֵתִים בְּרַחֲמִים רַבִּים
סוֹמֵךְ נוֹפְלִים, וְרוֹפֵא חוֹלִים, וּמַתִּיר אֲסוּרִים
וּמְקַיֵּם אֱמוּנָתוֹ לִישֵׁנֵי עָפָר.
מִי כָמוֹךָ, בַּעַל גְּבוּרוֹת, וּמִי דּוֹמֶה לָךְ
מֶלֶךְ, מֵמִית וּמְחַיֶּה וּמַצְמִיחַ יְשׁוּעָה.
וְנֶאֱמָן אַתָּה לְהַחֲיוֹת מֵתִים.

The מחיה follows a תשר״ק acrostic, with the last stanza
returning to the theme of the blessing.

All:

תָּמְכוּ כָּבוֹד נוֹחֲלֵי תְעוּדָה / שֻׁתְּפוּ בְּמַתָּן יְקָרָה וַחֲמוּדָה
רְצוּיָה חֲשׁוּקָה מִכֹּל כְּלִי חֶמְדָּה / קְרוּאָה בַּת מֶלֶךְ כְּבוּדָה.

צִיר נֶאֱמָן קָרְאַת לַעֲלוֹת / פָּנֶיךָ בֵּאֲרַתּוֹ חֲמוּרוֹת וְקַלּוֹת
עֳנָשִׁין וְאַזְהָרוֹת פְּרָטוֹת וּכְלָלוֹת / שְׂכַר הַמִּצְוֹת וְשָׁלוֹם גְּמוּלוֹת.

נֶמַתָּ לוֹ כֹּה תֹאמַר / מִלְפָחוֹת וּמִלְהוֹסִיף מֵאֲמָר
לַנָּשִׁים בִּלְשׁוֹן רַכָּה לוֹמַר / כְּבֶד הַדִּקְדּוּק לָאֲנָשִׁים לִגְמֹר.

יָרַד מִן הָהָר וְהִשְׁמִיעָם / טַעֲמֵי מֶתֶק וְאִמְרֵי נֹעַם
חָבְרוּ וְהֻשְׁווּ כְּאֶחָד בְּמַדָּעָם / זֹרְזוּ לְהַקְדִּים מַעֲשׂ לְמִשְׁמָעָם.

וּבַשְּׁלִישִׁי לְיוֹם הִתְקַדְּשָׁם בּוֹ / הִקְדִּים עַל יָדָם מֶלֶךְ בִּמְסִבּוֹ
דֶּרֶךְ תַּלְמִיד לְהַמְתִּין לְרַבּוֹ / גָּדְלָתּוֹ הִפְלִיא לְזֶרַע אוֹהֲבוֹ.

בְּנָסְעָם מִיַּם סוּף אֲגוּדִים / בְּרִיב וּמַצָּה נוֹסְעִים וְעוֹמְדִים
◂ אֲזַי בְּעֵת נָסְעוּ מֵרְפִידִים / אֶל סִינַי בָּאוּ כְּאֶחָד אֲחוּדִים.

All:

הַלְלוּיָהּ כִּי הוּא הָיָה וְיִהְיֶה / בְּגֶשֶׁם נְדָבוֹת אוֹתָנוּ יְחַיֶּה
◂ לְפָנָיו יְקַמֵּנוּ וְנִחְיֶה / וְצַדִּיק בֶּאֱמוּנָתוֹ יִחְיֶה.

בָּרוּךְ אַתָּה יהוה, מְחַיֵּה הַמֵּתִים.

משלש

The משלש has a more ambitious form than the two previous piyutim:
the author signed his name in the first letters of the stichs, the
fourth of which in each stanza is a biblical quote.

All:

שְׁלֵמִים בַּחֲנוּתָם נֶגֶד הָהֲדָרָה / שָׁוִים וּנְכוֹנִים בְּרוּחַ נִשְׁבָּרָה
שְׁמַעְתָּם חָקֵי עֲרוּכָה וּשְׁמֻרָה / שִׁמְעָה עַמִּי וַאֲדַבֵּרָה:

תהילים נ

תהלים עו
מִצְוֹת וְחֻקִּים דָּת וָדִין / מִשָּׁם לָמְדוּ מַאֲמַצֵּי הַדִּין
מֻדְשַׁן בֵּיתְךָ זָכוּ לְהֲדַדִין / מִשָּׁמַיִם הִשְׁמַעְתָּ דִּין:

חבקוק ג
עַד לֹא נִגְלָה לְמִצְקֵי אֶרֶץ / עָבַר וְזָרַח וְהוֹפִיעַ בָּאָרֶץ
עַמִּים מִשָּׁם נִפְרְצוּ פֶּרֶץ / עָמַד וַיְמֹדֶד אָרֶץ:

חבקוק ג
וּמֶרְכֶּבֶת קֹדֶשׁ אָתָה בְּמִצְעָד / וּלְעַם קְרוֹבוֹ מִסִּינַי נוֹעָד
וְעַמּוּדֵי תֵבֵל גָּעֲשׁוּ לְהֵרְעַד / וַיִּתְפֹּצְצוּ הַרְרֵי־עַד:

תהלים סח
נִקְבְּצוּ לְאֻמִּים וְגֶשׁ בְּשָׁמְעָם / נֶאֶסְפוּ לַקֶּסֶם לִשְׁאָלוּ מַה טַּעַם
נָאֵם הֵשִׁיבָם עַל מֶה הָרַעַם / נֹתֵן עֹז וְתַעֲצֻמוֹת לָעָם:

תהלים קיא
בְּנִתָּה מֵרָחוֹק לְנוֹחֲלֵי תְעוּדָה / בְּשָׁלֵם יָסַדְתָּ עַל אֶרֶץ אֲגֻדָּה
בְּכֵן נַעֲבָדְךָ בְּגִיל וּרְעָדָה / בְּסוֹד יְשָׁרִים וְעֵדָה:

חבקוק ג
רִדְתְּךָ לְסִינַי בְּאֵלִים בּוֹעֵרִים / רֶשֶׁף לְרַגְלֶךָ יָצָא בְהַדּוּרִים
רוֹעֲדִים נְמוֹגִים כָּל יְצוּרִים / רָאוּךָ יָחִילוּ הָרִים:

תהלים קלח
יִרְאָה וְחָלָה מִתְנַאֲה הָאָרֶץ / יִזְמָה פֶּן־תֵּהָפֵךְ לְתֹהוּ בְחָרֶץ
יָסְדוּ עַמּוּדֶיהָ בְּאָנְכִי בְּמֶרֶץ / יוֹדוּךָ יהוה כָּל־מַלְכֵי־אָרֶץ:

תהלים נ
צִבְאוֹת קֹדֶשׁ אֲחוּזִים בְּעָתָה / צֶלַע כְּגִיגִית עֲלֵיהֶם כְּפָפְתָּ
צְרוּפָה קִבְּלוּ בְּמָנוֹד וְאֵימָתָה / צוֹפִיָּה הֲלִיכוֹת בֵּיתָהּ:

תהלים סח
חָשׁוּ הָרִים לְקַבֵּל שְׁכִינָתוֹ / חֲפֵצִים לְהִתְעַלּוֹת בִּיקָר תִּפְאַרְתּוֹ
חָבַב חוֹרֵב מֵהֲרֵי אַדְמָתוֹ / חָמַד אֱלֹהִים לְשִׁבְתּוֹ:

תהלים צו
שמות יט
קָרָאתָ לְעֵנְו מֵרוֹם גְּבֹהִים / לְהַנְחִיל תְּעוּדָה לְעַם כְּמֵהִים
‹ מְאֹד נַעֲלֵיתָ עַל־כָּל־אֱלֹהִים: / וּמֹשֶׁה עָלָה אֶל הָאֱלֹהִים:

The שליח ציבור aloud, followed by the קהל:

תהלים קמו
יִמְלֹךְ יהוה לְעוֹלָם, אֱלֹהַיִךְ צִיּוֹן לְדֹר וָדֹר, הַלְלוּיָהּ:

תהלים כב
וְאַתָּה קָדוֹשׁ, יוֹשֵׁב תְּהִלּוֹת יִשְׂרָאֵל:

אֵל נָא.

This piyut is the parallel to "אָנֹכִי בְּשֵׁם" on page 710;
but rather than a "preview" of the Ten Commandments,
it offers praise to God for sustaining the world through the
Torah, and for graciously giving it to the people of Israel.

All:

אִם לֹא אֲמָרֶיךָ הַנְּעִימִים

חֻקּוֹת שָׁמַיִם וָאָרֶץ לֹא מִתְקַיְּמִים

וְהִנְחַלְתָּ מוֹרָשָׁה לִמְעוּטֵי עַמִּים

מֵאַהֲבָתְךָ אוֹתָם וּבִזְכֹר שְׁבוּעַת קְדוּמִים

וּמְאֹד תִּתְאַוֶּה לָמוֹ לִהְיוֹת שְׁלֵמִים

וּבְמִשְׁפְּטֵי חָקֶּיךָ לֵב וָדַעַת מְשִׂימִים

וּבְסוֹד יְרֵאֶיךָ יָשִׁיבוּ טְעָמִים

בְּרִיתְךָ לִנְצֹר לֶכֶת בְּדֶרֶךְ תְּמִים

וּבְעֵת הַשְׁמַעְתָּם חֻקֶּיךָ הַתְּמִימִים

עָמְדוּ בְּמוֹרָא כְּאֶחָד מֻשְׁלָמִים

וְנִגְלָה לָמוֹ רָז מַלְאֲכֵי מְרוֹמִים

עֲשִׂיָּה לִשְׁמִיעָה הֱיוֹת מַקְדִּימִים

וְנֵמַתָּ, מִי־יִתֵּן וְהָיָה לְבָבָם זֶה לְעוֹלָמִים

לְיִרְאָה אוֹתִי לְטוֹב לָהֶם כָּל הַיָּמִים

לוּ עַמִּי שׁוֹמֵעַ לִי וּבִדְרָכַי מְסַיְּמִים

וְיִצְדְּקוּ וְיִתְהַלְּלוּ בְּלִי הֱיוֹת אֲשֵׁמִים

כִּמְעַט מִפְּנֵיהֶם אַכְנִיעַ שׁוֹטְמִים

וְאָשִׁיב יָדִי עַל אוֹיְבִים וְקָמִים

יִשְׂרָאֵל נוֹשַׁע בַּיהוה תְּשׁוּעַת עוֹלָמִים

לֹא בוֹשִׁים וְלֹא נִכְלָמִים

וְאַתָּה אֲדוֹן הַצּוּר תָּמִים

בְּאוֹר פָּנֶיךָ יְהַלְּכוּן לְאֹרֶךְ יָמִים

פֶּתַח דְּבָרֶיךָ הָבִין הַבֵּינֵם בְּחֻכּוּמִים

ישעיה מה

וּתְחַכֶּם לִהְיוֹת חַיִּים וְקַיָּמִים
וּבְתוֹכְכֶם תִּשְׁכֹּן רָם עַל רָמִים.

The שליח ציבור aloud, followed by the קהל:

חַי וְקַיָּם נוֹרָא וּמָרוֹם וְקָדוֹשׁ.

שמעון בר יצחק בר אבון חזק, The author signed his name,
in the verses of this piyut, which describes the Tablets of the Law and
the Ten Commandments written upon them. The chorus "וַיָּקֶם עֵדוּת בְּיַעֲקֹב"
was possibly originally recited after every stanza (or every second stanza) but
Ashkenazi custom is to say it only twice – at the start and the end of the piyut.

The שליח ציבור aloud, followed by the קהל:

וַיָּקֶם עֵדוּת בְּיַעֲקֹב / וְתוֹרָה שָׂם בְּיִשְׂרָאֵל לְנִקֹּב
מוֹרָשָׁה קְהִלַּת יַעֲקֹב, קָדוֹשׁ.

דברים לג

All:

שְׁבוּיַת מָרוֹם לְקָחָהּ כְּהַיּוֹם / מִצְוֺתֶיהָ וְהוֹרִיוֹתֶיהָ מִפִּי אָיֹם
מִמִּדְבָּר נְתוּנָה לִיוֹצְאֵי פִדְיוֹם.

מַאֲמָר וְצִוּוּי וְעֹנֶשׁ וְאַזְהָרָה / חֹק וּמִשְׁפָּט בְּרִית וְתוֹרָה
נָעַם הֶגֶא דִבְּרוֹת עֲשָׂרָה.

עֲרוּכִים יַחַד זֶה אַחַר זֶה / וּצְמוּדִים מֶחֱזֶה אֶל מַחֱזֶה
לֻחֹת כְּתֻבִים מִזֶּה וּמִזֶּה.

וְהַמִּכְתָּב מִכְתַּב אֱלֹהִים לְאִשָּׁה / חֲקָקָם זֶה כְּנֶגֶד זֶה לְדָרְשָׁה
כֻּוַּנם וְהִתְוֻם חֲמִשָּׁה מוּל חֲמִשָּׁה.

נָעַם אָנֹכִי הַשְּׁמִיעַ בְּמַאֲמָר / כְּנֶגְדּוֹ לֹא תִרְצַח הִזְהִיר בְּמִשְׁמָר
זֶה עַל זֶה לְהָבִין וְלִגְמֹר.

בְּהִכָּשֵׁל יְצוּרִים לִשְׁפָּךְ דָּם / כְּאִלּוּ מְמַעֲטִים דְּמוּת בְּהֶזֵּידָם
כִּי בְּצֶלֶם אֱלֹהִים עָשָׂה אֶת־הָאָדָם:

בראשית ט

רָמַז לֹא־יִהְיֶה בַּשֵּׁנִי דִּבּוּר / כְּנֶגְדּוֹ לֹא־תִנְאָף הִזְהִיר לַצִּבּוּר
עַל אָפְנָיו דָּבָר דָּבוּר.

יַגִּיד וְיוֹכִיחַ עֲלֵי כוֹפְרִים / דּוֹמִים לְאִשָּׁה מְנָאֶפֶת מֵאֲחֵרִים

תַּחַת אִישָׁהּ תִּקַּח אֶת־זָרִים: יחזקאל טז

צַוֵּה לֹא תִשָּׂא לַשָּׁוְא שֵׁם כְּלָיוֹת חֵקֶר / כְּנֶגְדּוֹ לֹא תִגְנֹב הִזְהִיר לְהִתְיַקֵּר

הַגָּנֹב וְרָצֹחַ וְנָאֹף וְהִשָּׁבֵעַ לַשֶּׁקֶר.

חֻוֶּה זָכוֹר אֶת־יוֹם הַשַּׁבָּת / כְּנֶגְדּוֹ לֹא־תַעֲנֶה הִזְהִיר בִּמְשִׁיבַת

פֶּן תְּשַׁקֵּר וְתוֹצִיא דִּבַּת.

קְרִיאָתָם יוֹכִיחוּ לוֹ לְלָו לִדּוֹן / כָּל מְחַלֵּל יוֹם קֹדֶשׁ בְּזָדוֹן

כְּאִלּוּ מֵעִיד עֵדוּת שֶׁקֶר בָּאָדוֹן.

בְּשָׁמְרוֹ יְצִיר שַׁבָּת מְחַלֵּל / מֵעִיד כִּי לְשִׁשָּׁה עוֹלָם שִׁכְלֵל

וְאַתֶּם עֵדַי נְאֻם־יְהוה וַאֲנִי־אֵל: ישעיה מג

רָשַׁם מִצְוַת כַּבֵּד לְעַם נִבְרָא / אָב וָאֵם מְכַבֵּד בְּמוֹרָא

מִשְּׁמוּעָה רָעָה לֹא יִירָא.

אָמַר לֹא תַחְמֹד שָׁת לְנֶגְדּוֹ / בֵּית רֵעַ אֲמָתוֹ וְעַבְדּוֹ

שׁוֹרוֹ וַחֲמוֹרוֹ וְכָל כְּבוֹדוֹ.

בֵּאֵר מַאֲמָר לְמַאֲמָר לְמוּלוֹ / יַגִּיד עַל הַחוֹמֵד לְהַכְשִׁילוֹ

סוֹפוֹ לְהוֹלִיד בֵּן שֶׁהוּא מְקַלְלוֹ.

וְאֵלּוּ עֲשֶׂרֶת הַדִּבְּרוֹת הַכְּלוּלוֹת / נֶחֶרְתוּ עַל הַלֻּחוֹת הַמְעֻלּוֹת

וּמִפֶּה אֶל פֶּה הָשְׁמְעוּ בְקוֹלוֹת.

נְבוֹנִים שֶׁלָּהֲבוּ מִלַּהַב הַמֻּשְׁמָע / וְהַשְׁמִיעוּ אֵין יְכֹלֶת לִשְׁמֹעַ

קְרַב אַתָּה וּשְׁמָע: דברים ה

חַי הוֹדָה לַאֲשֶׁר אָמְרוּ / זְכוּ קְדוֹשִׁים וּמִשָּׁם נִתְאַשְּׁרוּ דברים ה

כְּנָם, הֵיטִיבוּ כָל־אֲשֶׁר דִּבֵּרוּ:

The שְׁלִיחַ צִבּוּר aloud, followed by the קהל:

וַיָּקֶם עֵדוּת בְּיַעֲקֹב / וְתוֹרָה שָׂם בְּיִשְׂרָאֵל לַנְקֹב

מוֹרָשָׁה קְהִלַּת יַעֲקֹב, קָדוֹשׁ. דברים לג

The שליח ציבור and the קהל (see rubric on page 712):

אֵל נָא, לְעוֹלָם תָּעֲרָץ וּלְעוֹלָם תָּקֻדַּשׁ
וּלְעוֹלְמֵי עוֹלָמִים תִּמְלֹךְ וְתִתְנַשֵּׂא
הָאֵל מֶלֶךְ נוֹרָא מָרוֹם וְקָדוֹשׁ
כִּי אַתָּה הוּא מֶלֶךְ מַלְכֵי הַמְּלָכִים.

מַלְכוּתוֹ נֶצַח / נוֹרְאוֹתָיו שִׂיחוּ / סַפְּרוּ עֻזּוֹ / פָּאֲרוּהוּ צְבָאָיו /
קַדְּשׁוּהוּ רוֹמְמוּהוּ / רָן שִׁיר / שֶׁבַח תֹּקֶף / תְּהִלּוֹת תִּפְאַרְתּוֹ.

The שליח ציבור aloud, followed by the קהל:

כַּאֲשֶׁר נִגְלֵיתָ לַאֲבוֹתֵינוּ בַּיּוֹם הַזֶּה
כֵּן נִזְכֶּה שְׁכִינָתְךָ לַחֲזֶה
וְנֹאמַר, הִנֵּה אֱלֹהֵינוּ זֶה, קָדוֹשׁ.

ישעיה כה

סדר

Like the piyut "אַלְפַּיִם שָׁנָה נִמְתַּקְתִּי בְחֵבּוּ" said on the first day (see page 712), this piyut also follows the Torah from Creation to מַעֲמַד הר סיני, with a slight shift in emphasis, devoting more space to the Patriarchs. The author signed his name, שמעון בר יצחק חזק ואמץ, in the first letters of the stanzas.

All:

משלי ח

וּבְכֵן, יהוה קָנָנִי רֵאשִׁית דַּרְכּוֹ:

שַׁעֲשׁוּעַ יוֹם יוֹם מֵרֹאשׁ יוֹם אֲמָנָה / קֶדֶם מִפְעָלָיו אַלְפַּיִם שָׁנָה
אָז רָאָה וַיְסַפְּרָהּ חֲקָרָהּ וְהֶכִינָהּ / בְּיָמִינוֹ חֲקָקָהּ וּבְחֵיקוֹ נְתָנָהּ
הֲלֹא חָכְמָה תִקְרָא וּתְבוּנָה / בְּרֹאשׁ מְרֹמִים קוֹלָהּ נָתָנָה
אֲלֵיכֶם אֶקְרָא בַּעֲלֵי אֱמוּנָה / שִׁמְעוּ כִּי נְגִידִים אֲדַבֵּר לְהָבִינָה
מִפְתַּח שְׂפָתַי מֵישָׁרִים וּנְכוֹנָה / בְּצֶדֶק אִמְרֵי פִי בְּלִי תֹאֲנָה
כֻּלָּם נְכֹחִים לִיוֹדְעֵי בִינָה / קְחוּ מוּסָרִי וְאַל־כֶּסֶף וּתְכוּנָה.

מִקַּדְמֵי קֶדֶם מֵרֹאשׁ נִסַּכְתִּי / בְּאֵין תְּהוֹם וּמַעֲיָן נִתְהַלָּלְתִּי
בְּטֶרֶם הַר וָגֶבַע נִתְחוֹלַלְתִּי / בְּהָכִינוֹ שָׁמַיִם שָׁם הָיִיתִי

בְּאַמְצוֹ שְׁחָקִים עִמּוֹ נִמְצֵאתִי / אֲנִי חָכְמָה עָרְמָה שָׁכַנְתִּי
מְשַׁחֲרַי יִמְצָאֻנְנִי וְאֹהֲבַי אָהֵבְתִּי / מֵחָרוּץ וּמִפָּז נִבְחָרָה תְּבוּאָתִי
בְּאֹרַח צְדָקָה וּמִשְׁפָּט הִתְהַלָּכְתִּי / יָסֻרוּ אֵלַי חֲסַר לֵב וּפֶתִי
לְלֹחֶם בְּלַחֲמִי וְלִשְׁתּוֹת יַיִן מָסָכְתִּי / כִּי עֹשֶׁר וְכָבוֹד נִמְצָא אִתִּי.

עֲצָתוֹ מֵרָחוֹק אָמֵן לְאָמְנִי / חֻקּוֹת שָׁמַיִם וָאָרֶץ שָׁם לְמַעֲנִי
רֵאשִׁית דַּרְכּוֹ בְּחֶסֶד קָנָנִי / מְצוּף דְּבַשׁ וְנֹפֶת הִמְתִּיקֵנִי
זָהָב וּפְנִינִים לֹא יַעַרְכֻנִי / כִּי כָל בֵּיתִי לָבֻשׁ שָׁנִי
לִוְיַת חֵן וְרִפְאוֹת נְתָנֵנִי / יָדַי וְכַפַּי לִפְרֹשׂ לֶעָנִי
פִּי פָתוּחַ בְּחָכְמָה וּבְשֵׂכֶל חִכְּמַנִי / וְתוֹרַת חֶסֶד עַל לְשׁוֹנִי
טָבוּחַ טִבְחִי וְעָרוּךְ שֻׁלְחָנִי / אֹרֶךְ יָמִים וְכָבוֹד בִּשְׂמֹאלִי וּבִימִינִי.

וּבַעֲצָתִי נוֹעַץ רוֹכֵב כְּרוּבִים / מְמַדֵּי אֶרֶץ שָׁם וְדָבַק וְגָבִים
שָׁמַיִם נָטָה וְשָׁם סִתְרוֹ עָבִים / שֶׁמֶשׁ הִזְרִיחַ וְצַר יָרֵחַ וְכוֹכָבִים
וְהִדְשִׁיא וְהִזְרִיעַ אִילָנוֹת וַעֲשָׂבִים / וְהִשְׁרִיץ דָּגִים עוֹפוֹת וַחֲגָבִים
וְחַיָּה וּבְהֵמָה וְכָל פָּרִים וְרַבִּים / וַיִּיצֶר בְּכַפּוֹ רֹאשׁ לְכָל נְצִיבִים
בְּהִבָּרְאוֹ כּוֹנְנוּ תֻּפִּים וּנְקָבִים / וּמְעַט מֵאֱלֹהִים חִסְּרוֹ בַּאֲהָבִים
וְכָבוֹד וְהָדָר עִטְּרוֹ בִּשְׂגוּבִים / וְהִמְשִׁילוֹ בְּמַעֲשָׂיו הָעֲצוּמִים וְהָרַבִּים.

נָעַם אֶבֶן יְקָרָה שָׁת מַסֵּכָתוֹ / בְּצַלְמוֹ רִקְּמוֹ וְהִפְאִיר תְּמוּנָתוֹ
וּמִקָּצֶה עַד קָצֶה הֵקִים קוֹמָתוֹ / וְחָלַק לוֹ מִשֵּׂכֶל תְּבוּנָתוֹ
וּבִמְלֵאת לָשׁוֹן הִפְלִיא דִּבְרָתוֹ / וַיִּקְרָא שֵׁמוֹת לְכָל בְּרִיתוֹ
וְעַל כָּל יְצוּרִים הָיְתָה אֵימָתוֹ / וּבְעֵדֶן גַּן הָיְתָה חֲנִיָּתוֹ
וּלְהַמְתִּיקֵנִי בְּפִיו הָיְתָה תַּאֲוָתוֹ / עֵקֶב הֱיוֹתוֹ רֹאשׁ עֲפָרוֹת אַדְמָתוֹ
חֻקּוֹתַי וְתוֹרוֹתַי לַהֲגוֹת בְּאִמְרָתוֹ / וְנָעַם מִשְׁפְּטֵי צִדְקִי לְהַחֲווֹתוֹ.

בְּשׁוּרִי מַעֲשֵׂהוּ זָר מַעֲשֵׂהוּ / לֹא שָׁמַר צִוּוּי וַיְפִירֵהוּ
בִּיקָר לֹא לָן וַיְגָרְשֵׁהוּ / נִמְשַׁל כַּבְּהֵמוֹת נִדְמָה מִקְרֵהוּ
בְּאָכְלוֹ מִן הָעֵץ אֲשֶׁר צִוָּהוּ / לְבִלְתִּי אֲכָל מִמֶּנּוּ וַלְטַעֲמֵהוּ
וְהִרְצֵיתִי אֲמָרַי לִפְנֵי בּוֹרְאֵהוּ / לֹא חָפַצְתִּי בּוֹ כִּי מְרִי הוּא

בְּמִפְקָד אֶחָד לֹא עָמַד לְקַיְּמֵהוּ / וּבְקוֹצוֹת תַּלְתַּלֵּי אֵיךְ יַעֲמָד הוּא
בַּחֲסַר לֵב יָמוּת בְּלִי לְהַחֲיֵהוּ / לֹא נוּכַל לְהִדָּבֵק אֲנִי וָהוּא.

רַבּוּ שָׁנִים וְהָלְכוּ דוֹרוֹת / אֲנִי הָיִיתִי אֲצוּרָה בִּמְרוֹמֵי דִירוֹת
בֵּין אֶרְאֶלֵּי טֹהַר אִמְרוֹתֵי טְהוֹרוֹת / וְעָמַד אִישׁ צַדִּיק תָּמִים בְּדוֹרוֹת
מְיַשֵּׁר מַעְגַּל וּמְסִלּוֹת יְשָׁרוֹת / אֶת הָאֱלֹהִים הִתְהַלֵּךְ בְּכוֹשָׁרוֹת
מְנַחֵם מִמַּעַשׂ וּמֵעֹצֶב מְאֵרוֹת / וּבְשֶׁטֶף זַעַם נֶחְלַץ מִצָּרוֹת
בְּצֵאתוֹ לָרְוָחָה מִתּוֹךְ מַסְגֵּרוֹת / הִקְרִיב קָרְבַּן מִנְחָה וּתְשׁוּרוֹת
מִכָּל חַיָּה וּבְהֵמָה וְעוֹפוֹת טְהוֹרוֹת / וְרָצָה לְדַבְּקוֹ בִי אִמְרוֹתֵי לְהוֹרוֹת.

יוֹם נִשְׁתַּכֵּר נִפְרְדָה תַאֲוָתוֹ / מִמַּטְעֵי כַרְמוֹ הָרָוֶה שְׁתִיָּתוֹ
וְנִתְגַּל בְּאָהֳלוֹ וְגֻלָּה נַבְלוּתוֹ / וּבְנוֹ נִכְנַס וְרָאָה עֶרְוָתוֹ
וַיִּיקֶץ מִיֵּינוֹ וְאֵרְרוּ בְּקִלְלָתוֹ / עֶבֶד עֲבָדִים לְאֶחָיו הֱיוֹתוֹ
בַּעֲשׂוֹתוֹ כָּכָה מֵאַסְתִּיו לִשְׂנֹאתוֹ / וְנָמַתִּי לְצוּרִי לֹא אֶחְפֹּץ קָרְבָּנוֹ
כִּי בְשִׁכְרוּתוֹ יָצָא מִדַּעְתּוֹ / וַיָּפֵר חֻקִּי וַיָּקְרַב מִיתָתוֹ
לֵץ הַיַּיִן הֹמֶה בִּשְׁתוֹתוֹ / כָּל שֹׁגֶה בּוֹ לֹא יַרְבֶּה חָכְמָתוֹ.

צֶדֶק לְעָשְׂרִים הֵעִיר מִמִּזְרָח / בּוֹרְאוֹ הִכִּיר לְשָׁלֹשׁ אֵיתָן הָאֶזְרָח
וְכִתֵּת וְשִׁבַּר אֱלִילֵי תֶרַח / וּמֵבִין חֲשֵׁכִים אוֹרוֹ זָרַח
וּמִבֵּית מוֹלַדְתּוֹ גָּלָה וּבָרַח / וְהִצְלִיחַ בְּלֶכְתּוֹ וְכַחֲבַצֶּלֶת פָּרַח
אֵשֶׁל נָטַע וְהָעוֹבְרִים הֶאֱרַח / וּבְקַצְוֵי אֶרֶץ רֵיחוֹ הֵרַח
וְתוֹעֵי דֶרֶךְ הִסְלִיל בָּאֹרַח / יִתֵּן לְפָנָיו גּוֹיִם וּמְלָכִים הַבְרַח
וְשָׁמַר תּוֹרוֹת וּבְמִצְוֹת טָרַח / וְגָבַר כְּצֵאת הַשֶּׁמֶשׁ מִן הַמִּזְרָח.

חֻבַּב וְנֶחְשַׁק בְּשָׁמְרוֹ אֱמוּנָה / בְּנִסְיוֹנוֹת עֶשֶׂר נִצְרַף לְבָחֳנָה
וּמָצָא שָׂכָר בִּטְנוֹ לְמֵאָה שָׁנָה / וְהִתְחִיל בְּמִצְוָה נִתְּנָה לִשְׁמֹנָה
וְנָם צוּר בָּא עֵת וְהִגִּיעָה עוֹנָה / אָמוֹן שַׁעֲשׁוּעִים לְהִנָּתֵן בְּמַתָּנָה
וְגַם אֲנִי נִרְצֵיתִי בוֹ לְהִתְחַתְּנָה / לוּלֵי נָאַם בַּמֶּה אֵדַע כִּי אִירָשֶׁנָּה
וְשָׁאַל אוֹת לְהוֹדִיעוֹ נְכוֹנָה / וְגָרַם גֵּרוּת אַרְבַּע מֵאוֹת שָׁנָה
בְּפָרֶךְ לְעַנּוֹת עֲדַת מִי מָנָה / אָז חָדַלְתִּי בָּאָרֶץ לִשְׁכֹּנָה.

קָם בְּנוֹ תַחְתָּיו וְהוּשַׁת לְשָׁרִים / בְּדַרְכֵי הוֹרוֹ הָלַךְ בְּמֵישָׁרִים
לַעֲשׂוֹת צְדָקָה וּמִשְׁפָּטִים יְשָׁרִים / וּכְקָרְבַּן נִיחֹחַ הֶעֱלָה בְּבֵרוּרִים
וְנִרְצָה כְּכָלִיל וְשַׁלְמֵי אֲמוּרִים / וְזָרַע וּמָצָא מֵאָה שְׁעָרִים
וְהִצְלִיחַ וְהִשְׂכִּיל וְהַנְּעִים אֲמָרִים / וְחָפֵץ לְהַגְדִּילוֹ בְּתוֹרַת מוּסָרִים
וְגַם אֲנִי אֲהַבְתִּיו חֲמַדְתִּיו מִנְּעוּרִים / לוּלֵי שְׁאָתוֹ פְּנֵי עוֹכֵר בָּעוֹכְרִים
וּבַעֲשָׁנוֹ נֶעֱשַׁן וְהִכְהָה מְאוֹרִים / בַּעֲבוּרוֹ נִמְנַעְתִּי לְהִוָּדַע בַּשְּׁעָרִים.

חֶבְיוֹן עֹז שָׁכַנְתִּי בְּמַחְמָד / לָאָרֶץ לֹא יָרַדְתִּי לְהִתְלַמַּד
וְעָמַד אִישׁ תָּם וְתַאֲוָתִי חָמַד / יָשַׁב אֹהָלִים עִתּוֹתִי לְהִתְמַד
בִּרְכָה יָרַשׁ וְלִגְבִּיר הָעֳמַד / זַרְעוֹ לְהַרְבּוֹת כַּחוֹל לֹא־יִמַּד
רוּחַ נְדִיבָה סְמָכַתְהוּ לְהִצָּמֵד / בְּתֻמּוֹ הָלַךְ וּבְכָשְׁרוֹ עָמַד
יוֹצְרוֹ אֲהֵבוֹ וּבְעֵינָיו נֶחְמַד / וַיֵּרָנִי הִנֵּה זֶה נָעִים וְנֶחְמָד
נָאֶה לוֹ בְּהֶגְיוֹנֵךְ לִלְמַד / יִתְמָךְ לִבּוֹ דְּבָרֶךְ וּבְסוֹדֶךְ יַעֲמַד.

זַךְ הָיָה וְנָבָר וְאִישׁ אֱמוּנָה / וְרָאוּי לְהִשְׁתַּעֲשֵׁעַ בְּמַתָּן צְפוּנָה
אֲבָל לֹא שָׁקַט וְלֹא הָפְנָה / בְּבֵית אָבִיו לֹא נָח מִתְּלוּנָה
אֶחָיו מִתְנַחֵם לְהָרְגוֹ בְּשִׂטְנָה / עָמַד מִפָּנָיו וַיֵּלֶךְ פֶּדֶנָה
בְּמַקְלוֹ עָבַר וַיָּבוֹא חָרָנָה / בְּאִשָּׁה שָׁמַר עֶשְׂרִים שָׁנָה
בְּגִדּוּל בָּנִים נִטְרַח בְּאֶמְנָה / נִמְכַּר פֹּרָת לְתַאֲלָה וְלַמְגִנָּה
בִּשְׁנֵי רְעָבוֹן יָרַד לְגָשְׁנָה / לָכֵן לֹא נָפְלָתִי בְּגוֹרָלוֹ לִמְנָה.

קָרַב מוֹעֵד וְהִגִּיעַ זְמַן / וְשָׂר בְּעָנְוִי עִם לֹא אַלְמָן
וַיָּקֶם מוֹשִׁיעַ רֹעֶה נֶאֱמָן / תְּחִלַּת צֵאתוֹ מִצְרֵי טָמָן
וַיַּךְ בְּמִצְרַיִם כָּל אֱלִיל וְחַמָּן / וַיִּכְחַד כָּל גִּבּוֹר שַׂר וּמִשְׁמָן
וְהִגִּיהַּ אוֹר וְהֵאִיר אַשְׁמָן / אֲסִירֵי עָנִי לְיַשַּׁע זְמַן
יָם הֶעֱבִירָם וְהִסִּיעָם לְתַחוּמָן / וְהֵגִיז לָמוֹ שְׂלָו וְהִמְטִירָם מָן
הִכָּה צוּר וַיָּזוּבוּ מֵימָן / וְאַוָּה לְהַנְחִילָם מַעֲשֵׂה יְדֵי אָמָן.

וּבִירַח הַשְּׁלִישִׁי לַחֲפֵשׁ בְּצֵאתָם / בָּאוּ לְחֹרֵב כָּל מַקְהֵלוֹתָם
וְנֶגֶד הָהָר הָיְתָה חֲנִיָּתָם / הִסְכִּימוּ דַעְתָּם וְהִשְׁווּ עֲצָתָם

וּמֹשֶׁה עָלָה וְהֹוּשַׁם כַּחֹותָם / וְנִצְטַוֶּה לֵךְ אֶל הָעָם וְקִדַּשְׁתָּם

הַיּוֹם וּמָחָר צַוֵּה פְרִישָׁתָם / וְיוֹם אֶחָד הוֹסִיף לְטַהֲרָתָם

וְסַדֵּר עִנְיָנָם וּמִצְוַת הַגְבָּלָתָם / וּבָנָה מִזְבֵּחַ וְכָרַת בְּרִיתָם

וְהֵקִים מַצֵּבוֹת כְּנֶגֶד שִׁבְטֵי תָם / וַיְקַדֵּשׁ אֶת־הָעָם וַיְכַבְּסוּ שִׂמְלֹתָם: שמות יט

אָז בַּשְּׁלִישִׁי בִּהְיוֹת בָּקְרוֹ / מֶלֶךְ בִּמְסִבּוֹ הוֹפִיעַ בִּיקָרוֹ

רִבְבֹתַיִם אַלְפֵי שִׁנְאָן מְשַׁנְּנֵי פְאֵרוֹ / וַיְהִי קֹלֹת וּבְרָקִים וְהִזְרִיחַ אוֹרוֹ

קוֹלוֹ בְּכֹחַ קוֹלוֹ בַּהֲדָרוֹ / וְרוּחַ סְעָרָה עָשָׂה דְבָרוֹ

וְעָנָן כָּבֵד כִּסָּה עַל הָרוֹ / וְהַצּוּרִים נִתְּצוּ הָרִים בָּעֶקְרוֹ

הוֹלֵךְ וְחָזֵק קוֹל שׁוֹפָרוֹ / חוֹצֵב לַהָבוֹת אֲרָזִים בְּשַׁבְּרוֹ

קוֹל יהוה יָחִיל מִדְבָּרוֹ / וְכֻלּוֹ אוֹמֵר כָּבוֹד בְּפָאֵר דְּבִירוֹ.

מִתְפָּאֶרֶת הָיִיתִי בְּיוֹם חֲתֻנָּתִי / הִנֵּה בָא קִצִּי וְהִגִּיעַ עִתִּי

לְהוֹדִיעַ יָפְיִי וּלְהַגִּיד תִּפְאַרְתִּי / יֵצֵא טִבְעִי וְתִתְעַלֶּה חֶפְתִּי

יֵדְעוּ הַכֹּל מַה מְּלַאכְתִּי / צֶדֶק וּמִשְׁפָּט בְּתוֹךְ נְתִיבָתִי

עֹמֶק חָכְמָתִי וְסוֹד בִּינָתִי / יָבִינוּ שְׂכָרִי עֻנְשִׁי וְאַזְהָרָתִי

עֶרֶךְ שֻׁלְחָנִי וְסֶגֶר מִסְגַּרְתִּי / תִּקּוּן אֶצְבְּעוֹתַי וְרֹב פְּעֻלָּתִי

כִּי עַד עַתָּה בַּמְּרוֹמִים שָׁכַנְתִּי / וְהַיּוֹם בָּאָדָם מַתָּנוֹת לָקָחְתִּי.

צִיר אֱמוּנִים נִתְעַלָּה בַּבְּחִירִים / כְּצַנַּת שֶׁלֶג בְּיוֹם קְצִירִים

חָכָם עָלָה לְעִיר גִּבֹּרִים / וַיֹּרֶד עֹז מִבְטְחָהּ לְהָדוּרִים

אֲמָרִים נְעִימִים מִפְּנִינִים יְקָרִים / וְקִבְּלָם מִימִין יוֹצֵר הָרִים

וְצִבְאוֹת קֹדֶשׁ עוֹנִים וְאוֹמְרִים / טֶרֶם נִשְׁמַע אָנוּ שׁוֹמְרִים

וְשָׁמְעוּ מִפִּיו עֲשֶׂרֶת הַדִּבְּרִים / וּפָחֲדוּ וְרָעֲדוּ מֵרְעָמִים כַּבִּירִים

וּפָתְחוּ וְעָנוּ כָּל הַיְצוּרִים / יהוה עֹז לְעַמּוֹ יִתֵּן וּמִשְׁפָּטִים יְשָׁרִים.

Some add:

וַיִּשְׂמְחוּ כָּל הָעָם / בְּשִׂמְחַת אִמְרֵי נֹעַם

וְנִתְמַנָּה צִיר רוֹעָם / וַיֵּרֶד מֹשֶׁה מִן־הָהָר אֶל־הָעָם: שמות יט

סדר דיברין

Like "אָתוּ מִצְוֹת וְחֻקִּים" (see page 719) in both form and content, this piyut describes the
Ten Commandments. The author has signed his name, שמעון בר יצחק חזק, in the last stanza.

The שליח ציבור aloud, followed by the קהל:

שמות יט

וּבְכֵן, וַיֵּרֶד מֹשֶׁה מִן־הָהָר אֶל־הָעָם:

All:

אַלּוּף מְסֻבָּל בְּהוֹד אֵפוֹדִים / בְּיָדָיו גְּלִילֵי זָהָב חֲמוּדִים

גָּרוֹן עָנֹק לְשׁוֹן לִמּוּדִים / דְּבָרִים דְּבוּרִים כְּאוֹפָן שְׁקוּדִים

הַמְשׁוּלִים לְשָׁלֹשׁ מַשְׁקִים נֶחֱמָדִים / וּבְפַחוֹת שֶׁבְּכֵלִים נִשְׁמָרִים וְעָמְדִים

זוֹנְחִים הַגַּבֹהַּ וְלַנָּמוּךְ יוֹרְדִים / חַיִּים וּרְפָאוֹת לְמוֹצְאֵיהֶם מַעֲמִידִים

טָהֹר בַּעֲלִיל שִׁבְעָתַיִם מְנֻקָּדִים / יְקָרִים מִזָּהָב וּמִפְּנִינִים נֶחֱמָדִים

כָּל חֲפָצִים לְנֶגְדָּם בַּל נִמְדָּדִים / לֶקַח טוֹב וּמוּסָר מַגִּידִים

מֶתֶק וּמַרְפֵּא לַעֲצָמוֹת וְגִידִים / נְתוּנִים מֵאֵשׁ וְכָאֵשׁ יוֹקְדִים

סַם חַיִּים לָהֶם מִתְכַּבְּדִים / עוֹזְבֵיהֶם עוֹזְבִים וְחוֹבְקֵיהֶם מְכַבְּדִים

פִּלְפּוּלָם בִּשְׁלֹשׁ עֶשְׂרֵה מִתְלַמְּדִים / צוֹרְפֵיהֶם מוֹשִׁיבִים בֵּין נְגִידִים

קוֹנֵיהֶם לְחַיֵּי עוֹלָם עֲתִידִים / רַב טוֹב הַצָּפוּן לַחֲסִידִים

שׁוֹמְרֵיהֶם יֻצְּלוּ מִכָּל פְּחָדִים / תּוֹמְכֵיהֶם מְאֻשָּׁרִים וּבוֹזֵיהֶם מְלֻפָּדִים.

◂ מְלֻפָּדִים לַפִּידִים וּבְרָקִים נוֹגְהִים / בְּתִתּוֹ קוֹל עֹז מִשְּׁמֵי גְבוֹהִים

All:

שמות כ

וַיְדַבֵּר אֱלֹהִים:

תַּחְתִּיּוֹת אֶרֶץ כַּדּוֹנַג נְמַקִּים / שַׂחוּ גְּבָעוֹת עוֹלָם וְהַמְּצוּקִים

רַבּוּ רְעָמִים וְגָבְרוּ זִקִּים / קוֹלֵי קוֹלוֹת מִשְׁנִים וַחֲזָקִים

צִפְצוּף הַדִּבּוּר כְּנִיצוֹצֵי בְרָקִים / פַּטִּישׁ מְפַצֵּץ סַלְעֵי נְקִיקִים

עוֹרֵךְ אַחַת וּשְׁתַּיִם מִתְחַלְּקִים / סוֹד יְרֵאִים וּמִשְׁפָּטִים צַדִּיקִים

נוֹתְנֵי קוֹל הַשּׁוֹפָר מִתְחַזְּקִים / מֹשֶׁה יְדַבֵּר וְהַכֹּל שׁוֹתְקִים

לְעַמּוֹ הִנְחִיל מִדְּבַשׁ מְתוּקִים / כֹּשֶׁר אֱמוּנַת עִתִּים חֲשׁוּקִים

יְדִיעַת חֹסֶן וִישׁוּעַת נְזִיקִים / טַעֲמֵי חָכְמָה וָדַעַת מְפִיקִים

חִנָּם נְתָנָם גּוֹזֵר וּמֵקִים / זְכֹם בְּמַתָּנָה לִבּוֹ דְבֵקִים
וְכָלוּ מַחֲמַדִּים וְחִכּוֹ מַמְתַקִּים / הַשְׁמִיעַ אָנֹכִי בְּרֹאשׁ פְּרָקִים
דֶּרֶךְ בַּעֲשׂוֹתוֹ בְּמַיִם עֲמֻקִים / גִּבּוֹר נִגְלָה וְנִלְחַם בִּמְצוּקִים
בְּתִתּוֹ בְּסִינַי דָּתוֹת וְחֻקִּים / אֲזַי כְּרַחֲמָן נִגְלָה מְשַׂחֲקִים.

◀ מִשְּׂחָקִים הַבָּרָקְתָּ נֹגַהּ / וְהִשְׁמַעְתָּ לְעַם כְּמֵהֶיךָ

שמות כ

All:

אָנֹכִי יהוה אֱלֹהֶיךָ:

אֶרֶץ עָשִׂיתִי וְאָדָם בָּרָאתִי / בְּרִיחַ וּדְלָתַיִם לַיָּם שַׂמְתִּי
גָּלִיתִי שַׁחַר וָבֹקֶר צִוֵּיתִי / דֶּרֶךְ לַחֲזִיז קֹלוֹת פִּלַּגְתִּי
הָאוֹר וְהַחֹשֶׁךְ בִּמְקוֹמָם שִׁכַּנְתִּי / וְהָאָרֶץ וּמְלֹאָהּ לִכְבוֹדִי יָצַרְתִּי
זְרִיחַת מְזָרוֹת בְּעִתָּם הוֹצֵאתִי / חֻקּוֹת שָׁמַיִם וָאָרֶץ מִשְׁטָרָם שַׂמְתִּי
טוֹפְלֵי שֶׁקֶר בְּשֶׁטֶף הֶאֱבַדְתִּי / יוֹרְדֵי בְקֵעָה לְשׁוֹנָם בָּלַלְתִּי
כְּדָרְלָעֹמֶר וְעוֹזְרָיו הִכֵּיתִי / לְעֵמֶק שָׁוֵה לַיְלָה חִלַּקְתִּי
מוֹרִיָּה עֲקֵדַת יָחִיד רָאִיתִי / נֶדֶר נָדַרְתִּי בִּי נִשְׁבַּעְתִּי
שַׂר אֵל מַלְאָךְ בְּעֶזְרוֹ הָיִיתִי / עַמּוֹ מִדַּבֵּר לְרוֹדְפוֹ הִזְהַרְתִּי
פָּתְרוֹסִים בְּעֶשֶׂר מַכּוֹת מָחַצְתִּי / צִבְאוֹתֵיכֶם בְּעֶצֶם הַיּוֹם גָּאַלְתִּי
קָרַעְתִּי יַם סוּף וְאֶתְכֶם הֶעֱבַרְתִּי / רְאִיתֶם בְּעֵינֵיכֶם אֲשֶׁר עָשִׂיתִי
שִׁדַּדְתִּי מִזֶּנֶב וְחֵילוֹ הֶחֱלַשְׁתִּי / שַׁבַּת קֹדֶשׁ לָכֶם הִנְחַלְתִּי
תַּרְגַּלְתִּי וּבְכַנְפֵי נֶשֶׁר נְשָׂאתִי / תֹּקֶף שָׁלֹשׁ מַתָּנוֹת לָכֶם נָתַתִּי.

◀ נָתַתִּי לְךָ תּוֹכְחוֹת מוּסָרִים / הִשָּׁמֵר לְבַל תִּטֶּה אַשּׁוּרִים

שמות כ

All:

לֹא־יִהְיֶה לְךָ אֱלֹהִים אֲחֵרִים:

תַּעְתְּעִים הֵמָּה מוּסָר הֲבָלִים / שַׁחַר אֵין לָמוֹ וְלֹא מוֹעִילִים
רָעֶה אֵפֶר לִבָּם הַתוּלִים / קֶצֶף מוֹסִיפִים וְחֵמָה מַגְדִּילִים
צֹרְפִים כֶּסֶף וּבַקָּנֶה שׁוֹקְלִים / פַּחֵי זָהָב מִכִּיס זָלִים
עַל כִּתְפָּם נוֹשְׂאִים וְסוֹבְלִים / סוֹגְדִים לוֹ וְאֵלָיו מִתְפַּלְלִים
נוֹטְעִים אֹרֶן וְגֶשֶׁם מַגְדִּילִים / מִקְצָתוֹ לָאֵשׁ וְחֶצְיוֹ לַפְּסִילִים

לֹא יָשִׁיבוּ לְלִבָּם וְאֵינָם מַשְׂכִּילִים / כִּי שְׁאֵרִיתוֹ שָׂרְפוּ לְגֶחָלִים

יִצְעֲקוּ אֵלָיו וְאֵינָם נִצּוֹלִים / טָחוּ עֵינֵיהֶם וְלִבּוֹתָם סְכָלִים

חַמָּנִים קְרוּאִים שִׁקּוּצִים וְגִלּוּלִים / וְנוֹחִים תְּעוּבִים אַטִּים וֶאֱלִילִים

וְחֵלֶק יַעֲקֹב יוֹצֵר הַכֹּל אֵל אֵלִים / הֲמוֹן מַיִם נוֹתֵן וּנְשִׂיאִים עוֹלִים

דְּבָרוֹ מֵקִים וַעֲצָתוֹ יַשְׁלִים / גּוֹעֵר בַּיָּם וַיֶּחֱמוּ גַלִּים

בּוֹ תִדְבָּקוּ וְעָדָיו הֱיוּ מְיַחֲלִים / אֹיְבֵיכֶם יַפִּיל חֲלָלִים חֲלָלִים.

‹ חֲלָלִים אֲפִיל כָּל שׁוֹכְחֵי הַשֵּׁם / הִשָּׁמֵר פֶּן תִּכָּשֵׁל וְתֶאֱשַׁם

All:

לֹא תִשָּׂא אֶת־שֵׁם:

שמות כ

אֲמִתִּי שְׁמוֹ הַמְפֹרָשׁ בְּשִׁבְעִים / בּוֹ נוֹסְדוּ אֲרָצוֹת וְנִטְּעוּ רְקִיעִים

גְּבוּלוֹת אֶרֶץ וְרוּחוֹת מְרֻבָּעִים / דָּבְקוּ בְּחוֹתָמוֹ הֱיוֹת נִקְבָּעִים

הַזְכֵּר עַל הַיָּם וְנַעֲשָׂה בְּקִיעִים / וְעַל הַמַּיִם אֶל הַכָּבוֹד הָרֵעִים

זֵכֶר קָדְשׁוֹ בּוֹ יָרוּצוּ נוֹשָׁעִים / חֹצֵב לֶהָבוֹת וּמְפוֹצֵץ סְלָעִים

טְהוֹר עֵינַיִם מֵרְאוֹת רָעִים / יְצוּרָיו בּוֹחֵן בְּכָל עִתִּים וּרְגָעִים

כַּלּוֹת בַּחֵמָה בּוֹ נִפְשָׁעִים / לְהָבִיא שֶׁבֶר לַחַטָּאִים וּפוֹשְׁעִים

מְפִירֵי חֹק וְלַשֶּׁקֶר נִשְׁבָּעִים / נִלְכָּדִים בַּעֲוֹנָם וּבְזְדוֹנָם נִתְבָּעִים

שׂוֹנְאֵי תוֹכָחוֹת וּמוּסָר פּוֹרְעִים / עֲבָרוֹת יוֹבְלוּ וְרֹגֶז שְׂבֵעִים

פּוֹקֵד עֲוֹן אָבוֹת עַל שְׁלֵשִׁים וְרִבֵּעִים / צוֹמֵת לַבְּקָרִים כָּל רְשָׁעִים

קַנּוֹא וְנֹקֵם וְקוֹבֵעַ קוֹבְעִים / רוֹאֶה וְצוֹפֶה טוֹבִים וְרָעִים

שָׁמֹר וְהִזָּהֵר מֵאֲרֶר פְּגָעִים / תִּתְיָרֵא מִלְּשֹׁא לַשָּׁוְא שֵׁם תְּמִים דֵּעִים.

‹ תְּמִים דֵּעִים דִּבֶּר בְּקָדְשׁוֹ / וְהִזָּהֵר עַל מוֹרָא מִקְדָּשׁוֹ

All:

שמות כ

זָכוֹר אֶת־יוֹם הַשַּׁבָּת לְקַדְּשׁוֹ:

תַּשְׁלוּם כָּל מַעַשׂ וּגְמַר מְלָאכָה / שַׁבָּת מְנוּחָה וְקִדּוּשׁ בְּרָכָה

רֶגֶל לְהָשִׁיב וּלְמַעֵט הֲלִיכָה / קָרוּי עֹנֶג לְכַבְּדוֹ כַּהֲלָכָה

צַעַד תְּחוּמָיו אַלְפַּיִם לֵלֵכָה / פְּסִיעָה גַסָּה בּוֹ בְּלִי לְהַלְּכָה

עֶרֶךְ הֲכָנָתוֹ בַּשִּׁשִּׁי לְעָרְכָה / סְעוּדוֹת שָׁלֹשׁ מִצְוָתוֹ עֲרוּכָה

נִכְפַּל בְּלַחְמוֹ לַעֲנָגָה וְרַכָּה / מִמְּרָה נָתַן כַּדָּת וְכַהֲלָכָה
לְאוֹת הוּשַׂם עָלָיו לְסָמְכָה / כִּי לְשִׁשָּׁה מְלַאכְתּוֹ נֶעֶרְכָה
יְצִיאוֹתָיו וּרְשִׁיּוֹתָיו בְּלִי לְהָפְכָה / טֹרַח מַשָּׂא בּוֹ לַחְשֹׂכָה
חִלּוּל מֵזִיד לְסָקְלָה לְמַשְׁכָה / זְכִירָה וּשְׁמִירָה עָדָיו תְּנוּכָה
וּמֵעֵין הָעוֹלָם הַבָּא מָתְקוֹ לְחַנְּכָה / הַנּוֹצְרוּ יְנֻצַּל מְשֻׁלָּשׁ מְבוּכָה
דִּין עָנְשׁוֹ וְאָזְהָרָתוֹ חֲתוּכָה / גְּמוּל מַשְׂכֻּרְתּוֹ מֵאִתִּי תְּמוּכָה
בֵּינִי וּבֵין אִם הַמְבֹרָכָה / אוֹת שַׂמְתִּי כִּי לִי הַמַּמְלָכָה.

◂ הַמַּמְלָכָה הַמְלִיכֵנִי כְּנָאֱמָךְ / וְתִזְכֶּה לְאֹרֶךְ יָמֶיךָ

All:

כַּבֵּד אֶת־אָבִיךָ וְאֶת־אִמֶּךָ:

אֹמֵן וּמֵינֶקֶת בָּךְ מִתְעַסְּקִים / בְּשֶׁלָּךְ תְּחִלָּה כְּאֵזוֹר דְּבֵקִים
גַּעֲיַת שָׁוְעַ וָתַחַן מְפִיקִים / דּוֹרְשִׁים לְצוּרָם הֱיוֹת בֵּן חוֹבְקִים
הִשְׁתַּפּוּ שְׁנֵיהֶם עִמּוֹ עֲסוּקִים / וְנוֹצַרְתָּ וְנוֹלַדְתָּ לְעִתֵּי חָקִים
זִכּוֹךְ וַהֲבִיאוּךְ בִּבְרִית לְהָקִים / חִבְּקוּךְ בְּרַכַּיִם וְשָׁדַיִם מֵינִיקִים
טֶרֶף חֻקֶּיךָ זָנִים וּמַשְׁקִים / יְגִיעַת עֲמָלָם עִמָּךְ מְחַלְּקִים
כֵּשֶׁר וּמוּסַר מְחַנְּכִים וּמְחַזְּקִים / לָשׁוֹן לְמוּדִים וּדְבָרִים עַתִּיקִים
מַתְקָנִים עֵזֶר וּלְהַשִּׂיאֲךָ זוֹקְקִים / נוֹשְׂאִים פֶּלֶל עֲבוּרְךָ וְלָאֵל זוֹעֲקִים
סָמְכֶם בְּמַאֲכָל וּבְמִשְׁתֶּה וּבְתַפְנוּקִים / עֲנָדֶם בִּכְסוּת נְקִיָּה בַּחֲשׁוּקִים
פְּנֵה לְגַעֲרָתָם לְבַל יְהוּ מְצִיקִים / צָפָה לְמוֹסְרָם וְלֹא תָרַדֵּף רֵיקִים
קַיֵּם כְּבוּדָם וּמוֹרָאָם כְּחָקִים / רַבּוֹת אֹרֶךְ יָמִים וּמָעוֹן מְנָקִים
שׁוּם לִכְבוּדוֹ וּלְמוֹרָאוֹ גּוֹזֵר וּמֵקִים / תַּחַת כֵּן הוֹדִיּהוּ מַלְכֵי אֲרָקִים.

◂ אֲרָקִים וּגְבוֹהִים יָסַד בְּפֶצַח / קַבֵּל מוֹרָאוֹ וְאַל תָּעֹז מֵצַח

All:

לֹא תִרְצָח:

תּוֹכַחַת אֱהֹב וּמוּסַר יְרֵאִים / שְׁמֹר וְהִזָּהֵר מִפְּתוּיֵי חַטָּאִים
רַגְלֵיהֶם רָצִים וְלָרַע מוּבָאִים / קֶשֶׁר קוֹשְׁרִים לְהַפִּיל חֲלָכָאִים
צָרִים בְּעָמְקֵי שְׁאוֹל קְרוּאִים / פּוֹעֶרֶת לִבְלִי חֹק בָּאִים

עֲצֶבֶת נוֹתְנִים וְכַשֵּׁל מַמְצִיאִים / שִׂפְתוֹתֵיהֶם אֹרֶב דָּם מְמַלְּאִים
נַחֲלַת אָוֶּלֶת יִנְחֲלוּ פְתָאִים / מְשׁוּבָתָם תַּהֲרֹג בְּתַחְלוּאִים
לֹא תֹאבֶה לַעֲצַת נִשְׁנָאִים / כִּי כֶחָצִיר יִמָּלוּ וּכְדִשְׁאִים
יְהִירִים אֲשֶׁר בְּרֶצַח חוֹטְאִים / טֹרַח גְּזַרְתָּם עֲלֵי מַשִּׂיאִים
חֲנֵפִים אֶרֶץ בְּדָם מְטַמְּאִים / זֹהַר שְׁכִינָתִי מִתּוֹכְכֶם מוֹצִיאִים
וְעַל יְדֵי חֲלָלִים הַנִּמְצָאִים / הָעֶגְלָה הָעֲרוּפָה בַּנַּחַל מְבִיאִים
דָּם שׁוֹפְכִים בְּשׁוֹגֵג בְּלֹא רוֹאִים / גּוֹלִים לְעָרֵי מִקְלָט הַנִּקְרָאִים
בַּהֲזִידָם לַהֲרֹג בְּצֶלֶם בְּרוּאִים / אַתָּה תְּבַעֵר הַדָּם לְעֵין כָּל רוֹאִים.

‹ רוֹאִים יָסֻרוּ לְהִשָּׁמֵר מֵאָף / שְׁמֹר מִצְוָה וְלַהֶבֶל אַל תִּשְׁאָף

All:
שמות כ

לֹא תִנְאָף:

אֵשֶׁת כְּסִילוּת הֹמִיָּה וְסוֹרֶרֶת / בֵּיתָהּ הַרְחֵק כִּי נַפְשׁוֹת עוֹכֶרֶת
גֶּחָלִים בַּחֵיק מַחְתָּה וּמַבְעֶרֶת / דְּרָכֶיהָ שְׁאוֹל וּמָוֶת עֹרֶרֶת
הוֹלֵךְ אַחֲרֶיהָ לַטֶּבַח מוֹסֶרֶת / וּכְעֶכֶס אֶל מוּסַר אֱוִיל מְיַסֶּרֶת
זַעַם מְרִיבָה וְעֶצֶב מְמַהֶרֶת / חֲמַת גֶּבֶר וְשִׂנְאָה מְעוֹרֶרֶת
טִיף נֹפֶת בִּשְׂפָתֶיהָ מְדַבֶּרֶת / יוֹם אַחֲרִיתָהּ כַּלַּעֲנָה מְמָרֶרֶת
כִּי אֵין הָאִישׁ בְּבֵיתוֹ אוֹמֶרֶת / לְיַד־שְׁעָרִים לְפִי־קָרֶת:
מַדָּע תִּקְרָא לַבִּינָה הַמְיַשֶּׁרֶת / נֶצַח עֵדִי עַד עָלַיִךְ מִשְׁמֶרֶת
שְׂמַח בְּאֵשֶׁת נְעוּרֶיךָ הַמְחֻבֶּרֶת / עִמָּהּ תִּתְרַפֵּק וְלֹא בְאַחֶרֶת
פּוֹצַת מֵעֵינְךָ חוּצָה עוֹבֶרֶת / צְמָחִים תַּרְבֶּה לְשֵׁם וּלְתִפְאֶרֶת
קַדֵּשׁ עַצְמְךָ בִּפְרִישׁוּת אַדֶּרֶת / רְצֵה לַעֲשׂוֹת מִשְׁמֶרֶת לְמִשְׁמֶרֶת
שְׁמַע מוּסָר וְעַנְדֵהוּ לְגַרְגֶּרֶת / תִּתֵּן לְרֹאשְׁךָ לִוְיַת חֵן וַעֲטֶרֶת.

‹ וַעֲטֶרֶת תִּנְחַל וּבִשְׁיבָה תָּנוּב / אִם תִּשְׁמֹר הוֹן מִלִּגְנֹב

All:
שמות כ

לֹא תִגְנֹב:

תִּתְעֵב מְתֵי גַנָּבִים וְסִיעָתָם / שׁוֹלְלִים וְחוֹמְסִים כָּל עִתָּם
רְחַק מֵעֹשֶׁק וֶהְיֵה תָם / קַשֵּׁט מַעֲבָדֶיךָ וְהַצְדֵּק אוֹתָם

צָפָה לַחֲכָמִים וְאֶלֶף אָרְחוֹתָם / פְּעֻלַּת צְדָקָה לְחַיִּים תְּבוּאָתָם

עִקְּשִׁים הַרְחֵק הַמְּעַקְּלִים נְתִיבָתָם / שִׂפְתוֹתֵיהֶם דּוֹלְקִים בְּלִבָּם רָעָתָם

נְכוֹנוּ שְׁפָטִים וּמַהֲלֻמוֹת לְגֵוָיתָם / מָדוֹן מְשַׁלְּחִים וּמַצָּה אַהֲבָתָם

לֹא יַחֲרֹכוּ רְמִיָּה צֵידָתָם / כִּי אָוֶן וְעָמָל תַּחַת שְׂפָתָם

יוֹם יִלְכְּדוּ בְגָדִים בְּהַוָּתָם / טוֹרְפִים בַּנַּעַר וּבַקְּדֵשִׁים חַיָּתָם

חוֹלְקִי עִם גַּנָּב שׂוֹנְאֵי נַפְשׁוֹתָם / זֶה דַּרְכָּם וְלַהֶבֶל אַחֲרִיתָם

וְאַל תֵּאָשֵׁר נִלְוֵי מַעְגְּלוֹתָם / הִזָּהֵר פֶּן תֵּלֵךְ בִּמְצוּדָתָם

דִּין אַרְבָּעָה וַחֲמִשָּׁה הַשְּׁלֵמָתָם / גְּנֵבָה אֵין לָמוֹ נִמְכָּרִים בִּגְנֵבָתָם

בְּנִי אַל תֵּלֵךְ בְּדֶרֶךְ אִתָּם / אֶת רַגְלְךָ מְנַע מִנְּתִיבָתָם.

‹ מִנְּתִיבָתָם חֲשֹׂךְ וְאַל תִּתְגַּנֶּה / וְרָעָה אֵלֶיךָ לֹא־תְאֻנֶּה

All:

לֹא־תַעֲנֶה:

שמות כ

אִמְרֵי כָזָב וּמַעַן כְּחָשִׁים / בְּנִיב שְׂפָתֶיךָ בַּל יְהוּ אֲרוּשִׁים

גַּם אֱוִילִים אֲשֶׁר מַחֲרִישִׁים / דּוֹמִים וְנֶחְשָׁבִים לְחַכְמֵי חֲרָשִׁים

הוֹלְכֵי רָכִיל שָׁלֹשׁ מְעַנְּשִׁים / וְנֶאֱמָנֵי רוּחַ מְכַסִּים וּמַחְשִׁים

זֶה חֵלֶק מַלְשִׁינִים הַמַּרְגִּישִׁים / חִצֵּי גִבּוֹר שְׁנוּנִים קָשִׁים

טוֹמְנִים פַּח כְּשַׁךְ יְקוּשִׁים / יוֹעֲצֵי מִרְמָה כָּזָב מְלַחֲשִׁים

כְּמַדְקְרוֹת חֶרֶב בּוֹטִים מְנַקְּשִׁים / לְשׁוֹן חֲכָמִים מַרְפֵּא מַגִּישִׁים

מִפְּרִי פִיהֶם יִשְׂבְּעוּ אֲנָשִׁים / נִרְגָּן דְּבָרָיו כְּמִתְלַהֲמִים חָשִׁים

שְׂפַת אֱמֶת יִכּוֹן בִּישִׁישִׁים / עַד אַרְגִּיעָה לְשׁוֹן טִפְּשִׁים

פּוֹשְׁקֵי שָׂפָה מְחִתָּה עֲנוּשִׁים / צָרוֹת רוֹדְפִים וְעֹנֶשׁ מְבַקְּשִׁים

קוּמָם לְהָעִיד חָמָס וְלֹא בוֹשִׁים / רוּחָם יוֹצִיאוּ כְּסִילִים אֱנוּשִׁים

שֶׁקֶר בַּהֲעִידָם נִזְמְמוּ בְּפֵרוּשִׁים / תַּעֲשֶׂה לָמוֹ כְּזִמּוֹתָם לְהָאֵשִׁים.

‹ לְהָאֵשִׁים מְנַע עַצְמְךָ לִתְמֹד / וְנֶצַח לְפָנַי תַּעֲמֹד

All:

לֹא תַחְמֹד:

שמות כ

שְׁכֶן רֵעֲךָ בֵּיתוֹ וְאָהֳלוֹ / מִקְנֵהוּ וְקִנְיָנוֹ וְכָל חֵילוֹ
עֲבָדוּ וַאֲמָתוֹ שָׂדֵהוּ וּגְבוּלוֹ / וְשׁוֹרוֹ וַחֲמֹרוֹ וְכָל אֲשֶׁר לוֹ
נָטְעוּ וְכַרְמוֹ גַּנּוֹ וּשְׁבִילוֹ / בְּעִירוֹ וְעֵצָיו פֵּרוֹתָיו וִיבוּלוֹ
רִכְבּוֹ וּפָרָשָׁיו יַעֲרוֹ וְכַרְמִלוֹ / יְקַר כַּסְפּוֹ וּזְהָבוֹ וְנֹעַם גְּדוֹלוֹ
צֹאנוֹ וַאֲלָפָיו מַשְׁקֵהוּ וּמַאֲכָלוֹ / חֶבְרָתוֹ וְכָל מַחֲמַדֵּי מִכְלָלוֹ
קָרוּץ מֵחֹמֶר מַה מּוֹעִילוֹ / חוֹמֵד וּמִתְאַוֶּה אֶת שֶׁאֵינוֹ שֶׁלּוֹ
זֶה שֶׁיֵּשׁ לוֹ אֵינוֹ שֶׁלּוֹ / קִנְיָן שֶׁאֵינוֹ שֶׁלּוֹ לָמָּה הוּא לוֹ
יָבִין וְיַשְׂכִּיל בְּדֵעוֹ וְשִׂכְלוֹ / יִשְׂמַח וְיָעֹז בְּמַתַּת גּוֹרָלוֹ.

‣ גּוֹרָלוֹ הִנְחִיל אֵל לִירֵאִים / בְּקֹלֹת וּבְרָקִים נוֹרָאִים

All:

שמות כ

וְכָל־הָעָם רֹאִים:

All:

וּבְכֵן, וּלְךָ תַּעֲלֶה קְדֻשָּׁה, כִּי אַתָּה קְדוֹשׁ יִשְׂרָאֵל וּמוֹשִׁיעַ.

Some congregations say the piyut וְכָל־הָעָם *(below) before* קדושה.
Many congregations omit it and continue with "נְקַדֵּשׁ אֶת שִׁמְךָ" *on page 349.*

סילוק

וְכָל־הָעָם רֹאִים אֶת הַנִּרְאֶה וְהַנִּשְׁמָע
וְשׁוֹמְעִים אֶת הַנִּשְׁמָע וְהַנִּרְאֶה
כְּשֶׁהַדִּבּוּר יוֹצֵא מִפִּי הַגְּבוּרָה / וְנֶחְצָב עַל הַלֻּחוֹת בְּתִפְאָרָה
קוֹל קוֹלֵי קוֹלוֹת וְרוּחַ סְעָרָה / וְלַפִּיד לַפִּידֵי לַפִּידִים אֵשׁ בֹּעֲרָה
קוֹל יהוה בַּכֹּחַ וְקוֹל יהוה בַּהֲדָרָה / מְפָרֵשׁ אֶת הַדִּבּוּר לְבָאֲרָה
יְסֹבְבֶנְהוּ יְבוֹנְנֵהוּ סִתְרֵי תוֹרָה / וַיַּרְא הָעָם וַיָּנֻעוּ לִבָּם לְשָׁבְרָה
וַיַּעַמְדוּ מֵרָחוֹק מִילִין שְׁנַיִם וְעֶשְׂרָה
וּמַלְאֲכֵי הַשָּׁרֵת יָרְדוּ לְסַיְּעָם מִשְּׁמֵי שִׁפְרָה
וּמַלְאֲכֵי צְבָאוֹת יִדּוֹן בַּהֲלִיכָה יִדּוֹן בַּחֲזִירָה
וְלֹא הֵם בִּלְבָד כִּי אִם עוֹטֶה אוֹרָה
שְׂמֹאלוֹ תַּחַת לְרֹאשִׁי וִימִינוֹ תְּחַבְּקֵנִי לְהַעֲזָרָה

וְנִשְׁתַּלְהֲבוּ מִכֹּחַ הָאֵשׁ וְרוּחַם עֲבָרָה

וְעָנְנִי כְבוֹד הַזִּילוּ טַלְלֵי אוֹרָה

אֶרֶץ רָעֲשָׁה וְגַם שָׁמַיִם נָטְפוּ לְחַשְׁרָה

גֶּשֶׁם נְדָבוֹת תָּנִיף אֱלֹהִים לְיָפָה וּבָרָה

נַחֲלָתְךָ וְנִלְאָה אַתָּה כּוֹנַנְתָּהּ לְשָׁמְרָה

וּכְמוֹצְאֵי שָׁלָל רַב שָׂשׂוּ בַּאֲמִירָה טְהוֹרָה

וְנַעֲשֶׂה וְנִשְׁמַע הַשְּׁמִיעוּ בַּאֲמִירָה

וְלֹא הָיָה בָהֶם כֹּחַ לְקַבֵּל יוֹתֵר מִדִּבְּרוֹת עֲשָׂרָה

וְנָמוּ לְרוֹעָם קְרַב אַתָּה וּשְׁמַע אֲמִירָה

כִּי אִם־יֹסְפִים אֲנַחְנוּ לִשְׁמֹעַ נָמוּת מְהֵרָה

וְרוּחַ הַקֹּדֶשׁ הוֹדָה לְדִבְרֵיהֶם בְּעֵינָיו לְיַשְּׁרָה

מִשָּׁם זָכוּ לְהַעֲמִיד נְבִיאִים לְהִתְאַשְּׁרָה

וְנָם מִי־יִתֵּן וְהָיָה לְבָבָם זֶה לָהֶם לְבָחֲרָה

אִלּוּ אֶפְשָׁר לְבַלַּע הַמָּוֶת וּלְהַעֲבִירָה

אֲבָל אִי אֶפְשָׁר שֶׁכְּבָר נִגְזְרָה גְּזֵרָה

וְעַל תְּנַאי כָּךְ עָמְדוּ לְקַבֵּל הַתּוֹרָה

אֲנִי אָמַרְתִּי אֱלֹהִים אַתֶּם לְהִתְפָּאֲרָה

חִבַּלְתֶּם מַעֲשֵׂיכֶם אָכֵן כְּאָדָם תְּמוּתוּן בְּעֶבְרָה

וּמֹשֶׁה מְזָרֵז וּמְפַיֵּס לְכָל שׁוּרָה וְשׁוּרָה

וְהַכָּתוּב מְשַׁבְּחוֹ וְהַחָכְמָה תָּעֹז לֶחָכָם יוֹתֵר מִשַּׁלִּיטִים עֲשָׂרָה

וְאוֹמֵר לָהֶם אַל תִּירְאוּ מִן הָאֵשׁ וּמִן הַסְּעָרָה

כִּי לְנַסּוֹת אֶתְכֶם בָּא וּלְגַדֵּל לָכֶם עֲטָרָה

וּבַעֲבוּר תִּהְיֶה עַל פְּנֵיכֶם יִרְאָה טְהוֹרָה

סִימָן טוֹב בְּאָדָם שֶׁהוּא בּוֹיְשָׁן וְרוּחוֹ נִשְׁבָּרָה

שֶׁכָּל מִי שֶׁהוּא עָנָו עִמּוֹ שְׁכִינָה שׁוֹרָה

אֶשְׁכֹּן אֶת־דַּכָּא וּשְׁפַל־רוּחַ לְעָזְרָה

אֶל־זֶה אַבִּיט אֶת־עָנִי וּנְכֵה־רוּחַ לְהַעֲתָרָה

אֲחַלְּצֵהוּ וַאֲכַבְּדֵהוּ עִמּוֹ אָנֹכִי בְצָרָה.

וְעָנָן נִכְנַס לִפְנִים מְשֻׁלָּשׁ מְחִיצוֹת

חֹשֶׁךְ עָנָן וַעֲרָפֶל נְחוּצוֹת

עָנָן לִפְנִים וַעֲרָפֶל לִפְנַי וְלִפְנִים וְחֹשֶׁךְ בַּחוּצוֹת

וְסִבֵּר לוֹ פָנִים לְהִתְרַצּוֹת

וְקִבְּלוּ עַל יָדוֹ שֵׁשׁ מֵאוֹת שָׁלֹשׁ עֶשְׂרֵה מִצְוֹת קְבוּצוֹת

וְנָתַן נַפְשׁוֹ עַל הַתּוֹרָה בְּדַעַת וּבְמַעֲצוֹת

וְלָכֵן נִקְרֵאת עַל שְׁמוֹ תַּלְתַּלֶּיהָ קְווּצוֹת

זִכְרוּ תּוֹרַת מֹשֶׁה עַבְדִּי עוֹמֵד בַּפְּרָצוֹת

אֲשֶׁר צִוִּיתִי אוֹתוֹ בְּחוֹרֵב הַר הַנִּבְחָר מֵהֲרֵי אֲרָצוֹת

חֻקִּים וּמִשְׁפָּטִים וְתוֹרוֹת לְחַיֶּיךָ נִמְלָצוֹת.

וְכָל הַדּוֹר הַהוּא אֲשֶׁר שָׁמְעוּ קוֹלוֹ / זָכוּ לִהְיוֹת כְּמַלְאֲכֵי זְבוּלוֹ

עָלָיו נִתְרַפְּקוּ וְחָיוּ בְּצִלּוֹ / וְנָתַן בְּתוֹכְכֶם מִשְׁכָּנוֹ וְאָהֳלוֹ

וְהוּרְבָּה לְהַרְאוֹתָם מוֹפְתֵי מִפְעָלוֹ / וְיָדוֹ הַחֲזָקָה וּכְבוֹדוֹ וְגָדְלוֹ

וּבְשׁוּב רוּחָם לְאוֹצַר מִכְלוֹלוֹ / לֹא שָׁלְטָה בִּבְשָׂרָם רִמָּה לְאָכְלוֹ

אַשְׁרֵיהֶם בָּעוֹלָם הַזֶּה הִדְרִיכָם שְׁבִילוֹ / וְלָעוֹלָם הַבָּא יֵאָסְפוּ לוֹ

וַעֲלֵיהֶם הַכָּתוּב אוֹמֵר מִלּוּלוֹ / אַשְׁרֵי הָעָם שֶׁכָּכָה לּוֹ

וּבַיּוֹם זֶה הִשְׁמִיעַ הוֹד קוֹלוֹ / וְכָל יוֹשְׁבֵי תֵבֵל פָּצְחוּ הִלּוּלוֹ

וּמַלְאֲכֵי מַעְלָה הַנְּעִימוּ מַהֲלָלוֹ / וּבְהֵיכָלוֹ כָּבוֹד אָמַר כֻּלּוֹ

שְׂרָפִים וְאוֹפַנִּים וְזִקֵּי חַשְׁמַלּוֹ / קְדֻשָּׁה וּתְהִלָּה קִדְּמוּ לְסַלְסְלוֹ

וְחַיּוֹת הַקֹּדֶשׁ אֲשֶׁר עֲלֵיהֶם סִבְּלוֹ / נִרְאִים נוֹשְׂאִים וְנִשָּׂאִים בְּחֵילוֹ

וּנְהַר דִּי־נוּר הָעוֹבֵר לְמוּלוֹ / נוֹתְנִים עֹז וּגְדֻלָּה לְהַלְלוֹ

וּמֵאָז מַקְדִּישִׁים חֶבֶל גּוֹרָלוֹ / יוֹם יוֹם יְנַשְּׂאוּהוּ וִירוֹמְמוּהוּ קָהֳלוֹ

חֵילֵי מַעְלָה אֵינָם מַעֲרִיצִים לוֹ / עַד יַקְדִּישׁוּהוּ הָעָם אֲשֶׁר בָּחַר לוֹ

אֵלּוּ אַחַר אֵלּוּ מַאֲדִירִים צִלְצוּלוֹ / וְשָׁלֹשׁ קְדֻשָּׁה יְשַׁלְּשׁוּ לוֹ

דָּרֵי מַעְלָה עִם דָּרֵי מַטָּה קוֹרְאִים וּמְשַׁלְּשִׁים לְהַקְדִּישׁ לוֹ.

Continue with "כַּכָּתוּב עַל יַד נְבִיאֶךָ" on page 349.

פיוט לחזרת הש"ץ של מוסף ביום שני של שבועות

אזהרות

On the second day, a long אזהרות piyut (see page 731) is not said;
instead a shorter piyut about the 613 mitzvot is recited. Composed by
an unknown author, the piyut might have been the first, introductory
stanza of a full אזהרות piyut; but if so, the original has been lost.

אַזְהָרַת רֵאשִׁית לְעַמְּךָ נָתַתָּ

מִצְוֹת עֲשֵׂה וּמִצְוֹת לֹא תַעֲשֶׂה

בְּמִסְפָּר בְּמִפְקָד הֵן שְׁלֹשׁ מֵאוֹת וְשִׁשִּׁים וְחָמֵשׁ

כְּנֶגֶד יְמוֹת הַחַמָּה

גַּם מִצְוֹת עֲשֵׂה מָאתַיִם וְאַרְבָּעִים וּשְׁמֹנֶה

כְּנֶגֶד אֵבָרִים שֶׁבָּאָדָם

דְּק וָחֶלֶד הֶעֱדֹתָ בָּנוּ עַל שָׁכְרָן וְעָנְשָׁן

הַחַיִּים וְהַטּוֹב וְהַמָּוֶת וְהָרָע

הוֹרֵיתָ לָנוּ עֲשֶׂרֶת הַדִּבְּרוֹת

וְקָשַׁרְתָּ לָנוּ עֲשָׂרָה כְתָרִים

וּבִשְׁנֵי לֻחוֹת חֲקַקְתָּם וּשְׁנֵי עוֹלָמוֹת הִנְחַלְתָּם

עַל יְדֵי נֶאֱמָן נְתַתָּם וּבֵין שְׁנֵי כְרֻבִים הִנַּחְתָּם

זֵרוּז מִקְרָא וְתַרְגּוּם תּוֹרָה וּנְבִיאִים שְׁמֹנָה

וּכְתוּבִים מְשֻׁלָּשִׁים אַחַד עָשָׂר

חִקְרֵי הֲלָכוֹת וּסְדָרִים שִׁשָּׁה

וַעֲלֵיהֶם תַּלְמוּד שְׁלֹשִׁים וְשִׁשָּׁה

טְעָמִים שֶׁלּוֹ שְׁלֹשֶׁת אֲלָפִים

וִיהִי שִׁירוֹ חֲמִשָּׁה וָאָלֶף

יְחִידָה נְתוּנָה לְשִׁשִּׁים רִבּוֹא

לְעָם אֲשֶׁר בָּחַר מִשִּׁבְעִים לְשׁוֹנוֹת

כְּתוּבָה בְּאוֹתִיּוֹת עֶשְׂרִים וּשְׁתַּיִם

וְגַם בַּשֵּׁם הַמְפֹרָשׁ בְּשִׁבְעִים וּשְׁתַּיִם

לְכָל אֶחָד וְאֶחָד שְׁלֹשָׁה כְתָרִים

כְּתוּבִים בְּאֶצְבַּע אֱלֹהִים מַעֲשֵׂה אָדוֹן

מֶלֶךְ הֲדָרָה בְּרֹב נוֹרָאוֹת

אַזְהָרָה בְּשֵׁם קָדְשׁוֹ וּבְשֵׁם יִשְׂרָאֵל יְכַנֶּה

נִקְרָא שְׁמוֹת שִׁבְעִים וְעַמּוֹ בָּחַר מִשִּׁבְעִים

וּשְׁמוֹ מְעֻלֶּה לְמַעְלָה מִשִּׁבְעִים

סִדְּרָהּ בְּסִימָנִים וּבְמַסּוֹרוֹת וּבְדִקְדּוּקֵי חֲקִירוֹת

בְּדִינֵי מָמוֹנוֹת וּבְדִינֵי נְפָשׁוֹת

עֲטִיפַת הַזֵּן צָהֳלָה וְרִנָּה יִרְאָה וּנְבוּאָה

הִגָּיוֹן וּמְלִיצָה תִּפְאֶרֶת וְשִׂמְחָה

פִּרְקֵי אַגָּדוֹת וְעֶרְכֵי עֲנִינוֹת

דִּקְדּוּקֵיהֶן וְדִקְדּוּקֵי סוֹפְרִים

צוּר כְּתָבָם בְּסוֹד שְׁלִישִׁים

וּנְתָנָם בְּאַהֲבָה לְזֶרַע הַמִּקְדָּשׁ

קַבָּלָה שְׁלִישִׁי בַּחֹדֶשׁ הַשְּׁלִישִׁי

וּנְתָנָהּ יַחַד לְזֶרַע יְשֻׁרוּן

רֵאשִׁית וְאַחֲרִית חָקוּק בְּתוֹכָהּ

וְהֵעִיד עֲלֵיהֶם שָׁמַיִם וָאָרֶץ

שִׁירָה פָּתַח עָנוּ עַל זֹאת וְאָמַר שִׁירוֹת הַרְבֵּה

וּפָץ וְאָמַר אֵין כָּאֵל יְשֻׁרוּן

תּוֹרָה תְמִימָה הִנְחִיל אָדוֹן לַשְּׁבָטִים

כְּדֵי לְהַכְנִיסָם בְּגַן עֵדֶן לְעוֹלְמֵי עוֹלָמִים

תּוֹרָה תְמִימָה נָתַתִּי לָכֶם עַמִּי וְנַחֲלָתִי

כְּדֵי שֶׁאֶתֵּן לָכֶם שָׂכָר טוֹב בָּעוֹלָם הַזֶּה וְחֵלֶק טוֹב לָעוֹלָם הַבָּא

דִּבְרֵי אֱמֶת וְחֻקֵּי צֶדֶק וְשֵׂכֶל טוֹב יִנְחֲלוּ עֹשֵׂיהֶם לְעוֹלָם וָעֶד.

Continue with "אָז שֵׁשׁ מֵאוֹת" on page 545.

הלכות תפילה

HALAKHA GUIDE

GUIDE TO SHAVUOT

SHAVUOT (6TH–7TH OF SIVAN)

1 When Shavuot falls on Friday, each household must prepare an *Eiruv Tavshilin* (page 5); this makes it permissible to prepare food on Friday for the Shabbat meals [שו״ע אור״ח, תקכז].

2 Candle lighting: Two blessings are said: (1) לְהַדְלִיק נֵר שֶׁל יוֹם טוֹב, and (2) שֶׁהֶחֱיָנוּ. On Friday night, the conclusion of the first blessing is: לְהַדְלִיק נֵר שֶׁל שַׁבָּת וְשֶׁל יוֹם טוֹב.

3 There is a widespread custom to decorate the synagogue with flowers or plants [רמ״א אור״ח, תצד:ג].

4 Ma'ariv: for Shabbat and Yom Tov. The custom is to begin Ma'ariv after nightfall [משנ״ב אור״ח, תצד:א]. Many congregations say the special verse for Yom Tov (וַיְדַבֵּר מֹשֶׁה), before saying the Amida for Yom Tov (page 63). This is followed by Full Kaddish, *Aleinu* and Mourner's Kaddish. It is customary to conclude with the singing of Adon Olam or Yigdal.

5 When Shavuot eve falls on Friday night, Ma'ariv is preceded by the last two psalms of Kabbalat Shabbat: יהוה מָלָךְ, גֵּאוּת לָבֵשׁ and מִזְמוֹר שִׁיר לְיוֹם הַשַּׁבָּת (page 41). בַּמֶּה מַדְלִיקִין is omitted. וְשָׁמְרוּ and the special verse for Yom Tov (וַיְדַבֵּר מֹשֶׁה) (page 61) precede the Yom Tov Amida, which is said with additions for Shabbat. After the Amida, the congregation says וַיְכֻלּוּ הַשָּׁמַיִם, and the *Shaliaḥ Tzibbur* says the abbreviated Repetition of the Amida as is customary on Shabbat eve [שו״ע אור״ח, תריט:ג]. When Shavuot eve falls on Motza'ei Shabbat, the congregation adds the paragraph וַתּוֹדִיעֵנוּ in the middle section of the Amida. Similarly, in Kiddush, the two blessings for Havdala are inserted prior to the blessing

שֶׁהֶחֱיָנוּ; thus the order of blessings is: wine, Kiddush, flame, Havdala, שֶׁהֶחֱיָנוּ (page 139).

6 When Shavuot eve falls on Friday night, Kiddush is said with additions for Shabbat.

7 The אר"י (Rabbi Isaac Luria) instituted the custom to stay awake all night and to say the *Tikkun Leil Shavuot*. Today most people who stay awake spend the night engaged in Torah study [משניב אויח, תצד: א]. (With regard to studying or reading the Ten Commandments, see law 11 below.)

8 Shaḥarit: for Shabbat and Yom Tov (page 217). The *Shaliaḥ Tzibbur* for Shaḥarit begins from the words הָאֵל בְּתַעֲצוּמוֹת עֻזֶּךָ (page 315). After *Barekhu*, the congregation says הַמֵּאִיר לָאָרֶץ or, if it is also Shabbat, הַכֹּל יוֹדוּךָ. The Amida for Yom Tov is said (page 347); if also Shabbat, one says the additions for Shabbat. The Repetition of the Amida is followed by Hallel and Full Kaddish. On the second day of Shavuot (in Israel on the first), *Megillat Rut* is read, followed by Mourner's Kaddish.

9 While the Torah is taken from the Ark, most congregations say the "Thirteen Attributes of Mercy" and a special supplication (page 381), except on Shabbat. After the Kohen has been called up, אַקְדָּמוּת are said (page 393) [משניב אויח, תצד: ב].

10 Torah Reading: first day – page 393; second day – page 471. Five men are called up, seven on Shabbat. Many congregations stand during the reading of the Ten Commandments (page 411). Maftir (both days): page 419. Haftara: first day – page 421; second day – page 485 [שו"ע אויח, תצד: א-ב]. By custom, an Aramaic poem, יַצִּיב פִּתְגָם, is said after the first two verses of the Haftara of the second day.

11 The Ten Commandments: The text of the Ten Commandments has two sets of cantillation notes known as *ta'am elyon* and *ta'am taḥton*. When read publicly, as in *Keriat HaTorah* on Shavuot (page 411), the reader follows *ta'am elyon*. When an individual reads or studies privately, for example at *Tikkun Leil Shavuot*, the individual follows *ta'am taḥton*.

12 The Haftara is followed by (*Yekum Purkan* on Shabbat, then) the prayers for the government and the State of Israel. On the first day, the *Shaliaḥ Tzibbur* says יָהּ אֵלִי וְגוֹאֲלִי (page 437). On the second day, *Yizkor* (page 503) is said, followed by אַב הָרַחֲמִים. On both days, the congregation says *Ashrei*, and the Torah scrolls are returned to the Ark. The *Shaliaḥ Tzibbur* says Half Kaddish.

13 Musaf: for Festivals (page 519). If also Shabbat, one says the additions for Shabbat. During the Repetition of the Amida, the Kohanim say *Birkat Kohanim*. The

Shaliaḥ Tzibbur says Full Kaddish. This is followed by *Ein Keloheinu* (page 565) and the conclusion of Musaf, as for Shabbat.

14 Minḥa: for Shabbat and Yom Tov (page 595). When the second day of Shavuot falls on Shabbat, the Torah is taken from the Ark and the beginning of the portion of the week is read (page 601). The Torah is returned to the Ark and the *Shaliaḥ Tzibbur* says Half Kaddish. The congregation says the Amida for Yom Tov (page 613).

MOTZA'EI SHAVUOT (8TH OF SIVAN)

15 Ma'ariv: for weekdays (page 631). In the fourth blessing of the Amida, the paragraph of אַתָּה חוֹנַנְתָּנוּ is said (page 647). Havdala is said over a cup of wine or grape juice; no blessing is made over spices or a flame [שו"ע או"ח, תרא: א].

16 If Motza'ei Shabbat, after the silent Amida, the *Shaliaḥ Tzibbur* says Half Kaddish and the congregation says וִיהִי נֹעַם and וְאַתָּה קָדוֹשׁ (pages 659–663) [רמ"א או"ח, רצה: א]. The *Shaliaḥ Tzibbur* then says Full Kaddish. Some have the custom to say וְיִתֶּן־לְךָ (page 665) [שם]. Havdala, begins at הִנֵּה אֵל יְשׁוּעָתִי, and blessings are recited over a cup of wine or grape juice, as well as spices and a flame [שו"ע או"ח, תרא: א]. The congregation says *Aleinu*, followed by Mourner's Kaddish.

17 Each month, one says *Kiddush Levana* (page 677) on seeing the New Moon at night. *Kiddush Levana* may be said from the eve of the fourth day of the new month until the middle day of the month. By custom, it is said on the first Motza'ei Shabbat that falls within the time span (including Motza'ei Shavuot), preferably outdoors with a *minyan*. [שו"ע ורמ"א או"ח, תכו].

A HALAKHIC GUIDE TO PRAYER
FOR VISITORS TO ISRAEL

General Rules
Public vs. Private Conduct

18 For halakhic purposes, the definition of "visitor" is one who intends to return to his place of origin within one year [משנ״ב, קי״ו: ה]. Unmarried students may be considered visitors as long as they are supported by their parents [שו״ת אגרות משה אור״ח ח״ב, קא].

19 In general, a visitor to Israel should continue to follow his or her customs in private. In public, however, one should avoid conduct that deviates from local practice [שו״ע אור״ח, תסח: ד; משנ״ב, שם: יד]. Hence, a visitor to Israel should generally pray in accordance with his non-Israeli customs. This rule is limited, however, to one's private prayers.

20 If one is serving as *Shaliaḥ Tzibbur*, one is required to pray in accordance with the local Israeli custom. This includes, for example, repeating the Amida according to Israeli practice: saying מוֹרִיד הַטָּל in the summer, and saying שִׂים שָׁלוֹם during Minḥa on Shabbat (page 623). This also includes saying *Ein Keloheinu* at the end of weekday Shaḥarit.

21 If one is serving as *Shaliaḥ Tzibbur* for Musaf on Yom Tov in a congregation of Israelis, in the silent Amida one should say the *Korbanot* as said outside Israel, but when repeating the Amida, say them following the Israeli practice [יום טוב שני כהלכתו, א (בשם שערי יצחק)].

22 Even if one is not serving as *Shaliaḥ Tzibbur*, a visitor praying with Israelis should say the following prayers, because of their public nature, following local Israeli custom:

a *Birkat Kohanim* is said daily in Shaḥarit and Musaf.

b In the Rabbis' Kaddish, the word קַדִּישָׁא is added after the words דִּי בְאַתְרָא.

Laws of Second Day Yom Tov – יום טוב שני של גלויות

23 Most authorities require a visitor to Israel to celebrate two days of Yom Tov [משנ״ב, תצו: יג]. Some hold that one should not publicly celebrate the second day, but say the festival prayers in private [שם]. Others permit organizing a public service for visitors on the second day of Yom Tov, and this has become the accepted practice. If, however, there are fewer than ten visitors, they should pray privately, rather than recruit Israeli residents to complete a *minyan* [אשי ישראל, טו: יח (בשם רש״ז אויערבאך)].

24 Some authorities rule that a visitor to Israel should celebrate only one day of Yom Tov, but, on the next day (Yom Tov outside Israel, but *Isru Ḥag* in Israel), one should abstain from labor and perform the מצוות עשה דאורייתא associated with Yom Tov [עיר הקודש והמקדש ח״ג, פ: יא]:

25 Some authorities rule that a visitor to Israel should celebrate only one day of Yom Tov. According to this view, the visitor should follow local Israeli practice without deviation [שו״ת חכם צבי, קסז].

26 If the second day of Shavuot outside Israel falls on Shabbat, a visitor to Israel may be called to the Torah, even though the portion being read is for Shabbat, not Yom Tov [אשי ישראל, לח: ל (בשם רש״ז אויערבאך)].

27 On a day when *Yizkor* is said in Israel, a visitor should not join, but should say *Yizkor* the following day with a *minyan* of visitors. If such a *minyan* will not be available, some rule that one should join with the Israelis [שו״ת רבבות אפרים ח״א, שמב: ב]; others rule that *Yizkor* be said in private the following day [שו״ת בצל החכמה ח״ד, קכ: א].

RABBIS' KADDISH

Mourner: Yitgadal ve-yitkadash shemeh raba. (*Cong:* Amen)
Be-alema di vera khir'uteh,
ve-yamlikh malkhuteh,
be-hayyeikhon, uv-yomeikhon, uv-hayyei de-khol beit Yisrael,
ba-agala uvi-zman kariv,
ve-imru Amen. (*Cong:* Amen)

All: Yeheh shemeh raba mevarakh le'alam ul-alemei alemaya.

Mourner: Yitbarakh ve-yishtabah ve-yitpa'ar ve-yitromam ve-yitnaseh
ve-yit-hadar ve-yit'aleh ve-yit-hallal
shemeh dekudsha, berikh hu. (*Cong:* Berikh hu)
Le-ela min kol birkhata ve-shirata,
tushbehata ve-nehemata,
da-amiran be-alema,
ve-imru, Amen. (*Cong:* Amen)

Al Yisrael, ve-al rabanan,
ve-al talmideihon, ve-al kol talmidei talmideihon,
ve-al kol man de-asekin be-oraita
di be-atra (*In Israel:* kadisha) ha-dein ve-di be-khol atar va-atar,
yeheh lehon ul-khon shelama raba,
hina ve-hisda, ve-rahamei,
ve-hayyei arikhei, um-zonei re-vihei,
u-furkana min kodam avuhon di vish-maya,
ve-imru Amen. (*Cong:* Amen)

Yeheh shelama raba min shemaya
ve-hayyim (tovim) aleinu ve-al kol Yisrael,
ve-imru Amen. (*Cong:* Amen)

*Bow, take three steps back, as if taking leave of the Divine Presence,
then bow, first left, then right, then center, while saying:*
Oseh shalom bim-romav,
hu ya'aseh ve-rahamav shalom aleinu, ve-al kol Yisrael,
ve-imru Amen. (*Cong:* Amen)

MOURNER'S KADDISH

Mourner: Yitgadal ve-yitkadash shemeh raba. (*Cong:* Amen)
Be-alema di vera khir'uteh,
ve-yamlikh malkhuteh,
be-ḥayyeikhon, uv-yomeikhon, uv-ḥayyei de-khol beit Yisrael,
ba-agala uvi-zman kariv,
ve-imru Amen. (*Cong:* Amen)

All: Yeheh shemeh raba mevarakh le'alam ul-alemei alemaya.

Mourner: Yitbarakh ve-yishtabaḥ ve-yitpa'ar ve-yitromam ve-yitnaseh
ve-yit-hadar ve-yit'aleh ve-yit-hallal
shemeh dekudsha, berikh hu. (*Cong:* Berikh hu)
Le-ela min kol birkhata ve-shirata,
tushbeḥata ve-neḥemata,
da-amiran be-alema,
ve-imru, Amen. (*Cong:* Amen)

Yeheh shelama raba min shemaya
ve-ḥayyim aleinu ve-al kol Yisrael,
ve-imru Amen. (*Cong:* Amen)

*Bow, take three steps back, as if taking leave of the Divine Presence,
then bow, first left, then right, then center, while saying:*
Oseh shalom bim-romav,
hu ya'aseh shalom aleinu, ve-al kol Yisrael,
ve-imru Amen. (*Cong:* Amen)

קוֹרֶן ירושלים